O·S Ordnance Survey

STREET ATLAS
Derbyshire

Contents

III Key to map symbols

IV Key to map pages

VI Administrative and post code boundaries

1 Street maps

266 Extra-large-scale maps of town centres

266 Chesterfield
267 Derby

268 Town maps

268 Mansfield
268 Nottingham
269 Stafford
269 Stoke-on-Trent

270 Index of hospitals, railway stations, schools, shopping centres, street names and universities

PHILIP'S

First edition published 1995
First colour edition published 1998 by

Ordnance Survey®   and George Philip Ltd
Romsey Road   an imprint of Reed Consumer Books Ltd
Maybush   Michelin House, 81 Fulham Road,
Southampton   London SW3 6RB
SO16 4GU   and Auckland and Melbourne

ISBN 0-540-07531-0 (hardback)
ISBN 0-540-07532-9 (spiral)

To the best of the Publishers' knowledge, the information in this
atlas was correct at the time of going to press. No responsibility
can be accepted for any errors or their consequences.

The representation in this atlas of a road, track or path is no
evidence of the existence of a right of way.

**The mapping between pages 1 and 269 (inclusive) in this atlas
is derived from Ordnance Survey® Large Scale and Landranger®
mapping, and revised using Land-line® data.**

Ordnance Survey, Land-line and Landranger are registered trade
marks of Ordnance Survey, the National Mapping Agency of Great
Britain.

Printed and bound in Spain by Cayfosa

Digital Data

The exceptionally high-quality mapping
found in this book is available as digital
data in TIFF format, which is easily
convertible to other bit-mapped (raster)
image formats.

The index is also available in digital form
as a standard database table. It contains
all the details found in the printed index
together with the National Grid reference
for the map square in which each entry
is named and feature codes for places
of interest in eight categories such as
education and health.

For further information and to discuss
your requirements, please contact the
Ordnance Survey Solutions Centre on
01703 792929.

Motorway (with junction number)		British Rail station	
Primary route (dual carriageway and single)		Metrolink station	
A road (dual carriageway and single)		Underground station	
B road (dual carriageway and single)		Docklands Light Railway station	
Minor road (dual carriageway and single)		Tyne and Wear Metro	
Other minor road		Private railway station	
Road under construction		Bus, coach station	
Pedestrianised area		Ambulance station	
County and Unitary Authority boundaries		Coastguard station	
Railway		Fire station	
Tramway, miniature railway		Police station	
Rural track, private road or narrow road in urban area		Accident and Emergency entrance to hospital	
Gate or obstruction to traffic (restrictions may not apply at all times or to all vehicles)		Hospital	
Path, bridleway, byway open to all traffic, road used as a public path		Church, place of worship	
The representation in this atlas of a road, track or path is no evidence of the existence of a right of way		Information centre (open all year)	
		Parking, Park and Ride	
Adjoining page indicators		Post Office	
		Important buildings, schools, colleges, universities and hospitals	
		Water name	
The map area within the pink band is shown at a larger scale on the page indicated by the red block and arrow		Stream	
		River or canal (minor and major)	
		Water	
		Tidal water	
		Woods	
		Houses	
		Non-Roman antiquity	
		Roman antiquity	

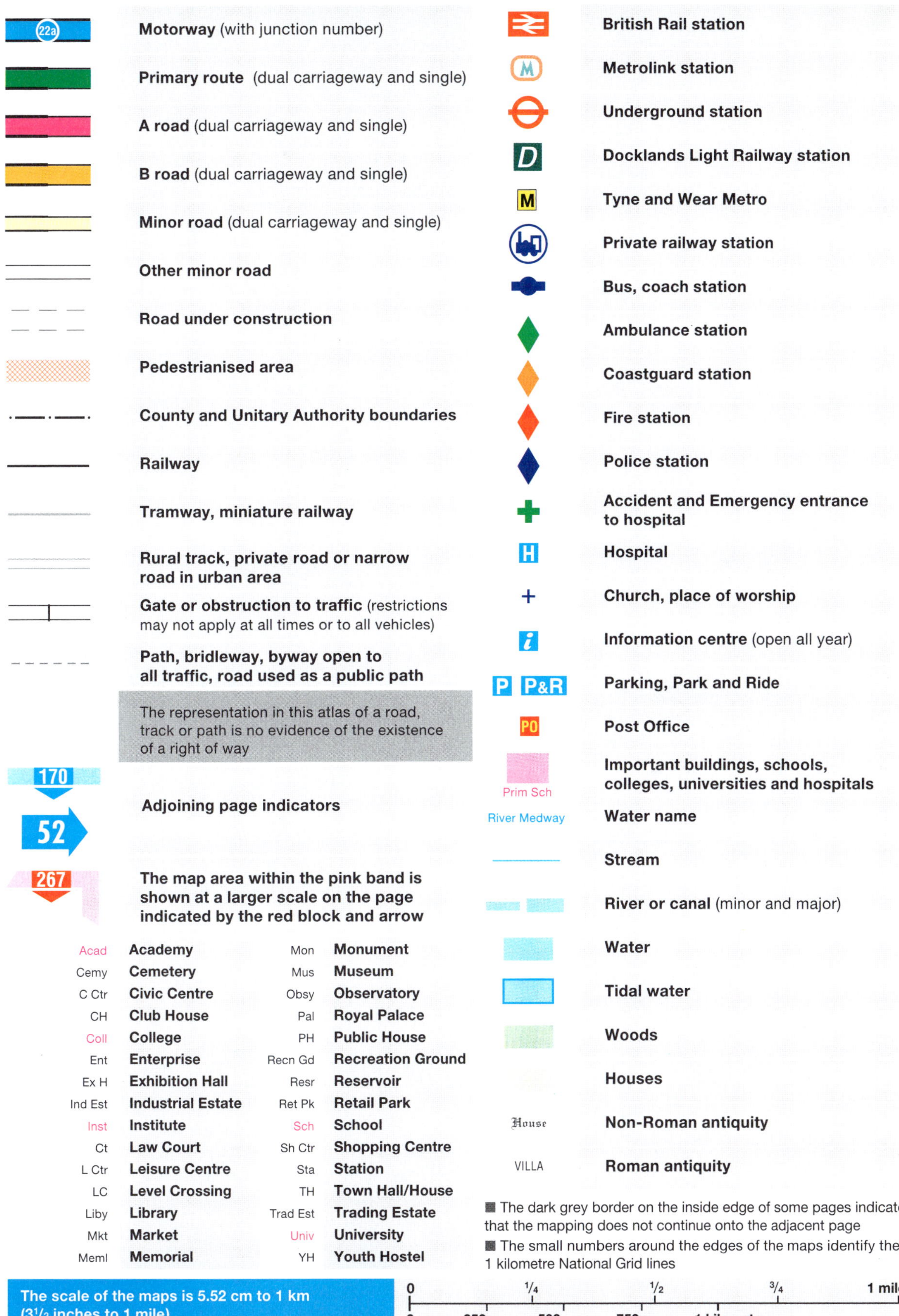

Acad	Academy	Mon	Monument
Cemy	Cemetery	Mus	Museum
C Ctr	Civic Centre	Obsy	Observatory
CH	Club House	Pal	Royal Palace
Coll	College	PH	Public House
Ent	Enterprise	Recn Gd	Recreation Ground
Ex H	Exhibition Hall	Resr	Reservoir
Ind Est	Industrial Estate	Ret Pk	Retail Park
Inst	Institute	Sch	School
Ct	Law Court	Sh Ctr	Shopping Centre
L Ctr	Leisure Centre	Sta	Station
LC	Level Crossing	TH	Town Hall/House
Liby	Library	Trad Est	Trading Estate
Mkt	Market	Univ	University
Meml	Memorial	YH	Youth Hostel

■ The dark grey border on the inside edge of some pages indicates that the mapping does not continue onto the adjacent page

■ The small numbers around the edges of the maps identify the 1 kilometre National Grid lines

The scale of the maps is 5.52 cm to 1 km (3½ inches to 1 mile)

0	¼	½	¾	1 mile
0	250m 500m 750m	1 kilometre		

The scale of the map on pages numbered in red is 11.04 cm to 1 km (7 inches to 1 mile)

0	220 yards	440 yards	660 yards	½ mile
0	125m 250m 375m	½ kilometre		

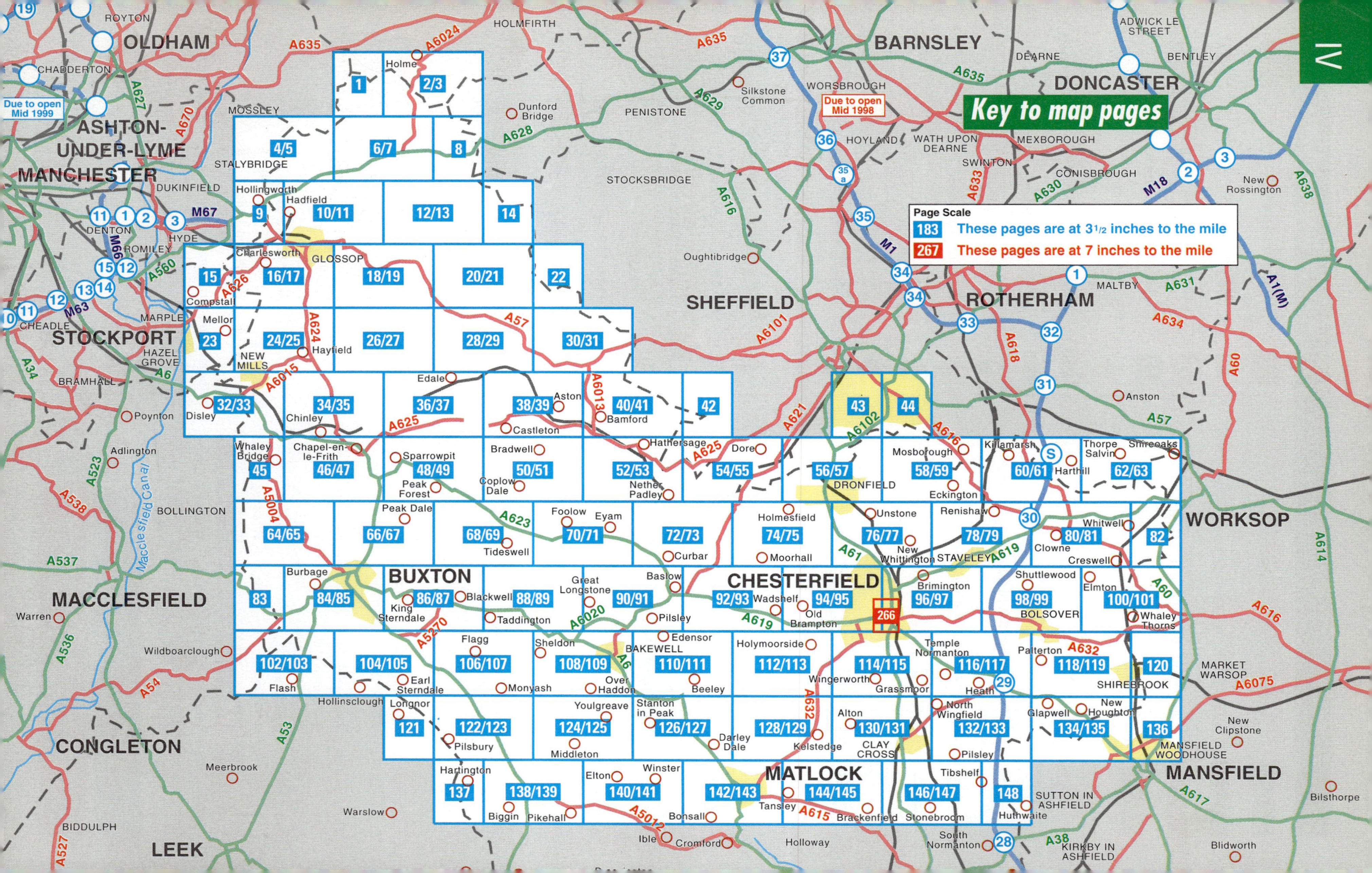
Key to map pages
Page Scale
183 These pages are at 3½ inches to the mile
267 These pages are at 7 inches to the mile
Due to open Mid 1999
Due to open Mid 1998
OLDHAM
ASHTON-UNDER-LYME
MANCHESTER
STOCKPORT
MACCLESFIELD
CONGLETON
LEEK
BARNSLEY
DONCASTER
SHEFFIELD
ROTHERHAM
WORKSOP
MANSFIELD
CHESTERFIELD
BUXTON
MATLOCK
BOLSOVER
DRONFIELD
STAVELEY
BAKEWELL
GLOSSOP
NEW MILLS
SHIREBROOK
MANSFIELD WOODHOUSE
CLAY CROSS
HOLMFIRTH
PENISTONE
STOCKSBRIDGE
STALYBRIDGE
MOSSLEY
HYDE
DUKINFIELD
DENTON
ROMILEY
MARPLE
HAZEL GROVE
BRAMHALL
CHEADLE
CHADDERTON
ROYTON
BOLLINGTON
BIDDULPH
WORSBROUGH
HOYLAND
WATH UPON DEARNE
MEXBOROUGH
SWINTON
CONISBROUGH
DEARNE
BENTLEY
ADWICK LE STREET
MALTBY
MARKET WARSOP
SUTTON IN ASHFIELD
KIRKBY IN ASHFIELD
Macclesfield Canal

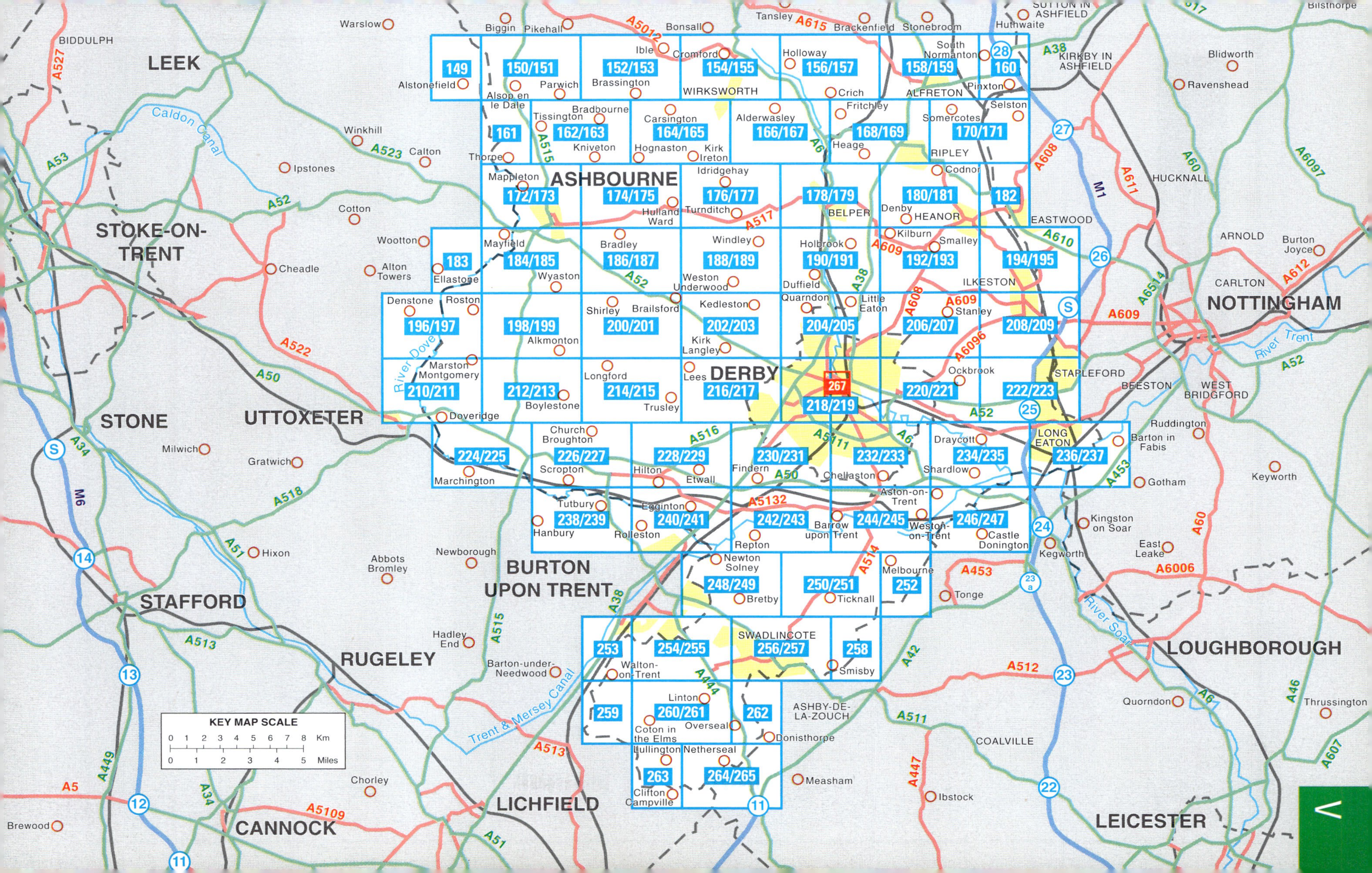

KEY MAP SCALE
Km
Miles
LEEK
STOKE-ON-TRENT
STONE
UTTOXETER
STAFFORD
RUGELEY
CANNOCK
LICHFIELD
BURTON UPON TRENT
ASHBOURNE
DERBY
NOTTINGHAM
LOUGHBOROUGH
LEICESTER
SWADLINCOTE
BELPER
HEANOR
ILKESTON
RIPLEY
ALFRETON
WIRKSWORTH
EASTWOOD
HUCKNALL
ARNOLD
CARLTON
BEESTON
STAPLEFORD
WEST BRIDGFORD
LONG EATON
ASHBY-DE-LA-ZOUCH
COALVILLE
KIRKBY IN ASHFIELD
SUTTON IN ASHFIELD
BIDDULPH
149
150/151
152/153
154/155
156/157
158/159
160
161
162/163
164/165
166/167
168/169
170/171
172/173
174/175
176/177
178/179
180/181
182
183
184/185
186/187
188/189
190/191
192/193
194/195
196/197
198/199
200/201
202/203
204/205
206/207
208/209
210/211
212/213
214/215
216/217
218/219
220/221
222/223
224/225
226/227
228/229
230/231
232/233
234/235
236/237
238/239
240/241
242/243
244/245
246/247
248/249
250/251
252
253
254/255
256/257
258
259
260/261
262
263
264/265
267
Warslow
Biggin
Pikehall
Bonsall
Tansley
Brackenfield
Stonebroom
Huthwaite
Bilsthorpe
Alstonefield
Alsop en le Dale
Parwich
Ible
Brassington
Cromford
Holloway
Crich
South Normanton
Pinxton
Bradbourne
Tissington
Kniveton
Carsington
Hognaston
Kirk Ireton
Alderwasley
Fritchley
Heage
Somercotes
Selston
Thorpe
Winkhill
Calton
Ipstones
Mappleton
Idridgehay
Turnditch
Hulland Ward
Codnor
Denby
Kilburn
Smalley
Cotton
Wootton
Alton Towers
Cheadle
Ellastone
Mayfield
Wyaston
Bradley
Windley
Weston Underwood
Holbrook
Duffield
Denstone
Roston
Shirley
Brailsford
Kedleston
Quarndon
Little Eaton
Stanley
Alkmonton
Kirk Langley
Marston Montgomery
Doveridge
Boylestone
Longford
Trusley
Lees
Ockbrook
Ravenshead
Bldworth
Burton Joyce
Church Broughton
Scropton
Marchington
Hilton
Etwall
Findern
Chellaston
Draycott
Shardlow
Aston-on-Trent
Ruddington
Barton in Fabis
Gotham
Keyworth
Milwich
Gratwich
Tutbury
Hanbury
Egginton
Rolleston
Repton
Barrow upon Trent
Weston-on-Trent
Castle Donington
Kingston on Soar
Kegworth
East Leake
Newborough
Abbots Bromley
Newton Solney
Bretby
Ticknall
Melbourne
Tonge
Hixon
Hadley End
Barton-under-Needwood
Walton-on-Trent
Smisby
Linton
Coton in the Elms
Overseal
Donisthorpe
Lullington
Netherseal
Clifton Campville
Measham
Ibstock
Quorndon
Thrussington
Chorley
Brewood
Caldon Canal
River Dove
River Trent
River Soar
Trent & Mersey Canal
M1
M6
A527
A53
A523
A52
A522
A50
A518
A34
A449
A5
A51
A513
A5109
A515
A38
A5012
A615
A6
A517
A609
A608
A6096
A610
A611
A6514
A612
A60
A6097
A453
A6006
A512
A46
A607
A42
A511
A447
A516
A5111
A5132
A514
A444
A38
A61
S
11
12
13
14
22
23
23a
24
25
26
27
28
V

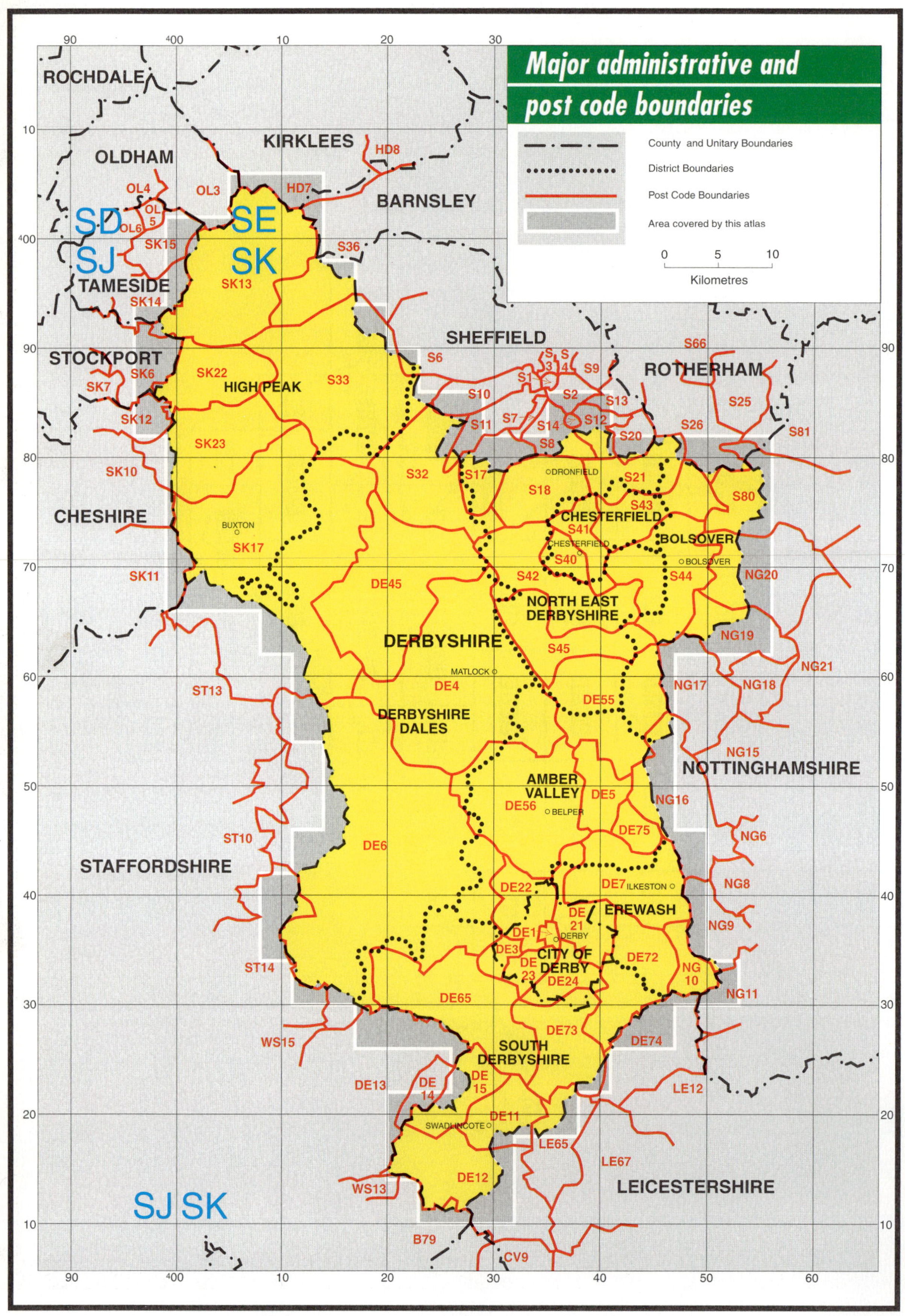

Major administrative and post code boundaries

— · — · —	County and Unitary Boundaries
· · · · · · ·	District Boundaries
———	Post Code Boundaries
▨	Area covered by this atlas

0   5   10
Kilometres

ROCHDALE

OLDHAM

KIRKLEES

BARNSLEY

HD8

OL4
OL5
OL6
OL3
HD7

SD
SJ

SE
SK

TAMESIDE

SK15
SK14
SK13

S36

STOCKPORT

SHEFFIELD

ROTHERHAM

SK6
SK7
SK12

SK22
HIGH PEAK
SK33

S6
S3 S14
S1
S9
S10
S5
S7
S2
S13
S25
S66

SK10

SK23

S11
S14
S12
S20
S26
S81

CHESHIRE

S32
S17
S8

DRONFIELD
S18
S21
S80

BUXTON
SK17

S43
CHESTERFIELD
S41
S40
CHESTERFIELD
BOLSOVER
BOLSOVER

SK11

DE45

S42
S44
NG20

DERBYSHIRE

NORTH EAST
DERBYSHIRE

NG19

S45

NG17
NG18
NG21

ST13

MATLOCK
DE4

DE55

NG15

DERBYSHIRE
DALES

NOTTINGHAMSHIRE

AMBER
VALLEY
DE5
NG16

ST10

DE56
BELPER

DE75
NG6

STAFFORDSHIRE

DE6

DE7 ILKESTON
NG8

DE22
NG9

ST14

DE1
DE21 DERBY
DE3
DE23
CITY OF
DERBY
DE24
EREWASH
DE72
NG10
NG11

DE65

DE73
DE74

WS15

SOUTH
DERBYSHIRE

DE13
DE14
DE15
DE11
LE12

SWADLINCOTE
LE65
LE67

SJ SK

WS13
DE12
LEICESTERSHIRE

B79

CV9

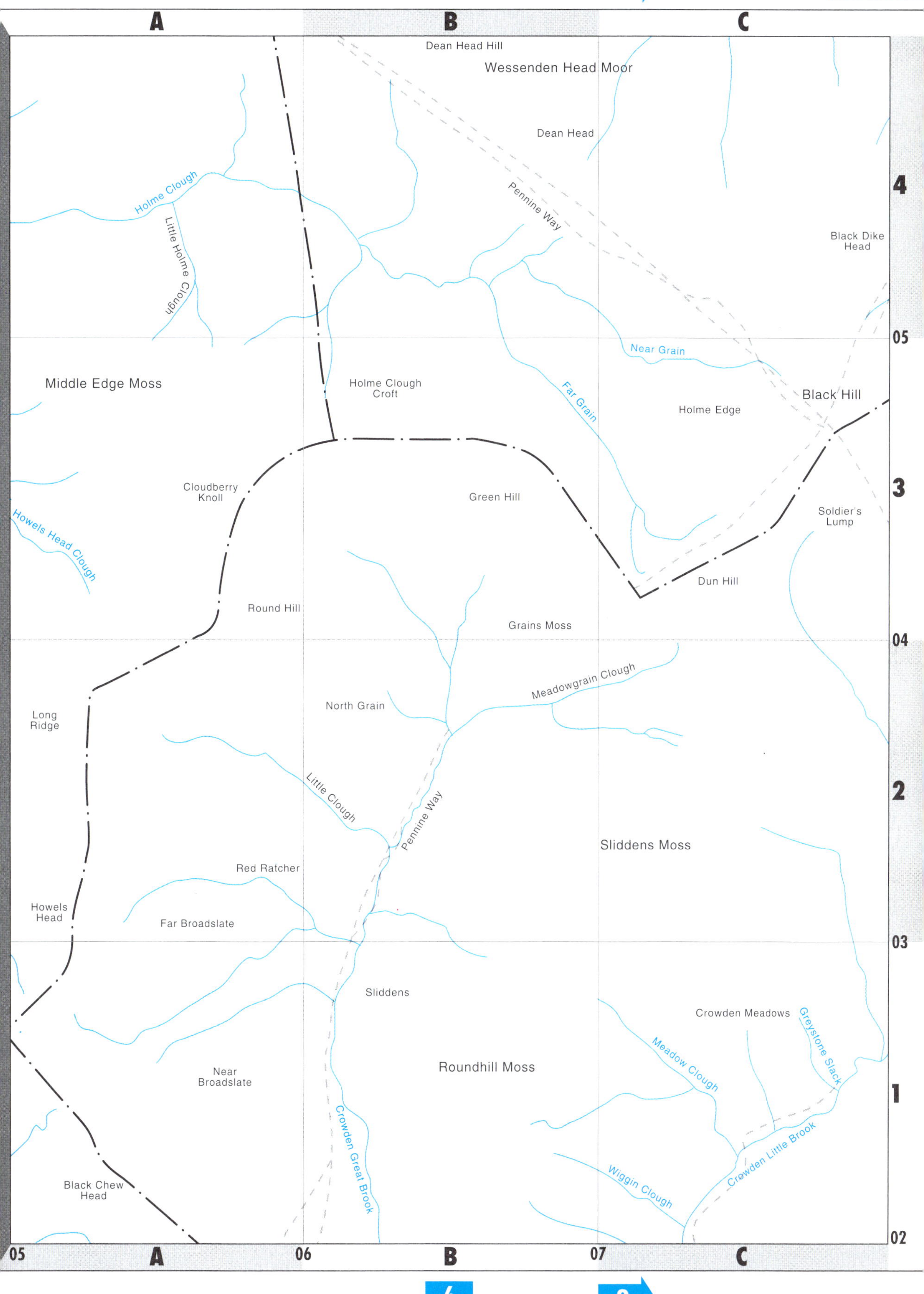

A   B   C

Dean Head Hill

Wessenden Head Moor

Dean Head

Pennine Way

4

Black Dike
Head

Holme Clough

Little Holme Clough

05

Middle Edge Moss

Holme Clough
Croft

Near Grain

Far Grain

Holme Edge

Black Hill

Howels Head Clough

Cloudberry
Knoll

Green Hill

3

Soldier's
Lump

Round Hill

Dun Hill

Grains Moss

04

Meadowgrain Clough

Long
Ridge

North Grain

Little Clough

Pennine Way

2

Sliddens Moss

Howels
Head

Red Ratcher

Far Broadslate

03

Sliddens

Crowden Meadows

Greystone Slack

Near
Broadslate

Roundhill Moss

Meadow Clough

1

Crowden Great Brook

Wiggin Clough

Crowden Little Brook

Black Chew
Head

02

05   A   06   B   07   C

6

2

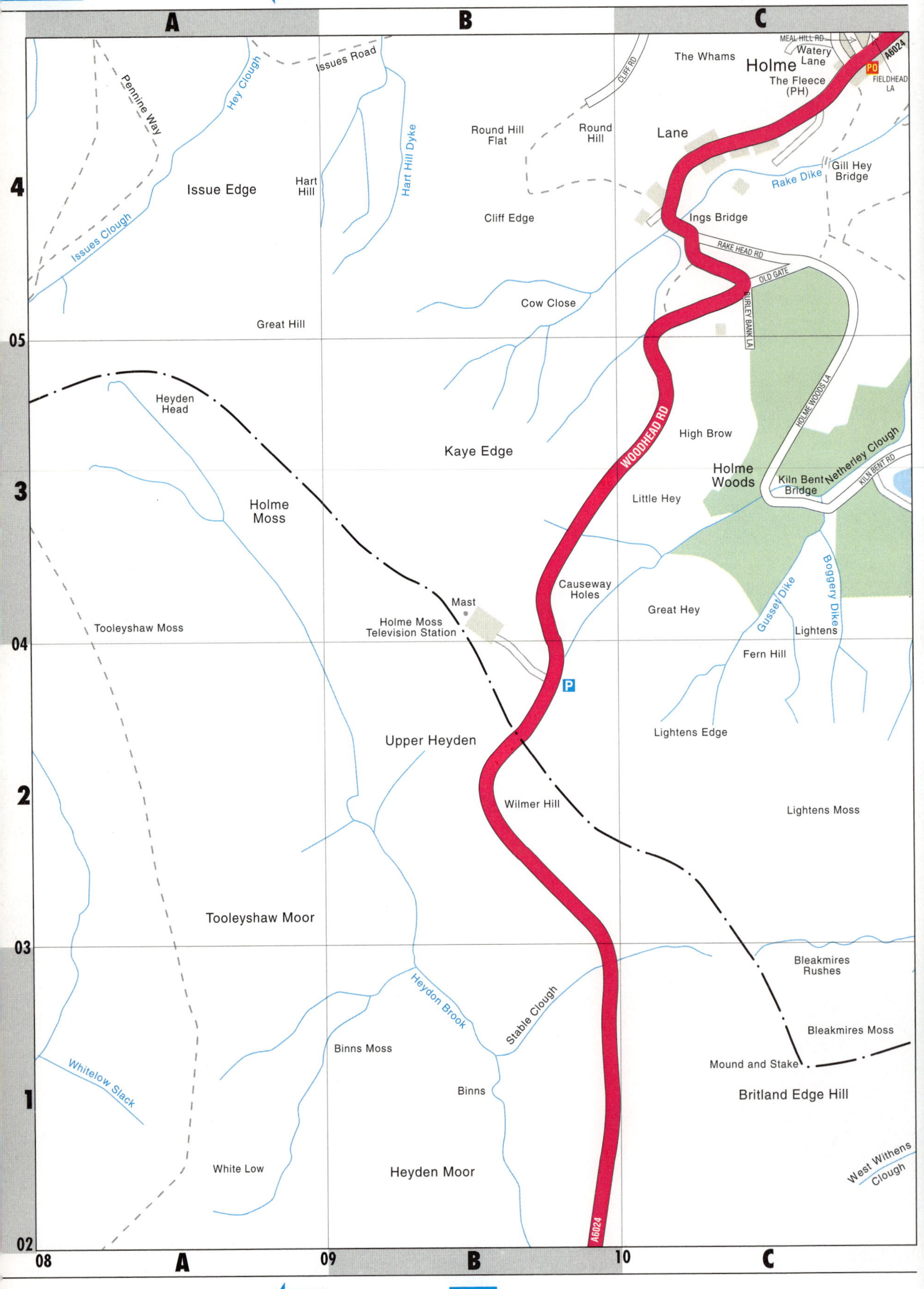

Pennine Way

Hey Clough

Issues Road

MEAL HILL RD

CLIFF RD

The Whams

Holme

Watery Lane

The Fleece (PH)

P O

FIELDHEAD LA

A6024

Lane

Round Hill Flat

Round Hill

Hart Hill Dyke

Hart Hill

Issue Edge

Gill Hey Bridge

Rake Dike

4

Issues Clough

Cliff Edge

Ings Bridge

RAKE HEAD RD

OLD GATE

Cow Close

High Brow

BURLEY BANK LA

Great Hill

HOLME WOODS LA

05

Holme Woods

Netherley Clough

Heyden Head

Kaye Edge

Kiln Bent Bridge

KILN BENT RD

Holme Moss

Little Hey

3

WOODHEAD RD

Gusset Dike

Boggery Dike

Tooleyshaw Moss

Causeway Holes

Great Hey

Lightens

Mast

Holme Moss Television Station

Fern Hill

04

P

Lightens Edge

Upper Heyden

Lightens Moss

Wilmer Hill

2

Tooleyshaw Moor

03

Bleakmires Rushes

Heydon Brook

Stable Clough

Bleakmires Moss

Binns Moss

Mound and Stake

Whitelow Slack

Binns

1

Britland Edge Hill

White Low

Heyden Moor

West Withens Clough

A6024

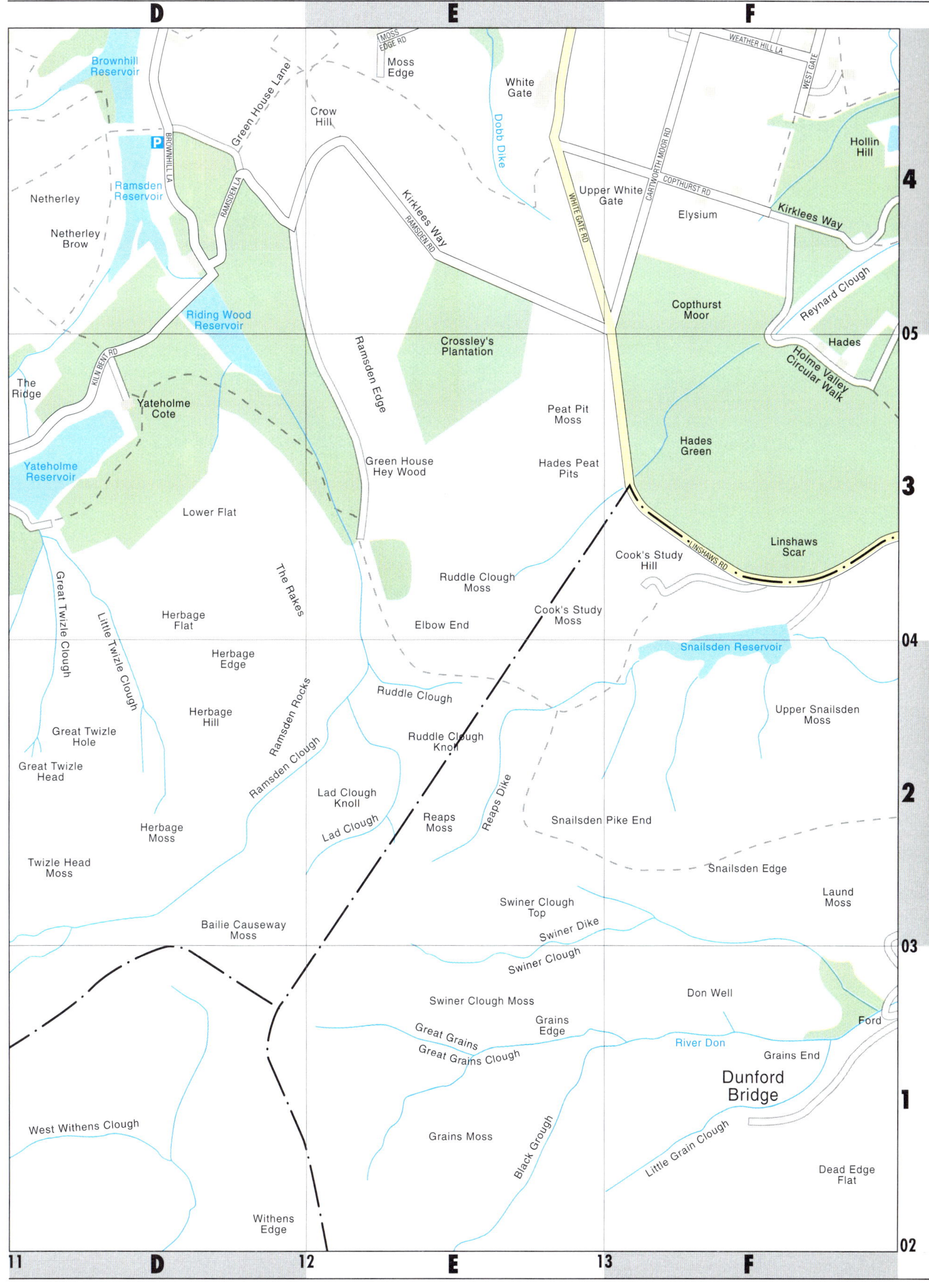

D
E
F

Brownhill Reservoir

Green House Lane

Moss Edge Rd

Moss Edge

Crow Hill

White Gate

Dobb Dike

WEATHER HILL LA

WEST GATE

P

Ramsden Reservoir

BROWNHILL LA

RAMSDEN LA

Kirklees Way

RAMSDEN RD

Upper White Gate

CARTWORTH MOOR RD

COPTHURST RD

Hollin Hill

Netherley

Netherley Brow

KILN BENT RD

Riding Wood Reservoir

Ramsden Edge

Crossley's Plantation

WHITE GATE RD

Elysium

Kirklees Way

Reynard Clough

The Ridge

Yateholme Cote

Green House Hey Wood

Peat Pit Moss

Copthurst Moor

Hades

Holme Valley Circular Walk

Hades Peat Pits

Yateholme Reservoir

Lower Flat

The Rakes

Ruddle Clough Moss

Cook's Study Hill

Hades Green

LINSHAWS RD

Linshaws Scar

Great Twizle Clough

Little Twizle Clough

Herbage Flat

Elbow End

Cook's Study Moss

Great Twizle Hole

Herbage Edge

Ramsden Rocks

Ruddle Clough

Snailsden Reservoir

Great Twizle Head

Herbage Hill

Ruddle Clough Knoll

Upper Snailsden Moss

Herbage Moss

Ramsden Clough

Lad Clough Knoll

Reaps Moss

Reaps Dike

Snailsden Pike End

Laund Moss

Twizle Head Moss

Lad Clough

Snailsden Edge

Bailie Causeway Moss

Swiner Clough Top

Swiner Dike

Swiner Clough

Swiner Clough Moss

Don Well

Ford

West Withens Clough

Great Grains

Great Grains Clough

Grains Edge

River Don

Grains End

Dunford Bridge

Grains Moss

Black Grough

Little Grain Clough

Dead Edge Flat

Withens Edge

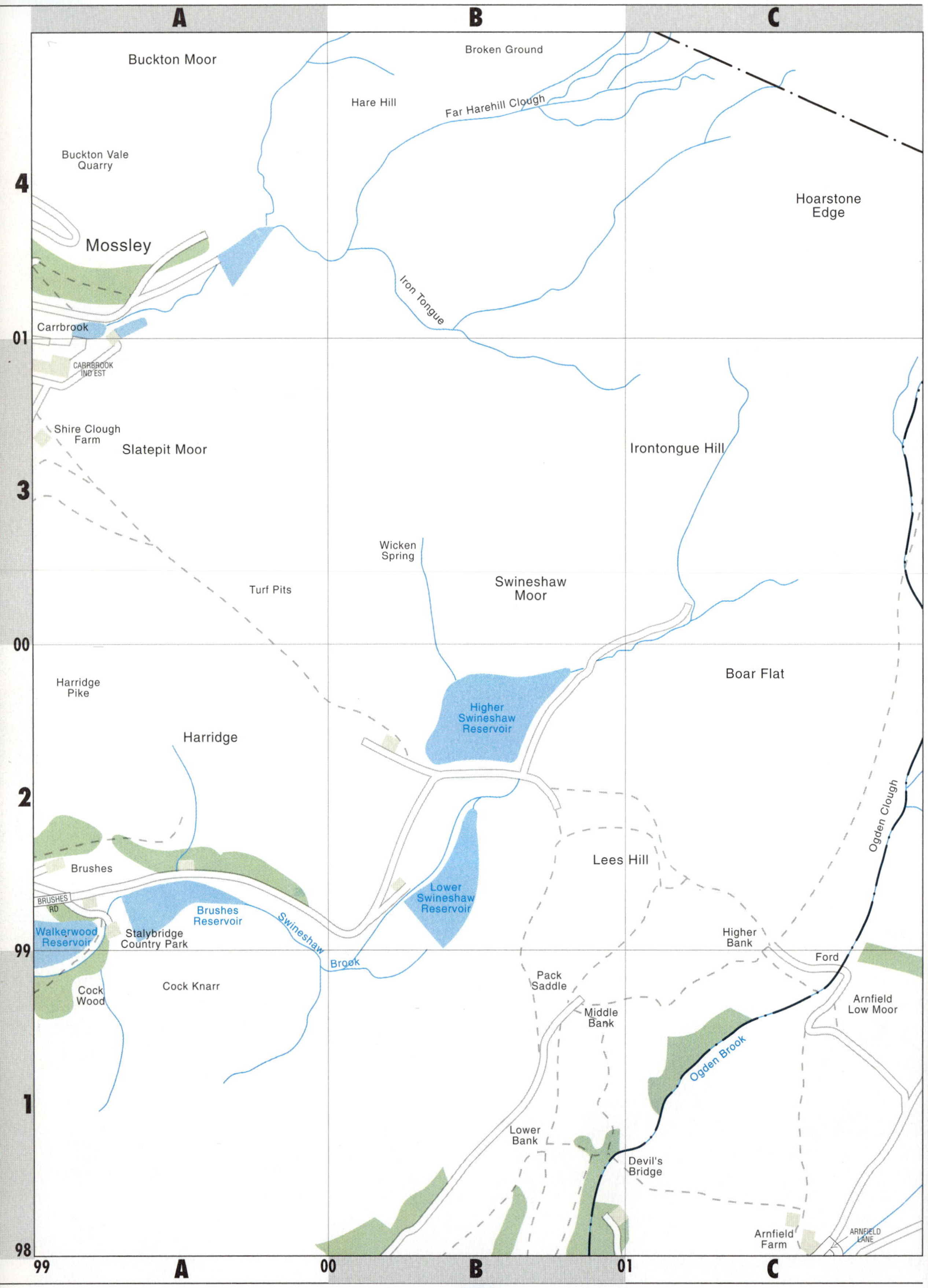

Buckton Moor

Broken Ground

Hare Hill

Far Harehill Clough

4

Hoarstone Edge

Buckton Vale Quarry

Mossley

Iron Tongue

Carrbrook

01

CARRBROOK IND EST

Shire Clough Farm

Slatepit Moor

Irontongue Hill

3

Wicken Spring

Turf Pits

Swineshaw Moor

00

Harridge Pike

Boar Flat

Harridge

Higher Swineshaw Reservoir

2

Brushes

Lees Hill

BRUSHES RD

Brushes Reservoir

Lower Swineshaw Reservoir

Walkerwood Reservoir

Stalybridge Country Park

Swineshaw

Higher Bank

99

Brook

Ford

Cock Wood

Cock Knarr

Pack Saddle

Arnfield Low Moor

Middle Bank

Ogden Clough

Ogden Brook

1

Lower Bank

Devil's Bridge

Arnfield Farm

ARNFIELD LANE

98

99   **A**   **00**   **B**   **01**   **C**

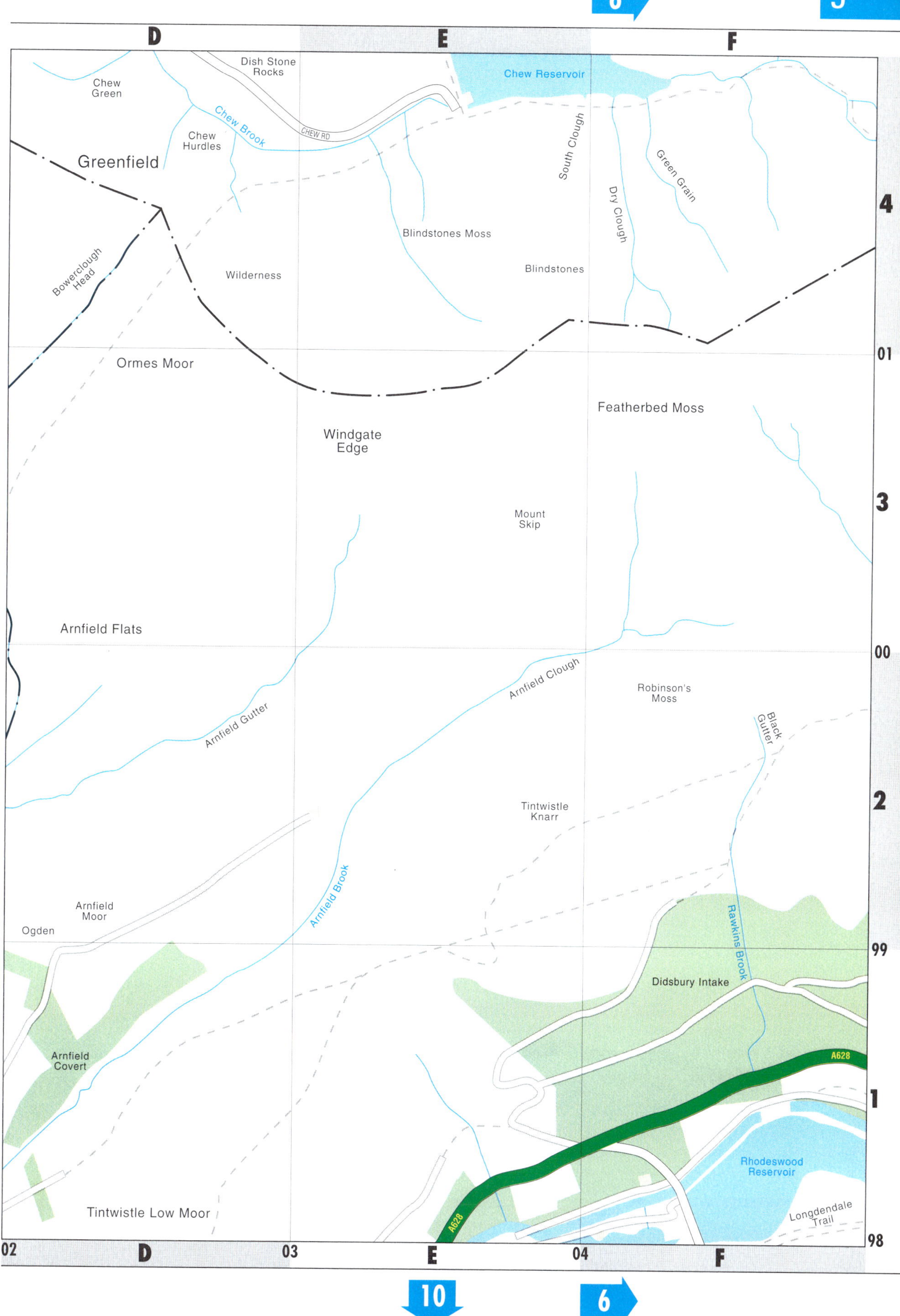

D

E

F

Chew
Green

Dish Stone
Rocks

Chew Reservoir

Chew Hurdles

Chew Brook

CHEW RD

South Clough

Green Grain

Greenfield

Dry Clough

4

Bowerclough
Head

Wilderness

Blindstones Moss

Blindstones

Ormes Moor

01

Featherbed Moss

Windgate
Edge

Mount
Skip

3

Arnfield Flats

Arnfield Clough

Robinson's
Moss

00

Arnfield Gutter

Black
Gutter

Tintwistle
Knarr

2

Arnfield
Moor

Arnfield Brook

Rawkins Brook

Ogden

99

Didsbury Intake

Arnfield
Covert

A628

Rhodeswood
Reservoir

1

Tintwistle Low Moor

A628

Longdendale
Trail

98

02

D

03

E

04

F

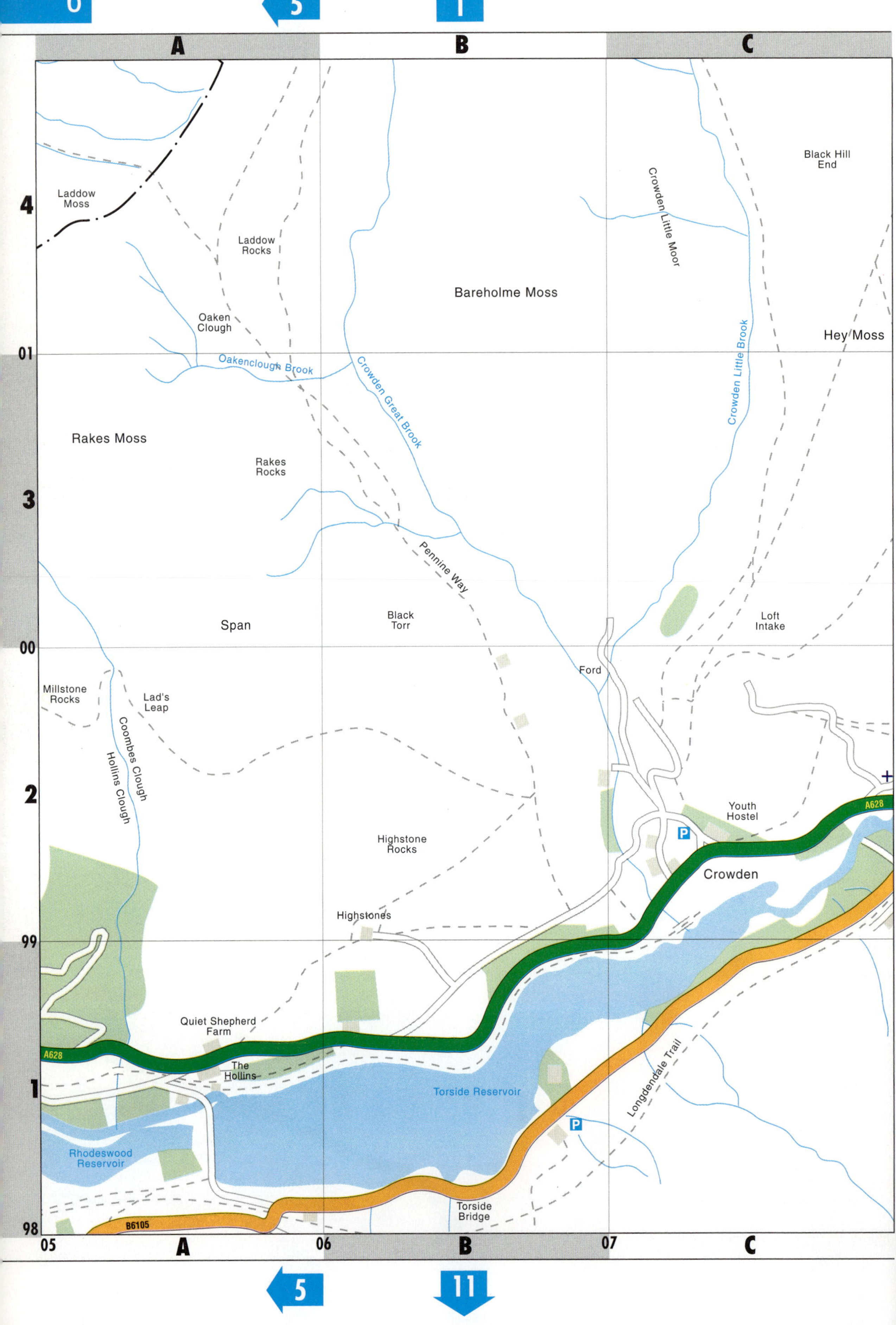

A B C

4

Laddow
Moss

Laddow
Rocks

Black Hill
End

Crowden Little Moor

Bareholme Moss

Oaken
Clough

01

Oakenclough Brook

Crowden Great Brook

Crowden Little Brook

Hey Moss

Rakes Moss

Rakes
Rocks

3

Pennine Way

Span

Black
Torr

Loft
Intake

00

Ford

Millstone
Rocks

Lad's
Leap

Coombes Clough

Hollins Clough

2

Youth
Hostel

A628

Crowden

P

Highstone
Rocks

Highstones

99

Quiet Shepherd
Farm

Longdendale Trail

A628

The
Hollins

1

Torside Reservoir

P

Rhodeswood
Reservoir

Torside
Bridge

98

05

B6105

A B C

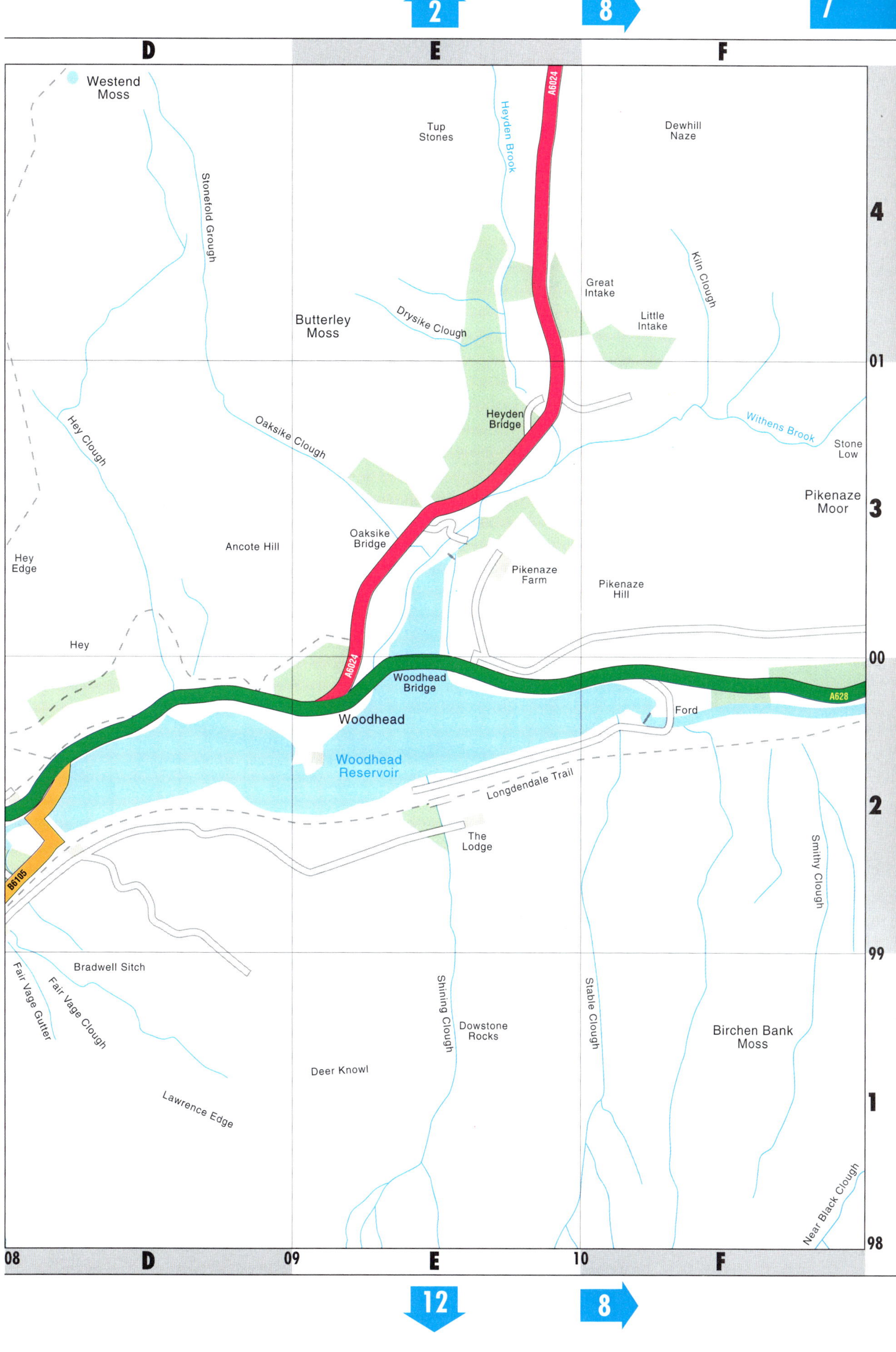
2
8
D
E
F
Westend Moss
Tup Stones
Heyden Brook
A6024
Dewhill Naze
Stonefold Grough
4
Kiln Clough
Great Intake
Little Intake
Butterley Moss
Drysike Clough
01
Heyden Bridge
Oaksike Clough
Hey Clough
Withens Brook
Stone Low
Pikenaze Moor
3
Oaksike Bridge
Ancote Hill
Hey Edge
Pikenaze Farm
Pikenaze Hill
Hey
00
Woodhead Bridge
A628
Ford
Woodhead
Woodhead Reservoir
Longdendale Trail
2
The Lodge
B6105
Smithy Clough
99
Bradwell Sitch
Fair Vage Gutter
Fair Vage Clough
Shining Clough
Dowstone Rocks
Stable Clough
Birchen Bank Moss
Deer Knowl
Lawrence Edge
1
Near Black Clough
98
08
09
10
12

7
3

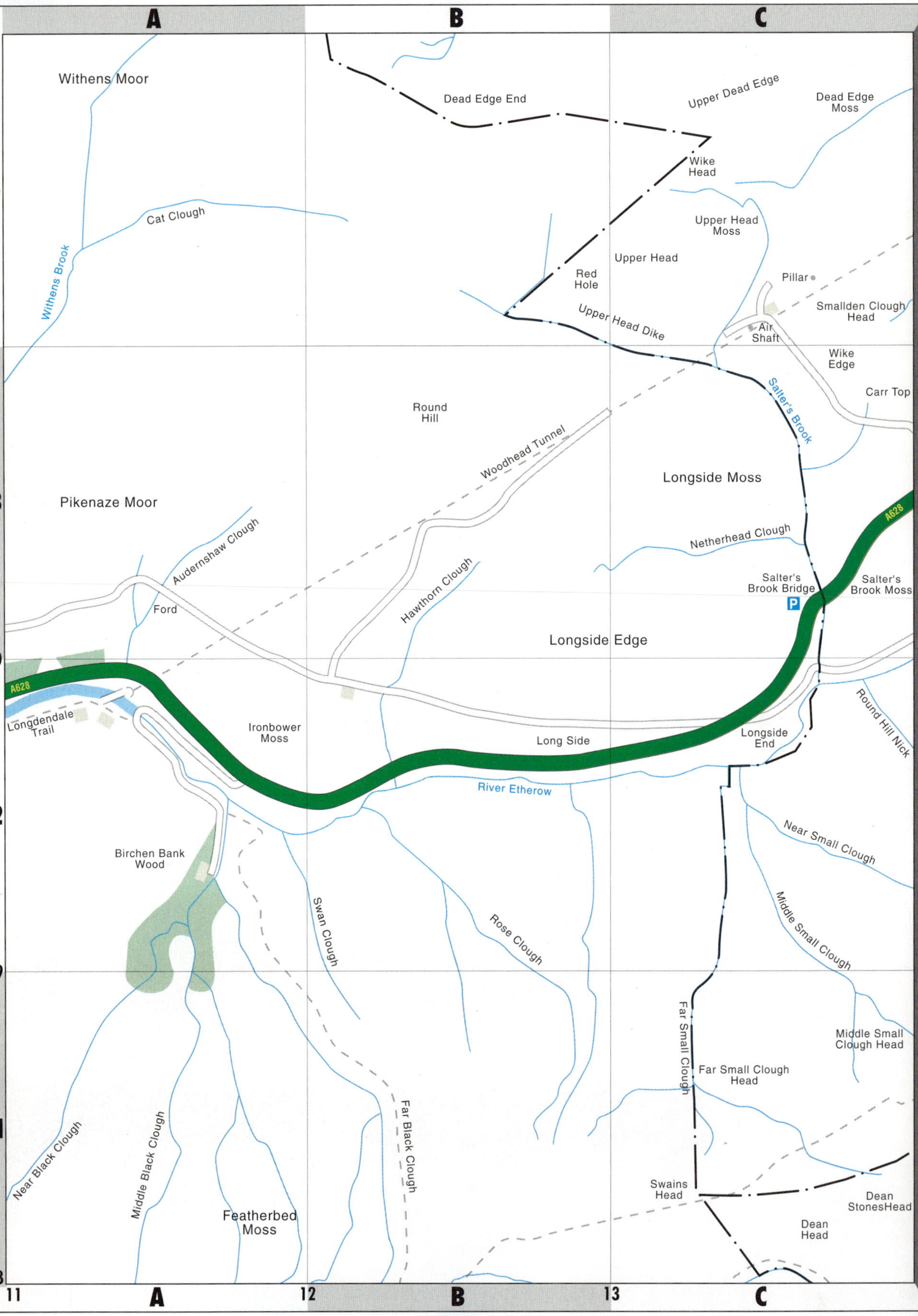

A
B
C

Withens Moor

Dead Edge End

Upper Dead Edge

Dead Edge Moss

4

Wike Head

Cat Clough

Upper Head Moss

Withens Brook

Upper Head

Pillar

Smallden Clough Head

Red Hole

01

Upper Head Dike

Air Shaft

Wike Edge

Salter's Brook

Carr Top

Round Hill

Woodhead Tunnel

Longside Moss

3

Pikenaze Moor

A628

Netherhead Clough

Audernshaw Clough

Hawthorn Clough

Salter's Brook Bridge

Salter's Brook Moss

Ford

P

Longside Edge

00

A628

Longdendale Trail

Ironbower Moss

Long Side

Longside End

Round Hill Nick

2

River Etherow

Birchen Bank Wood

Near Small Clough

Swan Clough

Rose Clough

Middle Small Clough

99

Far Small Clough

Middle Small Clough Head

Near Black Clough

Middle Black Clough

Far Black Clough

Far Small Clough Head

1

Swains Head

Dean StonesHead

Featherbed Moss

Dean Head

98

11
A
12
B
13
C

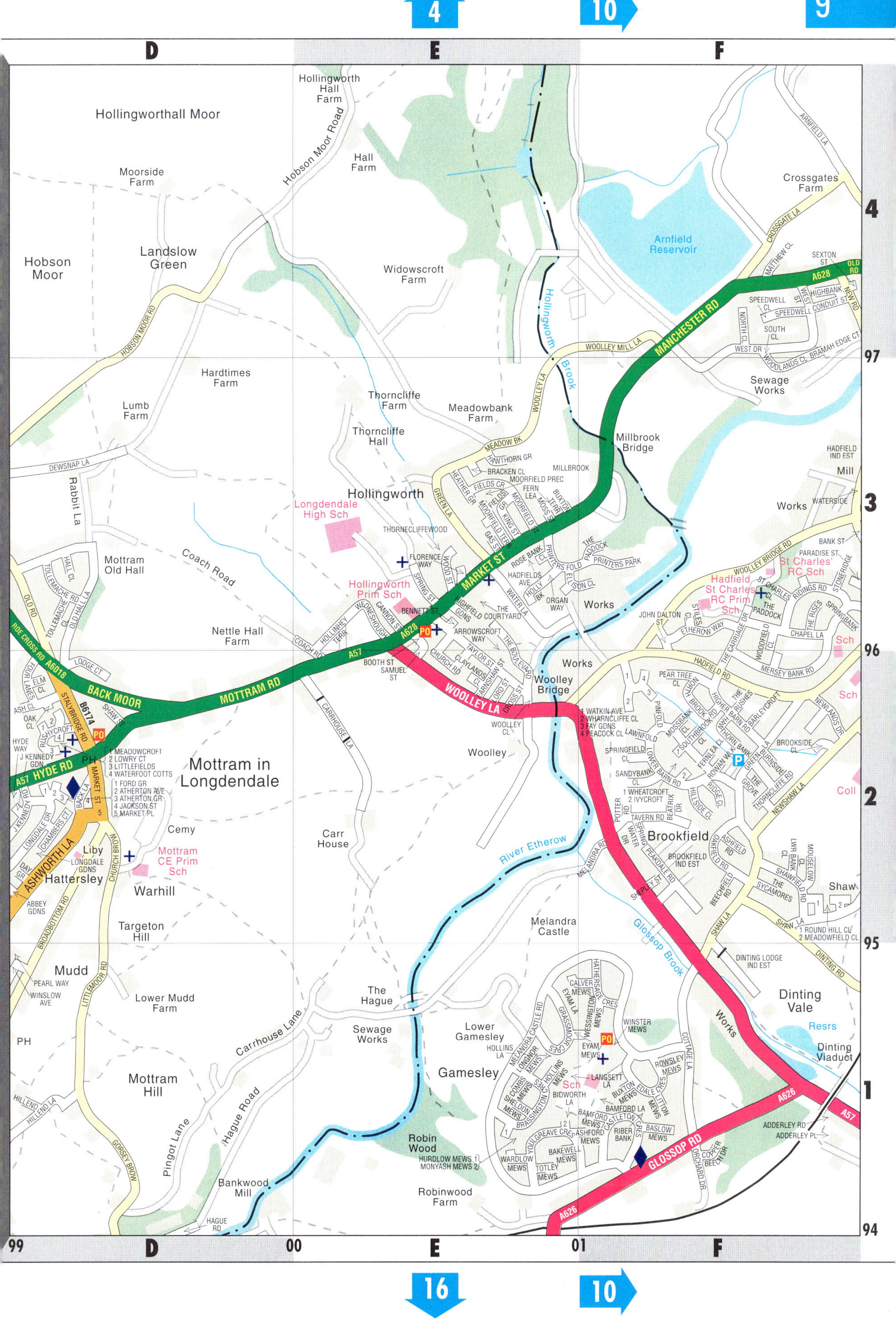
4
10
D
E
F
Hollingworthall Moor
Hollingworth Hall Farm
Hobson Moor Road
Hall Farm
Moorside Farm
Crossgates Farm
Arnfield Reservoir
Hobson Moor
Landslow Green
Widowscroft Farm
Hollingworth Brook
MANCHESTER RD
A628
WOOLLEY MILL LA
Hardtimes Farm
Lumb Farm
Thorncliffe Farm
Meadowbank Farm
Sewage Works
Thorncliffe Hall
Millbrook Bridge
DEWSNAP LA
Rabbit La
Hollingworth
Longdendale High Sch
Mill
Works
Mottram Old Hall
Coach Road
MARKET ST
St Charles' RC Sch
Hadfield St Charles RC Prim Sch
Hollingworth Prim Sch
Works
Nettle Hall Farm
A57
BACK MOOR
MOTTRAM RD
WOOLLEY LA
Woolley Bridge
Works
Sch
Sch
Mottram in Longdendale
Woolley
Coll
A57 HYDE RD
Cemy
Carr House
Brookfield
River Etherow
Liby
Hattersley
Mottram CE Prim Sch
Warhill
Targeton Hill
Melandra Castle
Glossop Brook
Shaw
Mudd
Lower Mudd Farm
The Hague
Dinting Vale
Resrs
Sewage Works
Lower Gamesley
Dinting Viaduct
Carrhouse Lane
Mottram Hill
Gamesley
Sch
Hague Road
Pingot Lane
Robin Wood
GLOSSOP RD
A626
Bankwood Mill
Robinwood Farm
99
00
01
94
95
96
97
1
2
3
4
16
10

9
5

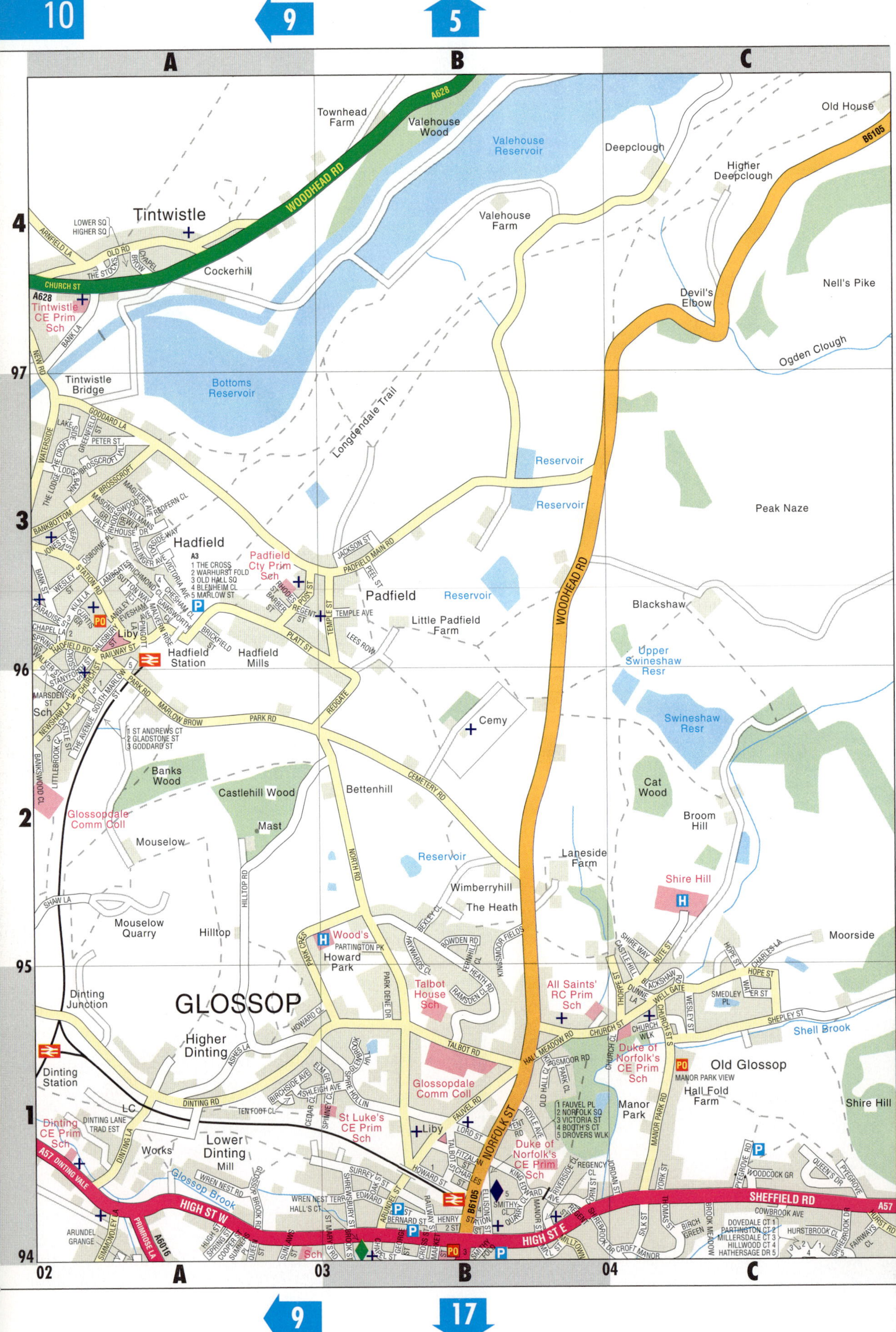
A
B
C
4
3
2
1
97
96
95
94
02
03
04
Tintwistle
Townhead Farm
Valehouse Wood
Valehouse Reservoir
Deepclough
Old House
Higher Deepclough
Valehouse Farm
Cockerhill
Tintwistle CE Prim Sch
Devil's Elbow
Nell's Pike
Ogden Clough
Tintwistle Bridge
Bottoms Reservoir
Longdendale Trail
Reservoir
Peak Naze
Hadfield
Padfield Cty Prim Sch
Padfield
Little Padfield Farm
Blackshaw
Upper Swineshaw Resr
Swineshaw Resr
Hadfield Station
Hadfield Mills
Cemy
Banks Wood
Castlehill Wood
Bettenhill
Cat Wood
Broom Hill
Glossopdale Comm Coll
Mouselow
Mast
Laneside Farm
Shire Hill
Wimberryhill
The Heath
Mouselow Quarry
Hilltop
Wood's
Howard Park
Moorside
Dinting Junction
GLOSSOP
Talbot House Sch
All Saints' RC Prim Sch
Shell Brook
Higher Dinting
Duke of Norfolk's CE Prim Sch
Old Glossop
Dinting Station
Hall Fold Farm
Manor Park
Lower Dinting Mill
St Luke's CE Prim Sch
Dinting CE Prim Sch
Works
Glossop Brook
WOODHEAD RD
A628
B6105
A57
SHEFFIELD RD
HIGH ST W
HIGH ST E
NORFOLK ST
CHURCH ST
1 THE CROSS
2 WARHURST FOLD
3 OLD HALL SQ
4 BLENHEIM CL
5 MARLOW ST
1 ST ANDREWS CT
2 GLADSTONE ST
3 GODDARD ST
1 FAUVEL PL
2 NORFOLK SQ
3 VICTORIA ST
4 BOOTH'S CT
5 DROVERS WLK
DOVEDALE CT 1
PARTINGTON CT 2
MILLERSDALE CT 3
HILLWOOD CT 4
HATHERSAGE DR 5

9
17

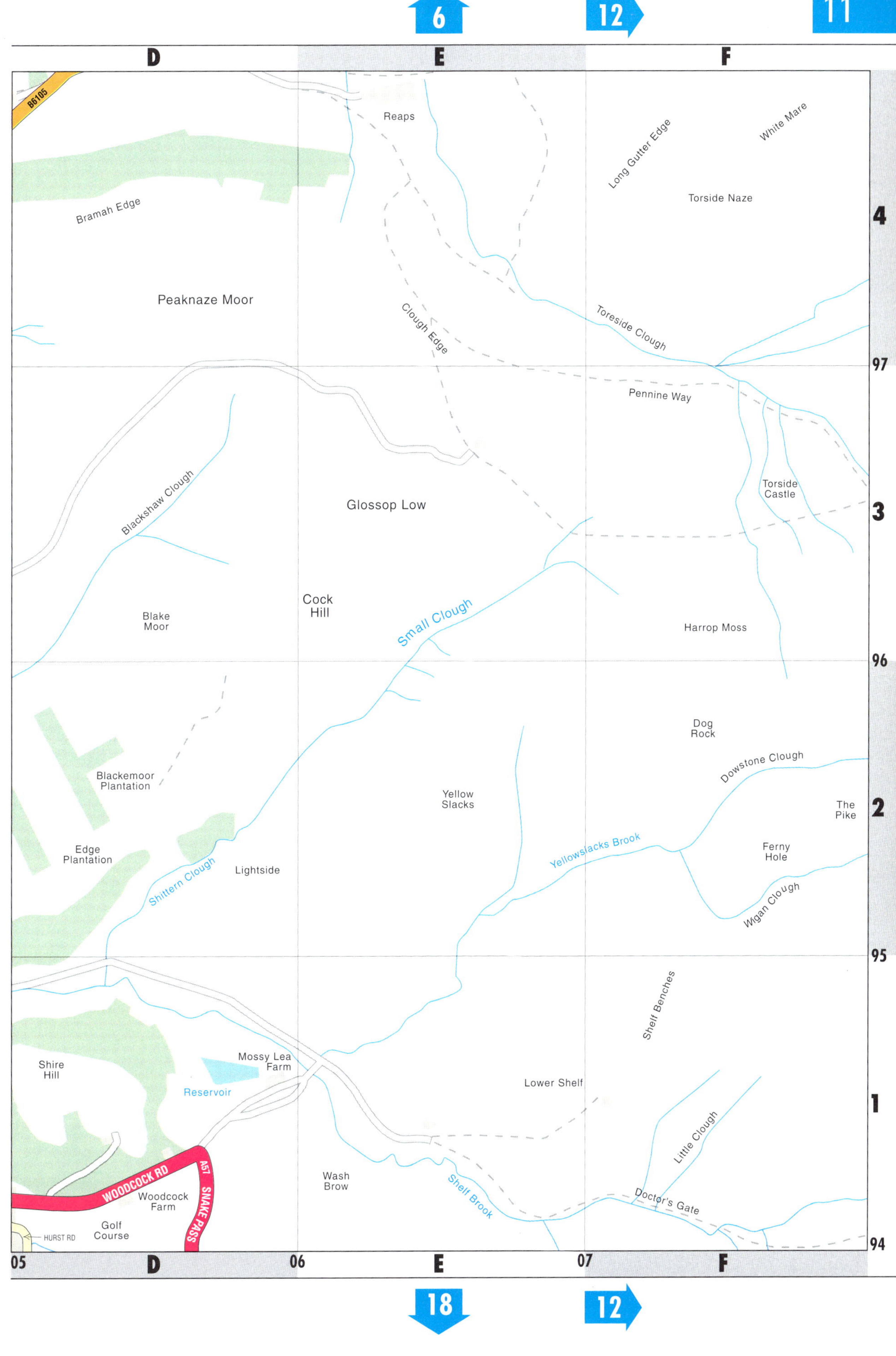

D
E
F

B6105

Bramah Edge

Reaps

Long Gutter Edge

White Mare

Torside Naze

4

Peaknaze Moor

Clough Edge

Toreside Clough

97

Pennine Way

Blackshaw Clough

Glossop Low

Torside
Castle

3

Cock
Hill

Blake
Moor

Small Clough

Harrop Moss

96

Blackemoor
Plantation

Dog
Rock

Dowstone Clough

Yellow
Slacks

The
Pike

2

Edge
Plantation

Shittern Clough

Lightside

Yellowslacks Brook

Ferny
Hole

Wigan Clough

95

Shelf Benches

Shire
Hill

Mossy Lea
Farm

Reservoir

Lower Shelf

Little Clough

1

WOODCOCK RD

A57 SNAKE PASS

Woodcock
Farm

Wash
Brow

Shelf Brook

Doctor's Gate

94

Golf
Course

HURST RD

05
D
06
E
07
F

A　　　　**B**　　　　**C**

Wildboar Clough

Round Hill

Shining Clough Moss

Near Black Clough

Bleaklow Meadows

4

Sykes Moor

97

Near Bleaklow Stones

Bleaklow

Wildboar Grain

Far Moss

3

Bleaklow Hill

Joseph Patch

Alport Head

Bleaklow Head

96

Wain Stones

Pennine Way

Dowstone Clough

Shelf Moss

2

Far Fork Grain

Near Fork Grain

Hern Stones

95

Shelf Moor

The Swamp

Grains in the Water

Lower Shelf Stones

Higher Shelf Stones

Hern Clough

Ashton Clough

1

Crooked Clough

Alport Low

White Clough

Devil's Dike

Gathering Hill

94

08　　　　**A**　　　　**09**　　　　**B**　　　　**10**　　　　**C**

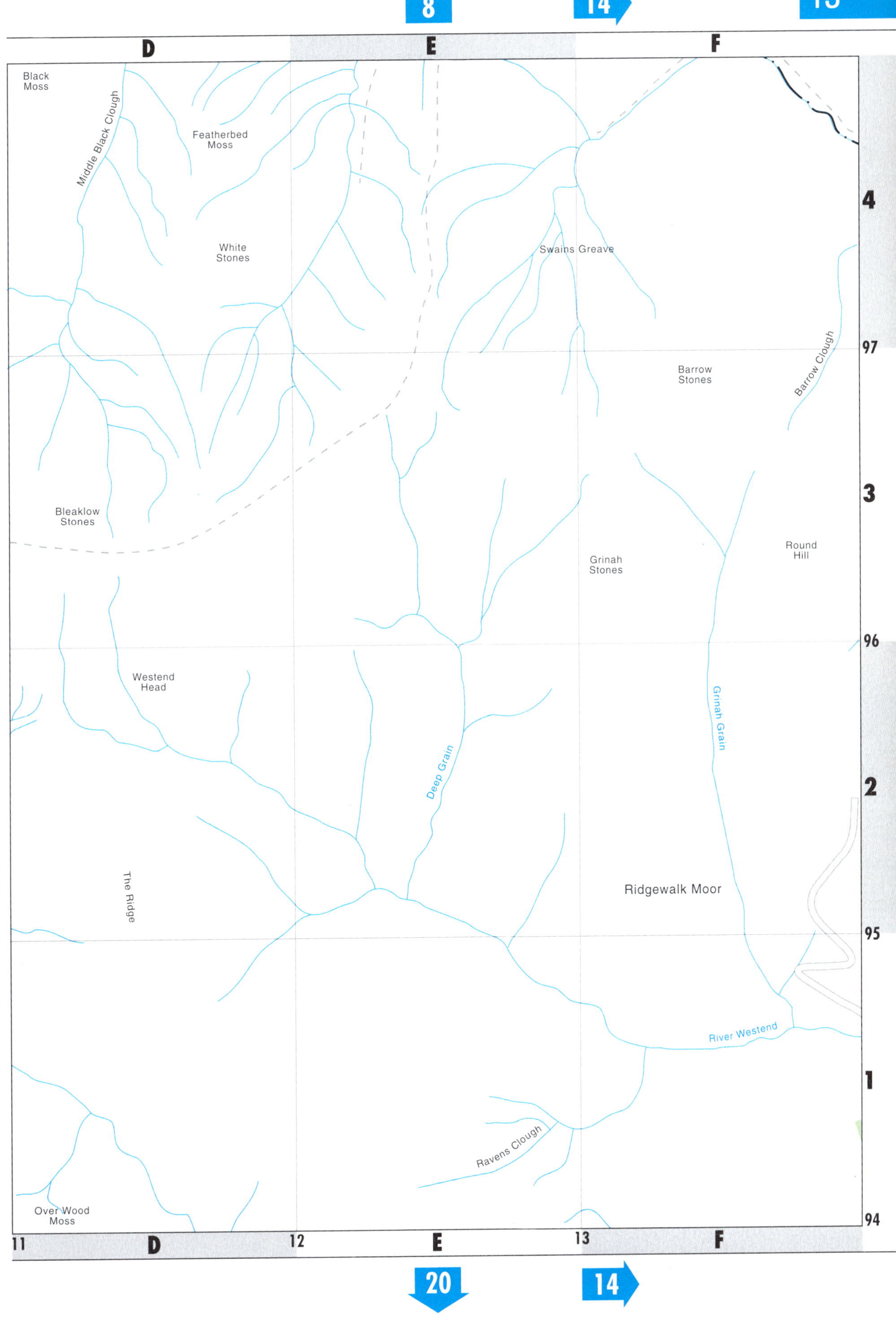

D

E

F

Black
Moss

Middle Black Clough

Featherbed
Moss

White
Stones

Swains Greave

4

Barrow Clough

Barrow
Stones

97

Bleaklow
Stones

3

Grinah
Stones

Round
Hill

96

Westend
Head

Grinah Grain

Deep Grain

2

The Ridge

Ridgewalk Moor

95

River Westend

1

Ravens Clough

Over Wood
Moss

94

13

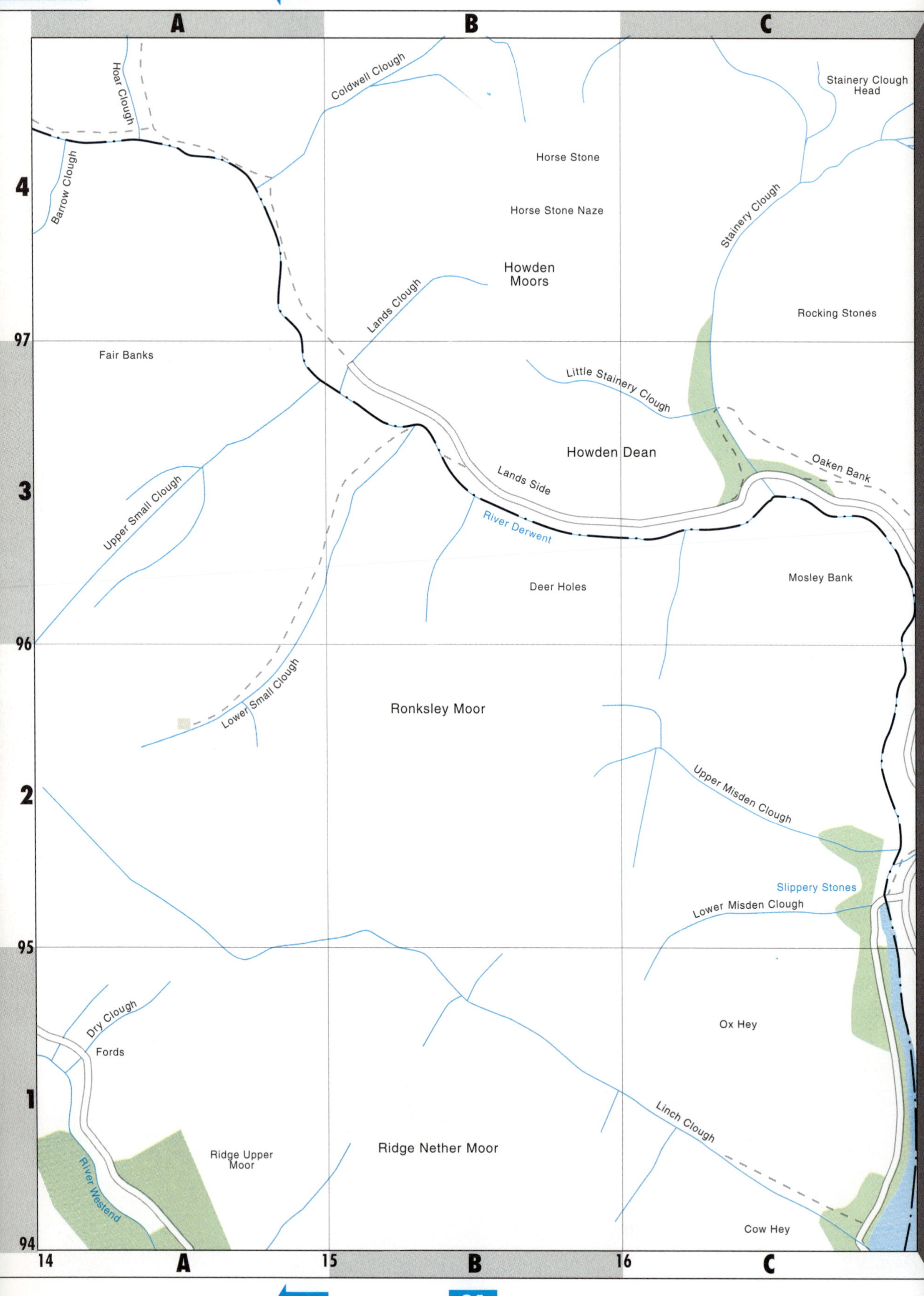
A
B
C
Hoar Clough
Coldwell Clough
Stainery Clough Head
Barrow Clough
4
Horse Stone
Horse Stone Naze
Stainery Clough
Howden Moors
Lands Clough
Rocking Stones
97
Fair Banks
Little Stainery Clough
Howden Dean
Oaken Bank
3
Lands Side
Upper Small Clough
River Derwent
Mosley Bank
Deer Holes
96
Lower Small Clough
Ronksley Moor
2
Upper Misden Clough
Slippery Stones
Lower Misden Clough
95
Dry Clough
Ox Hey
Fords
1
Linch Clough
Ridge Upper Moor
Ridge Nether Moor
River Westend
Cow Hey
94
14
A
15
B
16
C

13
21

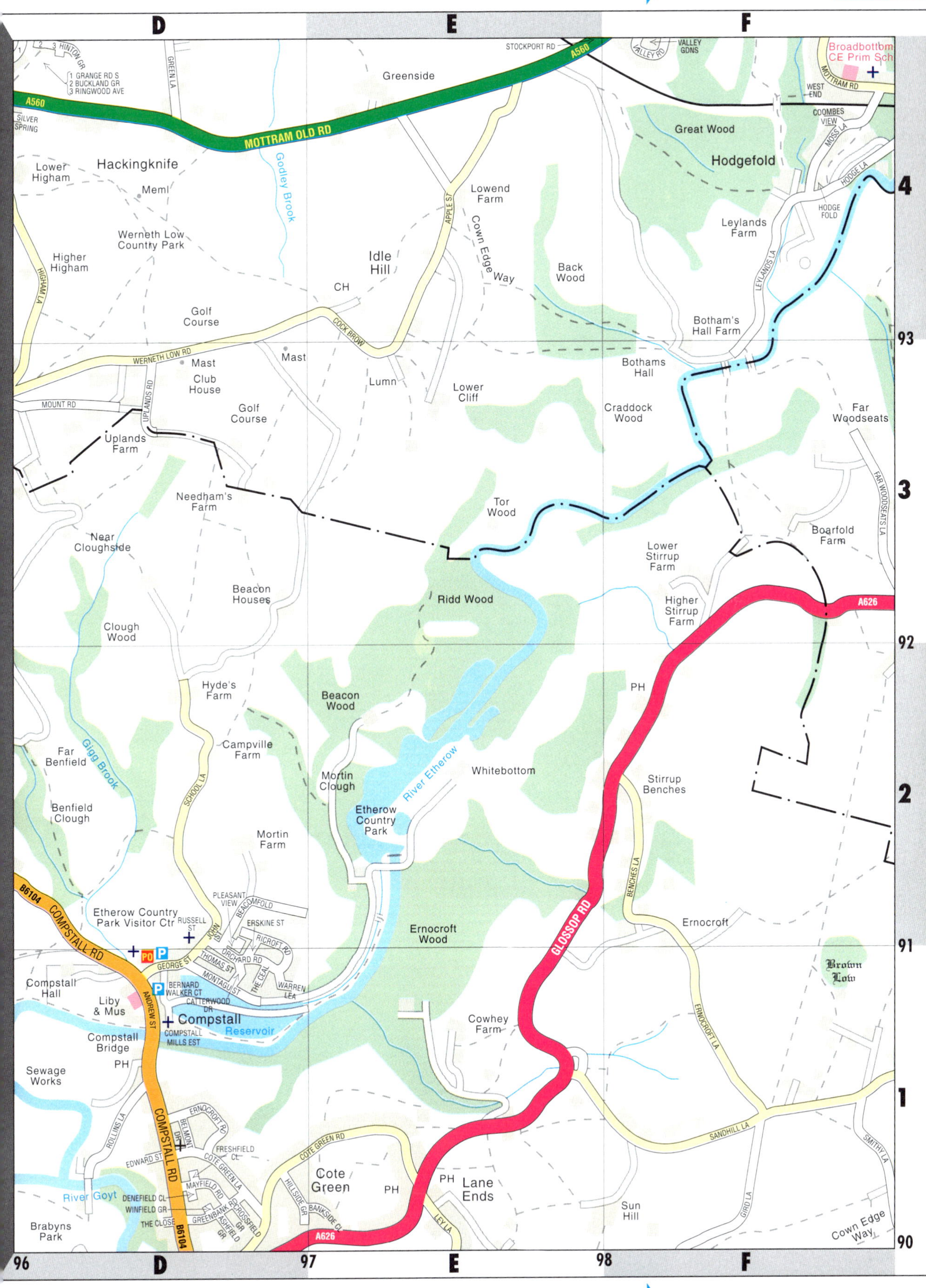
D
E
F
A560
MOTTRAM OLD RD
STOCKPORT RD
Greenside
Broadbottom CE Prim Sch
MOTTRAM RD
WEST END
COOMBES VIEW
MOSS LA
HODGE LA
HODGE FOLD
Great Wood
Hodgefold
Leylands Farm
LEYLANDS LA
GREEN LA
SILVER SPRING
1 GRANGE RD S
2 BUCKLAND GR
3 RINGWOOD AVE
HINTON GR
Lower Higham
Hackingknife
Meml
Godley Brook
Lowend Farm
APPLE ST
Cown Edge Way
Werneth Low Country Park
Higher Higham
HIGHAM LA
Idle Hill
CH
Back Wood
Golf Course
COCK BROW
Botham's Hall Farm
WERNETH LOW RD
Mast
Club House
Lumn
Lower Cliff
Bothams Hall
MOUNT RD
UPLANDS RD
Golf Course
Craddock Wood
Far Woodseats
Uplands Farm
Needham's Farm
Tor Wood
FAR WOODSEATS LA
Boarfold Farm
Near Cloughside
Lower Stirrup Farm
Beacon Houses
Ridd Wood
Higher Stirrup Farm
A626
Clough Wood
Hyde's Farm
PH
Beacon Wood
Campville Farm
Far Benfield
Gigg Brook
Mortin Clough
River Etherow
Whitebottom
Stirrup Benches
SCHOOL LA
Benfield Clough
Etherow Country Park
Mortin Farm
BENCHES LA
B6104
COMPSTALL RD
PLEASANT VIEW
BEACOMFOLD
Etherow Country Park Visitor Ctr
RUSSELL ST
JOHN ST
ERSKINE ST
Ernocroft
RICROFT RD
Ernocroft Wood
GLOSSOP RD
PO
GEORGE ST
THOMAS ST
ORCHARD RD
Brown Low
Compstall Hall
BERNARD WALKER CT
MONTAGUE ST
THE CEAL
WARREN LEA
CATTERWOOD DR
Liby & Mus
ANDREW ST
Compstall
Reservoir
COMPSTALL MILLS EST
Cowhey Farm
ERNOCROFT LA
Compstall Bridge
PH
Sewage Works
ROLLINS LA
ERNOCROFT RD
BELMONT DR
FRESHFIELD CL
SANDHILL LA
SMITHY LA
EDWARD ST
COTE GREEN LA
COTE GREEN RD
Cote Green
PH
Lane Ends
River Goyt
DENEFIELD CL
MAYFIELD RD
WINFIELD GR
GREENBANK RD
CROSSFIELD GR
ASHFIELD GR
HILLSIDE GR
BANKSIDE CL
LEY LA
Sun Hill
GIRD LA
Cown Edge Way
THE CLOSE
Brabyns Park
96
97
98
90
1
91
2
92
3
93
4

23
16

15
9

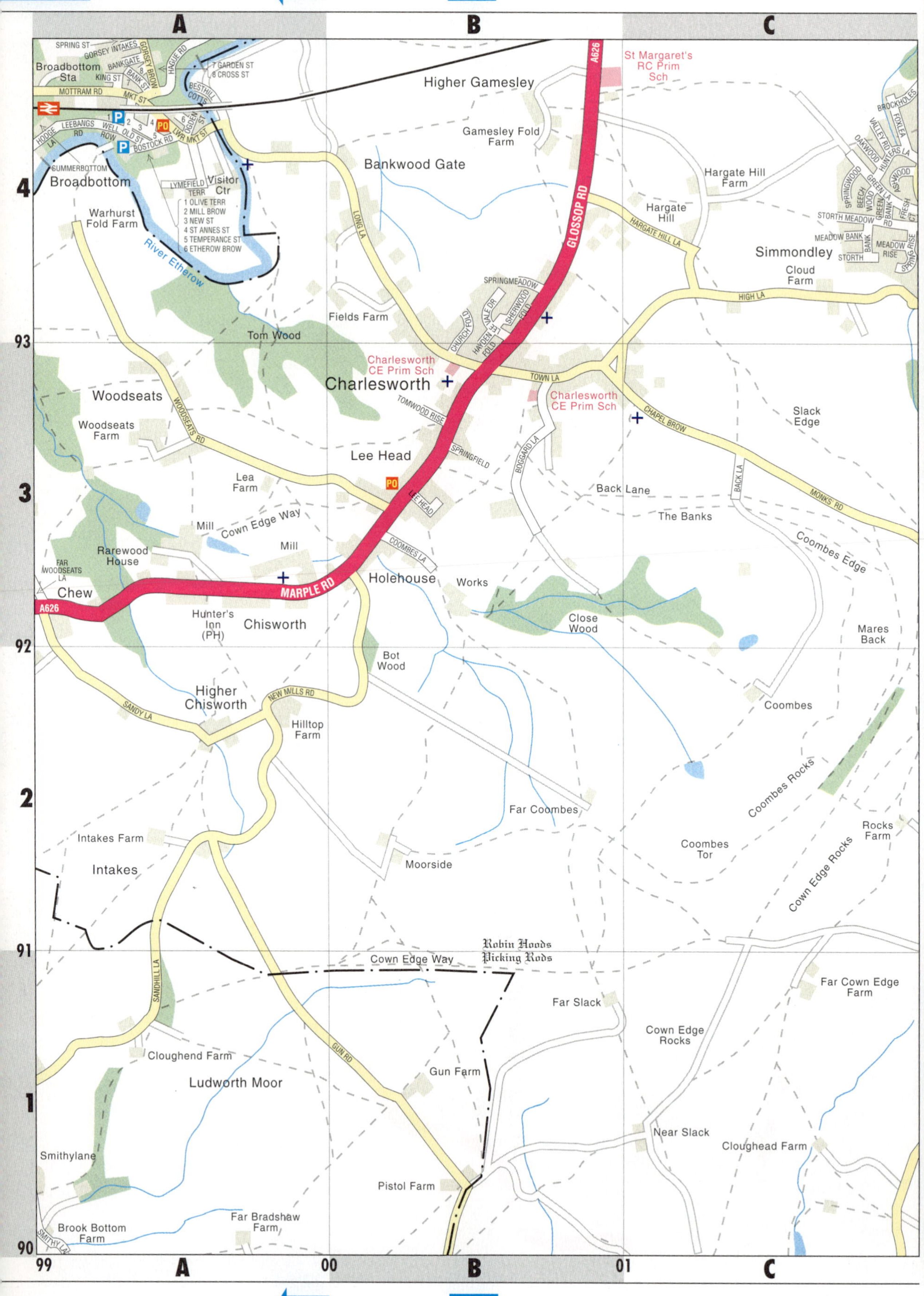
A
B
C
Broadbottom Sta
Broadbottom
SPRING ST
GORSEY INTAKES
BANKGATE
KING ST
GORSEY BROW
HAGUE RD
7 GARDEN ST
8 CROSS ST
MOTTRAM RD
MKT ST
BESTHILL COTTS
LEEBANGS RD
WELL ROW
OLD ST
BOSTOCK RD
LWR MKT ST
OGDEN ST
HODGE LA
SUMMERBOTTOM
LYMEFIELD TERR
Visitor Ctr
1 OLIVE TERR
2 MILL BROW
3 NEW ST
4 ST ANNES ST
5 TEMPERANCE ST
6 ETHEROW BROW
Warhurst Fold Farm
River Etherow
Higher Gamesley
Gamesley Fold Farm
Bankwood Gate
LONG LA
A626
GLOSSOP RD
St Margaret's RC Prim Sch
Hargate Hill Farm
Hargate Hill
HARGATE HILL LA
Simmondley
BROCKHOLES
FOXLEA
VALLEY RD
OAKWOOD
HUNTERS LA
SPRINGWOOD
BEECH WOOD
GREEN LA
ASHWOOD
STORTH MEADOW RD
MEADOW BANK
STORTH
MEADOW RISE
SPRING RISE
Cloud Farm
HIGH LA
SPRINGMEADOW
VALE DR
CHURCH FOLD
HAYDEN FOLD
SHERWOOD FOLD
Fields Farm
Tom Wood
Charlesworth CE Prim Sch
Charlesworth
TOWN LA
Charlesworth CE Prim Sch
CHAPEL BROW
Woodseats
Woodseats Farm
WOODSEATS RD
TOMWOOD RISE
Slack Edge
Lee Head
SPRINGFIELD
BOGGARD LA
BACK LA
Lea Farm
PO
LEE HEAD
Back Lane
The Banks
MONKS RD
Mill
Cown Edge Way
Mill
COOMBES LA
Coombes Edge
Rarewood House
FAR WOODSEATS LA
Chew
MARPLE RD
Holehouse
Works
A626
Hunter's Inn (PH)
Chisworth
Close Wood
Mares Back
Bot Wood
Higher Chisworth
NEW MILLS RD
SANDY LA
Hilltop Farm
Coombes
Coombes Rocks
Far Coombes
Intakes Farm
Rocks Farm
Intakes
Moorside
Coombes Tor
Cown Edge Rocks
Robin Hoods Picking Rods
Cown Edge Way
Far Cown Edge Farm
SANDHILL LA
Far Slack
Cown Edge Rocks
Cloughend Farm
Ludworth Moor
GUN RD
Gun Farm
Near Slack
Cloughead Farm
Smithylane
Pistol Farm
Brook Bottom Farm
Far Bradshaw Farm
SMITHY LA
4
93
3
92
2
91
1
90
99
00
01

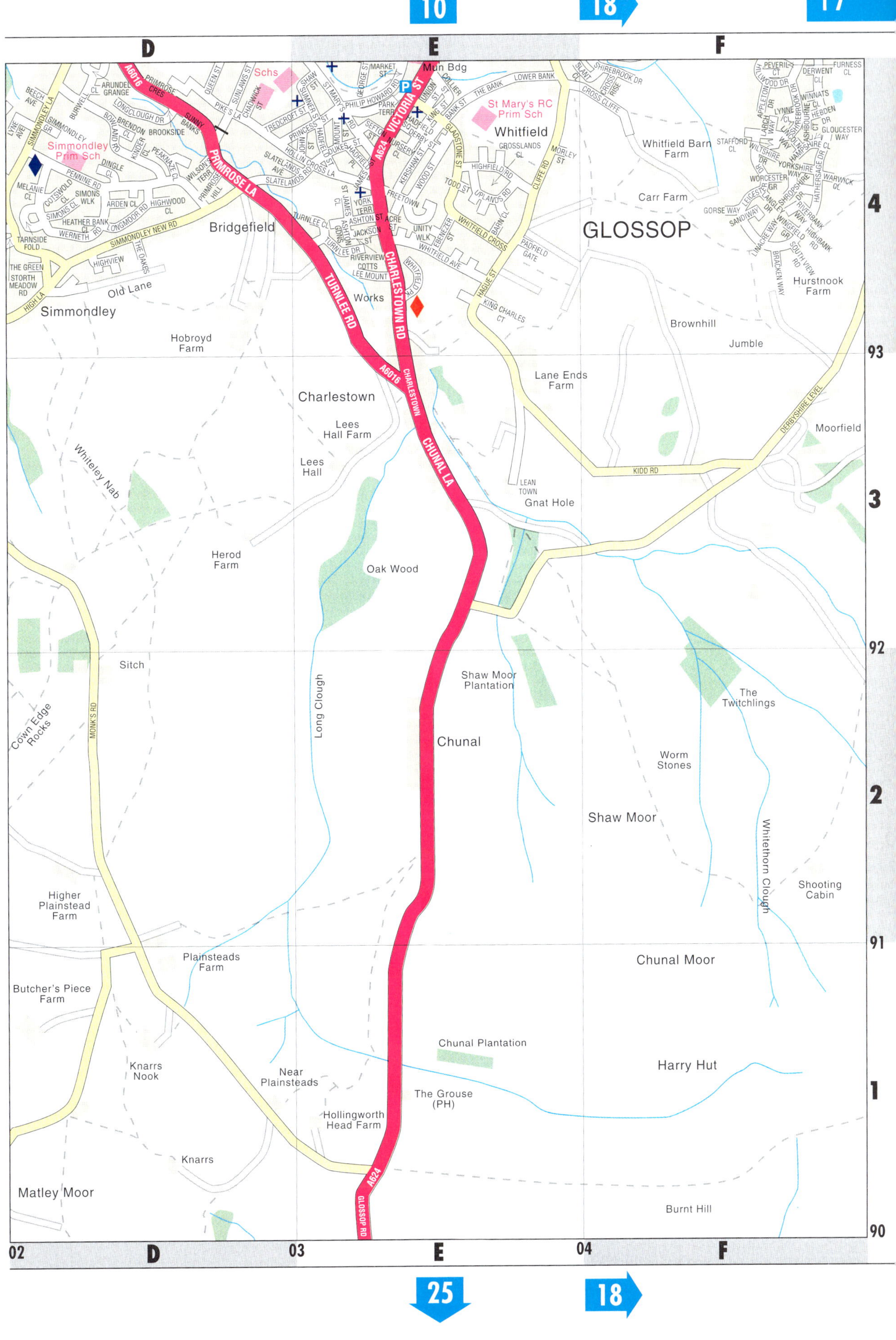
10
18
D
E
F
Schs
Mun Bdg
St Mary's RC
Prim Sch
Whitfield
Simmondley
Prim Sch
Whitfield Barn
Farm
Carr Farm
GLOSSOP
Bridgefield
Simmondley
Old Lane
Works
Hobroyd
Farm
Hurstnook
Farm
Brownhill
Jumble
Lane Ends
Farm
Charlestown
Lees
Hall Farm
Lees
Hall
Whiteley Nab
Moorfield
LEAN
TOWN
Gnat Hole
Herod
Farm
Oak Wood
Sitch
Shaw Moor
Plantation
The
Twitchlings
Cown Edge
Rocks
Long Clough
Chunal
Worm
Stones
Shaw Moor
Whitethorn Clough
Shooting
Cabin
Higher
Plainstead
Farm
Plainsteads
Farm
Chunal Moor
Butcher's Piece
Farm
Chunal Plantation
Knarrs
Nook
Near
Plainsteads
Harry Hut
The Grouse
(PH)
Hollingworth
Head Farm
Knarrs
Matley Moor
Burnt Hill
PRIMROSE LA
TURNLEE RD
CHARLESTOWN RD
VICTORIA ST
CHUNAL LA
A6016
A624
GLOSSOP RD
SIMMONDLEY NEW RD
KIDD RD
DERBYSHIRE LEVEL
MONK'S RD
CLIFFE RD
HAGUE ST
4
93
3
92
2
91
1
90
02
03
04
25
18

A   B   C

CH

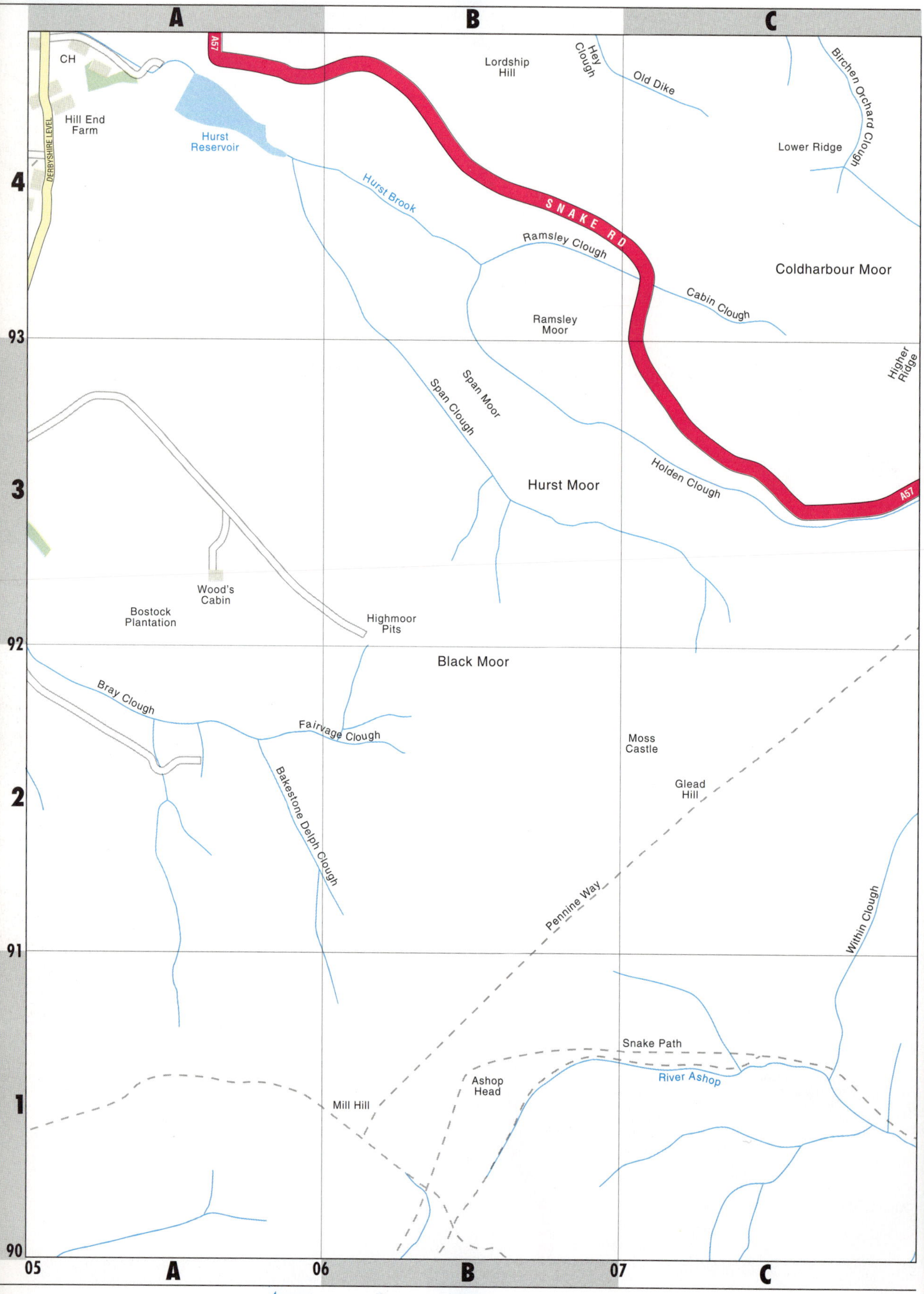

DERBYSHIRE LEVEL

Hill End
Farm

Hurst
Reservoir

A57

Lordship
Hill

Hey
Clough

Old Dike

Birchen Orchard Clough

Lower Ridge

4

Hurst Brook

S N A K E   R D

Ramsley Clough

Cabin Clough

Coldharbour Moor

93

Ramsley
Moor

Span Moor

Span Clough

Higher
Ridge

Hurst Moor

Holden Clough

3

A57

Wood's
Cabin

Bostock
Plantation

Highmoor
Pits

92

Black Moor

Bray Clough

Fairvage Clough

Moss
Castle

Glead
Hill

2

Bakestone Delph Clough

Within Clough

Pennine Way

91

Snake Path

River Ashop

Ashop
Head

1

Mill Hill

90

05   A   06   B   07   C

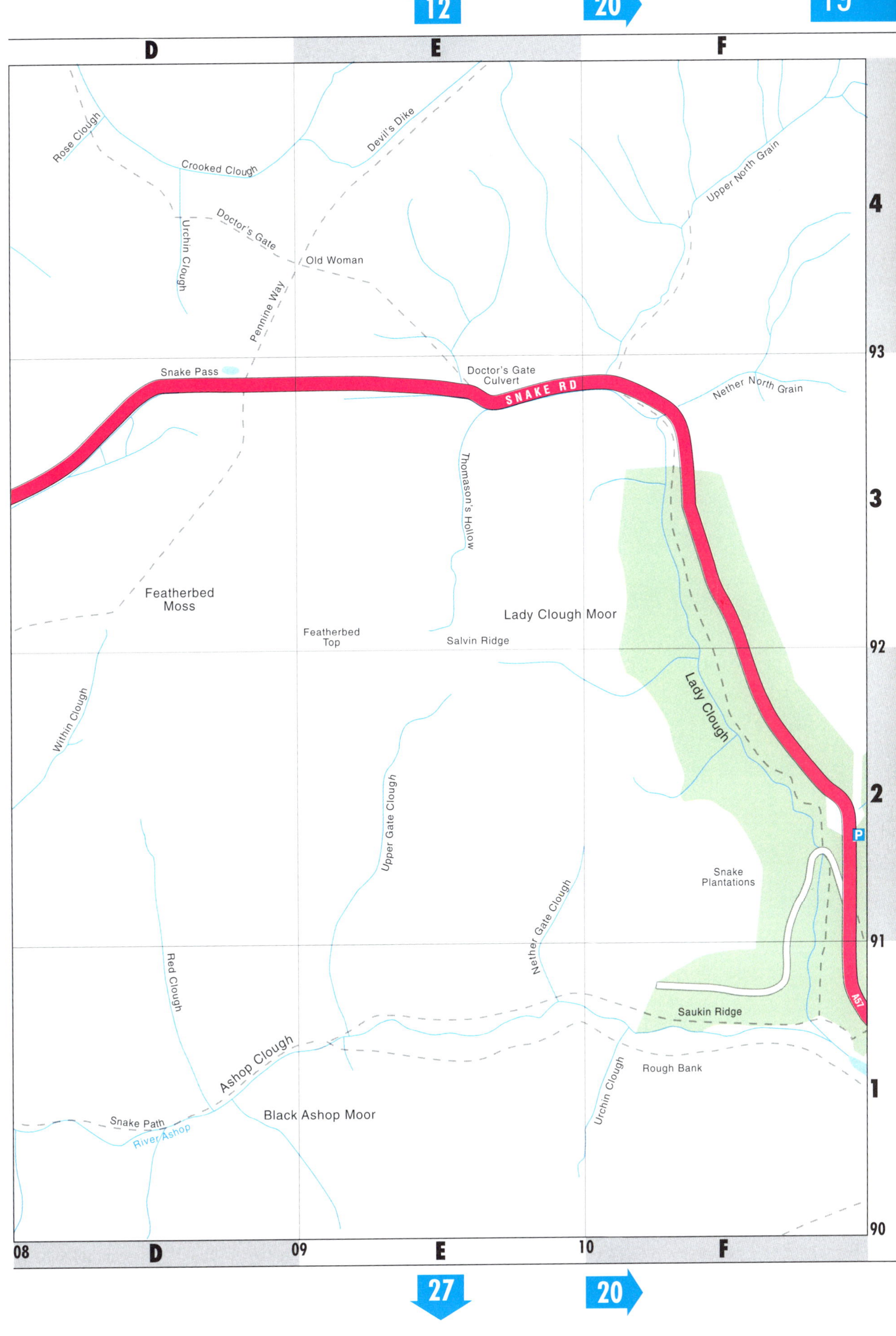

D
E
F

Rose Clough

Crooked Clough

Devil's Dike

Upper North Grain

4

Urchin Clough

Doctor's Gate

Old Woman

Pennine Way

93

Snake Pass

Doctor's Gate
Culvert

SNAKE RD

Nether North Grain

3

Thomason's Hollow

Featherbed
Moss

Lady Clough Moor

Lady Clough

Featherbed
Top

Salvin Ridge

92

Within Clough

Upper Gate Clough

2

P

Snake
Plantations

Nether Gate Clough

Red Clough

91

A57

Ashop Clough

Saukin Ridge

Urchin Clough

Rough Bank

1

Snake Path

Black Ashop Moor

River Ashop

90

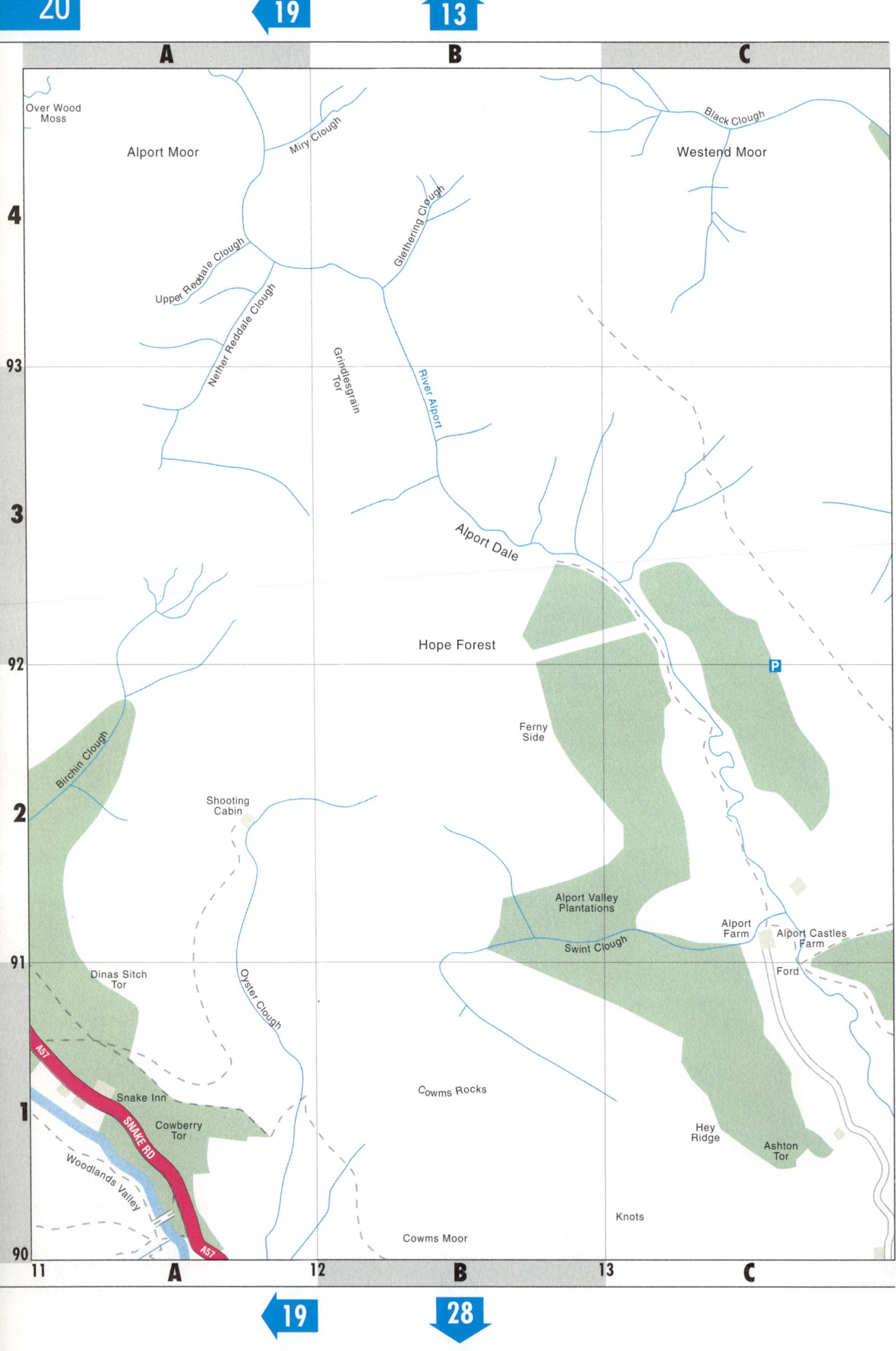

A   **B**   **C**

Over Wood Moss

Alport Moor

Miry Clough

Black Clough

Westend Moor

4

Upper Reddale Clough

Glethering Clough

Nether Reddale Clough

Grindlesgrain Tor

River Alport

93

3

Alport Dale

Hope Forest

92

P

Ferny Side

Birchin Clough

2

Shooting Cabin

Alport Valley Plantations

Alport Farm

Alport Castles Farm

Swint Clough

91

Dinas Sitch Tor

Oyster Clough

Ford

A57

Cowms Rocks

Hey Ridge

Snake Inn

1

Cowberry Tor

SNAKE RD

Ashton Tor

Woodlands Valley

Knots

A57

90

Cowms Moor

11   **A**   **12**   **B**   **13**   **C**

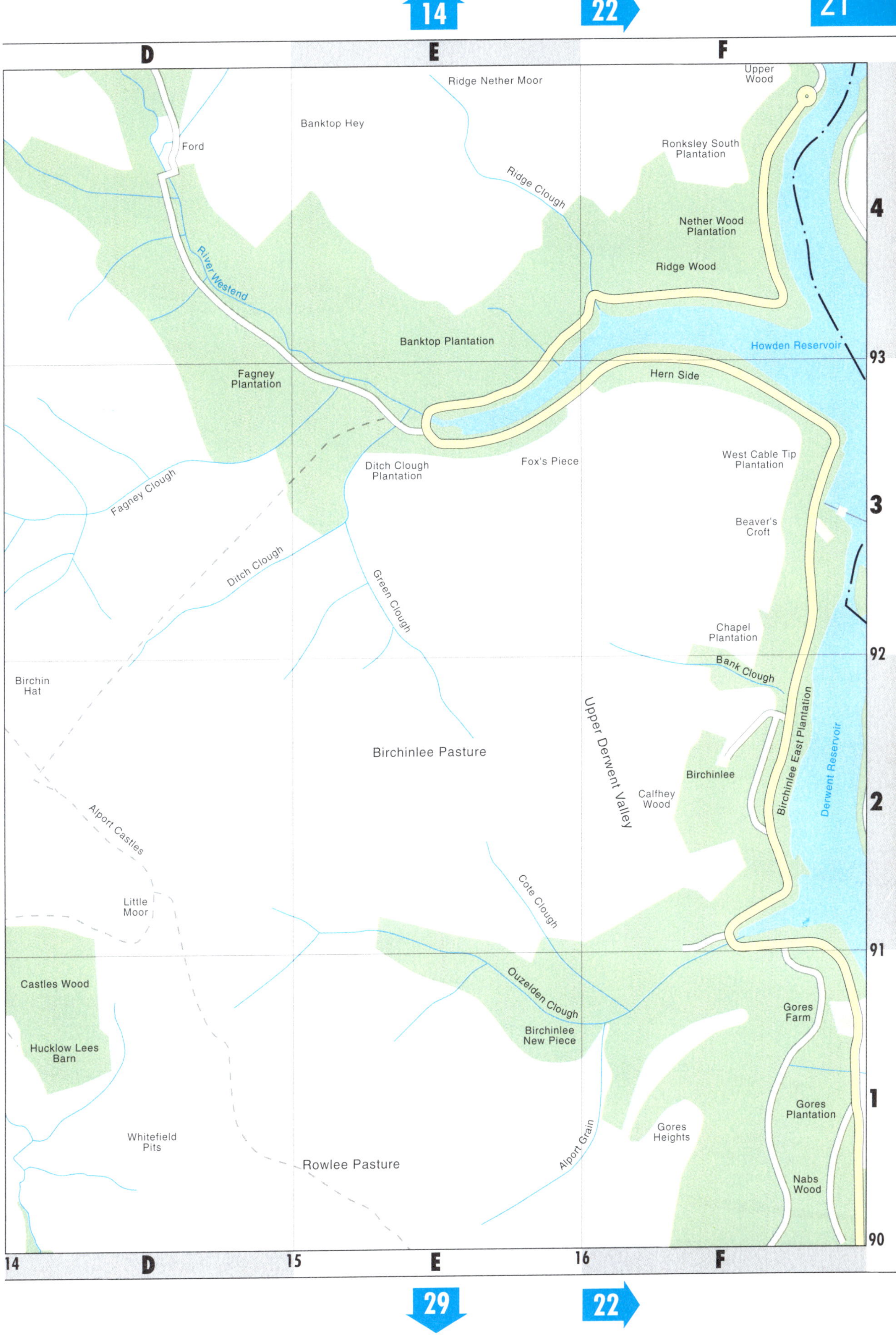

D
E
F

Upper Wood

Ridge Nether Moor

Banktop Hey

Ronksley South Plantation

Ford

Ridge Clough

Nether Wood Plantation

4

River Westend

Ridge Wood

Banktop Plantation

Howden Reservoir

93

Fagney Plantation

Hern Side

West Cable Tip Plantation

Ditch Clough Plantation

Fox's Piece

Beaver's Croft

3

Fagney Clough

Ditch Clough

Green Clough

Chapel Plantation

Bank Clough

92

Birchin Hat

Birchinlee Pasture

Upper Derwent Valley

Birchinlee East Plantation

Derwent Reservoir

Birchinlee

Calfhey Wood

2

Alport Castles

Little Moor

Cote Clough

91

Castles Wood

Ouzelden Clough

Gores Farm

Hucklow Lees Barn

Birchinlee New Piece

Gores Plantation

1

Whitefield Pits

Gores Heights

Alport Grain

Nabs Wood

Rowlee Pasture

90

14
D
15
E
16
F

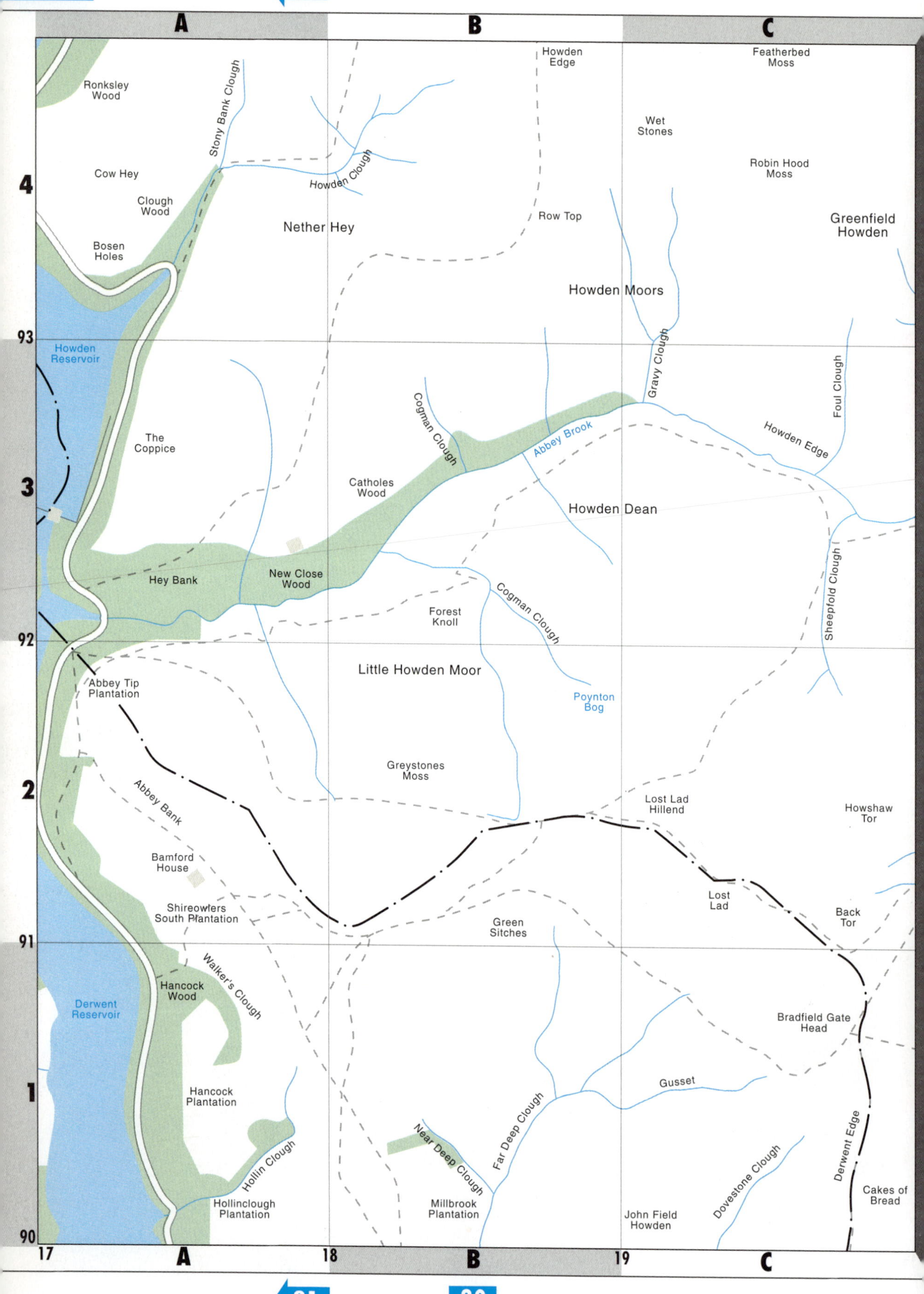

A B C

Ronksley
Wood

Howden
Edge

Featherbed
Moss

Stony Bank Clough

Wet
Stones

Cow Hey

4

Clough
Wood

Howden Clough

Robin Hood
Moss

Nether Hey

Row Top

Greenfield
Howden

Bosen
Holes

Howden Moors

93

Howden
Reservoir

Gravy Clough

Foul Clough

Cogman Clough

Abbey Brook

Howden Edge

The
Coppice

Catholes
Wood

Howden Dean

3

Sheepfold Clough

Hey Bank

New Close
Wood

Forest
Knoll

Cogman Clough

92

Little Howden Moor

Poynton
Bog

Abbey Tip
Plantation

Greystones
Moss

Abbey Bank

Lost Lad
Hillend

Howshaw
Tor

2

Bamford
House

Lost Lad

Back
Tor

Shireowlers
South Plantation

Green
Sitches

Walker's Clough

Bradfield Gate
Head

91

Derwent
Reservoir

Hancock
Wood

Gusset

1

Near Deep Clough

Far Deep Clough

Hancock
Plantation

Dovestone Clough

Derwent Edge

Hollin Clough

Millbrook
Plantation

John Field
Howden

Cakes of
Bread

Hollinclough
Plantation

90

17

A

18

B

19

C

15
24

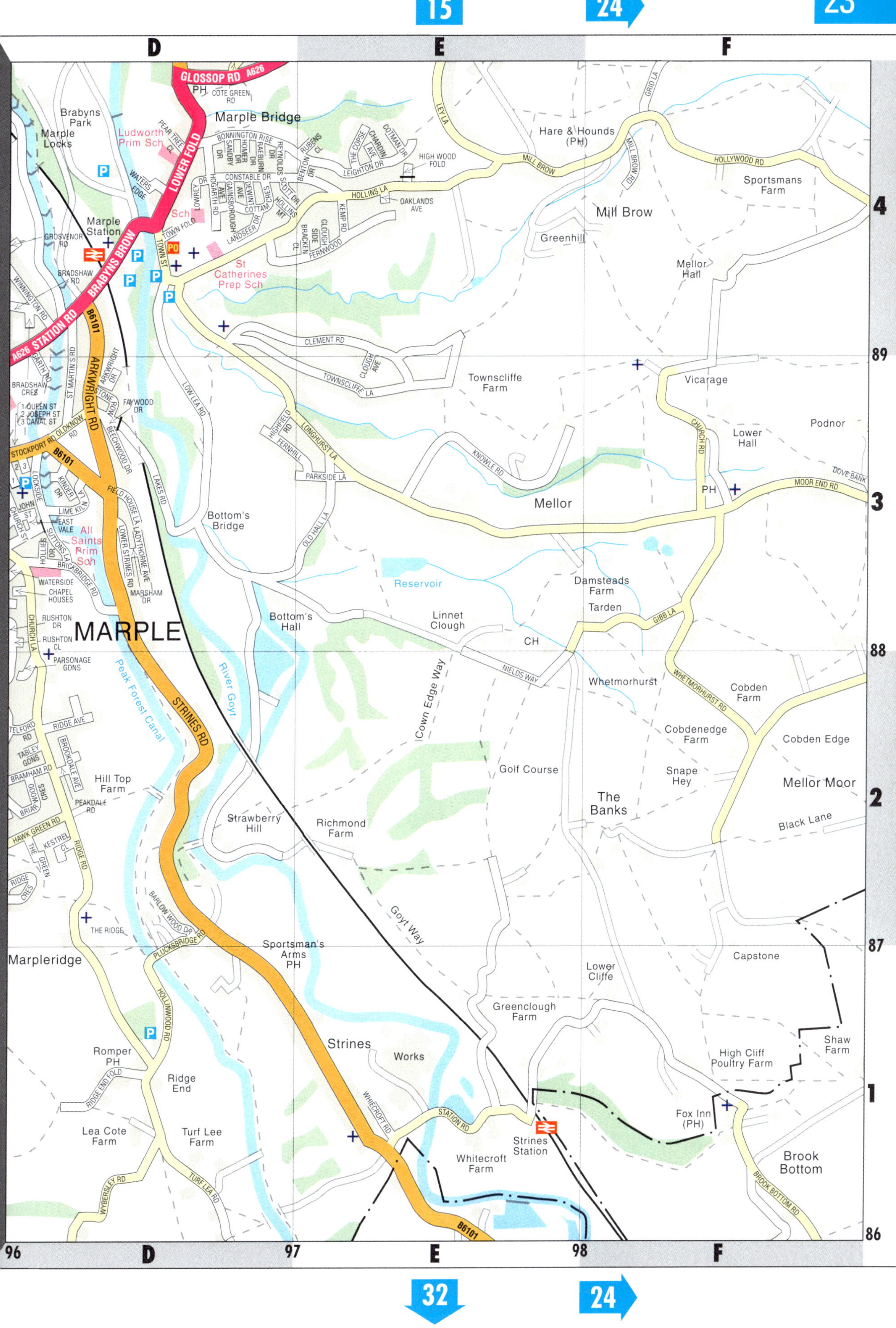
D
E
F
Marple Bridge
Brabyns Park
Marple Locks
Ludworth Prim Sch
Marple Station
St Catherines Prep Sch
GLOSSOP RD A626
LOWER FOLD
BRABYNS BROW
A626 STATION RD
Hare & Hounds (PH)
Mill Brow
Greenhill
Sportsmans Farm
Mellor Hall
Townscliffe Farm
Vicarage
Lower Hall
Podnor
Mellor
Bottom's Bridge
Reservoir
Damsteads Farm
Tarden
Bottom's Hall
Linnet Clough
CH
MARPLE
All Saints Prim Sch
Peak Forest Canal
River Goyt
STRINES RD
Whetmorhurst
Cobden Farm
Cobdenedge Farm
Cobden Edge
Snape Hey
Mellor Moor
Golf Course
The Banks
Black Lane
Hill Top Farm
Strawberry Hill
Richmond Farm
Cown Edge Way
Goyt Way
Marpleridge
Sportsman's Arms PH
Lower Cliffe
Capstone
Greenclough Farm
Strines
Works
Shaw Farm
High Cliff Poultry Farm
Romper PH
Ridge End
Fox Inn (PH)
Lea Cote Farm
Turf Lee Farm
Strines Station
Whitecroft Farm
Brook Bottom
4
89
3
88
2
87
1
86
96
97
98

32
24

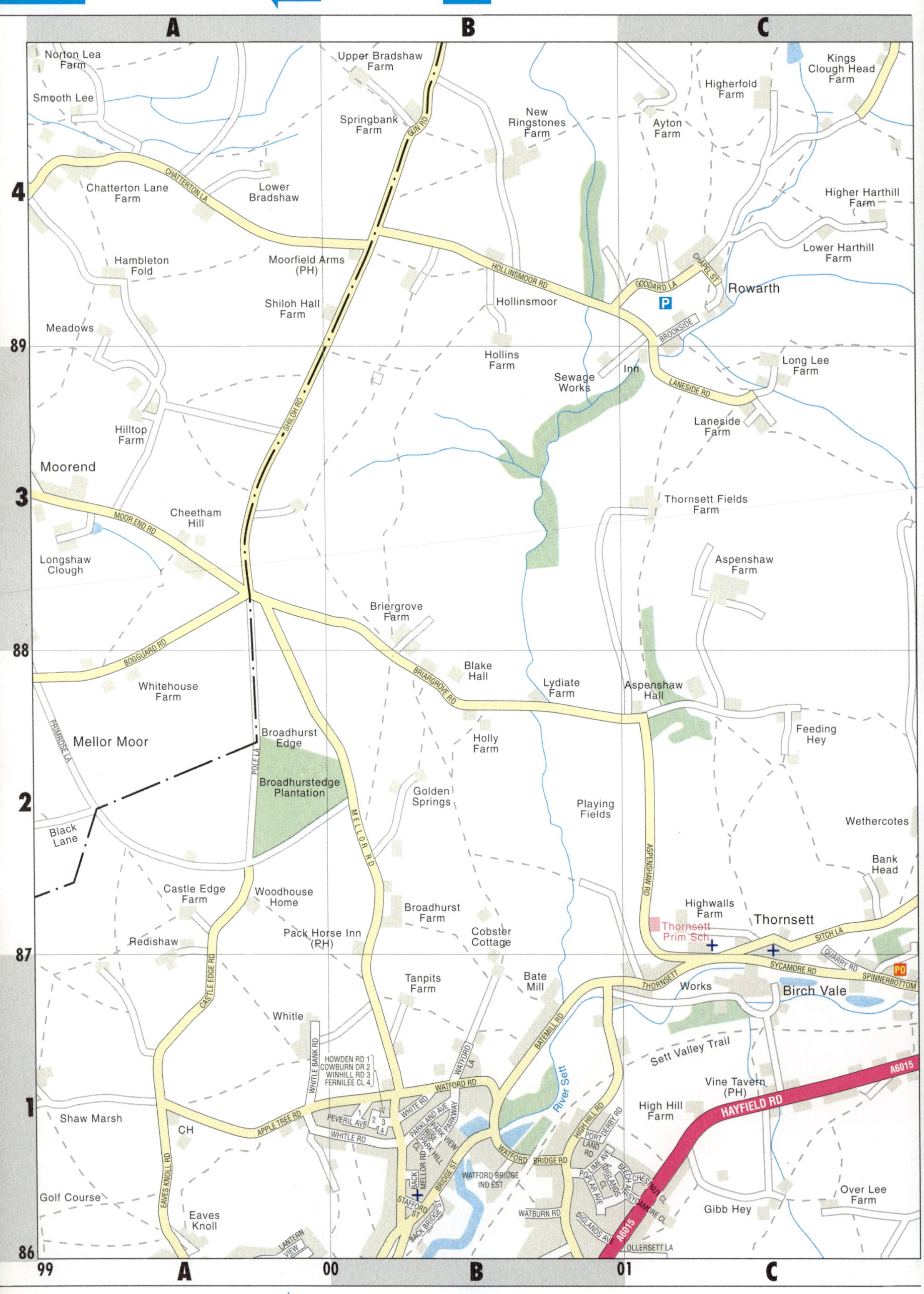
Norton Lea Farm
Smooth Lee
Upper Bradshaw Farm
Springbank Farm
New Ringstones Farm
Ayton Farm
Higherfold Farm
Kings Clough Head Farm
Chatterton Lane Farm
Lower Bradshaw
Higher Harthill Farm
Lower Harthill Farm
Hambleton Fold
Moorfield Arms (PH)
Hollinsmoor
Rowarth
Shiloh Hall Farm
Meadows
Hollins Farm
Sewage Works
Inn
Long Lee Farm
Laneside Farm
Hilltop Farm
Moorend
Cheetham Hill
Thornsett Fields Farm
Longshaw Clough
Aspenshaw Farm
Briergrove Farm
Blake Hall
Lydiate Farm
Aspenshaw Hall
Whitehouse Farm
Mellor Moor
Broadhurst Edge
Holly Farm
Feeding Hey
Broadhurstedge Plantation
Golden Springs
Playing Fields
Wethercotes
Black Lane
Bank Head
Castle Edge Farm
Woodhouse Home
Broadhurst Farm
Highwalls Farm
Thornsett
Thornsett Prim Sch
Redishaw
Pack Horse Inn (PH)
Cobster Cottage
Tanpits Farm
Bate Mill
Works
Birch Vale
Whitle
Sett Valley Trail
Vine Tavern (PH)
High Hill Farm
Shaw Marsh
CH
Golf Course
Eaves Knoll
Gibb Hey
Over Lee Farm
River Sett
Watford Bridge Ind Est
GUN RD
CHATTERTON LA
HOLLINSMOOR RD
GODDARD LA
CHAPEL ST
BROOKSIDE
LANESIDE RD
SHILOH RD
MOOR END RD
BOGGUARD RD
BRIARGROVE RD
PRIMROSE LA
POLE LA
MELLOR RD
ASPENSHAW RD
CASTLE EDGE RD
SITCH LA
QUARRY RD
SYCAMORE RD
SPINNERBOTTOM
THORNSETT
BATEMILL RD
HOWDEN RD 1
COWBURN DR 2
WINHILL RD 3
FERNILEE CL 4
WHITLE BANK RD
WATFORD RD
WATFORD LA
APPLE TREE RD
PEVERIL AVE
WHITLE RD
WHITE RD
PARKLAND AVE
PARK VIEW
PARKWAY
RISE
PARK HILL
MELLOR RD
BACK
BRIDGE ST
STAFFORD ST
BACK BRIDGE ST
WATFORD BRIDGE RD
HIGH HILL RD
DERBY RD
PORT LAND RD
LIME AVE
POPLAR AVE
DIGLANDS AVE
DIGLANDS CL
CHESTNUT CL
BEECH AVE
SYCAMORE CL
WATBURN RD
EAVES KNOLL RD
LANTERN VIEW
OLLERSETT LA
HAYFIELD RD
A6015
P
PO
A
B
C
4
3
2
1
89
88
87
86
99
00
01

23
16
23
33

17
26

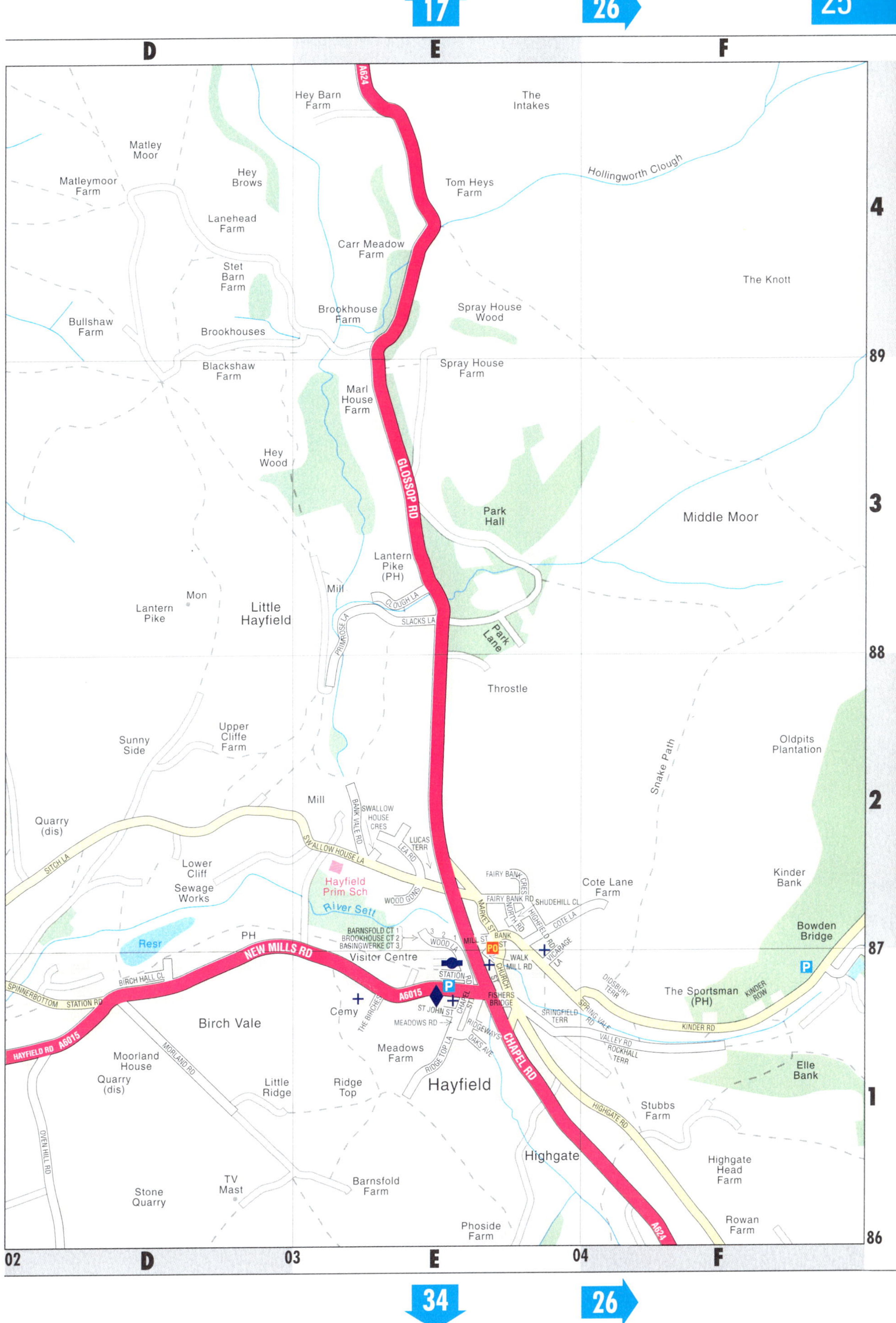
D
E
F
A624
Hey Barn Farm
The Intakes
Matley Moor
Matleymoor Farm
Hey Brows
Lanehead Farm
Tom Heys Farm
Hollingworth Clough
4
Carr Meadow Farm
Stet Barn Farm
The Knott
Bullshaw Farm
Brookhouse Farm
Spray House Wood
Brookhouses
Blackshaw Farm
Spray House Farm
89
Marl House Farm
Hey Wood
GLOSSOP RD
Park Hall
Middle Moor
3
Lantern Pike (PH)
Mon
Mill
Lantern Pike
Little Hayfield
CLOUGH LA
SLACKS LA
PRIMROSE LA
Park Lane
88
Throstle
Upper Cliffe Farm
Sunny Side
Snake Path
Oldpits Plantation
Mill
2
Quarry (dis)
BANK VALE RD
SWALLOW HOUSE CRES
LUCAS TERR
LEA RD
SITCH LA
SWALLOW HOUSE LA
Lower Cliff
Sewage Works
Hayfield Prim Sch
FAIRY BANK CRES
Cote Lane Farm
Kinder Bank
FAIRY BANK RD
SHUDEHILL CL
WOOD GDNS
River Sett
MARKET ST
NORTH RD
HIGHFIELD RD
COTE LA
Bowden Bridge
PH
BARNSFOLD CT
BROOKHOUSE CT
BASINGWERKE CT
WOOD LA
MILL ST
BANK ST
PO
VICARAGE LA
87
Resr
NEW MILLS RD
Visitor Centre
WALK MILL RD
P
BIRCH HALL CL
STATION RD
CHURCH ST
DIDSBURY TERR
The Sportsman (PH)
KINDER ROW
SPINNERBOTTOM
STATION RD
A6015
FISHERS BRIDGE
SPRING VALE RD
Cemy
THE BIRCHES
ST JOHN ST
CHAPEL ST
SPRINGFIELD TERR
KINDER RD
Birch Vale
MEADOWS RD
RIDGEWAYS
VALLEY RD
ROCKHALL TERR
HAYFIELD RD
A6015
OAKS AVE
MORLAND RD
Meadows Farm
RIDGE TOP LA
CHAPEL RD
Moorland House
Elle Bank
Quarry (dis)
Little Ridge
Ridge Top
Hayfield
1
HIGHGATE RD
Stubbs Farm
Highgate
Highgate Head Farm
OVEN HILL RD
TV Mast
Stone Quarry
Barnsfold Farm
Phoside Farm
Rowan Farm
A624
86
02
D
03
E
04
F

34
26

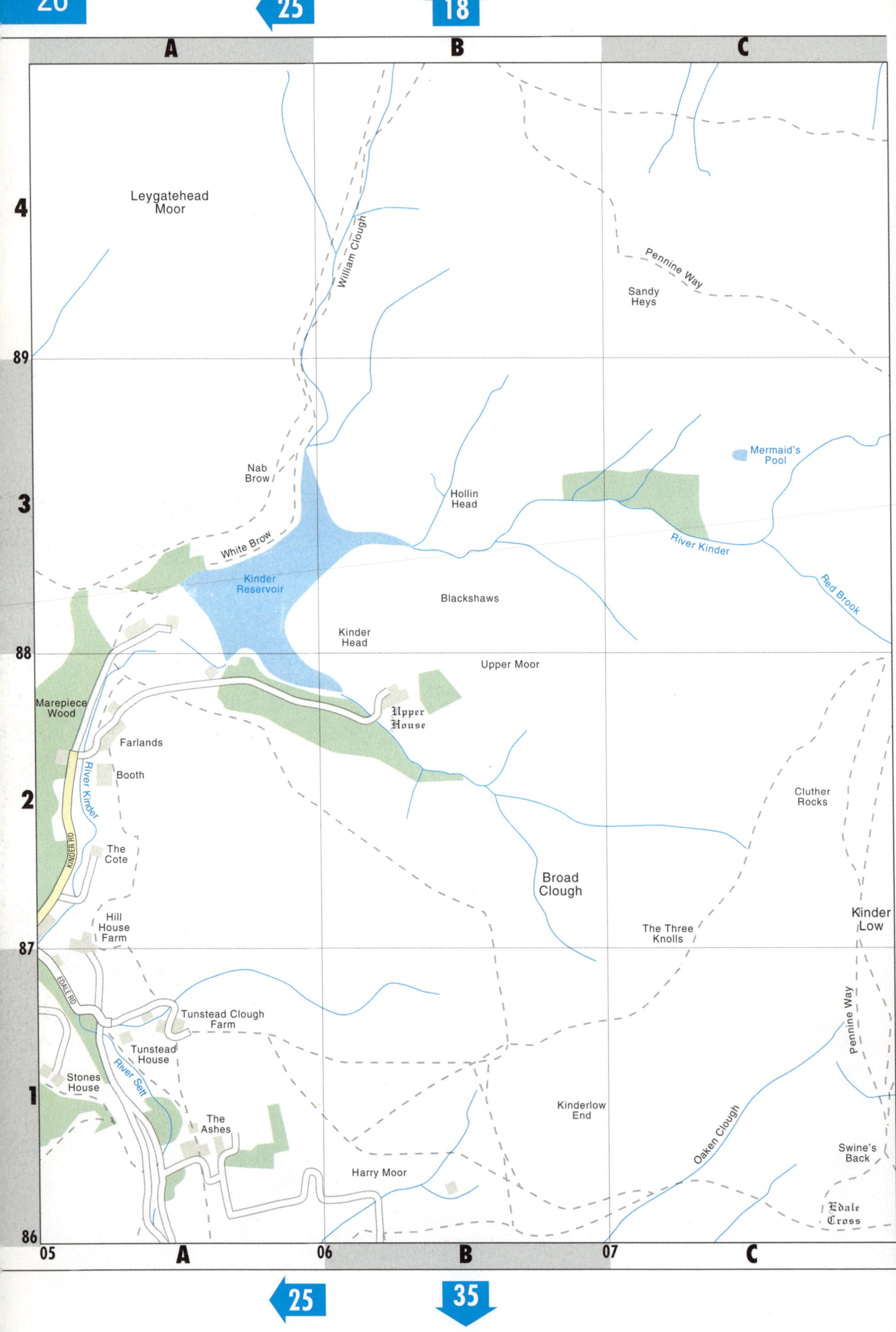

A
B
C

4

Leygatehead
Moor

William Clough

Pennine Way

Sandy
Heys

89

Mermaid's
Pool

Nab
Brow

Hollin
Head

3

River Kinder

White Brow

Kinder
Reservoir

Blackshaws

Red Brook

Kinder
Head

88

Upper Moor

Marepiece
Wood

Upper
House

Farlands

Cluther
Rocks

River Kinder

Booth

2

KINDER RD

The
Cote

Broad
Clough

Kinder
Low

Hill
House
Farm

The Three
Knolls

87

EDALE RD

Tunstead Clough
Farm

Pennine Way

Tunstead
House

Stones
House

1

Kinderlow
End

River Sett

The
Ashes

Oaken Clough

Swine's
Back

Harry Moor

Edale
Cross

86

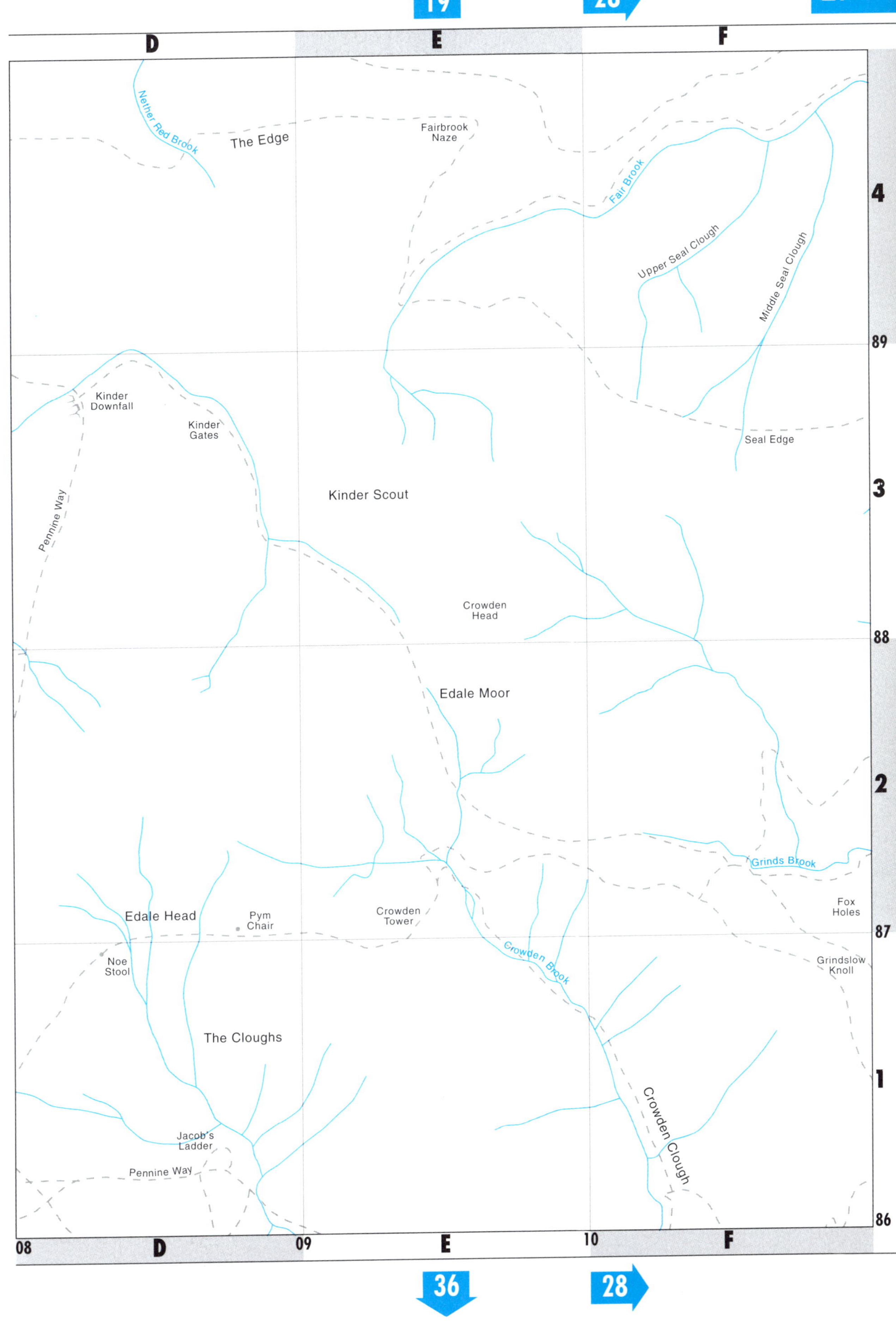

D   E   F

Nether Red Brook
The Edge
Fairbrook
Naze
Fair Brook
4
Upper Seal Clough
Middle Seal Clough
89
Kinder
Downfall
Kinder
Gates
Seal Edge
Pennine Way
Kinder Scout
3
Crowden
Head
88
Edale Moor
2
Grinds Brook
Edale Head
Pym
Chair
Crowden
Tower
Fox
Holes
87
Noe
Stool
Crowden Brook
Grindslow
Knoll
The Cloughs
1
Jacob's
Ladder
Crowden Clough
Pennine Way
86

08   D   09   E   10   F

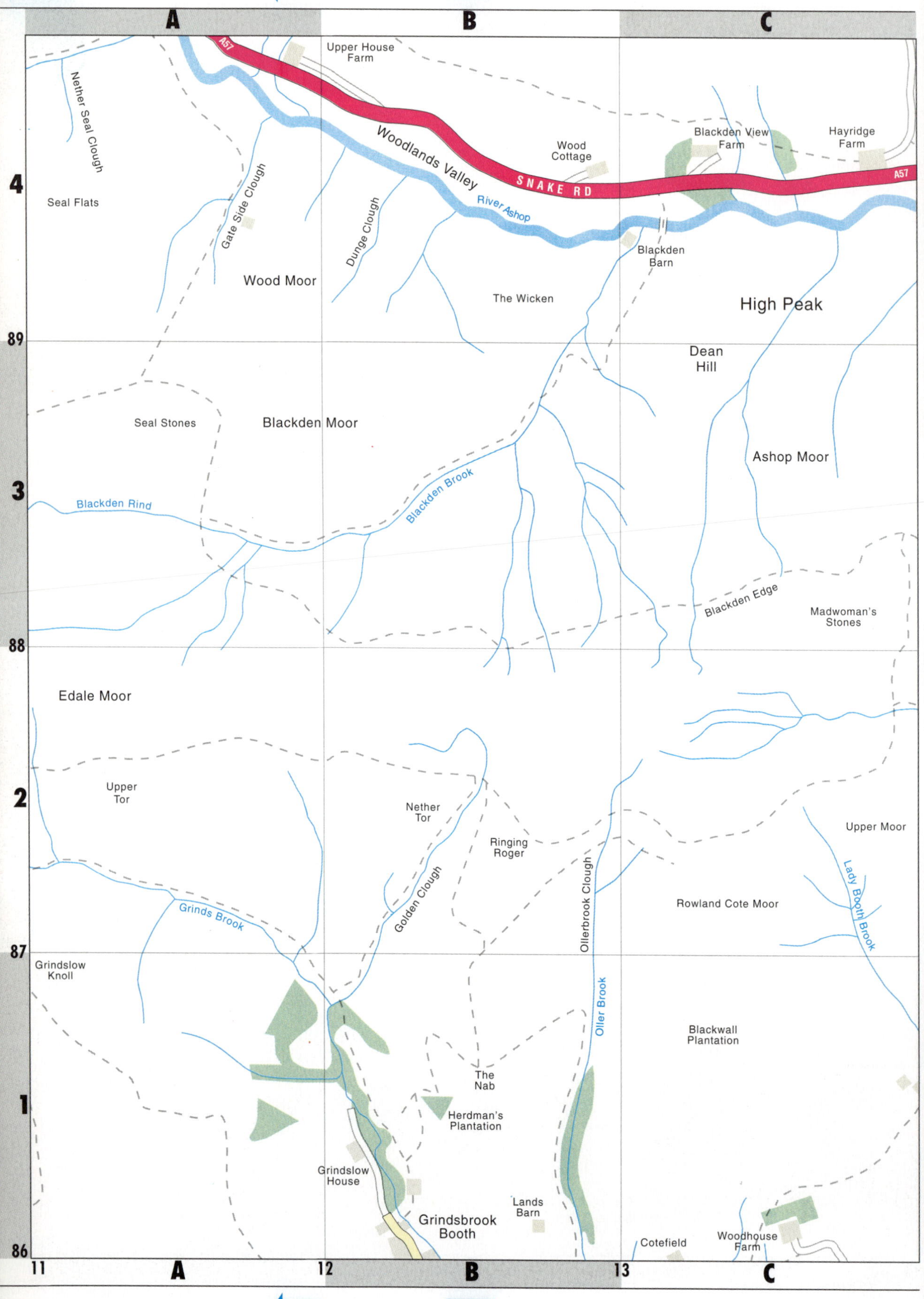

A57

Upper House Farm

Woodlands Valley

SNAKE RD

Wood Cottage

Blackden View Farm

Hayridge Farm

A57

Nether Seal Clough

Seal Flats

Gate Side Clough

Dunge Clough

River Ashop

Blackden Barn

4

Wood Moor

The Wicken

High Peak

Dean Hill

89

Seal Stones

Blackden Moor

Ashop Moor

3

Blackden Rind

Blackden Brook

Blackden Edge

Madwoman's Stones

88

Edale Moor

2

Upper Tor

Nether Tor

Ringing Roger

Upper Moor

Golden Clough

Ollerbrook Clough

Rowland Cote Moor

Lady Booth Brook

Grinds Brook

87

Grindslow Knoll

Oller Brook

Blackwall Plantation

1

The Nab

Herdman's Plantation

Grindslow House

Lands Barn

Cotefield

Woodhouse Farm

Grindsbrook Booth

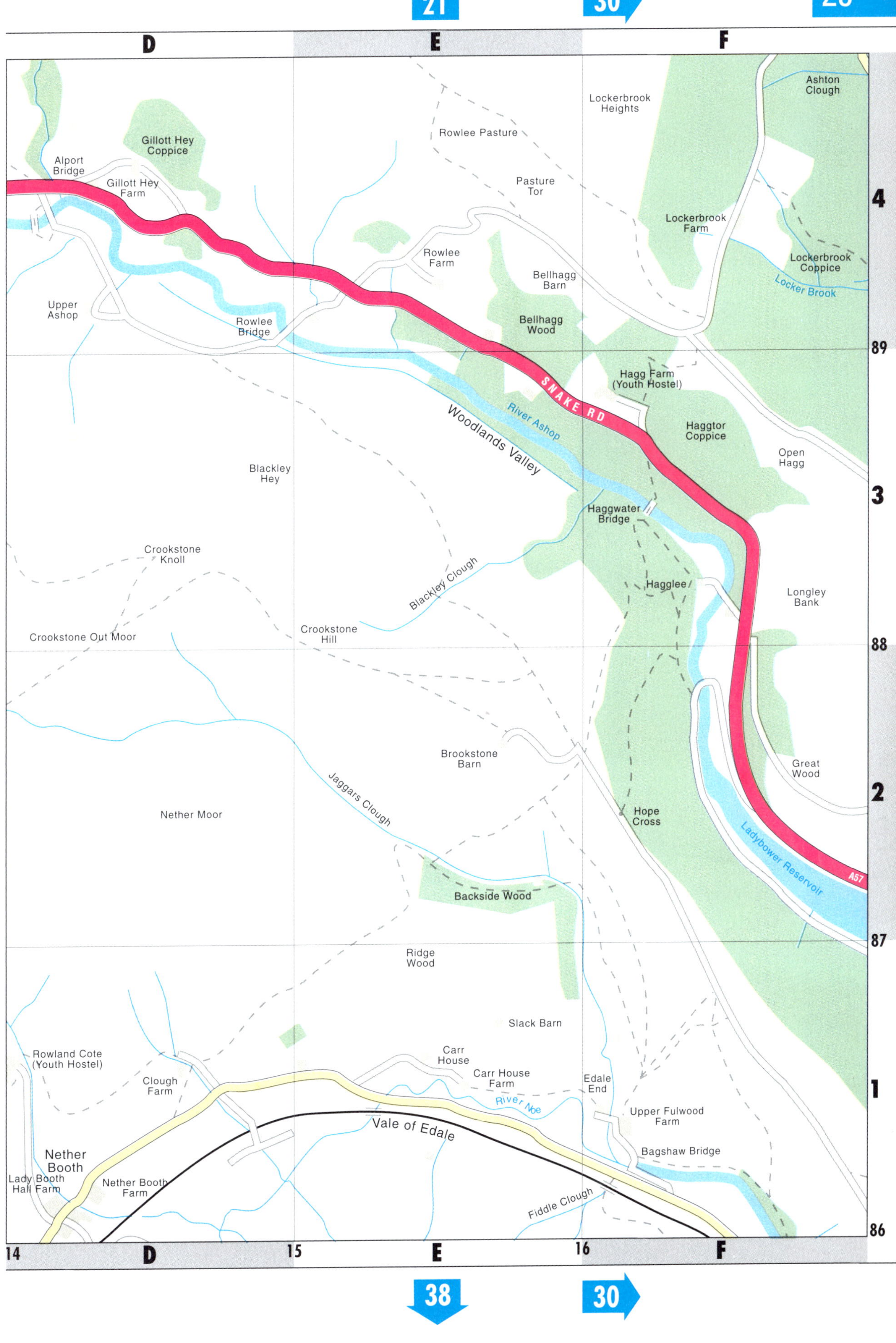
21
30
D
E
F
Ashton Clough
Lockerbrook Heights
Rowlee Pasture
Gillott Hey Coppice
Alport Bridge
Gillott Hey Farm
Pasture Tor
Lockerbrook Farm
Lockerbrook Coppice
Locker Brook
Rowlee Farm
Bellhagg Barn
Upper Ashop
Rowlee Bridge
Bellhagg Wood
4
89
Hagg Farm (Youth Hostel)
SNAKE RD
River Ashop
Woodlands Valley
Haggtor Coppice
Open Hagg
Blackley Hey
3
Haggwater Bridge
Crookstone Knoll
Hagglee
Longley Bank
Blackley Clough
Crookstone Out Moor
Crookstone Hill
88
Brookstone Barn
Great Wood
2
Jaggars Clough
Nether Moor
Hope Cross
Ladybower Reservoir
A57
Backside Wood
87
Ridge Wood
Slack Barn
Rowland Cote (Youth Hostel)
Carr House
Carr House Farm
Clough Farm
Edale End
1
River Noe
Upper Fulwood Farm
Vale of Edale
Bagshaw Bridge
Nether Booth
Lady Booth Hall Farm
Nether Booth Farm
Fiddle Clough
86
14
D
15
E
16
F
38
30

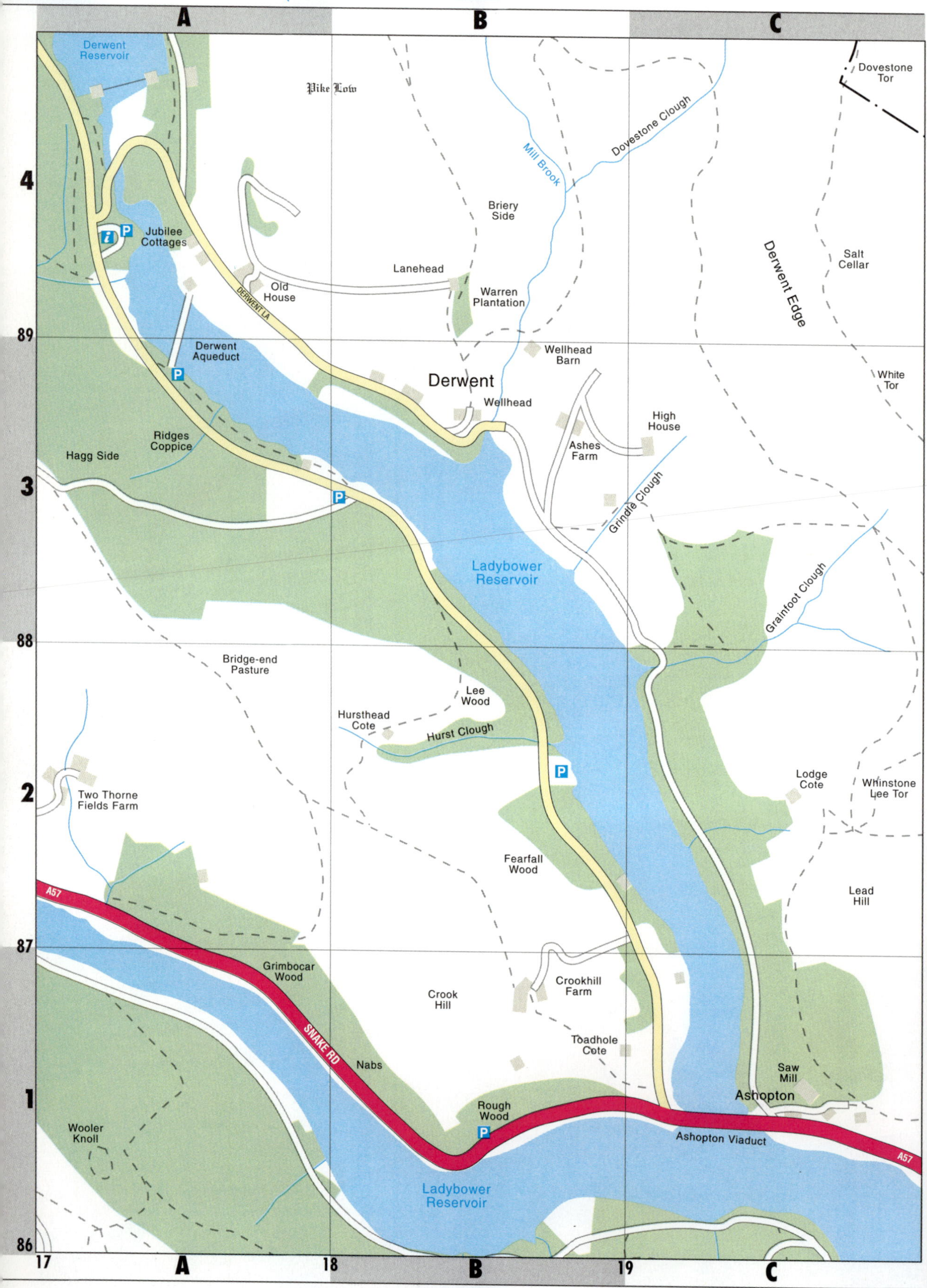

A B C

Derwent
Reservoir

Pike Low

Dovestone
Tor

Mill Brook

Dovestone Clough

4

Briery
Side

Derwent Edge

Salt
Cellar

Jubilee
Cottages

Lanehead

Old
House

Warren
Plantation

White
Tor

89

Derwent

Wellhead
Barn

Derwent
Aqueduct

Wellhead

High
House

Ridges
Coppice

Ashes
Farm

Hagg Side

DERWENT LA

3

Grindle Clough

Grainfoot Clough

Ladybower
Reservoir

88

Bridge-end
Pasture

Lee
Wood

Hursthead
Cote

Hurst Clough

2

Two Thorne
Fields Farm

Lodge
Cote

Whinstone
Lee Tor

Fearfall
Wood

Lead
Hill

A57

87

Grimbocar
Wood

Crookhill
Farm

SNAKE RD

Crook
Hill

Nabs

Toadhole
Cote

Saw
Mill

Ashopton

1

Wooler
Knoll

Rough
Wood

Ashopton Viaduct

A57

Ladybower
Reservoir

86

17 A 18 B 19 C

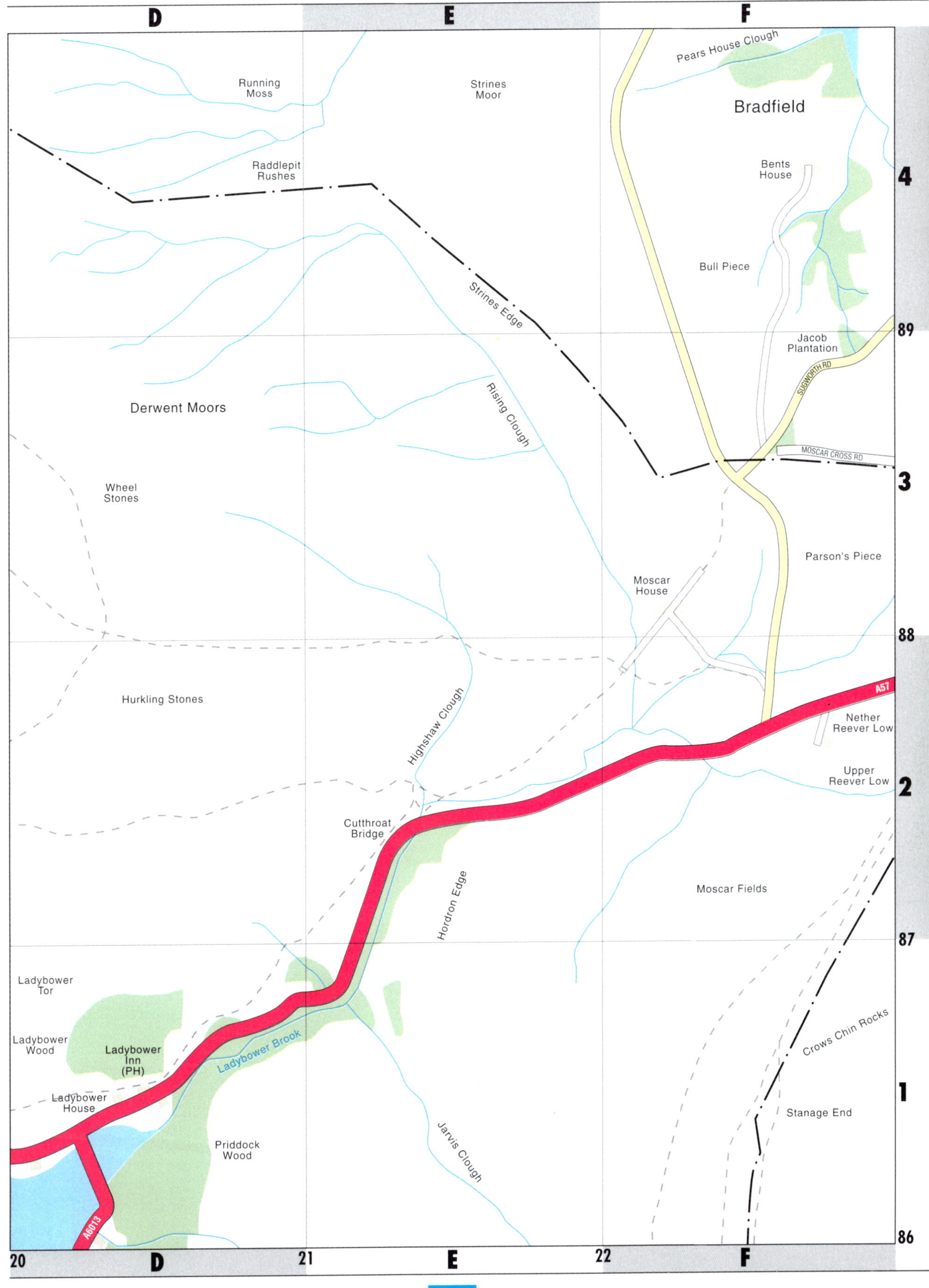

Pears House Clough

Bradfield

Running Moss

Strines Moor

Bents House

4

Raddlepit Rushes

Bull Piece

Jacob Plantation

89

Strines Edge

SIGSWORTH RD

Derwent Moors

Rising Clough

MOSCAR CROSS RD

3

Wheel Stones

Parson's Piece

Moscar House

88

Hurkling Stones

Highshaw Clough

A57

Nether Reever Low

Upper Reever Low

2

Cutthroat Bridge

Hordron Edge

Moscar Fields

87

Ladybower Tor

Crows Chin Rocks

Ladybower Wood

Ladybower Inn (PH)

Ladybower Brook

1

Ladybower House

Stanage End

Priddock Wood

Jarvis Clough

A6013

86

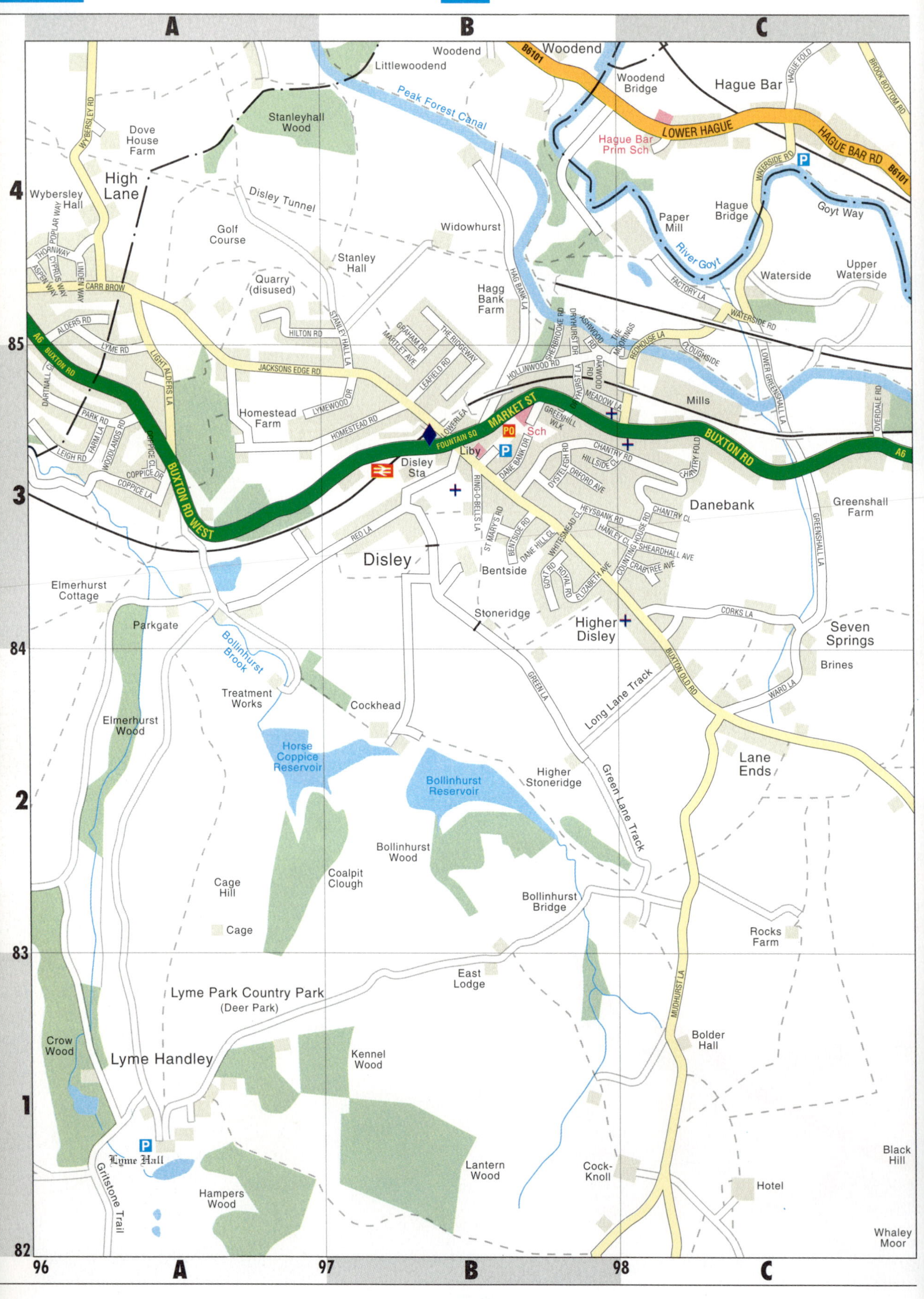

Woodend
Littlewoodend
Woodend
B6101 Woodend
Woodend Bridge
Hague Bar
Peak Forest Canal
LOWER HAGUE
HAGUE BAR RD B6101
Hague Bar Prim Sch
Hague Bridge
Goyt Way
Paper Mill
Upper Waterside
Waterside
River Goyt
WATERSIDE RD
Mills
High Lane
Wybersley Hall
Dove House Farm
Stanleyhall Wood
Disley Tunnel
Golf Course
Widowhurst
Hagg Bank Farm
Quarry (disused)
Stanley Hall
HILTON RD
Homestead Farm
JACKSONS EDGE RD
MARKET ST
FOUNTAIN SQ
Liby
PO
Sch
Greenhill WLK
Danebank
Disley Sta
Disley
RED LA
RING-O-BELLS LA
Bentside
Stoneridge
Higher Disley
Greenshall Farm
Seven Springs
Brines
Elmerhurst Cottage
Parkgate
Bollinhurst Brook
Treatment Works
Cockhead
Higher Stoneridge
Long Lane Track
Green Lane Track
Lane Ends
Elmerhurst Wood
Horse Coppice Reservoir
Bollinhurst Reservoir
Bollinhurst Wood
Coalpit Clough
Bollinhurst Bridge
Rocks Farm
Cage Hill
Cage
Lyme Park Country Park (Deer Park)
East Lodge
Bolder Hall
Crow Wood
Lyme Handley
Kennel Wood
Lyme Hall
Hampers Wood
Gritstone Trail
Lantern Wood
Cock-Knoll
Hotel
Black Hill
Whaley Moor

24
34

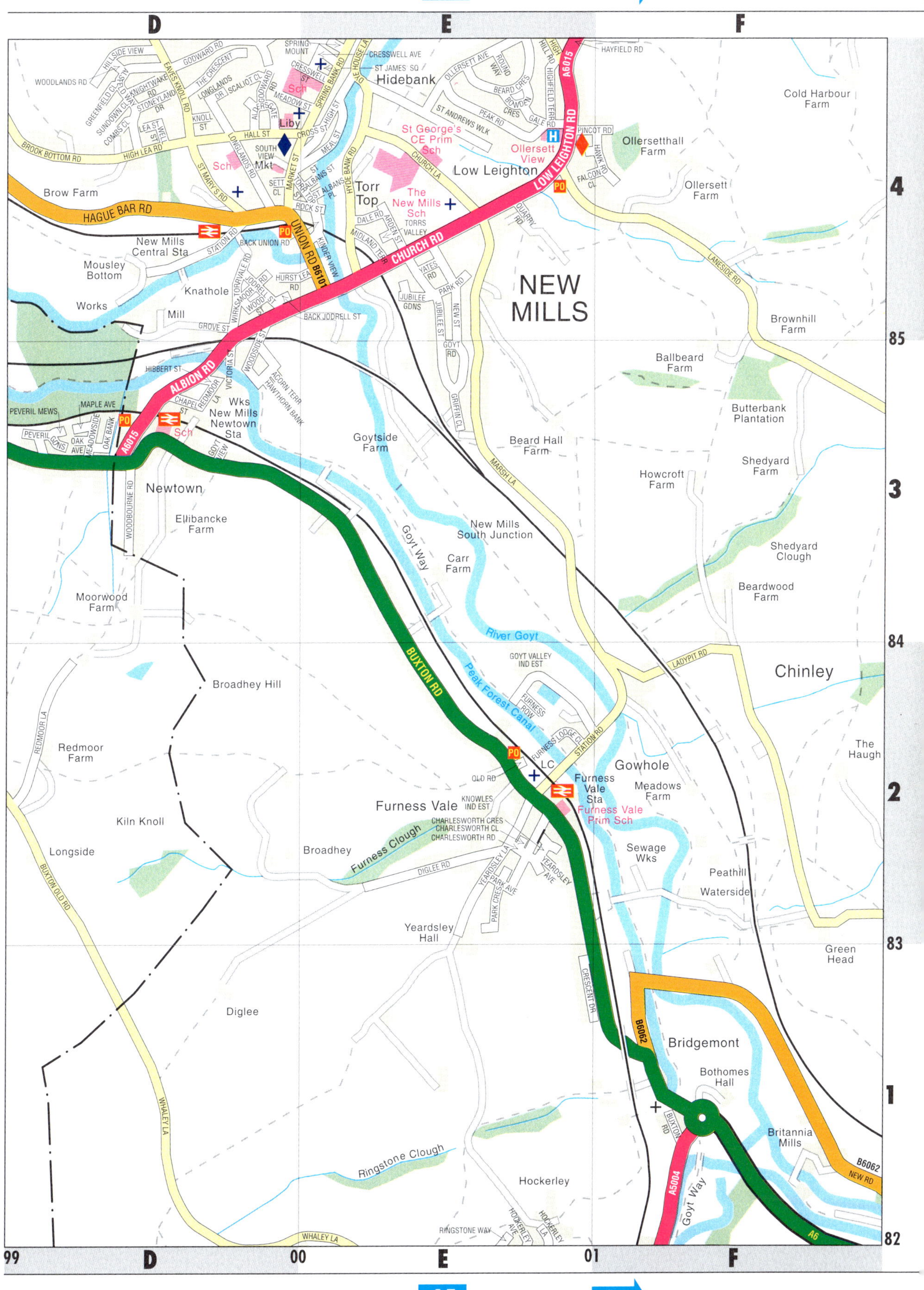

D
E
F
NEW MILLS
Hidebank
Low Leighton
Torr Top
Brow Farm
New Mills Central Sta
Mousley Bottom
Works
Knathole
Mill
Newtown
New Mills Newtown Sta
Ellibancke Farm
Moorwood Farm
Broadhey Hill
Redmoor Farm
Kiln Knoll
Longside
Diglee
Broadhey
Furness Vale
Furness Clough
Yeardsley Hall
Ringstone Clough
Hockerley
Goytside Farm
New Mills South Junction
Carr Farm
River Goyt
Peak Forest Canal
Goyt Way
BUXTON RD
Furness Vale Sta
Furness Vale Prim Sch
Gowhole
Meadows Farm
Sewage Wks
Peathill
Waterside
Bridgemont
Bothomes Hall
Britannia Mills
Chinley
Green Head
The Haugh
Beardwood Farm
Shedyard Clough
Shedyard Farm
Howcroft Farm
Beard Hall Farm
Butterbank Plantation
Ballbeard Farm
Brownhill Farm
Ollersett Farm
Ollersetthall Farm
Cold Harbour Farm
Ollersett View
St George's CE Prim Sch
The New Mills Sch
HAGUE BAR RD
CHURCH RD
ALBION RD
LOW LEIGHTON RD
UNION RD B6101
A6015
A5004
B6062
A6
LADYPIT RD
LANESIDE RD
MARSH LA
WHALEY LA
BUXTON OLD RD
85
84
83
82
4
3
2
1
99
00
01

45
34

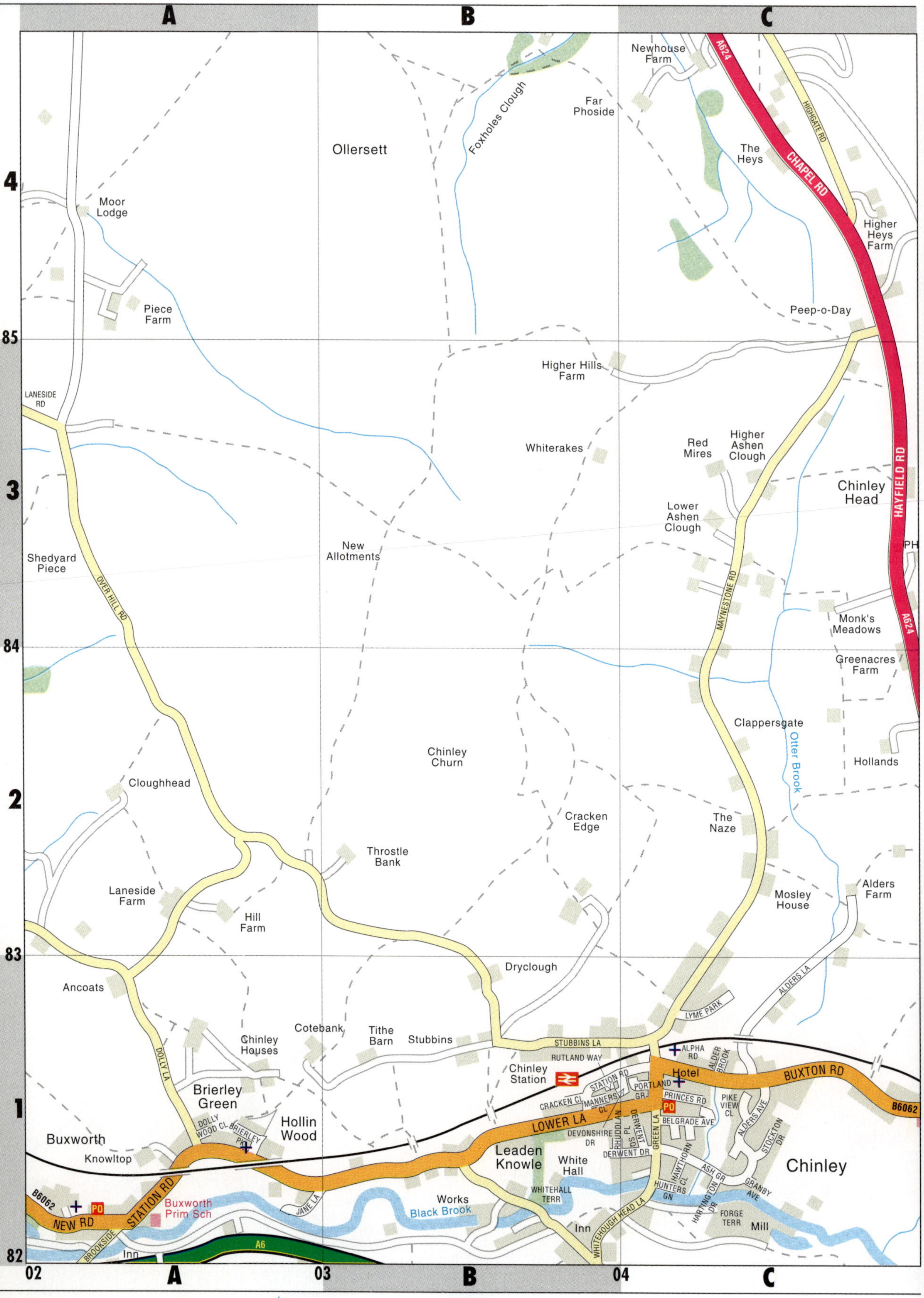

A | B | C

4

Newhouse Farm

Foxholes Clough

Far Phoside

Ollersett

The Heys

HIGHGATE RD

A624

CHAPEL RD

Higher Heys Farm

Moor Lodge

Peep-o-Day

85

Piece Farm

LANESIDE RD

Higher Hills Farm

HAYFIELD RD

A624

PH

Whiterakes

Red Mires

Higher Ashen Clough

Chinley Head

3

Shedyard Piece

DYER HILL RD

New Allotments

Lower Ashen Clough

Monk's Meadows

84

Greenacres Farm

Clappersgate

Hollands

Chinley Churn

Otter Brook

Cloughhead

Cracken Edge

The Naze

2

Laneside Farm

Hill Farm

Throstle Bank

Mosley House

Alders Farm

83

Ancoats

Dryclough

ALDERS LA

LYME PARK

Cotebank

Tithe Barn

Stubbins

STUBBINS LA

ALPHA RD

ALDER BROOK

BUXTON RD

Chinley Houses

RUTLAND WAY

STATION RD

Hotel

Brierley Green

DOLLY LA

Chinley Station

MANNERS RD

PORTLAND GRJ

PRINCES RD

PIKE VIEW CL

ALDERS AVE

Chinley

1

Buxworth

DOLLY WOOD CL

BRIERLEY PK

Hollin Wood

LOWER LA

CRACKEN CL

DEVONSHIRE DR

THE MEADOW

DERWENT DR

GREEN LA

BELGRADE AVE

HAWTHORN CL

ASH GR

STOCKTON DR

GRANBY AVE

B6062

Knowltop

Leaden Knowle

White Hall

WHITEHALL TERR

HUNTERS CL

HARTINGTON GN

FORGE TERR

Mill

B6062

NEW RD

STATION RD

BROOKSIDE

PO

Buxworth Prim Sch

JANE LA

Works

Black Brook

WHITEHOUGH HEAD LA

Inn

82

Inn

A6

02 | A | 03 | B | 04 | C

26
36

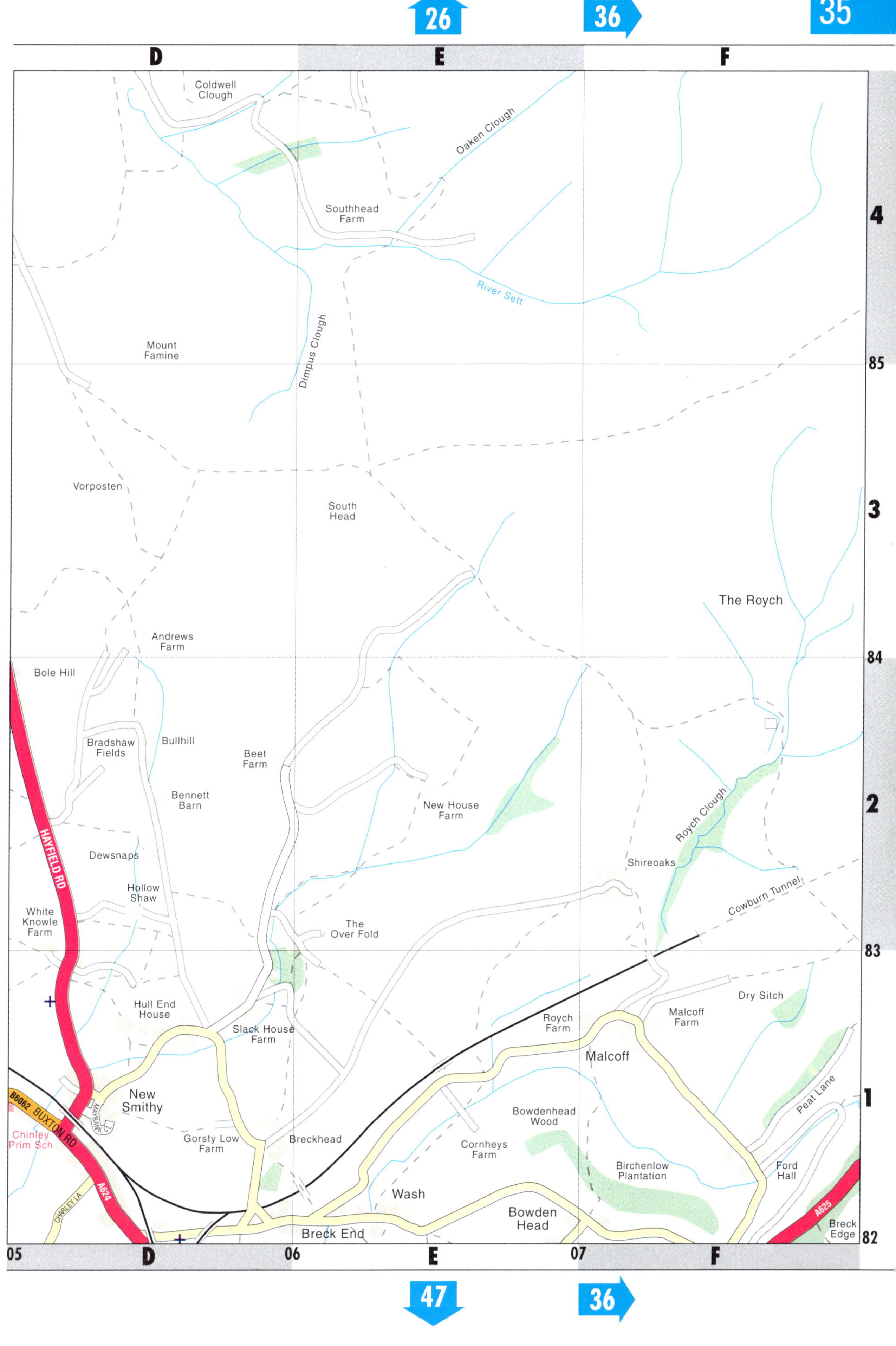
D
E
F
Coldwell Clough
Oaken Clough
Southhead Farm
River Sett
Mount Famine
Dimpus Clough
Vorposten
South Head
The Roych
Andrews Farm
Bole Hill
Bradshaw Fields
Bullhill
Beet Farm
Bennett Barn
New House Farm
Roych Clough
Dewsnaps
Shireoaks
Hollow Shaw
White Knowle Farm
The Over Fold
Cowburn Tunnel
HAYFIELD RD
Dry Sitch
Malcoff Farm
Hull End House
Roych Farm
Slack House Farm
Malcoff
New Smithy
Peat Lane
Bowdenhead Wood
B6062 BUXTON RD
Chinley Prim Sch
Gorsty Low Farm
Breckhead
Cornheys Farm
Birchenlow Plantation
Ford Hall
A624
CHARLEY LA
Wash
Bowden Head
A625
Breck Edge
Breck End
4
85
3
84
2
83
1
82
05
06
07

47
36

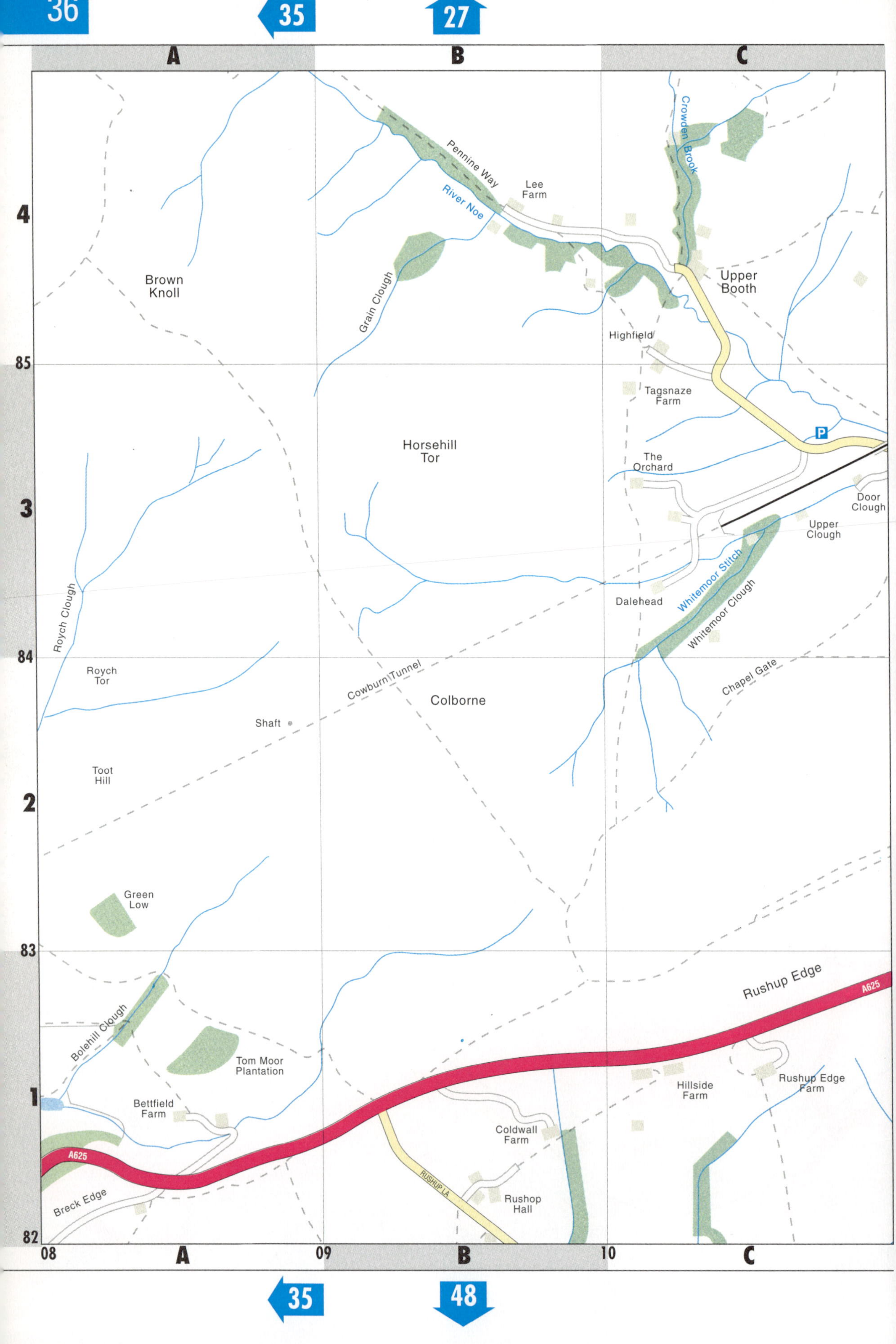

A   B   C

4

85

3

84

2

83

1

82

08   A   09   B   10   C

Brown
Knoll

Grain Clough

Roych Clough

Roych
Tor

Toot
Hill

Green
Low

Bolehill Clough

Tom Moor
Plantation

Bettfield
Farm

Breck Edge

A625

Horsehill
Tor

Cowburn Tunnel

Colborne

Shaft

RUSHUP LA

Coldwall
Farm

Rushop
Hall

Pennine Way

River Noe

Lee
Farm

Highfield

Tagsnaze
Farm

The
Orchard

Dalehead

Whitemoor Stitch

Whitemoor Clough

Crowden Brook

Upper
Booth

P

Door
Clough

Upper
Clough

Chapel Gate

Rushup Edge

A625

Hillside
Farm

Rushup Edge
Farm

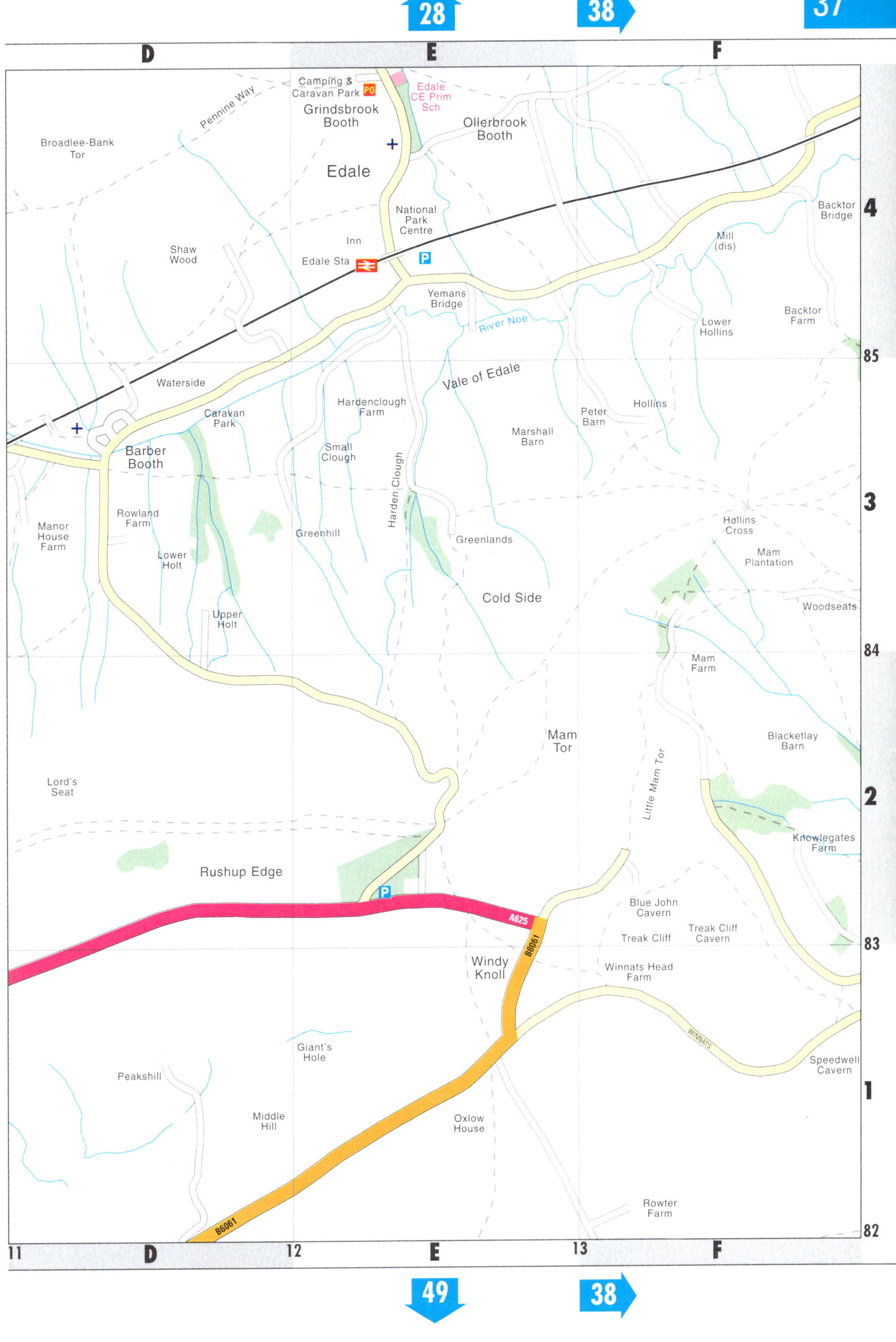

D   E   F

Pennine Way

Broadlee-Bank Tor

Camping & Caravan Park **PO**
Grindsbrook Booth
Edale CE Prim Sch
Ollerbrook Booth

Edale

National Park Centre

Shaw Wood

Inn
Edale Sta
Yemans Bridge

P

River Noe

Backtor Bridge

Mill (dis)

4

Lower Hollins

Backtor Farm

85

Waterside

Vale of Edale

Caravan Park

Hardenclough Farm

Barber Booth

Small Clough

Marshall Barn

Peter Barn

Hollins

Rowland Farm

Greenhill

Harden Clough

Greenlands

3

Manor House Farm

Lower Holt

Hollins Cross

Mam Plantation

Woodseats

Upper Holt

Cold Side

84

Mam Farm

Mam Tor

Blacketlay Barn

Lord's Seat

Little Mam Tor

2

Knowlegates Farm

Rushup Edge

P

Blue John Cavern

Treak Cliff

Treak Cliff Cavern

83

A625
Windy Knoll
B6061

Winnats Head Farm

WINNATS

Giant's Hole

Peakshill

Speedwell Cavern

1

Middle Hill

Oxlow House

Rowter Farm

B6061

82

11   D   12   E   13   F

37
29

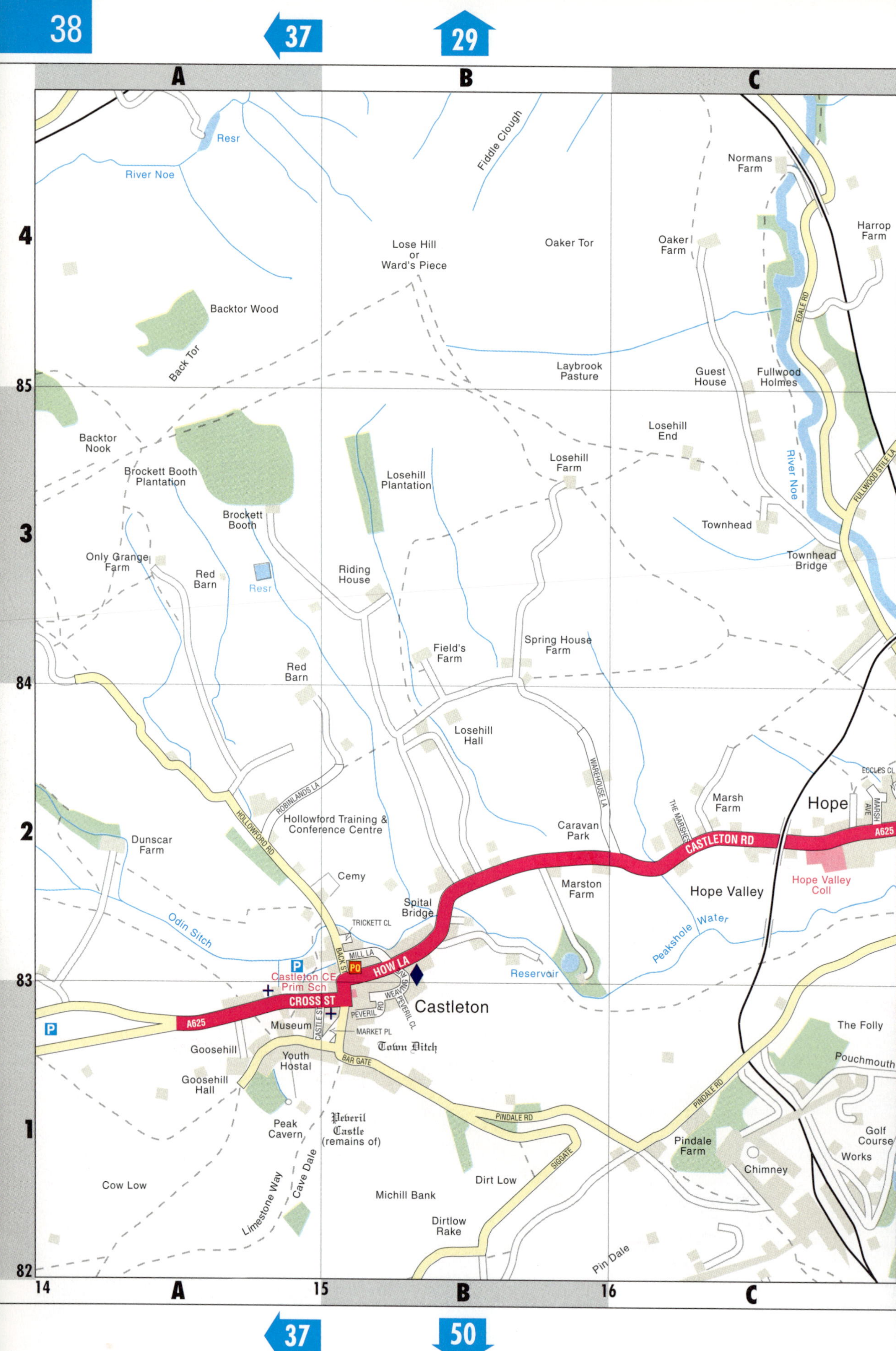
A
B
C
Resr
River Noe
Fiddle Clough
Normans Farm
Harrop Farm
Lose Hill or Ward's Piece
Oaker Tor
Oaker Farm
Backtor Wood
Back Tor
EDALE RD
Laybrook Pasture
Guest House
Fullwood Holmes
Backtor Nook
Losehill End
Brockett Booth Plantation
Losehill Plantation
Losehill Farm
River Noe
FULLWOOD STILE LA
Brockett Booth
Townhead
Only Grange Farm
Red Barn
Resr
Riding House
Townhead Bridge
Field's Farm
Spring House Farm
Red Barn
Losehill Hall
WAREHOUSE LA
ECCLES CL
ROBINLANDS LA
THE MARSHES
Marsh Farm
Hope
MARSH AVE
Hollowford Training & Conference Centre
Caravan Park
HOLLOWFORD RD
Dunscar Farm
CASTLETON RD
A625
Cemy
Marston Farm
Hope Valley
Hope Valley Coll
Spital Bridge
Odin Sitch
TRICKETT CL
Peakshole Water
MILL LA
BACK ST
HOW LA
PO
P
Castleton CE Prim Sch
Reservoir
CROSS ST
WEAVING
PEVERIL CL
PEVERIL RD
Castleton
A625
P
Museum
CASTLE ST
MARKET PL
The Folly
Town Ditch
Goosehill
Youth Hostal
BAR GATE
Pouchmouth
Goosehill Hall
PINDALE RD
Peveril Castle (remains of)
Peak Cavern
PINDALE RD
Golf Course
Pindale Farm
Works
SIGGATE
Chimney
Cave Dale
Cow Low
Dirt Low
Limestone Way
Michill Bank
Dirtlow Rake
Pin Dale
4
85
3
84
2
83
1
82
14
15
16

37
50

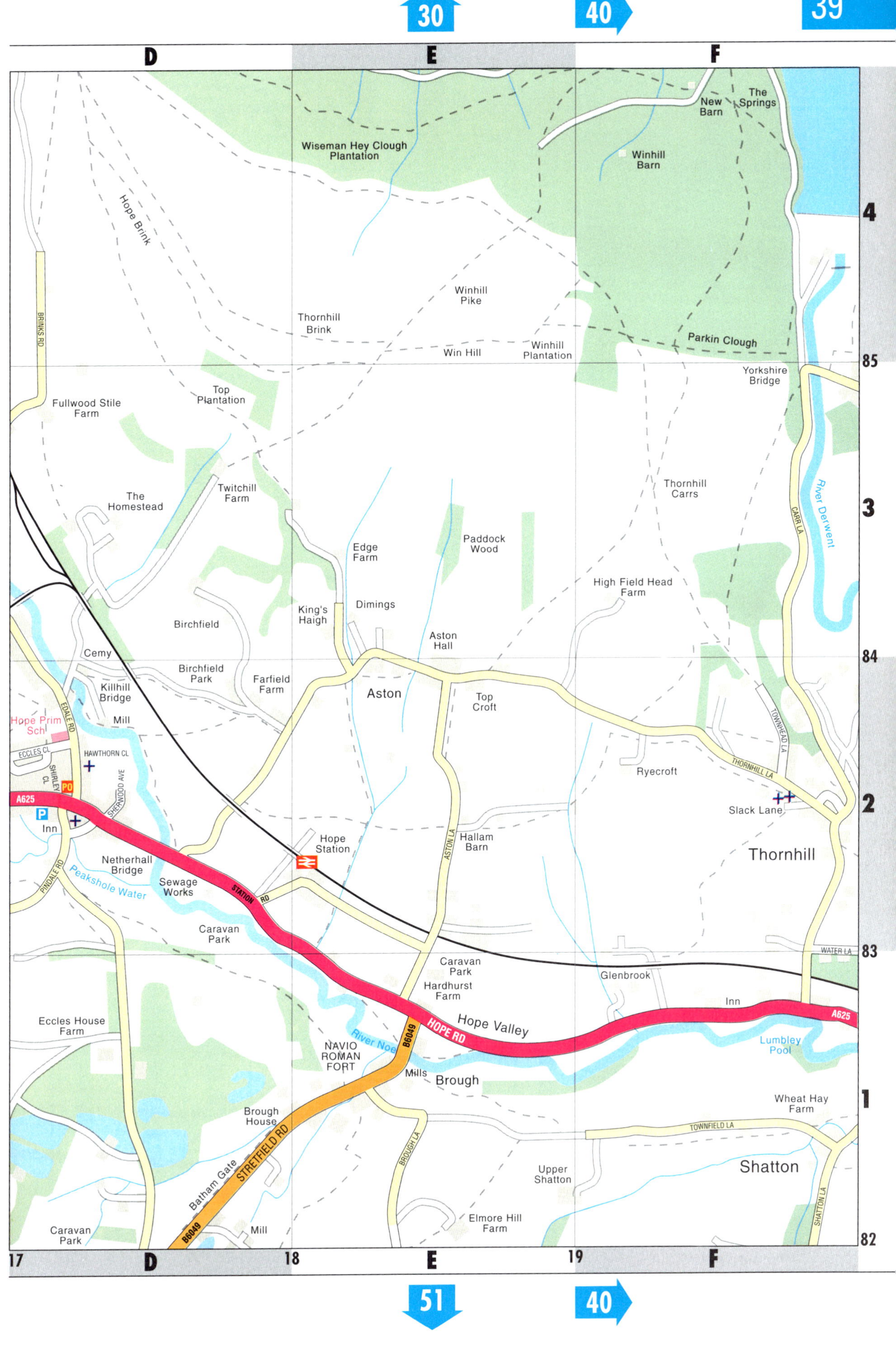
D
E
F
Wiseman Hey Clough Plantation
New Barn
The Springs
Winhill Barn
Hope Brink
BRINKS RD
Winhill Pike
Thornhill Brink
Win Hill
Winhill Plantation
Parkin Clough
Yorkshire Bridge
Fullwood Stile Farm
Top Plantation
Twitchill Farm
The Homestead
Thornhill Carrs
River Derwent
CARR LA
Edge Farm
Paddock Wood
High Field Head Farm
Birchfield
King's Haigh
Dimings
Aston Hall
Cemy
Birchfield Park
Farfield Farm
Killhill Bridge
Aston
Top Croft
Hope Prim Sch
Mill
EDALE RD
ECCLES CL
HAWTHORN CL
SHIRLEY CL
SHERWOOD AVE
TOWNHEAD LA
THORNHILL LA
Ryecroft
PO
A625
P
Inn
Slack Lane
Hope Station
Hallam Barn
ASTON LA
Thornhill
Netherhall Bridge
PINDALE RD
Peakshole Water
Sewage Works
STATION RD
Caravan Park
WATER LA
Caravan Park
Hardhurst Farm
Glenbrook
Inn
Eccles House Farm
Hope Valley
HOPE RD
A625
B6049
River Noe
NAVIO ROMAN FORT
Lumbley Pool
Mills
Brough
Wheat Hay Farm
Brough House
TOWNFIELD LA
BROUGH LA
Upper Shatton
Shatton
Batham Gate
STRETFIELD RD
SHATTON LA
Elmore Hill Farm
Caravan Park
Mill
B6049
4
85
3
84
2
83
1
82
17
18
19

39
31

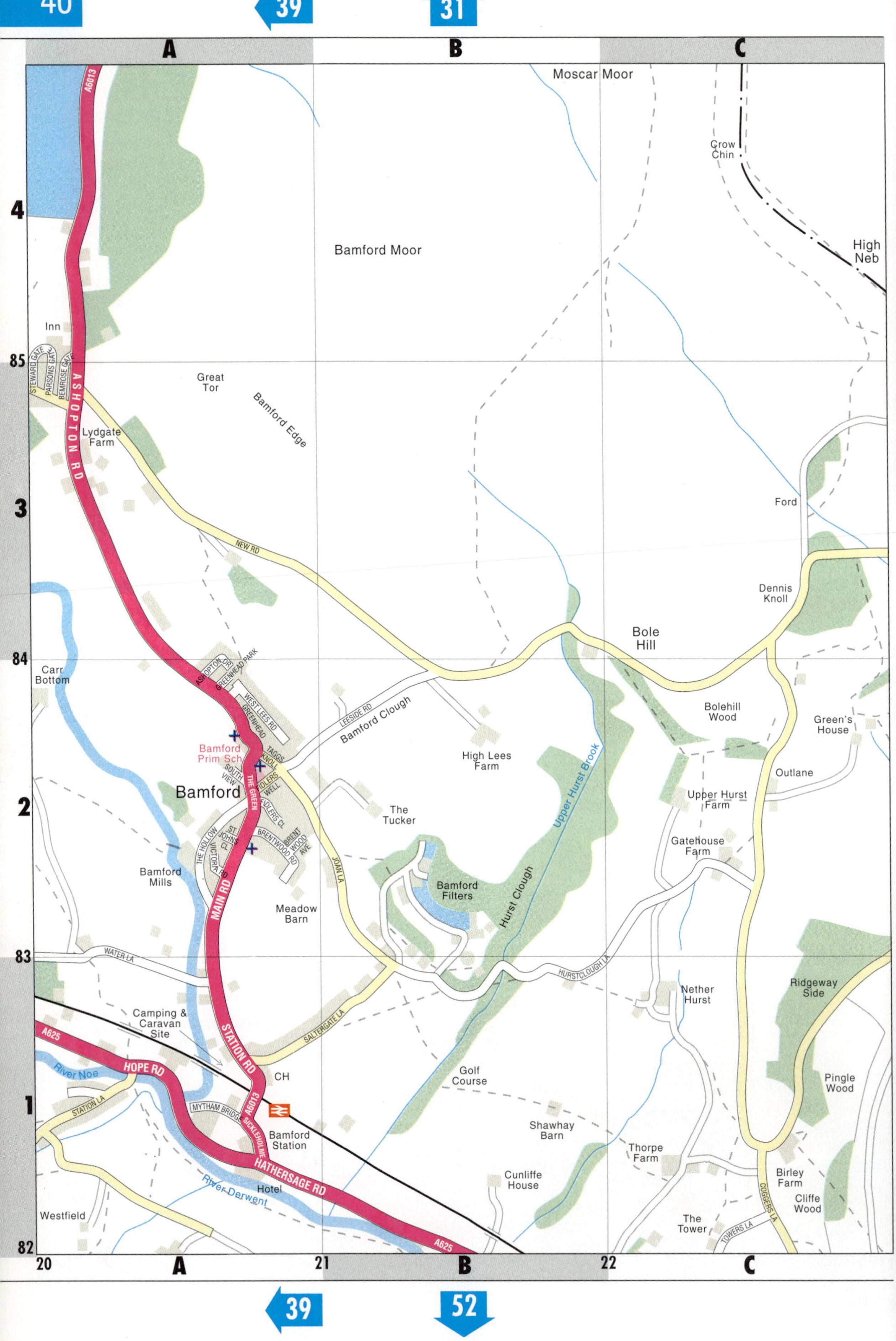
A
B
C
Moscar Moor
Crow Chin
High Neb
Bamford Moor
Inn
Great Tor
Bamford Edge
Lydgate Farm
ASHOPTON RD
A6013
STEWARD GATE
PARSONS GATE
BEMROSE GATE
NEW RD
Ford
Dennis Knoll
Bole Hill
Carr Bottom
ASHOPTON DR
GREENHEAD PARK
WEST LEES RD
GREENHEAD
LEESIDE RD
Bamford Clough
Bolehill Wood
Green's House
High Lees Farm
Bamford Prim Sch
TAGGS KNOLL
SOUTH VIEW
THE GREEN
FIDLERS WELL
FIDLERS CL
Bamford
Upper Hurst Brook
Outlane
Upper Hurst Farm
The Tucker
THE HOLLOW
ST JOHNS CL
VICTORIA RD
BRENTWOOD RD
BRENT WOOD AVE
JOAN LA
Gatehouse Farm
Bamford Mills
Bamford Filters
Hurst Clough
MAIN RD
Meadow Barn
WATER LA
HURSTCLOUGH LA
Nether Hurst
Ridgeway Side
Camping & Caravan Site
SALTERGATE LA
A625
HOPE RD
STATION RD
River Noe
CH
Golf Course
Pingle Wood
STATION LA
MYTHAM BRIDGE
SICKLEHOLME
Bamford Station
Shawhay Barn
Thorpe Farm
Birley Farm
HATHERSAGE RD
Cunliffe House
Cliffe Wood
River Derwent
Hotel
COGGERS LA
Westfield
The Tower
TOWERS LA
4
85
3
84
2
83
1
82
20
21
22

39
52

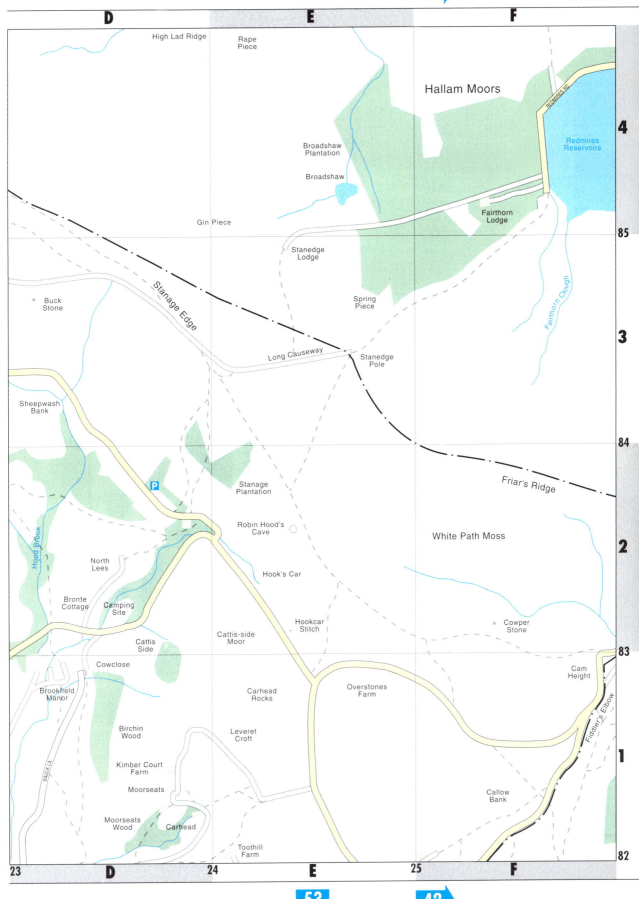

D
E
F
High Lad Ridge
Rape Piece
Hallam Moors
REDMIRES RD
Redmires Reservoirs
Broadshaw Plantation
Broadshaw
Fairthorn Lodge
Gin Piece
Stanedge Lodge
Stanage Edge
Buck Stone
Spring Piece
Fairthorn Clough
Long Causeway
Stanedge Pole
Sheepwash Bank
P
Stanage Plantation
Friar's Ridge
Robin Hood's Cave
White Path Moss
Hood Brook
North Lees
Hook's Car
Bronte Cottage
Camping Site
Hookcar Stitch
Cowper Stone
Cattis Side
Cattis-side Moor
Cowclose
Cam Height
Brookfield Manor
Carhead Rocks
Overstones Farm
Fiddler's Elbow
Birchin Wood
Leveret Croft
BAULK LA
Kimber Court Farm
Moorseats
Callow Bank
Moorseats Wood
Carhead
Toothill Farm
4
85
3
84
2
83
1
82
23
24
25

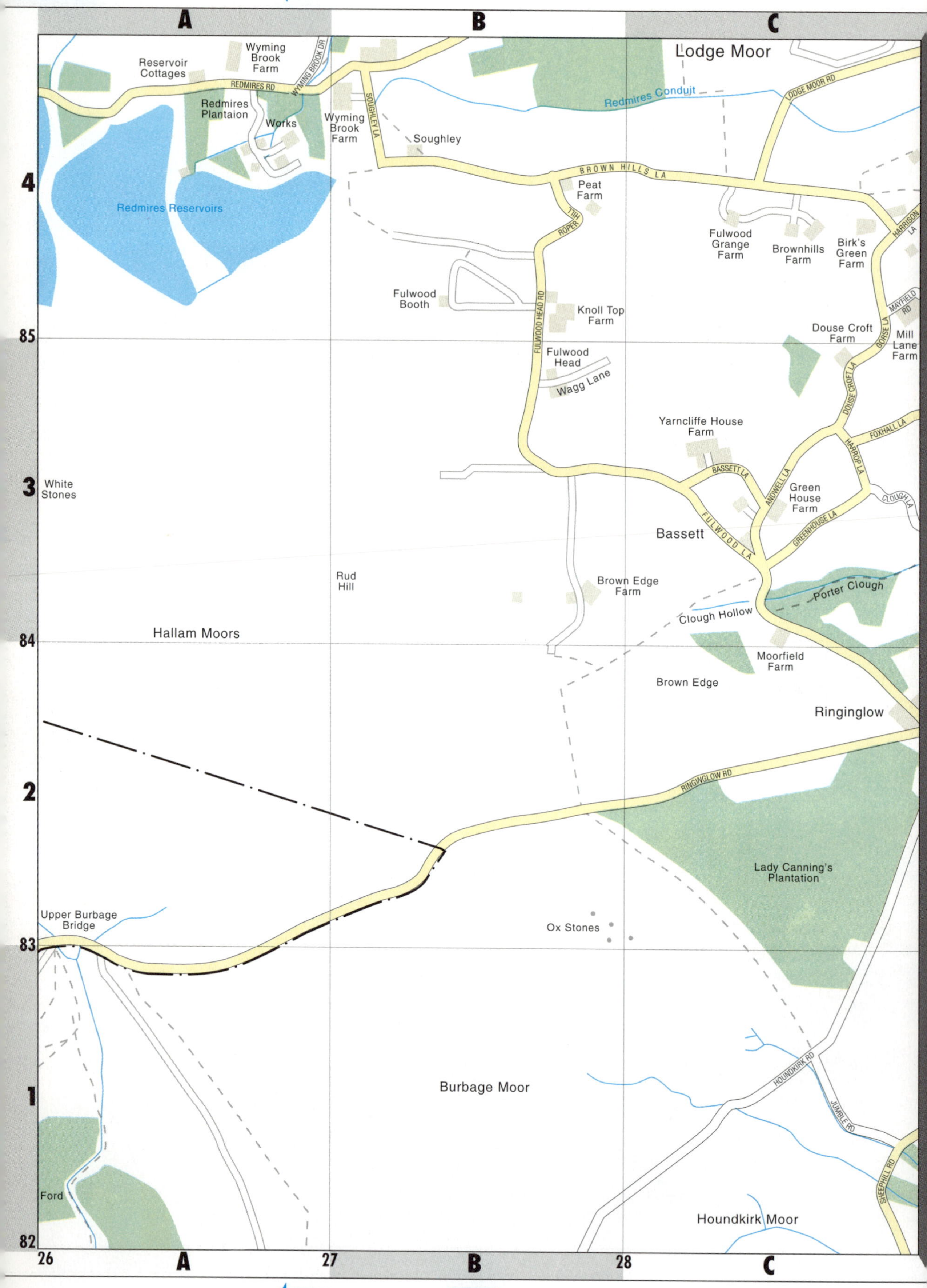

Lodge Moor

Reservoir Cottages

Wyming Brook Farm

REDMIRES RD

WYMING BROOK DR

Redmires Plantaion

Works

Wyming Brook Farm

SOUGHLEY LA

Soughley

Redmires Conduit

LODGE MOOR RD

4

Redmires Reservoirs

BROWN HILLS LA

Peat Farm

ROPER LA

Fulwood Grange Farm

Brownhills Farm

Birk's Green Farm

HARRISON LA

Fulwood Booth

FULWOOD HEAD RD

Knoll Top Farm

MAYFIELD RD

85

Douse Croft Farm

DOUSE CROFT LA

Mill Lane Farm

Fulwood Head

Wagg Lane

Yarncliffe House Farm

FOXHALL LA

HARROP LA

3 White Stones

BASSETT LA

ANGWELL LA

Green House Farm

CLOUGH LA

Rud Hill

FULWOOD LA

GREENHOUSE LA

Bassett

Brown Edge Farm

Porter Clough

84 Hallam Moors

Clough Hollow

Moorfield Farm

Brown Edge

Ringinglow

2

RINGINGLOW RD

Lady Canning's Plantation

Upper Burbage Bridge

Ox Stones

83

HOUNDKIRK RD

1

Burbage Moor

JUMBLE RD

Ford

SHEEPHILL RD

82

Houndkirk Moor

44

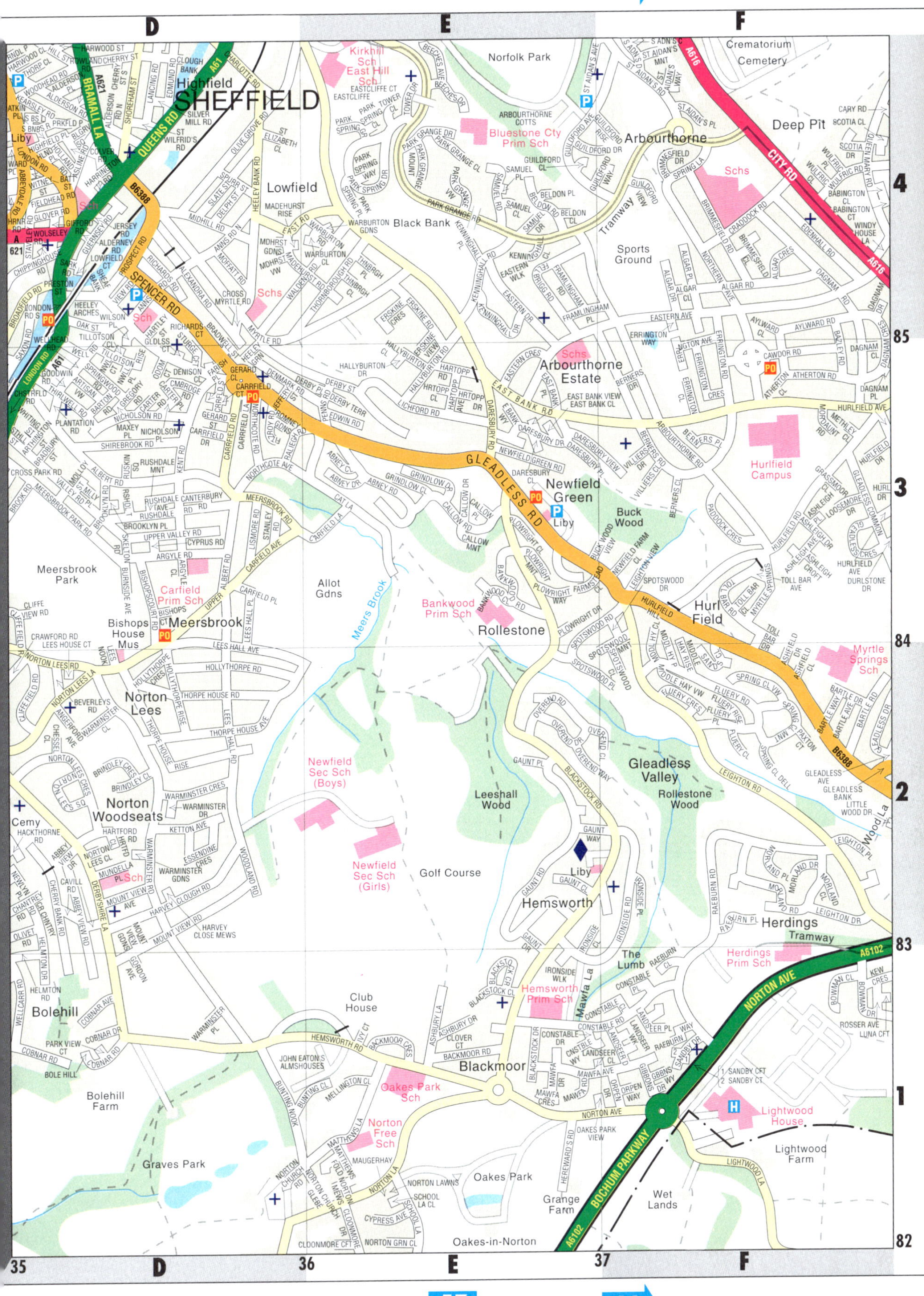
D
E
F
SHEFFIELD
Highfield
Norfolk Park
Crematorium
Cemetery
Deep Pit
Arbourthorne
Kirkhill Sch
East Hill Sch
Bluestone Cty Prim Sch
Schs
Lowfield
Black Bank
Sports Ground
Tramway
Arbourthorne Estate
Hurlfield Campus
Newfield Green
Liby
Buck Wood
Hurl Field
Meersbrook Park
Carfield Prim Sch
Allot Gdns
Meers Brook
Bankwood Prim Sch
Rollestone
Bishops House Mus
Meersbrook
Myrtle Springs Sch
Norton Lees
Newfield Sec Sch (Boys)
Leeshall Wood
Gleadless Valley
Rollestone Wood
Cemy
Norton Woodseats
Newfield Sec Sch (Girls)
Golf Course
Hemsworth
Herdings
Herdings Prim Sch
The Lumb
Club House
Hemsworth Prim Sch
Bolehill
Blackmoor
Oakes Park Sch
Lightwood House
Bolehill Farm
Norton Free Sch
Lightwood Farm
Graves Park
Oakes Park
Grange Farm
Wet Lands
Oakes-in-Norton
QUEENS RD
BRAMALL LA
SPENCER RD
GLEADLESS RD
CITY RD
NORTON AVE
BOCHUM PARKWAY
HEMSWORTH RD
EAST BANK RD
HURLFIELD AVE
A61
A621
A616
B6388
A6102
4
85
3
84
2
83
1
82
35
36
37

57

44

43

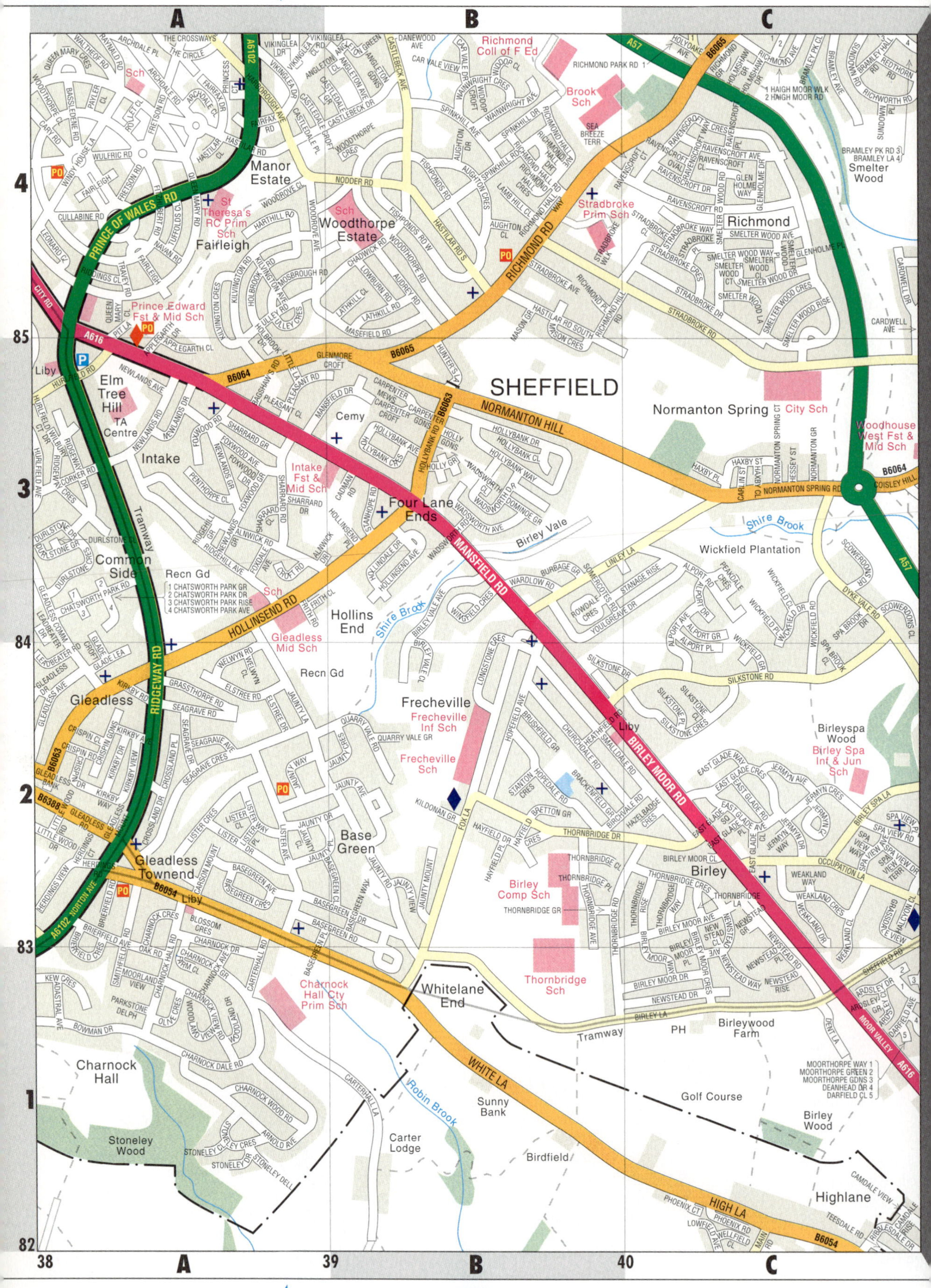

A
B
C
4
3
2
1
85
84
83
82
38
39
40
SHEFFIELD
Manor Estate
Woodthorpe Estate
Fairleigh
Richmond
Smelter Wood
Elm Tree Hill
Intake
Common Side
Normanton Spring
Four Lane Ends
Birley Vale
Wickfield Plantation
Hollins End
Gleadless
Frecheville
Base Green
Gleadless Townend
Birley
Birleyspa Wood
Whitelane End
Birleywood Farm
Charnock Hall
Stoneley Wood
Sunny Bank
Carter Lodge
Birdfield
Golf Course
Birley Wood
Highlane
Richmond Coll of F Ed
Brook Sch
St Theresa's RC Prim Sch
Stradbroke Prim Sch
Prince Edward Fst & Mid Sch
City Sch
Woodhouse West Fst & Mid Sch
Intake Fst & Mid Sch
Gleadless Mid Sch
Frecheville Inf Sch
Frecheville Sch
Birley Spa Inf & Jun Sch
Birley Comp Sch
Thornbridge Sch
Charnock Hall Cty Prim Sch
Cemy
Recn Gd
TA Centre
Liby
Tramway
PH
Shire Brook
Robin Brook
PRINCE OF WALES RD
RIDGEWAY RD
RICHMOND RD
NORMANTON HILL
MANSFIELD RD
BIRLEY MOOR RD
HOLLINSEND RD
WHITE LA
HIGH LA
SILKSTONE RD
THORNBRIDGE DR
NORMANTON SPRING RD
STRADBROKE RD
CITY RD
A57
A616
A6102
B6054
B6063
B6064
B6065
B6388

43

58

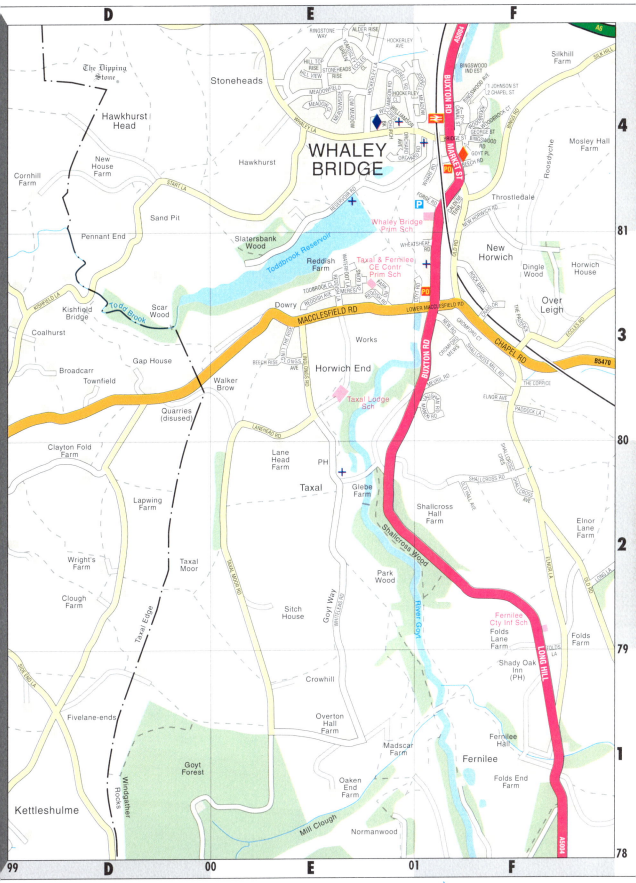

D E F

WHALEY BRIDGE

The Dipping Stone
Hawkhurst Head
Stoneheads
Hawkhurst
New House Farm
Cornhill Farm
Sand Pit
Pennant End
Slatersbank Wood
Toddbrook Reservoir
Reddish Farm
Kishfield Bridge
Todd Brook
Scar Wood
Dowry
Coalhurst
Broadcarr
Townfield
Gap House
Walker Brow
Works
Horwich End
Quarries (disused)
Taxal Lodge Sch
Whaley Bridge Prim Sch
Taxal & Fernilee CE Contr Prim Sch
Clayton Fold Farm
Lane Head Farm
PH
Taxal
Glebe Farm
Lapwing Farm
Wright's Farm
Taxal Moor
Clough Farm
Taxal Edge
Sitch House
Goyt Way
Park Wood
Shallcross Wood
River Goyt
Shallcross Hall Farm
Crowhill
Fivelane-ends
Overton Hall Farm
Madscar Farm
Goyt Forest
Windgather Rocks
Kettleshulme
Oaken End Farm
Mill Clough
Normanwood
Fernilee
Fernilee Hall
Folds End Farm
Shady Oak Inn (PH)
Folds Lane Farm
Fernilee Cty Inf Sch
Folds Farm
Elnor Lane Farm
Silkhill Farm
Mosley Hall Farm
Roosdyche
Throstledale
New Horwich
Dingle Wood
Horwich House
Over Leigh
Bingswood Ind Est

MACCLESFIELD RD
LOWER MACCLESFIELD RD
CHAPEL RD
BUXTON RD
MARKET ST
LONG HILL
A5004
A6
B5470
WHALEY LA
START LA
KISHFIELD LA
RESERVOIR RD
LANEHEAD RD
TAXAL MOOR RD
LINGLONGS RD
WHITELEAS RD
SIDE END LA
ELMOR LA
OLD RD
LONG LA
SHALLCROSS RD
SHALLCROSS MILL RD
BINGS RD
SILK HILL
ECCLES RD
NEW HORWICH RD

1 JOHNSON ST
2 CHAPEL ST

4
81
3
80
2
79
1
78

99 D 00 E 01 F

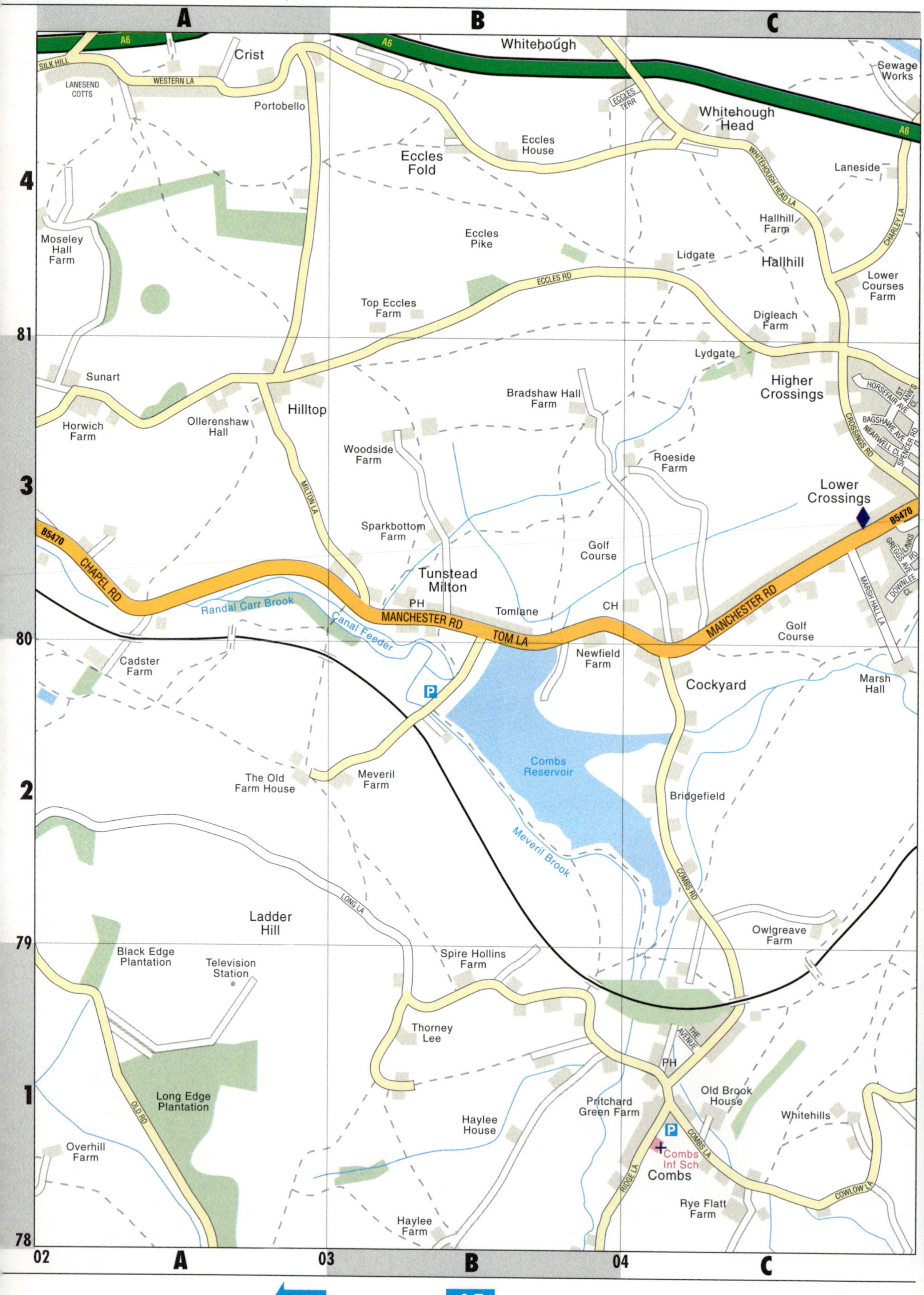

A B C

4

81

3

80

2

79

1

78

Silk Hill
Crist
A6
Western La
Lanesend Cotts
Portobello
Whitehough
A6
Whitehough Head
Eccles Terr
Sewage Works
A6
Eccles Fold
Eccles House
Laneside
Eccles Pike
Hallhill Farm
Whitehough Head La
Lidgate
Hallhill
Moseley Hall Farm
Top Eccles Farm
Eccles Rd
Lower Courses Farm
Charley La
Horsefair Ave
Digleach Farm
Higher Crossings
Sunart
Hilltop
Woodside Farm
Bradshaw Hall Farm
Lydgate
Higher Crossings
Horwich Farm
Ollerenshaw Hall
Roeside Farm
St Ann's
Nearwell Clough
Spencer Rd
Crossings Rd
Lower Crossings
B5470
Bagshawe Ave
Sparkbottom Farm
Golf Course
Gregg's Ave
Downlee Cl
B5470
Chapel Rd
Milton La
Tunstead Milton
PH
Tomlane
CH
Manchester Rd
Marsh Hall La
Randal Carr Brook
Manchester Rd
Tom La
Canal Feeder
Newfield Farm
Golf Course
Cadster Farm
P
Cockyard
Marsh Hall
The Old Farm House
Meveril Farm
Combs Reservoir
Bridgefield
Ladder Hill
Long La
Meveril Brook
Combs Rd
Owlgreave Farm
Black Edge Plantation
Television Station
Spire Hollins Farm
The Avenue
Long Edge Plantation
Old Rd
Thorney Lee
PH
Old Brook House
Pritchard Green Farm
Whitehills
Overhill Farm
Haylee House
Ridge La
P
Combs Inf Sch
Combs La
Combs
Rye Flatt Farm
Cowlow La
Haylee Farm

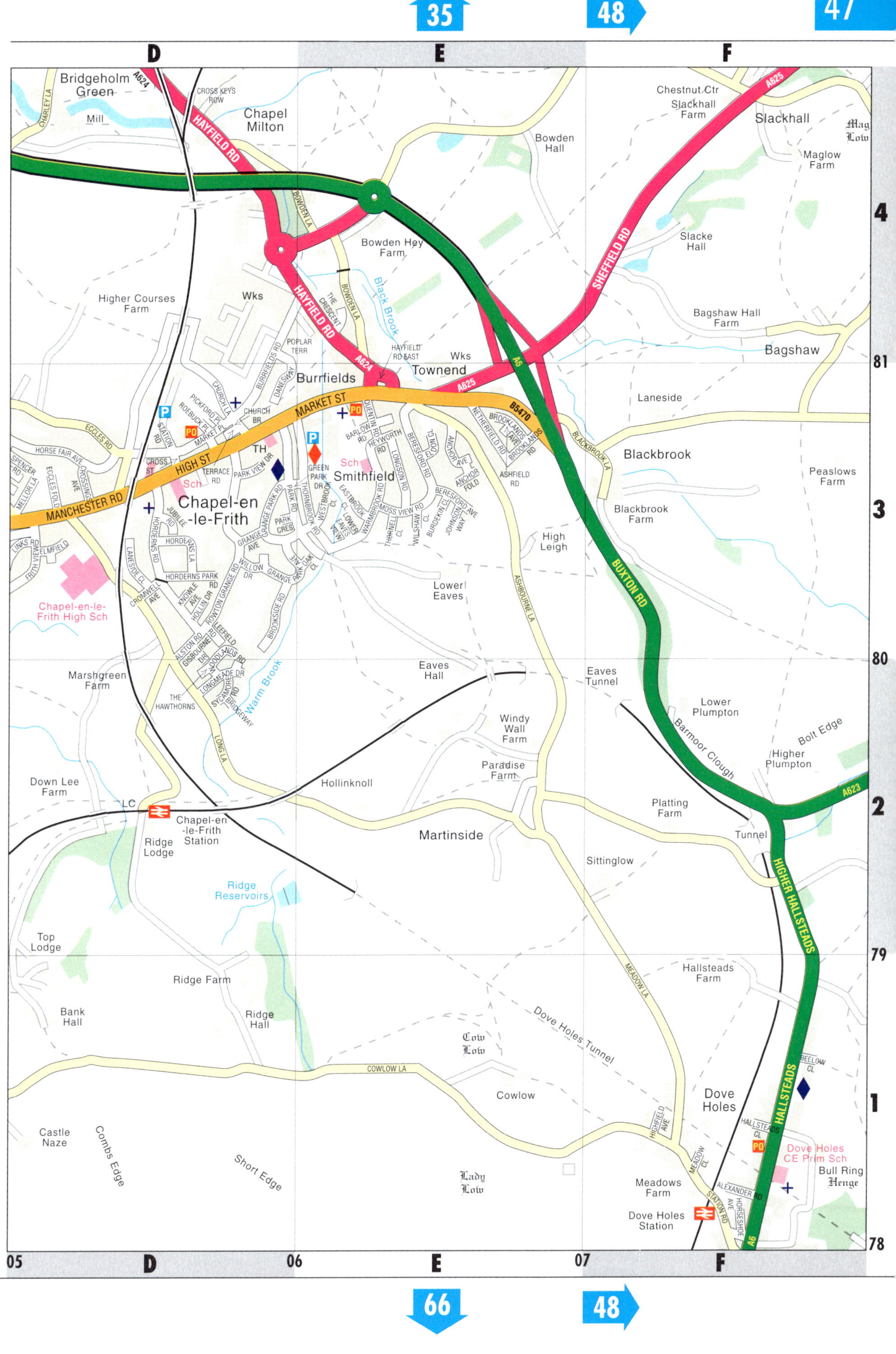
D
E
F
Bridgeholm Green
Mill
CHARLEY LA
A624
CROSS KEYS ROW
Chapel Milton
HAYFIELD RD
Bowden Hall
Chestnut Ctr
Slackhall Farm
A625
Slackhall
Mag Low
Maglow Farm
BOWDEN LA
Bowden Hey Farm
Slacke Hall
SHEFFIELD RD
Higher Courses Farm
Wks
THE CRESCENT
Black Brook
Bagshaw Hall Farm
Bagshaw
POPLAR TERR
HAYFIELD RD EAST
Wks
Townend
A6
Burrfields
Laneside
CHURCH LA
DANESWAY
BURRFIELDS RD
CHURCH BR
MARKET ST
B5470
Blackbrook
Peaslows Farm
STATION RD
PICKFORD PL
ROEBUCK PL
MARKET PL
ECCLES RD
HORSE FAIR AVE
CROSSINGS AVE
ECCLES FOLD
SPENCER RD
MELLOR LA
CROSS ST
HIGH ST
TERRACE RD
TH
PARK VIEW DR
Sch
Smithfield
GREEN PARK DR
BARLOW RD
QUENTIN RD
HEYWORTH RD
LONGSON RD
BERESFORD RD
ELDON CL
ANCHOR AVE
ANCHOR FOLD
NETHERFIELD RD
BROOKLANDS AVE
BROOKLANDS RD
ASHFIELD RD
BLACKBROOK LA
Blackbrook Farm
MANCHESTER RD
Sch
Chapel-en -le-Frith
JUBILEE RD
PARK RD
PARK CRES
GRANGE PARK RD
GRANGE AVE
THORNBROOK RD
WESTBROOK CL
EASTBROOK CL
LOWER EAVES VIEW
WARMBROOK RD
MOSS VIEW RD
THORNELL CL
WILSHAW CL
BURDEKIN CL
JOHNSON WAY
BERESFORD AVE
High Leigh
LINKS RD
FRITH VIEW
ELMFIELD
HORDERNS RD
HORDERNS LA
HORDERNS PARK RD
LANESIDE CL
CROMWELL AVE
KNOWLE AVE
HOLLIN DR
ROWTON GRANGE RD
WILLOW DR
GRANGE PARK AVE
OAK CL
BUXTON RD
Lower Eaves
ASHBOURNE LA
Chapel-en-le-Frith High Sch
BROOKSIDE RD
ALSTON RD
GISBOURNE DR
LEEFIELD RD
WOODLANDS RD
LONGMEADE DR
SYCAMORE RD
BRIDGEWAY
THE HAWTHORNS
Warm Brook
Marshgreen Farm
Eaves Hall
Eaves Tunnel
Lower Plumpton
Windy Wall Farm
Barmoor Clough
Bolt Edge
Higher Plumpton
Paradise Farm
LONG LA
Down Lee Farm
Hollinknoll
LC
Chapel-en -le-Frith Station
Platting Farm
A623
Ridge Lodge
Martinside
Tunnel
Sittinglow
HIGHER HALLSTEADS
Ridge Reservoirs
Top Lodge
Ridge Farm
Hallsteads Farm
MEADOW LA
Bank Hall
Ridge Hall
Dove Holes Tunnel
Cow Low
BEELOW CL
COWLOW LA
Cowlow
Dove Holes
HALLSTEADS
HIGHFIELD AVE
HALLSTEADS CL
Castle Naze
Combs Edge
Short Edge
Dove Holes CE Prim Sch
MEADOW CL
Lady Low
Meadows Farm
Bull Ring Henge
ALEXANDER RD
Dove Holes Station
STATION RD
HORSESHOE AVE
A6
4
81
3
80
2
79
1
78
05
06
07

47   36

A   B   C

4

Stonyford

Bella Vista

Rushup Farm

Whitelee

Gautries Side

Perryfoot

Pot Holes

Bull Pit

B6061

RUSHUP LA

81

Peaslows

Goldpiece Farm

Coalpit Hole

Perry Dale

Gautries Hill

Rake Vein

Peaslows Farm

Sparrowpit

BAGSHAW LA

B6061

The Wanted Inn (PH)

3

Bennett Edge Farm

Harratt Grange

Nether Barn

Higher Barmoor Farm

Haddock Low

80

Boltedge Farm

Bennettston Hall Hotel

Ebbing and Flowing Well

Middle Barmoor Farm

Pedlicote Farm

Chamberknoll

A623

Barmoor

A623

2

Barmoor Farm

Chamber Farm

Lower Barmoor Farm

Bee Low

Lower Bee Low

79

Lodesbarn

Ivy House

Ridgeclose Farm

Backlane Farm

Greenknoll Farm

1

Lodes Marsh

Laughman Tor

BATHAM GATE

Kemp's Hill

78

08   A   09   B   10   C

37
50

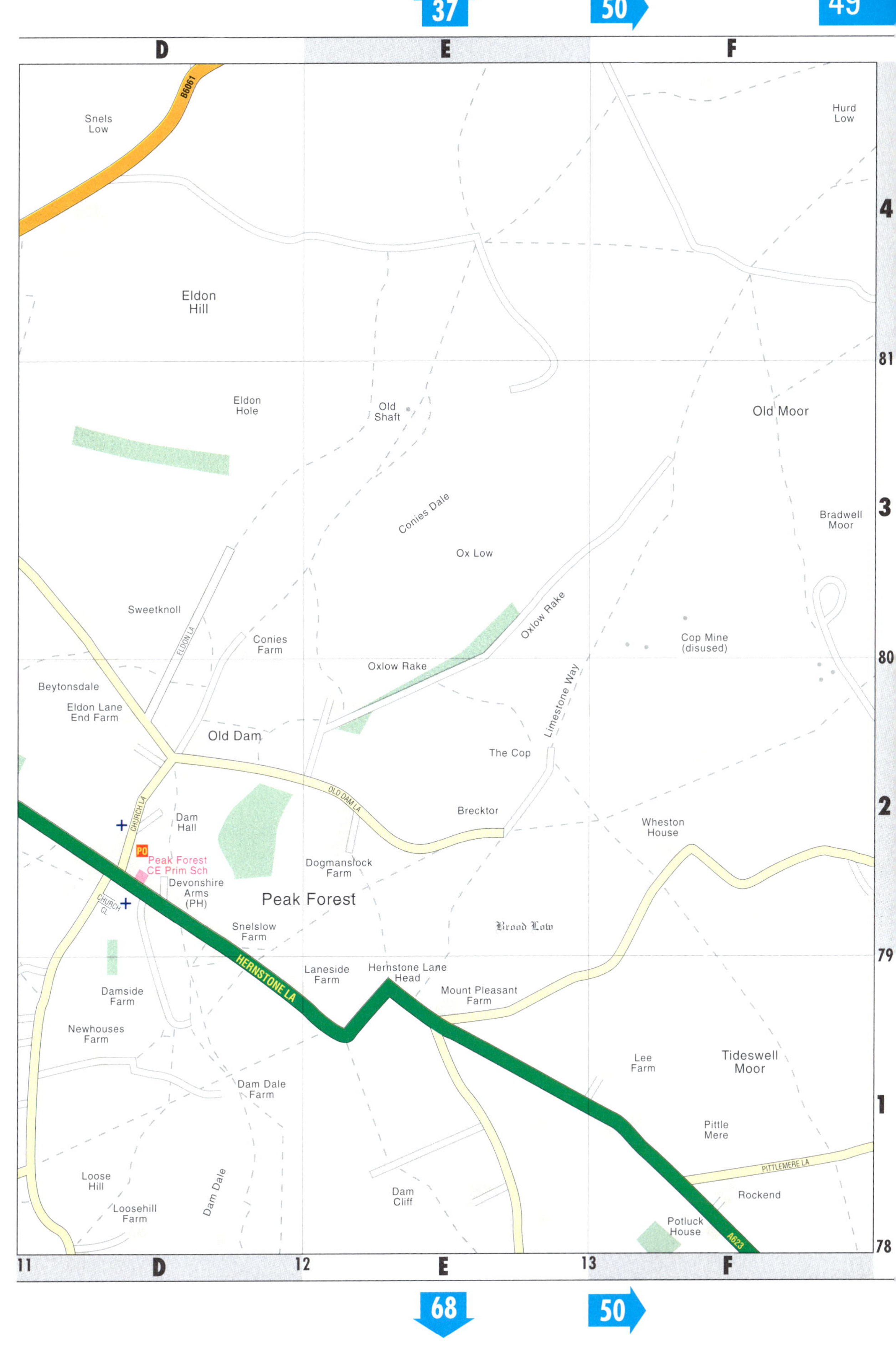
D
E
F
B6061
Snels Low
Hurd Low
4
Eldon Hill
81
Eldon Hole
Old Shaft
Old Moor
Conies Dale
3
Bradwell Moor
Ox Low
Oxlow Rake
Sweetknoll
ELDON LA
Conies Farm
Cop Mine (disused)
Oxlow Rake
80
Beytonsdale
Eldon Lane End Farm
Limestone Way
Old Dam
The Cop
OLD DAM LA
CHURCH LA
Dam Hall
Brecktor
2
Whetson House
PO
Peak Forest CE Prim Sch
Dogmanslock Farm
Devonshire Arms (PH)
CHURCH CL
Peak Forest
Snelslow Farm
Brood Low
79
HERNSTONE LA
Laneside Farm
Hernstone Lane Head
Damside Farm
Mount Pleasant Farm
Newhouses Farm
Lee Farm
Tideswell Moor
Dam Dale Farm
1
Pittle Mere
PITTLEMERE LA
Loose Hill
Dam Dale
Dam Cliff
Rockend
Loosehill Farm
Potluck House
A623
78
11
12
13

68
50

49
38

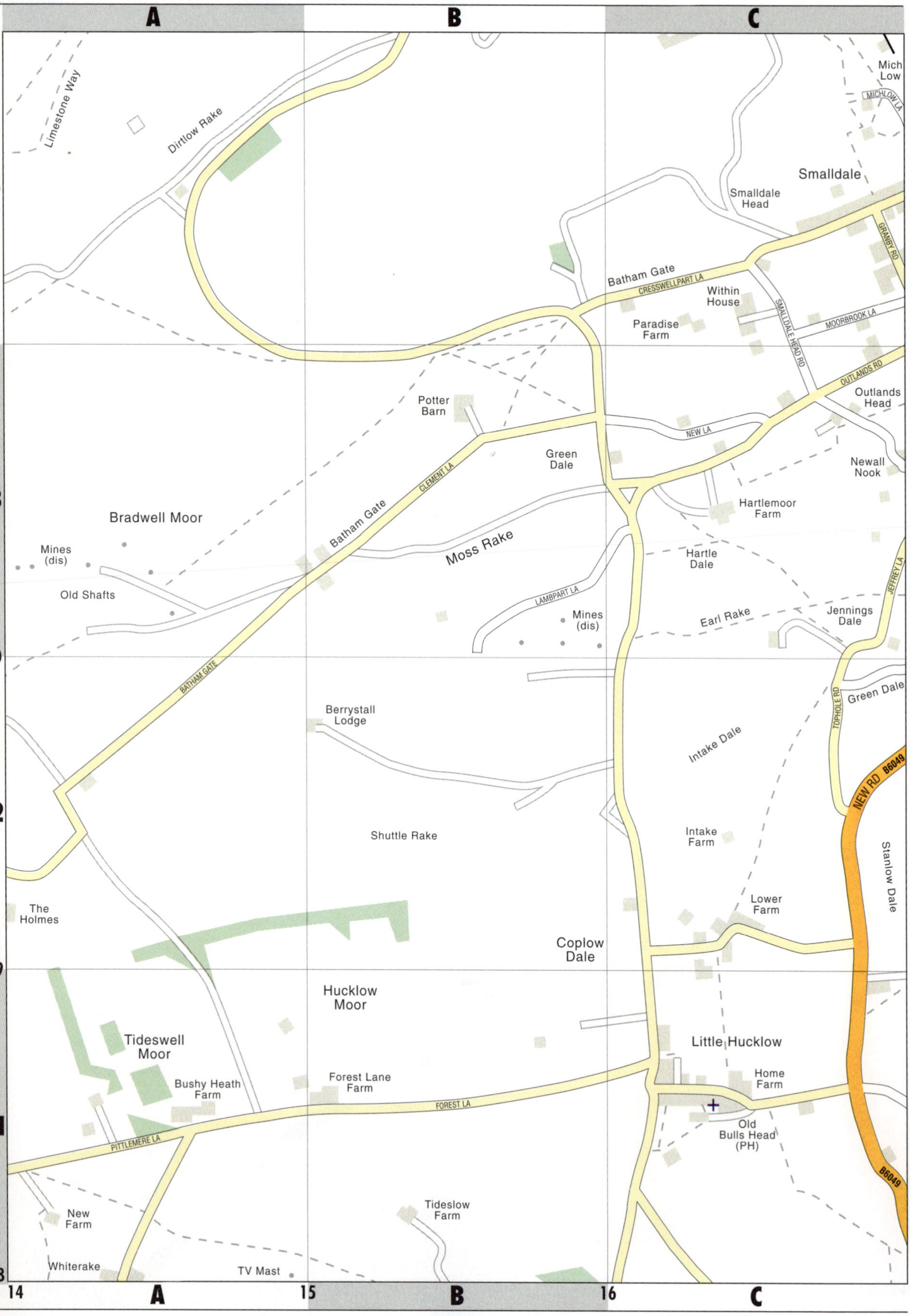

A　　　　　　　B　　　　　　　C

4

Limestone Way

Dirtlow Rake

Mich Low

MICHLOW LA

Smalldale

Smalldale Head

GRANBY RD

Batham Gate

CRESSWELLPART LA

Within House

MOORBROOK LA

SMALLDALE HEAD RD

Paradise Farm

81

OUTLANDS RD

Outlands Head

Potter Barn

NEW LA

Newall Nook

Green Dale

3

Bradwell Moor

CLEMENT LA

Hartlemoor Farm

Batham Gate

Moss Rake

Hartle Dale

Mines (dis)

LAMBPART LA

JEFFREY LA

Old Shafts

Earl Rake

Jennings Dale

Mines (dis)

TOPHOLE RD

80

Green Dale

Berrystall Lodge

BATHAM GATE

Intake Dale

NEW RD B6049

2

Shuttle Rake

Intake Farm

Stanlow Dale

The Holmes

Lower Farm

Coplow Dale

79

Hucklow Moor

Little Hucklow

Tideswell Moor

Home Farm

Bushy Heath Farm

Forest Lane Farm

Old Bulls Head (PH)

FOREST LA

1

PITTLEMERE LA

B6049

New Farm

Tideslow Farm

Whiterake

TV Mast

78

14　　　　A　　　　15　　　　B　　　　16　　　　C

49
69

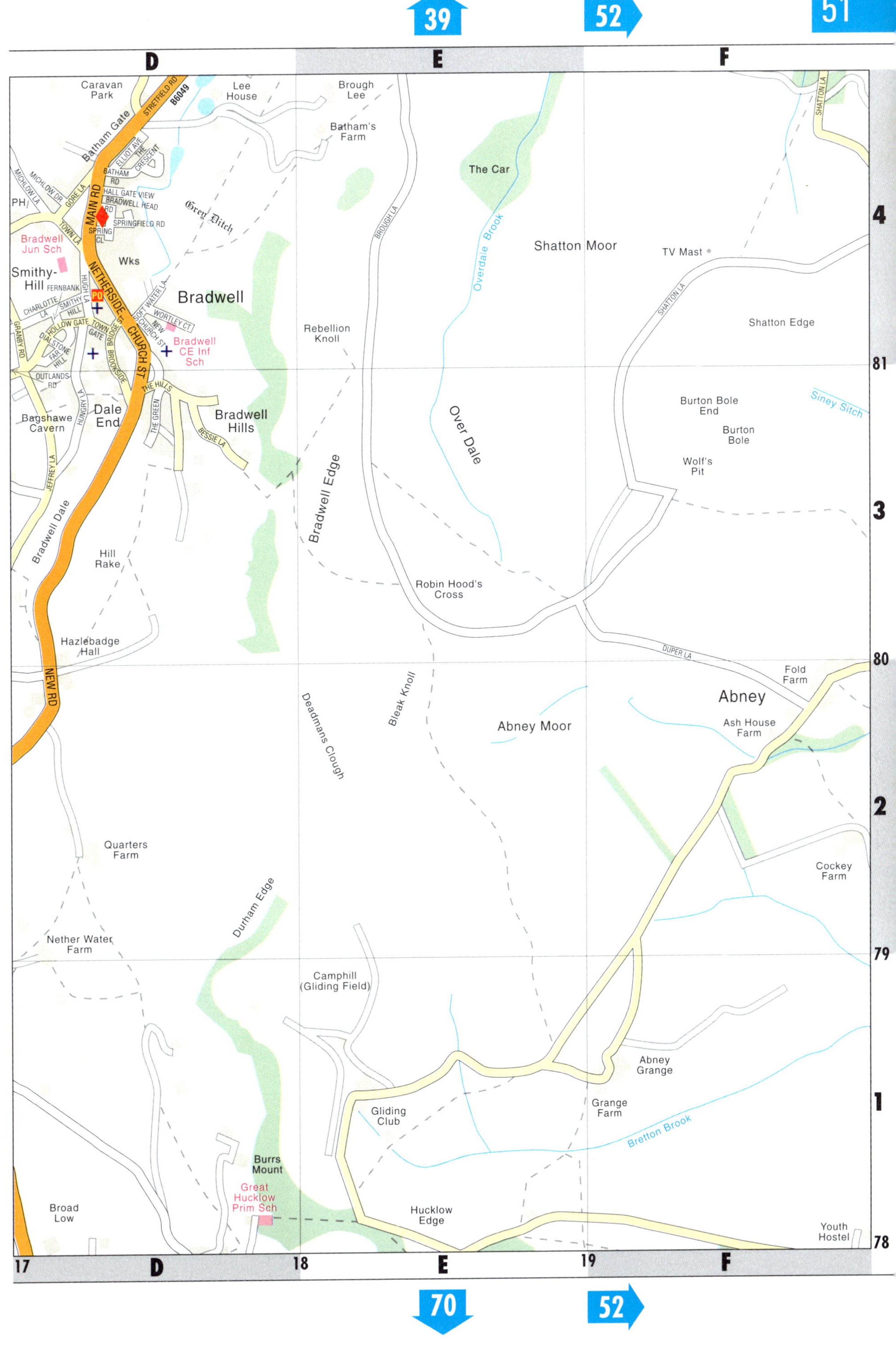
39
52
D
E
F
Caravan Park
Lee House
Brough Lee
Batham's Farm
Batham Gate
STRETFIELD RD
B6049
The Car
Grey Ditch
MAIN RD
Bradwell Jun Sch
Wks
Smithy-Hill
PH
Bradwell
NETHERSIDE
CHURCH ST
Bradwell CE Inf Sch
Shatton Moor
TV Mast
Overdale Brook
BROUGH LA
SHATTON LA
Shatton Edge
Rebellion Knoll
Bagshawe Cavern
Dale End
Bradwell Hills
BESSIE LA
THE GREEN
HUNGRY LA
JEFFREY LA
Over Dale
Burton Bole End
Burton Bole
Siney Sitch
Wolf's Pit
Bradwell Edge
Bradwell Dale
Hill Rake
Robin Hood's Cross
Hazlebadge Hall
NEW RD
DUPER LA
Fold Farm
Abney
Ash House Farm
Abney Moor
Bleak Knoll
Deadmans Clough
Quarters Farm
Cockey Farm
Durham Edge
Nether Water Farm
Camphill (Gliding Field)
Abney Grange
Gliding Club
Grange Farm
Bretton Brook
Burrs Mount
Great Hucklow Prim Sch
Broad Low
Hucklow Edge
Youth Hostel
4
81
3
80
2
79
1
78
17
18
19
70
52

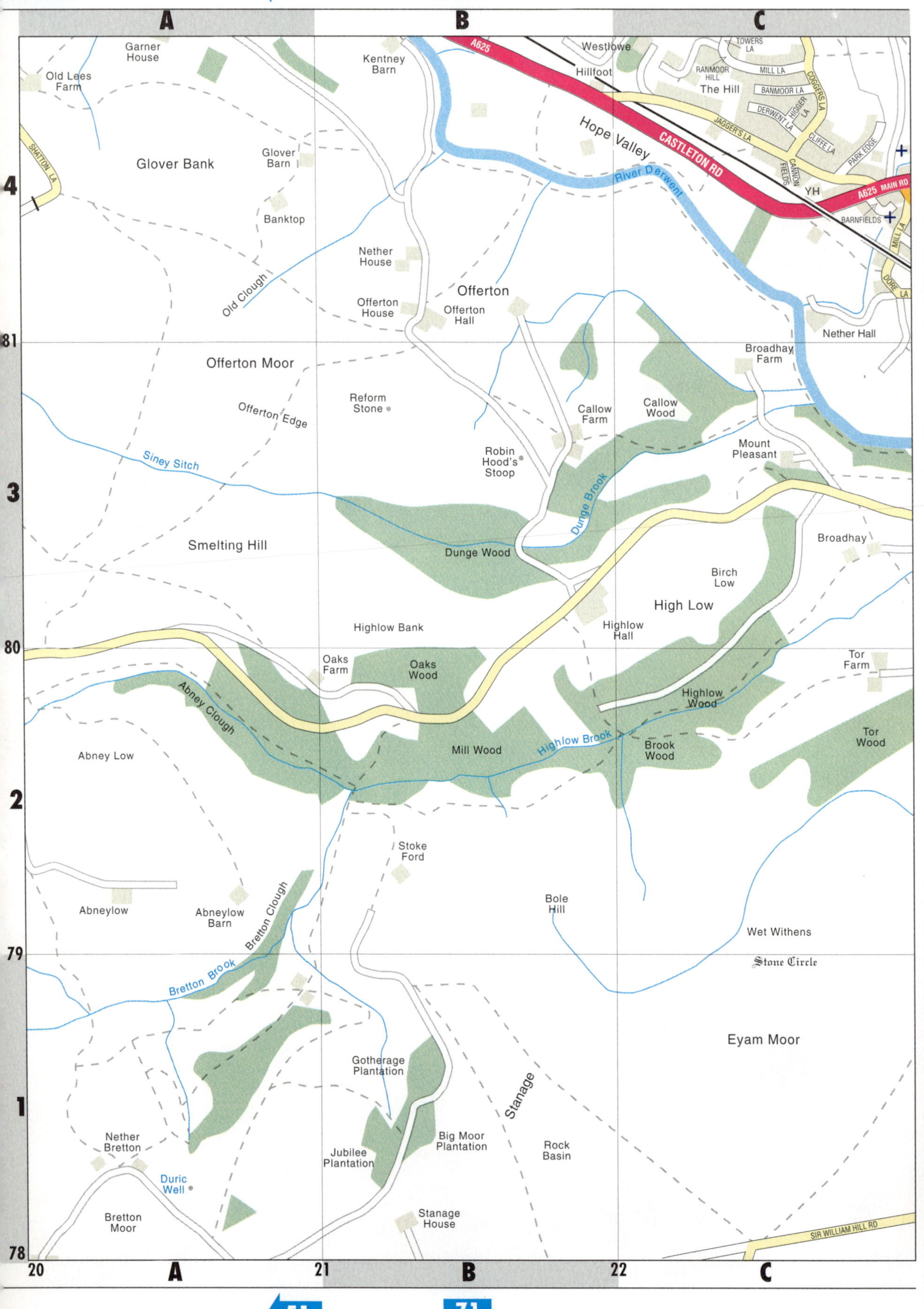

A   **B**   **C**

Garner House

Old Lees Farm

Glover Bank

Glover Barn

Banktop

Kentney Barn

Old Clough

Nether House

Offerton House

Offerton Hall

Offerton

Westlowe

Hillfoot

The Hill

A625

Hope Valley

River Derwent

CASTLETON RD

TOWERS LA

RANMOOR HILL

MILL LA

BANMOOR LA

COGGERS LA

DERWENT LA

HIDGER LA

CLIFFE LA

JAGGER'S LA

PARK EDGE

CANNON FIELDS

A625 MAIN RD

YH

BARNFIELDS

DORE LA

Nether Hall

4

Offerton Moor

Offerton Edge

Reform Stone

Siney Sitch

Smelting Hill

Robin Hood's Stoop

Callow Farm

Callow Wood

Broadhay Farm

Mount Pleasant

Dunge Brook

Dunge Wood

Birch Low

High Low

Broadhay

81

3

Highlow Bank

Oaks Farm

Oaks Wood

Abney Clough

Abney Low

Mill Wood

Highlow Brook

Highlow Hall

Highlow Wood

Brook Wood

Tor Farm

Tor Wood

80

2

Stoke Ford

Bole Hill

Wet Withens

Stone Circle

Abneylow

Abneylow Barn

Bretton Clough

Bretton Brook

79

Gotherage Plantation

Stanage

Eyam Moor

1

Nether Bretton

Duric Well

Jubilee Plantation

Big Moor Plantation

Rock Basin

Bretton Moor

Stanage House

SIR WILLIAM HILL RD

78

20   **A**   21   **B**   22   **C**

41
54

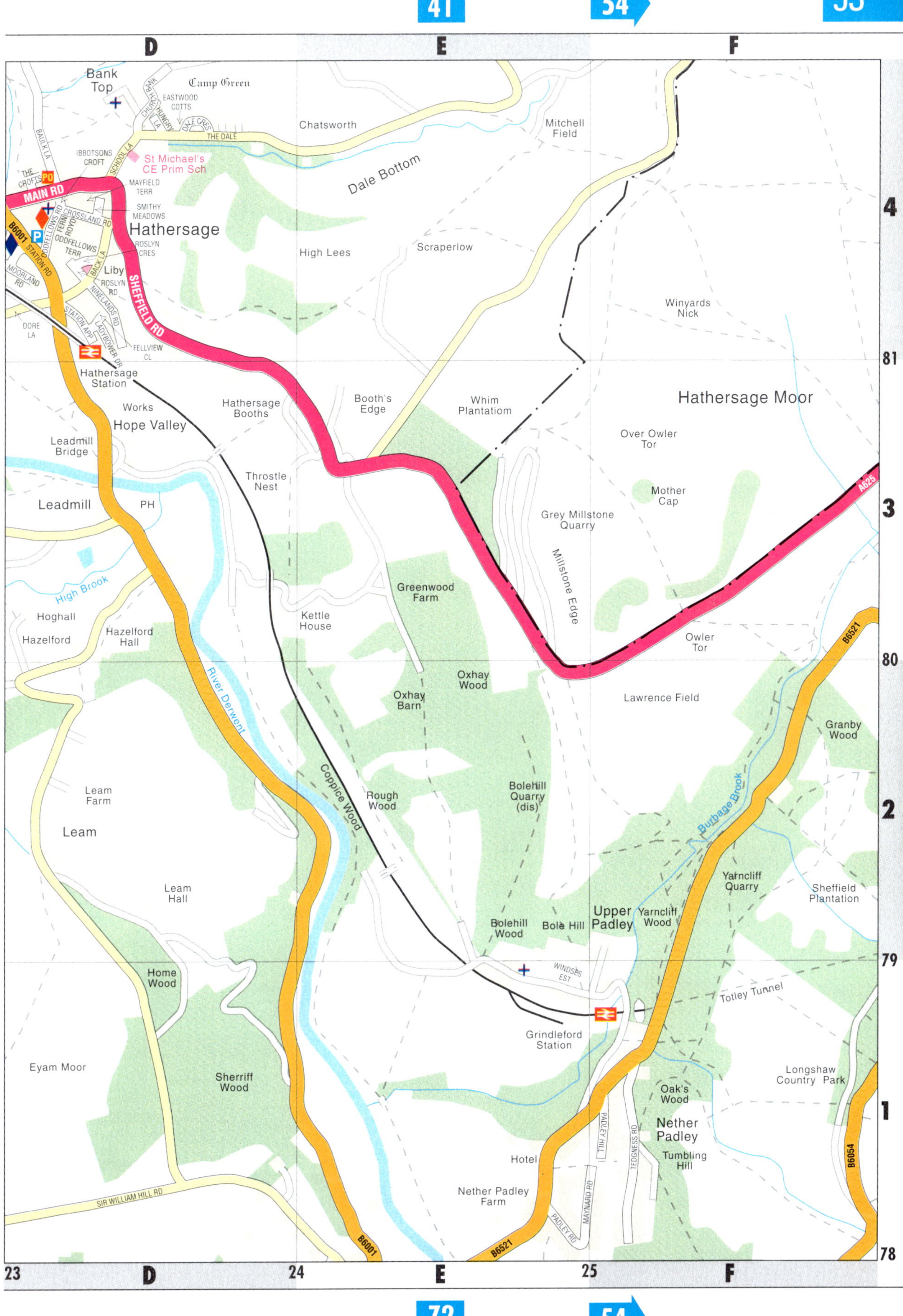
D
E
F
Bank Top
Camp Green
EASTWOOD COTTS
CHURCH BANK
HUNGRY LA
DALE CRES
THE DALE
BAULK LA
IBBOTSONS CROFT
SCHOOL LA
St Michael's CE Prim Sch
THE CROFTS
PO
MAIN RD
MAYFIELD TERR
SMITHY MEADOWS
CROSSLAND RD
ODDFELLOWS RD
FERN RD
ROYD
Hathersage
ROSLYN CRES
ODDFELLOWS TERR
BACK LA
Liby
ROSLYN RD
B6001
STATION RD
MOORLAND RD
NINELANDS RD
SHEFFIELD RD
STATION APP
DORE LA
LADYBOWER DR
FELLVIEW CL
Hathersage Station
Works
Hope Valley
Leadmill Bridge
Leadmill
PH
High Brook
Hoghall
Hazelford
Hazelford Hall
River Derwent
Leam Farm
Leam
Leam Hall
Home Wood
Eyam Moor
Sherriff Wood
SIR WILLIAM HILL RD
B6001
Chatsworth
Dale Bottom
High Lees
Scraperlow
Mitchell Field
Hathersage Booths
Booth's Edge
Whim Plantation
Throstle Nest
Kettle House
Greenwood Farm
Oxhay Wood
Oxhay Barn
Coppice Wood
Rough Wood
Bolehill Quarry (dis)
Bolehill Wood
Bole Hill
Upper Padley
WINDSES EST
Grindleford Station
Hotel
Nether Padley Farm
PADLEY RD
MAYNARD RD
PADLEY HILL
TEDGNESS RD
B6521
Winyards Nick
Hathersage Moor
Over Owler Tor
Mother Cap
Grey Millstone Quarry
Millstone Edge
A625
Owler Tor
Lawrence Field
B6521
Granby Wood
Burbage Brook
Yarncliff Quarry
Sheffield Plantation
Yarncliff Wood
Totley Tunnel
Longshaw Country Park
Oak's Wood
Nether Padley
Tumbling Hill
B6054
4
81
3
80
2
79
1
78
23
D
24
E
25
F

72
54

53
42

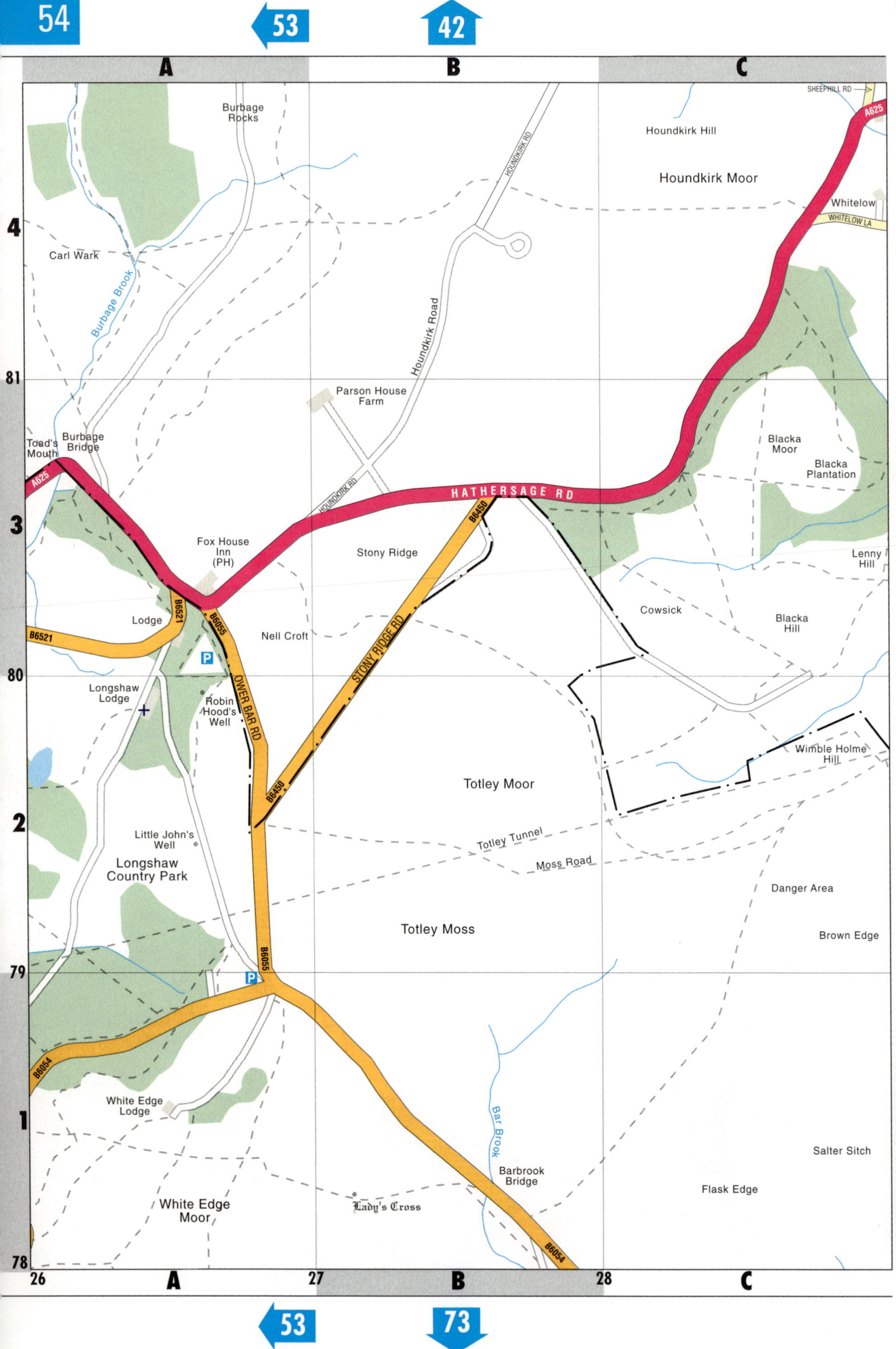

A **B** **C**

SHEEPHILL RD

A625

Houndkirk Hill

Houndkirk Moor

Whitelow

4

WHITELOW LA

Burbage Rocks

Carl Wark

Burbage Brook

HOUNDKIRK RD

81

Parson House Farm

Houndkirk Road

Blacka Moor

Blacka Plantation

Toad's Mouth

Burbage Bridge

A625

HATHERSAGE RD

B6450

Blacka Moor

Lenny Hill

3

Fox House Inn (PH)

Stony Ridge

HOUNDKIRK RD

Cowsick

Blacka Hill

Lodge

B6521

B6055

Nell Croft

STONY RIDGE RD

B6521

80

Longshaw Lodge

OWLER BAR RD

Robin Hood's Well

Wimble Holme Hill

Little John's Well

B6450

Totley Moor

2

Longshaw Country Park

Totley Tunnel

Moss Road

Danger Area

Brown Edge

Totley Moss

B6055

79

P

B6054

Bar Brook

White Edge Lodge

Salter Sitch

1

White Edge Moor

Lady's Cross

Barbrook Bridge

Flask Edge

B6054

78

26 **A** **27** **B** **28** **C**

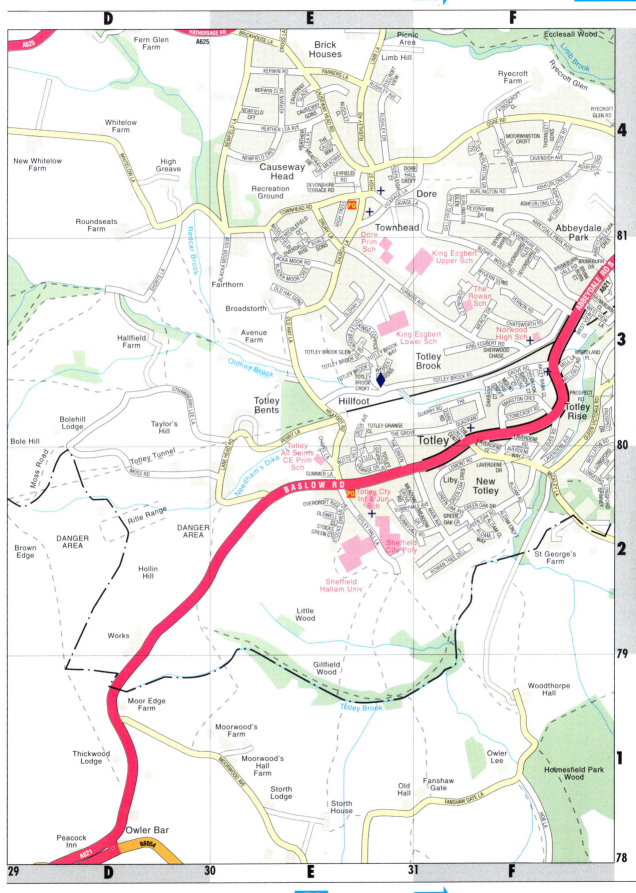
56

D E F

Fern Glen Farm
HATHERSAGE RD
A625
BRICKHOUSE LA
CROSS LA
Brick Houses
Picnic Area
Limb Hill
LIMB LA
Ecclesall Wood
Limb Brook
Ryecroft Farm
Ryecroft Glen
KERWIN RD
PARKERS LA
KERWIN CL
KERWIN DR
CAUSEWAY GLADE
CAUSEWAY GDNS
CAUSEWAY HEAD RD
RUSHLEY CL
RUSHLEY RD
RUSHLEY AVE
RYECROFT VIEW
RUSHLEY DR
NEWFIELD CFT
NEWFIELD LA
HEATHER LEA AVE
HEATHER LEA PL
THE CAUSEWAY
THE MEADWAY
MEADWAY DR
NEWFIELD CRES
Whitelow Farm
WHITELOW LA
New Whitelow Farm
High Greave
Causeway Head
Recreation Ground
LEYFIELD RD
DEVONSHIRE TERRACE RD
HIGH ST
RUSHLEIGH CT
DORE HALL CROFT
VICARAGE LA
SAVAGE LA
Dore
KINGSCROFT CL
DORE RD
MOORWINSTON CROFT
THORNSETT GDNS
VICTOR RD
RYECROFT GLEN RD
SOUTH CT
BURLINGTON CT
ASHFURLONG RD
CAVENDISH AVE
ASHFURLONG PK
ASHFURLONG CL
ASHFURLONG DR
BURLINGTON RD
BURLINGTON GLEN
BURLINGTON GR
DEVONSHIRE DR
GILLEYFIELD AVE
Abbeydale Park
ABBEYDALE PARK RISE
ABBEYDALE PARK CRES
Roundseats Farm
TOWNHEAD RD
HIGH TREES
PO
Townhead
MIDDLEFIELD CL
MIDDLEFIELD CFT
OVERDALE RISE
OVERDALE GDNS
DRURY LA
Dore Prim Sch
King Ecgbert Upper Sch
DEVONSHIRE GR
DEVONSHIRE GLEN
DEVONSHIRE CL
BUSHEY WOOD RD
BRINKBURN VALE RD
BRINKBURN DR
BRINKBURN CT
ABBEYDALE RD S
A621
Redcar Brook
BLACKA MOOR VIEW
SHORTS LA
BLACKA MOOR RD
BLACKA MOOR CRES
CHURCH LA
Fairthorn
WYVERN GDNS
The Rowan Sch
OLD HAY GDNS
FURNISS AVE
DURVALE CT
MERCIA DR
VERNON RD
Broadstorth
OLDHAY CL
CHATSWORTH RD
BRINKBURN CL
WEST VIEW
WEST VIEW CL
Hallfield Farm
Avenue Farm
OLD HAY LA
TOTLEY BROOK RD
KINGS COPPICE
King Ecgbert Lower Sch
Norwood High Sch
KING ECGBERT RD
SHERWOOD CHASE
WOODLAND PL
TOTLEY BROOK GLEN
TOTLEY BROOK GR
TOTLEY BROOK WAY
Totley Brook
MILL LA
MILLDALE RD
Oldhay Brook
TOTLEY BROOK CL
TOTLEY BROOK CROFT
WESSEX GDNS
TOTLEY BROOK RD
GROVE RD
GROVE HOUSE CT
LAYBROOK CT
AKLEY BANK CL
MOUNT FORD
OAKBANK CT
CROFT CT
MARSTON CRES
PROSPECT RD
STRAWBERRY LEE LA
Totley Bents
Hillfoot
HILLFOOT RD
QUARRY RD
TERREY RD
THE QUADRANT
STONECROFT RD
Totley Rise
QUEEN VICTORIA RD
PROSPECT DR
Bolehill Lodge
Taylor's Hill
PENNY LA
GROVE AVE
TOTLEY GRANGE CL
THE GROVE
THE CRES
CENT
Totley
LAVERDENE CL
LAVERDENE RD
LAVERDENE WAY
LAVERDENE AVE
GLOVER RD
WOLLATON RD
LONGFORD DR
Bole Hill
Moss Road
Totley Tunnel
MOSS RD
LANE HEAD RD
CHAPEL LA
Totley All Saints CE Prim Sch
BUTTS HILL
TOTLEY GRANGE DR
TOTLEY GRANGE RD
TOTLEY HALL CROFT
THE GREEN
LEMONT RD
LAVERDENE DR
Needham's Dike
SUMMER LA
Liby
GREEN OAK CRES
New Totley
ALDAM RD
MICKLEY LA
LONGFORD CL
LONGFORD RD
LONGFORD SPINNEY
BASLOW RD
PO
Totley Cty Inf & Jun Sch
MEADOW GROVE RD
OVERCROFT RISE
OLDWELL CL
STOCKS CL
STOCKS GREEN CT
STOCKS GREEN DR
TOTLEY HALL LA
SUNNYVALE AVE
SUNNYVALE RD
MEADOW GR
MAIN AVE
GREEN OAK AVE
GREEN OAK DR
GREEN OAK GR
GREEN OAK RD
ALDAM CL
ALDAM WAY
ALDAM CROFT
Rifle Range
DANGER AREA
DANGER AREA
Brown Edge
Sheffield City Poly
ROWAN TREE DELL
St George's Farm
Hollin Hill
Sheffield Hallam Univ
Little Wood
Works
Gillfield Wood
Woodthorpe Hall
Moor Edge Farm
Totley Brook
Moorwood's Farm
Moorwood's Hall Farm
MOORWOOD AVE
Thickwood Lodge
Owler Lee
Holmesfield Park Wood
Storth Lodge
Old Hall
Fanshaw Gate
FANSHAW GATE LA
Storth House
HOB LA
Owler Bar
Peacock Inn
A621
B6054

4 3 2 1
81 80 79 78

29 D 30 E 31 F

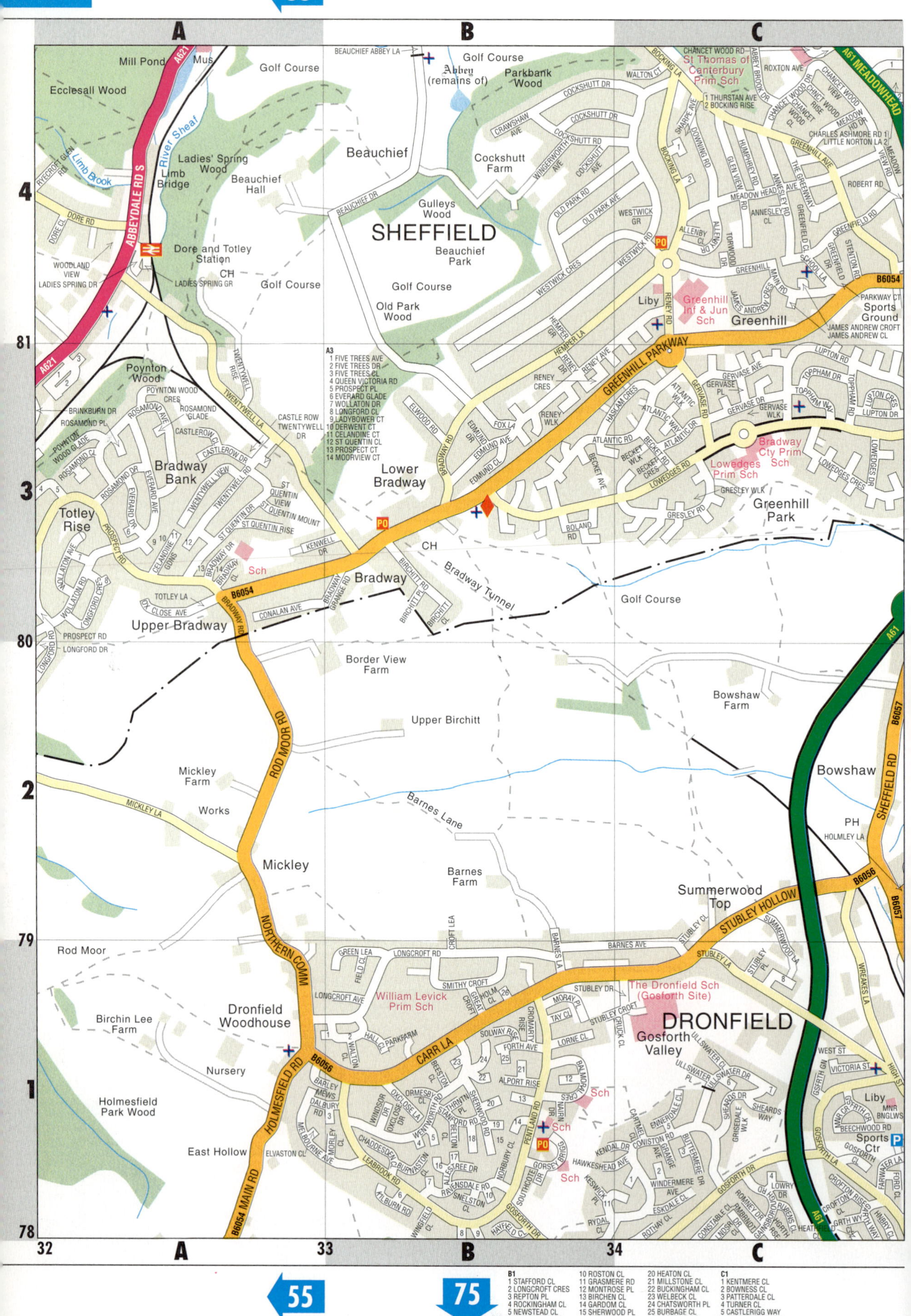

B1
1 STAFFORD CL
2 LONGCROFT CRES
3 REPTON PL
4 ROCKINGHAM CL
5 NEWSTEAD CL
6 MAPPERLEY RD
7 HAZELWOOD CL
8 BRADWELL CL
9 ASHFORD RD
10 ROSTON CL
11 GRASMERE RD
12 MONTROSE PL
13 BIRCHEN CL
14 GARDOM CL
15 SHERWOOD PL
16 INGLEBY CL
17 IVAN BROOK CL
18 ARUNDEL CL
19 LYNWOOD CL
20 HEATON CL
21 MILLSTONE CL
22 BUCKINGHAM CL
23 WELBECK CL
24 CHATSWORTH PL
25 BURBAGE CL
26 ORCHARD SQ

C1
1 KENTMERE CL
2 BOWNESS CL
3 PATTERDALE CL
4 TURNER CL
5 CASTLERIGG WAY
6 ULLSWATER PARK
7 SHEARDS CL
8 SUMMERWOOD PL

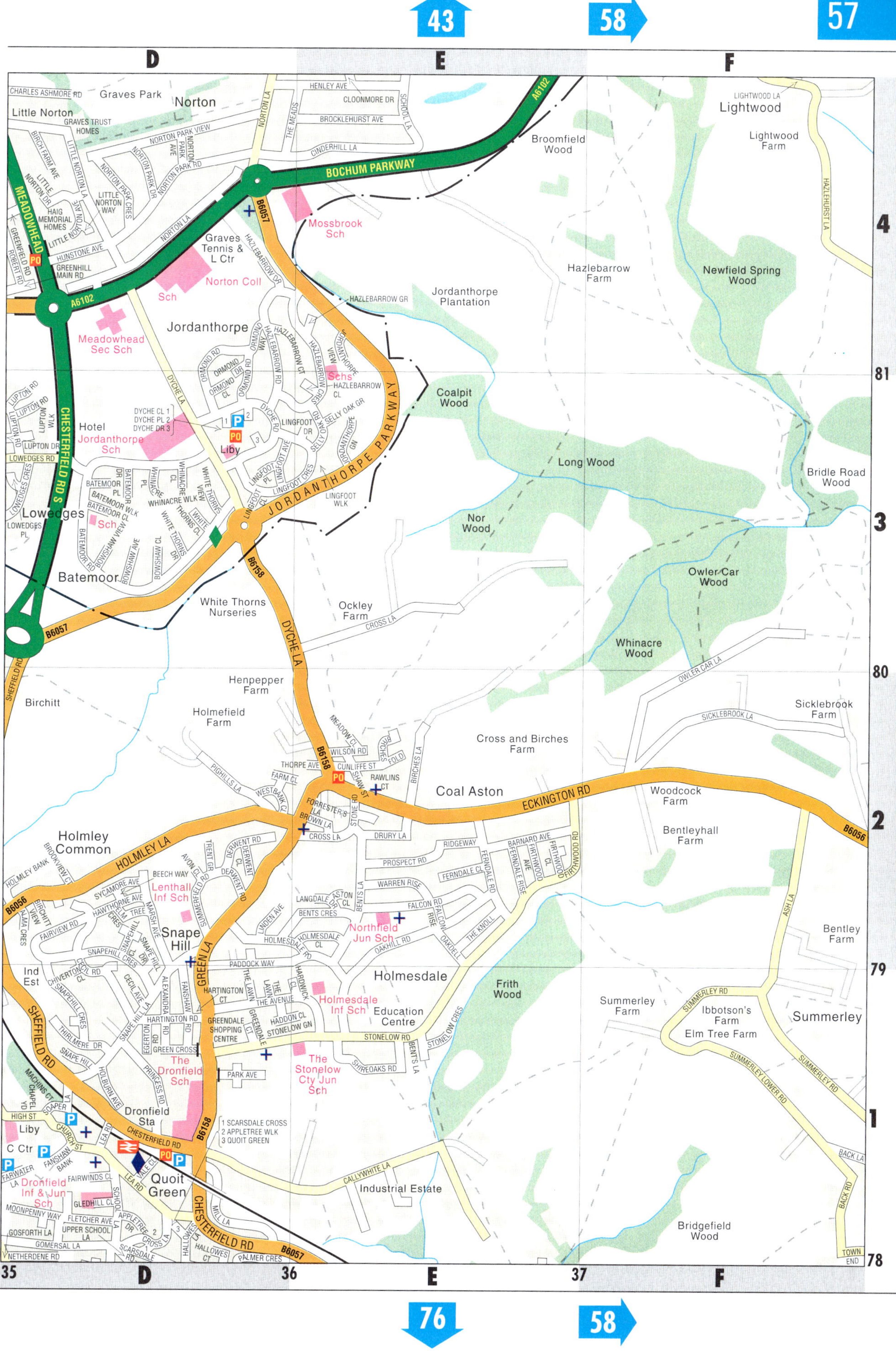
D
E
F
Graves Park
Norton
Little Norton
Lightwood
Lightwood Farm
Broomfield Wood
BOCHUM PARKWAY
A6102
MEADOWHEAD
Mossbrook Sch
Graves Tennis & L Ctr
Norton Coll
Sch
Hazlebarrow Farm
Newfield Spring Wood
Jordanthorpe Plantation
Jordanthorpe
Meadowhead Sec Sch
Coalpit Wood
Schs
CHESTERFIELD RD S
Hotel
Jordanthorpe Sch
Liby
JORDANTHORPE PARKWAY
Long Wood
Bridle Road Wood
Lowedges
Nor Wood
Batemoor
Owler Car Wood
White Thorns Nurseries
Ockley Farm
DYCHE LA
Whinacre Wood
B6057
B6158
Henpepper Farm
Birchitt
Holmefield Farm
Sicklebrook Farm
Cross and Birches Farm
Coal Aston
ECKINGTON RD
Woodcock Farm
Bentleyhall Farm
B6056
Holmley Common
HOLMLEY LA
Lenthall Inf Sch
Snape Hill
Northfield Jun Sch
Bentley Farm
Ind Est
Holmesdale
Frith Wood
Holmesdale Inf Sch
Education Centre
Summerley Farm
Ibbotson's Farm
Elm Tree Farm
Summerley
SHEFFIELD RD
The Dronfield Sch
The Stonelow Cty Jun Sch
Dronfield Sta
Liby
C Ctr
Quoit Green
Dronfield Inf & Jun Sch
Industrial Estate
Bridgefield Wood
CHESTERFIELD RD
1 SCARSDALE CROSS
2 APPLETREE WLK
3 QUOIT GREEN
4
81
3
80
2
79
1
78
35
36
37

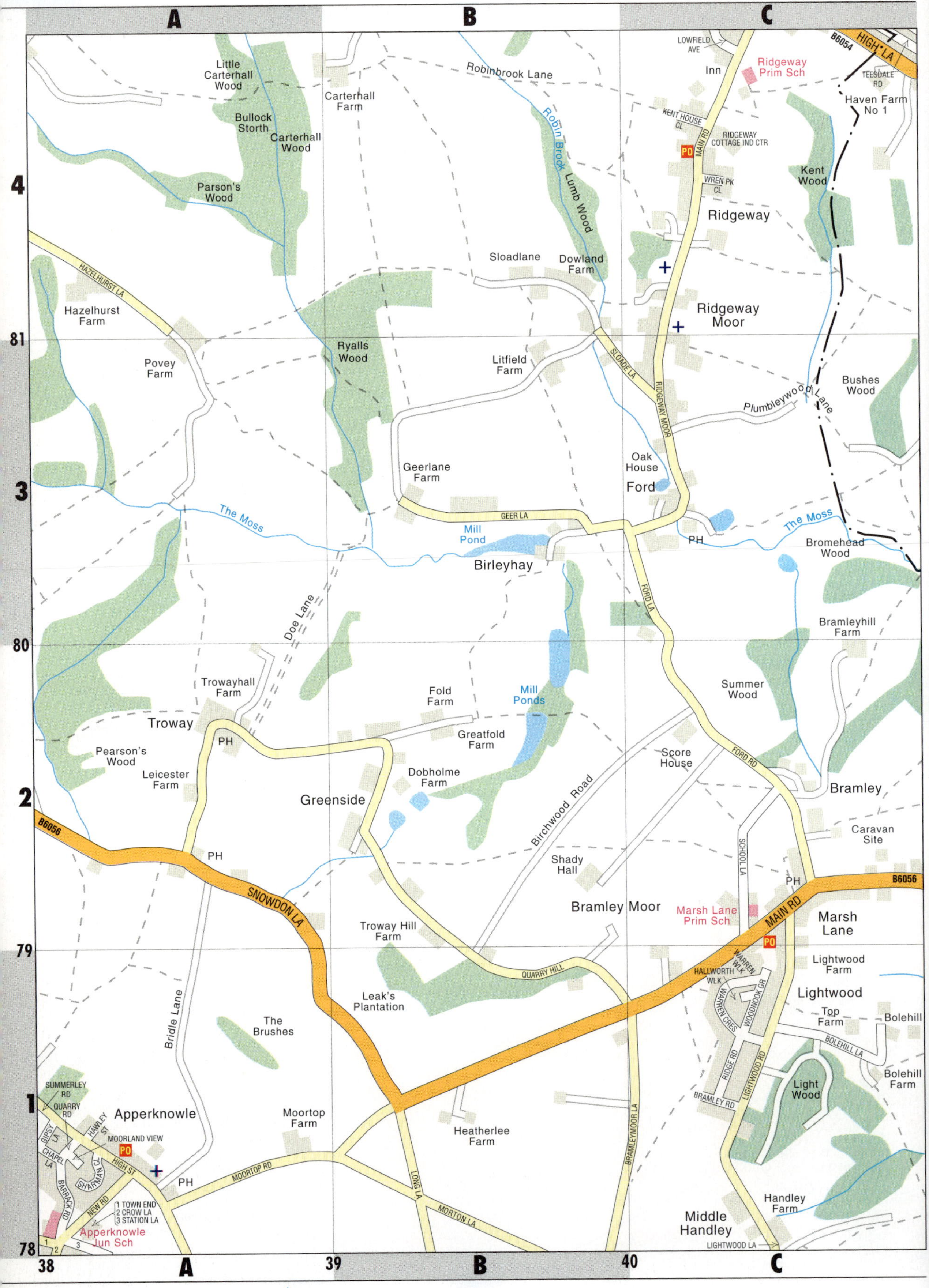
A
B
C
4
81
3
80
2
79
1
78
38
39
40
Little Carterhall Wood
Bullock Storth
Carterhall Wood
Parson's Wood
Carterhall Farm
Robinbrook Lane
Robin Brook
Lumb Wood
LOWFIELD AVE
Inn
Ridgeway Prim Sch
B6054
HIGH LA
TEESDALE RD
Haven Farm No 1
KENT HOUSE CL
RIDGEWAY COTTAGE IND CTR
MAIN RD
PO
WREN PK CL
Kent Wood
Ridgeway
Sloadlane
Dowland Farm
HAZELHURST LA
Hazelhurst Farm
Ridgeway Moor
Povey Farm
Ryalls Wood
Litfield Farm
SLOADE LA
Bushes Wood
Plumbleywood Lane
RIDGEWAY MOOR
Geerlane Farm
Oak House
Ford
GEER LA
The Moss
Mill Pond
PH
Bromehead Wood
Birleyhay
Doe Lane
FORD LA
Bramleyhill Farm
Trowayhall Farm
Fold Farm
Mill Ponds
Summer Wood
Troway
Greatfold Farm
Score House
PH
Pearson's Wood
Leicester Farm
Dobholme Farm
FORD RD
Birchwood Road
Bramley
Greenside
Caravan Site
B6056
SCHOOL LA
PH
Shady Hall
PH
SNOWDON LA
Bramley Moor
Marsh Lane Prim Sch
MAIN RD
Marsh Lane
Troway Hill Farm
PO
Lightwood Farm
WARREN WLK
HALLWORTH WLK
QUARRY HILL
Lightwood
WARREN CRES
WOODNOOK GR
Leak's Plantation
Top Farm
Bolehill
The Brushes
Bridle Lane
BOLEHILL LA
RIDGE RD
LIGHTWOOD RD
Bolehill Farm
Light Wood
SUMMERLEY RD
QUARRY RD
Apperknowle
BRAMLEY RD
Moortop Farm
HAWLEY ST
GIPSY LA
CHAPEL LA
MOORLAND VIEW
PO
Heatherlee Farm
HIGH ST
SHARMAN CL
PH
MOORTOP RD
BRAMLEYMOOR LA
LONG LA
BARRACK RD
NEW RD
1 TOWN END
2 CROW LA
3 STATION LA
MORTON LA
Handley Farm
Middle Handley
Apperknowle Jun Sch
LIGHTWOOD LA
1
2
3

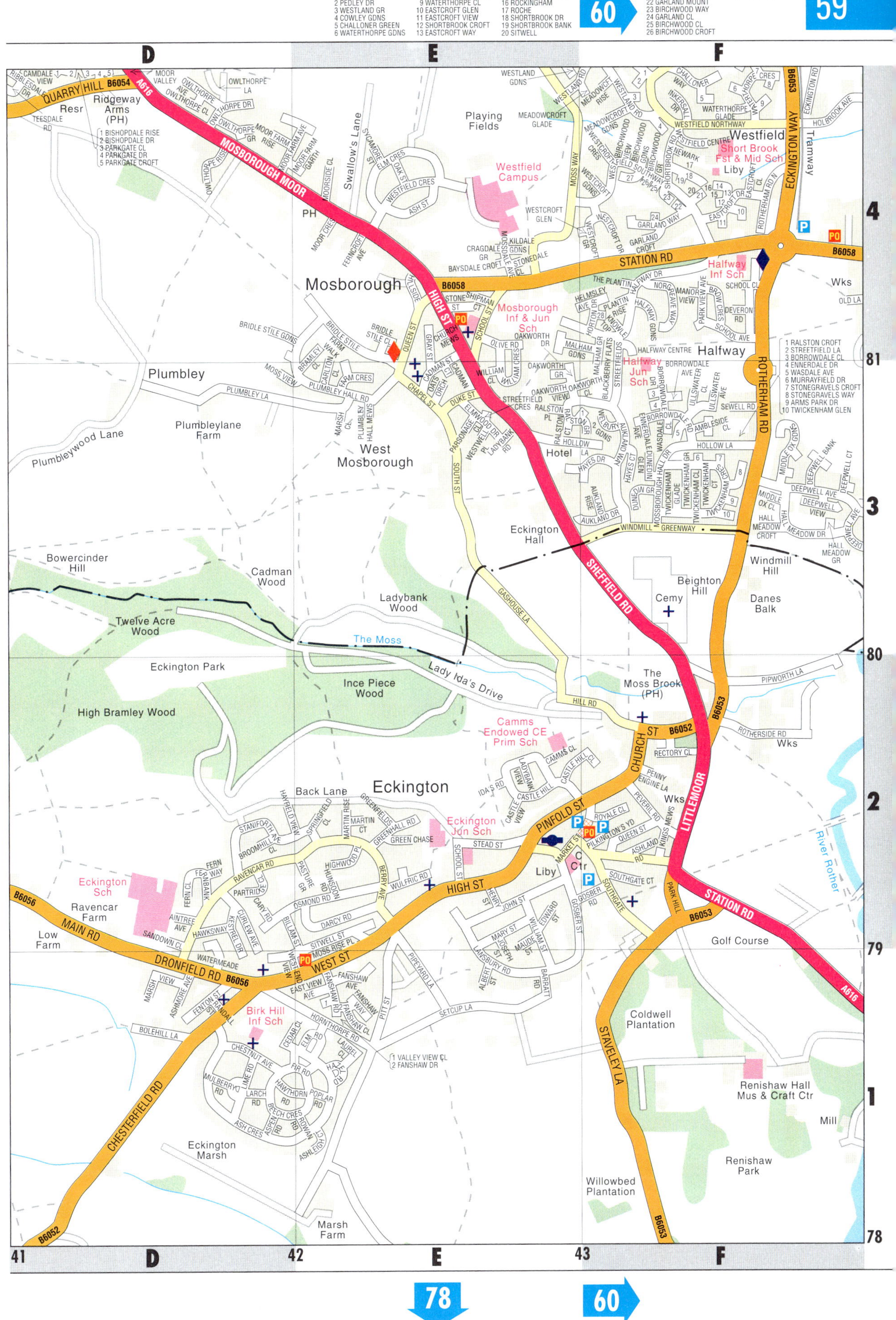
D
E
F
Mosborough
West Mosborough
Plumbley
Halfway
Westfield
Eckington
MOSBOROUGH MOOR
QUARRY HILL
B6054
A616
HIGH ST
SHEFFIELD RD
LITTLEMOOR
STATION RD
B6058
ROTHERHAM RD
ECKINGTON WAY
B6053
Tramway
Ridgeway Arms (PH)
Resr
Playing Fields
Westfield Campus
Short Brook Fst & Mid Sch
Liby
Halfway Inf Sch
Halfway Jun Sch
Mosborough Inf & Jun Sch
Hotel
Wks
Plumbleylane Farm
Plumbleywood Lane
Bowercinder Hill
Cadman Wood
Twelve Acre Wood
Ladybank Wood
The Moss
Eckington Park
High Bramley Wood
Ince Piece Wood
Lady Ida's Drive
Eckington Hall
Beighton Hill
Cemy
Windmill Hill
Danes Balk
The Moss Brook (PH)
Camms Endowed CE Prim Sch
Eckington Jun Sch
Eckington Sch
Ravencar Farm
Low Farm
Birk Hill Inf Sch
Back Lane
PINFOLD ST
CHURCH ST
B6052
DRONFIELD RD
B6056
MAIN RD
WEST ST
CHESTERFIELD RD
STAVELEY LA
Golf Course
Coldwell Plantation
Renishaw Hall Mus & Craft Ctr
Mill
Renishaw Park
Eckington Marsh
Marsh Farm
Willowbed Plantation
River Rother
1 BISHOPDALE RISE
2 BISHOPDALE DR
3 PARKGATE CL
4 PARKGATE DR
5 PARKGATE CROFT
1 RALSTON CROFT
2 STREETFIELD LA
3 BORROWDALE CL
4 ENNERDALE DR
5 WASDALE AVE
6 MURRAYFIELD DR
7 STONEGRAVELS CROFT
8 STONEGRAVELS WAY
9 ARMS PARK DR
10 TWICKENHAM GLEN
1 VALLEY VIEW CL
2 FANSHAW DR
4
81
3
80
2
79
1
78
41
42
43

59

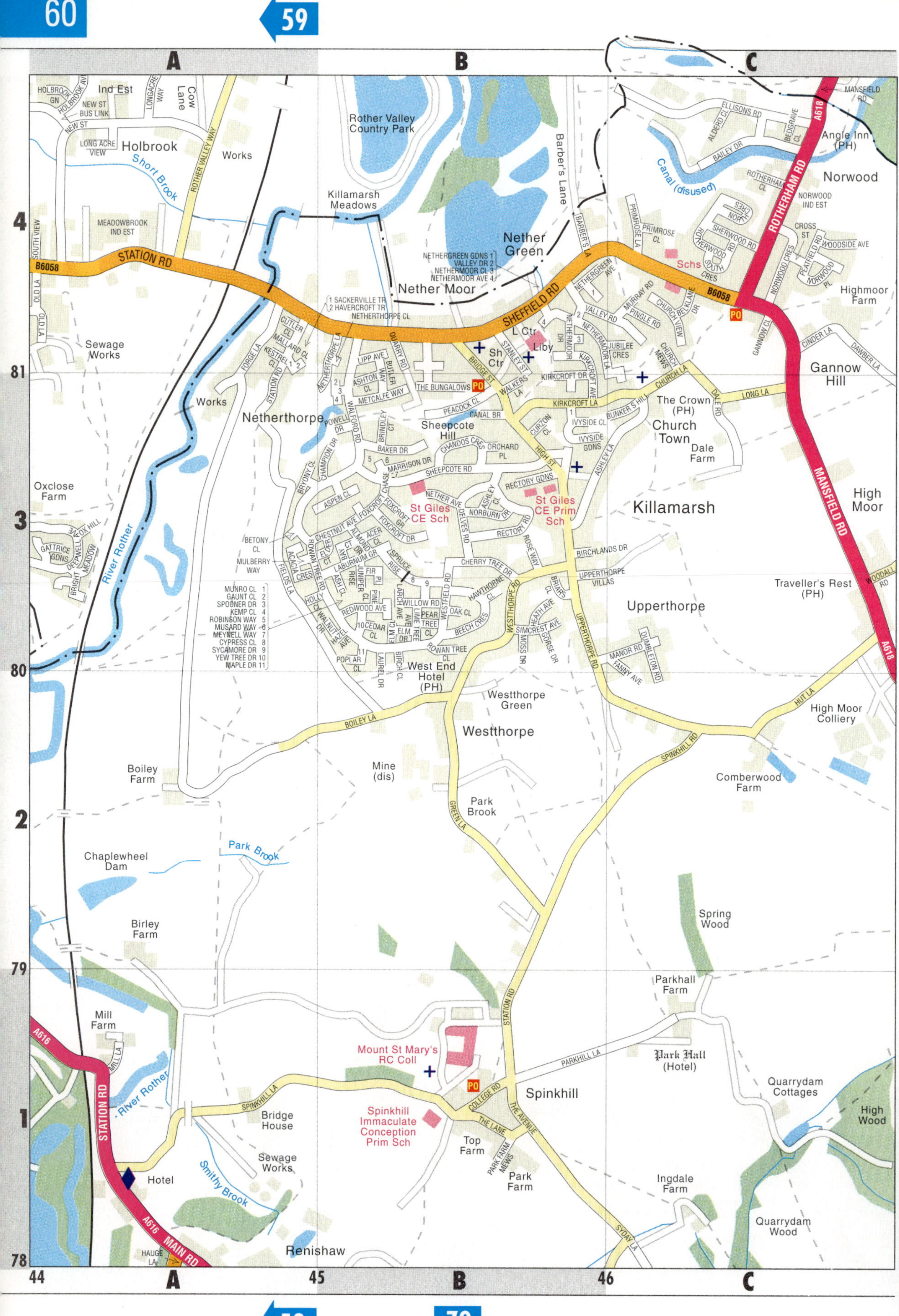

Holbrook
Ind Est
Cow Lane
Works
Rother Valley Country Park
Killamarsh Meadows
Barber's Lane
Norwood
Canal (disused)
Angle Inn (PH)
Norwood Ind Est
Nether Green
Nether Moor
Schs
Highmoor Farm
STATION RD
B6058
SHEFFIELD RD
ROTHERHAM RD
A618
Sewage Works
Meadowbrook Ind Est
Gannow Hill
L Ctr
Liby
Sh Ctr
Works
Netherthorpe
Sheepcote Hill
The Crown (PH)
Church Town
Dale Farm
Oxclose Farm
St Giles CE Sch
St Giles CE Prim Sch
Killamarsh
MANSFIELD RD
High Moor
River Rother
Traveller's Rest (PH)
Upperthorpe
West End Hotel (PH)
Westthorpe Green
Westthorpe
High Moor Colliery
Boiley Farm
Mine (dis)
Comberwood Farm
Park Brook
Chaplewheel Dam
Spring Wood
Birley Farm
Parkhall Farm
Mill Farm
Mount St Mary's RC Coll
Park Hall (Hotel)
Quarrydam Cottages
Spinkhill
High Wood
Bridge House
Spinkhill Immaculate Conception Prim Sch
Top Farm
Sewage Works
Hotel
Smithy Brook
Park Farm
Ingdale Farm
Quarrydam Wood
Renishaw
STATION RD
A616
MAIN RD
A
B
C
4
81
3
80
2
79
1
78
44
45
46

59
79

62

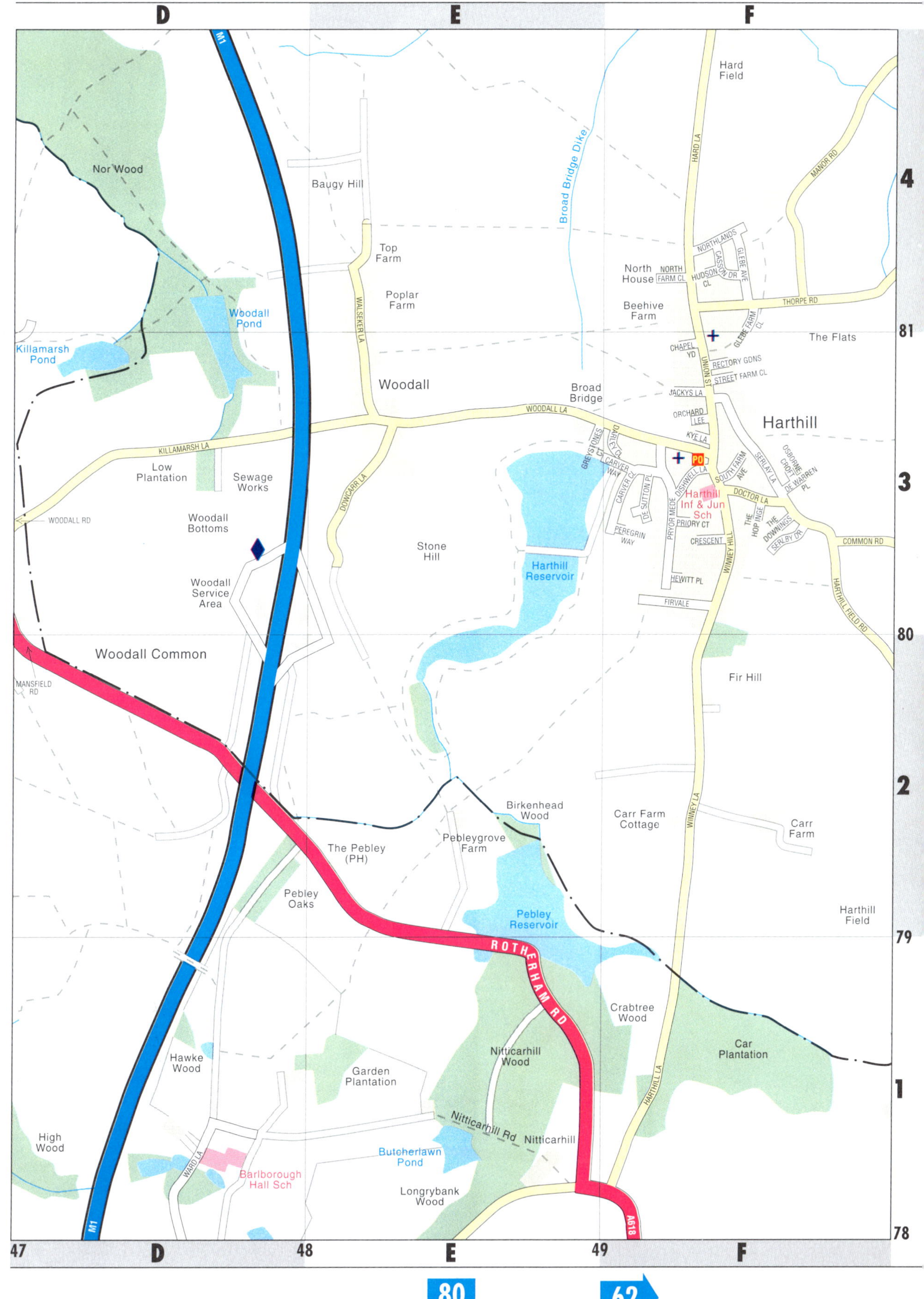
D
E
F
M1
Nor Wood
Baugy Hill
Hard Field
Broad Bridge Dike
HARD LA
MANOR RD
Top Farm
Poplar Farm
Woodall Pond
Killamarsh Pond
North House
NORTH FARM CL
NORTHLANDS
CASSON DR
GLEBE AVE
HUDSON CL
THORPE RD
Beehive Farm
GLEBE FARM CL
The Flats
CHAPEL YD
RECTORY GDNS
STREET FARM CL
UNION ST
WALSEKER LA
Woodall
Broad Bridge
JACKYS LA
WOODALL LA
ORCHARD LEE
KYE LA
Harthill
KILLAMARSH LA
Low Plantation
Sewage Works
GREYSTONES CT
DARLEY CL
CARVER WAY
CARVER CL
DE SUTTON PL
DISHWELL LA
SOUTH FARM AVE
SERLAY LA
OSBORNE CROFT
DE WARREN PL
DOWCARR LA
Harthill Inf & Jun Sch
DOCTOR LA
WOODALL RD
Woodall Bottoms
PRYOR MEDE
PRIORY CT
THE HOP INGE
THE DOWNINGS
SERLBY DR
COMMON RD
Stone Hill
PEREGRIN WAY
CRESCENT
Harthill Reservoir
Woodall Service Area
HEWITT PL
WINNEY HILL
FIRVALE
HARTHILL FIELD RD
Woodall Common
MANSFIELD RD
Fir Hill
Birkenhead Wood
Carr Farm Cottage
Carr Farm
WINNEY LA
Pebleygrove Farm
The Pebley (PH)
Pebley Oaks
Pebley Reservoir
Harthill Field
ROTHERHAM RD
Crabtree Wood
Car Plantation
Nitticarhill Wood
Hawke Wood
Garden Plantation
HARTHILL LA
Nitticarhill Rd
Nitticarhill
High Wood
Butcherlawn Pond
WARD LA
Barlborough Hall Sch
Longrybank Wood
A618
4
81
3
80
2
79
1
78
47
48
49

80
62

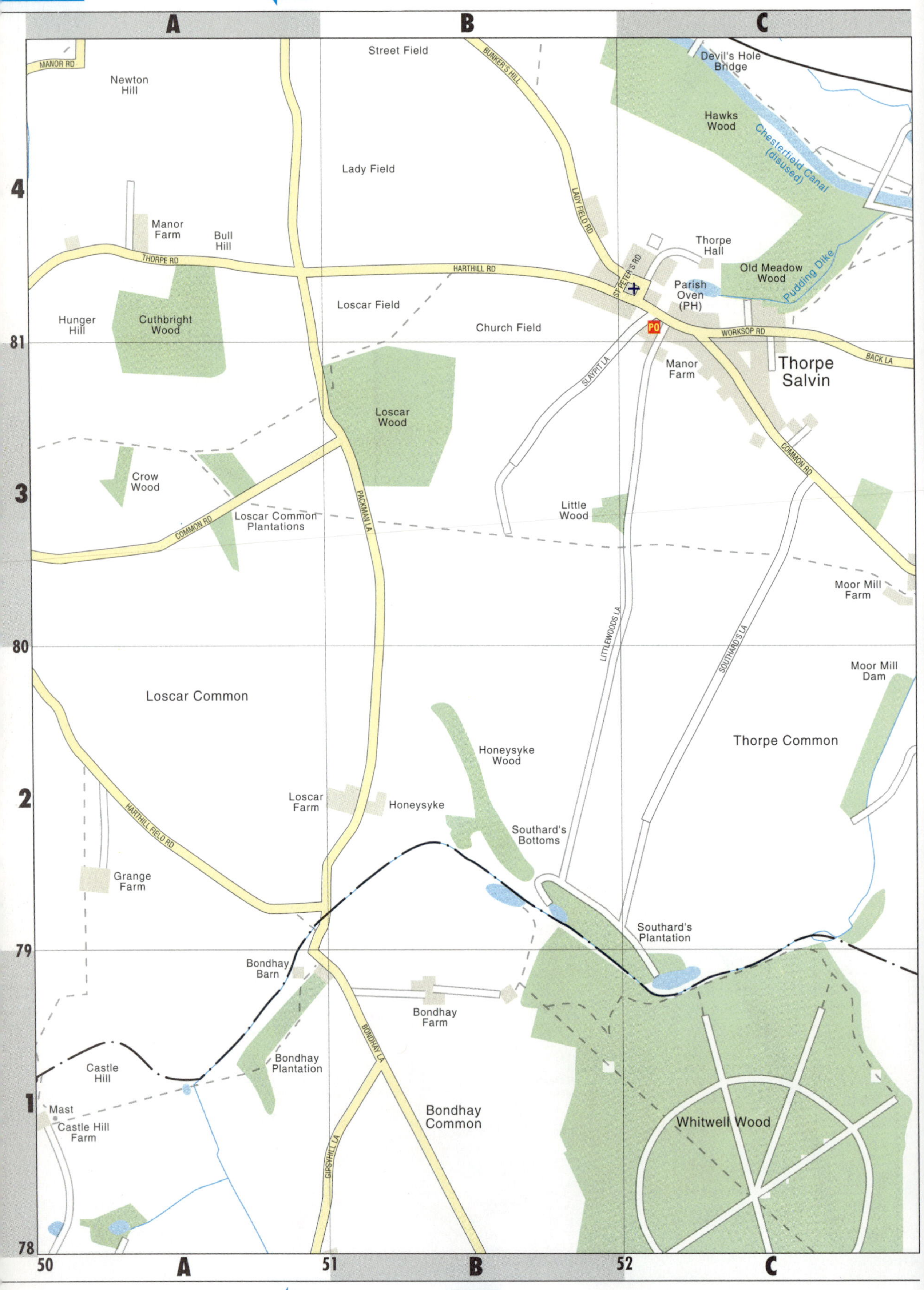

MANOR RD

Newton
Hill

Street Field

BUNKER'S HILL

Devil's Hole
Bridge

Hawks
Wood

Chesterfield Canal
(disused)

4

Lady Field

LADY FIELD RD

Manor
Farm

Bull
Hill

Thorpe Hall

Thorpe
Hall

Old Meadow
Wood

Pudding Dike

THORPE RD

HARTHILL RD

ST PETER'S RD

Parish
Oven
(PH)

Hunger
Hill

Loscar Field

Cuthbright
Wood

Church Field

PO

WORKSOP RD

BACK LA

81

Thorpe
Salvin

Loscar
Wood

SLAYPIT LA

Manor
Farm

COMMON RD

Crow
Wood

Loscar Common
Plantations

PACKMAN LA

Little
Wood

Moor Mill
Farm

COMMON RD

LITTLEWOODS LA

SOUTHARD'S LA

80

Moor Mill
Dam

Loscar Common

Thorpe Common

2

HARTHILL FIELD RD

Loscar
Farm

Honeysyke

Honeysyke
Wood

Southard's
Bottoms

Grange
Farm

Southard's
Plantation

79

Bondhay
Barn

BONDHAY LA

Bondhay
Farm

Castle
Hill

Bondhay
Plantation

1

Mast

Castle Hill
Farm

GIPSY HILL LA

Bondhay
Common

Whitwell Wood

78

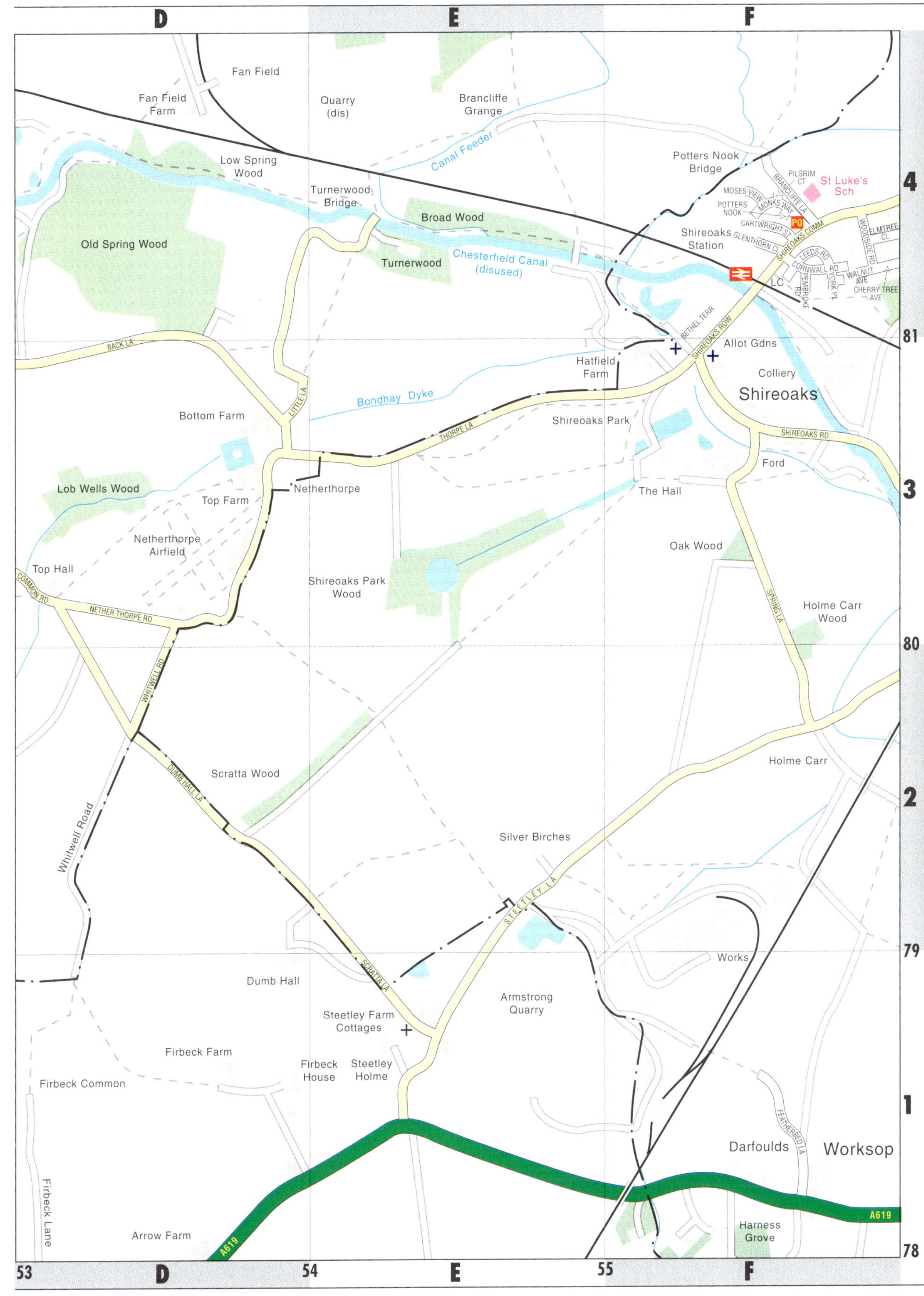

D
E
F
Fan Field
Fan Field Farm
Quarry (dis)
Brancliffe Grange
Canal Feeder
Low Spring Wood
Potters Nook Bridge
PILGRIM CT
St Luke's Sch
Turnerwood Bridge
MOSES VIEW
BRANCLIFFE LA
POTTERS NOOK
MONKS WAY
Broad Wood
CARTWRIGHT ST
PO
Old Spring Wood
Shireoaks Station
GLENTHORN CL
SHIREOAKS COMM
WOODSIDE RD
ELMTREE CL
Turnerwood
Chesterfield Canal (disused)
LEEDS RD
CORNWALL RD
WALNUT AVE
CHERRY TREE AVE
LC
PEMBROKE RD
YORK PL
BETHEL TERR
BACK LA
SHIREOAKS ROW
Allot Gdns
Hatfield Farm
Colliery
Shireoaks
Bondhay Dyke
LITTLE LA
Bottom Farm
THORPE LA
Shireoaks Park
SHIREOAKS RD
Ford
Netherthorpe
Lob Wells Wood
Top Farm
The Hall
Netherthorpe Airfield
Oak Wood
Top Hall
Shireoaks Park Wood
COMMON RD
NETHER THORPE RD
SPRING LA
Holme Carr Wood
WHITWELL RD
Scratta Wood
DUMB HALL LA
Holme Carr
Whitwell Road
Silver Birches
STEETLEY LA
Works
Dumb Hall
SCRATTA LA
Armstrong Quarry
Steetley Farm Cottages
Firbeck Farm
Firbeck House
Steetley Holme
Firbeck Common
FEATHERBED LA
Darfoulds
Worksop
Firbeck Lane
Arrow Farm
A619
Harness Grove
4
81
3
80
2
79
1
78
53
54
55

82

45

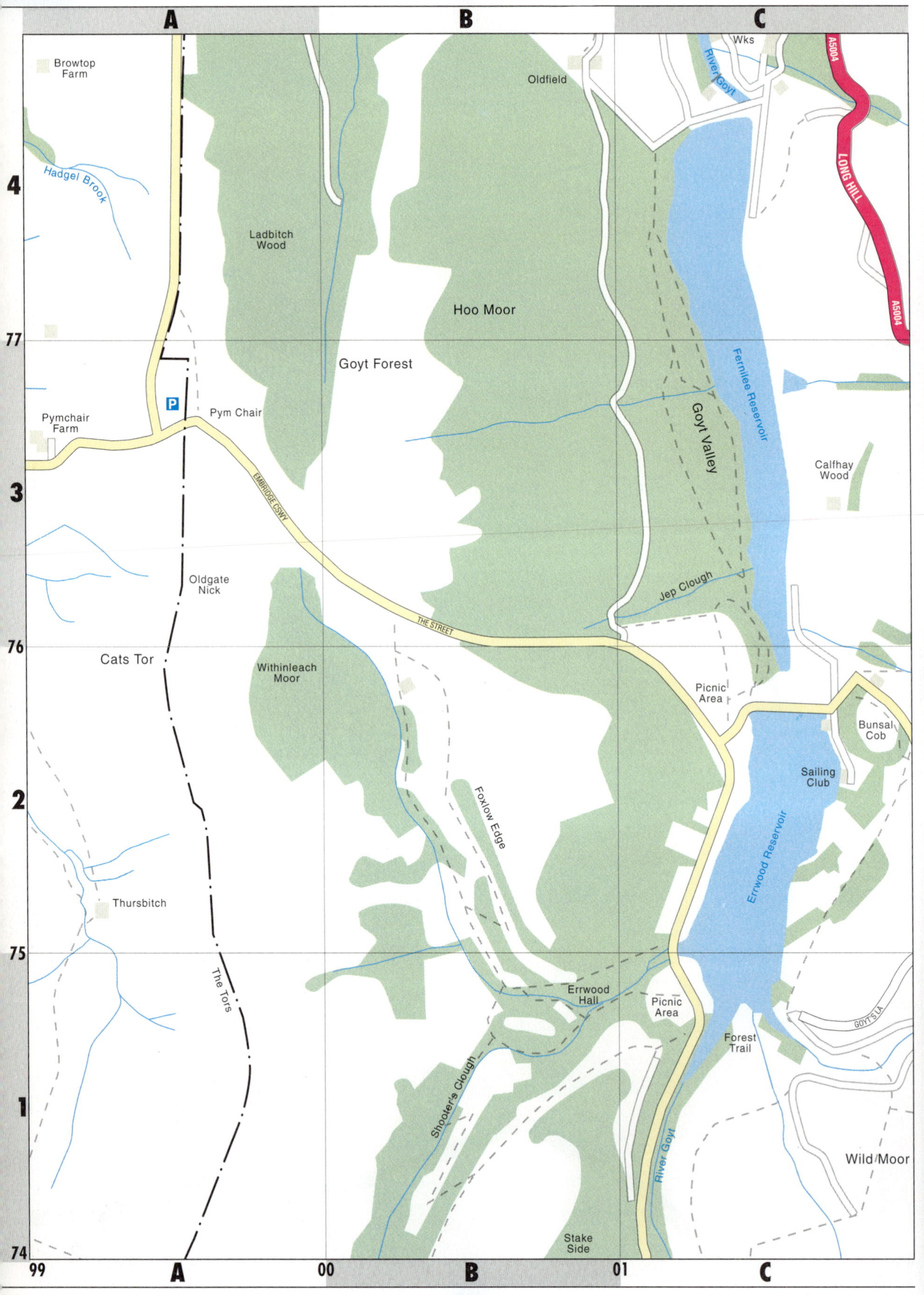
A
B
C
Browtop Farm
Oldfield
Wks
River Goyt
A5004
Hadgel Brook
LONG HILL
Ladbitch Wood
Hoo Moor
A5004
Goyt Forest
Fernilee Reservoir
Pymchair Farm
Pym Chair
Goyt Valley
Calfhay Wood
EMBRIDGE CSWY
Oldgate Nick
Jep Clough
THE STREET
Cats Tor
Withinleach Moor
Picnic Area
Bunsal Cob
Sailing Club
Foxlow Edge
Errwood Reservoir
Thursbitch
The Tors
Errwood Hall
Picnic Area
GOYT'S LA
Forest Trail
Shooter's Clough
River Goyt
Wild Moor
Stake Side
4
77
3
76
2
75
1
74
99
00
01

83

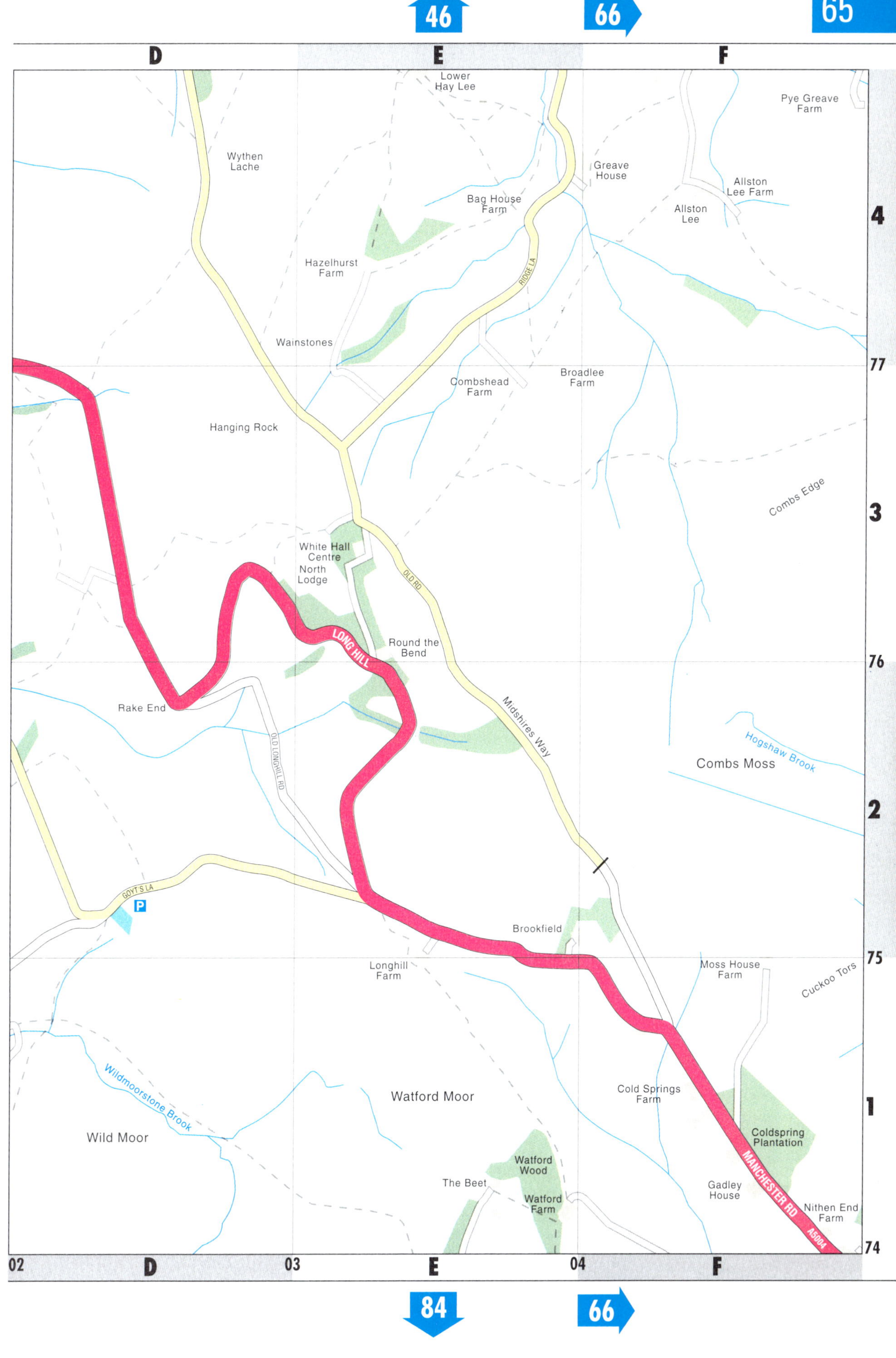
46
66
D
E
F
Lower Hay Lee
Pye Greave Farm
Wythen Lache
Greave House
Allston Lee Farm
Allston Lee
Bag House Farm
Hazelhurst Farm
RIDGE LA
Wainstones
Combshead Farm
Broadlee Farm
Hanging Rock
Combs Edge
White Hall Centre
North Lodge
OLD RD
Round the Bend
LONG HILL
Rake End
Midshires Way
OLD LONGHILL RD
Hogshaw Brook
Combs Moss
GOYT'S LA
P
Brookfield
Longhill Farm
Moss House Farm
Cuckoo Tors
Wildmoorstone Brook
Watford Moor
Cold Springs Farm
Wild Moor
Coldspring Plantation
Watford Wood
The Beet
Watford Farm
Gadley House
MANCHESTER RD
A5004
Nithen End Farm
4
77
3
76
2
75
1
74
02
D
03
E
04
F
84
66

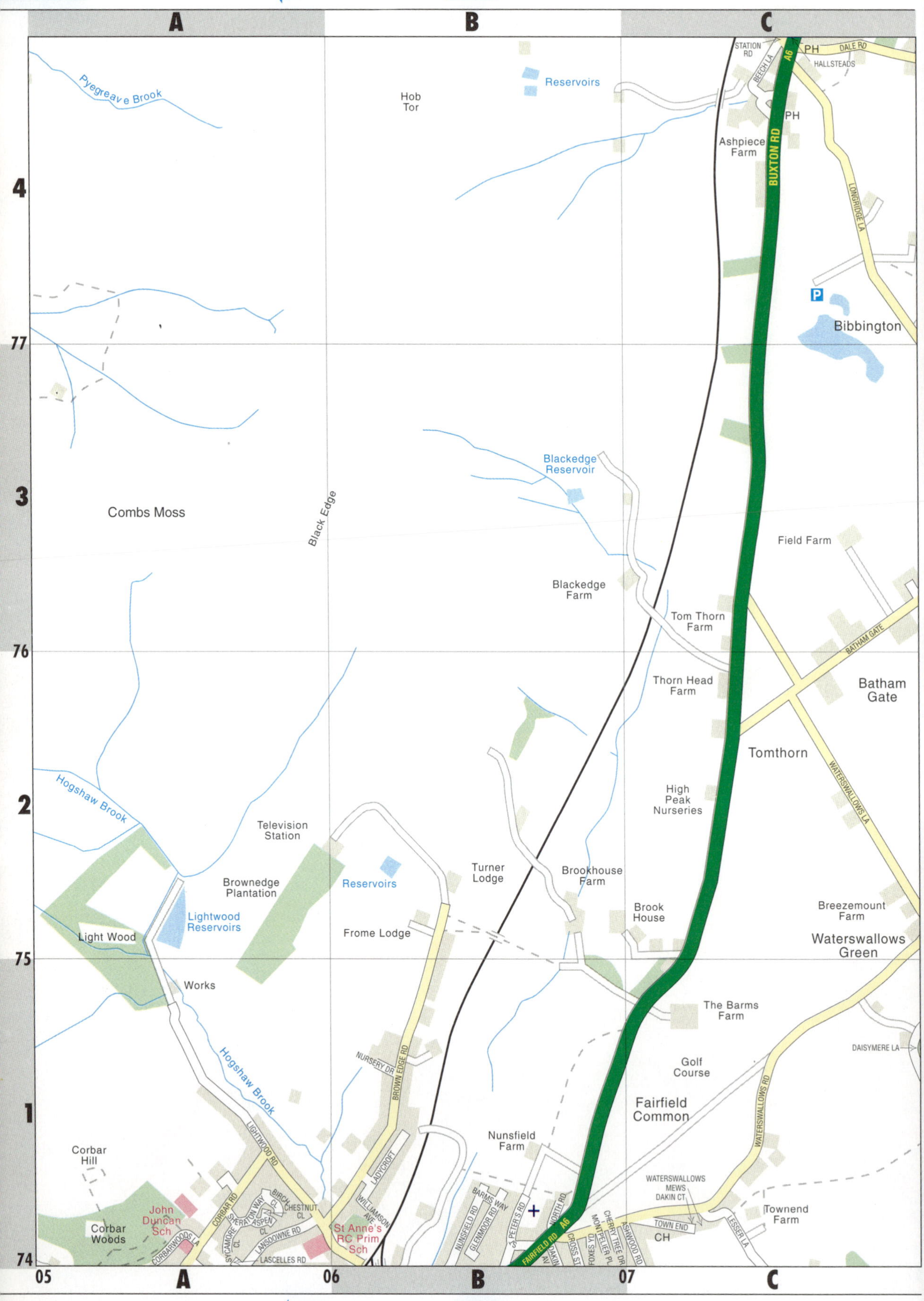

A B C

4

Pyegreave Brook

Hob Tor

Reservoirs

STATION RD
BEECH LA
A6
PH
DALE RD
HALLSTEADS

Ashpiece Farm

PH

BUXTON RD

LONGRIDGE LA

77

P

Bibbington

3

Combs Moss

Black Edge

Blackedge Reservoir

Blackedge Farm

Field Farm

Tom Thorn Farm

BATHAM GATE

76

Thorn Head Farm

Batham Gate

Tomthorn

High Peak Nurseries

WATERSWALLOWS LA

2

Hogshaw Brook

Television Station

Brownedge Plantation

Reservoirs

Turner Lodge

Brookhouse Farm

Breezemount Farm

Light Wood

Lightwood Reservoirs

Frome Lodge

Brook House

Waterswallows Green

75

Works

The Barms Farm

DAISYMERE LA

Hogshaw Brook

NURSERY DR

BROWN EDGE RD

Golf Course

WATERSWALLOWS RD

1

Corbar Hill

Nunsfield Farm

Fairfield Common

LIGHTWOOD RD

LADYCROFT

WILLIAMSON AVE

WATERSWALLOWS MEWS
DAKIN CT

Townend Farm

Corbar Woods

John Duncan Sch

CORBAR RD

KERATON WAY

BIRCH
ASPEN
CHESTNUT CL

SYCAMORE CL
LANSDOWNE RD
LASCELLES RD

St Anne's RC Prim Sch

BARMS WAY
NUNSFIELD RD
GLENMOOR RD
ST PETER'S RD
NORTH RD
CROSS ST
MONTPELIER PL
DA SWOD
CHERRY TREE DR
SHERWOOD RD

CH

FAIRFIELD RD
A6

TOWN END

LESSER LA

74

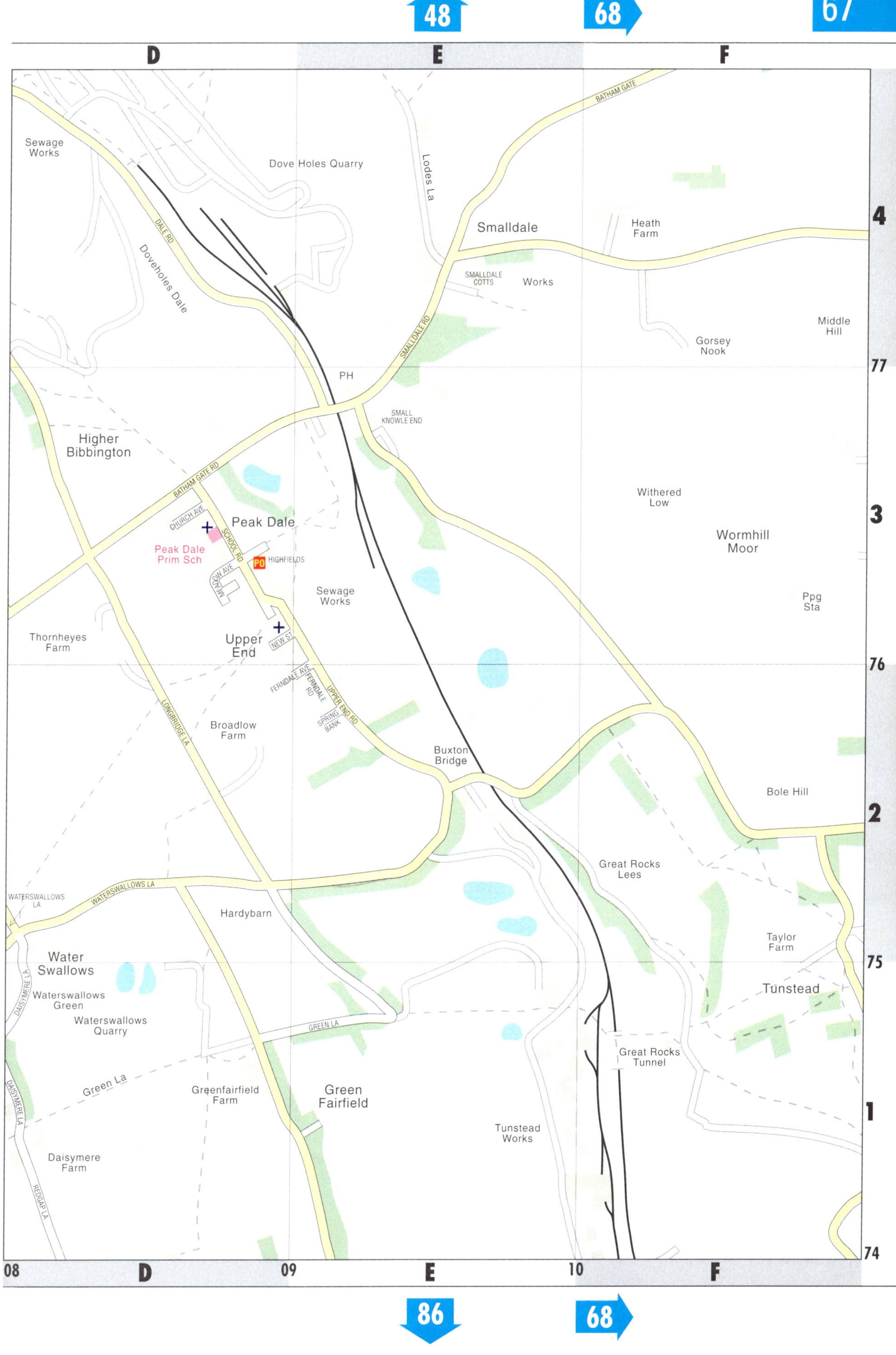

D
E
F

Sewage Works

Dove Holes Quarry

Lodes La

BATHAM GATE

Smalldale

Heath Farm

4

SMALLDALE COTTS

Works

Middle Hill

Gorsey Nook

SMALLDALE RD

DALE RD

Doveholes Dale

PH

77

SMALL KNOWLE END

Higher Bibbington

BATHAM GATE RD

CHURCH AVE

Withered Low

Wormhill Moor

3

Peak Dale

SCHOOL RD

Peak Dale Prim Sch

MEADOW AVE

PO HIGHFIELDS

Ppg Sta

Sewage Works

Thornheyes Farm

NEW ST

Upper End

FERNDALE AVE

FERNDALE RD

UPPER END RD

SPRING BANK

76

LONGRIDGE LA

Broadlow Farm

Buxton Bridge

Bole Hill

2

Great Rocks Lees

WATERSWALLOWS LA

Hardybarn

Taylor Farm

WATERSWALLOWS LA

DAISYMERE LA

Water Swallows

75

Tunstead

Waterswallows Green

Waterswallows Quarry

GREEN LA

Great Rocks Tunnel

Green La

Greenfairfield Farm

Green Fairfield

1

REDGAP LA

Daisymere Farm

Tunstead Works

08
D
09
E
10
F
74

67
49

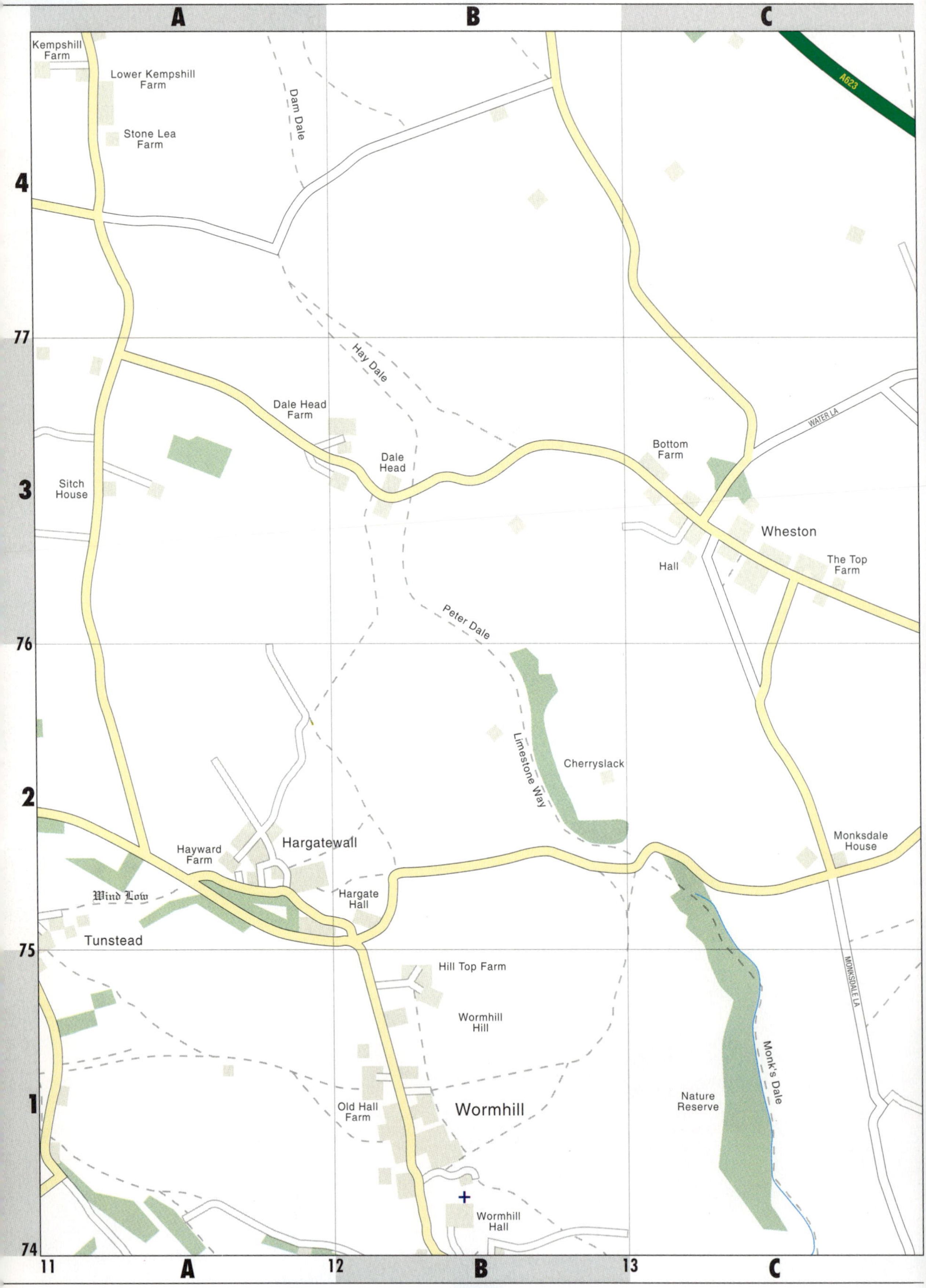

A   **B**   **C**

A623

Kempshill Farm

Lower Kempshill Farm

Stone Lea Farm

Dam Dale

4

77

Hay Dale

Dale Head Farm

Dale Head

Bottom Farm

WATER LA

3

Sitch House

Wheston

Hall

The Top Farm

76

Peter Dale

Limestone Way

Cherryslack

2

Hayward Farm

Hargatewall

Monksdale House

Wind Low

Hargate Hall

Tunstead

75

Hill Top Farm

Wormhill Hill

MONKSDALE LA

Monk's Dale

1

Old Hall Farm

Wormhill

Nature Reserve

Wormhill Hall

74

11   **A**   **12**   **B**   **13**   **C**

D E F

4

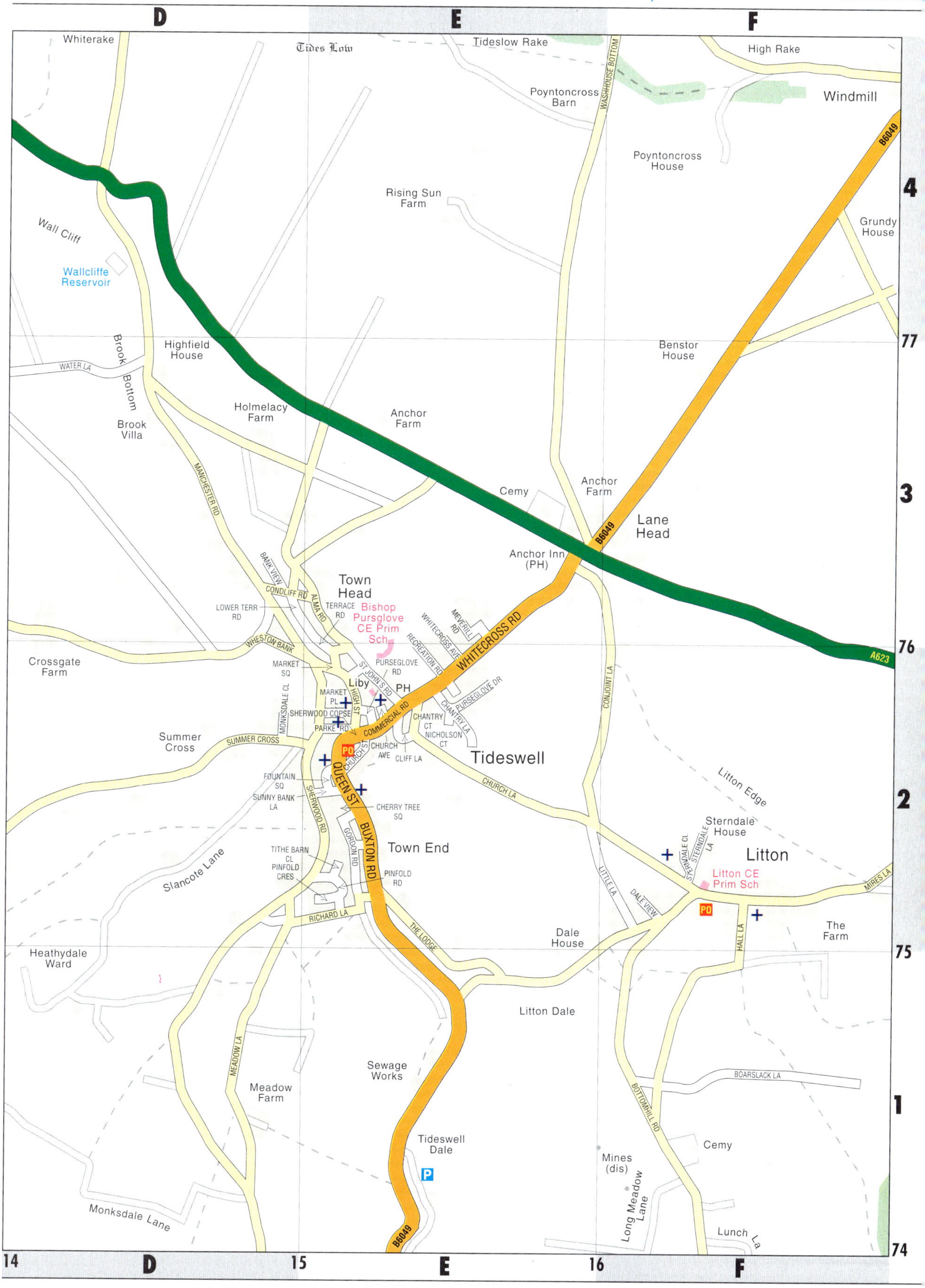

Whiterake

Tides Low

Tideslow Rake

High Rake

Windmill

Poyntoncross Barn

Poyntoncross House

Grundy House

Rising Sun Farm

Wall Cliff

Wallcliffe Reservoir

Benstor House

77

Highfield House

WATER LA

Brook Bottom

Brook Villa

Holmelacy Farm

Anchor Farm

MANCHESTER RD

Cemy

Anchor Farm

Lane Head

3

B6049

Anchor Inn (PH)

BANK VIEW

CONDLIFF RD

ALMA RD

Town Head

TERRACE

Bishop Pursglove CE Prim Sch

MILL RD

WHITECROSS RD

WHITECROSS AVE

RECREATION RD

LOWER TERR RD

WHESTON BANK

MARKET SQ

PURSEGLOVE RD

PURSEGLOVE DR

CONJOINT LA

76

Crossgate Farm

MONKSDALE CL

MARKET PL

SHERWOOD COPSE

PARKE RD

HIGH ST

ST JOHNS RD

Liby

PH

COMMERCIAL RD

CHANTRY CT

CHANTRY LA

NICHOLSON CT

CHURCH AVE

CLIFF LA

Tideswell

Litton Edge

Summer Cross

SUMMER CROSS

PO

CHURCH ST

CHURCH LA

Sterndale House

STERNDALE CL

STERNDALE LA

Litton

2

FOUNTAIN SQ

SUNNY BANK LA

QUEEN ST

SHERWOOD RD

GORDON RD

BUXTON RD

CHERRY TREE SQ

Town End

PINFOLD RD

LITTON LA

DALE VIEW

Litton CE Prim Sch

MIRES LA

TITHE BARN CL

PINFOLD CRES

RICHARD LA

HALL LA

PO

The Farm

Slancote Lane

Dale House

75

Heathydale Ward

THE LODGE

Litton Dale

MEADOW LA

Meadow Farm

Sewage Works

BOARSLACK LA

1

BOTTOMHILL RD

Cemy

Tideswell Dale

P

B6049

Mines (dis)

Long Meadow Lane

Lunch La

74

Monksdale Lane

14 D 15 E 16 F

B6049

A623

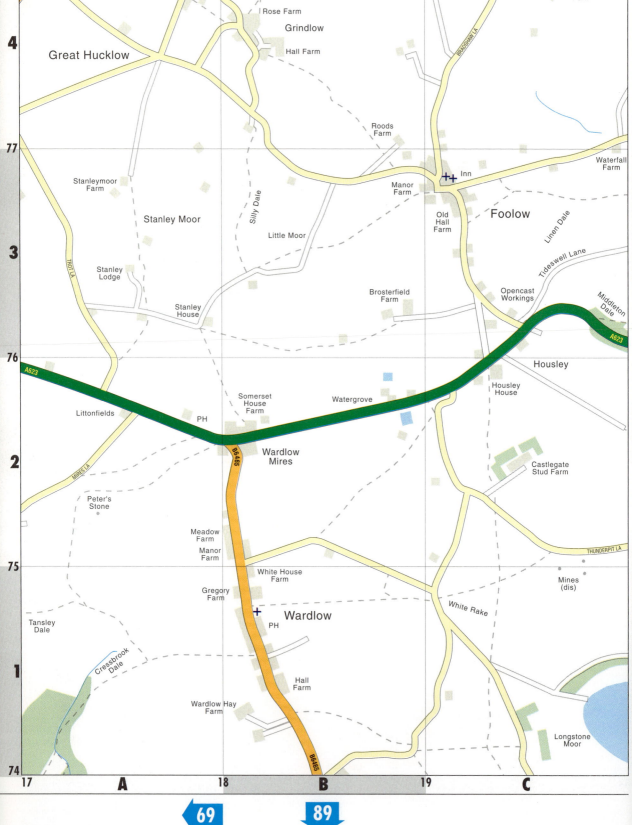

Bretton Mount

Shepherd's Park

Artis Farm

PH

Rose Farm

Grindlow

Hall Farm

Great Hucklow

Roods Farm

Waterfall Farm

Stanleymoor Farm

Inn

Manor Farm

Foolow

Stanley Moor

Silly Dale

Old Hall Farm

Linen Dale

Tideswell Lane

Little Moor

Stanley Lodge

Brosterfield Farm

Opencast Workings

Middleton Dale

A623

Stanley House

Housley

A623

Littonfields

Somerset House Farm

Watergrove

Housley House

PH

Wardlow Mires

Castlegate Stud Farm

Peter's Stone

B6465

Meadow Farm

Manor Farm

White House Farm

THUNDERPIT LA

Mines (dis)

Gregory Farm

Wardlow

White Rake

Tansley Dale

PH

Cressbrook Dale

Hall Farm

Longstone Moor

Wardlow Hay Farm

B6465

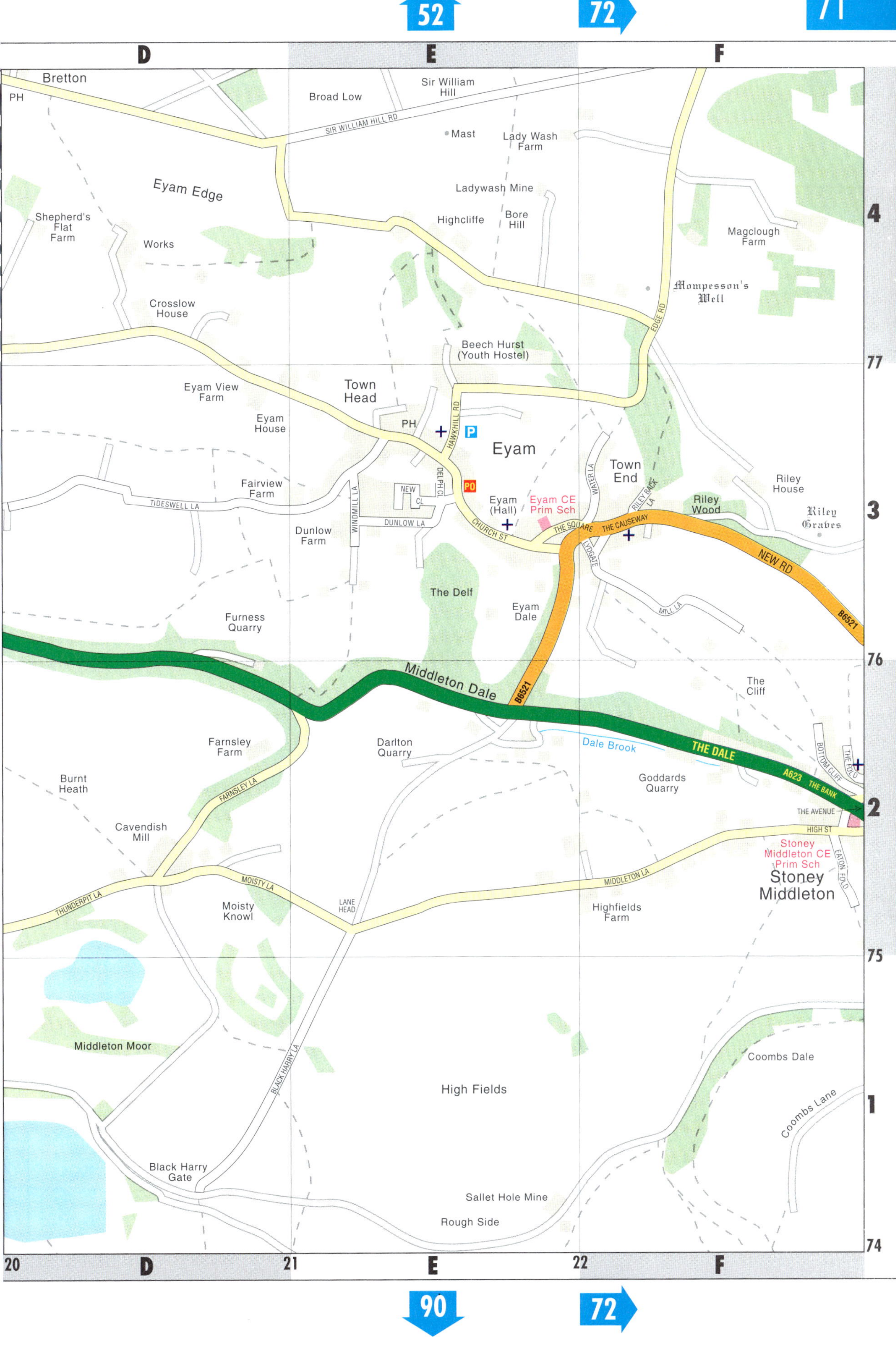
D
E
F
Bretton
PH
Broad Low
Sir William Hill
SIR WILLIAM HILL RD
Mast
Lady Wash Farm
Eyam Edge
Ladywash Mine
Shepherd's Flat Farm
Highcliffe
Bore Hill
Works
Magclough Farm
Mompesson's Well
Crosslow House
EDGE RD
Beech Hurst (Youth Hostel)
Eyam View Farm
Town Head
Eyam House
PH
HAWKHILL RD
Eyam
Town End
Fairview Farm
DELPH CL
PO
WATER LA
Riley House
TIDESWELL LA
NEW CL
Eyam (Hall)
Eyam CE Prim Sch
RILEY BACK LA
Riley Wood
Riley Graves
Dunlow Farm
WINDMILL LA
DUNLOW LA
CHURCH ST
THE SQUARE
THE CAUSEWAY
LYDGATE
NEW RD
The Delf
Eyam Dale
MILL LA
Furness Quarry
B6521
Middleton Dale
B6521
The Cliff
Farnsley Farm
Darlton Quarry
Dale Brook
THE DALE
BOTTOM CLIFF
THE FOLD
Burnt Heath
FARNSLEY LA
Goddards Quarry
A623 THE BANK
THE AVENUE
Cavendish Mill
HIGH ST
Stoney Middleton CE Prim Sch
EATON FOLD
MOISTY LA
MIDDLETON LA
Stoney Middleton
THUNDERPIT LA
Moisty Knowl
LANE HEAD
Highfields Farm
Middleton Moor
BLACK HARRY LA
Coombs Dale
High Fields
Coombs Lane
Black Harry Gate
Sallet Hole Mine
Rough Side
4
77
3
76
2
75
1
74
20
D
21
E
22
F

A B C

Grouse Inn
Hay Wood
Sir William Hotel (PH)
Grindleford Prim Sch
The Haywood
Mag Clough
Horse Hay Coppice
Grindleford
Resr
Goatscliff
Goatscliff Farm
Caravan Park
Stokehall Quarry
Stoke
Stoke Wood
Stoke Flat
Froggatt Edge
Top Riley
Derwent Farm
The Stables
Stoke Hall
Froggatt Bridge
Froggatt
Chequers Inn (PH)
Bee Wood
Middleton Plantation
Knouchley Farm
River Derwent
Curbar Edge
New Bridge
Ridding House Farm
Stoke Brook
Townend
Depot
Works
The Goit
Warren Lodge
Calver Sough
Hare Knoll
Coombsdale Quarry (dis)
Stocking Farm
Curbar
Caravan Park
Coombs Lane
Calver Low
Mill
Folds Farm
Calver
Curbar Prim Sch
The Bridge (PH)
Lane Farm
Baslow Edge
Calver Peak
TV Mast
Cliff Coll
Peak Pasture

4
77
3
76
2
75
1
74

23 24 25

A B C

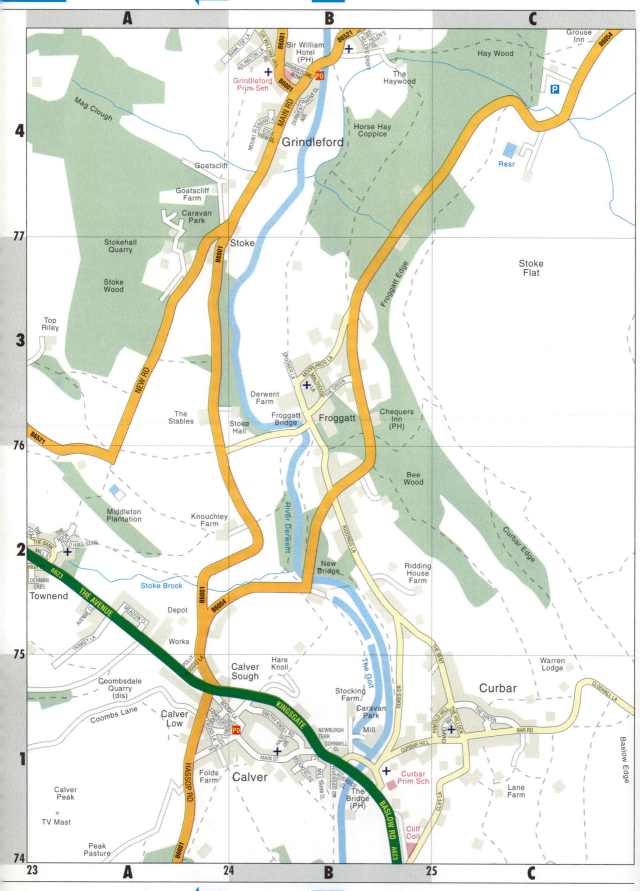

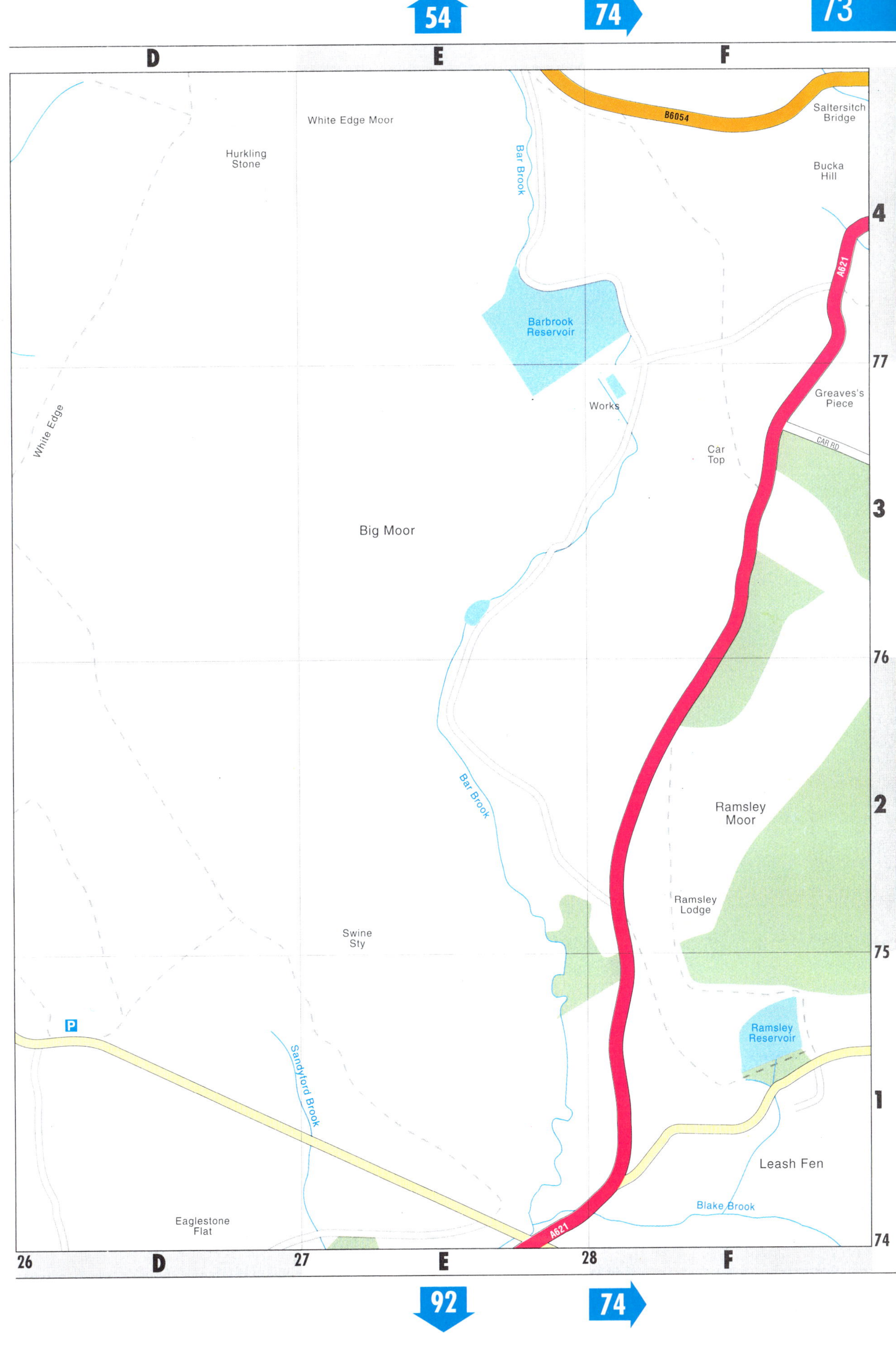
54
74
D
E
F
White Edge Moor
Hurkling
Stone
Bar Brook
B6054
Saltersitch
Bridge
Bucka
Hill
4
A621
Barbrook
Reservoir
77
Greaves's
Piece
Works
White Edge
Car
Top
CAR RD
3
Big Moor
76
Bar Brook
2
Ramsley
Moor
Ramsley
Lodge
Swine
Sty
75
P
Ramsley
Reservoir
Sandyford Brook
1
Leash Fen
Blake Brook
Eaglestone
Flat
A621
74
26
D
27
E
28
F
92
74

73
55

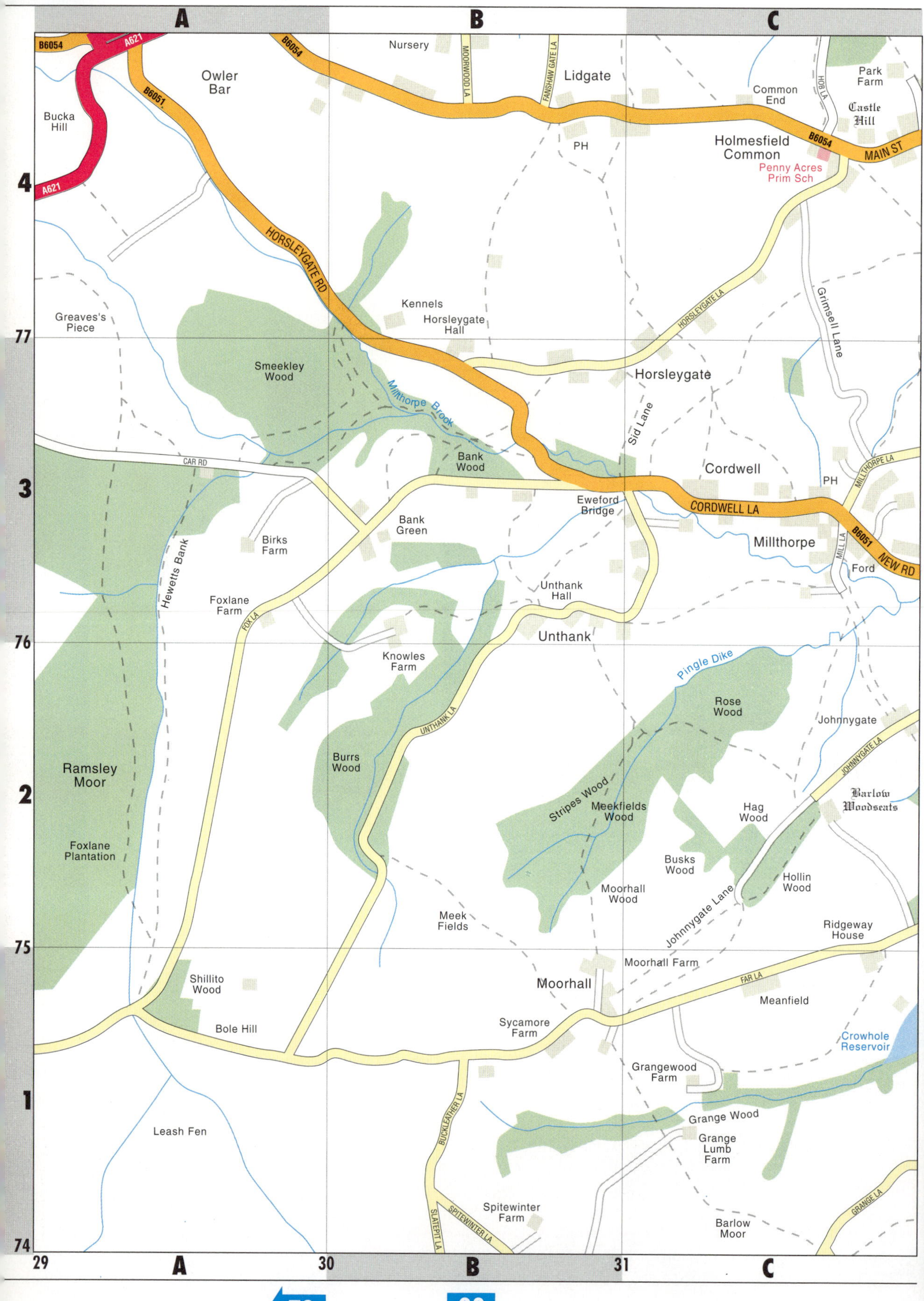
A
B
C
B6054
A621
B6051
Owler Bar
Bucka Hill
Nursery
MOORWOOD LA
FANSHAW GATE LA
Lidgate
Common End
HOB LA
Park Farm
Castle Hill
PH
Holmesfield Common
B6054
MAIN ST
Penny Acres Prim Sch
HORSLEYGATE RD
Kennels
Horsleygate Hall
Greaves's Piece
Smeekley Wood
HORSLEYGATE LA
Grimsell Lane
Horsleygate
Millthorpe Brook
Sid Lane
Bank Wood
CAR RD
Cordwell
PH
MILLTHORPE LA
Eweford Bridge
CORDWELL LA
Bank Green
Birks Farm
Hewetts Bank
Millthorpe
B6051
NEW RD
MILL LA
Ford
Foxlane Farm
FOX LA
Unthank Hall
Unthank
Knowles Farm
Pingle Dike
Rose Wood
Johnnygate
UNTHANK LA
JOHNNYGATE LA
Ramsley Moor
Burrs Wood
Stripes Wood
Meekfields Wood
Hag Wood
Barlow Woodseats
Foxlane Plantation
Busks Wood
Hollin Wood
Moorhall Wood
Johnnygate Lane
Meek Fields
Ridgeway House
Moorhall Farm
Shillito Wood
Moorhall
FAR LA
Meanfield
Bole Hill
Sycamore Farm
Crowhole Reservoir
Grangewood Farm
Grange Wood
BUCKLEATHER LA
Grange Lumb Farm
Leash Fen
Spitewinter Farm
SPITEWINTER LA
SLATEPIT LA
GRANGE LA
Barlow Moor
4
77
3
76
2
75
1
74
29
30
31

73
93

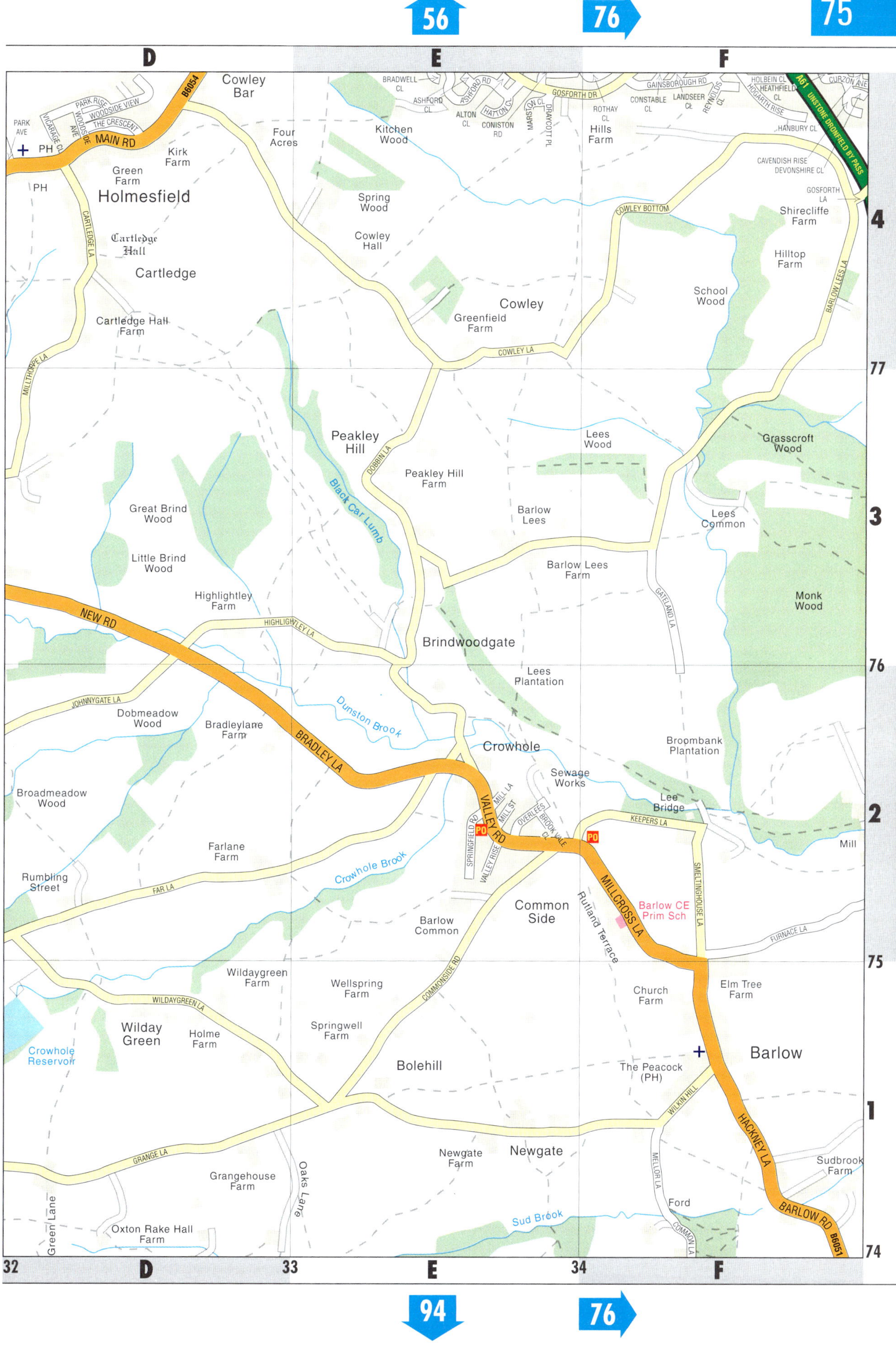
56
76
D
E
F
Cowley Bar
B6054
MAIN RD
PARK RISE
WOODSIDE VIEW
THE CRESCENT
WOODSIDE AVE
VICARAGE CL
PARK AVE
PH
Kirk Farm
Green Farm
Holmesfield
Four Acres
Kitchen Wood
BRADWELL CL
ASHFORD CL
ASHFORD RD
ALTON CL
HATTON CL
CONISTON RD
MARSTON CL
DRAYCOTT PL
GOSFORTH DR
ROTHAY CL
Hills Farm
GAINSBOROUGH RD
CONSTABLE CL
LANDSEER CL
REYNOLDS CL
HOLBEIN CL
HEATHFIELD CL
HOGARTH RISE
CURZON AVE
A61 UNSTONE DRONFIELD BY PASS
HANBURY CL
CAVENDISH RISE
DEVONSHIRE CL
GOSFORTH LA
Shirecliffe Farm
Hilltop Farm
PH
CARTLEDGE LA
Cartledge Hall
Cartledge
Spring Wood
Cowley Hall
COWLEY BOTTOM
School Wood
BARLOW LEES LA
Cartledge Hall Farm
Cowley
Greenfield Farm
COWLEY LA
MILLTHORPE LA
Peakley Hill
DOBBIN LA
Peakley Hill Farm
Lees Wood
Grasscroft Wood
Black Car Lumb
Barlow Lees
Lees Common
Great Brind Wood
Little Brind Wood
Barlow Lees Farm
GATELAND LA
Monk Wood
NEW RD
Highlightley Farm
HIGHLIGHTLEY LA
Brindwoodgate
Lees Plantation
JOHNNYGATE LA
Dobmeadow Wood
Bradleylane Farm
Dunston Brook
BRADLEY LA
Crowhole
Broombank Plantation
Broadmeadow Wood
Sewage Works
MILL LA
MILL ST
OVERLEES
BROOK VALE
Lee Bridge
KEEPERS LA
VALLEY RD
SPRINGFIELD RD
VALLEY RISE
PO
PO
Mill
Farlane Farm
Rumbling Street
Crowhole Brook
FAR LA
Common Side
Rutland Terrace
MILLCROSS LA
Barlow CE Prim Sch
SMELTINGHOUSE LA
FURNACE LA
Barlow Common
Wildaygreen Farm
Wellspring Farm
COMMONSIDE RD
Church Farm
Elm Tree Farm
WILDAYGREEN LA
Wilday Green
Holme Farm
Springwell Farm
Crowhole Reservoir
Bolehill
The Peacock (PH)
Barlow
WILKIN HILL
HACKNEY LA
GRANGE LA
Newgate Farm
Newgate
MELLOR LA
Sudbrook Farm
Grangehouse Farm
Oaks Lane
Green Lane
Oxton Rake Hall Farm
Sud Brook
Ford
COMMON LA
BARLOW RD
B6051
4
77
3
76
2
75
1
74
32
33
34
94
76

75
57

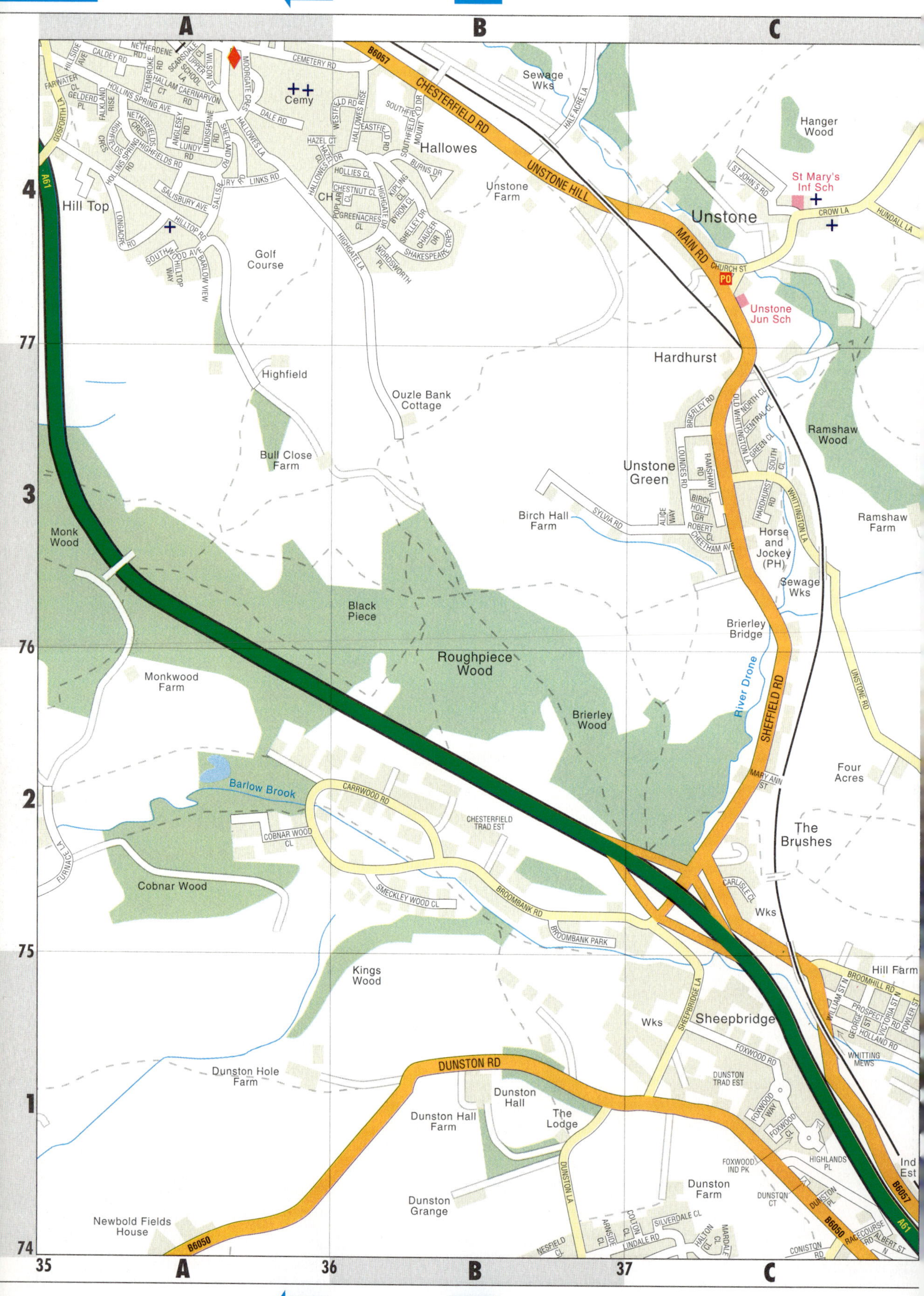
A
B
C
4
3
2
1
77
76
75
74
35
36
37
CALDEY RD
NETHERDENE RD
HILLSIDE AVE
FAIRVATER CL
GELDERD PL
GOSFORTH LA
FALKLAND RISE
HOLLINS SPRING AVE
PEMBROKE RD
HALLAM CT
SCARSDALE CL
UPPER SCHOOL LA
WILSON ST
CAERNARVON RD
MOORGATE CRES
CEMETERY RD
DALE RD
Cemy
B6057
CHESTERFIELD RD
UNSTONE HILL
Sewage Wks
HALF ACRE LA
Hanger Wood
NETHERFIELDS CRES
HIGHFIELDS RD
HOLLINS SPRING RD
ANGLESEY RD
LUNDY RD
LINDISFARNE RD
SHETLAND RD
HALLOWES LA
LINKS RD
SALISBURY AVE
HAZEL CT
WESTFIELD RD
HALLOWES RISE
EASTFIELD RD
SOUTHFIELD DR
MOUNT
Hallowes
BURNS DR
HOLLIES CL
CHESTNUT CL
KIPLING CL
BYRON CL
GREENACRES CL
SHELLEY DR
CHAUCER DR
SHAKESPEARE CRES
WORDSWORTH PL
HIGHGATE LA
HIGHGATE DR
POPLAR CL
HALLOWES CL
CH
Unstone Farm
ST JOHN'S RD
St Mary's Inf Sch
Unstone
CROW LA
HUNDALL LA
MAIN RD
CHURCH ST
PO
Unstone Jun Sch
A61
Hill Top
LONGACRE RD
HILLTOP RD
SOUTHWOOD AVE
HILLTOP WAY
BARLOW VIEW
Golf Course
Highfield
Ouzle Bank Cottage
Hardhurst
BRIERLEY RD
OLD WHITTINGTON LA
NORTH CL
CENTRAL CL
GREEN CL
SOUTH CL
Ramshaw Wood
Unstone Green
LOUNDES RD
RAMSHAW RD
BIRCH HOLT GR
ROBERT CL
CHETHAM AVE
ALICE WAY
HARDHURST RD
WHITTINGTON LA
Bull Close Farm
Birch Hall Farm
SYLVIA RD
Horse and Jockey (PH)
Ramshaw Farm
Monk Wood
Black Piece
Sewage Wks
Brierley Bridge
Roughpiece Wood
Monkwood Farm
River Drone
SHEFFIELD RD
UNSTONE RD
Brierley Wood
Four Acres
MARY ANN ST
Barlow Brook
CARRWOOD RD
CHESTERFIELD TRAD EST
The Brushes
COBNAR WOOD CL
FURNACE LA
Cobnar Wood
SMECKLEY WOOD CL
BROOMBANK RD
CARLISLE CL
Wks
BROOMBANK PARK
Hill Farm
BROOMHILL RD
Kings Wood
SHEEPBRIDGE LA
Wks
Sheepbridge
WILLIAM ST N
PROSPECT RD
GEORGE ST
VICTORIA ST N
HOLLAND RD
DOWLER ST
FOXWOOD RD
WHITTING MEWS
Dunston Hole Farm
DUNSTON RD
DUNSTON TRAD EST
Dunston Hall
The Lodge
FOXWOOD WAY
FOXWOOD CL
Dunston Hall Farm
FOXWOOD IND PK
HIGHLANDS PL
Ind Est
DUNSTON LA
Dunston Farm
DUNSTON CT
DUNSTON PL
B6057
Dunston Grange
Newbold Fields House
SILVERDALE CL
COLTON CL
ARNSIDE CL
LINDALE RD
HALTON CL
MARDALE CL
NESFIELD CL
B6050
RACECOURSE RD
ALBERT ST N
CONISTON RD

75
95

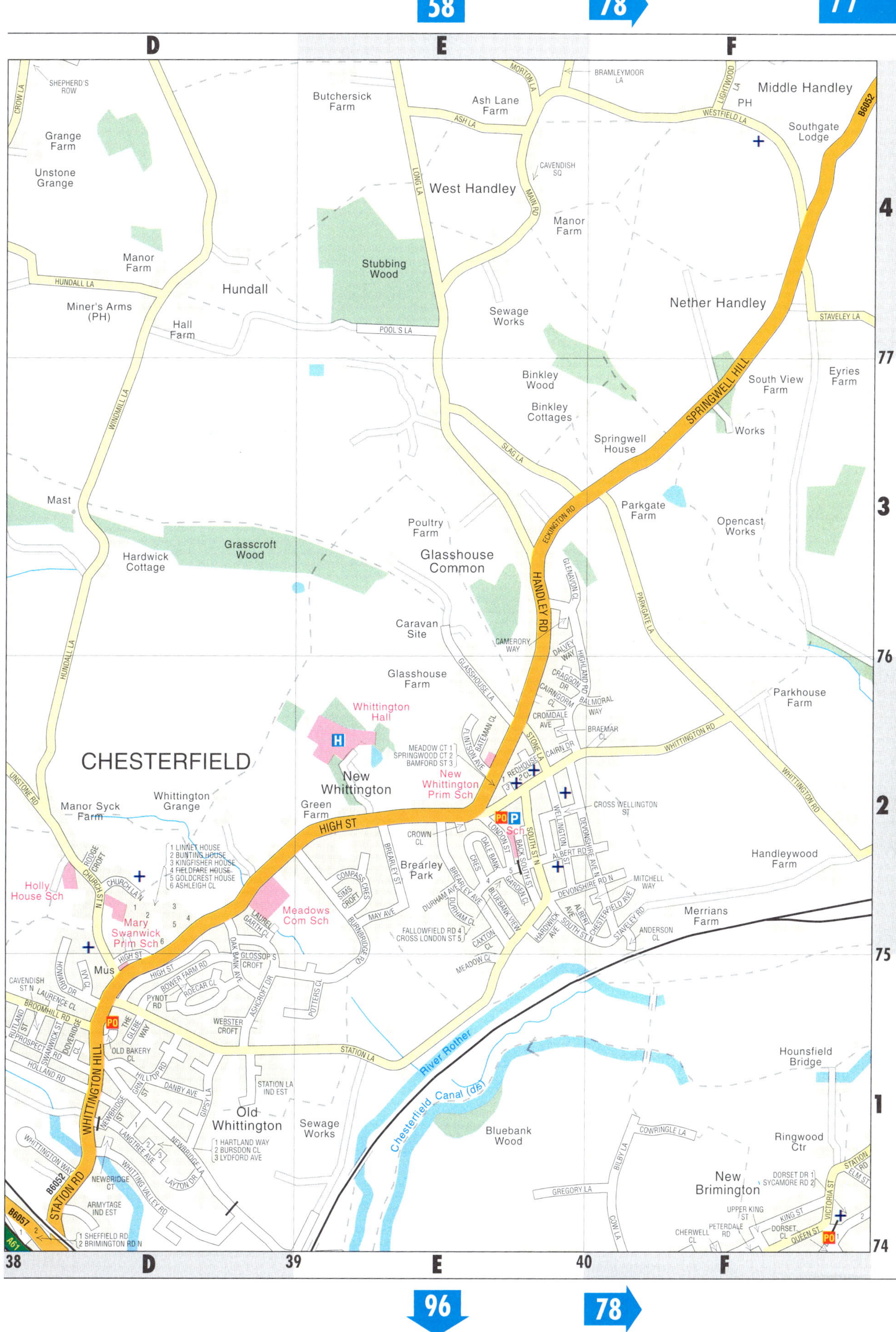
D
E
F
CHESTERFIELD
Middle Handley
West Handley
Nether Handley
Hundall
Glasshouse Common
New Whittington
Old Whittington
New Brimington
Butchersick Farm
Ash Lane Farm
Grange Farm
Unstone Grange
Manor Farm
Miner's Arms (PH)
Hall Farm
Stubbing Wood
Sewage Works
Binkley Wood
Binkley Cottages
Springwell House
Parkgate Farm
Opencast Works
South View Farm
Eyries Farm
Southgate Lodge
Works
Mast
Hardwick Cottage
Grasscroft Wood
Poultry Farm
Caravan Site
Glasshouse Farm
Whittington Hall
Parkhouse Farm
Manor Syck Farm
Whittington Grange
Green Farm
Brearley Park
Holly House Sch
Mary Swanwick Prim Sch
Meadows Com Sch
New Whittington Prim Sch
Handleywood Farm
Merrians Farm
Hounsfield Bridge
Bluebank Wood
Ringwood Ctr
River Rother
Chesterfield Canal (dis)
HIGH ST
HANDLEY RD
SPRINGWELL HILL
WHITTINGTON HILL
STATION RD
STATION LA
WHITTINGTON RD
PARKGATE LA
STAVELEY LA
HUNDALL LA
WINDMILL LA
LONG LA
MAIN RD
SLAG LA
ECKINGTON RD
POOL'S LA
ASH LA
MORTON LA
WESTFIELD LA
LIGHTWOOD LA
BRAMLEYMOOR LA
CAVENDISH SQ
SHEPHERD'S ROW
CROW LA
UNSTONE RD
B6052
B6057
A61
1 LINNET HOUSE
2 BUNTING HOUSE
3 KINGFISHER HOUSE
4 FIELDFARE HOUSE
5 GOLDCREST HOUSE
6 ASHLEIGH CL
MEADOW CT 1
SPRINGWOOD CT 2
BAMFORD ST 3
FALLOWFIELD RD 4
CROSS LONDON ST 5
1 HARTLAND WAY
2 BURSDON CL
3 LYDFORD AVE
1 SHEFFIELD RD
2 BRIMINGTON RD N
DORSET DR 1
SYCAMORE RD 2
38
39
40
74
75
76
77
1
2
3
4

77
59

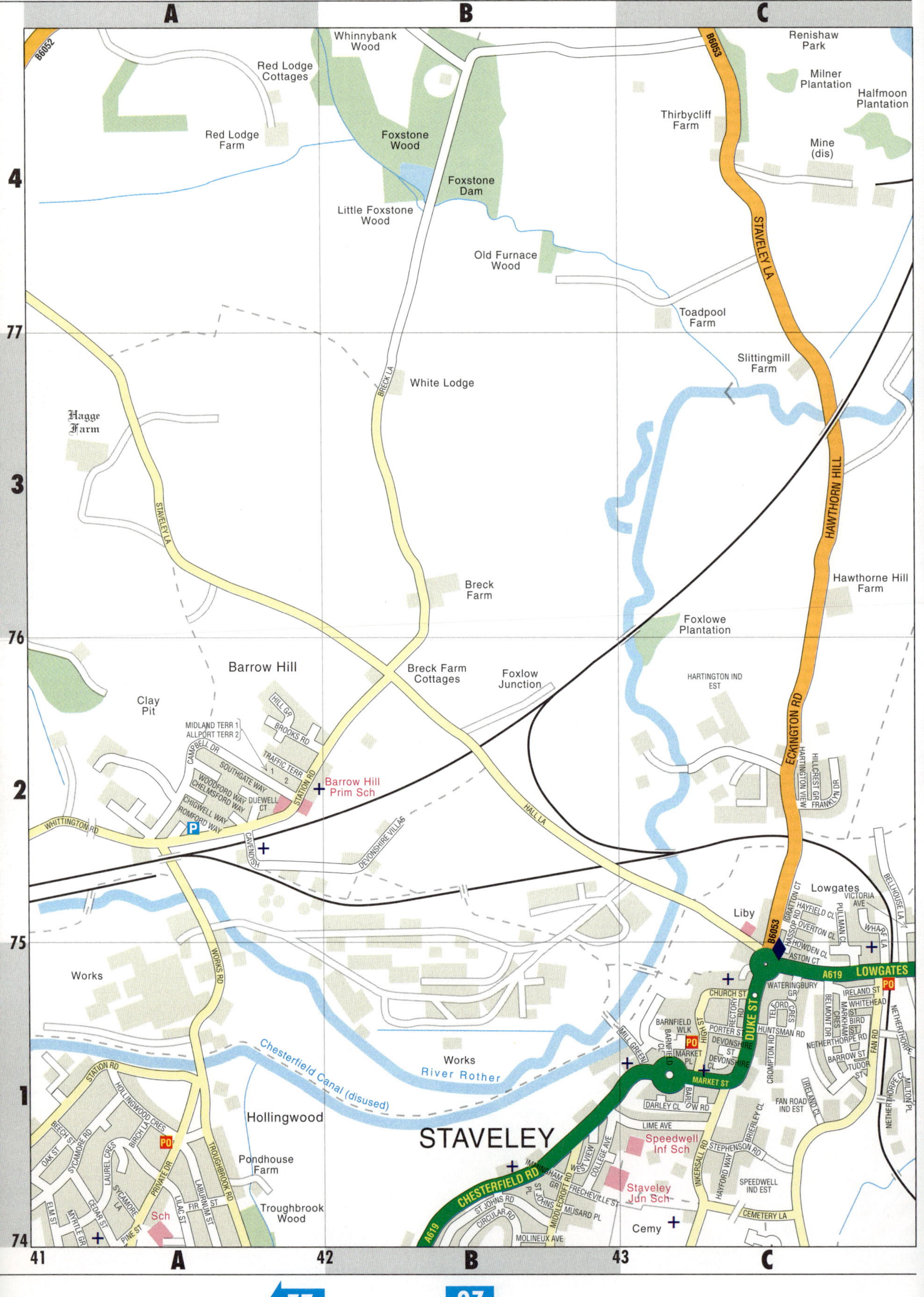
Whinnybank Wood
Red Lodge Cottages
Red Lodge Farm
Foxstone Wood
Foxstone Dam
Little Foxstone Wood
Old Furnace Wood
Renishaw Park
Milner Plantation
Halfmoon Plantation
Thirbycliff Farm
Mine (dis)
STAVELEY LA
Toadpool Farm
Slittingmill Farm
White Lodge
BRECK LA
Hagge Farm
HAWTHORN HILL
STAVELEY LA
Breck Farm
Hawthorne Hill Farm
Foxlowe Plantation
Barrow Hill
Breck Farm Cottages
Foxlow Junction
HARTINGTON IND EST
Clay Pit
ECKINGTON RD
Barrow Hill Prim Sch
HALL LA
WHITTINGTON RD
DEVONSHIRE VILLAS
Lowgates
Liby
LOWGATES
Works
WORKS RD
DUKE ST
Works
River Rother
Chesterfield Canal (disused)
MARKET ST
Hollingwood
STAVELEY
Speedwell Inf Sch
Staveley Jun Sch
Pondhouse Farm
Troughbrook Wood
CHESTERFIELD RD
Sch
Cemy
FAN ROAD IND EST
SPEEDWELL IND EST
CEMETERY LA
STATION RD
TROUGHBROOK RD
PRIVATE DR
B6052
B6053
A619
A
B
C
41
42
43
74
75
76
77
1
2
3
4

77
97

D E F

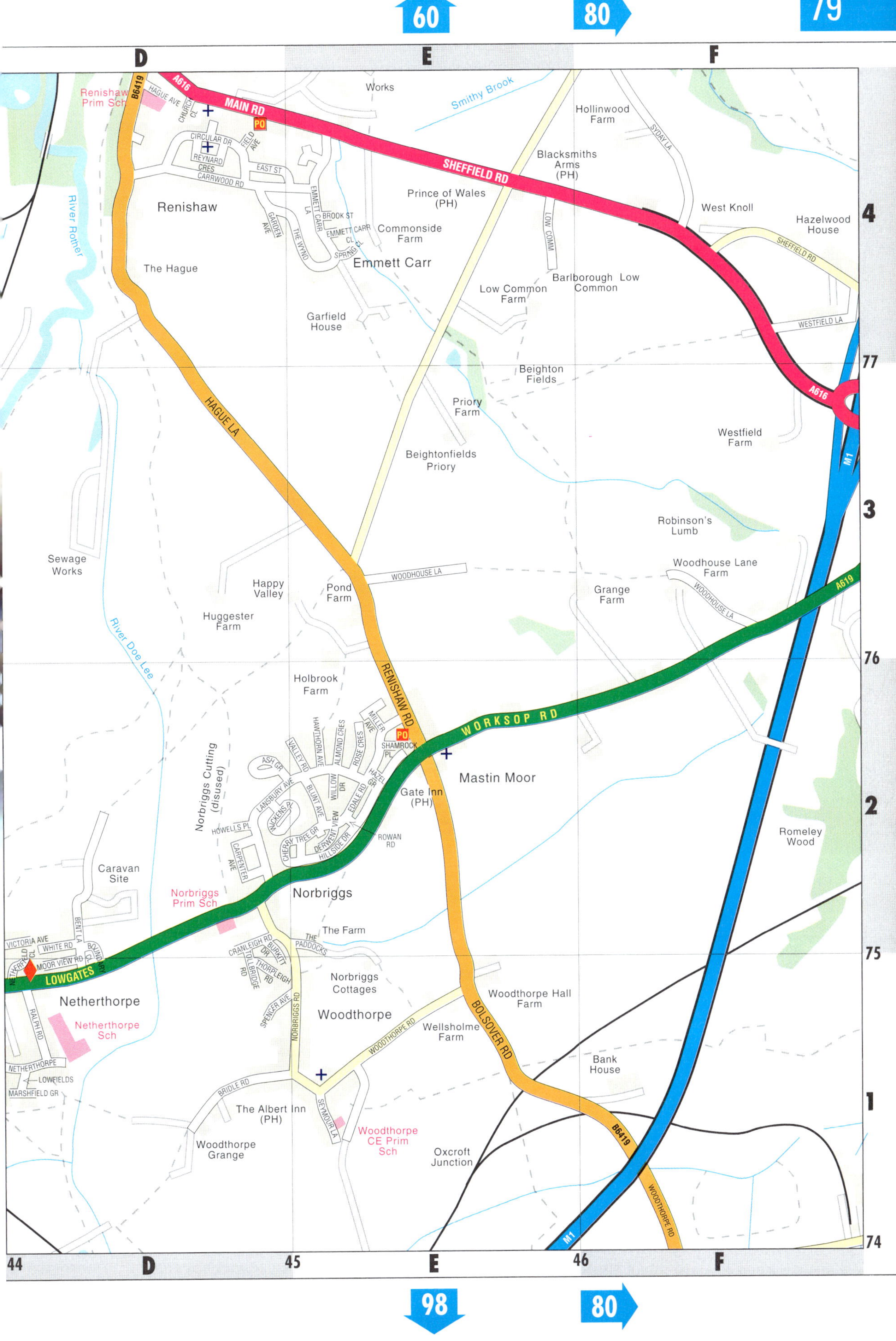
Renishaw Prim Sch
Works
Smithy Brook
Hollinwood Farm
Blacksmiths Arms (PH)
MAIN RD
SHEFFIELD RD
Prince of Wales (PH)
Renishaw
Commonside Farm
Emmett Carr
West Knoll
Hazelwood House
The Hague
Low Common Farm
Barlborough Low Common
Garfield House
Beighton Fields
Priory Farm
Westfield Farm
HAGUE LA
Beightonfields Priory
Robinson's Lumb
Sewage Works
Happy Valley
Pond Farm
WOODHOUSE LA
Woodhouse Lane Farm
Grange Farm
Huggester Farm
River Rother
River Doe Lee
Holbrook Farm
RENISHAW RD
WORKSOP RD
Mastin Moor
Gate Inn (PH)
Norbriggs Cutting (disused)
Caravan Site
Norbriggs
Norbriggs Prim Sch
Romeley Wood
The Farm
LOWGATES
Netherthorpe
Netherthorpe Sch
Norbriggs Cottages
Woodthorpe
Woodthorpe Hall Farm
Wellsholme Farm
BOLSOVER RD
WOODTHORPE RD
Bank House
The Albert Inn (PH)
Woodthorpe CE Prim Sch
Woodthorpe Grange
Oxcroft Junction
A616
A619
B6419
M1
77
76
75
74
4
3
2
1

44 D 45 E 46 F

79
61

A B C

4 77 3 76 2 75 1 74

Barlborough
Longrybank Wood
Coltsworth Lane
Speetley Plantation
Eastwood Cottage
Eastwood Farm
Whitebrick Moor
Speetley Farm
De Rodes Arms (PH)
Mill Farm
Van Dyk Hotel
Hawthorns Farm
Slayley Farm
Forrest's Plantation
Harlesthorpe
New Barlborough
Cemetery
Manor Farm
Barlborough Common
Golf Course
Heritage Com Sch
North Derbyshire Tertiary Coll
Clowne Linear Park
Hood Croft Farm
Clowne Jun & Inf Schs
Clowne Common
Clowne
Stanfree Farm
Milking Lane
Low Common Farm
Romeley Hall Farm
Sterry House Farm
High Ash Farm
Ringer Villa Farm
Ringer House
Appletree Inn (PH)
Stanfree Cottage
Congreave House
Border Farm
Grange Farm
Calow Farm

47 A 48 B 49 C

79
99

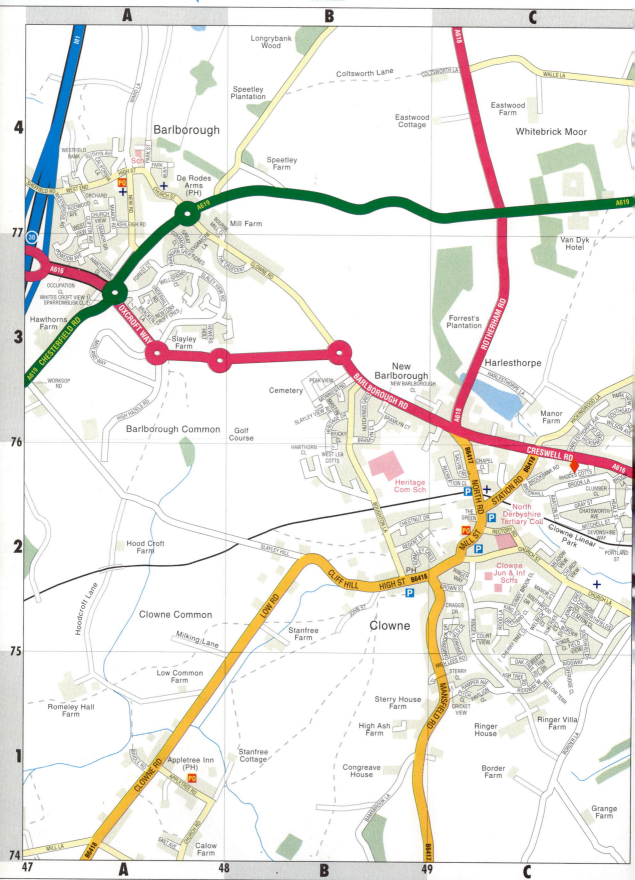

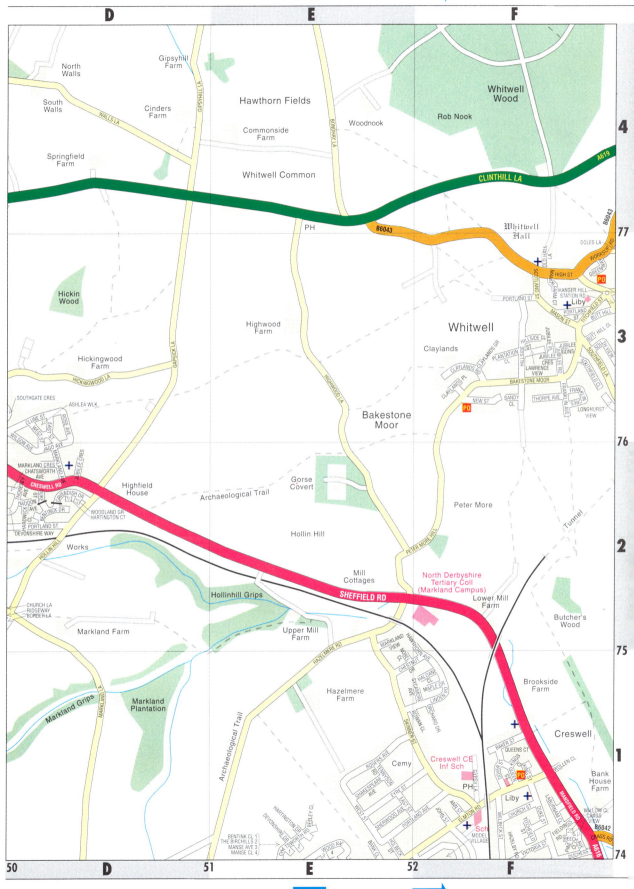

62
82
81

D E F

North Walls
Gipsyhill Farm
South Walls
Walls La
Cinders Farm
Gipsyhill La
Hawthorn Fields
Commonside Farm
Springfield Farm
Whitwell Common
Bondhay La
Woodnook
Rob Nook
Whitwell Wood
4
A619
Clinthill La
B6043
PH
B6043
Whitwell Hall
77
Doles La
Worksop Rd
Old Hall La
High St
Green
PO
Scotland St
Manor Farm Ct
Hanger Hill
Station Rd
Liby
Portland St
Mason St
Titchfield St
Butt Hill
Hickin Wood
Highwood Farm
Whitwell
Butt Hill Cl
3
Claylands
Claylands Gr
Hillside Cl
Jubilee Pl
Jubilee Gdns
South View
Southfield La
Plantation Cl
Hillside St
Jubilee Cres
Jubilee Rd
Lawrence View
Southfield Cl
Hickingwood Farm
Gapsick La
Hickingwood La
Claylands Rd
Claylands Pl
Bakestone Moor
Franklin Cres
Franklin Ave
Thorpe Ave
New St
Sandy Cl
PO
Longhurst View
Southgate Cres
Ashlea Wlk
Clune St
Rose Ave
West St
East St
Wilson Ave
Jago Ave
Highwood La
Bakestone Moor
76
Markland Cres
Chatsworth Ave
Markland Ave
Jubilee Cres
Creswell Rd
Thoresby Ave
Duke St
Cavendish Dr
Haddon Ave
Hardwick Cl
Bentinck Dr
Portland St
Devonshire Way
Woodland Gr
Hartington Ct
Highfield House
Archaeological Trail
Gorse Covert
Peter More
Tunnel
Hollin Hill
Peter More Hill
2
Works
Hollin Hill
Mill Cottages
North Derbyshire Tertiary Coll (Markland Campus)
Hollinhill Grips
Sheffield Rd
Lower Mill Farm
Church La
Ridgeway
Border La
Butcher's Wood
Markland Farm
Upper Mill Farm
Markland View
Hawthorn Ave
Noble Cl
Chestnut Dr
Haldane Cl
Maple Dr
Sycamore Ave
Linden Rd
75
Hazelmere Rd
Hazelmere Farm
Brookside Farm
Markland Grips
Markland La
Markland Plantation
Rowan Cl
Orchard Dr
Skinner St
Archaeological Trail
Creswell
1
Baker St
Queens Ct
Rogers Ave
Tennyson Rd
Cemy
Creswell CE Inf Sch
Dover St
Kings Ct
King St
Queen St
Wollen Cl
Bank House Farm
Shakespeare Ave
Eyre St
Gypsy La
PH
PO
West St
East St
Sherwood Ave
Portland Ave
John St
Ann St
Elmton Rd
Liby
Laburnam Cl
Duke St
Mansfield Rd
Willow Cl
Crags View
Hartington Dr
Devonshire Dr
Beeley Cl
Chatsworth Rd
Wood Ave
Bentink Cl 1
The Birchills 2
Manse Ave 3
Manse Cl 4
Bank Cl
Holbeck St
Sch
Model Village
Welbeck St
Church St
Titchfield St
Hazelby Rd
Victoria St
Fieldings Rd
Beech Ave
Pine Cl
Duchess
B6042
Crags Rd
A616
74

50 D 51 E 52 F

81
63

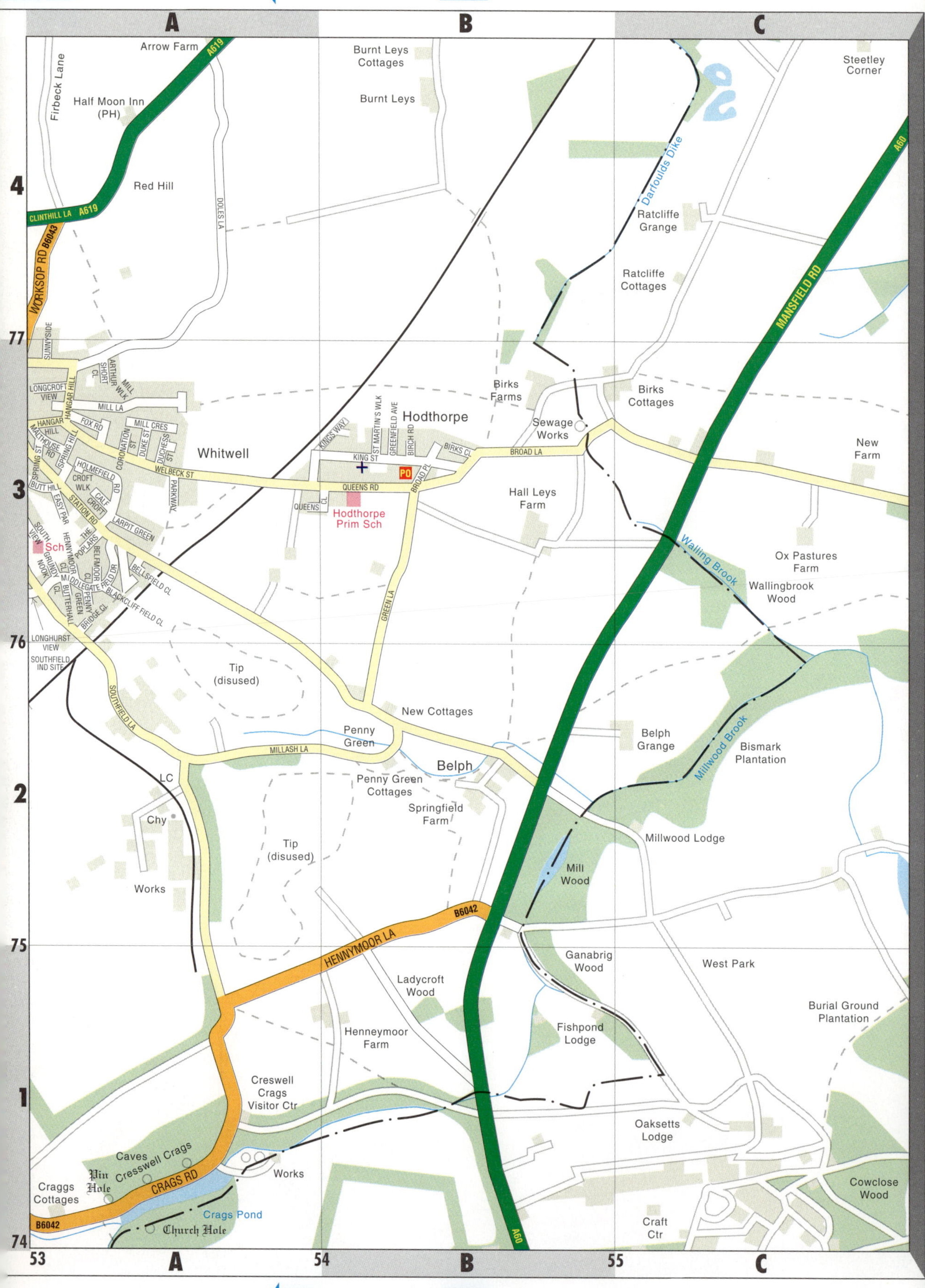
A
B
C
Arrow Farm
A619
Firbeck Lane
Half Moon Inn (PH)
Burnt Leys Cottages
Burnt Leys
Steetley Corner
Red Hill
CLINTHILL LA A619
DOLES LA
Darfoulds Dike
Ratcliffe Grange
Ratcliffe Cottages
A60
MANSFIELD RD
WORKSOP RD B6043
Hodthorpe
Whitwell
Birks Farms
Birks Cottages
Sewage Works
New Farm
BROAD LA
BIRKS CL
KING ST
QUEENS RD
Hodthorpe Prim Sch
Hall Leys Farm
Ox Pastures Farm
Walling Brook
Wallingbrook Wood
GREEN LA
Sch
Tip (disused)
New Cottages
Penny Green
MILLASH LA
Belph
Belph Grange
Bismark Plantation
Millwood Brook
Penny Green Cottages
Springfield Farm
LC
Chy
Millwood Lodge
Mill Wood
Works
Tip (disused)
HENNYMOOR LA
B6042
Ganabrig Wood
West Park
Ladycroft Wood
Henneymoor Farm
Fishpond Lodge
Burial Ground Plantation
Creswell Crags Visitor Ctr
Oaksetts Lodge
Caves
Cresswell Crags
Pin Hole
Works
Craggs Cottages
CRAGS RD
B6042
Crags Pond
Church Hole
Craft Ctr
Cowclose Wood
SOUTHFIELD LA
SOUTHFIELD IND SITE
LONGHURST VIEW
WELBECK ST
PARKWAY
77
76
75
74
4
3
2
1
53
54
55

81
101

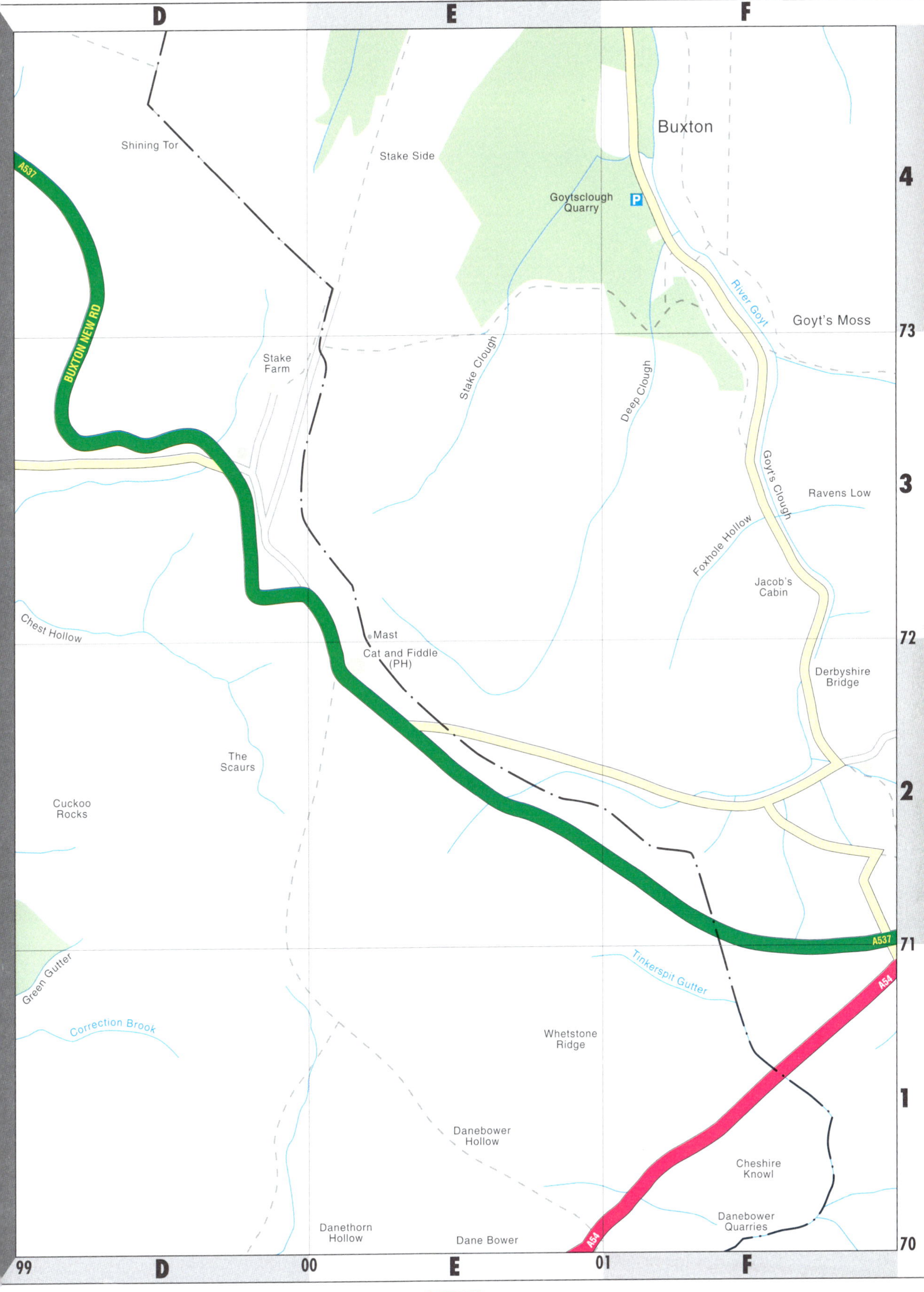
D
E
F
Shining Tor
Stake Side
Buxton
Goytsclough Quarry
P
River Goyt
Goyt's Moss
A537
BUXTON NEW RD
Stake Farm
Stake Clough
Deep Clough
Goyt's Clough
Ravens Low
Foxhole Hollow
Jacob's Cabin
Chest Hollow
Mast
Cat and Fiddle (PH)
Derbyshire Bridge
The Scaurs
Cuckoo Rocks
A537
Green Gutter
Tinkerspit Gutter
A54
Correction Brook
Whetstone Ridge
Danebower Hollow
Cheshire Knowl
Danebower Quarries
Danethorn Hollow
Dane Bower
A54
4
73
3
72
2
71
1
70
99
00
01

83
65

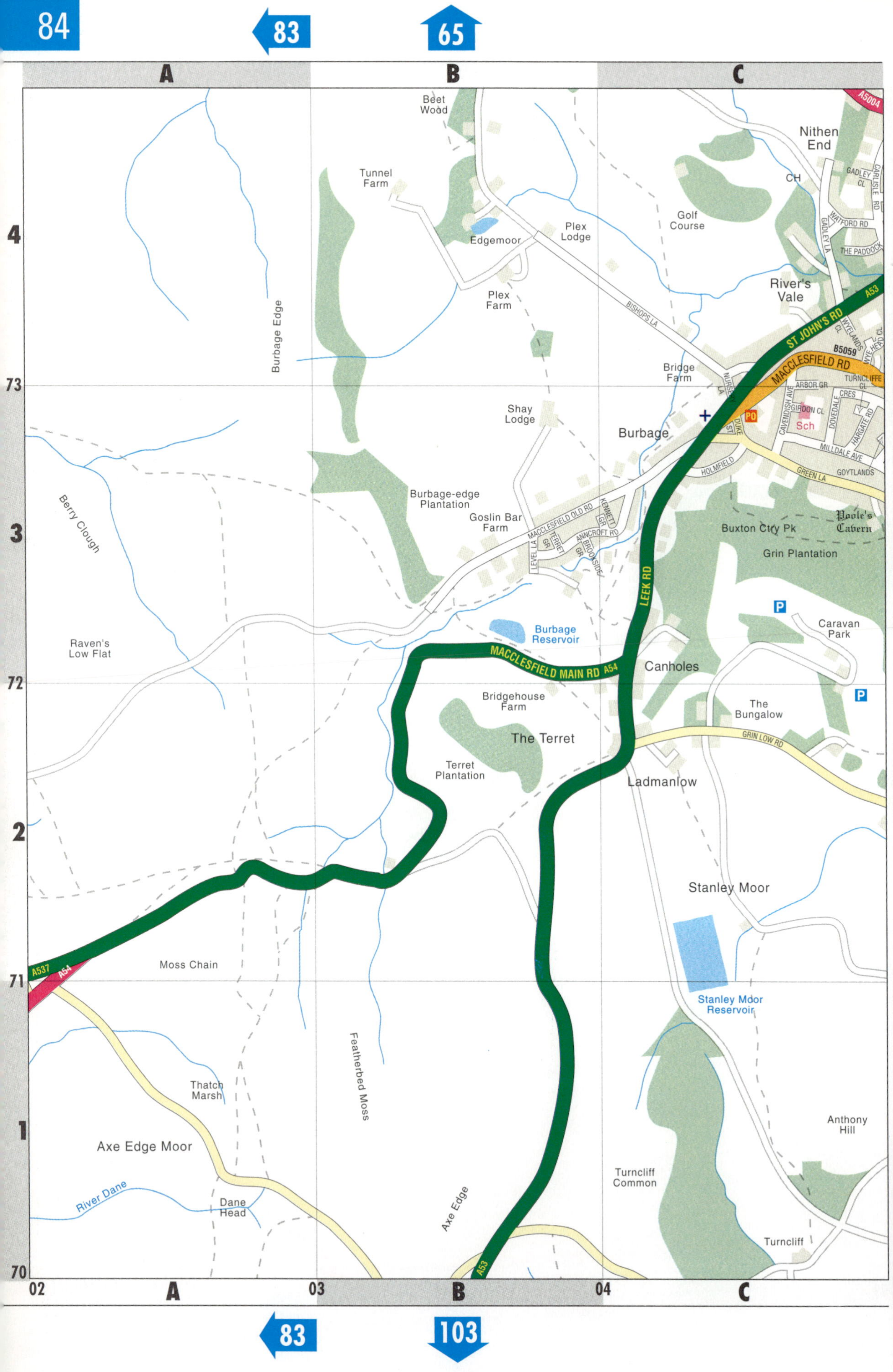
A
B
C
Beet Wood
Tunnel Farm
Edgemoor
Plex Lodge
Plex Farm
Golf Course
Nithen End
CH
River's Vale
A5004
A53
ST JOHN'S RD
B5059
MACCLESFIELD RD
BISHOPS LA
Burbage Edge
Bridge Farm
Shay Lodge
Burbage
Sch
Burbage-edge Plantation
Goslin Bar Farm
Buxton Ctry Pk
Poole's Cavern
Grin Plantation
Berry Clough
LEEK RD
Caravan Park
Raven's Low Flat
Burbage Reservoir
MACCLESFIELD MAIN RD A54
Canholes
Bridgehouse Farm
The Bungalow
The Terret
GRIN LOW RD
Terret Plantation
Ladmanlow
Stanley Moor
Moss Chain
A537
A54
Stanley Moor Reservoir
Featherbed Moss
Thatch Marsh
Anthony Hill
Axe Edge Moor
Turncliff Common
River Dane
Dane Head
Axe Edge
Turncliff
4
73
3
72
2
71
1
70
02
03
04

83
103

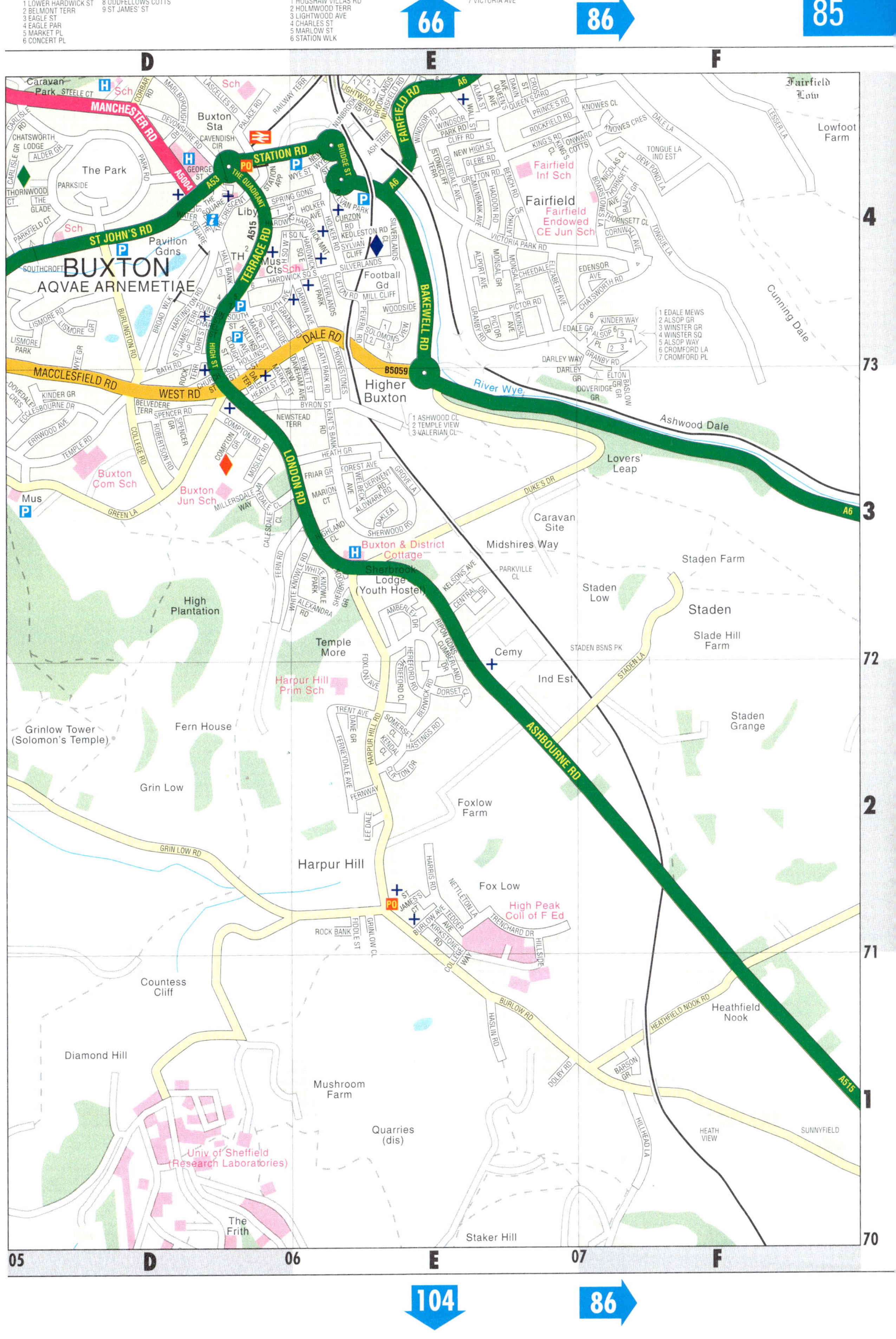

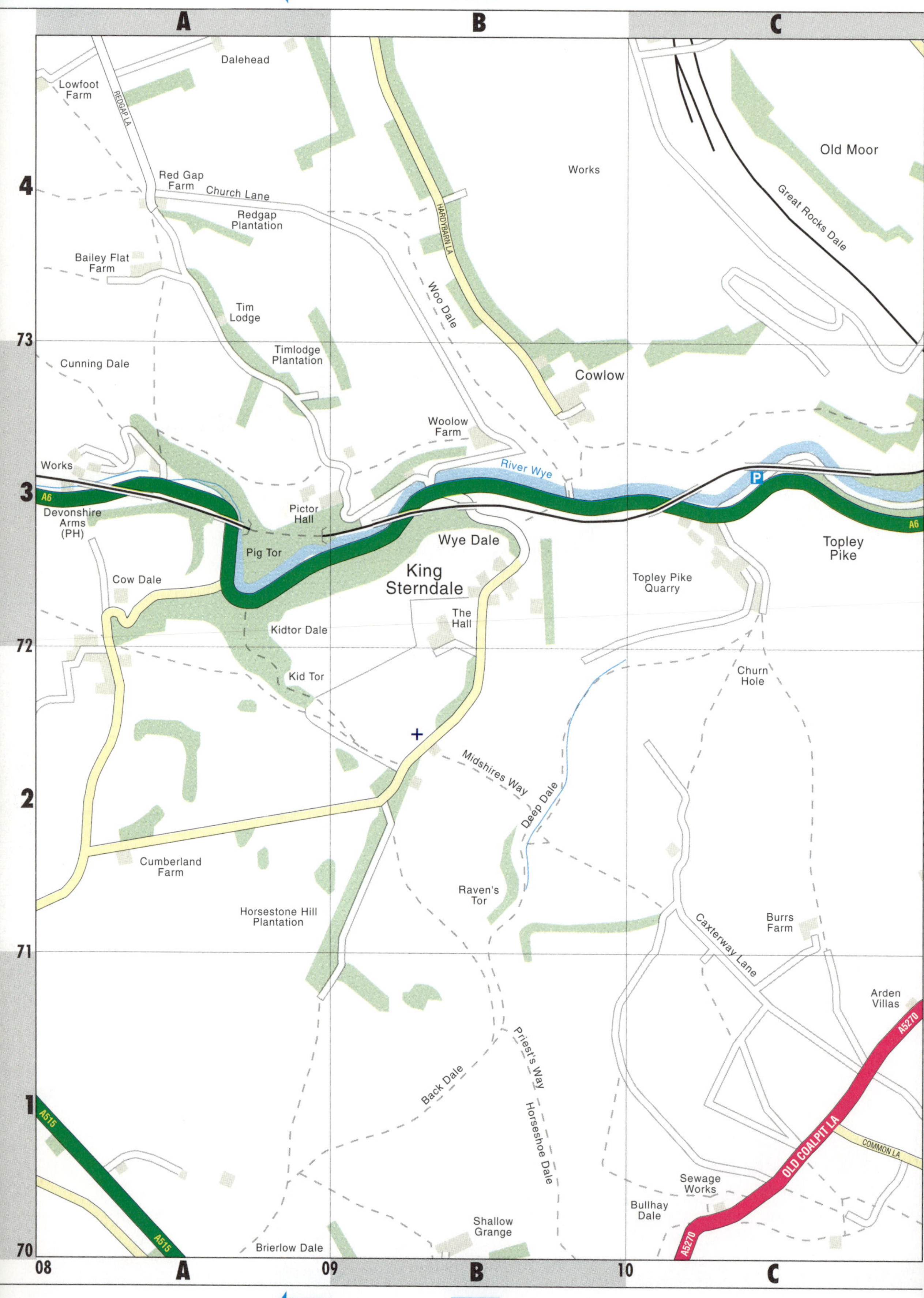

A   B   C

Dalehead

Lowfoot Farm

REDGAP LA

Red Gap Farm

Church Lane

Redgap Plantation

Works

4

HARDYBARN LA

Bailey Flat Farm

Tim Lodge

Woo Dale

Cowlow

Old Moor

Great Rocks Dale

73

Cunning Dale

Timlodge Plantation

Woolow Farm

River Wye

Works

3

A6

Devonshire Arms (PH)

Pictor Hall

Pig Tor

Wye Dale

King Sterndale

Topley Pike Quarry

P

Topley Pike

A6

Cow Dale

Kidtor Dale

The Hall

Kid Tor

72

Churn Hole

+

Midshires Way

Deep Dale

2

Cumberland Farm

Raven's Tor

Caxterway Lane

Burrs Farm

Horsestone Hill Plantation

71

Arden Villas

A5270

1

A515

Back Dale

Priest's Way

Horseshoe Dale

OLD COALPIT LA

COMMON LA

Sewage Works

Bullhay Dale

A5270

Shallow Grange

Brierlow Dale

70

08   A   09   B   10   C

68
88

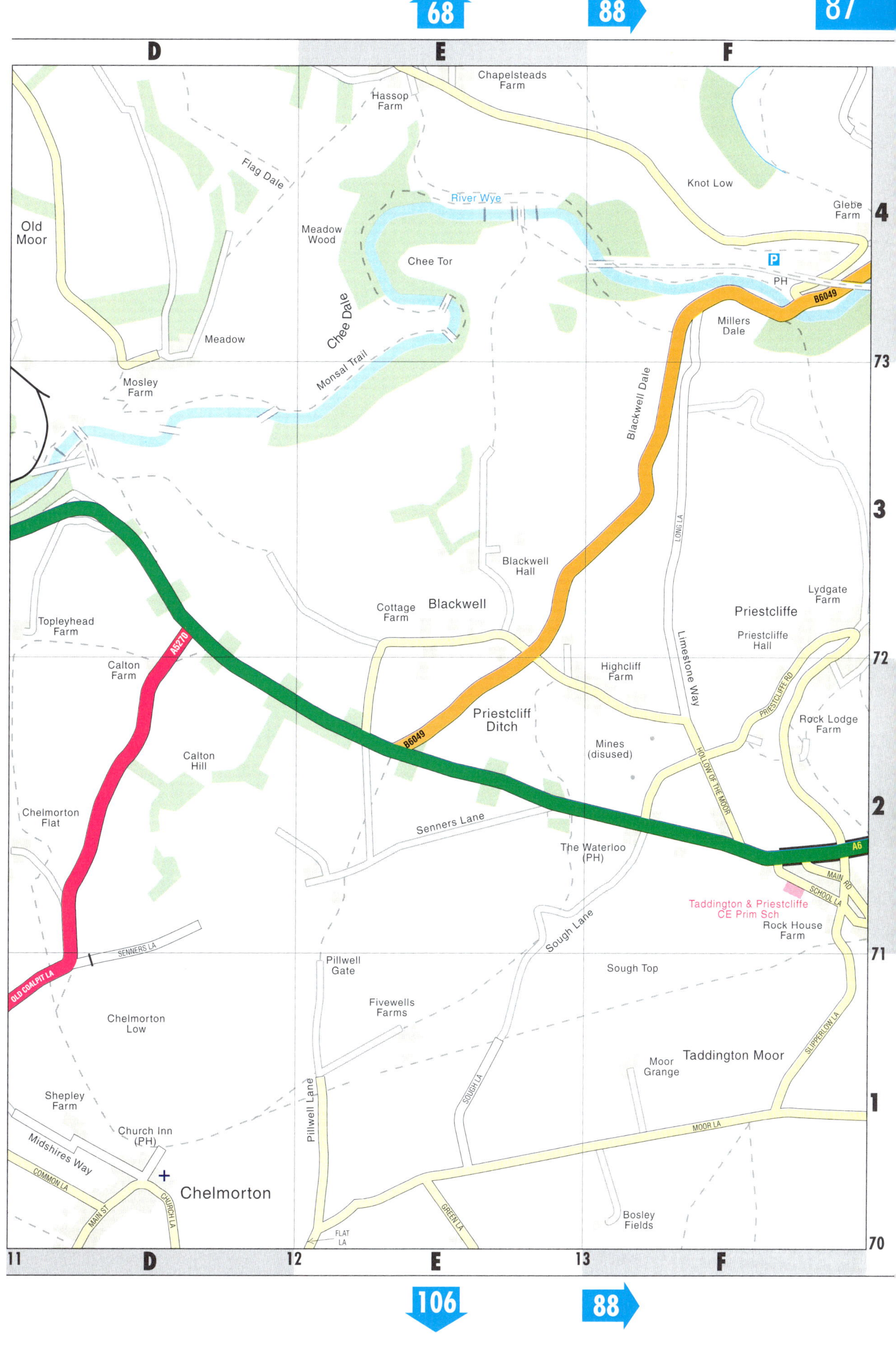
D
E
F
Chapelsteads Farm
Hassop Farm
Flag Dale
Knot Low
River Wye
Glebe Farm
Old Moor
Meadow Wood
Chee Tor
PH
B6049
Chee Dale
Millers Dale
Meadow
Monsal Trail
Mosley Farm
Blackwell Dale
LONG LA
Blackwell Hall
Cottage Farm
Blackwell
Lydgate Farm
Priestcliffe
Topleyhead Farm
A5270
Priestcliffe Hall
Calton Farm
Highcliff Farm
Limestone Way
PRIESTCLIFFE RD
Priestcliff Ditch
Rock Lodge Farm
B6049
Mines (disused)
Calton Hill
HOLLOW OF THE MOOR
Chelmorton Flat
Senners Lane
The Waterloo (PH)
A6
MAIN RD
SCHOOL LA
Taddington & Priestcliffe CE Prim Sch
Rock House Farm
Sough Lane
SENNERS LA
Pillwell Gate
Sough Top
OLD COALPIT LA
Chelmorton Low
Fivewells Farms
SLIPPERLOW LA
Moor Grange
Taddington Moor
Shepley Farm
Pillwell Lane
SOUGH LA
MOOR LA
Church Inn (PH)
Midshires Way
COMMON LA
Chelmorton
CHURCH LA
MAIN ST
GREEN LA
FLAT LA
Bosley Fields
4
73
3
72
2
71
1
70
11
D
12
E
13
F

106
88

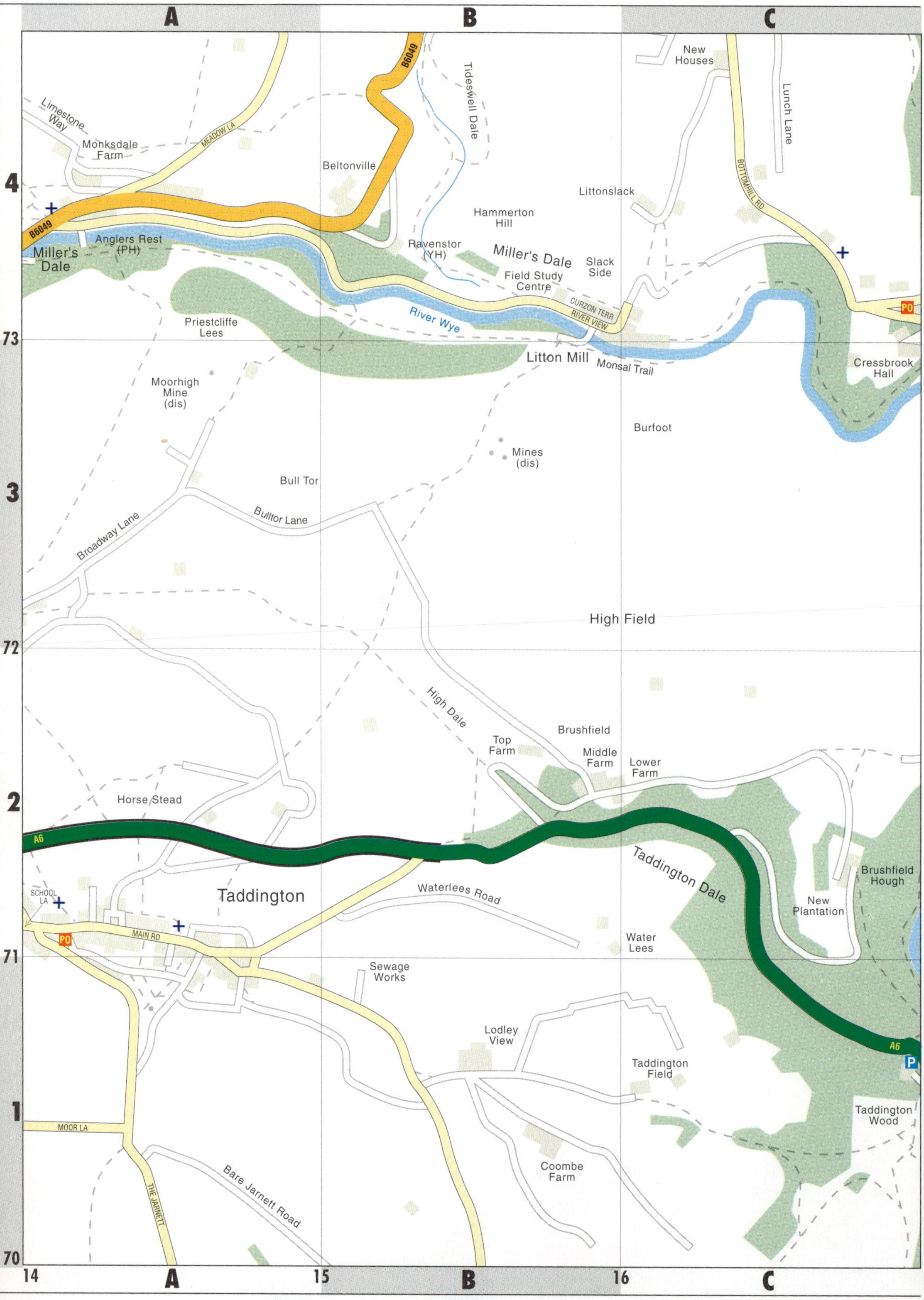

A　　　　　　　　B　　　　　　　　C

4

Limestone Way

Monksdale Farm

MEADOW LA

B6049

Beltonville

Tideswell Dale

New Houses

Littonslack

Lunch Lane

BOTTOMILL RD

Hammerton Hill

Miller's Dale

Slack Side

B6049

Miller's Dale

Anglers Rest (PH)

Ravenstor (YH)

Field Study Centre

CURZON TERR

RIVER VIEW

PO

73

Priestcliffe Lees

River Wye

Litton Mill

Monsal Trail

Cressbrook Hall

Moorhigh Mine (dis)

Burfoot

Mines (dis)

3

Bull Tor

Bulltor Lane

Broadway Lane

High Field

72

High Dale

Brushfield

Top Farm

Middle Farm

Lower Farm

Brushfield Hough

2

A6

Horse Stead

Taddington Dale

New Plantation

A6

Taddington

Waterlees Road

SCHOOL LA

Water Lees

P

PO

MAIN RD

71

Sewage Works

Lodley View

Taddington Field

Taddington Wood

1

MOOR LA

Bare Jarnett Road

THE JARNETT

Coombe Farm

70

14　　　　　　　15　　　　　　　16

A　　　　　　　　B　　　　　　　　C

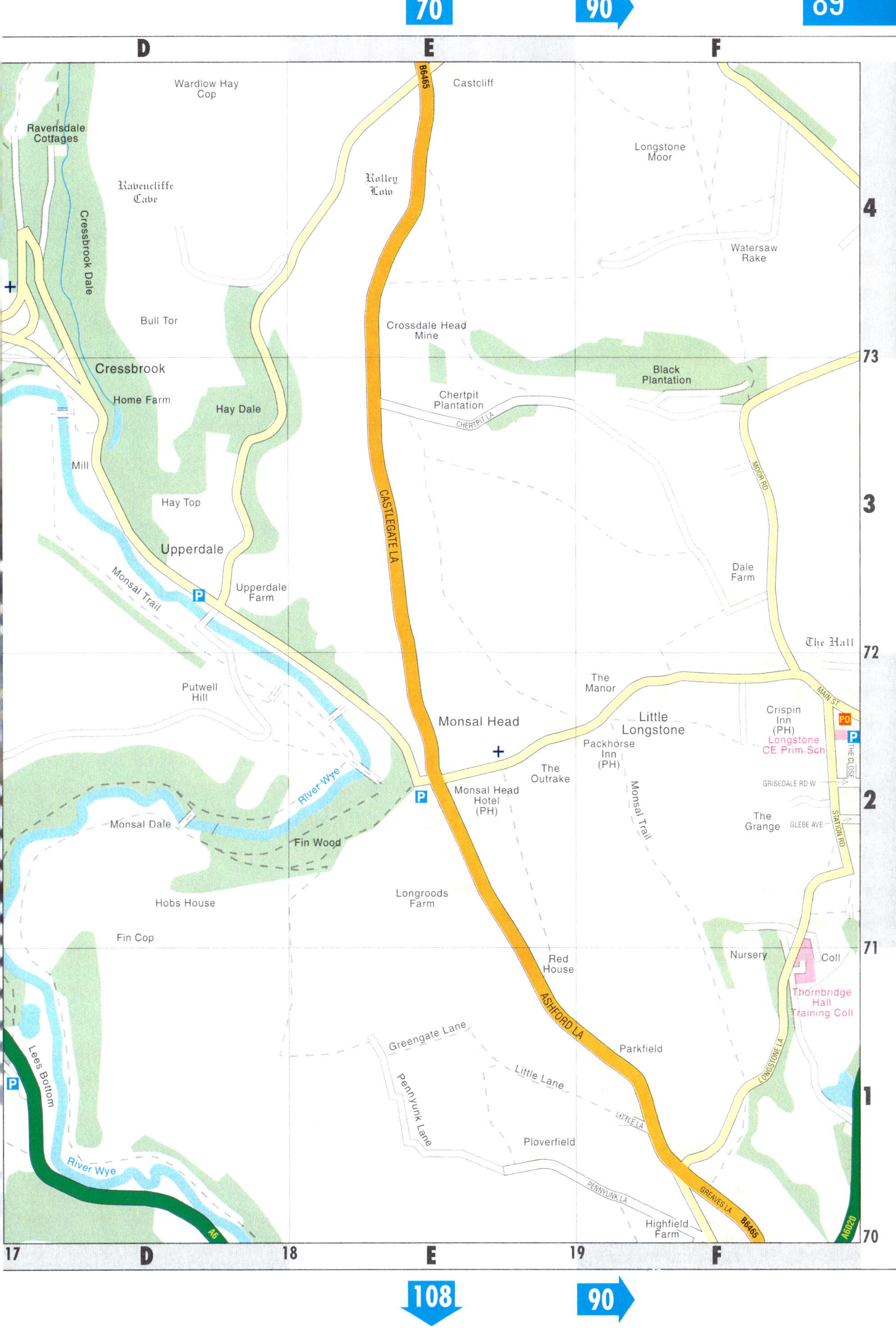
70
90
D
E
F
B6465
Castcliff
Wardlow Hay
Cop
Ravensdale
Cottages
Ravencliffe
Cave
Rolley
Low
Longstone
Moor
Cressbrook Dale
Watersaw
Rake
4
Bull Tor
Crossdale Head
Mine
73
Cressbrook
Black
Plantation
Home Farm
Chertpit
Plantation
CHERTPIT LA
Hay Dale
Mill
MOOR RD
Hay Top
3
CASTLEGATE LA
Upperdale
Dale
Farm
Monsal Trail
Upperdale
Farm
The Hall
72
Putwell
Hill
The
Manor
MAIN ST
Crispin
Inn
(PH)
Monsal Head
Little
Longstone
PO
Longstone
CE Prim Sch
Packhorse
Inn
(PH)
THE CLOSE
The
Outrake
GRISEDALE RD W
River Wye
Monsal Head
Hotel
(PH)
Monsal Trail
2
Monsal Dale
The
Grange
GLEBE AVE
STATION RD
Fin Wood
Longroods
Farm
Hobs House
Fin Cop
71
Nursery
Coll
Red
House
Thornbridge
Hall
Training Coll
ASHFORD LA
Greengate Lane
Parkfield
Lees Bottom
LONGSTONE LA
1
Little Lane
Pennyunk Lane
LITTLE LA
Ploverfield
River Wye
PENNYUNK LA
GREAVES LA
Highfield
Farm
B6465
A6
A6020
70
17
D
18
E
19
F
108
90

89 71

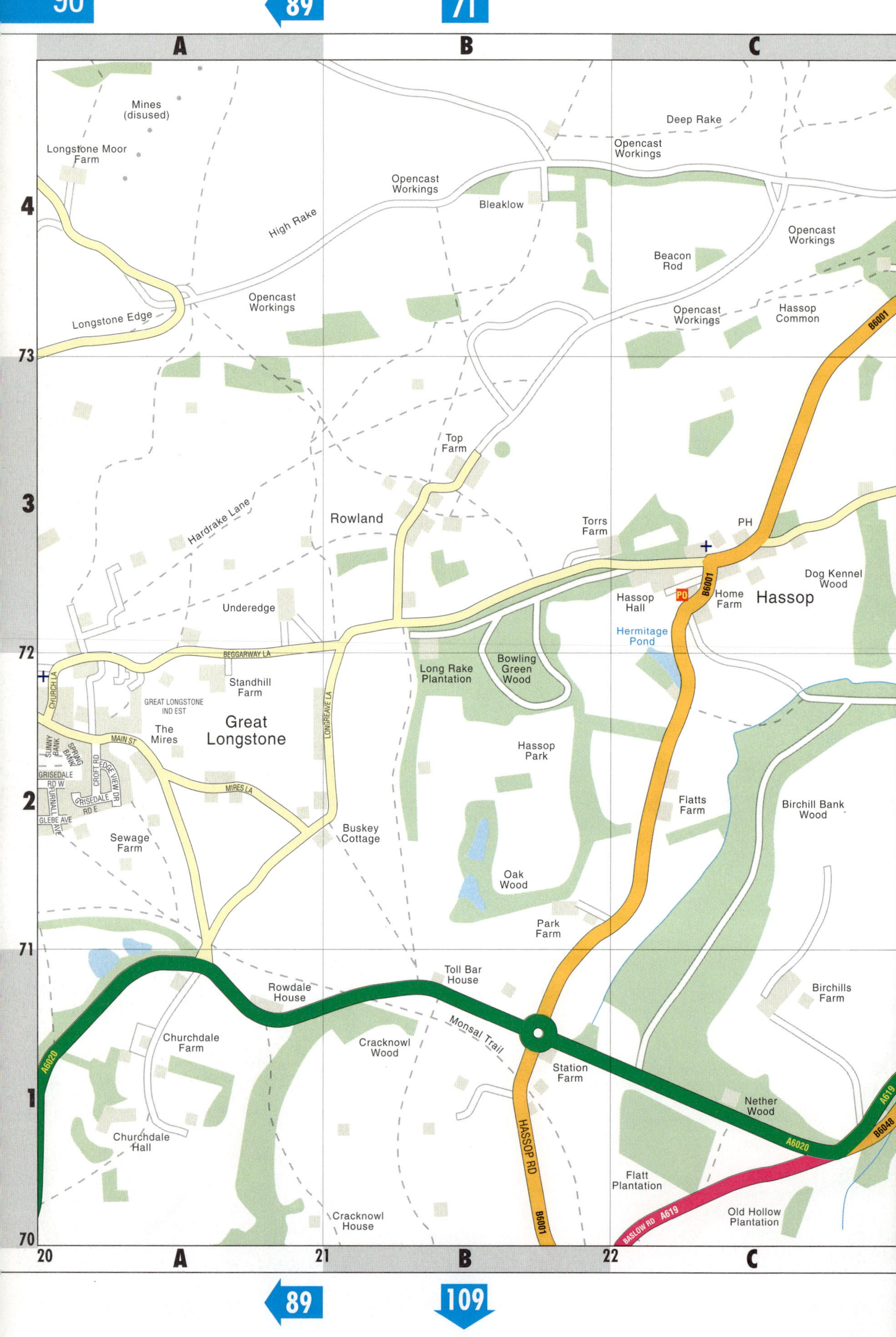

A
B
C
Mines (disused)
Longstone Moor Farm
Deep Rake
Opencast Workings
Opencast Workings
Bleaklow
High Rake
Opencast Workings
Beacon Rod
Opencast Workings
Longstone Edge
Opencast Workings
Hassop Common
B6001
Top Farm
Rowland
Hardrake Lane
Torrs Farm
PH
Dog Kennel Wood
Underedge
Hassop Hall
PO
B6001
Home Farm
Hassop
Hermitage Pond
BEGGARWAY LA
CHURCH LA
Standhill Farm
Long Rake Plantation
Bowling Green Wood
GREAT LONGSTONE IND EST
The Mires
Great Longstone
LONGREAVE LA
MAIN ST
Hassop Park
SUNNY BANK
SPRING BANK
CROFT RD
EDGE VIEW DR
GRISEDALE RD W
MIRES LA
FURNALL AVE
GRISEDALE RD E
GLEBE AVE
Flatts Farm
Birchill Bank Wood
Buskey Cottage
Sewage Farm
Oak Wood
Park Farm
Toll Bar House
Rowdale House
Birchills Farm
Monsal Trail
Churchdale Farm
Cracknowl Wood
A6020
Station Farm
Nether Wood
A619
B6048
A6020
Churchdale Hall
HASSOP RD
Flatt Plantation
B6001
Cracknowl House
BASLOW RD A619
Old Hollow Plantation
4
73
3
72
2
71
1
70
20
21
22

89 109

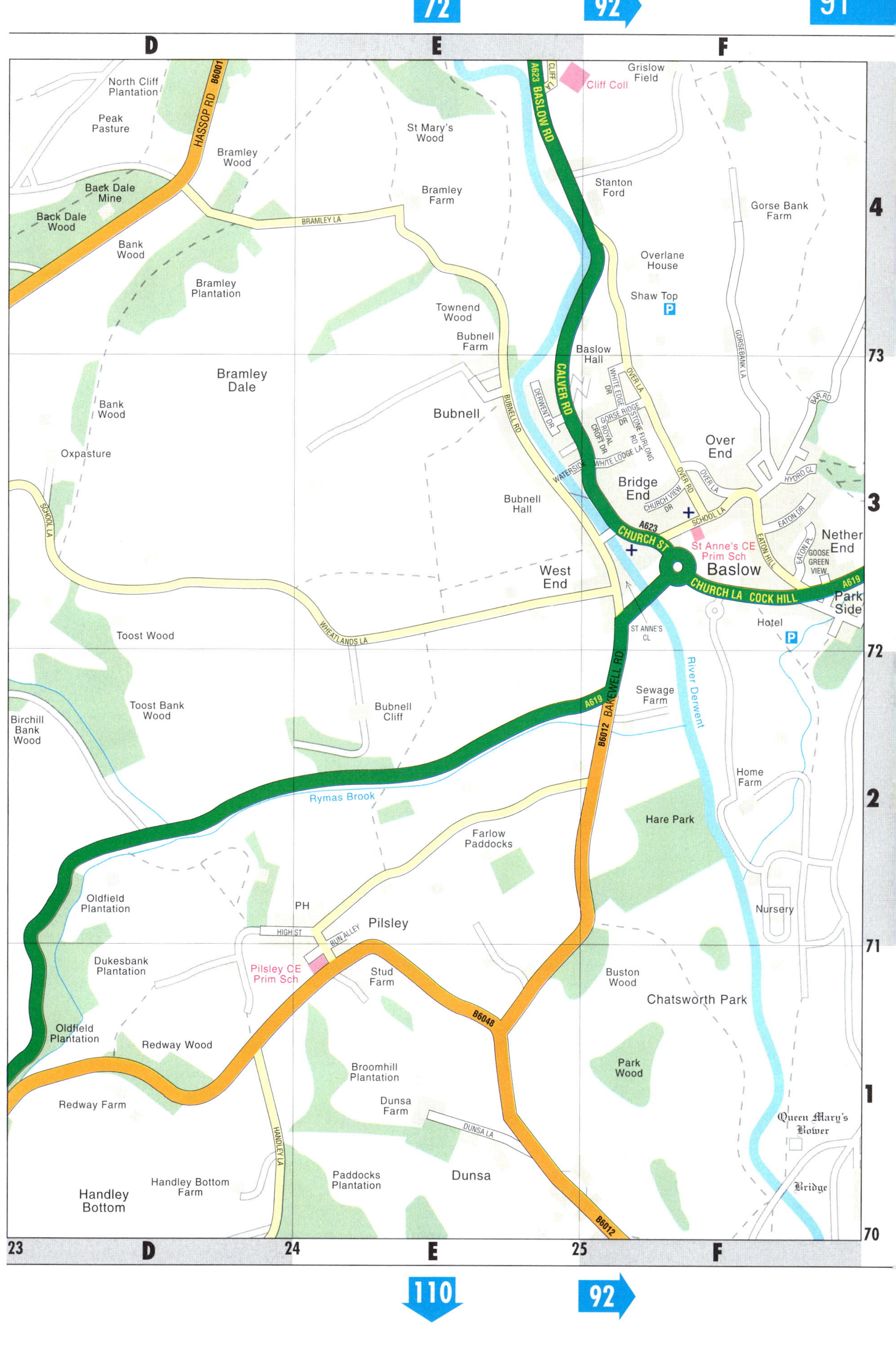
D
E
F
North Cliff Plantation
Peak Pasture
HASSOP RD B6001
Bramley Wood
Back Dale Mine
Back Dale Wood
Bank Wood
BRAMLEY LA
Bramley Plantation
St Mary's Wood
Bramley Farm
Townend Wood
Bubnell Farm
Bramley Dale
Bank Wood
Oxpasture
Bubnell
BUBNELL RD
SCHOOL LA
Bubnell Hall
West End
WHEATLANDS LA
Toost Wood
Toost Bank Wood
Birchill Bank Wood
Bubnell Cliff
Rymas Brook
A619
BAKEWELL RD
B6012
Farlow Paddocks
Oldfield Plantation
PH
Pilsley
HIGH ST
BUN ALLEY
Pilsley CE Prim Sch
Stud Farm
Dukesbank Plantation
Oldfield Plantation
Redway Wood
B6048
Broomhill Plantation
Redway Farm
Dunsa Farm
DUNSA LA
HANDLEY LA
Handley Bottom Farm
Paddocks Plantation
Dunsa
Handley Bottom
B6012
A623 BASLOW RD
CLIFF LA
Cliff Coll
Grislow Field
Stanton Ford
Gorse Bank Farm
Overlane House
Shaw Top
P
Baslow Hall
CALVER RD
DERWENT DR
WHITE EDGE DR
OVER LA
GORSE RIDGE DR
ROYAL CROFT DR
STONE FURLONG RD
WHITE LODGE LA
WATERSIDE
GORSEBANK LA
BAR RD
Over End
HYDRO CL
OVER RD
OVER LA
Bridge End
CHURCH VIEW DR
SCHOOL LA
EATON DR
A623
CHURCH ST
St Anne's CE Prim Sch
EATON HILL
EATON PL
GOOSE GREEN VIEW
Nether End
Baslow
CHURCH LA
COCK HILL
A619
Park Side
Hotel
P
ST ANNE'S CL
River Derwent
Sewage Farm
Home Farm
Hare Park
Nursery
Buston Wood
Chatsworth Park
Park Wood
Queen Mary's Bower
Bridge
4
73
3
72
2
71
1
70
23
24
25

91
73

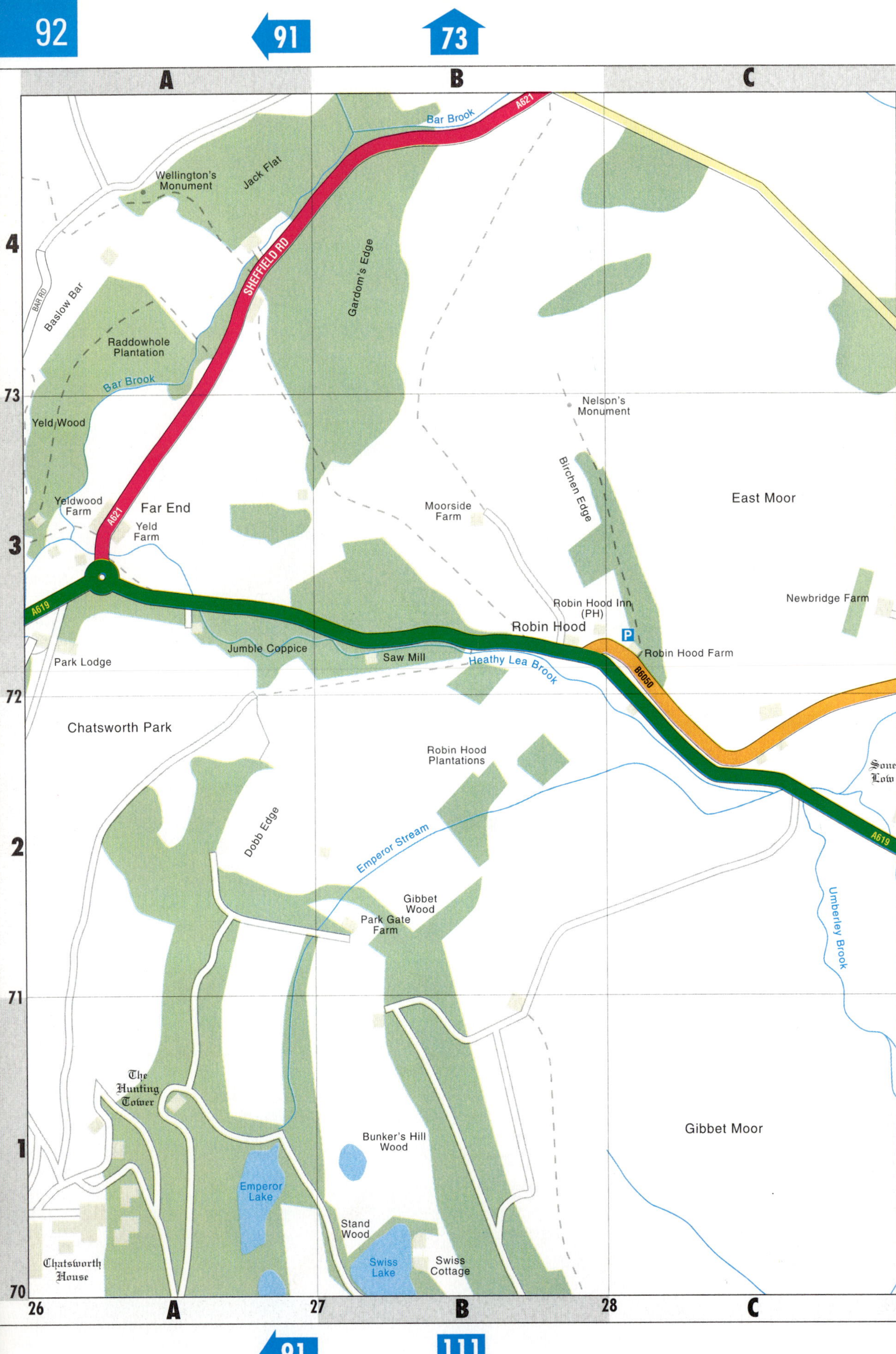

A B C

4

73

Bar Brook

A621

Wellington's
Monument

Jack Flat

SHEFFIELD RD

Gardom's Edge

Nelson's
Monument

Baslow Bar

BAR RD

Raddowhole
Plantation

Bar Brook

Birchen Edge

East Moor

Yeld Wood

Yeldwood
Farm

A621

Far End

Yeld
Farm

Moorside
Farm

Robin Hood Inn
(PH)

Newbridge Farm

3

A619

Robin Hood

P

Robin Hood Farm

Park Lodge

Jumble Coppice

Saw Mill

Heathy Lea Brook

B6050

72

Chatsworth Park

Robin Hood
Plantations

Sone
Low

Dobb Edge

Emperor Stream

Umberley Brook

A619

2

Gibbet
Wood

Park Gate
Farm

71

The
Hunting
Tower

Bunker's Hill
Wood

Gibbet Moor

1

Emperor
Lake

Stand
Wood

Chatsworth
House

Swiss
Lake

Swiss
Cottage

70

26 A 27 B 28 C

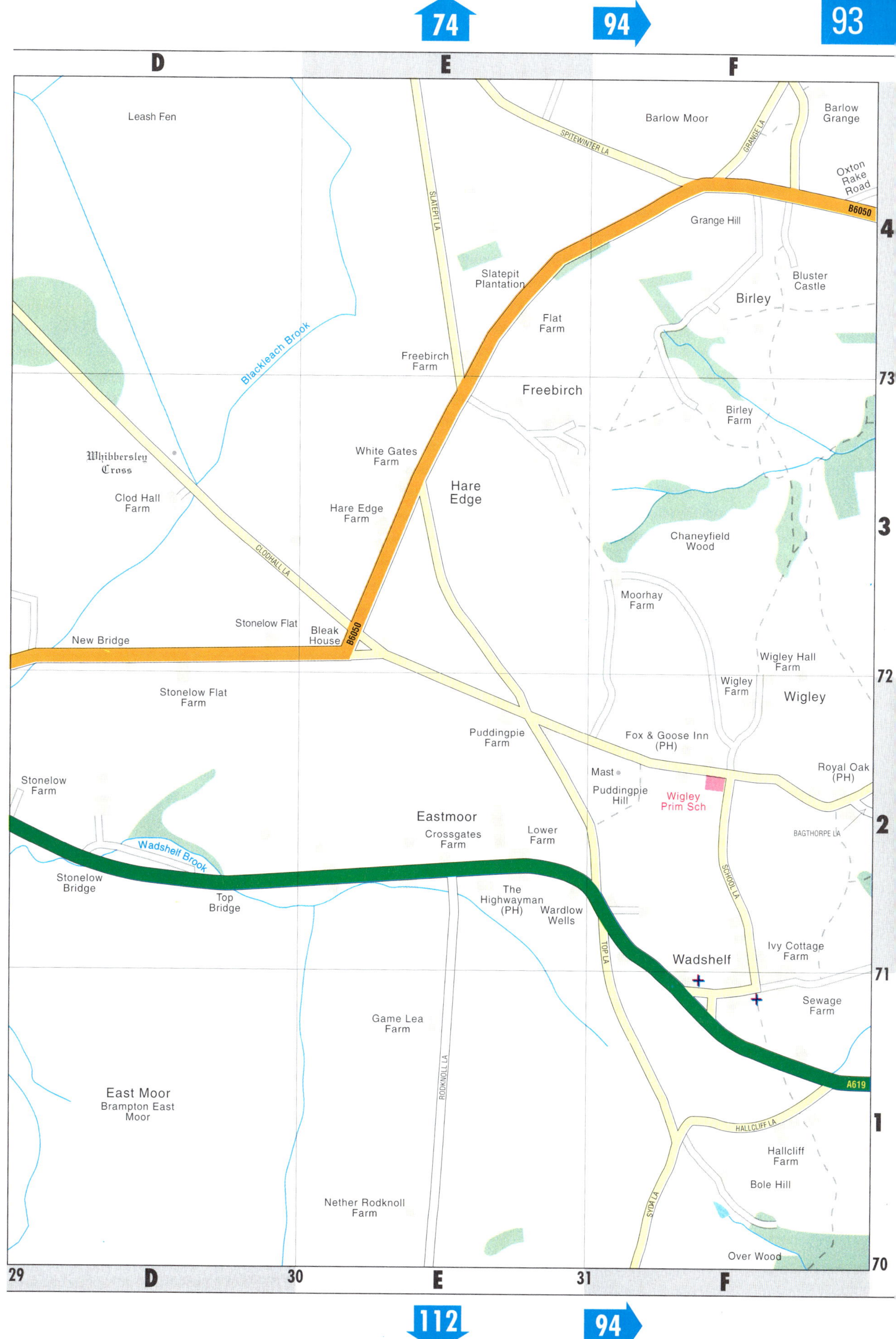
74
94
D
E
F
Leash Fen
Barlow Moor
Barlow Grange
SPITEWINTER LA
GRANGE LA
Oxton Rake Road
B6050
Grange Hill
4
SLATEPIT LA
Slatepit Plantation
Bluster Castle
Birley
Flat Farm
Blackleach Brook
Freebirch Farm
Freebirch
73
Birley Farm
Whibbersley Cross
White Gates Farm
Hare Edge
Clod Hall Farm
Hare Edge Farm
Chaneyfield Wood
3
CLODHALL LA
Moorhay Farm
Stonelow Flat
Bleak House
B6050
New Bridge
Wigley Hall Farm
72
Stonelow Flat Farm
Wigley Farm
Wigley
Puddingpie Farm
Fox & Goose Inn (PH)
Mast
Royal Oak (PH)
Stonelow Farm
Puddingpie Hill
Wigley Prim Sch
Eastmoor
2
Lower Farm
BAGTHORPE LA
Crossgates Farm
Wadshelf Brook
Stonelow Bridge
SCHOOL LA
Top Bridge
The Highwayman (PH)
Wardlow Wells
TOP LA
Ivy Cottage Farm
Wadshelf
71
Sewage Farm
Game Lea Farm
A619
RODKNOLL LA
East Moor
Brampton East Moor
1
HALLCLIFF LA
Hallcliff Farm
Bole Hill
SYDA LA
Nether Rodknoll Farm
Over Wood
70
29
D
30
E
31
F
112
94

93
75

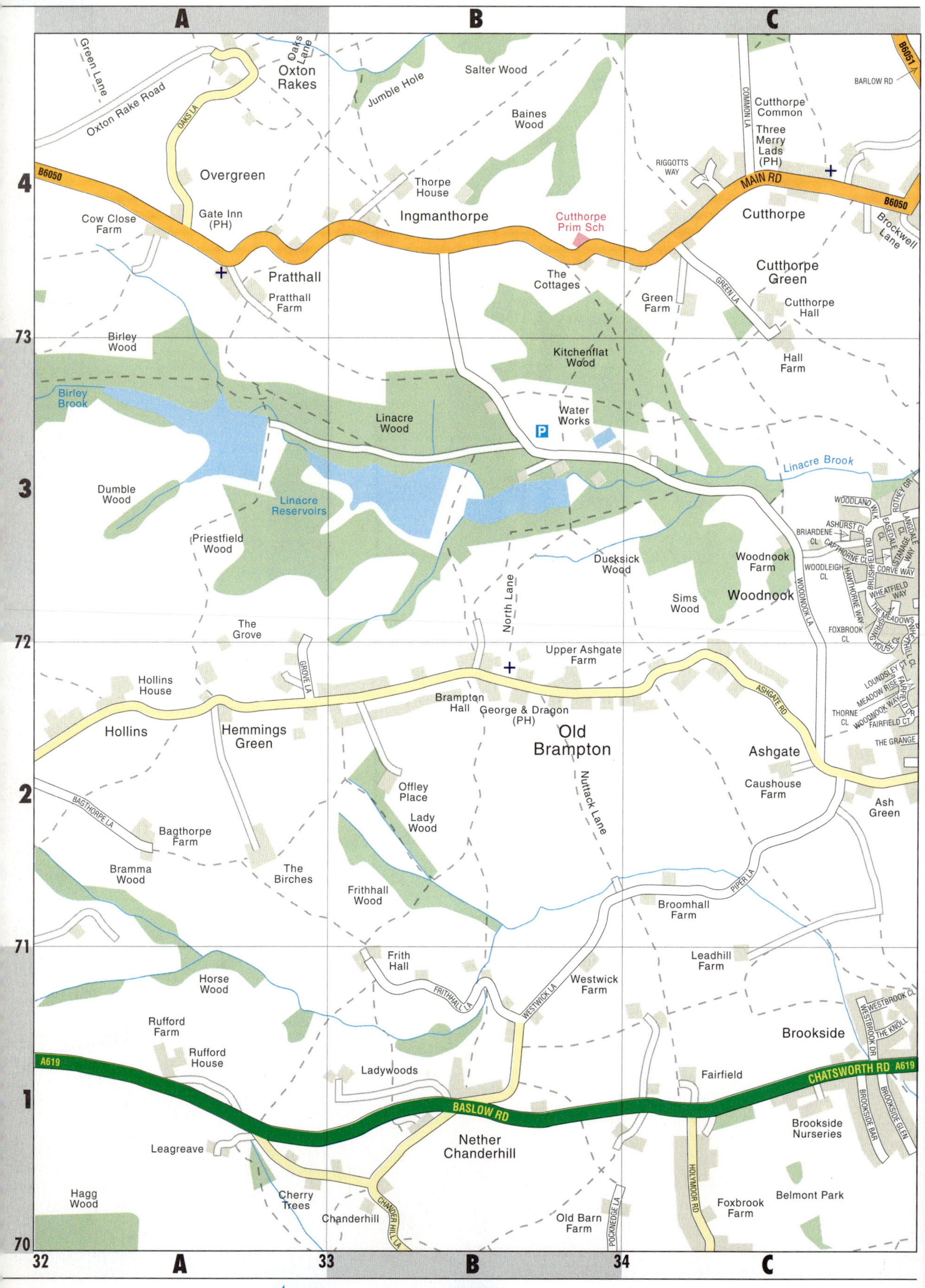
A
B
C
Green Lane
Oxton Rake Road
Oaks Lane
Oxton Rakes
Jumble Hole
Salter Wood
Baines Wood
OAKS LA
Overgreen
B6050
Cow Close Farm
Gate Inn (PH)
Thorpe House
Ingmanthorpe
Cutthorpe Prim Sch
Pratthall
Pratthall Farm
The Cottages
Green Farm
B6051
BARLOW RD
COMMON LA
Cutthorpe Common
Three Merry Lads (PH)
RIGGOTTS WAY
MAIN RD
Cutthorpe
Brockwell Lane
Cutthorpe Green
GREEN LA
Cutthorpe Hall
Hall Farm
Birley Wood
Kitchenflat Wood
Birley Brook
Linacre Wood
Water Works
Linacre Brook
Dumble Wood
Linacre Reservoirs
Priestfield Wood
Ducksick Wood
Woodnook Farm
Sims Wood
Woodnook
WOODNOOK LA
WOODLAND WLK
ROTHEY GR
ASHURST CL
BRIARDENE CL
CAPTHORNE CL
LANGDALE CL
EASEDALE CL
STANAGE WAY
WOODLEIGH CL
HAWTHORNE WAY
BRUSHFIELD RD
CORVE WAY
WHEATFIELD WAY
THE MEADOWS
FOXBROOK CL
SPRING HOUSE CL
North Lane
The Grove
Upper Ashgate Farm
GROVE LA
Hollins House
Hollins
Hemmings Green
Brampton Hall
George & Dragon (PH)
Old Brampton
ASHGATE RD
LOUNDSLEY CT
MEADOW RISE
WOODNOOK WAY
THORNE CL
FAIRFIELD CT
THE GRANGE
Ashgate
Caushouse Farm
Ash Green
Offley Place
Lady Wood
Nuttack Lane
BAGTHORPE LA
Bagthorpe Farm
Bramma Wood
The Birches
Frithhall Wood
PIPER LA
Broomhall Farm
Frith Hall
Horse Wood
Westwick Farm
Leadhill Farm
FRITHHALL LA
WESTWICK LA
Rufford Farm
Rufford House
WESTBROOK CL
WESTBROOK DR
THE KNOLL
Brookside
A619
Ladywoods
Fairfield
CHATSWORTH RD
BASLOW RD
BROOKSIDE DR
BROOKSIDE GLEN
BROOKSIDE BAR
Brookside Nurseries
Leagreave
Nether Chanderhill
Hagg Wood
Cherry Trees
CHANDER HILL LA
Chanderhill
Old Barn Farm
POCKNEDGE LA
HOLYMOOR RD
Foxbrook Farm
Belmont Park
4
73
3
72
2
71
1
70
32
33
34

93
113

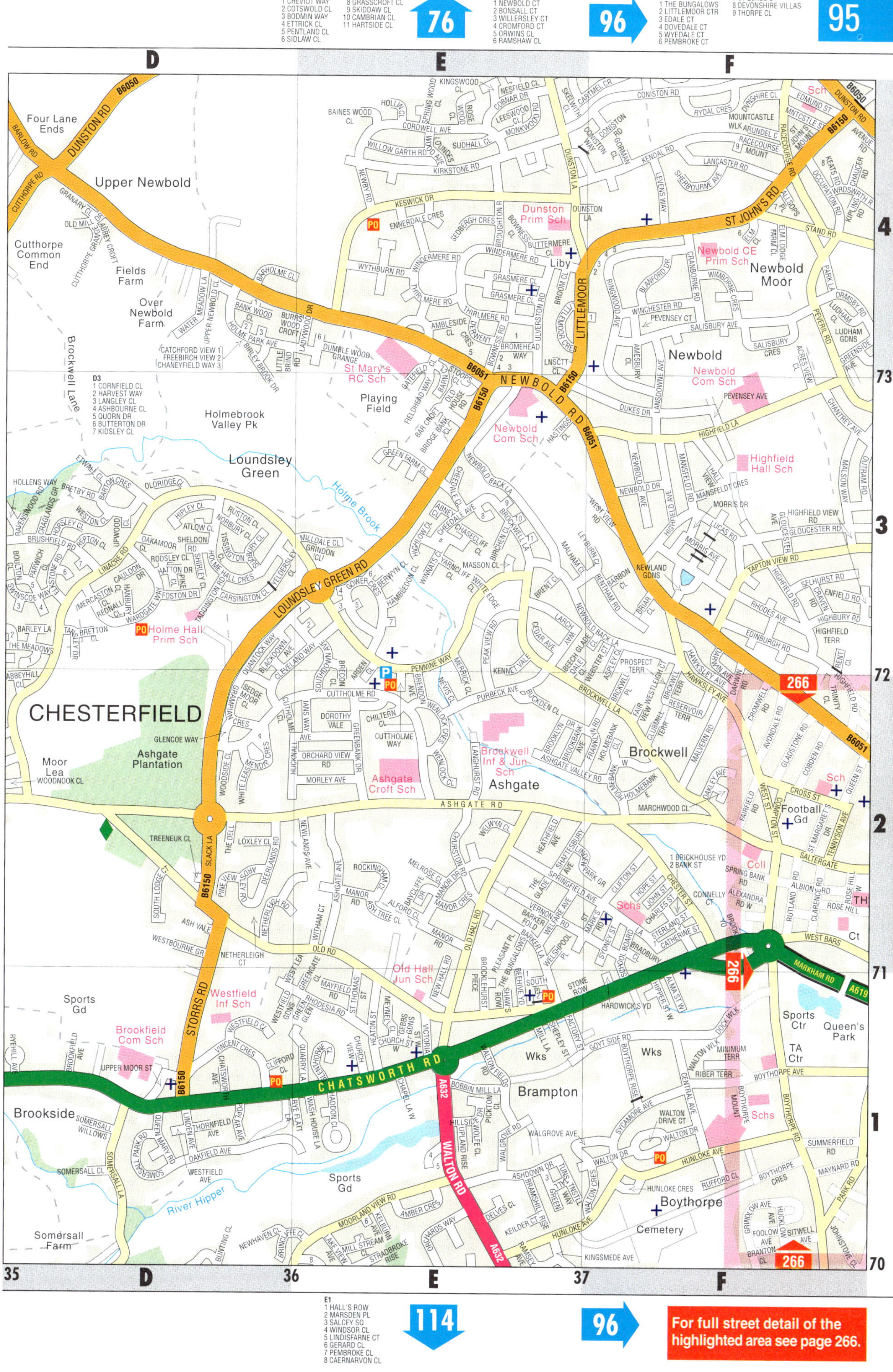

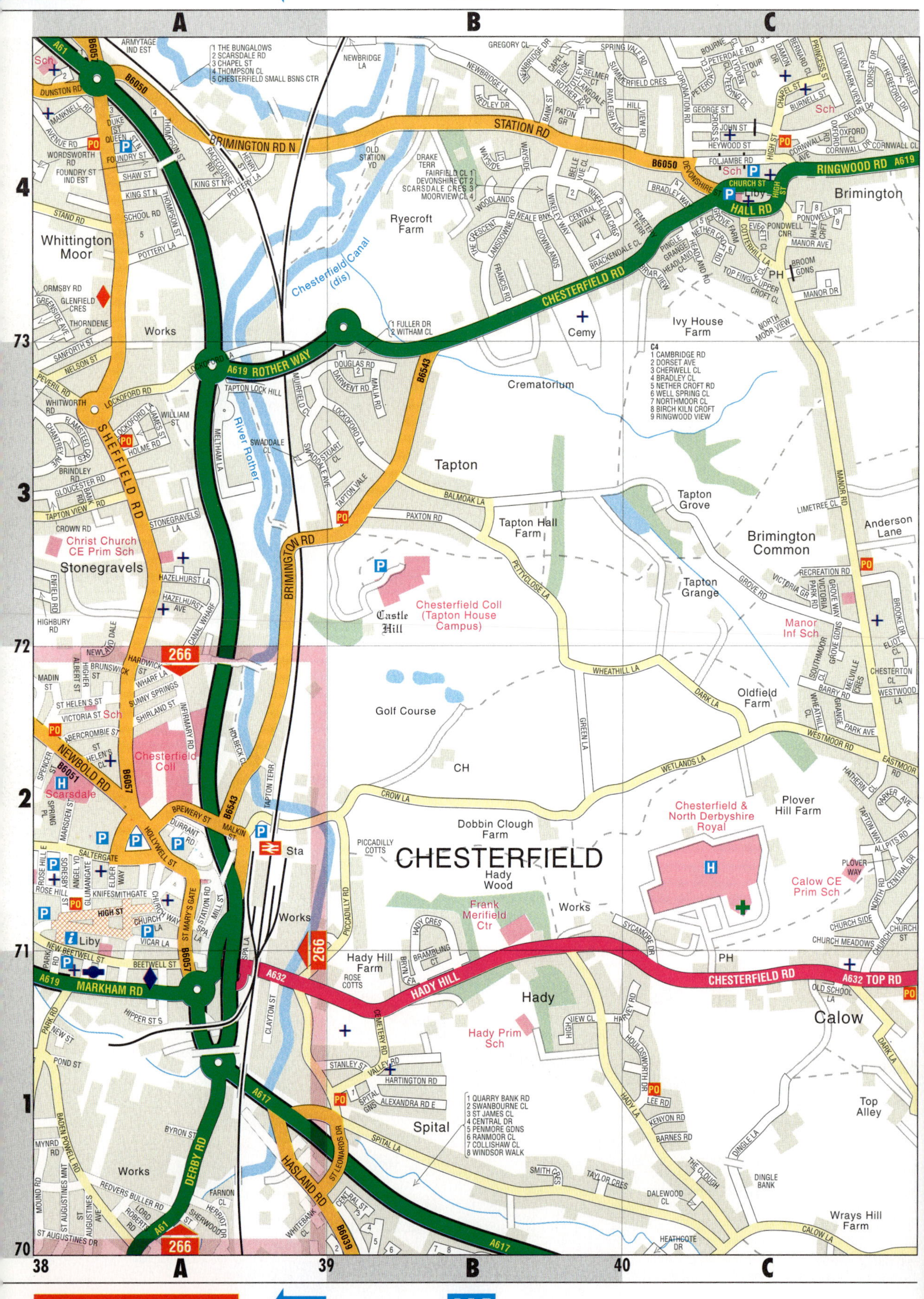

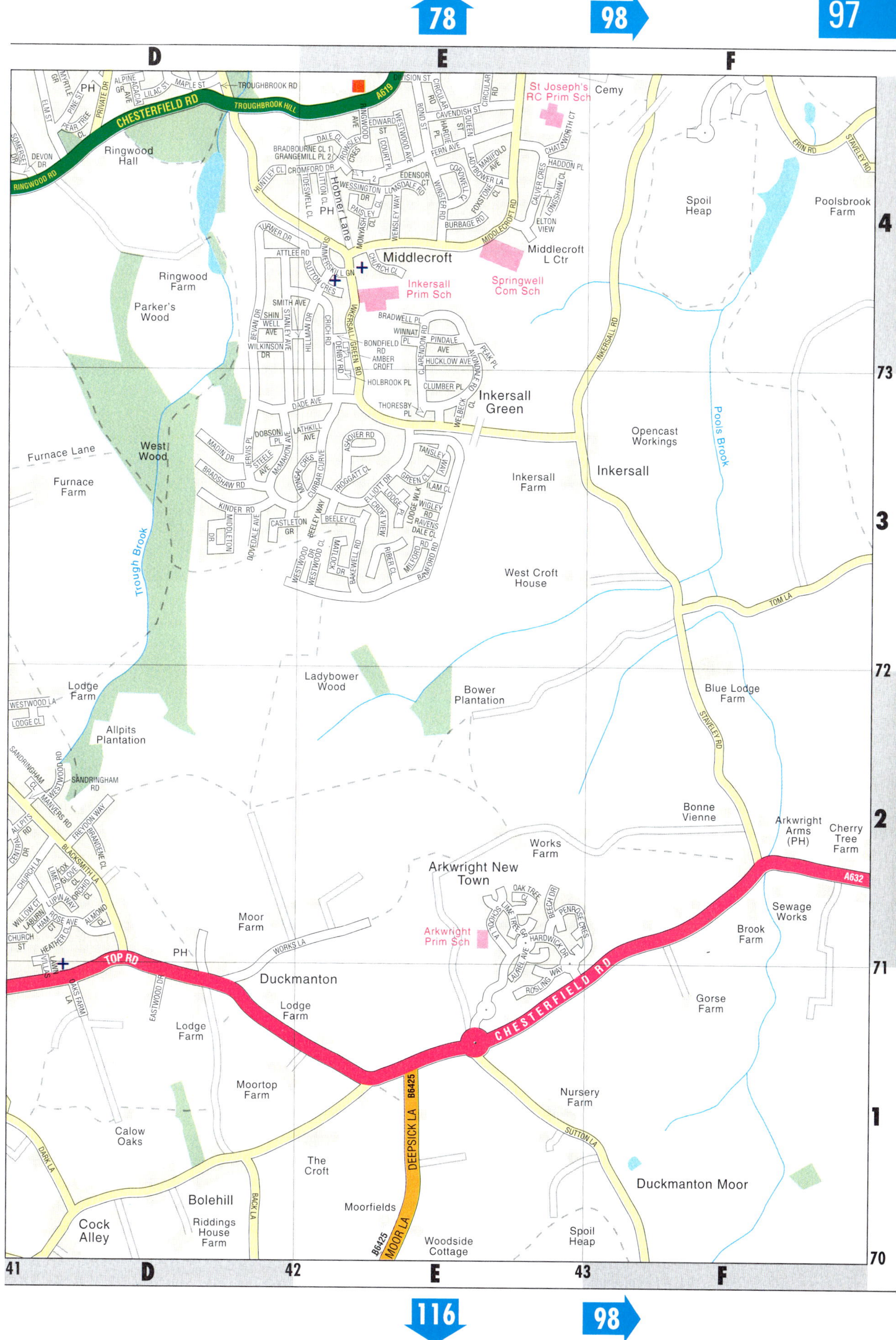

78
98
D
E
F
CHESTERFIELD RD
TROUGHBROOK RD
TROUGHBROOK HILL
A619
RINGWOOD RD
MAPLE ST
LILAC ST
ALPINE GR
ACACIA AVE
PH
PINE ST
PEAR TREE CL
MYRTLE GR
ELM ST
PRIVATE DR
DEVON DR
SOMERSET DR
Ringwood Hall
DIVISION ST
CIRCULAR RD
CAVENDISH ST
BOND ST
HARDIE PL
QUEEN ST
EDWARD ST
RINGWOOD AVE
WESTWOOD AVE
COURT PL
DALE CL
ROWSLEY CRES
BRADBOURNE CL
GRANGEMILL PL
HUNTLOY CL
CROMFORD DR
TIDESWELL CL
LITTON CL
Hobner Lane
WESSINGTON DR
EDENSOR CT
LONSDALE RD
PAISLEY CL
MONYASH CL
WENSLEY WAY
WINSTER RD
FERN AVE
LADYBOWER LA
CORDWELL CL
MANIFOLD AVE
FOXSTONE CL
BURBAGE RD
MIDDLECROFT RD
St Joseph's RC Prim Sch
Cemy
CHATSWORTH CT
HADDON PL
CALVER CRES
LONGSHAW CL
ELTON VIEW
ERIN RD
STAVELEY RD
Spoil Heap
Poolsbrook Farm
4
TURNER DR
ATTLEE RD
SUMMERSKILL GN
SUTTON CRES
CHURCH CL
Middlecroft
Middlecroft L Ctr
Inkersall Prim Sch
Springwell Com Sch
Ringwood Farm
Parker's Wood
SMITH AVE
SHIN WELL AVE
STANLEY AVE
BEVAN DR
WILKINSON DR
HILLMAN DR
CRICH RD
DENBY RD
INKERSALL GREEN RD
BRADWELL PL
WINNAT PL
BONDFIELD RD
AMBER CROFT
CLARENDON RD
PINDALE AVE
HUCKLOW AVE
PEAK PL
AVONDALE RD
HOLBROOK PL
CLUMBER PL
THORESBY PL
WELBECK CL
Inkersall Green
INKERSALL RD
73
DADE AVE
LATHKILL AVE
DOBSON PL
JERVIS PL
MADIN DR
STEELE AVE
McMAHON AVE
ASHOVER RD
TANSLEY WAY
Opencast Workings
Pools Brook
West Wood
Furnace Lane
Furnace Farm
BRADSHAW RD
MONSAL CRES
CURBAR CURVE
FROGGATT CL
GREEN CL
ILAM CL
ELLIOTT DR
LODGE PL
LODGE WLK
CROFT VIEW
WIGLEY RD
RAVENS DALE CL
Inkersall Farm
Inkersall
KINDER RD
MIDDLETON DR
DOVEDALE AVE
CASTLETON GR
BEELEY WAY
BEELEY CL
3
WESTWOOD DR
WESTWOOD CL
MATLOCK DR
BAKEWELL RD
RIBER CL
MILFORD RD
BAMFORD RD
Trough Brook
West Croft House
TOM LA
72
Ladybower Wood
Bower Plantation
Lodge Farm
Blue Lodge Farm
WESTWOOD LA
LODGE CL
Allpits Plantation
SANDRINGHAM CL
WESTWOOD RD
SANDRINGHAM RD
MANVERS RD
FREYDON WAY
BRANDENE CL
ALLPITS RD
CENTRAL DR
CHURCH LA
BLACKSMITH LA
FOX GLOVE CL
LIME CL
ORCHID CL
LUPIN WAY
WILLOW CT
LABURNUM CT
ROSE AVE
ALMOND CL
CHURCH ST
HEATHER CL
Bonne Vienne
2
Arkwright Arms (PH)
Cherry Tree Farm
Works Farm
Arkwright New Town
A632
OAK TREE CL
BEECH DR
SCHOOL LA
LIME TREE GR
PENROSE CRES
Arkwright Prim Sch
HARDWICK DR
LAUREL AVE
ROSLING WAY
Sewage Works
Brook Farm
Moor Farm
WORKS LA
TOP RD
PH
LAWN VILLAS
OAKS FARM LA
EASTWOOD DR
Duckmanton
71
CHESTERFIELD RD
Gorse Farm
Lodge Farm
Lodge Farm
B6425
Moortop Farm
Nursery Farm
1
SUTTON LA
Calow Oaks
DARK LA
DEEPSICK LA
The Croft
Duckmanton Moor
Bolehill
BACK LA
Cock Alley
Riddings House Farm
Moorfields
B6425
MOOR LA
Woodside Cottage
Spoil Heap
70
41
D
42
E
43
F
116
98

97
79

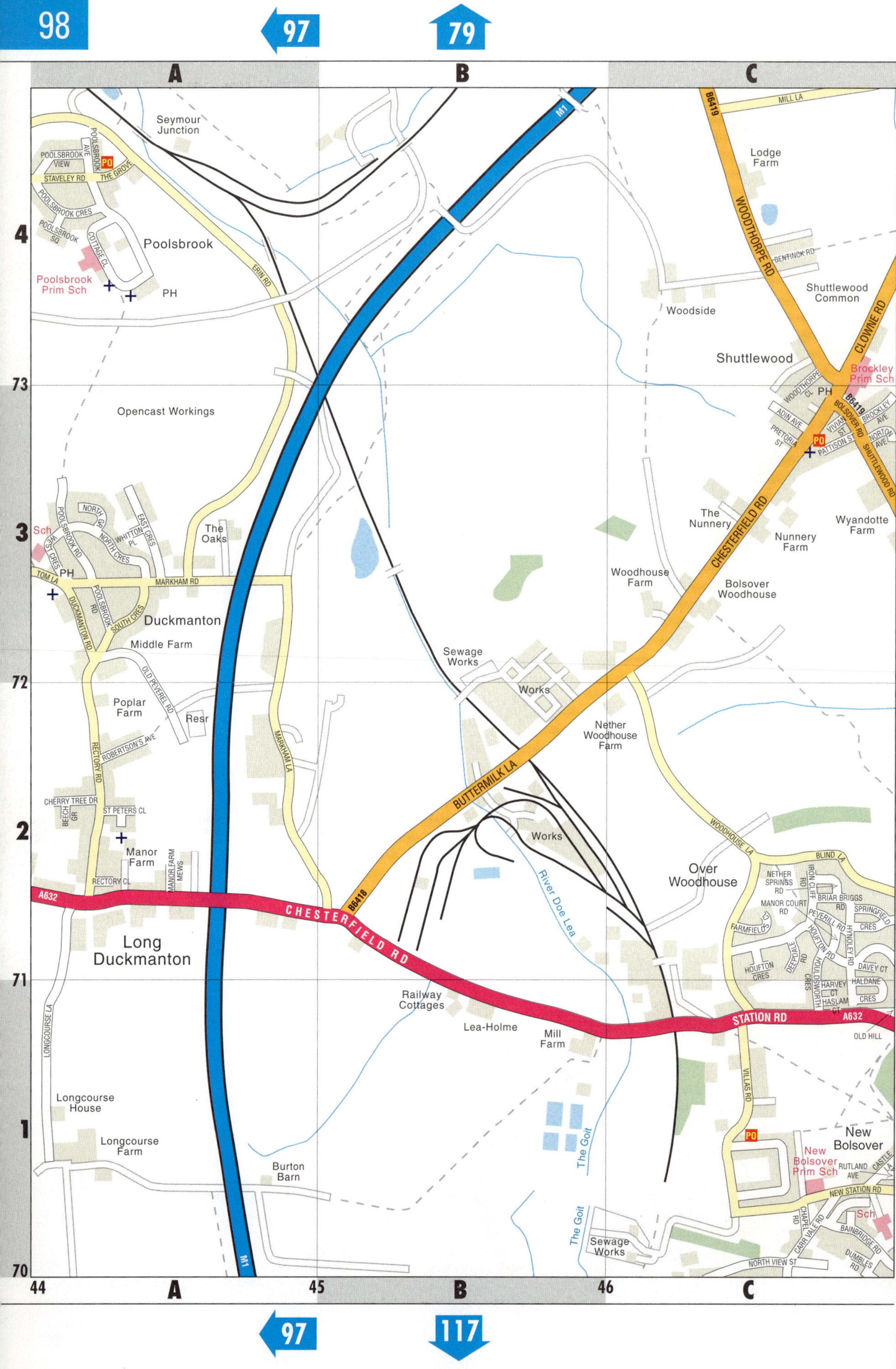
A
B
C
4
73
3
72
2
71
1
70
44
45
46
M1
MILL LA
B6419
Seymour Junction
POOLSBROOK AVE
POOLSBROOK VIEW
PO
STAVELEY RD
THE GROVE
POOLSBROOK CRES
POOLSBROOK SQ
COTTAGE CL
Poolsbrook
Poolsbrook Prim Sch
PH
ERIN RD
Lodge Farm
WOODTHORPE RD
BENTINCK RD
Shuttlewood Common
Woodside
CLOWNE RD
Shuttlewood
Brockley Prim Sch
WOODTHORPE CL
ADIN AVE
PRETORIA ST
VIVIAN ST
BOLSOVER RD
BROCKLEY AVE
PATTISON ST
NORTON AVE
SHUTTLEWOOD RD
Opencast Workings
Sch
NORTH GR
NORTH CRES
WHITTON PL
EAST CRES
POOLSBROOK RD
WEST CRES
TOM LA
MARKHAM RD
The Oaks
DUCKMANTON RD
SOUTH CRES
Duckmanton
Middle Farm
The Nunnery
Nunnery Farm
Wyandotte Farm
CHESTERFIELD RD
Woodhouse Farm
Bolsover Woodhouse
Sewage Works
Works
OLD PEVEREL RD
Poplar Farm
Resr
ROBERTSON'S AVE
RECTORY RD
MARKHAM LA
Nether Woodhouse Farm
BUTTERMILK LA
CHERRY TREE DR
BEECH GR
ST PETERS CL
Manor Farm
MANOR FARM MEWS
RECTORY CL
B6418
River Doe Lea
WOODHOUSE LA
BLIND LA
Over Woodhouse
NETHER SPRINGS RD
IRON CLIFF RD
BRIAR BRIGGS RD
MANOR COURT RD
SPRINGFIELD CRES
PEVERILL RD
FARMFIELD CL
HYNDLEY RD
HOUFTON RD
DEEPDALE RD
HOUFTON CRES
DAVEY CT
HOLLINGSWORTH CRES
HARVEY CT
HALDANE CRES
HASLAM CT
A632
CHESTERFIELD RD
Long Duckmanton
Railway Cottages
STATION RD
Lea-Holme
Mill Farm
OLD HILL
LONGCOURSE LA
Longcourse House
VILLAS RD
Longcourse Farm
The Goit
New Bolsover
New Bolsover Prim Sch
RUTLAND AVE
CASTLE LA
Burton Barn
NEW STATION RD
Sch
CHAPEL RD
CARR VALE RD
BAINBRIDGE RD
Sewage Works
NORTH VIEW ST
DUMBLES RD

97
117

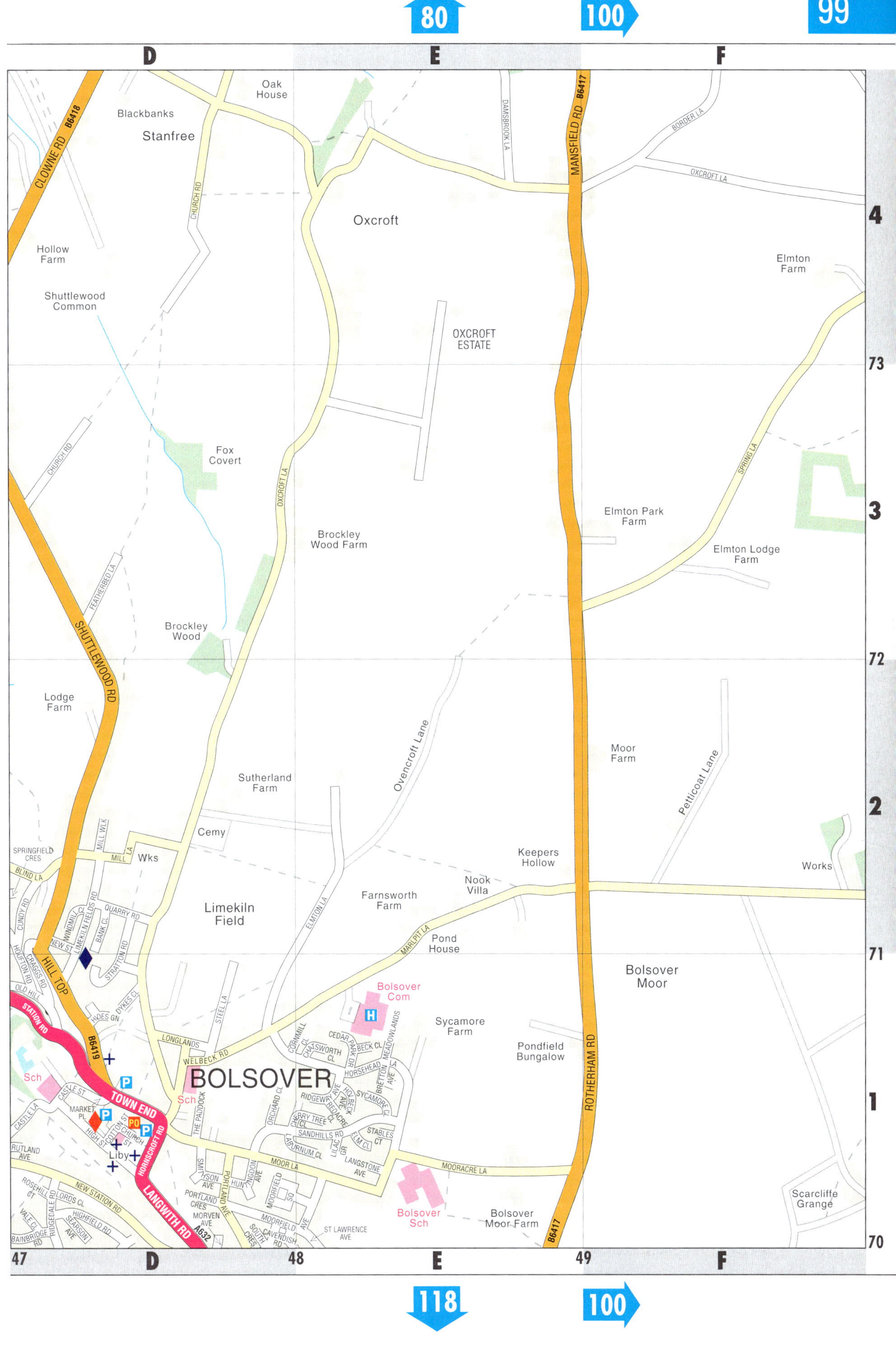

Blackbanks

Oak House

Stanfree

CLOWNE RD B6418

Hollow Farm

Shuttlewood Common

CHURCH RD

Oxcroft

DAMSBROOK LA

MANSFIELD RD B6417

BORDER LA

OXCROFT LA

Elmton Farm

4

OXCROFT ESTATE

73

CHURCH RD

FEATHERBED LA

Fox Covert

OXCROFT LA

Brockley Wood Farm

Elmton Park Farm

SPRING LA

Elmton Lodge Farm

3

Brockley Wood

SHUTTLEWOOD RD

Lodge Farm

72

Ovencroft Lane

Moor Farm

Petticoat Lane

2

Sutherland Farm

SPRINGFIELD CRES

BLIND LA

MILL WLK

MILL

Cemy

Wks

Keepers Hollow

Works

CUNDY RD

WINDMILL CL

RANK CL

QUARRY RD

Limekiln Field

ELMTON LA

Farnsworth Farm

Nook Villa

NEW STATION RD

STRATTON RD

HILL TOP

CRAGGS RD

OLD HILL

HYDES GN

DYKES CL

STELLA LA

LIMEKILN FIELDS RD

MARLPIT LA

Pond House

Bolsover Moor

71

STATION RD

B6419

LONGLANDS

Bolsover Com

H

Sycamore Farm

Pondfield Bungalow

ROTHERHAM RD

Sch

CASTLE ST

CASTLE LA

MARKET PL

TOWN END

P

PO

P

HORNSCROFT RD

Sch

WELBECK RD

THE PADDOCK

CORNMILL

CEDAR PARK DR

AINSWORTH CL

HORSEHEAD

BECK CL

MEADOWLANDS

BRETTON AVE

SYCAMORE

ORCHARD CL

RIDGEWAY

BEDACRE

SHERRY TREE CL

HIGH ST

Liby

ORCHARD CL

BEDACRE

ELM CL

STABLES CT

1

RUTLAND AVE

CASTLE LA

LANGWITH RD

A632

HIGH ST

CHURCH ST

SWS

PYSON AVE

PORTLAND AVE

HUNTINGTON AVE

MOORFIELD

MOOR LA

SANDHILLS RD

LILAC CL

LABURNUM CL

LANGSTONE AVE

MOORACRE LA

Bolsover Moor Farm

Scarcliffe Grange

ROSEHILL CT

VALE CL

BAINBRIDGE RD

LORDS CL

RIDGEDALE CL

HIGHFIELD RD

PEARSON AVE

NEW STATION RD

PORTLAND CRES

MORVEN AVE

MOORFIELD AVE

ST LAWRENCE AVE

CAVENDISH CRES

SOUTH AVE

Bolsover Sch

BOLSOVER

99
81

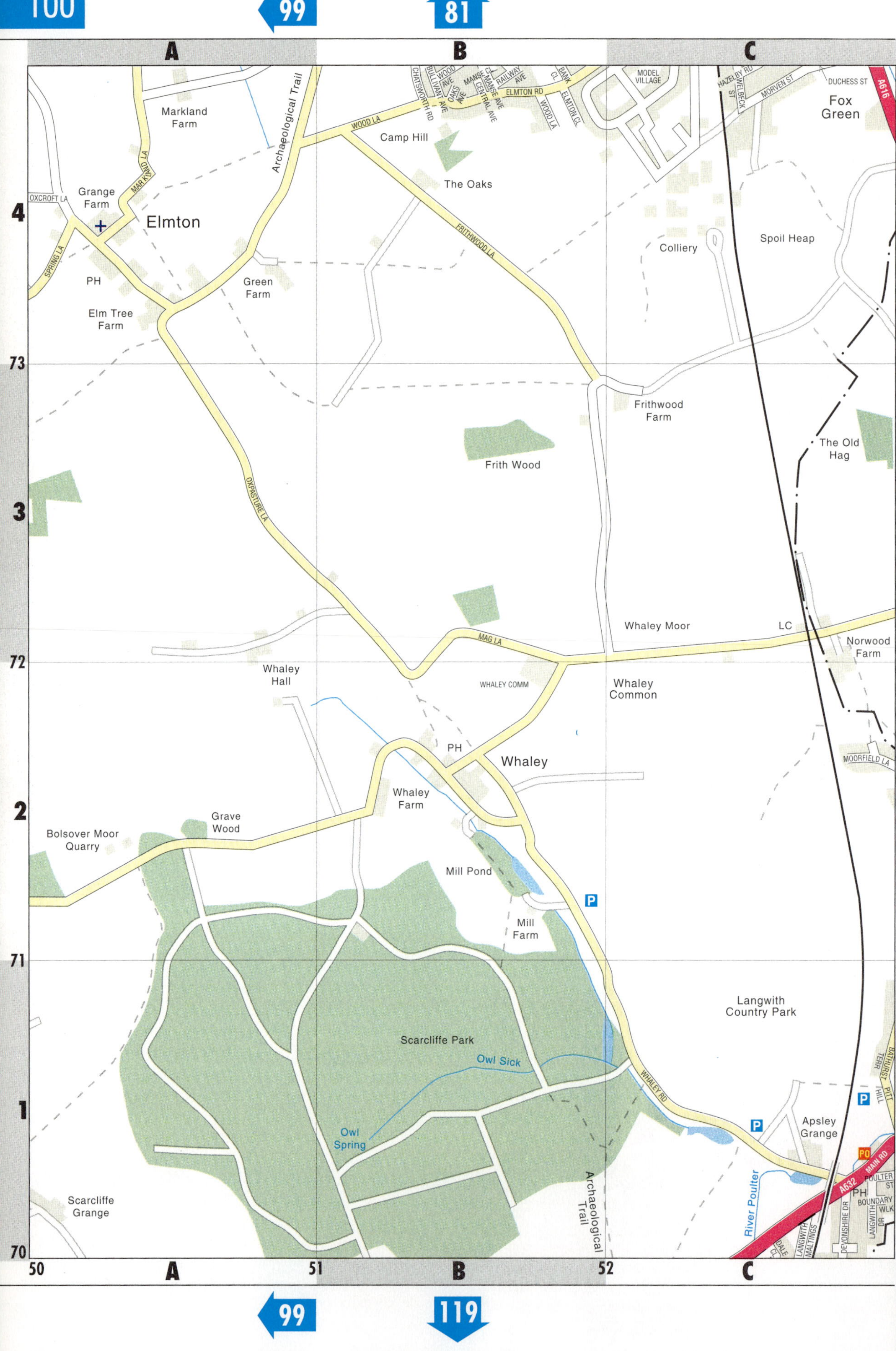
A
B
C
Markland Farm
Archaeological Trail
Grange Farm
Elmton
OXCROFT LA
MARKLAND LA
SPRING LA
PH
Elm Tree Farm
Green Farm
WOOD LA
Camp Hill
The Oaks
FRITHWOOD LA
CHATSWORTH RD
BULLIVANT AVE
OAKS AVE
WOOD AVE
MANSE CL
CENTRAL AVE
MANSE AVE
RAILWAY AVE
ELMTON RD
WOOD LA
BANK CL
ELMTON CL
MODEL VILLAGE
HAZELBY RD
WELBECK ST
MORVEN ST
DUCHESS ST
A616
Fox Green
Colliery
Spoil Heap
Frithwood Farm
The Old Hag
Frith Wood
OXPASTURE LA
MAG LA
Whaley Moor
LC
Norwood Farm
Whaley Hall
WHALEY COMM
Whaley Common
PH
Whaley
MOORFIELD LA
Whaley Farm
Grave Wood
Bolsover Moor Quarry
Mill Pond
P
Mill Farm
Langwith Country Park
Scarcliffe Park
Owl Sick
Owl Spring
WHALEY RD
Archaeological Trail
Apsley Grange
P
P
PO
A632
MAIN RD
PH
POULTER ST
BOUNDARY WLK
BATHURST TERR
PITT HILL
River Poulter
DEVONSHIRE DR
LANGWITH DR
LANGWITH MALTINGS
DALE CL
Scarcliffe Grange
4
73
3
72
2
71
1
70
50
51
52

99
119

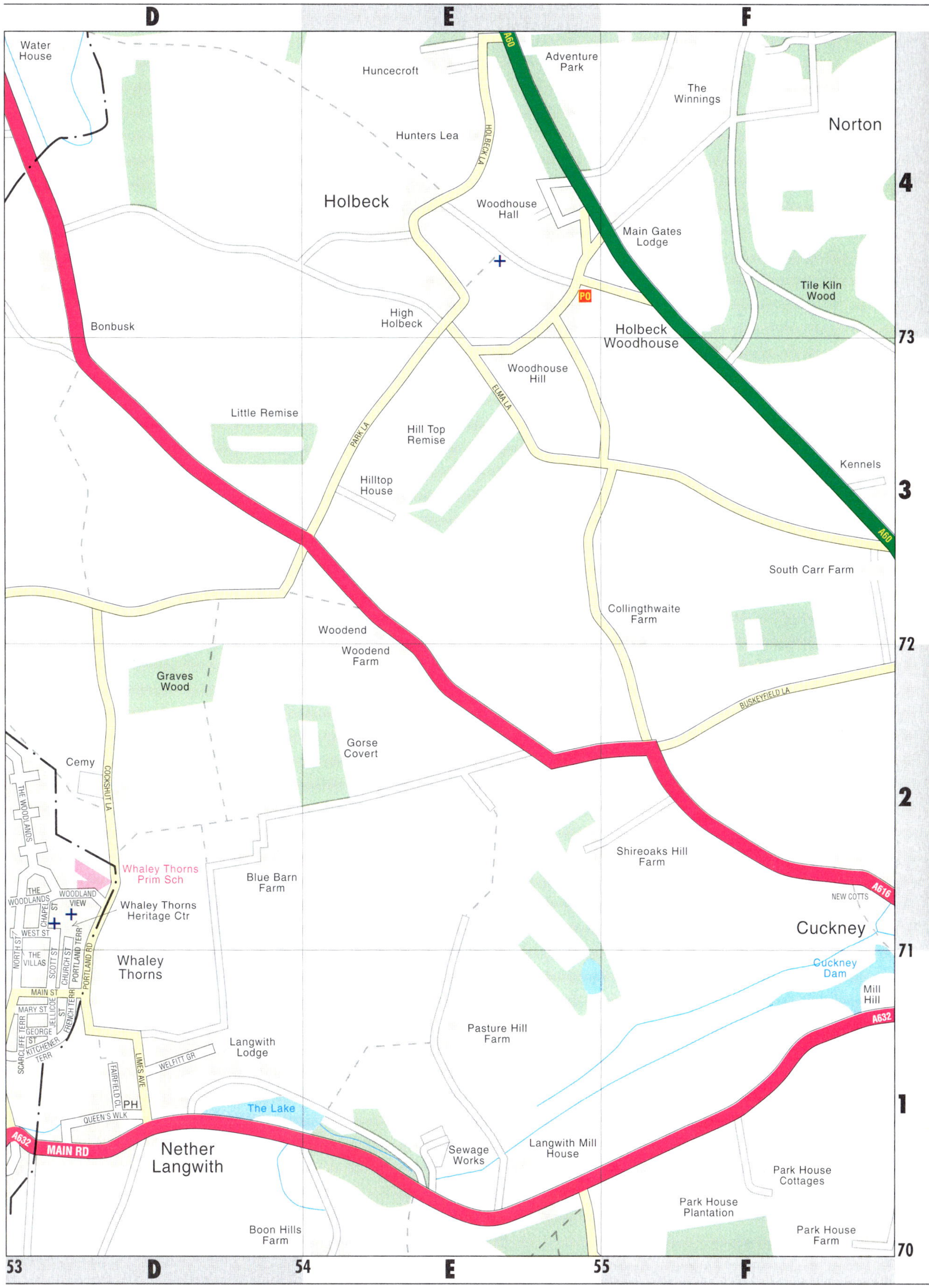

D E F

4

73

3

72

2

71

1

70

53 D 54 E 55 F

Water House

Huncecroft

Adventure Park

The Winnings

Norton

Hunters Lea

Holbeck

Woodhouse Hall

Main Gates Lodge

Tile Kiln Wood

PO

Holbeck Woodhouse

Bonbusk

High Holbeck

Woodhouse Hill

Little Remise

Hill Top Remise

ELMA LA

PARK LA

HOLBECK LA

A60

Kennels

Hilltop House

South Carr Farm

Collingthwaite Farm

A60

Woodend

Woodend Farm

Graves Wood

BUSKEYFIELD LA

Gorse Covert

Cemy

COCKSHUT LA

Shireoaks Hill Farm

A616

NEW COTTS

Cuckney

THE WOODLANDS

Whaley Thorns Prim Sch

WOODLAND VIEW

Blue Barn Farm

WOODLAND TERR

THE WOODLANDS

CHAPEL ST

Whaley Thorns Heritage Ctr

WEST ST

THE VILLAS

SCOTT ST

NORTH ST

CHURCH ST

PORTLAND TERR

PORTLAND RD

Whaley Thorns

Cuckney Dam

Mill Hill

A632

MARY ST

GEORGE ST

JELLICOE ST

FRENCH TERR

MAIN ST

LIMES AVE

Langwith Lodge

WELFITT GR

Pasture Hill Farm

SCARCLIFFE TERR

KITCHENER TERR

FAIRFIELD CL

PH

QUEEN'S WLK

The Lake

Sewage Works

Langwith Mill House

Park House Cottages

A632

MAIN RD

Nether Langwith

Boon Hills Farm

Park House Plantation

Park House Farm

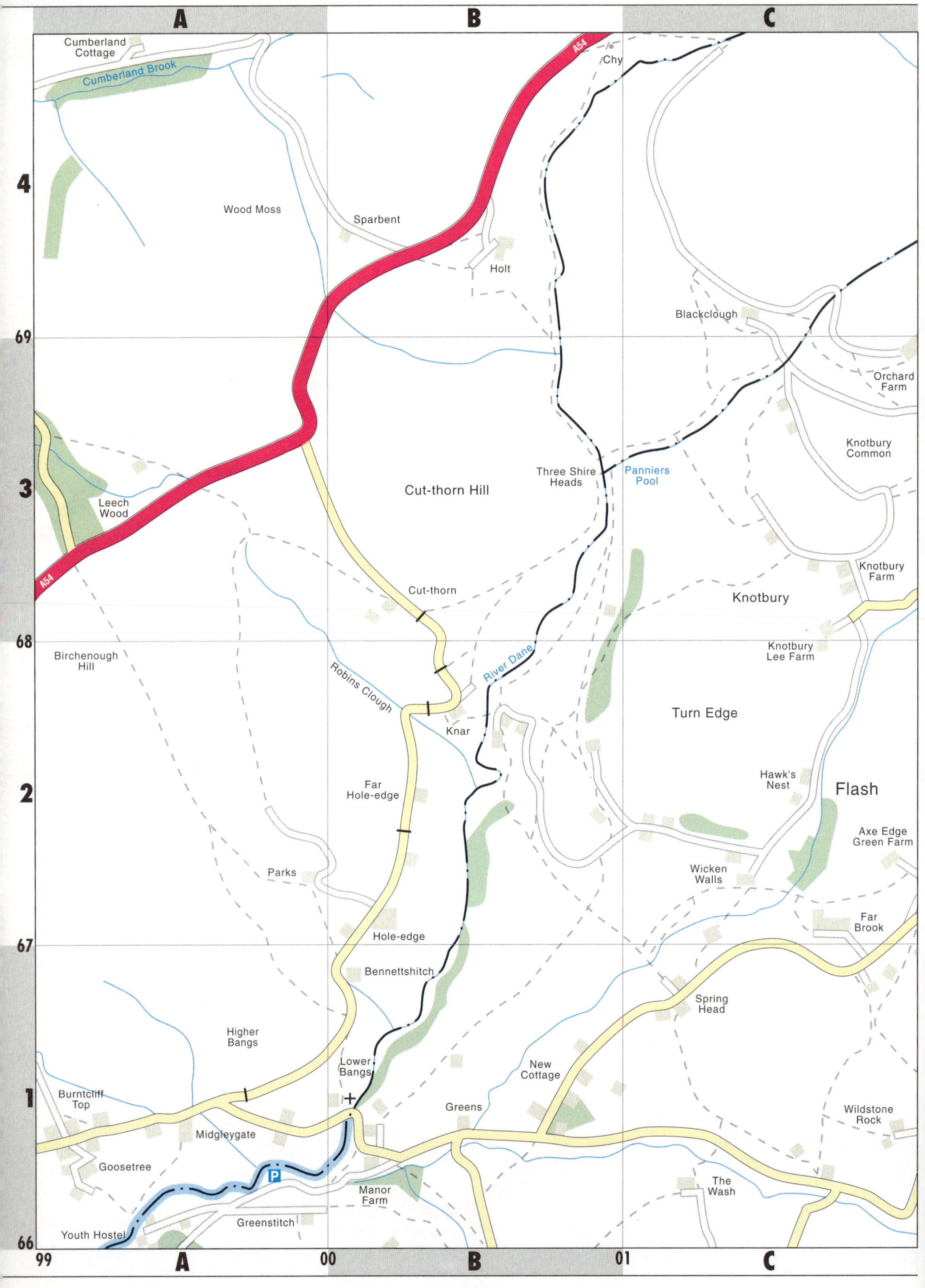

A · B · C

4

Cumberland Cottage

Cumberland Brook

Wood Moss

Sparbent

A54

Chy

Holt

Blackclough

Orchard Farm

69

Knotbury Common

3

Leech Wood

Cut-thorn Hill

Three Shire Heads

Panniers Pool

Knotbury

Knotbury Farm

A54

Cut-thorn

Knotbury Lee Farm

68

Birchenough Hill

Robins Clough

River Dane

Knar

Turn Edge

Far Hole-edge

Hawk's Nest

Flash

2

Parks

Axe Edge Green Farm

Wicken Walls

Far Brook

67

Hole-edge

Bennettshitch

Spring Head

Higher Bangs

Lower Bangs

New Cottage

Wildstone Rock

1

Burntcliff Top

Midgleygate

Greens

Goosetree

P

Manor Farm

The Wash

Greenstitch

66

Youth Hostel

99 A **00** B **01** C

84
104

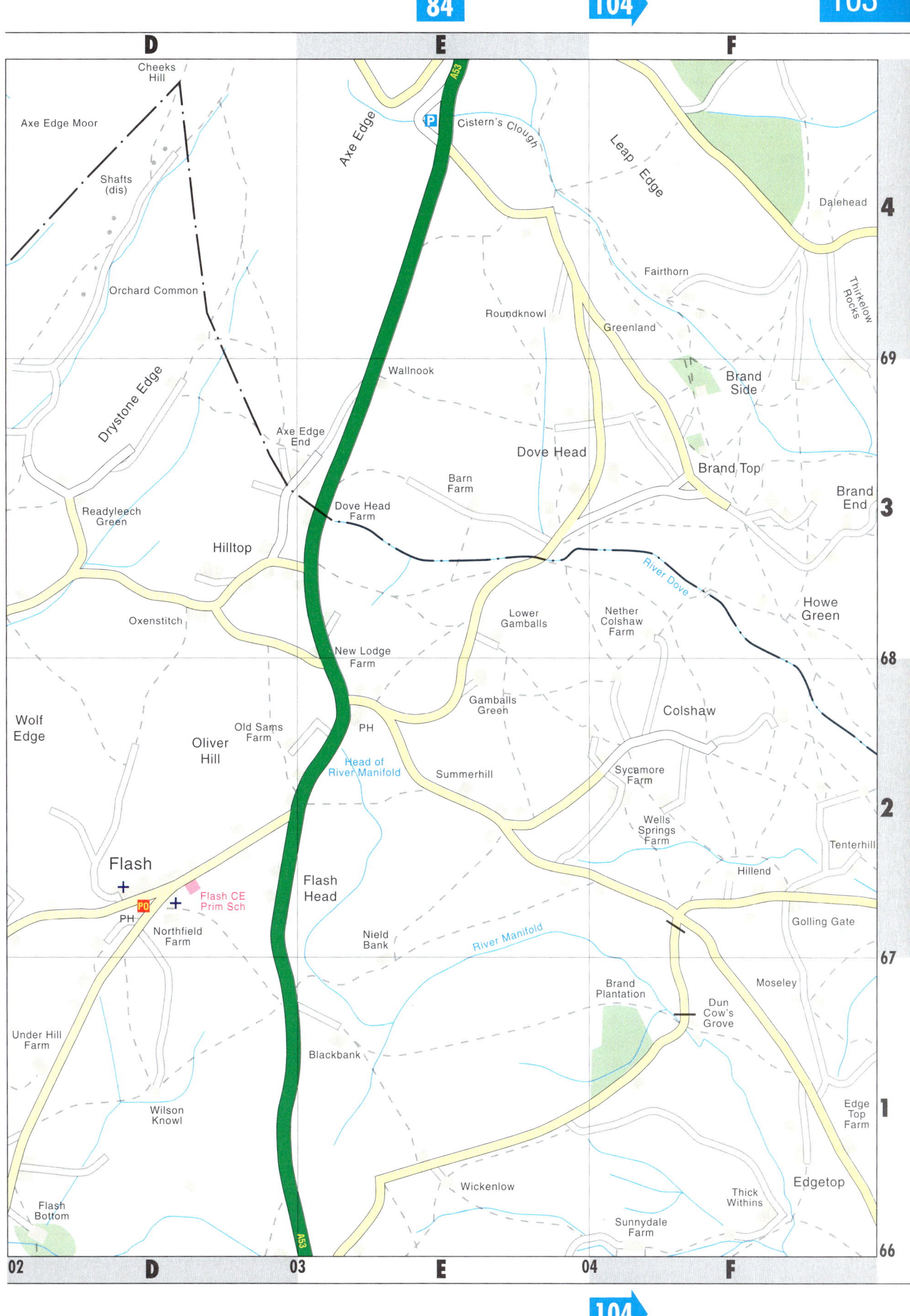
D
E
F
Cheeks Hill
Axe Edge Moor
Shafts (dis)
Orchard Common
Drystone Edge
Readyleech Green
Hilltop
Oxenstitch
Axe Edge End
Axe Edge
A53
Cistern's Clough
Leap Edge
Dalehead
Fairthorn
Thirkelow Rocks
Roundknowl
Greenland
Wallnook
Brand Side
Dove Head
Barn Farm
Dove Head Farm
Brand Top
Brand End
River Dove
Lower Gamballs
Nether Colshaw Farm
Howe Green
New Lodge Farm
Gamballs Green
Colshaw
Wolf Edge
Oliver Hill
Old Sams Farm
PH
Head of River Manifold
Summerhill
Sycamore Farm
Wells Springs Farm
Tenterhill
Hillend
Flash
Flash CE Prim Sch
PO
PH
Northfield Farm
Flash Head
Nield Bank
River Manifold
Golling Gate
Brand Plantation
Dun Cow's Grove
Moseley
Under Hill Farm
Blackbank
Wilson Knowl
Edge Top Farm
Wickenlow
Thick Withins
Edgetop
Flash Bottom
Sunnydale Farm
4
69
3
68
2
67
1
66
02
03
04

104

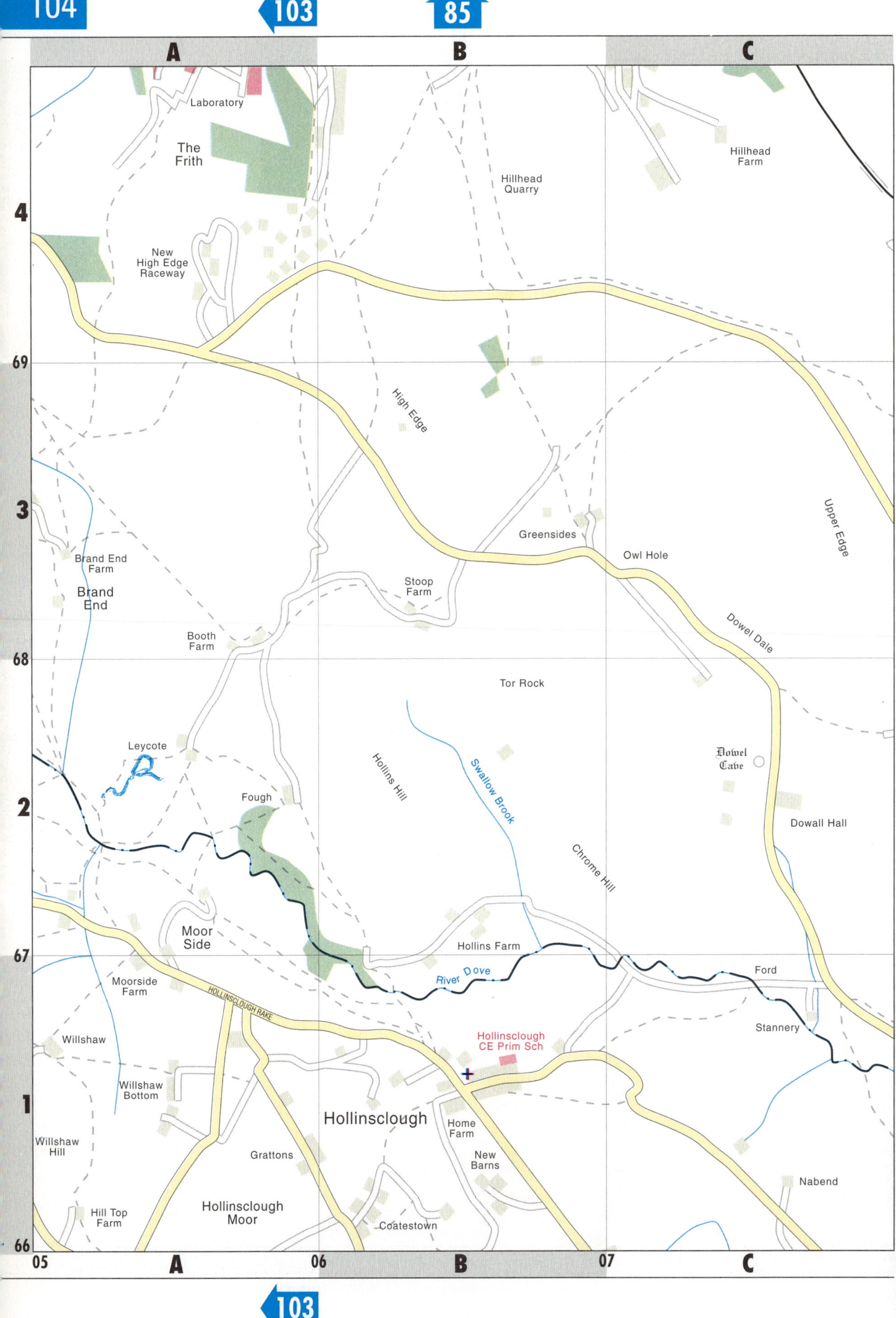

A   B   C

Laboratory

The Frith

Hillhead Quarry

Hillhead Farm

New High Edge Raceway

4

High Edge

69

Upper Edge

Brand End Farm

Brand End

3

Greensides

Owl Hole

Stoop Farm

Dowel Dale

Booth Farm

68

Tor Rock

Leycote

Hollins Hill

Swallow Brook

Dowel Cave

Dowall Hall

Fough

2

Chrome Hill

Moor Side

Hollins Farm

67

Ford

Moorside Farm

River Dove

Stannery

HOLLINSCLOUGH RAKE

Willshaw

Hollinsclough CE Prim Sch

Willshaw Bottom

1

Willshaw Hill

Hollinsclough

Home Farm

New Barns

Nabend

Grattons

Hill Top Farm

Hollinsclough Moor

Coatestown

66

05   A   06   B   07   C

86
106

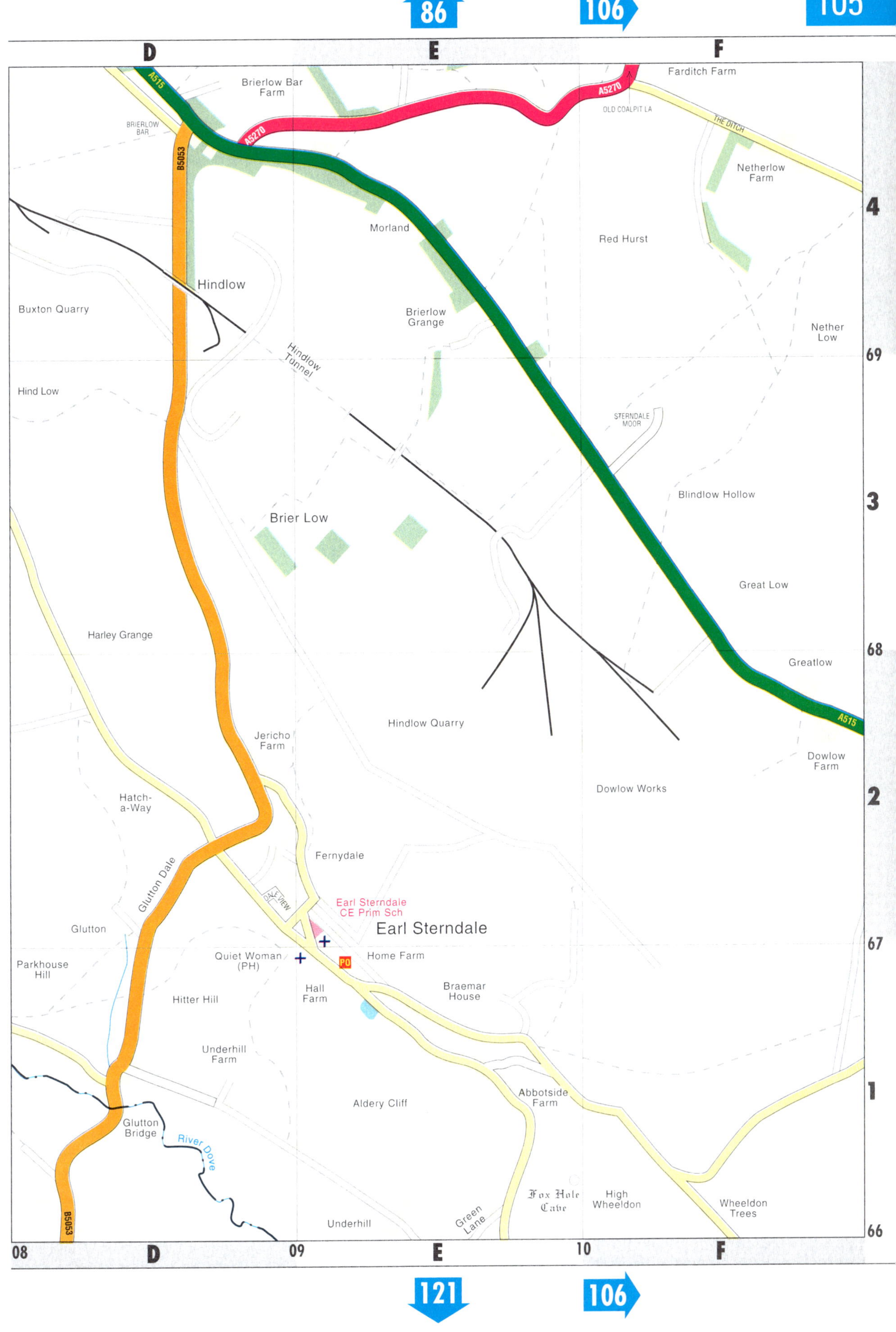
D
E
F
A515
A5270
B5053
Brierlow Bar Farm
BRIERLOW BAR
Farditch Farm
OLD COALPIT LA
THE DITCH
Netherlow Farm
Morland
Red Hurst
Hindlow
Buxton Quarry
Brierlow Grange
Nether Low
Hindlow Tunnel
Hind Low
STERNDALE MOOR
Blindlow Hollow
Brier Low
Great Low
Harley Grange
Greatlow
Hindlow Quarry
Jericho Farm
Dowlow Farm
Hatch-a-Way
Dowlow Works
Fernydale
Glutton Dale
Earl Sterndale CE Prim Sch
Earl Sterndale
Glutton
Quiet Woman (PH)
Home Farm
PO
Parkhouse Hill
Hall Farm
Braemar House
Hitter Hill
Underhill Farm
Abbotside Farm
Aldery Cliff
Glutton Bridge
River Dove
Fox Hole Cave
High Wheeldon
Wheeldon Trees
Green Lane
Underhill
4
69
3
68
2
67
1
66
08
09
10

121
106

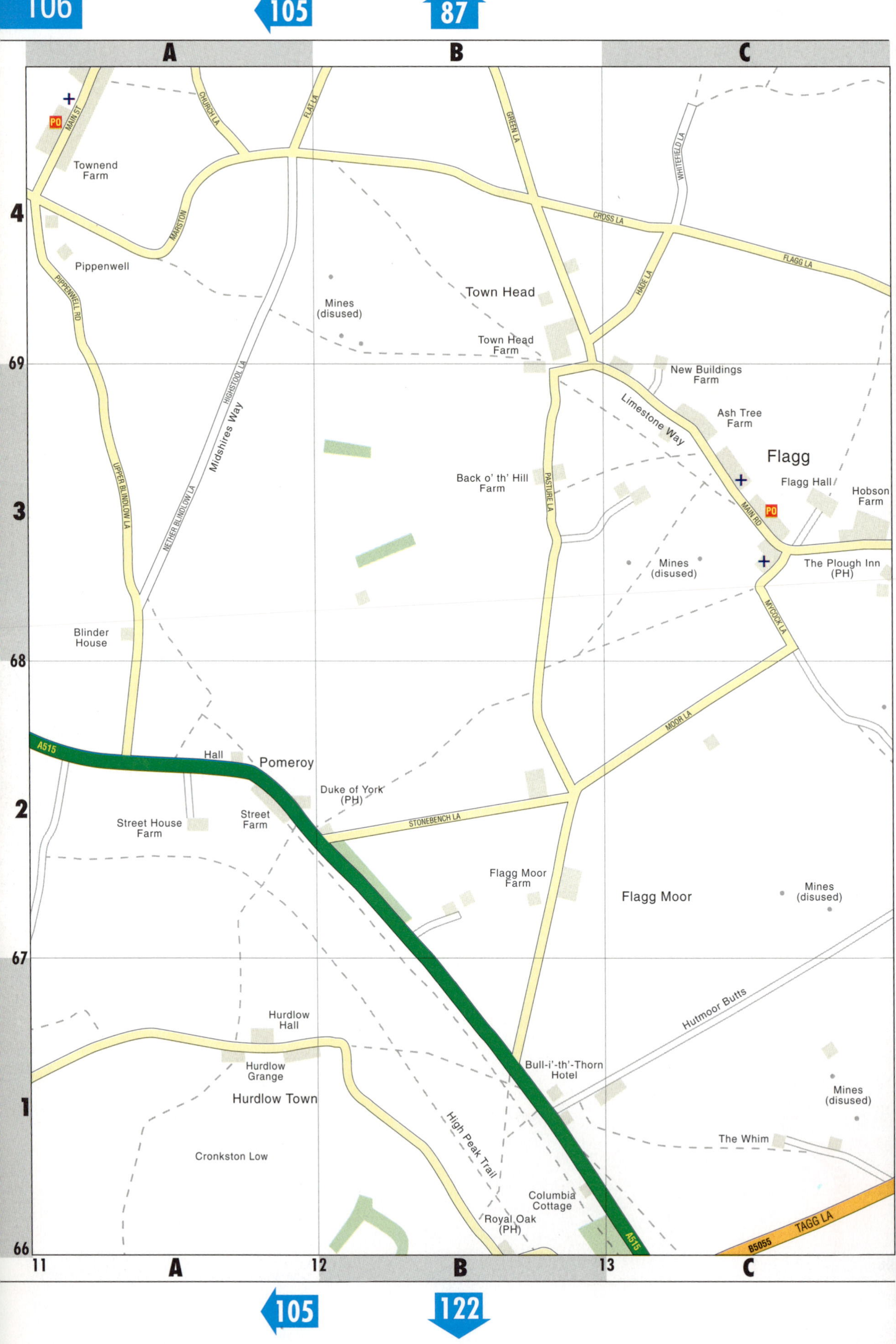

A · B · C

4

PO
Townend Farm
Pippenwell
CHURCH LA
FLAT LA
GREEN LA
CROSS LA
HABB LA
WHITEFIELD LA
FLAGG LA

69

Mines (disused)
Town Head
Town Head Farm
New Buildings Farm
Ash Tree Farm
Limestone Way
Flagg

3

MARSTON
HIGHSTOOL LA
NETHER BLUNDLOW LA
Midshires Way
UPPER BLUNDLOW LA
PIPPENWELL RD
Back o' th' Hill Farm
PASTURE LA
MAIN RD
PO
Flagg Hall
Hobson Farm
Mines (disused)
The Plough Inn (PH)

68

Blinder House
MYCOCK LA

2

A515
Hall
Pomeroy
Duke of York (PH)
Street House Farm
Street Farm
STONEBENCH LA
Flagg Moor Farm
Flagg Moor
MOOR LA
Mines (disused)

67

Hurdlow Hall
Hurdlow Grange
Hurdlow Town
Cronkston Low
High Peak Trail
Bull-i'-th'-Thorn Hotel
Hutmoor Butts
Mines (disused)
The Whim

1

Columbia Cottage
Royal Oak (PH)
A515
B5055
TAGG LA

66

11 · A · 12 · B · 13 · C

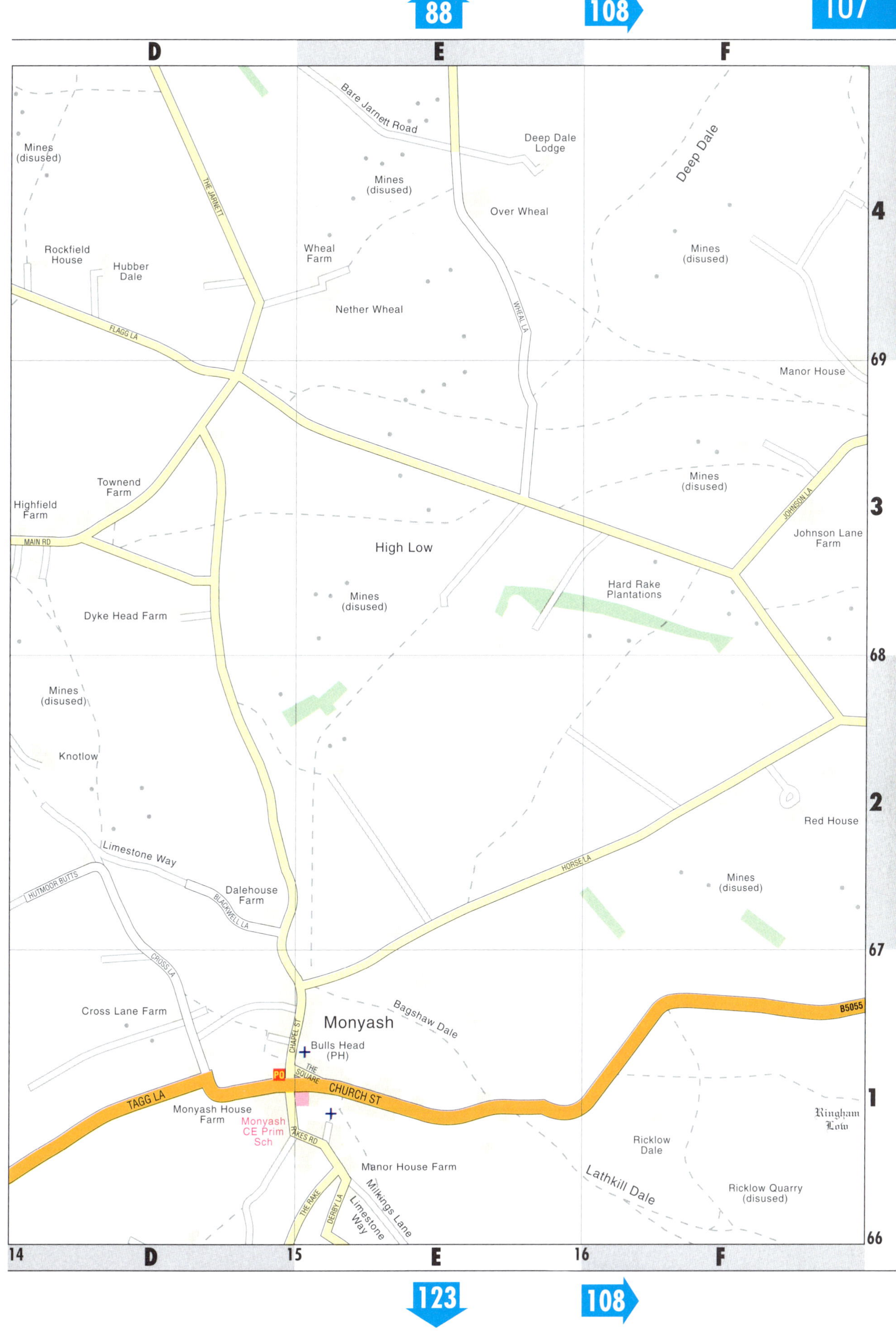
88
108
D
E
F
Bare Jarnett Road
Deep Dale Lodge
Deep Dale
Mines (disused)
Mines (disused)
Over Wheal
Mines (disused)
THE JARNETT
Wheal Farm
Rockfield House
Hubber Dale
Nether Wheal
WHEAL LA
FLAGG LA
4
69
Manor House
Mines (disused)
JOHNSON LA
Townend Farm
Highfield Farm
MAIN RD
3
High Low
Johnson Lane Farm
Hard Rake Plantations
Mines (disused)
Dyke Head Farm
68
Mines (disused)
Knotlow
2
Red House
Limestone Way
HORSE LA
Mines (disused)
HUTMOOR BUTTS
Dalehouse Farm
BLACKWELL LA
67
CROSS LA
Cross Lane Farm
Bagshaw Dale
Monyash
B5055
CHAPEL ST
Bulls Head (PH)
THE SQUARE
PO
CHURCH ST
TAGG LA
1
Monyash House Farm
Monyash CE Prim Sch
Ringham Low
RAKES RD
Ricklow Dale
Manor House Farm
Lathkill Dale
Ricklow Quarry (disused)
THE RAKE
DERBY LA
Milkings Lane
Limestone Way
66
14
D
15
E
16
F
123
108

107
89

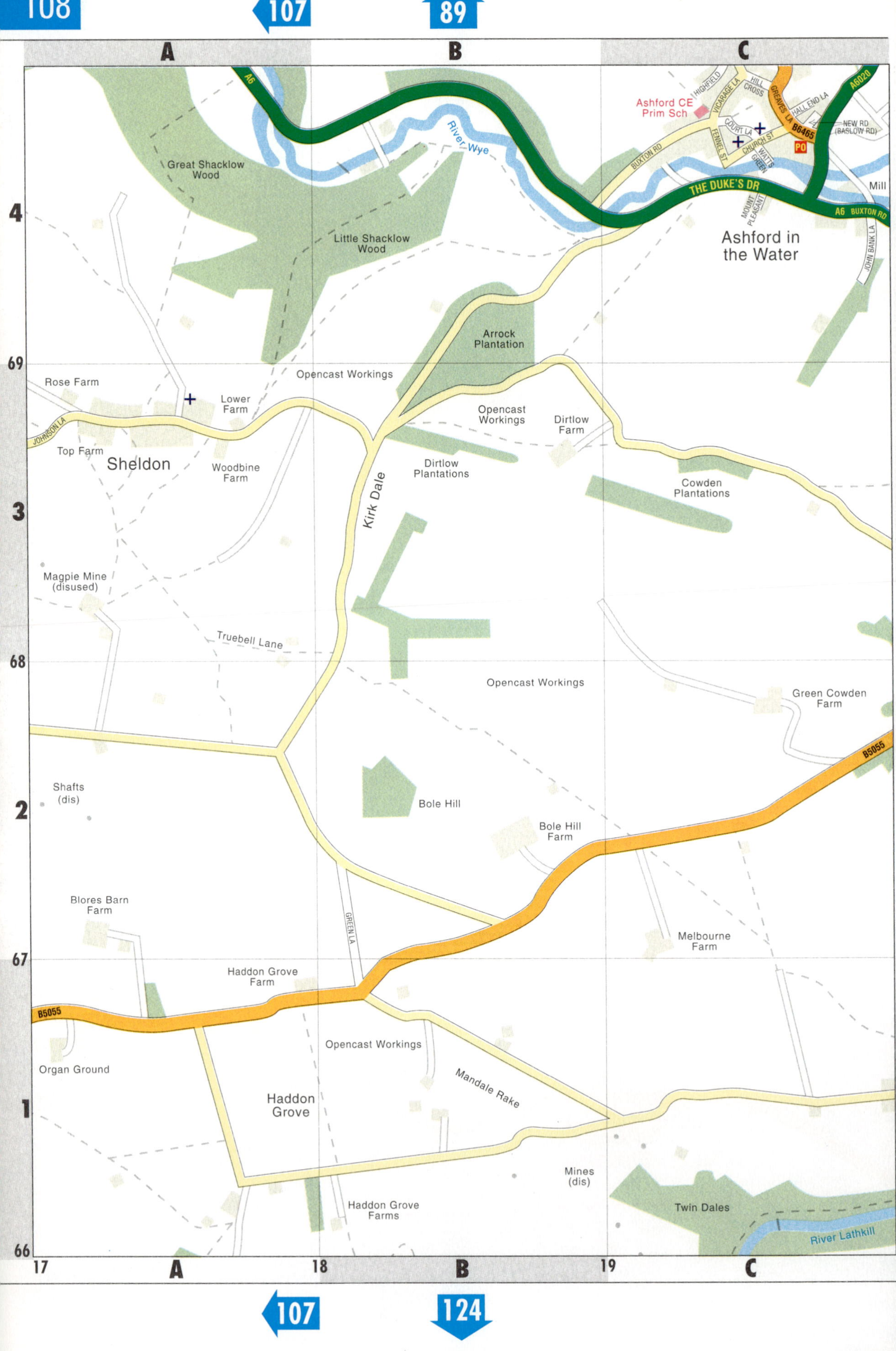
A
B
C
Great Shacklow Wood
Little Shacklow Wood
River Wye
A6
A6020
THE DUKE'S DR
A6 BUXTON RD
Ashford CE Prim Sch
HIGHFIELD
VICARAGE LA
HILL CROSS
GREAVES LA
HALL END LA
NEW RD (BASLOW RD)
B6465
COURT LA
FENNEL ST
CHURCH ST
WATTS GREEN
BUXTON RD
MOUNT PLEASANT
PO
Mill
JOHN BANK LA
Ashford in the Water
4
Arrock Plantation
69
Rose Farm
Opencast Workings
Lower Farm
JOHNSON LA
Opencast Workings
Dirtlow Farm
Top Farm
Sheldon
Woodbine Farm
Dirtlow Plantations
Kirk Dale
Cowden Plantations
3
Magpie Mine (disused)
Truebell Lane
68
Opencast Workings
Green Cowden Farm
B5055
Shafts (dis)
2
Bole Hill
Bole Hill Farm
Blores Barn Farm
GREEN LA
Melbourne Farm
67
Haddon Grove Farm
B5055
Opencast Workings
Organ Ground
Mandale Rake
1
Haddon Grove
Mines (dis)
Haddon Grove Farms
Twin Dales
River Lathkill
66
17
A
18
B
19
C

107
124

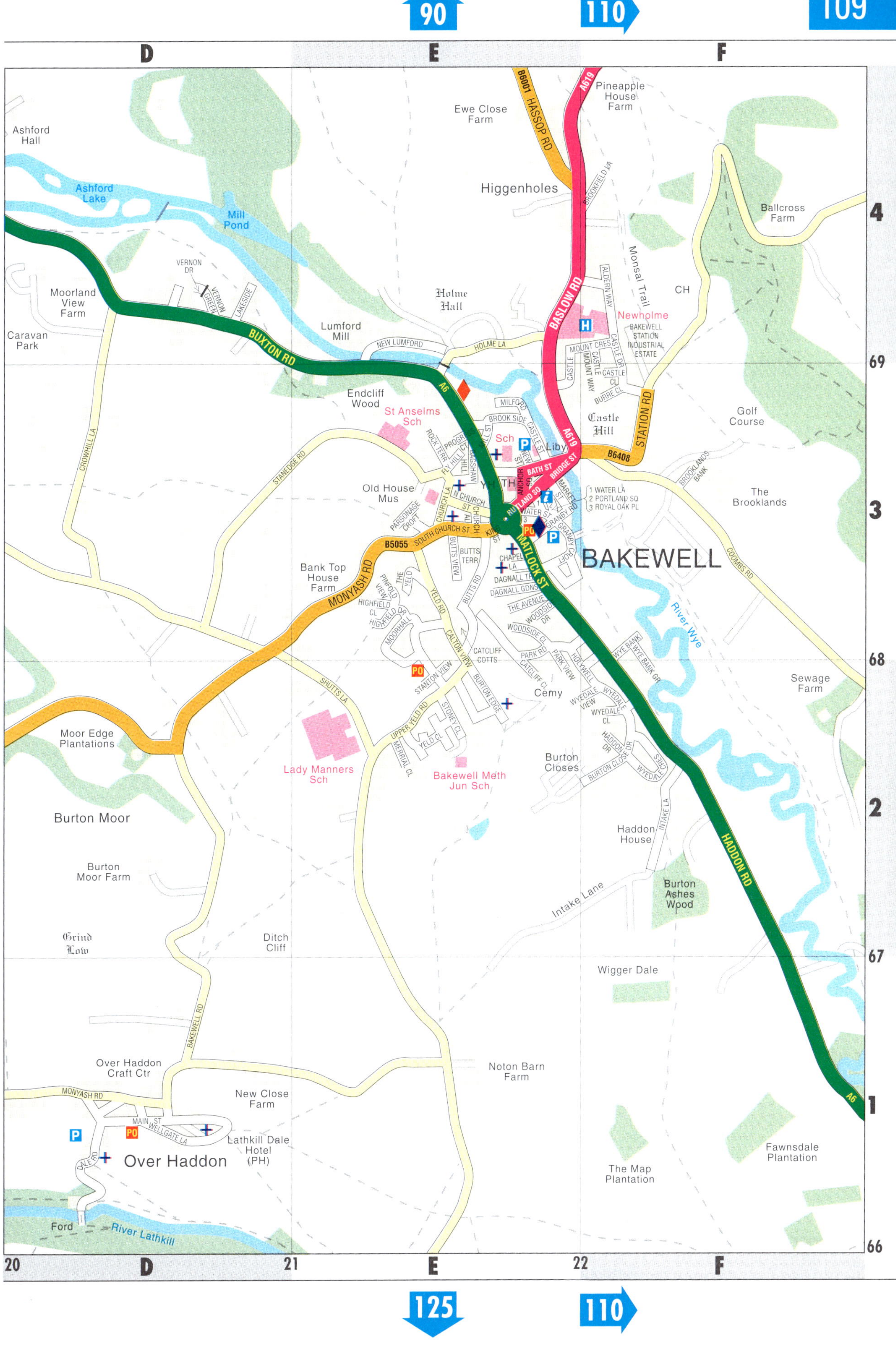
90
110
D
E
F
Ashford Hall
Ashford Lake
Mill Pond
Ewe Close Farm
Pineapple House Farm
Higgenholes
Ballcross Farm
Moorland View Farm
Caravan Park
Holme Hall
Lumford Mill
Monsal Trail
CH
Newholme
BAKEWELL STATION INDUSTRIAL ESTATE
BUXTON RD
BASLOW RD
HASSOP RD
HOLME LA
NEW LUMFORD
Endcliff Wood
St Anselms Sch
Castle Hill
STATION RD
Golf Course
Sch
Liby
Old House Mus
1 WATER LA
2 PORTLAND SQ
3 ROYAL OAK PL
The Brooklands
STANEDGE RD
CROWHILL LA
SOUTH CHURCH ST
MATLOCK ST
BAKEWELL
Bank Top House Farm
MONYASH RD
COOMBS RD
River Wye
Sewage Farm
Cemy
SHUTTS LA
Moor Edge Plantations
Lady Manners Sch
Bakewell Meth Jun Sch
Burton Closes
Burton Moor
Burton Moor Farm
Haddon House
HADDON RD
Burton Ashes Wood
Intake Lane
Grind Low
Ditch Cliff
Wigger Dale
BAKEWELL RD
Over Haddon Craft Ctr
Noton Barn Farm
New Close Farm
MONYASH RD
Lathkill Dale Hotel (PH)
Over Haddon
Fawnsdale Plantation
The Map Plantation
Ford
River Lathkill
4
69
3
68
2
67
1
66
20
21
22
125
110

109
91

A　　　　　　**B**　　　　　　**C**

Edensor

B6012

Handley La

Edensor Forest
Nursery

Chatsworth Park

4

Maud's
Plantation

Lindup Low

River Derwent

Moatless
Plantation

69

New Piece Wood

Long Gallery

Calton
Plantations

3

Calton Pastures

Calton Houses

Lees
Wood

Calton Lees Farm

Calton Lees

68

Manners
Wood

Coombs Rd

Coombs Farm

Beech Square
Plantation

Lindop Wood

Cook
Wood

Lees Moor Wood

2

Haddon Park Farm

Shadyside
Plantation

Park Rd

Rowsleymoor
Wood

67

Bank
Wood

Bowling Green
Farm

Aaron Hole
Plantation

Bouns
Corner

Shay Knowl

1

Haddon Park

A6

Park La

Sallowbed
Plantation

River Derwent

Haddon Hall

River Wye

Vicarage La

Devonshire Dr 1
Riverbank 2
Schofield Ct 3
Sunnybank 4
Hincley Ct 5

Parkside
Wood

Church La

St Katherine's La

Chatsworth Rd

B6012

Haddon
Barn

A6

66

23　　　　　**A**　　　　**24**　　　　**B**　　　　**25**　　　　**C**

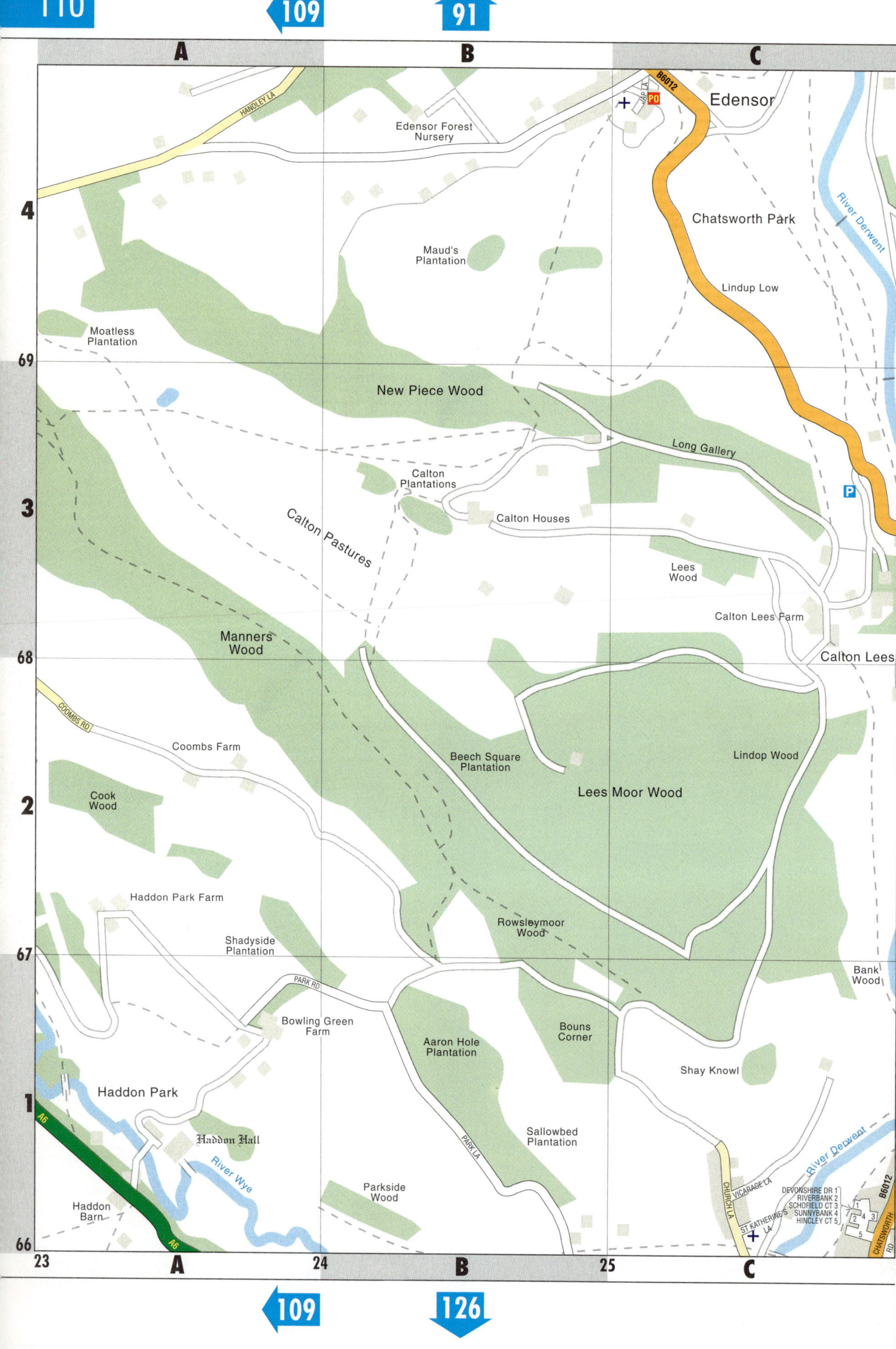

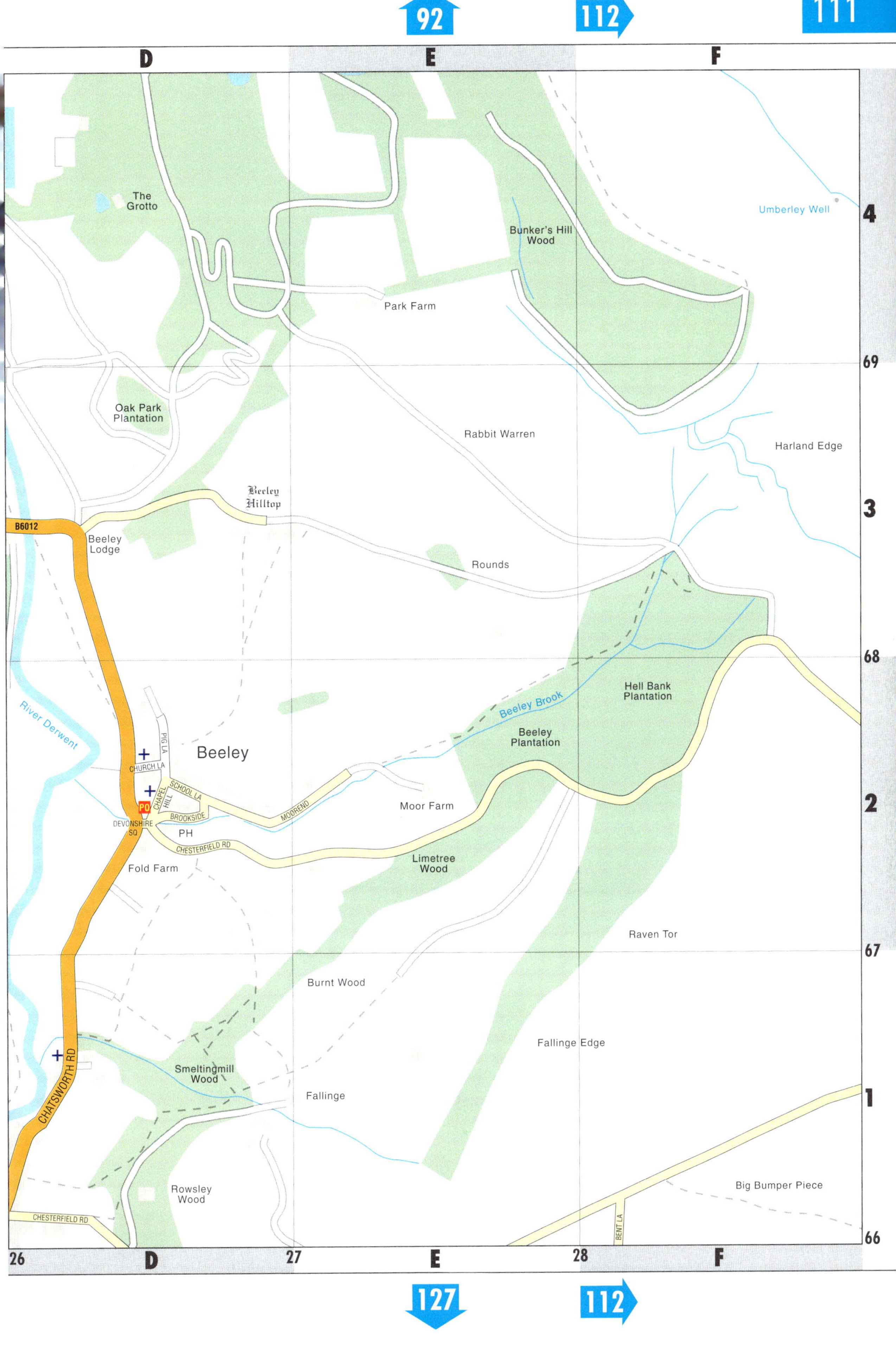
92
112
D
E
F
The Grotto
Bunker's Hill Wood
Umberley Well
Park Farm
Oak Park Plantation
Rabbit Warren
Harland Edge
Beeley Hilltop
B6012
Beeley Lodge
Rounds
Hell Bank Plantation
Beeley Brook
Beeley Plantation
River Derwent
Beeley
PIG LA
CHURCH LA
SCHOOL LA
CHAPEL HILL
PO
BROOKSIDE
MOOREND
Moor Farm
DEVONSHIRE SQ
PH
CHESTERFIELD RD
Limetree Wood
Fold Farm
Raven Tor
Burnt Wood
Fallinge Edge
CHATSWORTH RD
Smeltingmill Wood
Fallinge
Big Bumper Piece
Rowsley Wood
CHESTERFIELD RD
BENT LA
4
69
3
68
2
67
1
66
26
27
28
127
112

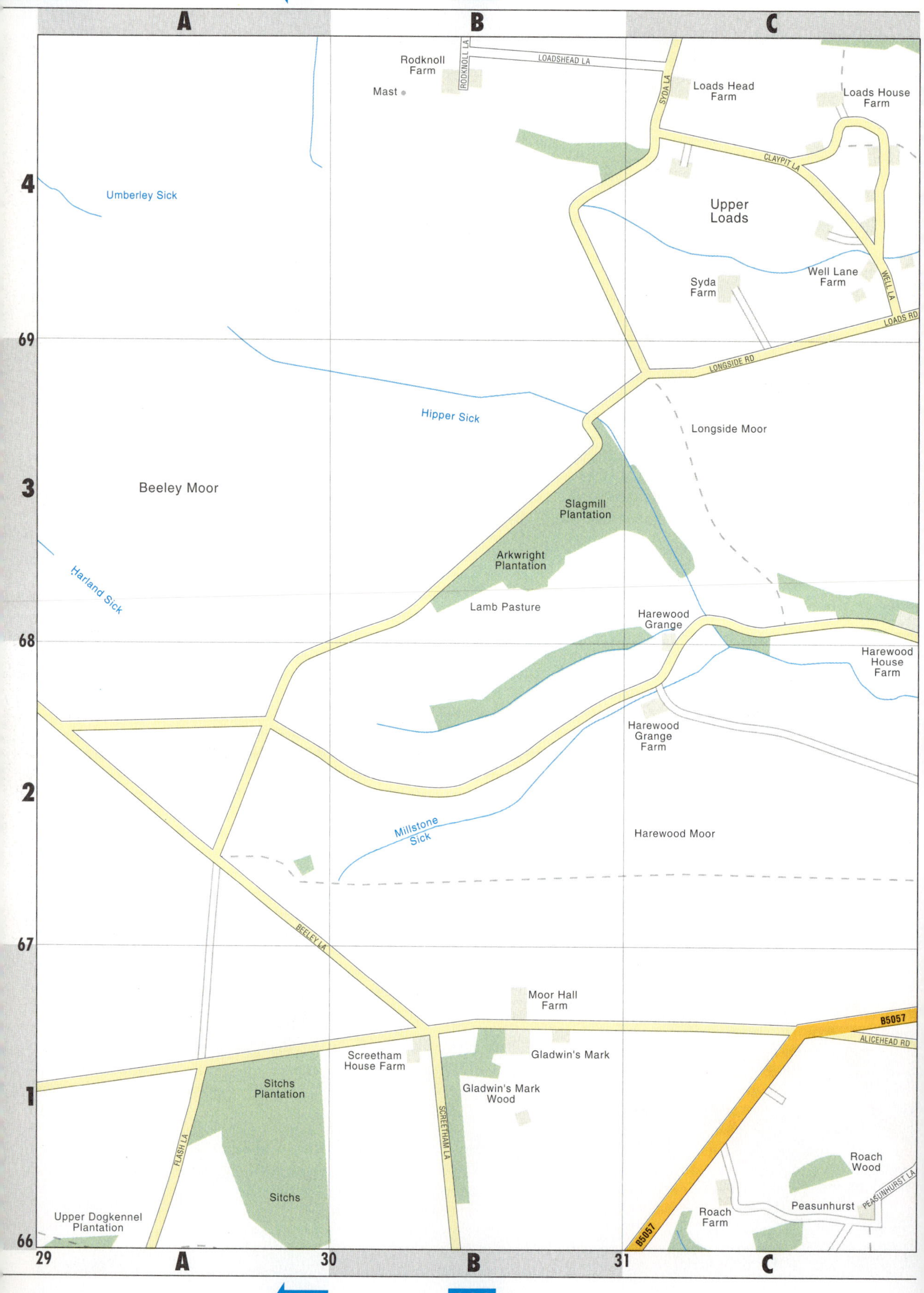

Rodknoll Farm

LOADSHEAD LA

RODKNOLL LA

SYDA LA

Loads Head Farm

Loads House Farm

Mast

4

Umberley Sick

CLAYPIT LA

Upper Loads

Well Lane Farm

Syda Farm

WELL LA

LOADS RD

69

Hipper Sick

LONGSIDE RD

Longside Moor

3

Beeley Moor

Slagmill Plantation

Arkwright Plantation

Harland Sick

Lamb Pasture

Harewood Grange

68

Harewood House Farm

Harewood Grange Farm

2

Millstone Sick

Harewood Moor

BEELEY LA

67

Moor Hall Farm

B5057

ALICEHEAD RD

Screetham House Farm

Gladwin's Mark

Sitchs Plantation

Gladwin's Mark Wood

1

HASH LA

SCREETHAM LA

Roach Wood

PEASUNHURST LA

Sitchs

Peasunhurst

Upper Dogkennel Plantation

Roach Farm

B5057

66

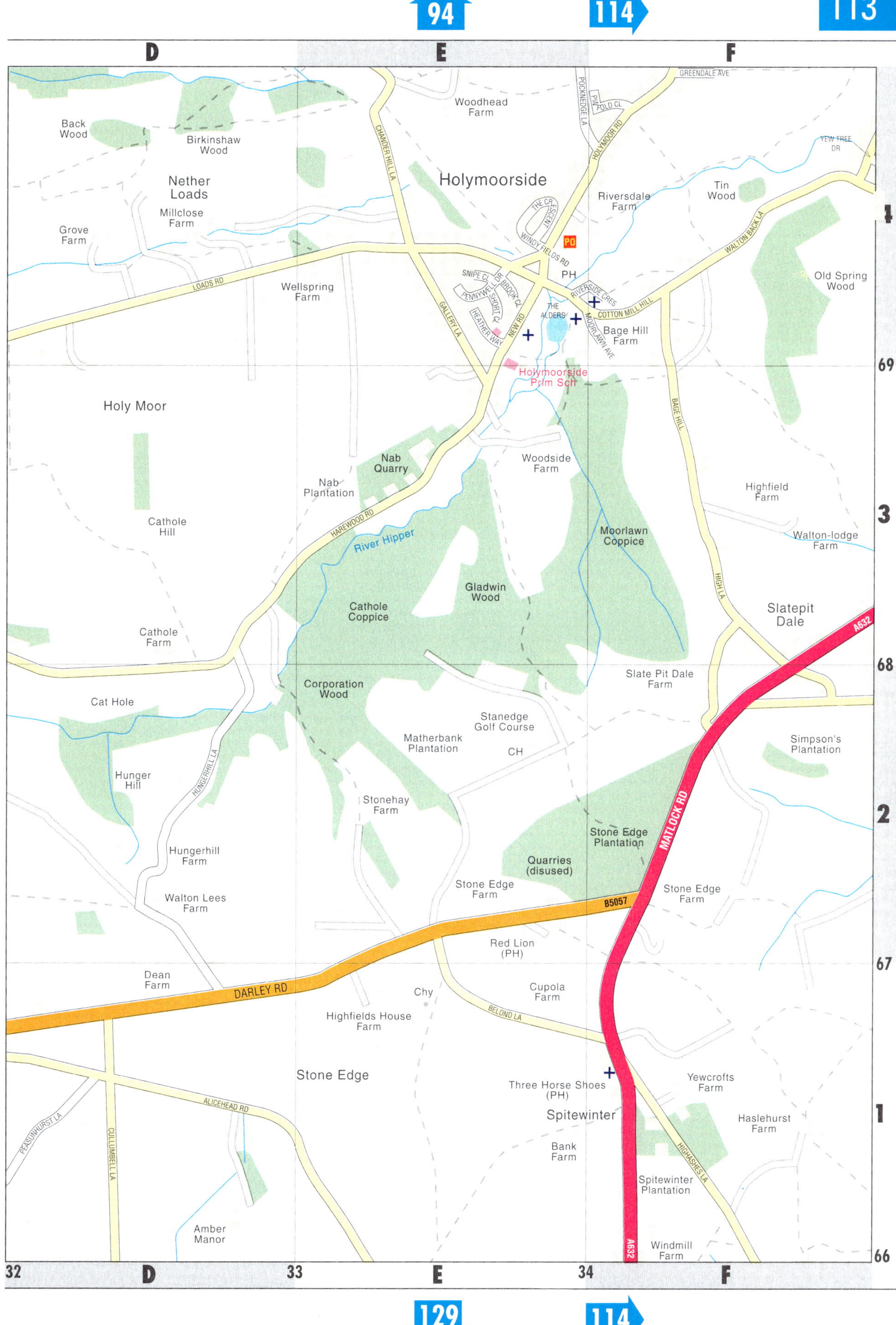
D
E
F
Back Wood
Birkinshaw Wood
Nether Loads
Millclose Farm
Grove Farm
Woodhead Farm
Holymoorside
Riversdale Farm
Tin Wood
Old Spring Wood
LOADS RD
Wellspring Farm
CHANDER HILL LA
GALLERY LA
NEW RD
HOLYMOOR RD
POCKNEDGE LA
GREENDALE AVE
YEW TREE DR
WALTON BACK LA
COTTON MILL HILL
RIVERSIDE CRES
MOORLAWN AVE
WINDY FIELDS RD
THE CRESCENT
SNIPE CL
BROOK CL
PENNYWELL DR
SHORT CL
HEATHER WAY
THE ALDERS
PO
PH
Bage Hill Farm
BAGE HILL
Holymoorside Prim Sch
Holy Moor
Woodside Farm
Nab Quarry
Nab Plantation
Highfield Farm
Cathole Hill
HAREWOOD RD
River Hipper
Moorlawn Coppice
Walton-lodge Farm
Gladwin Wood
Cathole Coppice
HIGH LA
Slatepit Dale
A632
Cathole Farm
Corporation Wood
Slate Pit Dale Farm
Cat Hole
Stanedge Golf Course
Matherbank Plantation
CH
Simpson's Plantation
Hunger Hill
HUNGERHILL LA
Stonehay Farm
MATLOCK RD
Stone Edge Plantation
Hungerhill Farm
Quarries (disused)
Stone Edge Farm
Stone Edge Farm
Walton Lees Farm
B5057
Red Lion (PH)
Dean Farm
DARLEY RD
Chy
Cupola Farm
Highfields House Farm
BELOND LA
Stone Edge
Three Horse Shoes (PH)
Yewcrofts Farm
Spitewinter
ALICEHEAD RD
PEASUNHURST LA
CULLUMBELL LA
Haslehurst Farm
Bank Farm
HIGHASHES LA
Spitewinter Plantation
Amber Manor
Windmill Farm
A632
4
69
3
68
2
67
1
66
32
33
34

113
95

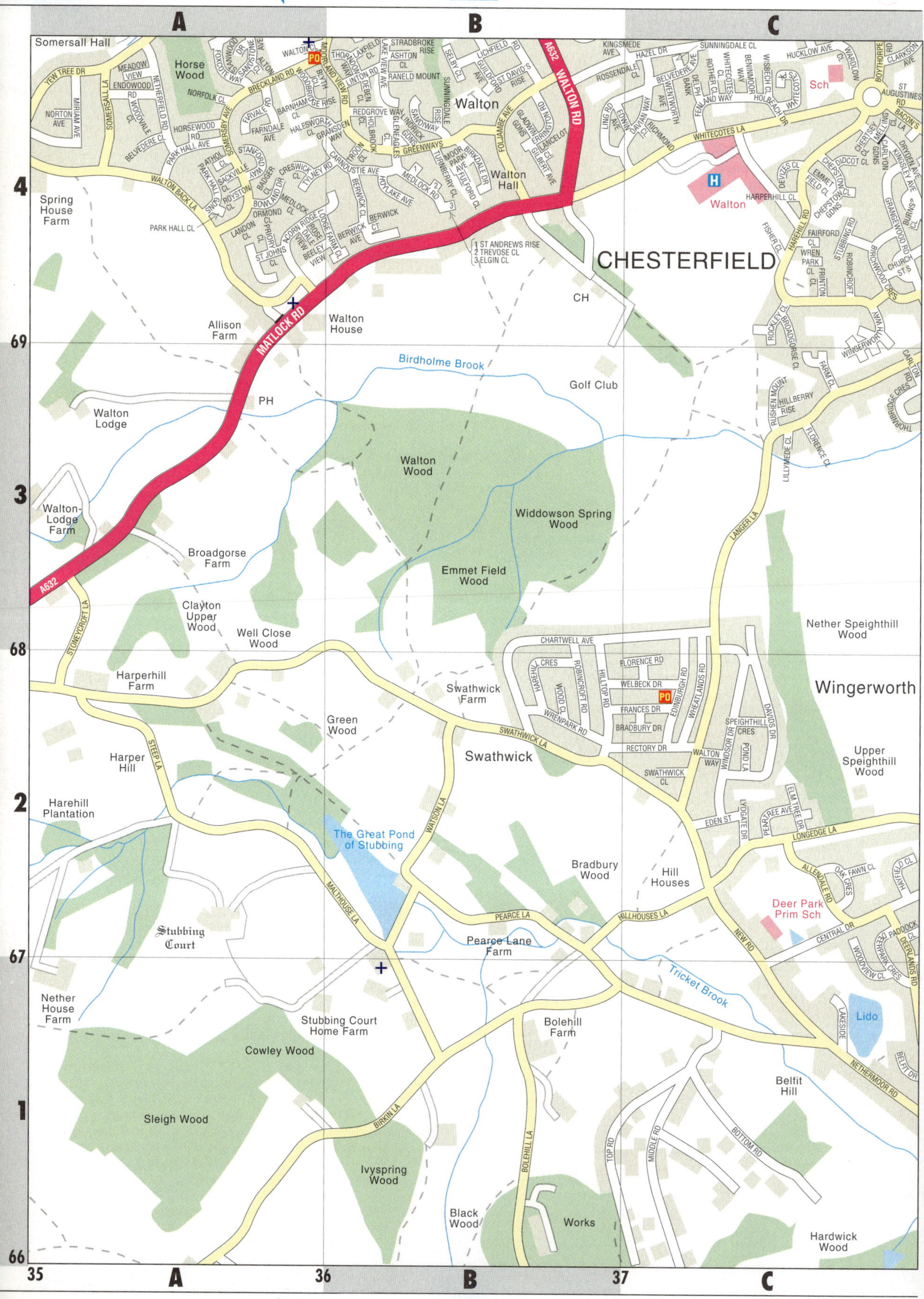
A
B
C
CHESTERFIELD
Walton
Walton Hall
Somersall Hall
Horse Wood
Spring House Farm
Allison Farm
Walton House
Birdholme Brook
Golf Club
Walton Lodge
Walton Wood
Walton-Lodge Farm
Widdowson Spring Wood
Broadgorse Farm
Emmet Field Wood
Clayton Upper Wood
Well Close Wood
Nether Speighthill Wood
Wingerworth
Harperhill Farm
Swathwick Farm
Green Wood
Harper Hill
Swathwick
Upper Speighthill Wood
Harehill Plantation
The Great Pond of Stubbing
Bradbury Wood
Hill Houses
Deer Park Prim Sch
Stubbing Court
Pearce Lane Farm
Tricket Brook
Nether House Farm
Stubbing Court Home Farm
Bolehill Farm
Lido
Cowley Wood
Belfit Hill
Sleigh Wood
Ivyspring Wood
Black Wood
Works
Hardwick Wood
Walton
Sch
CH
PH
PO
A632
WALTON RD
MATLOCK RD
WALTON BACK LA
WHITECOTES LA
SWATHWICK LA
LONGEDGE LA
MALTHOUSE LA
WATSON LA
PEARCE LA
HILLHOUSES LA
NEW RD
NETHERMOOR RD
BIRKIN LA
BOLEHILL LA
STEEP LA
STONEYCROFT LA
LANGER LA
TOP RD
MIDDLE RD
BOTTOM RD
CENTRAL DR
1 ST ANDREWS RISE
2 TREVOSE CL
3 ELGIN CL
69
68
67
66
4
3
2
1
35
36
37

113
130

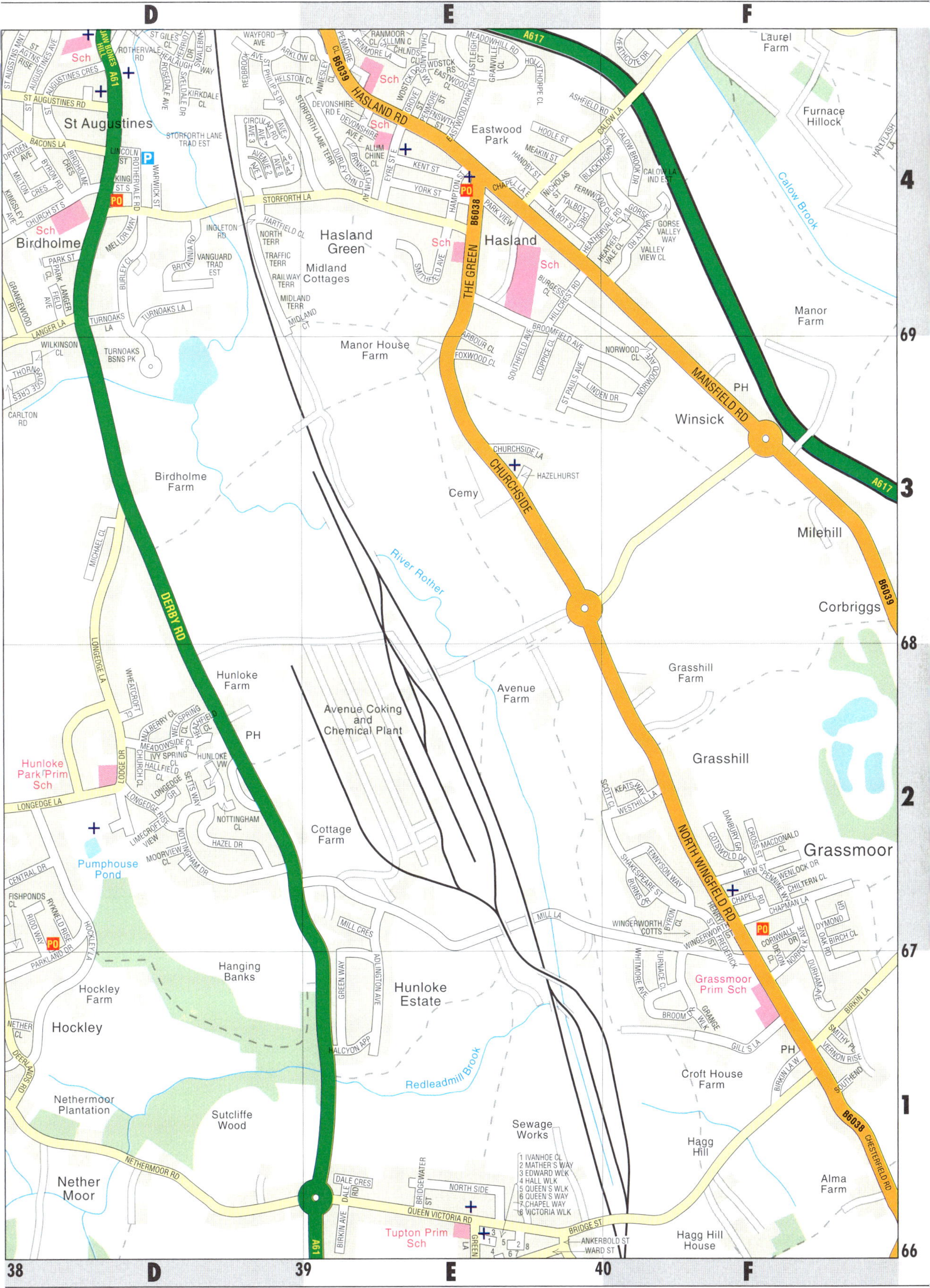
St Augustines
Birdholme
Hasland Green
Midland Cottages
Hasland
Eastwood Park
Manor House Farm
Birdholme Farm
Winsick
Milehill
Corbriggs
Cemy
River Rother
Calow Brook
Laurel Farm
Furnace Hillock
Manor Farm
Hunloke Farm
Avenue Coking and Chemical Plant
Avenue Farm
Grasshill Farm
Grasshill
Grassmoor
Cottage Farm
Hunloke Park Prim Sch
Pumphouse Pond
Hanging Banks
Hockley Farm
Hockley
Hunloke Estate
Grassmoor Prim Sch
Croft House Farm
Redleadmill Brook
Nethermoor Plantation
Sutcliffe Wood
Sewage Works
Hagg Hill
Nether Moor
Tupton Prim Sch
Hagg Hill House
Alma Farm
DERBY RD
MANSFIELD RD
CHURCHSIDE
THE GREEN
HASLAND RD
NORTH WINGFIELD RD
CHESTERFIELD RD
STORFORTH LA
NETHERMOOR RD
QUEEN VICTORIA RD
LONGEDGE LA
MILL LA
A61
A617
B6038
B6039
1 IVANHOE CL
2 MATHER'S WAY
3 EDWARD WLK
4 HALL WLK
5 QUEEN'S WLK
6 QUEEN'S WAY
7 CHAPEL WAY
8 VICTORIA WLK
D
E
F
38
39
40
1
2
3
4
66
67
68
69

115
97

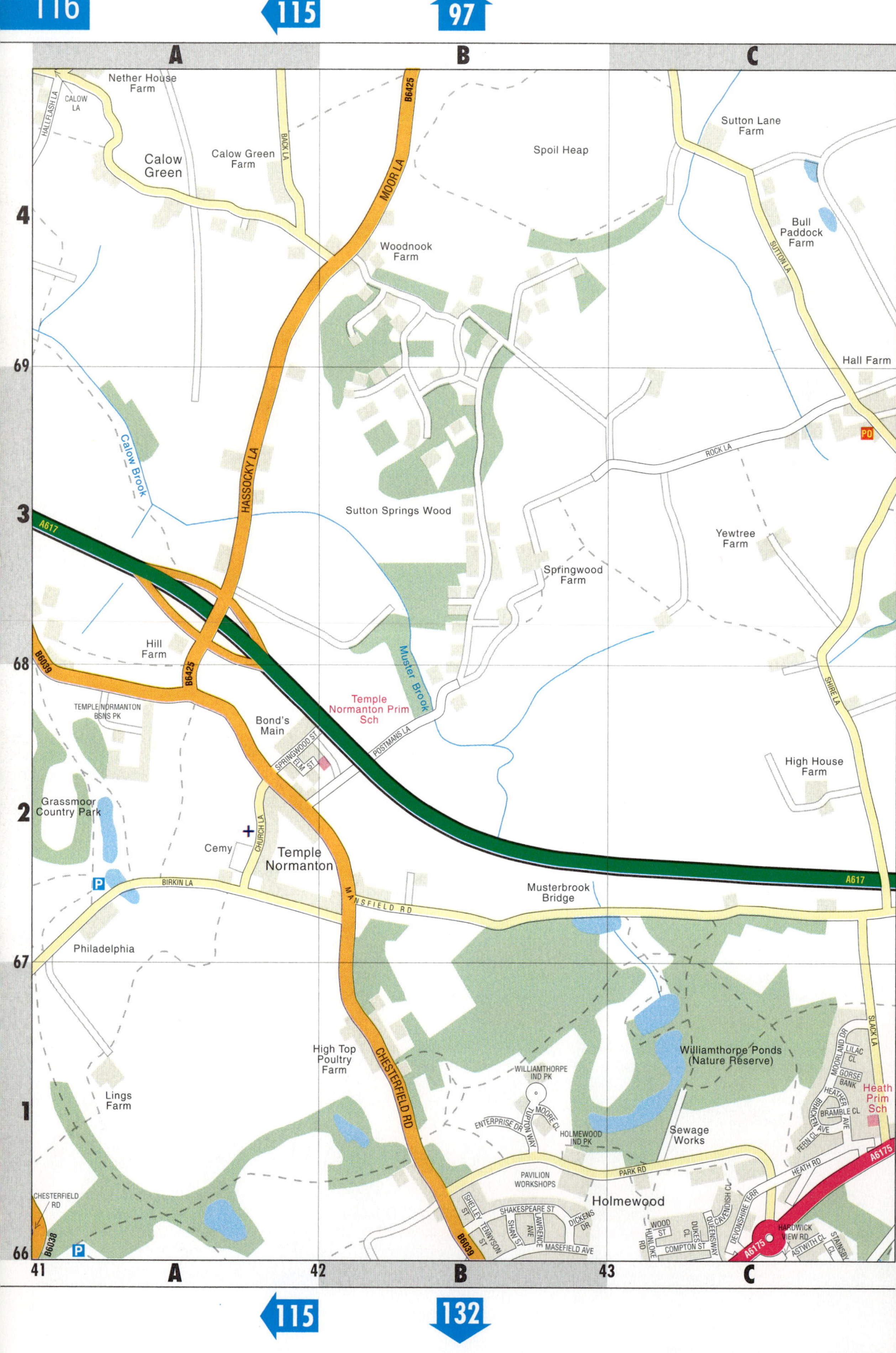
A
B
C
Nether House Farm
CALOW LA
HALFLASH LA
Calow Green
Calow Green Farm
BACK LA
B6425
MOOR LA
Spoil Heap
Sutton Lane Farm
Bull Paddock Farm
SUTTON LA
Woodnook Farm
4
69
Hall Farm
PO
ROCK LA
Calow Brook
HASSOCKY LA
Sutton Springs Wood
3
A617
Yewtree Farm
Springwood Farm
Hill Farm
Muster Brook
68
B6039
B6425
TEMPLE NORMANTON BSNS PK
Bond's Main
Temple Normanton Prim Sch
POSTMANS LA
SHIRE LA
SPRINGWOOD ST
ELM ST
High House Farm
Grassmoor Country Park
2
Cemy
CHURCH LA
Temple Normanton
P
BIRKIN LA
MANSFIELD RD
Musterbrook Bridge
A617
Philadelphia
67
SLACK LA
High Top Poultry Farm
CHESTERFIELD RD
Williamthorpe Ponds (Nature Reserve)
WILLIAMTHORPE IND PK
MOORLAND DR
LILAC CL
GORSE BANK
HEATHER AVE
Heath Prim Sch
Lings Farm
1
ENTERPRISE DR
TUPTON WAY
MOORE CL
HOLMEWOOD IND PK
Sewage Works
BRACKEN AVE
BRAMBLE CL
FERN CL
A6175
PAVILION WORKSHOPS
PARK RD
HEATH RD
CHESTERFIELD RD
Holmewood
CAVENDISH CL
DEVONSHIRE TERR
SHELLEY ST
SHAKESPEARE ST
DICKENS DR
WOOD ST
DUKES CL
QUEENSWAY
TENNYSON ST
SHAW ST
LAWRENCE AVE
HARDWICK VIEW RD
STAINSBY CL
MASEFIELD AVE
HUNLOKE RD
COMPTON ST
ASTWITH CL
A6175
66
B6038
P
B6039
41
42
43

115
132

98
118

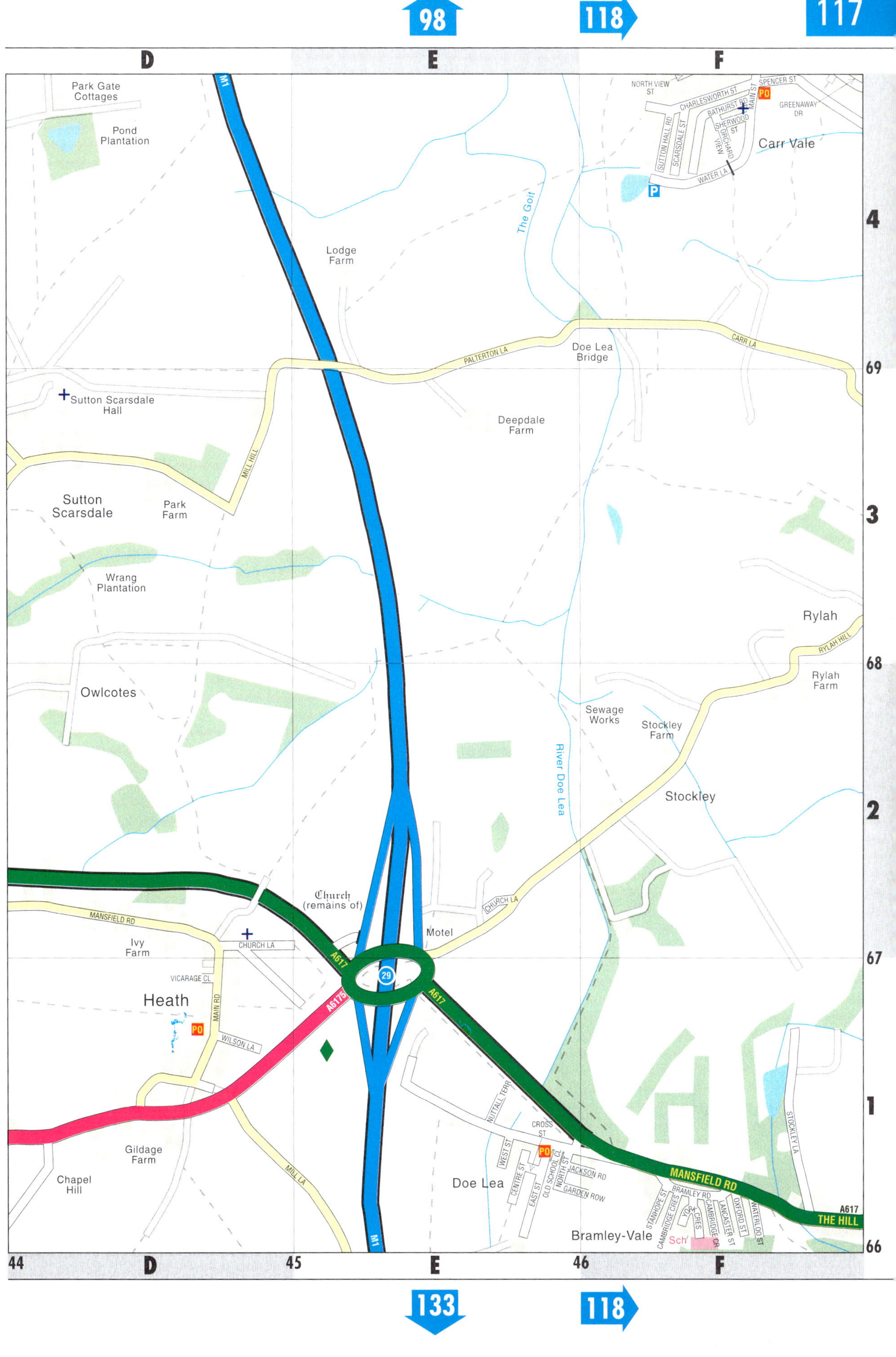
D
E
F
Park Gate Cottages
Pond Plantation
M1
Lodge Farm
The Goit
NORTH VIEW ST
CHARLESWORTH ST
SPENCER ST
PO
GREENAWAY DR
BATHURST RD
MAIN ST
SUTTON HALL RD
SCARSDALE ST
SHERWOOD ST
ORCHARD VIEW
WATER LA
Carr Vale
P
4
PALTERTON LA
Doe Lea Bridge
CARR LA
69
Sutton Scarsdale Hall
Deepdale Farm
MILL HILL
Sutton Scarsdale
Park Farm
3
Wrang Plantation
Rylah
RYLAH HILL
68
Rylah Farm
Owlcotes
Sewage Works
Stockley Farm
River Doe Lea
Stockley
2
Church (remains of)
CHURCH LA
MANSFIELD RD
Motel
Ivy Farm
CHURCH LA
67
VICARAGE CL
A617
29
A6175
Heath
MAIN RD
PO
WILSON LA
1
NUTTALL TERR
CROSS ST
STOCKLEY LA
Gildage Farm
WEST ST
PO
CENTRE ST
EAST ST
OLD SCHOOL CL
NORTH ST
JACKSON RD
GARDEN ROW
MANSFIELD RD
Chapel Hill
MILL LA
Doe Lea
STANHOPE ST
BRAMLEY RD
CAMBRIDGE CRES
YORK CRES
CAMBRIDGE DR
LANCASTER ST
OXFORD ST
WATERLOO ST
A617
THE HILL
Bramley-Vale
Sch
66
44
45
46

133
118

A   **B**   **C**

Greenway Dr
Brookfield Rd
New Station
Meadow
Avondale
Spital
Fairfield Rd
Cl
Ridgedale Rd
Valley Rd
CRICH LA
LININGTON
Eastern Ave
Stockley View
Cavendish Rd
Portland
Tower
Cres
Cavendish Rd
St Lawrence Ave
B6417
Cromwell Rd 1
Polyfields La 2
Owlcotes View
Crich View
Mount
Victoria St
Cross St
Nesbit St
Middle St
Selwyn St
Wells St
LANGWITH RD
A632
Darwood La
Sutton View
PH
West View
Hillstown
MOOR LA
The Meadows
Castle Gn
Pleasant Ave
Lidget La
Fox Hill
Fox Hill

4

Mansfield Rd
ROTHERHAM RD
Northfield La

69

Carr La
The Elms Farm
Scarcliffe
Sch
PO
PH
Main St
Station Rd
Wood La

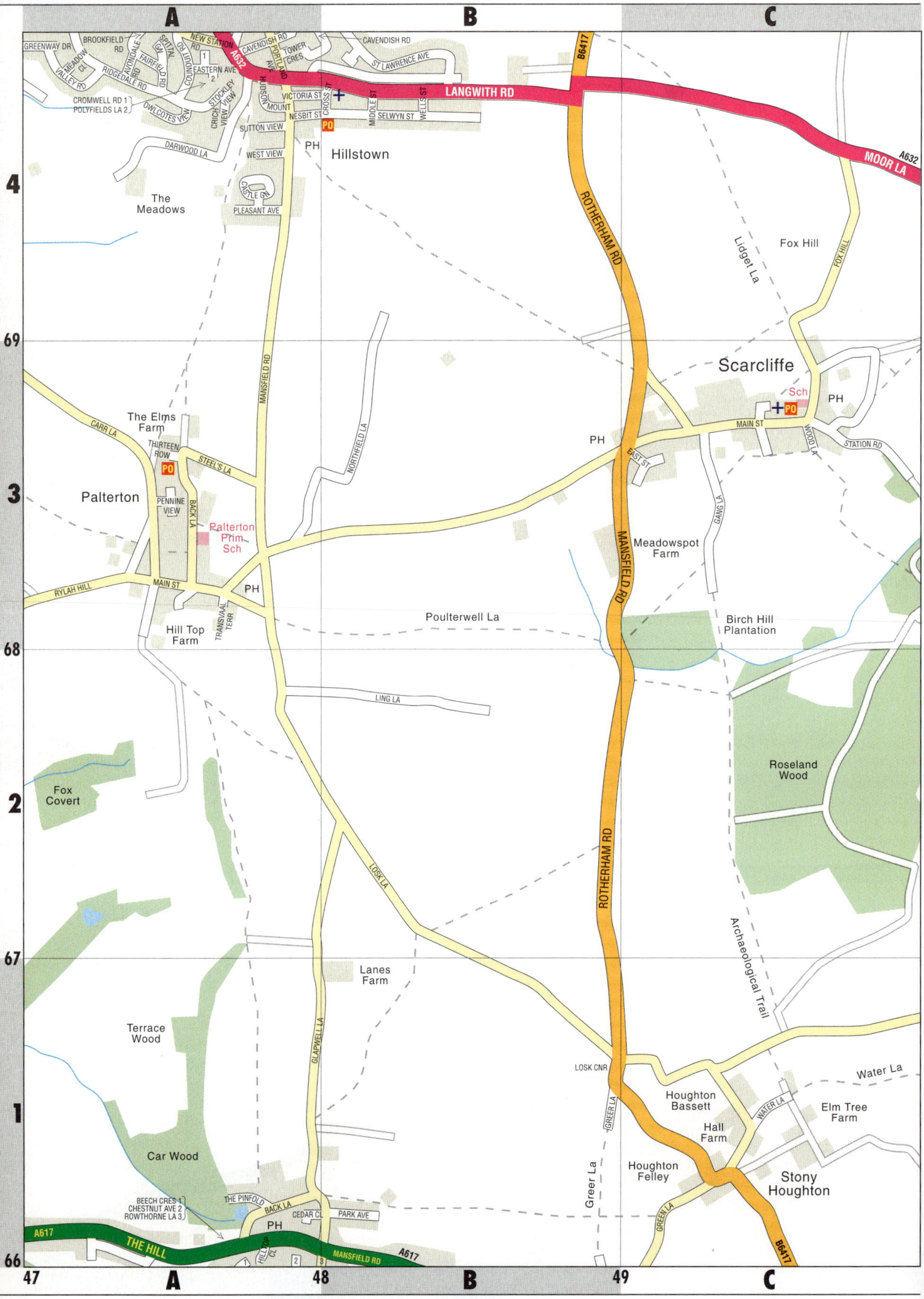

Thirteen Row
STEEL'S LA
PO
PH
East St
EAST ST
GANG LA
Palterton
Pennine View
BACK LA
Palterton Prim Sch
Mansfield Rd
Meadowspot Farm

3

RYLAH HILL
MAIN ST
PH
TRANSVAAL TERR
Poulterwell La
Birch Hill Plantation

Hill Top Farm

68

LING LA

Fox Covert
Roseland Wood

2

LOSK LA

GLAPWELL LA
ROTHERHAM RD
Archaeological Trail

67

Lanes Farm

Terrace Wood

LOSK CNR
Water La
Houghton Bassett
Elm Tree Farm
WATER LA

1

Car Wood
Hall Farm
GREER LA
Greer La
Houghton Felley
Stony Houghton
B6417

BEECH CRES 1
CHESTNUT AVE 2
ROWTHORNE LA 3
THE PINFOLD
BACK LA
CEDAR CL
PARK AVE
PH
A617
THE HILL
HILL TOP CL
Mansfield Rd
A617
GREEN LA

66

47   **A**   **48**   **B**   **49**   **C**

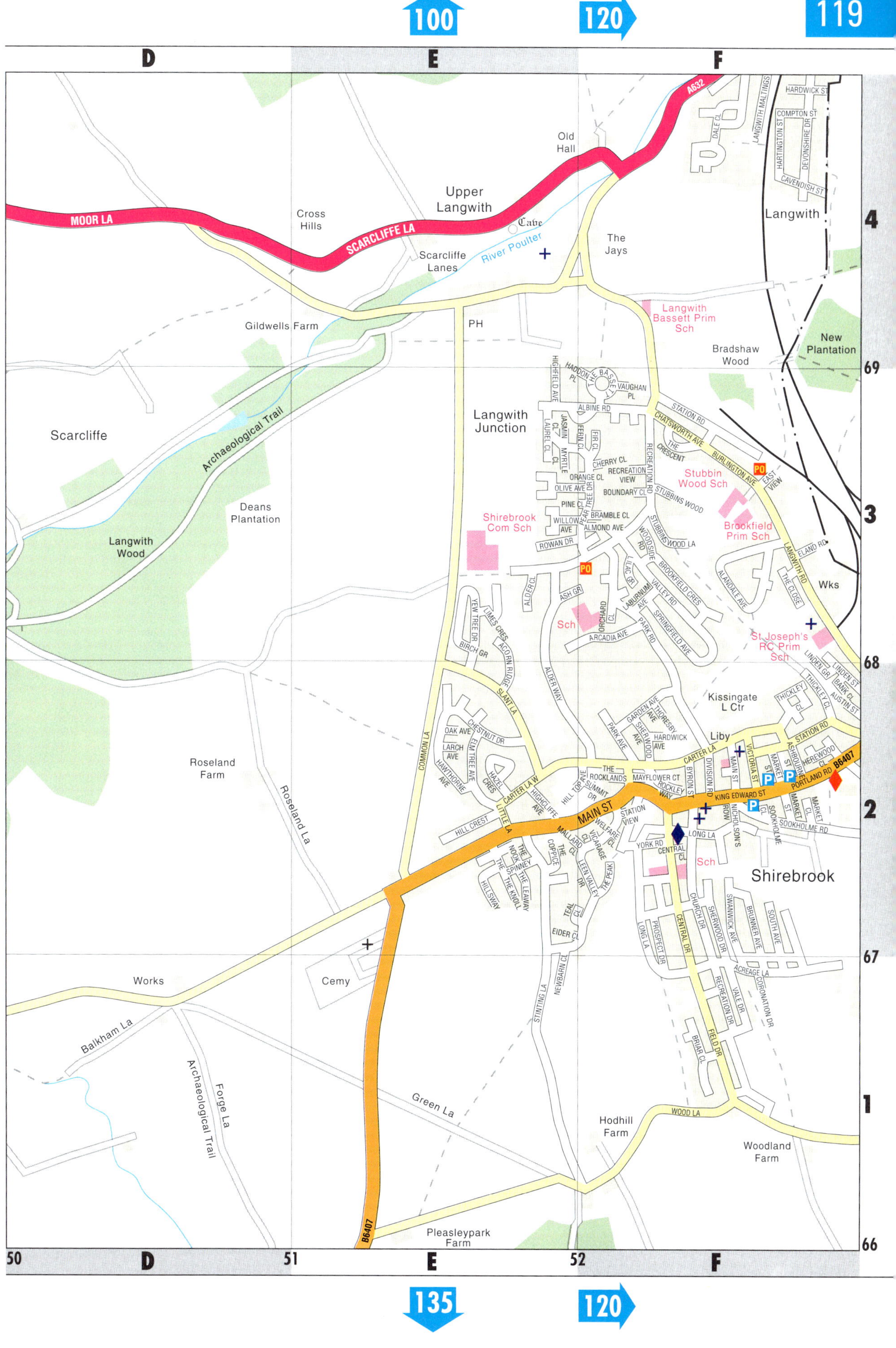
100
120
D
E
F
4
3
2
1
69
68
67
66
50
51
52
135
120
MOOR LA
SCARCLIFFE LA
A632
Old Hall
Upper Langwith
Cross Hills
Cave
River Poulter
Scarcliffe Lanes
The Jays
Langwith
HARDWICK ST
COMPTON ST
HARTINGTON ST
DEVONSHIRE DR
CAVENDISH ST
DALE CL
LANGWITH MALTINGS
Gildwells Farm
PH
Langwith Bassett Prim Sch
Bradshaw Wood
New Plantation
Scarcliffe
Archaeological Trail
Langwith Junction
Langwith Wood
Deans Plantation
HIGHFIELD AVE
HADDON PL
THE BASSETT
VAUGHAN PL
ALBINE RD
STATION RD
CHATSWORTH AVE
THE CRESCENT
BURLINGTON AVE
EAST VIEW
JASMIN CL
LAUREL CL
MYRTLE CL
FERN CL
FIR CL
CHERRY CL
RECREATION VIEW
RECREATION RD
ORANGE CL
OLIVE AVE
BOUNDARY CL
PEAR TREE DR
PINE CL
BRAMBLE CL
WILLOW AVE
ALMOND AVE
ROWAN DR
STUBBINS WOOD
STUBBINS WOOD LA
Stubbin Wood Sch
Brookfield Prim Sch
Shirebrook Com Sch
PO
WOODSIDE RD
LILAC GR
BROOKFIELD CRES
ALANDALE AVE
THE CLOSE
LANGWITH RD
ELAND RD
Wks
ALDER CL
ASH GR
Sch
ORCHARD CL
LABURNUM AVE
VALLEY RD
PARK RD
SPRINGFIELD AVE
ARCADIA AVE
St Joseph's RC Prim Sch
YEW TREE DR
LIMES CRES
ACORN RIDGE
BIRCH GR
ALDER WAY
SLANT LA
LINDEN GR
LINDEN ST
BANK CL
AUSTIN ST
THICKLEY CL
Kissingate L Ctr
GARDEN AVE
THORESBY AVE
SHERWOOD AVE
PARK AVE
HARDWICK AVE
Liby
STATION RD
CARTER LA
CHESTNUT DR
OAK AVE
LARCH AVE
ELM TREE AVE
HAWTHORNE AVE
HAZEL CRES
COMMON LA
Roseland Farm
Roseland La
THE ROCKLANDS
MAYFLOWER CT
ROCKLEY WAY
SUMMIT DR
HILL TOP AVE
DIVISION RD
BYRON ST
MAIN ST
VICTORIA ST
MARKET ST
ASHBOURNE ST
HEREWOOD CL
PORTLAND RD
B6407
KING EDWARD ST
CARTER LA W
HIGHCLIFFE AVE
LITTLE LA
HILL CREST
MAIN ST
WELFARE CL
STATION VIEW
VICARAGE CL
MALLARD CL
THE COPPICE
THE NOOK
SPINNEY
THE LEAWAY
THE KNOLL
HILLSWAY
LEEN VALLEY DR
THE PEAK
YORK RD
CENTRAL CL
LONG LA
NICHOLSON'S ROW
SOOKHOLME CL
SOOKHOLME RD
MARKET CL
Sch
Shirebrook
TEAL CL
EIDER CL
CHURCH DR
SHERWOOD DR
SWANWICK AVE
BRUNNER AVE
SOUTH AVE
PROSPECT DR
LONG LA
CENTRAL DR
ACREAGE LA
CORONATION DR
RECREATION DR
VALE DR
Works
Cemy
Balkham La
Archaeological Trail
Forge La
STINTING LA
NEWBARN CL
BRIAR CL
FIELD DR
Green La
Hodhill Farm
WOOD LA
Woodland Farm
Pleasleypark Farm
B6407

119
101

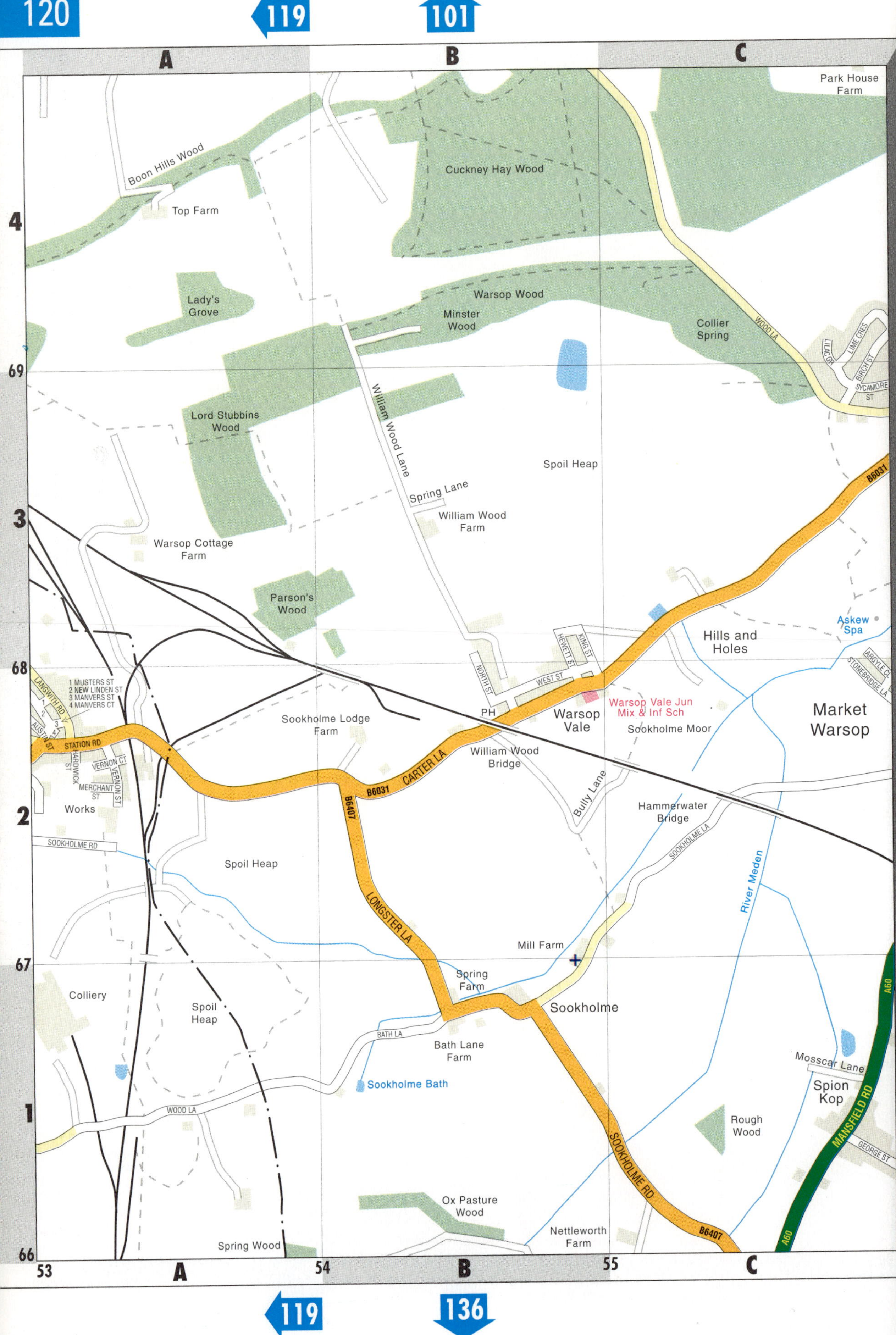
A
B
C
Park House Farm
Boon Hills Wood
Top Farm
Cuckney Hay Wood
Lady's Grove
Warsop Wood
Minster Wood
Collier Spring
WOOD LA
LILAC GR
LIME CRES
BIRCH ST
SYCAMORE ST
Lord Stubbins Wood
William Wood Lane
Spoil Heap
Spring Lane
William Wood Farm
B6031
Warsop Cottage Farm
Parson's Wood
Askew Spa
Hills and Holes
HEWETT ST
KING ST
NORTH ST
WEST ST
ARGYLE CL
STONEBRIDGE LA
1 MUSTERS ST
2 NEW LINDEN ST
3 MANVERS ST
4 MANVERS CT
LANGWITH RD
AUSTIN ST
STATION RD
Sookholme Lodge Farm
PH
Warsop Vale
Warsop Vale Jun Mix & Inf Sch
Sookholme Moor
Market Warsop
HARDWICK ST
VERNON CT
VERNON ST
MERCHANT ST
CARTER LA
B6031
William Wood Bridge
Bully Lane
Works
B6407
Hammerwater Bridge
SOOKHOLME RD
SOOKHOLME LA
Spoil Heap
River Meden
LONGSTER LA
Mill Farm
Spring Farm
Sookholme
Colliery
Spoil Heap
A60
BATH LA
Bath Lane Farm
Mosscar Lane
Sookholme Bath
Spion Kop
WOOD LA
Rough Wood
MANSFIELD RD
GEORGE ST
SOOKHOLME RD
Ox Pasture Wood
Nettleworth Farm
B6407
Spring Wood
A60
4
69
3
68
2
67
1
66
53
54
55

119
136

105
122

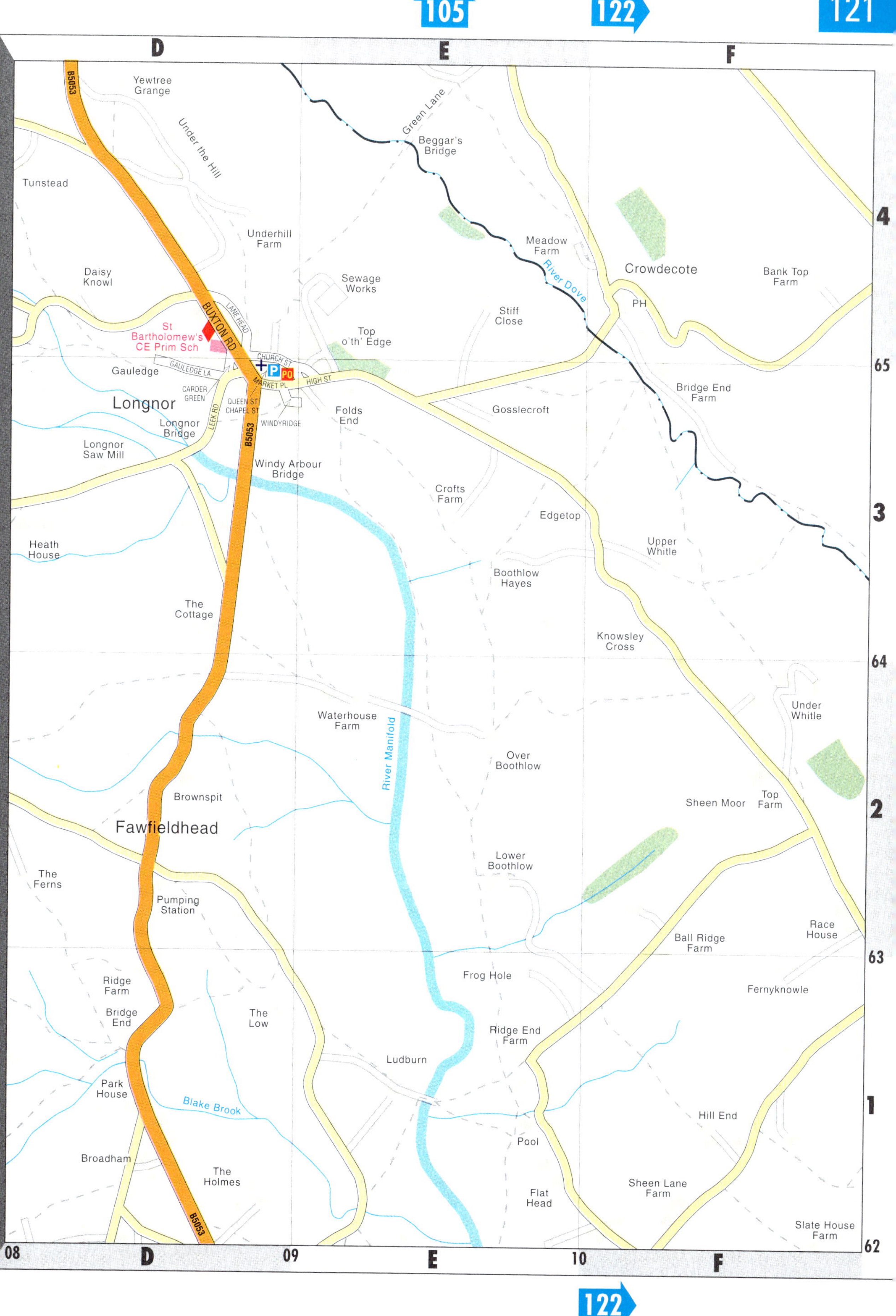
D
E
F
B5053
Yewtree Grange
Under the Hill
Green Lane
Beggar's Bridge
Tunstead
Underhill Farm
Meadow Farm
Daisy Knowl
Sewage Works
River Dove
Crowdecote
Bank Top Farm
PH
Stiff Close
BUXTON RD
LANE HEAD
St Bartholomew's CE Prim Sch
Top o'th' Edge
CHURCH ST
GAULEDGE LA
Gauledge
MARKET PL
HIGH ST
CARDER GREEN
QUEEN ST
CHAPEL ST
Longnor
LEEK RD
Longnor Bridge
WINDYRIDGE
Folds End
Gosslecroft
Bridge End Farm
Longnor Saw Mill
Windy Arbour Bridge
Crofts Farm
Edgetop
Heath House
Upper Whitle
Boothlow Hayes
The Cottage
Knowsley Cross
Waterhouse Farm
Under Whitle
River Manifold
Over Boothlow
Brownspit
Sheen Moor
Top Farm
Fawfieldhead
Lower Boothlow
The Ferns
Pumping Station
Ball Ridge Farm
Race House
Frog Hole
Fernyknowle
Ridge Farm
Bridge End
The Low
Ridge End Farm
Ludburn
Park House
Blake Brook
Hill End
Pool
Broadham
The Holmes
Flat Head
Sheen Lane Farm
Slate House Farm
4
65
3
64
2
63
1
62
08
09
10

122

121
106

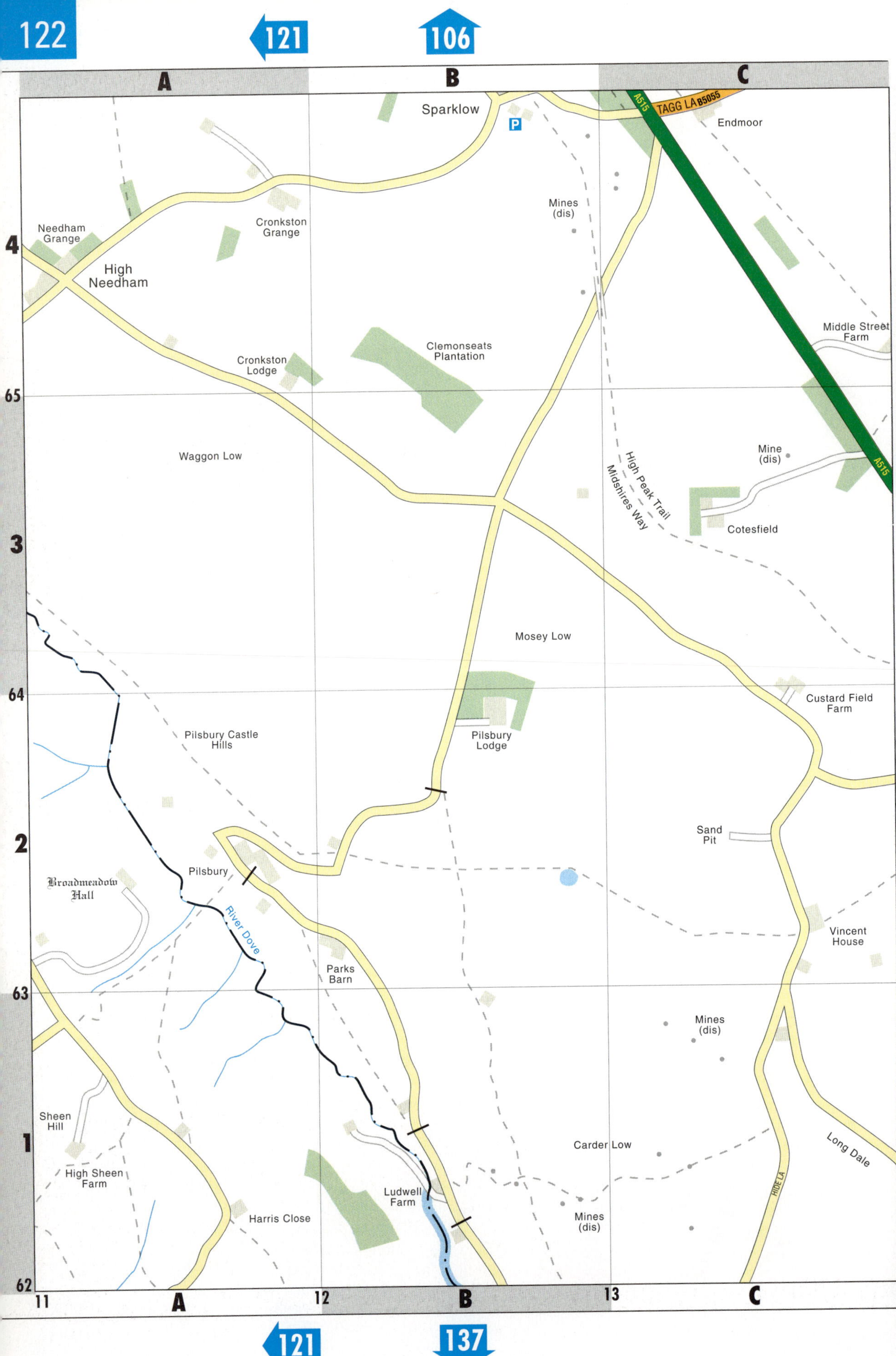
A
B
C
Sparklow
P
A515
TAGG LA B5055
Endmoor
Mines (dis)
Needham Grange
Cronkston Grange
High Needham
4
Middle Street Farm
Cronkston Lodge
Clemonseats Plantation
65
Waggon Low
Mine (dis)
A515
High Peak Trail
Midshires Way
Cotesfield
3
Mosey Low
64
Custard Field Farm
Pilsbury Castle Hills
Pilsbury Lodge
2
Sand Pit
Pilsbury
Broadmeadow Hall
River Dove
Vincent House
Parks Barn
63
Mines (dis)
Sheen Hill
1
Carder Low
Long Dale
High Sheen Farm
Ludwell Farm
HIDE LA
Harris Close
Mines (dis)
62
11
A
12
B
13
C

121
137

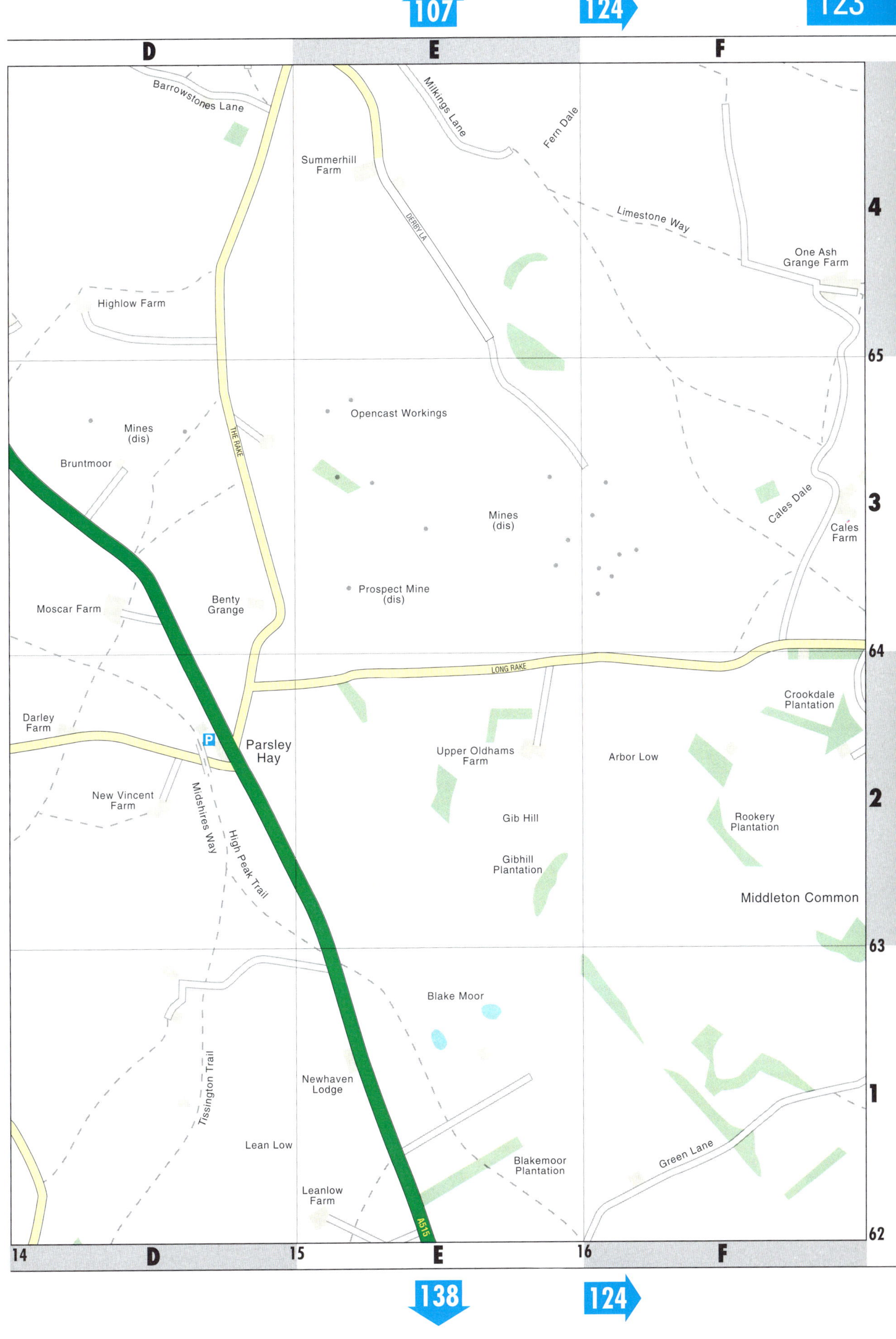
107
124
D
E
F
Barrowstones Lane
Milkings Lane
Fern Dale
Summerhill Farm
DERBY LA
Limestone Way
One Ash Grange Farm
Highlow Farm
4
65
Opencast Workings
Mines (dis)
THE RAKE
Bruntmoor
Mines (dis)
Cales Dale
Cales Farm
3
Moscar Farm
Benty Grange
Prospect Mine (dis)
LONG RAKE
64
Crookdale Plantation
Darley Farm
P
Parsley Hay
Upper Oldhams Farm
Arbor Low
New Vincent Farm
Midshires Way
High Peak Trail
Gib Hill
Rookery Plantation
2
Gibhill Plantation
Middleton Common
63
Blake Moor
Tissington Trail
Newhaven Lodge
1
Lean Low
Green Lane
Blakemoor Plantation
Leanlow Farm
A515
62
14
15
16
138
124

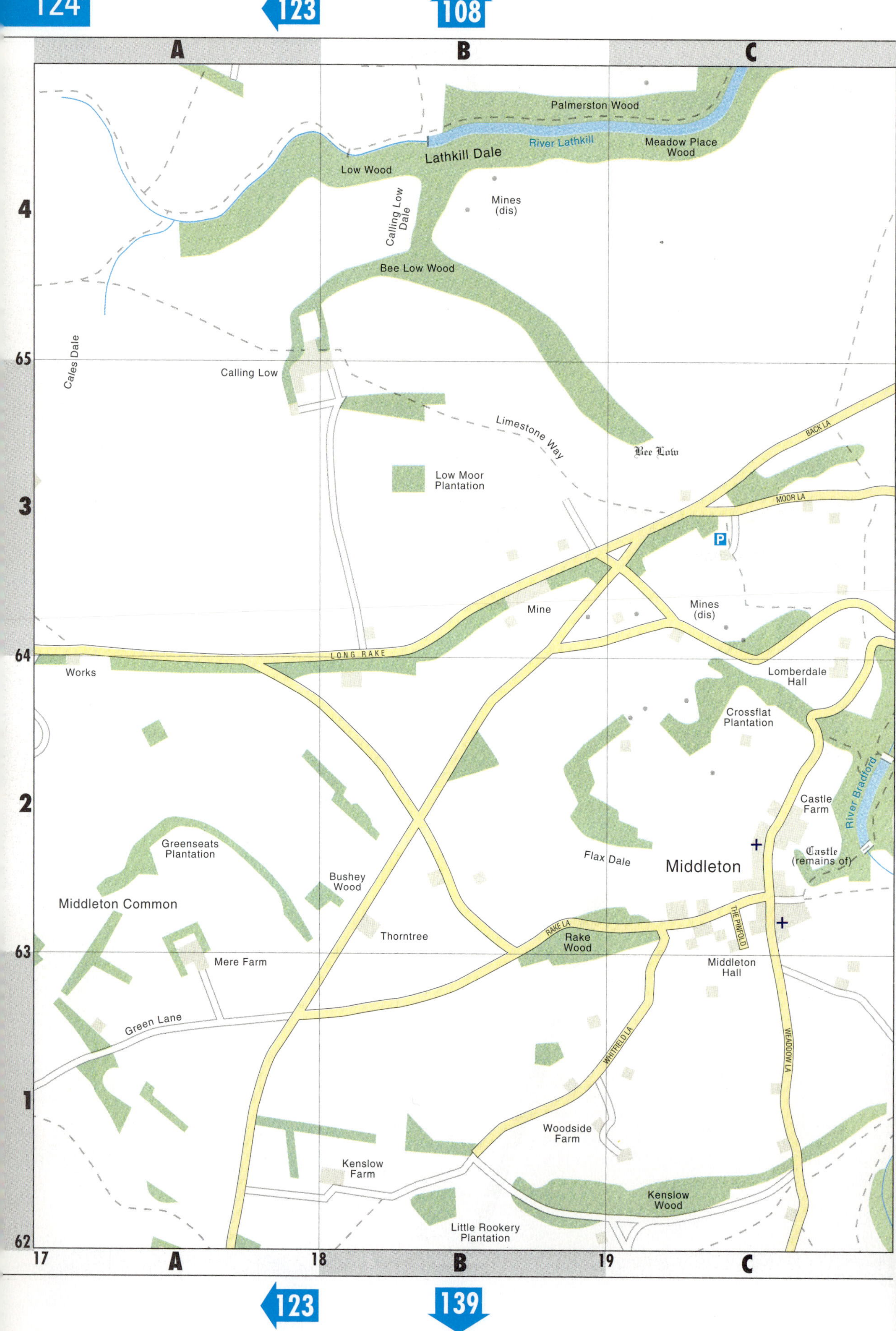

A   B   C

Palmerston Wood

River Lathkill

Meadow Place
Wood

Lathkill Dale

Low Wood

4

Mines
(dis)

Calling Low Dale

Bee Low Wood

Cales Dale

65

Calling Low

Limestone Way

Bee Low

BACK LA

MOOR LA

Low Moor
Plantation

3

P

Mine

Mines
(dis)

64

Works

LONG RAKE

Lomberdale
Hall

Crossflat
Plantation

River Bradford

2

Greenseats
Plantation

Flax Dale

Middleton

Castle
Farm

Castle
(remains of)

Middleton Common

Bushey
Wood

Thorntree

RAKE LA

Rake
Wood

THE PINFOLD

Middleton
Hall

63

Mere Farm

Green Lane

WHITFIELD LA

WEADOW LA

1

Woodside
Farm

Kenslow
Farm

Kenslow
Wood

62

Little Rookery
Plantation

17   A   18   B   19   C

109
126

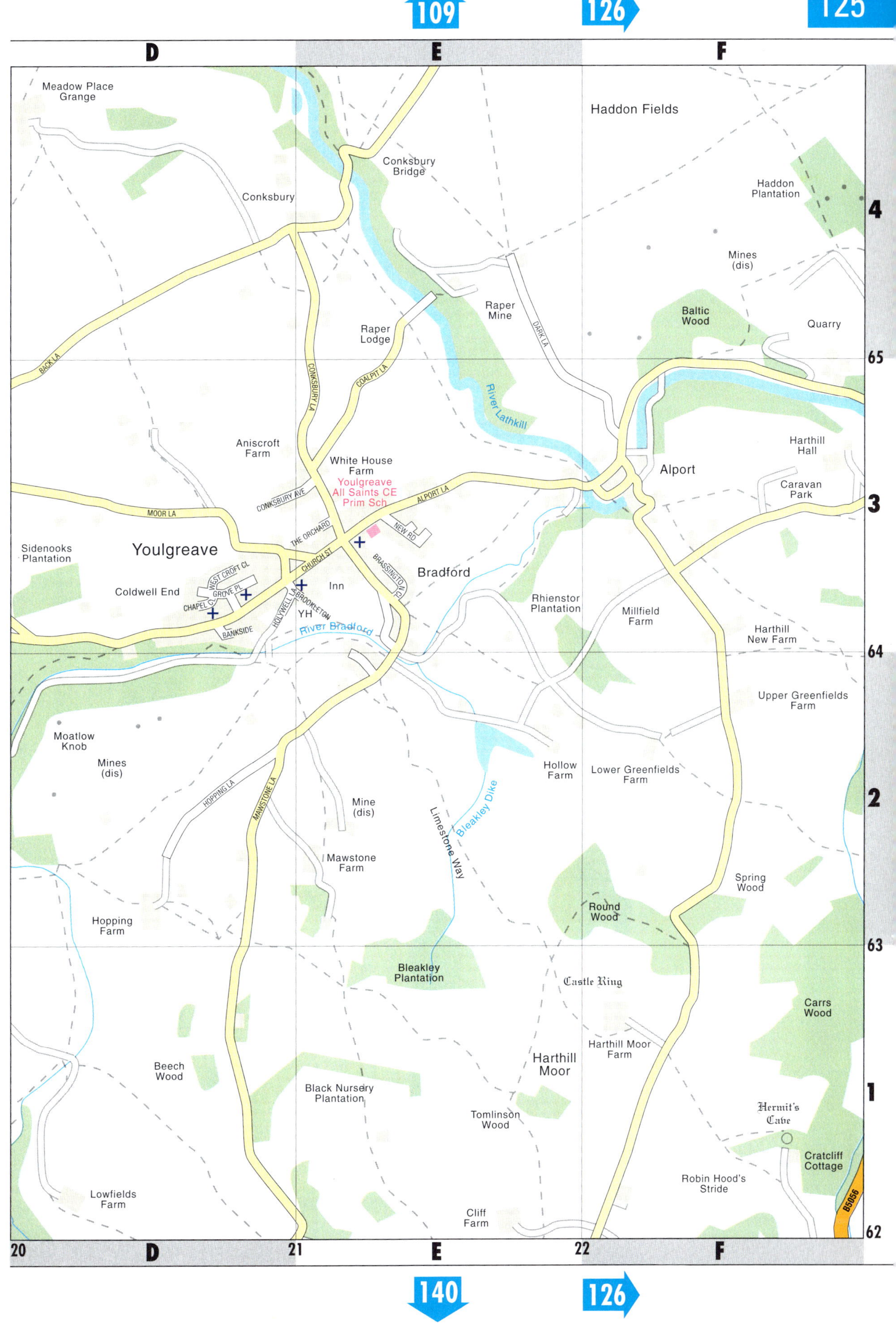
D
E
F
Meadow Place Grange
Conksbury
Conksbury Bridge
Haddon Fields
Haddon Plantation
Mines (dis)
Raper Mine
Raper Lodge
Baltic Wood
Quarry
BACK LA
CONKSBURY LA
COALPIT LA
DARK LA
River Lathkill
Aniscroft Farm
White House Farm
Youlgreave All Saints CE Prim Sch
Alport
Harthill Hall
Caravan Park
MOOR LA
CONKSBURY AVE
ALPORT LA
THE ORCHARD
NEW RD
Sidenooks Plantation
Youlgreave
CHURCH ST
WEST CROFT CL
GROVE PL
BRASSINGTON CL
Bradford
Coldwell End
Inn
CHAPEL CL
HOLYWELL LA
BROOKLETON
YH
BANKSIDE
River Bradford
Rhienstor Plantation
Millfield Farm
Harthill New Farm
Upper Greenfields Farm
Moatlow Knob
Mines (dis)
HOPPING LA
MAWSTONE LA
Mine (dis)
Limestone Way
Bleakley Dike
Hollow Farm
Lower Greenfields Farm
Mawstone Farm
Spring Wood
Hopping Farm
Round Wood
Bleakley Plantation
Castle Ring
Carrs Wood
Harthill Moor Farm
Beech Wood
Harthill Moor
Black Nursery Plantation
Tomlinson Wood
Hermit's Cave
Cratcliff Cottage
Robin Hood's Stride
Lowfields Farm
Cliff Farm
B5056
4
65
3
64
2
63
1
62
20
21
22

140
126

125
110

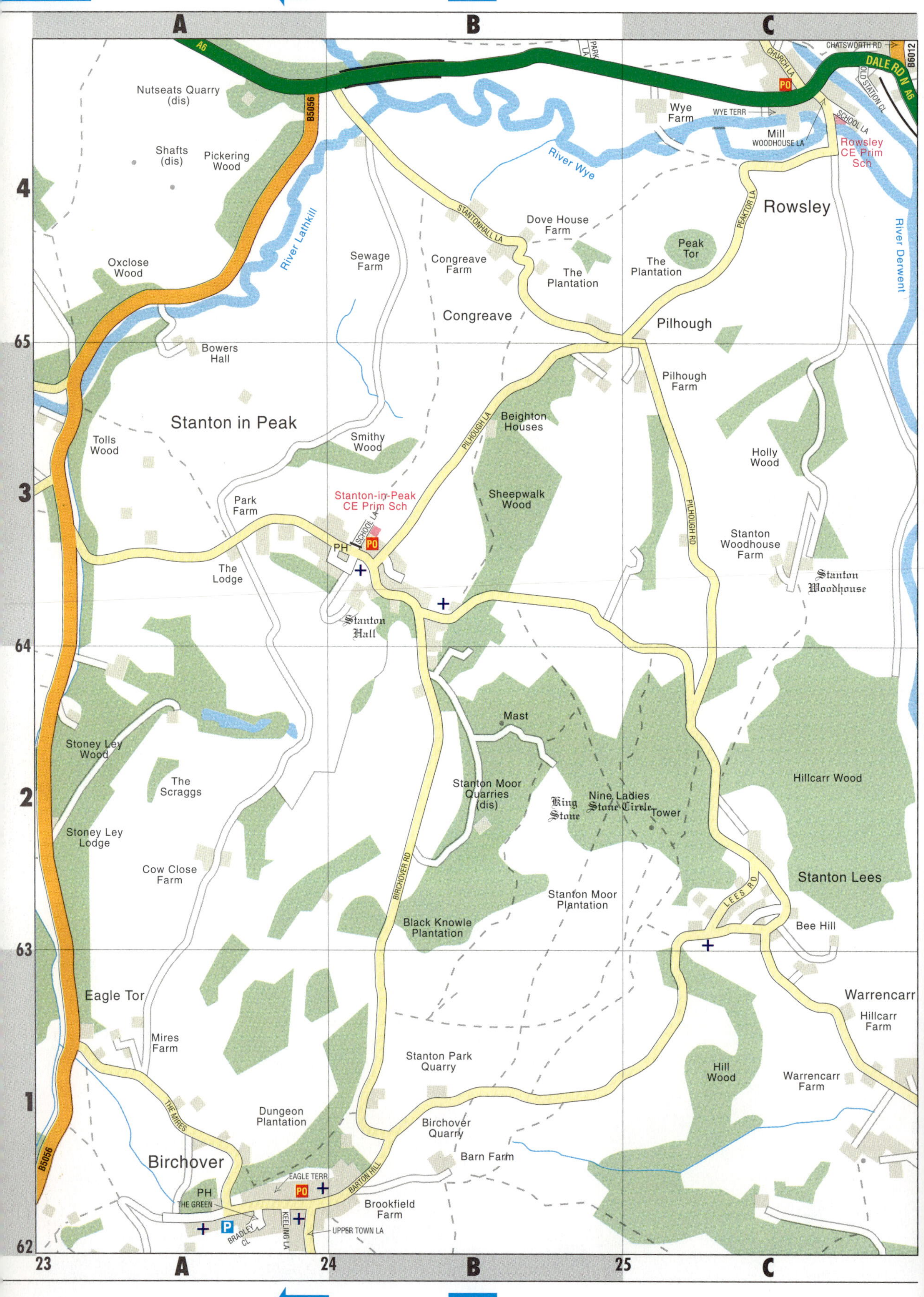
A
B
C
A6
B5056
Nutseats Quarry (dis)
Shafts (dis)
Pickering Wood
Oxclose Wood
River Lathkill
Bowers Hall
Stanton in Peak
Tolls Wood
Park Farm
The Lodge
Stoney Ley Wood
The Scraggs
Stoney Ley Lodge
Cow Close Farm
Eagle Tor
Mires Farm
THE MIRES
Dungeon Plantation
Birchover
PH
THE GREEN
EAGLE TERR
PO
BRADLEY CL
KEELING LA
UPPER TOWN LA
BARTON HILL
Brookfield Farm
Barn Farm
Birchover Quarry
Stanton Park Quarry
Black Knowle Plantation
BIRCHOVER RD
Stanton Moor Quarries (dis)
Mast
King Stone
Nine Ladies Stone Circle
Tower
Stanton Moor Plantation
Stanton Hall
PH
SCHOOL LA
PO
Stanton-in-Peak CE Prim Sch
Smithy Wood
Sewage Farm
STANTONHALL LA
Congreave Farm
Congreave
Dove House Farm
The Plantation
PILHOUGH LA
Beighton Houses
Sheepwalk Wood
River Wye
PARK LA
Wye Farm
WYE TERR
Mill
WOODHOUSE LA
CHURCH LA
CHATSWORTH RD
DALE RD N
B6012
OLD STATION CL
SCHOOL LA
Rowsley CE Prim Sch
Rowsley
PEAKTOR LA
Peak Tor
The Plantation
Pilhough
Pilhough Farm
PILHOUGH RD
Holly Wood
Stanton Woodhouse Farm
Stanton Woodhouse
River Derwent
Hillcarr Wood
Stanton Lees
LEES RD
Bee Hill
Warrencarr
Hillcarr Farm
Warrencarr Farm
Hill Wood
4
65
3
64
2
63
1
62
23
24
25

125
141

111
128

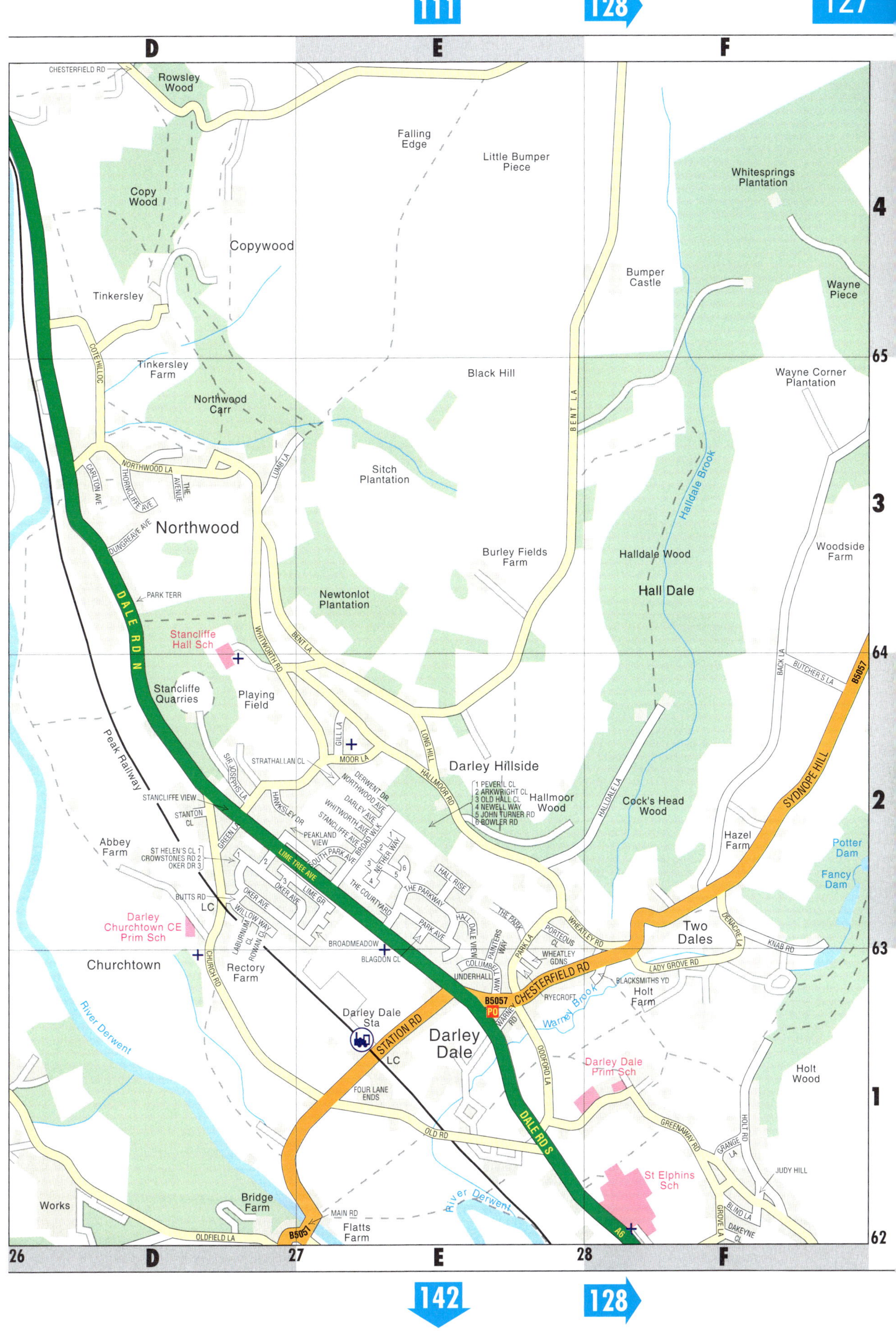
D
E
F
Rowsley Wood
Copy Wood
Copywood
Falling Edge
Little Bumper Piece
Whitesprings Plantation
Tinkersley
Tinkersley Farm
Northwood Carr
Bumper Castle
Wayne Piece
Black Hill
Wayne Corner Plantation
Sitch Plantation
Northwood
Burley Fields Farm
Halldale Wood
Hall Dale
Woodside Farm
Newtonlot Plantation
Stancliffe Hall Sch
Stancliffe Quarries
Playing Field
Peak Railway
Darley Hillside
Hallmoor Wood
Cock's Head Wood
Abbey Farm
Hazel Farm
Potter Dam
Fancy Dam
Darley Churchtown CE Prim Sch
Churchtown
Rectory Farm
Two Dales
Holt Farm
Darley Dale Sta
Darley Dale
Darley Dale Prim Sch
River Derwent
Holt Wood
St Elphins Sch
Works
Bridge Farm
Flatts Farm
DALE RD N
DALE RD S
CHESTERFIELD RD
STATION RD
SYDNOPE HILL
BENT LA
LIME TREE AVE
Halldale Brook
Warney Brook
1 PEVERIL CL
2 ARKWRIGHT CL
3 OLD HALL CL
4 NEWELL WAY
5 JOHN TURNER RD
6 BOWLER RD
ST HELEN'S CL 1
CROWSTONES RD 2
OKER DR 3
B5057
A6
PO
LC
4
3
2
1
65
64
63
62
26
27
28

142
128

127
112

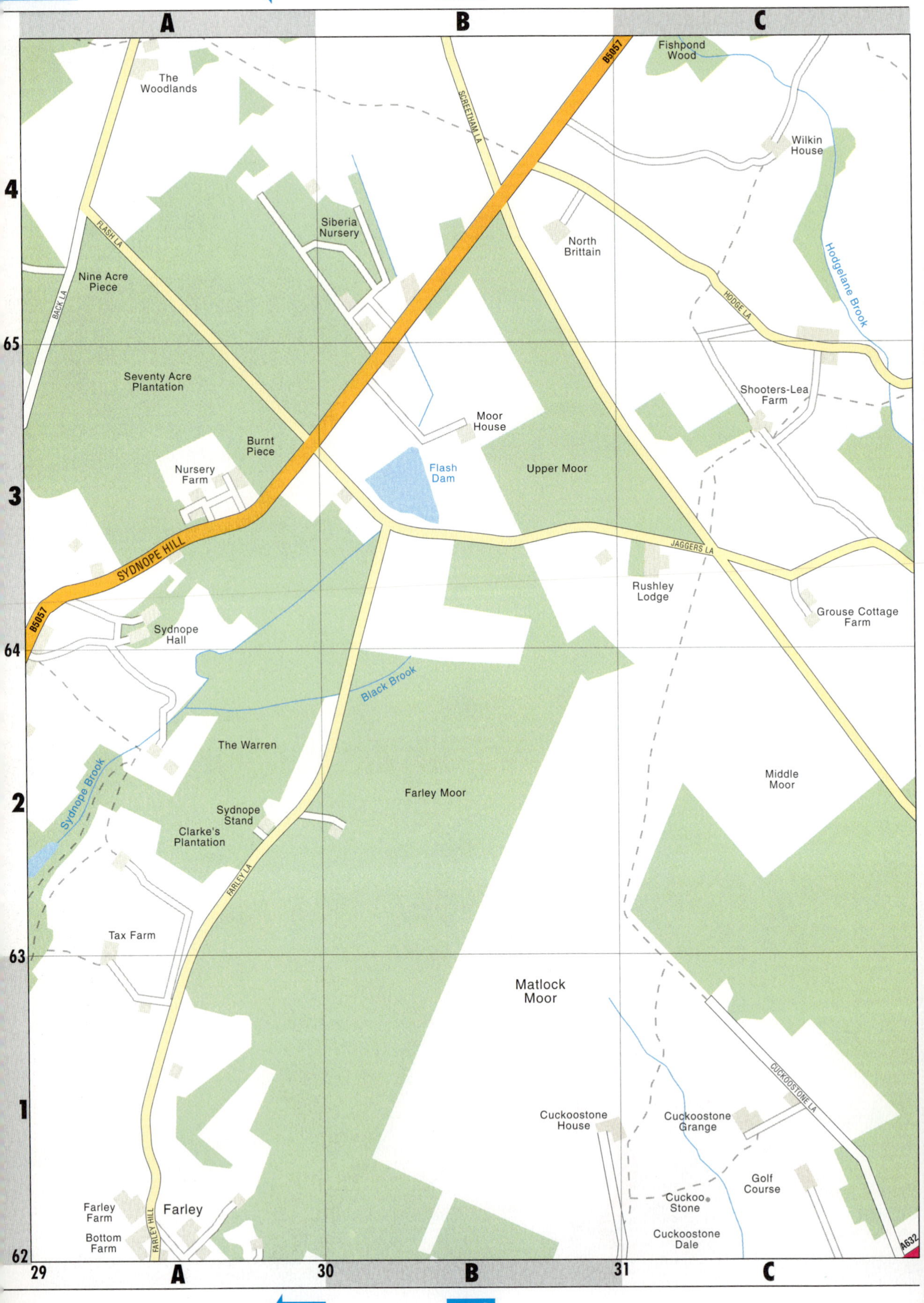
A
B
C
The Woodlands
Fishpond Wood
B5057
SCREETHAM LA
Wilkin House
4
FLASH LA
Siberia Nursery
North Brittain
Hodgelane Brook
Nine Acre Piece
BACK LA
HODGE LA
65
Seventy Acre Plantation
Moor House
Shooters-Lea Farm
Burnt Piece
Nursery Farm
Flash Dam
Upper Moor
3
JAGGERS LA
SYDNOPE HILL
Rushley Lodge
Grouse Cottage Farm
B5057
Sydnope Hall
64
Black Brook
The Warren
Middle Moor
Sydnope Brook
Farley Moor
2
Sydnope Stand
Clarke's Plantation
FARLEY LA
Tax Farm
63
Matlock Moor
CUCKOOSTONE LA
1
Cuckoostone House
Cuckoostone Grange
Golf Course
Cuckoo Stone
Farley Farm
Farley
Bottom Farm
FARLEY HILL
Cuckoostone Dale
A632
62
29
A
30
B
31
C

127
143

113

130

D E F

Alicehead Farm
Spancarr
Highashes Farm
Alicehead
Bunting Field
Alicehead Road Farm
ALICEHEAD RD
A632
HIGHASHES LA
Dryhurst Farm
SHEEPLEA LA
CULLUMBELL LA
4
Spancarr Farm
New Farm
BUNTINGFIELD LA
SWINGER LA
BIRKIN LA
Sheeplea House Farm
Thorntree Farm
Uppertown
LONG LA
Bath Lane Farm
65
HODGE LA
Well Six Farm
HARDWICK LA
Smalley Brook
Hardwick Farm
BATH LA
MATLOCK RD
Hall Moor Farm
BROCKHURST LA
Hardwick
Overend
Brockhurst
Whitefield Farm
Prestedge Farm
3
WHITEFIELD LA
OAKS LA
Peglant
Brockhurst Farm
Bath House Farm
Yew Tree Farm
JAGGERS LA
Henstone Cottage
Robridding
Hodgelane Brook
KELSTEDGE LA
CRIPTON LA
HILLTOP RD
64
Kelstedge Farm
PH
THE CAUSEWAY
ROBRIDDING RD
HILL RD
CHAPEL HILL
Vernonlane Farm
Marsh Brook
MARSH GREEN LA
B6036
WEST EDGE CL
Kelstedge
HILLSIDE
Marsh Green
Amber House
ASHOVER RD
PUDDING BAG LA
Quarry (dis)
Rattle
2
Ashover
AMBER LA
MOOR RD
MALTHOUSE LA
Wire Stone
West Edge
NARROWLEYS LA
Amberlane Farm
Ashover Prim Sch
PO
Amber Hill Cottage
YEW TREE CL
Eddlestow Hall Farm
P
DOVECOTES
Eddlestow Lot
Butts
River Amber
CHURCH ST
BUTTS RD
B6036
63
Bottom Moor
Quarry (dis)
Amber Hill Farm
Goss Hall
PH
HOCKLEY LA
Mill (dis)
Hollow Lane
Slack
Salter Lane
SLACK LA
Sycamore Farm
Greenend
Quarry (dis)
Back Lane
1
Top Slack Farm
HOLESTONE GATE RD
Amber Hill
Overton Cotts
Overton Hall
Lantlodge Wood
LANT LA
CHESTERFIELD RD A632
GIN LA
62

32 D 33 E 34 F

144
130

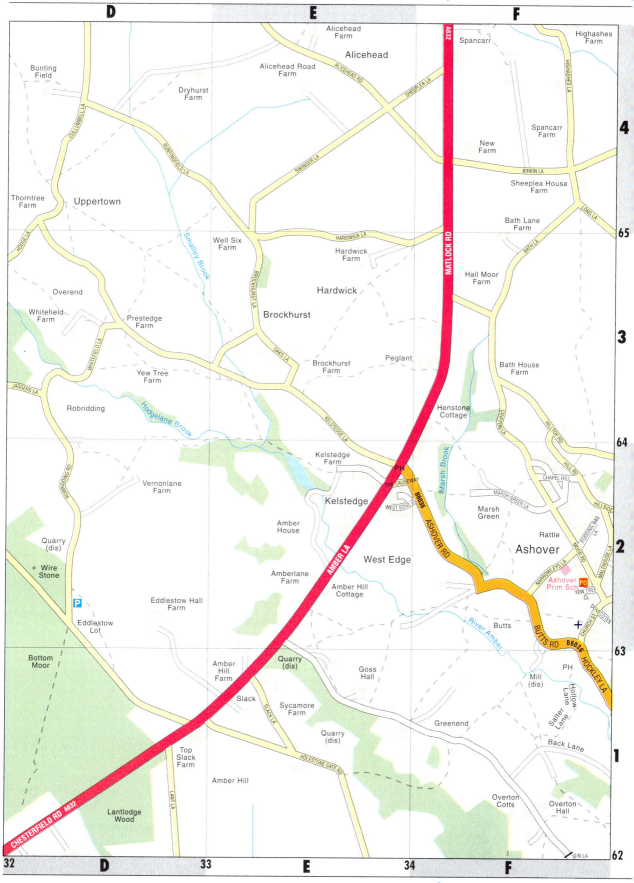

129
114

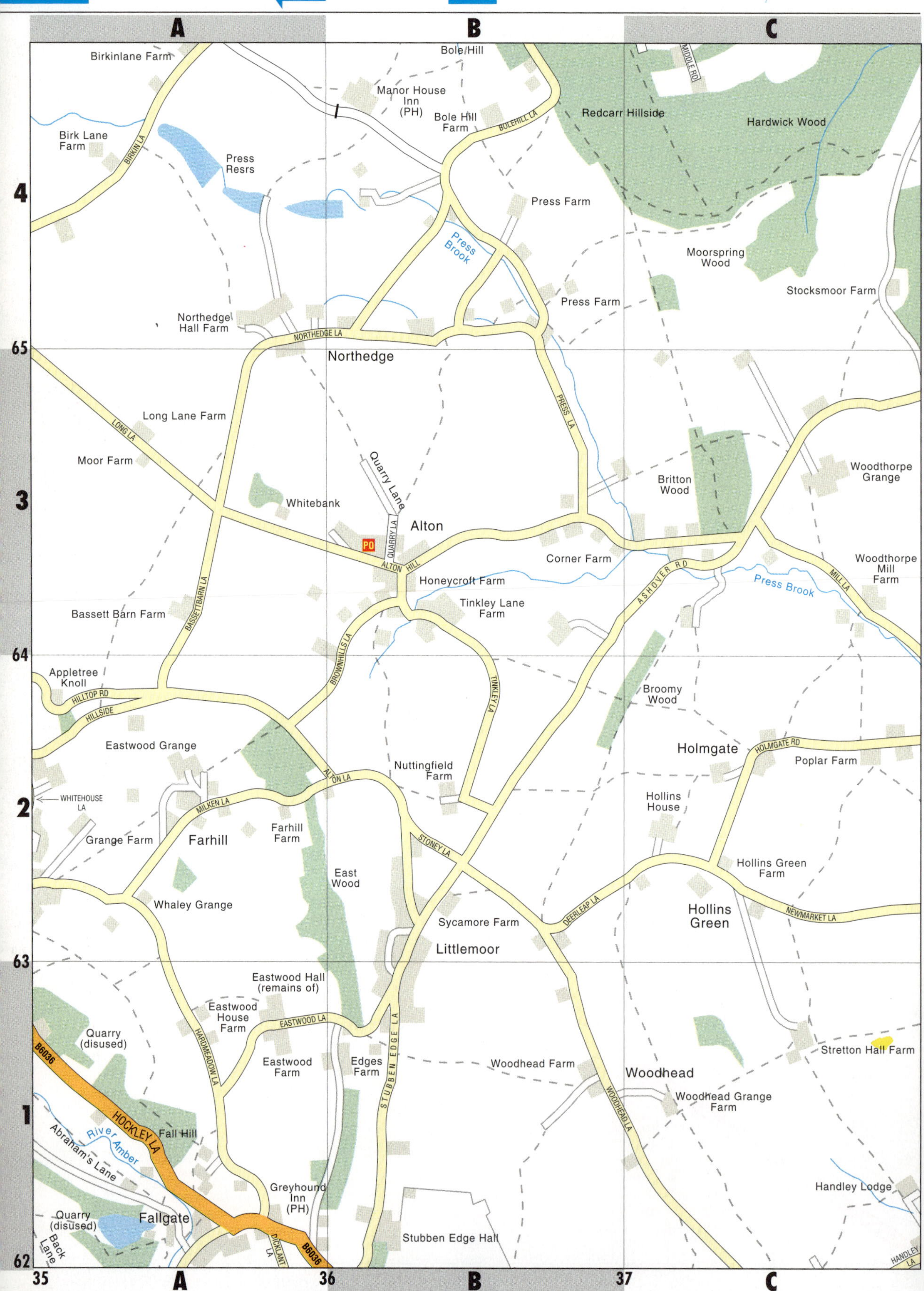
A
B
C
4
3
2
1
65
64
63
62
35
36
37
Birkinlane Farm
Bole Hill
Manor House Inn (PH)
Bole Hill Farm
BOLEHILL LA
Redcarr Hillside
Hardwick Wood
MIDDLE RD
Birk Lane Farm
BIRKIN LA
Press Resrs
Press Farm
Press Brook
Moorspring Wood
Stocksmoor Farm
Northedge Hall Farm
NORTHEDGE LA
Press Farm
Northedge
Long Lane Farm
LONG LA
PRESS LA
Moor Farm
Quarry Lane
Britton Wood
Woodthorpe Grange
Whitebank
Alton
QUARRY LA
PO
ALTON HILL
Corner Farm
ASHOVER RD
Woodthorpe Mill Farm
Honeycroft Farm
Press Brook
MILL LA
Tinkley Lane Farm
Bassett Barn Farm
BASSETTBARN LA
BROWNHILLS LA
TINKLEY LA
Appletree Knoll
HILLTOP RD
HILLSIDE
Broomy Wood
Eastwood Grange
Holmgate
HOLMGATE RD
Poplar Farm
Nuttingfield Farm
ALTON LA
WHITEHOUSE LA
MILKEN LA
Hollins House
Grange Farm
Farhill
Farhill Farm
STONEY LA
East Wood
Hollins Green Farm
Whaley Grange
DEERLEAP LA
Hollins Green
NEWMARKET LA
Sycamore Farm
Littlemoor
Eastwood Hall (remains of)
Eastwood House Farm
EASTWOOD LA
HARDMEADOW LA
Quarry (disused)
B6036
Eastwood Farm
Edges Farm
STUBBEN EDGE LA
Woodhead Farm
Woodhead
Stretton Hall Farm
Woodhead Grange Farm
WOODHEAD LA
HOCKLEY LA
Fall Hill
River Amber
Abraham's Lane
Greyhound Inn (PH)
Handley Lodge
Quarry (disused)
Fallgate
Back Lane
DICKLANT LA
B6036
Stubben Edge Hall
HANDLEY LA

129
145

D E F

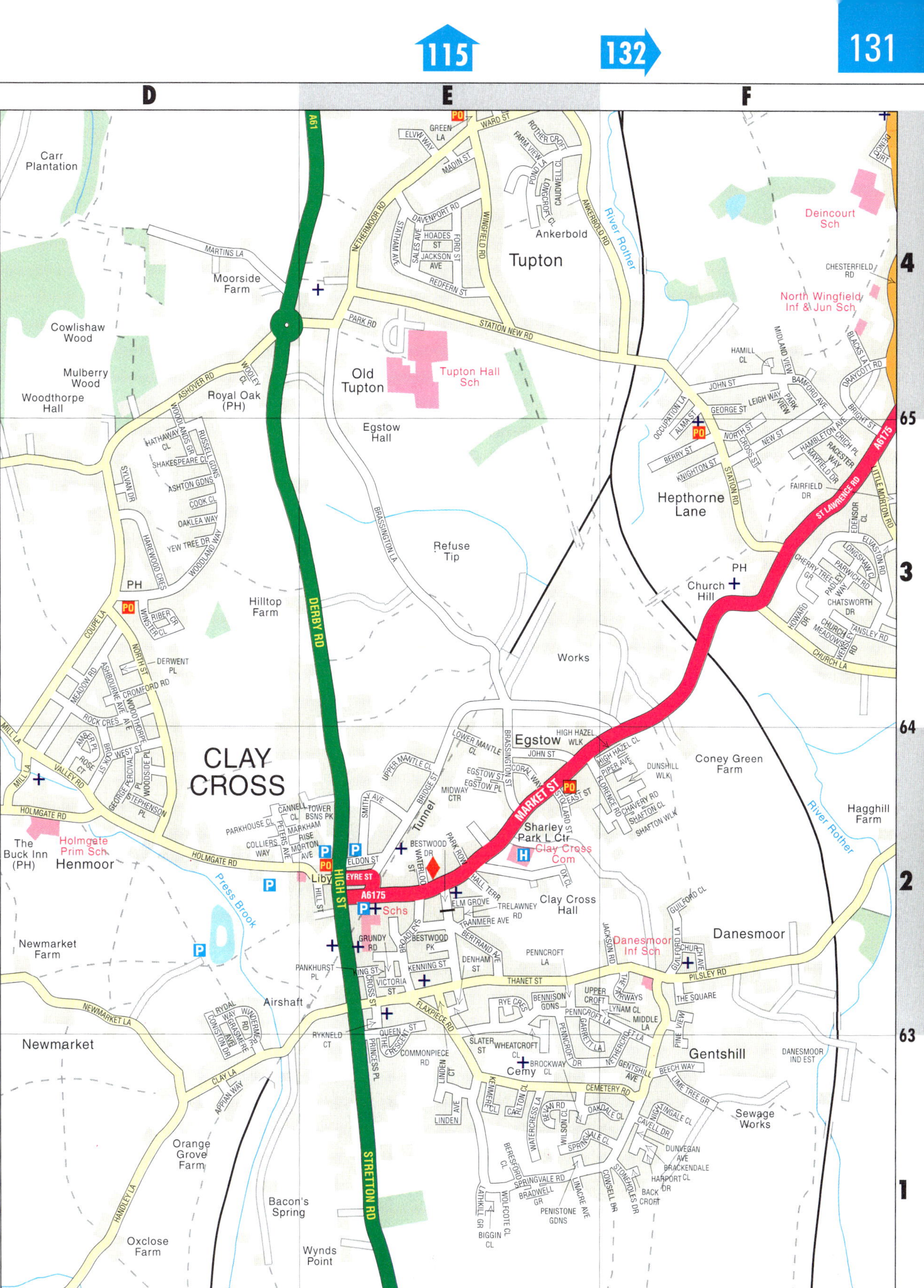
Carr Plantation
Moorside Farm
Cowlishaw Wood
Mulberry Wood
Woodthorpe Hall
Royal Oak (PH)
Old Tupton
Tupton Hall Sch
Egstow Hall
Tupton
Ankerbold
River Rother
Deincourt Sch
North Wingfield Inf & Jun Sch
Hepthorne Lane
Refuse Tip
Church Hill
Hilltop Farm
Works
CLAY CROSS
Egstow
Coney Green Farm
Hagghill Farm
Sharley Park L Ctr
Clay Cross Com
Clay Cross Hall
Danesmoor
Danesmoor Inf Sch
Holmgate Prim Sch
The Buck Inn (PH)
Henmoor
Press Brook
Newmarket Farm
Airshaft
Newmarket
Gentshill
Cemy
Sewage Works
Orange Grove Farm
Bacon's Spring
Wynds Point
Oxclose Farm
DERBY RD
HIGH ST
STRETTON RD
MARKET ST
ST LAWRENCE RD
STATION NEW RD
HOLMGATE RD
THANET ST
PILSLEY RD
NEWMARKET LA
CLAY LA
HANDLEY LA
A61
A6175
4
3
2
1
65
64
63
62
38
39
40

D E F

131
116

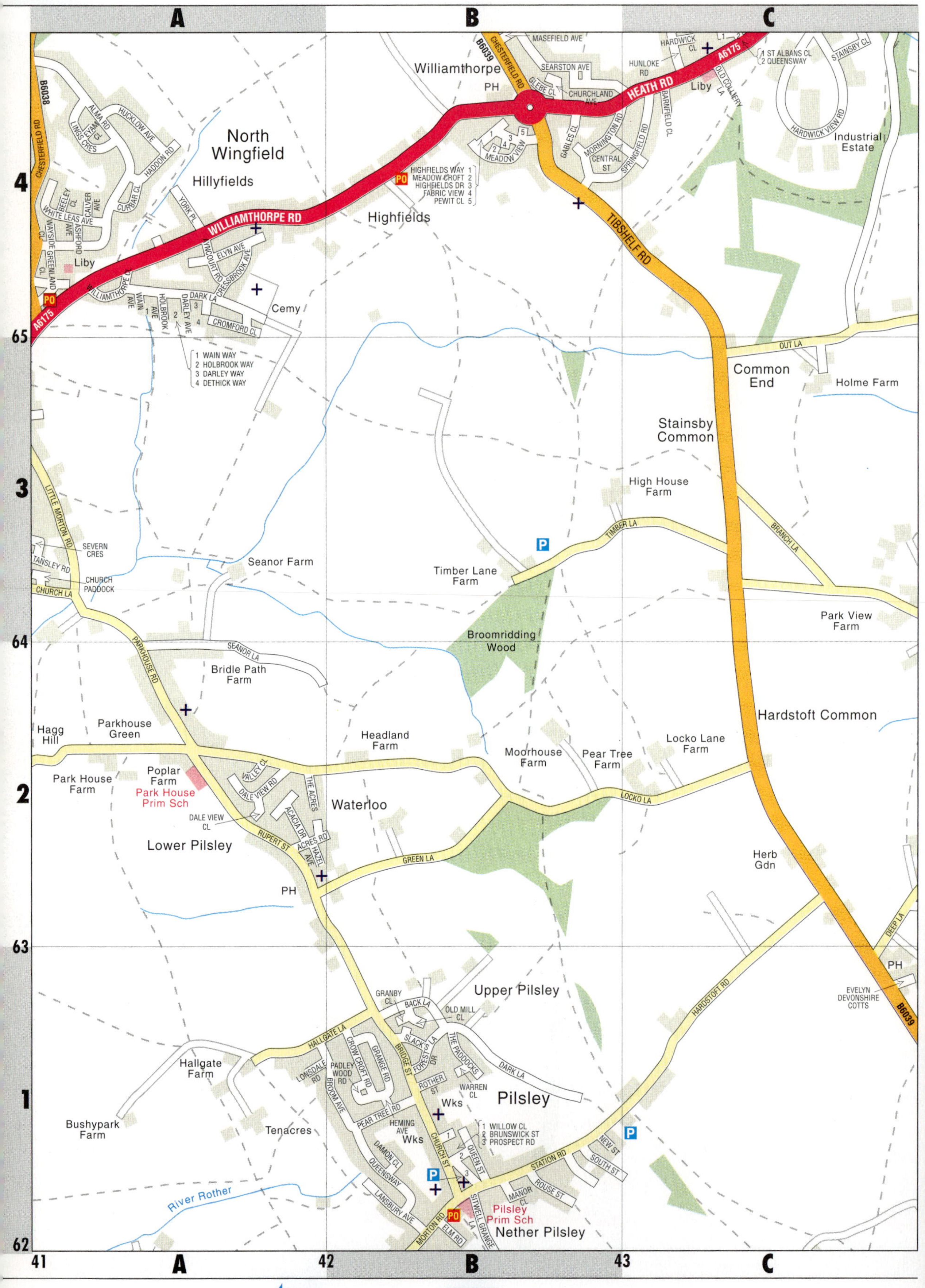
A
B
C
4
3
2
1
65
64
63
62
41
42
43
North Wingfield
Hillyfields
Williamthorpe
Highfields
Liby
Cemy
WILLIAMTHORPE RD
HEATH RD
A6175
B6038
B6039
CHESTERFIELD RD
TIBSHELF RD
Industrial Estate
Common End
Holme Farm
Stainsby Common
High House Farm
Timber Lane Farm
TIMBER LA
BRANCH LA
Park View Farm
Seanor Farm
Broomridding Wood
SEANOR LA
Bridle Path Farm
Hagg Hill
Parkhouse Green
Headland Farm
Moorhouse Farm
Pear Tree Farm
Locko Lane Farm
Hardstoft Common
Park House Farm
Poplar Farm
Park House Prim Sch
Waterloo
LOCKO LA
GREEN LA
Lower Pilsley
Herb Gdn
PH
Upper Pilsley
HARDSTOFT RD
DEEP LA
EVELYN DEVONSHIRE COTTS
Hallgate Farm
Pilsley
Bushypark Farm
Tenacres
Wks
River Rother
Pilsley Prim Sch
Nether Pilsley
STATION RD
1 WAIN WAY
2 HOLBROOK WAY
3 DARLEY WAY
4 DETHICK WAY
1 HIGHFIELDS WAY
2 MEADOW CROFT
3 HIGHFIELDS DR
4 FABRIC VIEW
5 PEWIT CL
1 ST ALBANS CL
2 QUEENSWAY
1 WILLOW CL
2 BRUNSWICK ST
3 PROSPECT RD

131
147

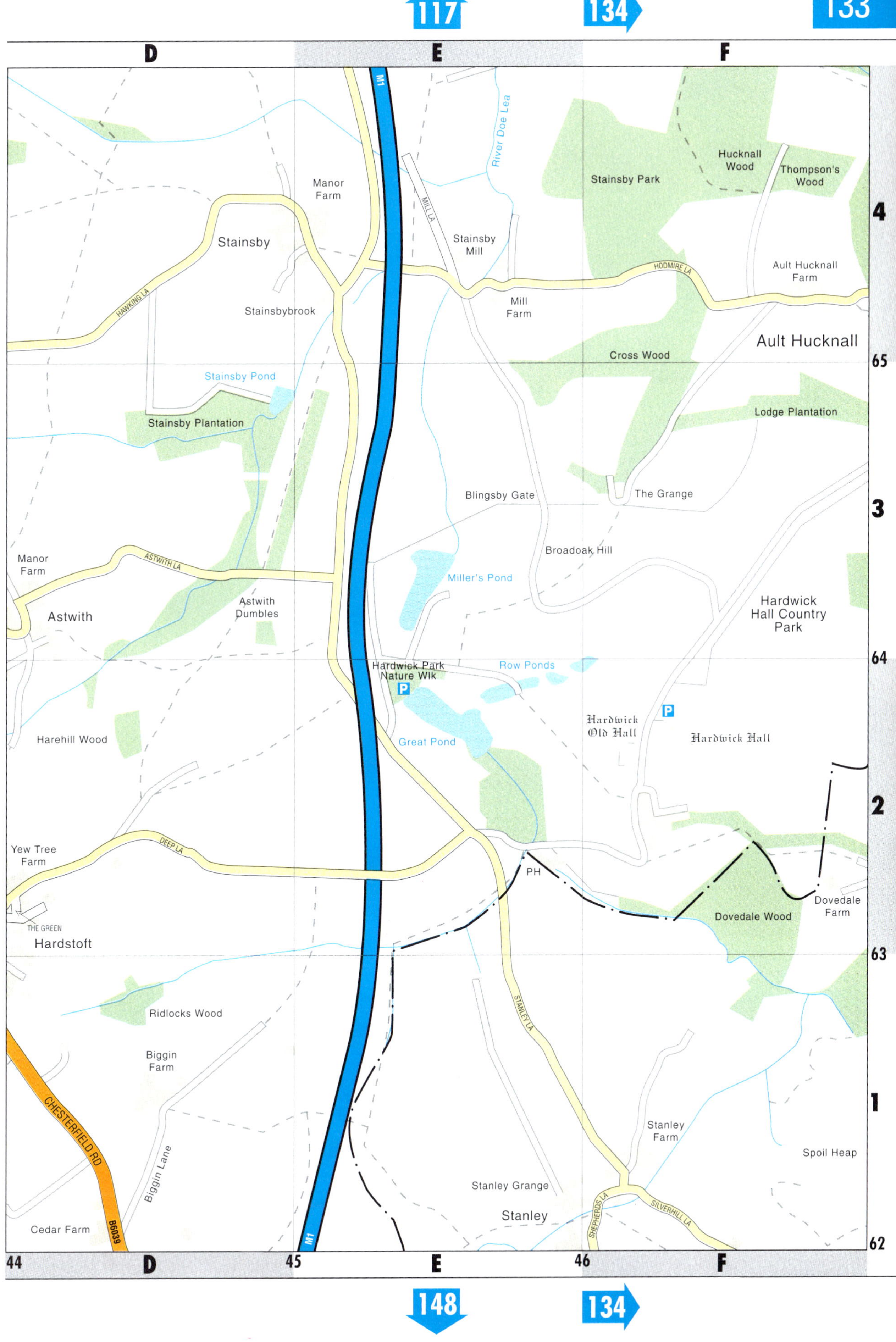
D
E
F
M1
Manor Farm
Stainsby
HAWKING LA
Stainsbybrook
River Doe Lea
MILL LA
Stainsby Mill
Mill Farm
HODMIRE LA
Stainsby Park
Hucknall Wood
Thompson's Wood
Ault Hucknall Farm
Ault Hucknall
Cross Wood
Lodge Plantation
Stainsby Pond
Stainsby Plantation
Blingsby Gate
The Grange
Broadoak Hill
Manor Farm
ASTWITH LA
Astwith
Astwith Dumbles
Miller's Pond
Hardwick Hall Country Park
Hardwick Park Nature Wlk
Row Ponds
Harehill Wood
Great Pond
Hardwick Old Hall
Hardwick Hall
Yew Tree Farm
DEEP LA
PH
Dovedale Farm
Dovedale Wood
THE GREEN
Hardstoft
Ridlocks Wood
STANLEY LA
Biggin Farm
CHESTERFIELD RD
Stanley Farm
Spoil Heap
Biggin Lane
Stanley Grange
Stanley
SHEPHERDS LA
SILVERHILL LA
Cedar Farm
B6039
4
65
3
64
2
63
1
62
44
45
46

Strickle Brook

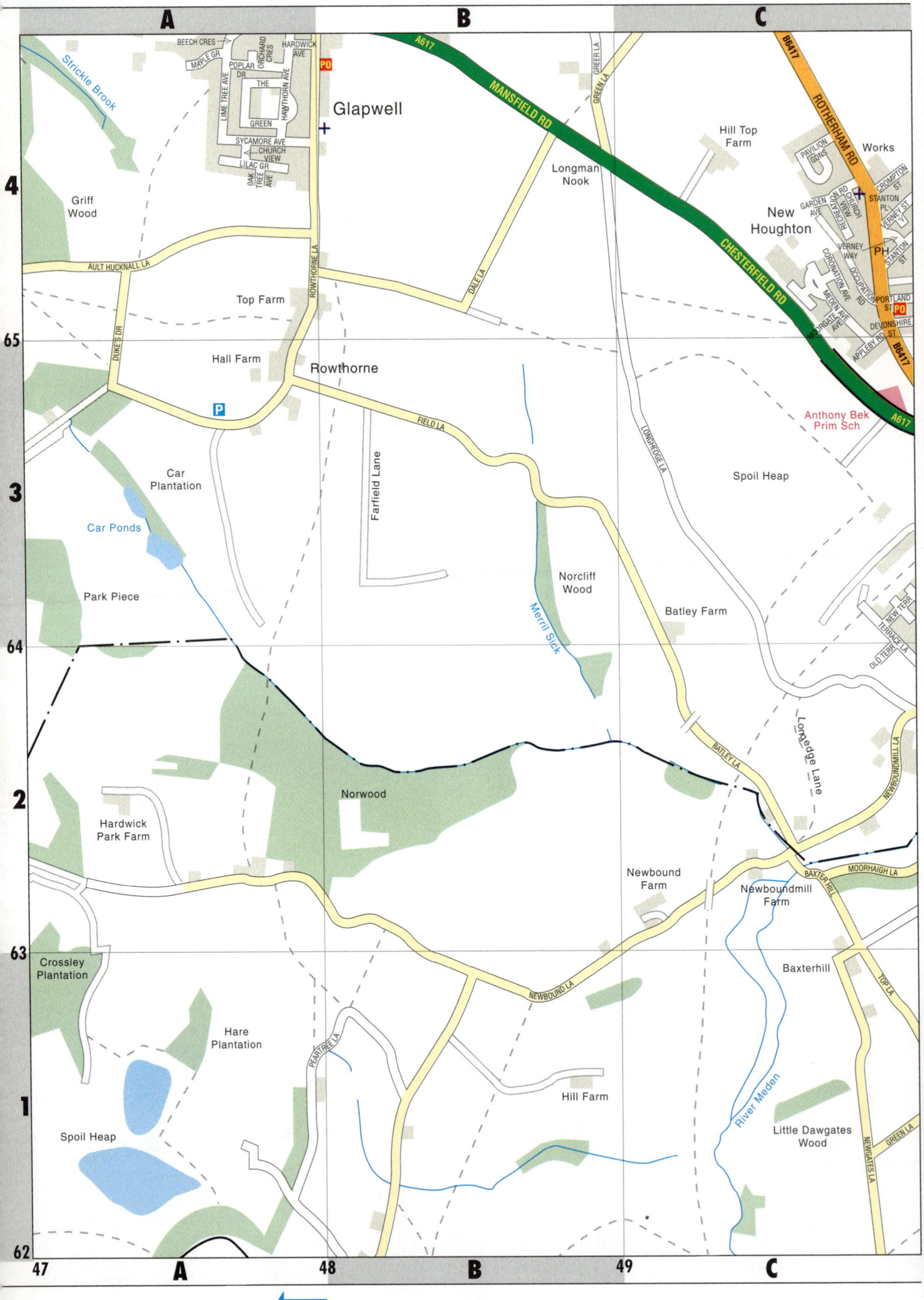

BEECH CRES
MAPLE GR
ORCHARD CRES
HARDWICK AVE
POPLAR DR
LIME TREE AVE
HAWTHORN AVE
THE GREEN
SYCAMORE AVE
CHURCH VIEW
LILAC GR
OAK TREE AVE
PO

Glapwell

A617
MANSFIELD RD

GREEN LA
GREER LA

Hill Top Farm

B6417
ROTHERHAM RD

Works

PAVILION GDNS

CROMPTON ST
STANTON PL
STANTON ST
VERNEY ST

New Houghton

Longman Nook

GARDEN AVE
CHURCH RD
ON RD
CLUMBER ST

CHESTERFIELD RD

VERNEY WAY
CORONATION AVE
OCCUPATION RD
STANTON ST

PH

MEDEN AVE
PORTGATE AVE
PORTLAND ST
PO
DEVONSHIRE ST
APPLEBY RD
B6417

Griff Wood

AULT HUCKNALL LA

4

Top Farm

ROWTHORNE LA

DALE LA

65

Hall Farm

Rowthorne

DUKE'S DR

A617

Anthony Bek Prim Sch

P

FIELD LA

Car Plantation

Farfield Lane

LONGRIDGE LA

Spoil Heap

3

Car Ponds

Merril Sick

Norcliff Wood

Batley Farm

NEW TERR

Park Piece

64

TERRACE LA
OLD TERR LA

Norwood

Hardwick Park Farm

BATLEY LA

Longedge Lane

NEWBOUNDMILL LA

2

Newbound Farm

MOORHAIGH LA

BAXTER HILL

Newboundmill Farm

63

Crossley Plantation

NEWBOUND LA

Baxterhill

TOP LA

Hare Plantation

PEARTREE LA

River Meden

Little Dawgates Wood

1

Spoil Heap

Hill Farm

GREEN LA
NEWGATES LA

62

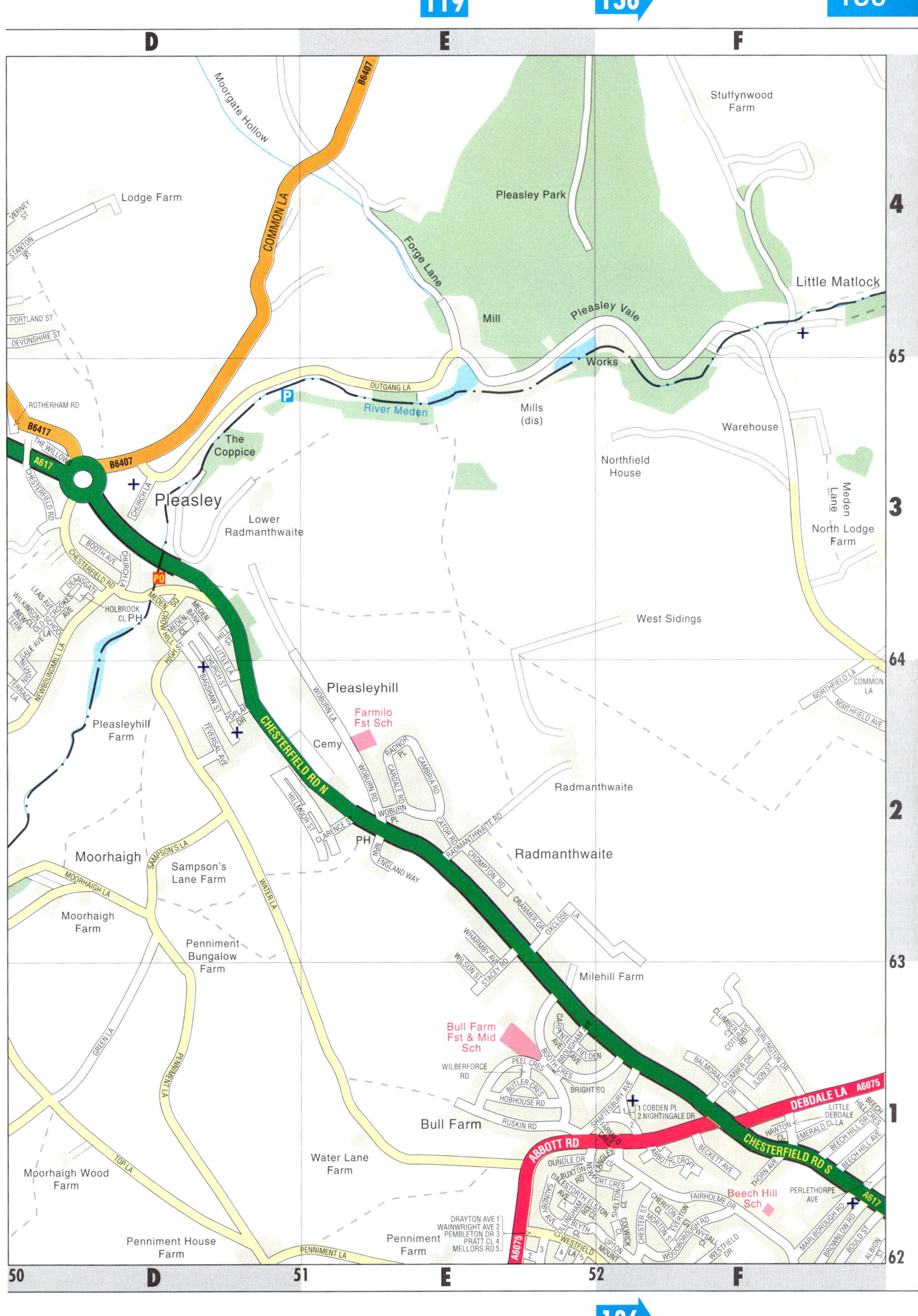
D
E
F
Stuffynwood Farm
Moorgate Hollow
B6407
Lodge Farm
Pleasley Park
COMMON LA
Forge Lane
Little Matlock
Mill
Pleasley Vale
PORTLAND ST
DEVONSHIRE ST
Works
OUTGANG LA
ROTHERHAM RD
River Meden
Mills (dis)
Warehouse
B6417
The Coppice
Northfield House
A617
B6407
Pleasley
Lower Radmanthwaite
Meden Lane
North Lodge Farm
West Sidings
Pleasleyhill
Farmilo Fst Sch
Pleasleyhill Farm
Cemy
CHESTERFIELD RD N
Radmanthwaite
Moorhaigh
Sampson's Lane Farm
Radmanthwaite
Moorhaigh Farm
Penniment Bungalow Farm
Milehill Farm
Bull Farm Fst & Mid Sch
Bull Farm
DEBDALE LA
A6075
ABBOTT RD
CHESTERFIELD RD S
Water Lane Farm
Moorhaigh Wood Farm
Beech Hill Sch
Penniment Farm
Penniment House Farm
PENNIMENT LA
4
65
3
64
2
63
1
62
50
51
52

135
120

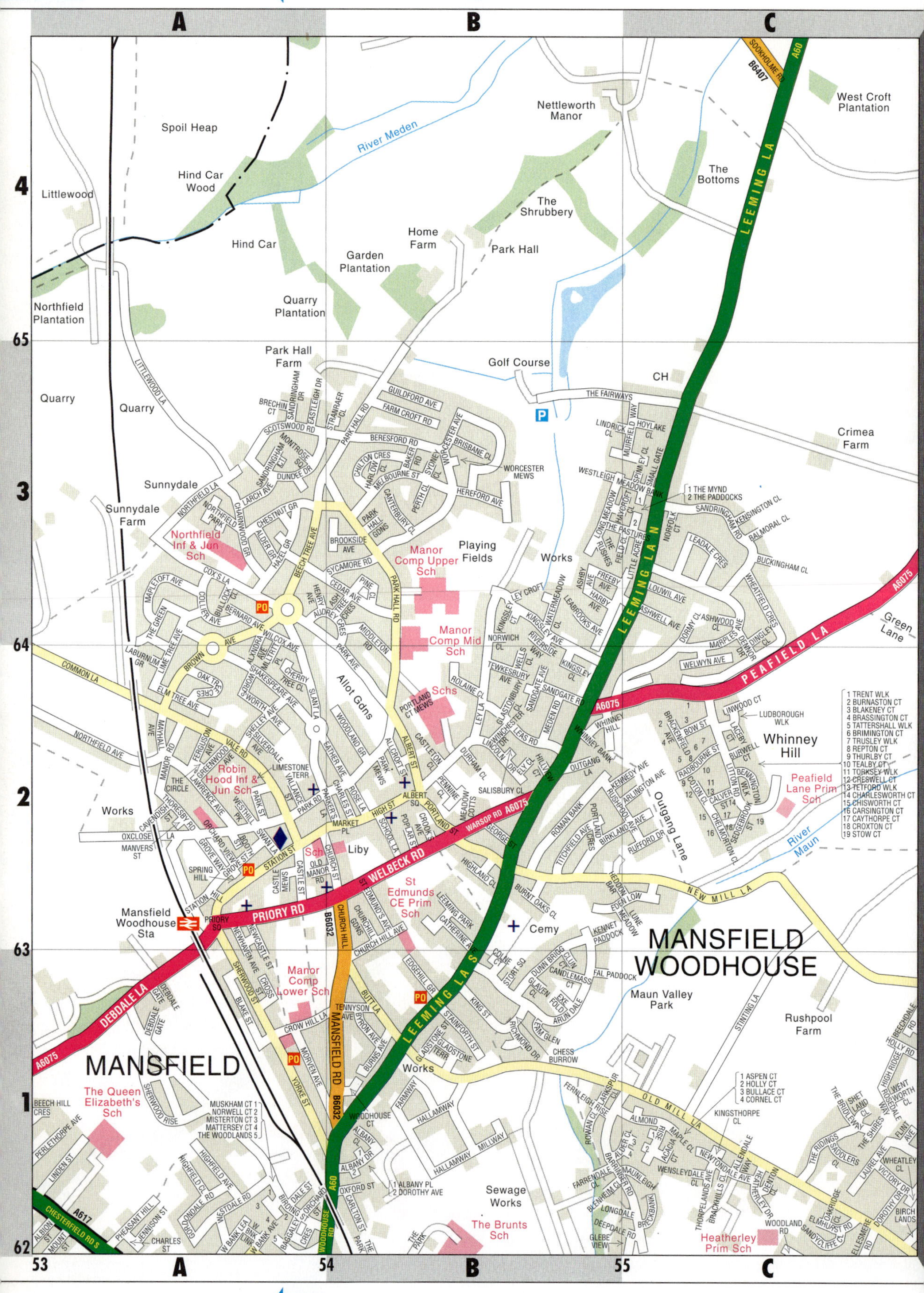
A
B
C
4
3
2
1
65
64
63
62
53
54
55
Spoil Heap
Hind Car Wood
Littlewood
Hind Car
River Meden
Garden Plantation
Home Farm
Park Hall
Nettleworth Manor
The Shrubbery
The Bottoms
West Croft Plantation
Northfield Plantation
Quarry Plantation
Park Hall Farm
Golf Course
CH
Quarry
Quarry
Crimea Farm
Sunnydale
Sunnydale Farm
LEEMING LA
A60
B6407
SOOKHOLME RD
THE FAIRWAYS
GUILDFORD AVE
FARM CROFT RD
BERESFORD RD
BRISBANE CL
WORCESTER AVE
WORCESTER MEWS
HEREFORD AVE
LINDRICK CL
HOYLAKE CL
MUIRFIELD WAY
WESTLEIGH
SMALL GATE
SPINNEY CL
1 THE MYND
2 THE PADDOCKS
SANDRINGHAM RD
KENSINGTON CL
BALMORAL CL
LEADALE CRES
BUCKINGHAM CL
NORFOLK CT
THE PASTURES
LITTLE ACRES
LONG MEADOW
Northfield Inf & Jun Sch
Manor Comp Upper Sch
Playing Fields
Works
Manor Comp Mid Sch
Schs
Allot Gdns
PORTLAND CT MEWS
COMMON LA
NORTHFIELD AVE
BEECH TREE AVE
PARK HALL RD
SCOTSWOOD RD
SANDRINGHAM DR
EASTLEIGH DR
STRANRAER CL
MONTROSE SQ
DUNDEE DR
CHESTNUT GR
LARCH AVE
CHARNWOOD GR
BROOKSIDE AVE
SYCAMORE RD
PINE CL
CEDAR AVE
MIDDLETON RD
PARK AVE
COX'S LA
MAPLEOFT AVE
BERNARD AVE
WILCOX AVE
BROWN AVE
LABURNUM GR
LIME TREE AVE
ELM TREE AVE
OAK TREE CRES
SHAKESPEARE AVE
SHELLEY AVE
SILVERDALE
SLANT LA
WOODLAND GR
CASTLETON CL
LEY CROFT
KINGSLEY AVE
NORWICH CL
TEWKESBURY AVE
ROLAINE CL
GLASTONBURY CL
SANDGATE AVE
SANDGATE RD
MEDEN RD
LEAS RD
WHINNEY HILL
WHINNEY BANK
LEABROOKS AVE
WATERMEADOW CL
LOUWIL AVE
ASHWELL AVE
ASHWOOD CL
MARPLES AVE
DORMY CL
WELWYN AVE
WHEATFIELD CRES
DINGLEY CL
DENNOR DR
PEAFIELD LA
A6075
Green Lane
LINWOOD CT
LUDBOROUGH WLK
Whinney Hill
1 TRENT WLK
2 BURNASTON CT
3 BLAKENEY CT
4 BRASSINGTON CT
5 TATTERSHALL WLK
6 BRIMINGTON CT
7 TRUSLEY WLK
8 REPTON CT
9 THURLBY CT
10 TEALBY CT
11 TORKSEY WLK
12 CRESWELL CT
13 TETFORD WLK
14 CHARLESWORTH CT
15 CHISWORTH CT
16 CARSINGTON CT
17 CAYTHORPE CT
18 CROXTON CT
19 STOW CT
Peafield Lane Prim Sch
River Maun
BRACKENFIELD AVE
BOW ST
RADBOURNE ST
CHELMORTON CL
SEDGEBROOK CL
KENNEDY AVE
ARLINGTON AVE
Outgang Lane
OUTGANG LA
RUFFORD DR
BIRKLAND AVE
ROMAN BANK
TITCHFIELD AVE
PORTLAND CRES
Works
OXCLOSE LA
MANVERS ST
CAVENDISH RD
THE CIRCLE
LAWRENCE AVE
ORCHARD WAY
GROVE WAY
SPRING HILL
STATION HILL
VALE RD
Robin Hood Inf & Jun Sch
LIMESTONE TERR
PARK RD
ALBERT ST
ALBERT SQ
HIGH ST
MARKET PL
SCHOOL LA
POPLAR ST
PORTLAND ST
WARSOP RD A6075
GEORGE ST
HIGHLAND CL
SALISBURY CL
DURHAM CL
PENNINE CL
MEADOW COTTS
Sch
Liby
STATION ST
WELBECK RD
PRIORY RD
PRIORY SQ
CASTLE ST
CHURCH ST
OLD MANOR RD
St Edmunds CE Prim Sch
CHURCH HILL
B6032
CHURCH HILL AVE
LEEMING PARK
CATHERINE AVE
BURNT OAKS CL
NEW MILL LA
Cemy
HEDDON BAR
EDEN LOW
LUNE MEADOW
KENNET PADDOCK
MANSFIELD WOODHOUSE
Mansfield Woodhouse Sta
DEBDALE LA
DEBDALE GATE
NEWHAVEN AVE
NEWCASTLE ST
SHERWOOD ST
BLAKE ST
Manor Comp Lower Sch
CROW HILL LA
MANSFIELD RD
TENNYSON AVE
BYRON AVE
BUTT LA
EDGEHILL GR
STAINFORTH ST
KING ST
GLADSTONE ST
GLADSTONE TERR
RICHMOND DR
CHESS BURROW
STORT SQ
COLNE CT
CANDLEMASS CT
ARUN DALE
FAL PADDOCK
Maun Valley Park
Rushpool Farm
STINTING LA
MANSFIELD
The Queen Elizabeth's Sch
BEECH HILL CRES
PERLETHORPE AVE
LINDEN ST
SHERWOOD RISE
MUSKHAM CT 1
NORWELL CT 2
MISTERTON CT 3
MATTERSEY CT 4
THE WOODLANDS 5
YORKE ST
MORVEN AVE
Works
WOODHOUSE CT
ALBANY DR
ALBANY CT
1 ALBANY PL
2 DOROTHY AVE
HALLAMWAY
MILLWAY
OXFORD ST
CARLTON ST
WOODHOUSE RD
Sewage Works
The Brunts Sch
FERNLEIGH RISE
LARKSPUR
OLD MILL LA
ALMOND RISE
MAPLE CL
NEWTONDALE AVE
ALLENDALE
KINGSTHORPE CL
1 ASPEN CT
2 HOLLY CT
3 BULLACE CT
4 CORNEL CT
WENSLEYDALE CL
THORPELANDS AVE
HEATHERLEY DR
DENTON CL
FARRENDALE CL
BLENHEIM CL
LONGDALE
DEEPDALE RD
GLEBE VIEW
BRECKBANK
Heatherley Prim Sch
WOODLAND RD
ELMHURST RD
OAKRIDGE CL
SADDLERS CL
THE RIDINGS
THE BRIDLEWAY
HIGH RIDGE
HOLLY RD
BEECHDALE RD
WENTWORTH CL
FLINT AVE
LAUREL AVE
WHEATLEY CL
VICTORY DR
DOROTHY DR
BIRCH LANDS
ELLESMERE RD
HIGHFIELD AVE
HIGHFIELD CL
WESTDALE RD
GOODALE RD
PHEASANT HILL
JENNISON ST
CHARLES ST
CHESTERFIELD RD S
A617
ALBION ST
MOUNT ST
DALE ST
W BANK AVE
BAGGALEY CRES
ORCHARD ST

135

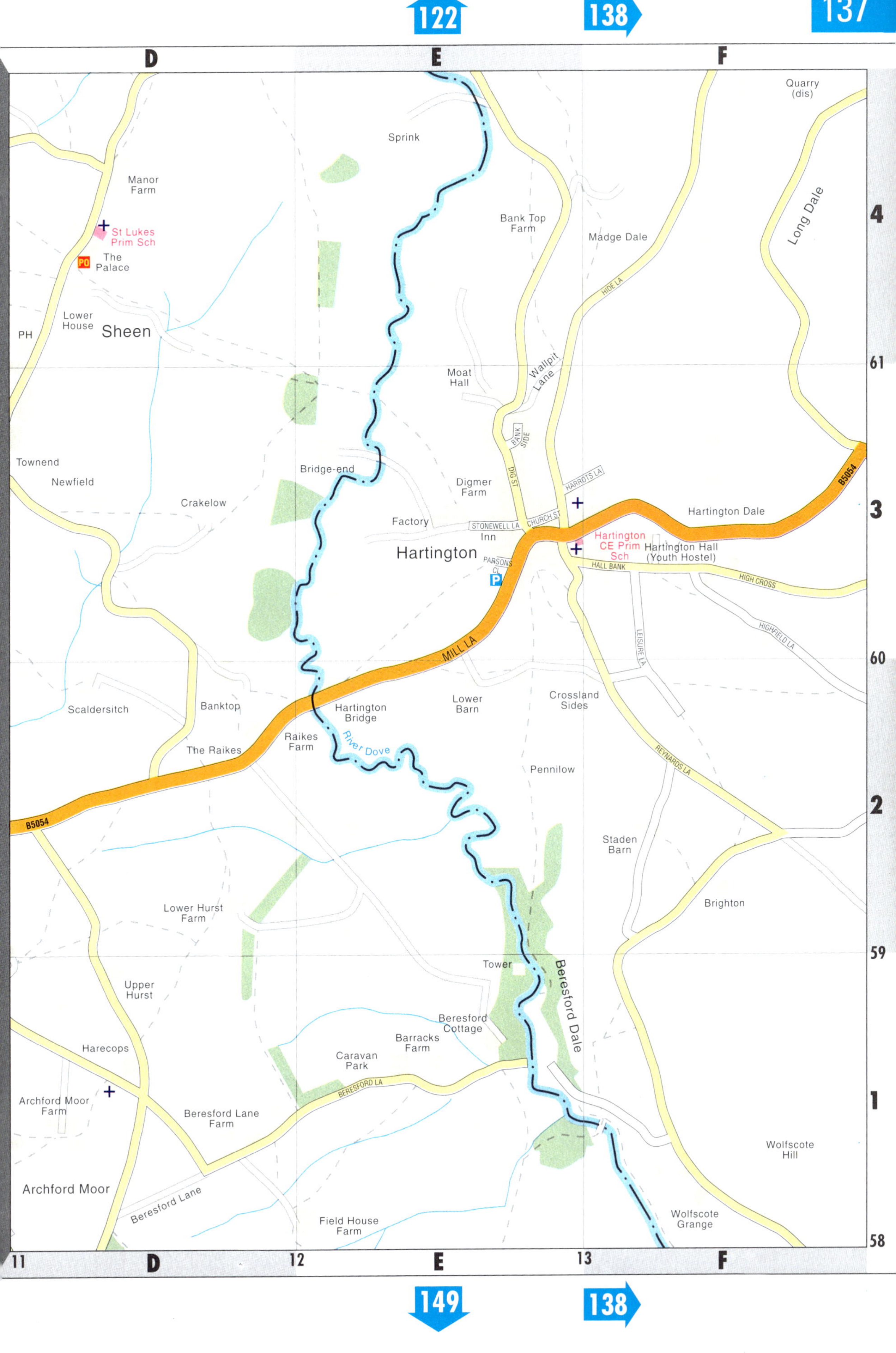

D
E
F

Quarry
(dis)

Sprink

Long Dale

Manor
Farm

4

✝ St Lukes
Prim Sch

Bank Top
Farm

Madge Dale

PO The
Palace

HIDE LA

Lower
House

Sheen

61

PH

Moat
Hall

Wallpit
Lane

BANK SIDE

DIG ST

HARROTS LA

B5054

Townend

Bridge-end

Digmer
Farm

Newfield

Crakelow

Factory

STONEWELL LA

CHURCH ST

✝

Hartington Dale

3

Hartington
CE Prim
Sch

Hartington Hall
(Youth Hostel)

Inn

Hartington

✝

PARSONS
CL

HALL BANK

HIGH CROSS

P

HIGHFIELD LA

Scaldersitch

Banktop

Lower
Barn

Crossland
Sides

LEISURE LA

60

Hartington
Bridge

The Raikes

Raikes
Farm

River Dove

Pennilow

REYNARDS LA

B5054

Staden
Barn

2

Lower Hurst
Farm

Brighton

59

Tower

Upper
Hurst

Beresford Dale

Harecops

Beresford
Cottage

Barracks
Farm

✝

Archford Moor
Farm

Caravan
Park

1

Beresford Lane
Farm

BERESFORD LA

Wolfscote
Hill

Archford Moor

Beresford Lane

Field House
Farm

Wolfscote
Grange

58

11
D
12
E
13
F

137
123

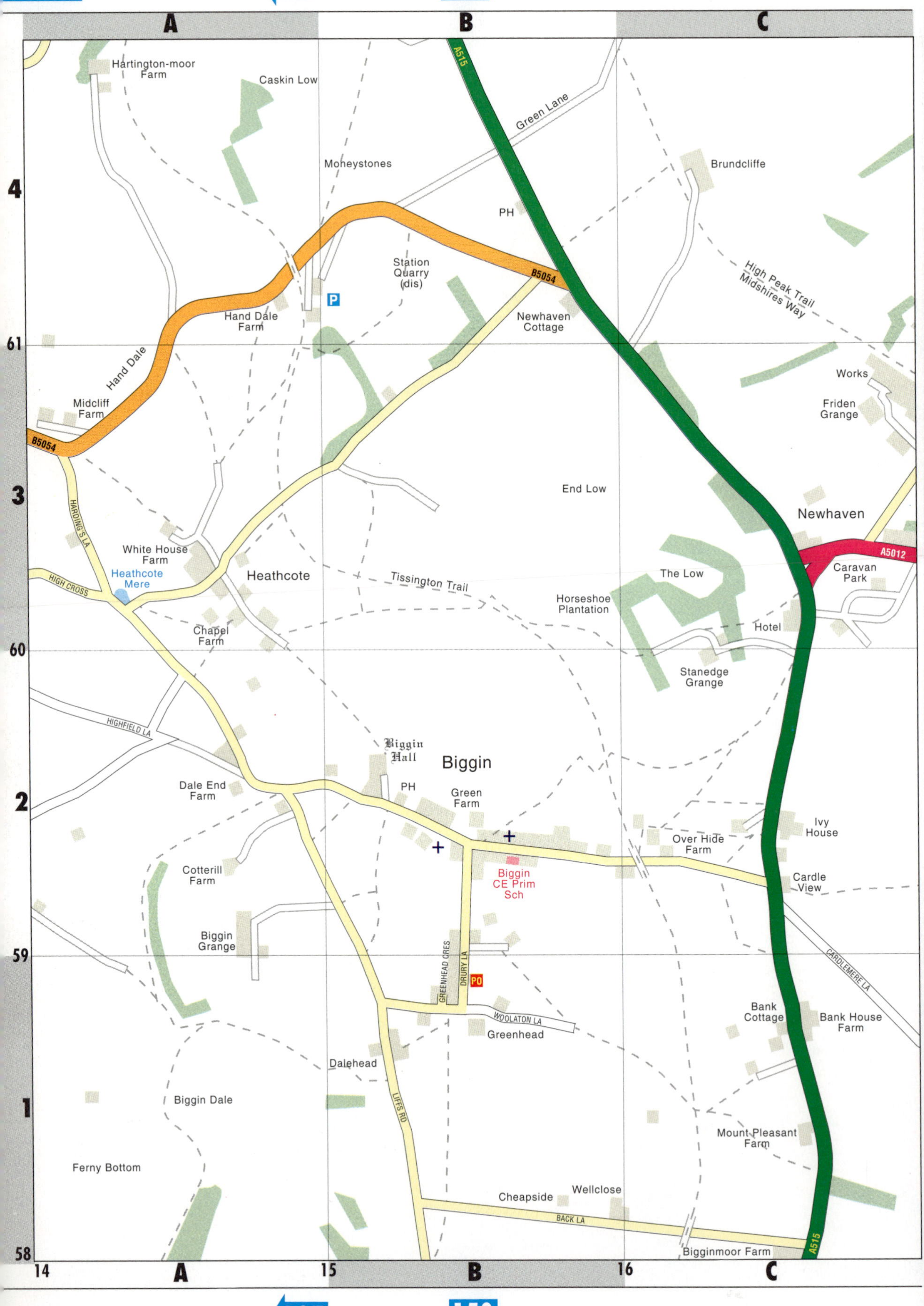
A
B
C
Hartington-moor Farm
Caskin Low
Green Lane
A515
Moneystones
Brundcliffe
PH
Station Quarry (dis)
B5054
High Peak Trail
Midshires Way
Hand Dale Farm
Newhaven Cottage
Hand Dale
Works
Midcliff Farm
Friden Grange
B5054
End Low
HARDING'S LA
Newhaven
White House Farm
A5012
Heathcote Mere
Heathcote
Tissington Trail
The Low
Caravan Park
HIGH CROSS
Horseshoe Plantation
Chapel Farm
Hotel
Stanedge Grange
HIGHFIELD LA
Biggin Hall
Biggin
Dale End Farm
PH
Green Farm
Ivy House
Over Hide Farm
Cotterill Farm
Biggin CE Prim Sch
Cardle View
Biggin Grange
CARDLEMERE LA
GREENHEAD CRES
DRURY LA
PO
WOOLATON LA
Greenhead
Bank Cottage
Bank House Farm
Dalehead
LIFFS RD
Biggin Dale
Mount Pleasant Farm
Ferny Bottom
Cheapside
Wellclose
BACK LA
Bigginmoor Farm
A515
4
61
3
60
2
59
1
58
14
15
16

137
150

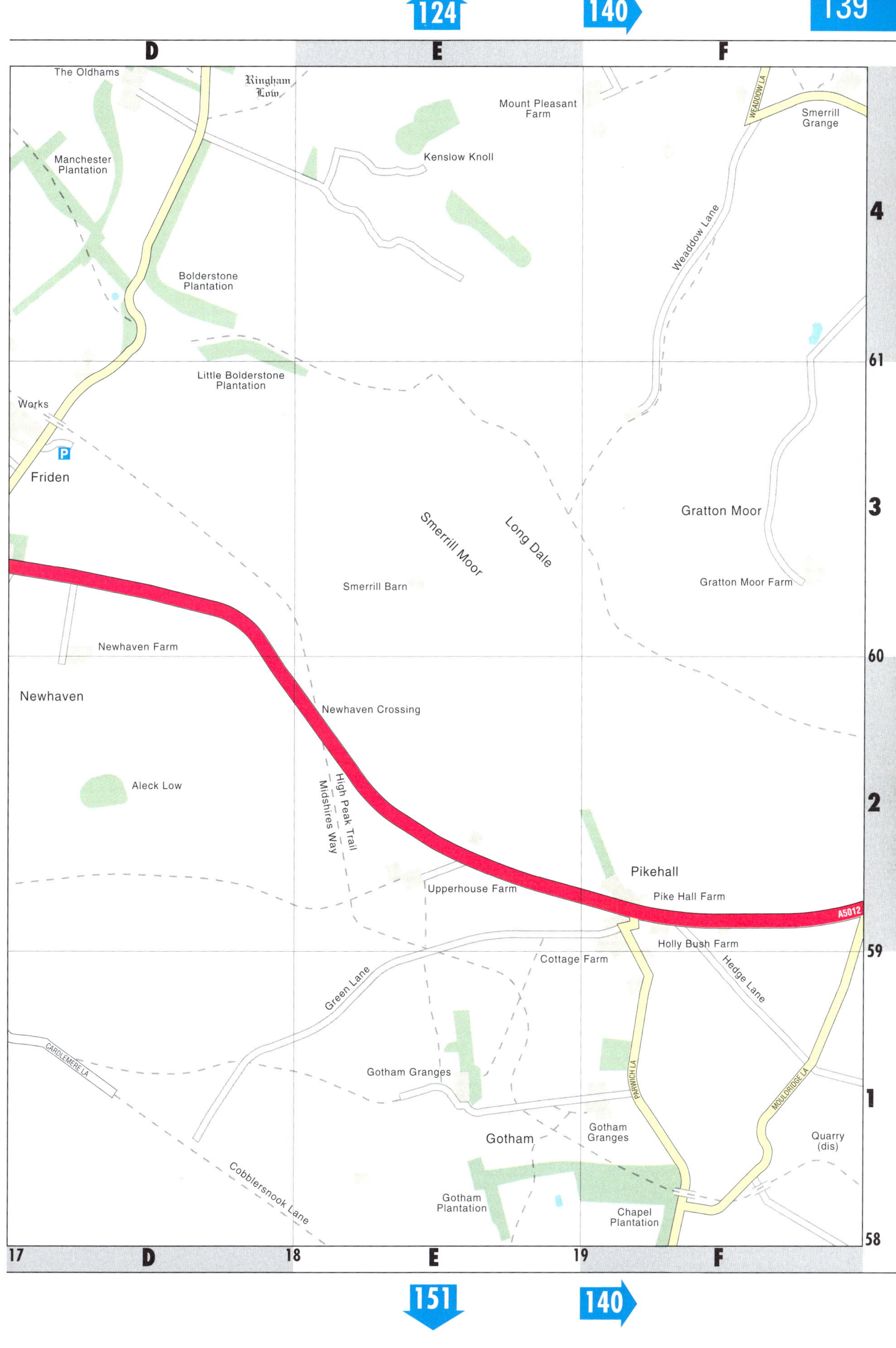

The Oldhams
Ringham Low

Manchester
Plantation

Bolderstone
Plantation

Mount Pleasant
Farm

Kenslow Knoll

Smerrill
Grange

Weaddow Lane

4

Little Bolderstone
Plantation

Works

Friden

P

61

Smerrill Moor

Long Dale

Gratton Moor

3

Smerrill Barn

Gratton Moor Farm

Newhaven Farm

60

Newhaven

Newhaven Crossing

Aleck Low

High Peak Trail
Midshires Way

2

Pikehall

Upperhouse Farm

Pike Hall Farm

A5012

Holly Bush Farm

59

Cottage Farm

Green Lane

Hedge Lane

CARDLEMERE LA

Gotham Granges

PARWICH LA

MOULDRIDGE LA

1

Gotham
Granges

Quarry
(dis)

Gotham

Cobblersnook Lane

Gotham
Plantation

Chapel
Plantation

58

139
125

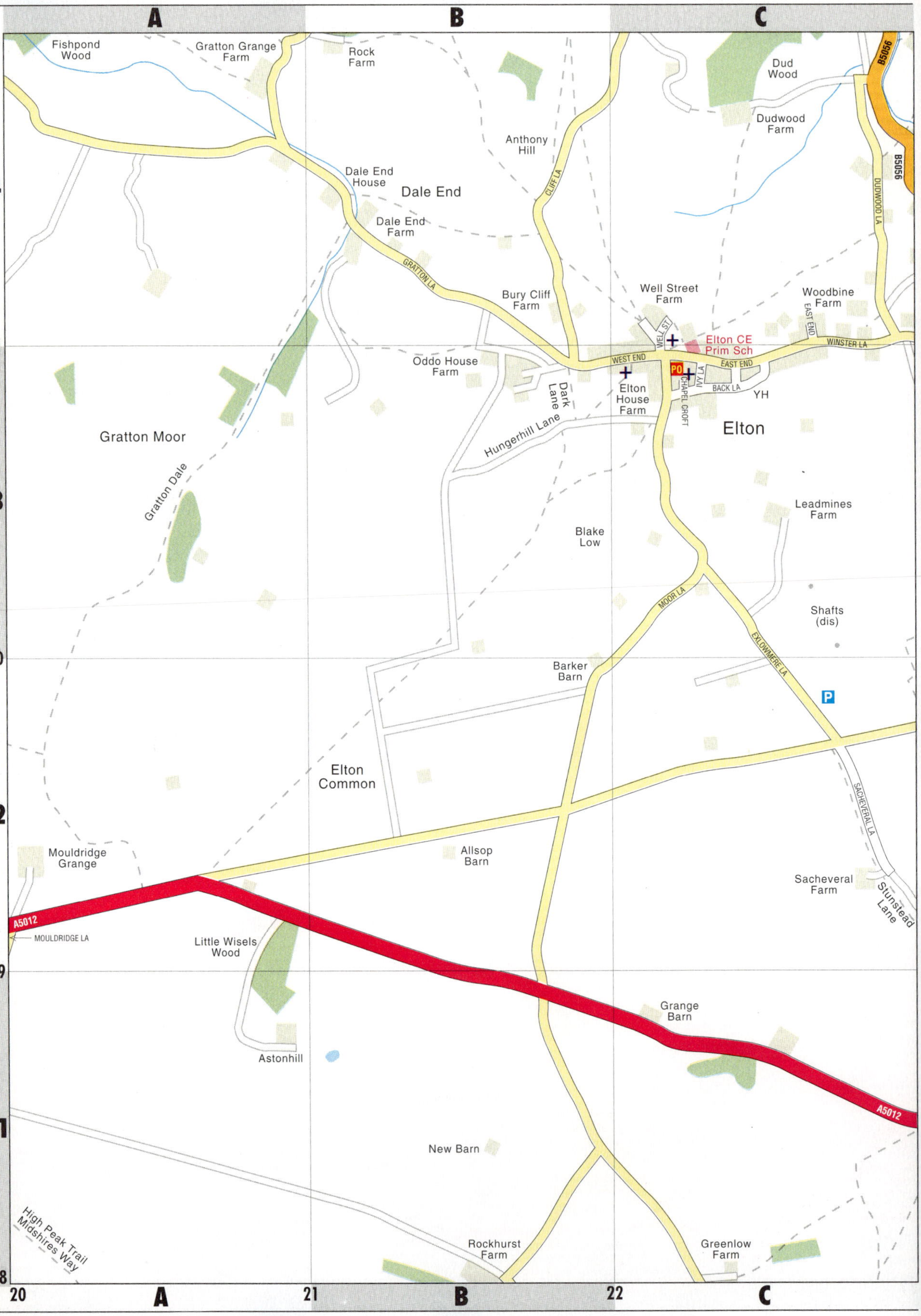

A **B** **C**

Fishpond Wood

Gratton Grange Farm

Rock Farm

Dud Wood

Dudwood Farm

B5056

B5056

DUDWOOD LA

Anthony Hill

CLIFF LA

Dale End House

Dale End

4

Dale End Farm

GRATTON LA

Bury Cliff Farm

Well Street Farm

Woodbine Farm

EAST END

Elton CE Prim Sch

WINSTER LA

61

Oddo House Farm

WEST END

PO

WELL ST

CHAPEL CROFT

BACK LA

EAST END

YH

Dark Lane

Elton House Farm

Gratton Moor

Hungerhill Lane

Elton

Gratton Dale

Blake Low

Leadmines Farm

3

Shafts (dis)

MOOR LA

60

Barker Barn

ELDONMERE LA

P

SACHEVERAL LA

Elton Common

Mouldridge Grange

Allsop Barn

Sacheveral Farm

2

Stunstead Lane

A5012

MOULDRIDGE LA

Little Wisels Wood

59

Grange Barn

Astonhill

A5012

1

New Barn

High Peak Trail Midshires Way

Rockhurst Farm

Greenlow Farm

58

20 **A** 21 **B** 22 **C**

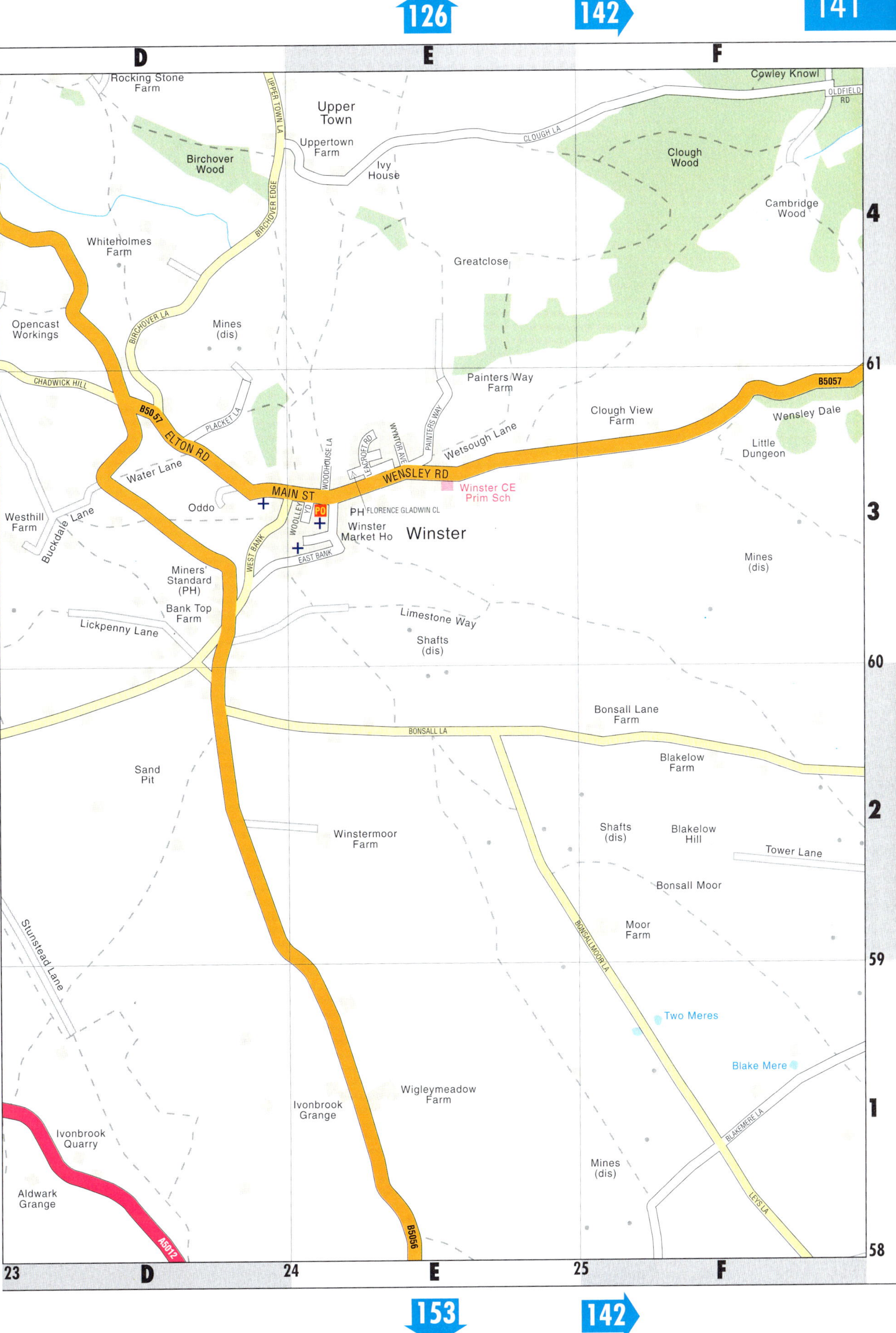
D
E
F
Rocking Stone Farm
Upper Town
UPPER TOWN LA
Uppertown Farm
Ivy House
Cowley Knowl
OLDFIELD RD
CLOUGH LA
Clough Wood
Birchover Wood
Cambridge Wood
BIRCHOVER EDGE
Whiteholmes Farm
Greatclose
Opencast Workings
Mines (dis)
BIRCHOVER LA
CHADWICK HILL
B5057
ELTON RD
PLACKET LA
Painters Way Farm
B5057
Wensley Dale
Clough View Farm
Little Dungeon
Wetsough Lane
WYNTOR AVE
PAINTERS WAY
LEACROFT RD
WOODHOUSE LA
Water Lane
MAIN ST
WENSLEY RD
Winster CE Prim Sch
Oddo
PO
PH
FLORENCE GLADWIN CL
Westhill Farm
Buckdale Lane
WOOLLEY YD
Winster Market Ho
Winster
WEST BANK
EAST BANK
Miners' Standard (PH)
Mines (dis)
Bank Top Farm
Lickpenny Lane
Limestone Way
Shafts (dis)
Bonsall Lane Farm
BONSALL LA
Blakelow Farm
Sand Pit
Shafts (dis)
Blakelow Hill
Winstermoor Farm
Tower Lane
Bonsall Moor
Moor Farm
BONSALLMOOR LA
Stunstead Lane
Two Meres
Blake Mere
Wigleymeadow Farm
Ivonbrook Grange
BLAKEMERE LA
Ivonbrook Quarry
Mines (dis)
LEYS LA
Aldwark Grange
A5012
B5056
4
61
3
60
2
59
1
58
23
D
24
E
25
F

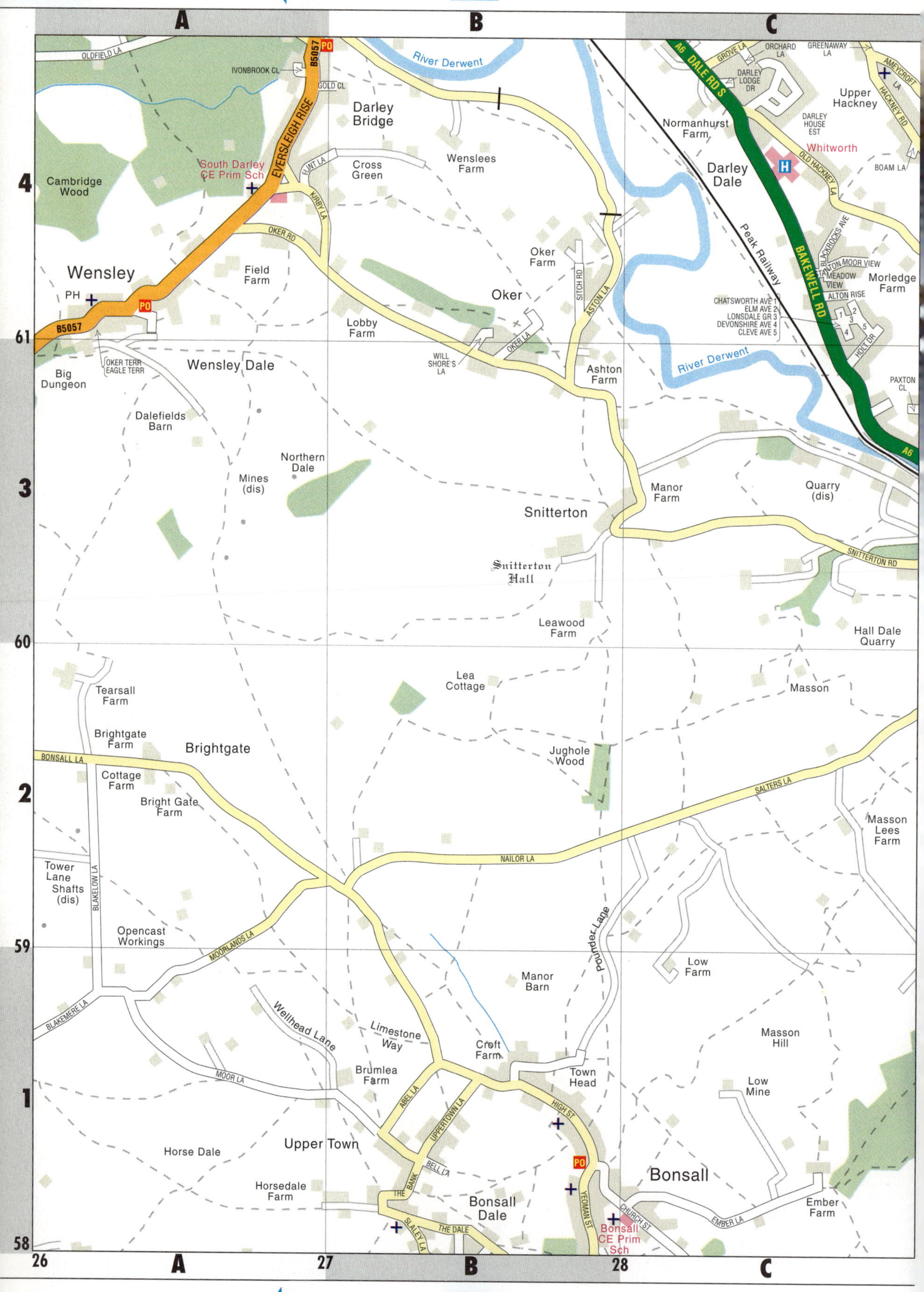

141
127

A
B
C

OLDFIELD LA

IVONBROOK CL

B5057

GOLD CL

River Derwent

A6 DALE RD S

GROVE LA

ORCHARD LA

GREENAWAY LA

DARLEY LODGE DR

DARLEY HOUSE EST

Upper Hackney

AMBERCROFT LA

HACKNEY RD

4

Cambridge Wood

South Darley CE Prim Sch

Darley Bridge

Cross Green

Wenslees Farm

Normanhurst Farm

Darley Dale

Whitworth

BOAM LA

EVERSLEIGH RISE

FLINT LA

KIRBY LA

H

OLD HACKNEY LA

BLACKROCKS AVE

TAYLON MOOR VIEW

MEADOW VIEW

ALTON RISE

Morledge Farm

Wensley

OKER RD

Field Farm

Oker Farm

SITCH RD

ASTON LA

CHATSWORTH AVE 1
ELM AVE 2
LONSDALE GR 3
DEVONSHIRE AVE 4
CLEVE AVE 5

PH

PO

B5057

Lobby Farm

Oker

OKER LA

1 2
3
4 5

HOLT DR

61

OKER TERR
EAGLE TERR

WILL SHORE'S LA

Ashton Farm

River Derwent

PAXTON CL

Big Dungeon

Wensley Dale

Dalefields Barn

Northern Dale

Mines (dis)

Snitterton

Manor Farm

Quarry (dis)

3

Snitterton Hall

SNITTERTON RD

Leawood Farm

Hall Dale Quarry

60

Lea Cottage

Masson

Tearsall Farm

Brightgate Farm

Brightgate

Jughole Wood

SALTERS LA

BONSALL LA

Cottage Farm

Bright Gate Farm

Masson Lees Farm

2

Tower Lane Shafts (dis)

BLAKELOW LA

NAILOR LA

Pounder Lane

Low Farm

Opencast Workings

MOORLANDS LA

59

Manor Barn

Masson Hill

BLAKEMERE LA

Wellhead Lane

Limestone Way

Croft Farm

Town Head

Low Mine

MOOR LA

ABEL LA

Brumlea Farm

HIGH ST

1

Horse Dale

UPPERTOWN LA

Bonsall

Upper Town

BELL LA

PO

YEOMAN ST

Horsedale Farm

THE BANK

Bonsall Dale

CHURCH ST

Ember Farm

58

THE DALE

SALTER LA

Bonsall CE Prim Sch

EMBER LA

26
A
27
B
28
C

128
144

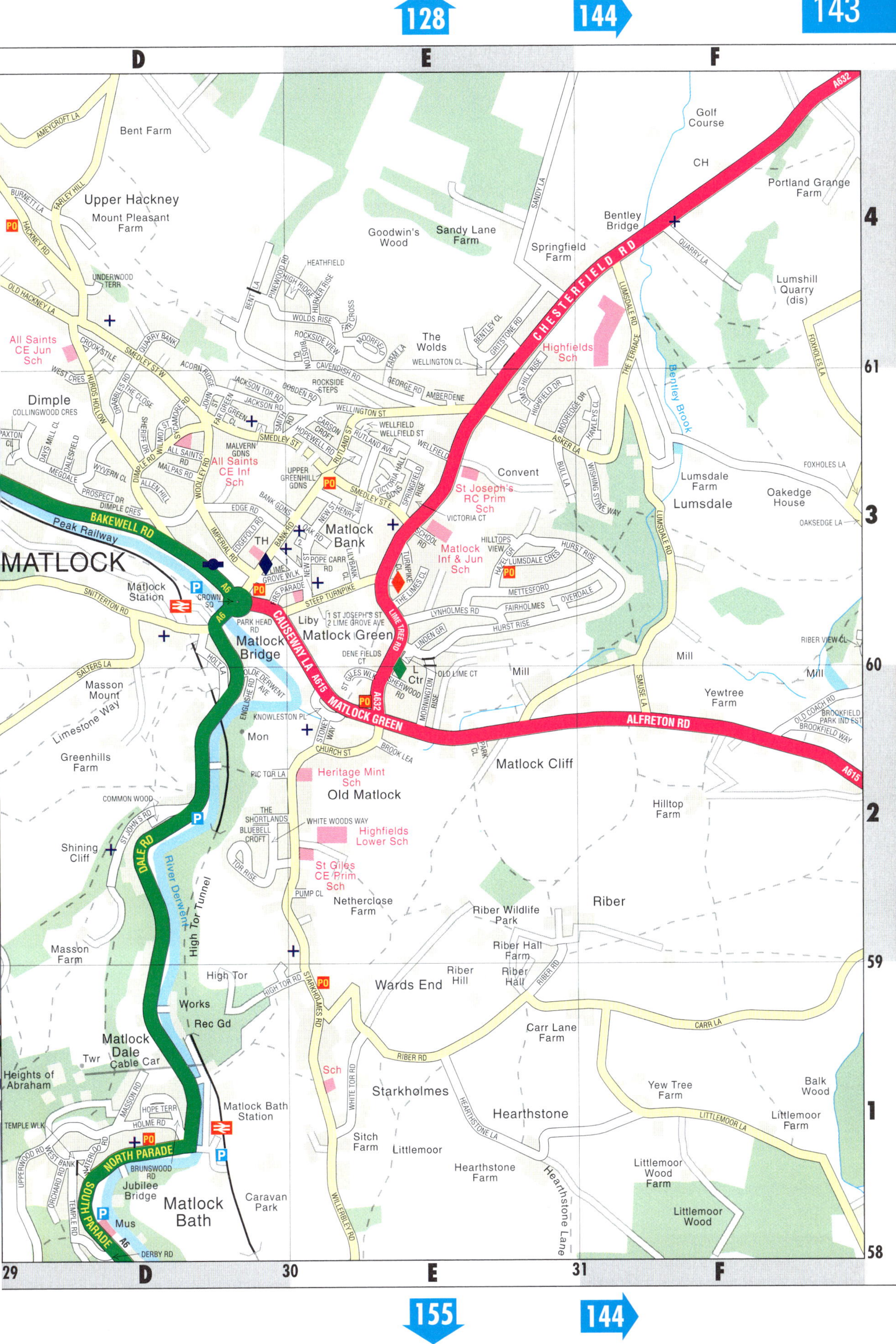
D
E
F
Golf Course
CH
Portland Grange Farm
Bent Farm
Upper Hackney
Mount Pleasant Farm
Goodwin's Wood
Sandy Lane Farm
Bentley Bridge
Springfield Farm
Lumshill Quarry (dis)
4
All Saints CE Jun Sch
The Wolds
Highfields Sch
CHESTERFIELD RD
A632
61
Dimple
Bentley Brook
Convent
St Joseph's RC Prim Sch
Lumsdale Farm
Lumsdale
Oakedge House
All Saints CE Inf Sch
3
BAKEWELL RD
Peak Railway
MATLOCK
Matlock Bank
Matlock Inf & Jun Sch
TH
Matlock Station
Liby
Matlock Green
Matlock Bridge
CAUSEWAY LA
A615
Ctr
Mill
Mill
60
Yewtree Farm
Masson Mount
Limestone Way
MATLOCK GREEN
ALFRETON RD
Mon
Greenhills Farm
Heritage Mint Sch
Old Matlock
Matlock Cliff
Hilltop Farm
2
Shining Cliff
DALE RD
River Derwent
Highfields Lower Sch
St Giles CE Prim Sch
High Tor Tunnel
Netherclose Farm
Riber Wildlife Park
Riber
Masson Farm
Riber Hall Farm
59
High Tor
Works
Rec Gd
Wards End
Riber Hill
Riber Hall
Carr Lane Farm
Matlock Dale
Twr
Cable Car
Heights of Abraham
Sch
Starkholmes
Hearthstone
Yew Tree Farm
Balk Wood
1
Matlock Bath Station
Littlemoor Farm
NORTH PARADE
Sitch Farm
Littlemoor
Hearthstone Farm
Hearthstone Lane
Littlemoor Wood Farm
Jubilee Bridge
Matlock Bath
Caravan Park
Mus
SOUTH PARADE
Littlemoor Wood
58
29
30
31

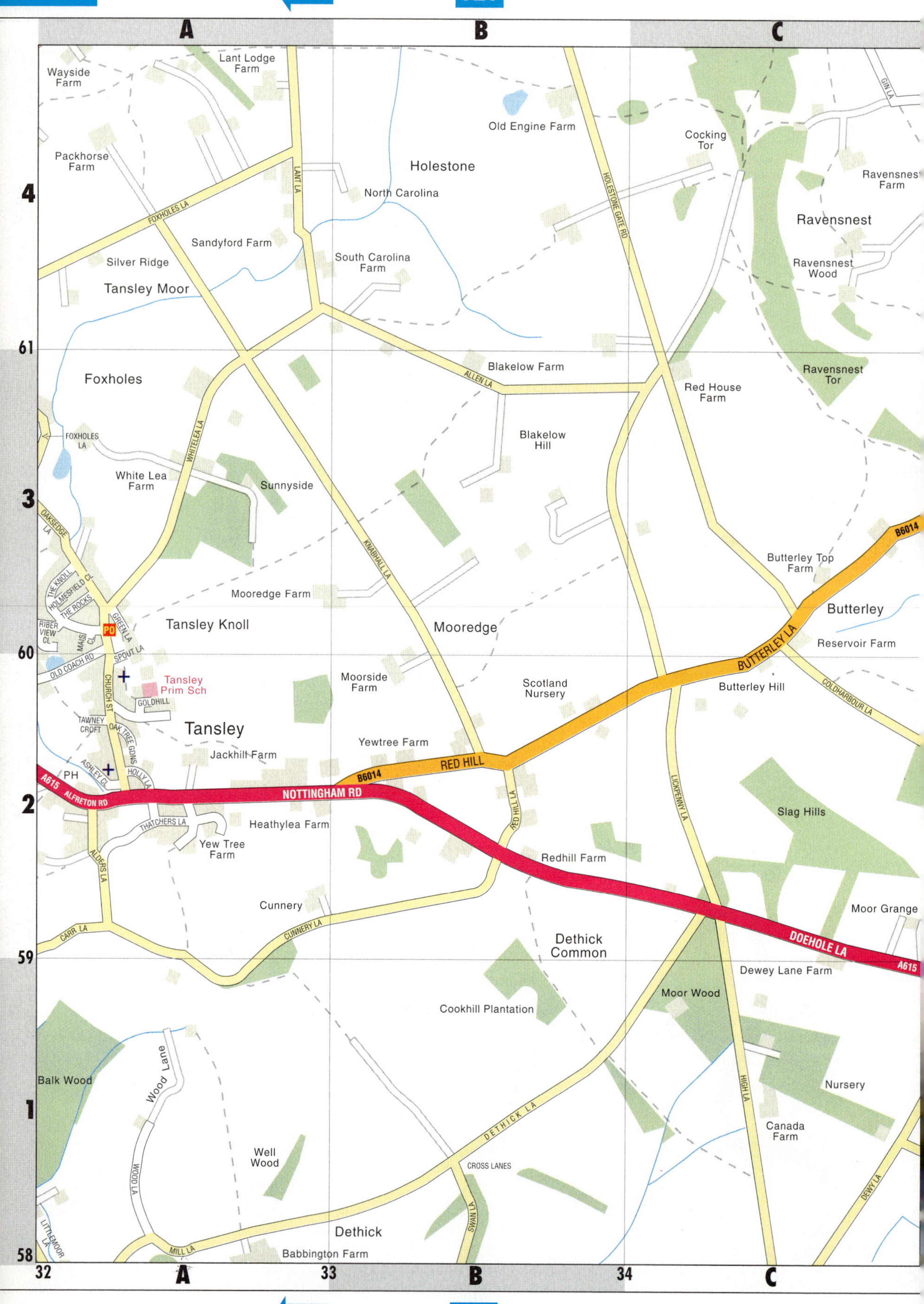

Wayside Farm
Lant Lodge Farm
Old Engine Farm
Cocking Tor
Ravensnest Farm
Packhorse Farm
Holestone
Ravensnest
North Carolina
FOXHOLES LA
LANT LA
South Carolina Farm
Silver Ridge
Sandyford Farm
Ravensnest Wood
Tansley Moor
Blakelow Farm
Red House Farm
Ravensnest Tor
HOLESTONE GATE RD
Foxholes
ALLEN LA
WHITELEA LA
Blakelow Hill
FOXHOLES LA
White Lea Farm
Sunnyside
Butterley Top Farm
B6014
Butterley
OAKEDGE LA
KNABHALL LA
BUTTERLEY LA
Reservoir Farm
Mooredge Farm
THE KNOLL
HOLMESFIELD CL
THE ROCKS
Tansley Knoll
Mooredge
Butterley Hill
COLDHARBOUR LA
RIBER VIEW CL
GREEN LA
PO
Moorside Farm
Scotland Nursery
OLD COACH RD
MAISL CL
SPOUT LA
Tansley Prim Sch
GOLDHILL
CHURCH ST
Yewtree Farm
RED HILL
B6014
LICKPENNY LA
Slag Hills
TAWNEY CROFT
OAK TREE GDNS
Tansley
Jackhill Farm
HOLLY LA
RED HILL LA
PH
A615
ALFRETON RD
NOTTINGHAM RD
ASHLEY CL
Heathylea Farm
Redhill Farm
Moor Grange
THATCHERS LA
Yew Tree Farm
DOEHOLE LA
A615
Dewey Lane Farm
ALDERS LA
Cunnery
Dethick Common
Moor Wood
Nursery
CARR LA
CUNNERY LA
HIGH LA
Cookhill Plantation
Canada Farm
Balk Wood
Wood Lane
DEWY LA
WOOD LA
Well Wood
DETHICK LA
LITTLEMOOR LA
CROSS LANES
SWAN LA
Dethick
MILL LA
Babbington Farm

130
146

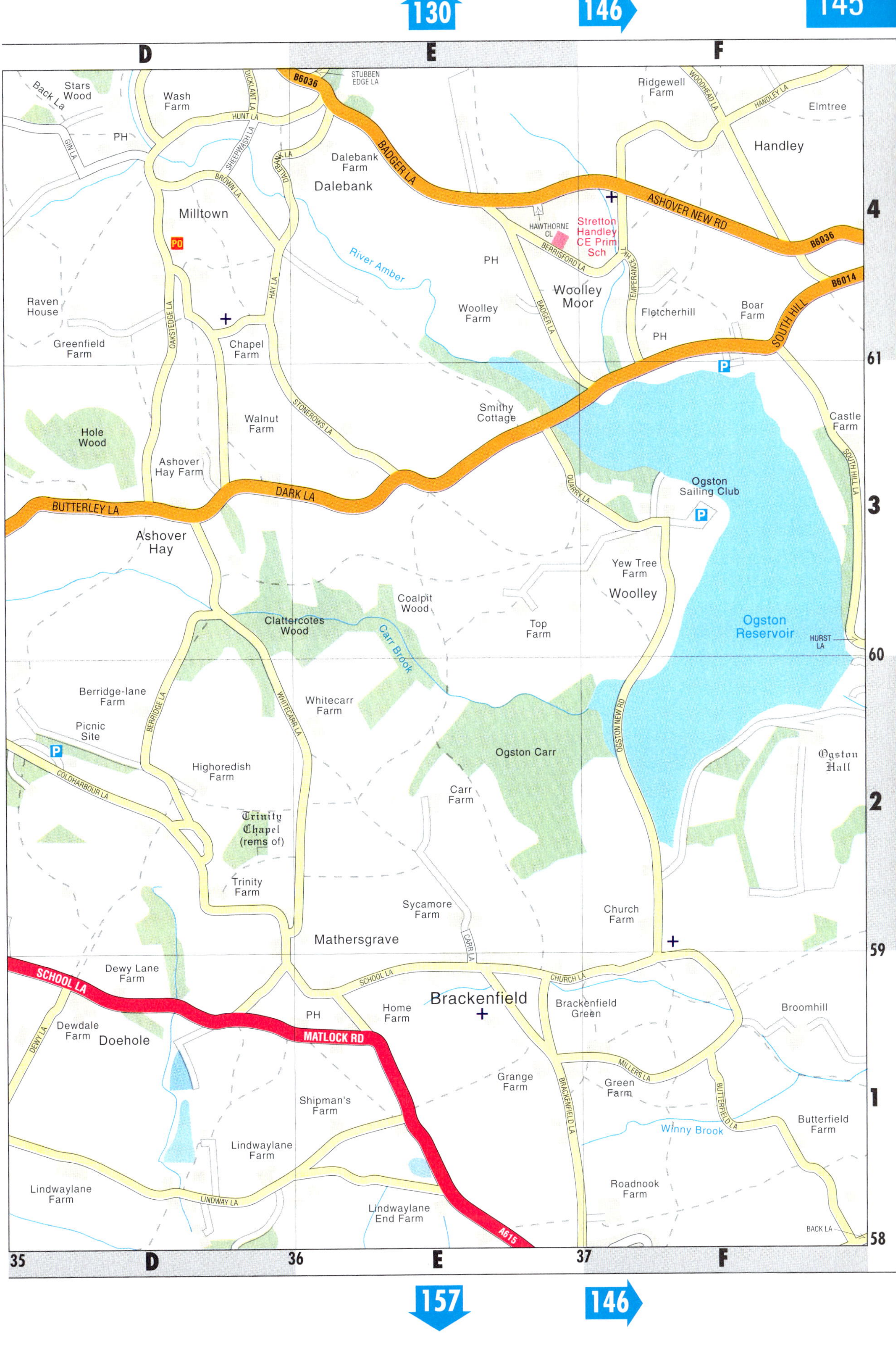
D
E
F
Back La
Stars Wood
Wash Farm
DICKLANT LA
HUNT LA
B6036
STUBBEN EDGE LA
PH
GIN LA
SHEEPWASH LA
DALEBANK LA
Dalebank Farm
Dalebank
BADGER LA
BROWN LA
Milltown
PO
Ridgewell Farm
WOODHEAD LA
HANDLEY LA
Elmtree
Handley
ASHOVER NEW RD
HAWTHORNE CL
Stretton Handley CE Prim Sch
BERRISFORD LA
River Amber
PH
Woolley Moor
Woolley Farm
BADGER LA
TEMPERANCE HILL
Fletcherhill
PH
Boar Farm
B6036
B6014
SOUTH HILL
HAY LA
Raven House
Greenfield Farm
OAKSTEDGE LA
Chapel Farm
4
61
Hole Wood
Walnut Farm
STONEROWS LA
Smithy Cottage
Castle Farm
SOUTH HILL LA
Ashover Hay Farm
BUTTERLEY LA
DARK LA
QUARRY LA
Ogston Sailing Club
3
Ashover Hay
Yew Tree Farm
Woolley
Coalpit Wood
Clattercotes Wood
Carr Brook
Top Farm
Ogston Reservoir
HURST LA
60
Berridge-lane Farm
BERRIDGE LA
WHITECARR LA
Whitecarr Farm
Picnic Site
P
COLDHARBOUR LA
Highoredish Farm
Ogston Carr
OGSTON NEW RD
Ogston Hall
Carr Farm
2
Trinity Chapel (rems of)
Trinity Farm
Sycamore Farm
Church Farm
Mathersgrave
CARR LA
59
SCHOOL LA
Dewy Lane Farm
SCHOOL LA
CHURCH LA
PH
Home Farm
Brackenfield
Brackenfield Green
Broomhill
Dewdale Farm
Doehole
DEWY LA
MATLOCK RD
MILLERS LA
Grange Farm
BRACKENFIELD LA
Green Farm
BUTTERFIELD LA
Shipman's Farm
Winny Brook
1
Butterfield Farm
Lindwaylane Farm
Lindwaylane Farm
LINDWAY LA
Lindwaylane End Farm
A615
Roadnook Farm
BACK LA
58
35
36
37

157
146

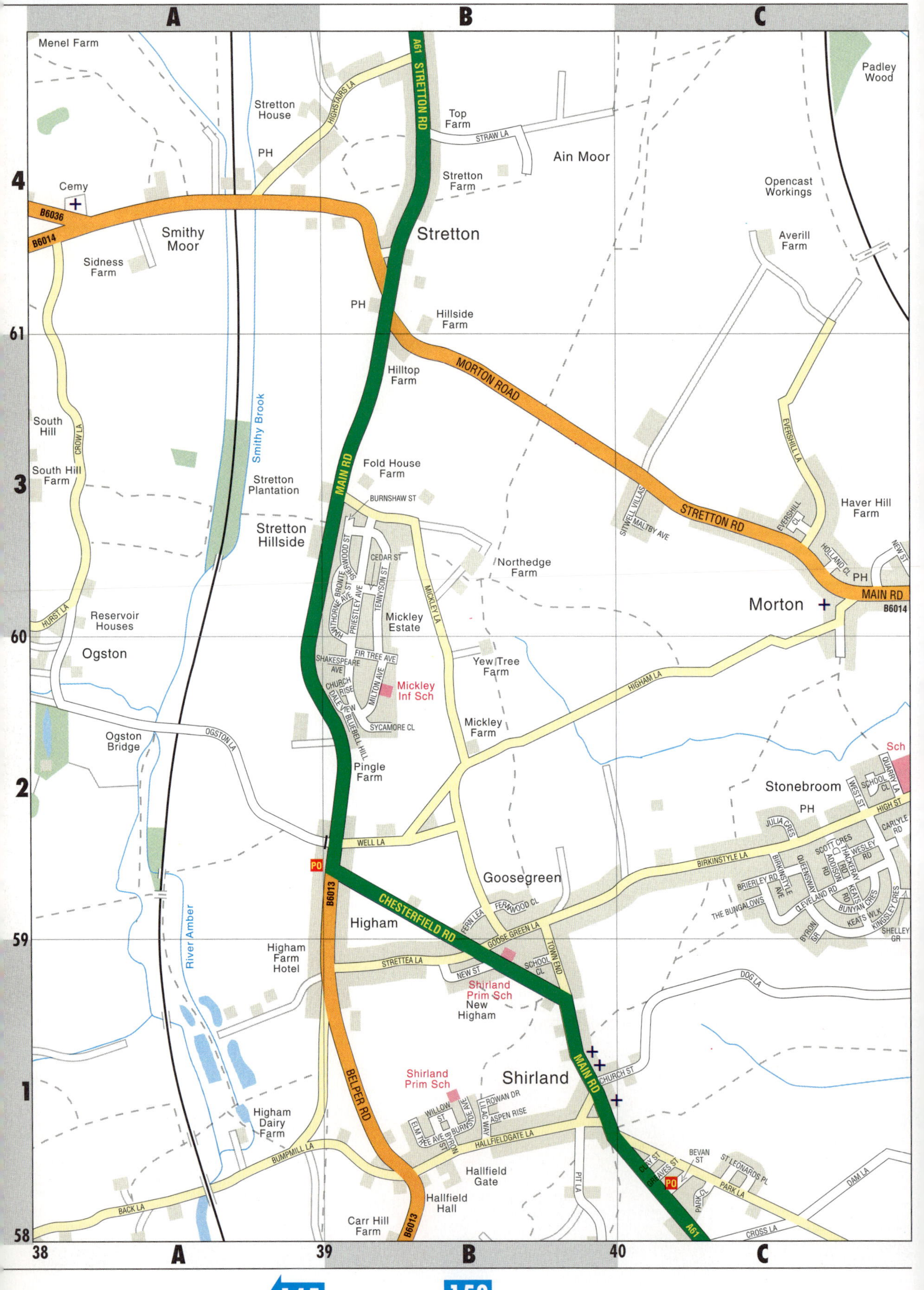

A   B   C

Menel Farm

Stretton House

PH

A61 STRETTON RD

Top Farm

STRAW LA

Ain Moor

Padley Wood

HIGHFIELDS LA

Opencast Workings

4

Cemy +

B6036

B6014

Smithy Moor

Sidness Farm

Stretton Farm

Stretton

Averill Farm

61

South Hill

Smithy Brook

PH

Hillside Farm

Hilltop Farm

MORTON ROAD

Eversmill LA

CROW LA

South Hill Farm

Stretton Plantation

MAIN RD

Fold House Farm

Burnshaw St

Northedge Farm

SITWELL VILLAS

MALTBY AVE

STRETTON RD

EVERSMILL CL

Haver Hill Farm

NEW ST

HOLLAND CL

HURST LA

Reservoir Houses

Stretton Hillside

HAWTHORNE AVE

BRONTE ST

SHERWOOD ST

PRIESTLEY AVE

TENNYSON ST

CEDAR ST

MICKLEY LA

PH

Morton +

MAIN RD

B6014

60

Ogston

Ogston Bridge

OGSTON LA

SHAKESPEARE AVE

FIR TREE AVE

CHURCH RISE

MILTON AVE

DALE VIEW

BLUEFELL HILL

Mickley Estate

Mickley Inf Sch

SYCAMORE CL

Yew Tree Farm

Mickley Farm

HIGHAM LA

Stonebroom

Sch

SCHOOL CL

QUARRY LA

WEST ST

HIGH ST

PH

2

River Amber

Pingle Farm

WELL LA

Goosegreen

BIRKINSTYLE LA

JULIA CRES

SCOTT CRES

BRIERLEY RD

QUEENSWAY

ADDISON RD

HACKETT

KEATS RD

WESLEY RD

CARLYLE RD

59

PO

B6013

CHESTERFIELD RD

Higham

FERN LEA

FERNWOOD CL

GOOSE GREEN LA

SCHOOL CL

TOWN END

THE BUNGALOWS

CLEVELAND RD

BUNYAN CRES

BYRON GR

KEATS WLK

KINGSLEY CRES

SHELLEY GR

Higham Farm Hotel

STRETTEA LA

NEW ST

Shirland Prim Sch

New Higham

DOG LA

1

Higham Dairy Farm

BELPER RD

Shirland Prim Sch

WILLOW ST

ELM TREE AVE

BURNS ST

ROWAN DR

LILAC WAY

ASPEN RISE

Shirland

MAIN RD

CHURCH ST

PIT LA

BEVAN ST

ST LEONARDS PL

HALLFIELDGATE LA

Hallfield Gate

REEVES ST

PARK LA

A61

PO

DAM LA

BUMPMILL LA

BACK LA

Hallfield Hall

Carr Hill Farm

B6013

Hallfield Gate

CROSS LA

58

38   A   39   B   40   C

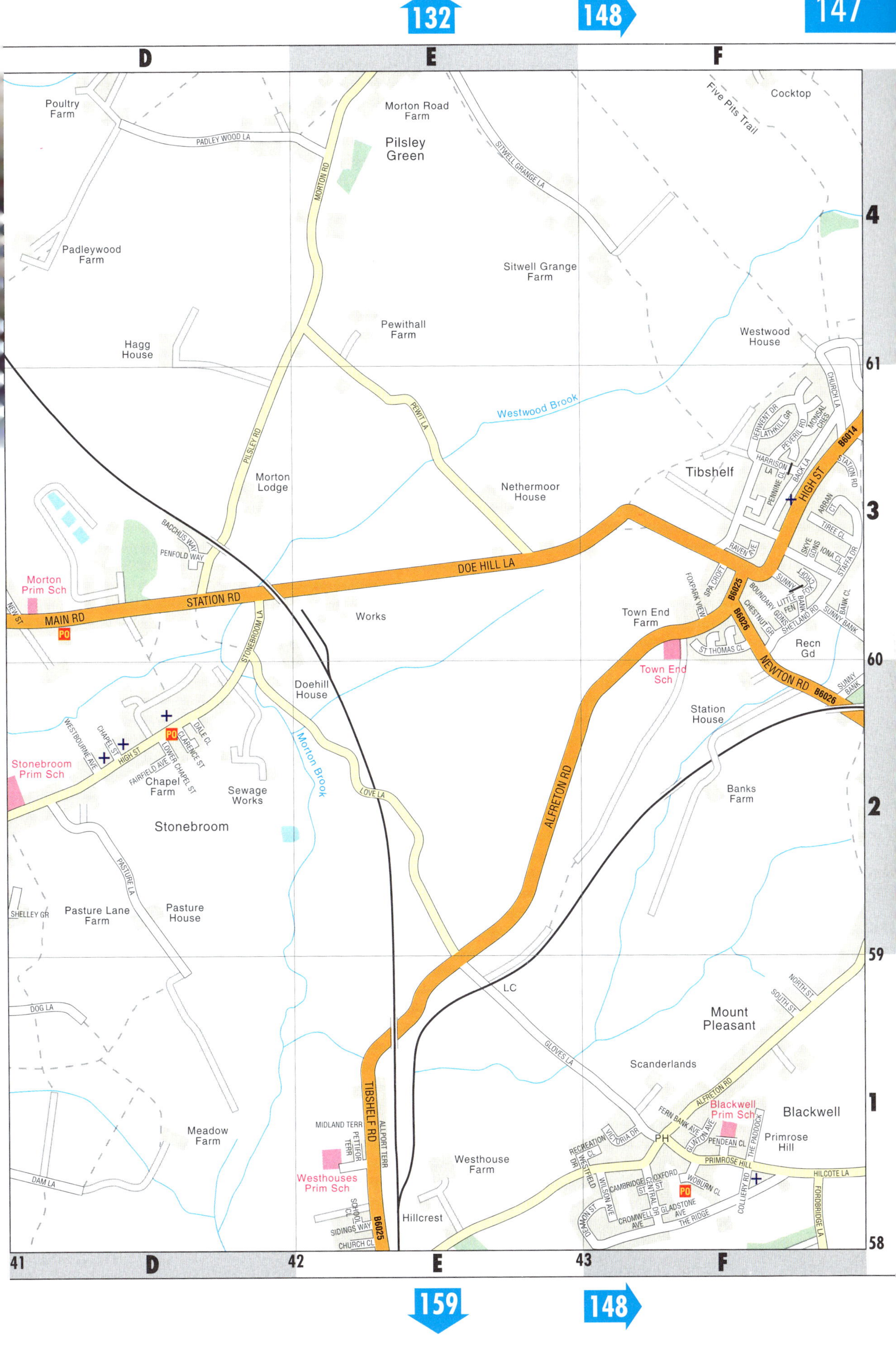

132
148
D
E
F
Poultry Farm
Morton Road Farm
Pilsley Green
Cocktop
Five Pits Trail
PADLEY WOOD LA
MORTON RD
SITWELL GRANGE LA
Padleywood Farm
Sitwell Grange Farm
Hagg House
Pewithall Farm
Westwood House
Westwood Brook
PEWIT LA
PILSLEY RD
Morton Lodge
Nethermoor House
Tibshelf
HIGH ST
B6014
STATION RD
CHURCH LA
BACK LA
HARRISON LA
PENNINE CL
PEVERIL RD
LATHKILL GR
DERWENT DR
MONSAL CRES
ARRAN CL
TIREE CL
SKYE GDNS
IONA CL
STAFFA DR
RAVEN AVE
SPA CROFT
FOXPARK VIEW
B6025
B6026
BOUNDARY GDNS
CHESTNUT GR
LITTLE FEN
SUNNY BANK
SHETLAND RD
SUNNY BANK CL
ST THOMAS CL
NEWTON RD
Recn Gd
BACCHUS WAY
PENFOLD WAY
DOE HILL LA
Morton Prim Sch
NEW ST
MAIN RD
STATION RD
PO
Works
Town End Farm
Town End Sch
STONEBROOM LA
Doehill House
Station House
WESTBOURNE AVE
CHAPEL ST
HIGH ST
DALE CL
CLARENCE ST
LOWER CHAPEL ST
FAIRFIELD AVE
Stonebroom Prim Sch
Chapel Farm
Sewage Works
Morton Brook
LOVE LA
ALFRETON RD
Banks Farm
Stonebroom
PASTURE LA
SHELLEY GR
Pasture Lane Farm
Pasture House
LC
DOG LA
NORTH ST
SOUTH ST
Mount Pleasant
GLOVES LA
Scanderlands
Meadow Farm
MIDLAND TERR
PETTIFOR TERR
ALLPORT TERR
TIBSHELF RD
Westhouse Farm
Westhouses Prim Sch
SCHOOL CL
SIDINGS WAY
CHURCH CL
B6025
Hillcrest
FERN BANK AVE
Blackwell Prim Sch
Blackwell
GLINTON AVE
THE PADDOCK
PENDEAN CL
PH
VICTORIA DR
RECREATION CL
WESTFIELD DR
Primrose Hill
PRIMROSE HILL
HILCOTE LA
FORDBRIDGE LA
WILSON AVE
CAMBRIDGE ST
CENTRAL DR
OXFORD ST
WOBURN CL
GLADSTONE AVE
THE RIDGE
COLLIERY RD
CROMWELL AVE
DEACON ST
4
61
3
60
2
59
1
58
41
42
43
159
148

147
133

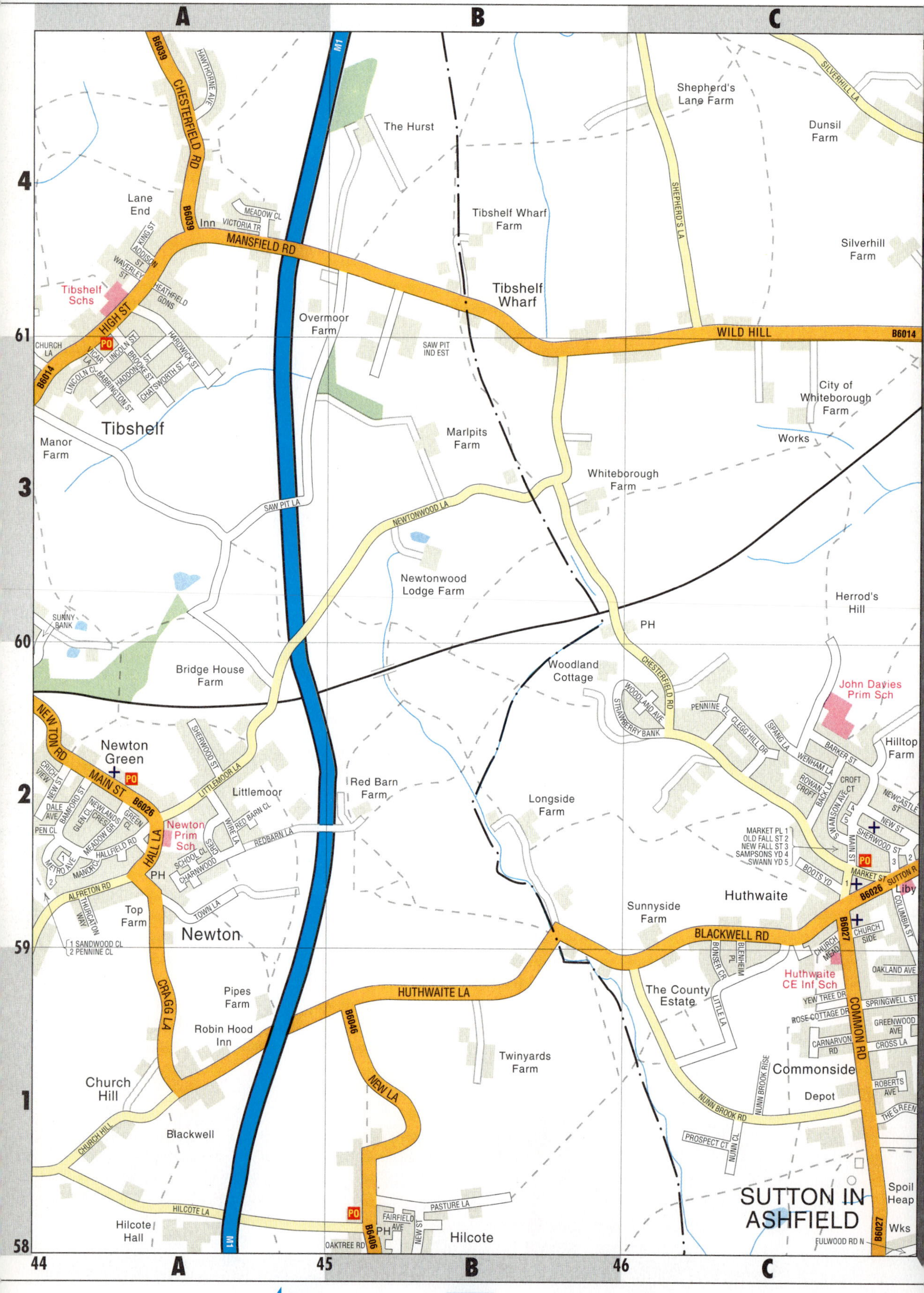
A
B
C
4
3
2
1
61
60
59
58
44
45
46
A
B
C
B6039
CHESTERFIELD RD
HAWTHORNE AVE
M1
The Hurst
Shepherd's Lane Farm
SILVERHILL LA
Dunsil Farm
Lane End
Inn
MEADOW CL
VICTORIA TR
B6039
KING ST
ADDISON ST
WAVERLEY ST
MANSFIELD RD
Tibshelf Wharf Farm
SHEPHERD'S LA
Silverhill Farm
Tibshelf Schs
HEATHFIELD GDNS
HIGH ST
PO
CHURCH LA
Overmoor Farm
Tibshelf Wharf
WILD HILL
B6014
SAW PIT IND EST
HARDWICK ST
LINCOLN ST
BROOKE ST
VICAR LA
HADDON ST
CHATSWORTH ST
LINCOLN CL
BABBINGTON ST
B6014
City of Whiteborough Farm
Tibshelf
Manor Farm
Marlpits Farm
Works
Whiteborough Farm
SAW PIT LA
NEWTONWOOD LA
Newtonwood Lodge Farm
Herrod's Hill
SUNNY BANK
PH
Woodland Cottage
Bridge House Farm
CHESTERFIELD RD
WOODLAND AVE
STRAWBERRY BANK
PENNINE CL
CLEGG HILL DR
SPANG LA
John Davies Prim Sch
NEW TON RD
Newton Green
PO
SHERWOOD ST
LITTLEMOOR LA
Red Barn Farm
BARKER ST
Hilltop Farm
WENHAM LA
ROWAN CROFT
BACK LA
CROFT CT
CRICH VIEW
NEW ST
MAIN ST
B6026
Littlemoor
Longside Farm
NEWCASTLE ST
DALE AVE
BAMFORD ST
GLEN CL
NEWLANDS CRES
MEADOW GR
GREEN CL
Newton Prim Sch
WIRE LA
RED BARN CL
REDBARN LA
MARKET PL 1
OLD FALL ST 2
NEW FALL ST 3
SAMPSONS YD 4
SWANN YD 5
SWANSON AVE
NEW ST
SHERWOOD ST
PEN CL
HALLFIELD RD
HALL LA
CRES
SCHOOL CL
MAIN ST
PO
METRO AVE
MANOR CL
PH
CHARNWOOD
BOOTS YD
MARKET ST
SUTTON R
ALFRETON RD
THURCATON WAY
Top Farm
TOWN LA
Huthwaite
B6026
Liby
COLUMBIA ST
Sunnyside Farm
CHURCH SIDE
Newton
BLACKWELL RD
B6027
CHURCH MEAD
1 SANDWOOD CL
2 PENNINE CL
BONSER CR
BLENHEIM PL
OAKLAND AVE
Huthwaite CE Inf Sch
CRAGG LA
Pipes Farm
HUTHWAITE LA
The County Estate
YEW TREE DR
SPRINGWELL ST
ROSE COTTAGE DR
LITTLE LA
GREENWOOD AVE
B6046
Robin Hood Inn
CARNARVON RD
COMMON RD
CROSS LA
Twinyards Farm
Commonside
Church Hill
NEW LA
NUNN BROOK RISE
ROBERTS AVE
Depot
NUNN BROOK RD
THE GREEN
Blackwell
CHURCH HILL
PROSPECT CT
NUNN CL
Spoil Heap
SUTTON IN ASHFIELD
HILCOTE LA
PASTURE LA
PO
FAIRFIELD AVE
Hilcote Hall
PH
NEW ST
Hilcote
B6027
Wks
M1
OAKTREE RD
B6406
FULWOOD RD N

147
160

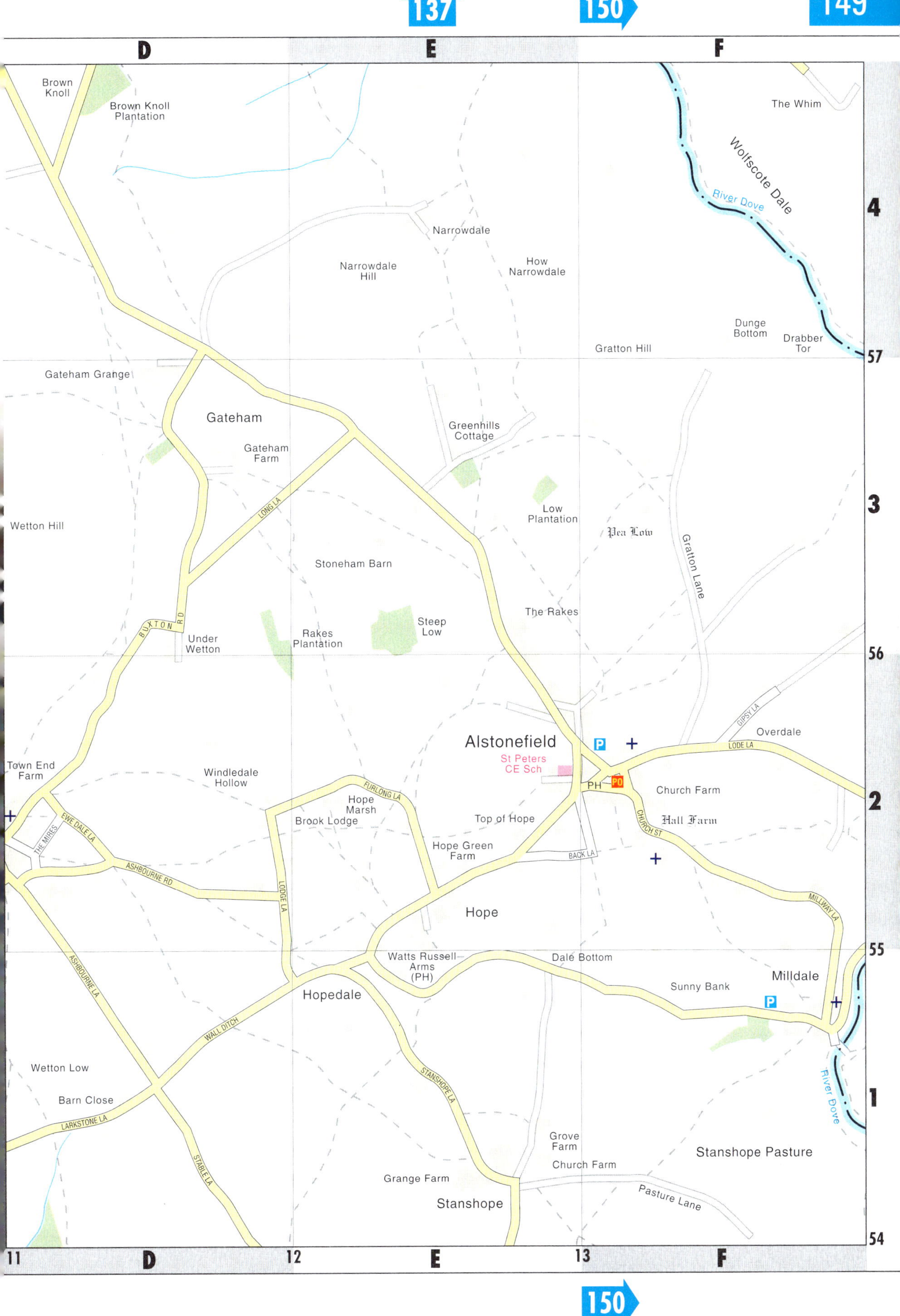
D
E
F
Brown Knoll
Brown Knoll Plantation
The Whim
Wolfscote Dale
River Dove
Narrowdale
Narrowdale Hill
How Narrowdale
Dunge Bottom
Drabber Tor
Gratton Hill
Gateham Grange
Gateham
Gateham Farm
Greenhills Cottage
Low Plantation
Pea Low
Gratton Lane
Wetton Hill
LONG LA
Stoneham Barn
Steep Low
Rakes Plantation
The Rakes
BUXTON RD
Under Wetton
Alstonefield
St Peters CE Sch
P
PH
PO
GIPSY LA
Overdale
LODE LA
Town End Farm
Windledale Hollow
Hope Marsh
FURLONG LA
Brook Lodge
Church Farm
Hall Farm
Top of Hope
CHURCH ST
EWE DALE LA
THE MIRES
ASHBOURNE RD
Hope Green Farm
BACK LA
LODGE LA
Hope
MILLWAY LA
ASHBOURNE LA
Watts Russell Arms (PH)
Dale Bottom
Hopedale
Sunny Bank
Milldale
WALL DITCH
Wetton Low
STANSHOPE LA
Barn Close
LARKSTONE LA
Grove Farm
Church Farm
Stanshope Pasture
STABLE LA
Grange Farm
Pasture Lane
Stanshope
4
57
3
56
2
55
1
54
11
12
13

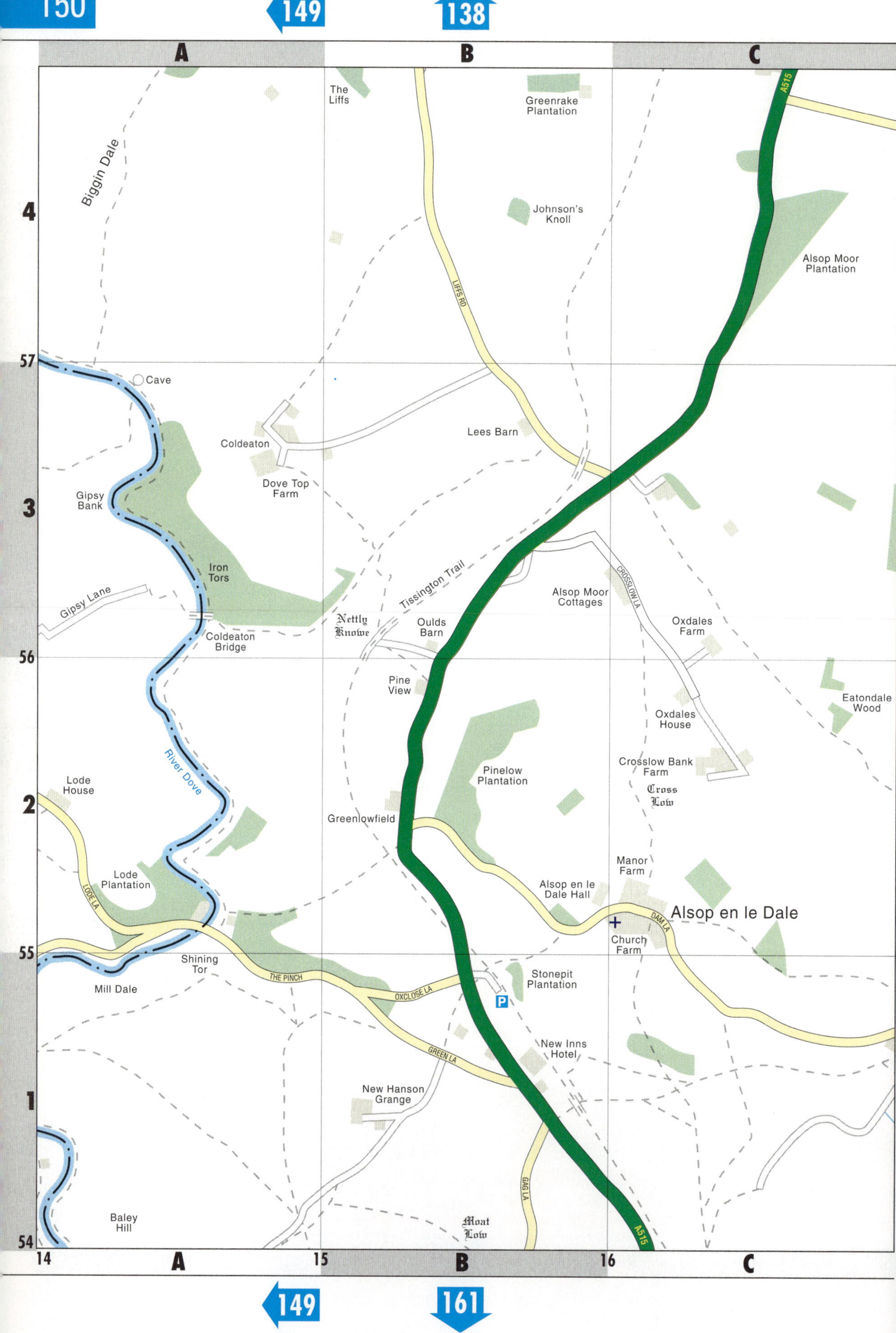

Biggin Dale

4

57

Cave

Coldeaton

Dove Top
Farm

Gipsy
Bank

3

Iron
Tors

Gipsy Lane

Coldeaton
Bridge

Nettly
Knowe

Oulds
Barn

56

Pine
View

River Dove

Lode
House

2

Lode
Plantation

Greenlowfield

LODE LA

Shining
Tor

55

THE PINCH

Mill Dale

OXCLOSE LA

GREEN LA

1

New Hanson
Grange

Baley
Hill

Moat
Low

54

The Liffs

Greenrake
Plantation

Johnson's
Knoll

LIFFS RD

Lees Barn

Tissington Trail

Alsop Moor
Cottages

Pinelow
Plantation

Alsop en le
Dale Hall

Stonepit
Plantation

P

New Inns
Hotel

GAG LA

A515

Alsop Moor
Plantation

CROSSLOW LA

Oxdales
Farm

Eatondale
Wood

Oxdales
House

Crosslow Bank
Farm

Cross
Low

Manor
Farm

DAM LA

Alsop en le Dale

Church
Farm

A515

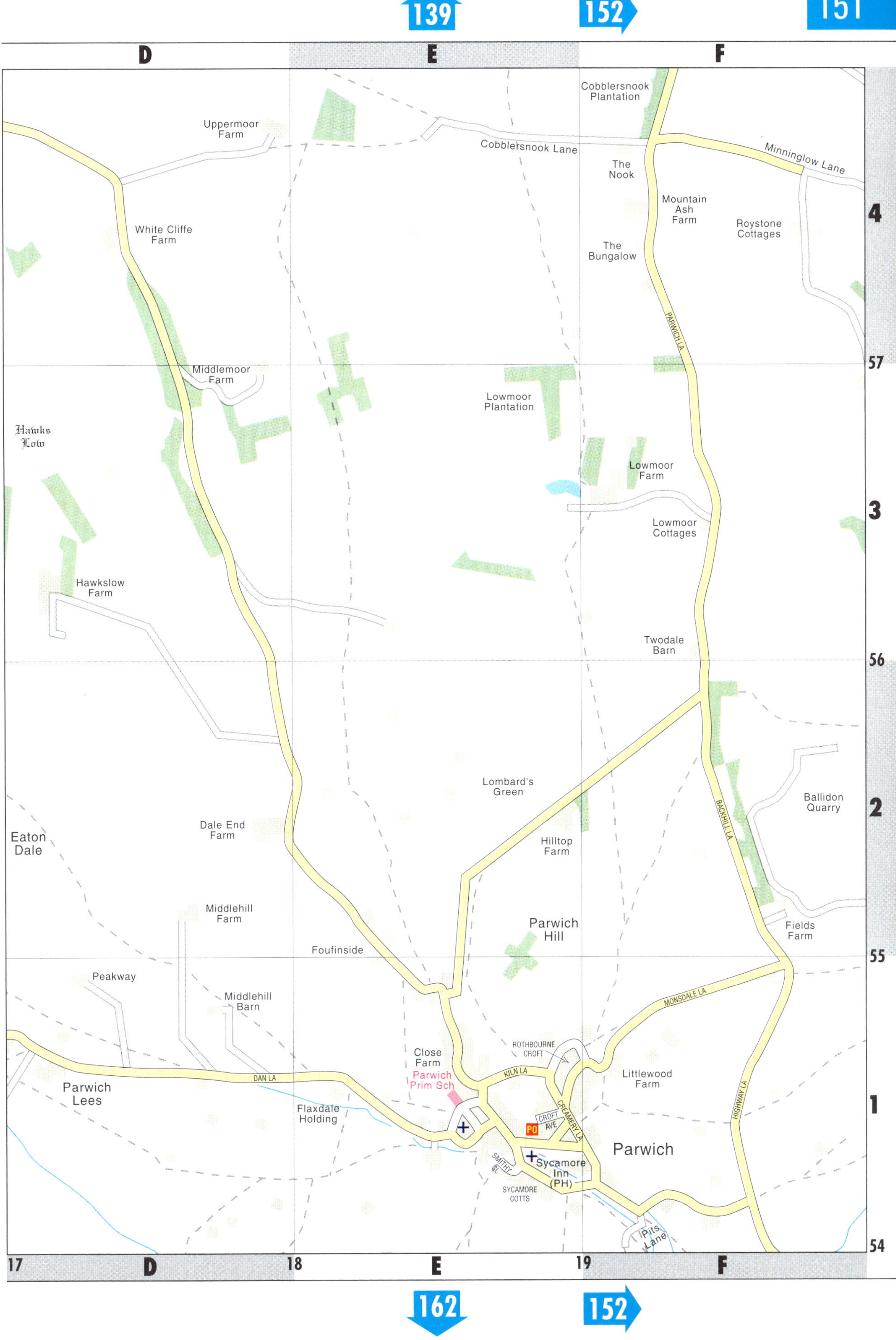
139
152
D
E
F
Cobblersnook Plantation
Uppermoor Farm
Cobblersnook Lane
Minninglow Lane
The Nook
Mountain Ash Farm
Roystone Cottages
White Cliffe Farm
The Bungalow
4
PARWICH LA
57
Middlemoor Farm
Lowmoor Plantation
Hawks Low
Lowmoor Farm
3
Lowmoor Cottages
Hawkslow Farm
Twodale Barn
56
Lombard's Green
Ballidon Quarry
2
BACKHILL LA
Eaton Dale
Dale End Farm
Hilltop Farm
Middlehill Farm
Parwich Hill
Fields Farm
Foufinside
55
Peakway
Middlehill Barn
MONSDALE LA
ROTHBOURNE CROFT
Close Farm
Parwich Prim Sch
KILN LA
Littlewood Farm
DAN LA
Parwich Lees
Flaxdale Holding
CREAMERY LA
CROFT AVE
PO
HIGHWAY LA
1
Parwich
SMITHY CL
Sycamore Inn (PH)
SYCAMORE COTTS
Pits Lane
54
17
18
19
162
152

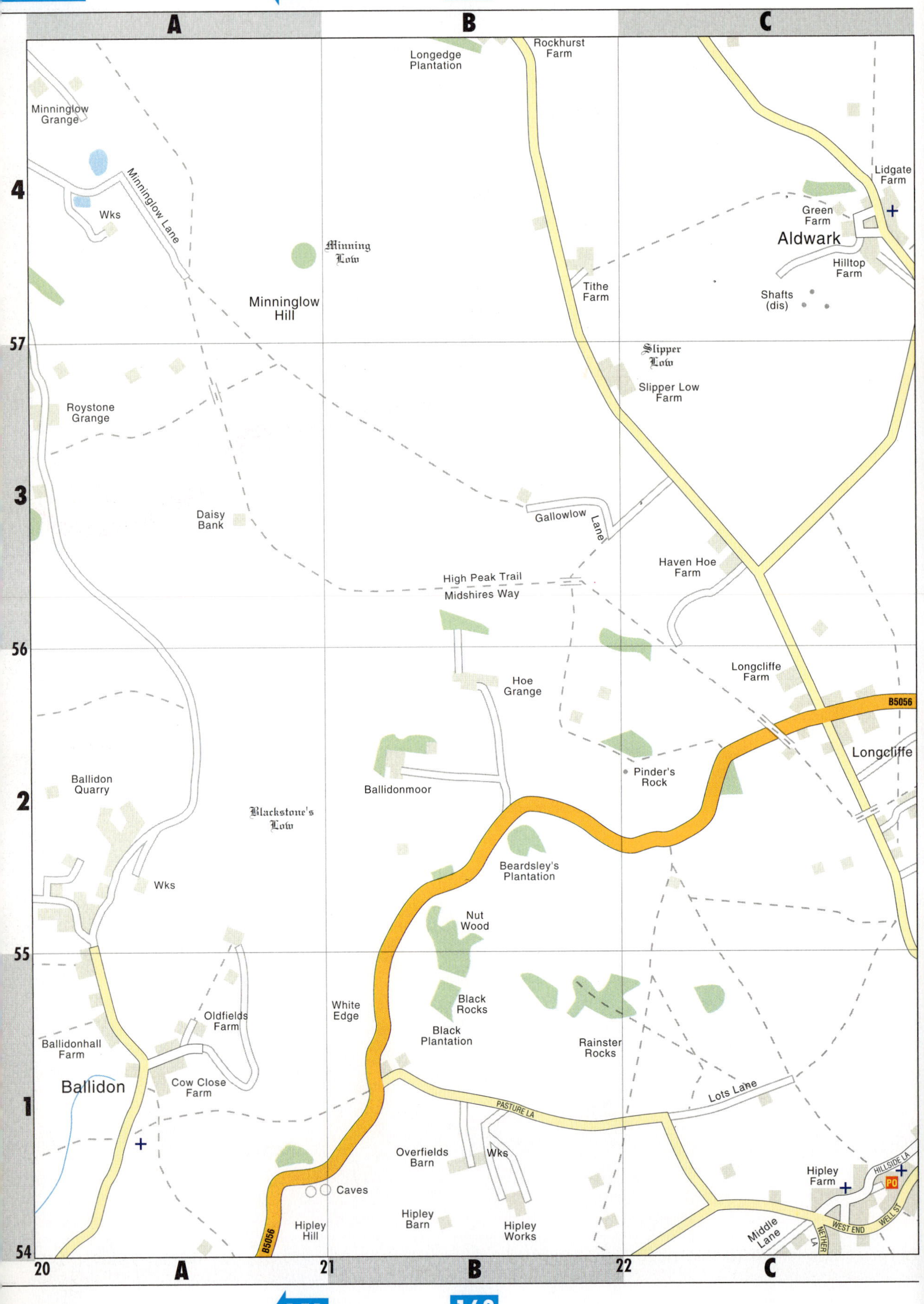
151
140
A
B
C
Rockhurst Farm
Longedge Plantation
Minninglow Grange
Minninglow Lane
Wks
Minning Low
Minninglow Hill
Lidgate Farm
Green Farm
Aldwark
Hilltop Farm
Tithe Farm
Shafts (dis)
4
57
Slipper Low
Slipper Low Farm
Roystone Grange
3
Daisy Bank
Gallowlow Lane
Haven Hoe Farm
High Peak Trail
Midshires Way
56
Hoe Grange
Longcliffe Farm
B5056
Longcliffe
Ballidon Quarry
Ballidonmoor
Pinder's Rock
2
Blackstone's Low
Beardsley's Plantation
Wks
Nut Wood
55
White Edge
Black Rocks
Oldfields Farm
Ballidonhall Farm
Black Plantation
Rainster Rocks
Ballidon
Cow Close Farm
Lots Lane
1
PASTURE LA
Overfields Barn
Wks
Hipley Farm
HILLSIDE LA
PO
Caves
Hipley Hill
Hipley Barn
Hipley Works
Middle Lane
NETHER LA
WEST END
WELL ST
B5056
54
20
21
22
A
B
C
151
163

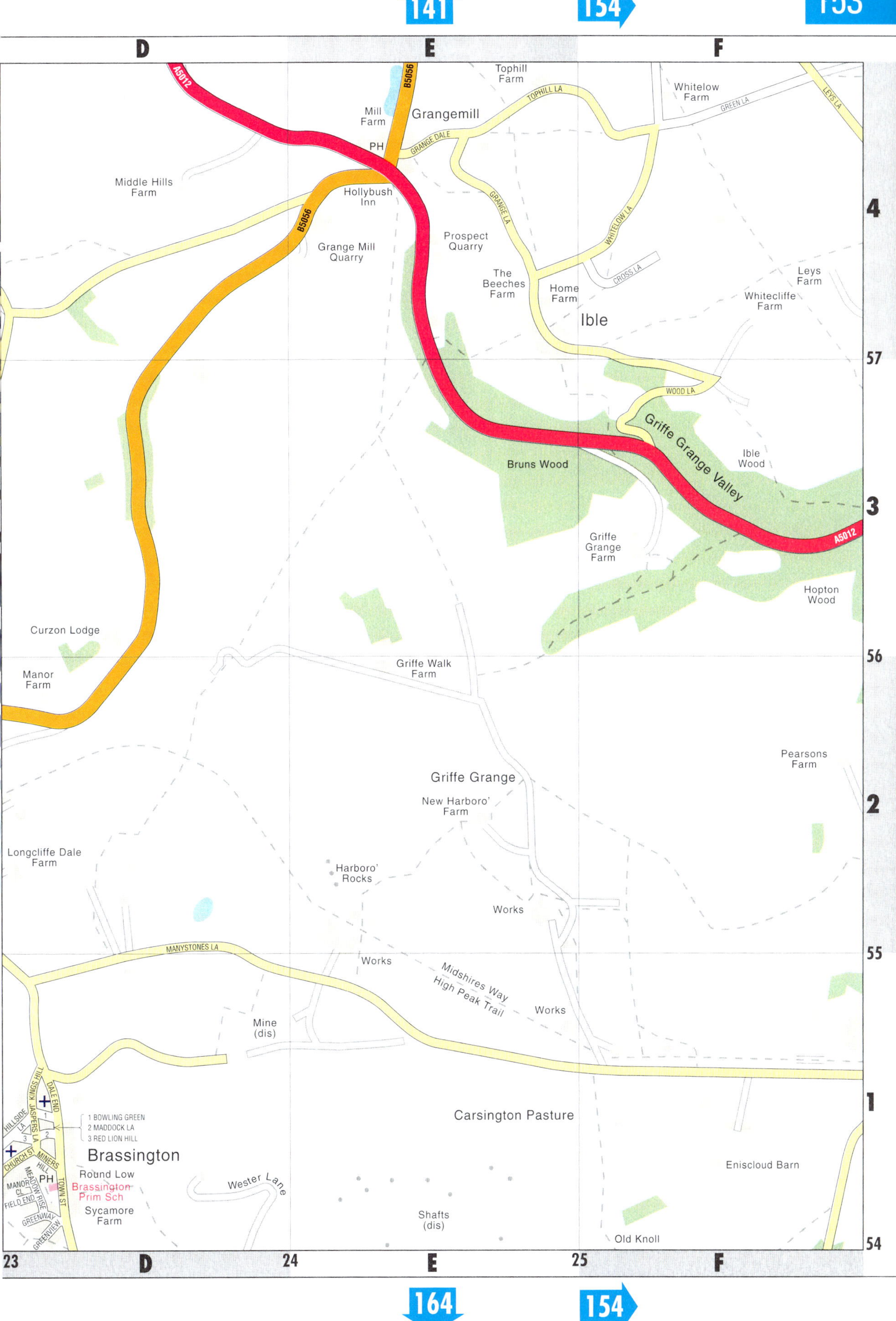
D
E
F
A5012
B5056
Tophill Farm
TOPHILL LA
Whitelow Farm
GREEN LA
LEYS LA
Mill Farm
Grangemill
GRANGE DALE
PH
Middle Hills Farm
Hollybush Inn
GRANGE LA
WHITELOW LA
Prospect Quarry
Grange Mill Quarry
The Beeches Farm
Home Farm
CROSS LA
Leys Farm
Whitecliffe Farm
Ible
4
57
WOOD LA
Griffe Grange Valley
Ible Wood
Bruns Wood
3
Griffe Grange Farm
Hopton Wood
Curzon Lodge
Manor Farm
Griffe Walk Farm
56
Pearsons Farm
Griffe Grange
New Harboro' Farm
2
Longcliffe Dale Farm
Harboro' Rocks
Works
MANYSTONES LA
55
Works
Midshires Way
High Peak Trail
Works
Mine (dis)
1
KINGS HILL
DALE END
HILLSIDE
JASPERS LA
1 BOWLING GREEN
2 MADDOCK LA
3 RED LION HILL
Carsington Pasture
Brassington
CHURCH ST
MINERS HILL
Round Low
Eniscloud Barn
MANOR CL
MEADOW RISE
TOWN ST
FIELD END
Brassington Prim Sch
Wester Lane
Sycamore Farm
GREENWAY
GREENVIEW
Shafts (dis)
Old Knoll
54
23
D
24
E
25
F

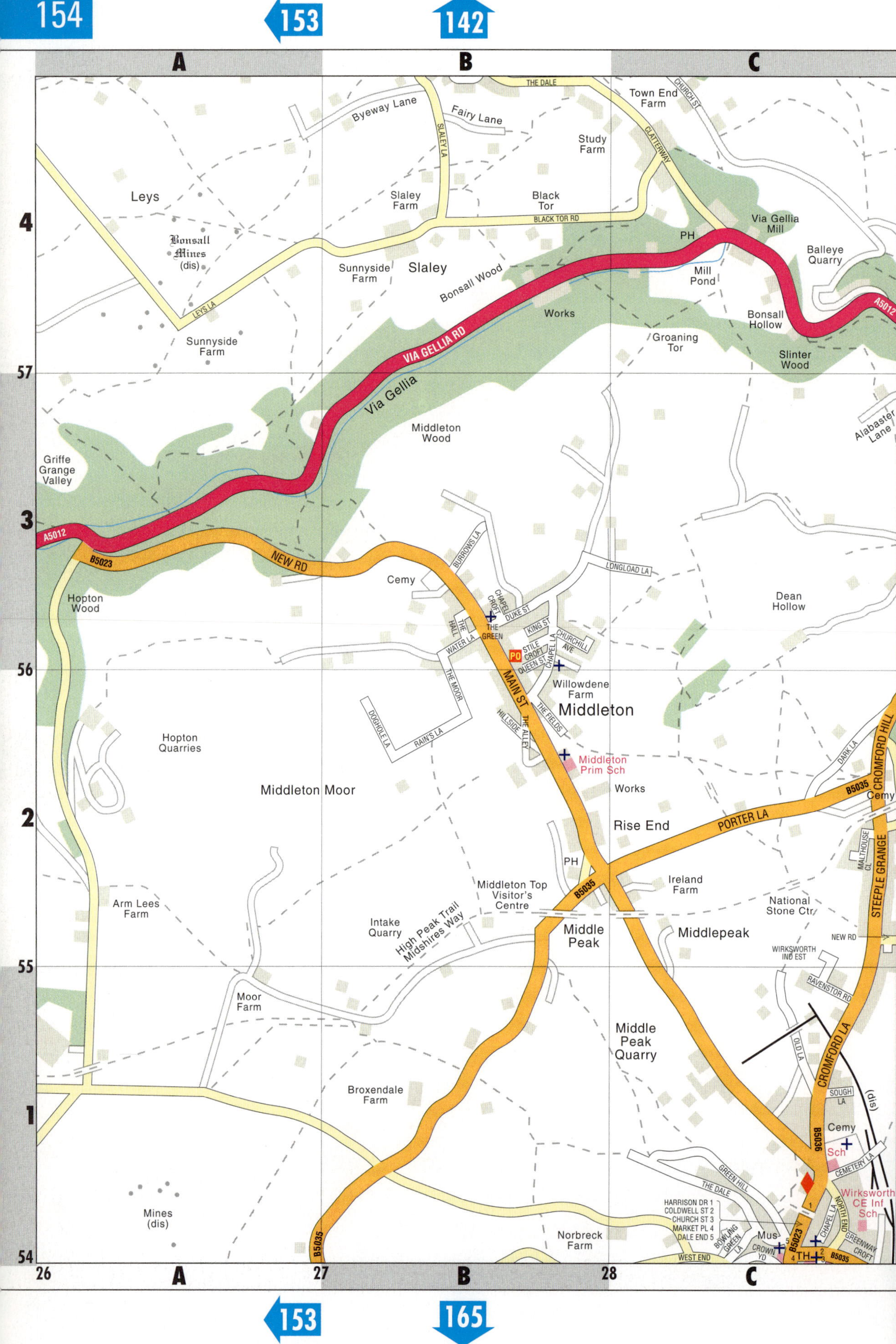
A
B
C
4
57
3
56
2
55
1
54
26
27
28
Leys
Bonsall Mines (dis)
Byeway Lane
Fairy Lane
SLALEY LA
THE DALE
Town End Farm
CHURCH ST
Study Farm
CLATTERWAY
Slaley Farm
Black Tor
BLACK TOR RD
Via Gellia Mill
Balleye Quarry
PH
Mill Pond
Sunnyside Farm
Slaley
Bonsall Wood
Works
LEYS LA
Sunnyside Farm
VIA GELLIA RD
Groaning Tor
Bonsall Hollow
Slinter Wood
A5012
Via Gellia
Middleton Wood
Alabaster Lane
Griffe Grange Valley
A5012
B5023
NEW RD
Cemy
BURROWS LA
LONGLOAD LA
Dean Hollow
Hopton Wood
CHAPEL CROFT
DUKE ST
THE HALL
THE GREEN
KING ST
WATER LA
PO
STILE CROFT
CHURCHILL AVE
QUEEN ST
CHAPEL LA
MAIN ST
THE MOOR
Willowdene Farm
Middleton
HILLSIDE
THE ALLEY
THE FIELDS
DOGHOLE LA
RAIN'S LA
Hopton Quarries
Middleton Prim Sch
DARK LA
CROMFORD HILL
Middleton Moor
Works
B5035
Cemy
Rise End
PORTER LA
MALTHOUSE CL
STEEPLE GRANGE
PH
B5035
Ireland Farm
Arm Lees Farm
Middleton Top Visitor's Centre
National Stone Ctr
Intake Quarry
High Peak Trail
Midshires Way
Middle Peak
Middlepeak
NEW RD
WIRKSWORTH IND EST
RAVENSTOR RD
Moor Farm
Middle Peak Quarry
OLD LA
CROMFORD LA
SOUGH LA
(dis)
Broxendale Farm
B5036
Cemy
Sch
CEMETERY LA
GREEN HILL
THE DALE
Wirksworth CE Inf Sch
Mines (dis)
HARRISON DR 1
COLDWELL ST 2
CHURCH ST 3
MARKET PL 4
DALE END 5
BOWLING GREEN LA
NORTH END
CHAPEL LA
B5035
Norbreck Farm
Mus
CROWN YD
B5023
TH
GREENWAY CROFT
B5035
WEST END

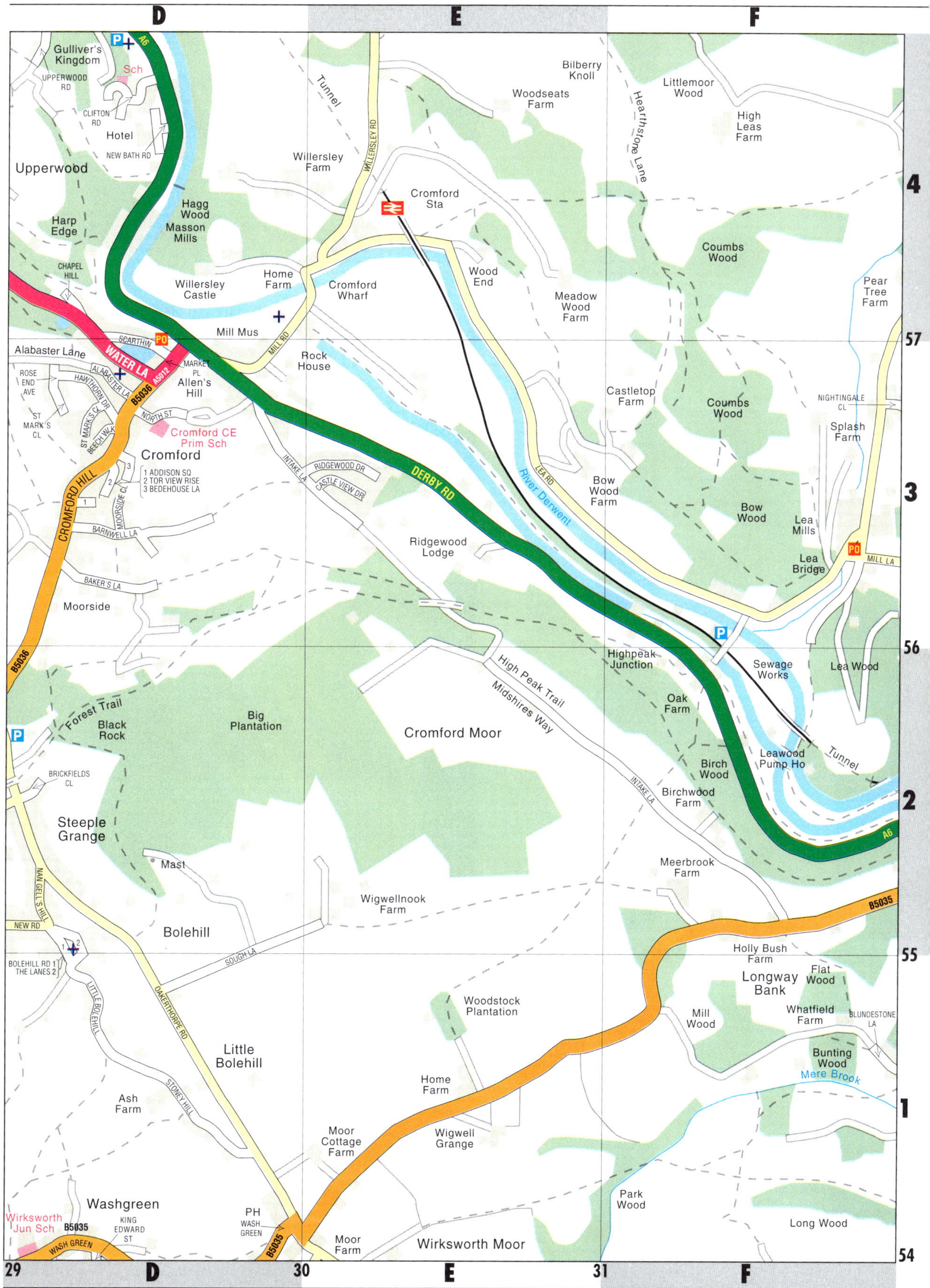
D
E
F
Gulliver's Kingdom
UPPERWOOD RD
Sch
CLIFTON RD
Hotel
NEW BATH RD
Upperwood
Harp Edge
Hagg Wood
Masson Mills
CHAPEL HILL
Willersley Castle
Home Farm
Cromford Wharf
Willersley Farm
WILLERSLEY RD
Tunnel
Cromford Sta
Woodseats Farm
Bilberry Knoll
Hearthstone Lane
Littlemoor Wood
High Leas Farm
Coumbs Wood
Pear Tree Farm
Wood End
Meadow Wood Farm
Mill Mus
MILL RD
Rock House
SCARTHIN
PO
WATER LA
A5012
MARKET PL
Allen's Hill
Alabaster Lane
ROSE END AVE
ALABASTER LA
HAWTHORN DR
ST MARK'S CL
ST MARK'S CL
BEECH WLK
B5036
NORTH ST
Cromford CE Prim Sch
Cromford
1 ADDISON SQ
2 TOR VIEW RISE
3 BEDEHOUSE LA
CROMFORD HILL
MOORSIDE CL
BARNWELL LA
BAKER'S LA
Moorside
INTAKE LA
RIDGEWOOD DR
CASTLE VIEW DR
DERBY RD
A6
Ridgewood Lodge
LEA RD
River Derwent
Castletop Farm
Coumbs Wood
NIGHTINGALE CL
Splash Farm
Bow Wood Farm
Bow Wood
Lea Mills
Lea Bridge
MILL LA
Highpeak Junction
Sewage Works
Lea Wood
Oak Farm
High Peak Trail
Midshires Way
Forest Trail
Black Rock
Big Plantation
Cromford Moor
Birch Wood
Leawood Pump Ho
Tunnel
BRICKFIELDS CL
Steeple Grange
Birchwood Farm
INTAKE LA
Mast
Meerbrook Farm
NAN GELL'S HILL
NEW RD
Wigwellnook Farm
B5035
Bolehill
SOUGH LA
Holly Bush Farm
BOLEHILL RD
THE LANES
LITTLE BOLEHILL
OAKERTHORPE RD
Longway Bank
Flat Wood
Woodstock Plantation
Mill Wood
Whatfield Farm
BLUNDESTONE LA
Little Bolehill
Bunting Wood
Mere Brook
Ash Farm
STONEY HILL
Home Farm
Moor Cottage Farm
Wigwell Grange
Washgreen
Park Wood
Wirksworth Jun Sch
KING EDWARD ST
PH
WASH GREEN
Long Wood
WASH GREEN
Moor Farm
Wirksworth Moor
4
57
3
56
2
55
1
54
29
30
31

155
144

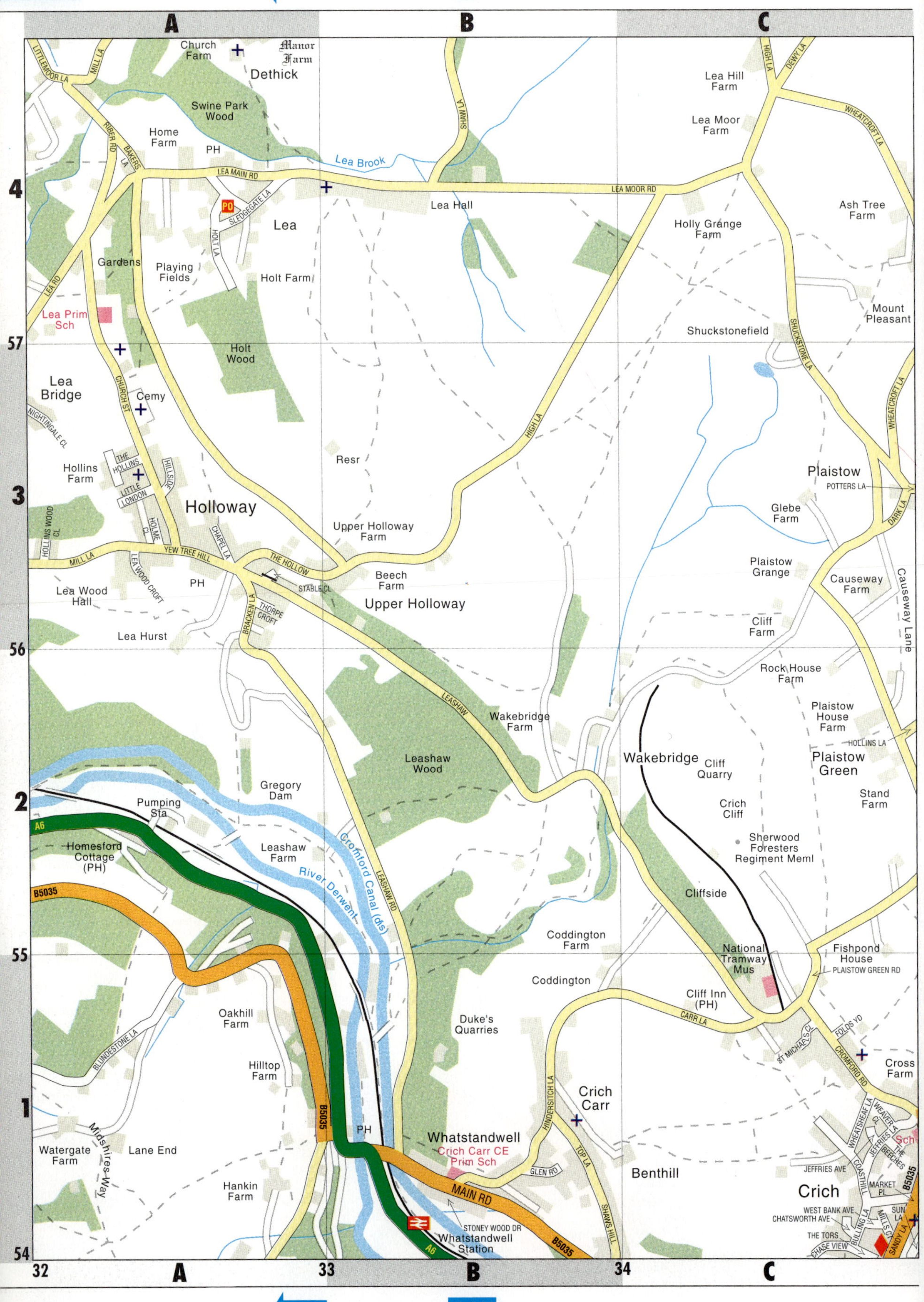
A
B
C
Church Farm
Manor Farm
Dethick
Swine Park Wood
Home Farm
PH
Lea Brook
LEA MAIN RD
LEA MOOR RD
Lea Hall
Lea
Holt Farm
Gardens
Playing Fields
Lea Prim Sch
Holt Wood
Lea Bridge
Cemy
Hollins Farm
Holloway
Resr
Upper Holloway Farm
Beech Farm
Upper Holloway
Lea Wood Hall
PH
Lea Hurst
Lea Hill Farm
Lea Moor Farm
Ash Tree Farm
Holly Grange Farm
Mount Pleasant
Shuckstonefield
Plaistow
POTTERS LA
Glebe Farm
Plaistow Grange
Causeway Farm
Causeway Lane
Cliff Farm
Rock House Farm
Plaistow House Farm
HOLLINS LA
Plaistow Green
Stand Farm
Wakebridge Farm
Wakebridge
Cliff Quarry
Crich Cliff
Sherwood Foresters Regiment Meml
Leashaw Wood
Gregory Dam
Pumping Sta
Homesford Cottage (PH)
Leashaw Farm
River Derwent
Cromford Canal (dis)
Cliffside
Coddington Farm
Coddington
National Tramway Mus
Fishpond House
PLAISTOW GREEN RD
Cliff Inn (PH)
CARR LA
Oakhill Farm
Duke's Quarries
Hilltop Farm
Crich Carr
Cross Farm
Watergate Farm
Lane End
Midshires Way
PH
Whatstandwell
Crich Carr CE Prim Sch
Hankin Farm
MAIN RD
STONEY WOOD DR
Whatstandwell Station
GLEN RD
Benthill
Crich
Sch
JEFFRIES AVE
MARKET PL
WEST BANK AVE
CHATSWORTH AVE
THE TORS
CHASE VIEW
A6
B5035
4
57
3
56
2
55
1
54
32
33
34

155
167

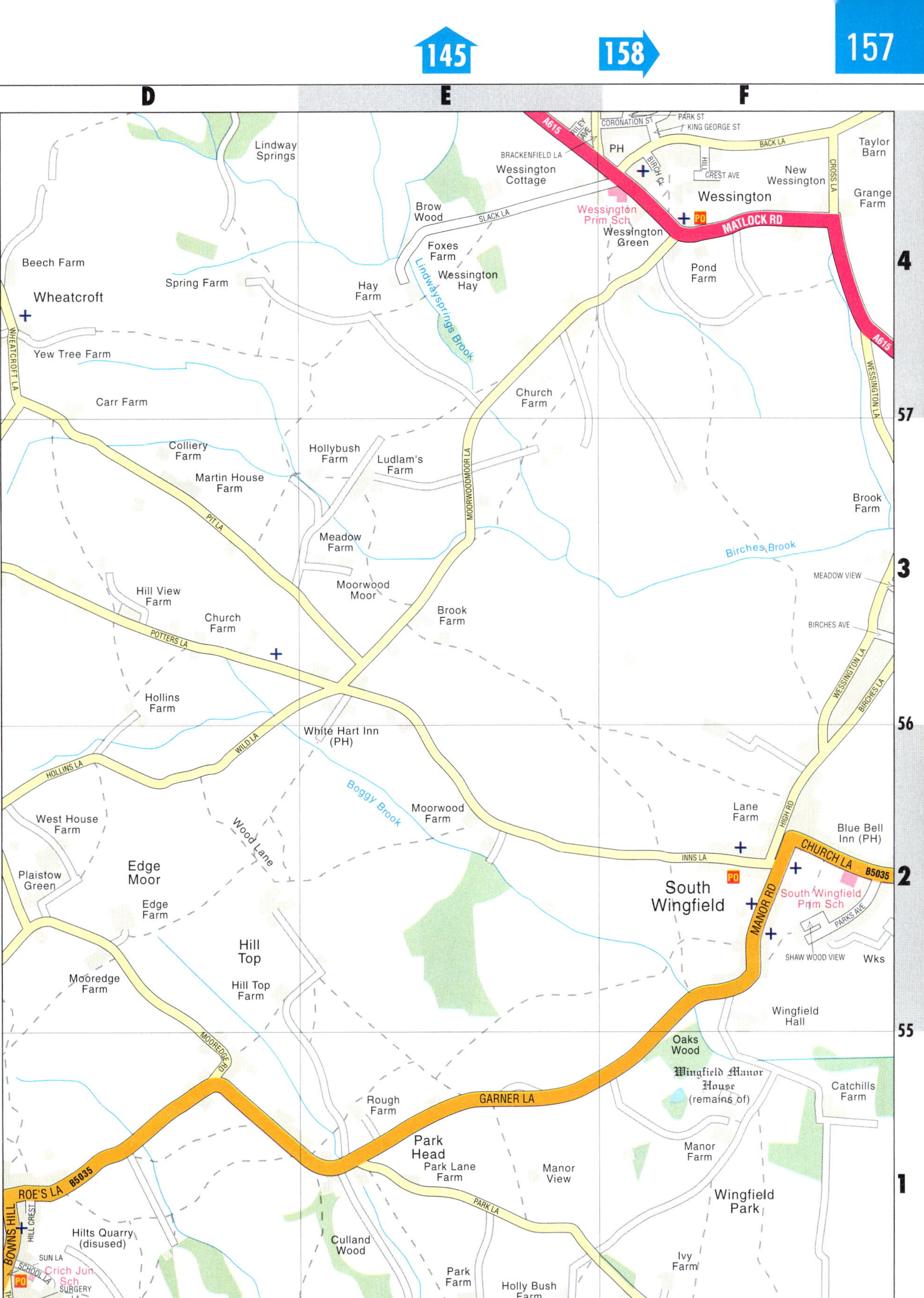

Lindway
Springs

Wessington Cottage

BRACKENFIELD LA

A615

CORONATION ST

PARK ST

KING GEORGE ST

BACK LA

Taylor
Barn

PH

Brow
Wood

SLACK LA

BIRCH CL

CREST AVE

New
Wessington

Wessington

Grange
Farm

Foxes
Farm

Wessington Prim Sch

Wessington
Green

PO

MATLOCK RD

Beech Farm

Spring Farm

Hay
Farm

Wessington
Hay

Pond
Farm

4

Wheatcroft

Lindwayssprings Brook

WESSINGTON LA

CROSS LA

Yew Tree Farm

Church
Farm

57

WHEATCROFT LA

Carr Farm

Colliery
Farm

Hollybush
Farm

Ludlam's
Farm

MOORWOODMOOR LA

Brook
Farm

Martin House
Farm

Meadow
View

PIT LA

Meadow
Farm

Birches Brook

BIRCHES AVE

3

Hill View
Farm

Moorwood
Moor

Church
Farm

POTTERS LA

Brook
Farm

WESSINGTON LA

BIRCHES LA

Hollins
Farm

White Hart Inn
(PH)

56

Boggy Brook

WILD LA

HOLLINS LA

Moorwood
Farm

Lane
Farm

HIGH RD

Blue Bell
Inn (PH)

West House
Farm

Wood Lane

INNS LA

CHURCH LA

B5035

2

Plaistow
Green

Edge
Moor

Edge
Farm

South
Wingfield

PO

South Wingfield
Prim Sch

MANOR RD

PARKS AVE

Hill
Top

SHAW WOOD VIEW

Wks

Mooredge
Farm

Hill Top
Farm

Wingfield
Hall

55

MOOREDGE RD

Oaks
Wood

Wingfield Manor
House
(remains of)

Catchills
Farm

Rough
Farm

GARNER LA

Manor
Farm

Park
Head

Park Lane
Farm

Manor
View

Wingfield
Park

1

ROE'S LA

B5035

HILL CREST

PARK LA

Ivy
Farm

BOND'S HILL

Hilts Quarry
(disused)

Culland
Wood

Park
Farm

Holly Bush
Farm

Coalburn
Farm

SUN LA

SCHOOL LA

Crich Jun
Sch

PO

SURGERY
LA

OULLAND VIEW

SPRINGFIELD CL

DIMPLE LA

THE COMMON

54

157
146

A   **B**   **C**

4

A61

CROSS LA

PARK LA

Sebastopol Farm

Adastra

Golf Course

CH

PIT LA

Upper Delves Farm

Shirland Lodge

Lower Delves Farm

Shirland Lodge Farm

B6013

Carr Hill

57

A615

MATLOCK RD

Amber Farm

Amber Hotel (PH)

Toadhole Furnace

Alfreton Brook

Hall's Plantation

CHESTERFIELD RD

B6025

WESSINGTON LA

Broom House

Brook Farm

3

BIRCHES AVE

BIRCHES LA

Dale Bridge

Long Plantation

Pond Wood

Dale House

Ufton Fields Farm

Wren Wood

ARTHUR ST

BISHOP ST

HARDY ST

CHARLES ST

HOWARD ST

56

LINBERY CL

Peacock Hotel

Lane Farm

Ufton Fields

BONSALL LA

CHURCH ST

B6006

Mill

HOLM LA

A615

B5035

Fourlane Ends

Alfreton Park

Alfreton L Ctr

NEW ST

PO

CHATSWORTH CL

KING ST

LINCOLN ST

2

B5035

River Amber

David's Hill

Oakerthorpe

Parkwood Sch

WINGFIELD RD

A615

BACK GOOKER LA

NUTTALL ST

INDEPENDENT HILL

NUTTALL CL

Anchor Inn (PH)

CH

DERBY RD

EWART LA

GLADSTONE ST

KING MEADOW

Hollybank House

Golf Course

A61

COLLIERY RD

DERWENT GR

Shaw Wood

Damstead Wood

55

Oakerthorpe Manor Farm

A38

Chestnut Farm

Hotel

Shaw Wood Farm

Lily Street Farm

DERBY RD

1

Longcroft

Lily Cottage

Sleetmoor House

B6179

JACKSON'S LA

B6013

Castle Hill

SLEETMOOR LA

54

A   39   **B**   40   **C**

38

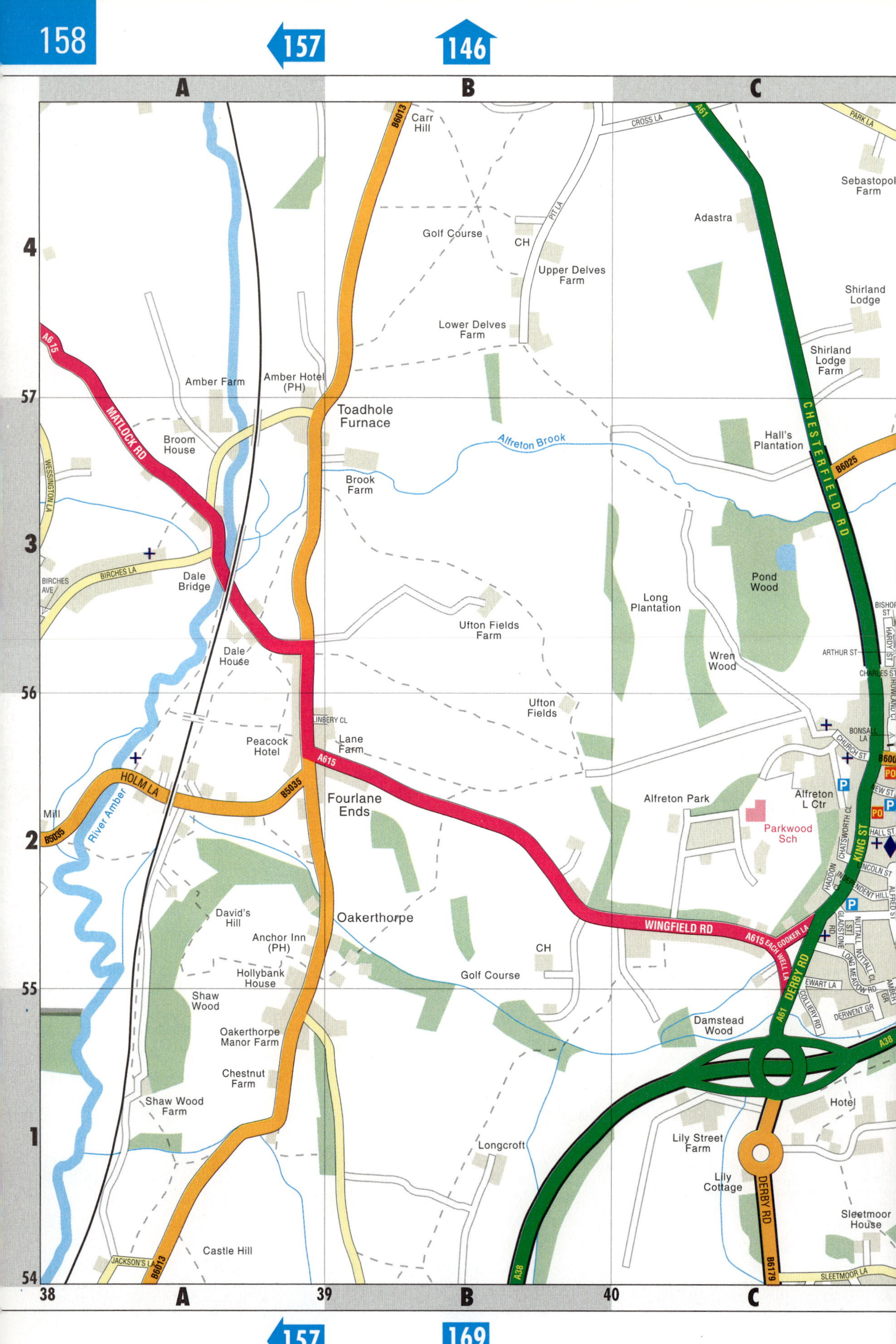

157
169

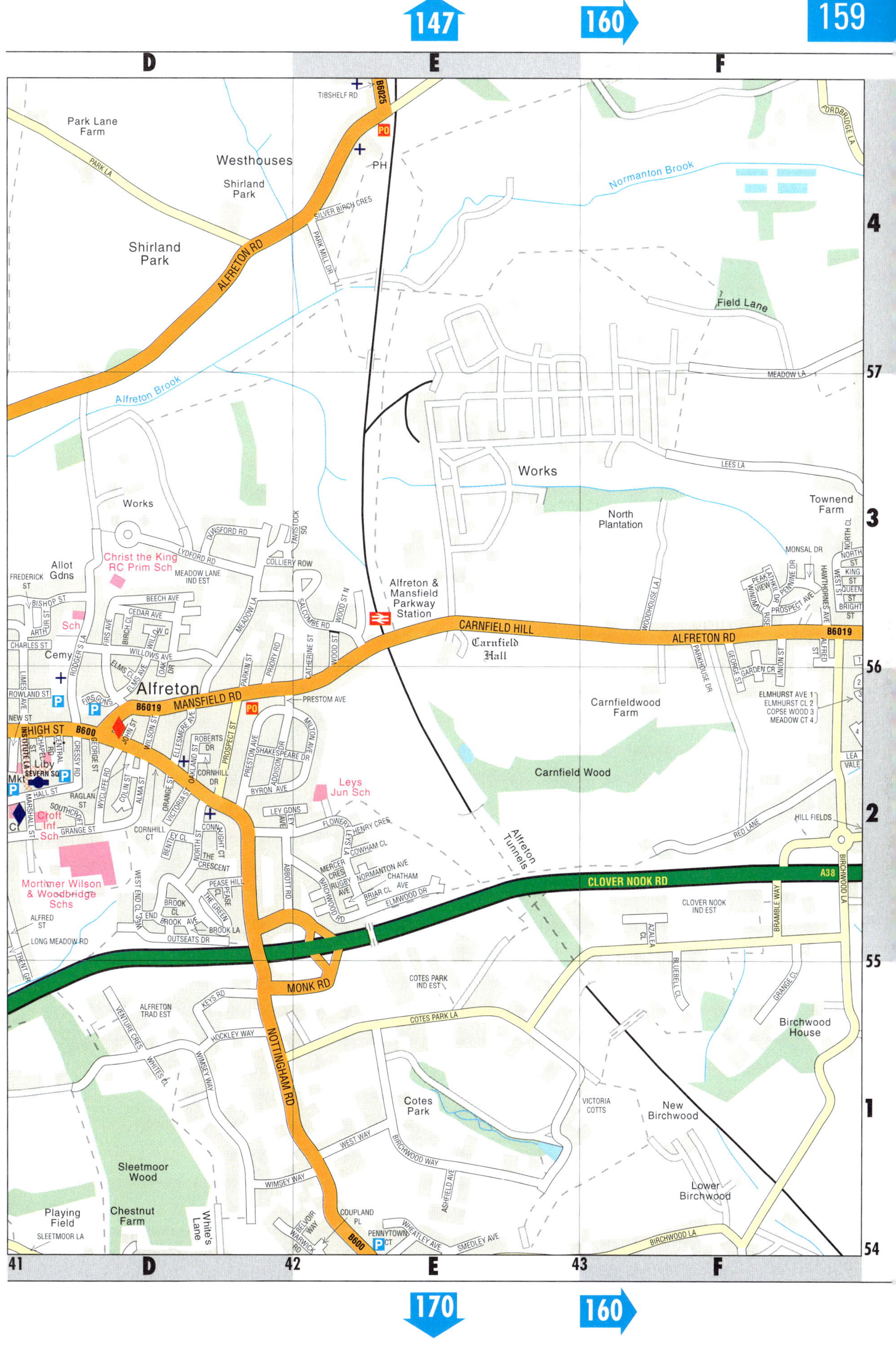
D
E
F
Park Lane Farm
Westhouses
Shirland Park
Shirland Park
PARK LA
ALFRETON RD
TIBSHELF RD
B6025
PO
PH
SILVER BIRCH CRES
PARK MILL DR
Normanton Brook
FORDBRIDGE LA
Field Lane
MEADOW LA
Alfreton Brook
Works
LEES LA
Works
Townend Farm
North Plantation
MONSAL DR
Christ the King RC Prim Sch
Allot Gdns
FREDERICK ST
MEADOW LANE IND EST
DUNSFORD RD
LYDFORD RD
COLLIERY ROW
TAVISTOCK SQ
Alfreton & Mansfield Parkway Station
CARNFIELD HILL
Carnfield Hall
ALFRETON RD
B6019
WOODHOUSE LA
PARKHOUSE DR
GEORGE ST
GARDEN CR
UNION ST
ALFRED ST
Cemy
Sch
Alfreton
MANSFIELD RD
B6019
HIGH ST
B600
PO
PRESTON AVE
Carnfieldwood Farm
ELMHURST AVE 1
ELMHURST CL 2
COPSE WOOD 3
MEADOW CT 4
LEA VALE
Carnfield Wood
Leys Jun Sch
Croft Inf Sch
Mortimer Wilson & Woodbridge Schs
Alfreton Tunnels
HILL FIELDS
RED LANE
CLOVER NOOK RD
A38
BIRCHWOOD LA
CLOVER NOOK IND EST
BRAMBLE WAY
AZALEA CL
BLUEBELL CL
GRANGE CL
MONK RD
NOTTINGHAM RD
ALFRETON TRAD EST
COTES PARK IND EST
COTES PARK LA
Birchwood House
Cotes Park
VICTORIA COTTS
New Birchwood
Lower Birchwood
BIRCHWOOD WAY
WEST WAY
WIMSEY WAY
HOCKLEY WAY
Sleetmoor Wood
Chestnut Farm
Playing Field
SLEETMOOR LA
White's Lane
COUPLAND PL
PENNYTOWN CT
WHEATLEY AVE
SMEDLEY AVE
BIRCHWOOD LA
B600
4
57
3
56
2
55
1
54
41
42
43

159
148

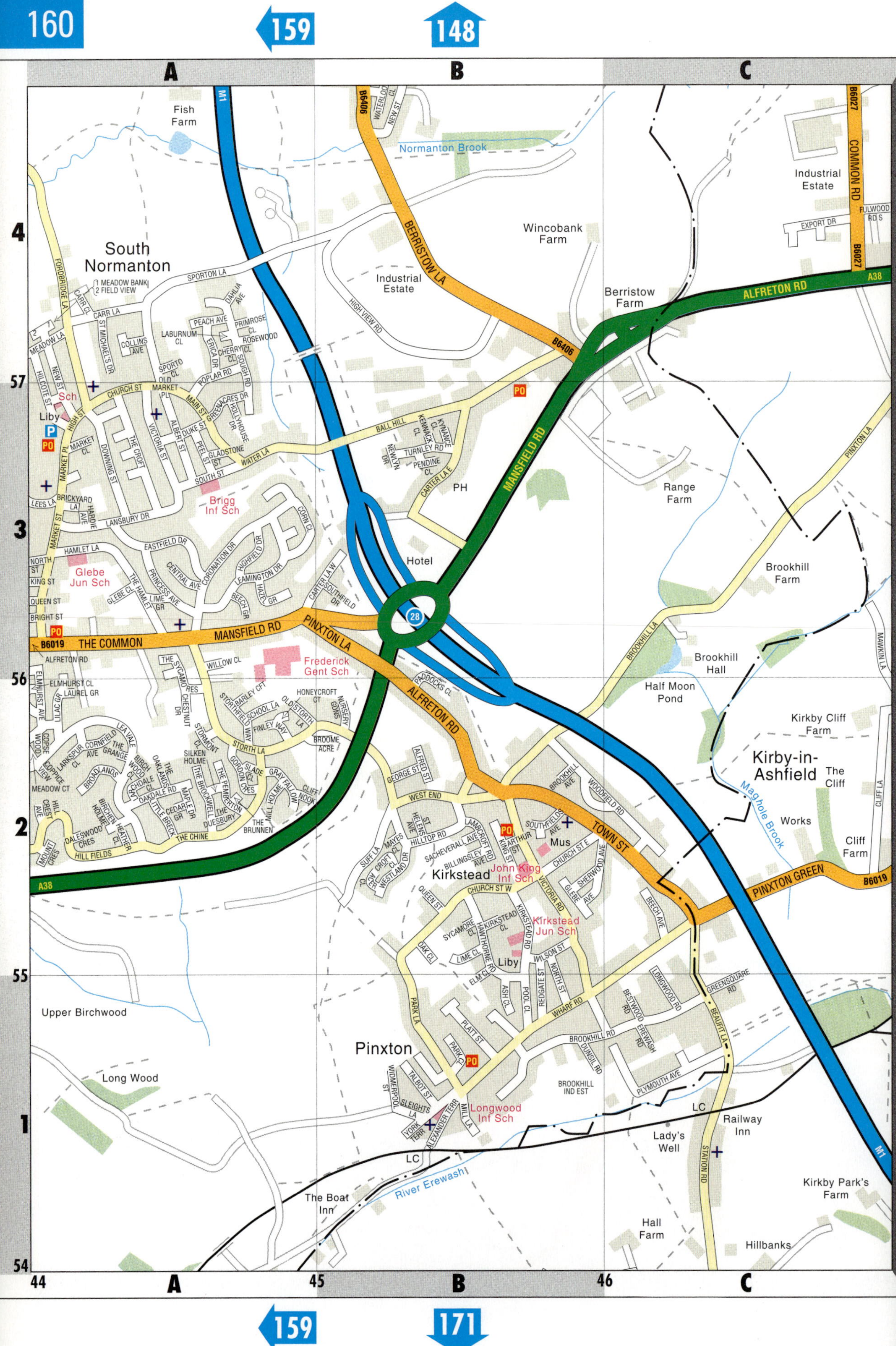
A
B
C
4
57
3
56
2
55
1
54
44
45
46
M1
B6406
Fish
Farm
Normanton Brook
Industrial
Estate
COMMON RD
B6027
FULWOOD
RD S
EXPORT DR
Wincobank
Farm
South
Normanton
BERRISTOW LA
Industrial
Estate
Berristow
Farm
ALFRETON RD
A38
FORDBRIDGE LA
1 MEADOW BANK
2 FIELD VIEW
SPORTON LA
HIGH VIEW RD
CARR CL
CARR LA
MEADOW LA
ST MICHAEL'S DR
COLLINS AVE
LABURNUM CL
PEACH AVE
DAHLIA AVE
PRIMROSE CL
ROSEWOOD
ERICA DR
CHERRY CL
SOUGH RD
POPLAR RD
SPORTO CL
OLD MARKET PL
GREENACRES DR
HOLLYHOUSE DR
CHURCH ST
MAIN ST
DUKE ST
ALBERT ST
PEEL ST
GLADSTONE ST
WATER LA
SOUTH ST
BALL HILL
KENNACK CL
KYNANCE CL
TURNLEY RD
NEWLYN DR
PENDINE CL
CARTER LA E
PO
MANSFIELD RD
Range
Farm
PINXTON LA
Sch
Liby
P
PO
HIGH ST
MARKET PL
MARKET CL
DOWNING ST
THE CROFT
VICTORIA ST
Brigg
Inf Sch
PH
NEW ST
HILCOTE ST
LEES LA
BRICKYARD LA
HARDIE AVE
LANSBURY DR
CORN CL
MARKET ST
EASTFIELD DR
CENTRAL AVE
CORONATION DR
HIGHFIELD DR
LEAMINGTON DR
HAZEL GR
BEECH GR
PRINCESS AVE
LIME GR
THE HAMLET
GLEBE CL
HAMLET LA
NORTH ST
KING ST
QUEEN ST
BRIGHT ST
Glebe
Jun Sch
CARTER LA W
SOUTHFIELD DR
Hotel
Brookhill
Farm
28
PO
B6019
THE COMMON
MANSFIELD RD
PINXTON LA
ALFRETON RD
Frederick
Gent Sch
WILLOW CL
THE SYCAMORES
CHESTNUT DR
BARLEY CFT
HONEYCROFT CT
NURSERY GDNS
SCHOOL LA
OLD STORTH LA
FINLEY WAY
STORTHFIELD WAY
BROOME ACRE
STORMONT CL
SILKEN HOLME
STORTH LA
GORDON CRES
SLADE CL
GRAY FALLOW
CLIFF NOOK
MILL HOLME
THE BRUNNEN
THE BROCKWELL
THE PEMBERTON
DUESBURY
THE CHINE
ELMHURST CL
LAUREL GR
LILAC GR
ELMHURST AVE
LEA VALE
CORNFIELD AVE
THE GRANGE
LARKSPUR CL
BROADLANDS
BIRCH WOOD
ACHDALE CL
OAKDALE RD
THE OAKLANDS
CEDAR GR
MAPLE DR
LITTLE BRECK
BIRCHEN HOLME
HEATHER CL
DALESWOOD CRES
HILL FIELDS
COPSE WOOD
COPPICE VIEW
MEADOW CT
HILL CREST AVE
MOUNT CRES
A38
Brookhill
Hall
Half Moon
Pond
BROOKHILL LA
MAWKIN LA
Kirkby Cliff
Farm
Kirby-in-
Ashfield
The
Cliff
Maghole Brook
CLIFF LA
Works
Cliff
Farm
PINXTON GREEN
B6019
PADDOCKS CL
GEORGE ST
ALFRED ST
WEST END
BROOKHILL AVE
WOODFIELD RD
TOWN ST
ST HELENS AVE
HILLTOP RD
LAMBCROFT RD
SACHEVERALL AVE
BILLINGSLEY AVE
KING ST
ARTHUR ST
SOUTHFIELDS AVE
PO
Mus
CHURCH ST E
SHERWOOD AVE
GLEBE AVE
SUFF LA
MAYES CL
CROFT CL
ACER CL
WESTLAND DR
Kirkstead
John King
Inf Sch
CHURCH ST W
QUEEN ST
VICTORIA RD
BEECH AVE
SYCAMORE CL
KIRKSTEAD CL
HAWTHORNE RD
KIRKSTEAD RD
Kirkstead
Jun Sch
OAK CL
LIME CL
Liby
WILSON ST
ELM CL
ASH CL
POOL CL
REDGATE ST
NORTH ST
WHARF RD
LONGWOOD RD
GREENSQUARE RD
BESTWOOD RD
EREWASH RD
BEAUFIT LA
Upper Birchwood
PARK LA
PLATT ST
BROOKHILL RD
DUNSIL RD
Pinxton
PARK CL
PO
PLYMOUTH AVE
BROOKHILL
IND EST
Long Wood
TALBOT ST
WIDMERPOOL ST
SLEIGHTS LA
YORK TERR
ALEXANDER TERR
MILL LA
Longwood
Inf Sch
LC
Railway
Inn
Lady's
Well
LC
STATION RD
River Erewash
The Boat
Inn
Kirkby Park's
Farm
Hall
Farm
Hillbanks
M1

159
171

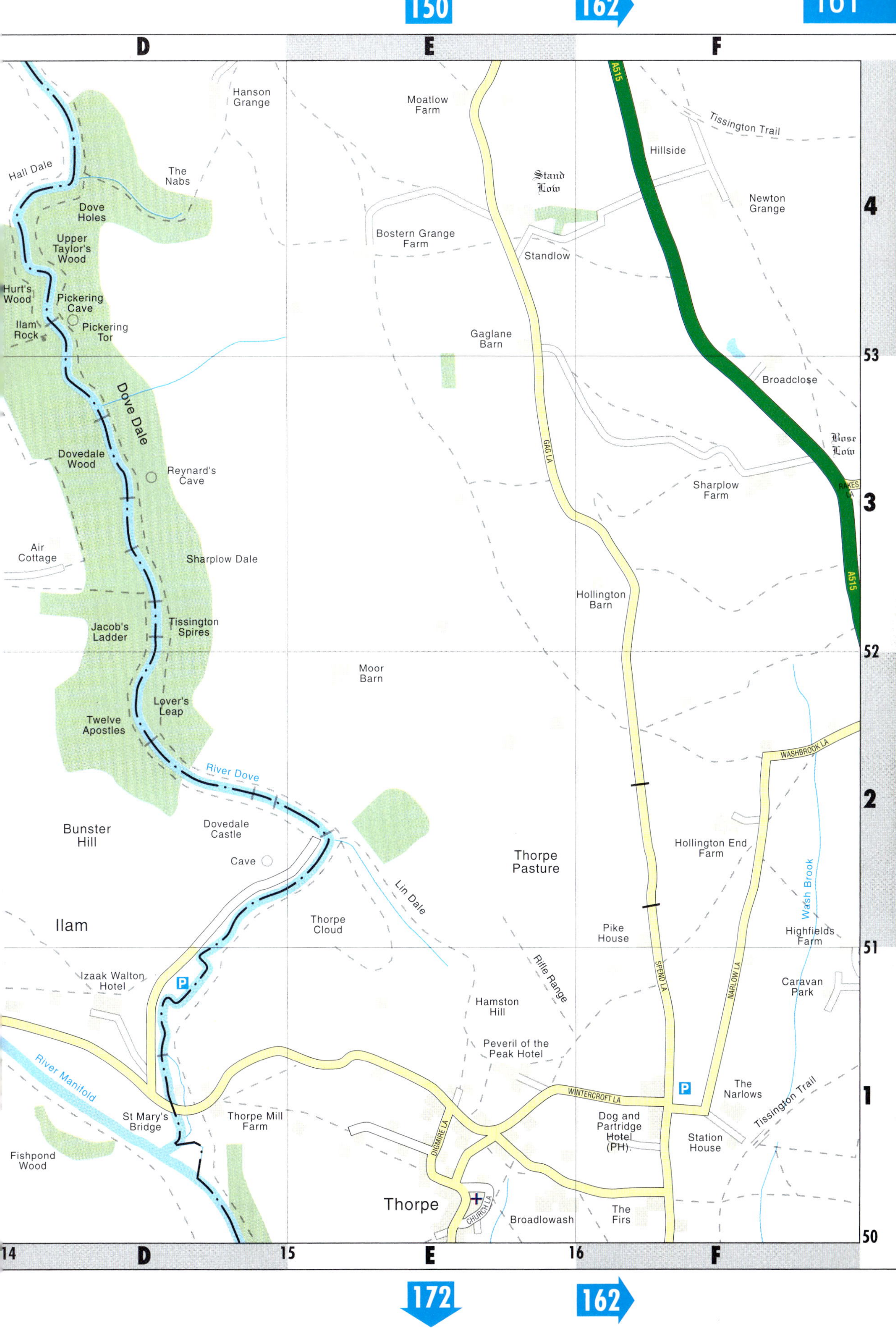
D
E
F
Hanson Grange
Moatlow Farm
Tissington Trail
Hillside
Hall Dale
The Nabs
Stand Low
Newton Grange
Dove Holes
Upper Taylor's Wood
Bostern Grange Farm
Standlow
Hurt's Wood
Pickering Cave
Ilam Rock
Pickering Tor
Gaglane Barn
Broadclose
Dove Dale
Rose Low
Dovedale Wood
Reynard's Cave
GAG LA
Sharplow Farm
RAKES LA
Air Cottage
Sharplow Dale
A515
Hollington Barn
Jacob's Ladder
Tissington Spires
Moor Barn
Lover's Leap
Twelve Apostles
WASHBROOK LA
River Dove
Bunster Hill
Dovedale Castle
Cave
Thorpe Pasture
Hollington End Farm
Lin Dale
Wash Brook
Ilam
Thorpe Cloud
Pike House
Highfields Farm
Izaak Walton Hotel
Rifle Range
SPEND LA
NARLOW LA
Caravan Park
Hamston Hill
Peveril of the Peak Hotel
River Manifold
WINTERCROFT LA
The Narrows
Tissington Trail
St Mary's Bridge
Thorpe Mill Farm
DIGMIRE LA
Dog and Partridge Hotel (PH)
Station House
Fishpond Wood
Thorpe
CHURCH LA
Broadlowash
The Firs
4
53
3
52
2
51
1
50
14
15
16

161
151

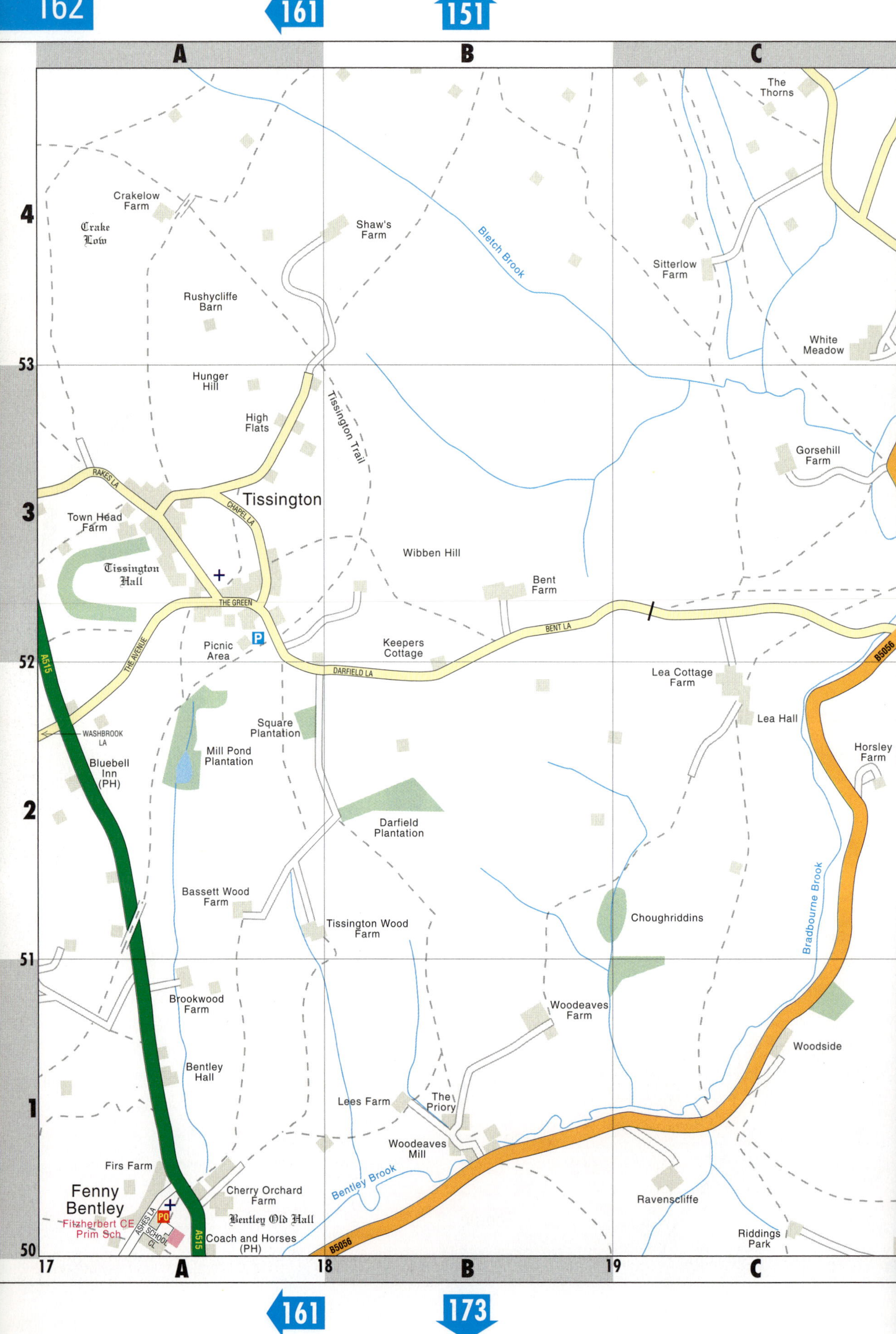
A
B
C
4
53
3
52
2
51
1
50
17
18
19
The Thorns
Crakelow Farm
Crake Low
Shaw's Farm
Bletch Brook
Sitterlow Farm
Rushycliffe Barn
White Meadow
Hunger Hill
Tissington Trail
High Flats
Gorsehill Farm
RAKES LA
Tissington
CHAPEL LA
Town Head Farm
Tissington Hall
Wibben Hill
Bent Farm
THE GREEN
BENT LA
Picnic Area
Keepers Cottage
THE AVENUE
A515
DARFIELD LA
Lea Cottage Farm
B5056
WASHBROOK LA
Square Plantation
Lea Hall
Mill Pond Plantation
Bluebell Inn (PH)
Horsley Farm
Darfield Plantation
Bassett Wood Farm
Bradbourne Brook
Tissington Wood Farm
Choughriddins
Brookwood Farm
Woodeaves Farm
Woodside
Bentley Hall
The Priory
Lees Farm
Woodeaves Mill
Firs Farm
Bentley Brook
Cherry Orchard Farm
Ravenscliffe
Fenny Bentley
ASHES LA
PO
Bentley Old Hall
Fitzherbert CE Prim Sch
SCHOOL CL
Coach and Horses (PH)
Riddings Park

161
173

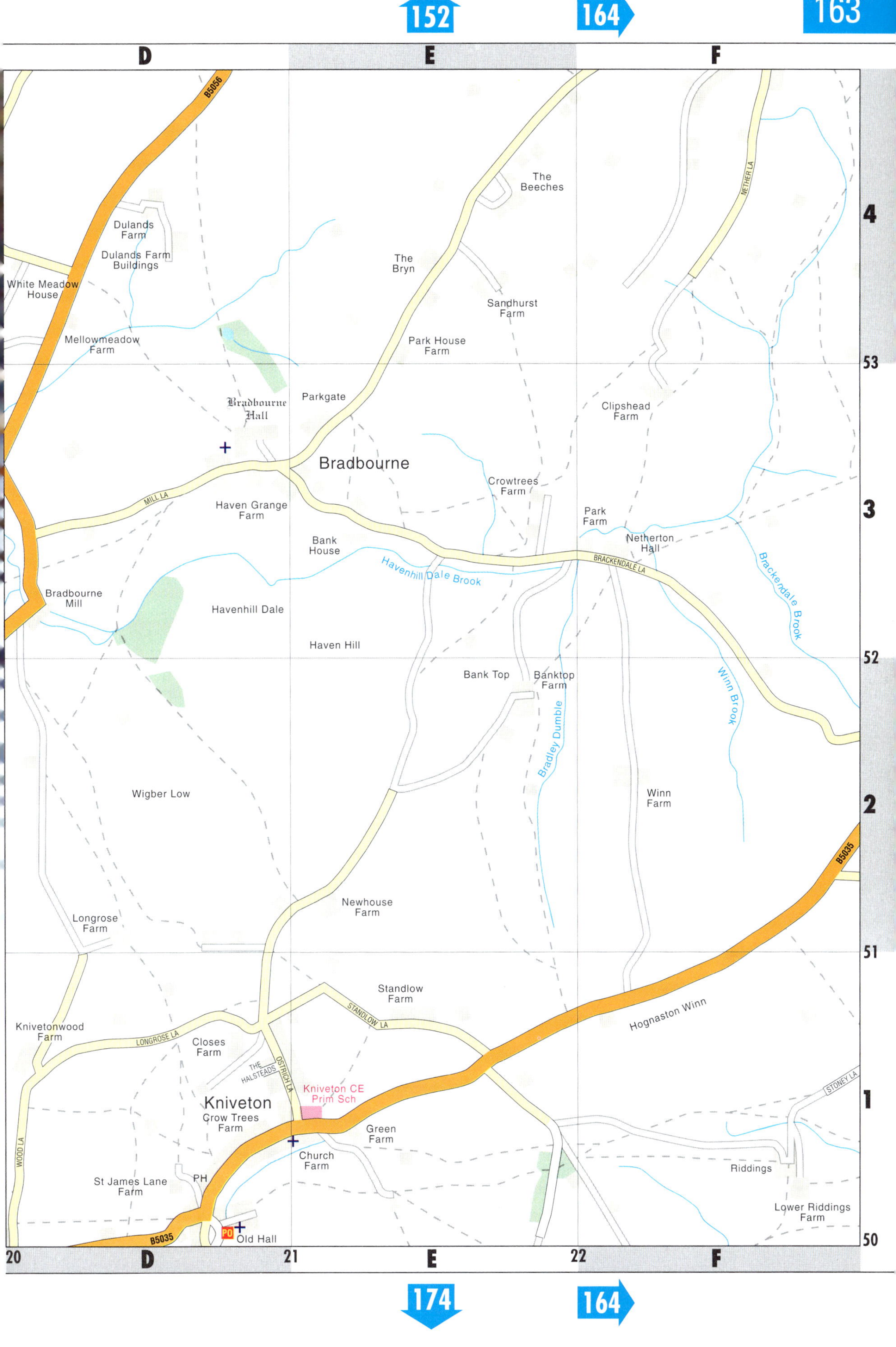
D
E
F
B5056
The Beeches
NETHER LA
4
Dulands Farm
Dulands Farm Buildings
The Bryn
White Meadow House
Sandhurst Farm
Mellowmeadow Farm
Park House Farm
53
Bradbourne Hall
Parkgate
Clipshead Farm
Bradbourne
Crowtrees Farm
MILL LA
Haven Grange Farm
3
Park Farm
Bank House
Netherton Hall
BRACKENDALE LA
Havenhill Dale Brook
Brackendale Brook
Bradbourne Mill
Havenhill Dale
Haven Hill
52
Bank Top
Banktop Farm
Winn Brook
Bradley Dumble
Wigber Low
2
Winn Farm
B5035
Newhouse Farm
Longrose Farm
51
Standlow Farm
Knivetonwood Farm
LONGROSE LA
Closes Farm
STANDLOW LA
Hognaston Winn
THE HALSTEADS
OSTRICH LA
Kniveton CE Prim Sch
Kniveton
STONEY LA
1
Crow Trees Farm
Green Farm
WOOD LA
Church Farm
Riddings
St James Lane Farm
PH
Lower Riddings Farm
PO
Old Hall
B5035
50
20
D
21
E
22
F

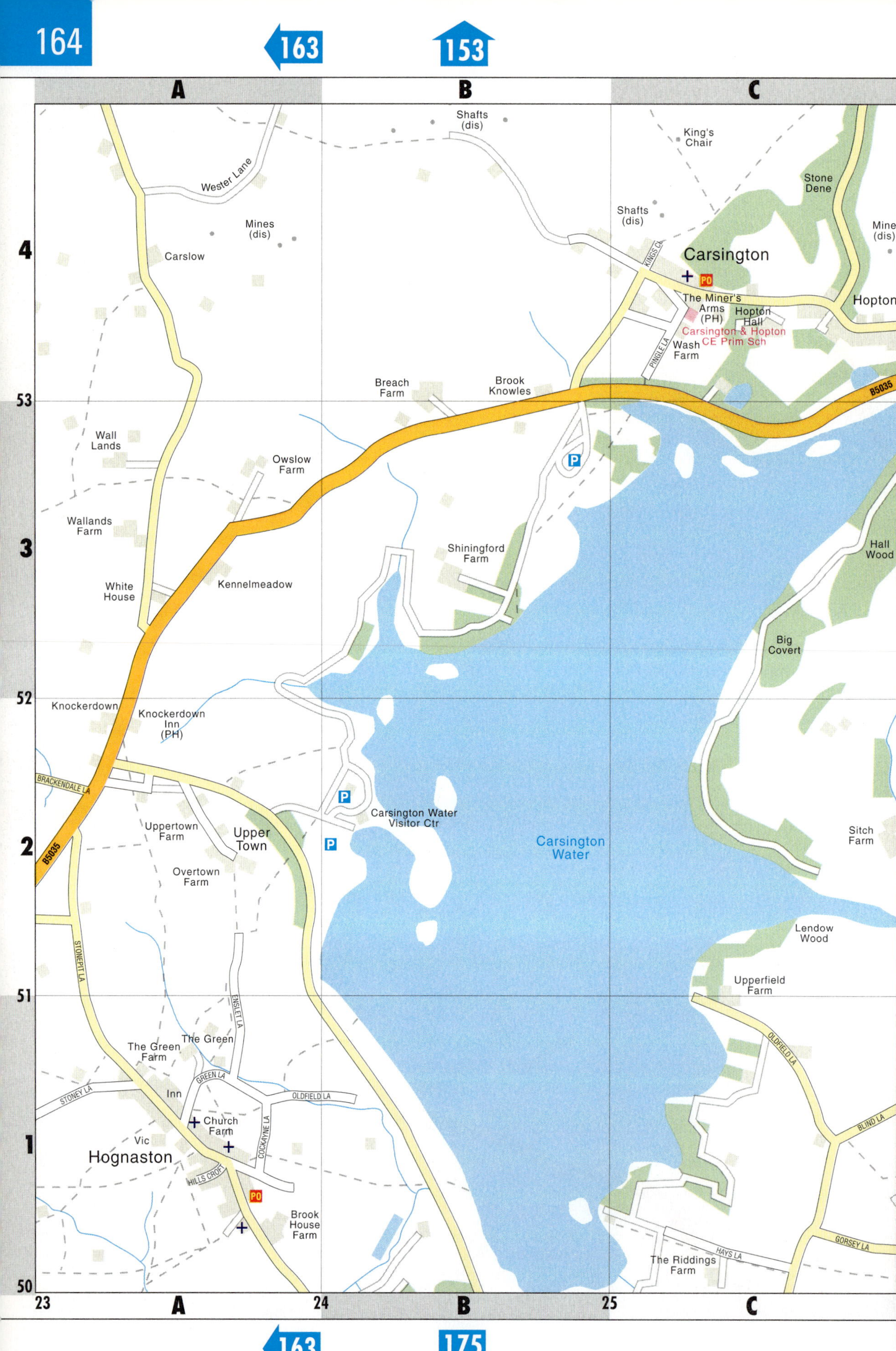
A
B
C
Shafts (dis)
King's Chair
Wester Lane
Stone Dene
Mines (dis)
Shafts (dis)
Mine (dis)
Carslow
Carsington
KINGS CL
PO
The Miner's Arms (PH)
Hopton Hall
Hopton
Carsington & Hopton CE Prim Sch
PINGLE LA
Wash Farm
Breach Farm
Brook Knowles
B5035
Wall Lands
Owslow Farm
P
Wallands Farm
Shiningford Farm
Hall Wood
White House
Kennelmeadow
Big Covert
Knockerdown
Knockerdown Inn (PH)
BRACKENDALE LA
P
Carsington Water Visitor Ctr
Uppertown Farm
Upper Town
P
Carsington Water
Sitch Farm
B5035
Overtown Farm
Lendow Wood
STONEPIT LA
Upperfield Farm
ENSLET LA
The Green
The Green Farm
OLDFIELD LA
GREEN LA
STONEY LA
Inn
OLDFIELD LA
Church Farm
COCKAYNE LA
BLIND LA
Vic
Hognaston
HILLS CROFT
PO
Brook House Farm
HAYS LA
GORSEY LA
The Riddings Farm
4
53
3
52
2
51
1
50
23
24
25

154

166

D E F

WIRKSWORTH
Yokecliffe
Godfreyhole
Godfreyhole Farm
Mines (dis)
Sycamore Farm
Yokecliffe Rake Mines (dis)
Summer Lane
Warmbrook
Stainsbro' Hall
Soldiers' Knoll
Sprink Wood
Pittywood Farm
Rough Pitty Side
Round Meadow Farm
Millers Green
Hob Hall
Hob Wood
Gorseybank
Recn Gd
Anthony Fell Sch
Sch
Hasker Farm
Catholе Wood
Callow Carr Farm
Upper House Farm
Stonebridge Farm
Sewage Works
River Ecclesbourne
DERBY RD
Callow
Callow Hall
Carr Bank
Sunnybank Wood
The Kennels
Callow Park Farm
Beighton Hill Farm
Parkhill Wood
Millbank Wood
Alton Manor Farm
Topshill Brook
Callow Moor Farm
Alton Manor
Windmill Farm
Moorside
Moorside Spring Farm
Topshill Farm
Moorside Farm
Alton Brook
Quarry Wood
Pearl Well Farm
Barley Hill
Ivy Cottage
Kirk Ireton CE Prim Sch
PH
Kirk Ireton
Alton Hall
Alton Farm
Town End Farm
Alton Mill Farm
B5035
B5023
STAINSBRO' LA
CALLOW LA
MILLERS GREEN
DARK LA
SITCH LA
MOOR LA
HALFMOON LA
TOPSHILL LA
WAPENTAKE LA
BLIND LA
TINKERLEY LA
WIRKSWORTH RD
GORSEY LA
MAIN ST
CHURCH CNR
RECTORY LA
HOB LA
BARNSLEY LA
BLACKWALL LA
WELL BANKS
PEATS CL
COFFIN LA
HEMPYD LA
CHURCH LEVEL
NETHER LA
BROAD WAY
WEST END
MARKET PL
THE CAUSEWAY
HAMMONDS CT
FOGGS ENTRY
ST JOHN'S ST
WARMBROOK
WOOD ST
COLDWELL ST
NETHER HALL GDNS
WIRKSWORTH
CANTERBURY RD
CANTERBURY TERR
1 BLIND LA
2 CHURCH ST
3 ST MARY'S GATE
WATER LA
BROOKLANDS AVE
GRIGGS GDNS
GORSEY BANK
LC
YOKECLIFFE HILL
YOKECLIFFE DR
YOKECLIFFE CRES
YOKECLIFFE AVE
WOODLANDS CL
COPSE CL
SUMMER LA
SUMMER DR
ARKWRIGHT ST
PILLAR BUTTS
PITTYWOOD RD
CRABTREE CL
RECREATION RD
MOUNTFORD AVE
OAT HILL
ECCLESBOURNE CL
IAN AVE
LADYFLATTS RD
STAFFORD CRES
KING GEORGE ST
WILLOWBATH LA
KINGSFIELD RD
JUBILEE CT
SLATER CRES
BOURNEBROOK AVE
KINGSFIELD IND EST
NURSERY CROFT
ADAM BEDE CRES
CINDER LA
SNOWFIELD VIEW
(dis)

4 3 2 1
53 52 51 50
26 27 28

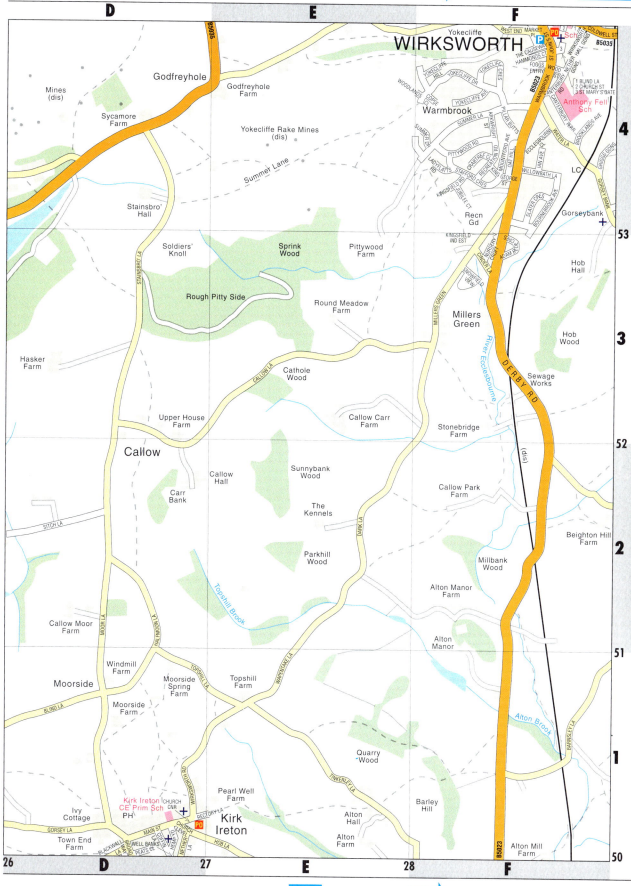

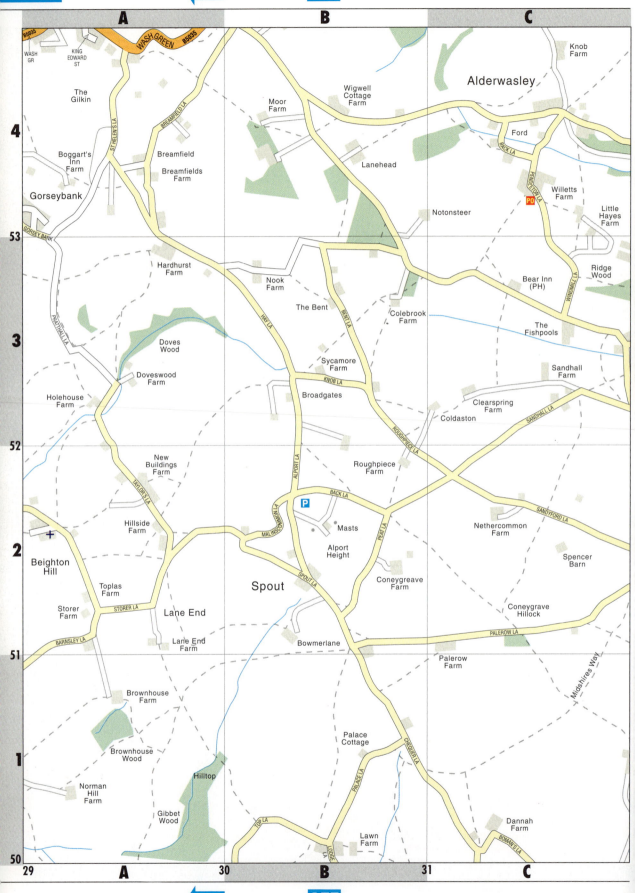

A

B

C

4

53

3

52

2

51

1

50

WASH GREEN B5035

B5035

WASH GR

KING EDWARD ST

The Gilkin

Boggart's Inn Farm

Breamfield

Breamfields Farm

Gorseybank

GORSEY BANK

ST HELEN'S LA

BREAMFIELD LA

Moor Farm

Wigwell Cottage Farm

Lanehead

Alderwasley

Knob Farm

Ford

BACK LA

PENDLETON LA

Notonsteer

PO

Willetts Farm

Little Hayes Farm

Hardhurst Farm

Nook Farm

The Bent

Colebrook Farm

Bear Inn (PH)

Ridge Wood

WINDMILL LA

The Fishpools

PRITHALL LA

Doves Wood

Doveswood Farm

Holehouse Farm

HAY LA

BENT LA

Sycamore Farm

Broadgates

KNOB LA

Sandhall Farm

Clearspring Farm

Coldaston

SANDHALL LA

New Buildings Farm

Roughpiece Farm

ROUGHPIECE LA

TAYLOR'S LA

ALPORT LA

P

BACK LA

Masts

Nethercommon Farm

SANDYFORD LA

Spencer Barn

Hillside Farm

MALINS COMMON LA

Alport Height

PEAT LA

Coneygreave Farm

Beighton Hill

Toplas Farm

STORER LA

Lane End

SPOUT LA

Spout

Coneygrave Hillock

Storer Farm

BARNSLEY LA

Lane End Farm

Bowmerlane

PALEROW LA

Palerow Farm

Midshires Way

Brownhouse Farm

Brownhouse Wood

Hilltop

Norman Hill Farm

Gibbet Wood

Palace Cottage

PALACE LA

CHERUER LA

Lawn Farm

Dannah Farm

BOMAN'S LA

TOP LA

LODGE LA

29

A

30

B

31

C

50

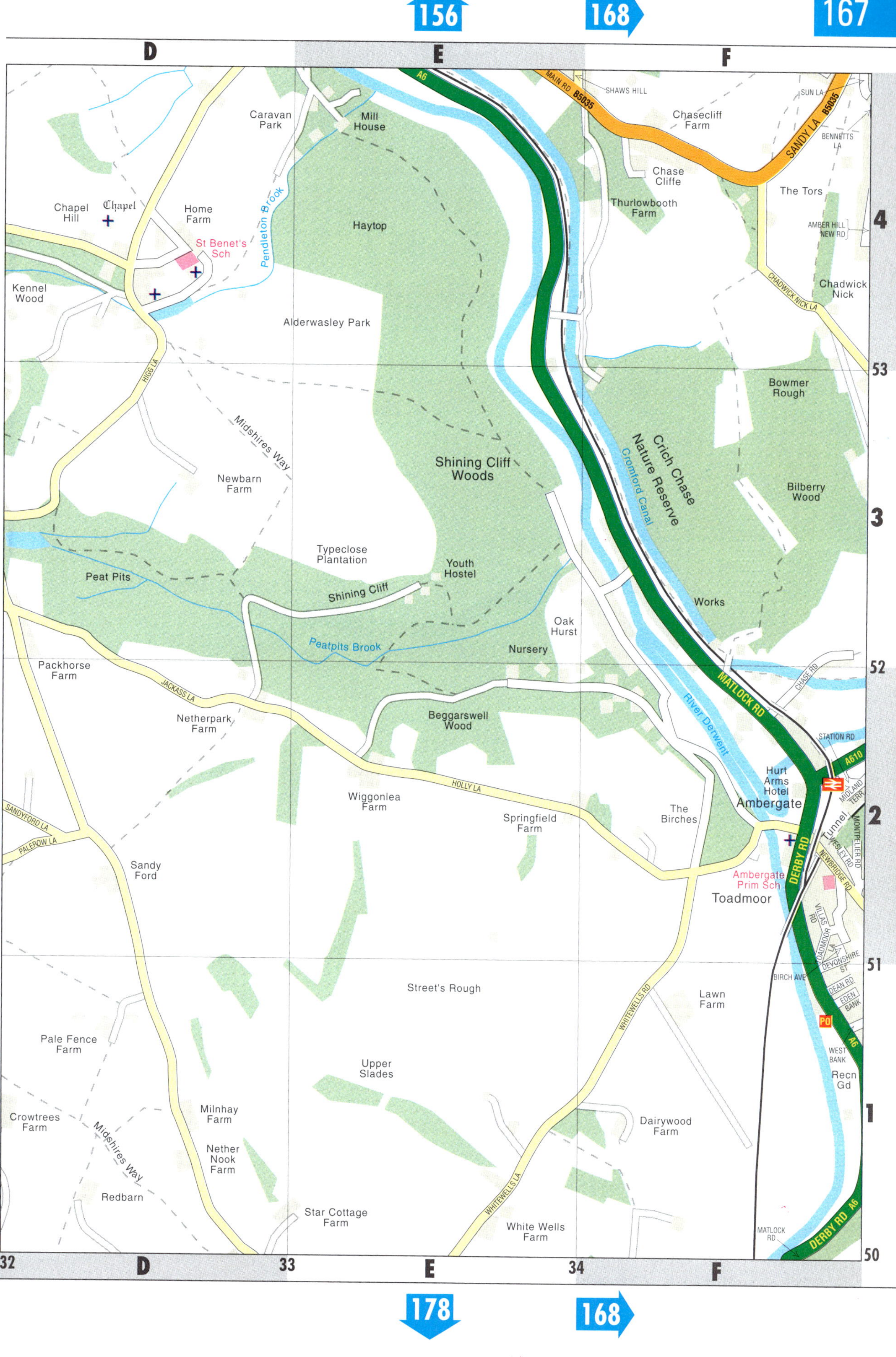
156
168
D
E
F
Caravan Park
Mill House
MAIN RD B5035
SHAWS HILL
Chasecliff Farm
SUN LA
SANDY LA B5035
BENNETTS LA
Chase Cliffe
Thurlowbooth Farm
The Tors
Chapel Hill
Chapel
Home Farm
St Benet's Sch
Pendleton Brook
Haytop
AMBER HILL NEW RD
4
CHADWICK NICK LA
Chadwick Nick
Kennel Wood
Alderwasley Park
A6
HIGG LA
53
Bowmer Rough
Midshires Way
Newbarn Farm
Shining Cliff Woods
Crich Chase Nature Reserve
Cromford Canal
Bilberry Wood
3
Typeclose Plantation
Youth Hostel
Peat Pits
Shining Cliff
Works
Oak Hurst
Peatpits Brook
Nursery
52
CHASE RD
Packhorse Farm
JACKASS LA
MATLOCK RD
Netherpark Farm
Beggarswell Wood
River Derwent
STATION RD
A610
Hurt Arms Hotel
Ambergate
SANDYFORD LA
PALEROW LA
HOLLY LA
Wiggonlea Farm
Springfield Farm
The Birches
Tunnel
MIDLAND TERR
2
MONTPELIER RD
WESLEY RD
NEWBRIDGE RD
DERBY RD
Sandy Ford
Ambergate Prim Sch
Toadmoor
VILLAS RD
TOADMOOR LA
DEVONSHIRE ST
51
BIRCH AVE
DEAN RD
EDEN BANK
Street's Rough
WHITEWELLS RD
Lawn Farm
PO
A6
Pale Fence Farm
WEST BANK
Upper Slades
Recn Gd
1
Crowtrees Farm
Milnhay Farm
Dairywood Farm
Midshires Way
Nether Nook Farm
Redbarn
WHITEWELLS LA
Star Cottage Farm
White Wells Farm
MATLOCK RD
DERBY RD A6
50
32
D
33
E
34
F
178
168

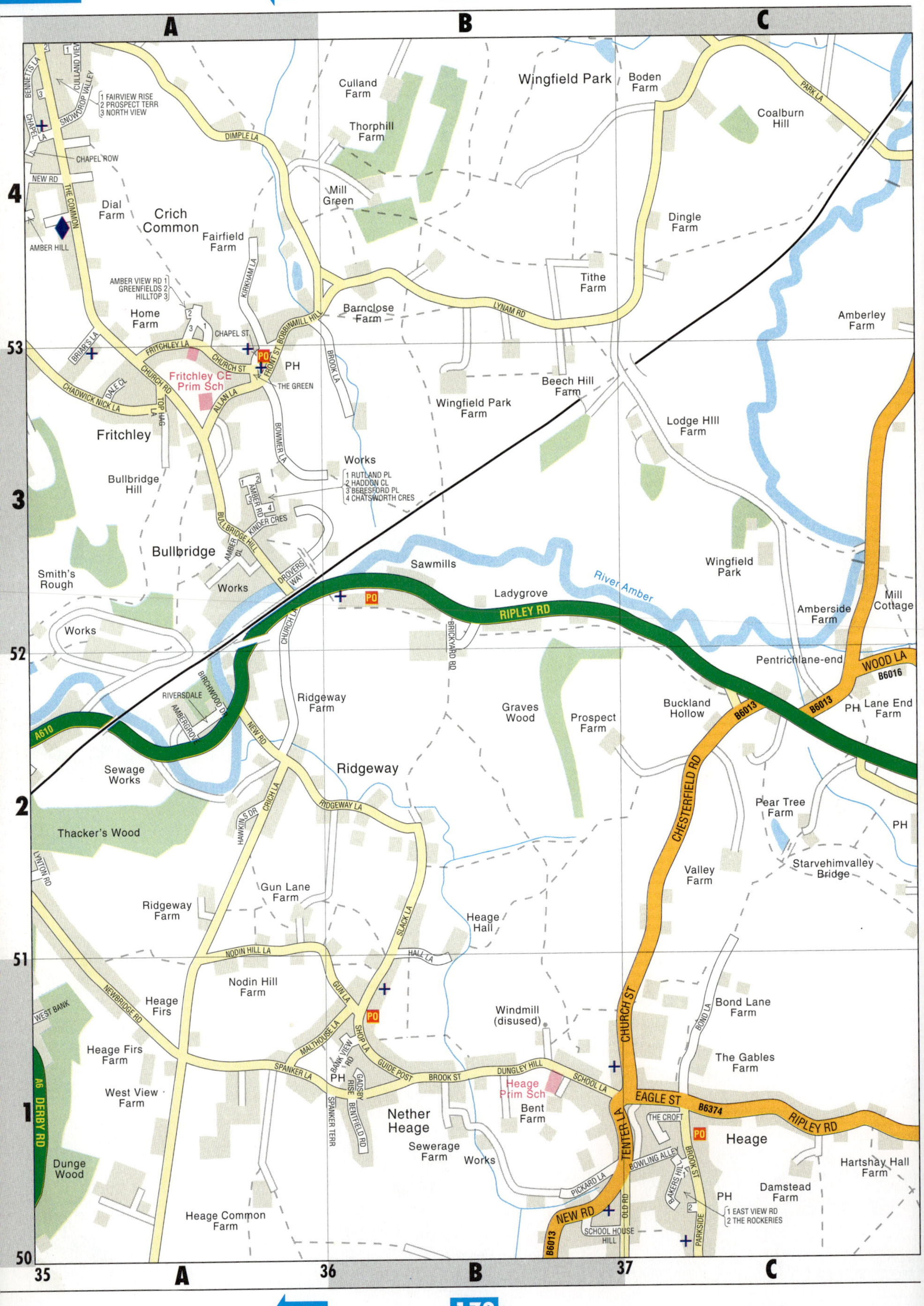

167 157

A B C

1 FAIRVIEW RISE
2 PROSPECT TERR
3 NORTH VIEW

Wingfield Park

Culland
Farm

Boden
Farm

Coalburn
Hill

Thorphill
Farm

Dimple La

Mill
Green

Dingle
Farm

Amberley
Farm

New Rd

Dial
Farm

Crich
Common

Fairfield
Farm

Chapel Row

Amber Hill

AMBER VIEW RD 1
GREENFIELDS 2
HILLTOP 3

Home
Farm

Chapel St

Barnclose
Farm

Lynam Rd

Tithe
Farm

53

Fritchley CE
Prim Sch

PH

The Green

Wingfield Park
Farm

Beech Hill
Farm

Lodge Hill
Farm

Fritchley

Brook La

Works

1 RUTLAND PL
2 HADDON CL
3 BERESFORD PL
4 CHATSWORTH CRES

Bullbridge
Hill

3

Bullbridge

Smith's
Rough

Works

Sawmills

Ladygrove

River Amber

Wingfield
Park

Amberside
Farm

Mill
Cottage

Ripley Rd

52

Works

A610

Riversdale

Ridgeway
Farm

Graves
Wood

Prospect
Farm

Buckland
Hollow

Pentrichlane-end

Wood La
B6016

Lane End
Farm

Sewage
Works

Ridgeway

Ridgeway La

Pear Tree
Farm

Starvehimvalley
Bridge

PH

2

Thacker's Wood

Chesterfield Rd

Valley
Farm

Ridgeway
Farm

Gun Lane
Farm

Heage
Hall

Hall La

Nodin Hill La

Nodin Hill
Farm

51

West Bank

Heage
Firs

Windmill
(disused)

Bond Lane
Farm

The Gables
Farm

Heage Firs
Farm

West View
Farm

Spanker La

PH

Guide Post

Brook St

Dungley Hill

Heage
Prim Sch

Eagle St

B6374

Heage

Ripley Rd

1

A6 Derby Rd

Nether
Heage

Bent
Farm

The Croft

PO

Hartshay Hall
Farm

Dunge
Wood

Sewerage
Farm

Works

Damstead
Farm

PH

Heage Common
Farm

Pickard La

New Rd

B6013

School House
Hill

Parkside

1 EAST VIEW RD
2 THE ROCKERIES

50

35 A 36 B 37 C

167 179

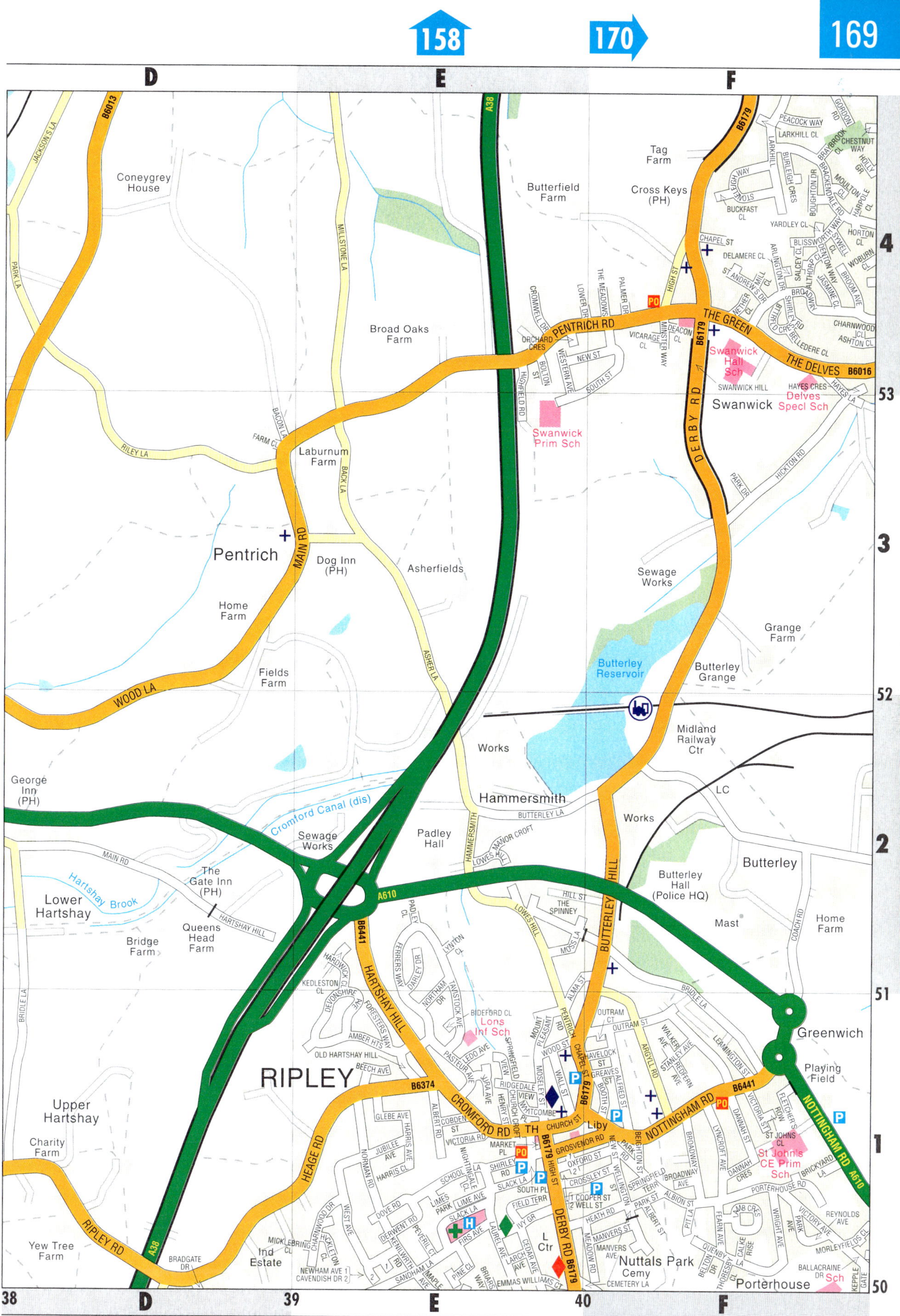

169
158
170
D
E
F
Coneygrey House
Butterfield Farm
Tag Farm
Cross Keys (PH)
Broad Oaks Farm
Laburnum Farm
Pentrich
Dog Inn (PH)
Asherfields
Home Farm
Fields Farm
Sewage Works
Grange Farm
Butterley Reservoir
Butterley Grange
Midland Railway Ctr
Works
Hammersmith
George Inn (PH)
Cromford Canal (dis)
Padley Hall
The Gate Inn (PH)
Lower Hartshay
Hartshay Brook
Queens Head Farm
Bridge Farm
Butterley
Butterley Hall (Police HQ)
Mast
Home Farm
Greenwich
Playing Field
RIPLEY
Upper Hartshay
Charity Farm
Yew Tree Farm
Ind Estate
Nuttals Park
Cemy
Porterhouse
Swanwick
Swanwick Hall Sch
Delves Specl Sch
Swanwick Prim Sch
Lons Inf Sch
St John's CE Prim Sch
LC
Liby
L Ctr
PENTRICH RD
THE GREEN
THE DELVES
DERBY RD
MAIN RD
WOOD LA
RILEY LA
PARK LA
JACKSON'S LA
MILLSTONE LA
BACK LA
ASHER LA
HAMMERSMITH
BUTTERLEY LA
BUTTERLEY HILL
HARTSHAY HILL
CROMFORD RD
NOTTINGHAM RD
HEAGE RD
RIPLEY RD
BRIDLE LA
HIGH ST
A38
A610
B6013
B6179
B6016
B6374
B6441
38
39
40
50
51
52
53
1
2
3
4

180
170

169
159

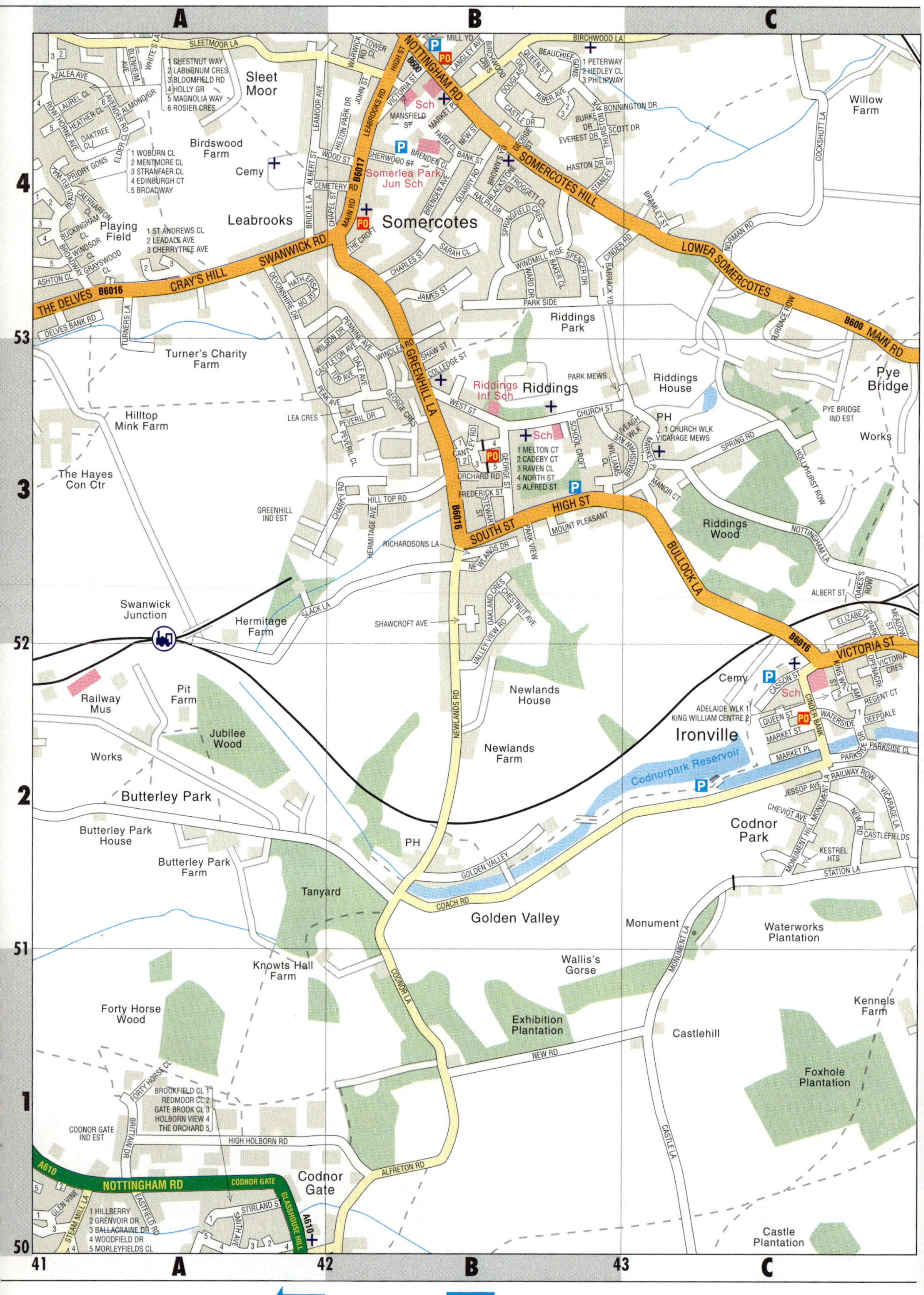
Sleet Moor
Birdswood Farm
Cemy
Leabrooks
Playing Field
Somercotes
Somerlea Park Jun Sch
Sch
Willow Farm
Riddings Park
Riddings
Riddings Inf Sch
Riddings House
Pye Bridge
PYE BRIDGE IND EST
Works
Turner's Charity Farm
Hilltop Mink Farm
The Hayes Con Ctr
GREENHILL IND EST
Riddings Wood
Swanwick Junction
Hermitage Farm
Railway Mus
Pit Farm
Jubilee Wood
Works
Newlands House
Newlands Farm
Ironville
Codnorpark Reservoir
Butterley Park
Butterley Park House
Butterley Park Farm
PH
Codnor Park
Tanyard
Golden Valley
Monument
Waterworks Plantation
Knowts Hall Farm
Wallis's Gorse
Forty Horse Wood
Exhibition Plantation
Castlehill
Kennels Farm
Foxhole Plantation
CODNOR GATE IND EST
Codnor Gate
Castle Plantation
THE DELVES
B6016
CRAY'S HILL
SWANWICK RD
NOTTINGHAM RD
SOMERCOTES HILL
LOWER SOMERCOTES
B600 MAIN RD
GREENHILL LA
SOUTH ST
HIGH ST
BULLOCK LA
VICTORIA ST
NEWLANDS RD
COACH RD
CODNOR LA
NEW RD
ALFRETON RD
A610
NOTTINGHAM RD
GLASSHOUSE HILL
HIGH HOLBORN RD
CASTLE LA
MONUMENT LA
STATION LA
1 CHESTNUT WAY
2 LABURNUM CRES
3 BLOOMFIELD RD
4 HOLLY GR
5 MAGNOLIA WAY
6 ROSIER CRES
1 WOBURN CL
2 MENTMORE CL
3 STRANFAER CL
4 EDINBURGH CT
5 BROADWAY
1 ST ANDREWS CL
2 LEADALE AVE
3 CHERRYTREE AVE
1 PETERWAY
2 HEDLEY CL
3 PHILIPWAY
1 MELTON CT
2 CADEBY CT
3 RAVEN CL
4 NORTH ST
5 ALFRED ST
1 CHURCH WLK
VICARAGE MEWS
ADELAIDE WLK 1
KING WILLIAM CENTRE 2
BROOKFIELD CL 1
REDMOOR CL 2
GATE BROOK CL 3
HOLBORN VIEW 4
THE ORCHARD 5
1 HILLBERRY
2 GRENVOIR DR
3 BALLACRAINE DR
4 WOODFIELD DR
5 MORLEYFIELDS CL
4
3
2
1
53
52
51
50
41
42
43
A
B
C

169
181

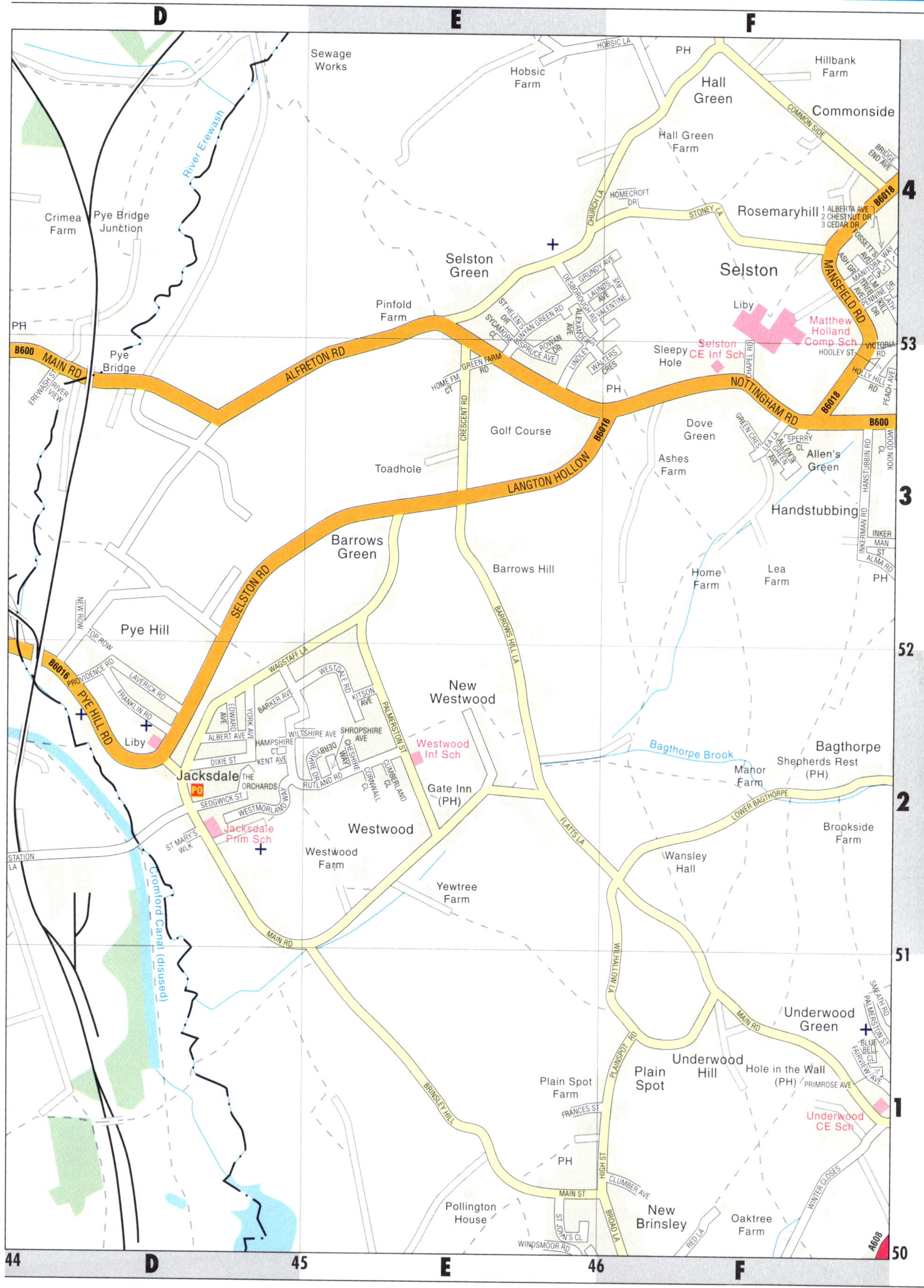
D
E
F
Sewage Works
Hobsic Farm
HOBSIC LA
PH
Hall Green
Hillbank Farm
Commonside
COMMON SIDE
Hall Green Farm
River Erewash
Crimea Farm
Pye Bridge Junction
HOMECROFT DR
CHURCH LA
STONEY LA
Rosemaryhill
1 ALBERTA AVE
2 CHESTNUT DR
3 CEDAR DR
B6018
Selston Green
Selston
Pinfold Farm
MANSFIELD RD
Liby
Matthew Holland Comp Sch
B600
MAIN RD
Pye Bridge
ALFRETON RD
Sleepy Hole
Selston CE Inf Sch
HOOLEY ST
NOTTINGHAM RD
B6016
Golf Course
Dove Green
Ashes Farm
Allen's Green
Toadhole
LANGTON HOLLOW
CRESCENT RD
Handstubbing
Barrows Green
Barrows Hill
SELSTON RD
Home Farm
Lea Farm
Pye Hill
BARROWS HILL LA
New Westwood
PYE HILL RD
WAGSTAFF LA
Westwood Inf Sch
Bagthorpe Brook
Bagthorpe
Shepherds Rest (PH)
Manor Farm
Jacksdale
PO
Gate Inn (PH)
Jacksdale Prim Sch
Westwood
LOWER BAGTHORPE
Brookside Farm
Westwood Farm
Wansley Hall
FLATTS LA
Cromford Canal (disused)
Yewtree Farm
MAIN RD
WILHALLOW LA
Underwood Green
Underwood Hill
Plain Spot
Hole in the Wall (PH)
Plain Spot Farm
Underwood CE Sch
BRINSLEY HILL
PH
New Brinsley
Oaktree Farm
Pollington House
A608
4
53
3
52
2
51
1
50
44
45
46

161

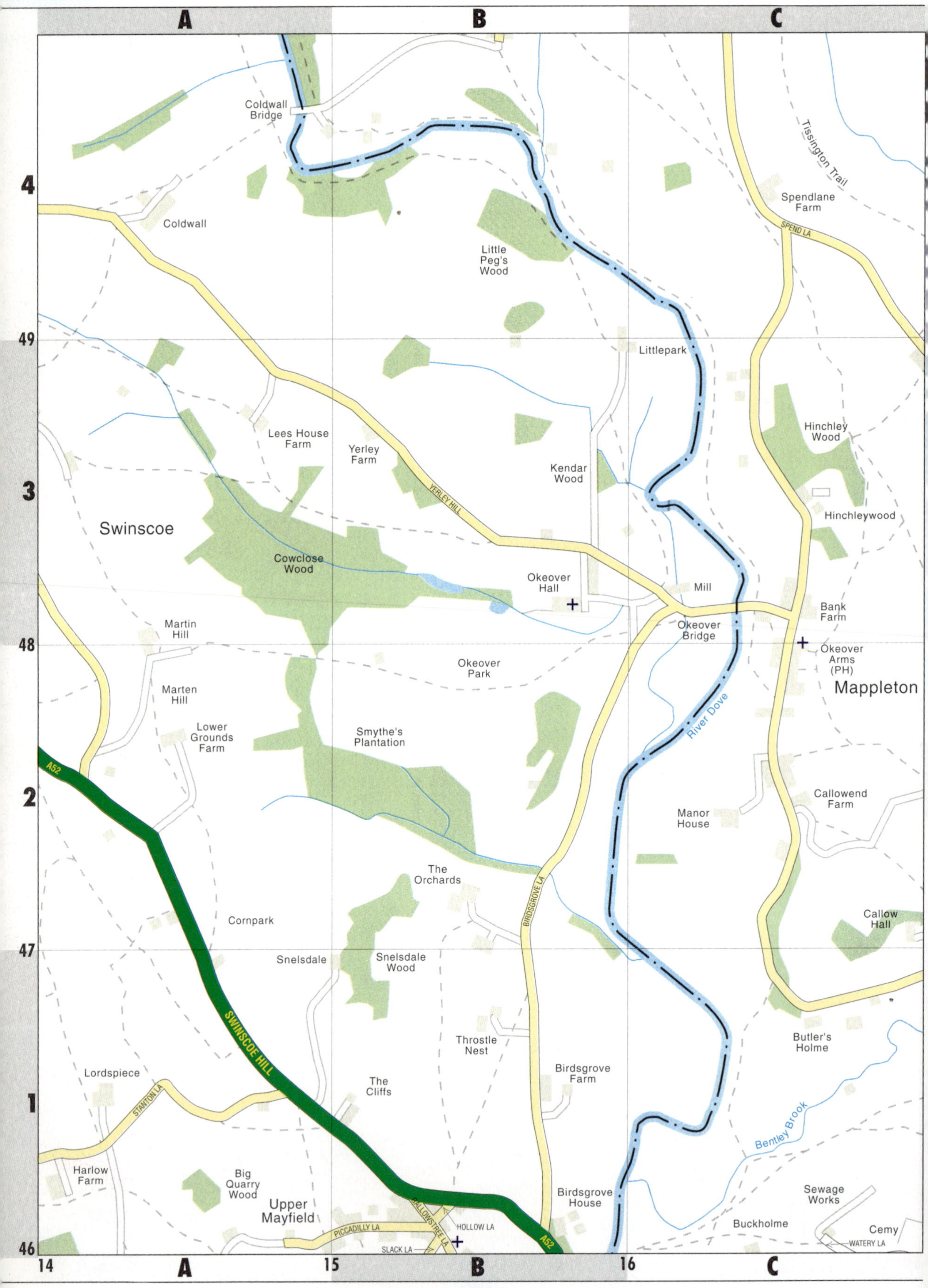
A
B
C
4
49
3
48
2
47
1
46
14
15
16
Coldwall Bridge
Coldwall
Little Peg's Wood
Tissington Trail
Spendlane Farm
SPEND LA
Littlepark
Lees House Farm
Yerley Farm
YERLEY HILL
Kendar Wood
Hinchley Wood
Hinchleywood
Swinscoe
Cowclose Wood
Okeover Hall
Mill
Bank Farm
Okeover Bridge
Okeover Arms (PH)
Mappleton
Martin Hill
Marten Hill
Okeover Park
River Dove
Lower Grounds Farm
Smythe's Plantation
A52
Callowend Farm
Manor House
The Orchards
BIRDSGROVE LA
Callow Hall
Cornpark
Snelsdale
Snelsdale Wood
SWINSCOE HILL
Throstle Nest
Butler's Holme
Lordspiece
Birdsgrove Farm
STANTON LA
The Cliffs
Bentley Brook
Harlow Farm
Big Quarry Wood
Upper Mayfield
Birdsgrove House
Sewage Works
Buckholme
Cemy
PICCADILLY LA
GALLOWSTREE LA
HOLLOW LA
SLACK LA
WATERY LA

184

162
174

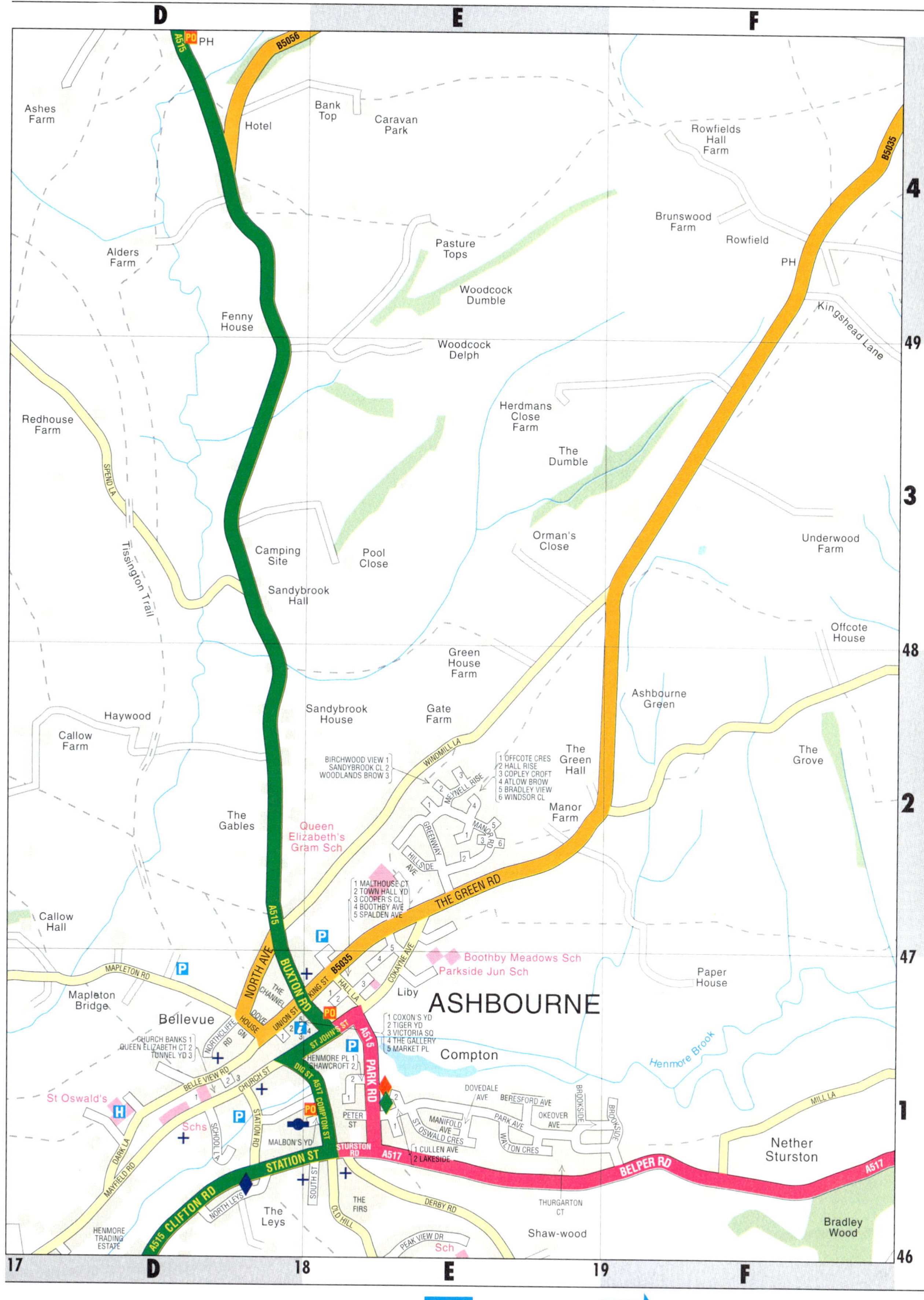
D
E
F
ASHBOURNE
Ashes Farm
Hotel
Bank Top
Caravan Park
Rowfields Hall Farm
Brunswood Farm
Rowfield
PH
Alders Farm
Pasture Tops
Woodcock Dumble
Fenny House
Woodcock Delph
Kingshead Lane
Redhouse Farm
Herdmans Close Farm
The Dumble
Tissington Trail
Camping Site
Pool Close
Orman's Close
Underwood Farm
Sandybrook Hall
Offcote House
Green House Farm
Ashbourne Green
Haywood
Callow Farm
Sandybrook House
Gate Farm
The Green Hall
The Grove
The Gables
Queen Elizabeth's Gram Sch
Manor Farm
Callow Hall
Boothby Meadows Sch
Parkside Jun Sch
Paper House
Mapleton Bridge
Bellevue
Liby
Compton
Henmore Brook
St Oswald's
Schs
Nether Sturston
The Leys
The Firs
Shaw-wood
Bradley Wood
Henmore Trading Estate
Sch
A515
B5056
B5035
A517
Spend La
Windmill La
The Green Rd
North Ave
Buxton Rd
Mapleton Rd
Park Rd
Station St
Clifton Rd
Belper Rd
Derby Rd
Mill La
Sturston Rd
Old Hill
South St
Compton St
Dig St
St John's St
Union St
King St
Church St
Belle View Rd
Cokayne Ave
Hall La
Dark La
Mayfield Rd
Station Rd
School La
North Leys
Peak View Dr
Dovedale Ave
Beresford Ave
Okeover Ave
Manifold Ave
Park Ave
Walton Cres
St Oswald Cres
Brookside
Thurgarton Ct
Peter St
Malbon's Yd
Northcliffe Rd
House Gn
The Channel
Dove
Greenway
Hillside Ave
Meynell Rise
Manor Rd
BIRCHWOOD VIEW 1
SANDYBROOK CL 2
WOODLANDS BROW 3
1 OFFCOTE CRES
2 HALL RISE
3 COPLEY CROFT
4 ATLOW BROW
5 BRADLEY VIEW
6 WINDSOR CL
1 MALTHOUSE CT
2 TOWN HALL YD
3 COOPER'S CL
4 BOOTHBY AVE
5 SPALDEN AVE
CHURCH BANKS 1
QUEEN ELIZABETH CT 2
TUNNEL YD 3
1 COXON'S YD
2 TIGER YD
3 VICTORIA SQ
4 THE GALLERY
5 MARKET PL
HENMORE PL 1
SHAWCROFT 2
1 CULLEN AVE
2 LAKESIDE
PO
PH
4
49
3
48
2
47
1
46
17
18
19

185
174

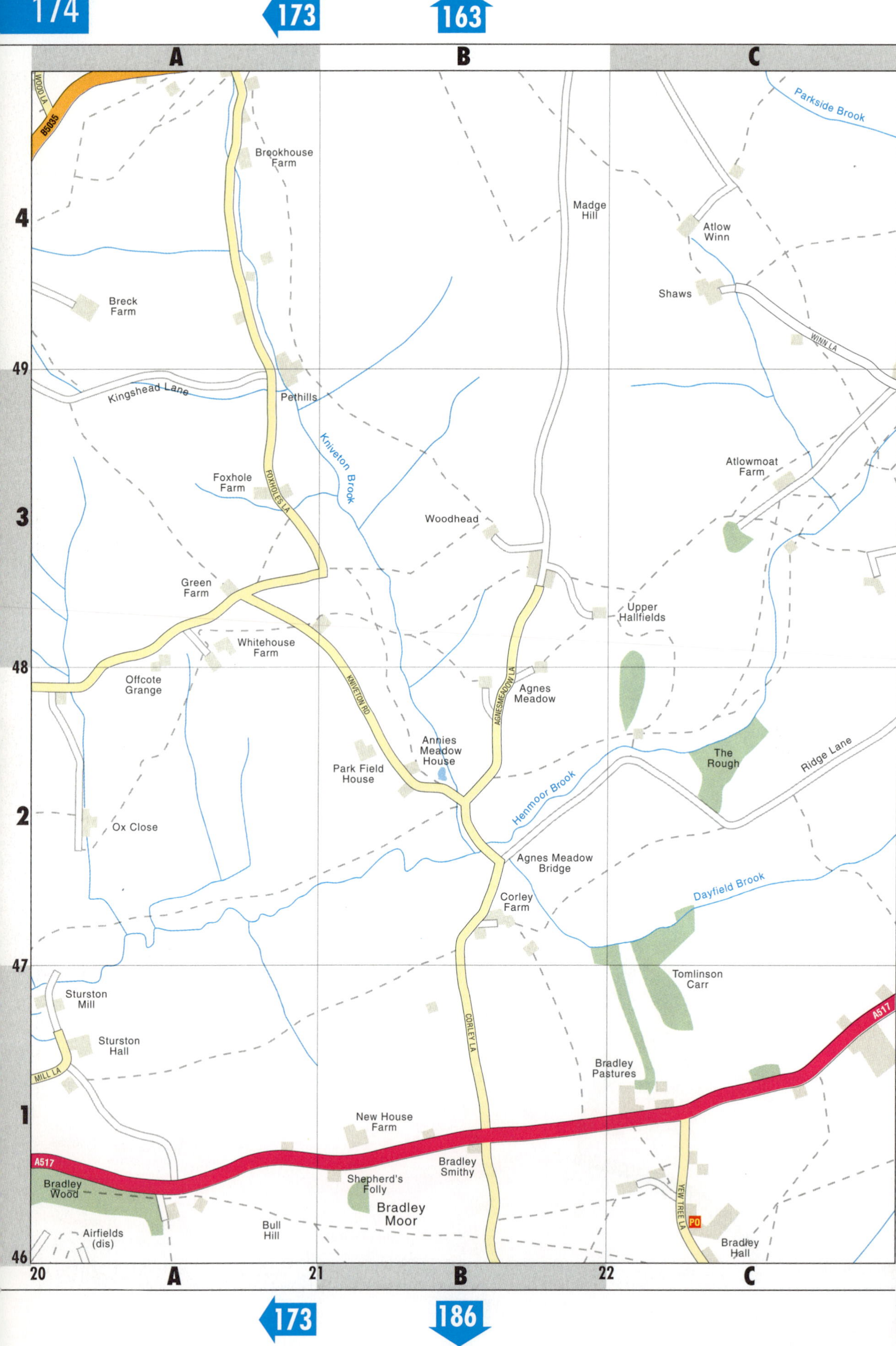
A
B
C
4
49
3
48
2
47
1
46
20
21
22
WOOD LA
B5035
Brookhouse Farm
Madge Hill
Parkside Brook
Atlow Winn
Breck Farm
Shaws
WINN LA
Kingshead Lane
Pethills
Kniveton Brook
Atlowmoat Farm
Foxhole Farm
FOXHOLES LA
Woodhead
Green Farm
Upper Hallfields
Whitehouse Farm
Offcote Grange
KNIVETON RD
AGNESMEADOW LA
Agnes Meadow
Annies Meadow House
Park Field House
The Rough
Ridge Lane
Henmoor Brook
Ox Close
Agnes Meadow Bridge
Dayfield Brook
Corley Farm
Tomlinson Carr
Sturston Mill
Sturston Hall
CORLEY LA
A517
MILL LA
Bradley Pastures
New House Farm
Bradley Smithy
Shepherd's Folly
Bradley Wood
Bradley Moor
YEW TREE LA
PO
Bull Hill
Airfields (dis)
Bradley Hall

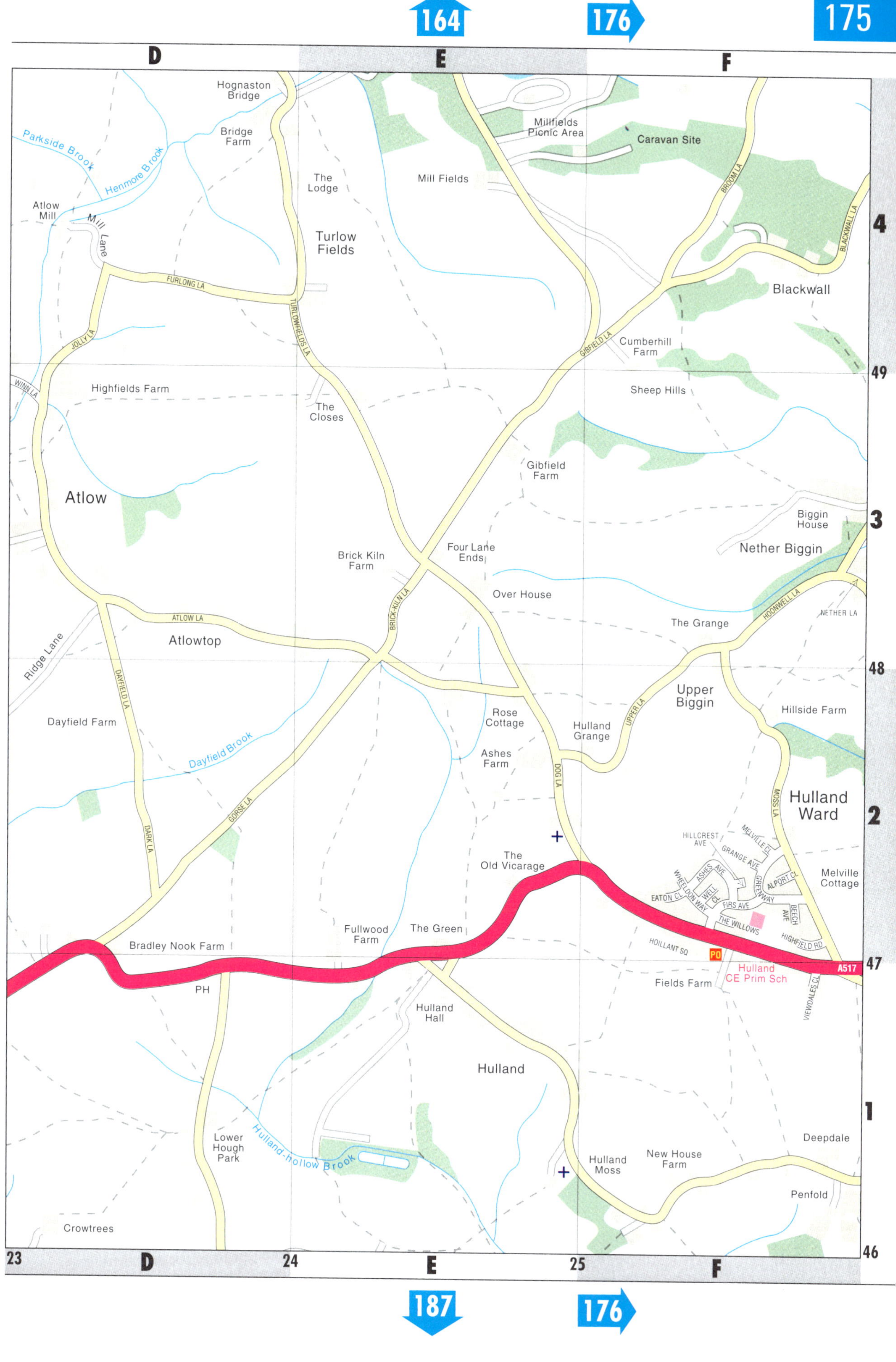

D E F

Parkside Brook
Henmore Brook
Hognaston Bridge
Bridge Farm
The Lodge
Mill Fields
Millfields Picnic Area
Caravan Site
BROOM LA

Atlow Mill
Mill Lane
FURLONG LA
Turlow Fields
Blackwall
BLACKWALL LA

JOLLY LA
WINN LA
Highfields Farm
The Closes
TURLOWFIELDS LA
GIBFIELD LA
Cumberhill Farm
Sheep Hills

4

49

Atlow
The Closes
Gibfield Farm
Biggin House
Nether Biggin

3

Ridge Lane
ATLOW LA
Atlowtop
BRICK KILN LA
Brick Kiln Farm
Four Lane Ends
Over House
The Grange
HOONWELL LA
NETHER LA

DAYFIELD LA
Dayfield Farm
Dayfield Brook
GORSE LA
Rose Cottage
Hulland Grange
Upper Biggin
UPPER LA
Hillside Farm

48

DARK LA
Ashes Farm
DOG LA
MOSS LA
Hulland Ward

2

The Old Vicarage
HILLCREST AVE
MELVILLE CL
Melville Cottage
GRANGE AVE
ASHES AVE
GREENWAY
ALPORT CL
WHEELDON WAY
FIRS AVE
EATON CL
WELL CL
BEECH AVE
THE WILLOWS

Bradley Nook Farm
Fullwood Farm
The Green
HOILLANT SQ
HIGHFIELD RD
PO
Hulland CE Prim Sch
A517

47

PH
Hulland Hall
Fields Farm
VIEWDALES CL

Lower Hough Park
Hulland-hollow Brook
Hulland
New House Farm
Deepdale

1

Hulland Moss
Penfold

Crowtrees

23 D 24 E 25 F 46

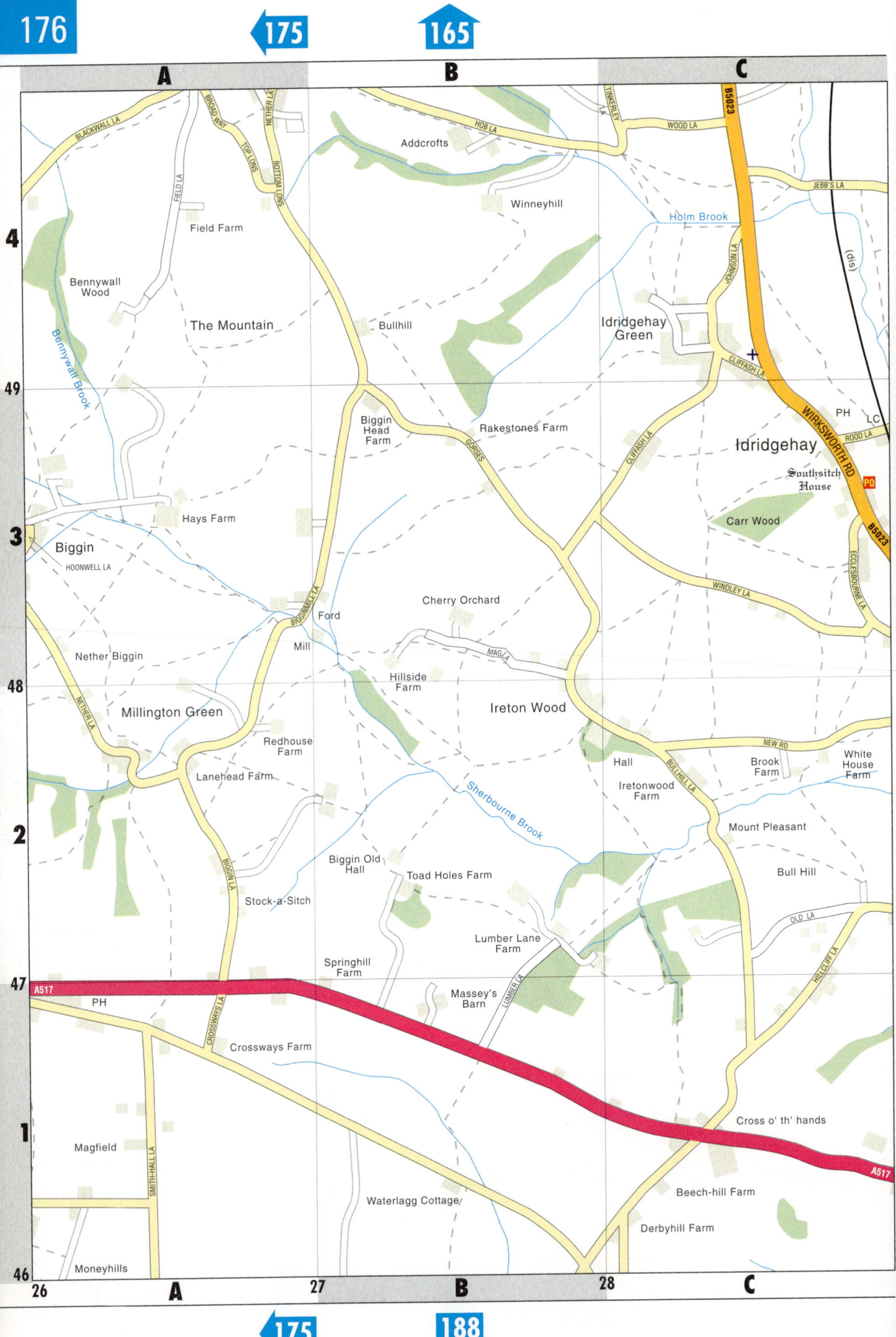

175
165

A   B   C

BLACKWALL LA
BROAD WAY
NETHER LA
TOP LYONS
BOTTOM LYONS
FIELD LA

4

Field Farm

Addcrofts

HOB LA

TINKERLEY
WOOD LA
B5023
JEBB'S LA

Winneyhill

Holm Brook

(dis)

Bennywall
Wood

The Mountain

Bullhill

Idridgehay
Green

CLIFFASH LA

Bennywall Brook

CLIFFASH LA

49

Biggin
Head
Farm

Rakestones Farm

GORSES

PH   LC

Idridgehay

WIRKSWORTH RD
ROOD LA

Hays Farm

Southsitch
House

ECCLESBOURNE LA

PO

3

Biggin

HOONWELL LA

Carr Wood

B5023

Cherry Orchard

WINDLEY LA

Nether Biggin

BIGGINMILL LA

Ford

Mill

MAG LA

Hillside
Farm

48

Millington Green

Ireton Wood

New Rd

Redhouse
Farm

NETHER LA

Hall

Brook
Farm

White
House
Farm

BULLHILL LA

Lanehead Farm

Iretonwood
Farm

Sherbourne Brook

Mount Pleasant

2

BIGGIN LA

Biggin Old
Hall

Bull Hill

Toad Holes Farm

Stock-a-Sitch

OLD LA

Lumber Lane
Farm

LUMBER LA

HILLCLIFF LA

47

A517

Springhill
Farm

Massey's
Barn

PH

CROSSWAYS LA

Crossways Farm

Cross o' th' hands

1

Magfield

SMITH-HALL LA

A517

Waterlagg Cottage

Beech-hill Farm

Derbyhill Farm

46

Moneyhills

26   A   27   B   28   C

175
188

166
178

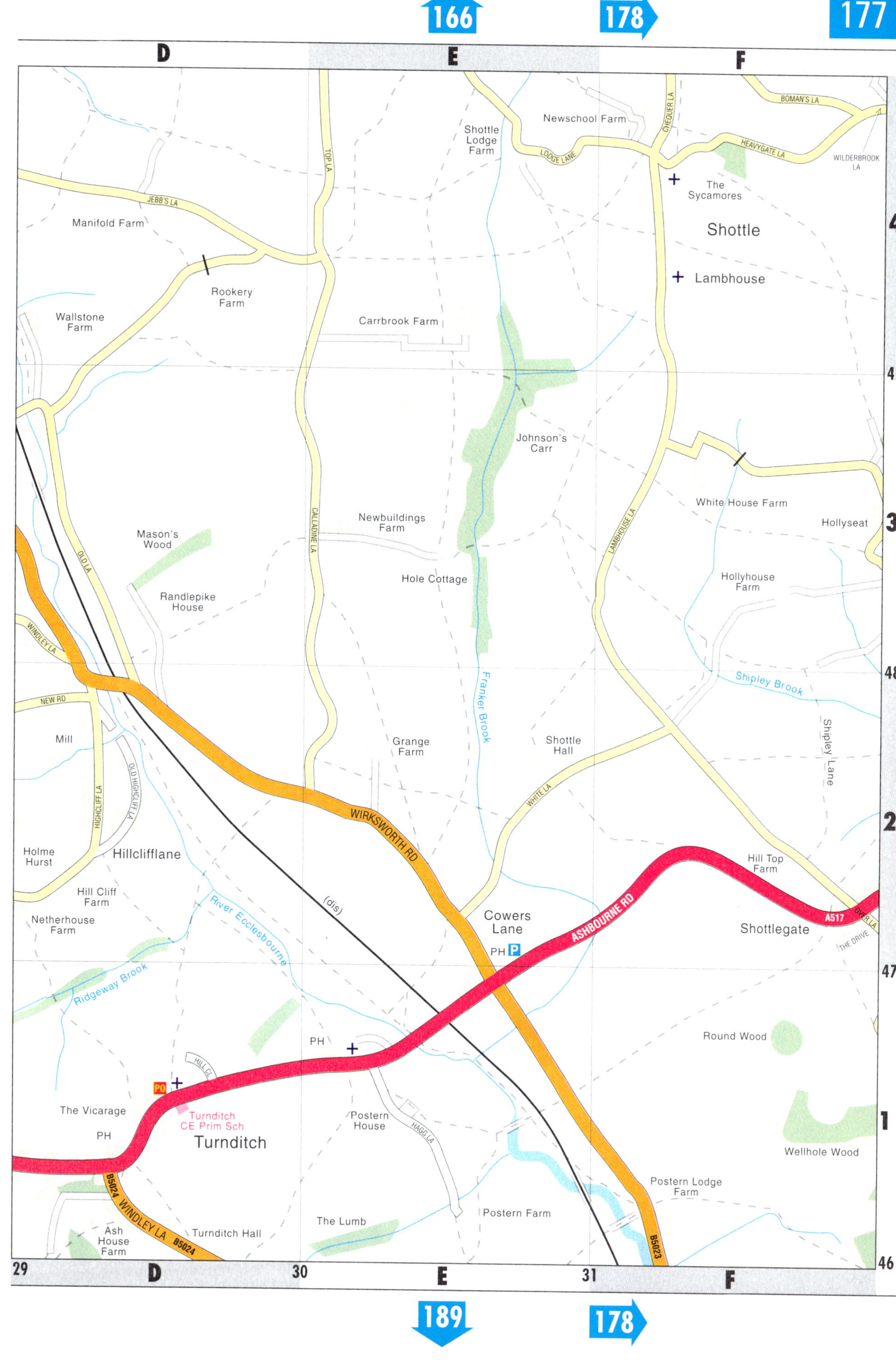
D
E
F
Newschool Farm
Shottle Lodge Farm
LODGE LANE
CHEQUER LA
BOMAN'S LA
HEAVYGATE LA
WILDERBROOK LA
The Sycamores
Shottle
Lambhouse
TOP LA
JEBB'S LA
Manifold Farm
Rookery Farm
Wallstone Farm
Carrbrook Farm
Johnson's Carr
White House Farm
Hollyseat
LAMBHOUSE LA
Newbuildings Farm
CALLADINE LA
Mason's Wood
OLD LA
Hole Cottage
Randlepike House
Hollyhouse Farm
WINDLEY LA
Shipley Brook
NEW RD
Franker Brook
Shipley Lane
Mill
Grange Farm
Shottle Hall
OLD HIGHCLIFF LA
HIGHCLIFF LA
WHITE LA
WIRKSWORTH RD
Holme Hurst
Hillclifflane
Hill Top Farm
Hill Cliff Farm
(dis)
River Ecclesbourne
Cowers Lane
ASHBOURNE RD
A517
OVER LA
Shottlegate
Netherhouse Farm
PH
THE DRIVE
Ridgeway Brook
Round Wood
PH
HILL CL
PO
The Vicarage
Turnditch CE Prim Sch
Postern House
PH
Turnditch
HAGG LA
Wellhole Wood
Postern Lodge Farm
B5024
WINDLEY LA
The Lumb
Postern Farm
Ash House Farm
Turnditch Hall
B5024
B5023
4
47
3
48
2
47
1
46
29
D
30
E
31
F

189
178

177
167

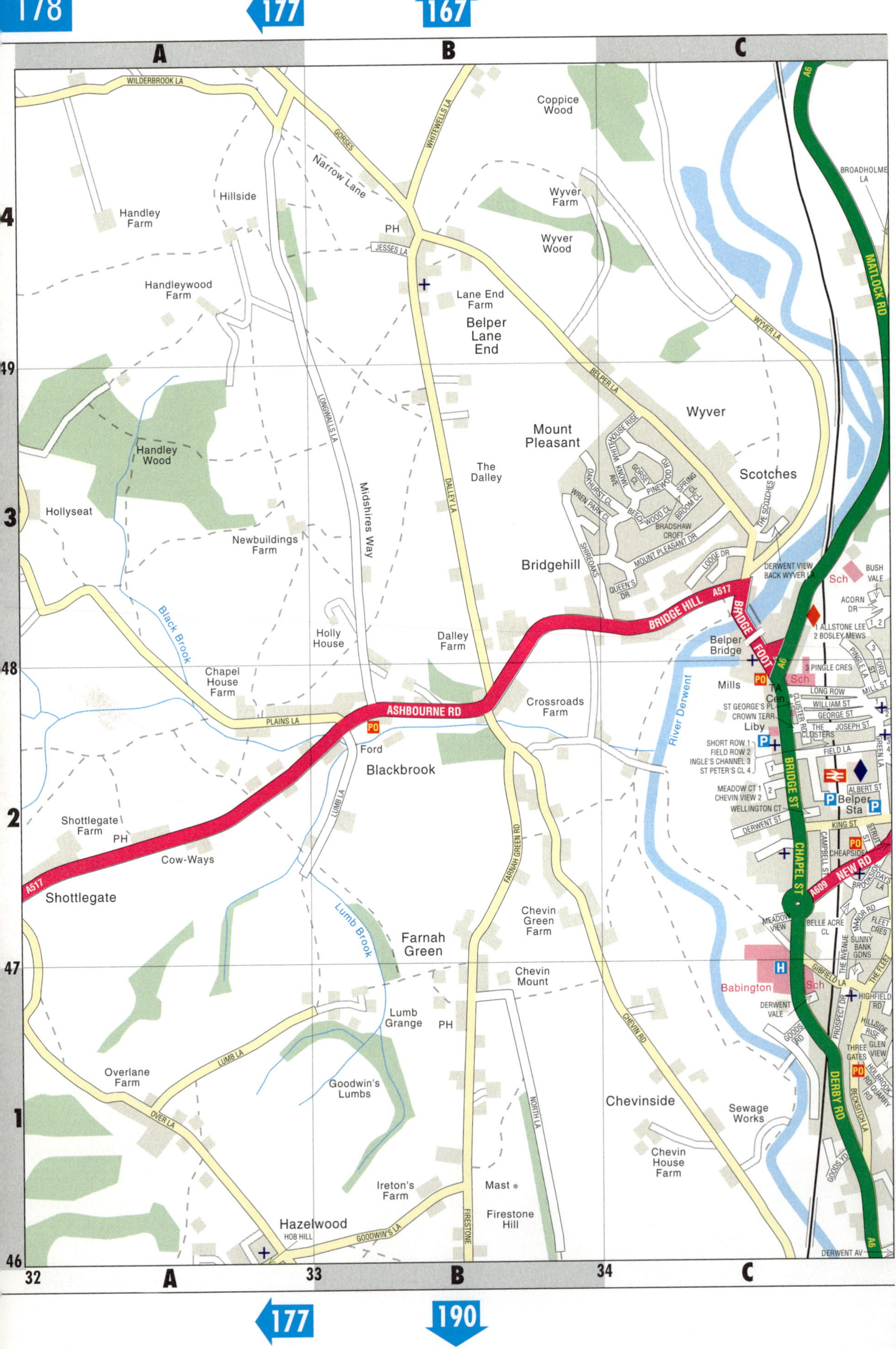
A
B
C
WILDERBROOK LA
GORSES
Narrow Lane
WHITEWELLS LA
Coppice Wood
Wyver Farm
Wyver Wood
BROADHOLME LA
Handley Farm
Hillside
PH
JESSES LA
Handleywood Farm
Lane End Farm
Belper Lane End
WYVER LA
MATLOCK RD
A6
BELPER LA
Wyver
Handley Wood
LONGWALLS LA
Mount Pleasant
The Dalley
DALLEY LA
Midshires Way
Scotches
THE SCOTCHES
Hollyseat
Newbuildings Farm
Bridgehill
BRADSHAW CROFT
MOUNT PLEASANT DR
LODGE DR
QUEEN'S DR
SHIREOAKS
WREN PARK CL
OAKHURST CL
DERWENT VIEW
BACK WYVER LA
Sch
BUSH VALE
ACORN DR
Black Brook
Holly House
Dalley Farm
BRIDGE HILL
A517
BRIDGE FOOT
Belper Bridge
1 ALLSTONE LEE
2 BOSLEY MEWS
PINGLE LA
3 PINGLE CRES
Chapel House Farm
Mills
PO
TA Cen
LONG ROW
WILLIAM ST
GEORGE ST
JOSEPH ST
MILL ST
ST GEORGE'S PL
CROWN TERR
Liby
THE CLUSTERS
PLAINS LA
ASHBOURNE RD
Crossroads Farm
River Derwent
SHORT ROW 1
FIELD ROW 2
INGLE'S CHANNEL 3
ST PETER'S CL 4
FIELD LA
Ford
Blackbrook
MEADOW CT 1
CHEVIN VIEW 2
ALBERT ST
Belper Sta
WELLINGTON CT
DERWENT ST
KING ST
BRIDGE ST
CHAPEL ST
LUMB LA
Shottlegate Farm
PH
CHEAPSIDE
CAMPBELL ST
NEW RD
A609
Cow-Ways
FARNAH GREEN RD
Shottlegate
Lumb Brook
Chevin Green Farm
MEADOW VIEW
BELLE ACRE CL
Farnah Green
Chevin Mount
H
Babington
GIBFIELD LA
THE AVENUE
HIGHFIELD RD
DERWENT VALE
Lumb Grange
PH
CHEVIN RD
GOODS RD
PROSPECT DR
THREE GATES
GLEN VIEW
Overlane Farm
LUMB LA
Goodwin's Lumbs
DERBY RD
OVER LA
NORTH LA
Chevinside
Sewage Works
Chevin House Farm
Ireton's Farm
Mast
Firestone Hill
FIRESTONE
Hazelwood
HOB HILL
GOODWIN'S LA
DERWENT AV
32
33
34
4
49
3
48
2
47
1
46

177
190

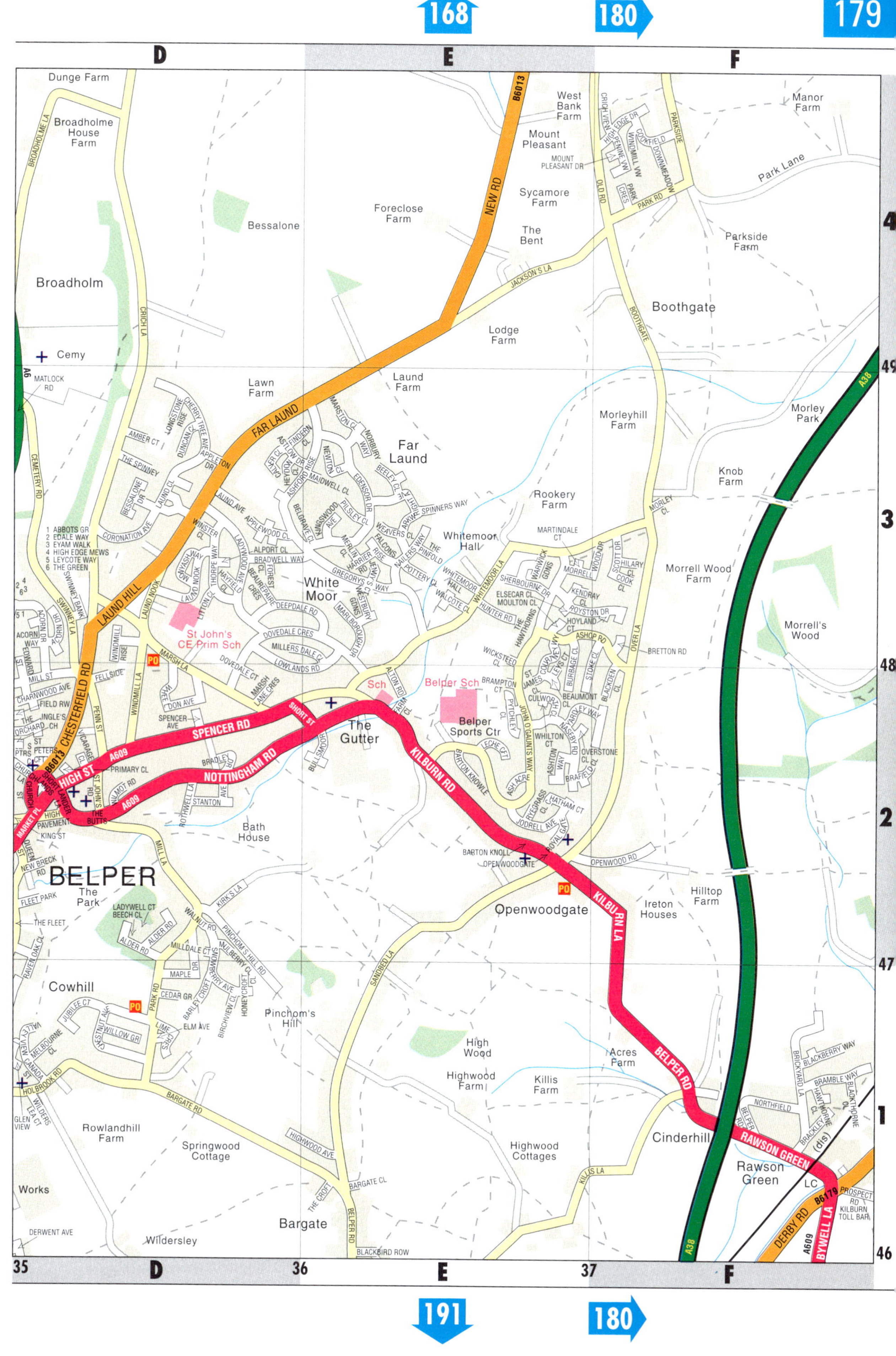
168
180
D
E
F
Dunge Farm
Broadholme House Farm
Broadholm
Bessalone
Foreclose Farm
West Bank Farm
Mount Pleasant
Sycamore Farm
The Bent
Manor Farm
Park Lane
Parkside Farm
Boothgate
Lodge Farm
Cemy
Lawn Farm
Laund Farm
Far Laund
Morleyhill Farm
Morley Park
Knob Farm
Rookery Farm
Whitemoor Hall
Morrell Wood Farm
Morrell's Wood
White Moor
St John's CE Prim Sch
Sch
Belper Sch
Belper Sports Ctr
The Gutter
Bath House
BELPER
The Park
Openwoodgate
Ireton Houses
Hilltop Farm
Cowhill
Pinchom's Hill
High Wood
Highwood Farm
Killis Farm
Acres Farm
Cinderhill
Rawson Green
Rowlandhill Farm
Springwood Cottage
Highwood Cottages
Works
Wildersley
Bargate
FAR LAUND
LAUND HILL
CHESTERFIELD RD
HIGH ST
SPENCER RD
NOTTINGHAM RD
KILBURN RD
KILBURN LA
BELPER RD
RAWSON GREEN
BYWELL LA
DERBY RD
NEW RD
B6013
B6179
A609
A38
A6
1 ABBOTS GR
2 EDALE WAY
3 EYAM WALK
4 HIGH EDGE MEWS
5 LEYCOTE WAY
6 THE GREEN
35
36
37
46
47
48
49
1
2
3
4
191
180

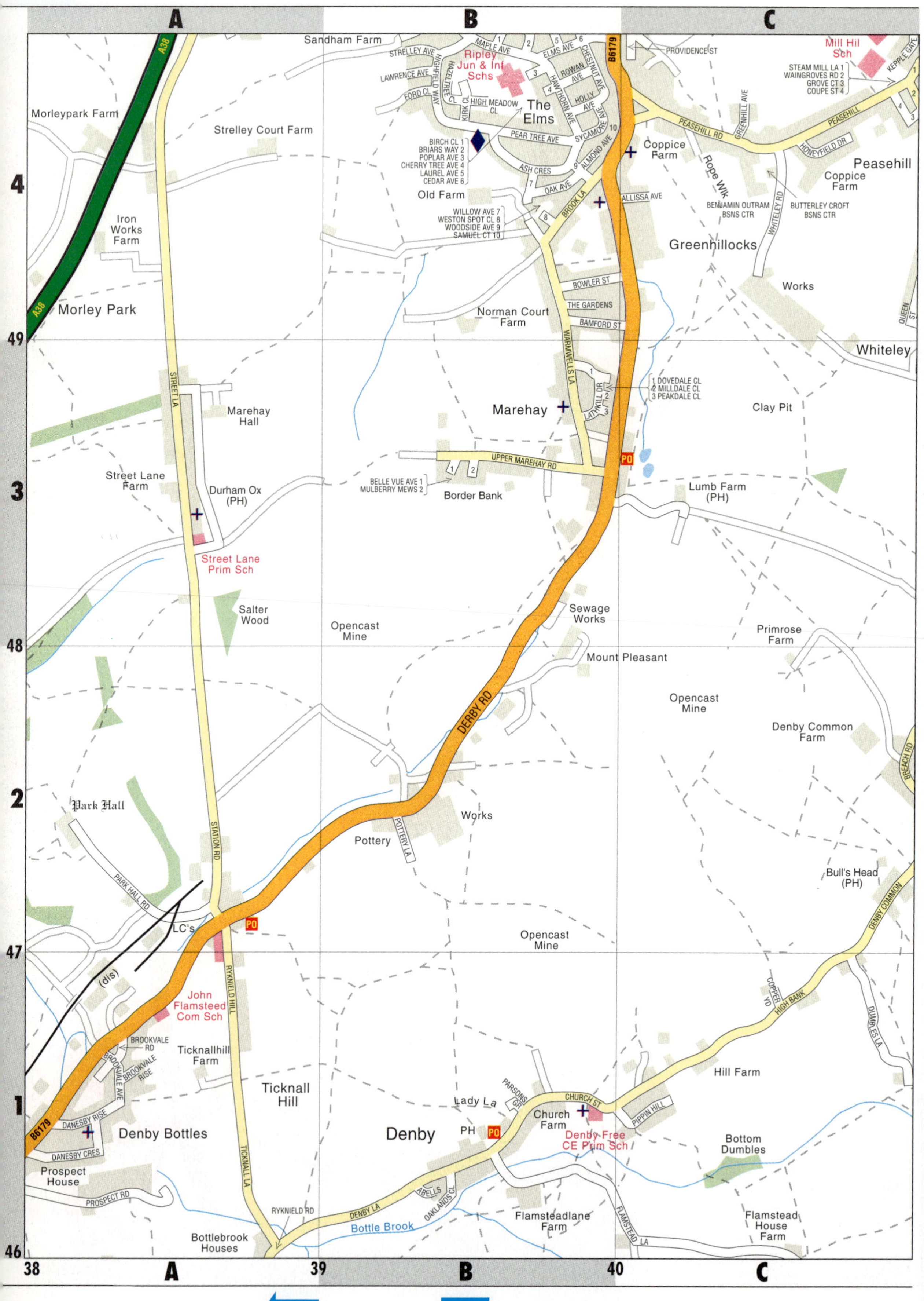

4

Morleypark Farm

Sandham Farm

Strelley Court Farm

A38

STRELLEY AVE
HIGHFIELD WAY
LAWRENCE AVE
FORD CL
HAZELTREE
KIRK CL
HIGH MEADOW CL
MAPLE AVE
ELMS AVE
CHESTNUT AVE
HAWTHORN AVE
ROWAN AVE
HOLLY AVE
SYCAMORE AVE

Ripley Jun & Inf Schs

The Elms

Providence St

Mill Hil Sch

STEAM MILL LA 1
WAINGROVES RD 2
GROVE CT 3
COUPE ST 4

KEPPLE GATE

Iron Works Farm

BIRCH CL 1
BRIARS WAY 2
POPLAR AVE 3
CHERRY TREE AVE 4
LAUREL AVE 5
CEDAR AVE 6

PEAR TREE AVE

Coppice Farm

Peasehill

Coppice Farm

PEASEHILL RD
GREENHILL AVE
HONEYFIELD DR
PEASEHILL

Old Farm

ASH CRES
OAK AVE
BROOK LA
ALMOND AVE
ALLISSA AVE

WILLOW AVE 7
WESTON SPOT CL 8
WOODSIDE AVE 9
SAMUEL CT 10

Rope Wlk

BENJAMIN OUTRAM BSNS CTR
WHITELEY RD
BUTTERLEY CROFT BSNS CTR

Morley Park

Greenhillocks

49

Norman Court Farm

BOWLER ST
THE GARDENS
BAMFORD ST

WARMWELLS LA

Works

Whiteley

QUEEN ST

Marehay Hall

Marehay

1 DOVEDALE CL
2 MILLDALE CL
3 PEAKDALE CL

Clay Pit

STREET LA
LATKILL DR

Street Lane Farm

UPPER MAREHAY RD

BELLE VUE AVE 1
MULBERRY MEWS 2

Border Bank

Lumb Farm (PH)

3

Durham Ox (PH)

Street Lane Prim Sch

Salter Wood

Opencast Mine

Sewage Works

Primrose Farm

48

Mount Pleasant

Opencast Mine

DERBY RD

Denby Common Farm

BEECH RD

2

Park Hall

Works

PARK HALL RD

STATION RD

Pottery

POTTERY LA

Bull's Head (PH)

DENBY COMMON

47

LC's

PO

Opencast Mine

(dis)

RYKNIELD HILL

John Flamsteed Com Sch

HIGH BANK

TO

DUMBLES LA

BROOKVALE RD
BROOKVALE AVE
BROOKVALE RISE

Ticknallhill Farm

Hill Farm

1

B6179

DANESBY RISE

Denby Bottles

TICKNALL LA

Ticknall Hill

Lady La

PARSONS GR

Church St
PIPPIN HILL

Denby

PH

PO

Church Farm

Denby Free CE Prim Sch

Bottom Dumbles

DANESBY CRES

Prospect House

PROSPECT RD

RYKNIELD RD

Bottle Brook

DENBY LA
ABELLS
OAKLANDS CL

FLAMSTEAD LA

Flamsteadlane Farm

Flamstead House Farm

46

Bottlebrook Houses

38   **A**   **39**   **B**   **40**   **C**

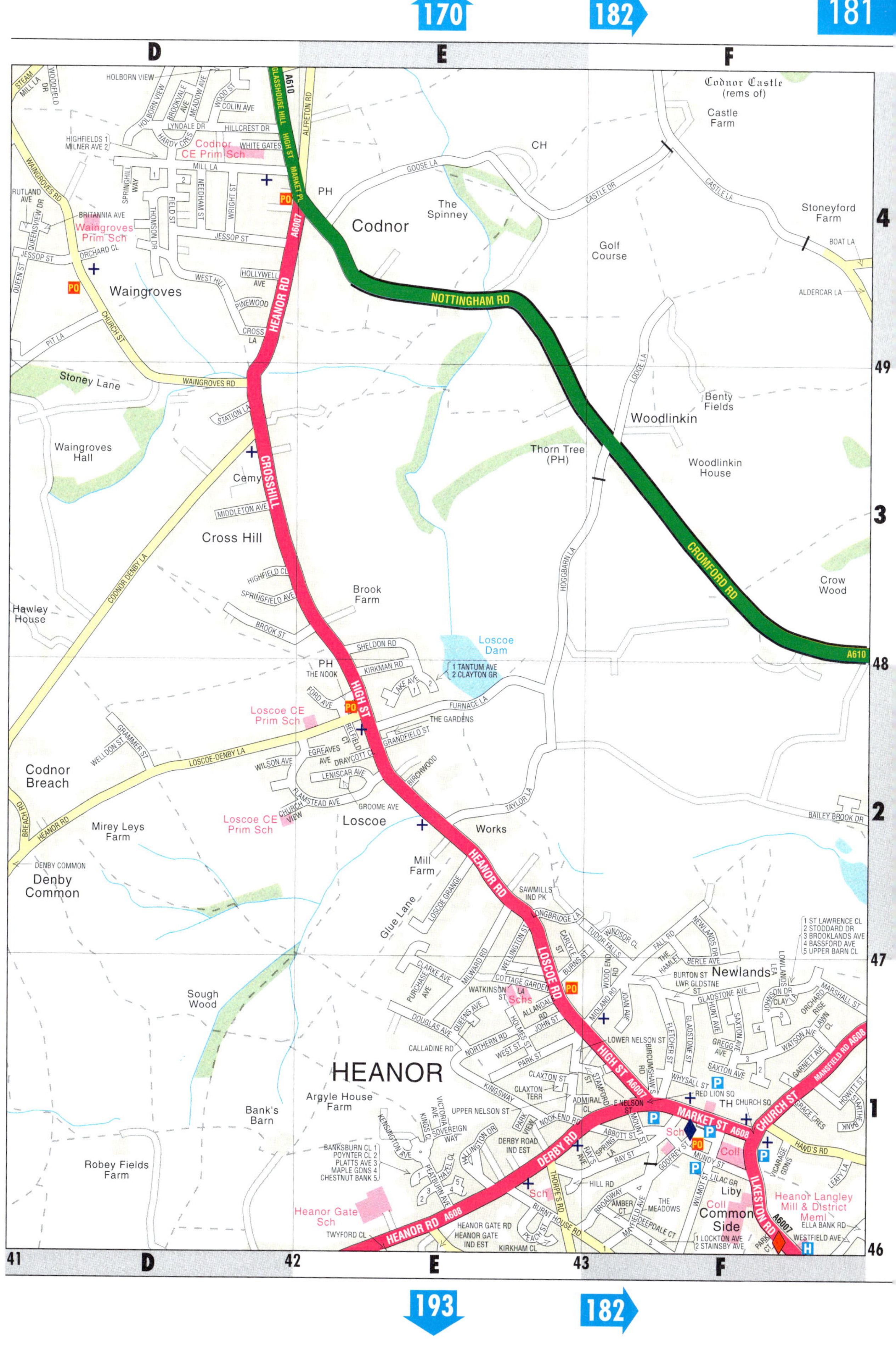
Codnor Castle (rems of)
Castle Farm
Codnor
Codnor CE Prim Sch
The Spinney
Stoneyford Farm
Golf Course
Waingroves
Waingroves Prim Sch
NOTTINGHAM RD
Stoney Lane
Waingroves Hall
Woodlinkin
Benty Fields
Woodlinkin House
Thorn Tree (PH)
Cross Hill
CROSSHILL
CROMFORD RD
Crow Wood
Hawley House
Brook Farm
Loscoe Dam
Loscoe CE Prim Sch
Codnor Breach
Mirey Leys Farm
Loscoe
Works
Mill Farm
Denby Common
Sough Wood
Newlands
HEANOR
Argyle House Farm
Bank's Barn
Robey Fields Farm
Heanor Gate Sch
Common Side
Heanor Langley Mill & District Meml
HEANOR RD
DERBY RD
MARKET ST
ILKESTON RD
LOSCOE RD
HIGH ST
MANSFIELD RD
CHURCH ST

181
171

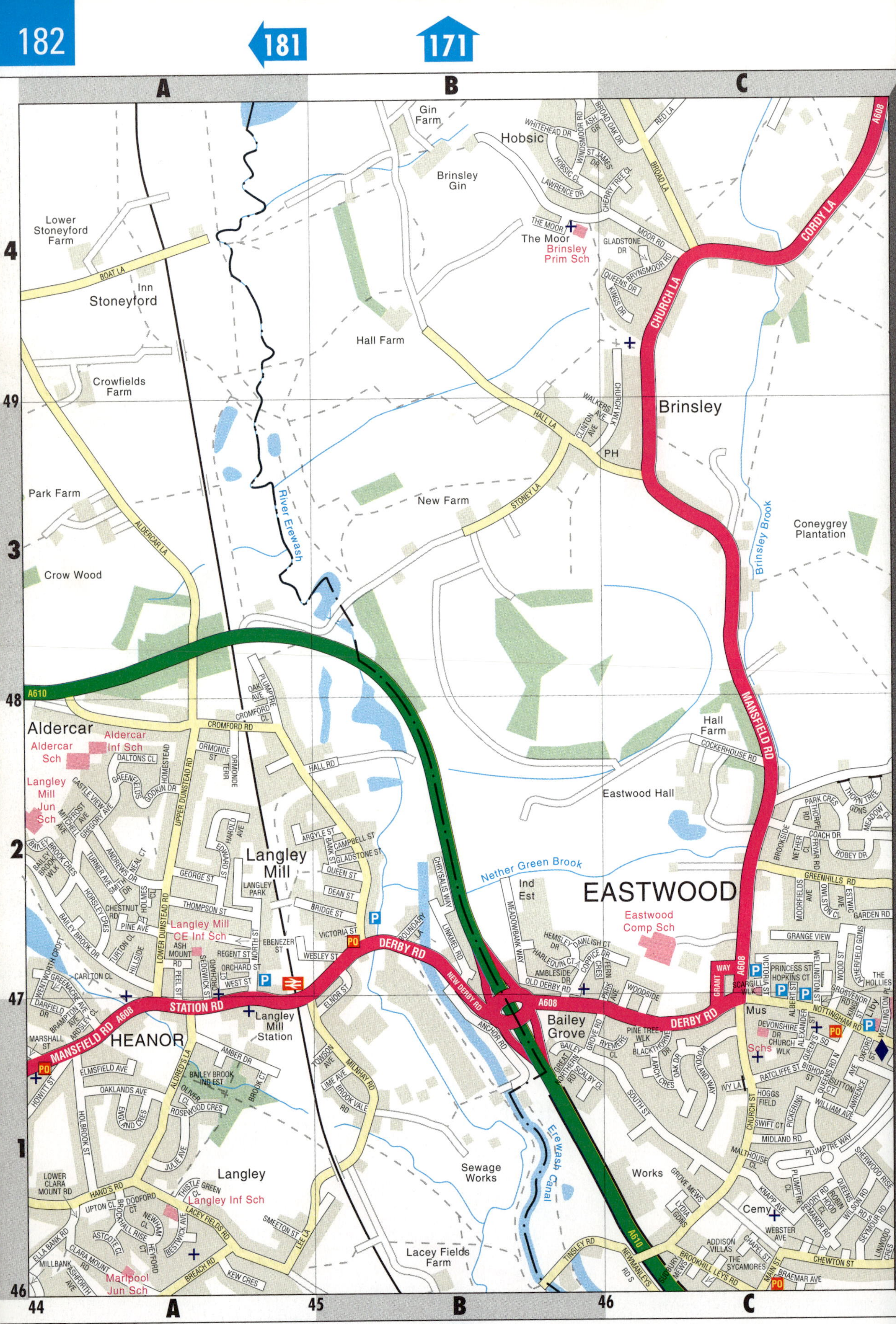
A
B
C
4
49
3
48
2
47
1
46
44
45
46
Gin Farm
Hobsic
Brinsley Gin
Lower Stoneyford Farm
BOAT LA
Inn
Stoneyford
The Moor
Brinsley Prim Sch
Hall Farm
Crowfields Farm
CHURCH LA
CORDY LA
A608
Brinsley
HALL LA
PH
Park Farm
River Erewash
New Farm
STONEY LA
Brinsley Brook
Coneygrey Plantation
ALDERCAR LA
Crow Wood
A610
Aldercar
Aldercar Sch
Aldercar Inf Sch
CROMFORD RD
Hall Farm
COCKERHOUSE RD
MANSFIELD RD
Langley Mill Jun Sch
HALL RD
Eastwood Hall
Langley Mill
Nether Green Brook
Ind Est
EASTWOOD
Eastwood Comp Sch
Langley Mill CE Inf Sch
DERBY RD
STATION RD
NEW DERBY RD
MANSFIELD RD
HEANOR
Langley Mill Station
Bailey Grove
Mus
Schs
Cemy
Sewage Works
Erewash Canal
Works
Langley
Langley Inf Sch
Lacey Fields Farm
Marlpool Jun Sch
NOTTINGHAM RD
GREENHILLS RD
CHEWTON ST
BRAEMAR AVE

181
194

184

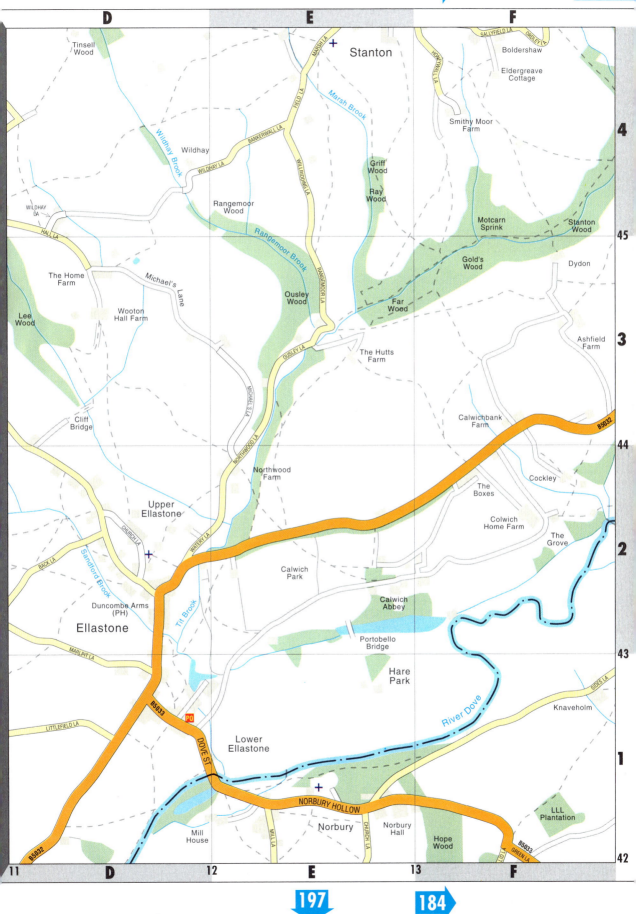

D
E
F
Tinsell Wood
Stanton
Boldershaw
Eldergreave Cottage
SALLYFIELD LA
ORDLEY LA
HONEYWALL LA
MARSH LA
Marsh Brook
FIELD LA
Smithy Moor Farm
BANKERWALL LA
Wildhay
Wildhay Brook
WILDHAY LA
WILLRIDDING LA
Griff Wood
Ray Wood
Rangemoor Wood
WILDHAY LA
HALL LA
Rangemoor Brook
Motcarn Sprink
Stanton Wood
Gold's Wood
Dydon
The Home Farm
Michael's Lane
RANGEMOOR LA
Ousley Wood
Far Wood
Lee Wood
Wooton Hall Farm
Ashfield Farm
OUSLEY LA
The Hutts Farm
MICHAEL'S LA
Cliff Bridge
Calwichbank Farm
B5032
NORTHWOOD LA
Northwood Farm
Cockley
The Boxes
Upper Ellastone
Colwich Home Farm
CHURCH LA
The Grove
WATERY LA
BACK LA
Sandford Brook
Calwich Park
Duncombe Arms (PH)
Tit Brook
Calwich Abbey
Ellastone
Portobello Bridge
MARLPIT LA
Hare Park
SIDES LA
B5033
Knaveholm
PO
River Dove
LITTLEFIELD LA
DOVE ST
Lower Ellastone
NORBURY HOLLOW
LLL Plantation
Mill House
MILL LA
Norbury
CHURCH LA
Norbury Hall
Hope Wood
B5033
GREEN LA
LID LA
B5032
4
45
3
44
2
43
1
42
11
12
13

197

184

183
172

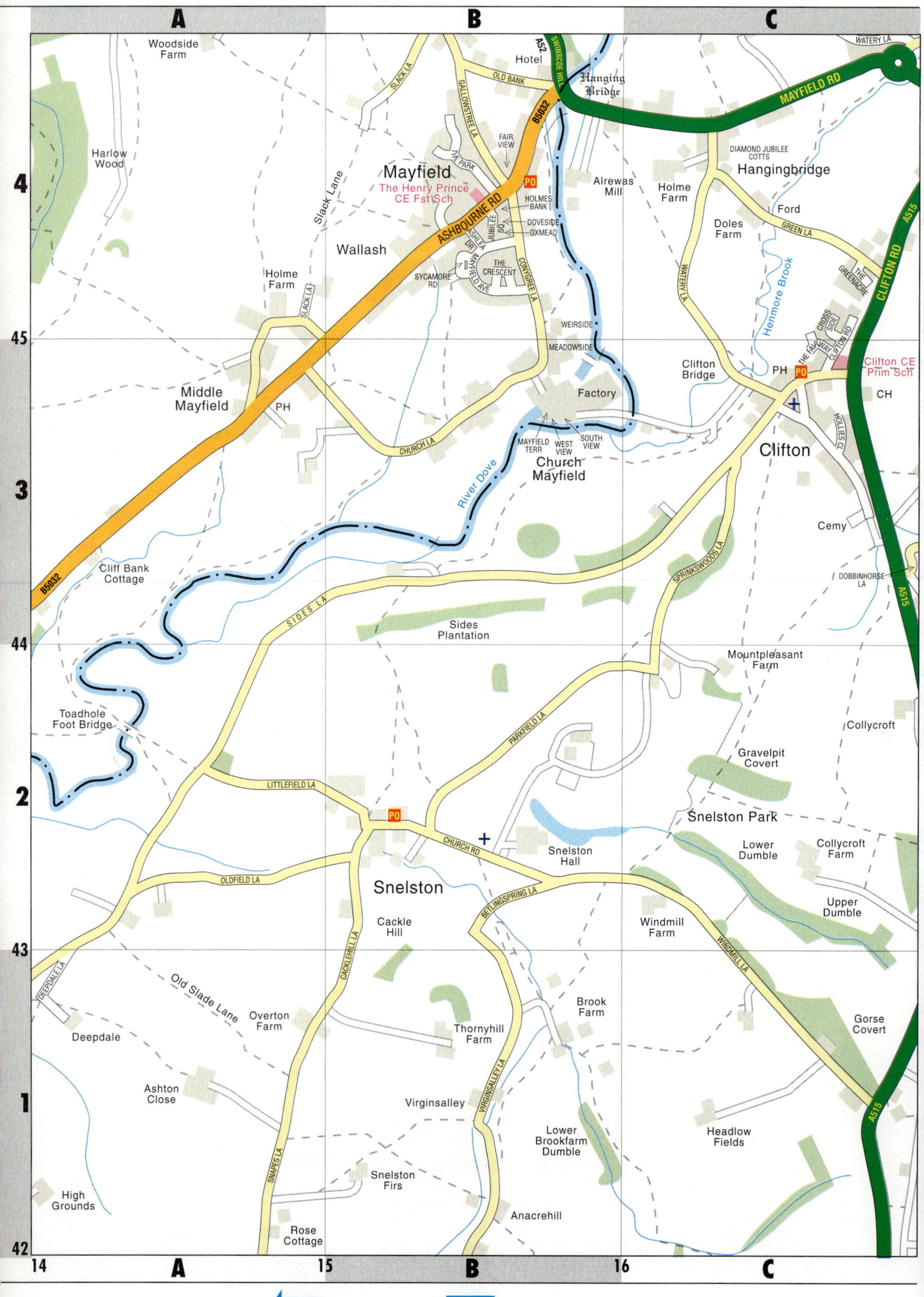
A
B
C
Woodside Farm
Hotel
Hanging Bridge
MAYFIELD RD
WATERY LA
Harlow Wood
Mayfield
The Henry Prince CE Fst Sch
Slack Lane
Wallash
ASHBOURNE RD
Alrewas Mill
Holme Farm
Hangingbridge
DIAMOND JUBILEE COTTS
Ford
Doles Farm
GREEN LA
Henmore Brook
CLIFTON RD
A515
Holme Farm
SLACK LA
WEIRSIDE
MEADOWSIDE
Clifton Bridge
PH
Clifton CE Prim Sch
CH
Factory
Middle Mayfield
PH
CHURCH LA
Clifton
Church Mayfield
River Dove
Cemy
Cliff Bank Cottage
B5032
SIDES LA
SPRINKSWOODS LA
DOBBINHORSE LA
Sides Plantation
Mountpleasant Farm
Toadhole Foot Bridge
PARKFIELD LA
Collycroft
Gravelpit Covert
LITTLEFIELD LA
Snelston Park
CHURCH RD
Snelston Hall
Lower Dumble
Collycroft Farm
OLDFIELD LA
Snelston
BETLINGSPRING LA
Upper Dumble
Cackle Hill
Windmill Farm
WINDMILL LA
DEEPDALE LA
Old Slade Lane
CACKLEHILL LA
Overton Farm
Brook Farm
Gorse Covert
Deepdale
Thornyhill Farm
Ashton Close
Virginsalley
VIRGINSALLEY LA
Lower Brookfarm Dumble
Headlow Fields
SNAPES LA
Snelston Firs
High Grounds
Rose Cottage
Anacrehill
4
45
3
44
2
43
1
42
14
15
16

183
198

173
186

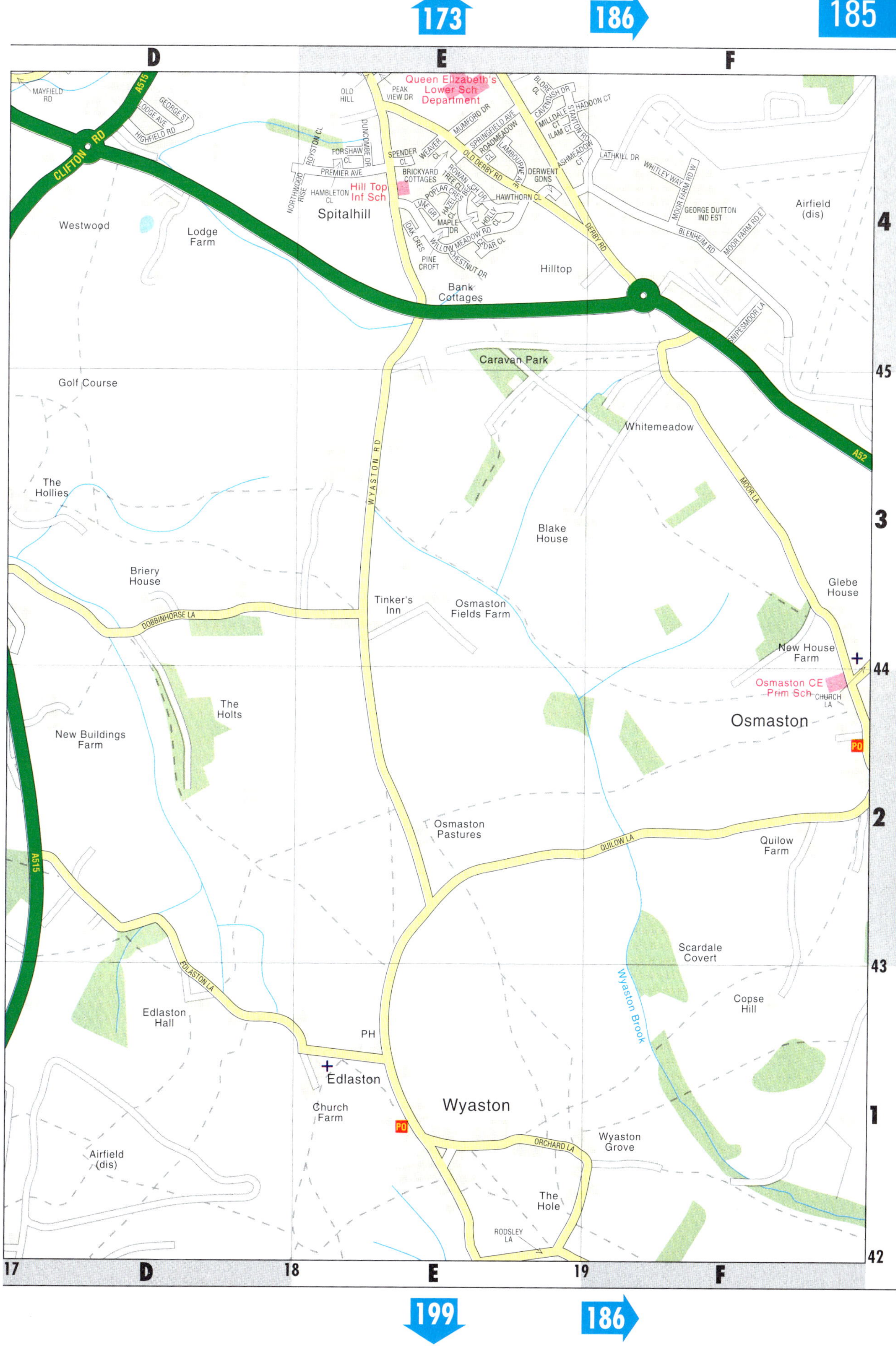
D
E
F
Queen Elizabeth's
Lower Sch
Department
Spitalhill
Hill Top
Inf Sch
Westwood
Lodge
Farm
Bank
Cottages
Hilltop
Airfield
(dis)
Caravan Park
Golf Course
Whitemeadow
The
Hollies
Blake
House
Briery
House
Tinker's
Inn
Osmaston
Fields Farm
Glebe
House
New House
Farm
Osmaston CE
Prim Sch
The
Holts
New Buildings
Farm
Osmaston
Osmaston
Pastures
Quilow
Farm
Scardale
Covert
Copse
Hill
Edlaston
Hall
PH
Edlaston
Church
Farm
Wyaston
Wyaston
Grove
Wyaston Brook
The
Hole
Airfield
(dis)
CLIFTON RD
A515
A52
WYASTON RD
DERBY RD
OLD DERBY RD
MOOR LA
DOBBINHORSE LA
QUILOW LA
EDLASTON LA
ORCHARD LA
RODSLEY LA
CHURCH LA
4
45
3
44
2
43
1
42
17
18
19

199
186

185
174

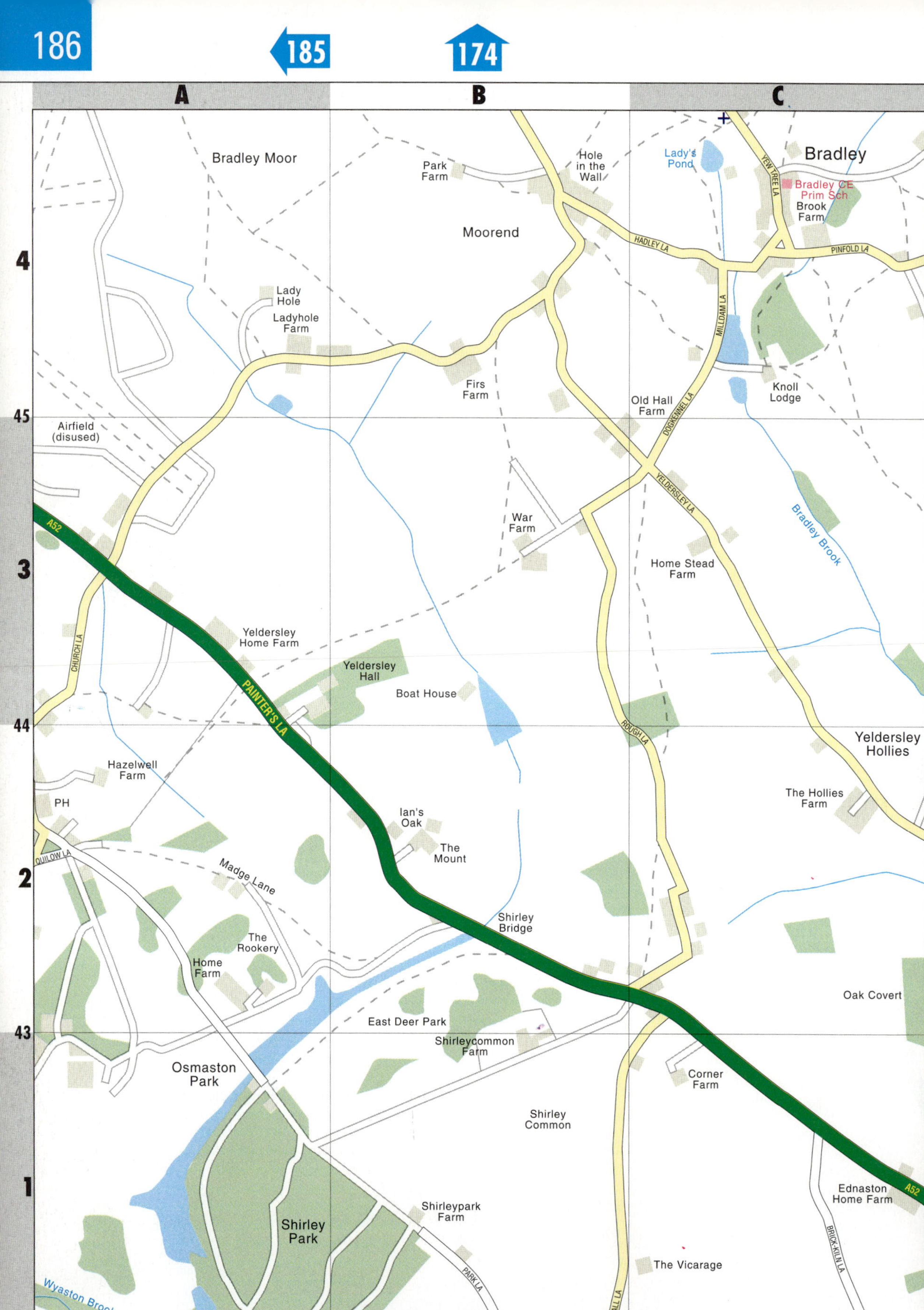

A B C

4

Bradley Moor

Park Farm

Hole in the Wall

Lady's Pond

YEW TREE LA

Bradley

Bradley CE Prim Sch

Brook Farm

Moorend

HADLEY LA

PINFOLD LA

Lady Hole

Ladyhole Farm

MILLDAM LA

Knoll Lodge

45

Airfield (disused)

Firs Farm

Old Hall Farm

DOGKENNEL LA

YELDERSLEY LA

Bradley Brook

A52

War Farm

Home Stead Farm

3

CHURCH LA

Yeldersley Home Farm

PAINTER'S LA

Yeldersley Hall

Boat House

ROUGH LA

Yeldersley Hollies

44

Hazelwell Farm

The Hollies Farm

PH

Ian's Oak

QUILOW LA

The Mount

Madge Lane

2

The Rookery

Home Farm

Shirley Bridge

Oak Covert

East Deer Park

43

Osmaston Park

Shirleycommon Farm

Corner Farm

Shirley Common

1

Shirley Park

Shirleypark Farm

Ednaston Home Farm

A52

BRICK-KILN LA

HALL LA

PARK LA

The Vicarage

42

Shirley House

Wyaston Brook

20 A 21 B 22 C

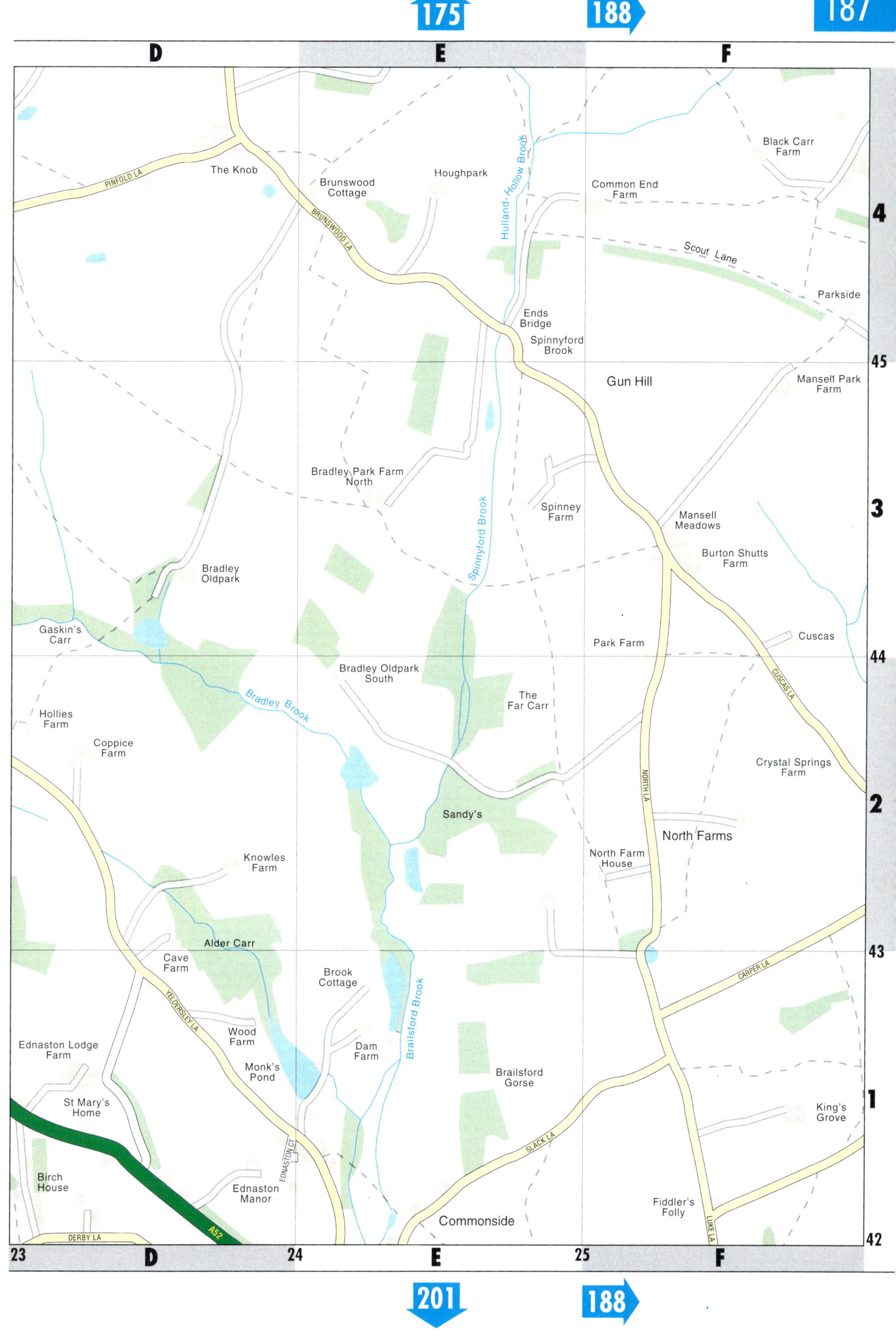
D
E
F
PINFOLD LA
The Knob
Brunswood Cottage
BRUNSWOOD LA
Houghpark
Hulland-Hollow Brook
Common End Farm
Black Carr Farm
Scout Lane
Parkside
Ends Bridge
Spinnyford Brook
Gun Hill
Mansell Park Farm
Bradley Park Farm North
Spinney Farm
Spinnyford Brook
Mansell Meadows
Burton Shutts Farm
Bradley Oldpark
Gaskin's Carr
Park Farm
Cuscas
CUSCAS LA
Bradley Oldpark South
The Far Carr
Bradley Brook
Hollies Farm
Coppice Farm
Crystal Springs Farm
NORTH LA
Sandy's
North Farms
North Farm House
Knowles Farm
Alder Carr
Cave Farm
Brook Cottage
CARPER LA
YELDERSLEY LA
Wood Farm
Dam Farm
Brailsford Brook
Ednaston Lodge Farm
Monk's Pond
Brailsford Gorse
St Mary's Home
King's Grove
SLACK LA
EDNASTON CT
Birch House
Ednaston Manor
Fiddler's Folly
Commonside
LUKE LA
A52
DERBY LA
4
45
3
44
2
43
1
42
23
24
25

A | B | C

4

Smith Hall Farm

Carrhall Farm

Waterlagg Brook

Works

The Carr

Blackbrook Farm

INTAKES LA

Pit (disused)

Mast

Common Farm

Hollinghurst

Herbalshaw Meadow Farm

The Clives

45

Blackbrook Farm

Redmiregap

Parkhill Farm

Muggintonlane End

Mansellpark

SMITH-HALL LA

Humblebee Hill

The Hollies

Black Brook

Sand Pit

Park Farm

Old Covert Farm

Highfields Farm

HIGHFIELD LA

3

Sand Pit

Sand Pit

Old Covert

Cock Inn (PH)

44

Shuckton Manor Farm

MERCASTON LA

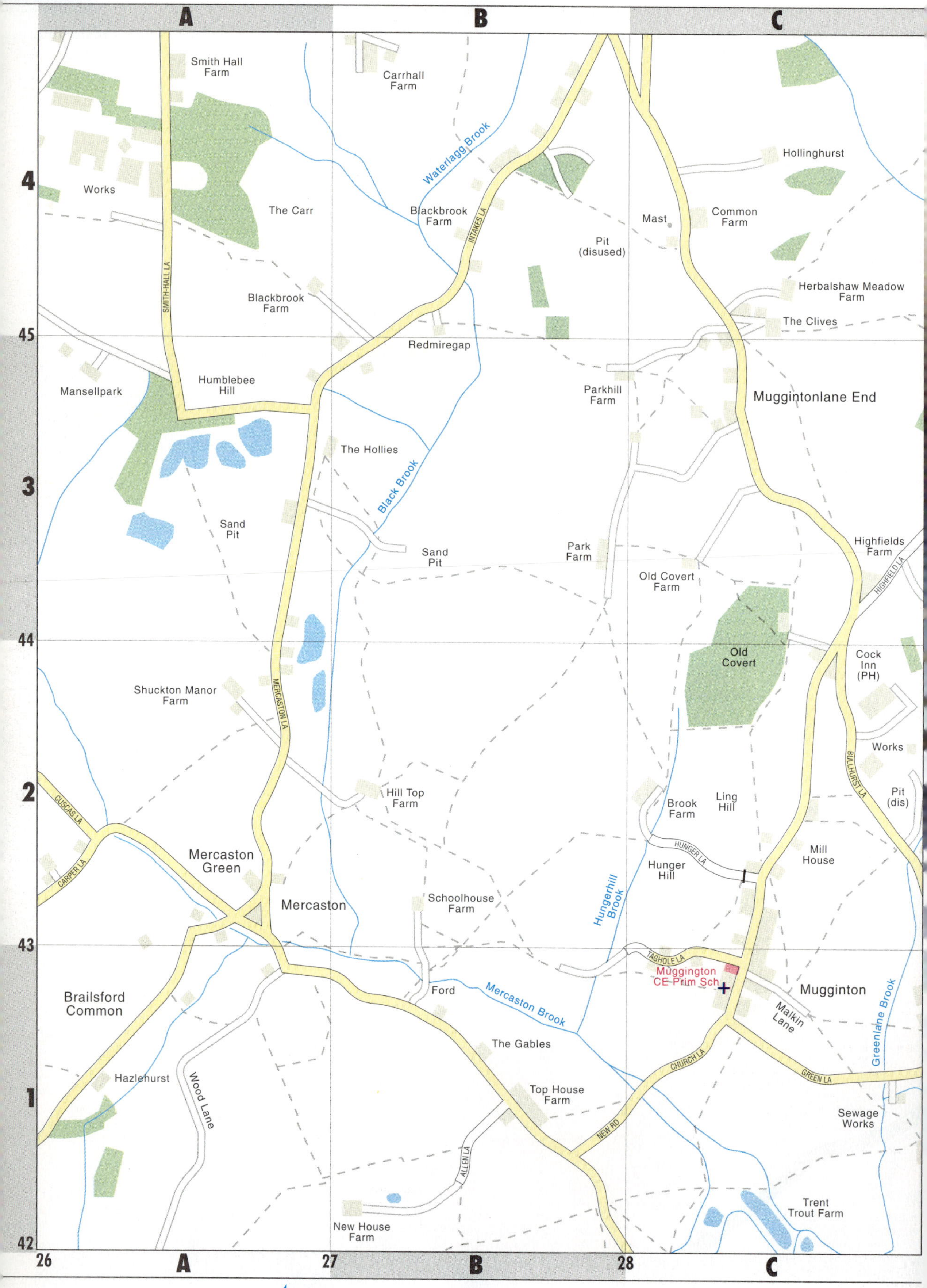

Works

BULLHURST LA

Pit (dis)

2

CUSCAS LA

Hill Top Farm

Brook Farm

Ling Hill

Mill House

Mercaston Green

CARPER LA

HUNGER LA

Hunger Hill

Mercaston

Schoolhouse Farm

Hungerhill Brook

43

TAGHOLE LA

Muggington CE-Prim Sch

Mugginton

Brailsford Common

Ford

Mercaston Brook

Malkin Lane

Greenlane Brook

The Gables

GREEN LA

1

Hazlehurst

Wood Lane

Top House Farm

CHURCH LA

NEW RD

Sewage Works

Trent Trout Farm

ALLEN LA

New House Farm

New Rd

42

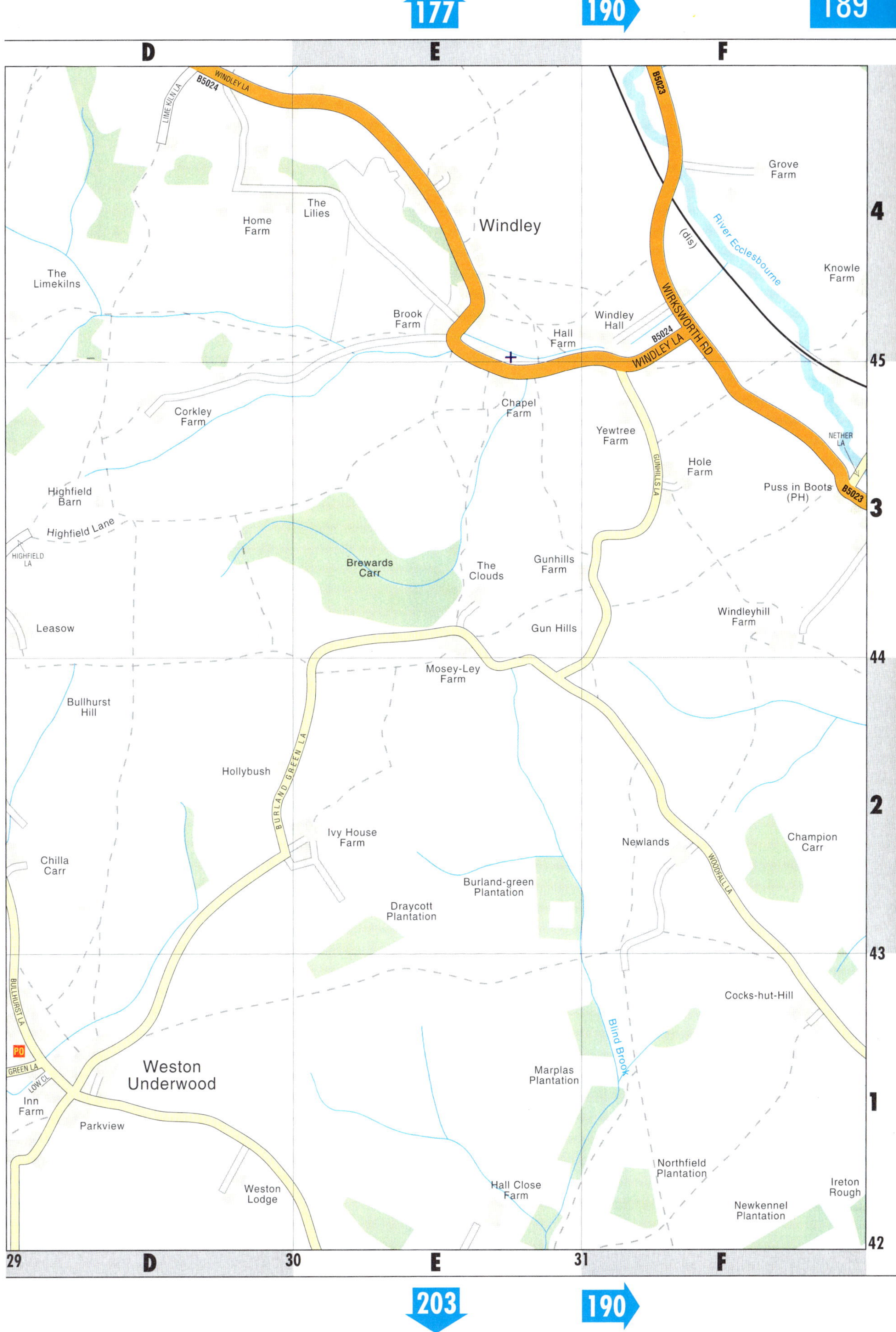

D
E
F

B5024 WINDLEY LA

LIME KILN LA

B5023

Grove
Farm

4

The
Lilies

Home
Farm

Windley

River Ecclesbourne

(dis)

Knowle
Farm

The
Limekilns

Brook
Farm

Windley
Hall

WIRKSWORTH RD

45

Hall
Farm

WINDLEY LA

B5024

Corkley
Farm

Chapel
Farm

Yewtree
Farm

Hole
Farm

NETHER
LA

Puss in Boots
(PH)

B5023

3

Highfield
Barn

GUNHILLS LA

Highfield Lane

HIGHFIELD
LA

Brewards
Carr

The
Clouds

Gunhills
Farm

Windleyhill
Farm

Leasow

Gun Hills

44

Bullhurst
Hill

Mosey-Ley
Farm

BURLAND GREEN LA

Hollybush

Newlands

WOODHALL LA

Champion
Carr

2

Chilla
Carr

Ivy House
Farm

Burland-green
Plantation

Draycott
Plantation

43

BULLHURST LA

Cocks-hut-Hill

Blind Brook

PO

GREEN LA

LOW G

Weston
Underwood

Marplas
Plantation

1

Inn
Farm

Parkview

Northfield
Plantation

Ireton
Rough

Weston
Lodge

Hall Close
Farm

Newkennel
Plantation

42

29
D
30
E
31
F

189
178

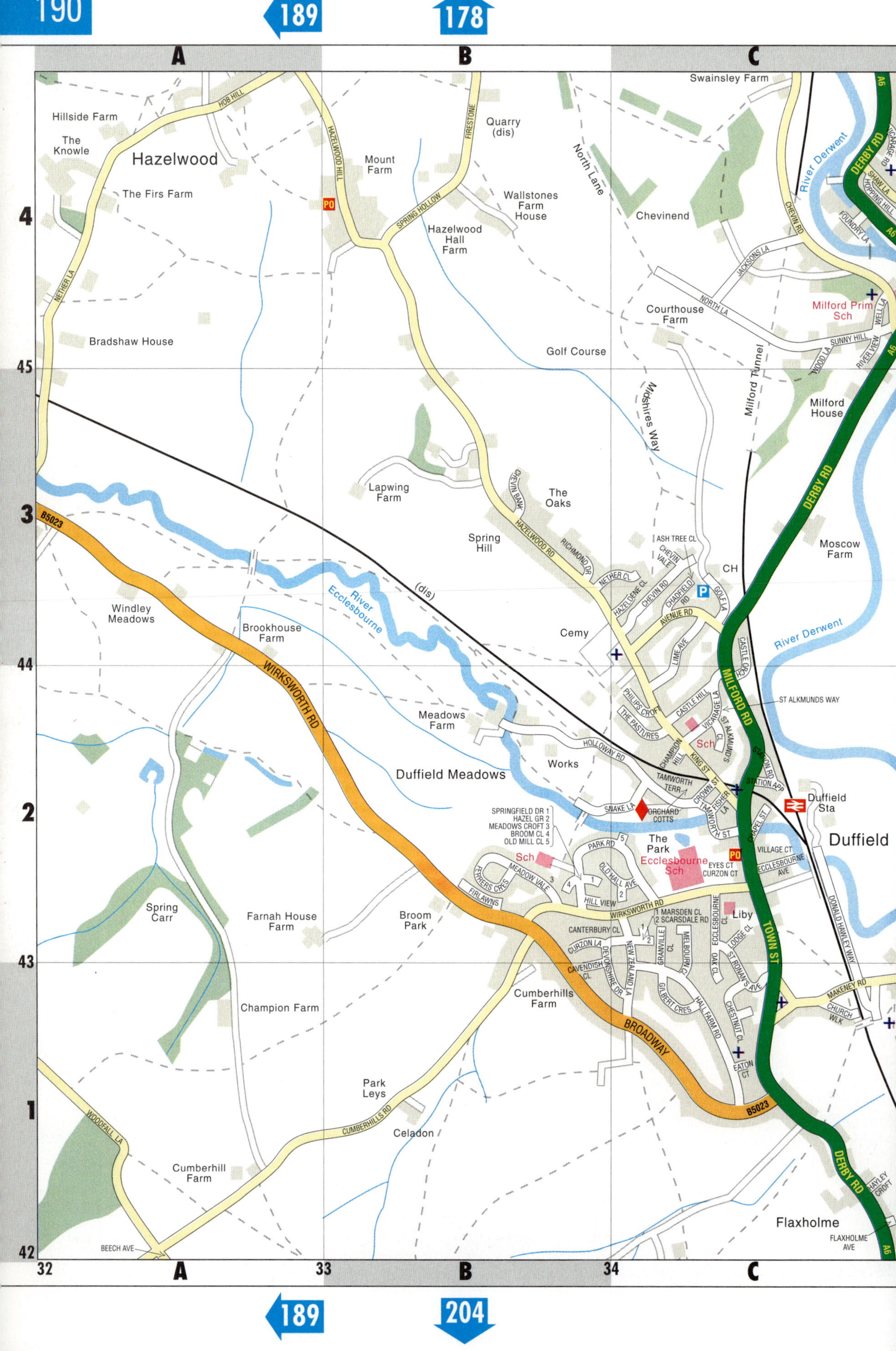
A
B
C
Swainsley Farm
Hillside Farm
The Knowle
Hazelwood
HOB HILL
HAZELWOOD HILL
FIRESTONE
Quarry (dis)
Mount Farm
PO
The Firs Farm
SPRING HOLLOW
Wallstones Farm House
Hazelwood Hall Farm
North Lane
Chevinend
River Derwent
DERBY RD
NETHER LA
Courthouse Farm
NORTH LA
JACKSONS LA
CHEVIN RD
Milford Prim Sch
Bradshaw House
Golf Course
Midshires Way
Milford Tunnel
Milford House
Lapwing Farm
The Oaks
CHEVIN BANK
HAZELWOOD RD
Spring Hill
RICHMOND DR
B5023
(dis)
River Ecclesbourne
ASH TREE CL
CHEVIN VALE
CH
Moscow Farm
Windley Meadows
Brookhouse Farm
Cemy
AVENUE RD
River Derwent
WIRKSWORTH RD
Meadows Farm
ST ALKMUNDS WAY
MILFORD RD
Works
HOLLOWAY RD
Duffield Meadows
Sch
KING ST
TAMWORTH TERR
STATION RD
STATION APP
Duffield Sta
SNAKE LA
ORCHARD COTTS
Duffield
SPRINGFIELD DR 1
HAZEL GR 2
MEADOWS CROFT 3
BROOM CL 4
OLD MILL CL 5
The Park
Ecclesbourne Sch
PARK RD
VILLAGE CT
EYES CT
CURZON CT
ECCLESBOURNE AVE
MEADOW VALE
FERRERS CRES
FIRLAWNS
HILL VIEW
OLD HALL AVE
Spring Carr
Farnah House Farm
Broom Park
1 MARSDEN CL
2 SCARSDALE RD
Liby
CANTERBURY CL
CURZON LA
CAVENDISH CL
DEVONSHIRE DR
NEW ZEALAND LA
GRANVILLE CL
MELBOURNE CL
ECCLESBOURNE CL
OAK CL
LODGE CL
ST RONAN'S AVE
TOWN ST
DONALD HAWLEY WAY
MAKENEY RD
CHURCH WLK
Cumberhills Farm
GILBERT CRES
HALL FARM RD
CHESTNUT CL
Champion Farm
BROADWAY
EATON CT
Park Leys
WOODFALL LA
CUMBERHILLS RD
Celadon
Cumberhill Farm
HAYLEY CROFT
Flaxholme
FLAXHOLME AVE
BEECH AVE
A6
4
45
3
44
2
43
1
42
32
33
34

189
204

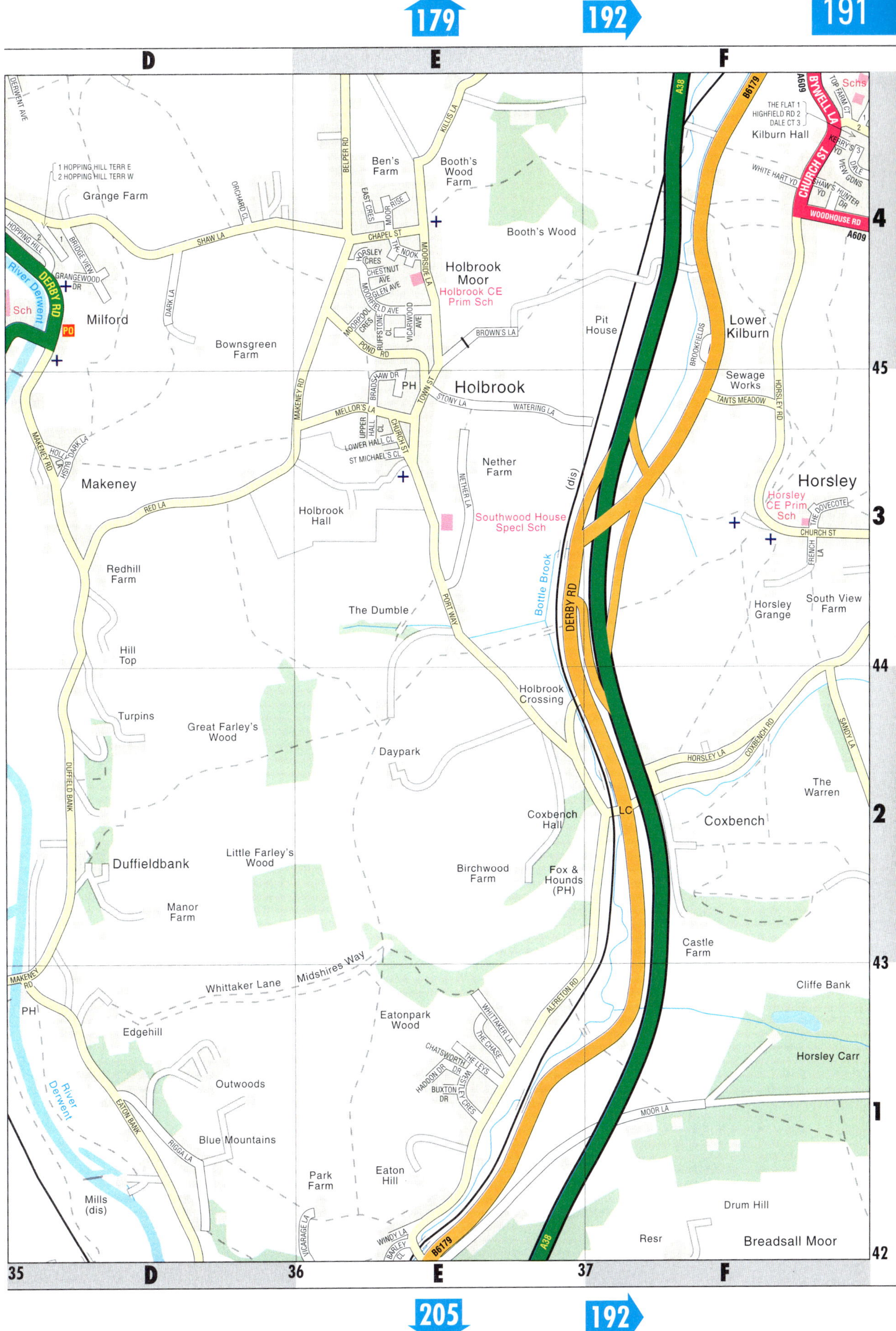
D
E
F
Milford
Makeney
Holbrook
Holbrook Moor
Holbrook CE Prim Sch
Lower Kilburn
Kilburn Hall
Horsley
Horsley CE Prim Sch
Coxbench
Duffieldbank
Grange Farm
Bownsgreen Farm
Ben's Farm
Booth's Wood Farm
Booth's Wood
Pit House
Sewage Works
Nether Farm
Holbrook Hall
Southwood House Specl Sch
Redhill Farm
Hill Top
The Dumble
Horsley Grange
South View Farm
Holbrook Crossing
Turpins
Great Farley's Wood
Daypark
The Warren
Coxbench Hall
Little Farley's Wood
Birchwood Farm
Fox & Hounds (PH)
Manor Farm
Castle Farm
Cliffe Bank
Whittaker Lane
Midshires Way
Eatonpark Wood
Edgehill
Horsley Carr
Outwoods
Blue Mountains
Park Farm
Eaton Hill
Mills (dis)
Drum Hill
Resr
Breadsall Moor
River Derwent
Bottle Brook
DERBY RD
A38
B6179
A609
SHAW LA
RED LA
MAKENEY RD
DUFFIELD BANK
EATON BANK
RIGGA LA
ALFRETON RD
MOOR LA
HORSLEY LA
COXBENCH RD
SANDY LA
HORSLEY RD
CHURCH ST
BYWELL LA
WOODHOUSE RD
PORT WAY
NETHER LA
STONY LA
WATERING LA
TOWN ST
MOORSIDE LA
KILLIS LA
BELPER RD
BROWN'S LA
BROOKFIELDS
TANTS MEADOW
1 HOPPING HILL TERR E
2 HOPPING HILL TERR W
THE FLAT 1
HIGHFIELD RD 2
DALE CT 3
Sch
Schs
PO
PH
LC
(dis)
4
45
3
44
2
43
1
42
35
36
37

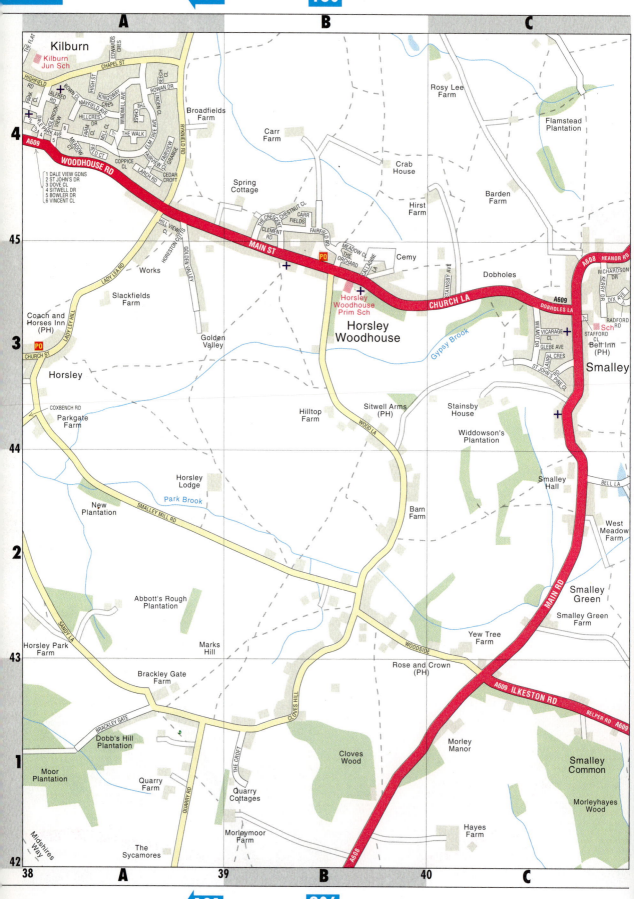
191
180
A
B
C
Kilburn
Kilburn Jun Sch
Broadfields Farm
Carr Farm
Rosy Lee Farm
Flamstead Plantation
Crab House
Spring Cottage
Hirst Farm
Barden Farm
WOODHOUSE RD
A609
1 DALE VIEW GDNS
2 ST JOHN'S DR
3 DOVE CL
4 SITWELL DR
5 BOWLER DR
6 VINCENT CL
MAIN ST
Works
Slackfields Farm
Cemy
Dobholes
CHURCH LA
Horsley Woodhouse Prim Sch
Horsley Woodhouse
Coach and Horses Inn (PH)
Golden Valley
Gypsy Brook
Horsley
Smalley
Bell Inn (PH)
Parkgate Farm
Hilltop Farm
Sitwell Arms (PH)
Stainsby House
Widdowson's Plantation
Horsley Lodge
Park Brook
New Plantation
Smalley Hall
Barn Farm
West Meadow Farm
Abbott's Rough Plantation
Smalley Green
Smalley Green Farm
Horsley Park Farm
Marks Hill
Yew Tree Farm
Rose and Crown (PH)
Brackley Gate Farm
ILKESTON RD
Dobb's Hill Plantation
Morley Manor
Cloves Wood
Smalley Common
Moor Plantation
Quarry Farm
Quarry Cottages
Morleyhayes Wood
Hayes Farm
Morleymoor Farm
Midshires Way
The Sycamores
38
39
40
42
43
44
45
1
2
3
4

181
194

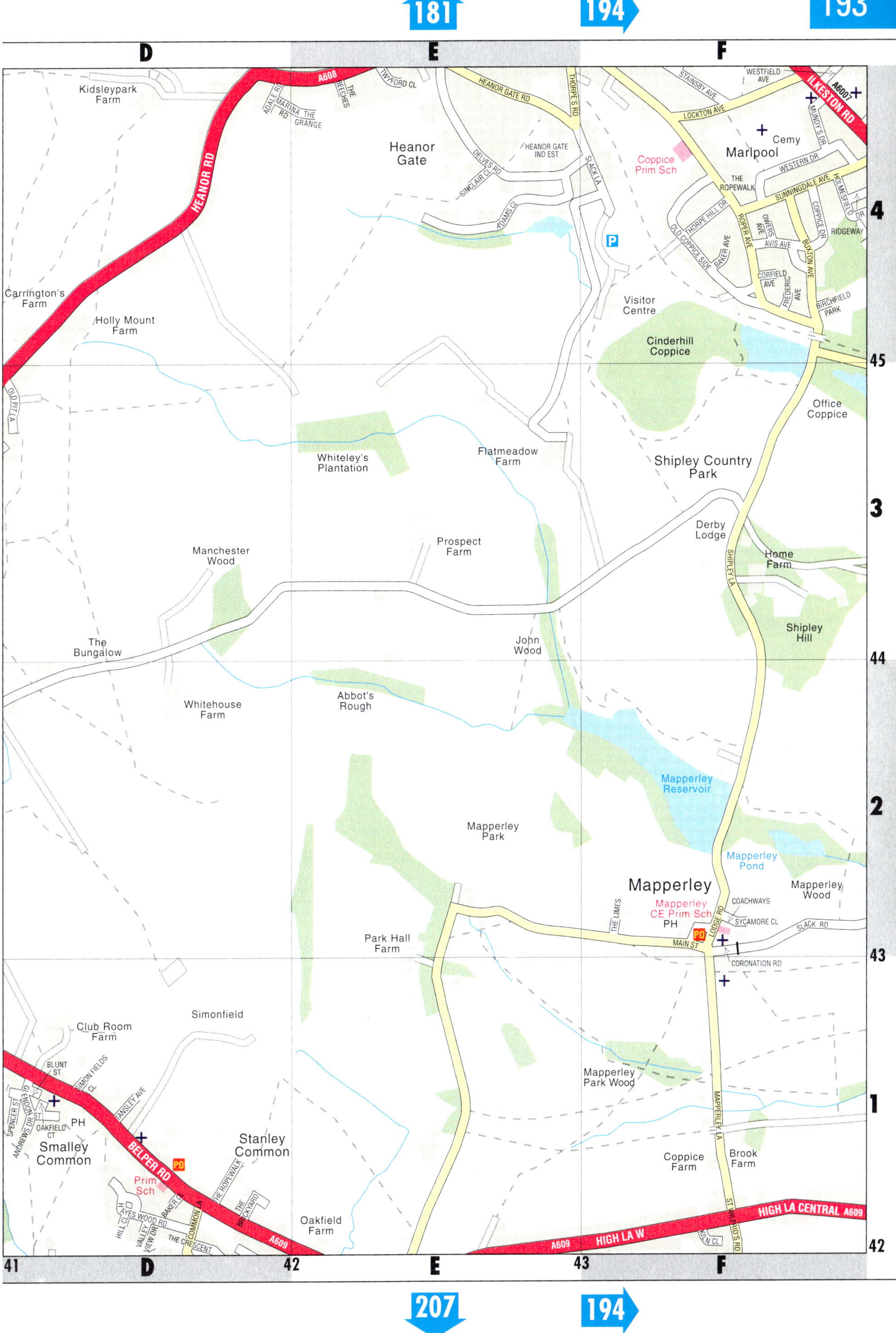
D
E
F
Kidsleypark Farm
A608
HEANOR RD
ADALE RD
MARINA RD
THE GRANGE
THE BEECHES
TWYFORD CL
HEANOR GATE RD
THORPE'S RD
Heanor Gate
HEANOR GATE IND EST
DELVES RD
SINCLAIR CL
ADAMS CL
SLACK LA
STAINSBY AVE
WESTFIELD AVE
LOCKTON AVE
ILKESTON RD
A6007
MUNDY'S DR
Cemy
Marlpool
Coppice Prim Sch
WESTERN DR
THE ROPEWALK
SUNNINGDALE AVE
HOLMESFIELD DR
THORPE HILL DR
OLD COPPICE SIDE
BAKER AVE
ROPER AVE
OWERS AVE
AVIS AVE
COPPICE DR
BUXTON AVE
RIDGEWAY
CORFIELD AVE
FREDERIC AVE
BIRCHFIELD PARK
P
Visitor Centre
Carrington's Farm
Holly Mount Farm
Cinderhill Coppice
45
OLD PIT LA
Office Coppice
Whiteley's Plantation
Flatmeadow Farm
Shipley Country Park
3
Derby Lodge
Prospect Farm
Manchester Wood
Home Farm
SHIPLEY LA
Shipley Hill
The Bungalow
John Wood
44
Whitehouse Farm
Abbot's Rough
Mapperley Reservoir
2
Mapperley Park
Mapperley Pond
Mapperley
Mapperley Wood
Mapperley CE Prim Sch
COACHWAYS
SYCAMORE CL
THE LIMES
PH
LODGE RD
SLACK RD
Park Hall Farm
PO
MAIN ST
CORONATION RD
43
Simonfield
Club Room Farm
BLUNT ST
SIMON FIELDS CL
GLENDON ST
SPENCER ST
ANDREWS DR
OAKFIELD CT
PH
TANSLEY AVE
Mapperley Park Wood
1
MAPPERLEY LA
Smalley Common
Stanley Common
BELPER RD
PO
Prim Sch
THE ROPEWALK
Coppice Farm
Brook Farm
HAYES WOOD RD
BAKER CL
HILL CL
VALLEY VIEW DR
COMMON LA
THE BRICKYARD
THE CRESCENT
A609
Oakfield Farm
A609
HIGH LA W
KILN CL
ST WILFRID'S RD
HIGH LA CENTRAL A609
42
41
D
42
E
43
F

207
194

A | B | C

4

ASHFORD HILL | BREACH RD | PO
Maripool Inf Sch
MILLBANK | THE OLD POND | WEST ST | PROSPECT RD | MILL RD
ILKESTON RD
RIDGEWY | A6007 | HARDY BARN
LOWER MAPER | HOLMESFIELD DR | HUFTON'S DR
1 SUNNINGDALE AVE
2 HUFTON'S DR
Hufton's Coppice
HASSOCK LA N
Algrave Hall Farm
Purdy House Farm

A610
NEWMANLEYS RD S
MAIN ST | NEWMANLEYS RD
BRAEMAR RD
Factory
Canal (disused)
LONG LA
The Shipley Boat (PH)

45

The Coppice Inn
THE FIELD
Shipley
Michael House - Rudolf Steiner Sch
PIT LA
HASSOCK LA S
LONG LA
Poplars Farm
Erewash Canal

A610

3

Shipley Lake
The American Adventure Theme Park
Cotmanhay Wood
THE COPSE
HARTINGTON PL 1
MILLERSDALE AVE 2
BIRCHOVER PL 3
CASTLETON AVE 4
DEVONSHIRE CL 5
BEAUVALE DR | EDALE | ICKNILD AV | LATHKILL AV
DALE | SKEVINGTON LA | OLUMBE
ASHFORD | DOVEDALE CL | MONSAL | DARLEY | SQ
DRONFIELD DR | DONNER CR | BOTANY DR
BERESFORD DR | BEAUVALE DR | SEAFORD WAY
Cotmanhay Inf & Jun Sch
HOPEWELL WK

44

Chapel Hill Farm | PO
WOODSIDE CRES
WOOD LA | LANGLEY AVE | COPPICE AVE | DRONFIELD | CHURCH DR
PEACOCK PL | ROSSENDALE | HENSHAW PL
CHURCH ST
BRIDGE ST | TRUE LA | MAIN ST
STRATFORD ST | RICHMOND AVE
Bennerley Fields Sch
CHAPEL CT
Cotmanhay
MOUNT PLEASANT | WESLEY ST | PRINCE ST
MILTON AVE | MILTON ST | BENNERLEY AVE
Bennerley Sch
Shipley Wood
Ilkeston Com
VICARAGE AVE | VICARAGE ST
ASH ST | MAY ST | MILTON ST | HORRIDGE ST | VERNON ST
HAWKINS | FISHER | RALEIGH | NELSON ST | ROPE | KEPPEL CT

2

Lodge Farm
Shipley Country Park
Shipley Common
SHIPLEY COMMON LA
RAYNEHAM RD | LANEWARD CL | GIMSON
AUDLEY CL
OAKHAM WAY
HEANOR RD
LITTON CL | STAPLETON RD | NORMAN ST | BRIGHT ST | LAMBERT ST
NORMAN CRES | TENNYSON ST | PRIMROSE
ARCHER ST | GRENVILLE | GRASS
1 DRAYCOTT CT | 2 BREADSALL CT | 3 HALLUM CT
PORTLAND RD | BOSWORAH AV | MOUNTBATTEN CT
DUKE ST
FARRIERS | CROFT | HOUGHTON CL | ELVEDEN DR | LILAC | HONINGHAM RD
WARWICK RD | ATHERTON RD | FOXTON CL | BARCLAY CT
SUMMERFIELDS WAY | THORPE ST | HADDON ST

43

Head House Farm
WAKEFIELD CROFT
HARLECH CL
MAINFIELD DR | PENTRIDGE DR | LANGMERE CL
MOUTH | WINDLEY CL
MILFORD CT | KEDLESTON CL
MONKTON | HIGHGATE DR | MILLBANK CL
SKIPTON CL | NEWSTEAD RD S | NEWSTEAD RD S
CHERITON DR | EMSWORTH CL
CLIFFORD CL | MORLEY ST | BROUGHTON | CLOSE
MAY SOUTH | CHARLOTTE ST | TRINITY CT | HADDON
Sch | Nurseries
BARBER PL | EBENEZER ST | VICTORIA | OAKBROOK | MUSKHAM AV | RISLEY CT
KITCHEN CL | EYRE'S GDNS | RED LAND | LANGLEY ST
BOATMANS CL | MANNING VIEW
REVILL CL | BARLING DR | HORSECROFT CL | WESTFIELD | HOLME | WHITEHEAD CL | PEVERIL DR | SPRINGFIELD GDN
Charlotte Inf Sch

1

The Brook
Mapperley Brook
WOOLISCROFT WAY | WATSHUCKER RD | ELLEY CT | MASON RD | STOPPARD CL | SUMMERFIELDS WAY | BOWES WELL RD
TURNBERRY CL
ILKESTON
Allotment Gardens
TATHAM'S LA
FACTORY LA | SPRING GARDEN TERR
GRANBY | BLOOMSGROVE | BARKER | SPRING GARDEN | ABBEY | GATE
BACK LA | RUTLAND ST | NORTHFIELD AV
LOWER BLOOMSGROVE RD
B6007
MANOR RD
MANNERS IND EST
BUXTON CT | BIRKDALE CL | FALCON CT | SHIPLEY CT
RUTLAND CT | MANNERS AVE | EREWASH | ELIZABETH ST | ORCHARD BSNS PK
MANNERS RD | PELHAM ST | BATH ST
STATION RD
A6096
MILL ST | MEADOW
West Hallam
PH | PO
HIGH LA CENTRAL | A609 | HIGH LA E
WILCOTE LA
Railway (disused)
Victoria CT
DRUMMOND RD | B6007 | BRISTO | NESFIELD RD | LORD ST | WILTON | ALBION ST | CHAPEL | ST
PELHAM ST | RUTLAND ST | OLIVER GRANBY ST
CHALONS WAY | A6007 | STATION RD
FLORENCE | GORDON | SHIPSTON | Sch | GRESLEY RD | CHAUCER ST | BYRON

42

44 | A | 45 | B | 46 | C

C1
1 BRUSSELS TERR
2 BURLEIGH ST
3 STAMFORD ST
4 ESSEX ST
5 DURHAM ST
6 NORTHGATE ST
7 WILTON ST
8 WEST TERR
9 NORTH ST
10 STATION CT
11 FULLWOOD AVE
12 PROVIDENCE PL
13 FULLWOOD ST
14 WHARNCLIFFE RD
15 JACKSON AVE
16 GREGORY ST
17 CHAPEL ST
18 LOWER CHAPEL ST
19 RIGLEY AVE

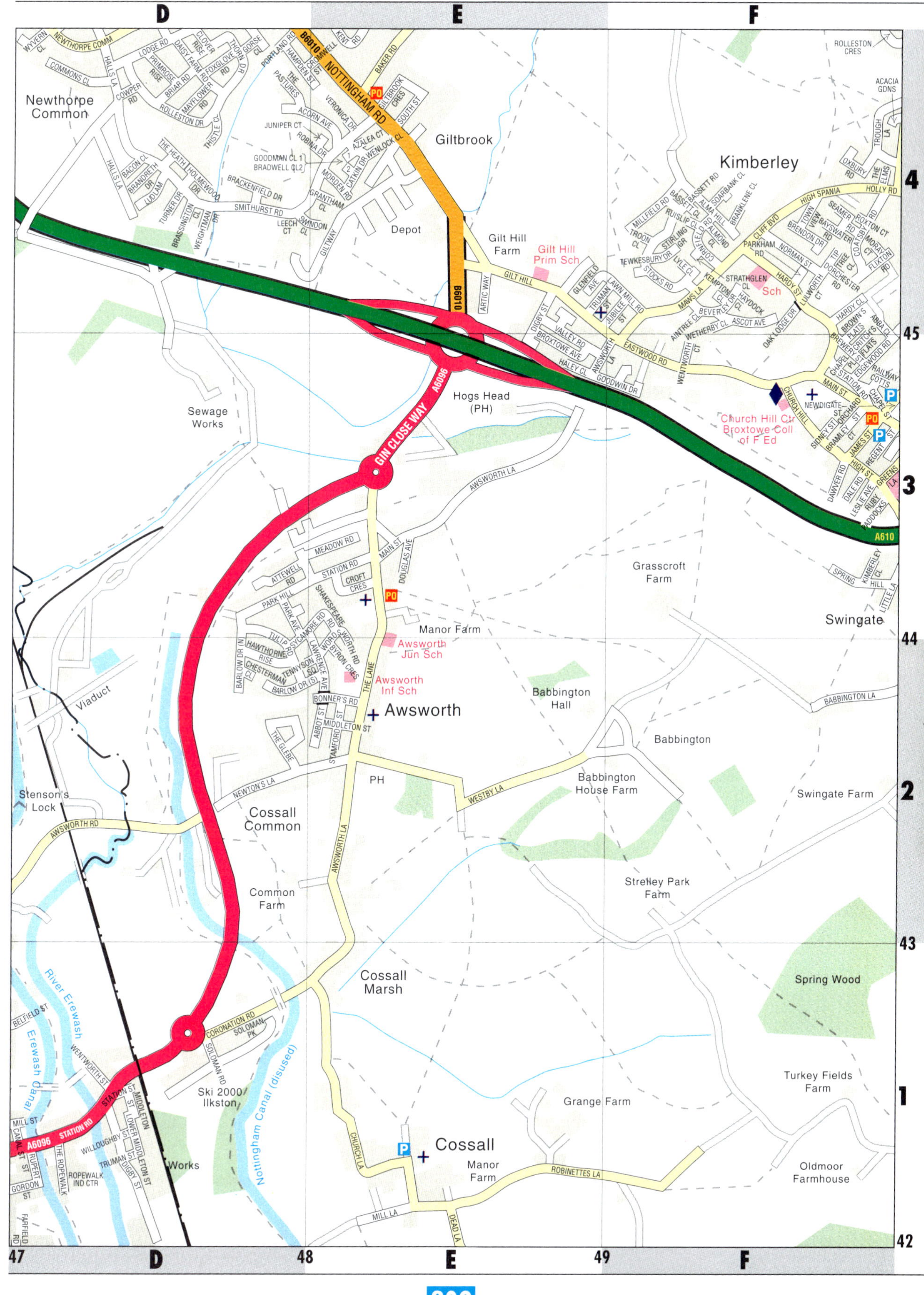

D
E
F
Newthorpe Common
Giltbrook
Kimberley
NOTTINGHAM RD
B6010
Depot
Gilt Hill Farm
Gilt Hill Prim Sch
Sch
Sewage Works
Hogs Head (PH)
GIN CLOSE WAY
A6096
Church Hill Ctr Broxtowe Coll of F Ed
A610
Grasscroft Farm
Swingate
Manor Farm
Awsworth Jun Sch
Awsworth Inf Sch
Awsworth
Babbington Hall
Babbington
Viaduct
Babbington House Farm
Swingate Farm
Stenson's Lock
PH
Cossall Common
Common Farm
Strelley Park Farm
Spring Wood
Cossall Marsh
River Erewash
Erewash Canal
Nottingham Canal (disused)
Ski 2000 Ilkston
Grange Farm
Turkey Fields Farm
Cossall
Manor Farm
Works
Oldmoor Farmhouse
ROBINETTES LA
4
45
3
44
2
43
1
42
47
48
49

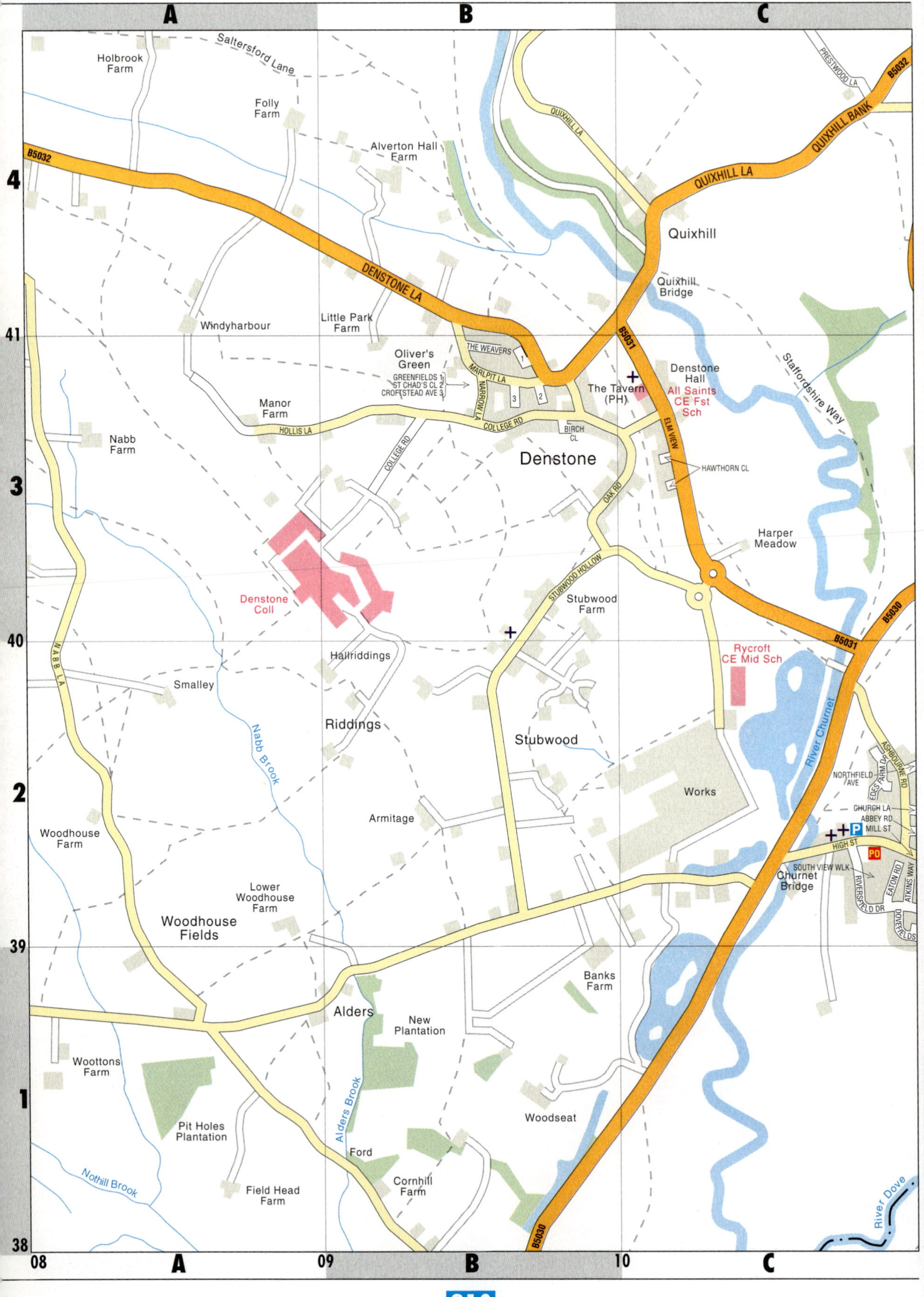
A
B
C
Holbrook Farm
Saltersford Lane
Folly Farm
Alverton Hall Farm
B5032
QUIXHILL LA
PRESTWOOD LA
QUIXHILL BANK
Quixhill
Quixhill Bridge
DENSTONE LA
Windyharbour
Little Park Farm
Oliver's Green
THE WEAVERS
MARLPIT LA
GREENFIELDS 1
ST CHAD'S CL 2
CROFTSTEAD AVE 3
NARROW LA
B5031
The Tavern (PH)
Denstone Hall
All Saints CE Fst Sch
Staffordshire Way
Manor Farm
HOLLIS LA
COLLEGE RD
BIRCH CL
ELM VIEW
HAWTHORN CL
Nabb Farm
Denstone
OAK RD
Harper Meadow
STUBWOOD HOLLOW
Stubwood Farm
Denstone Coll
Hallriddings
Rycroft CE Mid Sch
B5030
NABB LA
Smalley
Riddings
Stubwood
River Churnet
Nabb Brook
Works
NORTHFIELD AVE
EDES FARM DR
ASHBOURNE RD
CHURCH LA
ABBEY RD
MILL ST
HIGH ST
PO
SOUTH VIEW WLK
Churnet Bridge
RIVERSFIELD DR
EATON RD
ATKINS WAY
DOVEFIELDS
Armitage
Woodhouse Farm
Lower Woodhouse Farm
Woodhouse Fields
Banks Farm
Alders
New Plantation
Woottons Farm
Pit Holes Plantation
Woodseat
Alders Brook
Ford
Nothill Brook
Cornhill Farm
Field Head Farm
River Dove
4
41
3
40
2
39
1
38
08
09
10

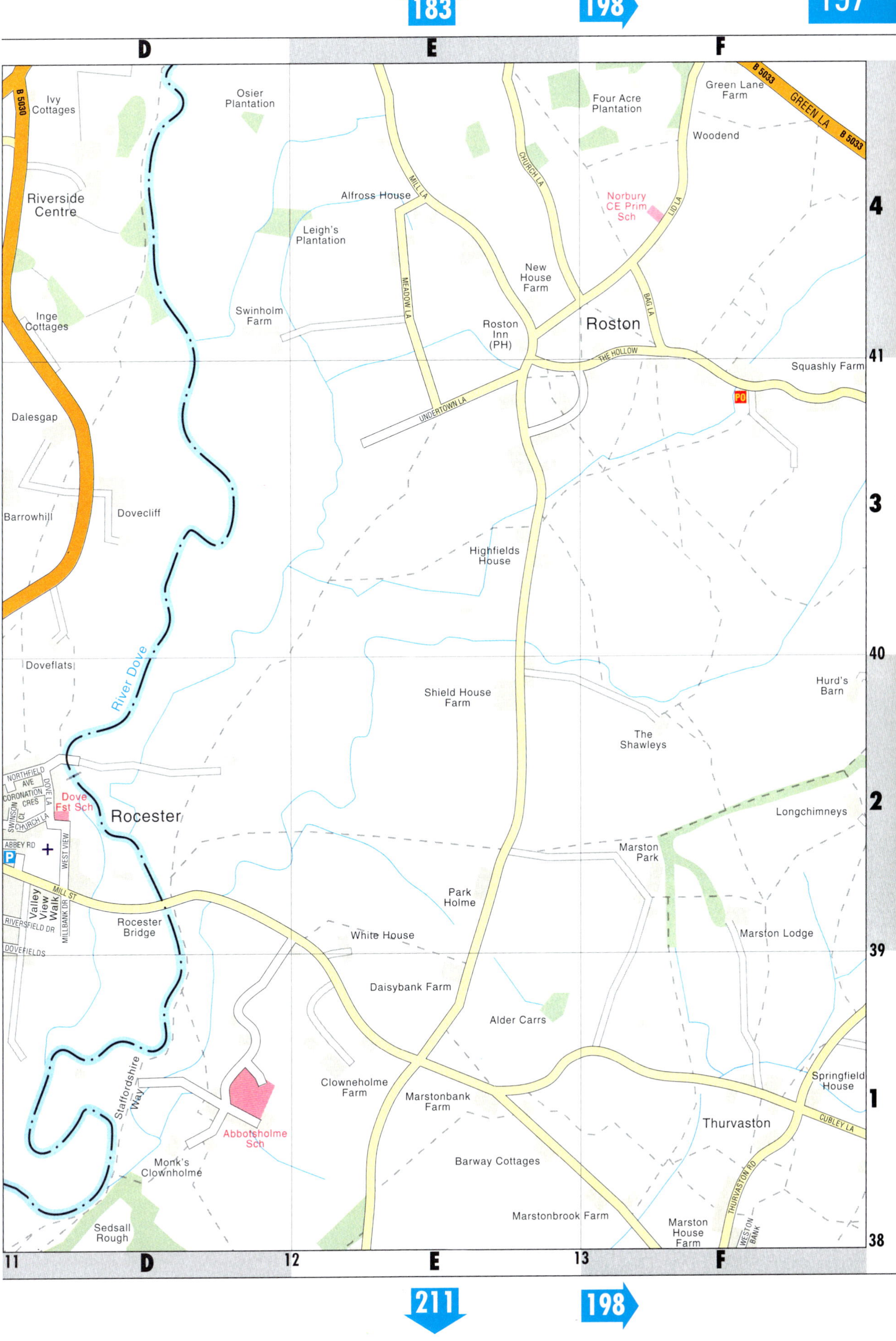
D
E
F
B 5030
Ivy Cottages
Osier Plantation
Four Acre Plantation
Green Lane Farm
B 5033
GREEN LA
B 5033
Woodend
Riverside Centre
Alfross House
MILL LA
CHURCH LA
Norbury CE Prim Sch
LID LA
Leigh's Plantation
MEADOW LA
New House Farm
Inge Cottages
Swinholm Farm
Roston Inn (PH)
Roston
BAG LA
THE HOLLOW
Squashly Farm
PO
Dalesgap
UNDERTOWN LA
Barrowhill
Dovecliff
Highfields House
Doveflats
River Dove
Shield House Farm
Hurd's Barn
The Shawleys
NORTHFIELD AVE
CORONATION CRES
DOVE LA
Dove Fst Sch
SWINSON CL
CHURCH LA
Rocester
Longchimneys
ABBEY RD
WEST VIEW
P
Marston Park
Park Holme
MILL ST
Valley View Walk
MILLBANK DR
RIVERSFIELD DR
Rocester Bridge
White House
Marston Lodge
DOVEFIELDS
Daisybank Farm
Alder Carrs
Staffordshire Way
Clowneholme Farm
Marstonbank Farm
Springfield House
Thurvaston
CUBLEY LA
Abbotsholme Sch
Monk's Clownholme
Barway Cottages
THURVASTON RD
Sedsall Rough
Marstonbrook Farm
Marston House Farm
WESTON BANK
4
41
3
40
2
39
1
38
11
12
13

A   B   C

Shepherdswood

Chapel House

B5033

GREEN LA

SNAPES LA

Queen Adelaide Arms (PH)

VIRGINSALLEY LA

Snelston Common

Cindershills Wood

Darley Moor

Old Queen Farm

Flat Covert

COCKSHEAD LA

B5033

A515

4

Common Farm

John Roe's Covert

Quarry (dis)

Grange Cottage

Top Stydd

41

Grange Farm

Manor House

Birchwood Park

Roston Common

Cubley Brook

3

Birchwoodmoor

Marstoncommon Farm

Cubley Wood Farm

40

Wood Hay Farm

Accession Wood

The Hollies

HOLLIES LA

Side Gate

Broad Lane

Sammy's Wood

2

Sandhills Farm

Cubley Covert

Whiterley

Holme Lea

Cubley Common

Cubley Cottage Farm

39

Gorse Covert

Common Farm

Mountpleasant Farm

1

Rough Grounds

Great Cubley

Birch Field Farm

The Spinney

Brookside Farm

SHAW LA

CUBLEY LA

A515

Howard Arms (PH)

DERBY LA

PO

LONG MEADOW

38

Cubley Fields Farm

14   A   15   B   16   C

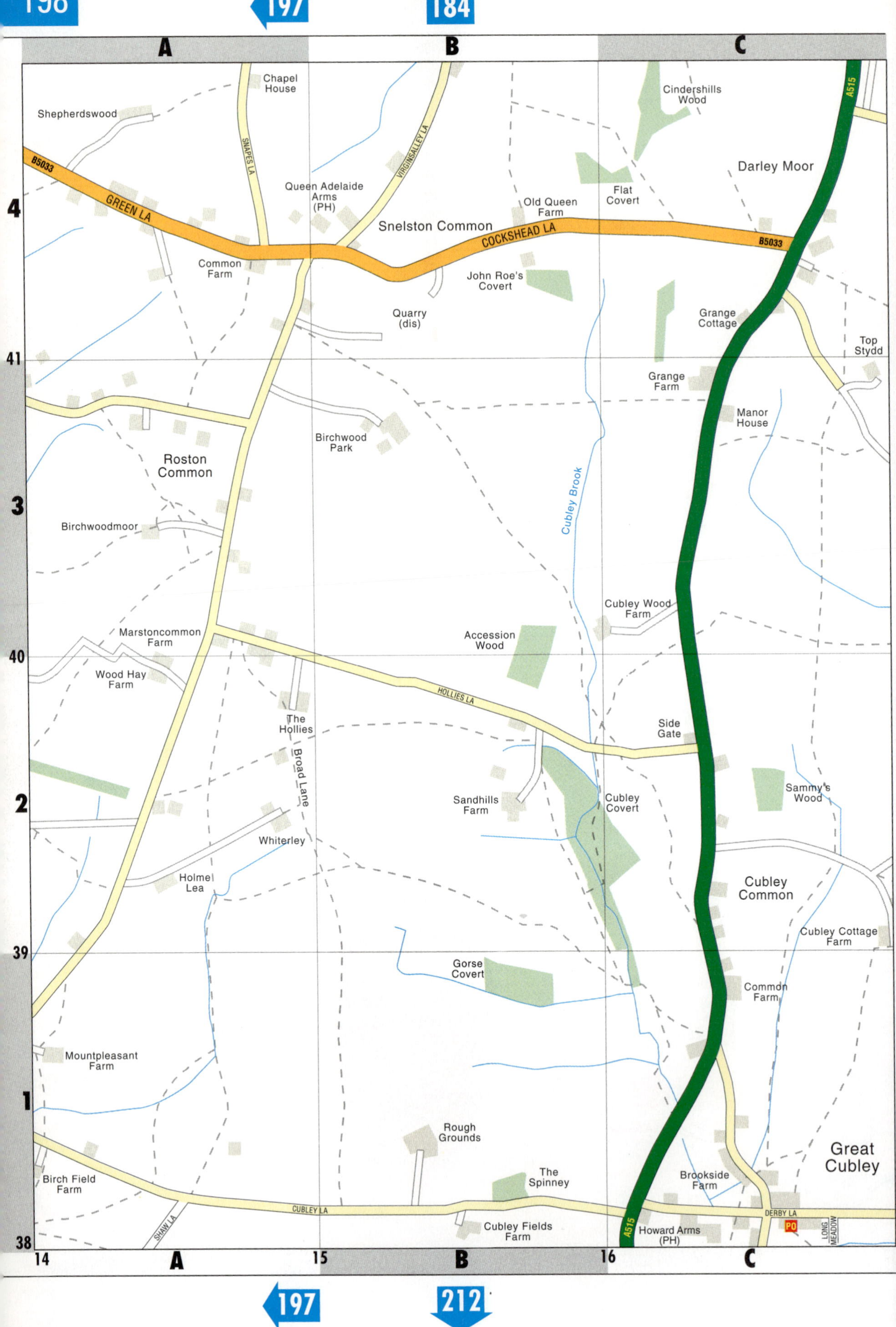

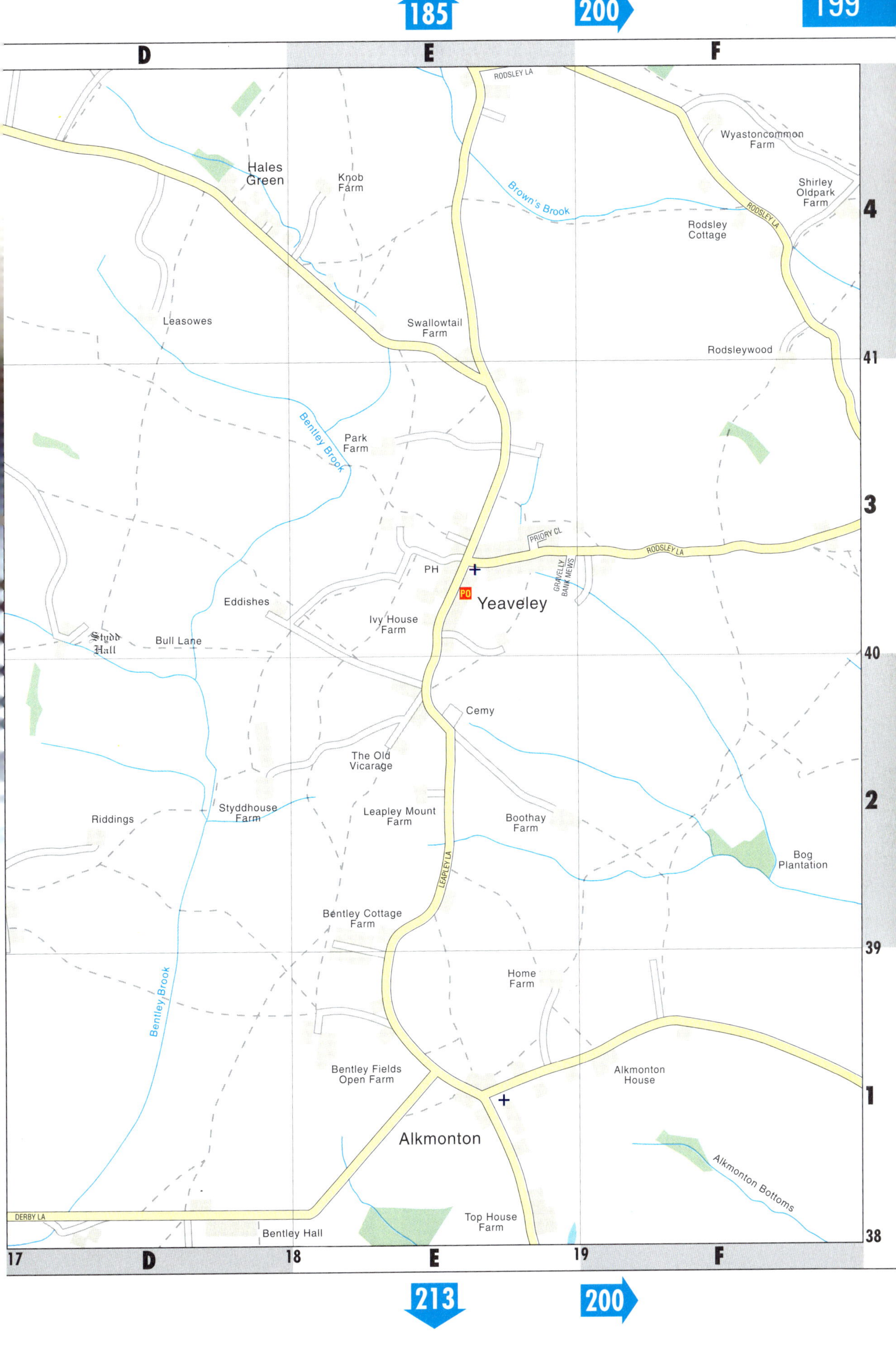

D | E | F

RODSLEY LA

Wyastoncommon Farm

Shirley Oldpark Farm

Hales Green

Knob Farm

Brown's Brook

Rodsley Cottage

RODSLEY LA

4

Leasowes

Swallowtail Farm

Rodsleywood

41

Bentley Brook

Park Farm

3

PRIORY CL

RODSLEY LA

PH

GRAVELLY BANK MEWS

PO

Yeaveley

Eddishes

Ivy House Farm

Studd Hall

Bull Lane

40

Cemy

The Old Vicarage

2

Riddings

Styddhouse Farm

Leapley Mount Farm

Boothay Farm

Bog Plantation

Bentley Cottage Farm

LEAPLEY LA

39

Bentley Brook

Home Farm

Alkmonton House

1

Bentley Fields Open Farm

Alkmonton

Alkmonton Bottoms

DERBY LA

Bentley Hall

Top House Farm

38

17 | D | 18 | E | 19 | F

199
186

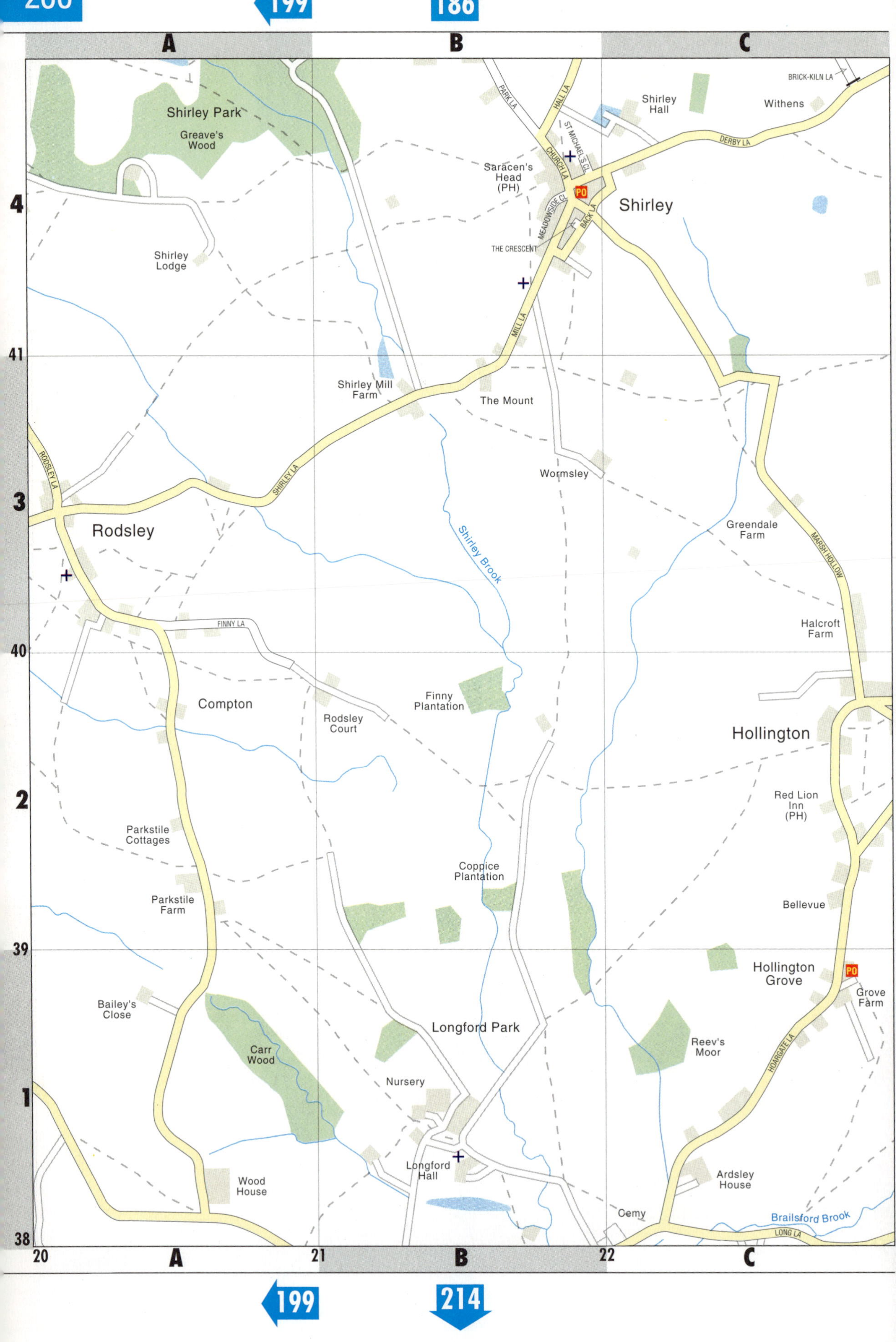
A
B
C
Shirley Park
Greave's Wood
Shirley Lodge
PARK LA
HALL LA
ST MICHAEL'S CL
CHURCH LA
Saracen's Head (PH)
PO
MEADOWSIDE CL
BACK LA
THE CRESCENT
Shirley
Shirley Hall
Withens
BRICK-KILN LA
DERBY LA
MILL LA
Shirley Mill Farm
The Mount
Wormsley
RODSLEY LA
SHIRLEY LA
Rodsley
Shirley Brook
Greendale Farm
MARSH HOLLOW
Halcroft Farm
FINNY LA
Compton
Rodsley Court
Finny Plantation
Hollington
Red Lion Inn (PH)
Parkstile Cottages
Coppice Plantation
Parkstile Farm
Bellevue
Hollington Grove
PO
Grove Farm
Bailey's Close
Carr Wood
Longford Park
Reev's Moor
HOARGATE LA
Nursery
Longford Hall
Wood House
Ardsley House
Cemy
Brailsford Brook
LONG LA
4
41
3
40
2
39
1
38
20
21
22

199
214

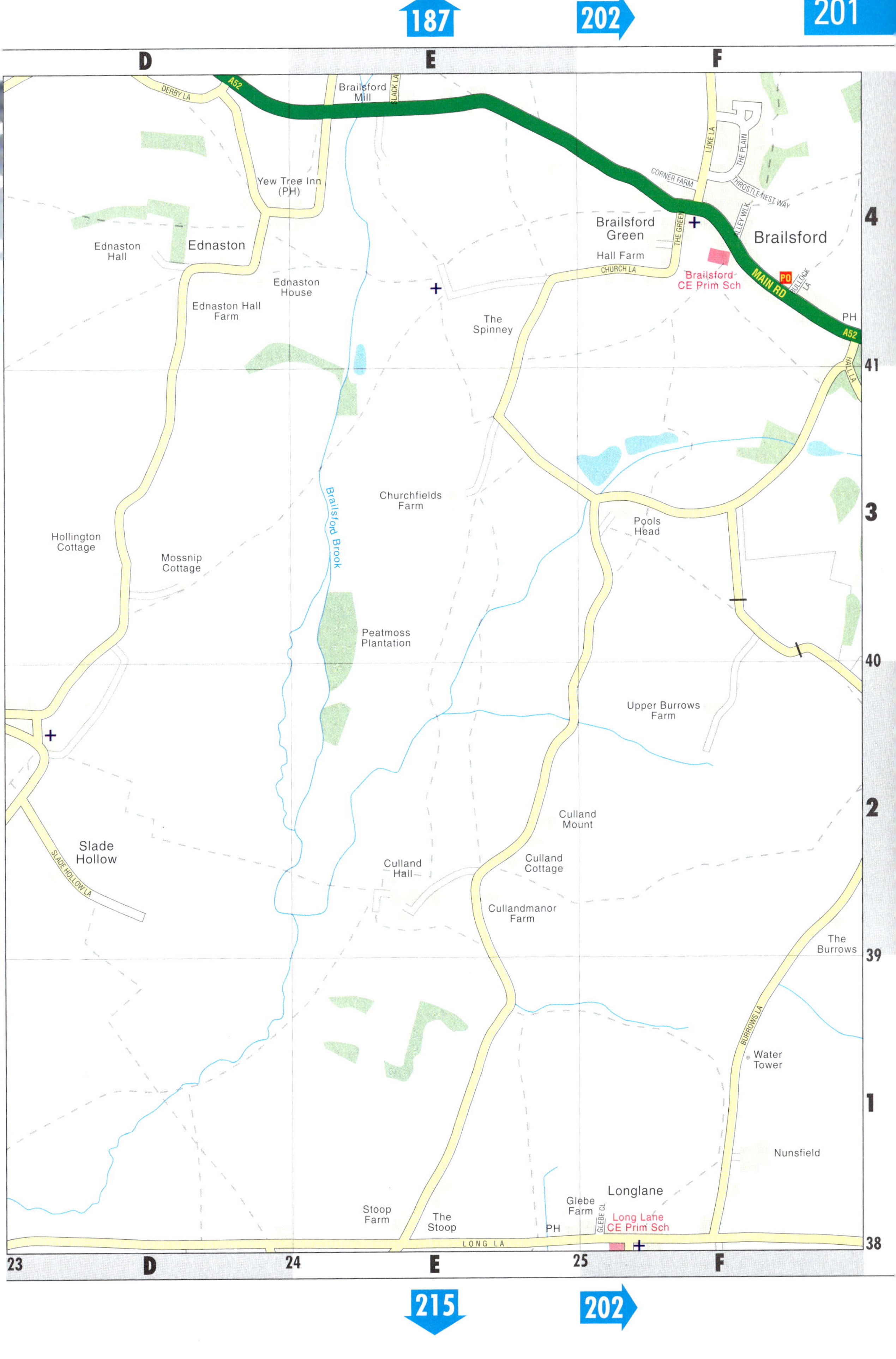
D
E
F
A52
DERBY LA
Brailsford Mill
SLACK LA
LUKE LA
THE PLAIN
CORNER FARM
THROSTLE NEST WAY
Yew Tree Inn (PH)
Brailsford Green
ALLEY WLK
THE GREEN
Brailsford
Ednaston Hall
Ednaston
Hall Farm
CHURCH LA
Brailsford CE Prim Sch
MAIN RD
PO
BULLOCK LA
Ednaston House
Ednaston Hall Farm
The Spinney
PH
HALL LA
4
41
Churchfields Farm
Brailsford Brook
Pools Head
3
Hollington Cottage
Mossnip Cottage
Peatmoss Plantation
40
Upper Burrows Farm
2
Slade Hollow
SLADE HOLLOW LA
Culland Mount
Culland Hall
Culland Cottage
Cullandmanor Farm
The Burrows
39
BURROWS LA
Water Tower
1
Nunsfield
Longlane
Glebe Farm
GLEBE CL
Long Lane CE Prim Sch
Stoop Farm
The Stoop
PH
LONG LA
38
23
D
24
E
25
F

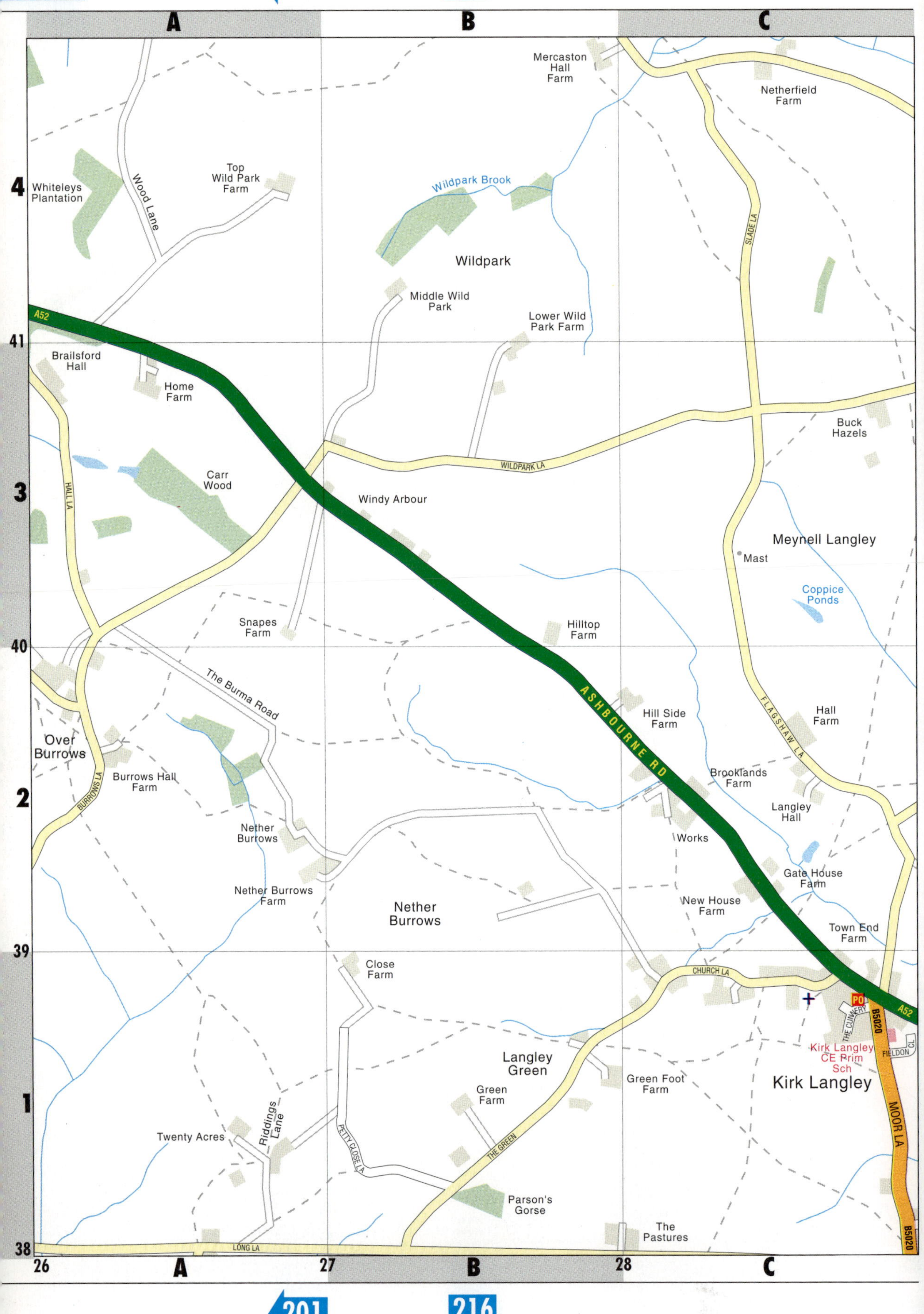

4

Whiteleys
Plantation

Wood Lane

Top Wild Park
Farm

Mercaston
Hall
Farm

Netherfield
Farm

Wildpark Brook

Wildpark

Slade La

Middle Wild
Park

Lower Wild
Park Farm

A52

41

Brailsford
Hall

Home
Farm

Wildpark La

Buck
Hazels

3

Hall La

Carr
Wood

Windy Arbour

Meynell Langley

Mast

Coppice
Ponds

Snapes
Farm

Hilltop
Farm

40

The Burma Road

Ashbourne Rd

Hall
Farm

Flagshaw La

Over
Burrows

Burrows Hall
Farm

Hill Side
Farm

Brooklands
Farm

Langley
Hall

Burrows La

2

Nether
Burrows

Works

Nether Burrows
Farm

Gate House
Farm

Nether
Burrows

New House
Farm

Town End
Farm

39

Close
Farm

Church La

A52

The Glebery

PO

B5020

Kirk Langley
CE Prim
Sch

Langley
Green

Green Foot
Farm

Kirk Langley

Riddings Lane

Green
Farm

Petty Close La

1

Twenty Acres

The Green

Moor La

Parson's
Gorse

The
Pastures

B5020

38

Long La

26
A
27
B
28
C

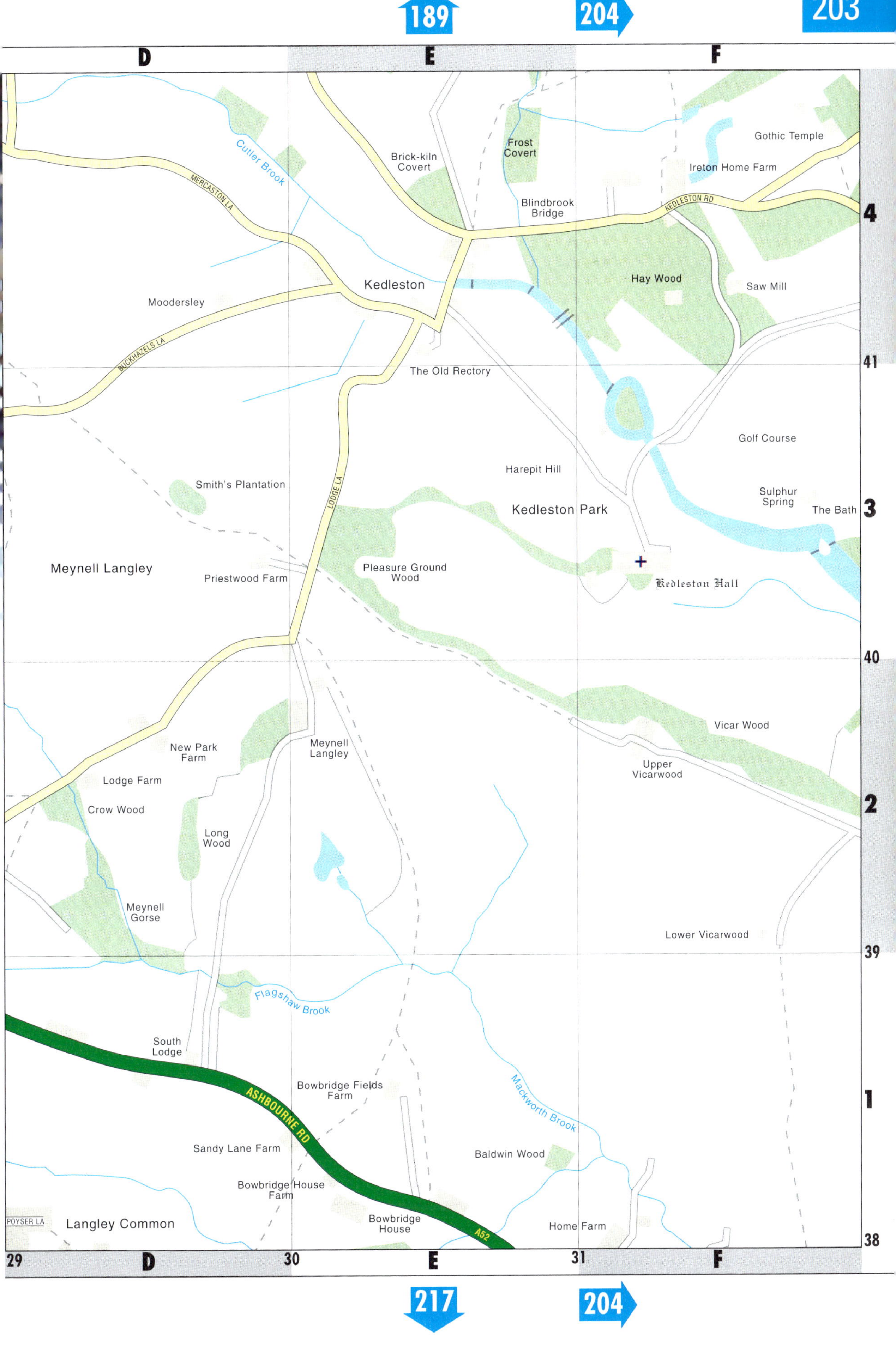

D E F

Gothic Temple

Cutler Brook

Brick-kiln Covert

Frost Covert

Ireton Home Farm

KEDLESTON RD

MERCASTON LA

Blindbrook Bridge

4

Hay Wood

Saw Mill

Kedleston

Moodersley

BUCKHAZELS LA

41

The Old Rectory

Golf Course

Harepit Hill

Smith's Plantation

LODGE LA

Kedleston Park

Sulphur Spring

The Bath

3

Meynell Langley

Priestwood Farm

Pleasure Ground Wood

Kedleston Hall

40

Vicar Wood

New Park Farm

Meynell Langley

Upper Vicarwood

Lodge Farm

Crow Wood

2

Long Wood

Meynell Gorse

Lower Vicarwood

39

Flagshaw Brook

South Lodge

ASHBOURNE RD

Bowbridge Fields Farm

Mackworth Brook

1

Sandy Lane Farm

Baldwin Wood

Bowbridge House Farm

POYSER LA

Langley Common

Bowbridge House

A52

Home Farm

38

29 D 30 E 31 F

203
190

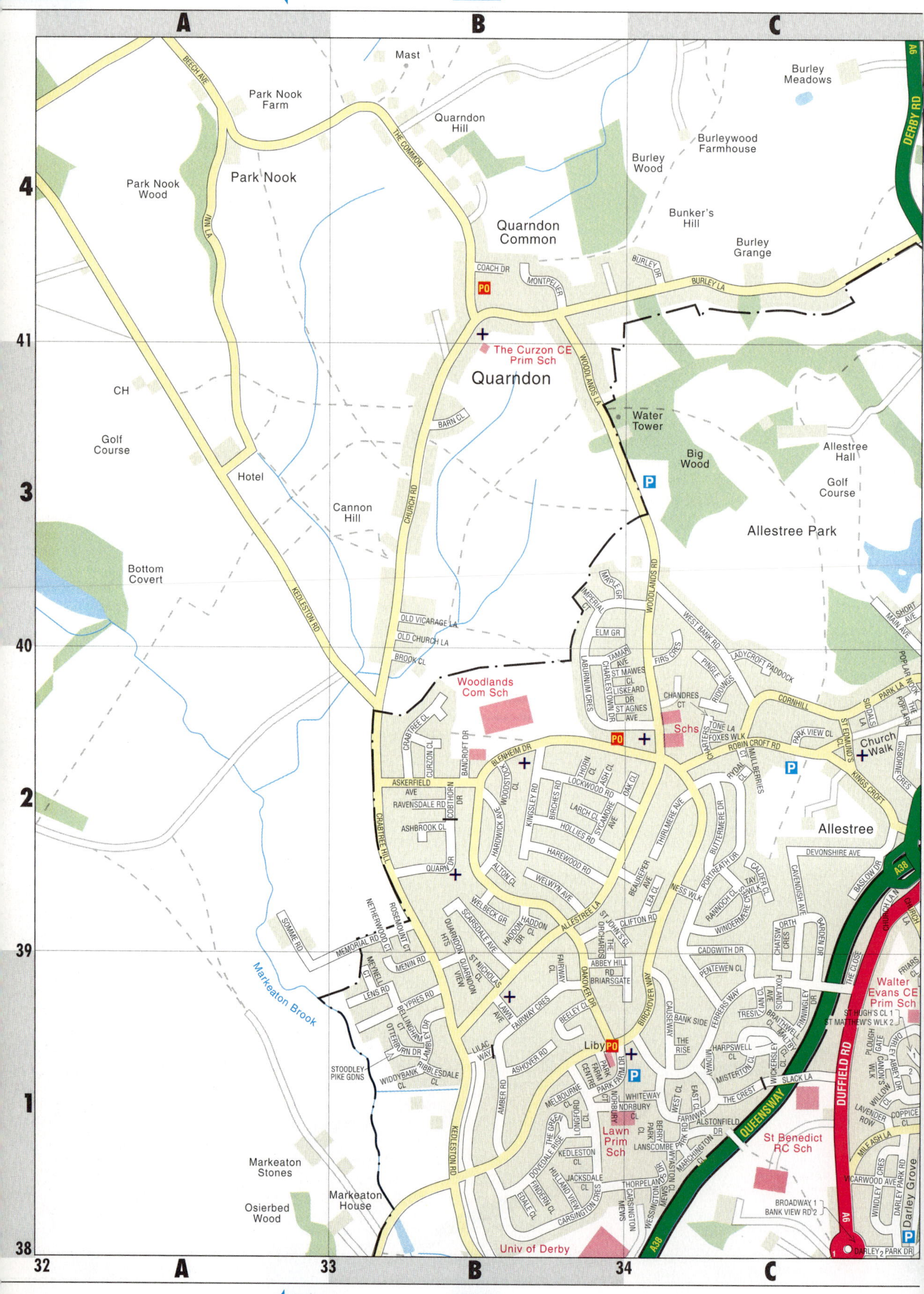
A
B
C
4
41
3
40
2
39
1
38
32
33
34
Mast
Park Nook Farm
Quarndon Hill
Burley Meadows
Burleywood Farmhouse
Burley Wood
Park Nook Wood
Park Nook
Bunker's Hill
Quarndon Common
Burley Grange
BEECH AVE
THE COMMON
INN LA
COACH DR
MONTPELIER
BURLEY DR
BURLEY LA
DERBY RD
A6
PO
The Curzon CE Prim Sch
Quarndon
WOODLANDS LA
CH
Golf Course
BARN CL
Water Tower
Big Wood
Allestree Hall
Golf Course
Hotel
Cannon Hill
CHURCH RD
P
Allestree Park
Bottom Covert
KEDLESTON RD
MAPLE GR
IMPERIAL CT
WOODLANDS RD
WEST BANK RD
SHORT AVE
MAIN AVE
OLD VICARAGE LA
OLD CHURCH LA
BROOK CL
ELM GR
FIRS CRES
TAMAR AVE
ST MAWES CL
LISKEARD DR
ST AGNES AVE
CHARLESTOWN DR
LABURNUM CRES
PINGLE
RIDDINGS
LADYCROFT PADDOCK
POPLAR NOOK
Woodlands Com Sch
CHANDRES CT
CORNHILL
PARK LA
SIDDALS LA
THE POPLARS
CRABTREE CL
CURZON CL
BANCROFT DR
Schs
TONE LA
FOXES WLK
PARK VIEW CL
ROBIN CROFT RD
ST EDMUND'S CL
Church Walk
GISBORNE CRES
BLENHEIM DR
WOODSTOCK CL
THORN CL
ASH CL
LOCKWOOD RD
OAK CL
RYDAL CL
MULLBERRIES
KINGS CROFT
ASKERFIELD AVE
RAVENSDALE RD
COBTHORN DR
KINGSLEY RD
BIRCHES RD
LARCH CL
SYCAMORE AVE
THIRLMERE AVE
BUTTERMERE DR
Allestree
ASHBROOK CL
CRABTREE HILL
HARDWICK AVE
HOLLIES RD
HAREWOOD RD
DEVONSHIRE AVE
QUARN DR
ALTON CL
WELWYN AVE
BEAUREPER AVE
PORTREATH DR
CALDER CL
TAY WLK
CAVENDISH AVE
BASLOW DR
A38
WELBECK GR
HADDON CL
HADDON DR
LEA CL
NESS WLK
RANNOCH CL
WINDERMERE CRES
CHURCH LA
NETHERWOOD CT
ROSEMOUNT CT
SOMME RD
QUARNDON HTS
SCARSDALE AVE
ALLESTREE LA
ST JOHN'S CL
CLIFTON RD
CHATSWORTH CRES
BARDEN DR
MEMORIAL RD
MENIN RD
ST NICHOLAS CL
QUARNDON VIEW
THE ORCHARDS
ABBEY HILL RD
BRIARSGATE
CADGWITH DR
PENTEWEN CL
THE CLOSE
FRIARS CL
METWELL CT
LENS RD
YPRES RD
FAIRWAY CL
OAKOVER DR
Walter Evans CE Prim Sch
Markeaton Brook
BELLINGHAM CT
LAWN AVE
FAIRWAY CRES
BEELEY CL
BIRCHOVER WAY
CAUSEWAY
BANK SIDE
FERRERS WAY
TRESILLIAN CL
FOXLANDS AVE
BRAITHWELL CL
FINNINGLEY DR
ST HUGH'S CL
ST MATTHEW'S WLK
OTTERBURN DR
LAMBLEY DR
LILAC WAY
ASHOVER RD
Liby
PARK FARM CENTRE
PARK FARM DR
THE RISE
HARPSWELL CL
MIDWAY
MISTERTON CL
WICKERSLEY CL
SLACK LA
PLOUGH GATE
CANON'S WLK
WILLOW CL
DARLEY ABBEY DR
STOODLEY PIKE GDNS
WIDDYBANK CL
RIBBLESDALE CL
AMBER RD
MELBOURNE CL
WHITEWAY
NORBURY CL
WEST CL
EAST CL
THE CREST
FARNWAY
QUEENSWAY
DUFFIELD RD
LAVENDER ROW
COPPICE CL
NORDBURY CL
Lawn Prim Sch
BERRY PARK CL
ALSTONFIELD DR
St Benedict RC Sch
MILE ASH LA
THE GREEN
DOVEDALE RISE
LONGFORD CL
KEDLESTON CL
LANSCOMBE PARK RD
MARCHINGTON CL
HULLAND VIEW
JACKSDALE CL
WYASTON CL
Markeaton Stones
Markeaton House
Osierbed Wood
EDALE CL
FINDERN CL
CARSINGTON CRES
THORPELANDS DR
CARSINGTON MEWS
WESSINGTON MEWS
CARWOOD AVE
WINDLEY CRES
DARLEY PARK RD
Darley Grove
BROADWAY
BANK VIEW RD
Univ of Derby
DARLEY PARK DR

203
218

191
206

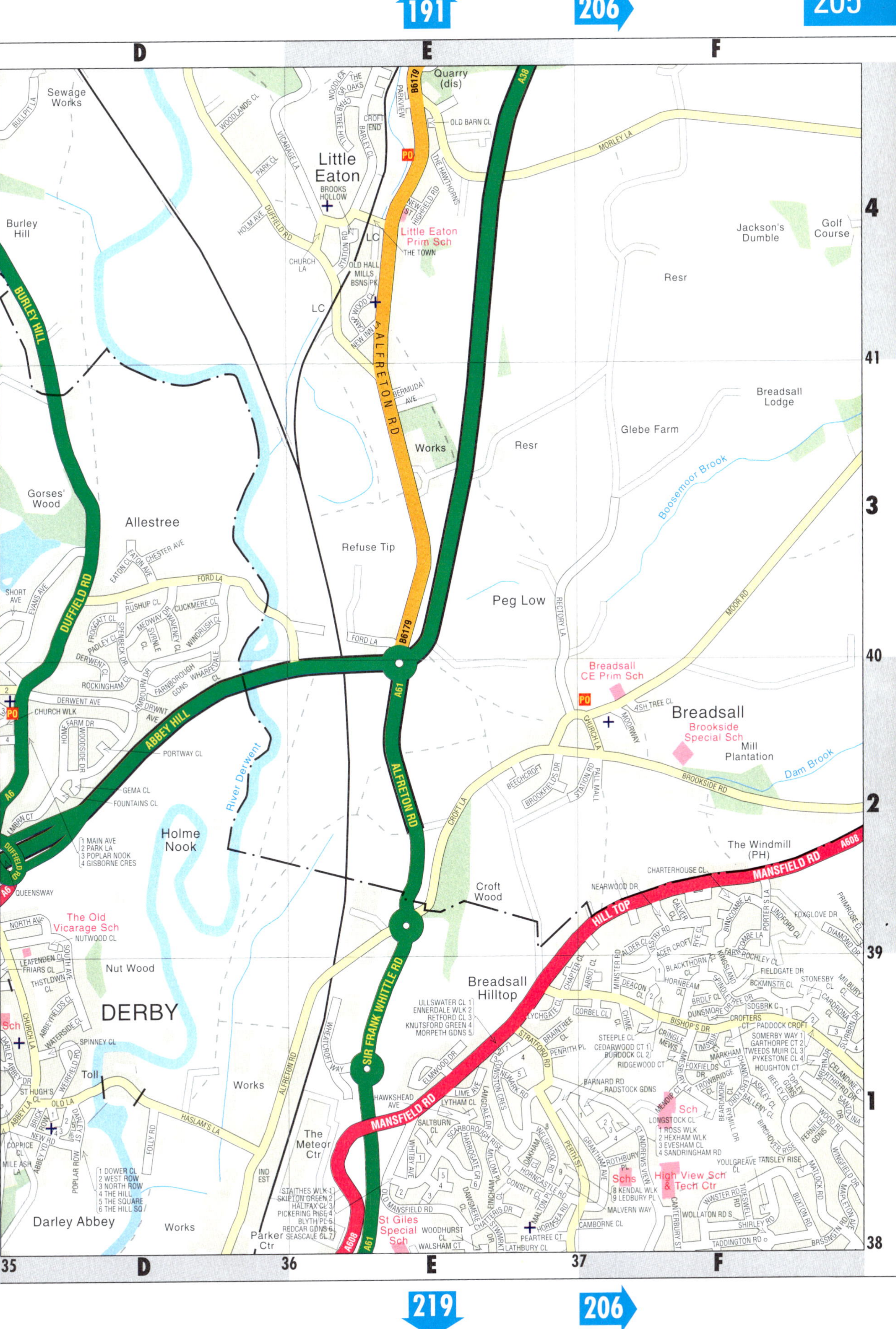
D
E
F
Sewage Works
Quarry (dis)
Little Eaton
Little Eaton Prim Sch
Burley Hill
Jackson's Dumble
Golf Course
Resr
Breadsall Lodge
Glebe Farm
Works
Boosemoor Brook
Gorses' Wood
Allestree
Refuse Tip
Peg Low
Breadsall CE Prim Sch
Breadsall
Brookside Special Sch
Mill Plantation
Dam Brook
River Derwent
Holme Nook
The Windmill (PH)
Croft Wood
The Old Vicarage Sch
Nut Wood
DERBY
Breadsall Hilltop
Toll
Works
The Meteor Ctr
Darley Abbey
Parker Ctr
St Giles Special Sch
High View Sch & Tech Ctr
ALFRETON RD
SIR FRANK WHITTLE RD
MANSFIELD RD
HILL TOP
ABBEY HILL
DUFFIELD RD
BURLEY HILL
MOOR RD
BROOKSIDE RD
A38
A61
A6
A608
B6179
4
3
2
1
41
40
39
38
35
36
37

219
206

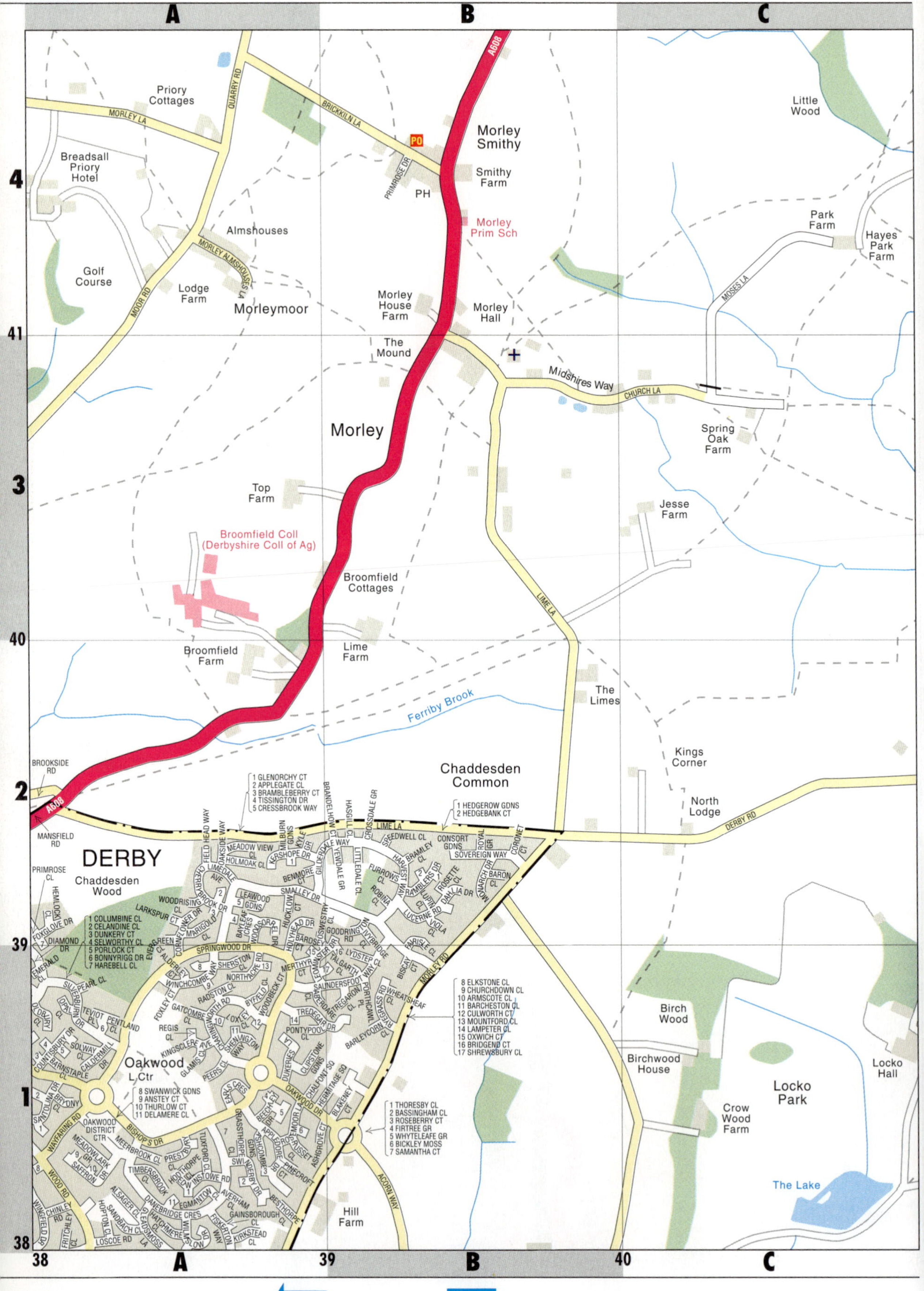

A   B   C

Priory
Cottages

MORLEY LA

QUARRY RD

BRICKKILN LA

PO

Morley
Smithy

Little
Wood

Breadsall
Priory
Hotel

PRIMROSE DR

PH

Smithy
Farm

Park
Farm

Hayes
Park
Farm

4

Almshouses

MORLEY ALMSHOUSES LA

Morley
Prim Sch

MOSES LA

MOOR RD

Golf
Course

Lodge
Farm

Morleymoor

Morley
House
Farm

Morley
Hall

41

The
Mound

Midshires Way

CHURCH LA

Spring
Oak
Farm

Morley

3

Top
Farm

Jesse
Farm

Broomfield Coll
(Derbyshire Coll of Ag)

Broomfield
Cottages

LIME LA

Broomfield
Farm

Lime
Farm

40

Ferriby Brook

The
Limes

Kings
Corner

BROOKSIDE
RD

A608

Chaddesden
Common

North
Lodge

DERBY RD

2

MANSFIELD
RD

1 GLENORCHY CT
2 APPLEGATE CL
3 BRAMBLEBERRY CT
4 TISSINGTON DR
5 CRESSBROOK WAY

1 HEDGEROW GDNS
2 HEDGEBANK CT

LIME LA

DERBY

PRIMROSE
CL

Chaddesden
Wood

FIELD HEAD WAY

MEADOW VIEW

OAKSIDE WAY

HOLMOAK CL

BENMORE

SMALLEY DR

FURROWS CL

ROBINS

CONSORT
GDNS

SOVEREIGN WAY

CORONET

ROYAL
GR

BARON

HEMLOCK

FOXGLOVE DR

1 COLUMBINE CL
2 CELANDINE CL
3 DUNKERY CT
4 SELWORTHY CL
5 PORLOCK CT
6 BONNYRIGG DR
7 HAREBELL CL

WOODRISING

LARKSPUR

LEAWOOD

BICKLOW DR

HOLYHEAD DR

BARDSEY

CALGARTH

QUARRY BANK

DALE DR

39

DIAMOND
DR

EMERALD

SILVERPEARL CL

GREEN

SPRINGWOOD DR

SHERSTON

NORTH

MERTHYR

SAUNDERSFOOT

PERTHWOMYL

MORLEY RD

8 ELKSTONE CL
9 CHURCHDOWN CL
10 ARMSCOTE CL
11 BARCHESTON CL
12 CULWORTH CT
13 MOUNTFORD CL
14 LAMPETER CL
15 OXWICH CT
16 BRIDGEND CT
17 SHREWSBURY CL

SOLWAY

CENTLAND

REGIS

KINGSCLERE

WINCHCOMBE

RADSTON CT

GATCOMBE

OXLEY

SHENINGTON

TREGARON

BARLEYCORN

Birch
Wood

SILVERBURN

TEVIOT

CALDERDALE

PEERS

FOXLEY

BYFLEET CL

WOODBECK CT

14

PONTYPOOL

CLIPSTONE

Birchwood
House

Locko
Hall

1

Oakwood
L. Ctr

BARNSTAPLE

KINGSCLERE

OAKWOOD DR

PINFOLD

Locko
Park

Crow
Wood
Farm

8 SWANWICK GDNS
9 ANSTEY CT
10 THURLOW CT
11 DELAMERE CL

BISHOP'S DR

BLAKENEY

ACORN WAY

1 THORESBY CL
2 BASSINGHAM CL
3 ROSEBERY CT
4 FIRTREE GR
5 WHYTELEAFE GR
6 BICKLEY MOSS
7 SAMANTHA CT

WAYFARING RD

OAKWOOD
DISTRICT
CTR

MEADOWLARK

MEETHBROOK CL

TUFFORD CL

PRESTHORPE

WOODTHORPE

TIMBERSBROOK

GAINSBOROUGH CL

The Lake

WOOD RD

WINGFIELD RD

FRITCHLEY

HIPTONLEA

SANDBACH CT

CLEARDENE

OAKBRIDGE CRES

TANSLEY

WEGNALTON

SWINSTOWE

BESTHORPE

Hill
Farm

LOSCOE RD

KIRKSTEAD
CL

38

38   A   39   B   40   C

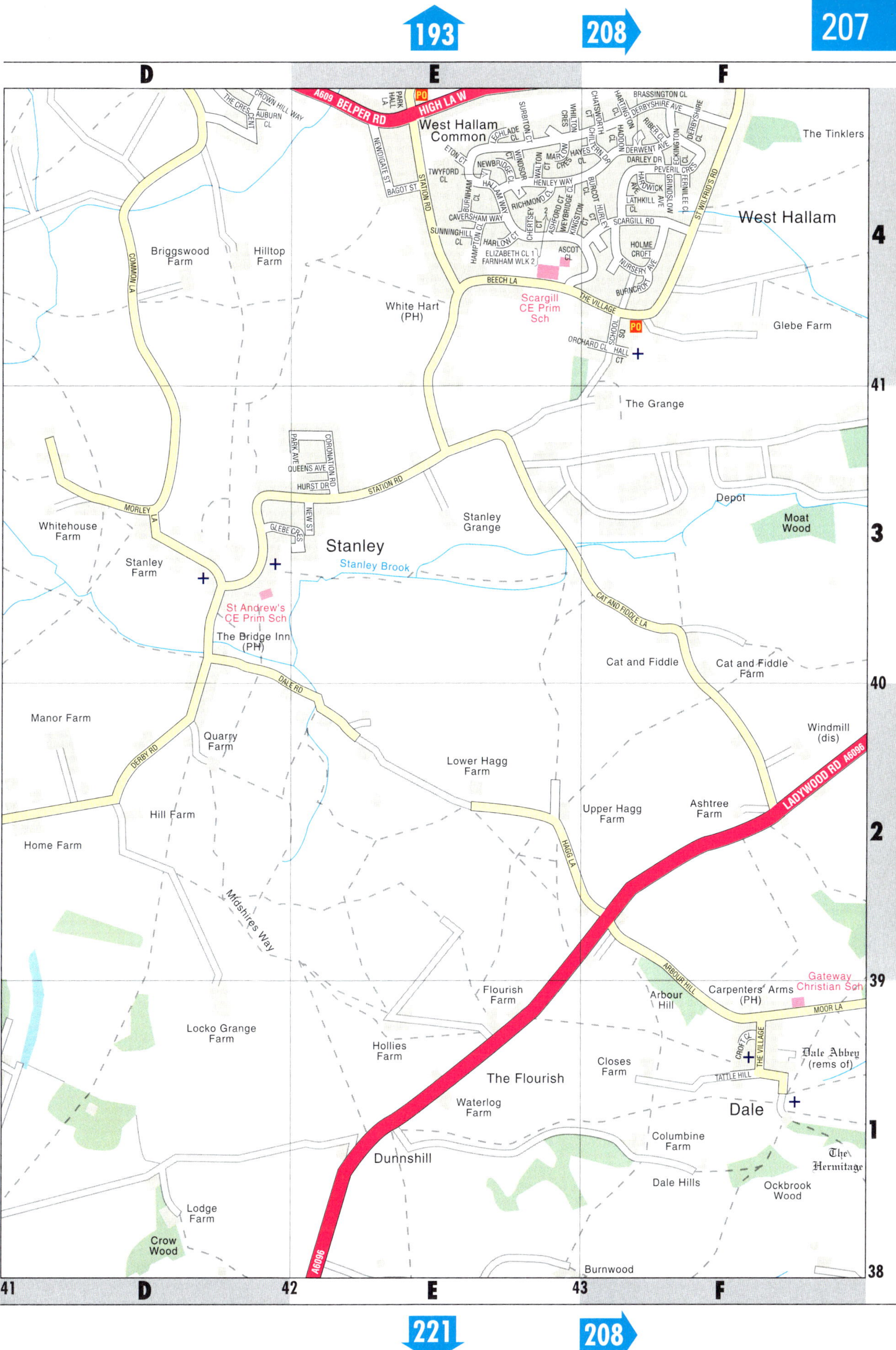

D
E
F

A609 BELPER RD
HIGH LA W

CROWN HILL WAY
THE CRESCENT
AUBURN CL

PARK HALL LA

West Hallam Common

The Tinklers

BRASSINGTON CL
CHATSWORTH CT
WHITTON CT
DERBYSHIRE AVE
HARTINGTON CL

West Hallam

ETON CT
NEWBRIDGE CL
WINDSOR
MAR CL
HAYES CL
RIBER CL
GRINDSLOW
TWYFORD CL
BURNHAM CL
HALL LAW WAY
HENLEY WAY
RICHMOND CL
DERWENT CL
DARLEY DR
PEVERIL CRES
FERNILEE CL
CAVERSHAM WAY
CHERTSEY
ASHFORD CT
WEYBRIDGE CT
HADDON CL
HARDWICK AVE
LATHKILL CL
SUNNINGHILL CL
HAMPTON CL
HARLOW CL
KINGSTON
SCARGILL RD
WILFRID'S RD
ELIZABETH CL 1
FARNHAM WLK 2
ASCOT CL
HOLME CROFT
BURNCROFT
NURSERY AVE

Briggswood Farm
Hilltop Farm

4

NEWGATE ST
BAGOT ST
STATION RD

BEECH LA

THE VILLAGE

White Hart (PH)

Scargill CE Prim Sch

ORCHARD CL
SCHOOL SQ
HALL CT

PO

Glebe Farm

41

The Grange

PARK AVE
QUEENS AVE
CORONATION RD
HURST DR
STATION RD
NEW ST
GLEBE CRES

Depot

Moat Wood

Whitehouse Farm

MORLEY LA

Stanley Grange

3

Stanley

Stanley Brook

Stanley Farm

St Andrew's CE Prim Sch

The Bridge Inn (PH)

CAT AND FIDDLE LA

Cat and Fiddle

Cat and Fiddle Farm

DALE RD

40

Manor Farm

Quarry Farm

Windmill (dis)

DERBY RD

Lower Hagg Farm

Upper Hagg Farm

Ashtree Farm

LADYWOOD RD A6096

Hill Farm

Home Farm

2

Midshires Way

HAGG LA

ARBOUR HILL

39

Flourish Farm

Arbour Hill

Carpenters Arms (PH)

Gateway Christian Sch

MOOR LA

Locko Grange Farm

Hollies Farm

Closes Farm

CROFT
THE VILLAGE

Dale Abbey (rems of)

TATTLE HILL

Dale

The Flourish

Waterlog Farm

Columbine Farm

The Hermitage

1

Crow Wood

Dunnshill

Dale Hills

Ockbrook Wood

Lodge Farm

Burnwood

A6096

38

207
194

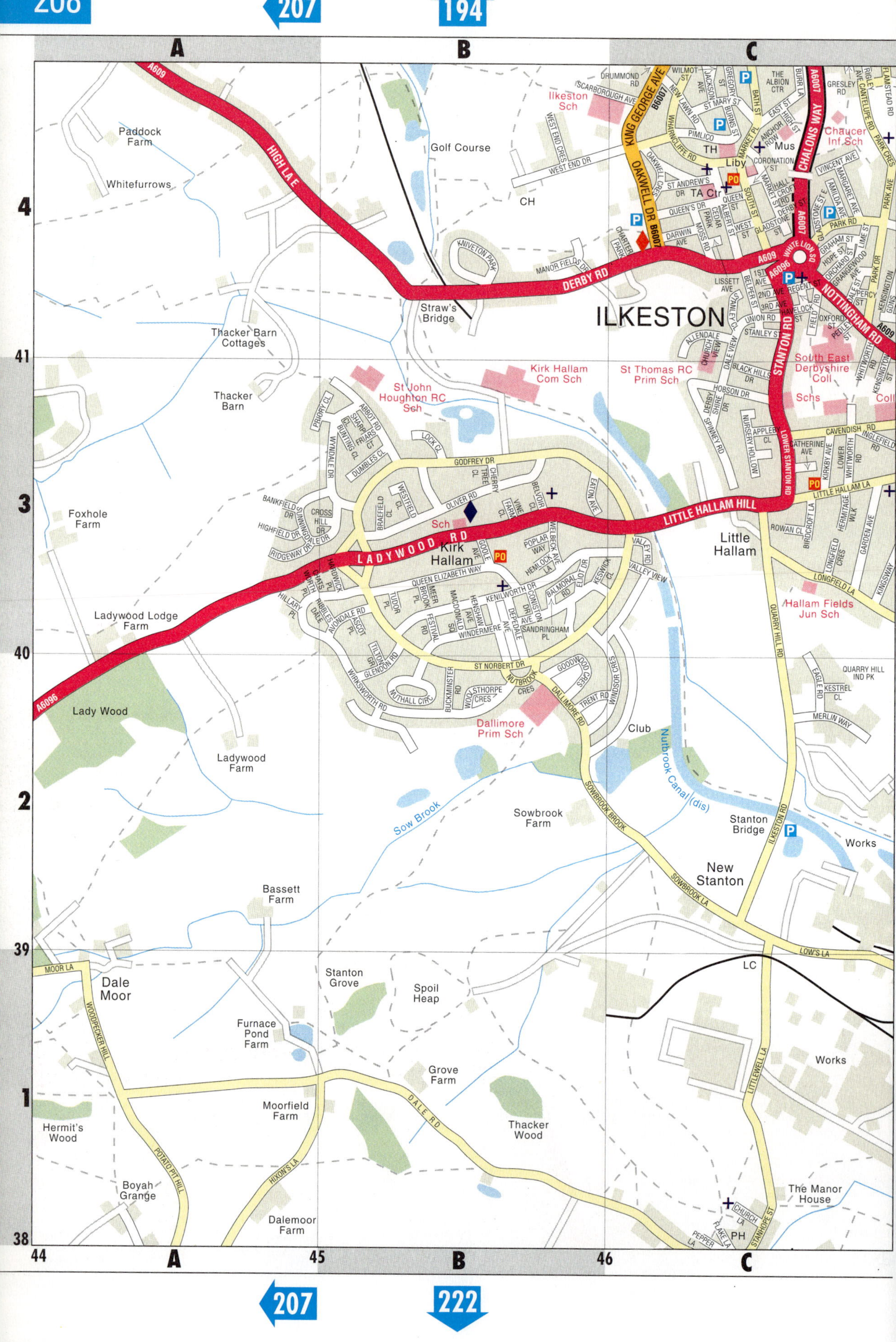
A
B
C
4
41
3
40
2
39
1
38
44
45
46
A609
HIGH LA E
Paddock Farm
Whitefurrows
Golf Course
CH
Straw's Bridge
DERBY RD
KNIVETON PARK
MANOR FIELDS DR
ILKESTON
Ilkeston Sch
KING GEORGE AVE
B6007
OAKWELL DR
WEST END DR
WEST END CRES
CHARTER PARK
DARWIN AVE
TH
Liby
Mus
TA Ctr
CORONATION ST
CHALONS WAY
A6007
WHITE LION SQ
NOTTINGHAM RD
Chaucer Inf Sch
PARK AVE
PARK DR
STANTON RD
LOWER STANTON RD
South East Derbyshire Coll
Schs
Coll
St Thomas RC Prim Sch
Kirk Hallam Com Sch
St John Houghton RC Sch
Thacker Barn Cottages
Thacker Barn
Foxhole Farm
GODFREY DR
OLIVER RD
LADYWOOD RD
Sch
Kirk Hallam
PO
LITTLE HALLAM HILL
Little Hallam
LITTLE HALLAM LA
LONGFIELD LA
Hallam Fields Jun Sch
QUARRY HILL RD
QUARRY HILL IND PK
MERLIN WAY
Ladywood Lodge Farm
A6096
Lady Wood
Ladywood Farm
ST NORBERT DR
Dallimore Prim Sch
Club
Nutbrook Canal (dis)
Sow Brook
Sowbrook Farm
SOWBROOK BROOK
SOWBROOK LA
Stanton Bridge
ILKESTON RD
New Stanton
Works
LOW'S LA
LC
Bassett Farm
MOOR LA
Dale Moor
WOODPECKER HILL
Stanton Grove
Spoil Heap
Furnace Pond Farm
Grove Farm
DALE RD
Moorfield Farm
Hermit's Wood
Thacker Wood
LITTLEWELL LA
Works
POTATO PIT HILL
Boyah Grange
HIXON'S LA
Dalemoor Farm
The Manor House
CHURCH LA
PH
STANHOPE ST
PEPPER LA
FLAKE LA

207
222

195

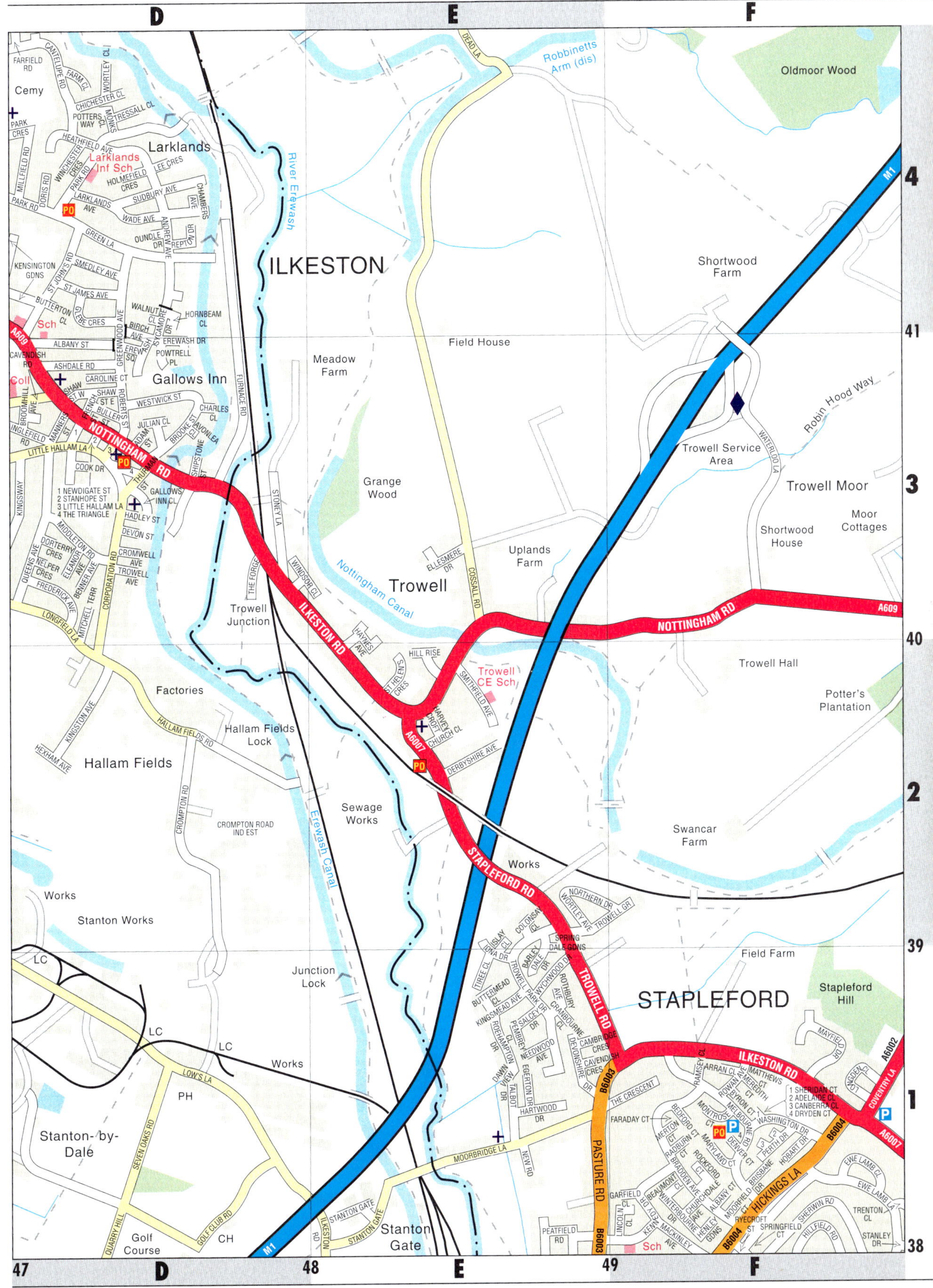
D
E
F
4
41
3
40
2
39
1
38
47
48
49
ILKESTON
STAPLEFORD
Larklands
Larklands Inf Sch
Cemy
Gallows Inn
Sch
Coll
PO
Oldmoor Wood
Robbinetts Arm (dis)
River Erewash
Shortwood Farm
Field House
Meadow Farm
Grange Wood
Trowell Service Area
Robin Hood Way
Trowell Moor
Moor Cottages
Shortwood House
Uplands Farm
Trowell
Nottingham Canal
Trowell Junction
NOTTINGHAM RD
A609
ILKESTON RD
A6007
Trowell Hall
Potter's Plantation
Trowell CE Sch
Factories
Hallam Fields Lock
Hallam Fields
Sewage Works
Erewash Canal
Swancar Farm
CROMPTON ROAD IND EST
Works
Stanton Works
STAPLEFORD RD
TROWELL RD
Field Farm
Stapleford Hill
Junction Lock
ILKESTON RD
LC
PH
Stanton-by-Dale
Golf Course
CH
Stanton Gate
M1
PASTURE RD
B6003
B6004
HICKINGS LA
A6002
COVENTRY LA
MOORBRIDGE LA
STANTON GATE
LOW'S LA
SEVEN OAKS RD
QUARRY HILL
GOLF CLUB RD
HALLAM FIELDS RD
KINGSTON AVE
HEXHAM AVE
CROMPTON RD
FURNACE RD
STONEY LA
COSSALL RD
DEAD LA
WATERLOO LA
CORPORATION RD
LONGFIELD LA
1 NEWDIGATE ST
2 STANHOPE ST
3 LITTLE HALLAM LA
4 THE TRIANGLE
1 SHERIDAN CT
2 ADELAIDE CL
3 CANBERRA CL
4 DRYDEN CT

223

196

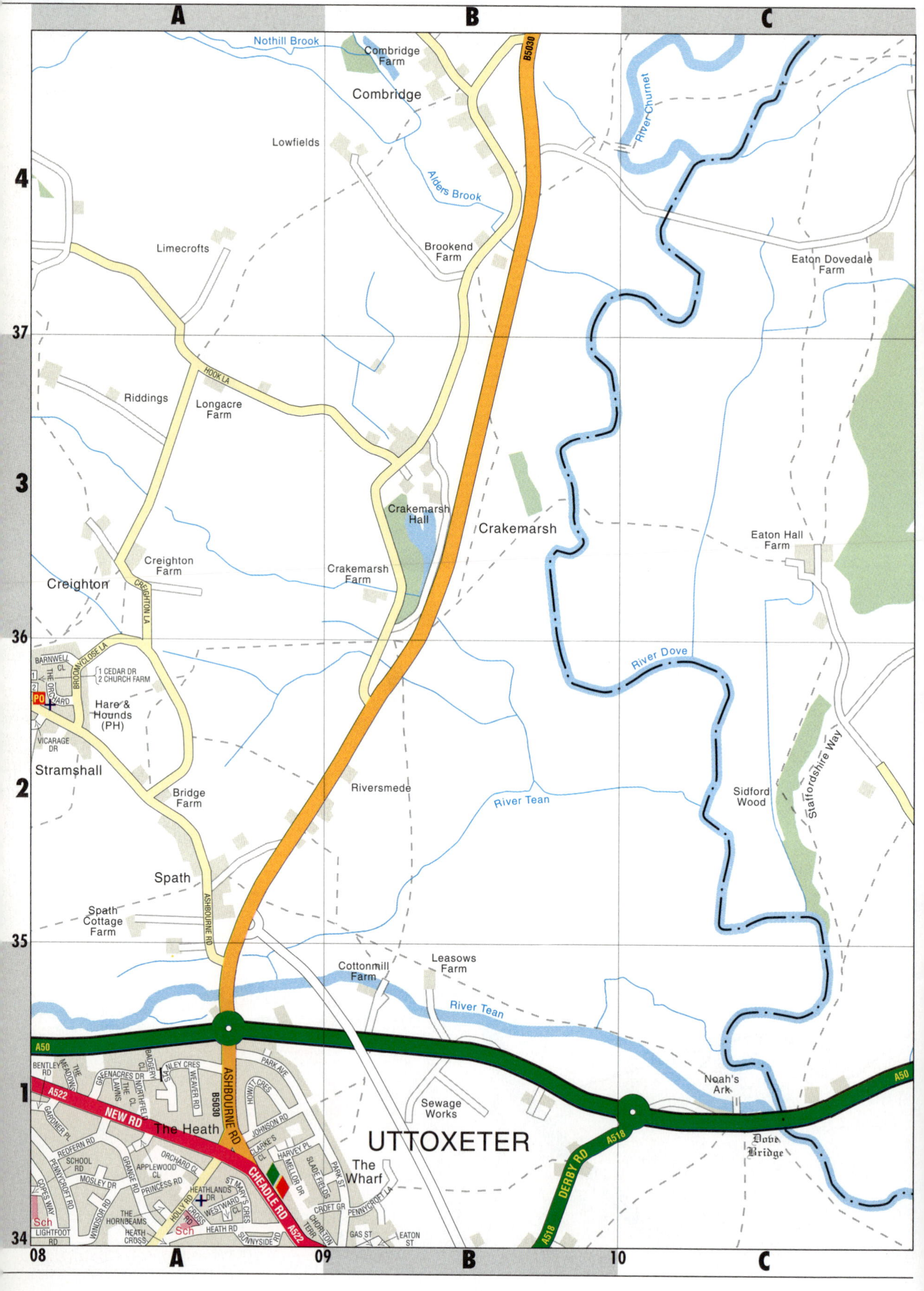

A   B   C

Nothill Brook

Combridge Farm

Combridge

Lowfields

4

Limecrofts

Brookend Farm

Alders Brook

River Churnet

B5030

Eaton Dovedale Farm

37

HOOK LA

Riddings

Longacre Farm

Creighton Farm

CREIGHTON LA

3

Crakemarsh Hall

Crakemarsh

Eaton Hall Farm

Creighton

Crakemarsh Farm

BROOMCLOSE LA

36

BARNWELL CL
THE ORCHARD
1 CEDAR DR
2 CHURCH FARM
PO

River Dove

Hare & Hounds (PH)

VICARAGE DR

Stramshall

Bridge Farm

Riversmede

River Tean

Sidford Wood

Staffordshire Way

2

Spath

ASHBOURNE RD

Spath Cottage Farm

35

Cottonmill Farm

Leasows Farm

River Tean

A50

A50

Noah's Ark

BENTLEY RD
THE MEADOWS
NILEY CRES
BADGERS
WEAVER RD
PARK AVE

ASHBOURNE RD

B5030

FINCH CRES

Dove Bridge

1

A522

NEW RD

The Heath

JOHNSON RD

CLARKE'S CL

Sewage Works

UTTOXETER

DERBY RD

A518

Dove Bridge

REDFERN RD
SCHOOL RD
MOSLEY DR
GRANGE RD
APPLEWOOD CL
PRINCESS RD
ORCHARD CL
HARVEY PL
SLADE FIELDS

CHEADLE RD

A522

The Wharf

PARK ST

COPES WAY
PENNYCROFT LA
GARDINER PL
LIGHTFOOT RD
THE HORNBEAMS
HEATH CROSS
HOLLY RD
HEATHLANDS DR
ST MARY'S CRES
MELLOR DR
WEST WARD CL
HEATH RD
SUNNYSIDE

A518

Sch

GAS ST

EATON ST

Sch

34

08   A   09   B   10   C

197
212

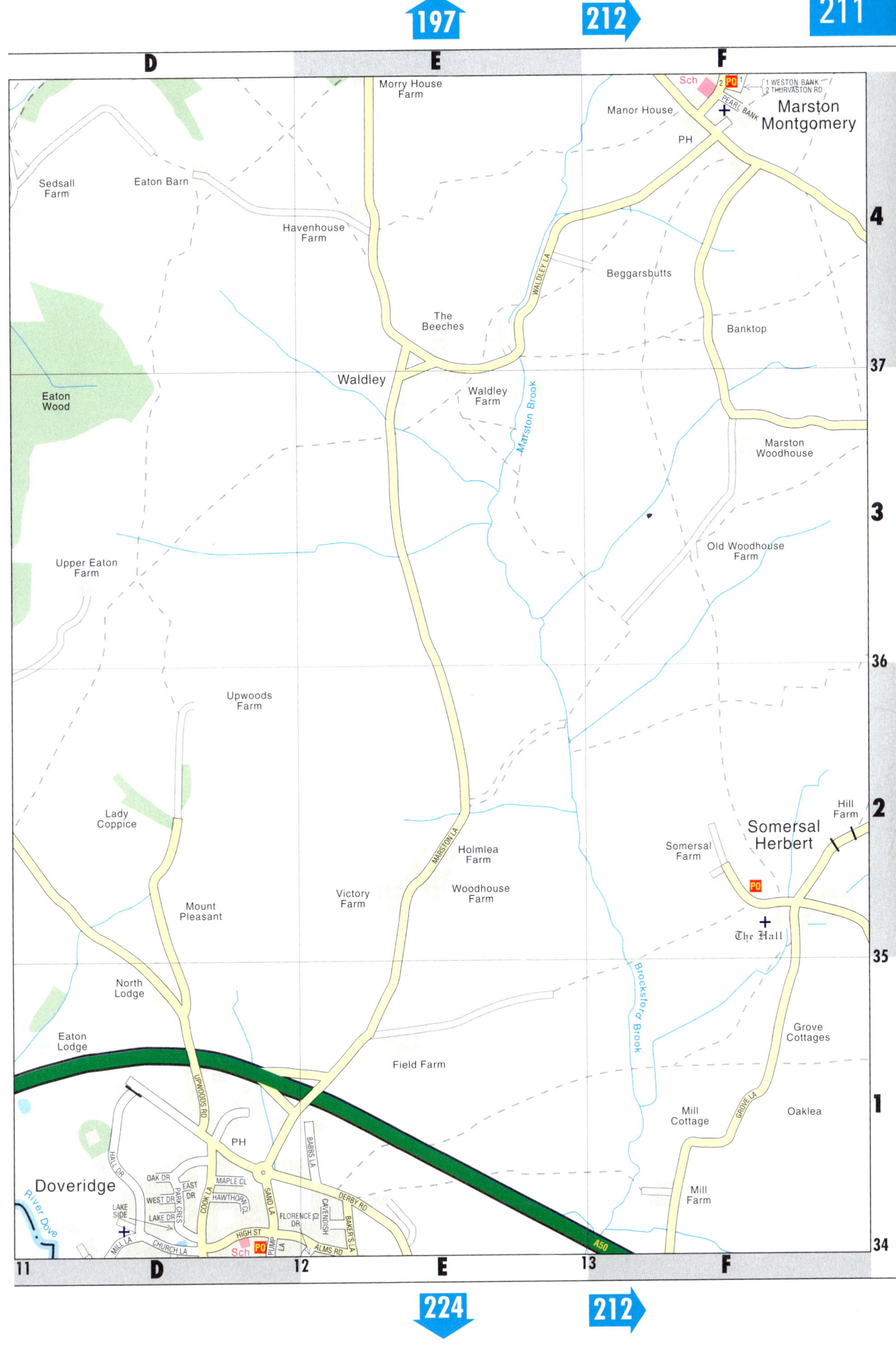
D
E
F
Morry House Farm
Sch
PO
1 WESTON BANK
2 THURVASTON RD
Manor House
PEARL BANK
Marston Montgomery
PH
Sedsall Farm
Eaton Barn
Havenhouse Farm
4
WALDLEY LA
Beggarsbutts
The Beeches
Banktop
37
Waldley
Eaton Wood
Waldley Farm
Marston Brook
Marston Woodhouse
3
Upper Eaton Farm
Old Woodhouse Farm
36
Upwoods Farm
Lady Coppice
2
Hill Farm
Somersal Herbert
Somersal Farm
MARSTON LA
Holmlea Farm
Victory Farm
Woodhouse Farm
Mount Pleasant
The Hall
35
North Lodge
Brocksford Brook
Grove Cottages
Eaton Lodge
Field Farm
1
UPWOODS RD
Mill Cottage
GROVE LA
Oaklea
PH
BABBS LA
HALL DR
Doveridge
OAK DR
EAST DR
MAPLE CL
WEST DR
PARK CRES
HAWTHORN CL
COOK LA
SAND LA
DERBY RD
Mill Farm
River Dove
LAKE SIDE
LAKE DR
FLORENCE DR
CAVENDISH CL
BAKER'S LA
HIGH ST
MILL LA
CHURCH LA
PUMP LA
ALMS RD
A50
34
11
12
13

224
212

211
198

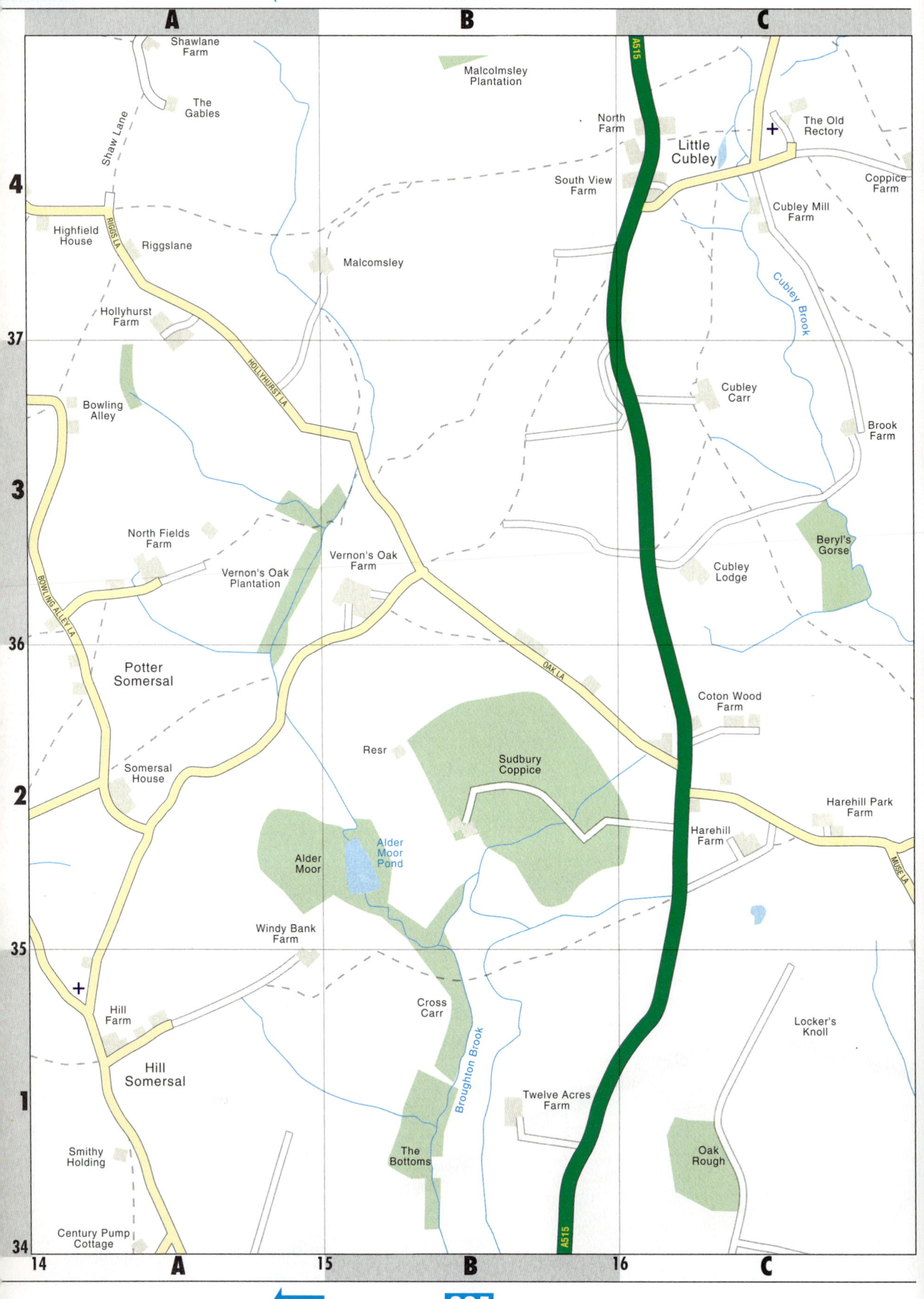
A
B
C
Shawlane Farm
The Gables
Shaw Lane
Malcolmsley Plantation
North Farm
Little Cubley
The Old Rectory
Coppice Farm
South View Farm
Cubley Mill Farm
A515
Highfield House
RIGGS LA
Riggslane
Malcomsley
Cubley Brook
Hollyhurst Farm
HOLLYHURST LA
Cubley Carr
Bowling Alley
Brook Farm
North Fields Farm
Beryl's Gorse
Vernon's Oak Farm
Vernon's Oak Plantation
Cubley Lodge
BOWLING ALLEY LA
Potter Somersal
OAK LA
Coton Wood Farm
Resr
Sudbury Coppice
Somersal House
Harehill Park Farm
Harehill Farm
Alder Moor
Alder Moor Pond
MUSE LA
Windy Bank Farm
Cross Carr
Locker's Knoll
Hill Farm
Hill Somersal
Broughton Brook
Twelve Acres Farm
Smithy Holding
The Bottoms
Oak Rough
Century Pump Cottage
4
37
3
36
2
35
1
34
14
15
16

211
225

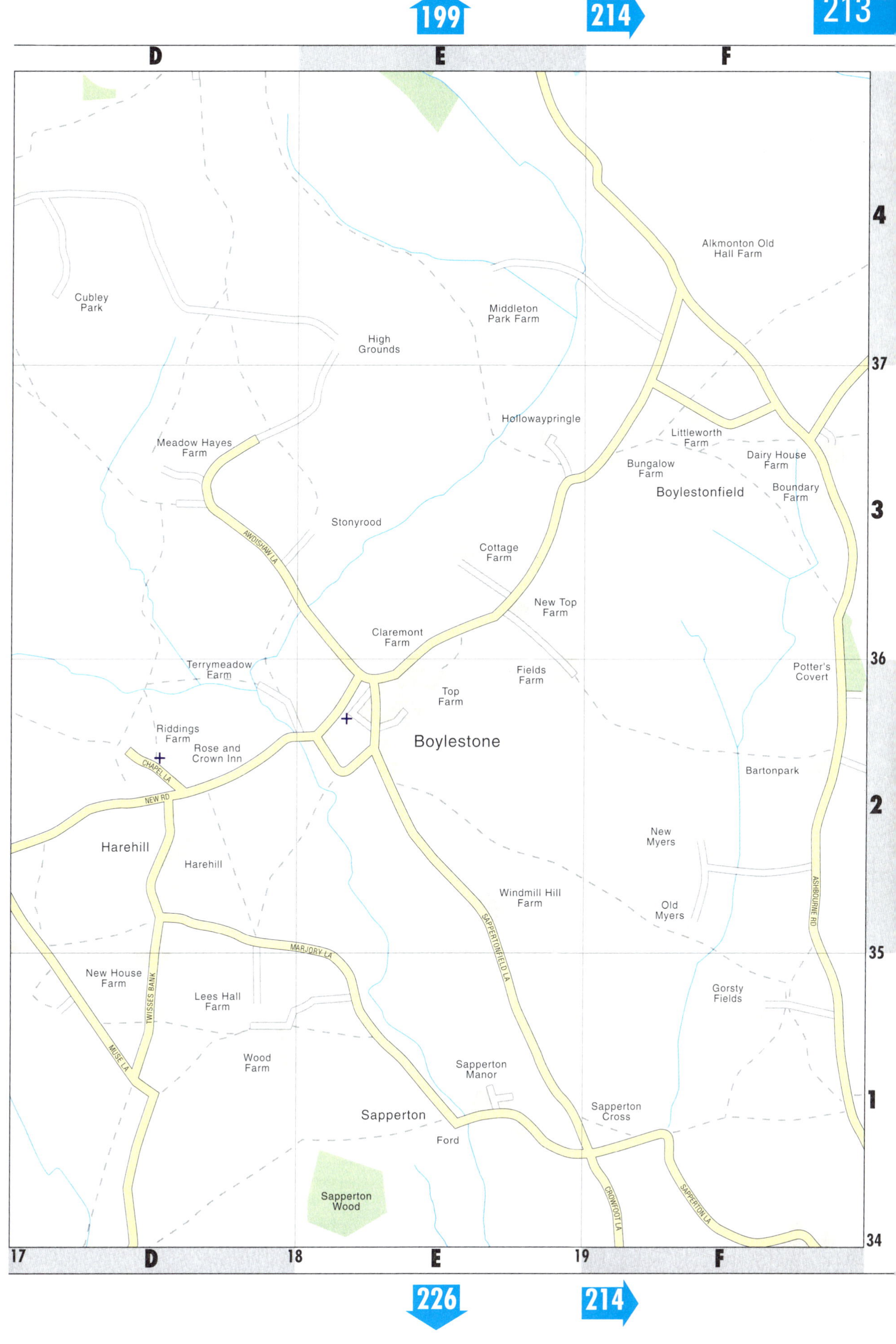

D
E
F

4

Alkmonton Old
Hall Farm

Cubley
Park

Middleton
Park Farm

37

High
Grounds

Hollowaypringle

Littleworth
Farm

Meadow Hayes
Farm

Bungalow
Farm

Dairy House
Farm

Boundary
Farm

Boylestonfield

3

AWDISHAW LA

Stonyrood

Cottage
Farm

New Top
Farm

Claremont
Farm

36

Terrymeadow
Farm

Top
Farm

Fields
Farm

Potter's
Covert

Boylestone

Riddings
Farm

Rose and
Crown Inn

CHAPEL LA

Bartonpark

NEW RD

2

Harehill

New
Myers

Harehill

Windmill Hill
Farm

Old
Myers

ASHBOURNE RD

SAPPERTONFIELD LA

MARJORY LA

35

New House
Farm

Gorsty
Fields

Lees Hall
Farm

TWISSES BANK

MUSE LA

Wood
Farm

Sapperton
Manor

Sapperton
Cross

1

Sapperton

Ford

CROWFOOT LA

SAPPERTON LA

Sapperton
Wood

34

17
D
18
E
19
F

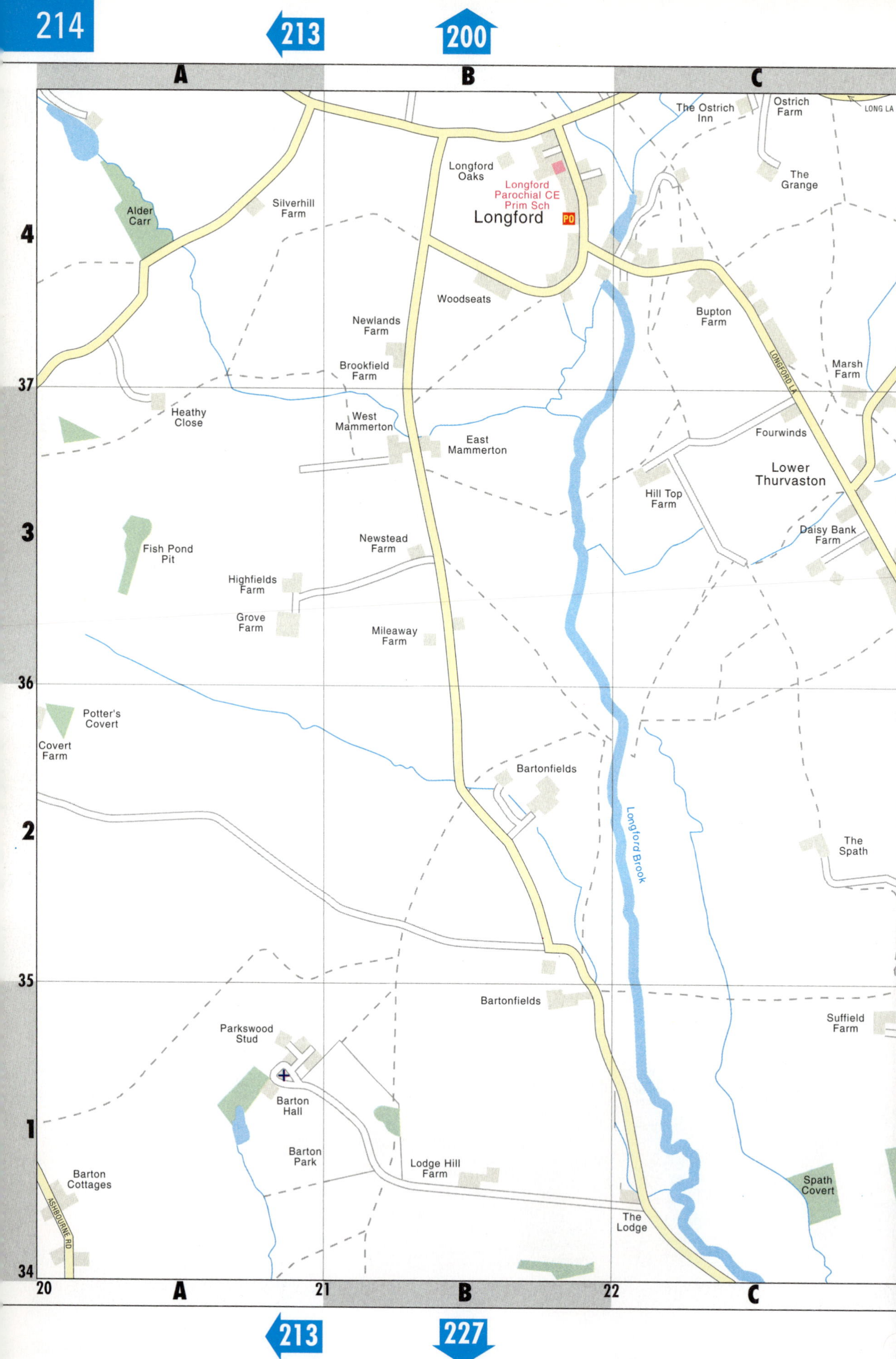
A   B   C

LONG LA

The Ostrich Inn

Ostrich Farm

Longford Oaks

The Grange

Longford Parochial CE Prim Sch

Silverhill Farm

Alder Carr

4

Longford PO

Woodseats

Bupton Farm

37

Newlands Farm

Brookfield Farm

LONGFORD LA

Marsh Farm

Heathy Close

West Mammerton

East Mammerton

Fourwinds

Lower Thurvaston

Hill Top Farm

3

Fish Pond Pit

Newstead Farm

Daisy Bank Farm

Highfields Farm

Grove Farm

Mileaway Farm

36

Potter's Covert

Covert Farm

Bartonfields

Longford Brook

2

The Spath

Bartonfields

35

Suffield Farm

Parkswood Stud

Barton Hall

1

Barton Park

Lodge Hill Farm

Spath Covert

Barton Cottages

ASHBOURNE RD

The Lodge

34

20   A   21   B   22   C

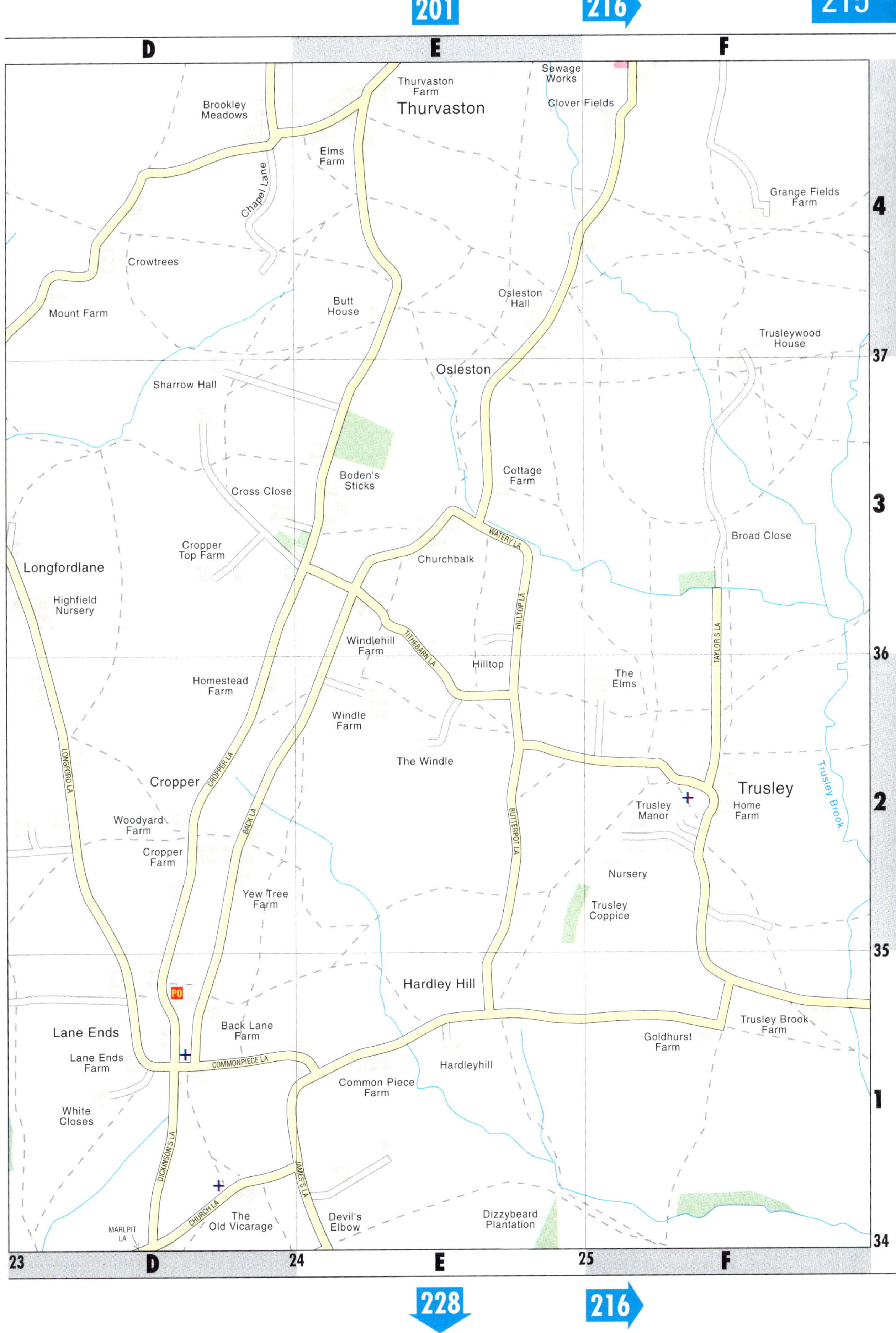

D E F

Brookley
Meadows

Thurvaston
Farm

Thurvaston

Sewage
Works

Clover Fields

Grange Fields
Farm

4

Chapel Lane

Elms
Farm

Crowtrees

Osleston
Hall

Trusleywood
House

Mount Farm

Butt
House

37

Sharrow Hall

Osleston

Boden's
Sticks

Cottage
Farm

Broad Close

Cross Close

3

Longfordlane

Cropper
Top Farm

Churchbalk

WATERY LA

HILLTOP LA

TAYLOR'S LA

Highfield
Nursery

Windlehill
Farm

TITHEBARN LA

Hilltop

The
Elms

36

Homestead
Farm

Windle
Farm

The Windle

Cropper

CROPPER LA

Trusley
Manor

Trusley

2

Woodyard
Farm

BACK LA

BUTTEROPT LA

Trusley
Home
Farm

LONGFORD LA

Cropper
Farm

Nursery

Yew Tree
Farm

Trusley
Coppice

35

PO

Hardley Hill

Lane Ends

Back Lane
Farm

Goldhurst
Farm

Trusley Brook
Farm

Lane Ends
Farm

COMMONPIECE LA

Hardleyhill

1

White
Closes

DICKINSON'S LA

Common Piece
Farm

JAMES'S LA

MARLPIT
LA

CHURCH LA

The
Old Vicarage

Devil's
Elbow

Dizzybeard
Plantation

34

Trusley Brook

23 D 24 E 25 F

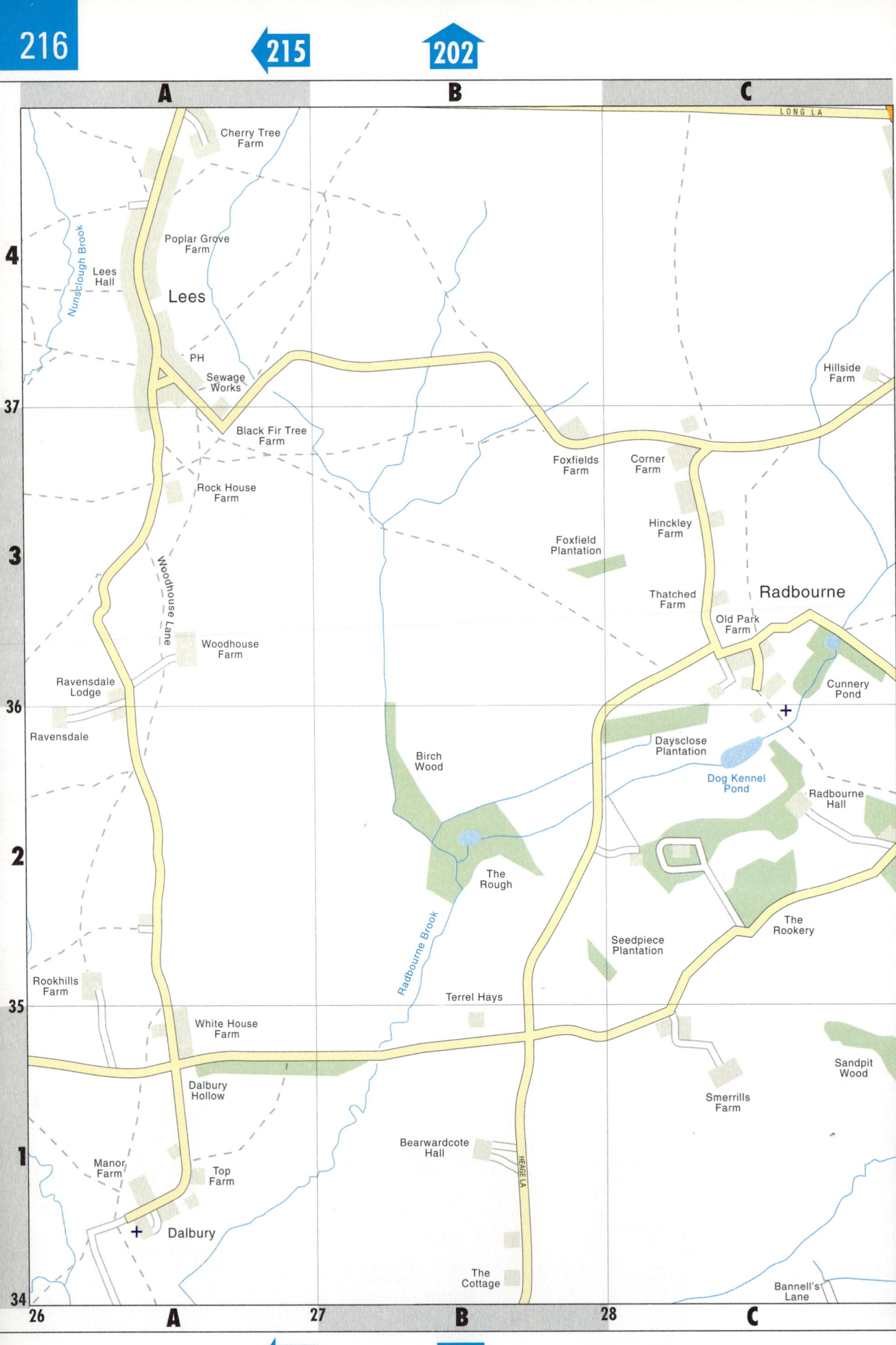

A   B   C

Cherry Tree
Farm

LONG LA

Nunsclough Brook

Poplar Grove
Farm

4

Lees
Hall

Lees

Hillside
Farm

PH

37

Sewage
Works

Black Fir Tree
Farm

Foxfields
Farm

Corner
Farm

Rock House
Farm

Foxfield
Plantation

Hinckley
Farm

Radbourne

3

Thatched
Farm

Woodhouse Lane

Old Park
Farm

Woodhouse
Farm

Cunnery
Pond

Ravensdale
Lodge

36

Birch
Wood

Daysclose
Plantation

Radbourne
Hall

Ravensdale

Dog Kennel
Pond

2

The
Rough

The
Rookery

Radbourne Brook

Seedpiece
Plantation

Rookhills
Farm

Sandpit
Wood

35

White House
Farm

Terrel Hays

Smerrills
Farm

Dalbury
Hollow

HEAGE LA

1

Manor
Farm

Bearwardcote
Hall

Top
Farm

Dalbury

The
Cottage

Bannell's
Lane

34

26   A   27   B   28   C

203

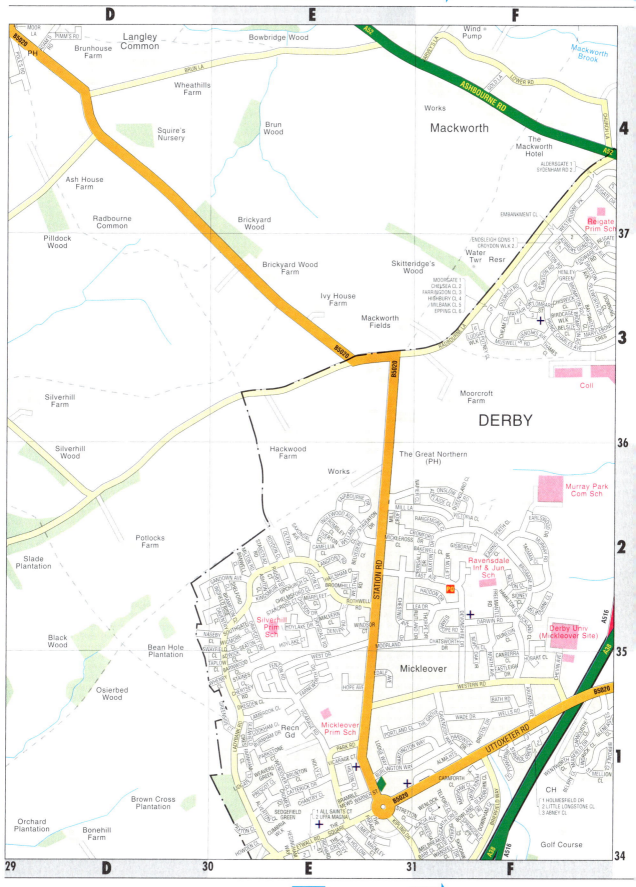
218

D E F

Langley Common
Brunhouse Farm
Bowbridge Wood
Wind Pump
Mackworth Brook
PH
B5020
MOOR LA
ADAM'S RD
PIMM'S RD
POLE'S RD
BRUN LA
A52
HARVEY'S LA
GOLD LA
LOWER RD
ASHBOURNE RD
CHURCH LA
Wheathills Farm
Works
Mackworth
Squire's Nursery
Brun Wood
The Mackworth Hotel
ALDERSGATE 1
SYDENHAM RD 2
Ash House Farm
EMBANKMENT CL
Reigate Prim Sch
REIGATE DR
REIGATE CL
Radbourne Common
Brickyard Wood
Pilldock Wood
ENDSLEIGH GDNS 1
CROYDON WLK 2
Water Twr
Resr
Brickyard Wood Farm
Skitteridge's Wood
MOORGATE 1
CHELSEA CL 2
FARRINGDON CL 3
HIGHBURY CL 4
MILBANK CL 5
EPPING CL 6
Ivy House Farm
Mackworth Fields
WESTBOURNE PK
FINCHLEY AVE
ADDISCOMBE GDNS
EDGWARE RD
ACTON RD
HENLEY GREEN
DRAYTON AVE
ISLEWORTH DR
DULWICH RD
BROMPTON RD
LOMBARD ST
CHISWICK CL
BIRDCAGE WLK
BAYSWATER CL
DOWNING CL
MAYFAIR CRES
CHEAM CL
BELSIZE CL
MARYLEBONE CRES
PRINCE CHARLES AVE
THAMES CL
SEVENOAKS AVE
MUSWELL RD
LUDGATE WLK
PUTNEY CL
RADBOURNE LA
Coll
Silverhill Farm
Moorcroft Farm
DERBY
Silverhill Wood
Hackwood Farm
The Great Northern (PH)
Works
Murray Park Com Sch
STATION RD
Potlocks Farm
Slade Plantation
Ravensdale Inf & Jun Sch
PO
Silverhill Prim Sch
Derby Univ (Mickleover Site)
Black Wood
Bean Hole Plantation
Mickleover
A516
A38
Osierbed Wood
WESTERN RD
UTTOXETER RD
Recn Gd
Mickleover Prim Sch
MOORLAND RD
CHATSWORTH DR
DARWIN RD
FAIRBOURNE DR
ONSLOW RD
QUEENSLAND CL
VICTORIA CL
MILL LA
MILL CROFT
RANGEMORE CL
CROMFORD DR
MICKLEROSS CL
BAKEWELL CL
GISBORNE CL
PERTH CL
EARLSWOOD DR
MURRAY RD
TASMAN CL
BRISBANE RD
HADDON DR
LEA DR
WINDSOR CT
WEST DR
HOPE AVE
PARK RD
VICARAGE CT
VICARAGE RD
LODGE WAY
HARTINGTON WAY
PORTLAND CL
THE GROVE
WADE DR
BATH RD
WELLS RD
BRISTOL DR
CARNFORTH CL
ALMA HTS
CH
1 HOLMESFIELD DR
2 LITTLE LONGSTONE CL
3 ABNEY CL
Golf Course
Brown Cross Plantation
Orchard Plantation
Bonehill Farm
1 ALL SAINTS CT
2 UFFA MAGNA
THE SQUARE
WARNER ST
THE PARADE
STRETTON CL
KIPLING DR
WENLOCK CL
BRIERFIELD WAY
DOWNHAM CL
LADYBANK RD
GREENSIDE CT
PAXTON CL
HOWDEN CL
MELBREAK CL
WENTWORTH CL
MELLION CL

4
37
3
36
2
35
1
34

29 D 30 E 31 F

230

218

217 204

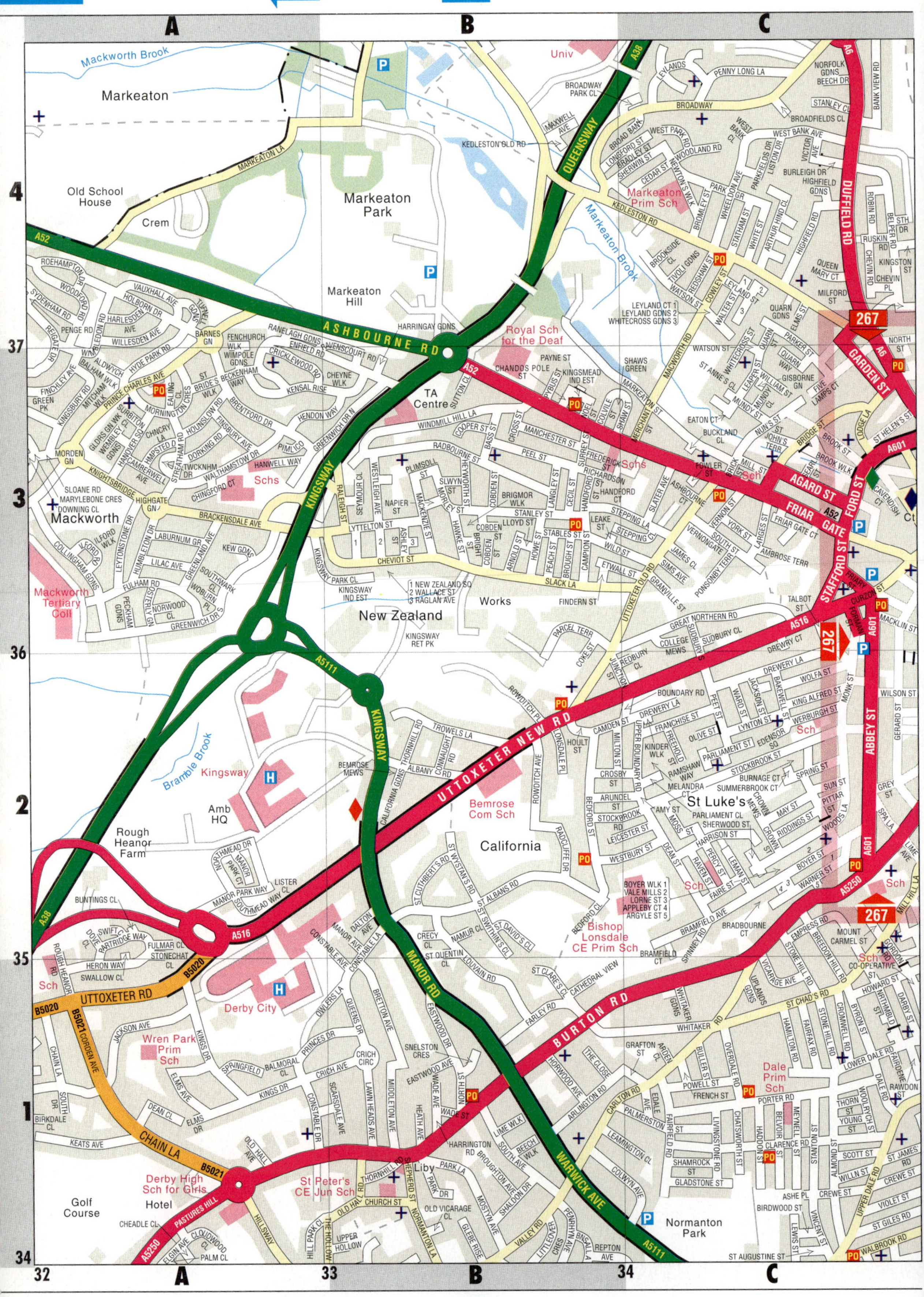
A
B
C
4
37
3
36
2
35
1
34
32
33
34
Mackworth Brook
Markeaton
Old School House
Crem
Markeaton Park
Markeaton Hill
Univ
QUEENSWAY
A38
A52
ASHBOURNE RD
KEDLESTON RD
Markeaton Brook
Markeaton Prim Sch
DUFFIELD RD
A6
Royal Sch for the Deaf
TA Centre
Mackworth
Mackworth Tertiary Coll
KINGSWAY
Schs
New Zealand
Works
AGARD ST
FRIAR GATE
FORD ST
STAFFORD ST
267
A601
A516
ABBEY ST
UTTOXETER NEW RD
A5111
Bramble Brook
Kingsway
Amb HQ
Rough Heanor Farm
Bemrose Com Sch
California
St Luke's
Bishop Lonsdale CE Prim Sch
Derby City
UTTOXETER RD
B5020
B5021
Wren Park Prim Sch
MANOR RD
BURTON RD
A5250
Dale Prim Sch
CHAIN LA
Derby High Sch for Girls
St Peter's CE Jun Sch
Golf Course
Hotel
PASTURES HILL
WARWICK AVE
Normanton Park
Sch
Ct

217 231

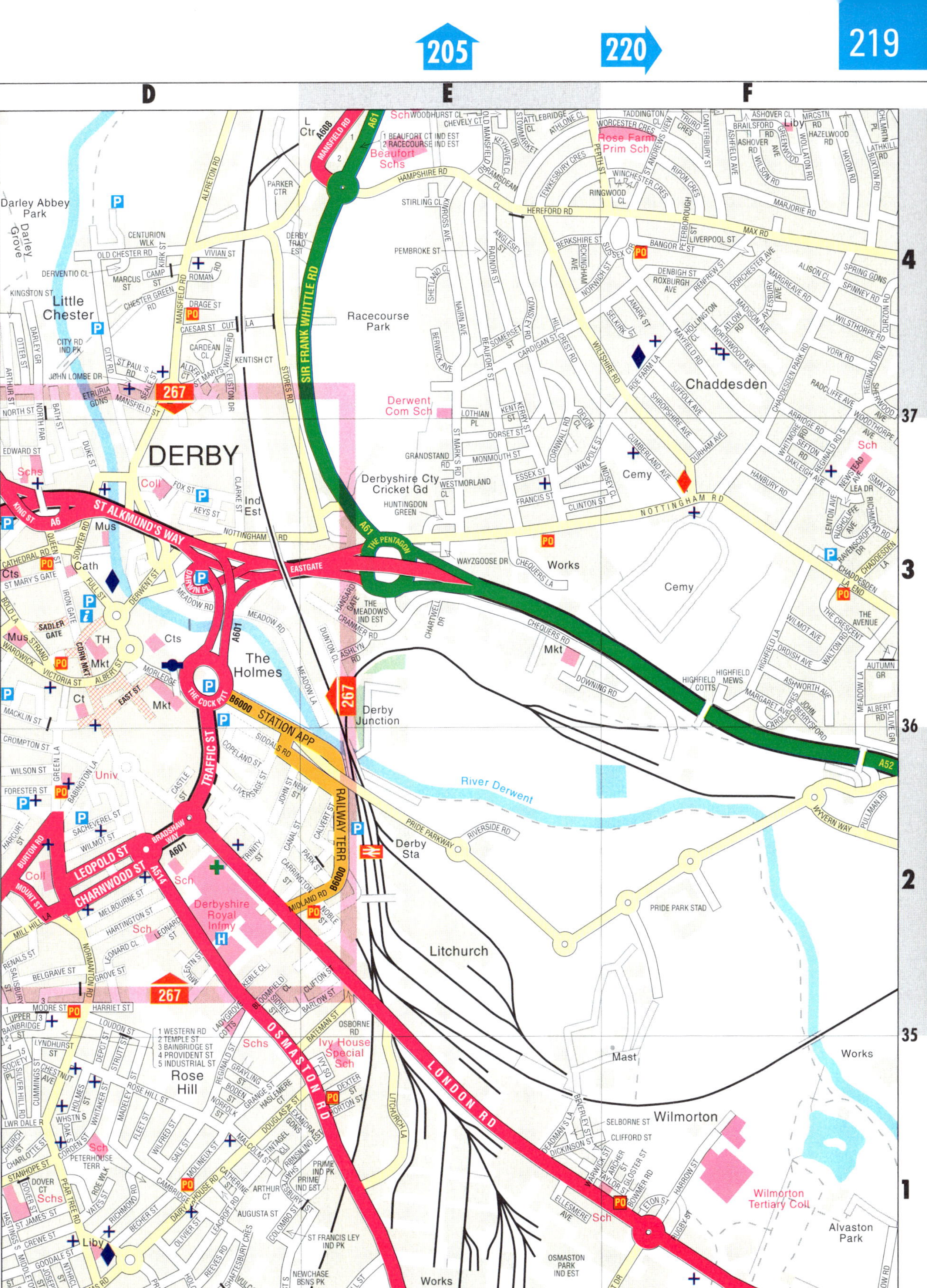

For full street detail of the highlighted area see page 267.

219
206

A
B
C
4
37
3
36
2
35
1
34
38
39
40
DERBY
Spondon
Cherrytree Hill
Chaddesden Park
Mossey Yard Plantation
Springfield Farm
South Lodge
Brunswood Farm
Spondon Wood
Lees Brook
Chaddesden Brook
Cavendish Close Inf & Jun Schs
Lees Brook Com Sch
Chaddesden Park Inf & Jun Schs
Cherry Tree Hill Inf & Jun Schs
Meadow Farm Com Prim Sch
Springfield Prim Sch
West Park Com Sch
Borrow Wood Inf & Jun Schs
Asterdale Prim Sch
Sch
Cemy
Liby
PO
The Wyvern
Water Reclamation Works
Sewage Works
Works
Nature Reserve
Electricity Generating Station
Chy
Mast
Spondon Sta
LC
River Derwent
A52
A6005
A5111
A6096
DERBY RD
NOTTINGHAM RD
BORROWASH BY-PASS
DALE RD
MOOR ST
SITWELL ST
WILLOWCROFT RD
RAYNESWAY
LOCKO RD
ACORN WAY
CELANESE RD
WEST SERVICE RD
EAST SERVICE RD
HOLME LA
STATION RD
CHURCH ST
LODGE LA
STONEY LA
BORROWASH RD
MAINE DR
ROOSEVELT AVE
PARKSIDE RD
MORLEY RD
WOOD RD
CHAPEL LA
MAX RD
LONGLEY LA
LOUSIE GREAVES LA
SANDCROFT RD
WEST RD
KIRK LEES AVE S
KIRK LEES AVE N
BORROWFIELD RD
CHAPEL ST

219
233

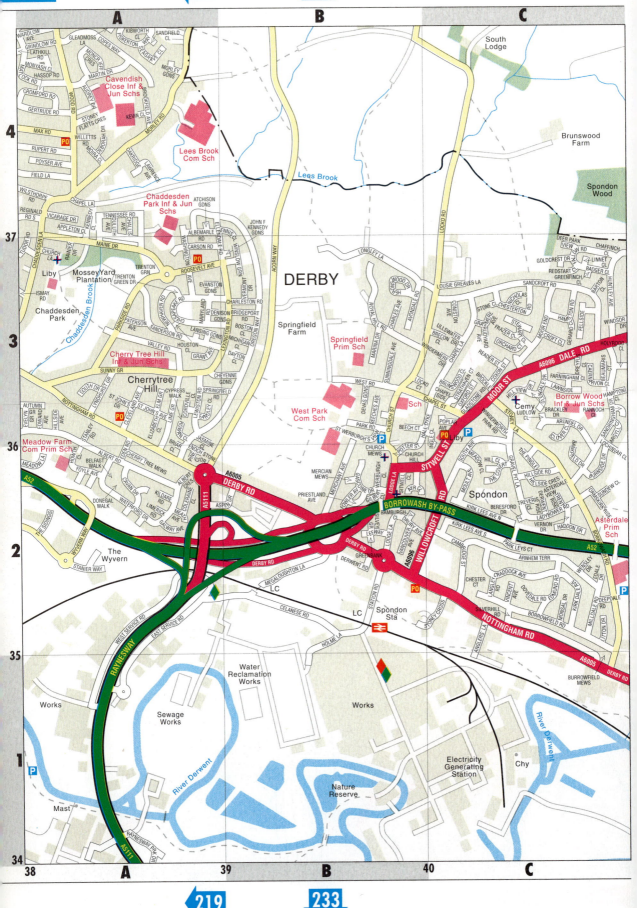

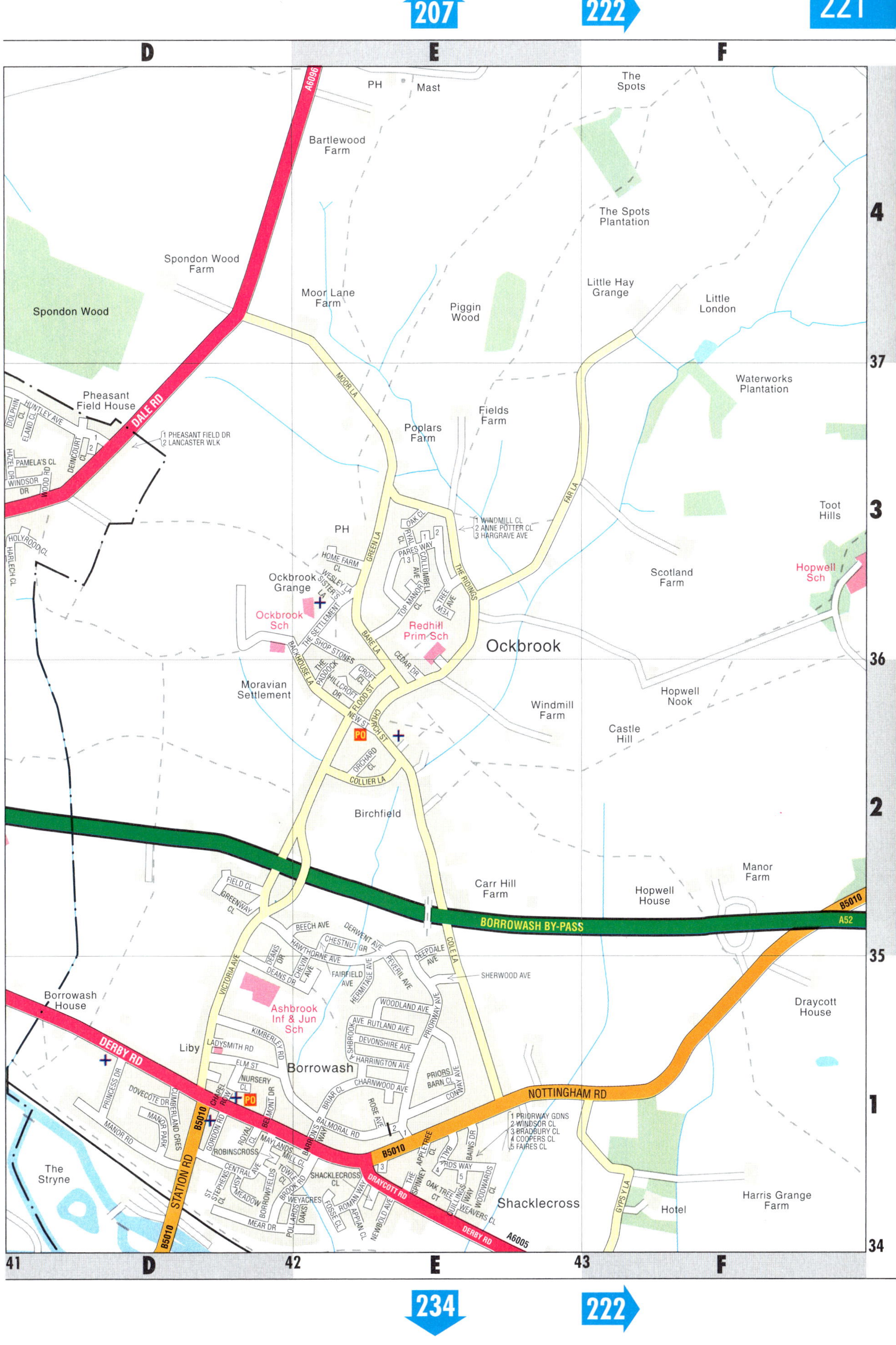
207
222
D
E
F
Spondon Wood
Spondon Wood Farm
Bartlewood Farm
PH
Mast
The Spots
The Spots Plantation
Moor Lane Farm
Piggin Wood
Little Hay Grange
Little London
Waterworks Plantation
Pheasant Field House
DALE RD
A6096
1 PHEASANT FIELD DR
2 LANCASTER WLK
Poplars Farm
Fields Farm
MOOR LA
FAR LA
Toot Hills
1 WINDMILL CL
2 ANNE POTTER CL
3 HARGRAVE AVE
Scotland Farm
Hopwell Sch
Ockbrook Grange
Ockbrook Sch
Redhill Prim Sch
Ockbrook
Moravian Settlement
Windmill Farm
Hopwell Nook
Castle Hill
Birchfield
Carr Hill Farm
Hopwell House
Manor Farm
BORROWASH BY-PASS
A52
B5010
Borrowash House
Ashbrook Inf & Jun Sch
Liby
Borrowash
Draycott House
SHERWOOD AVE
NOTTINGHAM RD
1 PRIORWAY GDNS
2 WINDSOR CL
3 BRADBURY CL
4 COOPERS CL
5 FAIRES CL
DERBY RD
DRAYCOTT RD
A6005
STATION RD
The Stryne
Shacklecross
Hotel
Harris Grange Farm
GYPSY LA
41
42
43
34
35
36
37
1
2
3
4
234
222

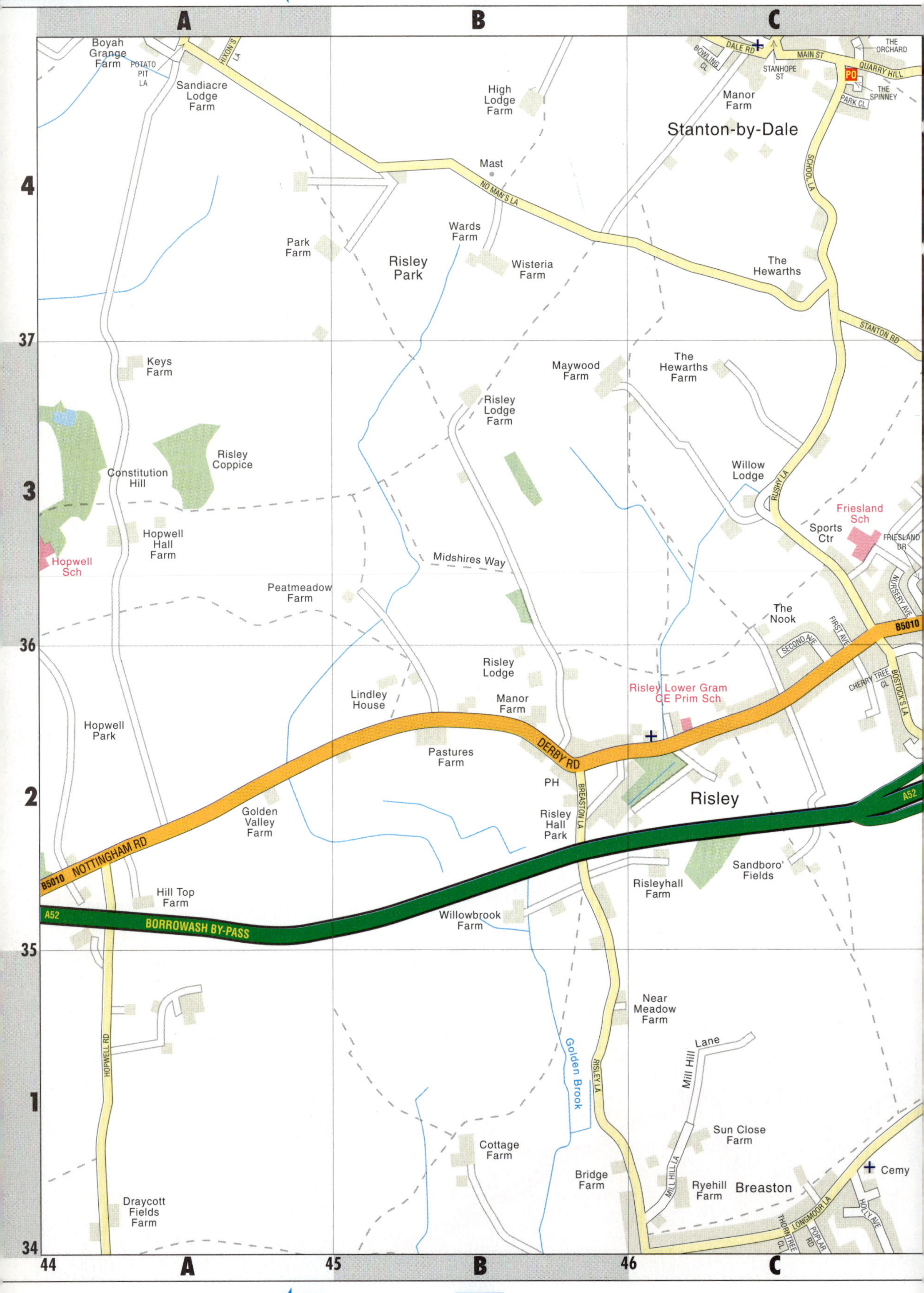

A B C

4

37

3

36

2

1

44 A 45 B 46 C

Boyah Grange Farm
POTATO PIT LA
NIXON'S LA
Sandiacre Lodge Farm
High Lodge Farm
Mast
DALE RD
BOWLING CL
Stanhope St
MAIN ST
THE ORCHARD
Manor Farm
QUARRY HILL
PO
PARK CL
THE SPINNEY
Stanton-by-Dale
SCHOOL LA
Wards Farm
Park Farm
Risley Park
Wisteria Farm
The Hewarths
STANTON RD
Keys Farm
Maywood Farm
The Hewarths Farm
Risley Lodge Farm
Willow Lodge
RUSHY LA
Friesland Sch
Constitution Hill
Risley Coppice
Sports Ctr
FRIESLAND DR
Hopwell Hall Farm
Hopwell Sch
Midshires Way
The Nook
FIRST AVE
SECOND AVE
Peatmeadow Farm
B5010
Risley Lodge
CHERRY TREE CL
BOSTOCK'S LA
Risley Lower Gram CE Prim Sch
Hopwell Park
Lindley House
Manor Farm
Pastures Farm
DERBY RD
PH
Risley
NURSERY AVE
Golden Valley Farm
A52
NOTTINGHAM RD
B5010
Risley Hall Park
BREASTON LA
Sandboro' Fields
Hill Top Farm
A52
BORROWASH BY-PASS
Willowbrook Farm
Risleyhall Farm
Near Meadow Farm
Mill Hill Lane
RISLEY LA
Golden Brook
MILL HILL LA
Sun Close Farm
Cemy
Draycott Fields Farm
Cottage Farm
Bridge Farm
Ryehill Farm
Breaston
THORNTREE CL
LONGMOOR LA
POPLAR RD
HOLLY AVE
HOPWELL RD

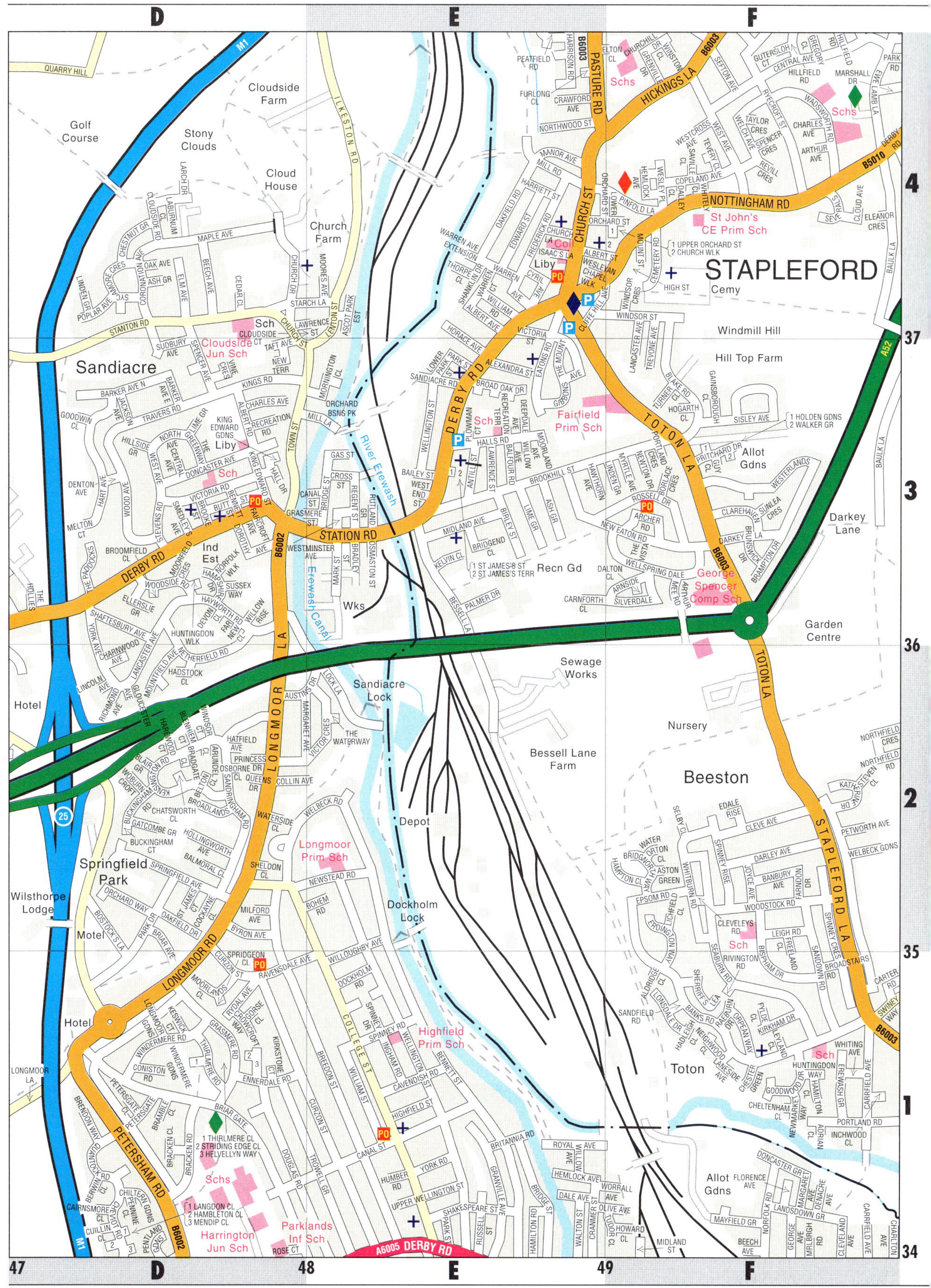

D · E · F

4

37

3

36

2

35

1

34

STAPLEFORD

Sandiacre

Beeston

Toton

Springfield Park

47 · 48 · 49

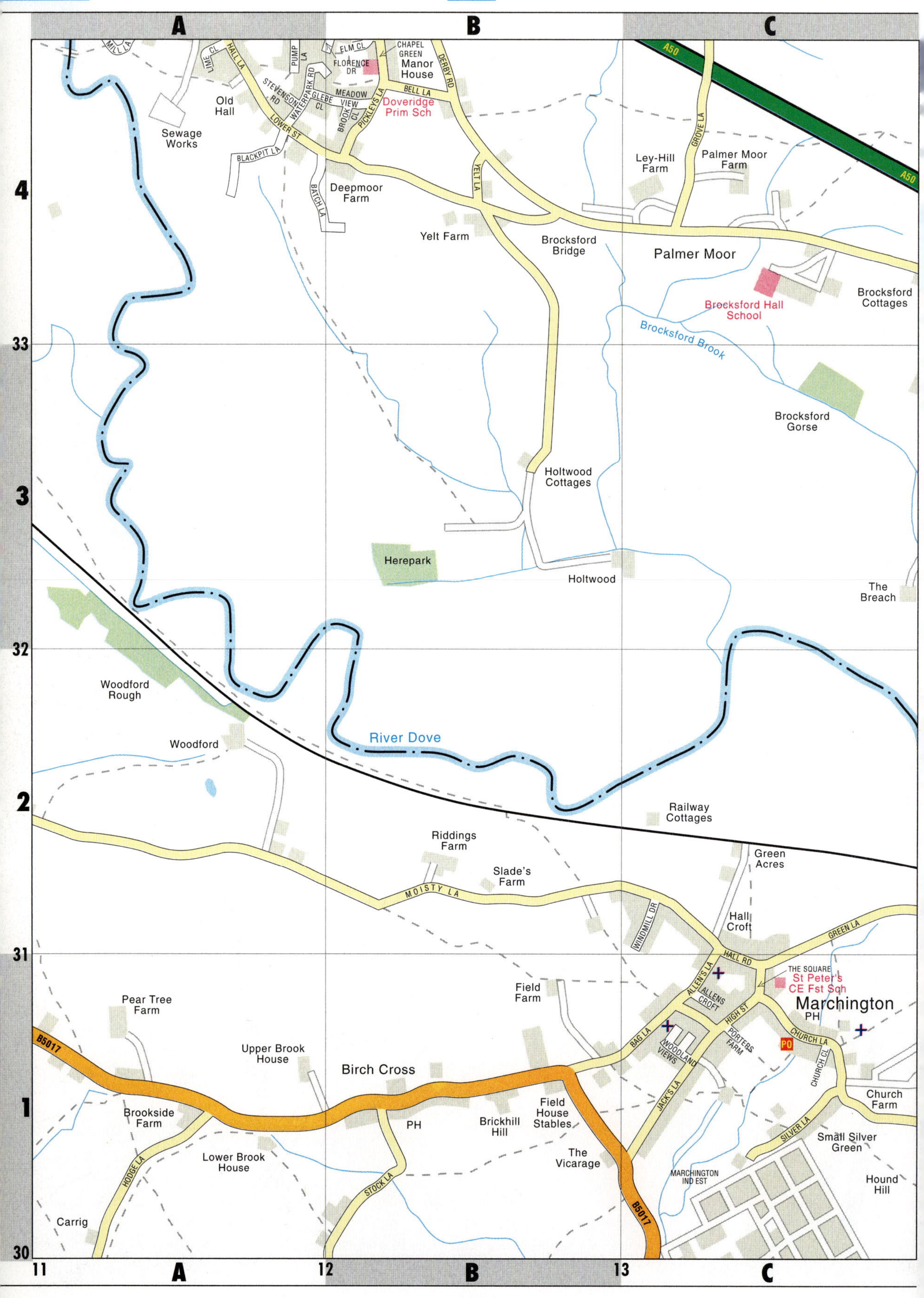
4
33
3
32
2
31
1
30
Chapel Green
Manor House
Elm Cl
Florence Dr
Pump La
Mill La
Lime Cl
Hall La
Derby Rd
Bell La
Meadow View
Glebe Cl
Stevenson Rd
Waterpark Rd
Brook Cl
Pickleys La
Doveridge Prim Sch
Old Hall
Sewage Works
Lower St
Blackpit La
Batch La
Deepmoor Farm
Yelt La
Yelt Farm
A50
Grove La
Ley-Hill Farm
Palmer Moor Farm
Brocksford Bridge
Palmer Moor
Brocksford Hall School
Brocksford Cottages
Brocksford Brook
Brocksford Gorse
Holtwood Cottages
Herepark
Holtwood
The Breach
River Dove
Woodford Rough
Woodford
Railway Cottages
Riddings Farm
Slade's Farm
Moisty La
Green Acres
Windmill Dr
Hall Croft
Green La
Hall Rd
The Square
St Peter's CE Fst Sch
Allen's La
Allens Croft
High St
Marchington
PH
Field Farm
Pear Tree Farm
B5017
Upper Brook House
Birch Cross
Bag La
Woodland Views
Porters Farm
Church La
PO
Church Cl
Church Farm
Brookside Farm
PH
Brickhill Hill
Field House Stables
Jack's La
Silver La
Small Silver Green
Lower Brook House
Hodge La
Stock La
The Vicarage
Marchington Ind Est
Hound Hill
Carrig

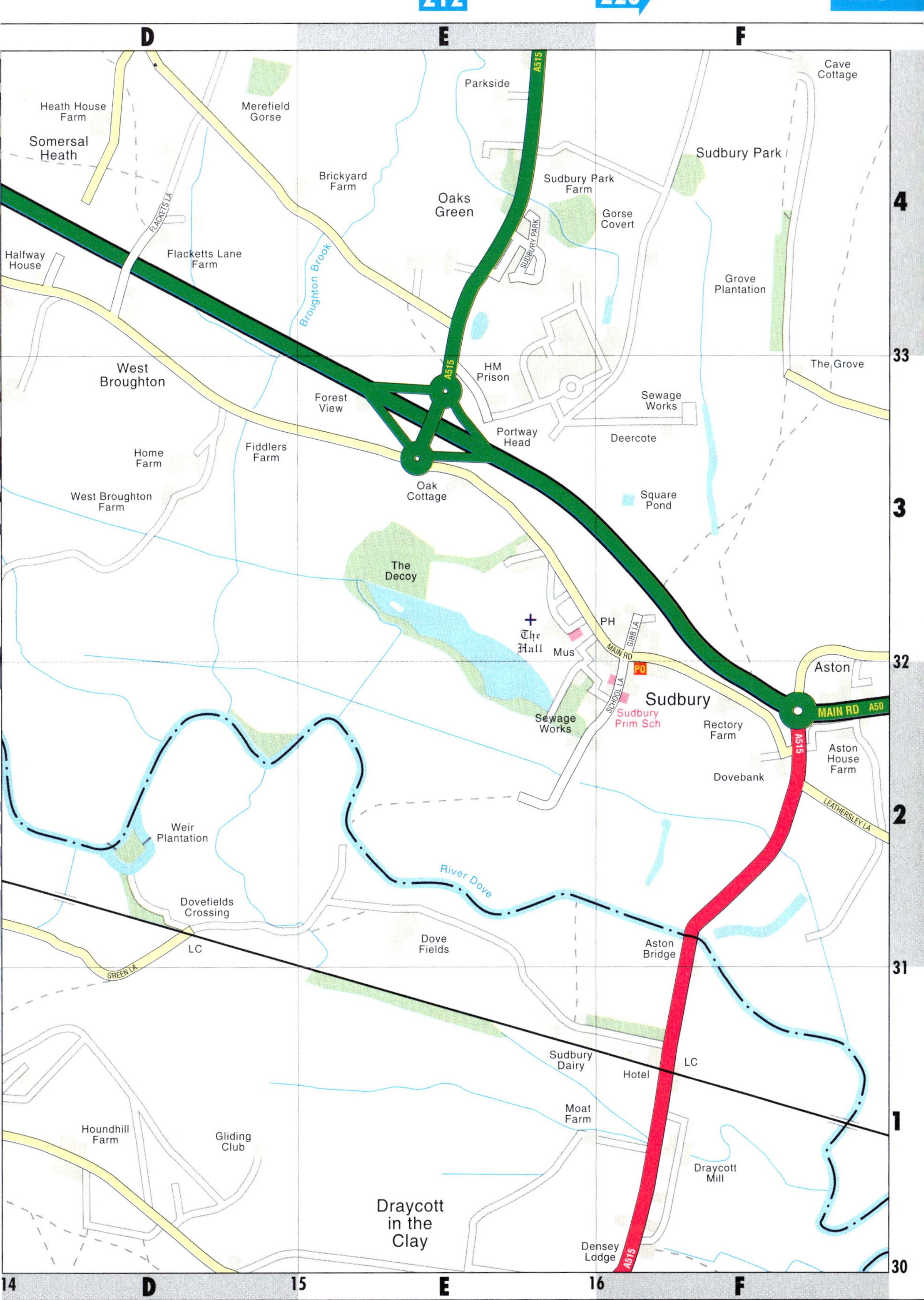
D
E
F
Heath House Farm
Somersal Heath
Merefield Gorse
Parkside
Cave Cottage
Sudbury Park
Brickyard Farm
Oaks Green
Sudbury Park Farm
Gorse Covert
Halfway House
Flacketts Lane Farm
FLACKETS LA
Broughton Brook
SUDBURY PARK
Grove Plantation
West Broughton
HM Prison
The Grove
Forest View
Sewage Works
Portway Head
Deercote
Home Farm
Fiddlers Farm
Oak Cottage
West Broughton Farm
Square Pond
The Decoy
The Hall
Mus
PH
GIBB LA
MAIN RD
PO
Aston
MAIN RD
A50
Sudbury
SCHOOL LA
Sudbury Prim Sch
Sewage Works
Rectory Farm
Aston House Farm
Dovebank
LEATHERSLEY LA
Weir Plantation
River Dove
Dovefields Crossing
Dove Fields
Aston Bridge
LC
GREEN LA
Sudbury Dairy
LC
Hotel
Moat Farm
Houndhill Farm
Gliding Club
Draycott Mill
Draycott in the Clay
Densey Lodge
A515
4
33
3
32
2
31
1
30
14
15
16

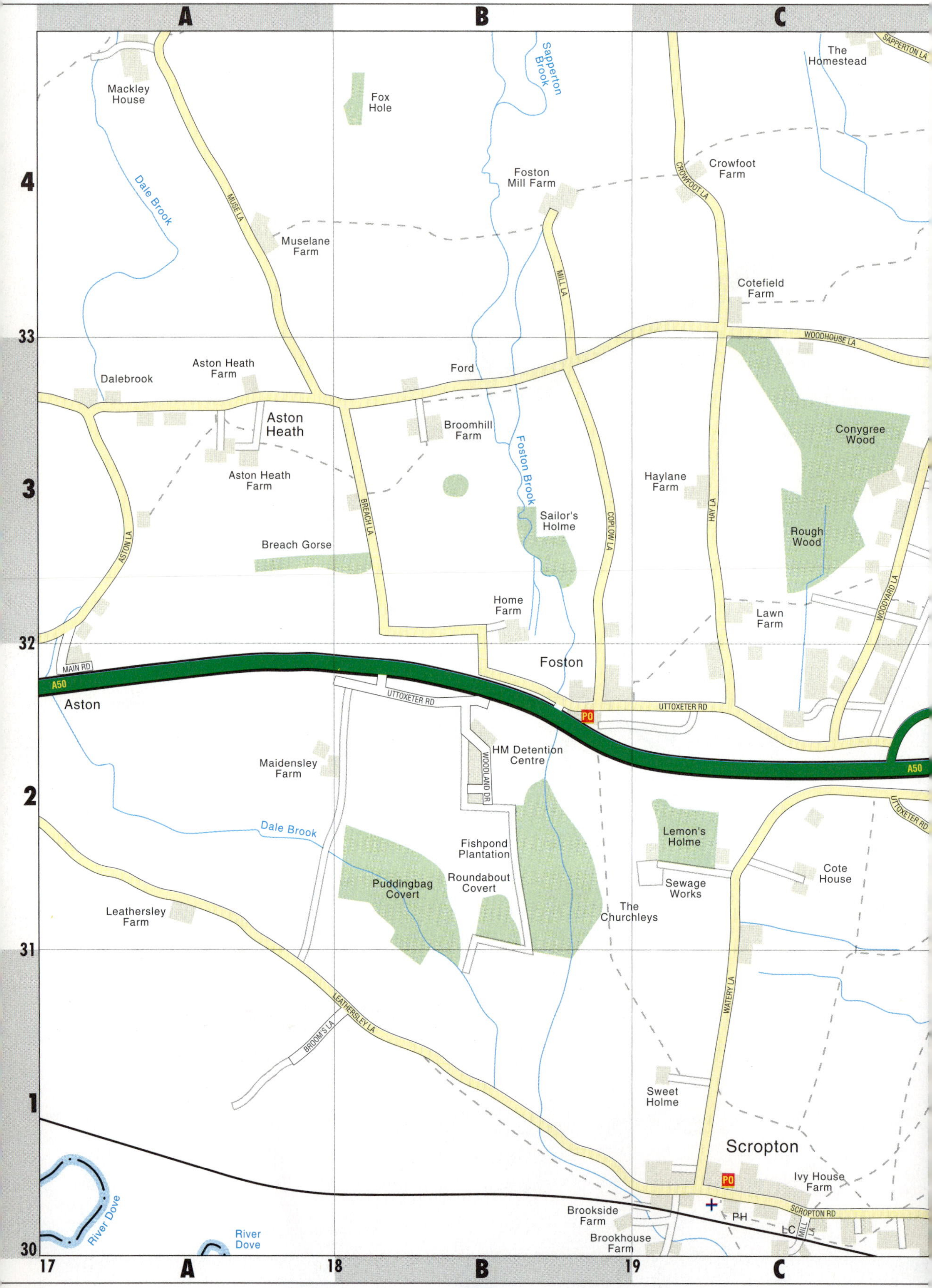

225
213

A **B** **C**

Sapperton Brook

The Homestead

Mackley House

Fox Hole

SAPPERTON LA

Crowfoot Farm

CROWFOOT LA

4

Dale Brook

MUSE LA

Muselane Farm

Foston Mill Farm

MILL LA

Cotefield Farm

WOODHOUSE LA

33

Dalebrook

Aston Heath Farm

Ford

Aston Heath

Broomhill Farm

Conygree Wood

ASTON LA

BREACH LA

Aston Heath Farm

Foston Brook

Sailor's Holme

Haylane Farm

HAY LA

Rough Wood

COPLOW LA

3

Breach Gorse

Home Farm

Lawn Farm

WOODYARD LA

32

MAIN RD

A50

Aston

UTTOXETER RD

Foston

PO

UTTOXETER RD

Maidensley Farm

HM Detention Centre

WOODLAND DR

Lemon's Holme

Cote House

A50

UTTOXETER RD

2

Dale Brook

Fishpond Plantation

Sewage Works

Puddingbag Covert

Roundabout Covert

The Churchleys

Leathersley Farm

WATERY LA

31

LEATHERSLEY LA

BROOM'S LA

Sweet Holme

1

Scropton

River Dove

PO

Ivy House Farm

SCROPTON RD

Brookside Farm

PH

MILL LA

LC 5

River Dove

Brookhouse Farm

30

17 **A** 18 **B** 19 **C**

225
238

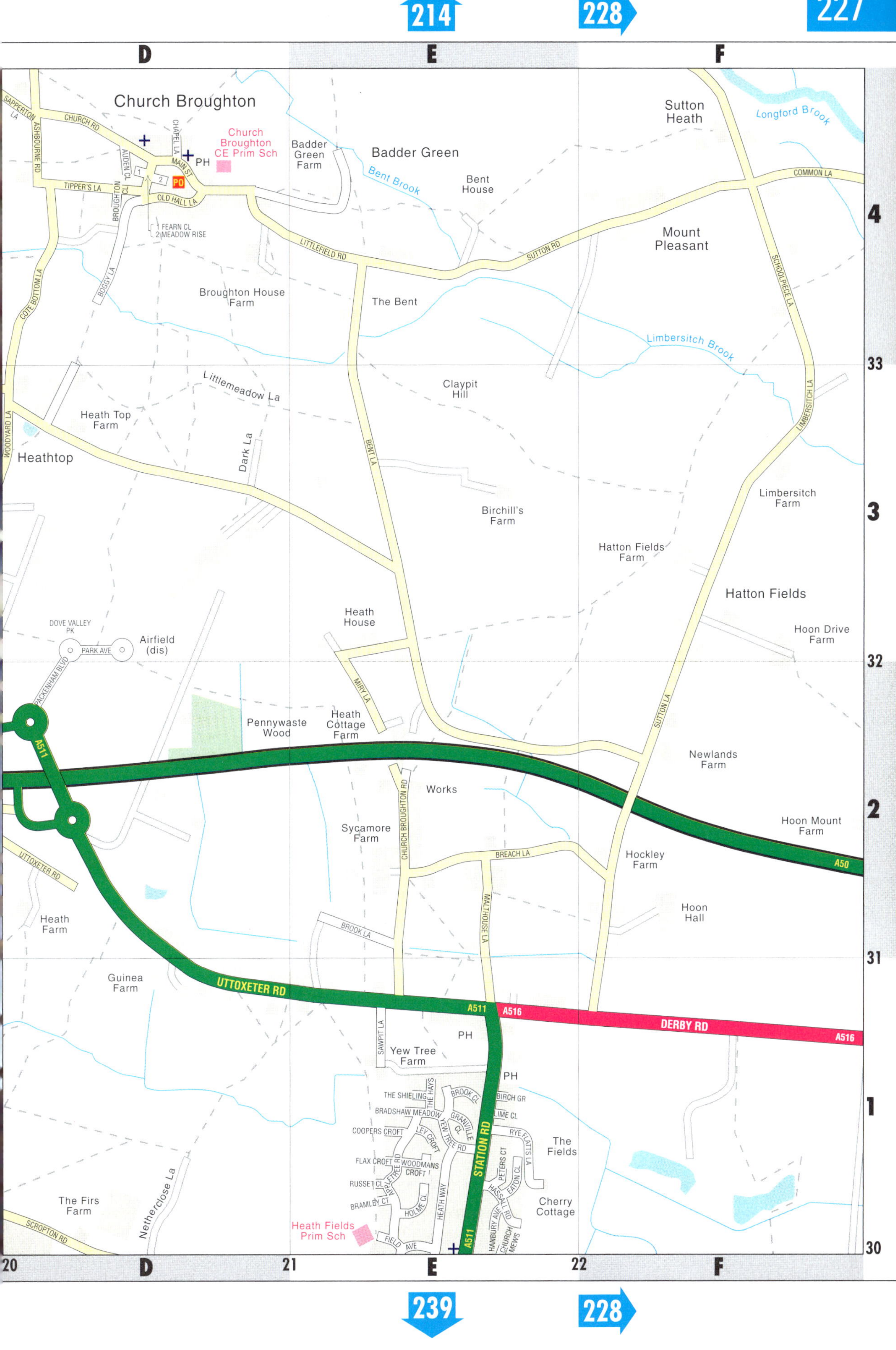
D
E
F
Church Broughton
Church Broughton CE Prim Sch
Badder Green Farm
Badder Green
Bent Brook
Bent House
Sutton Heath
Longford Brook
COMMON LA
SAPPERTON LA
CHURCH RD
ASHBOURNE RD
CHAPEL LA
AUDEN CL
MAIN ST
PH
PO
TIPPER'S LA
BROUGHTON CL
OLD HALL LA
1 FEARN CL
2 MEADOW RISE
LITTLEFIELD RD
SUTTON RD
Mount Pleasant
SCHOOLPIECE LA
COTE BOTTOM LA
BOGGY LA
Broughton House Farm
The Bent
Limbersitch Brook
Littlemeadow La
Claypit Hill
LIMBERSITCH LA
Heath Top Farm
WOODYARD LA
Heathtop
Dark La
BENT LA
Birchill's Farm
Limbersitch Farm
Hatton Fields Farm
Hatton Fields
Hoon Drive Farm
DOVE VALLEY PK
PARK AVE
Airfield (dis)
Heath House
PACKENHAM BLVD
MIRY LA
SUTTON LA
Pennywaste Wood
Heath Cottage Farm
Newlands Farm
A511
Works
CHURCH BROUGHTON RD
Sycamore Farm
Hoon Mount Farm
BREACH LA
Hockley Farm
A50
UTTOXETER RD
Heath Farm
MALTHOUSE LA
BROOK LA
Hoon Hall
Guinea Farm
UTTOXETER RD
A511
A516
DERBY RD
A516
SAWPIT LA
PH
Yew Tree Farm
PH
THE SHIELING
THE HAYS
BROOK CL
BIRCH GR
BRADSHAW MEADOW
GRANVILLE CL
LIME CL
COOPERS CROFT
LEY CROFT
YEW TREE RD
RYE FLATTS LA
STATION RD
The Fields
FLAX CROFT
WOODMANS CROFT
APPLETREE RD
PETERS CT
EATON CL
RUSSET CL
BRAMBLEY CT
HOLME CL
HEATH WAY
HASSALL RD
Cherry Cottage
The Firs Farm
Netherclose La
SCROPTON RD
Heath Fields Prim Sch
FIELD AVE
HANBURY AVE
CHURCH MEWS
4
33
3
32
2
31
1
30
20
21
22

227
215

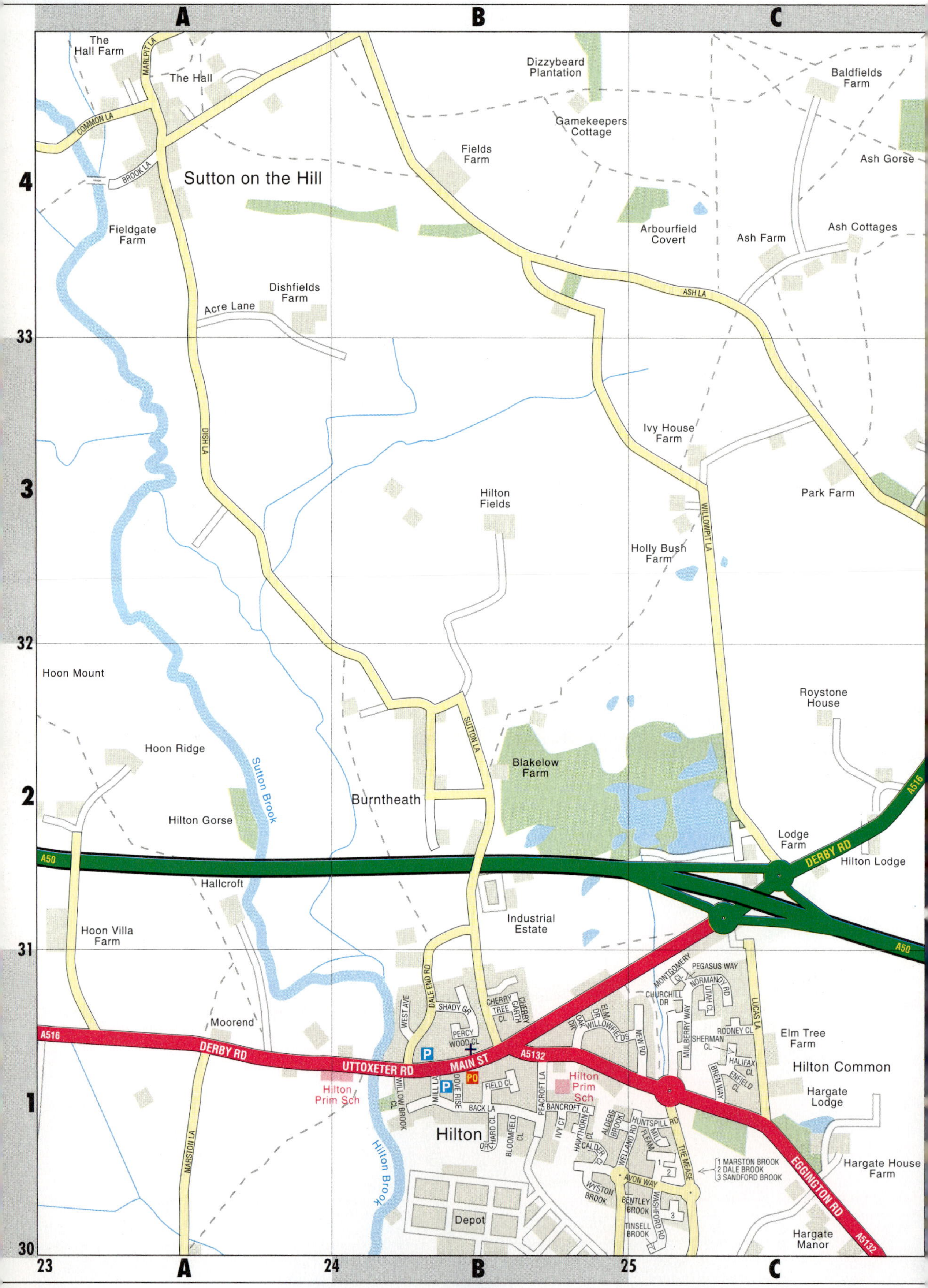

A   B   C

The Hall Farm

MARLPIT LA

The Hall

COMMON LA

BROOK LA

Sutton on the Hill

Fieldgate Farm

Dizzybeard Plantation

Gamekeepers Cottage

Fields Farm

Baldfields Farm

Ash Gorse

Arbourfield Covert

Ash Farm

Ash Cottages

ASH LA

Acre Lane

Dishfields Farm

4

DISH LA

33

Ivy House Farm

Park Farm

WILLOWPIT LA

Hilton Fields

3

Holly Bush Farm

Hoon Mount

Roystone House

32

Hoon Ridge

Sutton Brook

Blakelow Farm

SUTTON LA

Burntheath

Hilton Gorse

2

Lodge Farm

DERBY RD

A516

Hilton Lodge

A50

Hallcroft

A50

Hoon Villa Farm

Industrial Estate

31

DALE END RD

Montgomery CL

Pegasus Way

NORMAN CL

UTAH CL

Churchill DR

RODNEY CL

Elm Tree Farm

LUCAS LA

Hilton Common

Moorend

WEST AVE

SHADY GR

PERCY

CHERRY TREE CL

CHERRY GARTH CL

ELM DR

WILLOW CL DS

MULBERRY WAY

SHERMAN CL

HALIFAX CL

ENFIELD CL

BREN WAY

Hargate Lodge

A516

DERBY RD

UTTOXETER RD

MARSTON LA

WILLOW BROOK CL

MILL LA

MAIN ST

DOVE RISE

WOOD CL

P

PO

FIELD CL

A5132

Hilton Prim Sch

Hilton Common

Hargate Lodge

Hilton Prim Sch

BACK LA

ORCHARD CL

PEACROFT LA

BANCROFT CL

IVY CT

HAWTHORN CL

BLOOMFIELD CL

MCALOD CT

ALDERS BROOK

WELLAND RD

HUNTSPILL RD

WELLAND RD

MILL FLEAM

Hargate House Farm

EGGINGTON RD

THE MEASE

1 MARSTON BROOK
2 DALE BROOK
3 SANDFORD BROOK

1

Hilton

Hilton Brook

AVON WAY

WYSTON BROOK

BENTLEY BROOK

WASHFORD RD

TINSELL BROOK

Depot

Hargate Manor

A5132

30

23   A   24   B   25   C

227
240

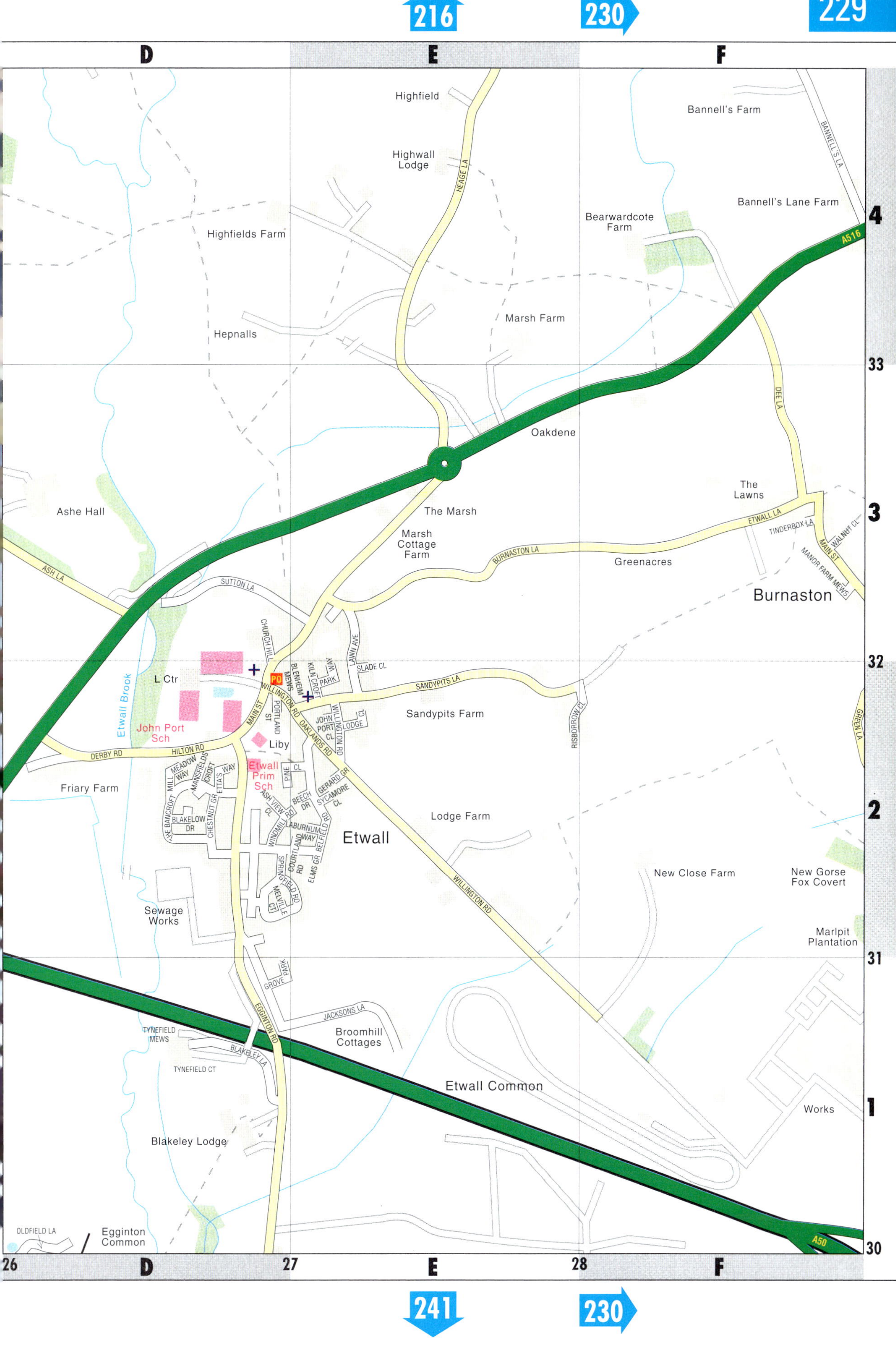

D E F

Highfield

Highwall Lodge

Bannell's Farm

BANNELL'S LA

Bearwardcote Farm

Bannell's Lane Farm

4

A516

Highfields Farm

Hepnalls

Marsh Farm

33

HEAGE LA

Oakdene

DEE LA

The Lawns

Ashe Hall

The Marsh

Marsh Cottage Farm

BURNASTON LA

Greenacres

ETWALL LA

MAIN ST

TINDERBOX LA

WALNUT CL

MANOR FARM MEWS

Burnaston

3

ASH LA

SUTTON LA

CHURCH HILL

LAWN AVE

SLADE CL

32

L Ctr

Etwall Brook

MAIN ST

PORTLAND ST

WILLINGTON RD

MEWS

BLENHEIM

KILN CROFT

PARK

ANVIL

SANDYPITS LA

Sandypits Farm

RISBORROW CL

GREEN LA

PO

John Port Sch

Liby

Etwall Prim Sch

HILTON RD

DERBY RD

PINE CL

BEECH DR

GERARD GR

SYCAMORE CL

OAKLANDS RD

JOHN PORT CL

WILLINGTON CL

LODGE CL

Friary Farm

Etwall

Lodge Farm

New Close Farm

New Gorse Fox Covert

2

MEADOW WAY

MARIGELDS CROFT

ETTA'S WAY

BLAKELOW DR

CHESTNUT GR

ASH VIEW RD

WINDMILL

LABURNUM WAY

COURTLAND DR

ELMS GR

BELFRY

SPRINGFIELD RD

MELVILLE CT

PARK GROVE

WILLINGTON RD

Marlpit Plantation

Sewage Works

31

EGGINTON RD

JACKSONS LA

Broomhill Cottages

Works

TYNEFIELD MEWS

BLAKELEY LA

Etwall Common

1

TYNEFIELD CT

Blakeley Lodge

OLDFIELD LA

Egginton Common

A50

30

26 D 27 E 28 F

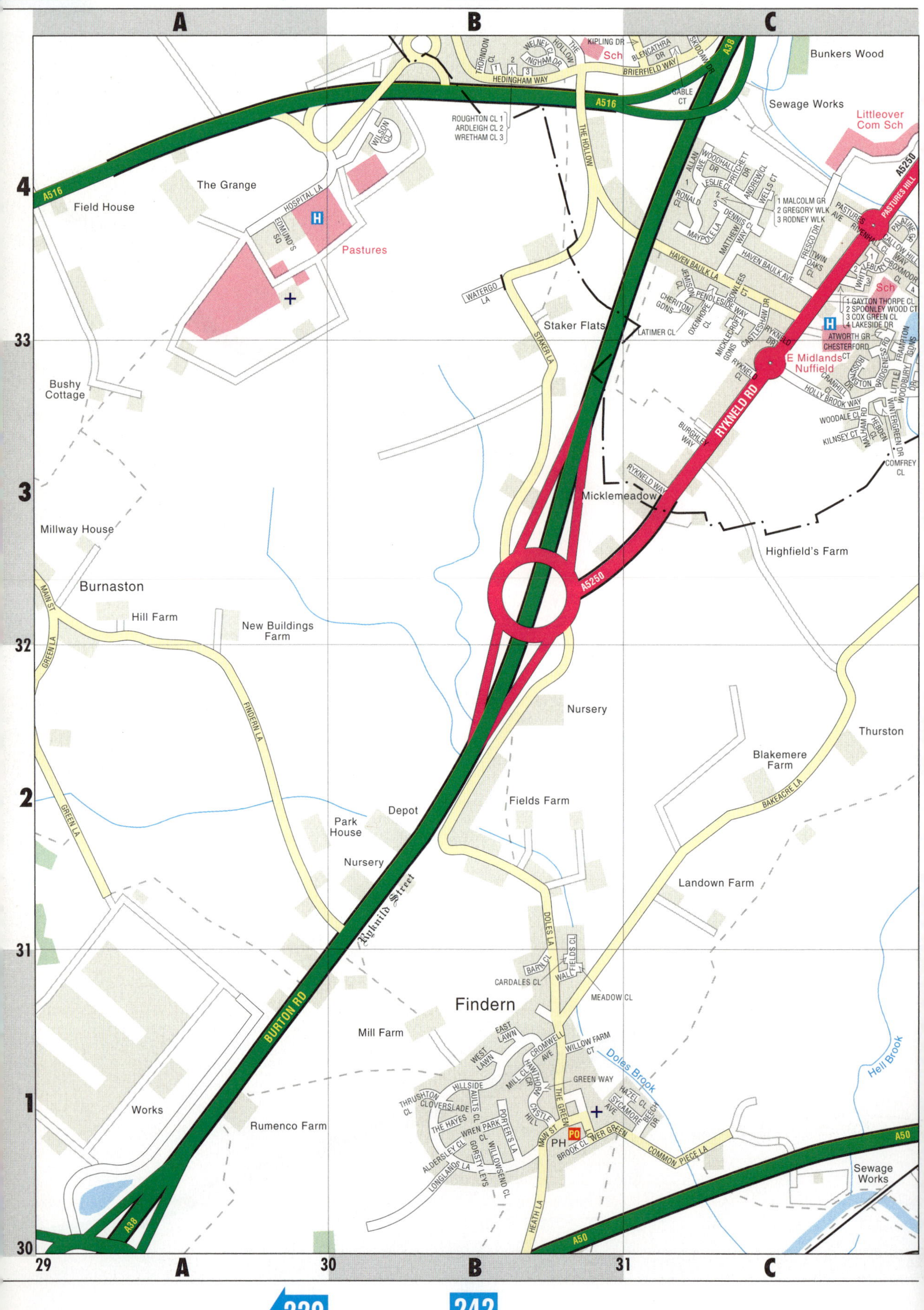

A   B   C

4

33

3

32

2

1

30

29   A   30   B   31   C

A Field House · The Grange · Hospital La · Pastures · Bushy Cottage · Millway House · Burnaston · Hill Farm · New Buildings Farm · Green La · Main St · Finmere La · Burton Rd · Rykniid Street · Park House · Nursery · Works · Rumenco Farm

B Thorndon · Welney Cl · Tingham Dr · The Hollow · Kipling Dr · Sch · Hedingham Way · A516 · Roughton Cl 1 · Ardleigh Cl 2 · Wretham Cl 3 · The Hollow · Watergo La · Staker Flats · Staker La · Latimer Cl · Micklemeadow · Depot · Fields Farm · Nursery · Doles La · Barn Cl · Wall · Fields Cl · Cardales Cl · Meadow Cl · Findern · Mill Farm · West Lawn · Cromwell Ave · Willow Farm Ct · Green Way · Doles Brook · Hillside Cl · Thrushton Cl · Cloverslade · The Hayes · Wren Park La · Aults Cl · Mill Cl · Hawthorn · Castle Hill · Porters La · The Green · Hazel Cl · Sycamore Ave · Main St · PH · PO · Brook Cl · Lower Green · Common Piece La · Aldersley La · Godsey Leys · Willowsend Cl · Longlands La · Heath La · A50

C Bunkers Wood · Sewage Works · Littleover Com Sch · A38 · Blencathra Dr · Brierfield Way · Gable Ct · A3250 · Allan Ave · Woodhall Dr · Pritchett Cl · Andrew Cl · Wells Cl · 1 Malcolm Gr · 2 Gregory Wlk · 3 Rodney Wlk · Leslie Cl · Ronald Cl · Dennis Cl · Pastures Ave · Pastures Hill · Maypole · Mathison Way · Rychnall · Haven Baulk La · Haven Baulk Ave · Whitfield · Sch · Nemisis · Pendleside Way · Oxenhope · 1 Gayton Thorpe Cl · 2 Spoonley Wood Cl · 3 Cox Green Cl · 4 Lakeside Dr · Cheriton Gdns · Micklecroft Gdns · Castlesward Dr · Atworth Gr · Chesterford · E Midlands Nuffield · Rykneld Rd · Holly Brook Way · Woodale Cl · Kilnsey Ct · Comfrey Cl · Burghley Way · Rykneld Way · Micklemeadow · Highfield's Farm · A3250 · Thurston · Blakemere Farm · Bakeacre La · Landown Farm · Hell Brook · A50 · Sewage Works

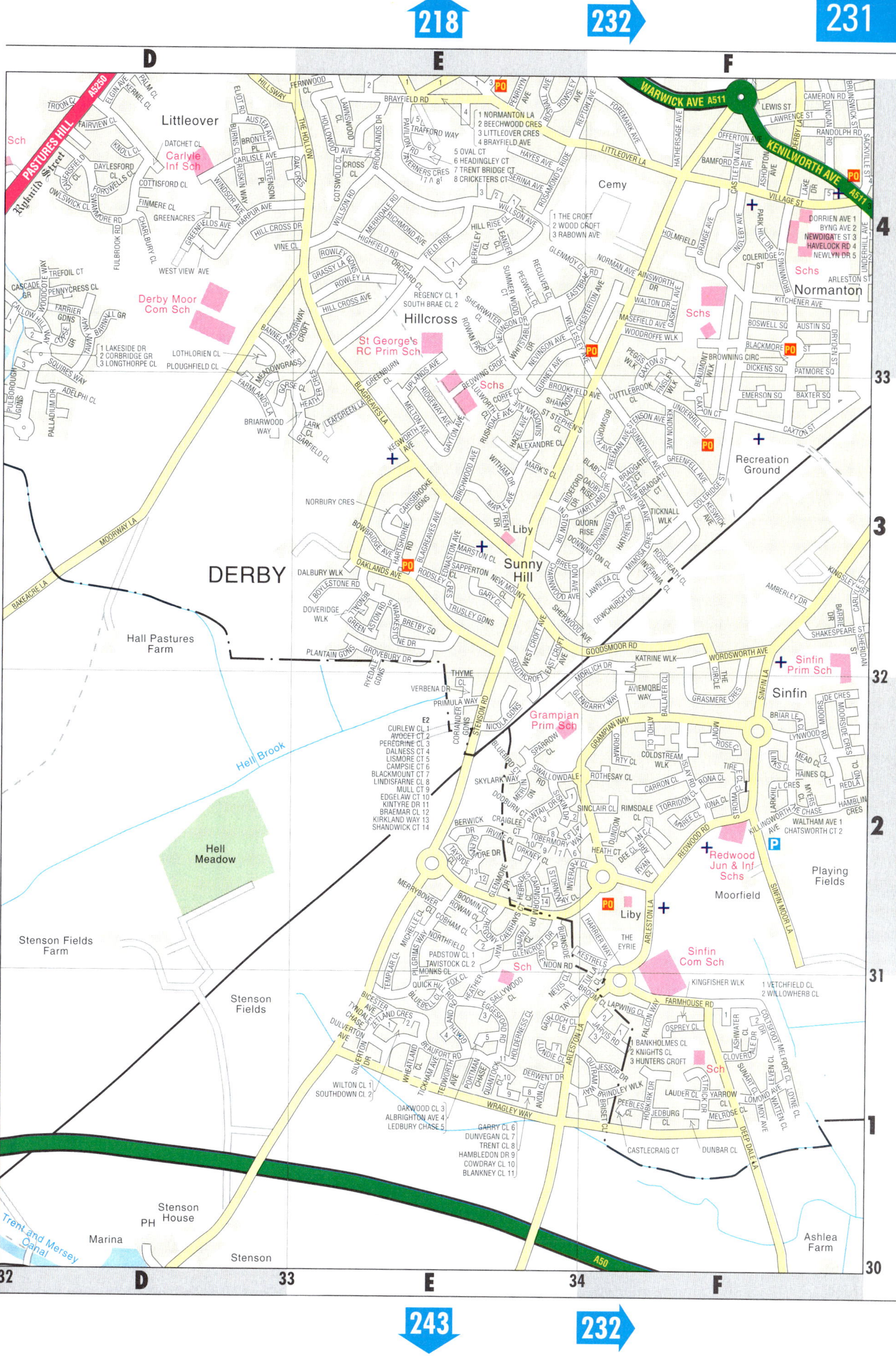
218
232
D
E
F
Littleover
Carlyle Inf Sch
Derby Moor Com Sch
Hillcross
St George's RC Prim Sch
Schs
Cemy
Normanton
Recreation Ground
DERBY
Sunny Hill
Liby
Hall Pastures Farm
Hell Brook
Hell Meadow
Stenson Fields Farm
Stenson Fields
Grampian Prim Sch
Sinfin
Sinfin Prim Sch
Redwood Jun & Inf Schs
Playing Fields
Moorfield
Sinfin Com Sch
Sch
Stenson House
PH
Marina
Trent and Mersey Canal
Stenson
Ashlea Farm
WARWICK AVE A511
KENILWORTH AVE A511
PASTURES HILL A5250
Ryknild Street
A50
1 NORMANTON LA
2 BEECHWOOD CRES
3 LITTLEOVER CRES
4 BRAYFIELD AVE
5 OVAL CT
6 HEADINGLEY CT
7 TRENT BRIDGE CT
8 CRICKETERS CT
1 THE CROFT
2 WOOD CROFT
3 RABOWN AVE
DORRIEN AVE 1
BYNG AVE 2
NEWDIGATE ST 3
HAVELOCK RD 4
NEWLYN DR 5
1 LAKESIDE DR
2 CORBRIDGE GR
3 LONGTHORPE CL
REGENCY CL 1
SOUTH BRAE CL 2
E2
CURLEW CL 1
AVOCET CT 2
PEREGRINE CL 3
DALNESS CT 4
LISMORE CT 5
CAMPSIE CT 6
BLACKMOUNT CT 7
LINDISFARNE CL 8
MULL CT 9
EDGELAW CT 10
KINTYRE DR 11
BRAEMAR CL 12
KIRKLAND WAY 13
SHANDWICK CT 14
WALTHAM AVE 1
CHATSWORTH CT 2
1 VETCHFIELD CL
2 WILLOWHERB CL
1 BANKHOLMES CL
2 KNIGHTS CL
3 HUNTERS CROFT
WILTON CL 1
SOUTHDOWN CL 2
OAKWOOD CL 3
ALBRIGHTON AVE 4
LEDBURY CHASE 5
GARRY CL 6
DUNVEGAN CL 7
TRENT CL 8
HAMBLEDON DR 9
COWDRAY CL 10
BLANKNEY CL 11
4
33
3
32
2
31
1
30
32
33
34
243
232

231
219

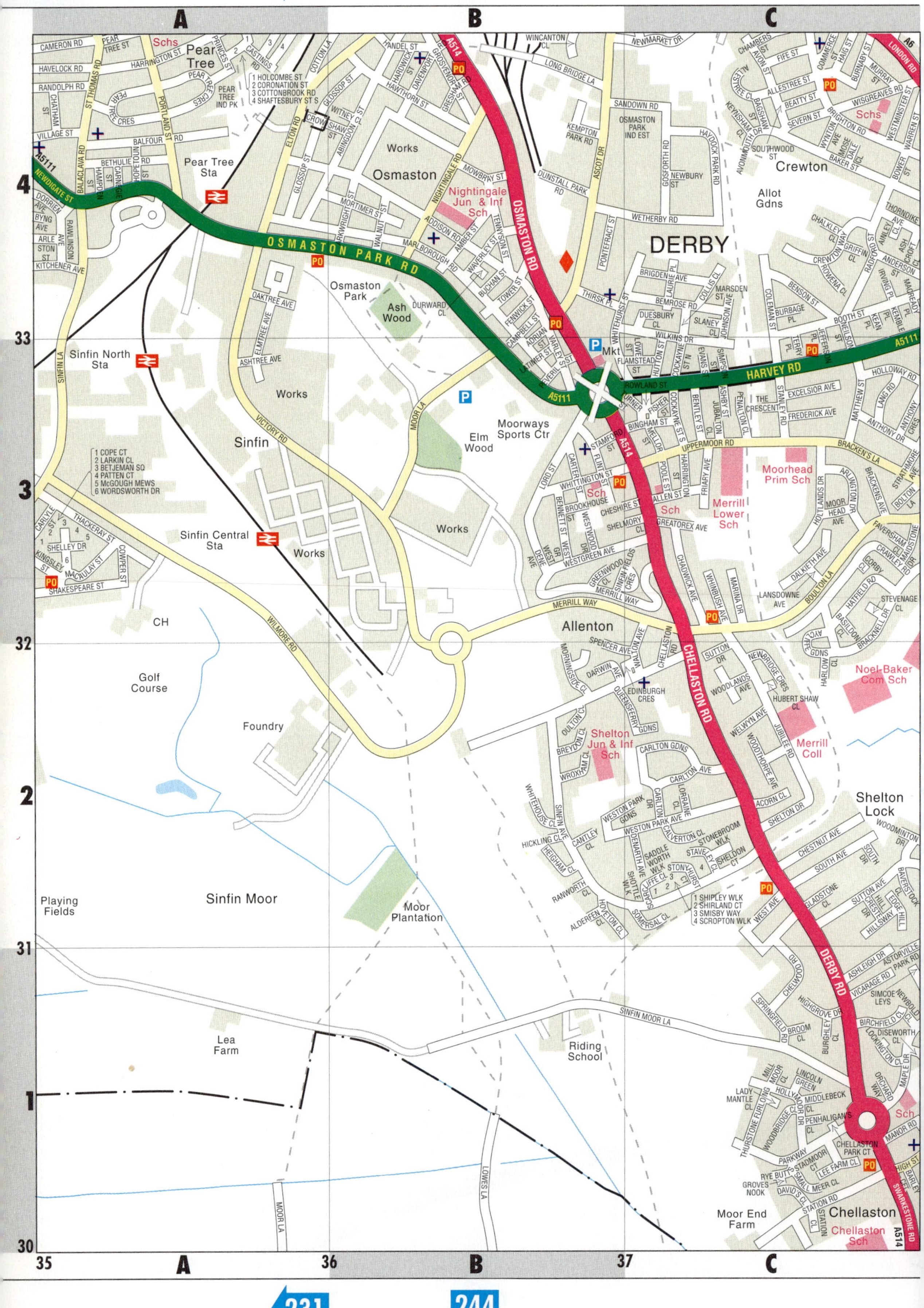
A
B
C
4
33
3
32
2
31
1
30
35
36
37
CAMERON RD
HAVELOCK RD
RANDOLPH RD
CHATHAM ST
VILLAGE ST
PEAR TREE ST
ST THOMAS RD
HARRINGTON ST
Schs
Pear Tree
PEAR TREE CRES
PEAR TREE IND PK
PORTLAND ST
BALFOUR RD
BETHULIE RD
HAMPDEN ST
CARNEGIE ST
HOPETOUN ST
PRINCES ST
CASTINGS RD
1 HOLCOMBE ST
2 CORONATION ST
3 COTTONBROOK RD
4 SHAFTESBURY ST S
COTTON LA
ELTON RD
GLOSSOP ST
CROWSHAW ST
WITNEY CL
ABINGDON CL
HANDEL ST
HARDWICK ST
DAVENPORT RD
GROSVENOR ST
GRESHAM RD
HAWTHORN ST
Works
Osmaston
MOWBRAY ST
NIGHTINGALE RD
Nightingale Jun & Inf Sch
MORTIMER ST
WALNUT ST
ADDISON RD
AMBER ST
MARLBOROUGH RD
TENNYSON ST
WAVERLEY ST
BUCHAN ST
TOWER ST
FENWICK ST
CAMPBELL ST
ADRIAN ST
VARLEY ST
LATIMER ST
BEVERLEY ST
A5111
NEWDIGATE ST
BALACLAVA RD
DORRIEN AVE
BYNG AVE
ARLESTON ST
RAWLINSON AVE
KITCHENER AVE
Pear Tree Sta
OSMASTON PARK RD
PO
Osmaston Park
Ash Wood
DURWARD CL
OAKTREE AVE
ELMTREE AVE
ASHTREE AVE
Sinfin North Sta
SINFIN LA
Works
MOOR LA
P
Elm Wood
Moorways Sports Ctr
Sinfin
VICTORY RD
1 COPE CT
2 LARKIN CL
3 BETJEMAN SQ
4 PATTEN CT
5 McGOUGH MEWS
6 WORDSWORTH DR
CARLYLE ST
THACKERAY ST
SHELLEY DR
KINGSLEY ST
MACAULAY ST
COWPER ST
SHAKESPEARE ST
Sinfin Central Sta
Works
Works
CH
WILMORE RD
Golf Course
Foundry
Playing Fields
Sinfin Moor
Moor Plantation
Lea Farm
SINFIN MOOR LA
Riding School
MOOR LA
LOWES LA
A514
OSMASTON RD
WINCANTON CL
NEWMARKET DR
LONG BRIDGE LA
SANDOWN RD
OSMASTON PARK IND EST
KEMPTON PARK RD
ASCOT DR
DUNSTALL PARK RD
GOSFORTH RD
NEWBURY ST
HAYDOCK PARK RD
PONTEFRACT ST
WETHERBY RD
DERBY
BRIGDEN AVE
LAURIE PL
COLLIS CL
THIRSK PL
MARSDEN ST
BEMROSE RD
DUESBURY CL
SLANEY CL
JOHNSON AVE
WHITEHURST ST
WILKINS DR
Mkt
FLAMSTEAD ST
ROWLAND ST
HARVEY RD
COLEMAN ST
BURBAGE PL
TERRY PL
JEFFERSON PL
NEILSON ST
BOOTH ST
KEAN PL
KEMBLE PL
MACREADY PL
CHAMBERS ST
AVON ST
FIFE ST
ALLESTREE ST
ALLESTREE CL
BAGSHAW ST
KEYNSHAM CL
AVONMOUTH DR
BEATTY ST
SEVERN ST
COMMERCE ST
HAIG ST
BURNABY ST
MURRAY ST
WISGREAVES RD
BRIGHTON RD
WYNTON AVE
MOSEDALE CL
BAKER ST
WESTMINSTER ST
WARREN ST
SOUTHWOOD ST
Crewton
BOWER ST
Allot Gdns
THORNDIKE AVE
CHALKLEY CL
CREWTON WAY
GRIFFIN CL
AINLEY CL
ASHCROFT CL
RADFORD ST
ANDERSON ST
IRVING PL
BENSON ST
ROWENA CL
LONDON RD
A6
HOLLOWAY RD
EXCELSIOR AVE
FREDERICK AVE
THE CRESCENT
MATTHEW ST
LANG RD
ANTHONY DR
ANTHONY CRES
STANLEY RD
PENALTON CL
ASHBY ST
JUBALTON CL
SIMPSON ST
BENTLEY ST
COCKAYNE ST
COCKAYNE ST N
EVANS ST
LOWE ST
HUTTON ST
TURNER ST
FISHER ST
BINGHAM ST
MELLOR ST
POOLE ST
HARRINGTON ST
UPPERMOOR RD
BRACKEN'S LA
STAMFORD ST
CARTER ST
FLINT ST
LORD ST
WHITTINGTON ST
Sch
BROOKHOUSE ST
BENNETT ST
WESTWOOD DR
CHESHIRE ST
ALLEN ST
SHELMORY CL
GREATOREX AVE
FRIARY AVE
Merrill Lower Sch
Moorhead Prim Sch
HOLTLANDS DR
MOORHEAD AVE
ARLINGTON DR
BRACKENS AVE
STRATHMORE AVE
BOLTON LA
FAVERSHAM CL
CRAWLEY RD
MAIDSTONE DR
CORBY CL
HATFIELD RD
STEVENAGE CL
BASILDON CL
BRACKNELL DR
DALKEITH AVE
BOULTON LA
LANSDOWNE AVE
DENE AVE
WEST GR
WESTGREEN AVE
GREENWOOD CL
SINFIN FIELDS CRES
MERRILL WAY
CHADWICK AVE
WHINBUSH AVE
MARINA DR
Allenton
SPENCER AVE
WALTON AVE
CHELLASTON RD
MORNINGSIDE CL
DARWIN AVE
EDINBURGH CRES
QUEENSFERRY GDNS
SUTTON DR
WOODLANDS AVE
NEWBRIDGE CRES
HUBERT SHAW CL
AYCLIFFE GDNS
HARLOW CL
Noel-Baker Com Sch
OULTON CL
BREYDON CL
WROXHAM CL
Shelton Jun & Inf Sch
CARLTON GDNS
CARLTON AVE
WELWYN AVE
JUBILEE RD
Merrill Coll
WOODTHORPE AVE
ACORN CL
SHELTON DR
LORRAINE CL
CARLTON DR
Shelton Lock
WOODMINTON DR
WHITEHOUSE CL
SINFIN AVE
HICKLING CL
HEIGHAM CL
CANTLEY CL
WESTON PARK GDNS
WESTON PARK AVE
CALVERTON CL
STONEBROOM WLK
STAVELEY CL
SHELDON CT
SADDLEWORTH WLK
DENARTH AVE
SHOTTLE WLK
STONYHURST CT
RANWORTH CL
ALDERFEN CL
HOVETON CL
SOMERSAL CL
1 SHIPLEY WLK
2 SHIRLAND CT
3 SMISBY WAY
4 SCROPTON WLK
WEST AVE
CHESTNUT AVE
SOUTH AVE
SOUTH DR
BAVERSTOCK CL
GLADSTONE CL
SUTTON AVE
HILLCREST DR
HILLSWAY
EDGE HILL
ASTORVILLE PARK RD
ASHLEIGH DR
VICARAGE RD
SIMCOE LEYS
NEWBOLD AVE
BIRCHFIELD CL
DISEWORTH CL
LOCKINGTON CL
MAPLE DR
ORCHARD WAY
DERBY RD
CHELWOOD RD
SPRINGFIELD RD
HIGHGROVE DR
BROOM CL
BURGHLEY CL
MILL MOOR CL
LINCOLN GREEN
LADY MANTLE CL
HOLLY MOOR DR
MIDDLEBECK CL
THURSTONE FURLONG
WOODBRIDGE CL
PENHALIGANS CL
CHELLASTON PARK CT
Sch
MANOR RD
HIGH ST
BARLEY CL
SWARKESTONE RD
PARKWAY
STADMOOR CT
LEE FARM CL
RYE BUTTS
SMALL MEER CL
GROVES NOOK
DAVID'S CL
STATION RD
STATION CL
Moor End Farm
Chellaston
Chellaston Sch

231
244

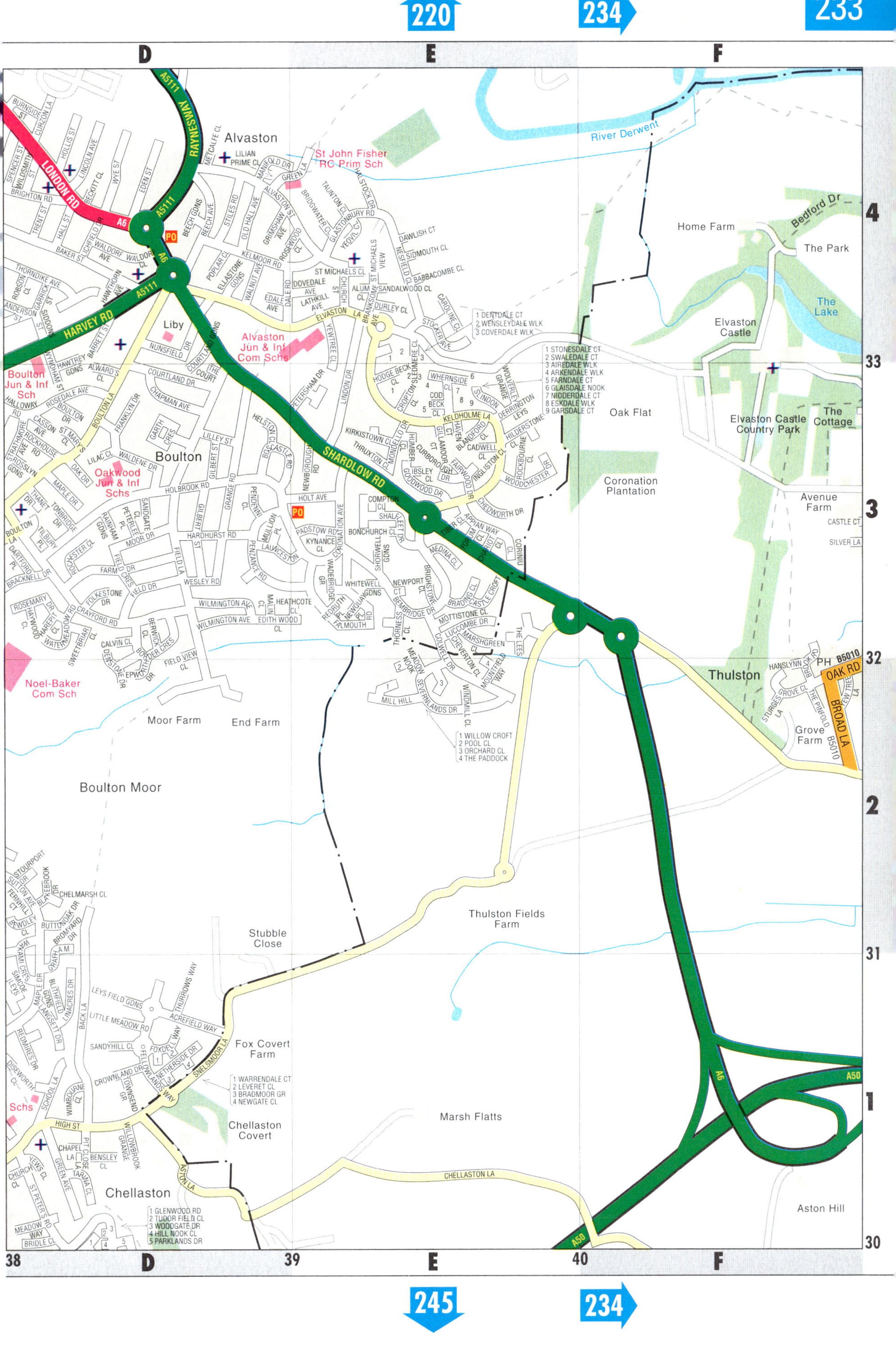
D
E
F
Alvaston
Boulton
Liby
Boulton Moor
Chellaston
Thulston
Elvaston Castle
Elvaston Castle Country Park
Home Farm
The Park
The Lake
The Cottage
Avenue Farm
Oak Flat
Coronation Plantation
River Derwent
St John Fisher RC Prim Sch
Alvaston Jun & Inf Com Schs
Boulton Jun & Inf Sch
Oakwood Jun & Inf Schs
Noel-Baker Com Sch
Schs
Moor Farm
End Farm
Stubble Close
Thulston Fields Farm
Fox Covert Farm
Chellaston Covert
Marsh Flatts
Grove Farm
Aston Hill
HARVEY RD
LONDON RD
RAYNESWAY
SHARDLOW RD
ELVASTON LA
CHELLASTON LA
SNELSMOOR LA
BROAD LA
OAK RD
HIGH ST
Bedford Dr
A6
A5111
A50
B5010
4
33
3
32
2
31
1
30
38
39
40

233
221

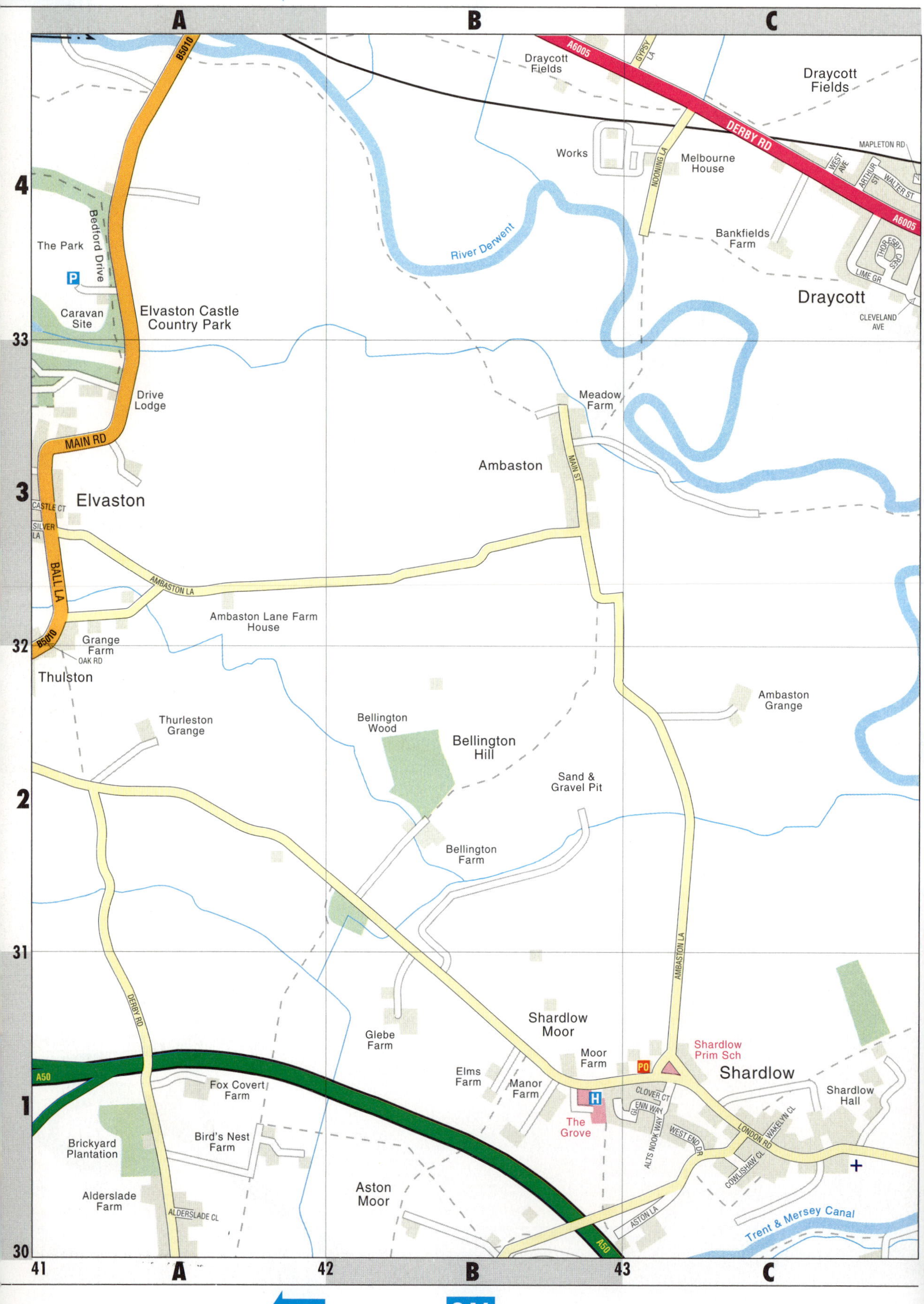
A
B
C
4
33
3
32
2
31
1
30
41
42
43
B5010
A6005
GYPSY LA
Draycott Fields
Draycott Fields
DERBY RD
MAPLETON RD
Works
Melbourne House
NOONING LA
WEST AVE
ARTHUR ST
WALTER ST
A6005
Bankfields Farm
THORESBY CRES
LIME GR
Draycott
CLEVELAND AVE
River Derwent
Bedford Drive
The Park
P
Caravan Site
Elvaston Castle Country Park
Drive Lodge
Meadow Farm
MAIN RD
Ambaston
MAIN ST
Elvaston
CASTLE CT
SILVER LA
BALL LA
AMBASTON LA
Ambaston Lane Farm House
B5010
Grange Farm
OAK RD
Thulston
Ambaston Grange
Thurleston Grange
Bellington Wood
Bellington Hill
Sand & Gravel Pit
Bellington Farm
AMBASTON LA
DERBY RD
Glebe Farm
Shardlow Moor
Moor Farm
PO
Shardlow Prim Sch
Shardlow
A50
Fox Covert Farm
Elms Farm
Manor Farm
H
CLOVER CT
GLENN WAY
The Grove
ALTS NOOK WAY
WEST END DR
LONDON RD
WAKELYN CL
Shardlow Hall
Brickyard Plantation
Bird's Nest Farm
COWLISHAW CL
Aston Moor
Alderslade Farm
ALDERSLADE CL
ASTON LA
A50
Trent & Mersey Canal

233
246

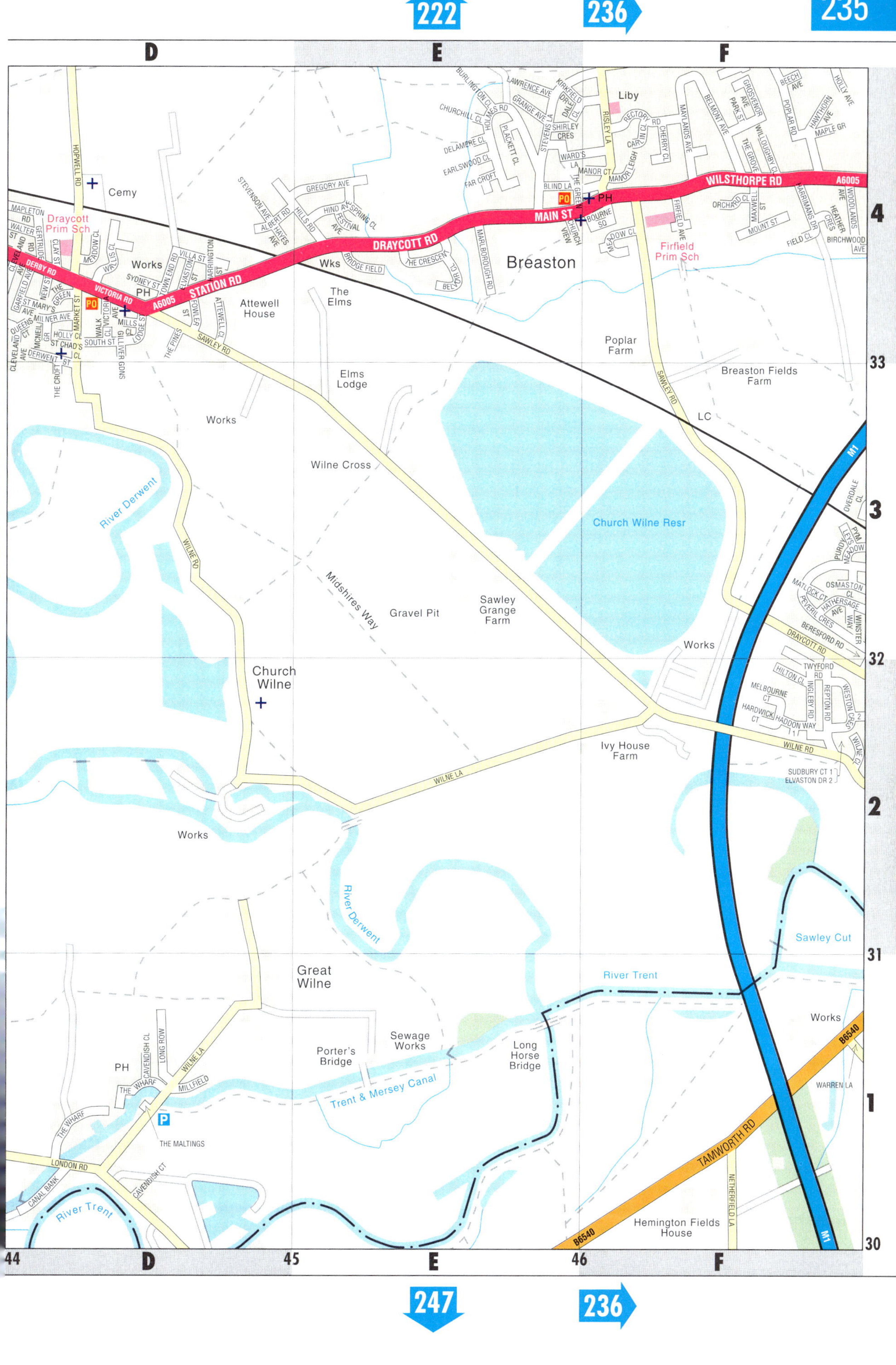

D
E
F

BURLINGTON AVE
LAWRENCE AVE
KIRKFIELD DR
Liby
BEECH AVE
HOLLY AVE
GROSVENOR AVE
PARK CL
POPLAR RD
HAWTHORN
MAPLE GR

CHURCHILL CL
MASS RD
GRANGE AVE
RISLEY LA
RECTORY RD
BELMONT AVE
WILLOUGHBY
THE GROVE
CHERRY CL

DELAMERE CL
STEVENS LA
SHIRLEY CRES
CAR

EARLSWOOD CL
FAR CROFT
MANOR CT
MANOR LEIGH

Cemy
MAPLETON RD
WALTER ST
CLAY ST
STEVENSON AVE
GREGORY AVE
ALBERT RD
HILLS RD
HIND RD
SPRING CL
FESTIVAL AVE
BLIND LA
WARD'S
THE GREEN
PO
PH
ORCHARD CL
HEATHER
MOUNT ST
FIELD CL
BIRCHWOOD AVE
WOODLANDS
4

Draycott Prim Sch
DERBY RD
VICTORIA RD
PO
STATION RD
A6005
DRAYCOTT RD
MAIN ST
WILSTHORPE RD
A6005
Works
Works
Wks
BRIDGE FIELD
THE CRESCENT
Breaston
MEADOW CL
Firfield Prim Sch

GARFIELD ST
ST MARY'S
NEW ST
MILNER AVE
QUEENS AVE
HOLLY CL
SOUTH ST
SAWLEY RD
THE ELMS
Attewell House
33

Works
Elms Lodge
Poplar Farm
Breaston Fields Farm

SAWLEY RD
LC

River Derwent
Wilne Cross
Church Wilne Resr
OVERDALE CL

WILNE RD
Midshires Way
Gravel Pit
Sawley Grange Farm
PURDY
PYM LA
MEADOW
OSMASTON CL
MATLOCK CV
HATHERSAGE AVE
PEVERIL CRES
BERESFORD RD
MINSTER
3

Church Wilne
Works
DRAYCOTT RD
TWYFORD RD
HILTON CL
INGLEBY RD
REPTON RD
WESTON CRES
WILNE
32

WILNE LA
Ivy House Farm
MELBOURNE CT
HARDWICK
HADDON WAY
WILNE RD
SUDBURY CT 1
ELVASTON DR 2

Works
2

Works
River Derwent
Sawley Cut
31

Great Wilne
River Trent
Works
B6540

PH
THE WHARF
CAVENDISH CL
LONG ROW
WILNE LA
MILLFIELD
Porter's Bridge
Sewage Works
Long Horse Bridge
WARREN LA
TAMWORTH RD
1

P
THE MALTINGS
Trent & Mersey Canal
NETHERFIELD LA

LONDON RD
CANAL BANK
CAVENDISH CT
River Trent
B6540
Hemington Fields House
30

44
D
45
E
46
F

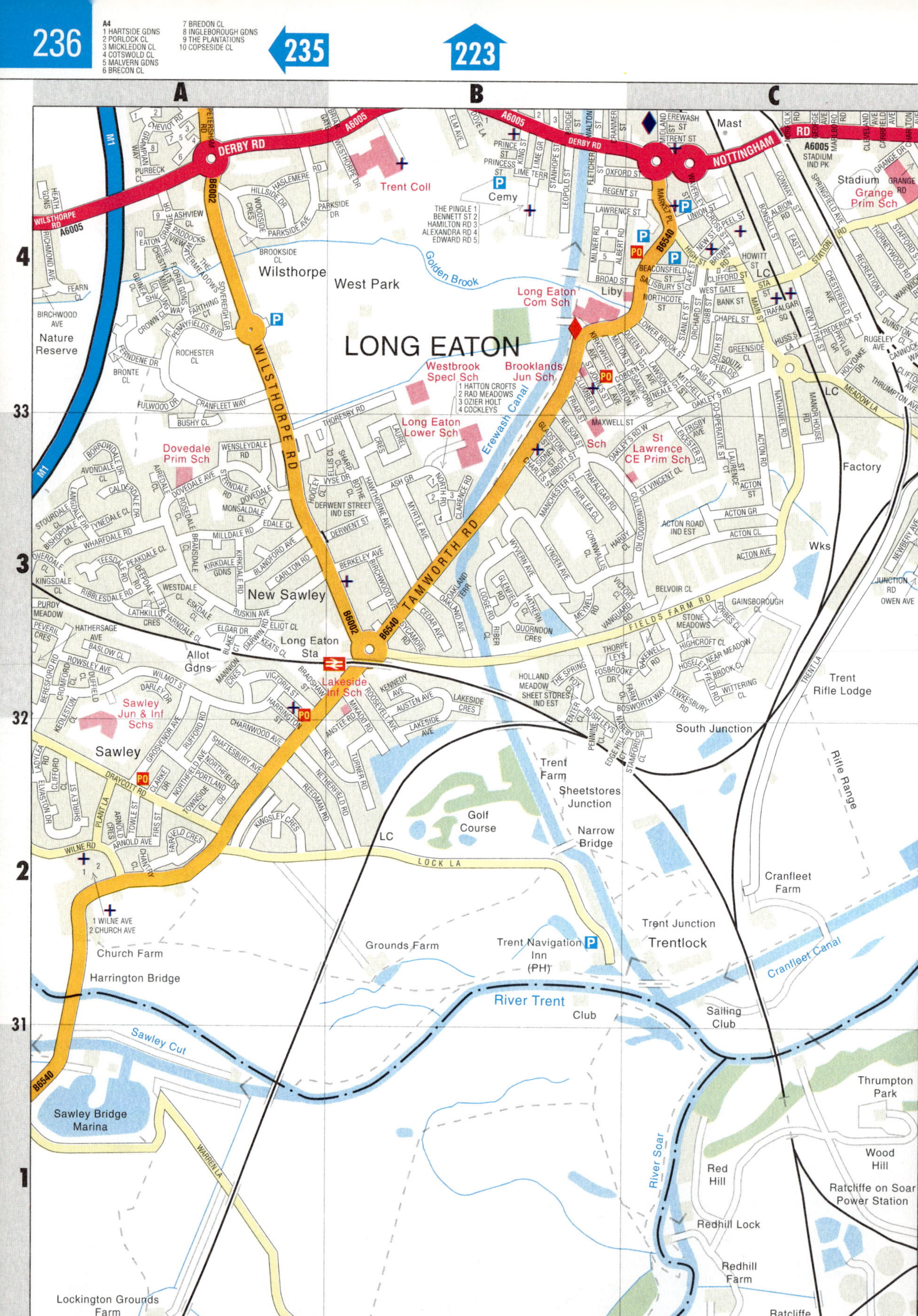

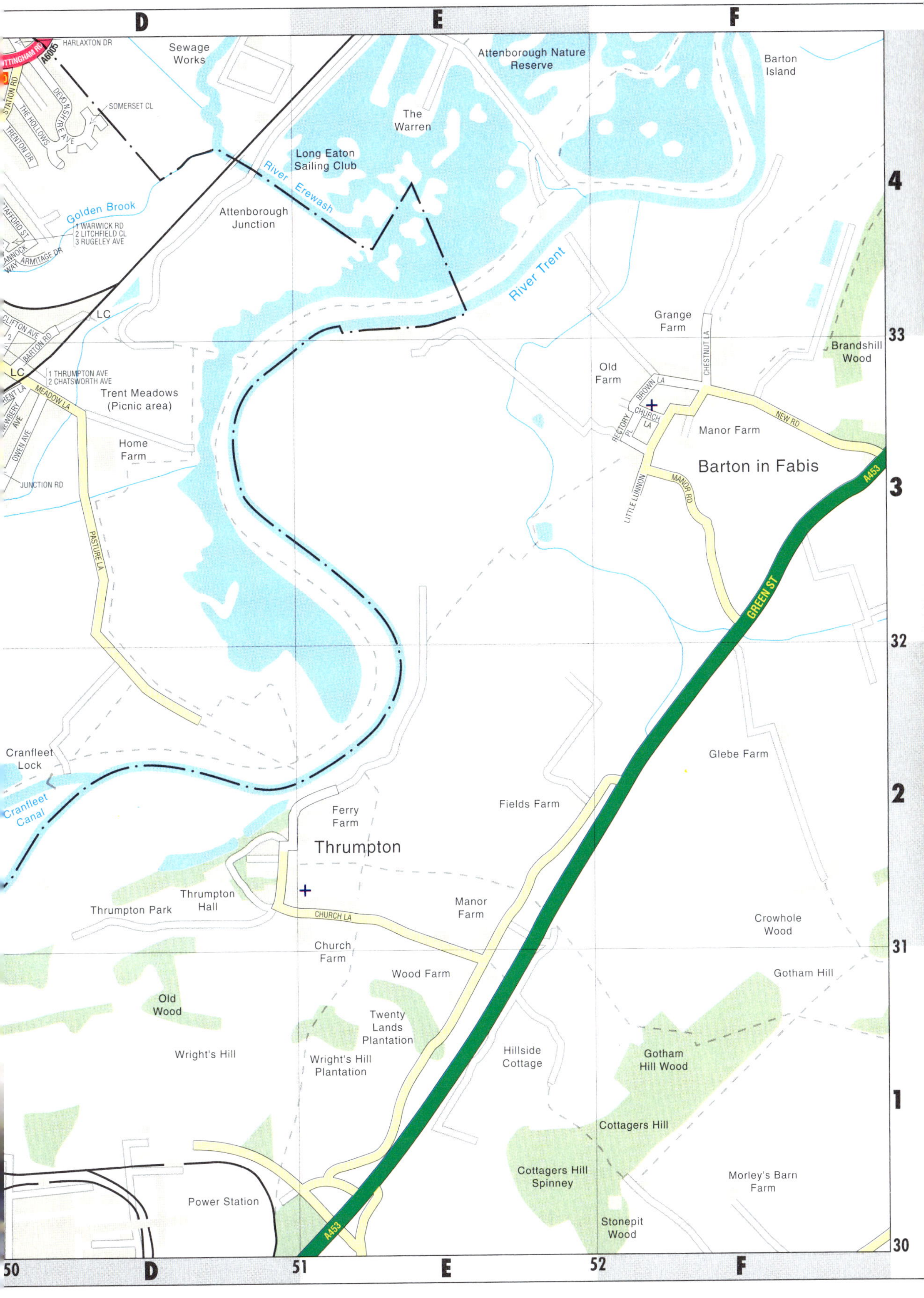
D
E
F
Sewage Works
HARLAXTON DR
SOMERSET CL
Attenborough Nature Reserve
Barton Island
The Warren
Long Eaton Sailing Club
River Erewash
Golden Brook
1 WARWICK RD
2 LITCHFIELD CL
3 RUGELEY AVE
Attenborough Junction
River Trent
LC
Grange Farm
CHESTNUT LA
Brandshill Wood
Old Farm
BROWN LA
CHURCH LA
RECTORY PL
NEW RD
1 THRUMPTON AVE
2 CHATSWORTH AVE
MEADOW LA
Trent Meadows (Picnic area)
Home Farm
Manor Farm
Barton in Fabis
LITTLE LUNNON
MANOR RD
A453
JUNCTION RD
PASTURE LA
GREEN ST
Cranfleet Lock
Cranfleet Canal
Glebe Farm
Ferry Farm
Fields Farm
Thrumpton
Thrumpton Hall
Thrumpton Park
CHURCH LA
Manor Farm
Crowhole Wood
Church Farm
Wood Farm
Gotham Hill
Old Wood
Twenty Lands Plantation
Wright's Hill
Wright's Hill Plantation
Hillside Cottage
Gotham Hill Wood
Cottagers Hill
Cottagers Hill Spinney
Morley's Barn Farm
Power Station
Stonepit Wood
4
33
3
32
2
31
1
30
50
51
52

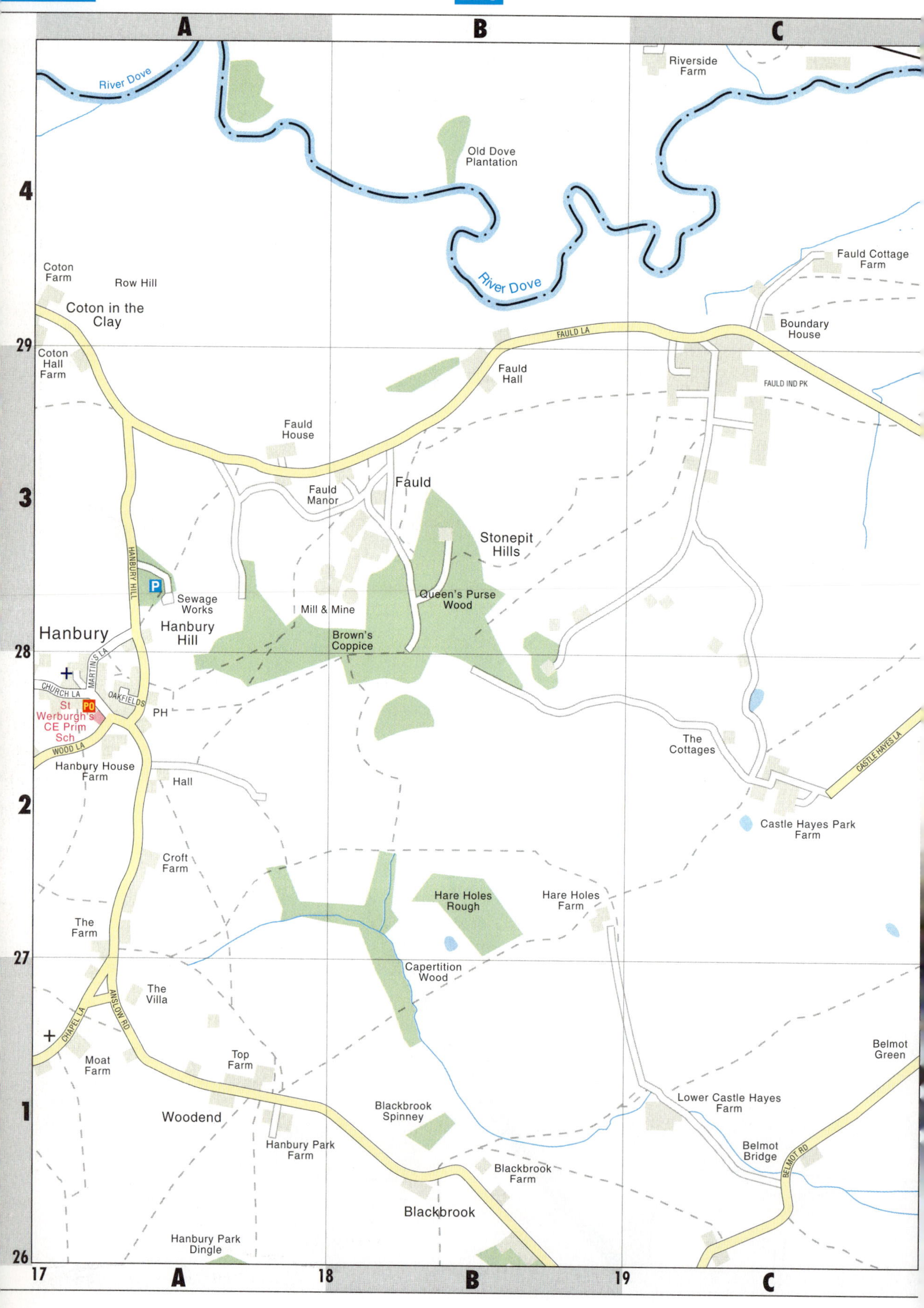

A   B   C

River Dove

Riverside
Farm

Old Dove
Plantation

River Dove

4

Fauld Cottage
Farm

Coton
Farm

Row Hill

Boundary
House

**Coton in the
Clay**

29

Coton
Hall
Farm

FAULD LA

FAULD IND PK

Fauld
Hall

Fauld
House

Fauld
Manor

Fauld

3

Stonepit
Hills

P

Sewage
Works

Queen's Purse
Wood

Hanbury

**Hanbury
Hill**

Mill & Mine

Brown's
Coppice

Hanbury

+

MARTIN'S LA

28

CHURCH LA

OAKFIELDS

St
Werburgh's
CE Prim
Sch

PO

PH

The
Cottages

WOOD LA

Hanbury House
Farm

Hall

Castle Hayes Park
Farm

CASTLE HAYES LA

Croft
Farm

2

The
Farm

Hare Holes
Rough

Hare Holes
Farm

27

Capertition
Wood

ANSLOW RD

The
Villa

CHAPEL LA

+

Belmot
Green

Moat
Farm

Top
Farm

Lower Castle Hayes
Farm

1

Woodend

Blackbrook
Spinney

Belmot
Bridge

Hanbury Park
Farm

BELMOT RD

Blackbrook
Farm

Hanbury Park
Dingle

Blackbrook

26

17   A   18   B   19   C

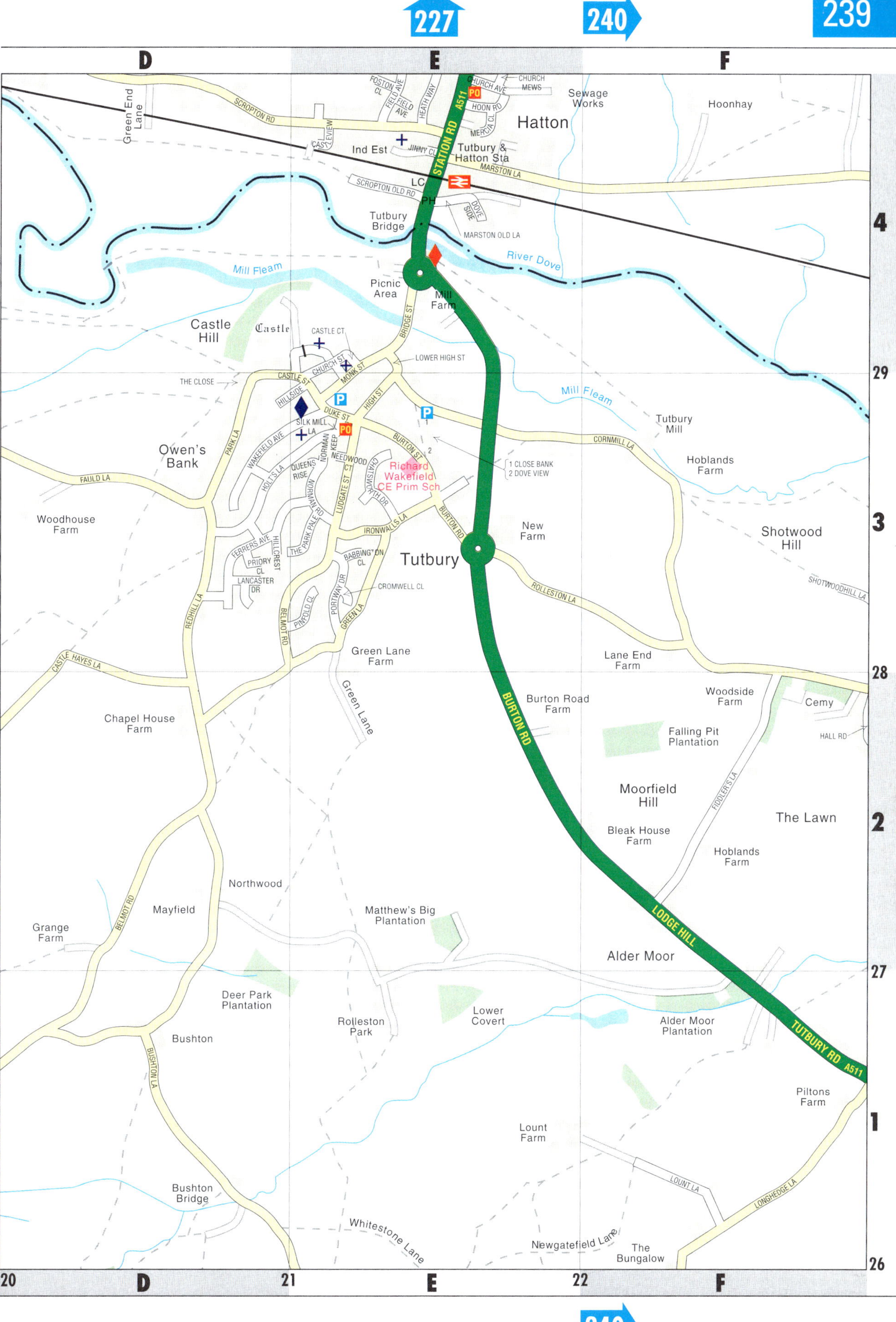
D
E
F
Hatton
Sewage Works
Hoonhay
Tutbury & Hatton Sta
Ind Est
STATION RD
A511
SCROPTON RD
SCROPTON OLD RD
MARSTON LA
MARSTON OLD LA
CHURCH AVE
CHURCH MEWS
HOON RD
MERCIA CL
JINNY CL
FOSTON CL
FIELD AVE
HEATH WAY
DOVE SIDE
Tutbury Bridge
River Dove
Mill Fleam
Picnic Area
Mill Farm
Castle Hill
Castle
CASTLE CT
CASTLE ST
CHURCH ST
MONK ST
LOWER HIGH ST
BRIDGE ST
HIGH ST
DUKE ST
THE CLOSE
HILLSIDE
SILK MILL LA
BURTON ST
1 CLOSE BANK
2 DOVE VIEW
Richard Wakefield CE Prim Sch
Owen's Bank
PARK LA
WAKEFIELD AVE
HOLTS LA
QUEENS RISE
NORMAN KEEP
NORMAN RD
NEEDWOOD CT
LUDGATE ST
CHATSWORTH DR
THE PARK PALE
IRONWALLS LA
FERRERS AVE
PRIORY CL
HILLCREST
LANCASTER DR
BABBINGTON CL
CROMWELL CL
PORTWAY DR
PINFOLD CL
GREEN LA
BELMOT RD
REDHILL LA
Tutbury
BURTON RD
CORNMILL LA
Tutbury Mill
Hoblands Farm
Shotwood Hill
SHOTWOODHILL LA
New Farm
ROLLESTON LA
Lane End Farm
FAULD LA
Woodhouse Farm
Green End Lane
Green Lane Farm
Green Lane
CASTLE HAYES LA
Chapel House Farm
Burton Road Farm
Woodside Farm
Cemy
HALL RD
Falling Pit Plantation
Moorfield Hill
FIDDLER'S LA
The Lawn
Bleak House Farm
Hoblands Farm
Northwood
Mayfield
Grange Farm
Matthew's Big Plantation
LODGE HILL
Alder Moor
Deer Park Plantation
Rolleston Park
Lower Covert
Alder Moor Plantation
TUTBURY RD
Bushton
BUSHTON LA
Piltons Farm
Lount Farm
LOUNT LA
LONGHEDGE LA
Bushton Bridge
Whitestone Lane
Newgatefield Lane
The Bungalow
PO
LC
PH
P
4
29
3
28
2
27
1
26
20
21
22

239
228

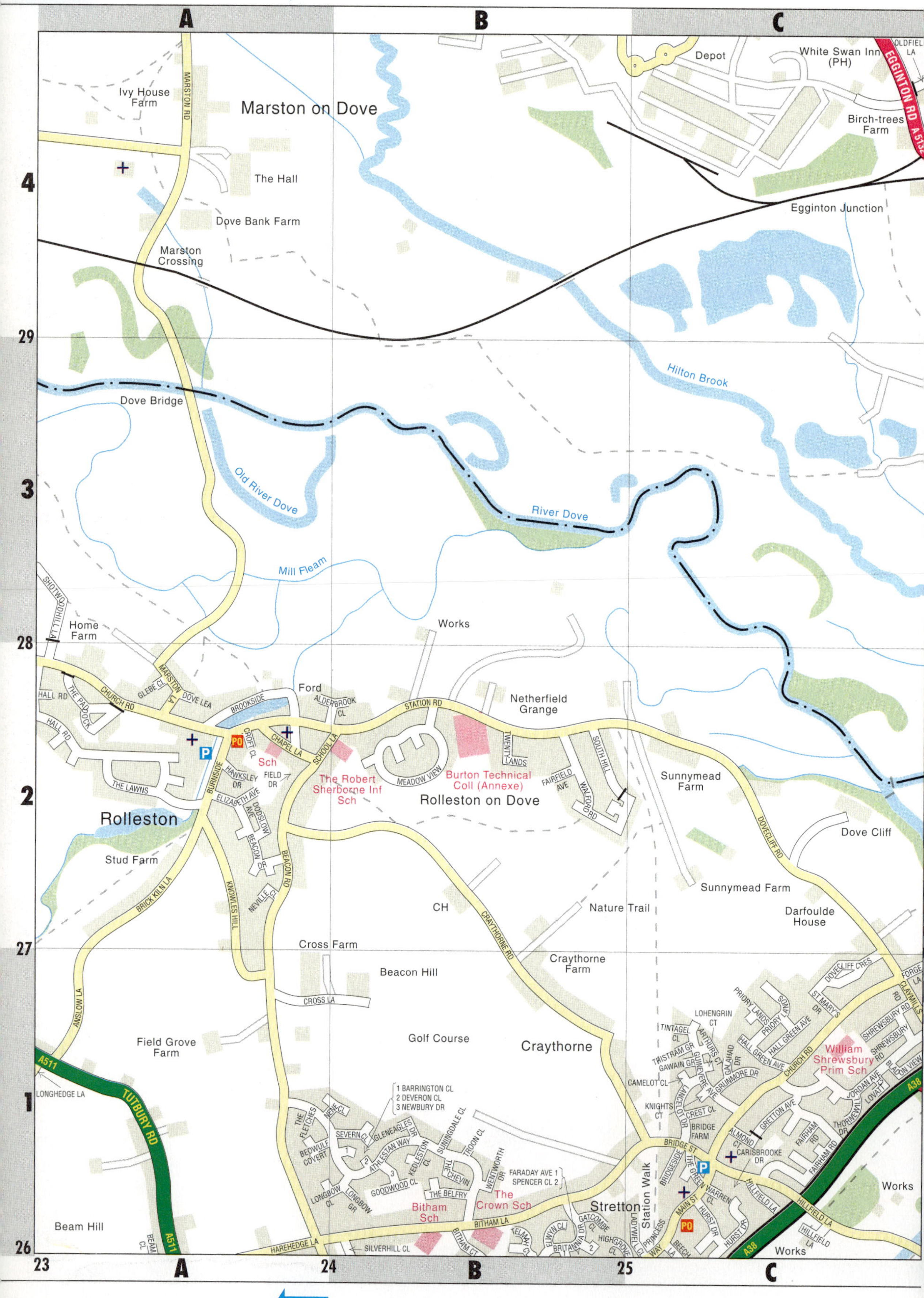
A
B
C
4
29
3
28
2
27
1
26
23
24
25
Ivy House Farm
Marston on Dove
MARSTON RD
The Hall
Dove Bank Farm
Marston Crossing
Depot
White Swan Inn (PH)
EGGINTON RD
Birch-trees Farm
Egginton Junction
Hilton Brook
Dove Bridge
Old River Dove
River Dove
Mill Fleam
Works
Home Farm
SHOTWOODHILL LA
HALL RD
THE PADDOCK
CHURCH RD
GLEBE CL
MARSTON LA
DOVE LEA
BROOKSIDE
Ford
ALDERBROOK CL
STATION RD
Netherfield Grange
CROFT CL
CHAPEL LA
SCHOOL LA
Sch
THE LAWNS
BURNSIDE
HAWKSLEY DR
FIELD DR
The Robert Sherborne Inf Sch
MEADOW VIEW
Burton Technical Coll (Annexe)
TWENTY LANDS
FAIRFIELD AVE
SOUTH HILL
WALFORD RD
Sunnymead Farm
Rolleston
ELIZABETH AVE
DODSLOW AVE
Rolleston on Dove
DOVECLIFF RD
Dove Cliff
Stud Farm
BEACON DR
BEACON RD
BRICK KILN LA
KNOWLES HILL
NEVILLE CL
CH
CRAYTHORNE RD
Nature Trail
Sunnymead Farm
Darfoulde House
Cross Farm
Craythorne Farm
Beacon Hill
CROSS LA
ANSLOW LA
Field Grove Farm
Golf Course
Craythorne
LOHENGRIN CT
TINTAGEL CL
TRISTRAM GR
GAWAIN GR
CAMELOT CL
KNIGHTS CT
PRIORY LANDS
HALL GREEN AVE
DOVECLIFF CRES
ST MARY'S DR
FORGE LA
CLAYMILLS RD
SHREWSBURY RD
William Shrewsbury Prim Sch
CHURCH RD
A511
LONGHEDGE LA
TUTBURY RD
1 BARRINGTON CL
2 DEVERON CL
3 NEWBURY DR
THE FLETCHES
NENE CL
SEVERN CL
GLENEAGLES DR
ATHLESTAN WAY
SUNINGDALE CL
TROON CL
BEOWULF COVERT
KEDLESTON CL
THE CHEVIN
WENTWORTH DR
FARADAY AVE 1
SPENCER CL 2
LONGBOW CL
LONGBOW GR
GOODWOOD CL
THE BELFRY
Bitham Sch
The Crown Sch
BITHAM LA
Stretton
Station Walk
BRIDGE ST
BRIDGESIDE
THE GREEN
WARREN CL
CARISBROOKE DR
GRETTON AVE
FAIRHAM RD
ALMOND CL
HILLFIELD LA
A38
Works
Beam Hill
BEAM CL
HAREHEDGE LA
SILVERHILL CL
BITHAM CT
ELMHURST CL
ELWYN CL
BRITANNIA DR
GATCOMBE CL
HIGHGROVE CL
LADYWELL CL
PRINCESS WAY
MAIN ST
HURST DR
BEECH LA
PO
P

239

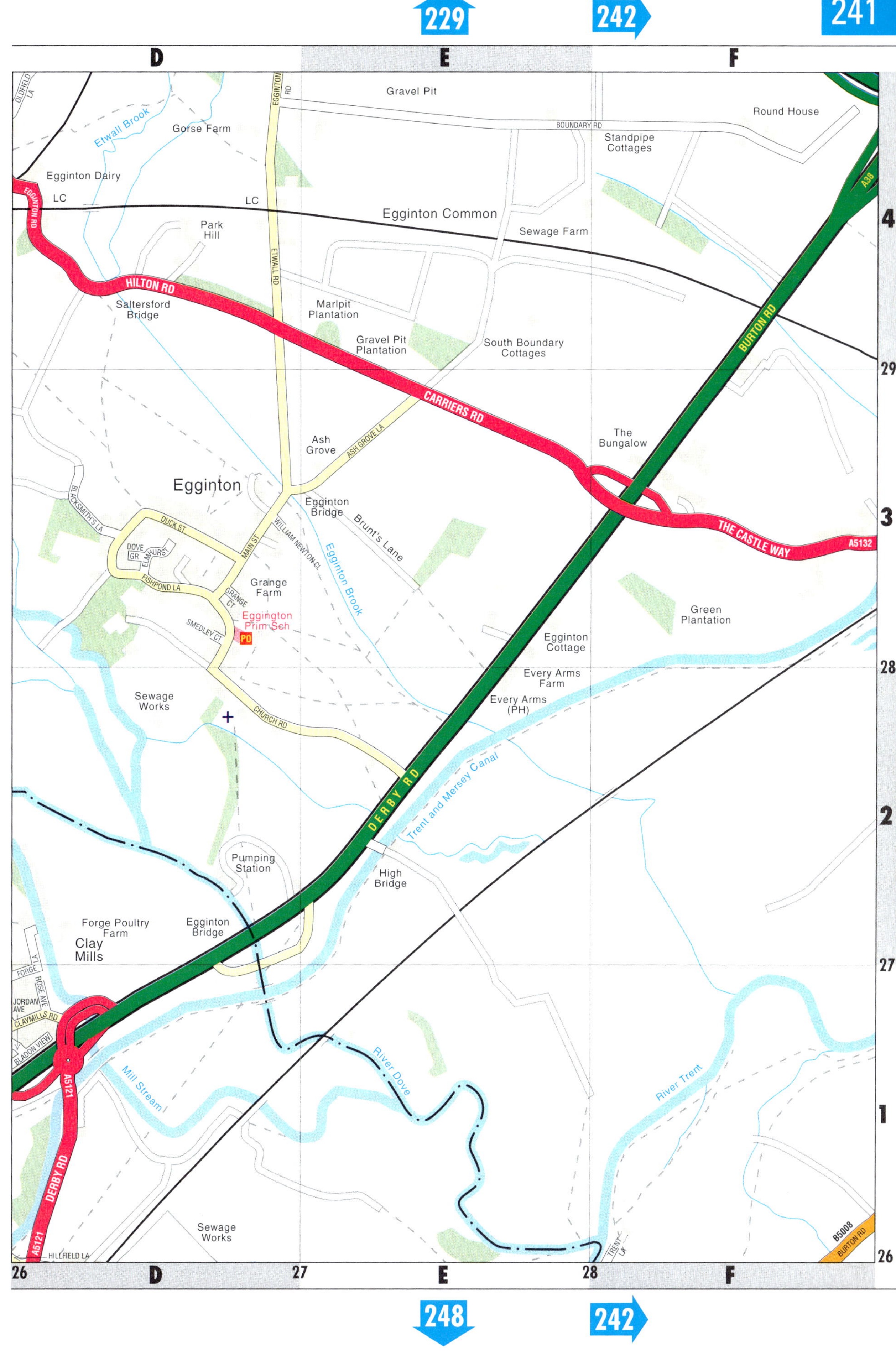
D
E
F
Gravel Pit
Round House
Gorse Farm
Etwall Brook
BOUNDARY RD
Standpipe Cottages
Egginton Dairy
LC
LC
A38
Egginton Common
Park Hill
Sewage Farm
HILTON RD
Saltersford Bridge
Marlpit Plantation
Gravel Pit Plantation
South Boundary Cottages
BURTON RD
CARRIERS RD
Ash Grove
ASH GROVE LA
The Bungalow
Egginton
Egginton Bridge
Brunt's Lane
BLACKSMITH'S LA
DUCK ST
MAIN ST
WILLIAM NEWTON CL
THE CASTLE WAY
A5132
Egginton Brook
FISHPOND LA
Grange Farm
GRANGE CT
Eggington Prim Sch
SMEDLEY CT
PO
Green Plantation
Egginton Cottage
Every Arms Farm
Every Arms (PH)
Sewage Works
CHURCH RD
Trent and Mersey Canal
DERBY RD
Pumping Station
High Bridge
Forge Poultry Farm
Egginton Bridge
Clay Mills
FORGE LA
ROSE AVE
JORDAN AVE
CLAYMILLS RD
BLADON VIEW
River Dove
Mill Stream
A5121
River Trent
DERBY RD
A5121
Sewage Works
HILLFIELD LA
TRENT LA
B5008
BURTON RD
EGGINTON RD
ETWALL RD
EGGINTON RD
OLDFIELD LA
4
29
3
28
2
27
1
26
26
27
28

241
230

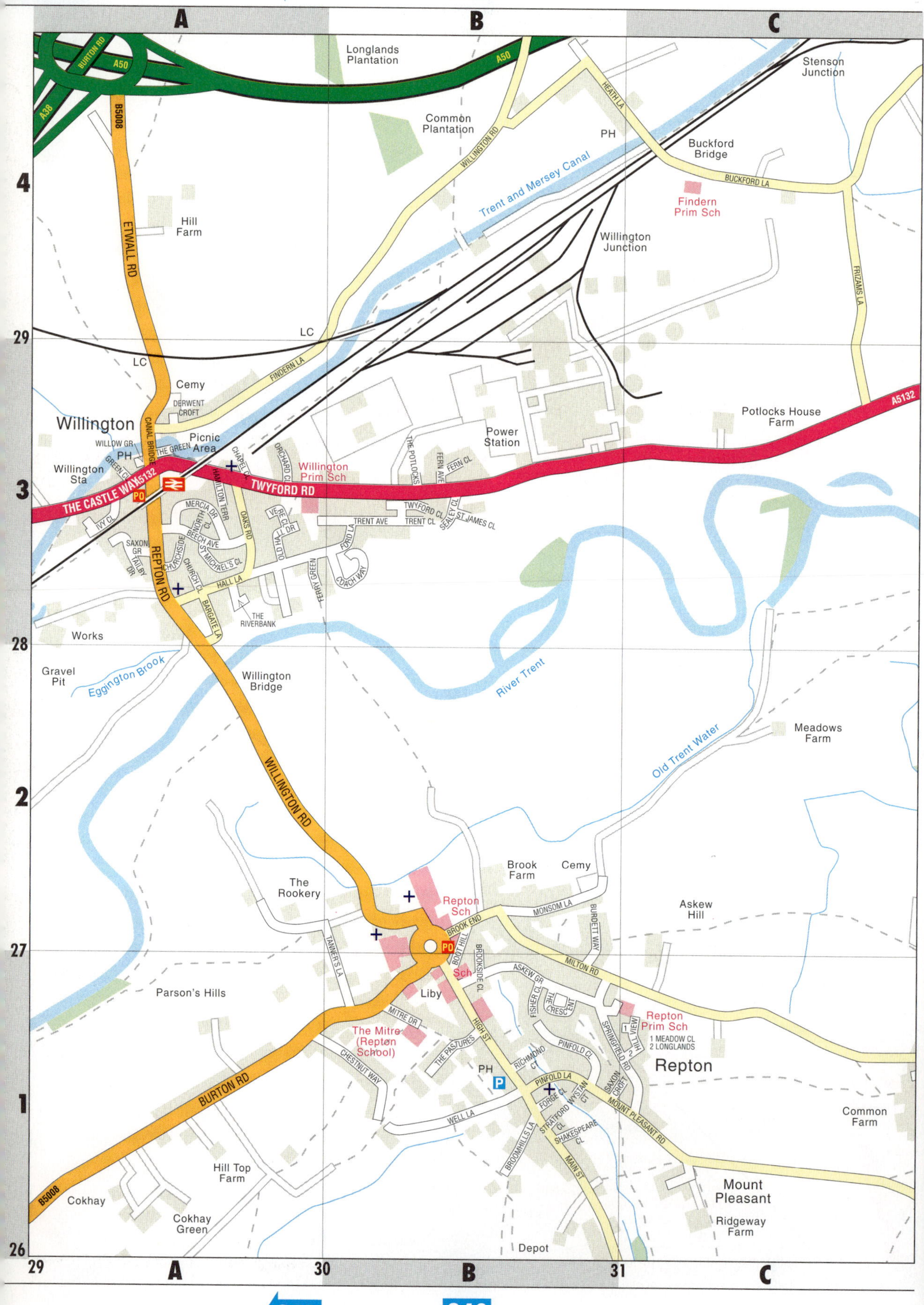
A
B
C
Longlands Plantation
Common Plantation
Stenson Junction
Buckford Bridge
Findern Prim Sch
Trent and Mersey Canal
Willington Junction
Hill Farm
ETWALL RD
B5008
A50
A38
BURTON RD
WILLINGTON RD
HEATH LA
BUCKFORD LA
FRIZAMS LA
PH
LC
FINDERN LA
Cemy
DERWENT CROFT
Willington
Picnic Area
Power Station
Potlocks House Farm
A5132
Willington Sta
Willington Prim Sch
THE CASTLE WAY
TWYFORD RD
CANAL BRIDGE
THE GREEN
WILLOW GR
GREEN CL
CHAPEL CL
ORCHARD CL
THE POTLOCKS
FERN AVE
FERN CL
TWYFORD CL
SEALEY CL
ST JAMES CL
TRENT AVE
TRENT CL
HAMILTON TERR
MERCIA DR
BEECH AVE
OAKS RD
ST MICHAEL'S CL
CHURCH CL
CHURCHSIDE
SAXON GR
TAILBY DR
IVY CL
REPTON RD
HALL LA
BARGATE LA
THE RIVERBANK
FERRY GREEN
FORD LA
COACH WAY
OLD HALL DR
Works
Gravel Pit
Eggington Brook
Willington Bridge
River Trent
Old Trent Water
Meadows Farm
WILLINGTON RD
The Rookery
Brook Farm
Cemy
Repton Sch
MONSOM LA
BURDETT WAY
Askew Hill
BROOK END
BOOT HILL
BROOKSIDE CL
TANNER'S LA
PO
Sch
Liby
MILTON RD
ASKEW GR
FISHER CL
THE CRESCENT
Repton Prim Sch
Parson's Hills
MITRE DR
The Mitre (Repton School)
HIGH ST
THE PASTURES
CHESTNUT WAY
PINFOLD CL
SPRINGFIELD RD
HILL VIEW
1 MEADOW CL
2 LONGLANDS
Repton
RICHMOND CT
PINFOLD LA
PH
P
BURTON RD
WELL LA
FORGE CL
STRATFORD CL
WYSTAN CT
SAXON CROFT
MOUNT PLEASANT RD
SHAKESPEARE CL
BROOMHILLS LA
MAIN ST
Common Farm
Mount Pleasant
Ridgeway Farm
Hill Top Farm
Cokhay
Cokhay Green
Depot
B5008
4
29
3
28
2
27
1
26
29
30
31

241
249

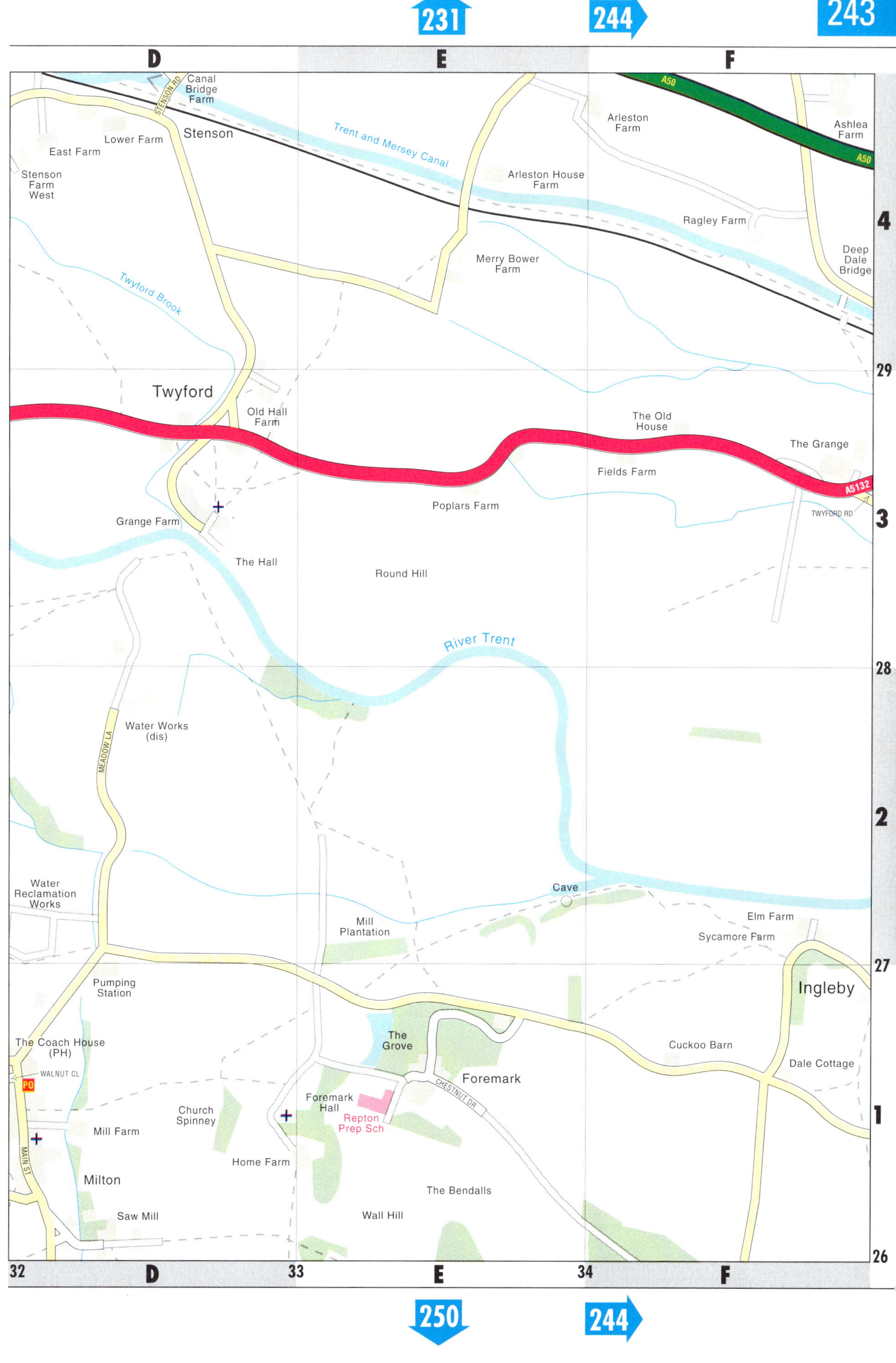
D
E
F
Canal Bridge Farm
STENSON RD
Stenson
Lower Farm
East Farm
Stenson Farm West
Trent and Mersey Canal
A50
Arleston Farm
Ashlea Farm
Arleston House Farm
Ragley Farm
Deep Dale Bridge
Merry Bower Farm
Twyford Brook
Twyford
Old Hall Farm
The Old House
The Grange
Fields Farm
A5132
Poplars Farm
TWYFORD RD
Grange Farm
The Hall
Round Hill
River Trent
Water Works (dis)
MEADOW LA
Water Reclamation Works
Cave
Mill Plantation
Elm Farm
Sycamore Farm
Pumping Station
Ingleby
The Grove
Cuckoo Barn
The Coach House (PH)
Dale Cottage
WALNUT CL
PO
Foremark
CHESTNUT DR
Foremark Hall
Church Spinney
Repton Prep Sch
Mill Farm
MAIN ST
Home Farm
Milton
The Bendalls
Saw Mill
Wall Hill
4
29
3
28
2
27
1
26
32
33
34

243
232

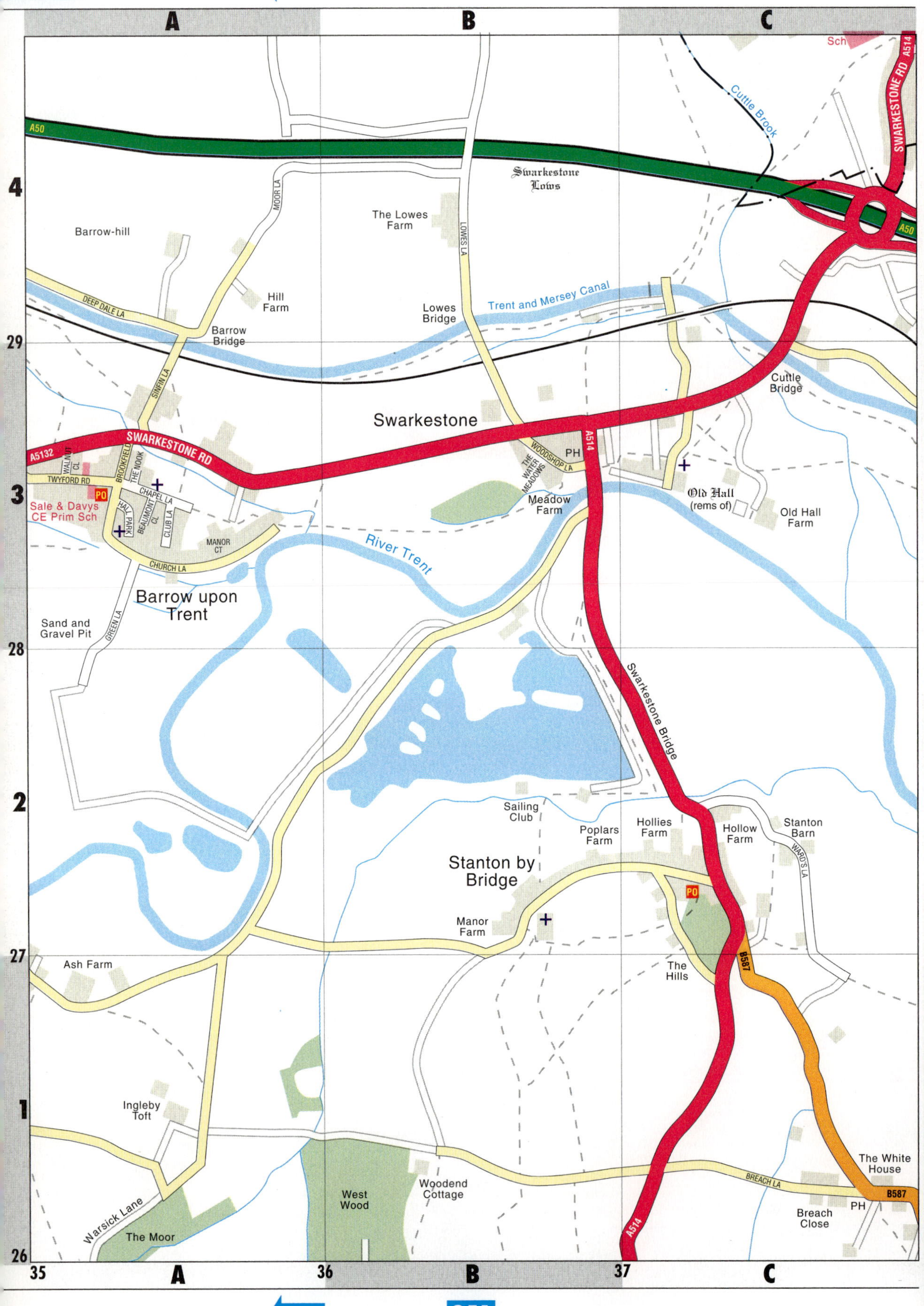
A
B
C
4
29
3
28
2
27
1
26
35
36
37
A50
A514
SWARKESTONE RD
Sch
Cuttle Brook
Swarkestone
Lows
The Lowes
Farm
Barrow-hill
MOOR LA
LOWES LA
Hill
Farm
DEEP DALE LA
Barrow
Bridge
Lowes
Bridge
Trent and Mersey Canal
Cuttle
Bridge
SINFIN LA
Swarkestone
A5132
SWARKESTONE RD
WALNUT CL
TWYFORD RD
BROOKFIELD
THE NOOK
CHAPEL LA
PO
Sale & Davys
CE Prim Sch
HALL PARK
BEAUMONT CL
CLUB LA
MANOR CT
CHURCH LA
WOODSHOP LA
THE WATER MEADOWS
PH
Meadow
Farm
Old Hall
(rems of)
Old Hall
Farm
River Trent
Barrow upon
Trent
Sand and
Gravel Pit
GREEN LA
Swarkestone Bridge
Sailing
Club
Poplars
Farm
Hollies
Farm
Hollow
Farm
Stanton
Barn
WARD'S LA
Stanton by
Bridge
PO
Manor
Farm
B587
The
Hills
Ash Farm
Ingleby
Toft
West
Wood
Woodend
Cottage
BREACH LA
The White
House
B587
PH
Breach
Close
Warsick Lane
The Moor
A514

233
246

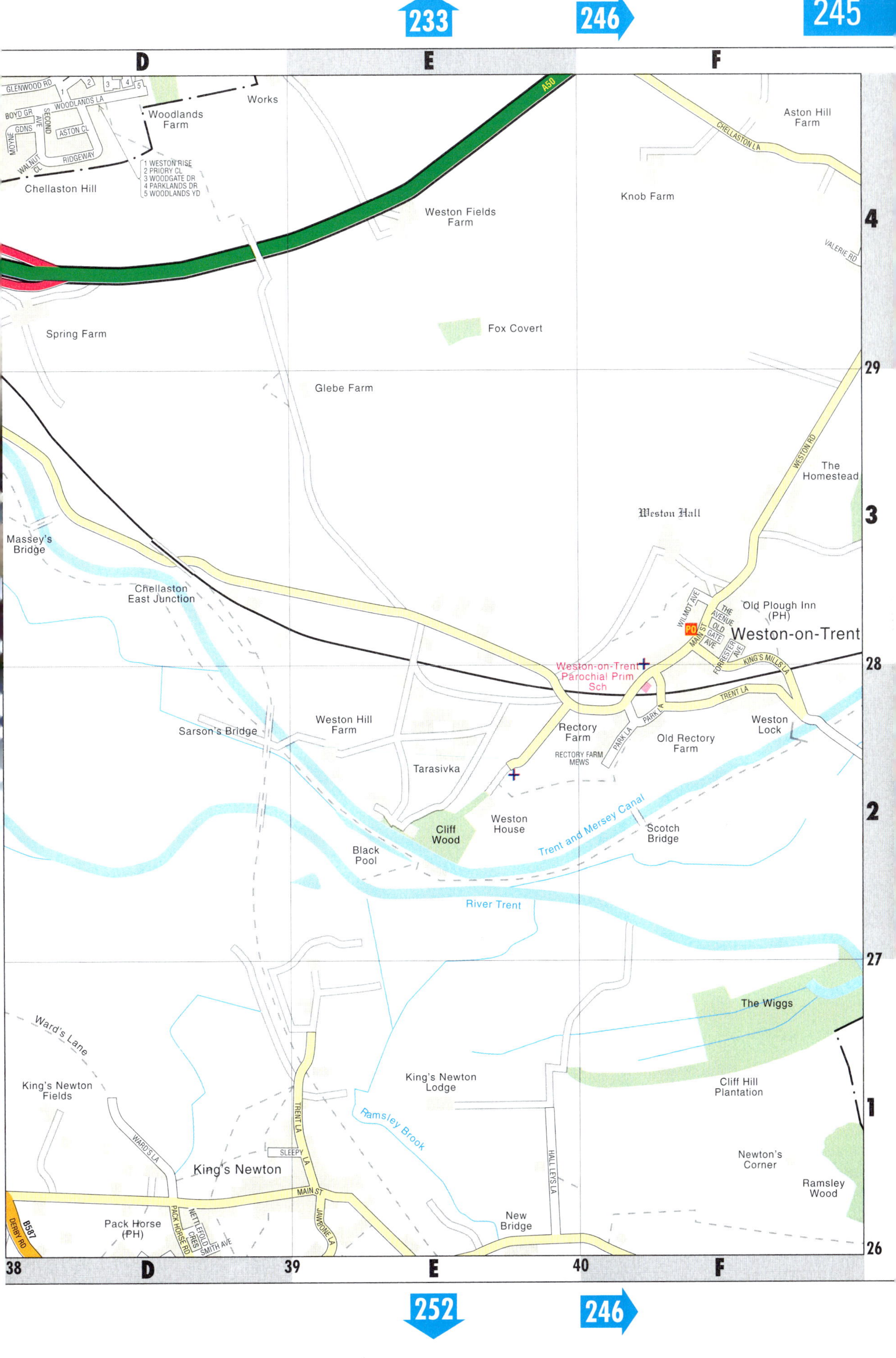
D
E
F
GLENWOOD RD
WOODLANDS LA
BOYD GR
GDNS
SECOND AVE
ASTON CL
MOYNE
WALNUT CL
RIDGEWAY
Works
Woodlands Farm
1 WESTON RISE
2 PRIORY CL
3 WOODGATE DR
4 PARKLANDS DR
5 WOODLANDS YD
Chellaston Hill
A50
CHELLASTON LA
Aston Hill Farm
Knob Farm
Weston Fields Farm
4
VALERIE RD
Spring Farm
Fox Covert
29
Glebe Farm
WESTON RD
The Homestead
Weston Hall
3
Massey's Bridge
Chellaston East Junction
WILMOT AVE
THE AVENUE
OLD GATE AVE
FORRESTER AVE
MAIN ST
PO
Old Plough Inn (PH)
Weston-on-Trent
KING'S MILLS LA
Weston-on-Trent Parochial Prim Sch
28
TRENT LA
PARK LA
Sarson's Bridge
Weston Hill Farm
Rectory Farm
RECTORY FARM MEWS
Old Rectory Farm
Weston Lock
Tarasivka
2
Cliff Wood
Weston House
Trent and Mersey Canal
Scotch Bridge
Black Pool
River Trent
27
The Wiggs
Ward's Lane
King's Newton Fields
King's Newton Lodge
Cliff Hill Plantation
1
Ramsley Brook
WARD'S LA
TRENT LA
SLEEPY LA
King's Newton
HALL LEYS LA
Newton's Corner
Ramsley Wood
MAIN ST
Pack Horse (PH)
PACK HORSE RD
NETTLEFOLD CRES
SMITH AVE
JAWBONE LA
New Bridge
B587
DERBY RD
26
38
D
39
E
40
F

252
246

245
234

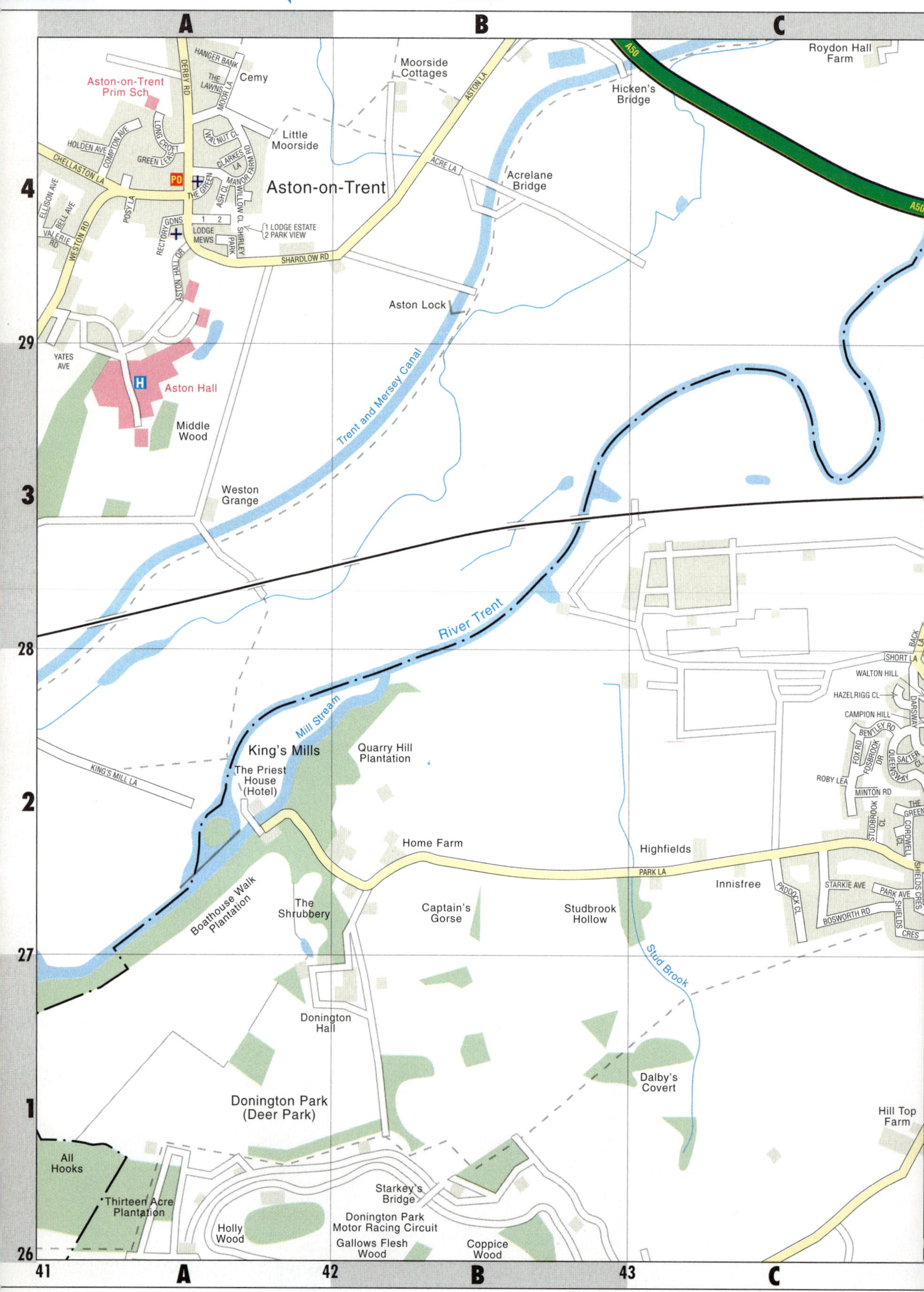
A
B
C
Aston-on-Trent
Aston-on-Trent Prim Sch
Cemy
Little Moorside
Moorside Cottages
Hicken's Bridge
Roydon Hall Farm
Acrelane Bridge
Aston Lock
Aston Hall
Middle Wood
Weston Grange
Trent and Mersey Canal
River Trent
Mill Stream
King's Mills
The Priest House (Hotel)
Quarry Hill Plantation
Home Farm
Highfields
Innisfree
Captain's Gorse
Studbrook Hollow
Boathouse Walk Plantation
The Shrubbery
Donington Hall
Stud Brook
Dalby's Covert
Donington Park (Deer Park)
Hill Top Farm
All Hooks
Thirteen Acre Plantation
Holly Wood
Starkey's Bridge
Donington Park Motor Racing Circuit
Gallows Flesh Wood
Coppice Wood
HANGER BANK
DERBY RD
THE LAWNS
MOOR LA
HOLDEN AVE
COMPTON AVE
LONG CROFT
GREEN LEAS
WALNUT CL
CLARKES LA
MANOR FARM RD
CHELLASTON LA
ELLISON AVE
BELL AVE
POSY LA
THE GREEN
ASH CL
WILLOW CL
SHIRLEY PARK
RECTORY GDNS
LODGE MEWS
1 LODGE ESTATE
2 PARK VIEW
VALERIE RD
WESTON RD
ASTON HALL DR
SHARDLOW RD
ASTON LA
ACRE LA
YATES AVE
KING'S MILL LA
PARK LA
A50
SHORT LA
BACK LA
WALTON HILL
HAZELRIGG CL
CAMPION HILL
DARSWAY
BENTLEY RD
FOX RD
FOSBROOK DR
SALTER CL
QUEENSWAY
ROBY LEA
MINTON RD
STUDBROOK CL
THE GREEN
CORDWELL CL
SHIELDS CRES
STARKIE AVE
PARK AVE
PADDOCK CL
BOSWORTH RD
4
29
3
28
2
27
1
26
41
42
43

245

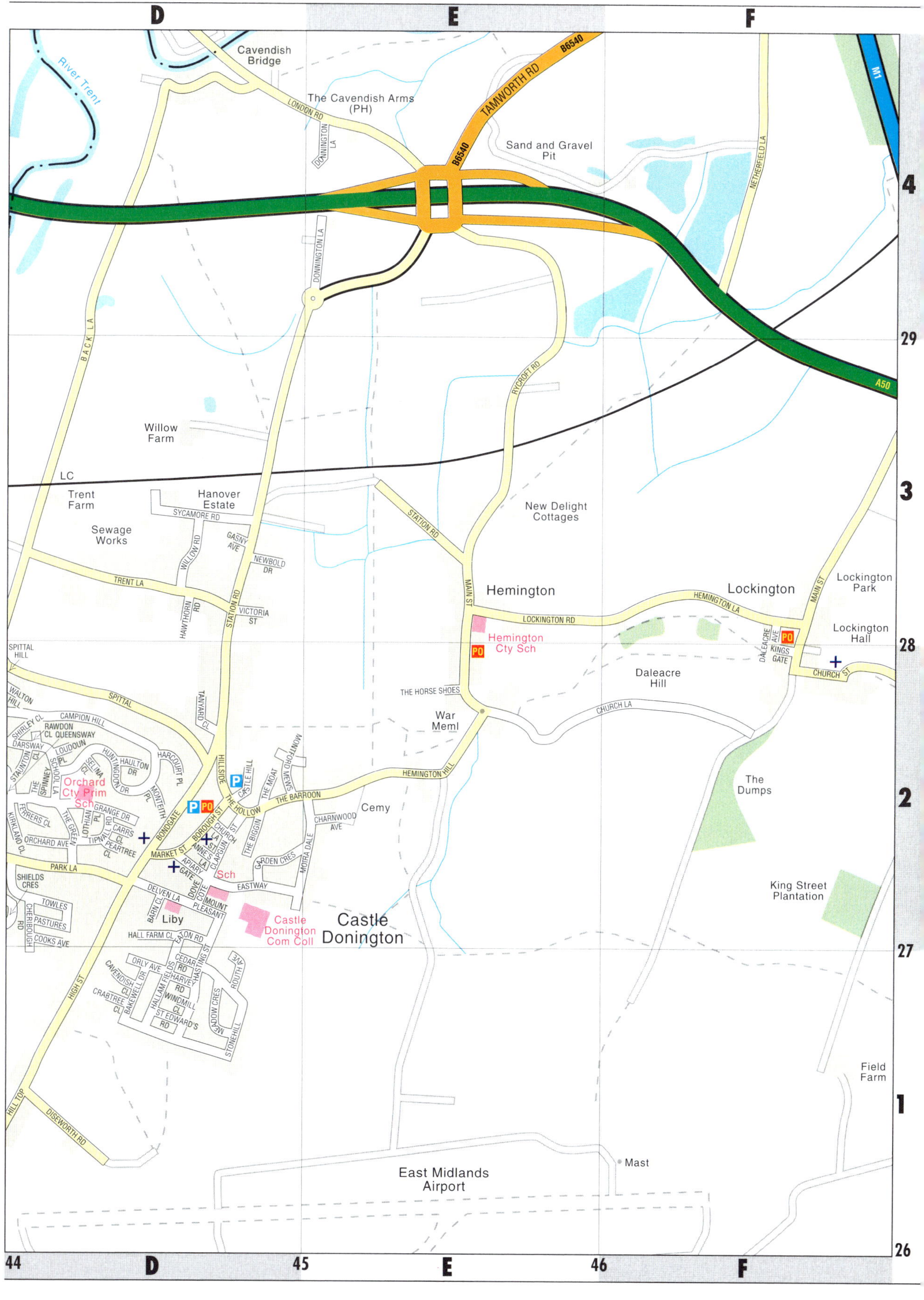
D
E
F
4
29
3
28
2
27
1
26
44
45
46
River Trent
Cavendish Bridge
The Cavendish Arms (PH)
LONDON RD
DONINGTON LA
TAMWORTH RD
B6540
Sand and Gravel Pit
NETHERFIELD LA
M1
A50
BACK LA
Willow Farm
LC
Trent Farm
Hanover Estate
SYCAMORE RD
Sewage Works
WILLOW RD
GASNY AVE
NEWBOLD DR
TRENT LA
HAWTHORN RD
STATION RD
VICTORIA ST
RYCROFT RD
New Delight Cottages
MAIN ST
Hemington
LOCKINGTON RD
Hemington Cty Sch
PO
Lockington
HEMINGTON LA
Lockington Park
Lockington Hall
DALEACRE AVE
KINGS GATE
CHURCH ST
Daleacre Hill
CHURCH LA
THE HORSE SHOES
War Meml
SPITTAL HILL
WALTON HILL
SPITTAL
CAMPION HILL
SHIRLEY CL
RAWDON CL
QUEENSWAY
DARSWAY
LOUDOUN PL
STAUNTON CL
THE SPINNEY
SCHOOL LA
SELINA CL
HUNTINGDON DR
HAULTON DR
HARCOURT PL
MONTEITH PL
TANYARD CL
HILLSIDE
CASTLE HILL
THE MOAT
MONTFORD MEWS
HEMINGTON HILL
THE BARROON
THE HOLLOW
Orchard Cty Prim Sch
P
FERRERS CL
THE GREEN
LOTHIAN PL
GRANGE DR
TIPNALL RD
CARRS CL
PEARTREE CL
KIRKLAND CL
ORCHARD AVE
BONDGATE
BOROUGH ST
CHURCH ST
ANNES CL
CLAPGUN ST
THE BIGGIN
CHARNWOOD AVE
Cemy
MARKET ST
APIARY GATE
MOIRA DALE
GARDEN CRES
Sch
EASTWAY
PARK LA
SHIELDS CRES
DELVEN LA
DOVECOTE
MOUNT PLEASANT
Castle Donington Com Coll
Castle Donington
TOWLES PASTURES
CHERIBOUGH RD
BARN CL
Liby
COOKS AVE
HALL FARM CL
EATON RD
HASTINGS ST
ORLY AVE
CEDAR RD
CAVENDISH CL
HARVEY RD
CRABTREE CL
BAKEWELL DR
HALLAM FIELDS
WINDMILL CL
ST EDWARD'S RD
MEADOW CRES
ROUTH AVE
STONEHILL
HIGH ST
HILL TOP
DISEWORTH RD
The Dumps
King Street Plantation
Field Farm
Mast
East Midlands Airport

241

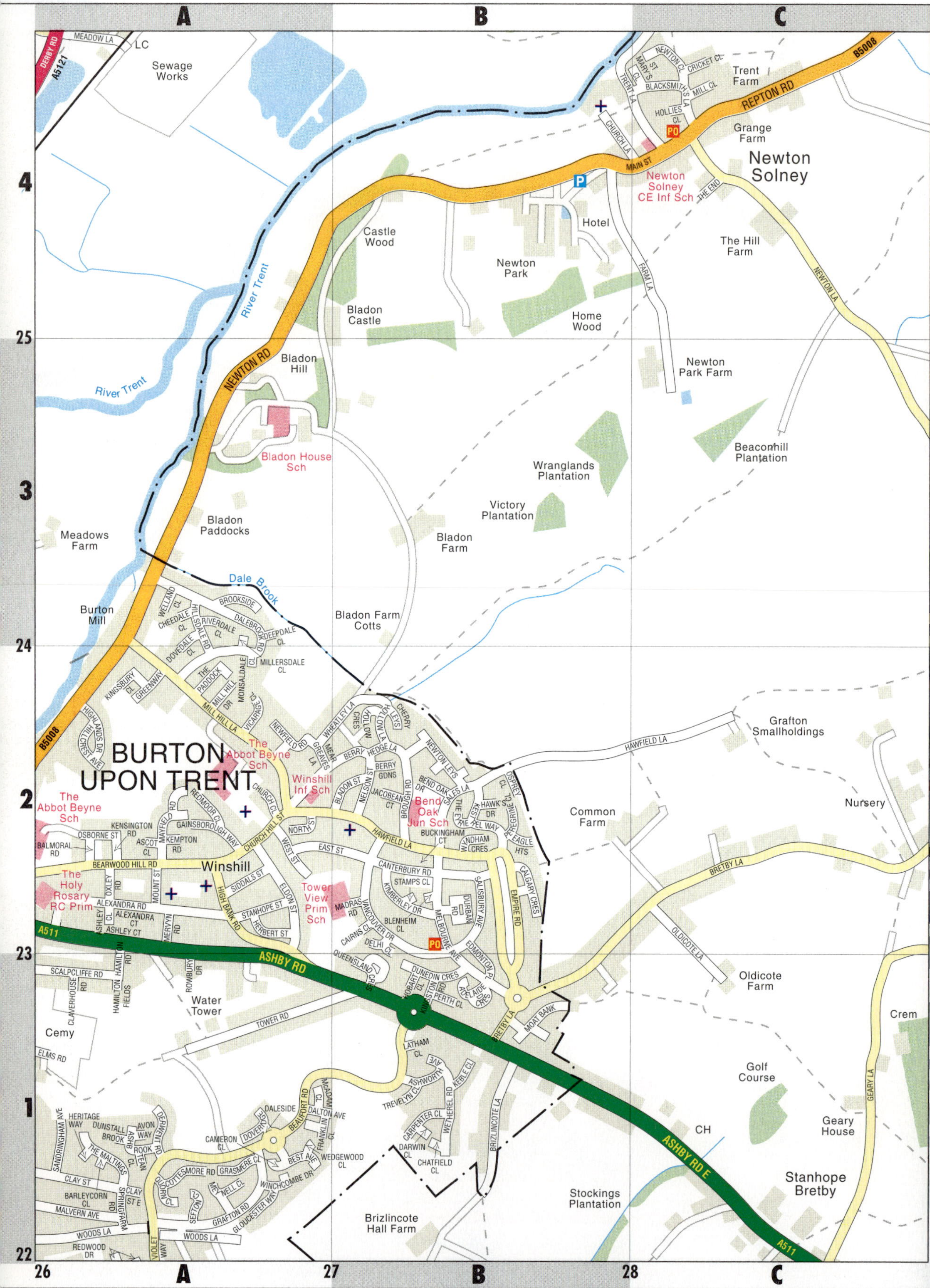

A
B
C
4
25
3
24
2
23
1
22
26
27
28
Sewage Works
LC
MEADOW LA
DERBY RD
A5121
River Trent
Castle Wood
Bladon Castle
Bladon Hill
NEWTON RD
Bladon House Sch
Bladon Paddocks
Meadows Farm
Burton Mill
Dale Brook
Bladon Farm Cotts
Bladon Farm
Victory Plantation
Wranglands Plantation
Newton Park
Home Wood
Hotel
FARM LA
Newton Park Farm
Beaconhill Plantation
The Hill Farm
NEWTON LA
Newton Solney
Newton Solney CE Inf Sch
THE END
Grange Farm
Trent Farm
REPTON RD
B5008
MAIN ST
CHURCH LA
TRENT LA
NEWTON CL
CRICKET CL
BLACKSMITHS LA
MILL CL
HOLLIES CL
PO
P
Grafton Smallholdings
HAWFIELD LA
Nursery
Common Farm
BRETBY LA
OLDICOTE LA
Oldicote Farm
Crem
Golf Course
GEARY LA
Geary House
Stanhope Bretby
CH
Stockings Plantation
Brizlincote Hall Farm
BRIZLINCOTE LA
ASHBY RD E
A511
ASHBY RD
BURTON UPON TRENT
Winshill
The Abbot Beyne Sch
Winshill Inf Sch
Bend Oak Jun Sch
Tower View Prim Sch
The Holy Rosary RC Prim
Water Tower
Cemy
TOWER RD
ELMS RD
MILL HILL LA
KINGSBURY CL
GREENWAY
BEARWOOD HILL RD
CHURCH HILL ST
HIGH BANK RD
EAST ST
NORTH ST
WEST ST
CANTERBURY RD
EMPIRE RD
SALISBURY AVE
CALGARY CRES
BRETBY LA
MOAT BANK
LATHAM CL
ASHWORTH AVE
KEBLE CL
TREVELYN CL
WETHEREL RD
CARPENTER CL
DARWIN CL
CHATFIELD CL
WEDGEWOOD CL
DALTON AVE
BEAUFORT RD
DALESIDE
CAMERON CL
GRASMERE CL
WINCHCOMBE DR
GLOUCESTER WAY
GRAFTON RD
SEFTON
COTTESMORE RD
WOODS LA
VIOLET WAY
REDWOOD DR
MALVERN AVE
BARLEYCORN CL
CLAY ST
SANDRINGHAM AVE
HERITAGE WAY
DUNSTALL BROOK
THE MALTINGS
SPRINGFARM RD
SCALPCLIFFE RD
CLAWERHOUSE RD
HAMILTON FIELDS
HAMILTON RD
ROWBURY DR
ALEXANDRA RD
ASHLEY CT
OXLEY RD
MOUNT ST
BALMORAL RD
OSBORNE ST
KENSINGTON RD
ASCOT CL
KEMPTON RD
GAINSBOROUGH WAY
REDMOOR CL
MAYFIELD RD
SIDDALS ST
STANHOPE ST
HERBERT ST
ELDON ST
MADRAS RD
VANCOUVER DR
CAIRNS CL
DELHI CL
QUEENSLAND CRES
DUNEDIN CRES
HOBART CL
KINGSTON DR
PERTH CL
ADELAIDE CRES
EDMONTON PL
BLENHEIM CL
KIMBERLEY DR
STAMPS CL
MELBOURNE AVE
DURBAN RD
BUCKINGHAM CT
WYNDHAM CRES
HAWFIELD LA
EAGLE HTS
PEREGRINE CL
OSPREY CL
KESTREL WAY
HAWK'S DR
THE EYRIE
SALES LA
BEND OAK DR
NEWTON LEYS
BROUGH RD
JACOBEAN CT
BERRY GDNS
BERRY HEDGE LA
NELSON ST
BLADON ST
MEAR GREAVES LA
WHEATLEY LA
HOLLOW CRES
CHERRY LEYS
NEWFIELD RD
VICARAGE CL
MONSALDALE CL
MILLERSDALE CL
DEEPDALE CL
DALEBROOK RD
RIVERDALE CL
BROOKSIDE
WELLAND CL
CHEEDALE CL
HILLSDALE RD
DOVEDALE CL
THE PADDOCK
MILL HILL DR
HIGHLANDS DR
HILLCREST AVE

255

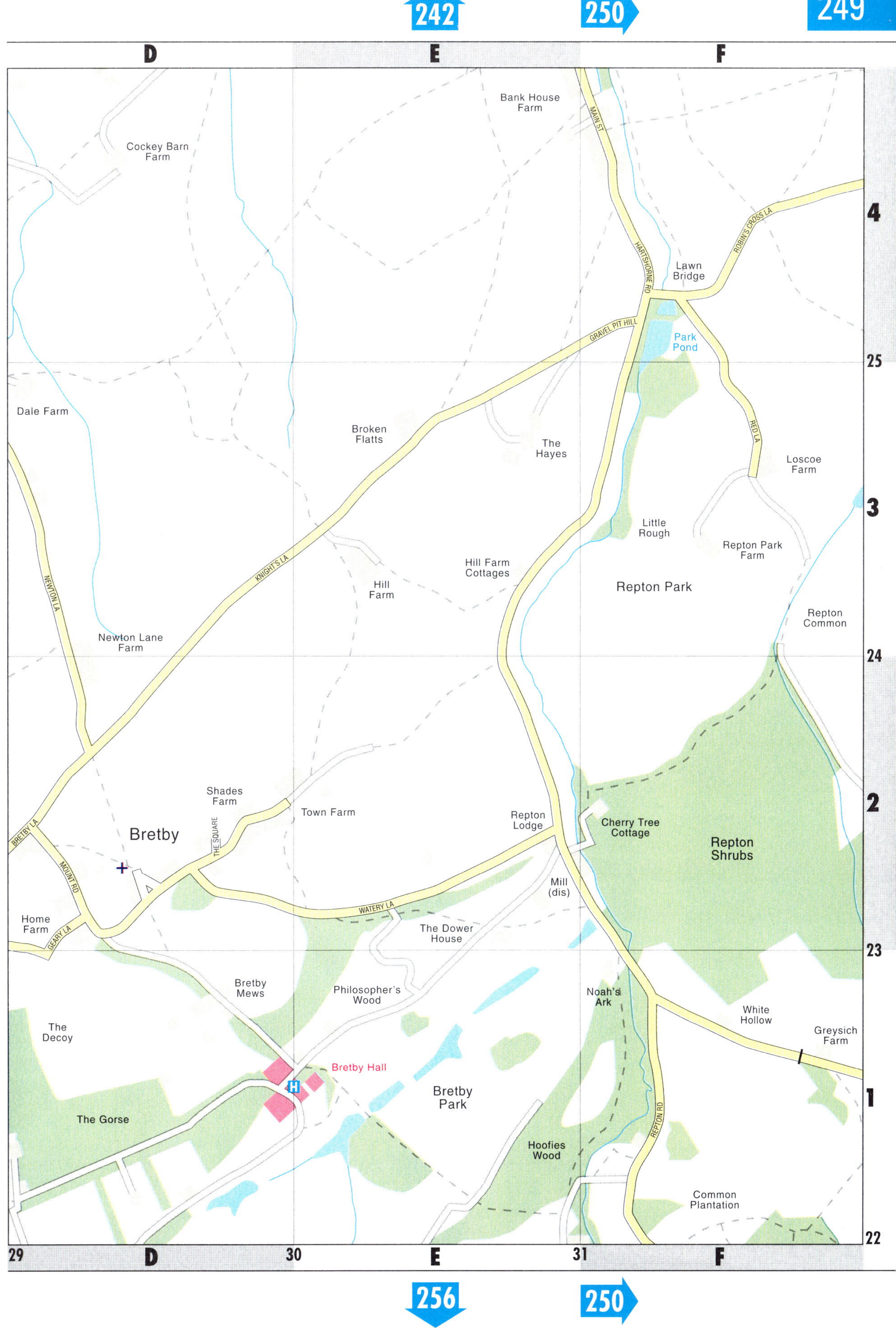

D
E
F

Bank House
Farm

MAIN ST

Cockey Barn
Farm

HARTSHORNE RD

ROBINS CROSS LA

Lawn
Bridge

4

GRAVEL PIT HILL

Park
Pond

RED LA

25

Dale Farm

Broken
Flatts

The Hayes

Loscoe
Farm

NEWTON LA

KNIGHT'S LA

Hill Farm
Cottages

Little
Rough

Repton Park
Farm

Repton
Common

3

Repton Park

Newton Lane
Farm

Hill
Farm

24

Shades
Farm

Town Farm

Repton
Lodge

Cherry Tree
Cottage

Repton
Shrubs

2

BRETBY LA

Bretby

THE SQUARE

MOUNT RD

Mill
(dis)

Home
Farm

GEARY LA

WATERY LA

The Dower
House

23

Bretby
Mews

Philosopher's
Wood

Noah's
Ark

White
Hollow

Greysich
Farm

The
Decoy

Bretby Hall

H

Bretby
Park

REPTON RD

1

The Gorse

Hoofies
Wood

Common
Plantation

22

29
D
30
E
31
F

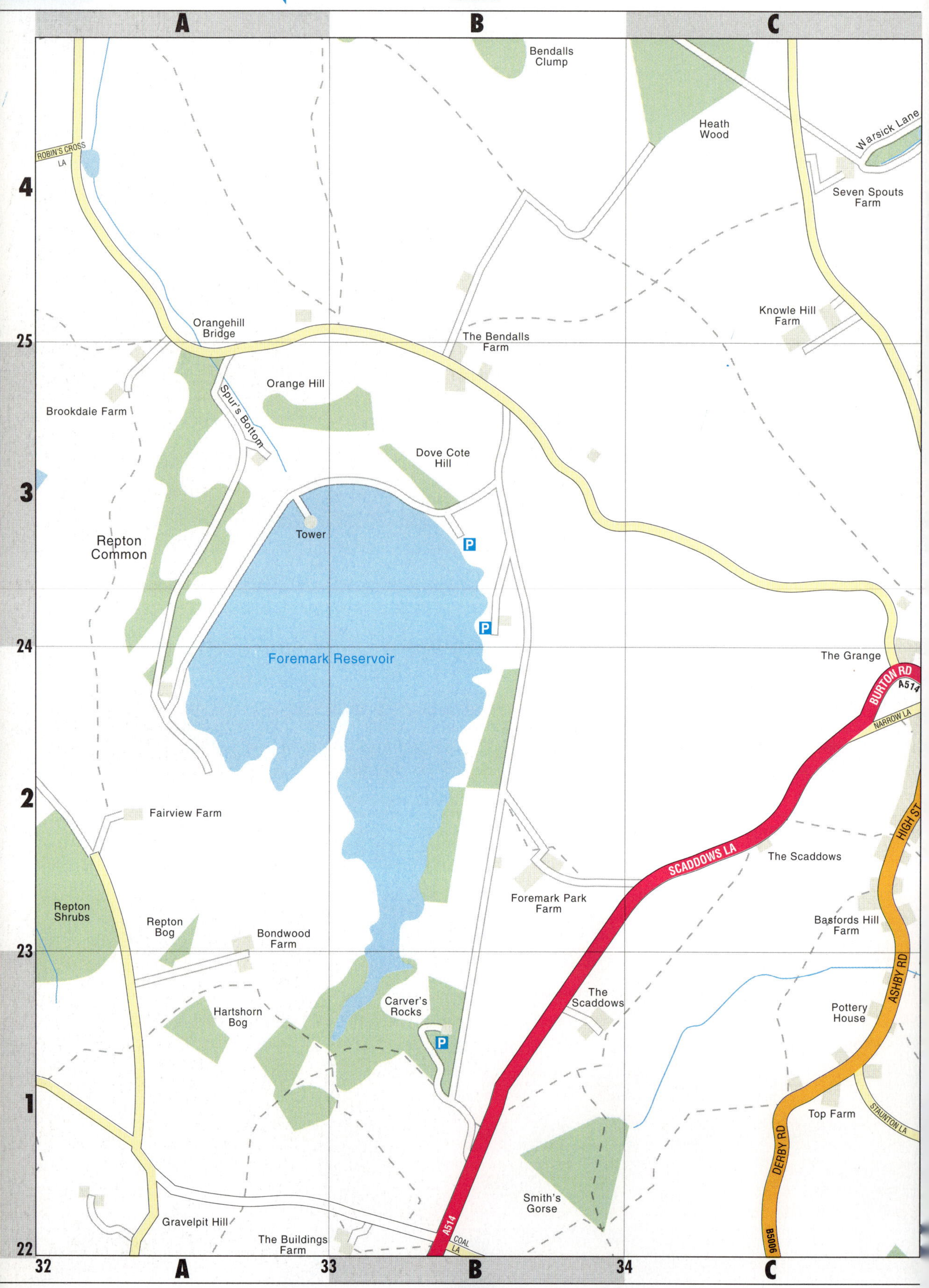

Bendalls
Clump

Heath
Wood

Warsick Lane

Seven Spouts
Farm

4

ROBIN'S CROSS
LA

Knowle Hill
Farm

Orangehill
Bridge

The Bendalls
Farm

25

Orange Hill

Brookdale Farm

SPUR'S BOTTOM

Dove Cote
Hill

3

Tower

P

Repton
Common

P

The Grange

BURTON RD
A514

24 Foremark Reservoir

NARROW LA

HIGH ST

2

Fairview Farm

SCADDOWS LA

The Scaddows

Repton
Shrubs

Basfords Hill
Farm

Repton
Bog

Bondwood
Farm

Foremark Park
Farm

ASHBY RD

23

The
Scaddows

Pottery
House

Hartshorn
Bog

Carver's
Rocks

P

DERBY RD

1

Top Farm

STAUNTON LA

Gravelpit Hill

Smith's
Gorse

B5006

22 The Buildings
Farm

A514

COAL
LA

32 A 33 B 34 C

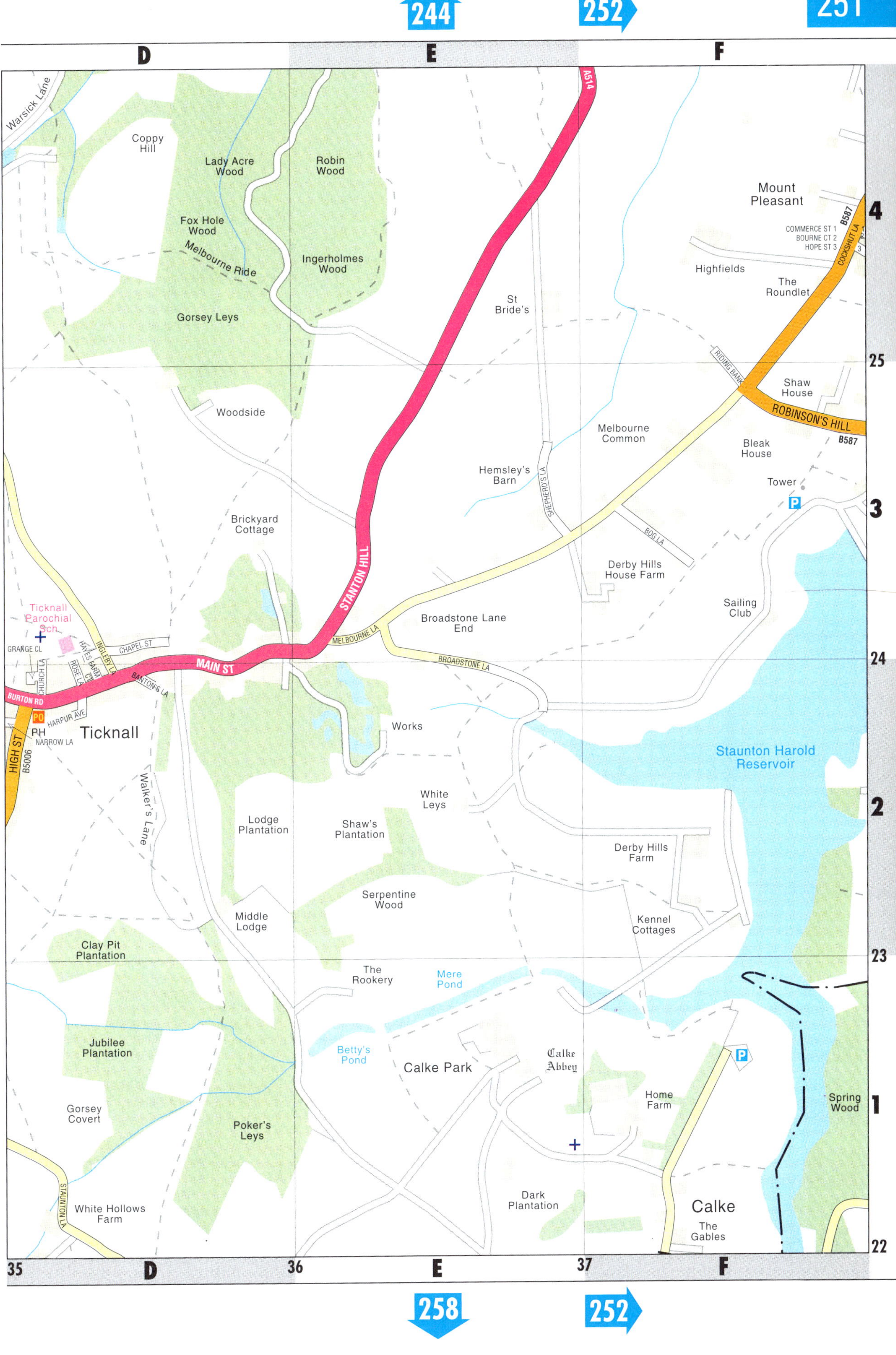
D
E
F
Warsick Lane
Coppy Hill
Lady Acre Wood
Robin Wood
Fox Hole Wood
Melbourne Ride
Ingerholmes Wood
Gorsey Leys
A514
St Bride's
Mount Pleasant
COMMERCE ST 1
BOURNE CT 2
HOPE ST 3
B587
COCKSHUT LA
Highfields
The Roundlet
RIDING BANK
Shaw House
ROBINSON'S HILL
B587
Woodside
Melbourne Common
Bleak House
Hemsley's Barn
SHEPHERD'S LA
Tower
Brickyard Cottage
BOG LA
Derby Hills House Farm
STANTON HILL
Ticknall Parochial Sch
Broadstone Lane End
Sailing Club
MELBOURNE LA
GRANGE CL
CHAPEL ST
INGLEBY LA
HAYES FARM CT
ROSE LA
CHURCH LA
MAIN ST
BANTON'S LA
BROADSTONE LA
BURTON RD
HARPUR AVE
PO
PH
NARROW LA
Ticknall
HIGH ST
B5006
Works
Staunton Harold Reservoir
Walker's Lane
White Leys
Lodge Plantation
Shaw's Plantation
Derby Hills Farm
Serpentine Wood
Middle Lodge
Kennel Cottages
Clay Pit Plantation
The Rookery
Mere Pond
Jubilee Plantation
Betty's Pond
Calke Park
Calke Abbey
Home Farm
Spring Wood
Gorsey Covert
Poker's Leys
STAUNTON LA
White Hollows Farm
Dark Plantation
Calke
The Gables
4
25
3
24
2
23
1
22
35
36
37

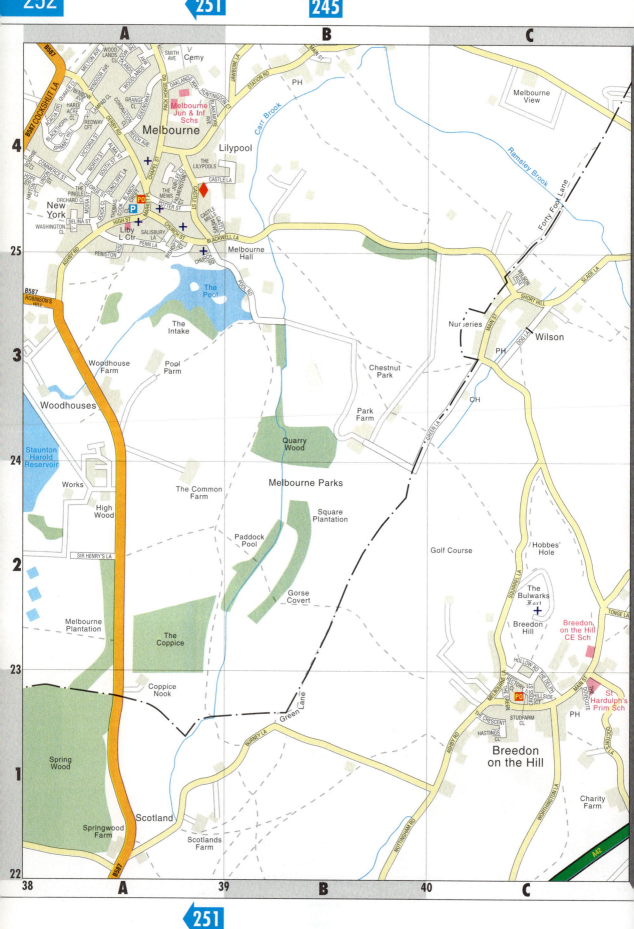

251
245

A
B
C
4
25
3
24
2
23
1
22
38
39
40
Melbourne
Melbourne Jun & Inf Schs
Cemy
Lilypool
New York
Liby
L Ctr
Melbourne Hall
The Pool
The Intake
Woodhouse Farm
Pool Farm
Woodhouses
Staunton Harold Reservoir
Works
High Wood
The Common Farm
Melbourne Parks
Quarry Wood
Chestnut Park
Park Farm
Square Plantation
Paddock Pool
Gorse Covert
Melbourne Plantation
The Coppice
Coppice Nook
Green Lane
Spring Wood
Springwood Farm
Scotland
Scotlands Farm
Carr Brook
Ramsley Brook
Melbourne View
Forty Foot Lane
Nurseries
Wilson
PH
CH
Golf Course
Hobbes' Hole
The Bulwarks
Fort
Breedon Hill
Breedon on the Hill CE Sch
St Hardulph's Prim Sch
Breedon on the Hill
Charity Farm
B587
COCKSHUT LA
ROBINSON'S HILL
SIR HENRY'S LA
ASHBY RD
PENISTON RISE
PENN LA
HIGH ST
BLACKWELL LA
POOL RD
CHURCH SQ
CASTLE ST
CASTLE LA
STATION RD
JAWBONE LA
MAIN ST
DERBY RD
PACK HORSE RD
SHORT HILL
SLADE LA
DOG LA
WILSON RISE
GREEN LA
SQUIRREL LA
TONGE LA
HOLLOW RD
THE DELPH
MELBOURNE LA
THE GREEN
THE CRESCENT
HASTINGS CL
STUDFARM CL
HILLSIDE CT
CROSS ST
RECTORY CL
THE DOVECOTE
DOCTOR'S LA
WORTHINGTON LA
NOTTINGHAM RD
BURNEY LA
A42

251

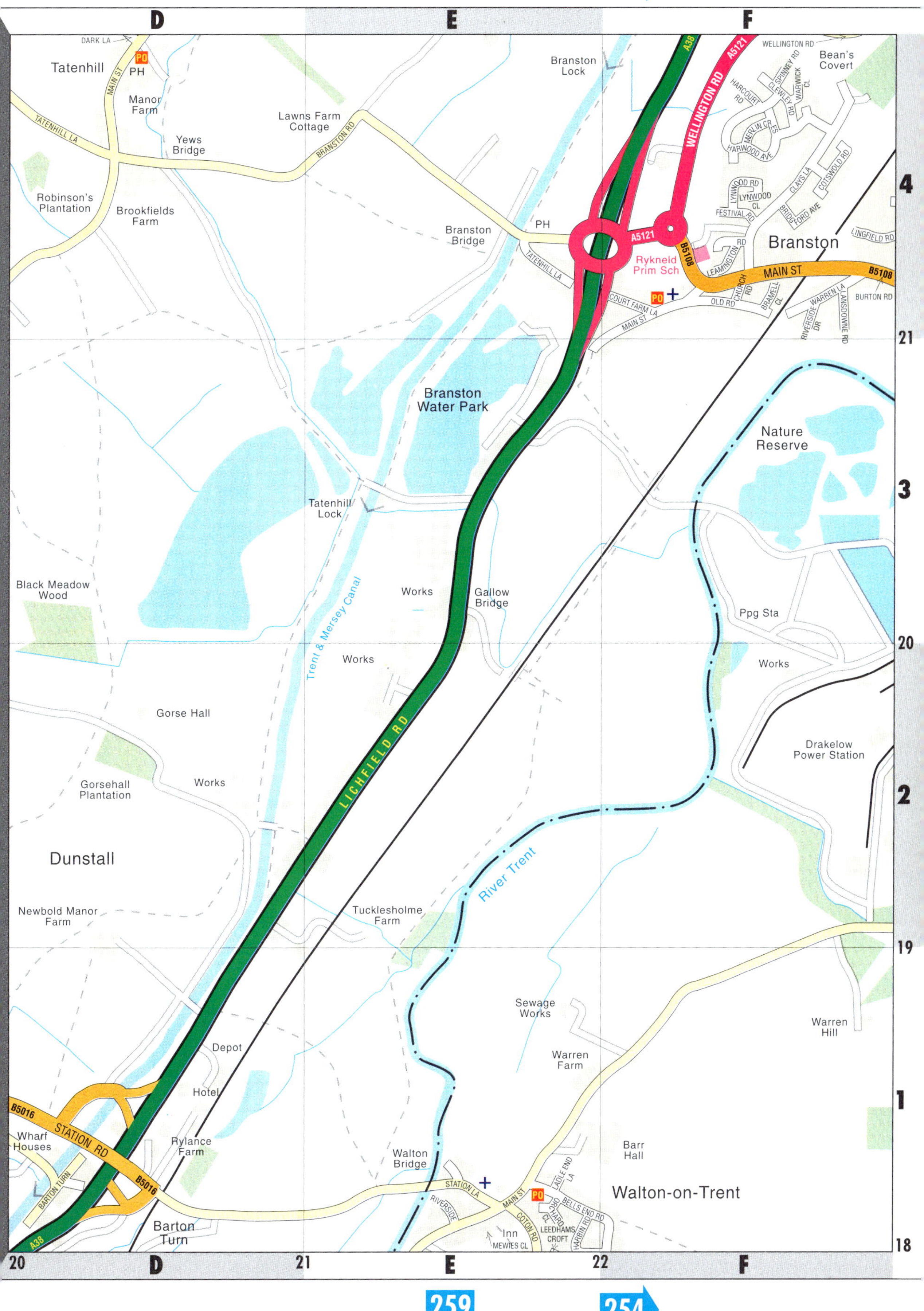
D
E
F
Tatenhill
Manor Farm
Yews Bridge
Lawns Farm Cottage
Branston Lock
Bean's Covert
Robinson's Plantation
Brookfields Farm
Branston Bridge
PH
Branston
Rykneld Prim Sch
Branston Water Park
Nature Reserve
Tatenhill Lock
Black Meadow Wood
Works
Gallow Bridge
Trent & Mersey Canal
Ppg Sta
Gorse Hall
Drakelow Power Station
Gorsehall Plantation
Dunstall
River Trent
Newbold Manor Farm
Tucklesholme Farm
Sewage Works
Warren Hill
Depot
Warren Farm
Hotel
Wharf Houses
Rylance Farm
Walton Bridge
Barr Hall
Walton-on-Trent
Barton Turn
Inn
LICHFIELD RD
WELLINGTON RD
MAIN ST
STATION RD
TATENHILL LA
BRANSTON RD
A38
A5121
B5108
B5016
4
3
2
1
21
20
19
18
22

253

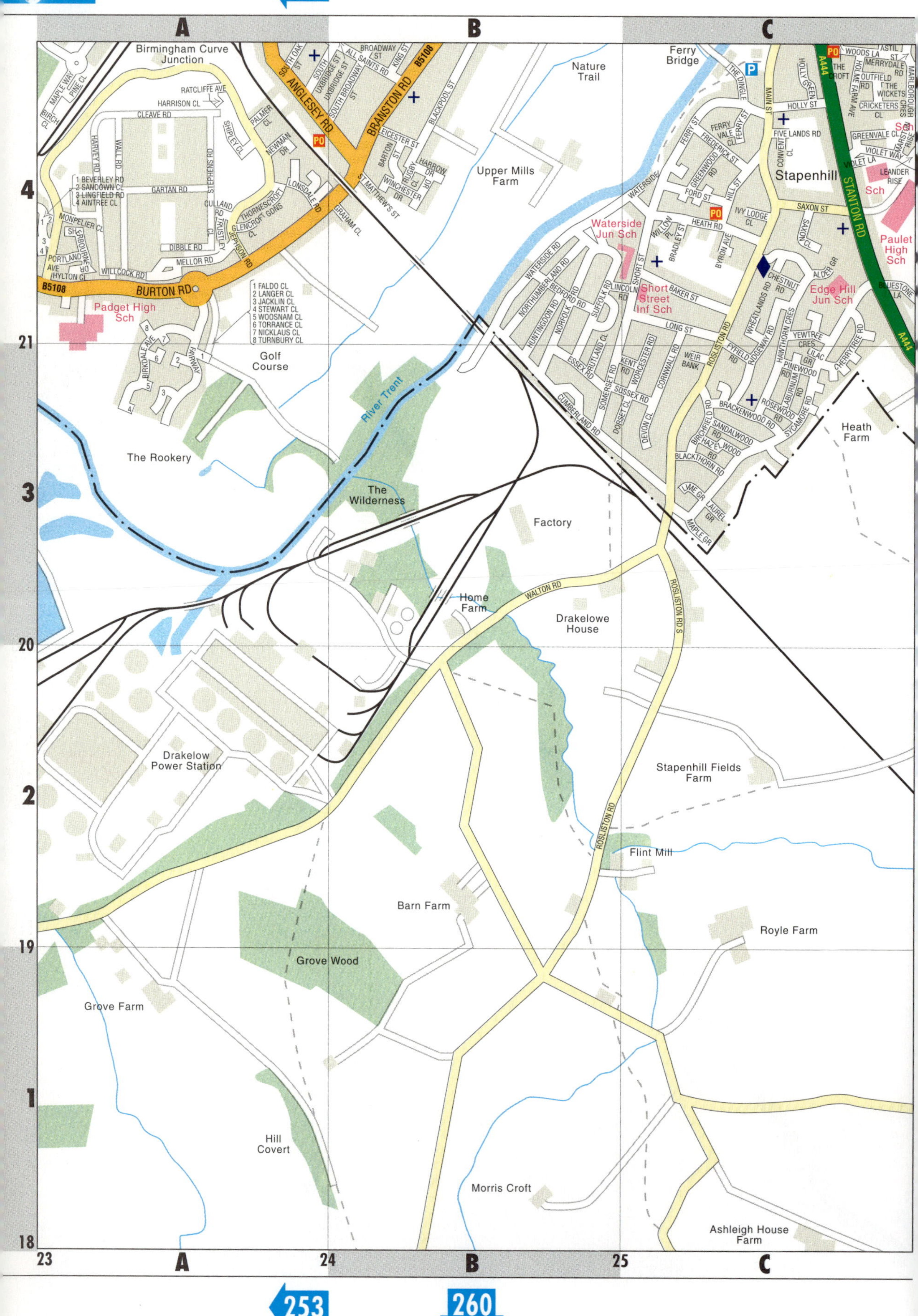

A
B
C
Birmingham Curve Junction
Ferry Bridge
Nature Trail
Upper Mills Farm
Stapenhill
Waterside Jun Sch
Short Street Inf Sch
Paulet High Sch
Edge Hill Jun Sch
Padget High Sch
Golf Course
River Trent
The Rookery
The Wilderness
Factory
Home Farm
Drakelowe House
Heath Farm
Drakelow Power Station
Stapenhill Fields Farm
Flint Mill
Barn Farm
Royle Farm
Grove Wood
Grove Farm
Hill Covert
Morris Croft
Ashleigh House Farm
BURTON RD
B5108
ANGLESEY RD
BRANSTON RD
STANTON RD
A444
WALTON RD
ROSLISTON RD
ROSLISTON RD S
MAIN ST
WATERSIDE RD
1 BEVERLEY RD
2 SANDOWN CL
3 LINGFIELD RD
4 AINTREE CL
1 FALDO CL
2 LANGER CL
3 JACKLIN CL
4 STEWART CL
5 WOOSNAM CL
6 TORRANCE CL
7 NICKLAUS CL
8 TURNBURY CL
23
24
25
4
21
3
20
2
19
1
18

253
260

248
256

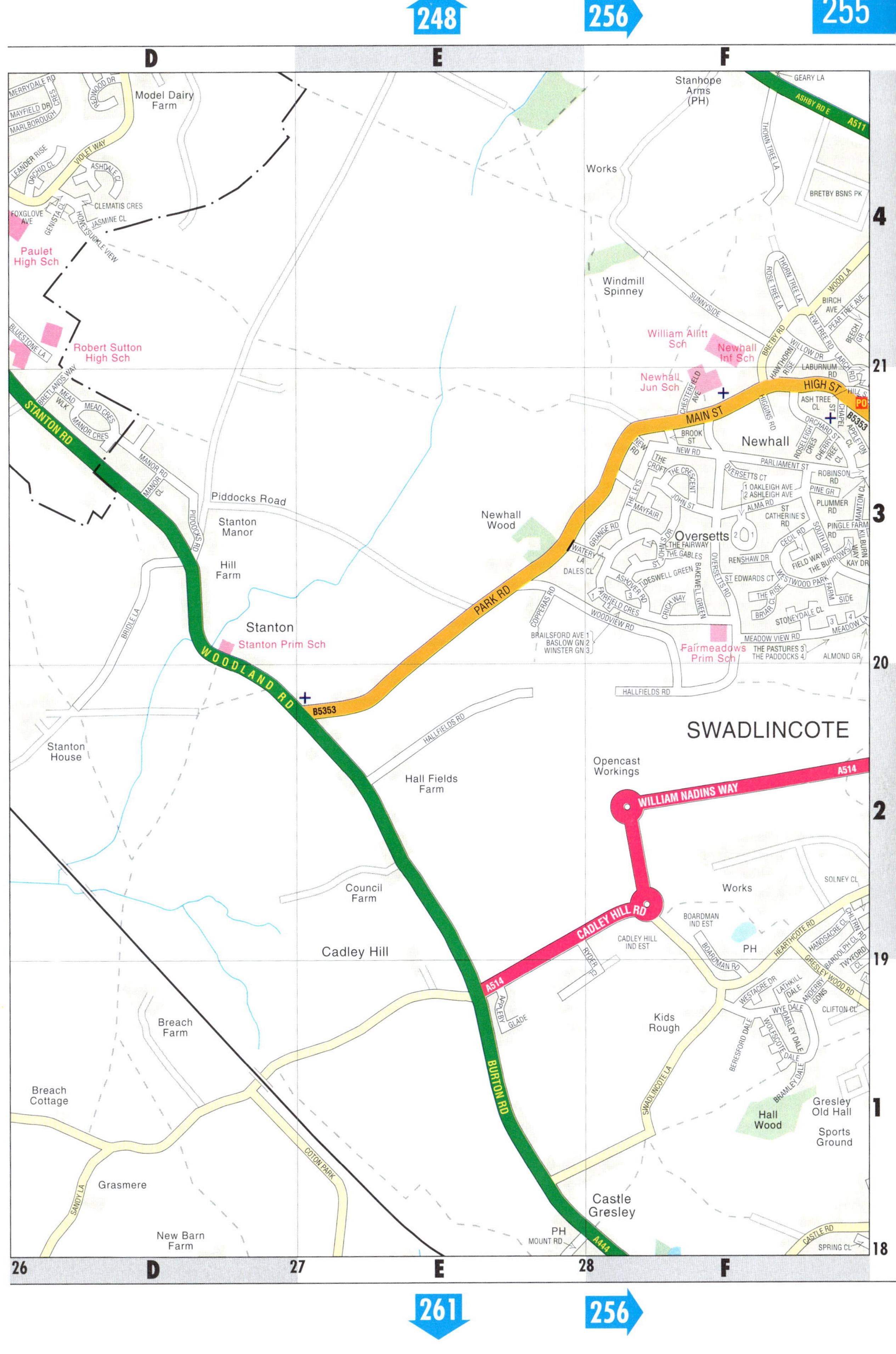
D
E
F
Model Dairy Farm
Stanhope Arms (PH)
Works
Paulet High Sch
Robert Sutton High Sch
Windmill Spinney
William Allitt Sch
Newhall Inf Sch
Newhall Jun Sch
Newhall
Oversetts
Newhall Wood
Piddocks Road
Stanton Manor
Hill Farm
Stanton
Stanton Prim Sch
Fairmeadows Prim Sch
SWADLINCOTE
Stanton House
Opencast Workings
Hall Fields Farm
Council Farm
Cadley Hill
Works
Kids Rough
Breach Farm
Breach Cottage
Grasmere
New Barn Farm
Castle Gresley
Hall Wood
Gresley Old Hall
Sports Ground
STANTON RD
WOODLAND RD
BURTON RD
PARK RD
MAIN ST
HIGH ST
B5353
WILLIAM NADINS WAY
CADLEY HILL RD
A514
A444
A511
ASHBY RD E
4
3
2
1
21
20
19
18
26
27
28

261
256

255
249

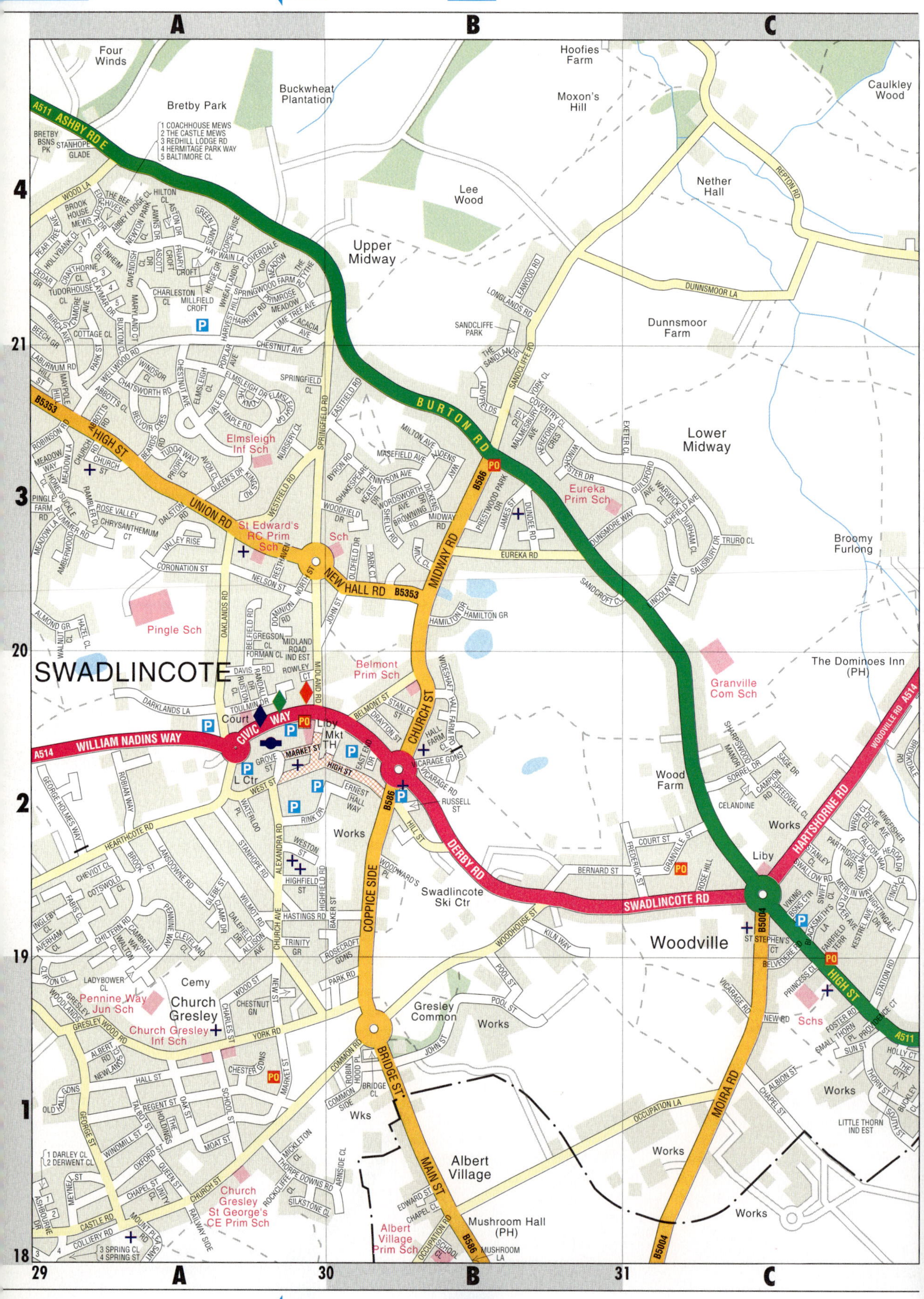
A
B
C
4
3
2
1
21
20
19
18
29
30
31
Four Winds
Bretby Park
Buckwheat Plantation
Hoofies Farm
Moxon's Hill
Caulkley Wood
A511 ASHBY RD E
BRETBY BSNS PK
1 COACHHOUSE MEWS
2 THE CASTLE MEWS
3 REDHILL LODGE RD
4 HERMITAGE PARK WAY
5 BALTIMORE CL
Lee Wood
Nether Hall
REPTON RD
Upper Midway
DUNNSMOOR LA
Dunnsmoor Farm
SANDCLIFFE PARK
BURTON RD
Lower Midway
Elmsleigh Inf Sch
Eureka Prim Sch
B5353
HIGH ST
UNION RD
St Edward's RC Prim Sch
Sch
NEW HALL RD
B5353
MIDWAY RD
B586
EUREKA RD
Broomy Furlong
CORONATION ST
NELSON ST
Pingle Sch
HAMILTON GR
SWADLINCOTE
Belmont Prim Sch
The Dominoes Inn (PH)
Granville Com Sch
A514
WILLIAM NADINS WAY
CIVIC WAY
Court
Liby
Mkt
TH
L Ctr
MARKET ST
HIGH ST
CHURCH ST
DERBY RD
Wood Farm
HARTSHORNE RD
WOODVILLE RD
A514
Works
Liby
Swadlincote Ski Ctr
SWADLINCOTE RD
COPPICE SIDE
B586
Woodville
B5004
HIGH ST
A511
Cemy
Church Gresley
Pennine Way Jun Sch
Church Gresley Inf Sch
Gresley Common
Works
Schs
BRIDGE ST
Wks
MOIRA RD
OCCUPATION LA
Works
LITTLE THORN IND EST
Albert Village
MAIN ST
Church Gresley St George's CE Prim Sch
Albert Village Prim Sch
Mushroom Hall (PH)
MUSHROOM LA
Works
B5004

255
262

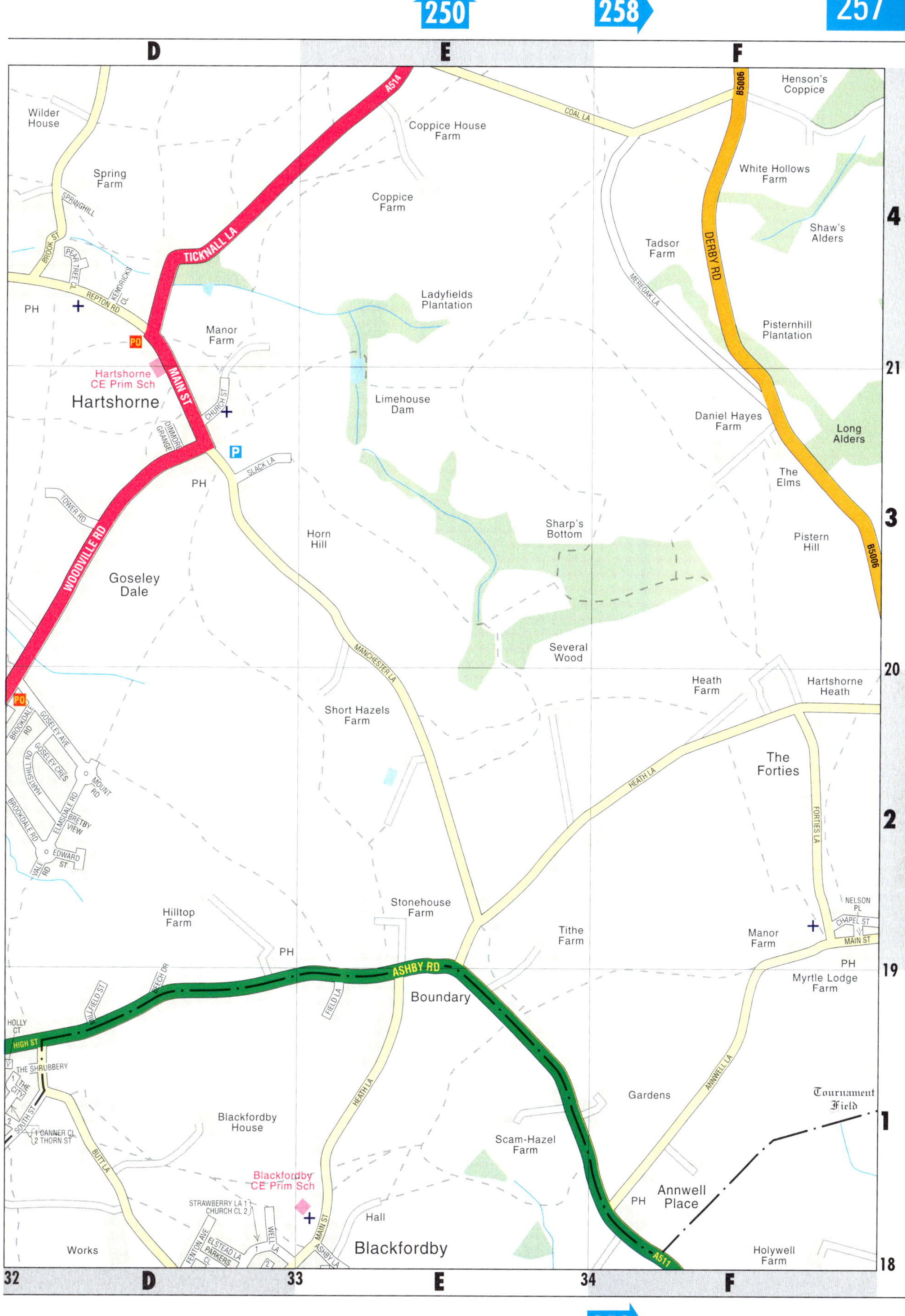
D
E
F
Wilder House
Spring Farm
SPRINGHILL
BROOK ST
PEAR TREE CL
KENDRICKS CL
REPTON RD
PH
PO
Hartshorne CE Prim Sch
Hartshorne
TICKNALL LA
A514
MAIN ST
Manor Farm
CHURCH ST
DIMMORE GRANGE
SLACK LA
PH
TOWER RD
WOODVILLE RD
Goseley Dale
Coppice House Farm
Coppice Farm
Ladyfields Plantation
Limehouse Dam
Horn Hill
MANCHESTER LA
COAL LA
B5006
Henson's Coppice
White Hollows Farm
Shaw's Alders
Tadsor Farm
DERBY RD
MEREOAK LA
Pisternhill Plantation
Daniel Hayes Farm
Long Alders
The Elms
Sharp's Bottom
Pistern Hill
Several Wood
Heath Farm
Hartshorne Heath
Short Hazels Farm
The Forties
HEATH LA
FORTIES LA
PO
BROOKDALE RD
GOSELEY AVE
GOSELEY CRES
HARTSHILL RD
MOUNT RD
ELMSDALE RD
BRETBY VIEW
EDWARD ST
VALE RD
Stonehouse Farm
Hilltop Farm
PH
Tithe Farm
Manor Farm
NELSON PL
CHAPEL ST
MAIN ST
PH
Myrtle Lodge Farm
ASHBY RD
Boundary
BEECH DR
MILLFIELD ST
HOLLY CT
HIGH ST
THE SHRUBBERY
THE CITY
SOUTH ST
1 CANNER CL
2 THORN ST
BUTT LA
FIELD LA
HEATH LA
Blackfordby House
Blackfordby CE Prim Sch
Gardens
ANNWELL LA
Tournament Field
Scam-Hazel Farm
Annwell Place
PH
STRAWBERRY LA 1
CHURCH CL 2
FENTON AVE
ELSTEAD LA
PARKERS CL
WELL LA
MAIN ST
ASHBY LA
Hall
Blackfordby
A511
Holywell Farm
Works
4
21
3
20
2
19
1
18
32
D
33
E
34
F

257
251

A
B
C
Standley's Barn
Archer's Alders
Heathend Plantation
Dimminsdale
Southwood House
Southwood
Southwood Farm
The Saracen's Head (PH)
Ley Farm
Heath End
CALLAN'S LA
Heath End Farm
Home Farm
Staunton Harold Hall Craft & Ferrous Ctr
Heath Farm
Staunton Harold Hall (Cheshire Home)
HEATH LA
The Coppice
Rough Heath
Lount
Pisternhill Plantation
Callan's Lane
Dogkennel Pool
Pisternhill Farm
South Wood
Southwood Farm
B5006
Wicket Nook
Mosley's Plantation
Old Parks Farm
Bryan's Coppice
Pistern Hills Farm East
Park Place
DERBY RD
Black Ditches
Smisby
CHAPEL ST
MAIN ST
Old Parks
Old Parks Farm
Lount Wood
Woodcote
Old Parks House
Gilwiskaw Brook
Western Old Parks Farm
SMISBY RD
B587
Eastern Old Parks
NOTTINGHAM RD
Cliftonthorpe
Ashby de la Zouch
B5006
Works
4
21
3
20
2
19
1
18
35
36
37

257

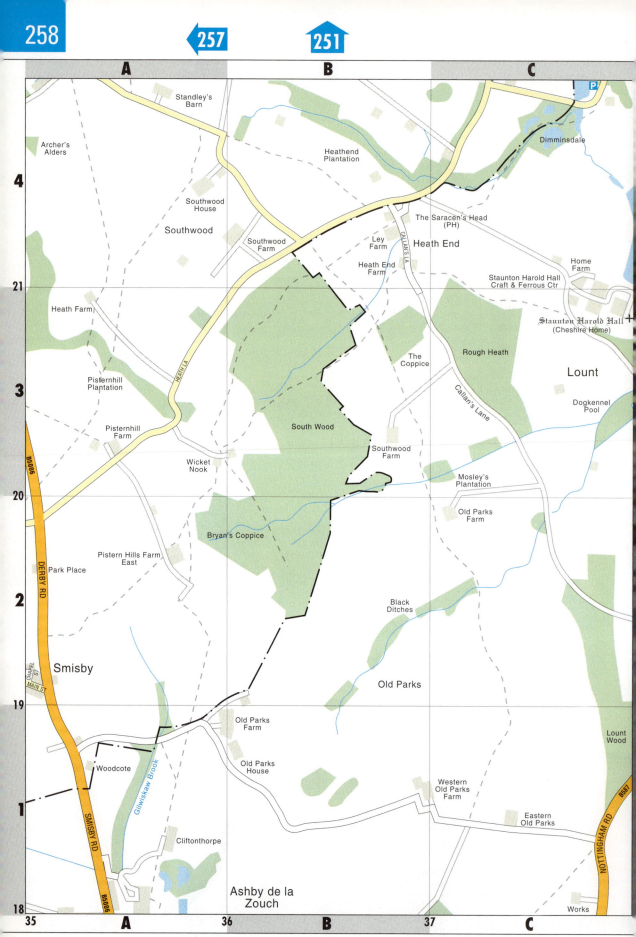

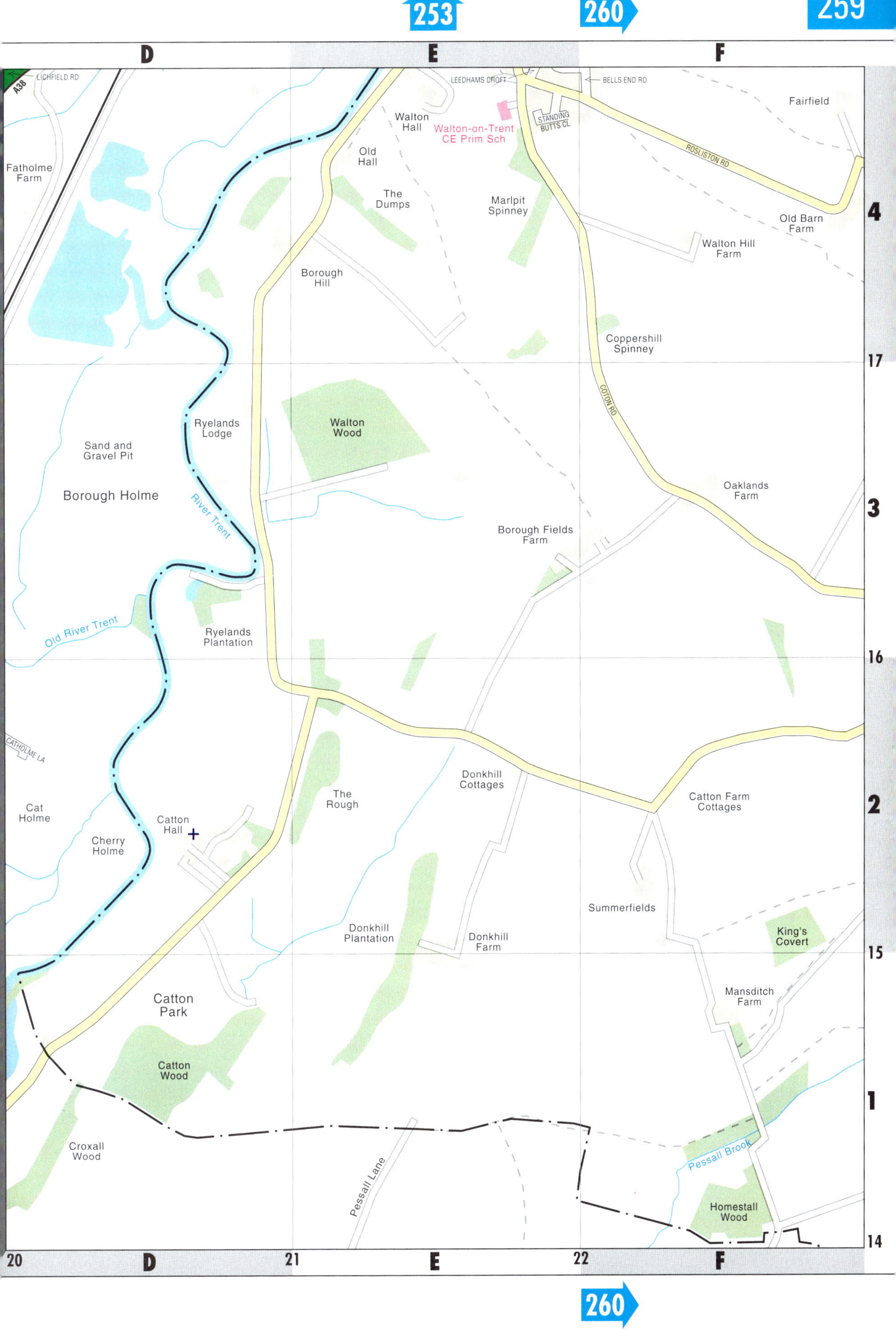

D E F

A38
LICHFIELD RD

Fatholme
Farm

Walton
Hall

Old
Hall

The
Dumps

Walton-on-Trent
CE Prim Sch

LEEDHAMS CROFT

BELLS END RD

STANDING
BUTTS CL

Fairfield

ROSLISTON RD

Marlpit
Spinney

Old Barn
Farm

Walton Hill
Farm

Borough
Hill

Coppershill
Spinney

4

17

Sand and
Gravel Pit

Ryelands
Lodge

Walton
Wood

COTTON RD

Oaklands
Farm

3

Borough Holme

River Trent

Borough Fields
Farm

Old River Trent

Ryelands
Plantation

16

CATHOLME LA

Cat
Holme

The
Rough

Donkhill
Cottages

Catton Farm
Cottages

2

Cherry
Holme

Catton
Hall

Summerfields

King's
Covert

Donkhill
Plantation

Donkhill
Farm

15

Mansditch
Farm

Catton
Park

Catton
Wood

1

Croxall
Wood

Pessall Lane

Pessall Brook

Homestall
Wood

14

20 D 21 E 22 F

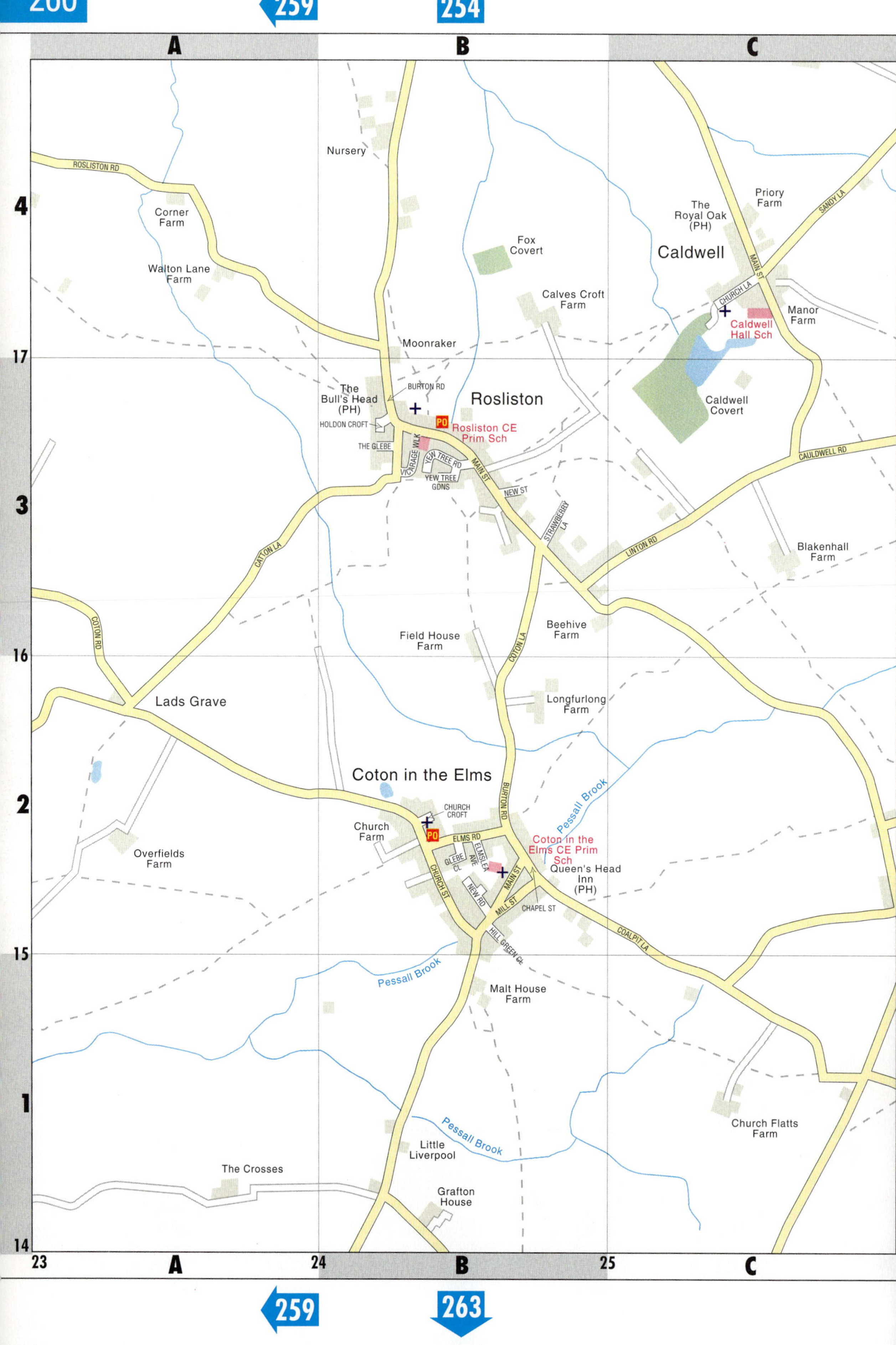

259
254
259
263

ROSLISTON RD

Corner
Farm

Walton Lane
Farm

Nursery

Fox
Covert

Calves Croft
Farm

The
Royal Oak
(PH)

Priory
Farm

SANDY LA

Caldwell

MAIN ST

CHURCH LA

Caldwell
Hall Sch

Manor
Farm

Moonraker

The
Bull's Head
(PH)

HOLDON CROFT

BURTON RD

Rosliston

Caldwell
Covert

CAULDWELL RD

THE GLEBE

VICARAGE WLK

YEW TREE RD

YEW TREE
GDNS

PO

Rosliston CE
Prim Sch

MAIN ST

NEW ST

STRAWBERRY LA

LINTON RD

Blakenhall
Farm

CATTON LA

COTON RD

Field House
Farm

COTON LA

Beehive
Farm

Lads Grave

Longfurlong
Farm

Pessall Brook

Coton in the Elms

Church
Farm

CHURCH
CROFT

PO

ELMS RD

ELMS LA

BURTON RD

Coton in the
Elms CE Prim
Sch

Overfields
Farm

GLEBE
CL

CHURCH ST

NEW RD

MAIN ST

MILL LA

CHAPEL ST

Queen's Head
Inn
(PH)

HILL GREEN CL

COALPIT LA

Pessall Brook

Malt House
Farm

Church Flatts
Farm

Pessall Brook

The Crosses

Little
Liverpool

Grafton
House

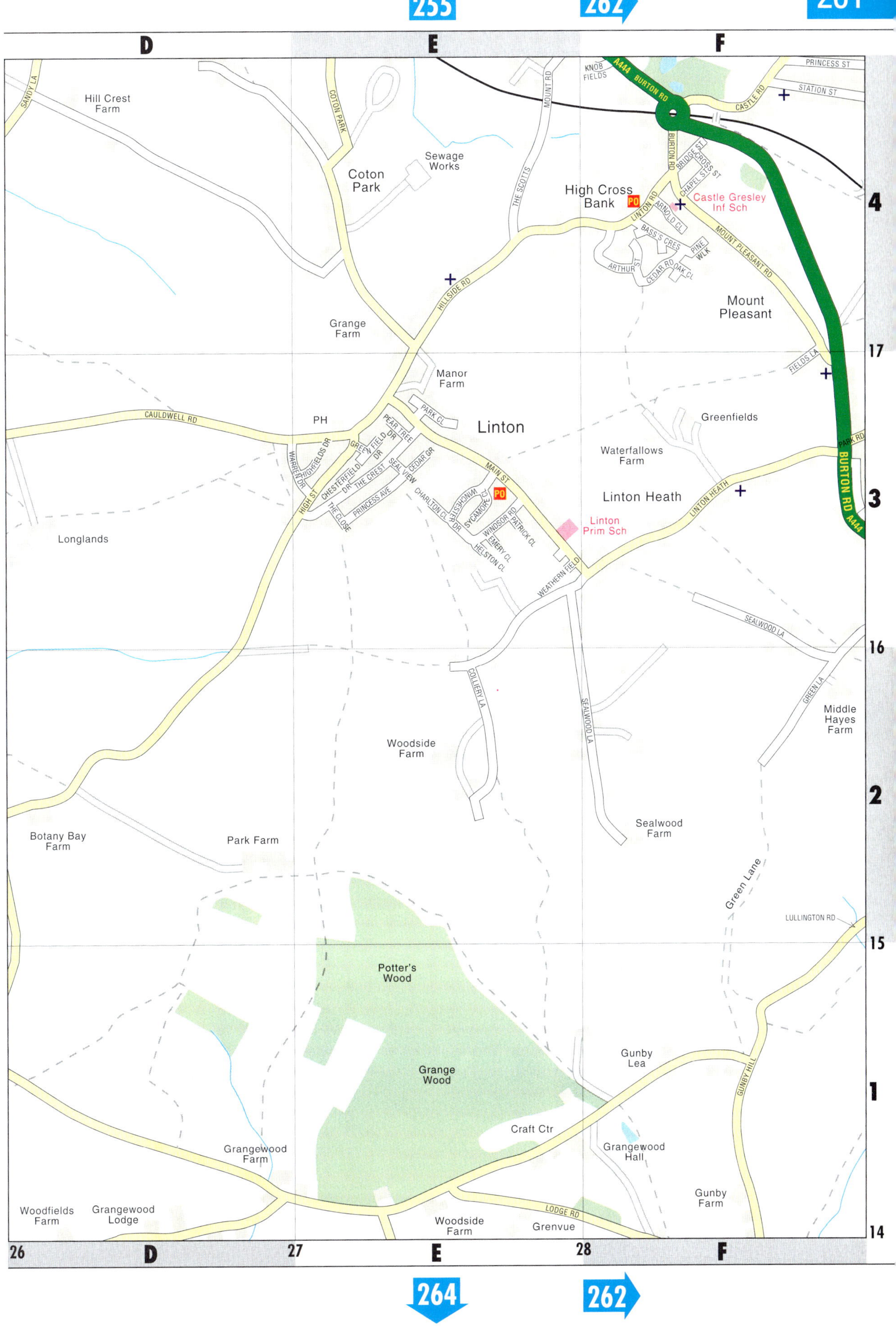

D E F

Hill Crest Farm

Coton Park

Sewage Works

KNOB FIELDS

A444 BURTON RD

PRINCESS ST

CASTLE RD

STATION ST

BURTON RD

BRIDGE ST

CROSS ST

CHAPEL ST

High Cross Bank PO

Castle Gresley Inf Sch

ARNOLD CL

BASS'S CRES

ARTHUR ST

CEDAR RD

OAK CL

PINE WLK

MOUNT PLEASANT RD

Mount Pleasant

4

THE SCOTTS

MOUNT RD

LINTON RD

HILLSIDE RD

Grange Farm

17

FIELDS LA

CAULDWELL RD

PH

Manor Farm

PARK CL

Linton

Greenfields

Waterfallows Farm

PARK RD

BURTON RD A444

WARREN DR

HIGHFIELDS DR

HIGH ST

CHESTERFIELD DR

THE CREST

GREEN FIELD DR

PEAR TREE

SEAL VIEW

CEDAR GR

CHARLTON CL

WILSHONIA DR

SYCAMORE

PATRICK CL

MAIN ST

PRINCESS AVE

THE CLOSE

WINDSOR RD

EMERY CL

HELSTON CL

PO

Linton Heath

Linton Prim Sch

LINTON HEATH

3

Longlands

WEATHERN FIELD

SEALWOOD LA

16

COLLIERY LA

SEALWOOD LA

GREEN LA

Middle Hayes Farm

Woodside Farm

Sealwood Farm

Green Lane

2

Botany Bay Farm

Park Farm

LULLINGTON RD

15

Potter's Wood

Gunby Lea

GUNBY HILL

1

Grange Wood

Craft Ctr

Grangewood Farm

Grangewood Hall

Gunby Farm

Woodfields Farm

Grangewood Lodge

Woodside Farm

Grenvue

LODGE RD

14

26 D 27 E 28 F

261
256

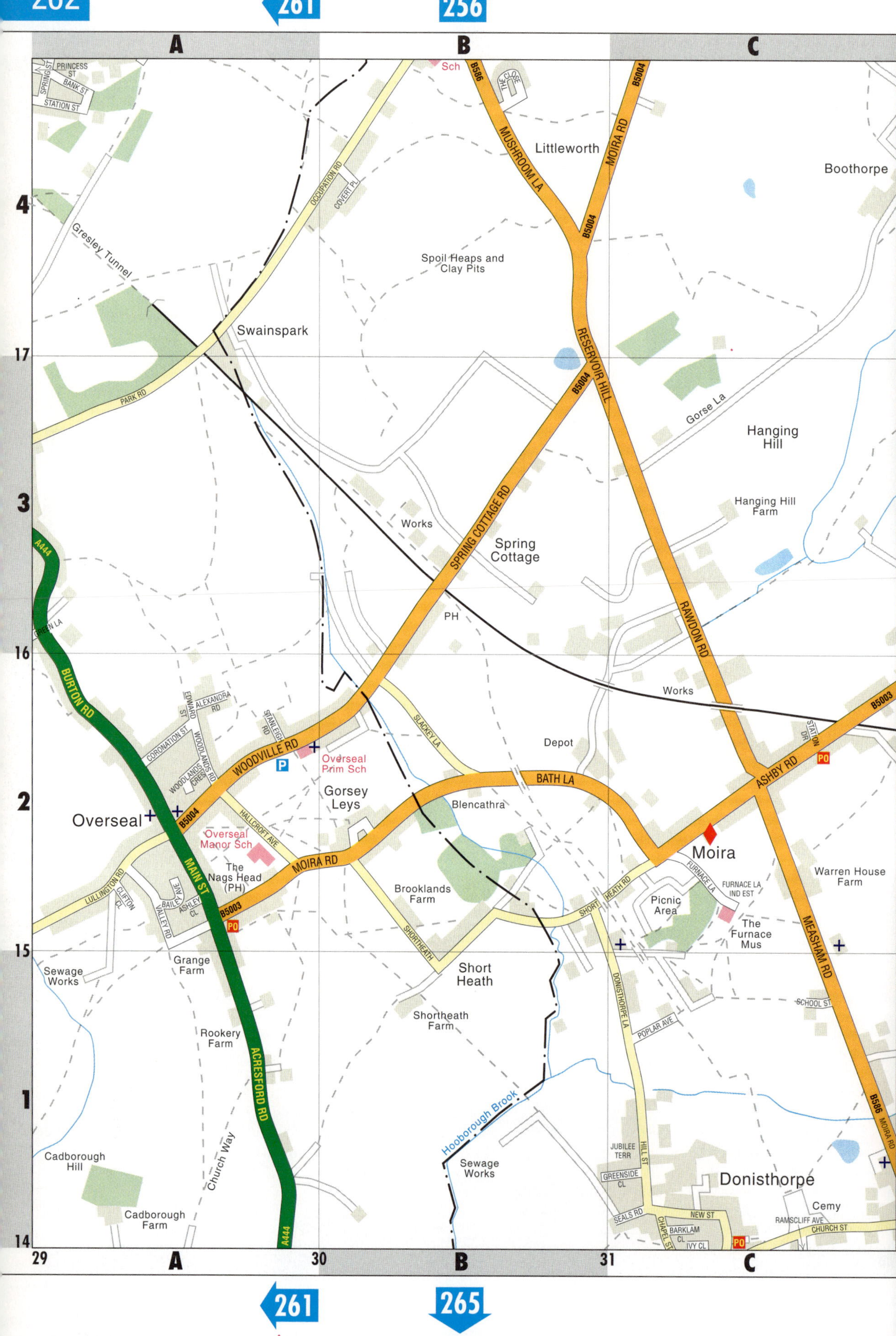
A
B
C
Littleworth
Boothorpe
Gresley Tunnel
Spoil Heaps and Clay Pits
Swainspark
Hanging Hill
Hanging Hill Farm
Works
Spring Cottage
PH
Works
Depot
Overseal Prim Sch
Gorsey Leys
Blencathra
Overseal
Overseal Manor Sch
The Nags Head (PH)
Moira
Warren House Farm
Brooklands Farm
Picnic Area
The Furnace Mus
FURNACE LA IND EST
Sewage Works
Grange Farm
Short Heath
Shortheath Farm
Rookery Farm
Hooborough Brook
Cadborough Hill
Cadborough Farm
Church Way
Sewage Works
Donisthorpe
Cemy
MUSHROOM LA
MOIRA RD
RESERVOIR HILL
SPRING COTTAGE RD
RAWDON RD
ASHBY RD
BATH LA
WOODVILLE RD
MOIRA RD
BURTON RD
MAIN ST
ACRESFORD RD
MEASHAM RD
Gorse La
OCCUPATION RD
COVERT PL
PARK RD
SLACKEY LA
SHORTHEATH
HALLCROFT AVE
LULLINGTON RD
DONISTHORPE LA
HILL ST
POPLAR AVE
SCHOOL ST
CHURCH ST
NEW ST
RAMSCLIFF AVE
SEALS RD
CHAPEL ST
JUBILEE TERR
GREENSIDE CL
BARKLAM CL
IVY CL
HEATH RD
SHORT
FURNACE LA
STATION DR
CORONATION ST
EDWARD ST
ALEXANDRA RD
WOODLANDS RD
WOODLANDS CRES
STANLEIGH RD
BAILEY AVE
ASHLEY CL
VALLEY RD
CLIFTON CL
GREEN LA
THE CLOSE
PRINCESS ST
BANK ST
STATION ST
SPRING ST
Sch
B586
B5004
B5003
A444
PO
P
4
17
3
16
2
15
1
14
29
30
31

261
265

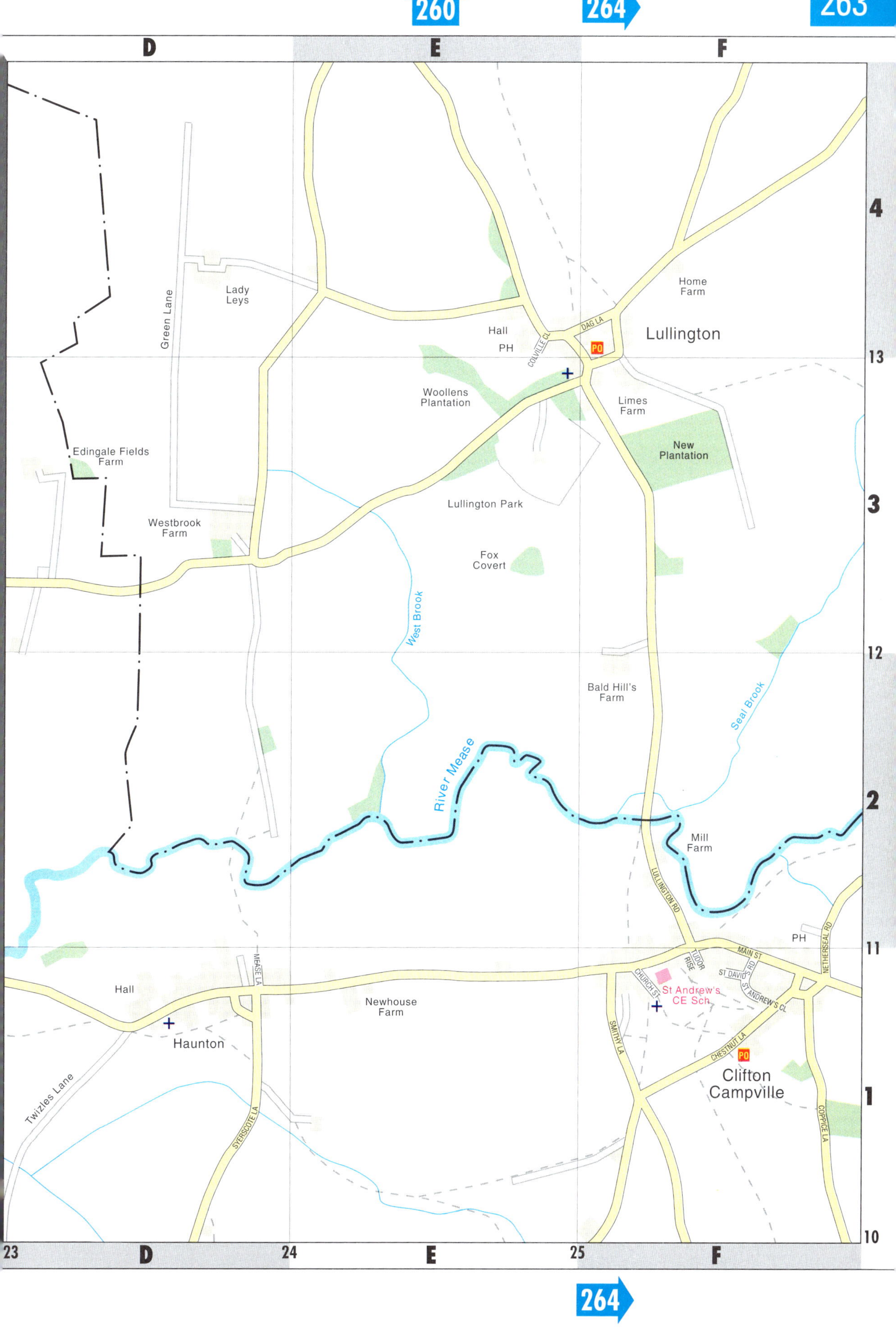

D
E
F

4

Home
Farm

Lullington

13

Green Lane

Lady
Leys

Hall
PH

PO

Woollens
Plantation

Limes
Farm

New
Plantation

Edingale Fields
Farm

Lullington Park

3

Westbrook
Farm

Fox
Covert

West Brook

12

Bald Hill's
Farm

Seal Brook

River Mease

2

Mill
Farm

PH

11

Hall

Newhouse
Farm

St Andrew's
CE Sch

MEASE LA

MAIN ST

TUDOR RISE

ST DAVID RD

ST ANDREW'S CL

NETHERSEAL RD

CHURCH ST

Twizles Lane

Haunton

SMITHY LA

CHESTNUT LA

PO

Clifton
Campville

1

SYERSCOTE LA

COPPICE LA

23
24
25

D
E
F

10

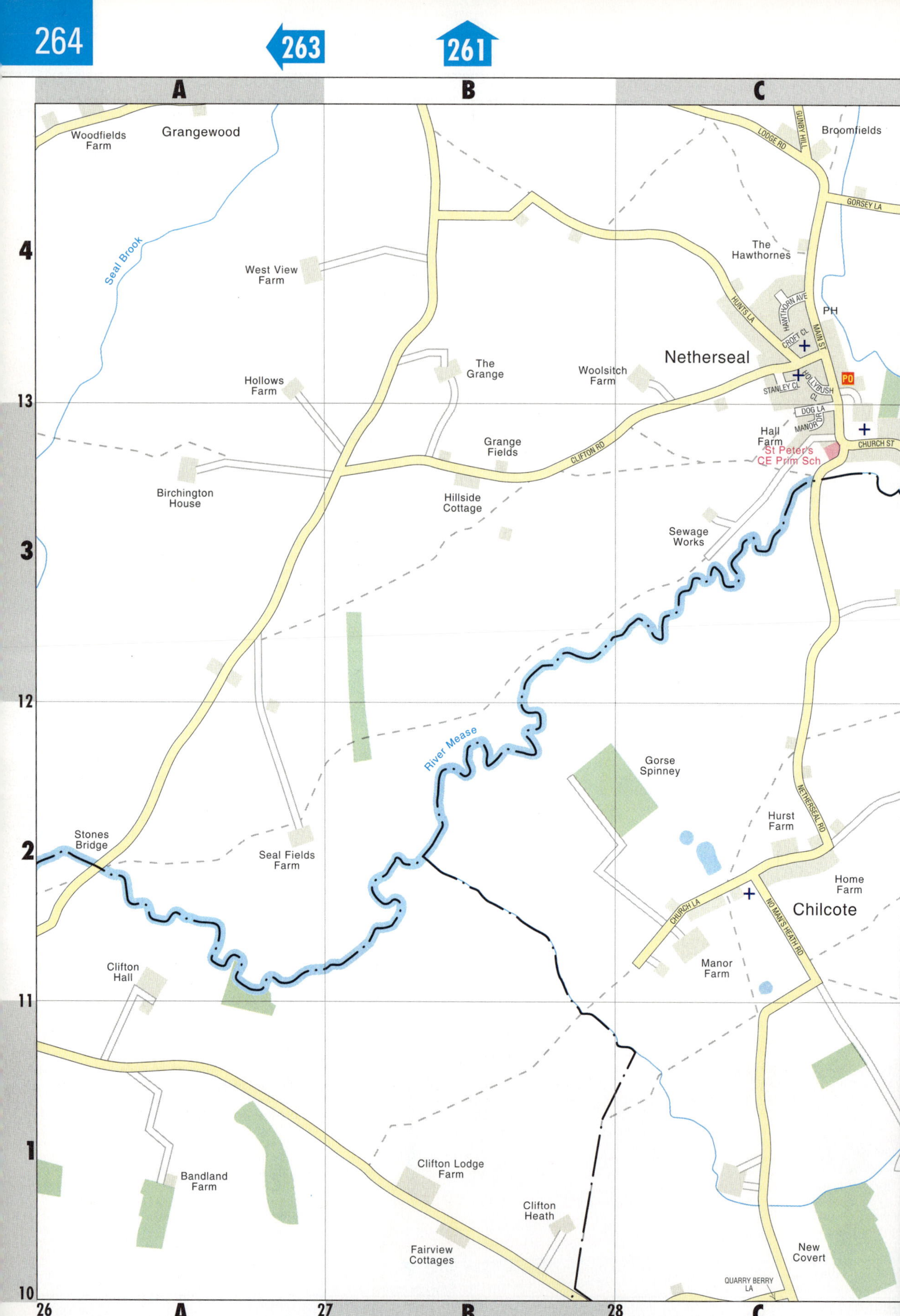
A
B
C
Woodfields Farm
Grangewood
Broomfields
LODGE RD
GUNBY HILL
GORSEY LA
Seal Brook
West View Farm
The Hawthornes
HAWTHORN AVE
HUNTS LA
MAIN ST
PH
CROFT CL
Netherseal
The Grange
Woolsitch Farm
Hollows Farm
HOLLYBUSH CL
STANLEY CL
PO
DOG LA
MANOR DR
Hall Farm
CHURCH ST
Grange Fields
CLIFTON RD
St Peter's CE Prim Sch
Birchington House
Hillside Cottage
Sewage Works
River Mease
Gorse Spinney
Hurst Farm
NETHERSEAL RD
Stones Bridge
Seal Fields Farm
Home Farm
Chilcote
CHURCH LA
NO MAN'S HEATH RD
Clifton Hall
Manor Farm
Bandland Farm
Clifton Lodge Farm
Clifton Heath
Fairview Cottages
New Covert
QUARRY BERRY LA
4
13
3
12
2
11
1
10
26
27
28

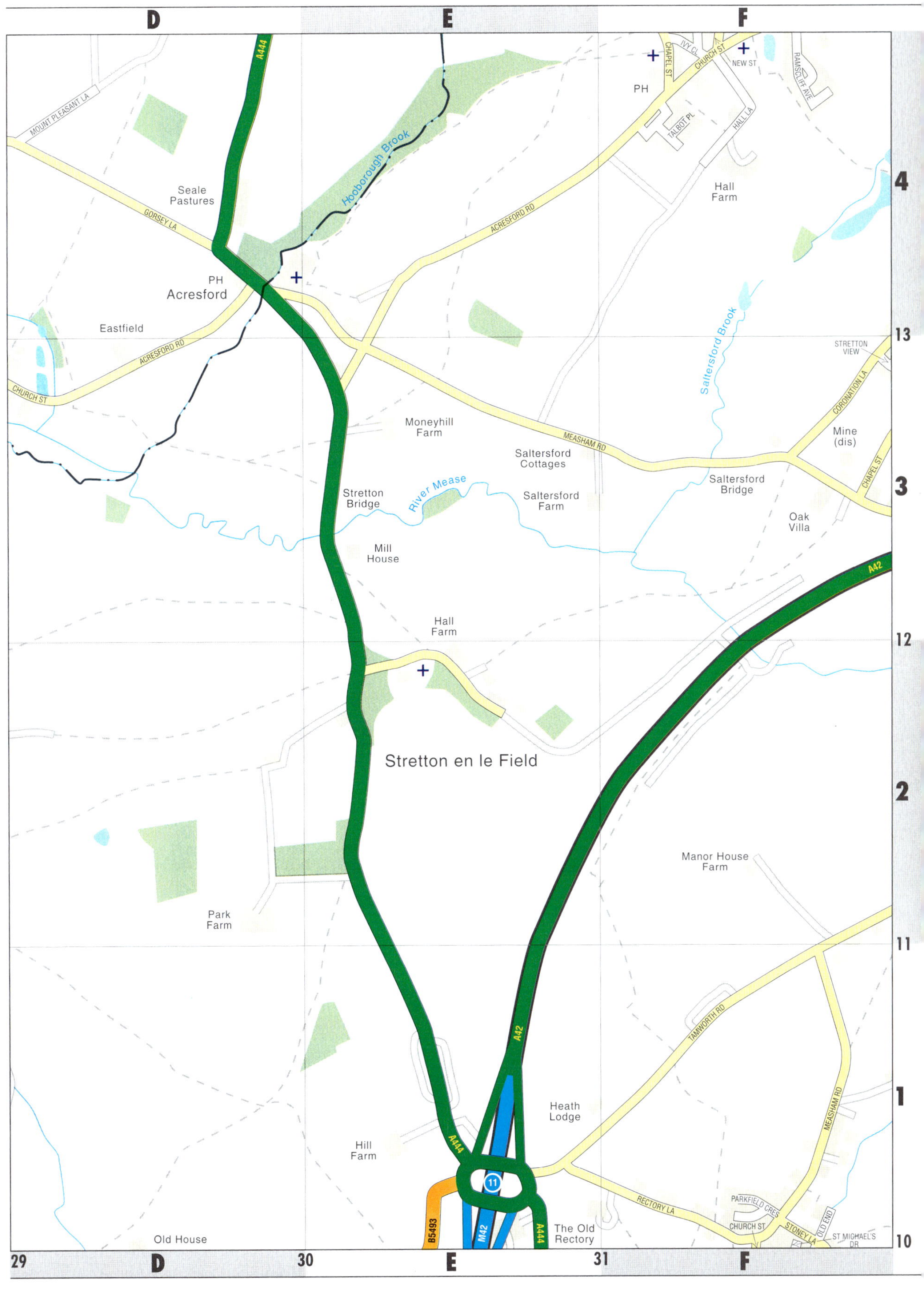
D
E
F
A444
MOUNT PLEASANT LA
Hooborough Brook
PH
CHAPEL ST
IVY CL
CHURCH ST
NEW ST
RAMSCLIFF AVE
TALBOT PL
HALL LA
Seale
Pastures
GORSEY LA
Hall
Farm
ACRESFORD RD
PH
Acresford
Eastfield
ACRESFORD RD
CHURCH ST
Saltersford Brook
STRETTON
VIEW
CORONATION LA
Moneyhill
Farm
MEASHAM RD
Mine
(dis)
Saltersford
Cottages
Stretton
Bridge
River Mease
Saltersford
Farm
Saltersford
Bridge
CHAPEL ST
Oak
Villa
Mill
House
A42
Hall
Farm
Stretton en le Field
Manor House
Farm
Park
Farm
TAMWORTH RD
A42
MEASHAM RD
Heath
Lodge
Hill
Farm
A444
11
RECTORY LA
PARKFIELD CRES
CHURCH ST
STONEY LA
OLD END
ST MICHAEL'S
DR
B5493
M42
A444
The Old
Rectory
Old House
4
13
3
12
2
11
1
10
29
D
30
E
31
F

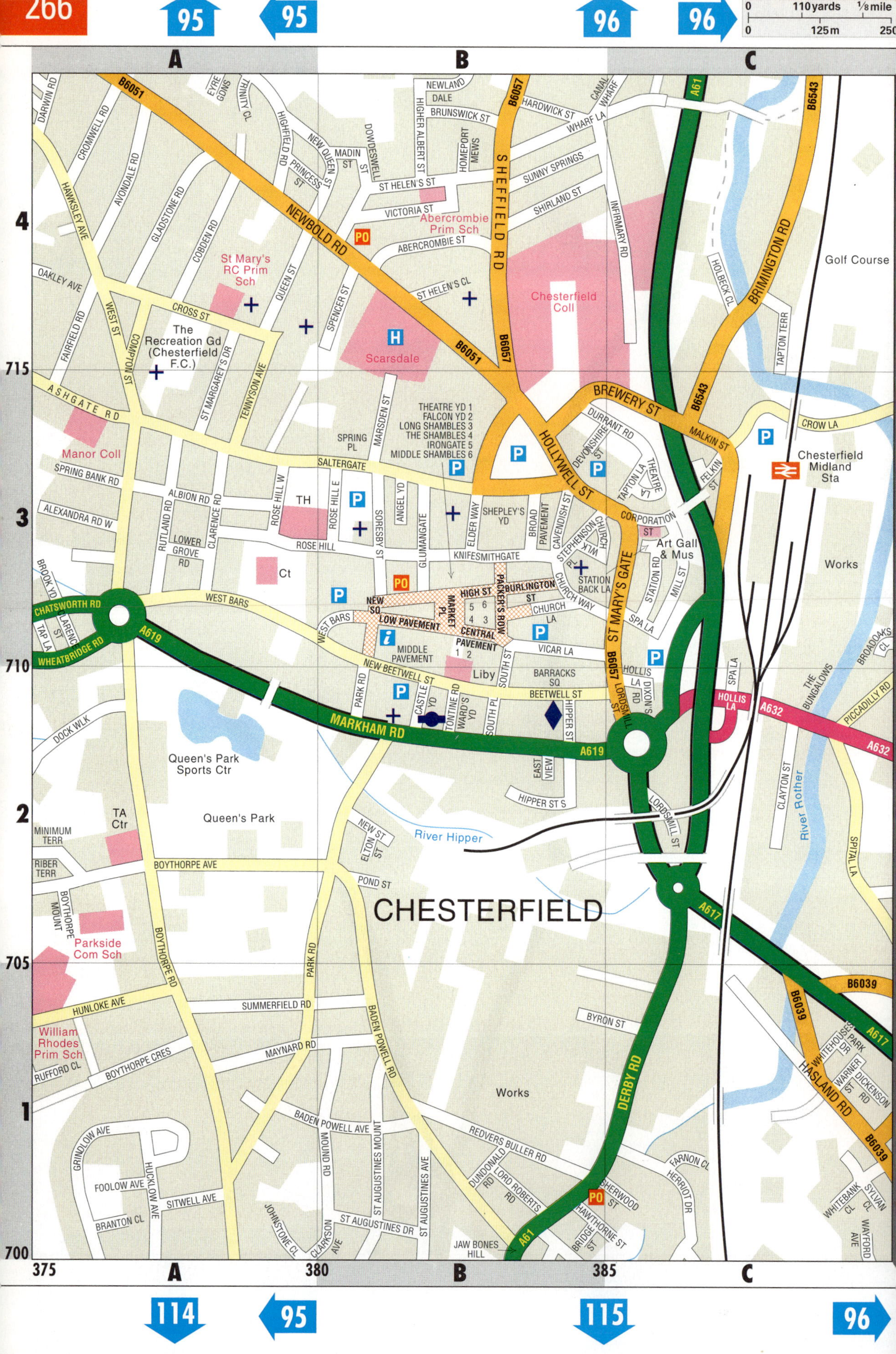
95
95
96
96
Scale: 7 inches to 1 mile
0
110 yards
1/8 mile
0
125 m
250
A
B
C
4
715
3
710
2
705
1
700
375
380
385
CHESTERFIELD
NEWBOLD RD
B6051
B6057
SHEFFIELD RD
HARDWICK ST
CANAL WHARF
WHARF LA
NEWLAND DALE
BRUNSWICK ST
HIGHER ALBERT ST
HOMEPORT MEWS
DOWDESWELL ST
MADIN ST
NEW QUEEN ST
PRINCESS ST
HIGHFIELD RD
TRINITY CL
EYRE GDNS
DARWIN RD
CROMWELL RD
AVONDALE RD
GLADSTONE RD
COBDEN RD
HAWKSLEY AVE
OAKLEY AVE
FAIRFIELD RD
WEST ST
COMPTON ST
CROSS ST
QUEEN ST
SPENCER ST
ST HELEN'S ST
VICTORIA ST
SUNNY SPRINGS
SHIRLAND ST
ABERCROMBIE ST
Abercrombie Prim Sch
ST HELEN'S CL
INFIRMARY RD
St Mary's RC Prim Sch
PO
H
Scarsdale
Chesterfield Coll
The Recreation Gd (Chesterfield F.C.)
ST MARGARET'S DR
TENNYSON AVE
ASHGATE RD
Manor Coll
SPRING BANK RD
ALBION RD
ALEXANDRA RD W
RUTLAND RD
LOWER GROVE RD
CLARENCE RD
ROSE HILL W
TH
ROSE HILL E
ROSE HILL
SPRING PL
MARSDEN ST
SALTERGATE
SORESBY ST
ANGEL YD
GLUMANGATE
THEATRE YD 1
FALCON YD 2
LONG SHAMBLES 3
THE SHAMBLES 4
IRONGATE 5
MIDDLE SHAMBLES 6
ELDER WAY
SHEPLEY'S YD
BROAD PAVEMENT
CAVENDISH ST
KNIFESMITHGATE
HOLLYWELL ST
BREWERY ST
DURRANT RD
DEVONSHIRE ST
TAPTON LA
THEATRE LA
CORPORATION ST
STEPHENSON PL
CHURCH WLK
Art Gall & Mus
STATION BACK LA
ST MARY'S GATE
STATION RD
MILL ST
SPA LA
B6543
MALKIN ST
FELKIN ST
CROW LA
Chesterfield Midland Sta
HOLBECK CL
BRIMINGTON RD
TAPTON TERR
Golf Course
Works
A61
Ct
BROOK YD
TAP LA
CLARENCE ST
CHATSWORTH RD
WHEATBRIDGE RD
A619
WEST BARS
NEW SQ
LOW PAVEMENT
MARKET PL
HIGH ST
BURLINGTON ST
PACKER'S ROW
CHURCH LA
CHURCH WAY
CENTRAL PAVEMENT
MIDDLE PAVEMENT
VICAR LA
NEW BEETWELL ST
Liby
SOUTH ST
BARRACKS SQ
BEETWELL ST
HOLLIS LA
DIXON'S RD
LORDSMILL ST
PARK RD
CASTLE YD
TONTINE RD
WARD'S YD
SOUTH PL
HIPPER ST
MARKHAM RD
A632
HOLLIS LA
DOCK WLK
Queen's Park Sports Ctr
Queen's Park
EAST VIEW
HIPPER ST S
LORDSMILL ST
CLAYTON ST
River Rother
THE BUNGALOWS
BROADOAKS CL
PICCADILLY RD
NEW ST
ELTON ST
River Hipper
POND ST
TA Ctr
MINIMUM TERR
RIBER TERR
BOYTHORPE MOUNT
BOYTHORPE AVE
BOYTHORPE RD
Parkside Com Sch
A617
SPITAL LA
B6039
HUNLOKE AVE
SUMMERFIELD RD
BADEN POWELL RD
BYRON ST
DERBY RD
William Rhodes Prim Sch
RUFFORD CL
BOYTHORPE CRES
MAYNARD RD
WHITEHOUSE DR
PARK
WARNER ST
DICKENSON RD
HASLAND RD
GRINDLOW AVE
FOOLOW AVE
HUCKLOW AVE
SITWELL AVE
BRANTON CL
BADEN POWELL AVE
MOUND RD
ST AUGUSTINES MOUNT
ST AUGUSTINES AVE
ST AUGUSTINES DR
JOHNSTONE CL
CLARKSON AVE
REDVERS BULLER RD
DUNDONALD RD
LORD ROBERTS RD
JAW BONES HILL
SHERWOOD ST
HAWTHORNE ST
BRIDGE ST
FARNON CL
HERRIOT DR
WHITEBANK CL
SYLVAN CL
WAYFORD AVE
114
95
115
96

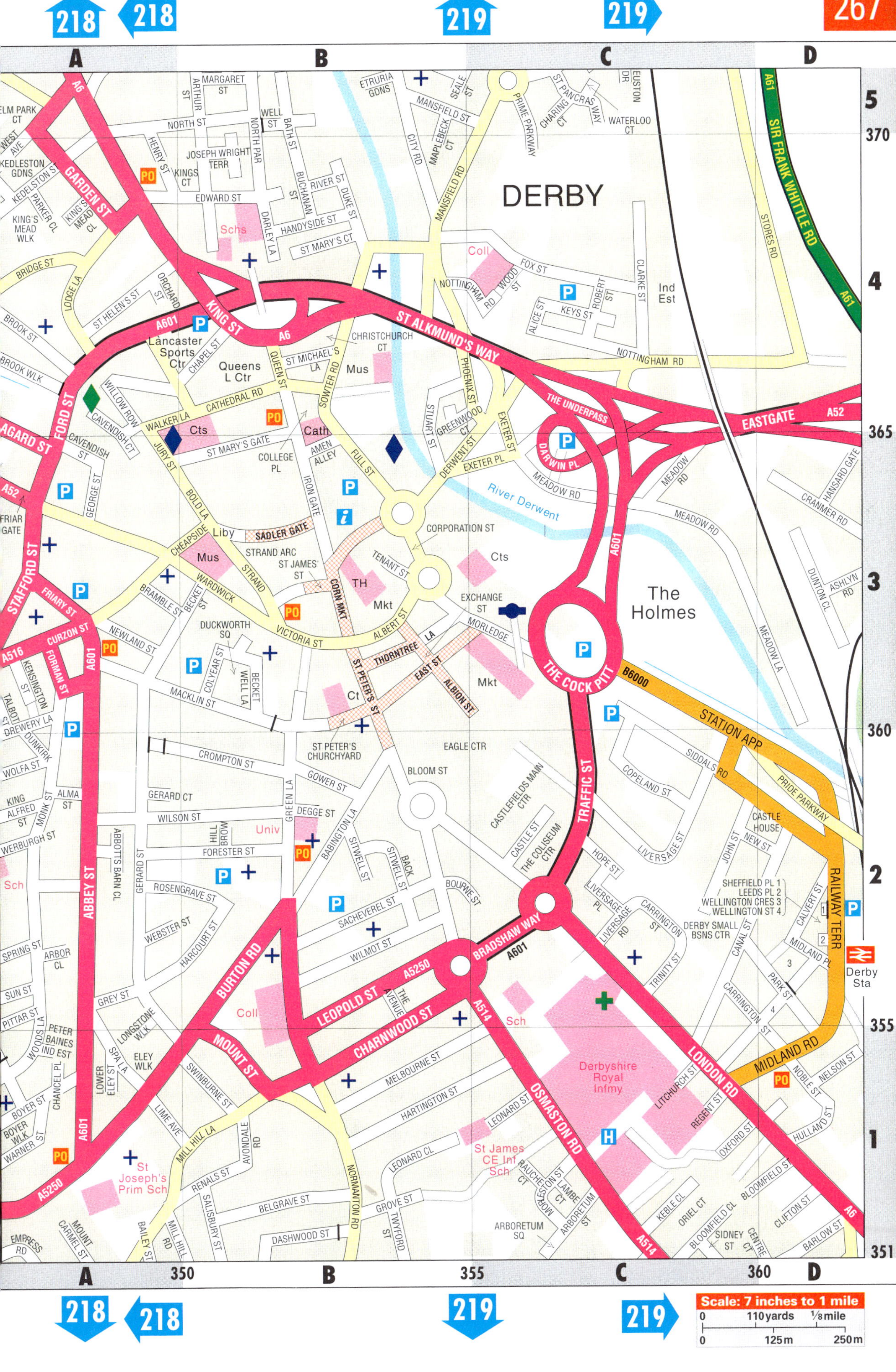
218
219
DERBY
The Holmes
River Derwent
ST ALKMUND'S WAY
THE UNDERPASS
EASTGATE
THE COCK PITT
TRAFFIC ST
STATION APP
RAILWAY TERR
MIDLAND RD
LONDON RD
OSMASTON RD
BRADSHAW WAY
CHARNWOOD ST
LEOPOLD ST
BURTON RD
MOUNT ST
ABBEY ST
STAFFORD ST
FORD ST
AGARD ST
GARDEN ST
KING ST
SIR FRANK WHITTLE RD
NOTTINGHAM RD
MANSFIELD RD
CORPORATION ST
VICTORIA ST
CORN MKT
ST PETER'S ST
Derbyshire Royal Infmy
Derby Sta
Queens L Ctr
Lancaster Sports Ctr
St James CE Inf Sch
St Joseph's Prim Sch
Ind Est
EAGLE CTR
DERBY SMALL BSNS CTR
SHEFFIELD PL 1
LEEDS PL 2
WELLINGTON CRES 3
WELLINGTON ST 4
350
355
360
351
365
370
A
B
C
D
1
2
3
4
5
Scale: 7 inches to 1 mile
110 yards
⅛ mile
125 m
250 m

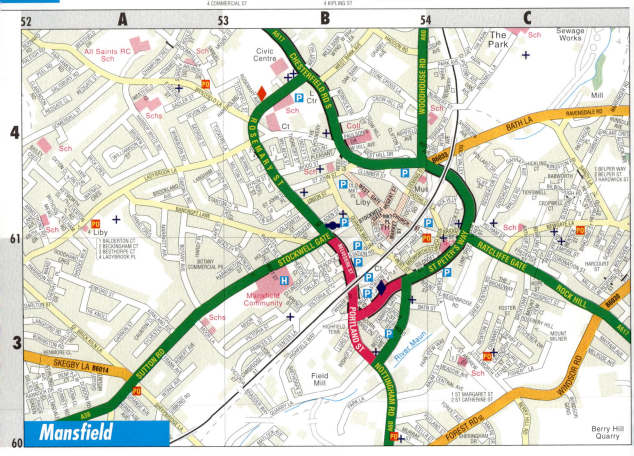

Mansfield

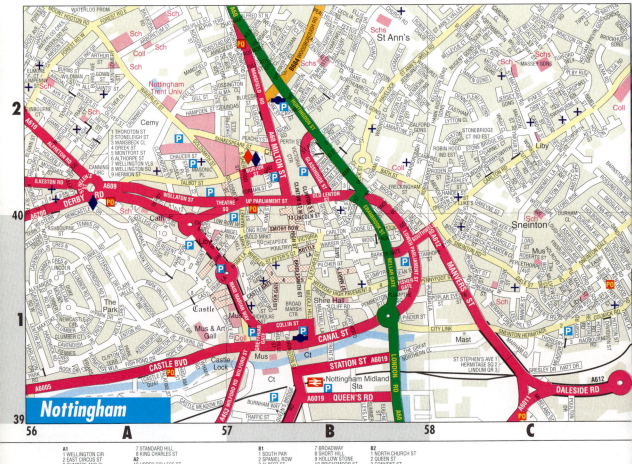

Nottingham

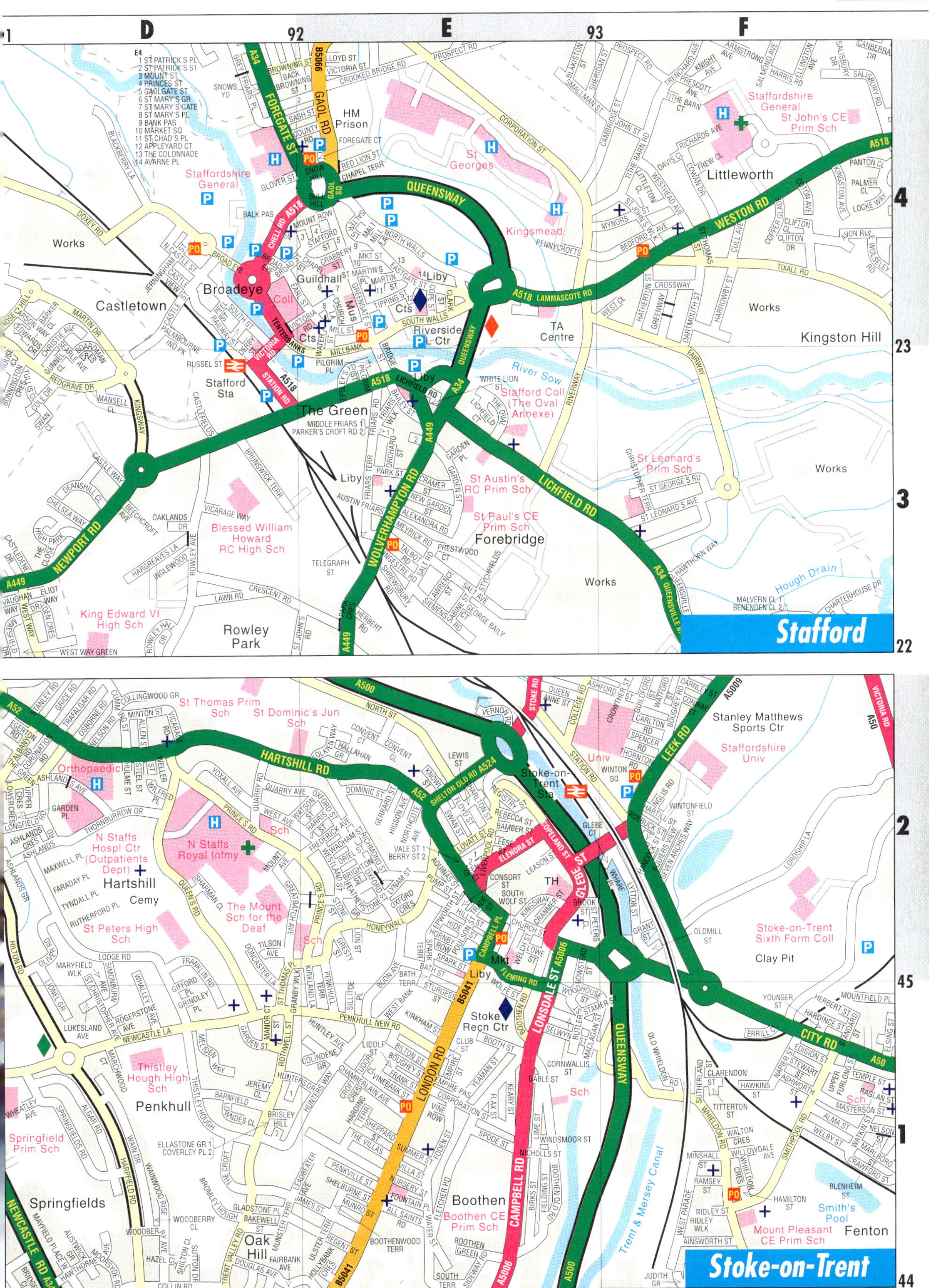
Stafford
Stoke-on-Trent
Broadeye
Castletown
Littleworth
Kingston Hill
Forebridge
The Green
Rowley Park
Staffordshire General
HM Prison
St Georges
Kingsmead
Guildhall
Riverside L Ctr
TA Centre
Stafford Sta
Stafford Coll (The Oval Annexe)
River Sow
St Leonard's Prim Sch
St Austin's RC Prim Sch
St Paul's CE Prim Sch
Blessed William Howard RC High Sch
King Edward VI High Sch
Hough Drain
Staffordshire General
St John's CE Prim Sch
Works
QUEENSWAY
WESTON RD
LICHFIELD RD
NEWPORT RD
WOLVERHAMPTON RD
FOREGATE ST
GAOL RD
Hartshill
Penkhull
Springfields
Oak Hill
Boothen
Fenton
Stoke-on-Trent Sta
Stanley Matthews Sports Ctr
Staffordshire Univ
Stoke-on-Trent Sixth Form Coll
Clay Pit
Orthopaedic
N Staffs Royal Infmy
N Staffs Hospl Ctr (Outpatients Dept)
St Thomas Prim Sch
St Dominic's Jun Sch
The Mount Sch for the Deaf
St Peters High Sch
Thistley Hough High Sch
Springfield Prim Sch
Stoke Recn Ctr
Boothen CE Prim Sch
Mount Pleasant CE Prim Sch
Smith's Pool
Trent & Mersey Canal
HARTSHILL RD
LONDON RD
CAMPBELL RD
LONSDALE ST
CITY RD
LEEK RD
NEWCASTLE RD

Index

Street names are listed alphabetically and show the locality, the Postcode District, the page number and a reference to the square in which the name falls on the map page

Cambridge Rd 1 Brimington S43 .. 96 C4

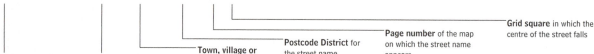

Full street name
This may have been abbreviated on the map

Location Number
If present, this indicates the street's position on a congested area of the map instead of the name

Town, village or locality in which the street falls.

Postcode District for the street name

Page number of the map on which the street name appears

Grid square in which the centre of the street falls

Schools, hospitals, sports centres, railway stations, shopping centres, industrial estates, public amenities and other places of interest are also listed. These are highlighted in magenta

Abbreviations used in the index

App **Approach**	Cl **Close**	Ent **Enterprise**	La **Lane**	Rdbt **Roundabout**
Arc **Arcade**	Comm **Common**	Espl **Esplanade**	N **North**	S **South**
Ave **Avenue**	Cnr **Corner**	Est **Estate**	Orch **Orchard**	Sq **Square**
Bvd **Boulevard**	Cotts **Cottages**	Gdns **Gardens**	Par **Parade**	Strs **Stairs**
Bldgs **Buildings**	Ct **Court**	Gn **Green**	Pk **Park**	Stps **Steps**
Bsns Pk **Business Park**	Ctyd **Courtyard**	Gr **Grove**	Pas **Passage**	St **Street, Saint**
Bsns Ctr **Business Centre**	Cres **Crescent**	Hts **Heights**	Pl **Place**	Terr **Terrace**
Bglws **Bungalows**	Dr **Drive**	Ho **House**	Prec **Precinct**	Trad Est **Trading Estate**
Cswy **Causeway**	Dro **Drove**	Ind Est **Industrial Estate**	Prom **Promenade**	Wlk **Walk**
Ctr **Centre**	E **East**	Intc **Interchange**	Ret Pk **Retail Park**	W **West**
Cir **Circus**	Emb **Embankment**	Junc **Junction**	Rd **Road**	Yd **Yard**

Town and village index

Abney 51 F2	Castle Donington 247 E2	Hayfield 25 E1
Aldercar 182 A2	Castleton 38 B1	Hazelwood 190 A4
Alderwasley 166 C4	Chapel-en-le-Frith 47 D3	Heage 168 C1
Alfreton 159 D2	Charlesworth 16 B3	Heanor 181 E1
Alkmonton 199 E1	Chelmorton 87 D1	Heath 117 D1
Alsop en le Dale 150 C2	Chesterfield 96 B2	High Lane 32 A4
Alstonefield 149 E2	Chinley 34 C1	Hilcote 148 B1
Alton 130 B3	Church Broughton 227 D4	Hilton 228 B1
Ambergate 167 F2	Clay Cross 131 D2	Hodthorpe 82 B3
Apperknowle 58 A1	Clifton 184 C3	Hognaston 164 A1
Ashbourne 173 E1	Clifton Campville 263 F1	Holbrook 191 E3
Ashby-de-la-Zouch 258 B1	Clowne 80 B2	Hollington 200 C2
Ashford in the Water 108 C4	Codnor 181 E4	Hollingworth 9 E3
Ashover 129 F2	Common Side 75 E2	Hollinsclough 104 B1
Aston-on-Trent 246 A4	Compstall 15 D1	Holloway 156 A3
Atlow 175 D3	Cossall 195 E1	Holme 2 C4
Ault Hucknall 133 F4	Coton in the Elms 260 B2	Holmesfield 75 D4
Awsworth 195 E2	Creswell 81 F1	Holmewood 116 C1
Bakewell 109 F3	Crich 156 C1	Holmoorside 113 E4
Ballidon 152 A1	Cromford 155 D3	Hope 38 C2
Bamford 40 A2	Curbar 72 C1	Horsley 191 F3
Barlborough 80 A4	Dale 207 F1	Hulland Ward 175 F2
Barlow 75 F1	Darley Dale 127 E1	Ible 153 F4
Barrow Hill 78 A2	Denby 180 B1	Idridgehay 176 C3
Barrow upon Trent 244 A4	Denstone 196 B3	Ilkeston 208 C4
Barton in Fabis 237 F3	Derby 219 D3	Ironville 170 C2
Barton Turn 253 D1	Disley 32 B3	Kilburn 192 A4
Baslow 91 F3	Donisthorpe 262 C1	Killamarsh 60 C3
Beeley 111 D2	Dore 55 F4	Kimberley 195 F4
Beeston 223 F2	Dove Holes 47 F1	Kirby-in-Ashfield 160 C2
Belper 179 D2	Doveridge 211 D1	Kirk Ireton 165 E1
Biggin 138 B2	Draycott 234 C4	Kirk Langley 202 C1
Birch Vale 25 D1	Dronfield 56 C1	Kniveton 163 D1
Birchover 126 A1	Duffield 190 C2	Langley Mill 182 A2
Blackfordby 257 E1	Earl Sterndale 105 E2	Langwith 119 F4
Blackwell 147 F1	Eastwood 182 C2	Linton 261 D3
Bolsover 99 D1	Eckington 59 E2	Little Eaton 205 E4
Bonsall 142 C1	Edale 37 E4	Litton 69 F2
Borrowash 221 E4	Eggington 241 D3	Lockington 247 F3
Boylestone 213 E2	Ellastone 183 D2	Lodge Moor 42 C4
Brackenfield 145 E1	Elton 140 C3	Long Duckmanton 98 A2
Bradbourne 163 E3	Elvaston 234 A3	Long Eaton 236 B4
Bradley 186 C4	Etwall 229 E2	Longford 214 B4
Bradwell 51 D4	Eyam 71 E3	Longnor 121 D2
Brailsford 201 F4	Fenton 269 F1	Lount 258 C3
Bramley-Vale 117 F1	Findern 230 B1	Lullington 263 F4
Branston 253 F4	Flagg 106 C3	Mackworth 217 F4
Brassington 153 D1	Fritchley 168 F2	Mansfield 136 A1
Breadsall 205 F2	Gamesley 9 E1	Mansfield 268
Breaston 235 E4	Glapwell 134 B4	Mansfield Woodhouse 136 C2
Breedon on the Hill 252 C1	Glossop 10 A1	Mapperley 193 F2
Bretby 249 D2	Grassmoor 115 F2	Marchington 224 C1
Brimington 96 C4	Great Cubley 198 C1	Market Warsop 120 C2
Brinsley 182 C3	Great Longstone 90 A2	Marple 23 D3
Broadbottom 16 A4	Grindleford 72 B4	Marsh Lane 58 C2
Bullbridge 168 A3	Hadfield 10 A3	Marston Montgomery 211 F4
Burnaston 229 F3	Hallam Moors 41 F4	Mastin Moor 79 E2
Burton upon Trent 248 A2	Hanbury 238 A3	Matlock 143 D3
Buxton 85 D4	Harthill 61 F3	Matlock Bath 143 D1
Caldwell 260 C4	Hartington 137 E3	Mayfield 184 B4
Callow 165 D2	Hartshorne 257 D3	Melbourne 252 A4
Calow 96 C3	Hassop 90 C3	Middleton 124 C2
Calver 72 B1	Hathersage 53 D4	Middleton
Carsington 164 C4	Hatton 239 E4	(Nr Wirksworth) 154 B2
Moira 262 C2	Spout 166 B2	
Monyash 107 E1	Stafford 269	
Morley 206 B3	Stanley 207 E3	
Morton 146 C3	Stanton 183 E4	
Mosborough 59 E4	Stanton in Peak 126 A3	
Mottram in Longdendale 9 D2	Stanton-by-Dale 222 C4	
Nether Heage 168 B1	Stapleford 223 F4	
Nether Langwith 101 D1	Staveley 78 B1	
Netherseal 264 C4	Stoke-on-Trent 269	
Neverthorpe 79 D1	Stonebroom 146 C2	
New Houghton 134 F4	Stoney Middleton 71 F2	
New Mills 33 E4	Stramshall 210 A2	
Newton 148 A2	Stretton 146 B4	
Newton Solney 248 C4	Stretton en le Field 265 E2	
North Wingfield 132 A4	Sudbury 225 F2	
Northwood 127 D3	Sutton in Ashfield 148 C1	
Nottingham 268	Sutton on the Hill 228 A4	
Ockbrook 221 E3	Swadlincote 256 A2	
Old Brampton 94 B2	Swanwick 169 F3	
Osmaston 185 F2	Swarkestone 244 B3	
Over Haddon 109 D1	Taddington 88 A2	
Overseal 262 A2	Tansley 144 A2	
Palterton 118 A3	Temple 116 A2	
Parwich 151 F1	Thornhill 39 F2	
Peak Dale 67 D3	Thorpe 161 E1	
Peak Forest 49 D2	Thorpe Salvin 62 C3	
Pentrich 169 D3	Thrumpton 237 E2	
Pilsley 132 B1	Thurvaston 215 E4	
Pinxton 160 B1	Tibshelf 148 A3	
Pleasley 135 D3	Ticknall 251 D2	
Poolsbrook 98 A4	Tideswell 69 E2	
Quarndon 204 B3	Tintwistle 10 A4	
Radmanthwaite 135 E2	Tissington 162 A3	
Renishaw 79 D4	Toadmoor 167 F2	
Repton 242 C1	Totley 55 F3	
Ridgeway 168 B2	Trowell 209 E3	
Ripley 169 E1	Trusley 215 F2	
Risley 222 C2	Tupton 131 E4	
Rocester 197 D2	Turnditch 177 D1	
Rodsley 200 A3	Tutbury 239 E3	
Rolleston 240 A2	Underwood Green 171 F1	
Rosliston 260 B3	Unstone 76 C4	
Roston 197 F4	Uttoxeter 210 B1	
Rowsley 126 C4	Walton-on-Trent 253 F1	
Sandiacre 223 D3	Wensley 142 A4	
Scarcliffe 118 C3	Wessington 157 F4	
Scropton 226 C1	West Hallam 207 F4	
Selston 171 F4	Weston Underwood 189 D1	
Shardlow 234 C1	Weston-on-Trent 245 F3	
Sheffield 43 D4	Westwood 171 E2	
Shipley 194 A3	Whaley Bridge 45 E4	
Shirebrook 119 F2	Whaley Thorns 101 D1	
Shireoaks 63 F3	Whitwell 81 F3	
Shirland 146 B1	Willington 242 A3	
Shirley 200 C4	Windley 189 E4	
Shottle 177 F4	Wingerworth 114 C2	
Smalley 192 C3	Winster 141 E3	
Smisby 258 A2	Wirksworth 165 F4	
Snelston 184 B2	Woodthorpe 79 E1	
Somercotes 170 B4	Woodville 256 C2	
Somersal Herbert 211 F2	Wyaston 185 E3	
South Normanton 160 A4	Yeaveley 199 E3	
South Wingfield 157 F2	Youlgreave 125 D3	
Spinkhill 60 B1		

1st Ave DE7 .... 208 C4
2nd Ave DE7 .... 208 C4
3rd Ave DE7 .... 208 C4
Abba Cl NG16 .... 195 F4
Abbey Brook Dr S8 ...... 56 C4
Abbey Croft S40 .... 95 D4
Abbey Gdns SK14 .... 9 D2
Abbey Hill
  Breadsall DE21, DE22 .... 205 D2
  Derby DE21, DE22 .... 205 D2
Abbey Hill Rd DE22 ...... 204 B1
Abbey La DE22 .... 205 D1
Abbey Lodge Cl DE11 .... 256 A4
Abbey St Derby DE1 ...... 267 A2
  Ilkeston DE7 .... 194 C1
Abbey View Dr S8 .... 43 D2
Abbey View Rd S8 .... 43 D2
Abbey Yd DE22 .... 205 D1
Abbeydale Park Cres S17 ... 55 F3
Abbeydale Park Rise S17 ... 55 F3
Abbeydale Rd S8 .... 43 D4
Abbeydale Rd S Dore S8 ... 56 A4
  Sheffield S17 .... 56 A4
Abbeyfields DE22 .... 205 D1
Abbeyhill Cl S40 .... 95 D2
Abbot Beyne Sch The
  DE15 .... 248 A2
Abbot Cl DE21 .... 205 F1
Abbot Rd DE7 .... 208 B3
Abbot St NG16 .... 195 E2
Abbots Gr DE56 .... 179 D3
Abbotsford Dr NG3 ...... 268 B2
Abbotsford Mews DE7 .... 194 B2
Abbott Rd DE55 .... 159 D2
Abbott St Heanor DE75 ... 181 F1
  Long Eaton NG10 .... 236 B3
Abbotts Barn Cl DE1 ..... 267 A2
Abbotts Cl DE11 .... 256 A3
Abbotts Croft NG19 ...... 135 F1
Abbotts Rd DE11 .... 256 A3
Abel La DE4 .... 142 B1
Abells DE5 .... 180 B1
Abercrombie Prim Sch
  S41 .... 266 B4
Abercrombie St S41 ...... 266 B4
Aberdare Cl DE21 .... 206 A1
Aberdeen St NG3 .... 268 C2
Abingdon Bsns Ctr The
  DE24 .... 219 E1
Abingdon St DE24 .... 232 B4
Abney Cl Chesterfield S40 ... 95 E3
  Derby DE3 .... 217 F1
  Sheffield S14 .... 43 E3
Abney Dr S14 .... 43 E3
Abney Rd S14 .... 43 E3
Acacia Ave Brimington S43 ... 97 D4
  Derby DE6 .... 217 F1
  Swadlincote DE11 .... 256 A4
Acacia Cres S21 .... 60 A3
Acacia Ct NG19 .... 136 C1
Acacia Dr
  Lower Pilsley S45 .... 132 A2
  Melbourne DE73 .... 252 A4
Acacia Gdns NG16 .... 195 F4
Acer Cl Killamarsh S21 .... 60 B3
  Pinxton NG16 .... 160 B2
Acer Croft DE21 .... 205 F2
Acorn Ave NG16 .... 195 E4
Acorn Bsns Pk NG18 .... 268 B3
Acorn Cl DE24 .... 232 C2
Acorn Dr DE56 .... 179 D3
Acorn Ridge
  Chesterfield S40 .... 114 A4
  Matlock DE4 .... 143 D3
  Shirebrook NG20 .... 119 E3
Acorn Terr SK22 .... 33 D3
Acorn Way Belper DE56 ... 179 D3
  Derby DE21 .... 220 B3
  Morley DE21 .... 220 B3
Acre La DE72 .... 246 B4
Acre St S14 .... 17 E4
Acreage La NG20 .... 119 F1
Acrefield Way DE73 ..... 233 D1
Acres Rd S45 .... 132 A2
Acres The S45 .... 132 A2
Acres View Cl S41 .... 95 F4
Acresford Rd
  Donisthorpe DE12 ...... 265 E4
  Nethersdale DE12 .... 265 D3
  Overseal DE12 .... 262 A1
Acton Ave NG10 .... 236 C3
Acton Cl NG10 .... 236 C3
Acton Gr NG10 .... 236 C3
Acton Rd Derby DE22 ... 217 F3
  Long Eaton NG10 .... 236 C3
Acton Road Ind Est NG10 .. 236 C3
Acton St NG10 .... 236 C3
Adale Rd DE7 .... 193 D4
Adam Bede Cres DE4 .... 165 F3
Adam St DE7 .... 209 D3
Adam's Rd DE6 .... 217 D4
Adams Cl DE75 .... 193 E4
Adams Ct DE7 .... 194 C2
Adastral Ave S41 .... 44 A1
Adderley Pl SK13 .... 9 F1
Adderley Rd SK13 .... 9 F1
Addison Dr DE55 .... 159 D2
Addison Rd Derby DE24 ... 232 B4
  Stonebroom DE55 ...... 146 C2
Addison Sq DE4 .... 155 D3
Addison St
  Nottingham NG1 .... 268 A2
  Tibshelf DE55 .... 148 A4
Addison Villas NG16 .... 182 C1
Adelaide Cl Derby DE3 ... 217 F2
  Stapleford NG9 .... 209 F1
Adelaide Cres DE15 ..... 248 B1

Adelaide Wlk NG16 ..... 170 C2
Adelphi Cl DE23 .... 231 D3
Adin Ave S44 .... 98 C3
Adlington Ave S42 ..... 115 E1
Adlington La S32 .... 72 B4
Admiral Cl DE75 .... 181 E1
Adrian Cl NG9 .... 223 F1
Adrian St DE24 .... 232 B3
Adwick Cl DE3 .... 217 E1
Agard St DE1 .... 218 C3
Agnesmeadow La DE6 ... 174 B2
Ainley Cl DE24 .... 232 C4
Ainsworth Dr DE23 .... 231 F4
Ainsworth St ST4 ...... 269 F1
Aintree Ave S21 .... 59 D2
Aintree Cl Branston DE14 ... 254 A4
  Kimberley NG16 .... 195 F4
Airedale Cl NG10 ...... 236 A3
Airedale Wlk DE24 .... 233 E3
Akley Bank Cl S17 .... 55 F3
Alabaster La DE4 .... 155 D3
Alandale Ave NG20 .... 119 F3
Albany Cl NG19 .... 136 B1
Albany Ct NG9 .... 209 F1
Albany Dr NG19 .... 136 B1
Albany Inf Sch NG9 .... 209 F1
Albany Jun & Inf Schs
  NG9 .... 223 F4
Albany Pl NG19 .... 136 B1
Albany Rd DE22 .... 218 B2
Albany St DE7 .... 209 D3
Albemarle Rd DE21 .... 220 A4
Albert Ave Chesterfield S43 .. 77 F2
  Stapleford NG9 .... 223 E4
  Westwood NG16 .... 171 D2
Albert Cres DE21 ...... 220 A2
Albert Rd Breaston DE72 .... 235 D4
  Chesterfield S43 .... 77 E2
  Derby DE21 .... 220 A2
  Long Eaton NG10 ..... 236 B4
  Ripley DE5 .... 169 E1
  Sandiacre NG10 .... 223 D3
  Sheffield S8 .... 43 D3
  Swadlincote DE11 ..... 256 A1
Albert St Belper DE56 ... 178 C2
  Derby DE1 .... 267 B3
  Eastwood NG16 ...... 182 C2
  Eckington S21 .... 59 E1
  Hadfield SK13 .... 10 A3
  Ilkeston DE7 .... 208 C4
  Ironville NG16 .... 170 C3
  Mansfield NG18 ...... 268 B3
  Mansfield Woodhouse
    NG19 .... 136 B2
  3 Nottingham NG1 ... 268 B1
  Ripley DE5 .... 169 F1
  Somercotes DE55 ..... 170 A4
  South Normanton DE55 ... 160 A3
  Stapleford NG9 .... 223 E4
Albert St N S41 .... 76 C1
Albert Village Prim Sch
  DE11 .... 256 B1
Alberta Rd NG16 ...... 171 F4
Albine Rd NG20 .... 119 F3
Albion Ctr The DE7 .... 208 C4
Albion Rd Chesterfield S40 .. 266 A3
  Long Eaton NG10 ..... 236 C4
  New Mills SK22 .... 33 D3
Albion St Derby DE1 .... 267 B3
  Ilkeston DE7 .... 194 C1
  Mansfield NG19 ...... 135 F1
  Ripley DE5 .... 169 F1
  Woodville DE11 .... 256 C1
Albrighton Ave DE24 ... 231 E1
Alcock Ave NG18 ...... 268 C4
Aldam Cl S17 .... 55 F2
Aldam Croft S17 .... 55 F2
Aldam Rd S17 .... 55 F2
Aldam Way S17 .... 55 F2
Alder Brook SK23 .... 34 C1
Alder Cl Derby DE21 .... 205 F2
  Mansfield NG19 ...... 136 C1
  Shirebrook NG20 ...... 119 E3
Alder Ct DE1 .... 219 D4
Alder Gr Burton u T DE15 ... 254 C4
  Buxton SK17 .... 85 D4
  Mansfield Woodhouse
    NG19 .... 136 A3
Alder Rd DE56 .... 179 D2
Alder Rise SK23 .... 45 E4
Alder Way NG20 .... 119 E2
Alderbrook Cl DE13 .... 240 C1
Aldercar Inf Sch NG16 .. 182 A2
Aldercar La NG16 ..... 182 A3
Aldercar Sch NG16 .... 182 A2
Alderd Cl S21 .... 60 C4
Alderfen Cl DE24 ...... 232 B2
Alderley Ct DE21 ...... 206 A1
Aldern Way DE45 ...... 109 F4
Alderney Rd S2 .... 43 D4
Alders Ave SK23 .... 34 C1
Alders Brook DE65 .... 228 B1
Alders La Chinley SK23 ... 34 C1
  Tansley DE4 .... 144 A2
Alders Rd SK6 .... 32 A4
Alders The S42 .... 113 E4
Aldersgate Derby DE22 ... 217 F4
  New Mills SK22 .... 33 D4
Aldersdale Cl DE72 .... 234 A1
Aldersley Cl DE65 ...... 230 B1
Alderson Pl S2 .... 43 D4
Alderson Rd S2 .... 43 D4
Alderson Rd N S2 .... 43 D4
Aldred's La DE75, NG16 ... 182 A1
Aldridge Cl NG9 .... 223 F1
Aldwark Rd SK17 .... 85 E3
Aldwych DE22 .... 218 A3
Alexander Ave NG16 ... 171 E4

Alexander Rd
  Dove Holes SK17 .... 47 F1
  Nottingham NG7 ...... 268 A1
Alexander St NG16 .... 182 C1
Alexander Terr NG16 ... 160 B1
Alexandra Ave NG19 ... 136 A3
Alexandra Ct DE15 .... 248 A2
Alexandra Gdns DE23 ... 219 E1
Alexandra Rd
  Burton u T DE15 ...... 248 A2
  Buxton SK17 .... 85 E3
  Dronfield S18 .... 57 D1
  Long Eaton NG10 ..... 236 B4
  Overseal DE12 .... 262 A2
  Sheffield S2 .... 43 D4
  Stafford ST17 .... 269 E3
  Swadlincote DE11 ..... 256 A2
Alexandra Rd E S41 ...... 96 B1
Alexandra Rd W S40 ... 266 A3
Alexandra St NG9 ..... 223 E3
Alexandre Cl DE23 .... 231 E3
Alford Cl S40 .... 95 E2
Alfred Cl NG3 .... 268 B2
Alfred Ct NG18 .... 268 B4
Alfred Rd DE56 .... 192 A4
Alfred St Alfreton DE55 ... 158 C2
  Pinxton NG16 .... 160 B2
  Ripley DE5 .... 169 F1
  Somercotes DE55 ..... 170 B3
  South Normanton DE55 ... 159 F3
Alfred St Central NG3 ... 268 B2
Alfred St N NG3 .... 268 B2
Alfred St S NG3 .... 268 C2
Alfreton L Ctr DE55 ... 158 C2
Alfreton & Mansfield
  Parkway Sta DE55 ... 159 E3
Alfreton Rd Blackwell DE55 ... 147 F1
  Breadsall DE21 .... 205 E3
  Codnor DE5 .... 170 B1
  Derby DE21 .... 205 E3
  Holbrook DE21 .... 191 E1
  Little Eaton DE21 ..... 205 E3
  Matlock DE4 .... 143 F2
  Nottingham NG7 ..... 268 A2
  Pinxton NG16 .... 160 B2
  Selston DE55, NG16 ... 171 E3
  Tansley DE4 .... 143 F2
  Tibshelf DE55 .... 147 E2
Alfreton Trad Est DE55 .. 159 D1
Algar Cl S2 .... 43 F4
Algar Cres S2 .... 43 F4
Algar Dr S2 .... 43 F4
Algar Pl S2 .... 43 F4
Algar Rd Sheffield S2 ..... 43 F4
  Stoke-on-T ST4 .... 269 D1
Alice St DE1 .... 267 C4
Alice Way S18 .... 76 C3
Alicehead Rd S45 ...... 113 D1
Alison Cl DE21 .... 219 F4
All Saints CE Fst Sch
  ST14 .... 196 C3
All Saints CE Inf Sch DE4 . 143 D3
All Saints CE Jun Sch
  DE4 .... 143 D4
All Saints Ct DE3 ...... 217 E1
All Saints Prim Sch SK6 ... 23 D3
All Saints RC Comp Sch
  NG18 .... 268 A4
All Saints Rd
  Burton u T DE14 ...... 254 B4
  Stoke-on-T ST4 .... 269 E1
All Saints' RC Prim Sch
  SK13 .... 10 B1
All Saints' Rd DE4 ..... 143 D4
All Saints' St NG7 ..... 268 A2
Allan Ave DE23 .... 230 C4
Allan La DE56 .... 168 A3
Allandale Rd DE75 .... 181 E1
Allcroft St NG19 ...... 136 B2
Allen Hill DE4 .... 143 D3
Allen La Ashover DE4 ... 144 B3
  Weston Underwood DE6 ... 188 B3
Allen St Derby DE24 ... 232 C3
  Stoke-on-T ST4 .... 269 D2
Allen's Green Ave NG16 ... 171 F3
Allen's La ST14 .... 224 C1
Allenby Cl S8 .... 56 C4
Allenby Dr S8 .... 56 C4
Allendale DE7 .... 208 C4
Allendale Rd S42 ..... 114 C2
Allendale Way NG19 ... 136 C1
Allenpark Inf Sch DE24 ... 232 B3
Allens Croft ST14 ..... 224 C1
Allenton Com Prim Sch
  DE24 .... 232 B3
Allestree Cl DE24 ..... 232 C4
Allestree Dr S18 .... 56 B1
Allestree La DE22 ..... 204 B2
Allestree St DE24 ..... 232 C4
Alley The DE4 .... 154 B2
Alley Wlk DE6 .... 201 F4
Allison Ave DE11 ..... 256 A2
Allissa Ave DE5 .... 180 C4
Allpits Rd S44 .... 96 C2
Allport Terr Barrow Hill S43 ... 78 A2
  Blackwell DE55 .... 147 E1
Allsops Pl S41 .... 95 F4
Allstone Lee DE56 .... 178 C3
Alma Cl NG3 .... 268 B2
Alma Cres S18 .... 57 D2
Alma Hill NG16 .... 195 F4
Alma Hts DE7 .... 217 F1
Alma Rd
  North Wingfield S42 ... 132 A4
  Nottingham NG3 ...... 268 C2
  Selston NG16 .... 171 F3
  Swadlincote DE11 ..... 255 F3
  Tideswell SK17 .... 69 C3

Alma St Alfreton DE55 ... 159 D2
  Buxton SK17 .... 85 E4
  Derby DE22 .... 267 A2
  Fenton ST4 .... 269 F1
  Melbourne DE73 ...... 252 A4
  North Wingfield S42 ... 131 F3
  Ripley DE5 .... 169 E2
Alma St W S40 .... 95 F1
Almond Ave Ripley DE5 ... 180 B4
  Shirebrook NG20 ...... 119 F3
Almond Cl Calow S44 ... 97 D2
  Kimberley NG16 ...... 195 F4
Almond Cres S43 .... 79 E2
Almond Ct DE13 ...... 240 C1
Almond Dr S21 .... 60 B3
Almond Gr
  Swadlincote DE11 ..... 256 A3
  Swanwick DE55 .... 170 A4
Almond Rise NG19 .... 136 C1
Alms Rd S21 .... 211 E1
Alnwick Dr S12 .... 44 A3
Alnwick Rd S12 .... 44 A3
Alpha St SK23 .... 34 C1
Alpha Terr NG1 .... 268 A2
Alpine Gr S43 .... 97 D4
Alport Ave Buxton SK17 ... 85 E4
  Sheffield S12 .... 44 C3
Alport Cl Belper DE56 ... 179 D3
  Hulland Ward DE6 ..... 175 F2
Alport Dr S12 .... 44 C3
Alport Gr S12 .... 44 C3
Alport Pl S12 .... 44 C3
Alport Rd S12 .... 44 C3
Alport Rise S18 .... 56 B1
Alsager Cl DE21 ...... 206 A1
Alsfeld Way SK22 .... 33 D4
Alsop Gr SK17 .... 85 F4
Alsop Pl S17 .... 85 F4
Alsop Way SK17 .... 85 F4
Alston Rd SK23 .... 47 D3
Alstonfield Dr DE22 .... 204 C1
Althorp Cl DE55 ...... 169 F4
Althorpe St NG7 ...... 268 A2
Alton Cl Chesterfield S40 ... 114 A4
  Derby DE22 .... 204 B2
  Dronfield S18 .... 75 E4
Alton Hill S42 .... 130 B3
Alton La S45 .... 130 B2
Alton Rd DE56 .... 179 E2
Alton Rise DE4 .... 142 C4
Alts Nook Way DE72 ... 234 C1
Alum Chine Cl S41 .... 115 E4
Alum Cl DE24 .... 233 E4
Alvaston Inf Sch DE24 ... 233 E3
Alvaston Jun Com Sch
  DE24 .... 233 E4
Alvaston St DE24 ..... 233 D4
Alvenor St DE7 .... 194 C1
Alverton Cl DE3 ...... 217 E1
Alward's Cl DE24 ..... 233 D3
Ambaston La
  Elvaston DE72 .... 234 A3
  Shardlow DE72 .... 234 C2
Amber Cl DE56 .... 168 A3
Amber Cres S40 .... 95 E1
Amber Croft S43 .... 97 E4
Amber Ct Belper DE56 ... 179 D3
  Heanor DE75 .... 181 F1
Amber Dr NG16 .... 182 A1
Amber Gr DE55 .... 158 C1
Amber Hill DE4 .... 168 A4
Amber Hts DE5 .... 169 E1
Amber La S45 .... 129 E2
Amber Pl S45 .... 131 D2
Amber Rd Bullbridge DE56 ... 168 A1
  Derby DE22 .... 204 B1
Amber St DE24 .... 232 B4
Amber View Rd DE56 ... 168 A4
Amberdene DE4 .... 143 E3
Ambergate Prim Sch
  DE56 .... 167 F2
Ambergate Sta DE56 .... 167 F2
Ambergrove DE56 .... 168 A2
Amberley Dr Buxton SK17 ... 85 E3
  Derby DE24 .... 231 F3
Amberwood DE11 .... 256 A3
Ambleside Cl
  Chesterfield S41 .... 95 E4
  Mosborough S20 .... 59 F3
Ambleside Dr NG16 ... 182 B2
Ambrose Terr DE1 .... 218 C3
Amen Alley DE1 .... 267 B3
American Adventure
  Theme Pk The DE75 ... 194 A3
Amesbury Cl S41 .... 95 F4
Amesbury La S41 ...... 205 F1
Ameycroft La DE4 .... 143 D4
Amilda Ave DE7 .... 208 C4
Amy St DE22 .... 218 C2
Anchor Ave SK23 .... 47 E3
Anchor Fold SK23 ...... 47 E3
Anchor Rd NG16 ...... 182 B1
Anchor Row DE7 ..... 208 C4
Anchor Sq DE45 ...... 109 E3
Anderby Gdns DE11 ... 255 F1
Anderson Cl S43 .... 77 F2
Anderson Sch The SK17 ... 85 D4
Anderson St DE24 .... 232 C4
Andrew Ave DE7 ..... 209 D4
Andrew Cl DE23 ..... 230 C4
Andrew St SK6 .... 15 D1
Andrews Dr
  Langley Mill NG16 .... 182 A2
  Stanley DE7 .... 193 D1
Andwell La S10 .... 42 C3
Angel Row NG1 .... 268 B1

Angel Yd S40 .... 266 B3
Angerford Ave S8 .... 43 D2
Anglers' La DE21 ...... 220 C2
Anglesey Rd
  Burton u T DE14 ...... 254 A4
  Dronfield S18 .... 76 A4
Anglesey St DE21 ..... 219 E4
Angleton Ave S2 .... 44 B4
Angleton Cl S2 .... 44 B4
Angleton Gdns S2 ...... 44 B4
Angleton Gn S2 .... 44 B4
Ankerbold Rd S42 .... 131 E4
Ann St S80 .... 81 F1
Anncroft Rd SK17 .... 84 B3
Anne Potter Cl DE72 ... 221 E3
Annesley Cl
  Chesterfield S41 .... 115 E4
  Sheffield S8 .... 56 C4
Annesley Gr NG1 ...... 268 B2
Annesley Rd S8 .... 56 C4
Anns Rd S2 .... 43 D4
Anns Rd N S2 .... 43 D4
Annwell La LE65 ...... 257 F1
Anslow La DE75, NG9 ... 240 A1
Anslow Rd DE13 ...... 238 A1
Anson Wlk DE7 .... 194 C2
Anstee Rd NG10 ..... 236 B3
Anstey Cl DE21 ...... 206 A1
Anstey Rise NG2 ..... 268 C2
Anthony Bek Prim Sch
  NG19 .... 134 C3
Anthony Cres DE24 ... 232 C3
Anthony Dr DE7 ..... 232 C3
Anthony Fell Sch DE4 ... 165 F4
Antill St NG9 .... 223 E3
Apiary Gate DE74 ..... 247 D2
Apperknowle Jun Sch S18 ... 58 A1
Appian Cl DE72 .... 221 E1
Appian Way
  Clay Cross S45 .... 131 E1
  Derby DE23 .... 233 E3
Apple St SK14 .... 15 E4
Apple Tree Rd SK22 ... 24 A1
Appleby Cl DE7 ...... 208 C3
Appleby Ct DE22 ..... 218 C2
Appleby Glade DE11 ... 255 E1
Appleby Rd NG19 .... 134 C3
Appledore Dr DE21 ... 206 A1
Applegarth Cl S12 ...... 44 A3
Applegarth Dr S12 ...... 44 A3
Applegate Cl DE21 ... 206 A2
Appleton Cl Derby DE21 ... 220 A4
  Swadlincote DE11 ..... 255 F3
Appleton Dr Belper DE56 ... 179 D3
  Glossop SK13 .... 17 F4
Appletree Cl DE72 .... 221 E1
Appletree Dr S18 .... 57 D1
Appletree Rd Bolsover S44 ... 80 A1
  Hatton DE65 .... 227 E3
Appletree Wlk S18 ...... 57 D1
Applewood Cl
  Belper DE56 .... 179 D3
  Uttoxeter ST14 .... 210 A1
Appleyard Ct **12** ST16 ... 269 E4
Aquinas St ST4 .... 269 E2
Arbor Cl DE22 .... 267 A2
Arbor Gr SK17 .... 84 C3
Arbor Low DE45 ...... 123 F2
Arboretum Prim Sch
  DE23 .... 219 D1
Arboretum Sch NG1 .... 268 A2
Arboretum Sq DE23 ... 267 C1
Arboretum St Derby DE23 .. 267 C1
  Nottingham NG1 ..... 268 A2
Arbour Cl S41 .... 115 E3
Arbour Hill DE7 ...... 207 F1
Arbourthorne Cotts S2 ... 43 E4
Arbourthorne Fst &
  Mid Sch S2 .... 43 E3
Arbourthorne Rd S2 ... 43 F3
Arcadia Ave NG20 .... 119 F3
Archdale Cl S2 .... 44 A4
Archdale Pl S2 .... 44 A4
Archdale Rd S2 .... 44 A4
Archer Rd NG9 .... 223 F3
Archer St Derby DE24 ... 219 F1
  Ilkeston DE7 .... 194 C2
Arden Cl Chesterfield S40 ... 95 E3
  Derby DE21 .... 218 C1
  Glossop SK13 .... 17 D4
Arden St SK22 .... 33 D4
Ardleigh Cl DE3 ...... 230 B4
Ardsley Cl Heanor DE75 ... 182 A1
  Sheffield S20 .... 44 C1
Ardsley Dr S20 .... 44 C1
Ardsley Gr S20 .... 44 C1
Ardsley Rd S40 .... 95 D2
Argyle Cl
  Market Warsop NG20 ... 120 C2
  Sheffield S8 .... 43 D3
Argyle Rd S8 .... 43 D3
Argyle St Derby DE22 ... 218 C2
  Langley Mill NG16 .... 182 B2
Argyll Cl DE21 .... 220 C3
Argyll Rd DE5 .... 169 F1
Arkendale Wlk DE24 ... 233 E3
Arklow Cl S41 .... 115 D4
Arkwright Ave DE56 ... 179 E3
Arkwright Cl DE4 ..... 127 E2
Arkwright Dr SK6 .... 23 D3
Arkwright Prim Sch S44 ... 97 E2
Arkwright Rd SK6 ...... 23 D3
Arkwright St Derby DE24 ... 232 B4
Wirksworth DE4 ...... 165 F4
Arleston La DE24 ..... 231 E1

Arleston St DE23 ... 231 F4
Arlington Ave NG19 ... 136 C2
Arlington Dr Derby DE24 ... 232 C3
Swanwick DE55 ... 169 F4
Arlington Rd DE23 ... 218 B1
Armitage Dr NG10 ... 237 D4
Arms Grove Prim Sch S2 ... 43 D4
Arms Park Dr S20 ... 59 F3
Armscote Cl DE21 ... 206 A1
Armstrong Ave ST 16 ... 269 F4
Armstrong Rd NG19 ... 268 A4
Armytage Ind Est S41 ... 77 D1
Arnfield La SK13 ... 9 F4
Arnhem Terr DE21 ... 220 C2
Arnold Ave
Long Eaton NG10 ... 236 A2
Sheffield S12 ... 44 A1
Arnold & Carlton Coll of F Ed NG1 ... 268 B1
Arnold Cl DE11 ... 261 F4
Arnold Cres NG10 ... 236 A2
Arnold St DE22 ... 218 B3
Arnside NG9 ... 223 F3
Arnside Cl
Chesterfield S41 ... 76 B1
Swadlincote DE11 ... 256 B1
Arran Cl Derby DE24 ... 231 F2
Stapleford NG9 ... 209 F1
Arran Ct DE55 ... 147 F3
Arridge Rd DE21 ... 219 F3
Arrowscroft Way SK14 ... 9 E3
Arthington St S8 ... 43 D3
Arthur Ave NG9 ... 223 F4
Arthur Ct DE23 ... 219 D1
Arthur Hind Cl DE22 ... 218 C4
Arthur Mee Ctr (Coll of F Ed) The NG9 ... 223 E4
Arthur Mee Rd NG9 ... 223 F3
Arthur Short Cl S80 ... 82 A3
Arthur St Alfreton DE55 ... 159 D3
Derby DE1 ... 267 B5
Draycott DE72 ... 234 C4
Linton DE11 ... 261 F4
Mansfield NG18 ... 268 C3
Nottingham NG7 ... 268 A2
Pinxton NG16 ... 160 B2
Arthurs Ct DE13 ... 240 C1
Artic Way NG16 ... 195 E4
Artisan View S8 ... 43 D3
Arun Dale NG19 ... 136 B1
Arundel Ave DE3 ... 217 F1
Arundel Cl Chesterfield S41 ... 95 F4
18 Dronfield S18 ... 56 B1
Sandiacre NG10 ... 223 D2
Arundel Dr Derby DE21 ... 220 C3
Mansfield NG19 ... 268 A4
Arundel Grange SK13 ... 17 D4
Arundel St Derby DE22 ... 218 B2
Glossop SK13 ... 10 B1
Nottingham NG7 ... 268 A2
Ascot Ave NG16 ... 195 F4
Ascot Cl
Burton u T DE15 ... 248 A2
West Hallam DE7 ... 207 E4
Ascot Dr DE24 ... 232 B4
Ascot Park Est NG10 ... 223 E4
Ascot Pl DE7 ... 208 B3
Ascott Dr DE11 ... 256 A4
Ash Acre DE56 ... 179 E2
Ash Cl Aston-on-T DE72 ... 246 A4
Derby DE22 ... 204 B2
Killamarsh S21 ... 60 B3
Mottram in L SK14 ... 9 D2
Pinxton NG16 ... 160 B1
Ash Cres Eckington S21 ... 59 D1
Ripley DE5 ... 180 B4
Ash Croft Prim Sch DE24 ... 231 F1
Ash Gr Brinsley NG16 ... 182 B4
Chinley SK23 ... 34 C1
Long Eaton NG10 ... 236 B3
Mastin Moor S43 ... 79 D2
Sandiacre NG10 ... 223 D4
Selston NG16 ... 171 F4
Shirebrook NG20 ... 119 E3
Stapleford NG9 ... 223 E3
Ash Grove La DE65 ... 241 E3
Ash La Eckington S18 ... 57 F2
Hilton DE65 ... 228 C4
Sutton on t H DE65 ... 228 C4
Unstone S18 ... 57 F2
West Handley S21 ... 77 E4
Ash Mount Rd NG16 ... 182 A2
Ash St Buxton SK17 ... 85 D3
Ilkeston DE7 ... 194 C2
Mosborough S20 ... 59 E4
Ash Terr SK17 ... 85 E4
Ash Tree Cl
Breadsall DE21 ... 205 F2
Chesterfield S40 ... 95 E2
Duffield DE56 ... 190 C3
Swadlincote DE11 ... 255 F3
Ash Tree Cres NG19 ... 136 B3
Ash Tree Rd S43 ... 80 C1
Ash Vale S40 ... 95 D2
Ash View Cl DE65 ... 229 D2
Ashbourne Ave S45 ... 131 D3
Ashbourne Cl 4 S40 ... 95 D3
Ashbourne Ct
Derby DE22 ... 218 C3
Glossop SK13 ... 17 F4
Ashbourne Dr DE11 ... 256 A1
Ashbourne La
Alstonefield DE6 ... 149 D1
Chapel-en-le-F SK23 ... 47 E3
Ashbourne Rd
Alstonefield DE6 ... 149 D2
Belper DE56 ... 178 B2
Buxton SK17 ... 85 E2
Church Broughton DE65 ... 213 F2
Derby DE22 ... 218 B4
Kirk Langley DE6 ... 202 B2
Mackworth DE22 ... 217 F4
Mayfield DE6 ... 184 B4
Rocester ST14 ... 196 C2
Shottle DE56 ... 177 E2
Turnditch DE56 ... 177 E2
Uttoxeter ST14 ... 210 A1
Ashbourne St
Nottingham NG7 ... 268 A2
Scarcliffe NG20 ... 119 F2
Ashbrook DE15 ... 248 A1
Ashbrook Ave DE72 ... 221 E1
Ashbrook Cl DE22 ... 204 B2
Ashbrook Inf & Jun Sch DE72 ... 221 D1
Ashbury Dr S8 ... 43 E1
Ashbury La S8 ... 43 E1
Ashby Ave NG19 ... 136 B3
Ashby La DE11 ... 257 E1
Ashby Rd
Blackfordby DE11, LE65 ... 257 E1
Breedon on t H DE73 ... 252 C1
Burton u T DE15 ... 248 A1
Melbourne DE73 ... 252 A3
Moira DE12 ... 262 C2
Ticknall DE73 ... 250 C1
Ashby Rd E DE15 ... 248 C1
Ashby St DE24 ... 232 C3
Ashcombe Gdns DE21 ... 206 A1
Ashcroft Cl DE24 ... 232 C4
Ashcroft Dr S41 ... 77 D1
Ashdale Cl DE15 ... 255 D4
Ashdale Rd DE7 ... 209 D3
Ashdown Dr S40 ... 95 E1
Ashe Pl DE23 ... 218 C1
Asher La DE5 ... 169 E3
Ashes Ave DE6 ... 175 F2
Ashes La
Fenny Bentley DE6 ... 162 A1
Glossop SK13 ... 10 A1
Ashfield Ave
Derby DE21 ... 219 F4
Mansfield NG18 ... 268 B4
Somercotes DE55 ... 159 E1
Ashfield Cl S12 ... 43 F2
Ashfield Dr S12 ... 43 F2
Ashfield Gr SK6 ... 15 D1
Ashfield Rd
Chapel-en-le-F SK23 ... 47 E3
Chesterfield S41 ... 115 E4
Hadfield SK13 ... 9 F2
Nottingham NG2 ... 268 C1
Ashford Ave S42 ... 132 A4
Ashford CE Prim Sch DE45 ... 108 C4
Ashford Cl S18 ... 75 E4
Ashford Ct DE7 ... 207 E4
Ashford La DE45 ... 89 E1
Ashford Mews SK13 ... 9 E1
Ashford Pl DE7 ... 194 C3
Ashford Rd S18 ... 75 E4
Ashford Rise DE56 ... 179 E3
Ashford St ST4 ... 269 F2
Ashforth Ave DE75 ... 182 A1
Ashforth St NG3 ... 268 B2
Ashfurlong Cl S17 ... 55 F4
Ashfurlong Dr S17 ... 55 F4
Ashfurlong Rd S17 ... 55 F4
Ashgate Ave S40 ... 95 E2
Ashgate Croft Sch S40 ... 95 E2
Ashgate Inf & Jun Sch DE22 ... 218 B3
Ashgate Rd
Chesterfield S40 ... 95 E2
Old Brampton S40 ... 95 E2
Ashgate Valley Rd S40 ... 95 E2
Ashgrove Ct DE21 ... 206 A1
Ashland Rd S21 ... 59 F2
Ashlands Ave ST4 ... 269 D2
Ashlands Cres ST4 ... 269 D2
Ashlands Rd ST4 ... 269 D2
Ashlea Dr DE6 ... 184 B4
Ashlea Wlk S43 ... 81 D3
Ashleigh Ave
Glossop SK13 ... 10 A1
Sheffield S12 ... 43 F3
Swadlincote DE11 ... 255 F3
Ashleigh Cl S41 ... 77 D2
Ashleigh Croft S12 ... 43 F3
Ashleigh Ct S21 ... 59 E1
Ashleigh Dr Derby DE73 ... 232 C1
Sheffield S12 ... 43 F3
Ashleigh Pl S12 ... 43 F3
Ashleigh Rd S43 ... 80 A4
Ashley Cl Killamarsh S21 ... 60 B3
Overseal DE12 ... 262 A2
Tansley DE4 ... 144 A2
Ashley Ct DE15 ... 248 A2
Ashley La S21 ... 60 B3
Ashley St Derby DE22 ... 218 B3
Nottingham NG3 ... 268 C2
Ashlyn Rd DE21 ... 267 D3
Ashmeadow DE72 ... 221 D1
Ashmeadow Ct DE6 ... 185 E4
Ashmore Ave S21 ... 59 D1
Ashop Rd DE56 ... 179 E3
Ashopton Ave DE23 ... 231 F4
Ashopton Dr S33 ... 40 A2
Ashopton Rd S33 ... 40 A3
Ashover Cl DE21 ... 219 F4
Ashover New Rd DE55 ... 145 F4
Ashover Prim Sch S45 ... 129 F2
Ashover Rd Alton S45 ... 130 C3
Ashover S45 ... 129 F2
Clay Cross S42 ... 130 C3
Derby, Allestree DE22 ... 204 B1
Derby, Chaddesden DE21 ... 219 F4
Staveley S43 ... 97 E3
Swadlincote DE11 ... 255 F3
Tupton S42 ... 131 D4
Ashton Cl Chesterfield S40 ... 114 B4
Derby DE3 ... 217 E2
Killamarsh S21 ... 60 B3
Swanwick DE55 ... 170 A4
Ashton Gdns Clay Cross S42 ... 131 D3
Glossop SK13 ... 17 E4
Ashton St SK13 ... 17 E4
Ashton Way DE56 ... 179 E2
Ashtree Ave DE24 ... 232 A3
Ashurst Cl S40 ... 94 C3
Ashview Cl NG10 ... 236 A4
Ashwater Cl DE24 ... 231 F1
Ashwell Ave NG19 ... 136 C3
Ashwood SK13 ... 16 C4
Ashwood Cl Buxton SK17 ... 85 E4
Mansfield Woodhouse NG19 ... 136 C3
Ashwood Rd Buxton SK17 ... 66 C1
Disley SK12 ... 32 B3
Ashworth Ave
Burton u T DE15 ... 248 B1
Derby DE21 ... 219 F3
Ashworth La SK14 ... 9 D2
Ashworth St ST4 ... 269 F1
Asker La DE4 ... 143 E3
Askerfield Ave DE22 ... 204 B2
Askew Gr DE65 ... 242 B1
Asline Rd S2 ... 43 D4
Aspen Cl Buxton SK17 ... 66 A1
Killamarsh S21 ... 60 B3
Aspen Ct NG19 ... 136 C1
Aspen Dr DE21 ... 220 B2
Aspen Rd S21 ... 59 D1
Aspen Rise DE55 ... 146 B1
Aspen Way SK6 ... 32 A4
Aspenshaw Rd SK22 ... 24 C2
Aspley Cl S40 ... 95 F3
Astcote Cl DE75 ... 182 A1
Asterdale Prim Sch DE21 ... 220 C2
Asterdale View DE21 ... 220 C2
Astil St DE15 ... 254 C4
Astlow Dr DE56 ... 179 D3
Aston Cl Derby DE73 ... 245 D4
Dronfield S18 ... 57 E2
Aston Ct Ilkeston DE7 ... 194 C1
Staveley S43 ... 78 C1
Aston Dr DE11 ... 256 A4
Aston Gn NG9 ... 223 F2
Aston Hall Dr DE72 ... 246 A4
Aston Hall Hospl DE72 ... 246 A3
Aston La Derby DE73 ... 233 D1
Hope S33 ... 39 E2
Shardlow DE72 ... 234 C1
Sudbury DE6 ... 226 A3
Wensley DE4 ... 142 B4
Aston Rd DE23 ... 231 E3
Aston-on-Trent Prim Sch DE72 ... 246 A4
Astorville Park Rd DE73 ... 232 C1
Astwith Cl S44 ... 116 C1
Astwith La S44, S45 ... 133 D3
Atchison Gdns DE21 ... 220 A4
Atherfield Gdns NG16 ... 182 C2
Atherton Ave SK14 ... 9 D2
Atherton Cl S2 ... 43 F3
Atherton Gr SK14 ... 9 D2
Atherton Rd Ilkeston DE7 ... 194 B2
Sheffield S2 ... 43 F3
Shipley DE7 ... 194 B2
Athlestan Way DE13 ... 240 B1
Athlone Cl DE21 ... 219 E4
Athol Cl Chesterfield S40 ... 114 A4
Derby DE24 ... 231 F2
Atkin Pl S2 ... 43 D4
Atkins Way ST14 ... 196 C2
Atlantic Dr S8 ... 56 C3
Atlantic Rd S8 ... 56 B3
Atlantic Way S8 ... 56 C3
Atlantic Wlk S8 ... 56 C3
Atlow Brow DE6 ... 173 E2
Atlow Cl S40 ... 95 D3
Atlow La DE6 ... 175 D3
Atlow Rd DE21 ... 219 F4
Attenborough Nature Reserve NG9 ... 237 E4
Attewell Cl DE72 ... 235 D4
Attewell Rd NG16 ... 195 D3
Attlebridge Cl DE21 ... 219 E4
Attlee Rd S43 ... 97 D4
Atworth Gr DE23 ... 230 C3
Auburn Cl DE7 ... 207 D4
Auckland Cl DE3 ... 217 F2
Auden Cl DE65 ... 227 D4
Audens Way DE11 ... 256 B3
Audley Cl DE7 ... 194 B2
Audrey Cres NG19 ... 136 B3
Audrey Dr DE21 ... 220 A4
Audrey Rd S13 ... 44 B4
Aughton Cl S13 ... 44 B4
Aughton Cres S13 ... 44 B4
Aughton Dr S13 ... 44 B4
Augusta St DE23 ... 219 D1
Aukland Dr S20 ... 59 F3
Aukland Rise S20 ... 59 F3
Aukland Way S20 ... 59 F3
Ault Hucknall La S44 ... 134 A4
Aults Cl DE65 ... 230 B1
Austen Ave Derby DE23 ... 231 D4
Long Eaton NG10 ... 236 B3
Austin Friars ST17 ... 269 E3
Austin Sq DE23 ... 231 F4
Austin St NG20 ... 120 A2
Austins Dr NG10 ... 223 D2
Austwick Gr ST4 ... 269 D1
Autumn Gr DE21 ... 219 F3
Avarne Pl 14 ST16 ... 269 E4
Avenue 1 S41 ... 115 D4
Avenue 2 S41 ... 115 D4
Avenue 3 S41 ... 115 D4
Avenue 4 S41 ... 115 D4
Avenue 5 S41 ... 115 D4
Avenue 6 S41 ... 115 D4
Avenue 7 S41 ... 115 D4
Avenue 8 S41 ... 115 D4
Avenue Cl S32 ... 72 A2
Avenue Rd Chesterfield S41 ... 96 A4
Duffield DE56 ... 190 C3
Avenue The Bakewell DE45 ... 109 E3
Belper DE56 ... 178 C1
Chapel-en-le-F SK23 ... 46 C1
Derby, Chaddesden DE21 ... 219 F3
Derby, The Holmes DE1 ... 267 B2
Dronfield S18 ... 57 D1
Hadfield SK13 ... 10 A2
Northwood DE4 ... 127 D3
Spinkhill S21 ... 60 B1
Stoney Middleton S32 ... 72 A2
Tissington DE6 ... 162 A3
Weston-on-T DE72 ... 245 F3
Averham Cl Derby DE21 ... 206 A1
Swadlincote DE11 ... 256 A2
Aviemore Way DE24 ... 231 F2
Avis Ave DE75 ... 193 F4
Avocet Ct 2 DE24 ... 231 E2
Avon Cl Derby DE24 ... 231 E1
Dronfield S18 ... 57 D2
Swadlincote DE11 ... 256 A3
Avon Rise ST 16 ... 269 F4
Avon St DE24 ... 232 C4
Avon Way Burton u T DE15 ... 248 A1
Hilton DE65 ... 228 C1
Avondale Cl NG10 ... 236 A3
Avondale Rd Bolsover S44 ... 118 A4
Chesterfield S40 ... 266 A4
Derby, Rose Hill DE23 ... 267 B1
Derby, Spondon DE21 ... 220 B3
Ilkeston DE7 ... 208 B3
Staveley S43 ... 97 E4
Avonlea Cl DE7 ... 209 D3
Avonmouth Dr DE24 ... 232 C4
Awdishaw La DE6 ... 213 E3
Awsworth Inf Sch NG16 ... 195 E2
Awsworth Jun Sch NG16 ... 195 E2
Awsworth La
Awsworth NG16 ... 195 E3
Cossall Marsh NG16 ... 195 E2
Kimberley NG16 ... 195 E3
Awsworth Rd DE7 ... 194 C1
Aycliffe Gdns DE24 ... 232 C2
Aylesbury Ave DE21 ... 219 F4
Aylward Cl S2 ... 43 F4
Aylward Rd S2 ... 43 F4
Ayncourt Rd S42 ... 132 A4
Ayr Cl DE21 ... 220 B2
Ayr St NG7 ... 268 A2
Azalea Ave DE55 ... 170 A4
Azalea Cl DE55 ... 159 F2
Azalea Ct NG16 ... 195 E4

Babbacombe Cl DE24 ... 233 E4
Babbington Cl DE13 ... 239 E3
Babbington La NG16 ... 195 F2
Babbington St DE55 ... 148 A3
Babbs La DE6 ... 211 E1
Babington Cl S2 ... 43 F4
Babington Ct S2 ... 43 F4
Babington Hospl DE56 ... 178 C1
Babington La DE1 ... 267 B2
Babworth Ct NG18 ... 268 C4
Bacchus Way DE55 ... 147 D3
Back Bridge St SK22 ... 24 B1
Back Browning St ST16 ... 269 D4
Back Croft S45 ... 131 F1
Back Jodrell St SK22 ... 33 D4
Back La Alderwasley DE56 ... 166 C4
Alstonefield DE6 ... 149 F2
Biggin SK17 ... 138 B1
Brackenfield DE55 ... 146 A1
Calow S44 ... 116 A4
Castle Donington DE74 ... 247 D3
Darley Dale DE4 ... 127 F2
Derby DE73 ... 233 D1
Ellastone DE6 ... 183 D2
Elton DE4 ... 140 C3
Glapwell S44 ... 118 A1
Glossop SK13 ... 16 C3
Hathersage S32 ... 53 D4
Hilton DE65 ... 228 B1
Ilkeston DE7 ... 194 C1
Mottram in L SK14 ... 9 D2
Palterton S44 ... 118 A3
Pentrich DE5 ... 169 E3
Pilsley S45 ... 132 B1
Shirley DE6 ... 200 B4
Spout DE56 ... 166 B2
Sutton in A NG17 ... 148 C2
Thorpe Salvin S80 ... 63 D3
Thurvaston DE6 ... 215 D2
Tibshelf DE55 ... 147 F3
Unstone S18 ... 57 F1
Wessington DE55 ... 157 F4
Youlgreave DE45 ... 125 D3
Back Mellor Rd SK22 ... 24 B1
Back Moor SK14 ... 9 D2
Back Rd S18 ... 57 F1
Back Sitwell St DE1 ... 267 B2
Back South St S43 ... 77 E2
Back St S33 ... 38 B2
Back Union Rd SK22 ... 33 E4
Back Wyver La DE56 ... 178 C3
Backhill La DE6 ... 151 D1
Backhouse La DE72 ... 221 E3
Backmoor Cres S8 ... 43 E1
Backmoor Rd S8 ... 43 E1
Bacon Cl NG16 ... 195 D4
Bacon La DE5 ... 169 D3
Bacons La S40 ... 115 D4
Baden Powell Ave S40 ... 266 B1
Baden Powell Rd S40 ... 266 B1
Badger Cl Chesterfield S40 ... 114 A4
Derby DE21 ... 220 C3
Badger La Ashover DE55 ... 145 E4
Stretton DE55 ... 145 E4
Badgery Cl ST14 ... 210 A1
Bag La Marchington ST14 ... 224 C1
Roston DE6 ... 197 F4
Bage Hill S42 ... 113 F3
Baggaley Cres NG19 ... 136 A1
Bagot St DE7 ... 207 E4
Bagshaw Hill DE45 ... 109 E3
Bagshaw La SK17 ... 48 A3
Bagshaw St Derby DE24 ... 232 C4
Pleasleyhill NG19 ... 135 D2
Bagshaw's Rd S12 ... 44 A3
Bagshawe Ave SK23 ... 46 C3
Bagshawe Cavern S33 ... 51 D3
Bagthorp La S42 ... 94 A2
Bagthorpe La S42 ... 94 A2
Bailey Ave DE12 ... 262 A2
Bailey Brook Cres NG16 ... 182 A2
Bailey Brook Dr NG16 ... 182 A2
Bailey Brook Ind Est DE75, NG16 ... 182 A1
Bailey Brook Wlk NG16 ... 182 A2
Bailey Cres NG19 ... 268 A4
Bailey Dr S21 ... 60 C4
Bailey Gr SK17 ... 85 F4
Bailey Grove Rd NG16 ... 182 B1
Bailey St Derby DE23 ... 267 A1
Stafford ST17 ... 269 E3
Stapleford NG9 ... 223 E3
Bainbridge Rd S44 ... 98 C2
Bainbridge St DE23 ... 219 D2
Baines Wood Cl S41 ... 95 E4
Bains Dr DE72 ... 221 E1
Bakeacre La DE65 ... 230 C2
Baker Ave DE75 ... 193 F4
Baker Cl Somercotes DE55 ... 170 B4
Stanley DE7 ... 193 D1
Baker Dr S21 ... 60 B3
Baker Rd NG19 ... 136 B3
Baker St Burton u T DE15 ... 254 C4
Creswell S80 ... 81 F1
Derby DE24 ... 232 C4
Ilkeston DE7 ... 194 C1
Swadlincote DE11 ... 256 B2
Baker's La Cromford DE4 ... 155 D3
Doveridge DE6 ... 211 E1
Bakers Hill DE56 ... 168 C1
Bakers La DE4 ... 156 A4
Bakestone Moor S80 ... 81 F3
Bakewell CE Inf Sch DE45 ... 109 E3
Bakewell Cl DE3 ... 217 F2
Bakewell Dr DE74 ... 247 D1
Bakewell Gn DE11 ... 255 F3
Bakewell Meth Jun Sch DE45 ... 109 E2
Bakewell Mews SK13 ... 9 E1
Bakewell Rd Baslow DE45 ... 91 F2
Buxton SK17 ... 85 E4
Darley Dale DE4 ... 142 C4
Long Eaton NG10 ... 236 C3
Matlock DE4 ... 143 D3
Over Haddon DE45 ... 109 D1
Staveley S43 ... 97 E3
Bakewell St Derby DE22 ... 218 C2
Stoke-on-T ST4 ... 269 D1
Balaclava Rd DE23 ... 232 A4
Balderton Ct NG19 ... 268 A4
Baldwin St NG7 ... 268 A2
Balfour Rd Derby DE23 ... 232 A4
Stapleford NG9 ... 223 E3
Balham Wlk DE22 ... 218 A3
Balk Pas ST16 ... 269 D4
Ball Hill DE55 ... 160 B3
Ball La DE72 ... 234 A3
Ballacraine Dr DE5 ... 169 F1
Ballards Way DE72 ... 221 E1
Ballater Cl DE24 ... 231 F2
Balleny Cl DE21 ... 205 F1
Balmoak La S41 ... 96 B3
Balmoral Cl Derby DE23 ... 218 A1
Mansfield Woodhouse NG19 ... 136 C3
Sandiacre NG10 ... 223 D2
Balmoral Cres S18 ... 56 B1
Balmoral Dr NG19 ... 135 F1
Balmoral Rd
Borrowash DE72 ... 221 E1
Burton u T DE15 ... 248 A2
Ilkeston DE7 ... 208 B3
Nottingham NG1 ... 268 A2
Balmoral Way S43 ... 77 F2
Baltimore Cl DE11 ... 256 A4
Bamber St ST4 ... 269 E2
Bamburgh Cl DE21 ... 220 B2
Bamford Ave Derby DE23 ... 231 F4
North Wingfield S42 ... 131 F4
Bamford La SK13 ... 9 F1
Bamford Mews SK13 ... 9 F1
Bamford Prim Sch S33 ... 40 A2
Bamford Rd S43 ... 97 E3
Bamford St
Chesterfield S43 ... 77 E2
Newton DE55 ... 148 A2
Ripley DE5 ... 180 B4
Bamford Sta S33 ... 40 A1

Bamsbrook La S43 80 B1
Banbury Ave NG9 223 F2
Bancroft Cl DE65 228 B1
Bancroft Dr DE22 204 B2
Bancroft La NG18 268 A4
Bancroft The DE65 229 D2
Bangor St DE21 219 F4
Bank Cl Bolsover S44 99 D2
Creswell S80 100 B4
Shirebrook NG20 119 F2
Tibshelf DE55 147 F3
Bank Gdns DE4 143 E3
Bank La SK13 10 A4
Bank Pas 9 ST16 269 E4
Bank Rd Chesterfield S41 96 A3
Matlock DE4 143 D3
Bank Side Derby DE22 204 C1
Hartington SK17 137 E3
Bank St Brimington S43 96 B4
Broadbottom SK14 16 A4
Chesterfield S40 95 F2
Glossop SK13 17 E4
Hadfield SK13 10 A3
Hayfield SK22 25 E2
Langley Mill NG16 182 B2
Long Eaton NG10 236 C4
Somercotes DE55 170 B4
Swadlincote DE11 262 A4
Bank The Bonsall DE4 142 B1
Glossop SK13 17 E4
Stoney Middleton S32 71 F2
Bank Top La S32 72 B4
Bank Vale Rd SK22 25 E2
Bank View SK17 69 D3
Bank View Rd Derby DE22 218 C4
Nether Heage DE56 168 B1
Bank Wood Cl S40 95 D4
Bankbottom SK13 10 A3
Bankerwall La DE6 183 E4
Bankfield Dr Derby DE21 220 C2
Ilkeston DE7 208 A3
Bankgate SK14 16 A4
Bankholmes Cl DE24 231 F1
Banks Rd NG9 223 F1
Banksburn Cl DE75 181 E1
Bankside DE45 125 D3
Bankside Cl SK6 15 E1
Bankswood Cl SK13 10 A2
Bankwood Cl S14 43 E3
Bankwood Prim Sch S14 43 E3
Bankwood Rd S14 43 E3
Banmoor La S32 52 C4
Bannell's La DE73 229 F4
Bannels Ave DE23 231 D4
Banton's La DE73 251 D2
Banwell Cl DE3 217 E2
Bar Croft S40 95 E3
Bar Gate S33 38 B1
Bar Rd Baslow DE45 91 F3
Curbar S32 72 C1
Barber Cl DE7 194 C2
Barber St SK13 10 A3
Barber's La S21 60 B4
Barbon Cl S40 95 F3
Barcheston Cl DE21 206 A1
Barclay Ct DE7 194 B2
Barden Dr DE22 204 C2
Bardolph Cl DE11 255 F2
Bardsey Ct DE21 206 A2
Bare La DE72 221 E3
Barf Cl DE3 217 F1
Bargate Cl DE56 179 E1
Bargate La DE65 242 A3
Bargate Rd DE56 179 D1
Barholme Cl S41 95 D4
Barker Ave NG16 171 D2
Barker Ave E NG10 223 D3
Barker Ave N NG10 223 D3
Barker Cl ST16 269 D4
Barker Fold S40 95 E2
Barker Gate Ilkeston DE7 194 C1
Nottingham NG1 268 B1
Barker La S40 95 E2
Barker St NG17 148 C2
Barklam Cl DE12 262 C1
Barlborough Hall Sch S43 61 D1
Barlborough Prim Sch S43 80 A4
Barlborough Rd S43 80 B3
Barley Cft Derby DE73 232 C1
South Normanton DE55 160 A2
Barley Cl DE21 205 E4
Barley Croft DE56 179 D1
Barley Dale Dr NG9 209 E1
Barley La S40 95 D3
Barleycorn Cl
Burton u T DE15 248 A1
Derby DE21 206 B1
Barleycroft SK13 9 F2
Barling Dr Ilkeston DE7 194 B1
Shipley DE7 194 B1
Barlow CE Prim Sch S18 75 F2
Barlow Dr N NG16 195 D2
Barlow Dr S NG16 195 D2
Barlow Lees La S18 75 F4
Barlow Rd Barlow S42 94 C4
Chapel-en-le-F SK23 47 E3
Staveley S43 78 C1
Barlow St DE1 267 D1
Barlow View S18 76 A4
Barlow Wood Dr SK6 23 D2
Barms Way SK17 66 B1
Barn Cl
Castle Donington DE74 247 D2
Chesterfield S40 95 E3
Findern DE65 230 B1
Glossop SK13 17 E4
Quarndon DE22 204 B3
Barnard Ave S18 57 E2
Barnard Rd DE21 205 E1
Barnes Ave S18 56 C1
Barnes Gn DE22 218 A4
Barnes La S18 56 B1
Barnes Rd S41 96 C1
Barnfield ST4 269 D1
Barnfield Cl
Holmewood S42 132 C4
Staveley S43 78 C1
Barnfield Wlk S43 78 C1
Barnfields S32 52 C4
Barnham Cl S40 114 A4
Barnhill Gr DE23 231 D4
Barnsfold Ct SK22 25 E2
Barnsley La
Idridgehay DE56 165 F1
Spout DE56 165 F1
Barnstaple Cl DE21 206 A1
Barnston Rd NG2 268 C2
Barnwell Cl ST14 210 A2
Barnwell La DE4 155 D3
Barnwood Cl DE3 217 E1
Baron Cl DE21 206 B2
Barrack Rd S18 58 A1
Barrack Yd DE55 170 B4
Barracks Sq S40 266 B2
Barratt Rd S21 59 E1
Barrett St DE24 233 D4
Barrie Dr DE24 231 F3
Barringer Rd NG19 136 B1
Barrington Cl DE13 240 B1
Barron's Way DE72 221 E1
Barroon The DE74 247 D2
Barrow Hill Prim Sch S43 78 A2
Barrow La DE73 244 B3
Barrow St S43 78 C1
Barrows Hill La NG16 171 E3
Barry Rd S43 96 C2
Barson Gr SK17 85 F1
Bartle Ave S12 43 F2
Bartle Dr S12 43 F2
Bartle Rd S12 43 F2
Bartle Way S12 43 F2
Barton Cl DE21 220 C3
Barton Cres S40 95 D3
Barton Hill DE4 126 B1
Barton Knoll DE56 179 E2
Barton Knowle DE56 179 E2
Barton Rd
Long Eaton NG10 237 D3
Sheffield S8 43 D3
Barton St Burton u T DE14 254 B4
Clowne S43 80 C2
Barton Turn DE13 253 D1
Basegreen Ave S12 44 A2
Basegreen Cl S12 44 B2
Basegreen Cres S12 44 A2
Basegreen Dr S12 44 B2
Basegreen Pl S12 44 A2
Basegreen Rd S12 44 B2
Basegreen Way S12 44 B2
Basildon Cl DE24 232 C3
Basingwerke Ct SK22 25 E2
Baslow Cl NG10 236 A3
Baslow Dr DE22 204 C2
Baslow Gn DE11 255 F3
Baslow Gr SK17 85 F3
Baslow Mews SK13 9 F1
Baslow Rd Bakewell DE45 109 E4
Curbar S32 72 B1
Holymoorside S42 94 B1
Totley S17 55 E2
Bass St DE22 218 B3
Bass's Cres DE11 261 F4
Bassett Cl NG16 195 F4
Bassett La S10 42 C3
Bassett Rd NG16 195 F4
Bassett The NG20 119 E3
Bassettbarn La S42 130 A3
Bassford Ave DE75 181 F1
Bassingham Cl DE21 206 A1
Bassledene Rd S2 44 A4
Batch La DE6 224 A4
Bateman Cl S43 77 E2
Bateman St DE23 219 E2
Batemill Rd SK22 24 B1
Batemoor Cl S8 57 D3
Batemoor Dr S8 57 D3
Batemoor Pl S8 57 D3
Batemoor Rd S8 57 D3
Batemoor Wlk S8 57 D3
Bath La Ashover S45 129 F3
Mansfield NG18 268 C4
Market Warsop NG19 120 B1
Moira DE12 262 B2
Bath Rd Buxton SK17 85 D3
Derby DE3 217 F1
Bath St Bakewell DE45 109 E3
Derby DE1 267 B4
Ilkeston DE7 194 C1
Mansfield NG18 268 B3
Nottingham NG1 268 B2
Stoke-on-T ST4 269 E2
Bath Terr ST4 269 E2
Batham Gate Bradwell SK17 50 A2
Peak Forest SK17 48 C1
Batham Gate Rd SK17 67 D3
Batham Rd S33 51 D4
Bathurst Rd S44 117 F4
Bathurst Terr NG20 100 C1
Batley La NG19 134 C2
Batt St S8 43 D4
Baulk La Beeston NG9 223 F4
Hathersage S32 41 D1
Baum's La NG18 268 C3
Baverstock Cl DE73 232 C2
Baxter Hill NG19 134 C2
Baxter Sq DE23 231 F3
Bay Ct S21 60 B3
Baycliffe Dr S40 95 E2
Bayleaf Cres DE21 206 A2
Baysdale Croft S20 59 E4
Bayswater Cl DE22 217 F3
Bayswater Rd NG16 195 F4
Bazley Rd S2 43 F3
Beacomfold SK6 15 D2
Beacon Dr DE13 240 A2
Beacon Hill Rise NG3 268 C2
Beacon Rd DE13 240 A2
Beaconsfield St NG10 236 C4
Beam Cl DE13 240 A1
Beard Cres SK22 33 E4
Beardall St 5 NG18 268 B4
Beardmore Cl DE21 205 F1
Beards Rd DE11 256 A3
Bearwood Hill Rd DE15 248 A2
Beast Market Hill NG1 268 B1
Beatrix Dr SK13 9 F2
Beatty St DE24 232 C4
Beatty Wlk DE7 194 C2
Beauchief Abbey La S8 56 B4
Beauchief Dr S17 56 B4
Beauchief Gdns DE55 170 B4
Beaufit La NG16 160 C1
Beaufort Ct Ind Est DE21 219 E4
Beaufort Inf & Jun Schs DE21 219 E4
Beaufort Rd
Burton u T DE15 248 A1
Derby DE24 231 E1
Beaufort St DE21 219 E4
Beaulieu Way DE55 170 A4
Beaumaris Ct DE21 220 C3
Beaumont Cl
Barrow u T DE73 244 A3
Belper DE56 179 E2
Stapleford NG9 209 F1
Beaumont St NG2 268 C1
Beaumont Wlk DE23 231 F3
Beaurepaire Cres DE56 179 D3
Beaureper Ave DE22 204 C2
Beauvale Dr DE7 194 C3
Beazley Ave NG18. 268 A4
Becher St DE23 219 D1
Beck Cl S44 99 E1
Beck Cres NG19 268 A4
Beck St NG3 268 B2
Beckenham Way DE22 218 A3
Becket Ave S8 56 B3
Becket Cres S8 56 C3
Becket Prim Sch DE22 218 C2
Becket Rd S8 56 C3
Becket St DE1 267 B3
Becket Well La DE1 267 B3
Becket Wlk S8 56 C3
Beckett Ave NG19 135 F1
Beckford Rd NG2 268 C1
Beckingham Ct NG19 268 A4
Beckitt Cl DE24 233 D4
Becksitch La DE56 178 C1
Bedehouse La DE4 155 D3
Bedford Ave ST 16 269 F4
Bedford Cl DE22 218 B2
Bedford Ct NG9 209 F1
Bedford Rd DE15 254 B4
Bedford St DE22 218 B2
Bedgrave Cl S21 60 C4
Bee Hives The DE11 256 A4
Beech Ave Alfreton DE55 159 D3
Borrowash DE72 221 E2
Breaston DE72 235 F4
Creswell S80 81 F1
Derby DE24 233 D4
Glossop SK13 17 D4
Hulland Ward DE6 175 F2
Long Eaton NG10 223 F1
Mansfield NG18 268 B3
Melbourne DE73 252 A4
New Mills SK22 24 B1
Pinxton NG16 160 C2
Quarndon DE22 204 A4
Ripley DE5 169 E1
Sandiacre NG10 223 D4
Willington DE65 242 A3
Beech Cl Belper DE56 179 D2
Kilburn DE56 192 A4
Beech Cres Eckington S21 59 D1
Glapwell S44 134 A4
Killamarsh S21 60 B3
Beech Ct DE21 220 B3
Beech Dr Ashbourne DE6 185 E4
Derby DE22 218 C4
Etwall DE65 229 E2
Findern DE65 230 C1
Long Duckmanton S44 97 E2
Woodville DE11 257 D1
Beech Gdns DE24 233 D4
Beech Gr
Long Duckmanton S44 98 A2
South Normanton DE55 160 A3
Swadlincote DE11 255 F4
Beech Hill Ave NG19 135 F1
Beech Hill Cres NG19 135 F1
Beech Hill Dr NG19 135 F1
Beech Hill Sch NG19 135 F1
Beech La Burton u T DE13 240 C1
Dove Holes SK17 66 C4
West Hallam DE7 207 E4
Beech Rd SK23 45 F4
Beech Rise SK23 45 E3
Beech St S43 78 A1
Beech Tree Ave NG19 136 A3
Beech Tree Dr S43 80 C1
Beech Way Clay Cross S45 131 F1
Dronfield S18 57 D2
Beech Wlk Cromford DE4 155 D3
Derby DE23 218 B1
Beechcroft DE21 205 E2
Beechcroft Ave ST17 269 D3
Beechdale Cl S40 95 E2
Beechdale Rd NG19 136 C1
Beeches Ave Derby DE21 220 B3
Sheffield S2 43 E4
Beeches Dr S2 43 E4
Beeches The Crich DE4 156 C1
Heanor DE75 193 E4
Beechfield Rd SK13 9 F2
Beechley Dr DE21 206 A1
Beechwood SK13 16 C4
Beechwood Cl DE56 178 C3
Beechwood Cres DE23 231 E4
Beechwood Dr SK6 23 D3
Beechwood Rd S18 56 C1
Beehive Yd S40 95 E1
Beeley Cl Belper DE56 179 E3
Creswell S80 81 E1
Derby, Allestree DE22 204 B1
Derby, Oakwood DE22 205 F1
North Wingfield S42 132 A4
Staveley S43 97 E3
Beeley La DE4 112 A2
Beeley View S40 114 A4
Beeley Way S43 97 E3
Below Cl SK17 47 F1
Beeston Cl S18 56 B1
Beetwell St S40 266 B2
Beggarway La DE45 90 A3
Beighton St DE5 169 F1
Beldon Cl S2 43 E4
Beldon Pl S2 43 E4
Beldon Rd S2 43 E4
Belfast Wlk DE21 220 A2
Belfield Ct DE75 181 E2
Belfield Rd Etwall DE65 229 E2
Swadlincote DE11 256 A3
Belfit Dr S42 114 C1
Belfmoor Cl S80 82 A3
Belfry Cl DE3 217 F1
Belfry The DE13 240 B1
Belgrade Ave SK23 34 C1
Belgrave Cl DE56 179 E3
Belgrave Sq S2 43 D4
Belgrave St DE23 267 B1
Belklane Dr S21 60 C4
Bell Ave DE72 246 A4
Bell La Bonsall DE4 142 B1
Doveridge DE6 224 B4
Bellar Gate NG1 268 B1
Belle Acre Cl DE56 178 C2
Belle View Rd DE6 173 D1
Belle Vue Ave DE5 180 B3
Belle Vue Cl S43 96 B4
Belledere Cl DE55 169 F4
Bellevue Ct NG3 268 C2
Bellhouse La S43 78 C2
Bellingham Ct DE22 204 B1
Bells End Rd DE12 253 E1
Bellsfield Cl S80 82 A3
Belmont Ave DE72 235 F4
Belmont Dr
Borrowash DE72 221 D1
Marple SK6 15 D1
Staveley S43 78 C1
Belmont Prim Sch DE11 256 B2
Belmont St DE11 256 B2
Belmont Terr 2 SK17 85 D4
Belmot Rd DE13 239 D2
Belond La S45 113 E1
Belper La DE56 178 C3
Belper Rd Ashbourne DE6 173 F1
Derby DE1 218 C4
Holbrook DE56 191 E4
Kilburn DE56 179 F1
Morley DE7 192 C1
Shirland DE55 146 B1
Stanley DE7 193 D1
West Hallam DE7 207 E4
Belper Sch DE56 179 E2
Belper Sports Ctr DE56 179 E2
Belper St Ilkeston DE7 208 C4
Mansfield NG18 268 C4
Belper Sta DE56 178 C2
Belper Way NG18 268 C4
Belsize Cl DE22 217 F3
Belton Cl Dronfield S18 56 B1
Sandiacre NG10 223 D2
Belton Dr DE5 169 F1
Belvedere Ave S40 114 C4
Belvedere Cl
Chesterfield S40 114 A4
Derby DE3 217 E2
Belvedere Rd DE11 256 C1
Belvedere St NG18 268 B3
Belvedere Terr SK17 85 D3
Belvoir Cl Breaston DE72 235 E4
Ilkeston DE7 208 B3
Long Eaton NG10 236 C3
Belvoir Cres DE11 256 A3
Belvoir Hill NG2 268 C1
Belvoir St DE23 218 C1
Belvoir Way DE55 159 E1
Bembridge Dr DE24 233 E3
Bemrose Com Sch DE22 218 B2
Bemrose Gate S33 40 A3
Bemrose Mews DE22 218 B2
Bemrose Rd DE24 232 C4
Benbow Ave DE73 252 A4
Bench Rd SK17 85 E4
Benches La SK14 15 F2
Bend Oak Dr DE15 248 B2
Bend Oak Jun Sch DE15 248 B2
Bendall Gn DE23 231 E3
Benenden Cl ST17 269 F3
Beninmoor Way S40 114 C4
Benjamin Outram Bsns Ctr DE5 180 C4
Benmore Ct DE21 205 E2
Benner Ave DE7 209 D3
Bennerley Ave DE7 194 C2
Bennerley Fields Sch DE7 194 C2
Bennerley Sch DE7 194 C2
Bennett St Buxton SK17 85 E3
Derby DE24 232 B3
Hollingworth SK14 9 E3
Long Eaton NG10 223 E1
Sandiacre NG10 223 D3
Bennetts La DE4 168 A4
Bennington Wlk NG19 136 C2
Bennison Gdns S45 131 E2
Bensley Cl DE73 233 D1
Benson St DE24 232 C4
Bent La
Church Broughton DE65 227 E3
Darley Dale DE4 127 E3
Matlock DE4 143 D4
Netherthorpe S43 79 D2
Northwood DE4 127 E3
Spout DE56 166 B3
Tissington DE6 162 B3
Wirksworth DE56 166 B3
Bent The S32 72 C2
Bent's La S18 57 E1
Bentfield Rd DE56 168 B1
Bentham Rd S40 95 F3
Bentick St NG18 268 C4
Bentinck Dr S43 81 D2
Bentinck Rd S44 98 C4
Bentink Cl S80 81 E1
Bentley Brook DE65 228 C1
Bentley Cl Alfreton DE55 159 D2
Matlock DE4 143 E4
Bentley Fields Open Farm DE6 199 E1
Bentley Rd
Castle Donington DE74 246 C2
Uttoxeter ST14 210 A1
Bentley St DE24 232 C3
Benton Dr SK6 23 E4
Bents Cres S18 57 E2
Bents La S18 57 E2
Bents Rd S17 55 E2
Bentside Rd SK12 32 B3
Beowulf Covert DE13 240 A1
Beresford Ave
Ashbourne DE6 173 E1
Chapel-en-le-F SK23 47 E3
Beresford Cl S45 131 E1
Beresford Dale DE11 255 F1
Beresford Dr Derby DE21 220 C2
Ilkeston DE7 194 C3
Beresford La SK17 137 E1
Beresford Pl DE56 168 A3
Beresford Rd
Chapel-en-le-F SK23 47 E3
Long Eaton NG10 236 A3
Mansfield Woodhouse NG19 136 B3
Beresford St NG18 268 C3
Berkeley Ave NG10 236 B3
Berkeley Cl DE23 231 E4
Berkshire St DE21 219 E4
Berle Ave DE75 181 F1
Bermuda Ave DE21 205 E3
Bernard Ave NG19 136 A3
Bernard Cl S43 96 C4
Bernard Rd NG19 268 A4
Bernard St Glossop SK13 10 B1
Swadlincote DE11 256 B2
Bernard Walker Ct SK6 15 D1
Berners Cl S2 43 F3
Berners Dr S2 43 F3
Berners Pl S2 43 F3
Berners Rd S2 43 F3
Berridge La S45 145 D2
Berrisford La DE55 145 E4
Berristow La DE55 160 B4
Berry Ave S21 59 E2
Berry Gdns DE15 248 B2
Berry Hedge La DE15 248 B2
Berry Hill Rd NG18 268 C3
Berry Park Cl DE22 204 C1
Berry St North Wingfield S42 131 F3
Stoke-on-T ST4 269 E2
Bertrand Ave S45 131 E2
Berwick Ave
Chesterfield S40 114 B4
Derby DE21 219 E4
Berwick Cl DE24 233 D3
Berwick Dr DE24 231 E2
Berwick Rd SK17 85 E2
Berwin Cl NG10 223 D1
Berwyn Cl S40 95 E3
Bessalone Dr DE56 179 D3
Bessell La Beeston NG9 223 E3
Stapleford NG9 223 E3
Bessie La S33 51 D3
Best Ave DE15 248 A1
Besthill Cotts SK14 16 A4
Besthorpe Cl DE21 206 A1
Besthorpe Ct NG19 268 A4
Bestwick Ave DE75 182 A1
Bestwood Dr S45 131 E2
Bestwood Pk S45 131 E2
Bestwood Rd NG16 160 C1
Bethel Terr S80 63 F3
Bethulie Rd DE23 232 A4
Betjeman Sq DE24 232 A3

Betlingspring La DE6 .... 184 B2
Betony Cl S21 .... 60 A3
Bevan Dr S43 .... 97 D4
Bevan Rd S45 .... 131 E1
Bevan St DE55 .... 146 C1
Beverley Dr NG16 .... 195 F4
Beverley Rd DE14 .... 254 A4
Beverley St DE24 .... 219 E1
Beverleys Rd S8 .... 43 D2
Bewdley Cl DE73 .... 233 D2
Bexley Cl SK13 .... 10 B2
Bicester Ave DE24 .... 231 E1
Bickley Moss DE21 .... 206 A1
Bideford Cl DE5 .... 169 E1
Bideford Dr DE23 .... 231 E3
Bidston Cl DE4 .... 143 E4
Bidworth La SK13 .... 9 E1
Biggin CE Prim Sch
SK17 .... 138 B2
Biggin Cl S45 .... 131 E1
Biggin La DE6 .... 176 A2
Biggin The DE74 .... 247 D2
Bigginmill La DE56 .... 176 B3
Bilby La S43 .... 77 F1
Billam St S21 .... 59 D2
Billingsley Ave NG16 .... 160 B2
Bilton St ST4 .... 269 E1
Bingham St DE24 .... 232 C3
Bings Rd SK23 .... 45 F4
Bingswood Ave SK23 .... 45 F4
Bingswood Ind Est SK23 .... 45 F4
Bingswood Rd SK23 .... 45 F4
Binscombe La DE21 .... 205 F2
Birch Ave Ilkeston DE7 .... 209 D4
Swadlincote DE11 .... 256 A4
Toadmoor DE56 .... 167 F2
Birch Cl Alfreton DE55 .... 159 D3
Branston DE14 .... 254 A4
Buxton SK17 .... 66 A1
Denstone ST14 .... 196 B3
Grassmoor S42 .... 115 F2
Killamarsh S21 .... 60 B3
Ripley DE5 .... 180 B4
Wessington DE55 .... 157 F4
Birch Farm Ave S8 .... 57 D4
Birch Gn SK13 .... 10 C1
Birch Gr Hatton DE65 .... 227 E1
Shirebrook NG20 .... 119 E3
Birch Hall Cl SK22 .... 25 D1
Birch Holt Gr S18 .... 76 C3
Birch Kiln Croft 8 S43 .... 96 C4
Birch La S43 .... 78 A1
Birch Rd S80 .... 82 B3
Birch St NG20 .... 120 C3
Birch View Ct DE1 .... 218 C4
Birchen Cl
Chesterfield S40 .... 95 E3
13 Dronfield S18 .... 56 B1
Birchen Holme DE55 .... 160 A2
Birches Ave DE55 .... 157 F3
Birches Fold S18 .... 57 E2
Birches La Dronfield S18 .... 57 E2
South Wingfield DE55 .... 158 A3
Birches Rd DE22 .... 204 B2
Birches The SK22 .... 25 E1
Birchfield Cl DE73 .... 232 C1
Birchfield Pk DE75 .... 193 F4
Birchfield Rd DE15 .... 254 C3
Birchills The S80 .... 81 E1
Birchitt Cl S17 .... 56 B3
Birchitt Pl S17 .... 56 B3
Birchitt Rd S17 .... 56 B3
Birchitt View S18 .... 57 D2
Birchlands NG19 .... 136 C1
Birchlands Dr S21 .... 60 B3
Birchover Edge DE4 .... 141 D4
Birchover La DE4 .... 141 D4
Birchover Pl DE7 .... 194 C3
Birchover Rd
Birchover DE4 .... 126 B2
Stanton in P DE4 .... 126 B2
Birchover Rise DE21 .... 205 F1
Birchover Way DE22 .... 204 C1
Birchside Ave SK13 .... 10 A1
Birchvale Rd S12 .... 44 C2
Birchview Cl DE56 .... 179 D1
Birchwood DE75 .... 181 E2
Birchwood Ave
Derby DE23 .... 231 E3
Long Eaton, Breaston
NG10 .... 236 A4
Long Eaton, New Sawley
NG10 .... 236 B3
Birchwood Cl
25 Mosborough S20 .... 59 F4
South Normanton DE55 .... 160 A2
Birchwood Cres
Chesterfield S40 .... 114 C4
Somercotes DE55 .... 170 B4
Birchwood Croft 26 S20 .... 59 F4
Birchwood Dr DE56 .... 168 A2
Birchwood Gdns S20 .... 59 F4
Birchwood Gr S20 .... 59 F4
Birchwood La
Pinxton DE55 .... 159 F2
Somercotes DE55 .... 159 F2
South Normanton DE55 .... 159 F2
Birchwood Rd DE55 .... 159 E2
Birchwood Rise 27 S20 .... 59 F4
Birchwood View
Ashbourne DE6 .... 173 E2
Mosborough S20 .... 59 F4
Birchwood Way
23 Mosborough S20 .... 59 F4
Somercotes DE55 .... 159 E1
Bircumshaw's Rd DE75 .... 181 F1
Bird St S43 .... 78 C1
Birdcage Wlk DE22 .... 217 F3
Birdcroft La DE7 .... 208 C3
Birdholme Cres S40 .... 115 D4
Birdholme Inf Sch S40 .... 115 D4
Birding St NG19 .... 136 A1
Birdsgrove La
Mayfield DE6 .... 172 B2
Swinscoe DE6 .... 172 B2
Birdwood St DE23 .... 218 C1
Birk Hill Inf Sch S21 .... 59 D1
Birkdale Cl Derby DE3 .... 218 A1
Ilkeston DE7 .... 194 B1
Birkdale Dr S40 .... 114 B4
Birkin Ave S42 .... 115 E1
Birkin La Grassmoor S42 .... 115 F1
Temple Normanton S42 .... 116 A2
Wingerworth S42 .... 114 B1
Birkin La W S42 .... 115 F1
Birkinstyle Ave DE55 .... 146 C2
Birkinstyle La DE55 .... 146 C2
Birkland Ave
Mansfield Woodhouse
NG19 .... 136 B2
Nottingham NG1 .... 268 B2
Birkland St NG18 .... 268 C4
Birks Cl S80 .... 82 B3
Birks St ST4 .... 269 E1
Birley Brook Dr S40 .... 95 D4
Birley Comp Sch S12 .... 44 B2
Birley La S12 .... 44 C1
Birley Moor Ave S12 .... 44 C2
Birley Moor Cl S12 .... 44 C2
Birley Moor Cres S12 .... 44 C1
Birley Moor Dr S12 .... 44 C1
Birley Moor Pl S12 .... 44 C1
Birley Moor Rd S12 .... 44 C2
Birley Moor Way S12 .... 44 C1
Birley Spa Inf & Jun Sch
S12 .... 44 C2
Birley Spa La S12 .... 44 C2
Birley St NG9 .... 223 E3
Birley Vale Ave S12 .... 44 B3
Birley Vale Cl S12 .... 44 B2
Biscay Ct DE21 .... 206 B1
Bishop Lonsdale CE Prim
Sch DE22 .... 218 C2
Bishop Pursglove CE Prim
Sch SK17 .... 69 E2
Bishop St Alfreton DE55 .... 159 D3
Eastwood NG16 .... 182 C1
Mansfield NG18 .... 268 B3
Bishop's Ct DE73 .... 252 A4
Bishop's Dr DE21 .... 205 F1
Bishopdale Cl NG10 .... 236 A3
Bishopdale Dr S20 .... 59 D4
Bishopdale Rise S20 .... 59 D4
Bishops Ct S8 .... 43 D3
Bishops House Mus S8 .... 43 D2
Bishops La SK17 .... 84 C4
Bishopscourt Rd S8 .... 43 D3
Bispham Dr NG9 .... 223 F1
Bitham Ct DE13 .... 240 B1
Bitham La DE13 .... 240 B1
Bitham Sch DE13 .... 240 B1
Blaby Cl DE23 .... 231 F3
Black Harry La S32 .... 71 D1
Black Hills Dr DE7 .... 208 C3
Black Tor Rd DE4 .... 154 B4
Blacka Moor Cres S17 .... 55 E3
Blacka Moor Rd S17 .... 55 E3
Blacka Moor View S17 .... 55 E3
Blackberry Flats S20 .... 59 F4
Blackberry La ST16 .... 269 D4
Blackberry Way DE56 .... 179 F1
Blackbird Row DE56 .... 179 E1
Blackbrook La SK23 .... 47 F3
Blackburn Pl DE7 .... 194 C2
Blackcliff Field Cl S80 .... 82 A3
Blackden Cl DE56 .... 179 F2
Blackdown Ave S40 .... 95 D3
Blackfordby CE Prim Sch
DE11 .... 257 E1
Blackmore St DE23 .... 231 F4
Blackmount Ct 7 DE24 .... 231 E2
Blackpit La DE6 .... 224 A4
Blackpool St DE14 .... 254 B4
Blackrocks Ave DE4 .... 142 C4
Blacks La S42 .... 131 F4
Blackshaw Rd SK13 .... 10 C1
Blacksmith La S44 .... 97 D2
Blacksmith's La
Egginton DE65 .... 241 D3
Newton Solney DE15 .... 248 C4
Woodville DE11 .... 256 C2
Blacksmiths Yd DE4 .... 127 F1
Blackstock Cl S14 .... 43 E1
Blackstock Cres S14 .... 43 E1
Blackstock Dr S14 .... 43 E1
Blackstock Rd S14 .... 43 E2
Blackstone Cl DE55 .... 170 B4
Blackthorn Cl
Chesterfield S41 .... 115 E4
Derby DE73 .... 205 F1
Melbourne DE73 .... 252 A4
Blackthorn Rd DE15 .... 254 C3
Blackthorne Cl DE56 .... 179 F1
Blackwall La DE56 .... 176 A4
Blackwell La
Melbourne DE73 .... 252 A4
Monyash DE45 .... 107 D2
Blackwell Prim Sch
DE55 .... 147 F1
Blackwell Rd NG17 .... 148 C2
Bladon House Sch
DE15 .... 248 A3
Bladon St DE15 .... 248 B2
Bladon View DE13 .... 241 D1
Blagdon Cl DE4 .... 127 E2
Blagreaves Ave DE23 .... 231 E3
Blagreaves La DE23 .... 231 E3
Blair Gr NG10 .... 223 D2
Blake Cres NG18 .... 268 C4
Blake Ct NG10 .... 236 A3
Blake Rd NG9 .... 223 F3
Blake St Ilkeston DE7 .... 194 C1
Mansfield Woodhouse
NG19 .... 136 A1
Blakebrook Dr DE73 .... 233 D2
Blakeley La DE65 .... 229 D1
Blakelow Dr DE65 .... 229 D2
Blakelow La DE4 .... 142 A2
Blakemere La DE4 .... 141 F1
Blakemore Ave DE73 .... 252 A4
Blakeney Ct Derby DE21 .... 206 B1
Mansfield Woodhouse
NG19 .... 136 C2
Blakiston St ST16 .... 269 E4
Blanch Croft DE73 .... 252 A4
Blandford Ave NG10 .... 236 A3
Blandford Cl DE24 .... 233 E3
Blanford Dr S41 .... 95 F4
Blankney Cl DE24 .... 231 E1
Bleasby St NG2 .... 268 C1
Blencathra Dr DE3 .... 230 C4
Blenheim Ave DE55 .... 170 A4
Blenheim Cl
Burton u T DE15 .... 248 B2
4 Hadfield SK13 .... 10 A3
Mansfield NG19 .... 136 B1
Swadlincote DE11 .... 256 A4
Blenheim Dr DE22 .... 204 B2
Blenheim Mews DE65 .... 229 E2
Blenheim Pl NG17 .... 148 C2
Blenheim Rd DE6 .... 185 F4
Blenheim St ST4 .... 269 F1
Blenheim Ct NG10 .... 223 D2
Blessed William Howard
RC High Sch ST17 .... 269 D3
Blind La Bolsover S44 .... 98 C2
Breaston DE72 .... 235 E4
Darley Dale DE4 .... 127 F1
Kirk Ireton DE6 .... 165 D1
Wirksworth DE4 .... 165 F4
Blissworth Way DE55 .... 169 F4
Blithfield Gdns DE73 .... 233 D1
Bloom St DE1 .... 267 B2
Bloomfield Cl Derby DE1 .... 267 C1
Hilton DE65 .... 228 B1
Bloomfield Rd DE55 .... 170 A4
Bloomfield St DE1 .... 267 D1
Bloomgrove Rd DE7 .... 194 C1
Blore Cl DE6 .... 185 E4
Blossom Cres S12 .... 44 A2
Blue Bell Hill Jun & Inf
Schs NG3 .... 268 C2
Blue Bell Hill Rd NG3 .... 268 C2
Blue John Cavern S33 .... 37 F2
Bluebank View S43 .... 77 E2
Bluebell Cl Derby DE24 .... 231 E1
Somercotes DE55 .... 159 F1
Underwood Green NG16 .... 171 F1
Bluebell Croft DE4 .... 143 D2
Bluebell Hill DE55 .... 146 B2
Bluebird Ct DE24 .... 231 E2
Bluecoat Cl NG1 .... 268 B2
Bluecoat St NG1 .... 268 B2
Bluestone Cty Prim Sch
S2 .... 43 E4
Bluestone La DE15 .... 255 D4
Blundestone La DE4 .... 156 A1
Blunt Ave S43 .... 79 E2
Blunt St DE7 .... 193 D1
Blyth Cl Chesterfield S40 .... 114 A4
Mansfield NG19 .... 135 E1
Blyth Pl DE21 .... 205 E1
Boam La DE4 .... 142 C4
Boardman Cres ST16 .... 269 D4
Boardman Ind Est
DE11 .... 255 F2
Boardman Rd DE11 .... 255 F1
Boarslack La SK17 .... 69 F1
Boarstones La SK17 .... 85 F4
Boat La NG16 .... 182 A4
Boatmans Cl DE7 .... 194 C1
Bobbin Mill La S40 .... 95 E1
Bobbinmill Hill DE56 .... 168 A4
Bochum Parkway S8 .... 57 E4
Bocking La S8 .... 56 C4
Bocking Rise S8 .... 56 C4
Boden St DE23 .... 219 D1
Bodmin Cl DE24 .... 231 E2
Bodmin Way 3 S40 .... 95 E3
Bog La DE73 .... 251 F3
Boggard La SK13 .... 16 B3
Boggard Rd SK6 .... 24 A3
Boggy La DE65 .... 227 D4
Bohem Rd NG10 .... 223 E2
Boiley La S21 .... 60 B2
Boland Rd S8 .... 56 B3
Bold La DE1 .... 267 B3
Bole Hill S8 .... 43 D1
Bolehill La Eckington S21 .... 59 D1
Marsh Lane S21 .... 58 C1
Northedge S42 .... 130 B4
Wingerworth S42 .... 114 B1
Bolehill Rd DE4 .... 155 D2
Bolsover CE Jun Sch S44 .... 99 D1
Bolsover Com Hospl S44 .... 99 E1
Bolsover Inf Sch S44 .... 99 D1
Bolsover Rd Bolsover S44 .... 98 C3
Mastin Moor S43 .... 79 E2
Bolsover Sch S44 .... 99 E1
Bolsover St NG18 .... 268 C3
Bolton St DE55 .... 169 E4
Boman's La DE56 .... 177 F4
Bonchurch Cl DE24 .... 233 E3
Bond La DE56 .... 168 C1
Bond St Nottingham NG2 .... 268 C1
Staveley S43 .... 97 E4
Bondfield Rd S43 .... 97 E4
Bondgate DE74 .... 247 D2
Bondhay La S80 .... 62 B1
Bonington Rd NG19 .... 268 A3
Bonner's Rd NG16 .... 195 E2
Bonnington Cres ST16 .... 269 D3
Bonnington Dr DE55 .... 170 B4
Bonnington Rise SK6 .... 23 D4
Bonnyrigg Dr DE21 .... 206 A1
Bonsall CE Prim Sch
DE4 .... 142 C1
Bonsall Ct 2 S41 .... 95 E4
Bonsall Dr DE3 .... 217 F2
Bonsall La Alfreton DE55 .... 158 C2
Bonsall DE4 .... 141 E2
Winster DE4 .... 141 E2
Bonsall St NG10 .... 236 C4
Bonsallmoor La DE4 .... 141 F1
Bonsalt Dr DE55 .... 170 B4
Bonser Cres NG17 .... 148 C1
Boon Ave ST4 .... 269 E2
Boot Hill DE65 .... 242 B2
Booth Ave NG19 .... 135 D3
Booth Cl NG3 .... 268 B2
Booth Cres NG19 .... 135 E1
Booth St Derby DE24 .... 232 C4
Hollingworth SK14 .... 9 E3
Mansfield Woodhouse
NG19 .... 136 A2
Ripley DE5 .... 169 F1
Stoke-on-T ST4 .... 269 E1
Booth's Ct SK13 .... 10 B1
Boothby Ave DE6 .... 173 E1
Boothby Meadows Sch
DE6 .... 173 E1
Boothen CE Prim Sch
ST4 .... 269 E1
Boothen Gn ST4 .... 269 E1
Boothen Old Rd ST4 .... 269 E1
Boothen Rd ST4 .... 269 E1
Boothenwood Terr ST4 .... 269 E1
Boothgate DE56 .... 179 F4
Boots Yd NG17 .... 148 C2
Border Cl S43 .... 80 C2
Border Cres DE24 .... 233 D3
Border La S80 .... 80 C1
Borlace Cres NG9 .... 223 F3
Borough St DE74 .... 247 D2
Borrow Wood Inf & Jun
Schs DE21 .... 220 C3
Borrowash By-pass
Borrowash DE72 .... 221 E2
Derby DE21 .... 220 B2
Risley DE72 .... 221 E2
Borrowash Rd DE21 .... 220 C2
Borrowdale Ave S20 .... 59 F3
Borrowdale Cl S20 .... 59 F3
Borrowdale Dr
Long Eaton NG10 .... 236 A3
Mosborough S20 .... 59 F3
Borrowdale Rd S20 .... 59 F3
Borrowfield Rd DE21 .... 220 C2
Borrowfields DE72 .... 221 D1
Boscastle Rd DE24 .... 233 D3
Boscowan Ct DE7 .... 194 C2
Bosley Mews DE56 .... 178 C3
Bosnall Ave DE23 .... 231 E4
Bostock Rd SK14 .... 16 A4
Bostock's La Risley NG10 .... 222 C2
Sandiacre NG10 .... 223 D2
Boston Cl DE21 .... 220 B3
Boston St NG1 .... 268 B2
Boswell Sq DE23 .... 231 F4
Bosworth Ave DE23 .... 231 F3
Bosworth Rd DE74 .... 246 C2
Bosworth Way NG10 .... 236 C3
Botany Ave NG18 .... 268 A3
Botany Commercial Pk
NG18 .... 268 A3
Botany Dr DE7 .... 194 C3
Bothe Cl NG10 .... 236 B3
Bottle La NG1 .... 268 B1
Bottom Cliff S32 .... 71 F2
Bottom Lons DE56 .... 176 A4
Bottom Rd S42 .... 114 C1
Bottomhill Rd SK17 .... 69 F1
Bough La S32 .... 72 A1
Boughey Rd ST4 .... 269 F2
Boughey St ST4 .... 269 E1
Boughton Dr DE55 .... 169 F4
Boughton La S43 .... 80 B2
Bould St NG19 .... 135 F1
Boulevard The SK14 .... 9 E2
Boulton Cl S40 .... 95 D3
Boulton Dr DE24 .... 233 D3
Boulton Inf Sch DE24 .... 233 D3
Boulton Jun Sch DE24 .... 233 D3
Boulton La
Derby, Allenton DE24 .... 232 C3
Derby, Boulton DE24 .... 233 D3
Boundary Cl
Netherthorpe S43 .... 79 D2
Shirebrook NG20 .... 119 F3
Boundary Gdns DE55 .... 147 F3
Boundary La NG16 .... 182 B2
Boundary Rd Derby DE22 .... 218 C2
Egginton DE65 .... 241 E4
Boundary Wlk NG20 .... 100 C1
Bourne Cl S43 .... 96 C4
Bourne Ct DE73 .... 251 F4
Bourne Mill Cl S43 .... 80 A4
Bourne Sq DE72 .... 235 F4
Bourne St DE1 .... 267 B2
Bournebrook Ave DE4 .... 165 F4
Bow St NG19 .... 136 C2
Bowbridge Ave DE23 .... 231 E3
Bowden Cres SK22 .... 33 E4
Bowden La SK23 .... 47 E4
Bowden Rd SK13 .... 10 B2
Bowdon Ave S43 .... 80 A3
Bower Farm Rd S41 .... 77 D1
Bower St DE24 .... 232 C4
Bowes Well Rd DE7 .... 194 C1
Bowland Cl DE3 .... 217 F1
Bowland Dr S40 .... 114 A4
Bowland Rd SK13 .... 17 D4
Bowlees Ct DE23 .... 230 C4
Bowler Dr DE56 .... 192 A4
Bowler Rd DE4 .... 127 E2
Bowler St DE5 .... 180 B4
Bowling Alley DE56 .... 168 C1
Bowling Alley La
Marston Montgomery DE6 .... 212 A3
Sudbury DE6 .... 212 A3
Bowling Cl DE7 .... 222 C4
Bowling Gn DE4 .... 153 D1
Bowling Green La DE4 .... 154 C1
Bowling St NG18 .... 268 C3
Bowman Cl S12 .... 43 F1
Bowman Dr S12 .... 44 A1
Bowmer La DE56 .... 168 A3
Bowmer Rd DE24 .... 219 F1
Bown Cl DE56 .... 192 A4
Bowness Cl
Chesterfield S41 .... 95 E4
2 Dronfield S18 .... 56 C1
Bowness Rd S41 .... 95 E4
Bowns Hill DE4 .... 157 D1
Bowshaw Ave S8 .... 57 D3
Bowshaw Cl S8 .... 57 D3
Bowshaw View S8 .... 57 D3
Bowstead St ST4 .... 269 E2
Boxmoor Cl DE23 .... 230 C4
Boyd Gr DE73 .... 245 D4
Boyer St DE22 .... 267 A1
Boyer Wlk DE22 .... 267 A1
Boylestone Rd DE23 .... 231 E3
Boythorpe Ave S40 .... 266 A2
Boythorpe Cres S40 .... 266 A1
Boythorpe Mount S40 .... 266 A2
Boythorpe Rd S40 .... 266 A2
Boythorpe Rise S40 .... 95 F1
Brabyns Brow SK6 .... 23 D4
Bracken Ave S44 .... 116 C1
Bracken Cl
Hollingworth SK14 .... 9 E3
Long Eaton NG10 .... 223 D1
Marple SK6 .... 23 E4
Bracken La
Barlborough S43 .... 80 A3
Holloway DE4 .... 156 A3
Bracken Rd NG10 .... 223 D1
Bracken Way SK13 .... 17 F4
Bracken's La DE24 .... 232 C3
Brackendale Cl
Brimington S43 .... 96 B4
Clay Cross S45 .... 131 F1
Brackendale La DE6 .... 163 F3
Brackendale Rd DE55 .... 169 F4
Brackenfield Ave NG19 .... 136 C2
Brackenfield Dr NG16 .... 195 D4
Brackenfield Gr S12 .... 44 B2
Brackenfield La
Brackenfield DE55 .... 145 E1
Wessington DE55 .... 157 E4
Brackenfield Specl Sch
NG10 .... 223 D1
Brackens Ave DE24 .... 232 C3
Brackensdale Ave DE22 .... 218 A3
Brackensdale Inf Sch
DE22 .... 218 A3
Brackensdale Jun Sch
DE22 .... 218 A3
Brackenwood Rd DE15 .... 254 C3
Brackhills Cl NG19 .... 136 C1
Brackley DE56 .... 179 F1
Brackley Dr DE21 .... 220 C3
Brackley Gate DE7 .... 192 A1
Bracknell Dr DE24 .... 232 C3
Bracton Dr NG3 .... 268 C2
Bradbourne Cl S43 .... 97 E4
Bradbourne Ct DE22 .... 218 C2
Bradbury Cl
Borrowash DE72 .... 221 E1
Chesterfield S40 .... 95 F2
Bradbury Dr S42 .... 114 C2
Bradbury St S8 .... 43 D3
Bradden Ave NG9 .... 209 F1
Bradder Way NG18 .... 268 B3
Bradgate Cl NG10 .... 223 D2
Bradgate Ct DE23 .... 231 F3
Bradgate Dr DE5 .... 169 D1
Brading Cl DE24 .... 233 E3
Bradley CE Prim Sch
DE6 .... 186 C4
Bradley Cl Birchover DE4 .... 126 A1
4 Brimington S43 .... 96 C4
Bradley Dr DE56 .... 179 D2
Bradley La S18 .... 75 E2
Bradley St
Burton u T DE15 .... 254 C4
Derby DE22 .... 218 C4
Sandiacre NG10 .... 223 E3
Bradley View DE6 .... 173 E2
Bradley Way S43 .... 96 C4
Bradmoor Gr DE73 .... 233 D1
Bradshaw Ave DE55 .... 170 C3
Bradshaw Cres SK6 .... 23 D4
Bradshaw Croft DE56 .... 178 C3
Bradshaw Dr DE56 .... 191 E3
Bradshaw La S32 .... 70 C4

Bradshaw Meadow DE65 ... 227 E1
Bradshaw Rd Marple SK6 ...... 23 D4
Staveley S43 ... 97 D3
Bradshaw St NG10 ... 236 A3
Bradshaw Way DE1 ... 267 C2
Bradway Cl S17 ... 56 A3
Bradway Cty Prim Sch S8 ... 56 C3
Bradway Dr S17 ... 56 A3
Bradway Grange Rd S17 ... 56 B3
Bradway Rd S17 ... 56 B3
Bradwell CE Inf Sch S33 ... 51 D4
Bradwell Cl Derby DE3 ... 217 F1
8 Dronfield S18 ... 56 B1
Eastwood NG16 ... 195 E4
Bradwell Gr S45 ... 131 E1
Bradwell Head Rd S33 ... 51 D4
Bradwell Jun Sch S33 ... 51 D4
Bradwell Pl S43 ... 97 E4
Bradwell St S2 ... 43 D3
Bradwell Way DE56 ... 179 D3
Braefield Cl DE7 ... 208 B3
Braemar Ave NG16 ... 182 C1
Braemar Cl Chesterfield S43 .. 77 E2
12 Derby DE24 ... 231 E2
Brafield Cl DE56 ... 179 E2
Brailsford Ave DE11 ... 255 F3
Brailsford CE Prim Sch DE6 ... 201 F4
Brailsford Rd DE21 ... 219 F4
Braintree Cl DE21 ... 205 E1
Braithwell Cl DE22 ... 204 C1
Bramah Edge Ct SK13 ... 9 F4
Bramall La S2 ... 43 D4
Bramble Cl
Holmewood S44 ... 116 C1
Long Eaton NG10 ... 223 D1
Shirebrook NG20 ... 119 F3
Bramble Mews DE3 ... 217 E1
Bramble St DE1 ... 267 A3
Bramble Way DE56 ... 179 F1
Brambleberry Ct DE21 ... 206 A2
Brambling Ct S41 ... 96 B1
Bramell Cl DE14 ... 253 F4
Bramfield Ave DE22 ... 218 C2
Bramfield Ct DE22 ... 218 C2
Bramham Rd SK6 ... 23 D2
Bramley Ave S13 ... 44 C4
Bramley Cl Derby DE21 ... 206 B2
Mosborough S20 ... 59 E4
Bramley Ct Hatton DE65 ... 227 E1
Kimberley NG16 ... 195 F3
Bramley Dale DE11 ... 255 F1
Bramley Hall Rd S13 ... 44 C4
Bramley La Baslow DE45 ... 91 E4
Hassop DE45 ... 91 E4
Sheffield S13 ... 44 C4
Bramley Park Cl S13 ... 44 C4
Bramley Park Rd S13 ... 44 C4
Bramley Rd
Bramley-Vale S44 ... 117 F1
Marsh Lane S21 ... 58 C1
Bramley St DE55 ... 170 C4
Bramley Vale Prim Sch S44 ... 117 F1
Bramleymoor La S21 ... 58 C1
Bramlyn Cl S43 ... 80 B3
Bramlyn Ct S43 ... 80 B3
Brampton Ave DE75 ... 182 A1
Brampton Cl DE3 ... 217 E2
Brampton Ct DE56 ... 179 E2
Brampton Dr NG9 ... 223 F3
Brampton Inf & Jun Sch S40 ... 95 F2
Bramshill Rise S40 ... 95 E1
Branch La S45 ... 132 C3
Brancliffe La S81 ... 63 F4
Brandelhow Ct DE21 ... 206 B2
Brandene Cl S44 ... 97 D2
Brandreth Dr NG16 ... 195 D4
Branklene Cl NG16 ... 195 F4
Branksome Ave DE24 ... 233 E4
Branksome Chine Ave S41 ... 115 E4
Bransdale Cl NG10 ... 236 A3
Branston Rd
Branston DE13 ... 253 E4
Burton u T DE14 ... 254 B4
Branston Water Pk DE14 ... 253 E3
Branton Cl S40 ... 266 A1
Brassington Cl
Eastwood NG16 ... 195 D4
West Hallam DE7 ... 207 F4
Youlgreave DE45 ... 125 E3
Brassington Cres SK13 ... 9 E1
Brassington Ct NG19 ... 136 C2
Brassington La S45 ... 131 E3
Brassington Prim Sch DE4 ... 153 D1
Brassington Rd DE21 ... 205 D4
Brassington St S45 ... 131 E2
Braybrook Cl DE55 ... 169 F4
Brayfield Ave DE23 ... 231 E4
Brayfield Rd DE23 ... 231 E4
Breach La Hatton DE65 ... 227 E2
Scropton DE6 ... 226 B3
Stanton by B DE73 ... 244 C1
Breach Rd Denby DE5 ... 181 D2
Heanor DE75 ... 194 A4
Breadsall CE Prim Sch DE21 ... 205 F2
Breadsall Ct DE7 ... 194 C2
Breadsall Hill Top Inf & Jun Sch DE21 ... 205 F1
Breamfield La DE56 ... 166 A4
Brearley Ave S43 ... 77 E2
Brearley St S41 ... 77 E2
Breaston La DE72 ... 222 B2
Brechin Ct NG19 ... 136 A3
Breck La S21, S43 ... 78 B3
Breckbank NG19 ... 136 C1
Breckland Rd S40 ... 114 A4
Brecon Cl
Chesterfield S40 ... 95 E3
Derby DE21 ... 220 C3
6 Long Eaton NG10 ... 236 A4
Bredon Cl 7 NG10 ... 236 A4
Breedon Ave DE23 ... 231 E3
Breedon Hill Rd DE23 ... 218 C2
Breedon on the Hill CE Sch DE73 ... 252 C2
Breedon St NG10 ... 223 E1
Bren Way DE65 ... 228 C1
Brenden Ave DE55 ... 170 B4
Brenden Cl DE55 ... 170 B4
Brendon Ave S40 ... 95 E2
Brendon Cl SK13 ... 17 D4
Brendon Dr NG16 ... 195 F4
Brendon Way NG10 ... 223 D1
Brent Cl S40 ... 95 E3
Brentford Dr DE22 ... 218 A3
Brentwood Ave S33 ... 40 A2
Brentwood Rd S33 ... 40 A2
Bretby Bsns Pk DE15 ... 255 F4
Bretby Hall Hospl DE15 ... 249 E1
Bretby La DE15 ... 248 C2
Bretby Rd
Chesterfield S40 ... 95 D3
Swadlincote DE11 ... 255 F4
Bretby Sq DE23 ... 231 E3
Bretby View DE11 ... 257 D2
Bretlands Way DE15 ... 255 D3
Bretton Ave Bolsover S44 ... 99 E1
Derby DE23 ... 218 B1
Bretton Cl S40 ... 95 D3
Bretton Gr S12 ... 44 B2
Bretton Rd DE56 ... 179 F3
Brewery St
Chesterfield S41 ... 266 C3
Kimberley NG16 ... 195 F3
Breydon Cl DE24 ... 232 B2
Briar Ave NG10 ... 223 D2
Briar Briggs Rd S44 ... 98 C2
Briar Cl Alfreton DE55 ... 159 E2
Borrowash DE72 ... 221 E1
Chesterfield S40 ... 95 F3
Derby DE21 ... 220 A2
Swadlincote DE11 ... 255 F3
Briar Gate NG10 ... 223 D1
Briar Lea Cl DE24 ... 231 F2
Briar Rd NG16 ... 195 D4
Briar View S43 ... 96 C4
Briar's La DE4 ... 168 A4
Briardene Cl S40 ... 94 C3
Briargrove Rd SK22 ... 24 B2
Briars Cl S21 ... 60 B3
Briars Way DE5 ... 180 B4
Briarsgate DE22 ... 204 B1
Briarwood Cres SK6 ... 23 D2
Briarwood Way DE23 ... 231 E3
Brick Kiln La
Mansfield NG19 ... 268 A4
Rolleston DE13 ... 240 A2
Brick Row DE22 ... 205 D1
Brick St DE1 ... 218 C3
Brick-kiln La
Brailsford DE6 ... 186 C1
Hulland Ward DE6 ... 175 E3
Brickbridge Rd SK6 ... 23 D3
Brickfield St SK13 ... 10 A3
Brickfields Cl DE4 ... 155 D2
Brickhouse La S17 ... 55 E4
Brickhouse Yd S40 ... 95 F2
Brickkiln La DE7 ... 206 B4
Bricky Cl S43 ... 80 B3
Brickyard Cotts DE6 ... 185 E4
Brickyard La
Kilburn DE56 ... 179 F1
Ripley DE5 ... 169 F1
South Normanton DE55 ... 160 A3
Brickyard Rd DE56 ... 168 B3
Brickyard The DE7 ... 193 D1
Bridge Bank Cl S40 ... 95 E3
Bridge Cl
Swadlincote DE11 ... 256 B1
Whitwell S80 ... 82 A3
Bridge End Ave NG16 ... 171 F4
Bridge Farm DE13 ... 240 C1
Bridge Field DE72 ... 235 E4
Bridge Foot DE56 ... 178 C3
Bridge Hill DE56 ... 178 C3
Bridge St Bakewell DE45 ... 109 E3
Belper DE56 ... 178 C2
Bradwell S33 ... 51 D4
Burton u T DE13 ... 240 C1
Buxton SK17 ... 85 E4
Chesterfield S40 ... 266 B1
Clay Cross S45 ... 131 E2
Derby DE1 ... 218 C3
Ilkeston DE7 ... 194 C2
Killamarsh S21 ... 60 B4
Langley Mill NG16 ... 182 B2
Linton DE11 ... 261 F4
Long Eaton NG10 ... 223 E1
Mansfield NG18 ... 268 C4
New Mills SK22 ... 24 B1
Pilsley S45 ... 132 B1
Sandiacre NG10 ... 223 E3
Stafford ST16 ... 269 E3
Swadlincote DE11 ... 256 B1
Tupton S42 ... 115 E1
Tutbury DE13 ... 239 E4
Whaley Bridge SK23 ... 45 F4
Bridge View DE56 ... 191 D4
Bridgend Cl NG9 ... 223 E3
Bridgend Ct DE21 ... 206 B1
Bridgeness Rd DE23 ... 230 C3
Bridgeport Rd DE21 ... 220 B3
Bridgeside DE13 ... 240 C1
Bridgett Cl ST4 ... 269 D1
Bridgewater St S42 ... 115 E1
Bridgeway SK23 ... 47 D2
Bridgford Ave DE14 ... 253 F4
Bridgnorth Way NG9 ... 223 F2
Bridgwater Cl DE24 ... 233 E4
Bridle Cl DE73 ... 233 D1
Bridle La
Ripley, Greenwich DE5 ... 169 F1
Ripley, Upper Hartshay DE5 ... 169 D1
Somercotes DE55 ... 170 A4
Swadlincote DE15 ... 255 D3
Bridle Rd Bolsover S44 ... 80 A1
Woodthorpe S43 ... 79 D1
Bridle Stile S20 ... 59 E4
Bridle Stile Cl S20 ... 59 E4
Bridle Stile Gdns S20 ... 59 D4
Bridlesmith Gate NG1 ... 268 B1
Bridleway The NG19 ... 136 C1
Brierfield Ave S12 ... 44 A2
Brierfield Cres S12 ... 44 A2
Brierfield Rd S12 ... 44 A2
Brierfield Way DE3 ... 230 C4
Brierley Cl S43 ... 78 C1
Brierley Pk SK23 ... 34 A1
Brierley Rd
Stonebroom DE55 ... 146 C2
Unstone S18 ... 76 C3
Brierlow Bar SK17 ... 105 D4
Brigden Ave DE24 ... 232 C4
Brigg Inf Sch DE55 ... 160 A3
Bright Meadow S20 ... 60 A3
Bright Sq NG19 ... 135 E1
Bright St Derby DE22 ... 218 B3
Ilkeston DE7 ... 194 C2
North Wingfield S42 ... 131 F3
South Normanton DE55 ... 159 F3
Brightmoor St 10 NG1 ... 268 B1
Brighton Rd DE24 ... 232 C4
Brighton St ST4 ... 269 E2
Brightstone Cl DE24 ... 233 E3
Brigmor Wlk DE22 ... 218 B3
Brimington Ct NG19 ... 136 C2
Brimington Jun Sch S43 ... 96 C4
Brimington Rd S41 ... 96 A3
Brimington Rd N S41 ... 96 A4
Brimmesfield Cl S2 ... 43 F4
Brimmesfield Dr S2 ... 43 F4
Brimmesfield Rd S2 ... 43 F4
Brincliffe Cl S40 ... 95 D1
Brindley Cl S8 ... 43 D2
Brindley Cres S8 ... 43 D2
Brindley Ct S21 ... 60 B3
Brindley Rd S41 ... 96 A3
Brindley Wlk DE24 ... 231 F1
Brinkburn Cl S17 ... 55 F3
Brinkburn Ct S17 ... 55 F3
Brinkburn Dr S17 ... 55 F3
Brinkburn Vale Rd S17 ... 55 F3
Brinks Rd S33 ... 39 D4
Brinsley Hill NG16 ... 171 E1
Brinsley Prim Sch NG16 ... 182 B4
Brisbane Cl NG19 ... 136 B3
Brisbane Dr NG9 ... 209 F1
Brisbane Rd DE3 ... 217 F2
Briset Cl DE24 ... 231 F1
Brisley Hill ST4 ... 269 D1
Bristol Dr DE3 ... 217 F1
Bristol Rd DE7 ... 194 C1
Britannia Ave DE5 ... 181 D4
Britannia Dr DE13 ... 240 B1
Britannia Rd
Chesterfield S40 ... 115 D4
Long Eaton NG10 ... 223 E1
Brittain Dr DE5 ... 170 A1
Britten Gdns NG3 ... 268 C2
Brizlincote La DE15 ... 248 B1
Broad Bank DE22 ... 218 C4
Broad Eye ST16 ... 269 D4
Broad La Brinsley NG16 ... 182 C4
Elvaston DE72 ... 233 F2
Hodthorpe S80 ... 82 B3
Broad Oak Dr
Brinsley NG16 ... 182 C4
Stapleford NG9 ... 223 E3
Broad Pavement S40 ... 266 B3
Broad Pl S80 ... 82 B3
Broad St Long Eaton NG10 ... 236 B4
Nottingham NG1 ... 268 B2
Stafford ST16 ... 269 D4
Broad Way DE56 ... 176 A4
Broad Wlk Buxton SK17 ... 85 D4
Darley Dale DE4 ... 127 E2
Broadbottom CE Prim Sch SK14 ... 15 F4
Broadbottom Rd SK14 ... 9 D2
Broadbottom Sta SK14 ... 16 A4
Broadfield Rd S8 ... 43 D4
Broadfields Cl DE22 ... 218 C4
Broadgorse Cl S40 ... 114 C4
Broadholme La DE56 ... 179 D4
Broadlands
Sandiacre NG10 ... 223 D2
South Normanton DE55 ... 160 A2
Broadleaf Cl DE21 ... 205 F1
Broadleys S45 ... 131 E2
Broadmeadow DE4 ... 127 E2
Broadoaks Cl S41 ... 266 C3
Broadstairs Rd NG9 ... 223 F1
Broadstone La DE73 ... 251 E2
Broadway Derby DE22 ... 218 C4
Duffield DE56 ... 190 C1
Heanor DE75 ... 181 F1
Ilkeston DE7 ... 194 C2
7 Nottingham NG1 ... 268 B1
Broadway continued
Ripley DE5 ... 169 F1
Swanwick DE55 ... 169 F4
Broadway Ave DE5 ... 169 F1
Broadway Park Cl DE22 ... 218 C4
Broadway St DE14 ... 254 B4
Broadway The NG18 ... 268 C3
Brockhall Rise DE75 ... 182 A1
Brockholes SK13 ... 16 C4
Brockhurst Gdns NG3 ... 268 C2
Brockhurst La S45 ... 129 E3
Brocklehurst Ave S8 ... 57 E4
Brocklehurst Piece S40 ... 95 E1
Brockley DE21 ... 220 C3
Brockley Ave S44 ... 98 C3
Brockley Prim Sch S44 ... 98 C4
Brockway Cl S45 ... 131 E1
Brockwell Inf & Jun Sch S40 ... 95 E2
Brockwell La S40 ... 95 F2
Brockwell Pl S40 ... 95 F2
Brockwell Terr S40 ... 95 F2
Brockwell The DE55 ... 160 A2
Bromehead Way S41 ... 95 E4
Bromley Hough ST4 ... 269 D1
Bromley Pl NG1 ... 268 A1
Bromley St DE22 ... 218 C4
Brompton Rd DE22 ... 217 F3
Bromyard Dr DE73 ... 233 D2
Bronte Cl NG10 ... 236 A4
Bronte Pl DE23 ... 231 D4
Bronte St DE55 ... 146 B3
Brook Ave DE55 ... 159 D2
Brook Bottom Rd SK22 ... 33 D4
Brook Cl Alfreton DE55 ... 159 D2
Doveridge DE6 ... 224 B4
Findern DE65 ... 230 B1
Hatton DE65 ... 227 E1
Holymoorside S42 ... 113 E4
Long Eaton NG10 ... 236 C3
Quarndon DE22 ... 204 B2
Brook Cotts DE7 ... 194 C2
Brook Ct NG16 ... 182 A1
Brook End DE65 ... 242 B2
Brook House Mews DE11 ... 256 A4
Brook La Alfreton DE55 ... 159 D2
Clowne S43 ... 80 C2
Crich DE56 ... 168 B3
Hatton DE65 ... 227 E2
Ripley DE5 ... 180 B4
Sutton on t H DE6 ... 228 A4
Brook Lea DE4 ... 143 E2
Brook Meadow SK13 ... 10 C1
Brook Rd Borrowash DE72 ... 221 E1
Elvaston DE72 ... 233 F2
Sheffield S8 ... 43 D3
Brook Sch S13 ... 44 B4
Brook Side DE45 ... 109 E3
Brook St Clay Cross S45 ... 131 D2
Derby DE1 ... 267 A4
Glossop SK13 ... 10 B1
Hartshorne DE11 ... 257 D4
Heage DE56 ... 168 C1
Heanor DE75 ... 181 D3
Nether Heage DE56 ... 168 B1
Nottingham NG1 ... 268 B2
Renishaw S21 ... 79 E4
Stoke-on-T ST4 ... 269 E2
Swadlincote, Church Gresley DE11 ... 256 A2
Swadlincote, Newhall DE11 ... 255 F3
Tibshelf DE55 ... 148 A3
Brook Vale Cl S18 ... 75 E2
Brook Vale Rd NG16 ... 182 B1
Brook Wlk DE1 ... 267 A4
Brook Yd S40 ... 266 A3
Brookbank Ave S40 ... 95 E2
Brookbank Rd S43 ... 80 C2
Brookdale Ave SK6 ... 23 D2
Brookdale Rd DE11 ... 257 D2
Brooke Dr S43 ... 96 C3
Brooke St Ilkeston DE7 ... 209 D3
Sandiacre NG10 ... 223 D3
Brookfield DE73 ... 244 A3
Brookfield Ave
Chesterfield S40 ... 95 D1
Derby, Chaddesden DE21 ... 220 A4
Derby, Littleover DE23 ... 231 E3
Brookfield Cl DE5 ... 170 A1
Brookfield Com Sch S40 ... 95 D1
Brookfield Cres NG20 ... 119 F3
Brookfield Ind Est SK13 ... 9 F2
Brookfield La DE45 ... 109 F4
Brookfield Park Ind Est DE4 ... 143 F2
Brookfield Prim Sch
Derby DE3 ... 230 B4
Shirebrook NG20 ... 119 F3
Brookfield Rd
Bolsover S44 ... 118 A4
Stoke-on-T ST4 ... 269 D1
Brookfield Way DE4 ... 143 F2
Brookfields Calver S32 ... 72 B1
Horsley DE56 ... 191 F4
Brookfields Dr DE21 ... 205 E2
Brookhill S43 ... 80 C2
Brookhill Ave NG16 ... 160 B2
Brookhill Ind Est NG16 ... 160 B1
Brookhill La NG16 ... 160 C3
Brookhill Leys Rd NG16 ... 182 C1
Brookhill Rd NG16 ... 160 B1
Brookhill St NG9 ... 223 E3
Brookhouse Ct SK22 ... 25 E2
Brookhouse St DE24 ... 232 B3
Brookland Ave NG18 ... 268 A4
Brooklands SK17 ... 85 E4
Brooklands Ave
Chapel-en-le-F SK23 ... 47 E3
Heanor DE75 ... 181 F1
Wirksworth DE4 ... 165 F4
Brooklands Bank DE45 ... 109 F3
Brooklands Dr DE23 ... 231 E4
Brooklands Inf Sch NG10 ... 236 B3
Brooklands Jun Sch NG10 ... 236 B4
Brooklands Rd SK23 ... 47 E3
Brookleton DE45 ... 125 E3
Brooklyn Dr S40 ... 95 E2
Brooklyn Pl S8 ... 43 D3
Brooklyn Rd S8 ... 43 D3
Brooks Hollow DE21 ... 205 E4
Brooks Rd S43 ... 78 A2
Brookside Ashbourne DE6 ... 173 E1
Beeley DE4 ... 111 D2
Belper DE56 ... 178 C2
Bradwell S33 ... 51 D4
Burton u T DE15 ... 248 A3
Buxworth SK23 ... 34 A1
Eastwood NG16 ... 182 C2
Glossop SK13 ... 17 D4
Rolleston DE13 ... 240 A2
Rowarth SK22 ... 24 C4
Brookside Ave NG19 ... 136 B3
Brookside Bar S40 ... 94 C1
Brookside Cl Derby DE1 ... 218 C4
Hadfield SK13 ... 9 F2
Long Eaton NG10 ... 236 A4
Repton DE65 ... 242 B1
Brookside Glen S40 ... 94 C1
Brookside Gr SK17 ... 84 B3
Brookside Rd
Breadsall DE21 ... 205 F2
Chapel-en-le-F SK23 ... 47 D3
Brookside Specl Sch DE21 ... 205 F2
Brookvale Ave Codnor DE5 ... 181 D4
Denby DE5 ... 180 A1
Brookvale Rd DE5 ... 180 A1
Brookvale Rise DE5 ... 180 A1
Brookview Ct S18 ... 57 D2
Broom Ave Pilsley S45 ... 132 B1
Swanwick DE55 ... 169 F4
Broom Cl Belper DE56 ... 178 C3
Chesterfield S41 ... 95 E4
Derby, Chellaston DE73 ... 232 C1
Derby, Sinfin DE73 ... 231 F1
Duffield DE56 ... 190 B2
Broom Dr S42 ... 115 F1
Broom Gdns S43 ... 96 C4
Broom La DE6 ... 175 F4
Broom's La DE6 ... 226 A1
Broombank Pk S18 ... 76 B2
Broombank Rd S18 ... 76 B2
Broome Acre DE55 ... 160 B2
Broomfield Ave S41 ... 115 E4
Broomfield Cl NG10 ... 223 D3
Broomfield Coll (Derbyshire Coll of Ag) DE7 ... 206 A3
Broomhill Ave DE7 ... 209 D3
Broomhill Cl Derby DE3 ... 217 E2
Eckington S21 ... 59 D2
Broomhill Fst Sch NG19 ... 268 A4
Broomhill La NG19 ... 268 A4
Broomhill Rd S41 ... 76 C1
Broomhills La DE65 ... 242 B1
Broomyclose La ST14 ... 210 A2
Brosscroft SK13 ... 10 A3
Brosscroft Village SK13 ... 10 A3
Brough La Bradwell S33 ... 51 E4
Shatton S33 ... 51 E4
Brough Rd DE15 ... 248 B2
Brough St DE22 ... 218 B3
Brougham Ave NG19 ... 135 E1
Broughton Ave DE23 ... 218 B1
Broughton Cl
Church Broughton DE65 ... 227 D4
Ilkeston DE7 ... 194 B1
Broughton Rd S41 ... 95 E4
Brow Cres S20 ... 59 F4
Brown Ave NG19 ... 136 A2
Brown Edge Rd SK17 ... 66 B1
Brown Hills La S10 ... 42 B4
Brown La Ashover S45 ... 145 D4
Barton in F NG11 ... 237 F3
Dronfield S18 ... 57 E2
Brown St NG19 ... 268 A4
Brown's Flats NG16 ... 195 F3
Brown's La DE56 ... 191 E4
Brown's Rd NG10 ... 236 C4
Brown's Yd DE55 ... 170 B4
Brownhill La HD7 ... 3 D4
Brownhills La S42 ... 130 B2
Browning Cir DE23 ... 231 F4
Browning Rd DE11 ... 256 B3
Browning St Derby DE23 ... 231 F4
3 Mansfield NG18 ... 268 B4
Stafford ST16 ... 269 D4
Brownlow Rd NG19 ... 135 F1
Broxtowe Ave NG16 ... 195 E3
Broxtowe Dr NG18 ... 268 C3
Brun La Kirk Langley DE6 ... 217 D4
Mackworth DE22 ... 217 D4
Brunnen The DE55 ... 160 A2
Brunner Ave NG20 ... 119 F2
Brunswick Dr NG9 ... 223 F3
Brunswick St
Chesterfield S41 ... 266 B4
Derby DE23 ... 231 F4
Pilsley S45 ... 132 B1
Brunswick Terr ST17 ... 269 D3

Brunswood Cl DE21 220 C3
Brunswood La DE6 187 E4
Brunswood Rd DE4 143 D1
Brunt St NG18 268 C3
Brunton Cl DE3 217 E1
Brunts Sch The NG19 136 B1
Brushes Rd SK15 4 A2
Brushfield Gr S12 44 B2
Brushfield Rd S40 94 C3
Brussels Terr 1 DE7 194 C1
Bryn Lea S41 96 B1
Brynsmoor Rd NG16 182 C4
Bryony Cl Derby DE21 206 A1
Killamarsh S21 60 A3
Bubnell Rd DE45 91 E3
Buchan St DE24 232 B4
Buchanan St DE1 267 B4
Buck Wood View S12 43 E3
Buckden Cl S40 95 E2
Buckfast Cl DE55 169 F4
Buckford La DE65 242 C4
Buckhazels La DE6 203 D4
Buckingham Ave DE21 219 E4
Buckingham Cl
22 Dronfield S18 56 B1
Mansfield Woodhouse NG19 136 C3
Swanwick DE55 170 A4
Buckingham Ct
Burton u T DE15 248 B2
Sandiacre NG10 223 D2
Buckingham Rd NG10 223 D2
Buckland Cl DE1 218 C3
Buckland Gr SK14 15 D4
Buckleather La S18 74 B1
Buckley Cl DE11 256 C1
Buckminster Cl DE21 205 F1
Buckminster Rd DE7 208 B2
Bull Farm Fst & Mid Sch NG19 135 E1
Bull Hill ST16 269 E4
Bull La DE4 143 E3
Bullace Ct NG19 136 C1
Bullbridge Hill DE56 168 A3
Buller St Derby DE23 218 C1
Ilkeston DE7 209 D3
Bullhill La DE56 176 C2
Bullhurst La DE6 188 C2
Bulling La DE4 156 C1
Bullivant Ave S80 100 B4
Bullivant St NG3 268 B2
Bullock Cl NG19 136 A3
Bullock La Brailsford DE6 201 F4
Ironville NG16 170 C3
Somercotes DE55 170 C3
Bullpit La DE56 205 D4
Bullsmoor DE56 179 E2
Bumpmill La DE55 146 A1
Bun Alley DE45 91 E2
Bungalows The
Chesterfield, Brampton S40 95 E2
Chesterfield, Hady S41 266 C2
1 Chesterfield, Newbold S41 95 F4
Chesterfield, Whittington Moor S41 96 A4
Killamarsh S21 60 B3
Stonebroom DE55 146 C2
Bunker S Hill S21 60 C3
Bunker's Hill S80 62 B4
Bunting Cl Chesterfield S40 95 D1
Ilkeston DE7 208 B3
Sheffield S8 43 D1
Bunting Ho S41 77 D2
Bunting Nook S8 43 D1
Buntingfield La S45 129 D4
Buntings Cl DE3 218 A2
Bunyan Cres DE55 146 C2
Bunyan Green Rd NG16 171 E4
Burbage Cl Belper DE56 179 E3
25 Dronfield S18 56 B1
Burbage Gr S12 44 B3
Burbage Pl DE24 232 C4
Burbage Prim Sch SK17 84 C3
Burbage Rd S43 97 E4
Burcot Cl DE7 207 F4
Burdekin Cl SK23 47 E3
Burdett Way DE65 242 B2
Burdock Cl DE21 205 F1
Burgess Cl S41 115 E4
Burghley Cl DE73 232 C1
Burghley Way DE23 230 C3
Burke Dr DE55 170 B4
Burkitt Dr S43 79 D2
Burland Green La DE6 189 D2
Burleigh Cres DE55 169 F4
Burleigh Dr DE22 218 C4
Burleigh St 2 DE7 194 C1
Burley Cl S40 115 D4
Burley Dr DE22 204 C4
Burley Hill DE22, DE56 205 D4
Burley La DE22 204 C4
Burlington Ave NG20 119 F3
Burlington Cl DE72 235 E4
Burlington Dr NG19 135 F1
Burlington Glen S17 55 F4
Burlington Gr S17 55 F4
Burlington Rd
Buxton SK17 85 D4
Derby DE22 217 F3
Dore S17 55 F4
Burlington St S40 266 B3
Burlington Way DE3 217 E1
Burlow Ave SK17 85 E2
Burlow Rd SK17 85 E1
Burnaby St DE24 232 C4
Burnage Ct DE22 218 C2
Burnaston Cl S18 56 B1
Burnaston Ct NG19 136 C2
Burnaston La DE65 229 E3
Burnbridge Rd S41 77 E2
Burncroft DE7 207 F4
Burnell St S43 96 C4
Burnett La DE4 143 D4
Burney La
Breedon on t H DE73 252 B1
Lount DE73 252 B1
Burnham Cl DE7 207 E4
Burnham Dr DE3 217 E1
Burnham Way NG2 268 B1
Burns Ave
Mansfield Woodhouse NG19 136 B1
Nottingham NG7 268 A2
Burns Cl Chesterfield S40 114 C4
Derby DE23 231 D4
Burns Dr Dronfield S18 76 B4
Grassmoor S42 115 F2
Burns St Ilkeston DE7 208 C4
Mansfield NG18 268 B4
Nottingham NG7 268 A2
Burnshaw St DE55 146 B3
Burnside Hadfield SK13 9 F2
Rolleston DE13 240 A2
Burnside Ave Sheffield S8 43 D3
Shirland DE55 146 B1
Burnside Cl DE24 231 E2
Burnside Dr DE21 220 C2
Burnside St DE24 233 D4
Burnt House Rd DE75 181 E1
Burnt Oaks Cl NG19 136 B2
Burr La DE7 194 C1
Burre Cl DE45 109 F3
Burrfields Rd SK23 47 D3
Burrowfield Mews DE21 220 C1
Burrows La
Brailsford DE6 201 F1
Middleton (Nr Wirksworth) DE4 154 B3
Trusley DE6 201 F1
Burrows The DE11 255 F3
Burrs Wood Croft S40 95 E4
Bursdon Cl S41 77 D1
Burton Close Dr DE45 109 F2
Burton Edge DE45 109 E2
Burton Rd Branston DE14 254 A4
Coton in t E DE12 260 B2
Derby DE23 218 B1
Findern DE65 230 B2
Linton DE11 255 E1
Overseal DE12 262 A2
Repton DE65 242 A1
Rosliston DE12 260 B3
Swadlincote DE11 256 B3
Ticknall DE73 250 C2
Tutbury DE13 239 E2
Willington DE65 241 F4
Burton St Heanor DE75 181 F1
Nottingham NG1 268 B2
Tutbury DE13 239 E3
Burton Tech Coll (Annexe) DE13 240 B2
Burwell Cl SK13 17 D4
Burwell Ct NG19 136 C2
Bush Vale DE56 178 C3
Bushey Wood Rd S17 55 F3
Bushton La
Burton u T DE13 239 D1
Tutbury DE13 239 D1
Bushy Cl NG10 236 A3
Buskeyfield La NG20 101 F2
Butcher's La DE4 127 F2
Bute St SK13 10 C2
Butler Cres NG19 135 E1
Butler St ST4 269 E1
Butler Way S21 60 B3
Butt Hill S80 81 F3
Butt Hill Cl S80 81 F3
Butt La Blackfordby DE11 257 D1
Mansfield Woodhouse NG19 136 B1
Butt St NG10 223 D3
Butterfield Cres DE55 169 F4
Butterfield La DE55 145 F1
Butterhall Cl S80 82 A3
Butterley Croft Bsns Ctr DE5 180 C4
Butterley Hill DE5 169 F2
Butterley La Ashover S45 144 C3
Ripley DE5 169 E2
Buttermead Cl NG9 209 E1
Buttermere Cl S41 95 E4
Buttermere Dr
Derby DE22 204 C2
Dronfield S18 56 C1
Buttermilk La Bolsover S44 98 B2
Long Duckmanton S44 98 B2
Butterpot La DE6 215 E2
Butterton Cl DE7 209 D4
Butterton Dr 6 S40 95 D3
Buttonoak Dr DE73 233 D2
Butts Hill S17 55 E2
Butts Rd Ashover S45 129 F2
Bakewell DE45 109 E3
Darley Dale DE4 127 D2
Butts Terr DE45 109 E3
Butts The DE56 179 D2
Butts View DE45 109 E3
Buxton Ave DE75 193 F4
Buxton Cl DE11 256 A4
Buxton Com Sch SK17 85 D3
Buxton Ct DE7 194 B1
Buxton Ctry Pk SK17 84 C3
Buxton & District Cottage Hospl SK17 85 E3
Buxton Dr Derby DE3 217 F2
Little Eaton DE21 191 E1
Buxton Inf Sch SK17 85 E4
Buxton Jun Sch SK17 85 D3
Buxton Mews SK13 9 F1
Buxton Micrarium Mus SK17 85 D4
Buxton Old Rd SK12 32 C2
Buxton Rd
Alstonefield DE6 149 D3
Ashbourne DE6 173 D1
Ashford in t W DE45 108 C4
Bakewell DE45 109 D4
Chapel-en-le-F SK23 47 E3
Chinley SK23 34 C1
Derby DE21 219 F4
Disley SK12 32 C3
Dove Holes SK17 66 C4
Furness Vale SK23 33 E2
High Lane SK6 32 A3
Longnor SK17 121 D4
Mansfield NG19 135 E1
New Mills SK23 33 E2
Tideswell SK17 69 E2
Buxton Rd W SK12 32 A3
Buxton Sta SK17 85 D4
Buxton Terr SK14 9 E3
Buxworth Prim Sch SK23 34 A1
Byfield Cl DE21 206 A1
Byng Ave DE23 231 F4
Byron Ave Alfreton DE55 159 D2
Burton u T DE15 254 C4
Long Eaton NG10 223 D2
Mansfield Woodhouse NG19 136 B1
Byron Cl Dronfield S18 76 B4
Grassmoor S42 115 F2
Byron Cres NG16 195 E2
Byron Ct NG9 209 F1
Byron Gr DE55 146 C2
Byron Rd Chesterfield S40 115 D4
Swadlincote DE11 256 B3
Byron St Buxton SK17 85 E3
Chesterfield S40 266 B1
Derby DE23 218 C1
Ilkeston DE7 194 C1
Mansfield NG18 268 B4
Shirebrook NG20 119 F2
Shirland DE55 146 B1
Bywell La DE56 179 F1

Cacklehill La DE6 184 B1
Cadeby Ct DE55 170 B3
Cadgwith Dr DE22 204 C2
Cadley Hill Ind Est DE11 255 F2
Cadley Hill Rd DE11 255 F2
Cadman Ct S20 59 E3
Cadman Rd S12 44 B3
Cadman St S20 59 E3
Cadwell Cl DE24 233 E3
Caerhays Ct DE24 231 E2
Caernarfon Cl DE55 170 A4
Caernarvon Cl
8 Chesterfield S40 95 E1
Derby DE21 220 C3
Caernarvon Rd S18 76 A4
Caesar St DE1 219 D4
Cairn Dr S43 77 E2
Cairngorm Cl S43 77 E2
Cairngorm Dr DE24 231 E2
Cairns Cl
Burton u T DE15 248 B2
Derby DE3 217 F2
Cairns St NG1 268 B2
Cairnsmore Cl NG10 223 D1
Caldene Terr SK23 45 F4
Calder Cl Derby DE22 204 C2
Hilton DE65 228 B1
Calderdale Dr NG10 236 A3
Caldermill Dr DE21 206 A1
Caldey Rd S18 76 A4
Caldwell Hall Sch DE12 260 C4
Calesdale Cl SK17 85 D3
Calf Croft S80 82 A3
Calgary Cres DE15 248 B2
California Gdns DE22 218 B2
California La S43 80 A4
Calke Abbey LE65 251 E1
Calke Rise DE5 169 F1
Calladine La
Horsley Woodhouse DE7 192 B3
Shottle DE56 177 E3
Calladine Rd DE75 181 E1
Callan's La LE65 258 B4
Callow Dr S2 43 E3
Callow Hill Way DE23 231 D4
Callow La Callow DE4 165 E3
Wirksworth DE4 165 E3
Callow Mount S14 43 E3
Callow Pl S14 43 E3
Callow Rd S14 43 E3
Callywhite La S18 57 E1
Calow Brook Dr S41 115 F4
Calow CE Prim Sch S44 96 C2
Calow La Calow S44 96 C1
Chesterfield S41 115 E4
Calow Lane Ind Est S41 115 F4
Calton View DE45 109 E3
Calver Ave S42 132 A4
Calver Cl Belper DE56 179 D3
Derby DE21 205 F2
Calver Cres S43 97 E4
Calver Mews SK13 9 F1
Calver Rd DE45 91 E3
Calver St NG19 136 C2
Calvert St DE1 267 D2
Calverton Cl DE24 232 C2
Calvin Cl DE24 233 D3
Camberwell Ave DE22 218 A3
Camborne Cl DE21 205 F1
Cambria Rd NG19 135 E2
Cambrian Cl 10 S40 95 E3
Cambrian Way DE11 256 A2
Cambridge Cres
Bramley-Vale S44 117 F1
Stapleford NG9 209 E1
Cambridge Rd
1 Brimington S43 96 C4
Sheffield S8 43 D3
Cambridge St
Blackwell DE55 147 F1
Derby, Rose Hill DE23 219 D1
Derby, Spondon DE21 220 C2
Mansfield NG18 268 B3
Stafford ST 16 269 F4
Camdale Rise S12 44 C1
Camdale View S12 44 C1
Camden Cl NG2 268 C1
Camden St DE22 218 B2
Camellia Cl DE3 217 E2
Camelot Cl DE13 240 C1
Cameron Cl DE15 248 A1
Cameron Rd DE23 231 F4
Camerory Way S43 77 E3
Camms Cl S21 59 E2
Camms Endowed CE Prim Sch S21 59 E2
Camp St DE1 219 D4
Camp Wood Cl DE21 205 E4
Campbell Dr S43 78 A2
Campbell Pl ST4 269 E2
Campbell Rd ST4 269 E1
Campbell St Belper DE56 178 C2
Derby DE24 232 B4
Langley Mill NG16 182 B2
Nottingham NG3 268 B2
Campion Hill DE74 247 D2
Campion Rd DE11 256 C2
Campion St DE22 218 B3
Campsie Ct 6 DE24 231 E2
Canada St DE56 179 D1
Canal Bank DE72 235 D1
Canal Br S21 60 B3
Canal Bridge DE65 242 A3
Canal Mus NG1 268 B1
Canal St Derby DE1 267 C2
Ilkeston DE7 195 D1
Long Eaton NG10 223 E1
Marple SK6 23 D3
Nottingham NG1 268 B1
Sandiacre NG10 223 E3
Whaley Bridge SK23 45 F4
Canal Wharf S41 96 A3
Canberra Cl Derby DE3 217 F1
Stapleford NG9 209 F1
Canberra Dr ST 16 269 F4
Candlemass Ct NG19 136 B1
Cannell Cl S45 131 D2
Canner Cl DE11 257 D1
Canning Cir NG7 268 A2
Cannock Way NG10 237 D4
Cannon Fields S32 52 C4
Cannon St SK14 9 E3
Canon Cl DE7 194 C3
Canon's Wlk DE22 204 C1
Cantelupe Rd DE7 209 D4
Canterbury Cl
Duffield DE56 190 C2
Mansfield Woodhouse NG19 136 B3
Canterbury Rd
Burton u T DE15 248 B2
Sheffield S8 43 D3
Wirksworth DE4 165 F4
Canterbury St DE21 219 F4
Canterbury Terr DE4 165 F4
Cantley Cl DE24 232 B2
Cantley Rd DE55 170 B3
Cape St NG18 268 A4
Capel Rise S43 96 B4
Capthorne Cl S40 94 C3
Car Rd S17 74 A3
Car Vale Dr S13 44 B4
Car Vale View S13 44 B4
Cardale Rd NG19 135 E2
Cardales Cl DE65 230 B1
Cardean Cl DE1 219 D4
Carder Gn SK17 121 D3
Cardiff St NG3 268 C2
Cardigan St DE21 219 E4
Cardinal Cl NG3 268 C2
Cardlemere La SK17 138 C1
Cardrona Cl DE21 205 F1
Cardwell Ave S13 44 C4
Cardwell Dr S13 44 C4
Carfield Ave S8 43 D3
Carfield La S8 43 E3
Carfield Pl S8 43 D3
Carfield Prim Sch S8 43 D3
Carisbrooke Dr DE13 240 C1
Carisbrooke Gdns DE23 231 E3
Carlin Cl DE72 235 F4
Carlin St S13 44 C3
Carlisle Ave DE23 231 D4
Carlisle Cl S41 76 C2
Carlisle Gr SK17 85 D4
Carlisle Rd SK17 84 C4
Carlton Ave Derby DE24 232 C2
Northwood DE4 127 D3
Carlton Cl Clay Cross S45 131 E1
Heanor DE75 182 A2
Mosborough S20 59 E3
Carlton Dr DE24 232 C2
Carlton Gdns DE24 232 C2
Carlton Rd
Chesterfield S40 115 D3
Derby DE23 218 C1
Long Eaton NG10 236 A3
Nottingham NG3 268 C2
Stoke-on-T ST4 269 F2
Carlton St
Mansfield Woodhouse NG19 136 B1
Nottingham NG1 268 B1
Carlyle Inf Sch DE23 231 D4
Carlyle Rd DE55 146 C2
Carlyle St Derby DE24 231 F3
Heanor DE75 181 E2
Carlyon Gdns S40 114 C4
Carnarvon Rd NG17 148 C1
Carnegie St DE23 232 A4
Carnfield Hall DE55 159 E3
Carnfield Hill DE55 159 E3
Carnforth Cl Derby DE3 217 F1
Stapleford NG9 223 E3
Carnoustie Ave S40 114 B4
Carnoustie Cl DE3 217 F1
Carol Cres DE21 219 F3
Caroline Cl DE24 233 E4
Caroline Ct DE7 209 D3
Carpenter Ave
Mansfield NG19 135 E1
Mastin Moor S43 79 D2
Carpenter Cl DE15 248 B1
Carpenter Croft S12 44 B3
Carpenter Gdns S12 44 B3
Carpenter Mews S12 44 B3
Carper La DE6 187 F1
Carr Brow SK6 32 A4
Carr Cl DE55 160 A4
Carr Fields DE7 192 B4
Carr La
Brackenfield DE55 145 E2
Crich DE4 156 C1
Matlock DE4 143 F1
Scarcliffe S44 117 F4
South Normanton DE55 160 A4
Thornhill S33 39 F3
Carr Vale Rd S44 98 C2
Carrbrook Ind Est SK15 4 A3
Carrfield Ave NG10 223 F1
Carrfield Ct S8 43 D3
Carrfield Dr S8 43 D3
Carrfield La S8 43 D3
Carrfield Rd S8 43 D3
Carrfield St S8 43 D3
Carrhouse La SK14 9 E2
Carriage Dr The SK13 9 F3
Carriers Rd DE65 241 E3
Carrington St Derby DE1 267 C2
Nottingham NG1 268 B1
Carron Cl DE24 231 F2
Carrs Cl DE74 247 D2
Carrwood Rd
Chesterfield S18 76 A2
Renishaw S21 79 D4
Carsington Cl S40 95 D3
Carsington Cres DE22 204 B1
Carsington Ct NG19 136 C2
Carsington & Hopton CE Prim Sch DE4 164 C4
Carsington Mews DE22 204 C1
Carsington Water Visitor Ctr DE6 164 B2
Carson Croft DE4 143 E3
Carson Mount S12 44 A2
Carson Rd DE21 220 A3
Carson Way ST16 269 D4
Carter La
Shirebrook NG20 119 F2
Warsop Vale NG20 120 B2
Carter La E DE55 160 B3
Carter La W
Shirebrook NG20 119 E2
South Normanton DE55 160 B3
Carter Pl S8 43 D3
Carter Rd Beeston NG9 223 F1
Sheffield S8 43 D3
Carter St DE24 232 B3
Carterhall La S12 44 B1
Carterhall Rd S12 44 A1
Cartledge La S18 75 D4
Cartmel Cl S18 56 C1
Cartmel Cres S41 95 F4
Cartworth Moor Rd HD7 3 F4
Cartwright St S81 63 F4
Carver Cl S26 61 F3
Carver Way S26 61 F3
Cary Rd Eckington S21 59 D2
Sheffield S2 44 A4
Cascade Gr DE23 231 D4
Casson Ave DE24 233 D3
Casson Dr S26 61 F4
Casson St NG16 170 C2
Castings Rd DE23 232 A4
Castle Bvd NG7 268 A1
Castle Cl DE45 109 F3
Castle Croft DE24 233 E3
Castle Ct Elvaston DE72 234 A3
Tutbury DE13 239 E4
Castle Donington Com Coll DE74 247 D2
Castle Dr Bakewell DE45 109 F4
Codnor NG16 181 F4
Somercotes DE55 170 B4
Castle Edge Rd SK22 24 A1
Castle Gate NG1 268 B1
Castle Gn S44 118 A4
Castle Gr NG7 268 A1
Castle Gresley Inf Sch DE11 261 F4
Castle Hayes La DE13 239 D3

Castle Hill
Castle Donington DE74 247 D2
Duffield DE56 190 C2
Eckington S21 59 E2
Findern DE65 230 B1
Glossop SK13 10 C1
Castle Hill Cl S21 59 E2
Castle Ho DE1 267 D2
Castle La
Bolsover S44 99 D1
Ironville NG16 170 C1
Melbourne DE73 252 A4
Castle Meadow Rd NG7 268 A1
Castle Mews
Mansfield Woodhouse
NG19 136 A2
Melbourne DE73 252 A4
Castle Mews The DE11 256 A4
Castle Mills DE73 252 A4
Castle Mount Cres DE45 109 E4
Castle Mount Way DE45 109 F4
Castle Mus & Art Gall
NG1 268 A1
Castle Orch DE56 190 C2
Castle Pl NG1 268 A1
Castle Quay NG7 268 A1
Castle Rd Nottingham NG1 268 B1
Swadlincote DE11 255 F1
Castle Row S17 56 A3
Castle St Bakewell DE45 109 E3
Bolsover S44 99 D1
Castleton S33 38 A1
Derby DE1 267 C2
Hadfield SK13 10 A2
Mansfield NG18 268 B4
Mansfield Woodhouse
NG19 136 A2
Melbourne DE73 252 A4
Nottingham NG2 268 C1
Stafford ST16 269 D4
Tutbury DE13 239 E3
Castle View Aldercar NG16 182 A2
Eckington S21 59 E2
Stafford ST16 269 D4
Castle View Dr DE4 155 E3
Castle Way ST16 269 D3
Castle Way The DE65 241 F3
Castle Yd S40 266 B2
Castlebeck Ave S2 44 B4
Castlebeck Dr S2 44 B4
Castlecraig Ct DE24 231 F1
Castledale Croft S2 44 A4
Castledale Gr S2 44 B4
Castledale Pl S2 44 A4
Castledene Dr ST16 269 D3
Castlefields Ironville NG16 170 C2
Stafford ST16 269 D3
Castlegate La DE45 89 E3
Castlerigg Way 5 S18 56 C1
Castlerow Cl S17 56 A3
Castlerow Dr S17 56 A3
Castleshaw Dr DE23 230 C4
Castleton Ave Derby DE23 231 F4
Ilkeston DE7 194 C3
Somercotes DE55 170 B3
Castleton CE Prim Sch
S33 38 B1
Castleton Cl NG19 136 B2
Castleton Cres SK13 9 F1
Castleton Gr S43 97 D3
Castleton Rd
Hathersage S32 52 C4
Hope S33 38 C2
Castleview DE65 239 E4
Cat & Fiddle La DE7 207 F3
Cat La S8 43 E3
Catchford View S40 95 D4
Catcliff Cl DE45 109 E2
Catcliff Cotts DE45 109 E3
Cathedral Rd DE1 267 B4
Cathedral View DE22 218 B1
Catherine Ave
Ilkeston DE7 208 C3
Mansfield Woodhouse
NG19 136 B2
Catherine St
Alfreton DE55 159 E2
Chesterfield S40 95 F2
Derby DE23 219 D1
Catholme La DE13 259 D2
Catkin Dr NG16 195 E4
Cator Rd NG19 135 E2
Catterick Dr DE3 217 E1
Catterwood Dr SK6 15 D1
Catton La Rosliston DE12 260 A3
Walton-on-T DE12 260 A3
Caudwell Cl S42 131 E4
Cauldon Dr S40 95 D3
Cauldwell Rd
Caldwell DE12 261 D3
Linton DE12 261 D3
Caunton Cl NG18 268 A3
Causeway DE22 204 C1
Causeway Gdns S17 55 E4
Causeway Head Rd S17 55 E4
Causeway La DE4 143 E3
Causeway The
Ashover S45 129 E2
Dore S17 55 E4
Eyam S32 71 F3
Wirksworth DE4 165 F4
Cavan Dr DE21 220 A2
Cavell Dr S45 131 F1
Cavendish Ave
Buxton SK17 84 C3
Derby DE22 204 C2
Dore S17 55 F4
Cavendish Cir SK17 85 D4
Cavendish Cl
Castle Donington DE74 247 D1
Doveridge DE6 211 E1
Duffield DE56 190 B1
Holmewood S42 116 C1
Shardlow DE72 235 D1
Swadlincote DE11 256 A4
Cavendish Close Inf &
Jun Schs DE21 220 A4
Cavendish Cres NG9 209 E1
Cavendish Cres N NG7 268 A1
Cavendish Cres S NG7 268 A1
Cavendish Ct Derby DE1 267 A4
Shardlow DE72 235 D1
Cavendish Dr
Ashbourne DE6 185 E4
Clowne S43 81 D2
Ripley DE5 169 E1
Cavendish Hospl The
SK17 85 D4
Cavendish Jun Sch S41 95 F4
Cavendish Pk DE4 143 E4
Cavendish Pl S43 78 A2
Cavendish Rd
Bolsover S44 99 D1
Ilkeston DE7 208 C3
Long Eaton NG10 223 E1
Matlock DE4 143 E3
Cavendish Rd E NG7 268 A1
Cavendish Rd W NG7 268 A1
Cavendish Rise S18 75 F4
Cavendish Sq S21 77 E4
Cavendish St
Chesterfield S40 266 B3
Derby DE1 267 A3
Langwith NG20 119 F4
Mansfield NG18 268 C3
Mansfield Woodhouse
NG19 136 A2
Staveley S43 97 E4
Cavendish St N S41 77 D1
Cavendish Way DE3 217 F1
Caversfield Cl DE23 231 D4
Caversham Way DE7 207 E4
Cavill Rd S8 43 D2
Cawdor Rd S2 43 F3
Caxton Cl S43 77 E2
Caxton St
Derby, Littleover DE23 231 F3
Derby, Normanton DE23 231 F4
Caythorpe Ct NG19 136 C2
Ceal The SK6 15 D1
Cecil Ave S18 57 D1
Cecil Rd Dronfield S18 57 D1
Swadlincote DE11 255 F3
Cecil St DE22 218 B3
Cedar Ave Alfreton DE55 159 D3
Chesterfield S40 95 E3
Long Eaton NG10 236 B3
Mansfield Woodhouse
NG19 136 B3
Ripley DE5 169 E1
Cedar Cl Ashbourne DE6 185 E4
Eckington S21 59 D1
Glapwell S44 118 A1
Glossop SK13 10 A1
Killamarsh S21 60 B3
Sandiacre NG10 223 D4
Cedar Croft DE56 192 A4
Cedar Dr Ockbrook DE72 221 E2
Selston NG16 171 F4
Stramshall ST14 210 A2
Cedar Gr Belper DE56 179 D1
Linton DE12 261 E3
South Normanton DE55 160 A2
Swadlincote DE11 256 A4
Cedar Park Dr S44 99 E1
Cedar Pk DE7 208 C4
Cedar Rd
Castle Donington DE74 247 D1
Linton DE11 261 F4
Cedar St Brimington S43 78 A1
Derby DE22 218 C4
Mansfield NG18 268 C3
Shirland DE55 146 B3
Cedarwood Ct DE21 205 F1
Celandine Cl DE21 206 A1
Celandine Ct 11 S17 56 A3
Celandine Gdns S17 56 A3
Celandine Pl DE11 256 C2
Celanese Rd DE21 220 B2
Cemetery La Ripley DE5 169 F1
Staveley S43 78 C1
Wirksworth DE4 154 C1
Cemetery Rd Belper DE56 179 D3
Chesterfield S41 96 B1
Clay Cross S45 131 F1
Dronfield S18 76 A4
Glossop SK13 10 B2
Somercotes DE55 170 B4
Stapleford NG9 223 F4
Cemetery Terr S43 96 C4
Central Ave
Borrowash DE72 221 D1
Chesterfield S40 95 F1
Creswell S80 100 B4
Mansfield NG18 268 C3
Sandiacre NG10 223 D3
South Normanton DE55 160 A3
Stapleford NG9 223 F4
Central Cl
Shirebrook NG20 119 F2
Unstone S18 76 C3
Central Dr Blackwell DE55 147 F1
Buxton SK17 85 E3
Calow S44 96 C2
Chesterfield S41 96 B1
Shirebrook NG20 119 F2
Central Dr continued
Wingerworth S42 114 C2
Central Pavement S40 266 B3
Central Rd DE55 159 D2
Central St Chesterfield S41 96 B1
Holmewood S42 132 C4
Nottingham NG3 268 C2
Central Wlk S43 96 B4
Centre Ct DE1 267 C1
Centre St S44 117 E1
Centurion Wlk DE1 219 D4
Chaddesden Cl S18 56 B1
Chaddesden La DE21 220 A3
Chaddesden Lane End
DE21 219 F3
Chaddesden Park Inf &
Jun Schs DE21 220 A4
Chaddesden Park Rd
DE21 219 F4
Chadfield Rd DE56 190 C3
Chadwick Ave DE24 232 C3
Chadwick Hill DE4 141 D3
Chadwick Nick La DE4 167 F4
Chadwick Rd S13 44 B4
Chadwick St SK13 17 D4
Chaffinch Cl DE21 220 C3
Chain La DE3 218 A1
Chalfont Sq DE21 206 A1
Chalkley Cl DE24 232 C4
Challands Cl S41 115 E4
Challands Way S41 115 E4
Challis Ave DE21 220 A4
Challoner Gn 5 S20 59 F4
Challoner Way S20 59 F4
Chalons Cl DE7 194 C1
Chalons Way DE7 208 C4
Chamberlain Ave ST4 269 E1
Chambers Ave DE7 209 D4
Chambers Ct SK14 9 D2
Chambers St DE24 219 F1
Champion Ave DE7 194 B2
Champion Cres NG19 268 A4
Champion Dr S21 60 B3
Champion Hill DE56 190 C2
Chancel Pl DE22 267 A1
Chancery La DE22 218 A3
Chancet Wood Cl S8 56 C4
Chancet Wood Dr S8 56 C4
Chancet Wood Rd S8 56 C4
Chancet Wood Rise S8 56 C4
Chancet Wood View S8 56 C4
Chander Hill La S42 113 E4
Chandlers Ford DE21 205 F1
Chandos Cres S21 60 B3
Chandos Pole St DE22 218 B3
Chandres Ct DE22 204 C2
Chaneyfield Way S40 95 D4
Channel The DE6 173 D1
Chantrey Ave S41 96 A3
Chantrey Rd S8 43 D2
Chantry Cl Derby DE73 217 E1
Disley SK12 32 C3
Long Eaton NG10 236 A2
Chantry Ct SK17 69 E2
Chantry Fold SK12 32 C3
Chantry La SK17 69 E2
Chantry Rd SK12 32 B3
Chapel Bar NG1 268 A1
Chapel Brow
Charlesworth SK13 16 C3
Tintwistle SK13 10 A4
Chapel Cl Clowne S43 80 C2
Moira DE11 256 B1
Willington DE65 242 A3
Youlgreave DE45 125 D3
Chapel Croft Elton DE4 140 C3
Middleton (Nr Wirksworth)
DE4 154 B3
Chapel Ct DE7 194 C2
Chapel Gn DE6 224 B4
Chapel Hill Ashover S45 129 F2
Beeley DE4 111 D2
Cromford DE4 155 D4
Chapel Houses SK6 23 D3
Chapel La Apperknowle S18 58 A1
Bakewell DE45 109 E3
Barrow u T DE73 244 A3
Boylestone DE6 213 D2
Church Broughton DE65 227 D4
Crich DE4 168 A4
Derby, Chaddesden DE21 220 A4
Derby, Chellaston DE73 233 D1
Derby, Spondon DE21 220 C3
Hadfield SK13 9 F3
Hanbury DE13 238 A1
Holloway DE4 156 A3
Middleton (Nr Wirksworth)
DE4 154 B3
Rolleston DE13 240 A2
Tissington DE6 162 A3
Totley S17 55 E2
Wirksworth DE4 154 C1
Chapel La E S41 115 E4
Chapel La W S40 95 E1
Chapel Pl NG16 195 F3
Chapel Rd Bolsover S44 98 C2
Grassmoor S42 115 F2
Hayfield SK22 25 E1
Selston NG16 171 F3
Whaley Bridge SK23 45 F3
Chapel Row
Borrowash DE72 221 D1
Crich DE4 168 A4
Chapel Side DE21 220 C3
Chapel St Alfreton DE55 159 D2
Belper DE56 178 C2
Brimington S43 96 C4
Buxton SK17 85 D4
Chapel St continued
Chesterfield S41 96 A4
Coton in t E DE12 260 B2
Derby, Spondon DE21 220 C3
Derby, The Holmes DE1 267 B4
Donisthorpe DE12 265 F4
Duffield DE56 190 C2
Eastwood NG16 182 C1
Fritchley DE56 168 A3
Glossop SK13 10 B1
Hayfield SK22 25 E1
Heanor DE75 194 A4
Holbrook DE56 191 E4
17 Ilkeston DE7 194 C1
Kilburn DE56 192 A4
Kimberley NG16 195 F3
Linton DE11 261 F4
Long Eaton NG10 236 C4
Longnor SK17 121 D3
Melbourne DE73 252 A4
Monyash DE45 107 D1
Mosborough S20 59 E3
New Mills SK22 33 D3
Ripley DE5 169 E1
Rowarth SK22 24 C4
Smisby LE65 257 F2
Somercotes DE55 170 B4
Stafford ST16 269 E4
Stonebroom DE55 147 D2
Stretton en le F DE12 265 F3
Swadlincote, Church Gresley
DE11 256 A1
Swadlincote, Newhall DE12 255 F3
Swanwick DE55 169 F4
Ticknall DE73 251 D3
Whaley Bridge SK23 45 F4
Whaley Thorns NG20 101 D2
Woodville DE11 256 C1
Chapel Terr ST16 269 E4
Chapel Way S42 115 E1
Chapel Wlk S32 72 C1
Chapel Yd Dronfield S18 57 D1
Harthill S26 61 F3
Chapel-en-le-Frith CE Inf
Sch SK23 47 D3
Chapel-en-le-Frith High
Sch SK23 47 D3
Chapel-en-le-Frith Sta
SK23 47 D2
Chapman Ave DE24 233 D3
Chapman La S42 115 F2
Chapter Cl DE21 205 E1
Chardin Ave SK6 23 E4
Charing Ct DE1 267 C5
Charingworth Rd DE21 206 A1
Chariot Cl DE24 233 E3
Charity Rd DE55 170 B3
Charlbury Cl DE23 231 D4
Charles Ashmore Rd S8 57 D4
Charles Ave Derby DE21 220 B3
Sandiacre NG10 223 D3
Stapleford NG9 223 F4
Charles Cl DE7 209 D3
Charles La SK13 10 C2
Charles St Alfreton DE55 159 D3
4 Buxton SK17 85 E4
Chesterfield S40 95 F2
Glossop SK13 10 B1
Long Eaton NG10 236 B3
Mansfield NG19 136 A1
Mansfield Woodhouse
NG19 136 B2
Somercotes DE55 170 B4
Swadlincote DE11 256 A1
Charleston Cl DE11 256 A4
Charleston Rd DE21 220 B3
Charlestown SK13 17 E3
Charlestown Dr DE22 204 B2
Charlestown Rd SK13 17 E4
Charlesworth CE Prim Sch
SK13 16 B3
Charlesworth Cl SK23 33 E2
Charlesworth Cres SK23 33 E2
Charlesworth Ct NG19 136 C2
Charlesworth Rd SK23 33 E2
Charlesworth St S44 117 F4
Charley La SK23 47 D4
Charlotte Inf Sch DE7 194 C1
Charlotte La S33 51 D4
Charlotte Rd S2 43 D4
Charlotte St DE23 219 D1
Charlton Ave NG10 223 F1
Charlton Cl DE12 261 E3
Charlton St ST4 269 E2
Charnock Ave S12 44 A1
Charnock Cres S12 44 A2
Charnock Dale Rd S12 44 A1
Charnock Dr S12 44 A2
Charnock Gr S12 44 A1
Charnock Hall Cty Prim
Sch S12 44 A1
Charnock Hall Rd S12 44 A1
Charnock View Rd S12 44 A1
Charnock Wood Rd S12 44 A1
Charnwood Ave
Belper DE56 179 D2
Borrowash DE72 221 E1
Castle Donington DE74 247 E2
Derby DE23 231 E3
Long Eaton NG10 236 A2
Sandiacre NG10 223 D2
Charnwood Cl DE55 169 F4
Charnwood Cres DE55 148 A2
Charnwood Dr DE5 169 E1
Charnwood Gr NG19 136 A3
Charnwood St DE1 267 B1
Charter Pk DE7 208 C4
Charterhouse Cl DE21 205 F2
Charterhouse Dr ST17 269 F3
Charterstone La DE22 204 C2
Chartwell Ave S42 114 B3
Chartwell Dr DE21 219 E3
Chase Rd DE56 167 F2
Chase The Derby DE24 231 F2
Kilburn DE56 192 A4
Little Eaton DE21 191 E1
Chase View DE4 156 C1
Chasecliff Cl S40 95 E3
Chatfield Cl DE15 248 B1
Chatham Ave DE55 159 E2
Chatham Ct DE56 179 E2
Chatham St Derby DE23 232 A4
Nottingham NG1 268 B2
Chatsworth Ave
Chesterfield S40 95 D1
Clowne S43 80 C2
Crich DE4 156 C1
Darley Dale DE4 142 C4
Long Eaton NG10 237 D3
Shirebrook NG20 119 F3
Chatsworth Cl
Alfreton DE55 158 C2
Bolsover S44 99 E1
Sandiacre NG10 223 D2
Chatsworth Cres
Bullbridge DE56 168 A3
Derby DE22 204 C2
Chatsworth Ct Derby DE24 231 F2
Staveley S43 97 E4
West Hallam DE7 207 F4
Chatsworth Dr Derby DE3 217 F2
Little Eaton DE21 191 E1
North Wingfield S42 131 F3
Tutbury DE13 239 E3
Chatsworth Lodge SK17 85 D4
Chatsworth Park Ave S12 44 A3
Chatsworth Park Dr S12 44 A3
Chatsworth Park Gr S12 44 A3
Chatsworth Park Rd S12 44 A3
Chatsworth Park Rise S12 44 A3
Chatsworth Pl
24 Dronfield S18 56 B1
Ilkeston DE7 208 A3
Chatsworth Rd Buxton SK17 85 F4
Chesterfield S40 95 E1
Creswell S80 81 E1
Dore S17 55 F3
Rowsley DE4 111 D1
Swadlincote DE11 256 A3
Chatsworth St Derby DE23 218 C1
Tibshelf DE55 148 A3
Chatteris Dr DE21 205 E1
Chatterton La SK6 24 A4
Chaucer Dr S18 76 B4
Chaucer Inf Sch DE7 208 C4
Chaucer Jun Sch DE7 194 C1
Chaucer Rd S41 95 F4
Chaucer St Ilkeston DE7 194 C1
Mansfield NG18 268 B4
Nottingham NG1 268 A2
Chavery Rd S45 131 F2
Cheadle Cl DE23 218 A1
Cheadle Rd ST14 210 A1
Cheam Cl DE22 217 F3
Cheapside Belper DE56 178 C2
Derby DE1 267 B3
Nottingham NG1 268 B1
Chedworth Cl NG3 268 C2
Chedworth Dr DE24 233 E3
Cheedale SK17 85 E4
Cheedale Ave S40 95 E3
Cheedale Cl
Burton u T DE15 248 A3
Chesterfield S40 95 E3
Cheetham Ave S18 76 C3
Chell Rd ST16 269 D4
Chellaston Inf Sch DE73 233 D1
Chellaston Jun Sch
DE73 232 C1
Chellaston La DE73 233 E1
Chellaston Park Ct DE73 232 C1
Chellaston Rd DE24 232 C2
Chellaston Sch DE73 232 C1
Chelmarsh Cl DE73 233 D2
Chelmorton Cl NG19 136 C2
Chelmorton Pl DE21 219 F4
Chelmsford Cl DE3 217 E2
Chelmsford Way S43 78 A2
Chelsea Cl DE22 217 F3
Chelsea Way ST16 269 D3
Cheltenham Cl NG9 223 F1
Chelwood Rd DE73 232 C1
Chepstow Cl S40 114 C4
Chepstow Gdns S40 114 C4
Chequer La DE56 166 B1
Chequers La DE21 219 E3
Chequers Rd DE21 219 E3
Cheribough Rd DE74 247 D2
Cheriton Cl NG19 135 F1
Cheriton Dr DE7 194 B2
Cheriton Gdns DE23 230 C4
Cherry Bank Rd S8 43 D2
Cherry Cl Breaston DE72 235 F4
Shirebrook NG20 119 F3
South Normanton DE55 160 A4
Cherry Garth DE65 228 B1
Cherry Gr NG18 268 A3
Cherry Leys DE15 248 B2
Cherry St S2 43 D4
Cherry St S S2 43 D4
Cherry Tree Ave
Belper DE56 179 D3
Ripley DE5 180 B4

Cherry Tree Ave continued
Shireoaks S81 63 F4
Cherry Tree Cl
Barlborough S43 80 A4
Bolsover S44 99 E1
Brinsley NG16 182 C4
Hilton DE65 228 B1
Ilkeston DE7 208 B3
Mansfield Woodhouse NG19 136 A2
Risley NG10 222 C2
Swadlincote DE11 255 F3
Cherry Tree Dr
Buxton SK17 66 B1
Killamarsh S21 60 B3
Long Duckmanton S44 98 A2
Cherry Tree Gr
Mastin Moor S43 79 E2
North Wingfield S42 131 F3
Cherry Tree Hill Inf & Jun Schs DE21 220 A3
Cherry Tree Mews DE21 220 A2
Cherry Tree Sq SK17 69 E2
Cherrybrook Dr DE21 206 A2
Cherrytree Ave DE55 170 A4
Cherrytree Rd DE15 254 C4
Chertpit La DE45 89 E3
Chertsey Cl S40 114 C4
Chertsey Ct DE7 207 E4
Chertsey Rd DE3 217 E1
Cherwell Cl S43 77 F1
Chesapeake Rd DE21 220 A3
Chesham Cl SK13 10 A3
Cheshire St DE24 232 C3
Cheshire Way NG16 171 E2
Chess Burrow NG19 136 B1
Chessel Cl S8 43 D2
Chester Ave DE22 205 D3
Chester Ct DE21 220 C2
Chester Gdns DE11 256 A1
Chester Gn NG9 223 F1
Chester Green Rd DE1 219 D4
Chester St
Chesterfield S40 95 F2
Mansfield NG19 135 F1
Chesterfield Ave
Chesterfield S43 77 F2
Long Eaton NG10 236 C4
Swadlincote DE11 255 F3
Chesterfield Coll S41 266 B4
Chesterfield Coll (Tapton House Campus) S41 96 B3
Chesterfield Dr DE12 261 E3
Chesterfield Midland Sta S41 266 C3
Chesterfield & North Derbyshire Royal Hospl S44 96 C2
Chesterfield Rd
Alfreton DE55 158 C3
Barlborough S43 80 A3
Beeley DE4 111 D2
Belper DE56 179 D2
Bolsover S44 98 C3
Brimington, Middlecroft S43 97 D4
Brimington, Tapton S43 96 B4
Calow S44 96 C1
Darley Dale DE4 127 E1
Dronfield S18 57 D1
Eckington S21 59 D1
Grassmoor S42 115 F1
Hardstoft DE55 133 D1
Heage DE56 168 C2
Holmewood S42 116 B1
Long Duckmanton S44 98 B2
Matlock DE4 143 E4
New Houghton NG19 134 C4
North Wingfield S42 132 A4
Pleasley NG19 135 D3
Rowsley DE4 111 D1
Sheffield S8 43 D3
Shirland DE55 146 B2
Sutton in A NG17 148 C2
Unstone S21 59 D1
Chesterfield Rd N NG19 135 E2
Chesterfield Rd S
Mansfield NG18 268 B4
Sheffield S8 57 D3
Chesterfield Small Bsns Ctr S41 96 A4
Chesterfield Trad Est S18 76 B2
Chesterford Ct DE23 230 C3
Chesterman Cl NG16 195 D2
Chesterton Ave DE23 231 F4
Chesterton Cl S43 96 C2
Chesterton Rd DE21 220 C3
Chestnut Ave Belper DE56 179 D1
Derby, Chellaston DE73 232 C2
Derby, Mickleover DE73 217 E2
Derby, Rose Hill DE23 219 D1
Eckington S21 59 D1
Holbrook DE56 191 E4
Killamarsh S21 60 B3
Ripley DE5 180 B4
Somercotes DE55 170 B3
Swadlincote DE11 256 A3
Chestnut Bank DE75 181 E1
Chestnut Cl
Buxton SK17 66 A1
Dronfield S18 76 B4
Duffield DE56 190 C1
Horsley Woodhouse DE7 192 B4
New Mills SK22 24 C1
Chestnut Ctr SK23 47 F4
Chestnut Dr
Ashbourne DE6 185 E4
Clowne S43 80 B2
Creswell S80 81 F1
Repton DE65 243 E1
Selston NG16 171 F4
Shirebrook NG20 119 E2
South Normanton DE55 160 A2
Chestnut Gn DE11 256 A1
Chestnut Gr
Borrowash DE72 221 E2
Etwall DE65 229 D2
Mansfield Woodhouse NG19 136 A3
Sandiacre NG10 223 D4
Tibshelf DE55 147 F3
Chestnut La
Barton in F NG11 237 F3
Clifton Campville B79 263 F1
Chestnut Rd
Burton u T DE15 254 C4
Langley Mill NG16 182 A2
Chestnut Way Repton DE65 242 B1
Swanwick DE55 170 A4
Chestnuts The NG10 236 A4
Chevely Ct DE21 219 E4
Cheverton Cl DE24 233 E3
Chevin Ave
Borrowash DE72 221 E1
Derby DE72 217 F1
Chevin Bank DE56 190 B3
Chevin Pl DE1 218 C4
Chevin Rd
Belper, Chevinside DE56 178 C1
Belper, Milford DE56 190 C4
Derby DE1 218 C4
Duffield DE56 190 C3
Chevin The DE13 240 B1
Chevin Vale DE56 190 C3
Chevin View DE56 178 C2
Cheviot Ave NG16 170 C2
Cheviot Cl DE11 256 A2
Cheviot Rd NG10 223 D1
Cheviot St DE22 218 B3
Cheviot Way 1 S40 95 E3
Chew Rd OL3 5 E4
Chewton St NG16 182 C1
Cheyenne Gdns DE21 220 B3
Cheyne Wlk DE22 218 B3
Chichester Cl DE7 209 D4
Chilson Dr DE3 217 E2
Chiltern Cl
Chesterfield S40 95 E2
Grassmoor S42 115 F2
Chiltern Dr DE7 207 F4
Chiltern Gdns NG10 223 D1
Chiltern Rd DE11 256 A2
Chilton Cres NG19 136 B3
Chime Cl DE21 205 F1
Chine The DE55 160 A2
Chingford Ct DE22 218 A3
Chinley Prim Sch SK23 35 D1
Chinley Rd DE21 206 A1
Chinley Sta SK23 34 B1
Chippinghouse Rd S8 43 D4
Chiswick Cl DE22 217 F3
Chisworth Ct NG19 136 C2
Chiverton Cl S18 57 D1
Chorlton Terr ST14 210 B1
Christ Church CE Prim Sch S41 96 A3
Christ the King RC Prim Sch DE55 159 D3
Christchurch Ct DE1 267 B4
Christie Ave ST16 269 D4
Christopher Terr ST17 269 F3
Chrysalis Way NG16 182 B2
Chrysanthemum Ct DE11 256 A3
Chunal La SK13 17 E3
Church Alley DE45 109 E3
Church Ave Clay Cross S45 131 F2
Hatton DE65 239 E4
Long Eaton NG10 236 A2
Peak Dale SK17 67 D3
Swadlincote DE11 256 A2
Tideswell SK17 69 E2
Church Bank S32 53 D4
Church Banks DE6 173 D1
Church Bk SK23 45 E4
Church Broughton CE Prim Sch DE65 227 D4
Church Broughton Rd DE65 227 E2
Church Brow
Chapel-en-le-F SK23 47 D3
Mottram in L SK14 9 D2
Church Cl
Blackfordby DE11 257 D1
Blackwell DE55 147 E1
Burton u T DE15 248 A2
Clowne S43 80 C2
Derby DE73 233 D1
Glossop SK13 10 C1
Marchington ST14 224 C1
Nottingham NG3 268 B2
Peak Forest SK17 49 D2
Renishaw S21 79 D4
Staveley S43 97 E4
Trowell NG9 209 E2
Willington DE65 242 A3
Wingerworth S42 115 D2
Church Cnr DE6 165 D1
Church Croft
Coton in t E DE12 260 B2
Ripley DE5 169 E1
Church Dr Ilkeston DE7 194 B2
Sandiacre NG10 223 D4
Shirebrook NG20 119 F2
Church Farm ST14 210 A2
Church Fold SK13 16 B4
Church Gresley Inf Sch DE11 256 A1
Church Gresley St George's CE Prim Sch DE11 256 A1
Church Hill Derby DE21 220 B2
Etwall DE65 229 D3
Kimberley NG16 195 F3
Mansfield Woodhouse NG19 136 B2
Newton DE55 148 A1
Church Hill Ave NG19 136 B2
Church Hill Ctr Broxtowe Coll of F Ed NG16 195 F3
Church Hill St DE15 248 A2
Church La
Bakewell DE45 109 E3
Barrow u T DE73 244 A3
Barton in F NG11 237 F3
Baslow DE45 91 F3
Beeley DE4 111 D2
Belper DE56 179 D2
Brackenfield DE55 145 E1
Brailsford DE6 201 F4
Breadsall DE21 205 F2
Brinsley NG16 182 C4
Caldwell DE12 260 C4
Calow S44 97 D2
Castle Donington DE74 247 D2
Chapel-en-le-F SK23 47 D3
Chelmorton SK17 106 A4
Chesterfield S40 266 B3
Chilcote DE12 264 C2
Clowne S43 80 C2
Cossall NG16 195 E1
Derby, Chaddesden DE21 220 A3
Derby, Darley Abbey DE22 205 D1
Dore S17 55 E3
Doveridge DE6 211 D1
Ellastone DE6 183 D2
Fritchley DE56 168 A3
Great Longstone DE45 90 A2
Hanbury DE13 238 A2
Heath S44 117 D2
Hemington DE74 247 F2
Horsley Woodhouse DE7 192 C3
Killamarsh S21 60 C3
Kirk Langley DE6 202 C1
Little Eaton DE21 205 E4
Mackworth DE22 217 F4
Mansfield NG18 268 C3
Marchington ST14 224 C1
Marple SK6 23 D3
Mayfield DE6 184 B3
Morley DE7 206 C3
New Mills SK22 33 E4
Newton Solney DE15 248 B4
North Wingfield S42 131 F3
Osmaston DE6 186 A3
Peak Forest SK17 49 D2
Pleasley NG19 135 D3
Rocester ST14 197 D2
Roston DE6 197 E4
Rowsley DE4 110 C1
Selston NG16 171 E4
Shirley DE6 200 B4
South Wingfield DE55 157 F2
Stafford ST16 269 E4
Stanton-by-D DE7 208 C1
Stapleford NG9 223 E4
Stockley S44 117 E2
Sutton on t H DE6 215 D1
Temple Normanton S42 116 A2
Thorpe DE6 161 E1
Thrumpton NG11 237 E2
Tibshelf DE55 147 F3
Ticknall DE73 251 D2
Tideswell SK17 69 E2
Weston Underwood DE6 188 C1
Church La N
Chesterfield S41 77 D2
Derby DE22 204 C2
Church Level DE6 165 D1
Church Mead NG17 148 C2
Church Meadows
Calow S44 96 C2
North Wingfield S42 131 F3
Church Mews
Derby DE21 220 B2
Hatton DE65 227 E1
Killamarsh S21 60 C4
Mosborough S20 59 E4
Church Paddock S45 132 A3
Church Rd
Bolsover, Shuttlewood S44 99 D3
Bolsover, Stanfree S44 99 D4
Branston DE14 253 F4
Burton u T DE13 240 C1
Church Broughton DE65 227 D4
Darley Dale DE4 127 D1
Eggington DE65 241 D2
Fritchley DE56 168 A3
Hollingworth SK14 9 E2
Marple SK6 23 F3
New Mills SK22 33 E4
Nottingham NG3 268 B2
Quarndon DE22 204 B3
Rolleston DE13 240 A2
Snelston DE6 184 B2
Swadlincote DE11 256 A3
Church Rise DE55 146 B2
Church Side Calow S44 96 C2
Mansfield NG18 268 C3
Sutton in A NG17 148 C2
Church Sq Heanor DE75 181 F1
Melbourne DE73 252 A3
Church St Alfreton DE55 158 C2
Alstonefield DE6 149 F2
Ashbourne DE6 173 D1
Ashford in t W DE45 108 C4
Ashover S45 129 F2
Barlborough S43 80 A4
Baslow DE45 91 F3
Belper DE56 179 D2
Bolsover S44 99 D1
Bonsall DE4 142 B1
Bradwell S33 51 D4
Brassington DE4 153 D1
Brimington S43 96 C4
Buxton SK17 85 D3
Calow S44 96 C2
Clifton Campville B79 263 F1
Clowne S43 80 C2
Coton in t E DE12 260 B2
Creswell S80 81 F1
Denby DE5 180 B1
Derby, Alvaston DE24 233 E4
Derby, Littleover DE23 218 B1
Derby, Rose Hill DE23 219 D1
Derby, Spondon DE21 220 B3
Donisthorpe DE12 262 C1
Dronfield S18 57 D1
Eastwood NG16 182 C1
Eckington S21 59 F2
Eyam S32 71 E3
Fritchley DE56 168 A3
Glossop SK13 10 B1
Hadfield SK13 10 A2
Hartington SK17 137 E3
Hartshorne DE11 257 D3
Hayfield SK22 25 E1
Heage DE56 168 C2
Heanor DE75 181 F1
Holbrook DE56 191 E3
Holloway DE4 156 A3
Horsley DE21 191 F3
Ilkeston DE7 194 C2
Kilburn DE56 191 F4
Lockington DE74 247 F2
Longnor SK17 121 D3
Mansfield NG18, NG19 268 B4
Mansfield Woodhouse NG19 136 B2
Marple SK6 23 D3
Matlock DE4 143 E2
Melbourne DE73 252 A4
Monyash DE45 107 E1
Netherseal DE12 264 C3
Ockbrook DE72 221 E2
Pilsley S45 132 B1
Pleasleyhill NG19 135 D2
Ripley, Greenwich DE5 169 E1
Ripley, Waingroves DE5 181 D4
Sandiacre NG10 223 D4
Shirland DE55 146 B1
Somercotes DE55 170 B3
South Normanton DE55 160 A3
Stapleford NG9 223 E4
Staveley S43 78 C1
Stoke-on-T ST4 269 E2
Stretton en le F DE12 265 F1
Swadlincote, Church Gresley DE11 256 A1
Swadlincote, Lower Midway DE11 256 B2
Swadlincote, Newhall DE11 256 A3
Tansley DE4 144 A2
Tideswell SK17 69 E2
Tintwistle SK13 10 A4
Tutbury DE13 239 E4
Unstone S18 76 C4
Whaley Thorns NG20 101 D1
Wirksworth DE4 165 F4
Youlgreave DE45 125 E3
Church St E NG16 160 B2
Church St N S41 77 D2
Church St S
Chesterfield S40 115 D4
Glossop SK13 10 C1
Church St W
Chesterfield S40 95 E1
Pinxton NG16 160 B2
Church View
Barlborough S43 80 A4
Breaston DE72 235 E4
Chesterfield S40 95 E1
Clowne S43 80 C2
Glapwell S44 134 A4
Heanor DE75 181 D2
Ilkeston DE7 208 C4
Killamarsh S21 60 C4
New Houghton NG19 134 C4
Church View Dr DE45 91 F3
Church Way S40 266 B3
Church Wlk Brinsley NG16 182 C4
Chesterfield S40 266 B3
Derby DE22 205 D2
Duffield DE56 190 C1
Eastwood NG16 182 C1
Glossop SK13 10 C1
Somercotes DE55 170 C3
Stapleford NG9 223 F4
Churchdale Ave NG9 209 F1
Churchdale Rd S12 44 B2
Churchdown Cl DE21 206 A1
Churchill Ave DE4 154 B3
Churchill Cl DE72 235 E4
Churchill Dr Hilton DE65 228 C1
Stapleford NG9 223 F4
Churchill Gdns NG19 136 B2
Churchland Ave S42 132 B4
Churchside Grassmoor S41 115 E3
Willington DE65 242 A3
Churchside La S41 115 E3
Churston Rd S40 95 E2
Cinder Bank NG16 170 C2
Cinder La Killamarsh S21 60 C4
Wirksworth DE4 165 F3
Cinder Rd DE55 170 B4
Cinderhill La S8 57 E4
Circle The Derby DE24 231 F3
Mansfield Woodhouse NG19 136 A2
Sheffield S2 44 A4
Circular Dr S21 79 D4
Circular Rd
Chesterfield S40 115 D4
Staveley S43 78 B1
City Link NG1 268 C1
City Rd Derby DE1 219 D4
Fenton ST4 269 F1
Sheffield S2 43 F4
Stoke-on-T ST4 269 F1
City Rd Ind Pk DE1 219 D4
City Sch S13 44 C3
City The Woodville DE11 256 C1
Woodville DE11 257 D1
Civic Way DE11 256 A2
Clamp Dr DE11 256 A2
Clapgun St DE74 247 D2
Clara Mount Rd DE75 182 A1
Clare Valley NG7 268 A1
Clarehaven NG9 223 F3
Clarence Rd
Chesterfield S40 266 A3
Derby DE23 218 C1
Long Eaton NG10 236 B3
Clarence St
Chesterfield S40 266 A3
Mansfield NG18 268 B3
Nottingham NG3 268 C2
Pleasleyhill NG19 135 E2
Stonebroom DE55 147 D2
Clarendon Coll NG1 268 A2
Clarendon Rd
Mansfield NG19 268 A4
Staveley S43 97 E4
Clarendon St
Fenton ST4 269 F1
Nottingham NG1 268 A2
Clark St ST16 269 E4
Clarke Ave DE75 181 E1
Clarke Dr NG10 236 A2
Clarke St DE1 267 C4
Clarke's Cl ST14 210 A1
Clarkes La DE72 246 A4
Clarkson Ave S40 266 B1
Clatterway DE4 154 C4
Claverhouse Rd DE15 248 A1
Claxton St DE75 181 E1
Claxton Terr DE75 181 E1
Clay Cross Com Hospl S45 131 E2
Clay Cross Inf & Jun Sch S45 131 E2
Clay La Clay Cross S45 131 D1
Heanor DE75 181 F1
Clay St
Burton u T DE15 248 A1
Draycott DE72 235 D4
Shirland DE55 146 C1
Clay St E DE15 248 A1
Claye St NG10 236 C4
Claylands Cl SK14 9 E2
Claylands Gr S80 81 F3
Claylands Pl S80 81 F3
Claylands Rd S80 81 F3
Claymar Dr DE11 256 A4
Claymills Rd DE13 241 D1
Claypit La S42 112 C4
Clays La DE14 253 F4
Clayton Gr DE75 181 E2
Clayton St S41 266 C2
Cleave Rd DE14 254 A4
Clegg Hill Dr NG17 148 C2
Clematis Cres DE15 255 D4
Clement La S33 50 B3
Clement Rd
Horsley Woodhouse DE7 192 B4
Marple SK6 23 E4
Clerkson St 5 NG18 268 B3
Clerkson's Alley NG18 268 B4
Cleve Ave Beeston NG9 223 F2
Darley Dale DE4 142 C4
Cleveland Ave Derby DE21 220 A3
Draycott DE72 235 D4
Long Eaton NG10 223 F1
Cleveland Cl DE11 256 A2
Cleveland Rd DE55 146 C2
Cleveland Way S40 95 E3
Cleveleys Rd NG9 223 F2
Clewley Rd DE14 253 F4
Cliff Bvd NG16 195 F4
Cliff Coll S32 91 F4
Cliff La Curbar S32 72 C1
Elton DE4 140 B4
Kirby-in-A NG16 160 C2
Tideswell SK17 69 E2
Cliff Nook DE55 160 A2
Cliff Rd Buxton SK17 85 E4
Holme HD7 2 C4
Nottingham NG1 268 B1
Cliff St NG18 268 C4
Cliffash La DE56 176 C3
Cliffe Field Rd S8 43 D2
Cliffe Hill Ave NG9 223 E4
Cliffe La S32 52 C4
Cliffe Rd SK13 17 E4
Cliffe View Rd S8 43 D3
Clifford Cl
Chesterfield S40 95 D1
Long Eaton NG10 236 A2

Clifford St Derby DE24 219 E1
Long Eaton NG10 236 C4
Clifton Ave
Barlborough S43 80 A4
Long Eaton NG10 237 D4
Clifton CE Prim Sch
DE6 184 C3
Clifton Cl Overseal DE12 262 A2
Stafford ST 16 269 F4
Swadlincote DE11 256 A1
Clifton Dr Buxton SK17 85 E2
Derby DE3 217 F2
Stafford ST 16 269 F4
Clifton Pl NG18 268 B4
Clifton Rd Ashbourne DE6 185 D4
Buxton SK17 85 E4
Clifton DE6 184 C3
Derby DE22 204 C2
Matlock Bath DE4 155 D4
Netherseal DE12 264 B3
Clifton St
Chesterfield S40 95 F2
Derby DE1 267 D1
Clifton Terr NG7 268 A1
Clinthill La S80 81 F4
Clinton Ave NG16 182 B3
Clinton St DE21 219 E3
Clinton St E NG1 268 B2
Clinton St W NG1 268 B2
Clipstone Ave
Mansfield NG18 268 C4
Nottingham NG1 268 A2
Clipstone Gdns DE21 206 A1
Clodhall La Curbar S32 72 C1
Old Brampton S32, S42 93 D3
Cloonmore Croft S8 43 E1
Cloonmore Dr S8 43 E1
Close Bank DE13 239 E3
Close The
Derby, Allestree DE23 204 C1
Derby, Rose Hill DE23 218 B1
Great Longstone DE45 89 F2
Linton DE12 261 E3
Marple SK6 15 D1
Matlock DE4 143 D3
Moira DE11 262 B4
Shirebrook NG20 119 F3
Stafford ST16 269 D3
Tutbury DE13 239 D3
Cloud Ave NG9 223 F4
Cloudside Ct NG10 223 D4
Cloudside Jun Sch NG10 223 D4
Cloudside Rd NG10 223 D4
Cloudwood Cl DE23 218 A1
Clough Ave SK6 23 E3
Clough Bank S2 43 D4
Clough La Birchover DE4 141 E4
Little Hayfield SK22 25 E3
Lodge Moor S10 42 C3
Wensley DE4 141 E4
Clough Side SK6 23 E4
Clough St SK17 85 D4
Clough The S41 96 C1
Cloughside SK12 32 C3
Clover Cl DE21 220 C3
Clover Ct Shardlow DE72 234 C1
Sheffield S8 43 E1
Clover Nook Ind Est
DE55 159 F2
Clover Nook Rd
Pinxton DE55 159 F2
Somercotes DE55 159 F2
South Normanton DE55 159 F2
Clover Rise NG16 195 D4
Cloverdale DE11 256 A4
Cloverdale Dr DE24 231 F1
Cloverslade DE65 230 B1
Cloves Hill Morley DE7 192 B1
Smalley DE7 192 B1
Clowne Jun & Inf Schs
S43 80 C2
Clowne Rd
Barlborough S43 80 B3
Bolsover S44 99 D4
Club La DE73 244 A3
Club St ST4 269 E1
Clubmill Terr S40 95 F2
Clumber Ave NG16 171 F1
Clumber Cl S43 80 C2
Clumber Cres N NG7 268 A1
Clumber Cres S NG7 268 A1
Clumber Ct Ilkeston DE7 194 C3
Mansfield NG19 135 F1
Nottingham NG7 268 A1
Clumber Dr NG19 135 F1
Clumber Pl S43 97 E3
Clumber Rd E NG7 268 A1
Clumber Rd W NG7 268 A1
Clumber St
Long Eaton NG10 236 B4
Mansfield NG18 268 B4
13 Nottingham NG3 268 B2
Clun Ct NG19 136 B1
Clune St S43 81 D3
Cluster Rd DE56 178 C2
Clusters The DE56 178 C2
Co-operative St
Derby DE23 218 C1
Long Eaton NG10 236 C3
Coach Dr Eastwood NG16 182 C2
Quarndon DE22 204 B4
Coach Rd Hollingworth SK14 9 E3
Ironville DE5 170 B2
Ironville NG16 170 B2
Ripley DE5 169 F2
Somercotes DE55 170 B2
Coach Way DE65 242 B3
Coachhouse Mews DE11 256 A4
Coachways DE7 193 F2
Coal La Hartshorne DE11 257 E4
Ticknall DE11 257 E4
Coalpit La
Coton in t E DE12 260 C2
Youlgreave DE45 125 E3
Coasthill DE4 156 C1
Coatsby Rd NG16 195 F4
Cobden Pl NG19 135 F1
Cobden Rd
Chesterfield S40 266 A4
Matlock DE4 143 E3
Cobden St Derby DE22 218 B3
Long Eaton NG10 236 C4
Ripley DE5 169 E1
Cobham Cl DE24 231 E2
Cobnar Ave S8 43 D1
Cobnar Dr Chesterfield S41 95 E4
Sheffield S8 43 D1
Cobnar Rd S8 43 D1
Cobnar Wood Cl S18 76 A2
Cobthorn Dr DE22 204 B2
Cock Brow SK14 15 E4
Cock Hill DE45 91 F3
Cock Pitt The DE1 267 C3
Cockayne Cl NG10 223 D2
Cockayne La DE6 164 A1
Cockayne St N DE24 232 C3
Cockayne St S DE24 232 C3
Cockerhouse Rd NG16 182 C2
Cockleys NG10 236 B3
Cockshead La DE6 198 B4
Cockshut La
Holbeck NG20 101 D2
Melbourne DE73 251 F4
Whaley Thorns NG20 101 D2
Cockshutt Ave S8 56 B4
Cockshutt Dr S8 56 B4
Cockshutt La DE55 170 C4
Cockshutt Rd S8 56 B4
Cod Beck Cl DE24 233 E3
Codnor CE Prim Sch
DE5 181 D4
Codnor Denby La
Codnor DE5 181 D3
Denby DE5 181 D3
Codnor Gate DE5 170 A1
Codnor Gate Ind Est DE5 170 A1
Codnor La DE5 170 B1
Coffin La DE6 165 D1
Coggers La S32 52 C4
Coisley Hill S13 44 C3
Cokayne Ave DE6 173 E1
Coke St DE22 218 B3
Coldharbour La S45 145 D2
Coldstream Wlk DE24 231 F2
Coldwell St DE4 154 C1
Cole Dr ST16 269 D3
Cole La DE72 221 E2
Coleman St DE24 232 C4
Coleraine Cl DE21 220 A2
Coleridge St
Derby, Littleover DE23 231 F3
Derby, Normanton DE23 231 F4
Colin Ave DE5 181 D4
Colin St DE55 159 D2
Colindene Gr ST4 269 E1
Coliseum Ctr The DE1 267 C2
Colledge St DE55 170 B3
College Mews DE1 218 C3
College Pl DE1 267 B4
College Rd Buxton SK17 85 D3
Denstone ST14 196 B3
Spinkhill S21 60 B1
College St
Long Eaton NG10 223 E1
Nottingham NG1 268 A1
College Way SK17 85 E1
Collier Ave NG19 136 A3
Collier La DE72 221 E2
Collier St SK13 17 E4
Colliers Way S45 131 D2
Colliery La DE12 261 E2
Colliery Rd Alfreton DE55 158 C1
Blackwell DE55 147 F1
Swadlincote DE11 256 A1
Colliery Row DE55 159 D3
Collin Ave NG10 223 D2
Collin Rd ST4 269 D1
Collin St NG1 268 B1
Collingham Gdns DE22 218 A3
Collingham Rd NG19 135 E1
Collingwood Cres DE4 143 D3
Collingwood Gr ST4 269 D2
Collingwood Rd NG10 236 C3
Collins Ave DE55 160 A4
Collis Cl DE24 232 C4
Collishaw Cl S41 115 E4
Collumbell Ave DE72 221 E3
Colne Ct NG19 136 B1
Colombo St DE23 219 D1
Colonnade The 13 ST16 269 E4
Colonsay Cl NG9 209 E2
Colton Cl S41 76 C1
Coltsfoot Dr DE24 231 F1
Coltsworth La S43 80 C4
Columbell Way DE4 127 E1
Columbia St NG17 148 C2
Columbine Cl DE21 206 A1
Colver Rd S2 43 D4
Colvile St DE22 218 B3
Colville Ct DE12 263 E4
Colville St NG1 268 A2
Colwell Dr DE24 233 E3
Colwick Cl NG19 135 F1
Colwyn Ave DE23 218 B1
Colyear St DE1 267 B3
Combs Cl SK22 33 D4
Combs Inf Sch SK23 46 C1
Combs La SK23 46 C1
Combs Mews SK13 9 E1
Combs Rd SK23 46 C2
Comfrey Cl DE23 230 C3
Commerce St Derby DE24 232 C4
Melbourne DE73 252 A4
Commercial Gate NG18 268 B3
Commercial Rd SK17 69 E2
Commercial Row S32 72 B4
Commercial St 4 NG18 268 B3
Common La
Chelmorton SK17 87 D1
Mansfield Woodhouse
NG19 136 A2
Old Brampton S42 94 C4
Pleasley NG20 119 E2
Scarcliffe NG20 119 E2
Shirebrook NG20 119 E2
Stanley DE7 207 D4
Sutton on t H DE6 228 A4
Common Piece La DE65 230 C1
Common Rd Harthill S26 62 A3
Sutton in A NG17 148 C1
Swadlincote DE11 256 B1
Thorpe Salvin S80 62 C3
Common Side
Selston NG16 171 F4
Swadlincote DE11 256 B1
Common The Crich DE4 168 A4
Quarndon DE22 204 B4
South Normanton DE55 160 A3
Common Wood DE4 143 D2
Commonpiece La DE6 215 D1
Commonpiece Rd S45 131 E2
Commons Cl NG16 195 D4
Commonside Rd S18 75 E1
Compass Cres S41 77 E2
Compstall Mills Est SK6 15 D1
Compstall Rd Compstall SK6 15 D2
Marple SK6 15 D1
Compton Ave DE72 246 A4
Compton Cl DE24 233 E3
Compton Gr SK17 85 D3
Compton Rd SK17 85 D3
Compton St
Ashbourne DE6 173 E1
Chesterfield S40 266 A4
Holmewood S42 116 C1
Langwith NG20 119 F4
Comyn Gdns NG3 268 B2
Conalan Ave S17 56 A3
Concert Pl 6 SK17 85 D4
Condliff Rd SK17 69 D3
Conduit St SK13 9 F4
Coniston Ave DE21 220 C3
Coniston Cres DE21 205 E1
Coniston Dr
Clay Cross S45 131 D1
Ilkeston DE7 208 B3
Coniston Rd
Chesterfield S41 95 F4
Dronfield S18 56 C1
Long Eaton NG10 223 D1
Coniston Way S41 95 F4
Conksbury Ave DE45 125 E3
Conksbury La DE45 125 E3
Connaught Ct DE55 159 D2
Connaught Rd DE22 218 B2
Connelly Ct S40 95 F2
Consett Cl DE21 205 E1
Consort Gdns DE21 206 B2
Consort St ST4 269 E2
Constable Ave DE23 218 B1
Constable Cl Dronfield S18 56 C1
Sheffield S14 43 F1
Constable Dr Derby DE23 218 A1
Marple SK6 23 D4
Sheffield S14 43 E1
Constable La DE23 218 B2
Constable Pl S14 43 F1
Constable Rd S14 43 E1
Constable Way S14 43 E1
Convent Cl
Burton u T DE15 254 C4
Stoke-on-T ST4 269 E2
Convent Ct ST4 269 E2
Convent St 3 NG1 268 B2
Conway Ave DE72 221 E1
Conway St
Long Eaton NG10 236 C4
Stoke-on-T ST4 269 F2
Conygree La DE6 184 B4
Cook Cl Belper DE56 179 F3
Clay Cross S42 131 D3
Cook Dr DE7 209 D3
Cook La DE6 211 D1
Cookfield DE56 179 F4
Cookham Cl DE3 217 E1
Cooks Ave DE74 247 D2
Coombes La SK13 16 B3
Coombes View SK14 15 F4
Coombs Rd DE45 109 F3
Cooper St Derby DE22 218 B3
Glossop SK13 10 A1
Ripley DE5 169 E1
Cooper's Cl DE6 173 E1
Coopers Cl DE72 221 E1
Coopers Croft DE65 227 E1
Cope Ct DE24 232 A3
Cope St ST16 269 E4
Copeland Ave NG9 223 F4
Copeland St Derby DE1 267 C2
Stoke-on-T ST4 269 E2
Copes Way Derby DE21 220 A4
Uttoxeter ST14 210 A1
Copley Croft DE6 173 E2
Coplow La DE6 226 B3
Copper Beech Dr SK13 9 F1
Copper Glade ST 16 269 F4
Copper Yd DE5 180 C1
Copperas Rd DE11 255 E3
Coppice Ave DE7 194 B3
Coppice Cl
Chesterfield S41 115 E3
Derby DE22 204 C1
Disley SK12 32 A3
Kilburn DE56 192 A4
Coppice Dr Disley SK12 32 A3
Eastwood NG16 182 B2
Heanor DE75 193 F4
Coppice La
Clifton Campville B79 263 F1
Disley SK12 32 A3
Coppice Prim Sch DE75 193 F4
Coppice Side DE11 256 B2
Coppice The
Shirebrook NG20 119 E2
Whaley Bridge SK23 45 F3
Coppice View DE55 160 A2
Copse Cl DE4 165 F4
Copse Gr DE23 231 D4
Copse Rise DE11 256 A4
Copse The Ilkeston DE7 194 B3
Marple SK6 23 E4
Copseside Cl 10 NG10 236 A4
Copsewood DE55 160 A2
Copthorne Inf Sch DE55 159 D3
Copthurst Rd HD7 3 F4
Coral Way S45 131 E2
Corbar Rd SK17 66 A1
Corbarwoods La SK17 66 A1
Corbel Cl DE21 205 F1
Corbridge Gr DE23 231 D4
Corden Ave DE3 218 A1
Corden St DE23 219 D1
Cordville Cl DE21 220 A3
Cordwell Ave S41 95 E4
Cordwell Cl
Castle Donington DE74 246 C2
Staveley S43 97 E4
Cordwell La S18 74 C3
Cordy La Brinsley NG16 182 C4
Selston NG16 182 C4
Corfe Cl DE23 231 E3
Corfield Ave DE75 193 F4
Coriander Gdns DE23 231 E2
Corinium Cl DE24 233 E3
Corker Rd S12 44 A3
Corks La SK12 32 C3
Corley La DE6 174 B1
Corn Cl DE55 160 A3
Corn Mkt DE1 267 B3
Corn St SK13 10 B1
Corner Farm DE6 201 F4
Cornfield Ave DE55 160 A2
Cornfield CE Inf Sch
DE75 181 E1
Cornfield Cl 1 S40 95 D3
Cornfield Rd NG16 195 F4
Cornflower Dr DE21 206 A2
Cornhill DE22 204 C2
Cornhill Dr DE55 159 D2
Cornmill Cl Bolsover S44 99 D1
Calver S32 72 B1
Cornmill La DE13 239 F3
Cornwall Ave
Brimington S43 96 C4
Buxton SK17 85 F4
Cornwall Cl
Brimington S43 96 C4
Westwood NG16 171 E2
Cornwall Dr Brimington S43 96 C4
Grassmoor S42 115 F2
Cornwall Rd
Burton u T DE15 254 C3
Derby DE21 219 E3
Shireoaks S81 63 F4
Cornwallis Cl NG10 236 B3
Cornwallis St ST4 269 E1
Coronation Ave
Belper DE56 179 D3
Derby DE24 233 E3
New Houghton NG19 134 C4
Sandiacre NG10 223 D4
Coronation Cl DE73 252 A4
Coronation Cres ST14 197 D2
Coronation Dr
Shirebrook NG20 119 F1
South Normanton DE55 160 A3
Coronation La DE12 265 F3
Coronation Rd
Brimington S43 96 C4
Cossall NG16 195 D1
Mapperley DE7 193 F2
Stanley DE7 207 E3
Stoke-on-T ST4 269 D2
Coronation St
Derby DE23 232 A4
Ilkeston DE7 208 C4
Mansfield NG18 268 C3
Overseal DE12 262 A2
Swadlincote DE11 256 A3
Whitwell S80 82 A3
Coronet Ct DE21 206 B2
Corporation Rd DE7 209 D3
Corporation St
Chesterfield S41 266 C3
Derby DE1 267 B3
6 Mansfield NG18 268 B4
Stafford ST16 269 E4
Stoke-on-T ST4 269 E1
Corve Way S40 94 C3
Cosby Rd NG2 268 C1
Cossall Rd Cossall NG9 209 E3
Trowell NG9 209 E3
Cote Bottom La DE65 227 D4
Cote Green La SK6 15 D1
Cote Green Rd SK6 15 E1
Cote Hilloc DE4 127 D3
Cote La SK22 25 E2
Cotes Park Ind Est DE55 159 E1
Cotes Park La DE55 159 E1
Cotgrave Rd NG19 135 F1
Cotman Dr SK6 23 E4
Cotmanhay Inf & Jun Sch
DE7 194 C3
Cotmanhay Rd DE7 194 C2
Coton Ave ST 16 269 F4
Coton Cl NG19 136 C2
Coton in the Elms CE
Prim Sch DE12 260 B2
Coton La DE12 260 B3
Coton Pk DE11 255 E1
Coton Rd Derby DE23 219 D1
Walton- u-T DE12 259 F3
Cotswold Cl
2 Chesterfield S40 95 E3
Derby DE23 231 E4
Glossop SK13 17 D4
4 Long Eaton NG10 236 A4
Swadlincote DE11 256 A2
Cotswold Dr S42 115 F2
Cotswold Rd DE14 253 F4
Cottage Cl Ilkeston DE7 194 B2
Poolsbrook S43 98 A4
Swadlincote DE11 256 A4
Cottage Garden La DE75 181 E1
Cottage La SK13 9 F1
Cottam Cres SK6 23 D4
Cotterhill La S43 96 C4
Cottesmore Rd DE15 248 A1
Cottisford Cl DE23 231 D4
Cotton La DE24 219 E1
Cotton Mill Hill S42 113 F4
Cotton St S44 99 D1
Counduit Rd S44 118 A4
Counting House Rd SK12 32 C3
Countisbury Dr DE21 206 A1
County Rd ST16 269 E4
Coupe La S42, S45 131 D3
Coupe St DE5 180 C4
Coupland Pl DE55 159 E1
Court Farm La DE14 253 F4
Court La DE45 108 C4
Court Pl S43 97 E4
Court St DE11 256 C2
Court The DE24 233 D3
Court View S43 80 C2
Courtland Dr DE24 233 D3
Courtland Gdns DE24 233 D4
Courtland Rd DE65 229 E2
Courtney Way DE56 179 E3
Courtyard The
Darley Dale DE4 127 E2
Hollingworth SK14 9 E3
Coventry Cl DE11 256 B3
Coventry La NG9 209 F1
Coverdale Wlk DE24 233 E4
Coverley Pl ST4 269 D1
Covert Pl DE11 262 B4
Covert The DE21 220 C2
Cow La S43 77 F1
Cowan Dr ST16 269 F4
Cowan St NG1 268 B2
Cowbrook Ave SK13 10 C1
Cowburn Dr SK22 24 B1
Cowdray Cl DE24 231 E1
Cowham Cl DE55 159 E2
Cowley Bottom S18 75 F4
Cowley Gdns 4 S20 59 F4
Cowley La S18 75 E4
Cowley St DE22 218 C4
Cowlishaw Cl DE72 234 C1
Cowlow La SK17 47 E1
Cowper Rd NG16 195 D4
Cowper St DE24 232 A3
Cowringle La S43 77 F1
Cowsell Dr S45 131 F1
Cowsley Rd DE21 219 E4
Cox Green Cl DE23 230 C4
Cox Green Ct DE23 230 C4
Cox's La NG19 136 A3
Coxbench Rd DE21 191 F2
Coxon St DE21 220 C3
Coxon's Yd DE6 173 D1
Coyt Rd SK23 45 F3
Crab Tree Hill DE21 205 E4
Crabbery St ST16 269 E4
Crabtree Ave SK12 32 C3
Crabtree Cl
Castle Donington DE74 247 D1
Derby DE22 204 B2
Wirksworth DE4 165 F4
Crabtree Hill DE21 204 B2
Cracken Cl SK23 34 B1
Craddock Ave DE21 220 C2
Craddock Rd S2 43 F4
Cragdale Gr S20 59 E4
Cragg La DE55 148 A1
Craggon Dr S43 77 E2
Craggs Dr S43 80 C2
Craggs Rd S44 99 D1
Craglands Gr S40 95 D3
Crags Rd S80 82 A1
Crags View S80 81 F1
Craig Dr SK23 45 F3
Craig St NG10 236 C4
Craiglee Ct DE24 231 E2
Craigs Gn NG18 268 A3
Cramer St ST17 269 E3

Cranborne Rd S41 95 F4
Cranbourne Cl NG9 209 E1
Cranbrook St NG1 268 B1
Cranfleet Way NG10 236 A4
Cranhill Cl DE23 230 C3
Cranleigh Rd S43 79 D2
Cranmer Gr NG19 135 E2
Cranmer Rd DE21 267 D3
Cranmer St Ilkeston DE7 194 C1
Long Eaton NG10 223 E1
Stoke-on-T ST4 269 E2
Craven Rd S41 95 F3
Crawford Ave NG9 223 E4
Crawford Rd S8 43 D2
Crawford St ST4 269 F1
Crawley Rd DE24 232 C3
Crawshaw Ave S8 56 B4
Cray's Hill DE55 170 A4
Crayford Rd DE24 233 D3
Craythorne Cl DE11 256 A4
Craythorne Rd
Burton u T DE13 240 B2
Rolleston DE13 240 B2
Creamery La DE6 151 E1
Crecy Cl DE22 218 B2
Creighton La ST14 210 A3
Crescent S26 61 F3
Crescent Dr SK23 33 E1
Crescent Rd Selston NG16 171 E3
Stafford ST17 269 D3
Crescent The
Alfreton DE55 159 D2
Barlborough S43 80 B3
Bradwell S33 51 D4
Breaston DE72 235 E4
Breedon on t H DE73 252 C1
Brimington S43 96 B4
Buxton SK17 85 D4
Chapel-en-le-F SK23 47 E4
Clay Cross S45 131 E1
Derby, Boulton DE24 232 C3
Derby, Chaddesden DE21 219 F3
Holmesfield S18 75 D4
Holymoorside S42 113 E4
Horsley Woodhouse DE7 192 B4
Mayfield DE6 184 B4
New Mills SK22 33 D4
Repton DE65 242 B1
Shirebrook NG20 119 F3
Shirley DE6 200 B4
Stanley DE7 207 D4
Stapleford NG9 209 F1
Swadlincote DE11 255 F3
Totley S17 55 F3
Cressbrook Ave S42 132 A4
Cressbrook Way DE21 206 A2
Cresswell Ave SK22 33 E4
Cresswell St SK22 33 E4
Cresswellpart La S33 50 C4
Cressy Rd DE55 159 D2
Crest Cl DE13 240 C1
Crest The Derby DE22 204 C1
Linton DE12 261 E3
Creswell CE Inf Sch S80 81 F1
Creswell CE Jun Sch S80 81 F1
Creswell Crags Visitor Ctr S80 82 A1
Creswell Ct NG19 136 C2
Creswell Rd S43 80 C2
Creswick Cl S40 114 A4
Crewe St DE23 218 C1
Crewton Way DE24 232 C4
Crich Ave DE23 218 B1
Crich Carr CE Prim Sch DE4 156 B1
Crich CE Inf Sch DE4 156 C1
Crich Cir DE23 218 B1
Crich Jun Sch DE4 157 D1
Crich La Belper DE56 179 D4
Ridgeway DE56 168 A2
Crich Pl S42 131 F3
Crich Rd S43 97 E4
Crich View
Bolsover S44 118 A4
Heage DE56 179 F4
Newton DE55 148 A2
Crich Way DE11 255 F3
Cricket Cl DE15 248 C4
Cricket View S43 80 C1
Cricketers Cl DE15 254 C4
Cricketers Ct DE23 231 E4
Cricklewood Rd DE22 218 A3
Cringle Mews DE21 205 F1
Cripton La S45 129 F3
Crispin Cl S12 44 A2
Crispin Dr S12 44 A2
Crispin Gdns S12 44 A2
Crispin Rd S12 44 A2
Critch's Flats NG16 195 F3
Critchley St DE7 194 C1
Croft Ave DE6 151 E1
Croft Cl Dale DE7 207 F1
Derby DE21 220 C3
Netherseal DE12 264 C4
Ockbrook DE72 221 E2
Pinxton NG16 160 B2
Rolleston DE13 240 A2
Croft Cres
Awsworth NG16 195 E3
Stoke-on-T ST4 269 E1
Croft Ct NG17 148 C2
Croft End DE21 205 E4
Croft Gr ST14 210 B1
Croft Inf Sch DE55 159 D2
Croft La DE21 205 E2
Croft Lea S18 56 B1
Croft Manor SK13 10 C1
Croft Rd
Great Longstone DE45 90 A2
Sheffield S12 44 A3
Croft The Belper DE56 179 E1
Burton u T DE15 254 C4
Derby DE72 231 E4
Draycott DE72 235 D3
Hadfield SK13 10 A3
Heage DE56 168 C1
Morley DE7 192 B1
Somercotes DE55 170 B4
South Normanton DE55 160 A3
Stoke-on-T ST4 269 D1
Swadlincote DE11 255 F3
Croft View S43 97 E3
Croft Wlk S80 82 A3
Crofters Ct DE21 205 F1
Crofton Cl S18 56 C1
Crofton Rise S18 56 C1
Crofts The S32 53 D4
Croftstead Ave ST14 196 B3
Cromarty Cl DE24 231 F2
Cromarty Rise S18 56 B1
Cromdale Ave S43 77 E2
Cromer Cl DE3 217 E1
Cromford CE Prim Sch DE4 155 D3
Cromford Cl
Aldercar NG16 182 A2
Long Eaton NG10 236 A3
North Wingfield S42 132 A4
Cromford Ct
4 Chesterfield S41 95 E4
Whaley Bridge SK23 45 F3
Cromford Dr Derby DE3 217 F2
Staveley S43 97 E4
Cromford Hill DE4 155 D3
Cromford La Buxton SK17 85 F4
Wirksworth DE4 154 C1
Cromford Mews SK23 45 F3
Cromford Pl SK17 85 F4
Cromford Rd
Aldercar NG16 181 F3
Clay Cross S45 131 D3
Crich DE4 156 C1
Derby DE21 220 A4
Langley Mill NG16 182 A2
Ripley DE5 169 E1
Cromford Sta DE4 155 E4
Cromford Wharf DE4 155 E4
Crompton Rd
Ilkeston DE7 209 D2
Radmanthwaite NG19 135 E2
Crompton St Derby DE1 267 B2
New Houghton NG19 134 C4
Cromwell Ave
Blackwell DE55 147 F1
Chapel-en-le-F SK23 47 D3
Findern DE65 230 B1
Ilkeston DE7 209 D3
Cromwell Cl DE13 239 E3
Cromwell Dr DE55 169 E4
Cromwell Rd Bolsover S44 118 A4
Chesterfield S40 266 A4
Derby DE23 218 C1
Cromwell St
Eastwood NG16 195 E4
Mansfield NG18 268 C3
Nottingham NG7 268 A2
Crook Stile DE4 143 D4
Crook's Ave NG19 136 B2
Crooked Bridge Rd ST16 269 E4
Crookes Ave NG19 135 D3
Cropper La DE6 215 D2
Cropton Cl DE24 233 E3
Cropwell Ct NG18 268 C4
Cropwell Gn NG3 268 C2
Crosby St DE22 218 B2
Cross Chantrey Rd S8 43 D2
Cross Cl DE23 231 E4
Cross Cliffe SK13 17 F4
Cross Keys Row SK23 47 D4
Cross La Calver S32 72 A1
Codnor DE5 181 D4
Dore S17 55 E4
Dronfield, Coal Aston S18 57 E2
Dronfield, Quoit Green S18 57 D1
Flagg SK17 106 C4
Ible DE4 153 F4
Monyash DE45 107 D1
Rolleston DE13 240 A1
Shirland DE55 158 C4
Sutton in A NG17 148 C1
Wessington DE55 157 F4
Cross Lanes DE4 144 B1
Cross London St S43 77 E2
Cross Myrtle Rd S2 43 D4
Cross Park Rd S8 43 D3
Cross Rd ST14 210 A1
Cross Rise SK13 17 F4
Cross Side DE6 184 C4
Cross St Bolsover S44 118 B4
Bramley-Vale S44 117 E1
Breedon on t H DE73 252 C1
Brimington S43 96 C4
Broadbottom SK14 16 A4
Buxton SK17 85 E4
Castleton S33 38 A1
Chapel-en-le-F SK23 47 D3
Chesterfield S40 266 A4
Clay Cross S45 131 E2
Derby DE22 218 B3
Grassmoor S42 115 F2
Hadfield SK13 10 A3
Hollingworth SK14 9 E2
Killamarsh S21 60 C4
Cross St continued
Linton DE11 261 F4
Long Eaton NG10 236 C4
Mansfield Woodhouse NG19 136 A1
New Mills SK22 33 E4
North Wingfield S42 131 F3
Sandiacre NG10 223 E3
Cross The 1 SK13 10 A3
Cross Wellington St S43 77 E2
Crossdale Gr DE21 206 B2
Crossfield Gr SK6 15 D1
Crossgate La SK13 9 F4
Crosshill DE5 181 D3
Crosshill Dr DE7 208 B3
Crossings Ave SK23 47 D3
Crossings Rd SK23 46 C3
Crossland Dr S12 44 A2
Crossland Pl S12 44 A2
Crossland Rd S32 53 D4
Crosslands Cl SK13 17 E4
Crossley St DE5 169 E1
Crosslow La DE6 150 C3
Crossway ST 16 269 F4
Crossways La DE6 176 A1
Crossways The S2 44 A4
Crow Croft Rd S45 132 B1
Crow Hill NG19 135 D3
Crow Hill Ct NG18 268 B4
Crow Hill Dr NG18 268 B4
Crow Hill La NG19 136 A1
Crow La Chesterfield S41 96 B2
Stretton DE55 146 A3
Unstone S18 76 C4
Crowcroft Way NG10 223 D1
Crowestones SK17 85 E3
Crowfoot La DE65 226 C4
Crowhill La DE45 109 D3
Crown Cl Chesterfield S43 77 E2
Long Eaton NG10 236 A4
Crown Hill Way DE7 207 D4
Crown Mews DE22 218 C2
Crown Rd S41 96 A3
Crown Specl Sch The DE13 240 B1
Crown Sq DE4 143 D3
Crown St Clowne S43 80 C2
Derby DE22 218 C2
Duffield DE56 190 C2
Crown Terr DE56 178 C2
Crown Yd DE4 154 C1
Crownland Dr DE73 233 D1
Crowshaw St DE24 232 A4
Crowstones Rd DE4 127 D2
Crowther St ST4 269 F2
Croxton Ct NG19 136 C2
Croydon Wlk DE22 217 F3
Cruck Cl S18 56 C1
Cubley La Great Cubley DE6 198 B1
Marston Montgomery DE6 198 B1
Cuckmere Cl DE22 205 D3
Cuckoostone La DE4 128 C1
Cuillin Cl NG10 223 D1
Cull Ave ST 16 269 F4
Cullabine Rd S2 44 A4
Culland Rd DE14 254 A4
Culland View DE4 168 A4
Cullen Ave DE6 173 E1
Cullumbell La S45 129 D4
Culworth Cl DE56 179 E2
Culworth Ct DE21 206 A1
Cumberhills Rd DE56 190 B1
Cumberland Ave DE21 219 F3
Cumberland Cl NG16 171 E2
Cumberland Cres DE72 221 D1
Cumberland Dr SK17 85 E2
Cumberland Pl 3 NG1 268 A1
Cumberland Rd DE15 254 B3
Cumbria Wlk DE3 217 E1
Cumming St ST4 269 D2
Cummings St DE23 219 D1
Cundy Rd S44 99 D2
Cunliffe St S18 57 E2
Cunnery La DE4 144 A2
Cunnery The DE6 202 C1
Curbar Cl S42 132 A4
Curbar Curve S43 97 E3
Curbar Hill S32 72 B1
Curbar Prim Sch S32 72 B1
Curborough Dr DE24 233 E3
Curlew Ave S21 59 D2
Curlew Cl 1 DE24 231 E2
Curtis Gr SK13 10 A3
Curzon Ave S18 75 F4
Curzon CE Prim Sch The DE22 204 B3
Curzon Cl Derby DE22 204 B2
Killamarsh S21 60 B3
Curzon Ct Duffield DE56 190 C2
Nottingham NG3 268 B2
Curzon La Derby DE24 233 D4
Duffield DE56 190 B2
Curzon Rd Buxton SK17 85 E4
Derby DE21 219 F4
Curzon St Derby DE1 267 A3
Long Eaton NG10 223 D1
Nottingham NG3 268 B2
Curzon Terr SK17 88 B4
Cuscas La DE6 187 F2
Cut La DE1 219 D4
Cutholme Cl S40 95 D2
Cutler Cl S21 60 A4
Cuttholme Rd S40 95 E2
Cuttholme Way S40 95 E2
Cutthorpe Grange S40 95 D4
Cutthorpe Prim Sch S42 94 B4
Cutthorpe Rd S40 95 D4
Cuttlebrook Cl DE23 231 F3
Cypress Ave S8 43 E1
Cypress Cl S21 60 B3
Cypress Wlk DE21 220 A3
Cyprus Rd S8 43 D3
Cyprus Way SK6 32 A4
Cyril Ave NG9 223 E4
D H Lawrence Mus NG16 182 C2
Dade Ave S43 97 E3
Dag La DE12 263 F4
Dagnall Gdns DE45 109 E3
Dagnall Terr DE45 109 E3
Dagnam Cl S2 43 F3
Dagnam Cres S2 43 F3
Dagnam Dr S2 43 F4
Dagnam Pl S2 43 F3
Dagnam Rd S2 43 F4
Dahlia Ave DE55 160 A4
Dahlia Dr DE21 206 B2
Dairy House Rd DE23 219 D1
Daisy Farm Rd NG16 195 D4
Daisymere La SK17 67 D1
Dakeyne Cl DE4 127 F1
Dakeyne St NG3 268 C2
Dakin Ave SK17 85 E4
Dakin Ct SK17 66 C1
Dalbury Rd S18 56 B1
Dalbury Wlk DE23 231 E3
Dale Ave Long Eaton NG10 223 E1
Newton DE55 148 A2
Somercotes DE55 170 B3
Dale Bank Cres S43 77 E2
Dale Brook DE65 228 C1
Dale Cl Breaston DE72 235 E4
Fritchley DE56 168 A3
Langwith NG20 119 F4
Staveley S43 97 E4
Stonebroom DE55 147 D2
Whaley Thorns NG20 100 C1
Dale Cres Hathersage S32 53 D4
Tupton S42 115 E1
Dale Ct DE56 191 F4
Dale End Brassington DE4 153 D1
Wirksworth DE4 154 C1
Dale End Rd DE65 228 B1
Dale Gr NG2 268 C1
Dale La Ault Hucknall S44 134 B4
Buxton SK17 85 F4
Dale Park Ave DE56 192 A4
Dale Prim Sch DE23 218 C1
Dale Rd Buxton SK17 85 E4
Dale DE21 221 D3
Derby, Alvaston DE24 233 D4
Derby, Rose Hill DE23 218 C1
Derby, Spondon DE21 220 C3
Dove Holes SK17 66 C4
Dove Holes SK17 67 D4
Dronfield S18 76 A4
Killamarsh S21 60 C3
Kimberley NG16 195 F3
Matlock Bath DE4 143 D2
New Mills SK22 33 E4
Over Haddon DE45 109 D1
Stanley DE7 207 E2
Stanton-by-D DE7 208 B1
Tupton S42 115 E1
Dale Rd N Darley Dale DE4 127 D3
Northwood DE4 127 D3
Rowsley DE4 126 C4
Dale Rd S DE4 127 E1
Dale Side SK17 85 D4
Dale St Ilkeston DE7 208 C4
Mansfield NG19 136 A1
Nottingham NG2 268 C1
Dale Terr SK17 85 D3
Dale The Bonsall DE4 142 B1
Hathersage S32 53 D4
Stoney Middleton S32 71 F2
Wirksworth DE4 154 C1
Dale View
Earl Sterndale SK17 105 D2
Ilkeston DE7 208 C4
Litton SK17 69 F2
Shirland DE55 146 B2
Dale View Cl S45 132 A2
Dale View Gdns DE56 191 F4
Dale View Rd S45 132 A2
Daleacre Ave DE74 247 F3
Dalebank La S45 145 D4
Dalebrook Rd DE15 248 A3
Dalefield Dr DE11 256 A2
Dales Cl DE11 255 F3
Dalesfield DE4 143 D3
Daleside DE15 248 A1
Dalestorth Ave NG19 135 E1
Daleswood Cres DE55 160 A2
Dalewood Cl S41 96 C1
Dalkieth Ave DE24 232 C3
Dallas St NG18 268 B3
Dalley Cl NG9 223 F4
Dalley La DE56 178 B3
Dallimore Prim Sch DE7 208 B2
Dallimore Rd DE7 208 B2
Dalness Ct 4 DE24 231 E2
Dalston Rd DE11 256 A3
Dalton Ave
Burton u T DE15 248 A1
Derby DE22 218 B2
Dalton Cl NG9 223 F3
Daltons Cl NG16 182 A2
Dalvey Way S43 77 E3
Dam La Alsop en le D DE6 150 C2
Shirland DE55 146 C1
Dame Flogan St 6 NG18 268 B3
Damon Cl S45 132 B1
Damon Dr S43 96 C4
Damsbrook Dr S43 80 C2
Dan La DE6 151 D1
Danbury Gr S42 115 F2
Danby Ave S41 77 D1
Dane Bank Dr SK12 32 B3
Dane Cl NG3 268 B2
Dane Gr SK17 85 E2
Dane Hill Cl SK12 32 B3
Danebridge Cres DE21 206 A1
Danesby Cres DE5 180 A1
Danesby Rise DE5 180 A1
Danesmoor Ind Est S45 131 F1
Danesmoor Inf Sch S45 131 F2
Danesway SK23 47 D3
Danewood Ave S2 44 B4
Daniel Cres NG18 268 A4
Dannah Cres DE5 169 F1
Dannah St DE5 169 F1
Darby St DE23 218 C1
Darcy Rd S21 59 E2
Daresbury Cl S2 43 E3
Daresbury Dr S2 43 E3
Daresbury Pl S2 43 E3
Daresbury Rd S2 43 E3
Daresbury View S2 43 E3
Darfield Ave S20 44 C1
Darfield Cl S20 44 C1
Darfield Dr DE75 182 A1
Darfield La DE6 162 B2
Dark La Ashbourne DE6 173 D1
Ashover DE55 145 E3
Bradley DE6 175 D2
Callow DE4 165 E2
Calow S44 96 C1
Chesterfield S44 96 C2
Crich DE4 156 C3
Cromford DE4 154 C2
Holbrook DE56 191 D4
North Wingfield S42 132 A4
Pilsley S45 132 B1
Tatenhill DE13 253 D4
Youlgreave DE45 125 E4
Darkey La NG9 223 F3
Darklands La DE11 256 A2
Darley Abbey Dr DE22 204 C1
Darley Ave Beeston NG9 223 F2
Darley Dale DE4 127 E2
North Wingfield S42 132 A4
Darley Churchtown CE Prim Sch DE4 127 D2
Darley Cl Harthill S26 61 F3
Staveley S43 78 C1
Swadlincote DE11 256 A1
Darley Dale DE11 255 F1
Darley Dale Prim Sch DE4 127 F1
Darley Dale Sta DE4 127 E1
Darley Dr
Long Eaton NG10 236 A3
Ripley DE5 169 E2
West Hallam DE7 207 F4
Darley Gr Buxton SK17 85 E3
Derby DE1 219 D4
Darley House Est DE4 142 C4
Darley La DE1 267 B4
Darley Lodge Dr DE4 142 C4
Darley Park Dr DE22 204 C1
Darley Park Rd DE22 204 C1
Darley Rd S45 113 D1
Darley Sq DE7 194 C3
Darley St DE22 205 D1
Darley Way Buxton SK17 85 F4
North Wingfield S42 132 A4
Darlton St NG19 268 A3
Darnley St ST4 269 F2
Darsway DE74 246 C2
Dartford Pl DE24 233 D3
Dartmouth St ST 16 269 F4
Dartnall Cl SK12 32 A3
Darwent Rd S41 96 B3
Darwin Ave Buxton SK17 85 E4
Chesterfield S40 95 F3
Derby DE24 232 B2
Ilkeston DE7 208 C4
Darwin Cl DE15 248 B1
Darwin Pl DE1 267 C3
Darwin Rd
Chesterfield S40 266 A4
Derby DE3 217 F2
Long Eaton NG10 236 A3
Darwood La S44 118 A4
Dashwood St DE23 267 B1
Datchet Cl DE23 231 D4
Daveham Ave SK17 85 E3
Davenport Rd Derby DE24 232 B4
Tupton S42 131 E4
Daventry Cl DE3 217 E2
Davey Ct S44 98 C2
Davey Rd NG18 268 B4
Davian Way S40 114 C4
David's Cl DE73 232 C1
Davids Dr S42 114 C2
Davidson St NG2 268 C1
Davis Cl ST16 269 F4
Davis Rd DE11 256 A2
Dawber La S21 60 C4
Dawlish Ct Derby DE24 233 E4
Eastwood NG16 182 B2
Dawn View NG9 209 E1
Dawsmere Cl DE21 205 E1
Dawver Rd NG16 195 F3
Day Gr SK14 9 D2
Dayfield La DE6 175 D2
Daylesford Cl DE23 231 D4
Days La DE56 178 C2
Days Mill Cl DE4 143 D3
Dayton Cl DE21 220 B3
De Sutton Pl S26 61 F3
De Warren Pl S26 61 F3
Deacon Cl Derby DE21 205 F1
Swanwick DE55 169 F4

Dead La NG16 195 E1
Deadman's La DE24 219 E1
Deamon St DE55 147 F1
Dean Cl DE23 218 A1
Dean Rd DE56 167 F1
Dean St Derby DE22 218 C2
Langley Mill NG16 182 B2
Nottingham NG1 268 B1
Deanhead Dr S20 44 C1
Deans Dr DE72 221 D1
Deansgate NG19 135 D3
Deanshill Cl ST16 269 D3
Debdale Gate NG19 136 A1
Debdale La NG19 136 A1
Deben Cl S40 114 B4
Deborah Dr DE21 220 A4
Dee Cl DE24 231 F2
Dee La DE65 229 F3
Deep Dale La
Barrow u T DE73 244 A4
Derby DE24, DE73 231 F1
Deep La S45 133 D2
Deepdale NG16 170 C2
Deepdale Ave
Borrowash DE72 221 E1
Stapleford NG9 223 E3
Deepdale Cl DE15 248 A3
Deepdale Ct DE75 181 F1
Deepdale La DE6 184 A1
Deepdale Rd
Belper DE56 179 D3
Bolsover S44 98 C2
Derby DE21 220 C2
Long Eaton NG10 236 A3
Mansfield NG19 136 C1
Deepsick La S44 97 E1
Deepwell Ave
Killamarsh S20 60 A3
Mosborough S20 59 F3
Deepwell Bank S20 59 F3
Deepwell Ct S20 59 F3
Deepwell View S20 59 F3
Deer Park Prim Sch S42 114 C2
Deer Park View DE21 220 C3
Deerlands Rd
Chesterfield S40 95 D2
Wingerworth S42 114 C1
Deerleap La S42 130 B2
Deerpark Cres S42 114 C2
Degge St DE1 267 B2
Deincourt Cl DE21 221 D3
Deincourt Cres S42 131 F4
Deincourt Sch S42 131 F4
Delamere Cl
Breaston DE72 235 E4
Derby DE21 206 A1
Swanwick DE55 169 F4
Delamere Dr NG18 268 C3
Delhi Cl DE15 248 B2
Dell The S40 95 D2
Delph Bank S40 114 C4
Delph Cl S32 71 E3
Delph St S2 43 D4
Delph The DE73 252 C1
Delven La DE74 247 D2
Delves Bank Rd DE55 170 A4
Delves Cl S40 95 E1
Delves Rd Heanor DE75 193 E4
Shipley DE75 193 E4
Delves Specl Sch DE55 169 F4
Delves The DE55 169 F4
Denacre Ave NG10 223 F1
Denacre La DE4 127 F2
Denarth Ave DE24 232 C2
Denbigh St DE21 219 F4
Denby Comm DE5 180 C2
Denby Free CE Prim Sch DE5 180 B1
Denby La DE5 180 B1
Denby Rd S43 97 E4
Dene Fields Ct DE4 143 E3
Denefield Cl SK6 15 D1
Denham St S45 131 E2
Denison Cl S8 43 D3
Denison Gdns DE21 220 A3
Denman Cres S32 72 A2
Denmark Rd S2 43 D3
Dennett Cl NG3 268 C2
Dennis Cl DE23 230 C4
Dennor Dr NG19 136 C3
Denstone Coll ST14 196 A3
Denstone Dr DE24 233 D2
Denstone La ST14 196 B4
Denstone Rd NG3 268 C2
Dent La S12 44 C1
Dentdale Ct DE24 233 E4
Denton Ave NG10 223 D3
Denton Cl NG19 136 C1
Denton Way DE55 169 F4
Denver Ct NG9 209 F1
Denver Rd DE3 217 E2
Depedale Ave DE7 208 B3
Depot St DE23 219 D1
Derby Cath DE1 267 B4
Derby City Hospl DE23 218 A1
Derby High Sch DE23 218 A1
Derby Ind Gram Sch for Boys DE23 230 C4
Derby La Brailsford DE6 201 D4
Derby DE23 231 F4
Great Cubley DE6 198 C1
Monyash DE45 123 E4
Shirley DE6 200 C4
Derby Moor Com Sch DE23 231 D4
Derby Pl S2 43 E3
Derby Rd
Alderwasley DE56 167 F1
Derby Rd continued
Alfreton DE55 158 C2
Ambergate DE56 167 F2
Ashbourne DE6 185 F4
Aston-on-T DE72 234 A1
Belper DE56 190 C4
Borrowash DE21, DE72 221 D1
Burton u T DE13 241 D1
Chesterfield S40 115 D3
Clay Cross S45 131 E3
Cromford DE4 155 E3
Dale DE21 206 C2
Denby DE5 180 B2
Derby, Chellaston DE73 232 C1
Derby, Spondon DE21 220 B2
Doveridge DE6 211 E1
Draycott DE72 234 C4
Duffield DE56 190 C1
Eastwood NG16 182 C1
Eggington DE65 241 E2
Elvaston DE72 234 A1
Hatton DE65 227 F1
Heanor DE75 181 E1
Hilton DE65 228 C2
Horsley DE21 191 E3
Ilkeston DE7 208 B4
Kilburn DE56 179 F1
Langley Mill NG16 182 B2
Long Eaton NG10 236 A4
Marston on D DE65 228 A1
Melbourne DE73 252 A4
New Mills SK22 24 B1
Nottingham NG7 268 A2
Ripley DE5 180 B2
Risley DE72 222 B2
Sandiacre NG10 223 D3
Smisby LE65 258 A2
Stanley DE7 207 D2
Stapleford NG9 223 E3
Swadlincote DE11 256 B2
Swanwick DE5, DE55 169 F3
Ticknall DE11 257 F4
Tupton S45 131 E3
Uttoxeter ST14 210 B1
Wingerworth S42 115 D3
Wirksworth DE4 165 F3
Derby Rd Ind Est NG10 223 D3
Derby Road Ind Est DE75 181 E1
Derby Small Bsns Ctr DE1 267 C2
Derby St Glossop SK13 17 E4
Ilkeston DE7 208 C4
Mansfield NG18 268 C3
Nottingham NG1 268 A2
Sheffield S2 43 E3
Stafford ST16 269 D4
Derby Sta DE1 219 E2
Derby Terr S2 43 E3
Derby Trad Est DE21 219 D4
Derby Univ (Mickleover Site) DE3 217 F2
Derbyshire Ave
Trowell NG9 209 E2
West Hallam DE7 207 F4
Derbyshire Cl DE7 207 F4
Derbyshire Cty Cricket Gd DE21 219 E3
Derbyshire Dr
Ilkeston DE7 208 C3
Westwood NG16 171 E2
Derbyshire La S8 43 D2
Derbyshire Level SK13 17 F3
Derbyshire Royal Infmy DE1 267 C1
Derrington Leys DE24 233 E3
Derventio Cl DE1 219 D4
Derwent Ave
Belper DE56 179 D1
Borrowash DE72 221 E2
Derby DE72 205 D2
Grindleford S32 72 B4
Ilkeston DE7 194 B1
West Hallam DE7 207 F4
Derwent Cl Derby DE22 205 D2
Dronfield S18 57 D2
Glossop SK13 17 F4
Grindleford S32 72 B4
Swadlincote DE11 256 A1
Derwent Com Sch DE21 219 E4
Derwent Cres S41 95 E4
Derwent Croft DE65 242 A3
Derwent Ct 10 S17 56 A3
Derwent Dr Baslow DE45 91 E3
Chinley SK23 34 C1
Darley Dale DE4 127 E2
Derby DE24 231 E1
Tibshelf DE55 147 F3
Derwent Gdns DE6 185 E4
Derwent Gr DE55 158 C1
Derwent La Derwent S33 30 A4
Hathersage S32 52 C4
Derwent Pl S45 131 D3
Derwent Rd
Burton u T DE15 248 A1
Buxton SK17 85 E3
Derby DE21 220 B2
Dronfield S18 57 D2
Ripley DE5 169 E1
Derwent Rise DE21 220 C2
Derwent Sq SK23 34 C1
Derwent St Belper DE56 178 C2
Derby DE1 267 B3
Draycott DE72 235 D4
Long Eaton NG10 236 B3
Derwent Street Ind Est NG10 236 B3
Derwent Vale DE56 178 C1
Derwent View
Belper DE56 178 C3
Mastin Moor S43 79 E2
Desborough Rd NG16 171 E4
Dethick La DE4 144 B1
Dethick Way S42 132 A4
Devas Gdns DE21 220 B3
Deveron Cl DE13 240 B1
Deveron Rd S20 59 F4
Devizes Cl S40 114 C4
Devon Cl Burton u T DE15 254 C3
Derby DE21 219 E3
Grassmoor S42 115 F1
Sandiacre NG10 223 D3
Devon Dr Brimington S43 96 C4
Mansfield NG19 268 A4
Devon Park View S43 96 C4
Devon St Ilkeston DE7 209 D3
Nottingham NG3 268 C2
Devonish Royal Hospl The SK17 85 D4
Devonshire Ave
Borrowash DE72 221 E1
Darley Dale DE4 142 C4
Derby DE22 204 C2
Long Eaton NG10 237 D4
Devonshire Ave E S41 115 E4
Devonshire Ave N S43 77 F2
Devonshire Cl
Chesterfield S41 95 F4
Dore S17 55 F3
Dronfield S18 75 F4
Ilkeston DE7 194 C3
Staveley S43 78 C1
Devonshire Ct S43 96 B4
Devonshire Dr Chinley SK23 34 B1
Creswell S80 81 E1
Derby DE3 217 F2
Dore S17 55 F4
Duffield DE56 190 B1
Eastwood NG16 182 C1
Langwith NG20 119 F4
Rowsley DE4 110 C1
Somercotes DE55 170 A4
Stapleford NG9 209 E1
Devonshire Glen S17 55 F3
Devonshire Gr S17 55 F3
Devonshire Rd Buxton SK17 85 D4
Dore S17 55 F3
Devonshire Rd E S41 115 E4
Devonshire Rd N S43 77 E2
Devonshire Sq DE4 111 D2
Devonshire St
Brimington S43 96 C4
Chesterfield S41 266 B3
New Houghton NG19 135 D4
Staveley S43 78 C1
Toadmoor DE56 167 F2
Devonshire Terr S42 116 C1
Devonshire Terrace Rd S17 55 E4
Devonshire Villas
Barrow Hill S43 78 B2
8 Chesterfield S41 95 F4
Devonshire Way S43 81 D2
Dew Pond La SK17 85 E4
Dewchurch Dr DE23 231 F3
Dewint Ave SK6 23 D4
Dewsnap La SK14 9 D3
Dewy La Ashover DE4 144 C1
Crich DE4 144 C1
Dexter St DE23 219 E1
Dialstone S33 51 D4
Diamond Dr DE21 205 F2
Diamond Jubilee Cotts DE6 184 C4
Dibble Rd DE14 254 A4
Dickens Dr Holmewood S42 116 B1
Swadlincote DE11 256 B3
Dickens Sq DE23 231 F4
Dickenson Rd S41 266 C1
Dickinson St DE24 219 E1
Dickinson's La DE6 215 D1
Dicklant La S45 145 D4
Didcot Cl S40 114 C4
Didsbury Terr SK22 25 F1
Dig St Ashbourne DE6 173 E1
Hartington SK17 137 E3
Digby St Cossall DE7 195 D1
Kimberley NG16 195 E4
Diglands Ave SK22 24 B1
Diglands Cl SK22 24 B1
Diglee Rd SK23 33 E2
Digmire La DE6 161 E1
Dimple Cres DE4 143 D3
Dimple La DE4 168 A4
Dimple Rd DE4 143 D3
Dingle Bank S44 96 C1
Dingle Cl SK13 17 D4
Dingle La S44 96 C1
Dingle The DE15 254 C4
Dingley Cl NG19 136 C3
Dinmore Grange DE11 257 D3
Dinting CE Prim Sch SK13 10 A1
Dinting La SK13 10 A1
Dinting Lane Trad Est SK13 10 A1
Dinting Lodge Ind Est SK13 9 F1
Dinting Rd SK13 10 A1
Dinting Sta SK13 10 A1
Dinting Vale SK13 10 A1
Diseworth Rd DE74 247 D1
Dish La DE65 228 A3
Dishwell La S26 61 F3
Disley Cty Prim Sch SK12 32 B3
Disley Sta SK12 32 B3
Ditch The SK17 105 F4
Division Rd NG20 119 F2
Division St S43 97 E4
Dix Ave DE7 192 C3
Dixie St NG16 171 D2
Dixon's Rd S41 266 C2
Dobbin La S18 75 E3
Dobbinhorse La DE6 185 D3
Dobholes La DE7 192 C3
Dobson Pl S43 97 D3
Dock Wlk S40 266 A2
Dockholm Rd NG10 223 E1
Doctor La S26 61 F3
Doctor's La DE74 252 C1
Dodburn Ct DE24 231 E2
Dodford Ct DE75 182 A1
Dodslow Ave DE13 240 A2
Doe Hill La DE55 147 E3
Doehole La DE4 144 C2
Dog La
Breedon on t H DE73 252 C3
Hulland Ward DE6 175 E2
Netherseal DE12 264 C3
Stonebroom DE55 146 C1
Doghole La DE4 154 B2
Dogkennel La DE6 186 C4
Dolby Rd SK17 85 E1
Doles La Findern DE65 230 B2
Whitwell S80 82 A4
Dolly La Brierley Green SK23 34 A1
Whaley Bridge SK23 33 F2
Dolly Wood Cl SK23 34 A1
Dolphin Cl DE21 221 D3
Dominic St ST4 269 E2
Dominion Rd DE11 256 A3
Dominoe Gr S12 44 B3
Donald Hawley Way DE56 190 C2
Doncaster Ave NG10 223 D3
Doncaster Gr NG10 223 F1
Doncaster La ST4 269 D2
Donegal Wlk DE21 220 A2
Donington Park Motor Racing Circuit DE74 246 B1
Donisthorpe La DE12 262 C1
Donner Cres DE7 194 C3
Donnington Cl DE23 231 F3
Donnington Dr DE23 231 F3
Donnington La DE74 247 E4
Dorchester Ave DE21 219 F4
Dorchester Rd NG16 195 F4
Dore Cl S17 56 A4
Dore Hall Croft S17 55 E4
Dore La S32 53 D4
Dore Prim Sch S17 55 E3
Dore Rd S17 55 F4
Dore & Totley Sta S17 56 A4
Doris Rd DE7 209 D4
Dorking Rd DE22 218 A3
Dormy Cl NG19 136 C3
Dorothy Ave
Mansfield Woodhouse NG19 136 B1
Sandiacre NG10 223 D3
Dorothy Dr NG19 136 C1
Dorothy Vale S40 95 E2
Dorrien Ave DE23 232 A4
Dorset Ave 2 S43 96 C4
Dorset Cl Brimington S43 77 F1
Burton u T DE15 254 C3
Buxton SK17 85 F2
Dorset Dr S43 96 C4
Dorset St DE21 219 E3
Dorterry Cres DE7 209 D3
Douglas Ave
Awsworth NG16 195 E3
Heanor DE75 181 E1
Stoke-on-T ST4 269 D1
Douglas Rd
Chesterfield S41 96 B3
Long Eaton NG10 223 D1
Somercotes DE55 170 B4
Douglas St DE23 219 D1
Douse Croft La S10 42 C3
Dove Bk SK6 23 F3
Dove Cl Derby DE3 218 A2
Kilburn DE56 192 A4
Woodville DE11 256 C2
Dove Fst Sch ST14 197 D2
Dove Gr DE65 241 D3
Dove Holes CE Prim Sch SK17 47 F1
Dove Holes Sta SK17 47 F1
Dove House Gn DE6 173 D1
Dove La Long Eaton NG10 236 B4
Rocester ST14 197 D2
Dove Lea DE13 240 A2
Dove Rd DE5 169 E1
Dove Rise DE65 228 B1
Dove Side DE65 239 E4
Dove St DE6 183 D1
Dove Valley Pk DE65 227 D3
Dove View DE13 239 E3
Dovecliff Cres DE13 240 C1
Dovecliff Rd
Burton u T DE13 240 C2
Rolleston DE13 240 C2
Dovecote DE74 247 D2
Dovecote Dr DE72 221 D1
Dovecote The
Breedon on t H DE73 252 C1
Horsley DE21 191 F3
Dovecotes S45 129 F2
Dovedale Ave
Ashbourne DE6 173 E1
Derby DE24 233 E4
Long Eaton NG10 236 A3
Staveley S43 97 D3
Dovedale Cir DE7 194 C3
Dovedale Cl
Burton u T DE15 248 A3
Ripley DE5 180 B3
Dovedale Cres
Belper DE56 179 D3
Buxton SK17 84 C3
Dovedale Ct Belper DE56 179 D2
4 Chesterfield S41 95 F4
Glossop SK13 10 C1
Long Eaton NG10 236 A3
Dovedale Prim Sch NG10 236 A3
Dovedale Rd DE21 220 C2
Dovedale Rise DE22 204 B1
Dovefields ST14 196 C2
Dover Ct DE23 219 D1
Dover St Creswell S80 81 F1
Derby DE23 219 D1
Doveridge DE15 248 A1
Doveridge Cl S41 77 D1
Doveridge Cty Jun Mix & Inf Sch DE6 211 D1
Doveridge Gr SK17 85 F3
Doveridge Prim Sch DE6 224 B4
Doveridge Wlk DE23 231 E3
Doveside DE6 184 B4
Dowcarr La S26 61 E3
Dowdeswell St S41 266 B4
Dower Cl DE22 205 D1
Downham Cl DE3 217 F1
Downing Cl DE22 217 F3
Downing Rd Derby DE21 219 E3
Sheffield S8 56 C4
Downing St DE55 160 A3
Downings The S26 61 F3
Downlands S43 96 B4
Downlee Cl SK23 46 C3
Downmeadow DE56 179 F4
Dowson St NG3 268 C2
Doxey Rd ST16 269 D4
Dr John Bingham Prim Sch S8 57 D3
Drabbles Rd DE4 143 D3
Drage St DE1 219 D4
Drake Terr S43 96 B4
Draycott Cl DE75 181 E2
Draycott Ct DE7 194 C2
Draycott Dr DE3 217 E2
Draycott Pl S18 75 E4
Draycott Prim Sch DE72 235 D4
Draycott Rd
Borrowash DE72 221 E1
Breaston DE72 235 E4
Long Eaton NG10 236 A2
North Wingfield S42 131 F4
Drayton Ave Derby DE22 217 F3
Mansfield NG19 135 E1
Drayton St DE11 256 B2
Dresden Cl DE3 217 E1
Drewery La DE22 218 C2
Drewry Ct DE1 218 C3
Dreyfus Cl DE21 220 C3
Drive The DE56 177 F2
Dronfield Inf & Jun Sch S18 57 D1
Dronfield Pl DE7 194 C3
Dronfield Rd S21 59 D1
Dronfield Sch (Gosforth Site) The S18 56 C1
Dronfield Sch The S18 57 D1
Dronfield Sta S18 57 D1
Drovers Way DE56 168 A3
Drovers Wlk SK13 10 B1
Drummond Rd DE7 194 C1
Drury Ave DE21 220 B2
Drury La Biggin SK17 138 B1
Dore S17 55 E4
Dronfield S18 57 E2
Dryden Ave S40 115 D4
Dryden Cres ST17 269 D3
Dryden Ct NG9 209 F1
Dryden St Derby DE23 231 F4
Nottingham NG1 268 A2
Dryhurst Dr SK12 32 B3
Dryhurst La SK12 32 B3
Drysdale Rd DE3 217 E2
Duchess St Creswell S80 81 F1
Whitwell S80 82 A3
Duck St DE65 241 D3
Duckmanton Prim Sch S44 98 A3
Duckmanton Rd S44 98 A3
Duckworth Sq DE1 267 B3
Dudwood La DE4 140 C4
Duesbury Cl DE24 232 C4
Duesbury The DE55 160 A2
Duewell Ct S43 78 A2
Duffield Bank DE56 191 D2
Duffield Cl NG10 236 A3
Duffield Rd
Derby, Allestree DE22 205 D3
Derby, Darley Abbey DE22 204 C1
Little Eaton DE21 205 D3
Duffield Sta DE56 190 C2
Duke of Norfolk's CE Prim Sch Glossop SK13 10 B1
Glossop, Old Glossop SK13 10 C1
Duke St Buxton SK17 84 C3
Chesterfield S41 96 A4
Clowne S43 81 D2
Creswell S80 81 F1
Derby DE1 267 B4
Ilkeston DE7 194 C2
Middleton (Nr Wirksworth) DE4 154 B3
Mosborough S20 59 E3
South Normanton DE55 160 A3
Staveley S43 78 C1
Whitwell S80 82 A3

Duke William Mount NG7 268 A1
Duke's Dr
Ault Hucknall S44 134 A4
Buxton SK17 85 E3
Duke's Dr The DE45 108 C4
Dukeries Ct S43 80 C1
Dukeries La DE21 206 A1
Dukes Cl S42 116 C1
Dukes Dr Chesterfield S41 95 F3
Curbar S32 72 B1
Dukes Pl DE7 194 C2
Dukes St SK13 17 E4
Duluth Ave DE21 220 A4
Dulverton Ave DE24 231 E1
Dulwich Rd DE22 217 F3
Dumb Hall La
Shireoaks S80 63 D2
Thorpe Salvin S80 63 D2
Dumble Wood Grange S40 95 E4
Dumbles Cl DE7 208 B3
Dumbles La DE5 180 C1
Dumbles Rd S44 98 C2
Dumbleton Rd S21 60 C3
Dunbar Cl DE24 231 F1
Duncan Cl DE56 179 D3
Duncan Rd DE23 231 F4
Duncliffe La DE73 252 A4
Duncombe Dr DE6 185 E4
Dundas Cl NG1 268 B2
Dundee Dr NG19 136 A3
Dundee Rd DE11 256 B3
Dundonald Rd S40 266 B1
Dunedin Cl DE3 217 F2
Dunedin Cres DE15 248 B1
Dunedin Glen S20 59 F3
Dunedin Gr S20 59 F3
Dungley Hill DE56 168 B1
Dungreave Ave DE4 127 D3
Dunkery Ct DE21 206 A1
Dunkirk DE22 267 A2
Dunlow La S32 71 E3
Dunn Brigg NG19 136 B1
Dunne La SK13 10 C1
Dunnett Rd NG18 268 A3
Dunnsmoor La DE11 256 C4
Dunoon Cl DE24 231 F2
Dunoon Rd NG18 268 A3
Dunsa La DE45 91 E1
Dunsford Rd DE55 159 D3
Dunshill Wlk S45 131 F2
Dunsil Rd NG16 160 B1
Dunsmore Dr DE21 205 F1
Dunsmore Way DE11 256 B3
Dunstall Brook DE15 248 A1
Dunstall Park Rd DE24 232 B4
Dunston Cl NG10 236 C4
Dunston Ct S41 76 C1
Dunston La S41 95 E4
Dunston Pl S41 76 C1
Dunston Prim Sch S41 95 E4
Dunston Rd S41 76 B1
Dunston Trad Est S41 76 C1
Dunton Cl DE21 267 D3
Dunvegan Ave S45 131 F1
Dunvegan Cl DE24 231 E1
Duper La S32 51 F3
Durban Rd DE15 248 B2
Durham Ave
Chesterfield S43 77 E2
Derby DE21 219 F3
Grassmoor S42 115 F1
Nottingham NG2 268 C1
Durham Cl
Chesterfield S43 77 E2
Mansfield Woodhouse NG19 136 B2
Nottingham NG2 268 C1
Swadlincote DE11 256 C3
Durham St 5 DE7 194 C1
Durley Chine Dr S41 115 E4
Durley Cl DE24 233 E4
Durlstone Cl S12 44 A3
Durlstone Cres S12 44 A3
Durlstone Dr S12 44 A3
Durlstone Gr S12 44 A3
Durrant Rd S41 266 B3
Durvale Ct S17 55 F3
Durward Cl DE24 232 B4
Dyche Cl S8 57 D3
Dyche Dr S8 57 D3
Dyche La Dronfield S18 57 D3
Sheffield S8 57 D3
Dyche Pl S8 57 D3
Dyche Rd S8 57 D3
Dye House La SK22 33 E4
Dyke Vale Rd S12 44 C3
Dykes Cl S44 99 D1
Dymond Gr S42 115 F2
Dystelegh Rd SK12 32 B3

Each Well La DE55 158 C2
Eagle Ctr DE1 267 B2
Eagle Hts DE15 248 B2
Eagle Par 4 SK17 85 D4
Eagle Rd DE7 208 C2
Eagle St 3 Buxton SK17 85 D4
Heage DE56 168 C1
Eagle Terr Birchover DE4 126 A1
Wensley DE4 142 A4
Ealing Cl DE22 218 A3
Eardley Cl DE21 220 A3
Earl St ST16 269 E4
Earl Sterndale CE Prim Sch SK17 105 E2
Earls Cres DE21 206 A1
Earlswood Cl DE72 235 E4
Earlswood Dr DE3 217 F2
Earnshaw St SK14 9 E2
Easedale Cl S40 94 C3
East Ave Bolsover S44 80 A1
Derby DE3 217 F2
East Bank DE4 141 E3
East Bank Cl S2 43 E3
East Bank Pl S2 43 E3
East Bank Rd S2 43 E3
East Bank View S2 43 E3
East Bank Way S2 43 E3
East Circus St 2 NG1 268 A1
East Cl DE22 204 C1
East Cres Holbrook DE56 191 E4
Long Duckmanton S44 98 A3
East Croft Ave DE23 231 E3
East Dr DE6 211 D1
East End DE4 140 C3
East End Dr DE11 256 B2
East Glade Ave S12 44 C2
East Glade Cl S12 44 C2
East Glade Cres S12 44 C2
East Glade Pl S12 44 C2
East Glade Rd S12 44 C2
East Glade Sq S12 44 C2
East Glade Way S12 44 C2
East Hill Sch S2 43 E4
East Lawn DE65 230 B1
East Midlands Airport DE74 247 E1
East Midlands Nuffield Hospl DE23 230 C3
East Nelson St DE75 181 F1
East Rd S2 43 D4
East Service Rd DE21 220 A2
East St Bramley-Vale S44 117 E1
Burton u T DE15 248 B2
Clay Cross S45 131 E2
Clowne S43 81 D3
Creswell S80 81 E1
Derby DE1 267 B3
Heanor DE75 194 A4
Ilkeston DE7 208 C4
Long Eaton NG10 236 C4
Nottingham NG1 268 B2
Renishaw S21 79 D4
Scarcliffe S44 118 C3
East Vale SK6 23 D3
East View Chesterfield S40 266 B2
Shirebrook NG20 119 F3
East View Ave S21 59 E1
East View Rd DE56 168 C1
Eastbrae Rd DE23 231 E4
Eastbrook Cl SK23 47 E3
Eastcliffe S2 43 E4
Eastcliffe Ct S2 43 E4
Eastcroft Cl S20 59 F4
Eastcroft Dr S20 59 F4
Eastcroft Glen 10 S20 59 F4
Eastcroft View 11 S20 59 F4
Eastcroft Way 13 S20 59 F4
Eastern Ave Bolsover S44 118 A4
Sheffield S2 43 F4
Eastern Cres S2 43 E3
Eastern Dr S2 43 E4
Eastern Wlk S2 43 E4
Eastfield Dr DE55 160 A3
Eastfield Rd Dronfield S18 76 B4
Ripley DE5 170 A1
Swadlincote DE11 256 B3
Eastgate DE21 267 D4
Eastgate St ST16 269 E4
Eastham Cl NG3 268 C2
Eastleigh Ct S41 115 E4
Eastleigh Dr Derby DE3 217 F1
Mansfield Woodhouse NG19 136 A3
Eastmoor Rd S43 96 C2
Eastway DE74 247 D2
Eastwood Ave DE23 218 B1
Eastwood Cl S41 115 E4
Eastwood Comp Sch NG16 182 C2
Eastwood Cotts S32 53 D4
Eastwood Dr Callow S44 97 D1
Derby DE23 218 B1
Eastwood Jun & Inf Schs NG16 182 C2
Eastwood La S45 130 A1
Eastwood Park Dr S41 115 E4
Eastwood Rd NG16 195 F3
Easy Par S80 82 A3
Eather Ave NG19 136 B2
Eaton Ave Derby DE22 205 D3
Ilkeston DE7 208 B3
Eaton Bank DE56 191 D1
Eaton Cl Derby DE65 205 D3
Hatton DE65 227 E1
Hulland Ward DE6 175 F2
Eaton Ct Derby DE1 218 C3
Duffield DE56 190 C1
Eaton Dr DE45 91 E3
Eaton Fold S32 71 F2
Eaton Grange Dr NG10 236 A4
Eaton Hill DE45 91 F3
Eaton Pl DE45 91 F3
Eaton Rd
Castle Donington DE74 247 D2
Rocester ST14 196 C2
Eaton St ST14 210 B1
Eatons Rd NG9 223 E3
Eaves Knoll Rd SK22 33 D4
Ebenezer St Glossop SK13 17 E4
Ilkeston DE7 194 C2
Langley Mill NG16 182 A2
Eccles Cl Hope S33 39 D2
Whaley Bridge SK23 45 E4
Eccles Fold SK23 47 D3
Eccles Rd
Chapel-en-le-F, Higher Crossings SK23 47 D3
Chapel-en-le-F, Hilltop SK23 46 B4
Whaley Bridge SK23 45 F3
Eccles Terr SK23 46 B4
Ecclesbourne Ave DE56 190 C2
Ecclesbourne Cl
Duffield DE56 190 C2
Wirksworth DE4 165 F4
Ecclesbourne Dr SK17 85 D3
Ecclesbourne La DE56 176 C3
Ecclesbourne Sch DE56 190 C2
Eckington Cl DE7 207 F4
Eckington Jun Sch S21 59 E2
Eckington Rd Dronfield S18 57 E2
Eckington S18 57 E2
Mosborough S20 59 F4
Staveley S43 78 C2
Unstone S43 77 E3
Eckington Sch S21 59 D2
Eckington Way S20 59 F4
Eclipse Yd NG18 268 B4
Edale Ave
Derby, Alvaston DE24 233 D4
Derby, Mickleover DE3 217 E1
Derby, Rose Hill DE23 218 C1
Edale CE Prim Sch S33 37 E4
Edale Cl Derby DE22 204 B1
Long Eaton NG10 236 A3
Edale Cres SK13 9 F1
Edale Ct 3 S41 95 F4
Edale Dr DE21 220 C2
Edale Gr SK17 85 F4
Edale Rd Hayfield SK22 26 A1
Hope S33 38 C4
Mastin Moor S43 79 E2
Edale Rise NG9 223 F2
Edale Sq DE7 194 C3
Edale Sta S33 37 E4
Edale Way DE56 179 D3
Eden Bank DE56 167 F1
Eden Low NG19 136 C2
Eden Rd DE21 220 A2
Eden St Derby DE24 233 D4
Wingerworth S42 114 C2
Edenhall Rd S2 43 F4
Edensor Ave SK17 85 F4
Edensor Cl S42 131 F3
Edensor Ct S43 97 E4
Edensor Dr DE56 179 E3
Edensor Sq DE22 218 C2
Edes Farm Dr ST14 196 C2
Edgar Ave NG18 268 C4
Edge Hill DE73 232 C2
Edge Hill Ct NG10 236 B2
Edge Hill Jun Sch DE15 254 C4
Edge Rd Eyam S32 71 F4
Matlock DE4 143 D3
Edge View Cl S32 72 B4
Edge View Dr DE45 90 A2
Edgecote Dr DE11 256 A4
Edgefold Rd DE4 143 D3
Edgehill Gr NG19 136 B1
Edgelaw Ct 10 DE24 231 E2
Edgewood Rd NG16 195 F3
Edgware Rd DE22 217 F3
Edinburgh Cres DE24 232 C2
Edinburgh Ct DE55 170 A4
Edinburgh Rd
Chesterfield S41 95 F3
Wingerworth S42 114 C2
Edision St ST4 269 F1
Edith Wood Cl DE24 233 D3
Edlaston La DE6 185 D1
Edmonton Pl DE15 248 B1
Edmund Ave S17 56 B3
Edmund Cl S17 56 B3
Edmund Dr S17 56 B3
Edmund Rd Derby DE21 220 C2
Sheffield S2 43 D4
Edmund St S41 95 F4
Edmund's Sq DE3 230 A4
Ednaston Ave DE23 231 E3
Edward Ave Derby DE21 220 A3
Westwood NG16 171 D2
Edward Rd NG10 236 B4
Edward St Aldercar NG16 182 A2
Belper DE56 179 D2
Derby DE1 267 B4
Eckington S21 59 E2
Glossop SK13 10 B1
Hartshorne DE11 257 D2
Marple SK6 15 D1
Moira DE11 256 B1
Overseal DE12 262 A2
Stapleford NG9 223 E4
Staveley S43 97 E4
Edward Wlk S42 115 E1
Edwards Cres DE56 192 A4
Edwards Dr ST16 269 D4
Edwin Ave S40 114 B4
Edwin Rd S2 43 E3
Edwinstowe Rd DE21 206 A1
Egerton Dr NG9 209 E1
Egerton Rd Dronfield S18 57 D1
Stoke-on-T ST4 269 D2
Eggesford Rd DE24 231 E1
Eggington Prim Sch DE65 241 D3
Eggington Rd DE65 228 C1
Egginton Rd DE65 229 D1
Egmanton Cl DE21 206 A1
Egreaves Ave DE75 181 E2
Egstow Pl S45 131 E2
Egstow St S45 131 E2
Ehlinger Ave SK13 10 A3
Eider Cl NG20 119 E2
Eland Cl DE21 221 D3
Eland Rd NG20 119 F3
Elder Cl DE55 170 A4
Elder Ct S21 60 B3
Elder Way S40 266 B3
Eldon Cl SK23 47 E3
Eldon La SK17 49 D3
Eldon St Burton u T DE15 248 A2
Clay Cross S45 131 E2
Eleanor Ave DE7 209 D3
Eleanor Cres NG9 223 F4
Elenora St ST4 269 E2
Eley Cl DE7 194 B1
Eley Wlk DE22 267 A1
Elford Rise NG2 268 C2
Elgar Dr NG10 236 A3
Elgin Ave DE23 218 A1
Elgin Cl S40 114 B4
Eliot Cl Calow S43 96 C3
Long Eaton NG10 236 A3
Eliot Dr DE7 208 B3
Eliot Rd DE23 231 D4
Eliot Way ST17 269 D3
Elizabeth Ave Buxton SK17 85 E4
Disley SK12 32 B3
Rolleston DE13 240 A2
Elizabeth Cl Derby DE21 220 A3
West Hallam DE7 207 E4
Elizabeth Ct DE7 194 B1
Elizabeth Pk NG16 170 C3
Elkstone Cl DE21 206 A1
Elkstone Rd S40 95 D3
Ella Bank Rd DE75 182 A1
Ellastone Gdns DE24 233 D4
Ellastone Gr ST4 269 D1
Ellendale Rd DE21 220 A4
Ellerslie Gr NG10 223 D3
Ellesmere Ave
Alfreton DE55 159 D2
Derby DE24 219 E1
Ellesmere Dr NG9 209 E3
Ellington Ave ST 16 269 F4
Elliot Ave S33 51 D4
Elliott Dr S43 97 E3
Elliott St NG7 268 A2
Ellis Cl NG10 236 B3
Ellis Ct NG3 268 B2
Ellison Ave DE72 246 A4
Ellison Cl SK14 9 E3
Ellison St SK13 10 B1
Elm Ave Belper DE56 179 D1
Darley Dale DE4 142 C4
Long Eaton NG10 236 B4
Sandiacre NG10 223 D4
Elm Cl Bolsover S44 99 E1
Chesterfield S41 95 F4
Doveridge DE6 224 B4
Killamarsh S21 60 B3
Mottram in L SK14 9 D2
Pinxton NG16 160 B2
Elm Cres S20 59 E4
Elm Dr Hilton DE65 228 B1
Killamarsh S21 60 B3
Elm Gr Clay Cross S45 131 E2
Derby, Allestree DE22 204 B3
Derby, Cherrytree Hill DE21 220 A3
Glossop SK13 10 B1
Elm Lodge Farm Cl S41 95 F4
Elm Park Ct DE1 267 A5
Elm Rd Eckington S21 59 E1
Pilsley S45 132 B1
Elm St Borrowash DE72 221 D1
Brimington S43 97 D4
Temple Normanton S42 116 A2
Elm Tree Ave Kilburn DE56 192 A4
Mansfield Woodhouse NG19 136 A2
Shirebrook NG20 119 E2
Shirland DE55 146 B1
Elm Tree Cres S18 57 D2
Elm Tree Dr S42 114 C2
Elm Tree St NG18 268 C4
Elm View ST14 196 C3
Elma La NG20 101 E3
Elmfield SK23 47 D3
Elmhurst DE65 241 D3
Elmhurst Ave DE55 160 A2
Elmhurst Cl DE55 160 A2
Elmhurst Rd NG19 136 C1
Elmore Ct NG7 268 A2
Elms Ave Alfreton DE55 159 D2
Derby DE23 218 A1
Ripley DE5 180 B4
Elms Cl DE55 159 D2
Elms Dr DE23 218 A1
Elms Gr DE65 229 E2
Elms Rd Burton u T DE15 248 A1
Coton in t E DE12 260 B2
Elms St DE1 218 C4
Elms The NG16 195 F4
Elmsdale Rd DE11 257 D2
Elmsfield Ave DE75 182 A1
Elmslea Ave DE12 260 B2
Elmsleigh Cl DE11 256 A3
Elmsleigh Dr DE11 256 A3
Elmsleigh Gr DE11 256 A3
Elmsleigh Inf Sch DE11 256 A3
Elmton Cl Clowne S43 80 C2
Creswell S80 100 B4
Elmton La S44 99 E2
Elmton Rd S80 81 F1
Elmtree Ave Derby DE24 232 A4
Selston NG16 171 F4
Elmtree Cl S81 63 F4
Elmwood Dr Derby DE21 205 E1
Mosborough S20 59 E3
Elnor Ave SK23 45 F3
Elnor La SK23 45 F2
Elnor St NG16 182 B2
Elsecar Cl DE56 179 E3
Elsing St ST4 269 F1
Elstead La DE11 257 D1
Elston Cl NG19 135 E1
Elstree Dr S12 44 A2
Elstree Rd S12 44 A2
Elton CE Prim Sch DE4 140 C3
Elton Cl NG9 223 E4
Elton Gr SK17 85 F3
Elton Rd Derby DE24 232 A4
Winster DE4 141 D3
Elton St S40 266 B2
Elton View S43 97 E4
Elvaston Castle DE21 233 F4
Elvaston Castle Ctry Pk DE21 233 F3
Elvaston Cl S18 56 A1
Elvaston Dr NG10 236 A2
Elvaston La DE24 233 E4
Elvaston Rd S42 131 F3
Elvaston St DE72 235 D4
Elveden Dr DE7 194 B2
Elvin Way S42 131 E4
Elwood Rd S17 56 B3
Elwyn Cl DE13 240 B1
Ely Cl
Mansfield Woodhouse NG19 136 B2
Swadlincote DE11 256 B3
Elyn Ave S42 132 A4
Embankment Cl DE22 217 F4
Ember La DE4 142 C1
Embridge Causeway SK10, SK17 64 A3
Emerald Cl Derby DE21 206 A1
Mansfield NG19 135 F1
Emerson Sq DE23 231 F3
Emery Cl DE12 261 E3
Emmas Williams Ct DE5 169 E1
Emmet Field Cl S40 114 C4
Emmett Carr Cl S21 79 E4
Emmett Carr La S21 79 E4
Empire Pas ST4 269 E1
Empire Rd DE15 248 B2
Empire St Mansfield NG18 268 C3
Stoke-on-T ST4 269 E1
Empress Rd DE23 267 A1
Emsworth Cl DE7 194 B2
Ena Ave NG2 268 C2
End The DE15 248 C4
Endowood Rd S40 114 A4
Endsleigh Gdns DE22 217 F3
Enfield Cl DE65 228 C1
Enfield Rd Chesterfield S41 96 A3
Derby DE22 218 A3
England Cres DE75 182 A1
English Martyrs RC Prim Sch NG10 223 D1
Englishe Rd DE4 143 D2
Ennerdale Ave S20 59 F3
Ennerdale Cl S18 56 C1
Ennerdale Cres S41 95 E4
Ennerdale Dr S20 59 F3
Ennerdale Rd NG10 223 D1
Ennerdale Wlk DE21 205 E1
Ennis Cl DE21 220 B4
Enoch Stone Dr DE21 220 A2
Enslet La DE6 164 A2
Enterprise Dr S42 116 B1
Epping Cl DE22 217 F3
Epsley's Yd ST16 269 E3
Epsom Rd NG9 223 F2
Epworth Dr DE24 233 D2
Epworth St ST4 269 E2
Erdington Way NG9 223 F2
Erewash Ct DE7 194 B1
Erewash Dr DE7 209 D3
Erewash Gr NG9 223 F1
Erewash Mus DE7 208 C4
Erewash Rd NG16 160 C1
Erewash Sq DE7 209 D3
Erewash St Aldercar DE55 171 D3
Long Eaton NG10 236 C4
Erica Dr DE55 160 A4
Erin Rd S43 98 A4
Ernest Hall Way DE11 256 B2
Ernocroft La SK6 15 F1
Ernocroft Rd SK6 15 D1
Errill Cl ST4 269 F1
Errington Ave S2 43 F3
Errington Cl S2 43 F3
Errington Cres S2 43 F3
Errington Rd
Chesterfield S40 114 B4
Sheffield S2 43 F3
Errington Way S2 43 F4
Errwood Ave SK17 85 D3
Erskine Cres S2 43 E4
Erskine Rd S2 43 E4
Erskine St SK6 15 D2
Erskine View S2 43 E4
Eskdale Cl Dronfield S18 56 C1
Long Eaton NG10 236 A3
Eskdale Wlk DE24 233 E3
Essendine Cres S8 43 D2
Essex Rd DE15 254 B3
Essex St Derby DE21 219 E3
4 Ilkeston DE7 194 C1
Estwic Ave NG16 182 C2
Ethel Wainwright Fst & Mid Schs NG19 268 A4
Etherow Brow SK14 16 A4
Etherow Ctry Pk SK6 15 E2
Etherow Ctry Pk Visitor Ctr SK6 15 D2
Etherow Way SK13 9 F3

Eton Ct DE7 207 E4
Eton St DE24 219 F1
Etruria Gdns DE1 267 B5
Etta's Way DE65 229 D2
Ettrick Cl 4 S40 95 E3
Ettrick Dr DE24 231 F1
Etwall Cl S40 95 D3
Etwall La DE65 229 F3
Etwall Prim Sch DE65 229 D2
Etwall Rd Derby DE3 217 E1
Eggington DE65 241 D4
Willington DE65 242 A4
Etwall St DE22 218 C3
Eugene St NG2 268 B1
Eureka Prim Sch DE11 256 B3
Eureka Rd DE11 256 B3
Euston Dr DE1 267 C5
Evans Ave DE22 205 D3
Evans St DE24 232 C3
Evanston Gdns DE21 220 A3
Evelyn Devonshire Cotts S45 132 C1
Evelyn Gr DE21 220 A3
Evelyn St Fenton ST4 269 F1
Nottingham NG2 268 C1
Everard Ave S17 56 A3
Everard Dr S17 56 A3
Everard Glade 6 S17 56 A3
Everest Dr DE55 170 B4
Everett Cl S43 96 C4
Evergreen Cl DE21 206 A2
Evershill Cl DE55 146 C3
Evershill La DE55 146 C3
Eversleigh Rise DE4 142 A4
Everton St NG19 135 F1
Evesham Ave SK13 10 A3
Evesham Cl DE21 205 F1
Ewart La DE55 158 C2
Ewe Dale La DE6 149 D2
Ewe Lamb Cl NG9 209 F1
Ewe Lamb La NG9 209 F1
Excelsior Ave DE24 232 C3
Exchange St DE1 267 B3
Exe Fold NG19 136 B1
Exeter Cl DE11 256 C3
Exeter Pl DE1 267 C3
Exeter St DE1 267 C4
Exlowmere La DE4 140 C3
Export Dr NG17 160 C4
Eyam CE Prim Sch S32 71 E3
Eyam Cl S42 132 A4
Eyam (Hall) S32 71 E3
Eyam La SK13 9 E1
Eyam Mews SK13 9 F1
Eyam Wlk DE56 179 D3
Eyes Ct DE56 190 C2
Eyre Gdns S40 266 A4
Eyre St Clay Cross S45 131 E2
Creswell S80 81 E1
Nottingham NG2 268 C1
Eyre St E S41 115 E4
Eyre's Gdns DE7 194 C1
Eyrie The
Burton u T DE15 248 B2
Derby DE24 231 F1

Fabis Cl DE11 256 A2
Fabric View S42 132 B4
Factory La Disley SK12 32 C4
Ilkeston DE7 194 C1
Factory St S40 95 E1
Fair Lea Cl NG10 236 B3
Fair View Chesterfield S40 95 F2
Mayfield DE6 184 B4
Fairbank Ave ST4 269 E1
Fairbourne Dr DE3 217 E2
Fairburn Croft Cres S43 80 A3
Faircroft Ave NG10 223 D3
Fairdene DE23 218 C1
Faire St DE22 218 C2
Faires Cl DE72 221 E1
Fairfax Dr S2 44 A4
Fairfax Rd DE23 218 C1
Fairfield Ave
Borrowash DE72 221 E2
Hilcote DE55 148 B1
Rolleston DE13 240 B2
Stonebroom DE55 147 D2
Fairfield Cl Brimington S43 96 B4
Nether Langwith NG20 101 D1
Fairfield Cres
Long Eaton NG10 236 A2
Swadlincote DE11 255 F3
Fairfield Ct S40 94 C2
Fairfield Dr S40 94 C2
Fairfield Endowed CE Jun Sch SK17 85 F4
Fairfield Inf Sch SK17 85 E4
Fairfield Prim Sch NG9 223 E3
Fairfield Rd Bolsover S44 118 A4
Buxton SK17 85 E4
Chesterfield S40 266 A4
Derby DE23 218 C1
Horsley Woodhouse DE7 192 B4
Fairfield Terr DE11 256 C2
Fairford Cl S40 114 C4
Fairham Rd DE13 240 C1
Fairholme Dr NG19 135 F1
Fairholmes DE4 143 E3
Fairisle Cl DE21 206 B2
Fairleigh S2 44 A4
Fairmeadows Prim Sch DE11 255 F3
Fairview Ave NG16 171 F1
Fairview Cl Derby DE23 231 D4
Kilburn DE56 192 A4
Fairview Grange DE56 192 A4
Fairview Rd S18 57 D2
Fairview Rise DE4 168 A4
Fairway Branston DE14 254 A4
Stafford ST16, ST17 269 F3
Fairway Cl DE22 204 B1
Fairway Cres DE22 204 B1
Fairway The Clifton DE6 184 C3
Swadlincote DE11 255 F3
Fairways Cl SK13 10 C1
Fairways The
Clay Cross S45 131 F2
Mansfield Woodhouse NG19 136 B3
Fairwinds Cl S18 57 D1
Fairwood Dr DE24 233 E3
Fairy Bank Cres SK22 25 E2
Fairy Bank Rd SK22 25 E2
Fal Paddock NG19 136 B1
Falcon Cl SK22 33 E4
Falcon Ct DE7 194 B1
Falcon Rd S18 57 E2
Falcon Rise S18 57 E2
Falcon Way Derby DE24 231 F1
Woodville DE11 256 C2
Falcon Yd S40 266 B3
Falcons Rise DE56 179 E3
Faldo Cl DE14 254 A3
Falkland Rise S18 76 A4
Fall Rd DE75 181 F2
Fallow Rd DE21 220 C3
Fallowfield Rd S43 77 E2
Falmouth Rd DE24 233 E3
Fan Rd S43 78 C1
Fan Road Ind Est S43 78 C1
Fanny Ave S21 60 C3
Fanshaw Ave S21 59 E1
Fanshaw Bank S18 57 D1
Fanshaw Cl S21 59 E1
Fanshaw Dr S21 59 E1
Fanshaw Gate La S18 55 F1
Fanshaw Rd Dronfield S18 57 D1
Eckington S21 59 E1
Fanshaw Way S21 59 E1
Far Croft DE72 235 E4
Far Cross DE4 143 E4
Far Green DE4 143 D3
Far Hill S33 51 D4
Far La Common Side S18 75 D2
Ockbrook DE72 221 E3
Far Laund DE56 179 D3
Far New Cl NG10 223 D3
Far Woodseats La SK13 15 F3
Faraday Ave DE13 240 B1
Faraday Ct NG9 209 F1
Faraday Pl ST4 269 D2
Farfield Rd DE7 209 D4
Farish Pl S2 43 D3
Farley Hill DE4 143 D4
Farley La DE4 128 A1
Farley Rd DE23 218 B1
Farm Cl Belper DE56 179 E2
Chesterfield S40 114 C3
Dronfield S18 57 D2
Ilkeston DE7 209 D4
Kilburn DE56 192 A4
Long Eaton NG10 236 C3
Pentrich DE5 169 D3
Sheffield S12 44 A1
Somercotes DE55 170 B4
Farm Cres S20 59 E3
Farm Croft Rd NG19 136 B3
Farm Dr DE24 233 D3
Farm La Disley SK12 32 A3
Matlock DE4 143 E4
Newton Solney DE15 248 C4
Farm Side DE11 255 F3
Farm St DE22 218 C2
Farm View S42 131 E4
Farm Wlk S20 59 E4
Farmfields Cl S44 98 C2
Farmhouse Rd DE24 231 F1
Farmilo Cres NG19 135 F1
Farmilo Fst Sch NG19 135 E2
Farmlands La DE23 231 D3
Farmstead Cl S14 43 E3
Farmway NG19 136 B1
Farnah Green Rd DE56 178 B2
Farnborough Gdns DE22 205 D2
Farncombe La DE21 205 F2
Farndale Ave S40 114 A4
Farndale Cl NG10 236 A3
Farndale Ct DE24 233 E3
Farndon Dr NG9 223 F2
Farndon Way NG19 268 A4
Farneworth Rd DE3 217 E1
Farnham Cl DE3 217 E1
Farnham Wlk DE7 207 E4
Farningham Cl DE21 220 C3
Farnon Cl S40 266 C1
Farnsley La S32 71 D2
Farnsworth St S41 115 E4
Farnway DE22 204 C1
Farrendale Cl NG19 136 B1
Farrier Gdns DE23 231 D4
Farriers Croft DE7 194 B2
Farringdon Cl DE22 217 F3
Farthing Ct NG10 236 A4
Farwater Cl S18 76 A4
Farwater La S18 56 C1
Fauld Ind Pk DE13 238 C3
Fauld La Hanbury DE13 238 B4
Tutbury, Fauld DE13 238 B4
Tutbury, Owen's Bank DE13 239 D3
Fauvel Pl SK13 10 B1
Fauvel Rd SK13 10 B1
Faversham Cl DE24 232 C3
Fawn Cl S42 114 C2
Fay Gdns SK13 9 F2
Faywood Dr SK6 23 D3
Fearn Ave DE5 169 F1
Fearn Cl
Church Broughton DE65 227 D4
Long Eaton DE72 236 A4
Featherbed La
Bolsover S44 99 D3
Worksop S80 63 F1
Featherstone Gr ST4 269 E2
Felkin St S41 266 C3
Fellbrigg Rd S2 43 E4
Fellowlands Way DE73 233 D1
Fellside Belper DE56 179 D2
Derby DE21 220 C3
Fellview Cl S32 53 D4
Fenchurch Wlk DE22 218 A4
Fenland Way S40 114 C4
Fennel St DE45 108 C4
Fenton Ave DE11 257 D1
Fenton Rd DE3 217 E1
Fenton St S21 59 D1
Fenwick St DE24 232 B4
Ferguson Ave NG19 136 A2
Fern Ave Staveley S43 97 E4
Willington DE65 242 B3
Fern Bank Ave DE55 147 F1
Fern Cl Eckington S21 59 D2
Holmewood S44 116 C1
Shirebrook NG20 119 F3
Willington DE65 242 B3
Fern Cres NG16 182 B2
Fern Lea Hollingworth SK14 9 E3
Shirland DE55 146 B2
Fern Rd SK17 85 D3
Fern Royd S32 53 D4
Fern Way S21 59 D2
Fernbank S33 51 D4
Fernbank Dr S21 59 D2
Ferncroft Ave S20 59 E4
Ferndale Ave SK17 67 E2
Ferndale Cl S18 57 E2
Ferndale Rd Dronfield S18 57 E2
Peak Dale SK17 67 E2
Ferndale Rise S18 57 E2
Ferndene Dr NG10 236 A4
Ferneydale Ave SK17 85 E2
Fernhill SK6 23 D3
Fernhill Cl SK13 10 B2
Fernhill Ct DE73 233 D2
Fernilee Cl New Mills SK22 24 B1
West Hallam DE7 207 F4
Fernilee Cty Inf Sch SK23 45 F2
Fernilee Gdns DE21 205 D4
Fernlea Cl SK13 9 F2
Fernleigh Rise NG19 136 B1
Fernway SK17 85 E2
Fernwood SK6 23 E4
Fernwood Cl
Chesterfield S41 115 F4
Derby DE23 231 E4
Shirland DE55 146 B2
Ferrers Ave DE13 239 D3
Ferrers Cl DE74 247 D2
Ferrers Cres DE56 190 B2
Ferrers Way Derby DE22 204 C1
Ripley DE5 169 E2
Ferry Gn DE65 242 A3
Ferry St DE15 254 C4
Ferry Vale Cl DE15 254 C4
Festival Ave DE72 235 E4
Festival Rd Branston DE14 253 F4
Ilkeston DE7 208 B3
Festus Cl NG3 268 B2
Fiddle St SK17 85 E2
Fiddler's La DE13 239 F2
Fidlers Cl S33 40 A2
Fidlers Well S33 40 A2
Field Ave Hatton DE65 239 E4
Renishaw S21 79 D4
Field Cl Borrowash DE72 221 D2
Breaston DE72 235 F4
Dronfield S18 56 B1
Hilton DE65 228 B1
Mansfield Woodhouse NG19 136 B3
Field Cres DE24 233 D3
Field Ct DE56 192 A4
Field Dr Derby DE24 233 D3
Rolleston DE13 240 A2
Shirebrook NG20 119 F1
Field End DE4 153 D1
Field Head Way DE21 206 A2
Field House Inf Sch DE7 208 C3
Field House La SK6 23 D3
Field La
Ault Hucknall NG19, S44 134 B3
Belper DE56 178 C2
Blackfordby DE11 257 E1
Derby, Boulton DE24 233 D3
Derby, Chaddesden DE21 220 A4
Kirk Ireton DE56 176 A4
Stanton DE6 183 E4
Field Rd DE7 208 C4
Field Rise DE23 231 E4
Field Row DE56 178 C2
Field St DE5 181 D4
Field Terr DE5 169 E1
Field The DE75 194 A3
Field View Clowne S43 80 C2
South Normanton DE55 160 A4
Field View Cl DE24 233 D3
Field Way DE11 255 F3
Fielden Ave NG19 135 E1
Fieldfare Ho S41 77 D2
Fieldgate Dr DE21 205 F1
Fieldhead La HD7 2 C4
Fieldhead Rd S8 43 D4
Fieldhead Way S40 95 E3
Fielding St ST4 269 E1
Fieldings Rd S80 81 F1
Fieldon Cl DE6 202 C1
Fields Cres SK14 9 E3
Fields Farm Rd NG10 236 C3
Fields Gr SK14 9 E3
Fields La Killamarsh S21 60 A3
Linton DE11 261 F3
Fields The DE4 154 B2
Fiennes Cres NG7 268 A1
Fife St DE24 232 C4
Finch Cl DE11 256 C2
Fincham Cl DE21 205 E1
Finchley Ave DE22 217 F3
Findern Cl Belper DE56 179 E3
Derby DE22 204 B1
Findern La
Burnaston DE65 230 A2
Willington DE65 242 A3
Findern Prim Sch DE65 242 C4
Findern St DE22 218 B3
Finley Way DE55 160 A2
Finmere Cl DE23 231 D4
Finningley Dr DE22 204 C1
Finny La DE6 200 A3
Finsbury Ave Derby DE22 218 A3
Nottingham NG2 268 C1
Finsley Wlk DE23 231 F3
Fir Cl NG20 119 E3
Fir Pl S21 60 B3
Fir Rd S21 59 E1
Fir St S43 78 A1
Fir Tree Ave DE55 146 B2
Firestone DE56 178 B1
Firfield Ave DE72 235 F4
Firfield Prim Sch DE72 235 F4
Firlawns DE56 190 B2
Firs Ave Alfreton DE55 159 D3
Hulland Ward DE6 175 F2
Ripley DE5 169 E1
Firs Cres DE22 204 C2
Firs Estate Prim Sch DE22 218 C2
Firs Gdns DE55 159 D2
Firs Par DE4 143 E3
Firs St NG10 236 A2
Firs The DE6 173 E1
First Ave NG10 222 C3
Firthwood Ave S18 57 E2
Firthwood Cl S18 57 E2
Firthwood Rd S18 57 E2
Firtree Gr DE21 206 A1
Firvale S26 61 F3
Firvale Rd S40 114 A4
Fish Pond Dr NG7 268 A1
Fisher Cl Chesterfield S40 114 C4
Repton DE65 242 B1
Fisher Ct DE7 194 C2
Fisher Gate NG1 268 B1
Fisher La Duffield DE56 190 C2
Mansfield NG18 268 C3
Fisher St DE24 232 C3
Fishers Bridge SK22 25 E1
Fishpond La DE65 241 D3
Fishponds Cl S42 115 D2
Fishponds Rd S13 44 B4
Fishponds Rd W S13 44 B4
Fiskerton Way DE21 206 A1
Fitzalan St SK13 10 B1
Fitzherbert CE Prim Sch DE6 162 A1
Fitzhubert Rd S2 44 A4
Fitzroy Rd S2 43 D3
Five Lamps Ct DE1 218 C3
Five Lands Rd DE15 254 C4
Five Trees Ave 1 S17 56 A3
Five Trees Cl 3 S17 56 A3
Five Trees Dr 2 S17 56 A3
Flackets La Doveridge DE6 225 D4
Sudbury DE6 225 D4
Flagg La SK17 106 C4
Flagshaw La DE6 202 C2
Flake La DE7 208 C1
Flamstead Ave DE75 181 E2
Flamstead La DE5 180 C1
Flamstead Rd DE7 194 C1
Flamstead St DE24 232 C3
Flamsteed Cres S41 96 A3
Flash CE Prim Sch SK17 103 D2
Flash La DE4 128 A4
Flat La SK17 106 B4
Flat The DE56 191 F4
Flatts La NG16 171 E2
Flax Croft DE65 227 E1
Flax St ST4 269 E1
Flaxholme Ave DE56 190 C1
Flaxpiece Rd S45 131 E2
Fleet Cres DE56 178 C2
Fleet Pk DE56 179 D2
Fleet St DE23 219 D1
Fleet The DE56 178 C2
Fleming Rd ST4 269 E2
Fletcher Ave S18 57 D1
Fletcher Gate NG1 268 B1
Fletcher Rd ST4 269 E1
Fletcher St Heanor DE75 181 F1
Long Eaton NG10 236 B4
Fletcher's Row DE5 169 F1
Fletches The DE13 240 A1
Flewitt Gdns NG3 268 C2
Flint Ave NG19 136 C1
Flint La DE4 142 A4
Flint St DE24 232 B3
Flintson Ave S43 77 E2
Flixton Rd NG16 195 F4
Flood St DE72 221 E2
Florence Ave NG10 223 F1
Florence Cl S40 114 C3
Florence Ct DE7 194 C1
Florence Dr DE6 211 E1
Florence Gladwin Cl DE4 141 E3
Florence Rd
Clay Cross S45 131 F2
Wingerworth S42 114 C2
Florence Way SK14 9 E3
Florin Gdns NG10 236 A4
Flowery Leys La DE55 159 E2
Floyd St ST4 269 E2
Fluery Cl S14 43 F2
Fluery Cres S14 43 F2
Fluery Pl S14 43 F2
Fluery Rd S14 43 F2
Fluery Rise S14 43 F2
Fly Hill DE45 109 E3
Foden St ST4 269 E1
Foggs Entry DE4 165 F4
Fold The S32 71 F2
Folds La SK23 45 F2
Folds Yd DE4 156 C1
Foljambe Ave S40 114 B4
Foljambe Rd S43 96 C4
Folkestone Dr DE24 233 D3
Folly Rd DE22 205 D1
Fontaine Pl ST4 269 E1
Foolow Ave S40 266 A1
Forbes Cl NG10 236 C3
Ford Ave DE75 181 E2
Ford Cl Dronfield S18 56 C1
Ripley DE5 180 B4
Ford Gr SK14 9 D2
Ford La Derby DE65 205 D3
Ford S12 58 C3
Willington DE65 242 B3
Ford Rd S21 58 C2
Ford St Belper DE56 178 C2
Burton u T DE15 254 C4
Derby DE1 218 C3
Tupton S42 131 E4
Fordbridge La DE55 160 A4
Fordwells Cl DE23 231 D4
Foregate Ct ST16 269 E4
Foregate St ST16 269 D4
Foremark Ave DE23 231 F4
Forest Ave Buxton SK17 85 E3
Mansfield NG18 268 C3
Forest Cl DE56 179 D3
Forest Ct S43 80 A3
Forest Dr S45 132 B1
Forest Fields Coll NG3 268 C2
Forest La SK17 50 B1
Forest Rd NG18 268 C3
Forest Rd E NG1 268 A2
Forest Rd W NG7 268 A2
Forester St DE1 267 B2
Foresters Way DE5 169 E1
Forge Cl DE65 242 B1
Forge La Burton u T DE13 241 D1
Killamarsh S21 60 A4
Forge Rd SK23 45 F4
Forge Terr SK23 34 C1
Forge The NG9 209 D3
Forman Cl DE11 256 A2
Forman St Derby DE1 267 A3
Nottingham NG1 268 B2
Forrester Ave DE72 245 F3
Forrester's La S18 57 E2
Forshaw Cl DE6 185 E4
Forth Ave S18 56 B1
Forties La LE65 257 F2
Forty Horse Cl DE5 170 A1
Forum Cl DE24 233 E3
Fosbrook Dr DE74 246 C2
Fosbrooke Dr NG10 236 B3
Fosse Cl DE72 221 E1
Fossett's Ave NG16 171 F4
Foster Rd DE11 256 C1
Foster St NG18 268 C3
Foston Cl DE65 239 E4
Foston Dr S40 95 D3
Foundry La DE56 190 C4
Foundry St S41 96 A4
Foundry Street Ind Est S41 96 A4
Fountain Sq Disley SK12 32 B3
Tideswell SK17 69 E2
Fountain St SK17 85 D4
Fountains Cl DE22 205 D2
Four Lane Ends DE4 127 E1
Four Lanes SK14 9 D2
Fowler Ave DE21 220 B2
Fowler St Chesterfield S41 76 C1
Derby DE22 218 C3
Draycott DE72 235 D4
Fox Cl Derby DE24 231 E1
Long Eaton NG10 236 B3
Fox Croft DE55 147 F3
Fox Hill S44 118 C4
Fox La Holmesfield S18 74 A3
Sheffield, Frecheville S12 44 B2
Sheffield, Lower Bradway S18 56 B3
Fox Rd
Castle Donington DE74 246 C2
Whitwell S80 82 A3
Fox St DE21 267 C4
Foxbrook Cl S40 94 C3
Foxcote Way S40 114 A4
Foxcroft Chase S21 60 B3
Foxcroft Dr S21 60 B3
Foxcroft Gr S21 60 B3
Foxdale Ave S12 44 A3
Foxdell Way DE73 233 D1
Foxes Cl NG7 268 A1
Foxes Wlk DE22 204 C2

Foxes Yd SK17 .... 66 B1
Foxfields Dr DE21 .... 205 F1
Foxglove Ave DE15 .... 255 D4
Foxglove Cl S44 .... 97 D2
Foxglove Rd NG16 .... 195 D4
Foxhall La S10 .... 42 C3
Foxholes La Kniveton DE6 .. 174 A3
Tansley DE4 .... 144 A4
Foxlands Ave DE22 .... 204 C1
Foxlea SK13 .... 16 C4
Foxley Ct DE21 .... 206 A1
Foxpark View DE55 .... 147 F3
Foxstone Cl S43 .... 97 E4
Foxwood Ave S12 .... 44 A3
Foxwood Cl
  Chesterfield, Hasland S41 .... 115 E3
  Chesterfield, Sheepbridge
  S41 .... 76 C1
Foxwood Dr S12 .... 44 A3
Foxwood Gr S12 .... 44 A3
Foxwood Ind Pk S41 .... 76 C1
Foxwood Rd
  Chesterfield S41 .... 76 C1
  Sheffield S12 .... 44 A3
Foxwood Way S41 .... 76 C1
Foyle Ave DE21 .... 220 A2
Framlingham Pl S2 .... 43 E4
Framlingham Rd S2 .... 43 E4
Frampton Gdns DE23 ..... 230 C3
Frances Dr S42 .... 114 C2
Frances St NG16 .... 171 E1
Franchise St DE22 .... 218 C2
Francis Rd S43 .... 96 B4
Francis St Derby DE21 ..... 219 E3
  Nottingham NG7 .... 268 A2
Frank Ave NG18 .... 268 A3
Frank Merifield Ctr S41 ...... 96 B2
Frank St ST4 .... 269 E1
Franklin Ave S80 .... 81 F3
Franklin Cl DE15 .... 248 A1
Franklin Cres S80 .... 81 F3
Franklin Rd
  Stoke-on-T ST4 .... 269 D2
  Westwood NG16 .... 171 D2
Franklyn Dr Derby DE24 .. 233 D3
  Staveley S43 .... 78 C2
Franklyn Rd S40 .... 95 F2
Frazer Cl S43 .... 220 C3
Frecheville Inf Sch S12 ...... 44 B2
Frecheville Sch S12 .... 44 B2
Frecheville St S43 .... 78 B1
Freckingham St NG1 ...... 268 B1
Frederic Ave DE75 .... 193 F4
Frederick Ave Derby DE24 .. 232 C3
  Ilkeston DE7 .... 209 D3
  Stoke-on-T ST4 .... 269 E2
Frederick Gent Sch DE55 .. 160 A3
Frederick Harrison Inf
Sch NG9 .... 223 F4
Frederick Rd NG9 .... 223 E4
Frederick St Alfreton DE55 .. 159 D3
  Burton u T DE15 .... 254 C4
  Derby DE22 .... 218 B3
  Grassmoor S42 .... 115 F2
  Long Eaton NG10 .... 236 C4
  Mansfield NG18 .... 268 C3
  Somercotes DE55 .... 170 B3
  Swadlincote DE11 .... 256 C2
Freebirch View S40 .... 95 D4
Freeby Ave NG19 .... 136 B3
Freehold St DE22 .... 218 C2
Freeland Cl NG9 .... 223 F2
Freeman Ave DE23 .... 231 F3
Freemantle Rd DE3 .... 217 F2
Freesia Cl DE24 .... 217 F1
Freetown SK13 .... 17 E4
French La DE21 .... 191 F3
French St Derby DE23 ..... 218 C1
  Ilkeston DE7 .... 209 D3
French Terr NG20 .... 101 D1
Fresco Dr DE23 .... 230 C4
Fresh Ct SK13 .... 16 C4
Freshfield Cl SK6 .... 15 D1
Fretson Rd S2 .... 44 A4
Frew Cl ST16 .... 269 F4
Freydon Way S44 .... 97 D2
Friar Gate DE1 .... 218 C3
Friar Gate Ct DE1 .... 218 C3
Friar Gate House Sch
  DE1 .... 218 C3
Friar Gr SK17 .... 85 E3
Friar La NG1 .... 268 A1
Friar St NG10 .... 236 B4
Friars Cl DE22 .... 205 D1
Friars Ct Ilkeston DE7 ...... 208 B3
  Nottingham NG1 .... 268 A1
Friars' Rd ST17 .... 269 E3
Friars' Terr ST17 .... 269 E3
Friars' Wlk ST17 .... 269 E3
Friary Ave DE24 .... 232 C3
Friary Croft DE11 .... 256 A4
Friary St DE1 .... 267 A4
Friesland Dr NG10 .... 222 C3
Friesland Sch NG10 .... 222 C3
Frinton Cl S40 .... 114 C4
Frisby Ave NG10 .... 236 C3
Fritchley CE Prim Sch
  DE56 .... 168 A3
Fritchley Cl DE21 .... 206 A1
Fritchley La DE56 .... 168 A4
Frith Cl S12 .... 44 A3
Frith Gr NG19 .... 268 A4
Frith Rd S12 .... 44 A3
Frith View SK23 .... 47 D3
Frithhall La S42 .... 94 B1
Frithwood La S80 .... 100 B4
Frizams La DE65 .... 242 C4
Froggatt Cl Derby DE22 .. 205 D3
  Staveley S43 .... 97 E3
Froggett Cl DE55 .... 170 B4
Frogmore St NG1 .... 268 B2
Front St DE56 .... 168 A3
Frost Ave NG16 .... 182 A2
Fryar Rd NG16 .... 182 C2
Fulbrook Rd DE23 .... 231 D4
Fulford Cl S40 .... 114 B4
Fulforth St NG1 .... 268 B2
Fulham Rd DE22 .... 218 A3
Full St DE1 .... 267 B3
Fuller Dr S41 .... 96 B3
Fullwood Ave **11** DE7 ...... 194 C1
Fullwood St **13** DE7 .... 194 C1
Fulmar Cl DE3 .... 218 A2
Fulwood Dr NG10 .... 236 A4
Fulwood Head Rd S10 ..... 42 B4
Fulwood La S10 .... 42 C3
Fulwood Rd N NG17 ...... 148 C1
Fulwood Rd S NG17 ...... 160 C4
Furlong Cl NG9 .... 223 E4
Furlong La
  Alstonefield DE6 .... 149 E2
  Atlow DE6 .... 175 D4
Furnace Cl S42 .... 115 F1
Furnace La Barlow S18 ..... 75 F2
  Heanor DE75 .... 181 E2
  Moira DE12 .... 262 C2
Furnace La Ind Est DE12 ... 262 C2
Furnace Mus The DE12 ..... 262 C2
Furnace Rd DE7 .... 209 D3
Furnace Row DE55 .... 170 C4
Furnall Ave DE45 .... 90 A2
Furness Cl SK13 .... 17 F4
Furness Lodge CI SK23 .... 33 E2
Furness Row SK23 .... 33 E2
Furness Vale Prim Sch
  SK23 .... 33 E2
Furness Vale Sta SK23 .... 33 E2
Furniss Ave S17 .... 55 E3
Furrows Cl DE21 .... 206 B2
Fyfield Rd DE15 .... 254 C3
Fylde Cl NG9 .... 223 F1

Gable Ct DE3 .... 230 C4
Gable St ST4 .... 269 E1
Gables Cl S42 .... 132 B4
Gables The DE11 .... 255 F3
Gadley Cl SK17 .... 84 C4
Gadley La SK17 .... 84 C4
Gadsby Rise DE56 .... 168 B1
Gag La DE6 .... 161 E3
Gainborough Cl DE21 ... 206 A1
Gainsborough Ave SK6 .... 23 D4
Gainsborough Cl
  Long Eaton NG10 .... 236 C3
  Stapleford NG9 .... 223 F3
Gainsborough Rd S18 ..... 75 F4
Gainsborough Way DE15 .. 248 A2
Gairloch Cl DE24 .... 231 E1
Galahad Dr DE13 .... 240 C1
Gale Rd SK22 .... 33 E4
Gallery La S42 .... 113 E4
Gallery The DE6 .... 173 E1
Gallows Inn Cl DE7 ...... 209 D3
Gallowstree La DE6 ...... 184 B4
Galway Ave DE21 .... 220 A2
Gamble St NG7 .... 268 A2
Gamesley Cty Prim Sch
  SK13 .... 9 F1
Gang La S44 .... 118 C3
Gannow Cl S21 .... 60 C4
Gaol Rd ST16 .... 269 E4
Gaol Sq ST16 .... 269 E4
Gaolgate St 5 ST16 .... 269 E4
Gapsick La S43 .... 81 D3
Garden Ave Ilkeston DE7 .. 208 C3
  New Houghton NG19 .... 134 C4
  Renishaw S21 .... 79 D4
  Shirebrook NG20 .... 119 F2
Garden Cl S43 .... 77 E2
Garden Cr DE55 .... 159 F2
Garden Cres DE74 .... 247 D2
Garden Pl Stafford ST17 .. 269 F3
  Stoke-on-T ST4 .... 269 D2
Garden Rd Eastwood NG16 .. 182 C2
2 Mansfield NG18 .... 268 B3
Garden Row S44 .... 117 E1
Garden St
  Broadbottom SK14 .... 16 A4
  Derby DE1 .... 267 A4
  Stafford ST17 .... 269 E3
  Stoke-on-T ST4 .... 269 D1
Gardens The Heanor DE75 .. 181 E2
  Ripley DE5 .... 180 B4
Gardner Pl ST14 .... 210 A1
Gardom Cl **14** S18 .... 56 B1
Garfield Ave DE72 .... 235 D4
Garfield Cl Derby DE21 .... 231 E3
  Stapleford NG9 .... 209 F1
Garland Cl **24** S20 .... 59 F4
Garland Croft S20 .... 59 F4
Garland Mount **22** S20 ..... 59 F4
Garland Way S20 .... 59 F4
Garner La DE4, DE55 ...... 157 E1
Garnet Ct NG3 .... 268 C2
Garnett Ave DE75 .... 181 F1
Garnon St NG18 .... 268 A3
Garratt Ave NG18 .... 268 C4
Garrett La S45 .... 131 E1
Garrick St DE24 .... 233 D4
Garry Cl DE24 .... 231 E1
Garsdale Ct DE24 .... 233 E3
Gartan Rd DE14 .... 254 A4
Garth Cres DE24 .... 233 D3
Garth Rd SK6 .... 23 D3
Garth Way S18 .... 56 C1
Garth Way Cl S18 .... 56 C1
Garthorpe Ct DE21 ...... 205 F1
Gartrice Gdns S20 .... 60 A3
Gary Cl DE23 .... 231 E3
Gas St Hollingworth SK14 ..... 9 E3
  Sandiacre NG10 .... 223 E3
  Uttoxeter ST14 .... 210 B1
Gascoine Dr DE21 .... 220 B2
Gashouse La Eckington S21 ... 59 E3
  Mosborough S21 .... 59 E3
Gaskell Ave DE23 .... 231 F4
Gasny Ave DE74 .... 247 D3
Gatcombe Cl
  Burton u T DE13 .... 240 B1
  Derby DE21 .... 206 A1
Gatcombe Gr NG10 ...... 223 D2
Gate Brook Cl DE5 .... 170 A1
Gatefield Cl S40 .... 95 E4
Gateland La S18 .... 75 F3
Gateway Christian Sch
  DE7 .... 207 F1
Gattrice Gdns S20 .... 60 A3
Gauledge La SK17 .... 121 D3
Gaunt Cl Killamarsh S21 .... 60 B3
  Sheffield S31 .... 43 E2
Gaunt Dr S14 .... 43 E2
Gaunt Pl S14 .... 43 E2
Gaunt Rd S14 .... 43 E2
Gaunt Way S14 .... 43 E2
Gawain Gr DE13 .... 240 C1
Gawsworth Cl SK13 .... 10 A3
Gayton Ave S8 .... 56 C3
Gayton Ave DE23 .... 231 E3
Gayton Com Jun Sch
  DE23 .... 231 E3
Gayton Thorpe Cl DE23 .. 230 C4
Geary La DE55 .... 148 C1
Gebbs Gdns S40 .... 95 E1
Gedling Gr NG7 .... 268 A2
Gedling St NG1 .... 268 B1
Geen St ST4 .... 269 E2
Geer La S21 .... 58 B3
Gelderd Pl S18 .... 76 A4
Gema Cl DE22 .... 205 D2
Genista Cl DE15 .... 255 D4
Gentshill Ave S45 .... 131 F1
George Ave NG10 .... 223 F1
George Baily Ct ST17 .... 269 E3
George Cres DE55 .... 170 B3
George Dutton Ind Est
  DE6 .... 185 F4
George Holmes Way DE11 .. 256 A2
George Percival Pl S45 .. 131 D2
George Rd DE4 .... 143 E3
George Spencer Comp
Sch NG9 .... 223 F3
George St Alfreton DE55 .. 159 D2
  Ashbourne DE6 .... 185 D4
  Belper DE56 .... 178 C2
  Brimington S43 .... 96 C4
  Buxton SK17 .... 85 D4
  Chesterfield S43 .... 76 C1
  Compstall SK6 .... 15 D1
  Derby DE1 .... 267 A3
  Glossop SK13 .... 17 E4
  Langley Mill NG16 .... 182 A2
  Mansfield NG18, NG19 .. 268 A4
  Mansfield Woodhouse
  NG19 .... 136 B2
  Market Warsop NG20 ... 120 C1
  Melbourne DE73 .... 252 A4
  North Wingfield S42 ..... 131 F4
  Nottingham NG1 .... 268 B2
  Pinxton NG16 .... 160 B2
  Riddings DE55 .... 170 B3
  Somercotes DE55 .... 170 B4
  South Normanton DE55 .. 159 F3
  Swadlincote DE11 .... 256 A1
  Whaley Bridge SK23 ...... 45 F4
  Whaley Thorns NG20 .... 101 D1
Gerard Cl
  6 Chesterfield S40 ...... 95 E1
  Derby DE21 .... 220 C3
  Sheffield S8 .... 43 D3
Gerard Ct DE1 .... 267 A2
Gerard Gr DE65 .... 229 E2
Gerard St Derby DE1 ...... 267 A2
  Sheffield S8 .... 43 D3
Gerrard St ST4 .... 269 E2
Gertrude Rd Derby DE21 .. 220 A4
  Draycott DE72 .... 235 D4
Gervase Ave S8 .... 56 C3
Gervase Dr S8 .... 56 C3
Gervase Pl S8 .... 56 C3
Gervase Rd S8 .... 56 C3
Gervase Wlk S8 .... 56 C3
Gibb La Marple SK6 .... 23 F3
  Sudbury DE6 .... 225 F3
Gibb St NG10 .... 236 C4
Gibbons Ave NG9 .... 223 E3
Gibbons Dr S14 .... 43 F1
Gibbons Rd NG18 .... 268 A3
Gibbons Way S14 .... 43 F1
Gibfield La Belper DE56 ... 178 C1
  Hognaston DE6 .... 175 D3
  Kirk Ireton DE6 .... 175 E3
Gifford Pl ST4 .... 269 D1
Gifford Rd S8 .... 43 D4
Gilbert Ave S40 .... 114 B4
Gilbert Cl DE21 .... 220 B2
Gilbert Cres DE56 .... 190 C1
Gilbert Heathcote Inf Sch
  S41 .... 96 A4
Gilbert St DE24 .... 233 D3
Gilcroft St NG18 .... 268 C3
Gilderdale Way DE21 .... 206 A2
Gill La DE4 .... 127 E2
Gill St NG1 .... 268 A2
Gill's La S42 .... 115 F1
Gillamoor Ct DE24 .... 233 E3
Gilleyfield Ave S17 .... 55 F4
Gillies The NG19 .... 268 A3
Gilliver Gdns DE72 ...... 235 D4
Gillot St DE75 .... 194 A4
Gilt Hill NG16 .... 195 E4
Gilt Hill Prim Sch NG16 .... 195 E4
Giltbrook Cres NG16 .... 195 E4
Giltway NG16 .... 195 E4
Gimson Cl DE7 .... 194 B2
Gin Close Way
  Awsworth NG16 .... 195 E3
  Kimberley NG16 .... 195 E3
Gin La S45 .... 144 C4
Gipsy La Alstonefield DE6 .. 149 F2
  Apperknowle S18 .... 58 A1
  Chesterfield S41 .... 77 D1
Gipsyhill La S80 .... 81 D4
Gird La S6 .... 15 F1
Girdon Cl SK17 .... 84 C3
Gisborne Cl DE3 .... 217 F2
Gisborne Cres DE22 ..... 204 C3
Gisborne Gr DE1 .... 218 C3
Gisbourne Dr SK23 .... 47 D3
Glade Cl S40 .... 95 F3
Glade Croft S12 .... 44 A2
Glade Lea S12 .... 44 A2
Glade The Buxton SK17 .... 85 D4
  Chesterfield S40 .... 95 F3
Gladstone Ave
  Blackwell DE55 .... 147 F1
  Heanor DE75 .... 181 F1
Gladstone Cl DE73 .... 232 C2
Gladstone Dr NG16 ...... 182 C4
Gladstone Pl ST4 .... 269 D1
Gladstone Rd
  Alfreton DE55 .... 158 C2
  Chesterfield S40 .... 266 A4
  Derby DE21 .... 220 C3
Gladstone St Derby DE23 .. 218 C1
  Glossop SK13 .... 17 E4
  Hadfield SK13 .... 10 A2
  Heanor DE75 .... 181 F1
  Ilkeston DE7 .... 208 C4
  Langley Mill NG16 .... 182 B2
  Long Eaton NG10 .... 236 B3
  Mansfield NG18 .... 268 C4
  Mansfield Woodhouse NG19 .. 136 B1
  South Normanton DE55 .. 160 A3
Gladstone St E DE7 ...... 208 C4
Gladstone Terr NG19 ... 136 B1
Gladwin Gdns S40 .... 114 B4
Glaisdale Nook DE24 .... 233 E3
Glamis Cl DE21 .... 206 A1
Glapwell La S44 .... 118 A1
Glasshouse Hill DE5 ..... 181 D4
Glasshouse La S43 .... 77 E2
Glasshouse St NG1 ...... 268 B2
Glastonbury Cl NG19 ... 136 B2
Glastonbury Rd DE24 ... 233 E4
Glaven Cl NG19 .... 136 B1
Gleadless Ave S12 .... 44 A2
Gleadless Bank S12 .... 43 F2
Gleadless Comm S12 ..... 44 A3
Gleadless Cres S12 .... 43 F3
Gleadless Ct S2 .... 43 D3
Gleadless Dr S12 .... 43 F2
Gleadless Fst Sch S12 ...... 44 A3
Gleadless Mid Sch S12 ..... 44 A3
Gleadless Mount S12 .... 44 A2
Gleadless Rd S2 .... 43 E3
Glebe Ave
  Great Longstone DE45 ... 90 A2
  Harthill S26 .... 61 F4
  Pinxton NG16 .... 160 B2
  Ripley DE5 .... 169 E1
  Smalley DE7 .... 192 C3
Glebe Cl Coton in t E DE12 .. 260 B2
  Doveridge DE6 .... 224 A4
  Holmewood S42 .... 132 B4
  Rolleston DE13 .... 240 A2
  South Normanton DE55 .. 160 A3
  Thurvaston DE6 .... 201 F1
Glebe Cres Ilkeston DE7 ... 209 D4
  Stanley DE7 .... 207 D3
Glebe Ct ST4 .... 269 F2
Glebe Farm Cl S26 .... 61 F4
Glebe Jun Sch DE55 ..... 160 A3
Glebe Rd SK17 .... 85 E4
Glebe Rise DE23 .... 218 B1
Glebe St Stoke-on-T ST4 .. 269 E2
  Swadlincote DE11 .... 256 A2
Glebe The
  Awsworth NG16 .... 195 D2
  Rosliston DE12 .... 260 B3
Glebe Way The S41 .... 77 D1
Gledhill Cl S18 .... 57 D1
Glen Ave DE56 .... 191 E4
Glen Cl DE55 .... 148 A2
Glen Rd DE4 .... 156 B1
Glen View DE56 .... 178 C1
Glen View Rd S8 .... 56 C4
Glen Vine DE5 .... 170 A1
Glenavon Cl S43 .... 77 E3
Glenbrook Hill SK13 ...... 10 B1
Glencoe Way S40 .... 95 D2
Glencroft Dr DE24 .... 231 E2
Glendale Dr DE21 .... 220 C3
Glendon Rd Derby DE24 .. 231 E2
  Ilkeston DE7 .... 208 B2
Glendon St DE7 .... 193 D1
Gleneagles Cl
  Chesterfield S40 .... 114 B4
  Derby DE3 .... 217 F1
Gleneagles Dr DE13 ..... 240 B1
Glenfield Ave NG16 ...... 195 E4
Glenfield Cres
  Chesterfield S41 .... 96 A4
  Derby DE3 .... 217 E1
Glenfield Rd NG10 .... 236 B3
Glengarry Way DE24 .... 231 F2
Glenholme Dr S13 .... 44 C4
Glenholme Pl S13 .... 44 C4
Glenholme Way S13 ...... 44 C4
Glenmoor Rd SK17 .... 66 B1
Glenmore Croft S12 ..... 44 B3
Glenmore Dr DE24 ...... 231 E2
Glenmoy Cl DE23 .... 231 E4
Glenn Way DE72 .... 234 C1
Glenorchy Ct DE21 ...... 206 A2
Glenthorn Cl S81 .... 63 F4
Glenthorne Cl S40 .... 95 E1
Glenwood Rd DE73 ...... 245 D4
Glinton Ave DE55 .... 147 F1
Glossop Brook Rd SK13 ... 10 A1
Glossop Central Sta SK13 ... 10 B1
Glossop Rd
  Charlesworth SK13 .... 16 B4
  Gamesley SK13 .... 9 F1
  Little Hayfield SK22 ...... 25 E3
  Marple SK6 .... 15 E2
Glossop St DE24 .... 232 A4
Glossop's Croft S41 .... 77 D1
Glossopdale Comm Coll
  Glossop SK13 .... 10 B1
  Hadfield SK13 .... 10 A2
Gloster St DE24 .... 219 F1
Gloucester Ave
  Chesterfield S41 .... 95 F3
  Sandiacre NG10 .... 223 D2
Gloucester Rd S41 .... 95 F3
Gloucester Way
  Burton u T DE15 .... 248 A1
  Glossop SK13 .... 17 F4
Glover Rd Sheffield S8 .... 43 D4
  Totley S17 .... 55 F3
Glover St ST16 .... 269 D4
Gloves La DE55 .... 147 E1
Glumangate S40 .... 266 B3
Goathland Rd DE24 ...... 231 E1
Goddard La Hadfield SK13 ... 10 A3
  Rowarth SK22 .... 24 C4
Goddard Rd SK13 .... 10 A2
Godfrey Dr DE7 .... 208 B3
Godfrey St DE75 .... 181 F1
Godkin Dr NG16 .... 182 A2
Godward Rd SK22 .... 33 D4
Gold Cl DE4 .... 142 A4
Gold La DE22 .... 217 F4
Goldcrest Dr DE21 ...... 220 C3
Goldcrest Ho S41 .... 77 D2
Golden Valley
  Horsley Woodhouse DE7 .. 192 A3
  Somercotes DE55 .... 170 B2
Golders Green Wlk DE22 .. 218 A3
Goldhill DE4 .... 144 A2
Goldsmith St
  Mansfield NG18 .... 268 B4
  Nottingham NG1 .... 268 A2
Golf Club Rd DE7 .... 209 D1
Golf La DE56 .... 190 C3
Gomersal La S18 .... 57 D1
Goodacre St NG18 .... 268 C4
Goodale St DE23 .... 219 D1
Goodhand Cres NG18 ... 268 A3
Goodman Cl NG16 .... 195 E4
Goodrington Rd DE21 ... 206 B2
Goods Rd DE56 .... 178 C1
Goods Yd S41 .... 178 C1
Goodsmoor Rd DE23 .... 231 F3
Goodwin Cl NG10 .... 223 D3
Goodwin Dr NG16 .... 195 F3
Goodwin Rd S8 .... 43 D3
Goodwin St NG7 .... 268 A2
Goodwin's La DE56 ...... 178 B1
Goodwood Cl DE13 ...... 240 B1
Goodwood Cres DE7 .... 208 B2
Goodwood Dr
  Beeston NG9 .... 223 F1
  Derby DE24 .... 233 E3
Gooker La DE55 .... 158 C2
Goole Rd DE7 .... 208 B3
Goose Gate NG1 .... 268 B1
Goose Green La DE55 .. 146 B2
Goose Green View DE45 .. 91 F3
Goose La DE5 .... 181 E4
Gordon Ave S8 .... 43 D1
Gordon Cres DE55 ...... 160 A2
Gordon Rd
  Borrowash DE72 .... 221 D1
  Derby DE23 .... 218 C2
  Nottingham NG3 .... 268 C2
  Swanwick DE55 .... 169 F4
  Tideswell SK17 .... 69 E2
Gordon St DE7 .... 195 D1
Gordondale Rd NG19 ... 136 A1
Gore La S33 .... 51 D4
Gorman Cl S41 .... 95 F4
Gorse Bank S44 .... 116 C1
Gorse La Derby DE23 .... 231 E3
  Eastwood NG16 .... 195 D4
  Long Eaton NG10 .... 223 D1
Gorse St S21 .... 60 B3
Gorse La Bradley DE6 .... 175 D2
  Lodge Moor S10 .... 42 C4
Gorse Ridge Dr DE45 .... 91 F3
Gorse Valley Rd S41 ..... 115 F4
Gorse Valley Way S41 ... 115 F4
Gorse Way SK13 .... 17 F4
Gorsebank La DE45 .... 91 F4
Gorses Alderwasley DE56 .. 178 B4
  Idridgehay DE56 .... 176 B3

Gorsey Bank DE4	165	F4
Gorsey Brigg S8	56	C4
Gorsey Brow S14	9	D1
Gorsey Cl DE56	178	C3
Gorsey Intakes S14	16	A4
Gorsey La Kirk Ireton DE6	165	D1
Netherseal DE12	265	D4
Gorseybrigg Inf Sch S18	56	B1
Gorseybrigg Jun Sch S18	56	B1
Gorsty Leys DE65	230	B1
Gosber Rd S21	59	F2
Gosber St S21	59	E2
Goseley Ave DE11	257	D2
Goseley Cres DE11	257	D2
Gosforth Cl S18	56	C1
Gosforth Cres S18	56	C1
Gosforth Dr S18	56	C1
Gosforth Gn S18	56	C1
Gosforth La S18	56	C1
Gosforth Rd DE24	232	C4
Gower Ave S40	95	E3
Gower St DE1	267	B2
Goyt Pl SK23	45	F4
Goyt Rd Disley SK12	32	B3
New Mills SK22	33	E3
Goyt Side Rd S40	95	F1
Goyt Valley Ind Est SK23	33	E2
Goyt View SK22	33	D3
Goyt's La SK17	65	D2
Goytlands SK17	84	C3
Grace Cres DE75	181	F1
Grafham Cl DE73	233	D2
Grafton Rd DE15	248	A1
Grafton St DE23	218	C1
Graham Cl DE14	254	B4
Graham Dr SK12	32	B3
Graham St DE7	208	C4
Grammer St DE5	181	D2
Grampian Cres S40	95	D2
Grampian Prim Sch DE24	231	E2
Grampian Way		
Derby DE24	231	F2
Long Eaton NG10	236	A4
Granary Cl S40	95	D4
Granby Ave Chinley SK23	34	C1
Mansfield NG18	268	B4
Granby Cl S45	132	B1
Granby Croft DE45	109	E3
Granby Jun Sch DE7	194	C2
Granby Rd Bakewell DE45	109	E3
Bradwell S33	50	C4
Buxton SK17	85	E4
Granby St DE7	194	C1
Granby Wlk ST4	269	D1
Grandfield St DE75	181	E2
Grandstand Rd DE21	219	E3
Grange Ave Breaston DE72	235	E4
Chapel-en-le-F SK23	47	D3
Derby DE72	231	F4
Dronfield S18	56	C1
Hulland Ward DE6	175	F2
Mansfield NG18	268	A3
Grange Cl Melbourne DE73	252	A4
Somercotes DE55	159	F1
Ticknall DE73	251	D2
Grange Ct DE65	241	D3
Grange Dale DE4	153	E4
Grange Dr		
Castle Donington DE74	247	D2
Long Eaton NG10	236	C4
Grange La Barlow S18	75	D1
Darley Dale DE4	127	F1
Ible DE4	153	E4
Grange Park Ave		
Calow S43	96	C2
Chapel-en-le-F SK23	47	D3
Grange Park Rd SK23	47	D3
Grange Prim Sch NG10	236	C4
Grange Rd Buxton SK17	85	E4
Derby DE24	233	D3
Long Eaton NG10	236	C4
Pilsley S45	132	B1
Swadlincote DE11	255	F3
Uttoxeter ST14	210	A1
Grange Rd S SK14	15	D4
Grange St Alfreton DE55	159	D2
Derby DE23	219	D1
Grange The		
Old Brampton S40	94	C2
Smalley DE75	193	E4
South Normanton DE55	160	A2
Grange View NG16	182	C2
Grange Wlk S42	115	F1
Grangemill Pl S43	97	E4
Grangewood Ave DE7	208	C4
Grangewood Dr DE56	191	D4
Grangewood Rd S40	114	C4
Gransden Way S40	114	B4
Grant Ave DE21	220	A3
Grant St ST4	269	F2
Grant Way NG16	182	C2
Grantham Ave DE21	205	F1
Grantham Cl NG16	195	E4
Granville Ave NG10	223	E1
Granville Cl		
Chesterfield S41	115	E4
Duffield DE56	190	C2
Hatton DE65	227	E1
Granville Com Sch DE11	256	C2
Granville St Derby DE1	218	C3
Swadlincote DE11	256	C2
Grasmere Ave		
Clay Cross S45	131	D2
Derby DE21	220	C3
Grasmere Cl		
Burton u T DE15	248	A1
Chesterfield S41	95	E4
Grasmere Cres DE24	231	F2

Grasmere Rd		
11 Dronfield S18	56	B1
Long Eaton NG10	223	D1
Grasmere St NG10	223	D3
Grass St DE7	194	C2
Grasscroft Cl 8 S40	95	E3
Grassdale View S12	44	C2
Grassmoor Cl S12	43	F3
Grassmoor Cres S13	9	E1
Grassmoor Ctry Pk S42	116	A2
Grassmoor Prim Sch S42	115	F1
Grassthorpe Cl DE21	206	A1
Grassthorpe Rd S12	44	A2
Gratton Ct S43	78	C2
Gratton La DE4	140	B4
Gravel Pit Hill DE65	249	F4
Gravel Pit La DE21	220	C2
Gravelly Bank Mews DE6	199	E3
Graves Tennis & L Ctr S8	57	D4
Graves Trust Homes S8	57	D4
Gray Fallow DE55	160	A2
Gray St Clowne S43	80	C2
Mosborough S20	59	E4
Grayling St DE23	219	D1
Grayswood Cl DE55	170	A4
Great Central Rd NG18	268	C3
Great Common Cl S43	80	A3
Great Croft S18	56	B1
Great Freeman St NG3	268	B2
Great Hucklow Prim Sch SK17	51	D1
Great Longstone Ind Est DE45	90	A2
Great Northern Cl The NG2	268	B1
Great Northern Rd		
Derby DE1	218	C3
Eastwood NG16	182	B1
Greatbatch Ave ST4	269	D2
Greatorex Ave DE24	232	C3
Greaves La DE45	108	C4
Greaves St Ripley DE5	169	F1
Shirland DE55	146	C1
Greek St NG7	268	A2
Green Ave DE73	233	D1
Green Bank S13	16	C4
Green Chase S21	59	E2
Green Cl Matlock DE4	143	D3
Newton DE55	148	A2
Staveley S43	97	E3
Unstone S18	76	C3
Willington DE65	242	A4
Green Cres NG16	171	F3
Green Cross S18	57	D1
Green Farm Cl S40	95	E3
Green Farm Rd NG16	171	E3
Green Glen S40	95	E1
Green Hill DE4	154	C1
Green Inf Sch The DE55	160	A3
Green La Bakewell DE45	108	B2
Barlborough S21	60	B2
Barrow u T DE73	244	A3
Belper DE56	178	C2
Bonsall DE4	153	F4
Breedon on t H DE73	252	C3
Burnaston DE65	230	A2
Buxton SK17	85	D3
Chelmorton SK17	106	B4
Chesterfield S41	96	B2
Chinley SK23	34	C1
Clifton DE6	184	C4
Darley Dale DE4	127	D2
Derby, Alvaston DE24	233	E4
Derby, The Holmes DE1	267	B2
Disley SK12	32	B2
Dronfield S18	57	D1
Glossop SK13	16	C4
Hackingknife SK14	15	D4
Hadfield SK13	9	F2
Hodthorpe S80	82	B3
Hognaston DE6	164	A1
Hollingworth SK14	9	E3
Ilkeston DE7	209	D4
Killamarsh S21	60	B2
Mansfield NG19	135	D1
Marchington ST14	225	D1
Ockbrook DE72	221	E3
Old Brampton S42	94	C4
Overseal DE12	261	F2
Pilsley S45	132	B2
Pleasley S44	134	B4
Roston DE6	198	A4
Tansley DE4	144	A3
Tissington DE6	150	B1
Tupton S42	115	E1
Tutbury DE13	239	E3
Water Swallows SK17	67	E1
Weston Underwood DE6	188	C1
Green Lands DE11	256	A4
Green Lea S18	56	B1
Green Leas DE72	246	A4
Green Oak Ave S17	55	F2
Green Oak Cres S17	55	F2
Green Oak Dr S17	55	F2
Green Oak Gr S17	55	F2
Green Oak Rd S17	55	F2
Green Park Dr SK23	47	D3
Green Pk DE22	218	A3
Green Rd The DE6	173	E2
Green St Barton in F NG11	237	F3
Chesterfield S41	77	D1
Green The Alfreton DE55	159	D2
Aston-on-T DE72	246	A4
Bamford S33	40	A2
Belper DE56	179	D3
Birchover DE4	126	A1
Bradwell S33	51	D3
Brailsford DE6	201	F4

Green The continued		
Breaston DE72	235	E4
Breedon on t H DE73	252	C1
Burton u T DE13	240	C1
Castle Donington DE74	247	D2
Chesterfield S41	115	E4
Clowne S43	80	C2
Curbar S32	72	C1
Derby, Allestree DE22	204	B1
Derby, Mickleover DE74	217	E1
Draycott DE72	235	D4
Findern DE65	230	B1
Fritchley DE56	168	A3
Froggatt S32	72	B3
Glapwell S44	134	A4
Glossop SK13	17	D4
Hardstoft S45	133	D2
Kirk Langley DE6	202	B1
Mansfield Woodhouse NG19	136	A3
Marple SK6	23	D2
Middleton (Nr Wirksworth) DE4	154	B3
Stoke-on-T ST4	269	D2
Sutton in A NG17	148	C1
Swanwick DE55	169	F4
Tissington DE6	162	A3
Totley S17	55	E2
Willington DE65	242	A3
Green Way Findern DE65	230	B1
Wingerworth S42	115	E1
Greenacre DE75	182	A2
Greenacre The DE6	184	C4
Greenacres DE23	231	D4
Greenacres Cl S18	76	B4
Greenacres Dr		
South Normanton DE55	160	A3
Uttoxeter ST14	210	A1
Greenaway Rd DE4	127	F1
Greenbank DE21	220	B2
Greenbank Dr S40	95	E2
Greenbank Rd SK6	15	D1
Greendale Ave S42	113	F4
Greendale Ct S18	57	D1
Greendale Sh Ctr S18	57	D1
Greenfell Ave DE23	231	F3
Greenfield Ave S80	82	B3
Greenfield Cl		
New Mills SK22	33	D4
Sheffield S8	56	C4
Greenfield Dr Linton DE12	261	E4
Sheffield S8	56	C4
Greenfield Rd S8	56	C4
Greenfield St SK13	10	A3
Greenfields Aldercar NG16	182	A2
Denstone ST14	196	B3
Eckington S21	59	E2
Fritchley DE4	168	A4
Greenfields Ave DE23	231	D4
Greenfinch Cl DE21	220	C3
Greengate Cl S40	95	E1
Greengate St ST16	269	E4
Greenhall Rd S21	59	E2
Greenhead S33	40	A2
Greenhead Cres SK17	138	B1
Greenhead Pk S33	40	A2
Greenhill Ave Ripley DE5	180	C4
Sheffield S8	56	C4
Greenhill Ind Est DE55	170	A3
Greenhill Inf & Jun Sch S8	56	C4
Greenhill La DE55	170	B3
Greenhill Main Rd S8	56	C4
Greenhill Parkway S8	56	C3
Greenhill Wlk SK12	32	B3
Greenhills Rd NG16	182	C2
Greenhouse La S10	42	C3
Greenland Ave DE22	218	A3
Greenland Cl S42	132	A4
Greens Ct DE7	194	B1
Greens La NG16	195	F3
Greenshall La SK12	32	C3
Greenside Ave S41	96	A4
Greenside Cl		
Donisthorpe DE12	262	C1
Long Eaton NG10	236	C4
Greenside Ct DE3	217	E1
Greensquare Rd NG16	160	C1
Greenvale Cl DE15	254	C4
Greenview DE4	153	D1
Greenway Ashbourne DE6	173	E2
Brassington DE4	153	D1
Burton u T DE15	248	A2
Hulland Ward DE6	175	F2
Stafford ST 16	269	F4
Whitwell S80	81	F3
Greenway Cl DE72	221	D2
Greenway Croft DE4	154	C1
Greenway Dr S44	118	A4
Greenway The		
Sandiacre NG10	223	D3
Sheffield S8	56	C4
Greenways NG10	114	B4
Greenwich Dr N DE22	218	B3
Greenwich Dr S DE22	218	A3
Greenwood Ave		
Derby DE21	219	F4
Ilkeston DE7	209	D4
Mansfield Woodhouse NG19	136	A2
Sutton in A NG17	148	C1
Greenwood Cl DE24	232	B3
Greenwood Ct DE11	267	B4
Greenwood Rd DE15	254	C4
Greer La S44	118	B1
Gregg Ave DE75	181	F1
Greggs Ave SK23	46	C3

Gregory Ave		
Aldercar NG16	182	A2
Breaston DE72	235	E4
Langley Mill NG16	182	A2
Gregory La Brimington S43	96	B4
Stapleford NG9	223	F4
Gregory La S43	77	E1
Gregory Rd S8	43	D3
Gregory St DE7	208	C4
Gregory Wlk DE23	230	C4
Gregorys Way DE56	179	E3
Gregson Cl DE11	256	A3
Grenville Dr Ilkeston DE7	194	C2
Stapleford NG9	223	F4
Grenvoir Dr DE5	170	A1
Gresham Rd DE24	232	B4
Gresley Dr NG2	268	C1
Gresley Rd Ilkeston DE7	194	C1
Sheffield S8	56	C3
Gresley Wlk S8	56	C3
Gresley Wood Rd DE11	256	A1
Gresley Woodlands DE11	256	A1
Gresty St ST4	269	E2
Gretton Ave DE13	240	C1
Gretton Rd S17	85	E4
Grey Friars' Pl ST16	269	D4
Grey St DE22	267	A2
Greyfriar Gate NG1	268	B1
Greystones Ct S26	61	E3
Grice Rd ST4	269	D2
Griffin Cl Derby DE24	232	C4
New Mills SK22	33	E3
Griggs Gdns DE4	165	F4
Grimshaw Ave DE24	233	D4
Grin Low Rd SK17	85	D2
Grindleford Prim Sch S32	72	B4
Grindleford Sta S32	53	F1
Grindley Pl ST4	269	D1
Grindlow Ave S40	266	A1
Grindlow Cl S14	43	E3
Grindlow Dr S2	43	E3
Grindlow Rd DE21	220	A4
Grindon Cl S40	95	E3
Grindslow Ave DE7	207	F4
Grinlow Cl SK17	85	E2
Grisedale Rd E DE45	90	A2
Grisedale Rd W DE45	90	A2
Grisedale Wlk S18	56	C1
Gritstone Rd DE4	143	E4
Groome Ave DE75	181	E2
Grosvenor Ave		
Breaston DE72	235	F4
Long Eaton NG10	236	A2
Grosvenor Rd		
Eastwood NG16	182	C1
Marple SK6	23	D4
Ripley DE5	169	E1
Grosvenor St DE24	232	B4
Grove Ave		
Nottingham NG7	268	A2
Totley S17	55	E3
Grove Cl DE72	233	F2
Grove Ct DE5	180	C4
Grove Farm Cl S43	96	C4
Grove Gdns S43	96	C3
Grove Hospl The DE72	234	B1
Grove House Ct S17	55	F3
Grove La Buxton SK17	85	E3
Darley Dale DE4	127	F1
Doveridge DE6	224	C4
Old Brampton S42	94	A2
Somersal Herbert DE6	211	F1
Grove Mews NG16	182	C1
Grove Pk DE65	229	D1
Grove Pl DE45	125	D3
Grove Rd Calow S43	96	C3
Totley S17	55	F3
Grove St Chesterfield S41	115	E4
Derby DE21	267	B1
3 Mansfield NG18	268	B3
Mansfield Woodhouse NG19	136	A2
New Mills SK22	33	D4
Swadlincote DE11	256	A2
Grove The Breaston DE72	235	F4
Derby DE72	217	F1
Hadfield SK13	9	F2
Poolsbrook S43	98	A4
Totley S17	55	E3
Grove Way Calow S43	96	C3
Mansfield Woodhouse NG19	136	A2
Grovebury Dr DE23	231	E3
Groves Nook DE73	232	C1
Grundy Ave NG16	171	E4
Grundy Nook S80	82	A3
Grundy Rd S45	131	E2
Grunmore Dr DE13	240	C1
Guernsey Rd S2	43	D4
Guide Post DE56	168	B1
Guildford Ave		
Chesterfield S40	114	B4
Mansfield Woodhouse NG19	136	B3
Sheffield S2	43	E4
Swadlincote DE11	256	C3
Guildford Cl S2	43	E4
Guildford Dr S2	43	E4
Guildford Rise S2	43	E4
Guildford St ST4	269	F2
Guildford View S2	43	E4
Guildford Way S2	43	E4
Guilford Cl S45	131	F2
Guilford La S45	131	F2
Guinea Cl NG10	236	A4
Guinevere Ave DE13	240	C1
Gulliver's Kingdom DE4	155	D4
Gun La DE56	168	B1
Gun Rd Charlesworth SK6	16	B1
Marple SK6	16	B1
Gunby Hill DE12	261	F1

Gunhills La DE56	189	F3
Gunnel Cl ST16	269	D3
Gurney Ave DE23	231	E3
Gutersloh Ct NG9	223	F4
Guy Cl NG9	223	F3
Gypsy La Creswell S80	81	F1
Draycott DE72	221	F1
Hackney La S18	75	F1
Hackney Rd DE4	143	D4
Hackthorne Rd S8	43	D2
Haddon Cl Alfreton DE55	158	C2
Bullbridge DE56	168	A3
Chesterfield S40	95	E1
Derby DE22	204	B2
Dronfield S18	57	D1
West Hallam DE7	207	F4
Haddon Ct DE6	185	E4
Haddon Dr Bakewell DE45	109	F2
Derby, Allestree DE3	204	B2
Derby, Mickleover DE3	217	F2
Derby, Spondon DE21	220	C2
Little Eaton DE21	191	E1
Haddon Hall DE45	110	A1
Haddon Nurseries DE7	194	C2
Haddon Pl Shirebrook NG20	119	E3
Staveley S43	97	E4
Haddon Rd Bakewell DE45	109	F2
Buxton SK17	85	E4
Mansfield NG18	268	B4
North Wingfield S42	132	A4
Haddon St Derby DE23	218	C1
Ilkeston DE7	194	C2
Tibshelf DE55	148	A3
Haddon Way NG10	235	F2
Hade La SK17	106	C4
Hadfield Ind Est SK13	9	F3
Hadfield Inf Sch SK13	9	F3
Hadfield Pl SK13	17	E4
Hadfield Rd SK13	9	F2
Hadfield Sq SK13	17	E4
Hadfield St SK13	17	E4
Hadfield St Andrew's CE Jun Sch SK13	9	F2
Hadfield St Charles RC Prim Sch SK13	9	F3
Hadfield Sta SK13	10	A3
Hadfields Ave SK14	9	F3
Hadleigh Cl NG9	223	F1
Hadley La DE6	186	C4
Hadley St DE7	209	D3
Hadstock Ct NG10	223	D2
Hady Cres S41	96	B2
Hady Hill S41	96	B1
Hady La S41	96	B1
Hady Prim Sch S41	96	B1
Hag Bank La SK12	32	B4
Hagg La Dale DE7	207	E2
Windley DE56	177	E1
Hague Ave S21	79	D4
Hague Bar Prim Sch SK22	32	C4
Hague Bar Rd SK22	33	D4
Hague Fold SK22	32	C4
Hague La S21	79	D3
Hague Rd SK14	16	A4
Hague St SK13	17	E4
Haig Meml Homes S8	57	D4
Haig St DE24	232	C4
Haigh Moor Rd S13	44	C4
Haigh Moor Wlk S13	44	C4
Hailsham Cl DE3	217	E2
Haines Cl DE24	231	F2
Halcyon App S42	115	E1
Halcyon Cl S12	44	C2
Haldane Cl S80	81	F1
Haldane Cres S44	98	C1
Halesworth Cl S40	114	A4
Haley Cl NG16	195	E3
Half Acre La S18	76	B4
Half Croft S43	96	C4
Halfmoon La Callow DE6	165	D2
Kirk Ireton DE6	165	D2
Halfway Ctr S20	59	F4
Halfway Dr S20	59	F4
Halfway Gdns S20	59	F4
Halfway Inf Sch S20	59	F4
Halfway Jun Sch S20	59	F3
Halifax Cl Derby DE65	205	E1
Hilton DE65	228	C1
Halifax Pl 6 NG1	268	B1
Hall Bank Buxton SK17	85	D4
Hartington SK17	137	F3
Hall Cl Dronfield S18	56	B1
Mottram in L SK14	9	D3
Hall Ct DE7	207	F4
Hall Dale View DE4	127	E2
Hall Dr Doveridge DE6	211	D1
Mottram in L SK14	9	D3
Sandiacre NG10	223	D3
Hall Dyke DE21	220	B3
Hall End La DE45	108	C4
Hall Farm Cl		
Castle Donington DE74	247	D2
Swadlincote DE11	256	B2
Hall Farm Rd		
Duffield DE56	190	C1
Swadlincote DE11	256	B2
Hall Gate View S33	51	D4
Hall Green Ave DE13	240	C1
Hall La Ashbourne DE6	173	E1
Brailsford DE6	202	A3
Brinsley NG16	182	B3
Donisthorpe DE12	265	F4
Doveridge DE6	224	A4

Hall La continued
Litton SK17 ... 69 F2
Nether Heage DE56 ... 168 B2
Newton DE55 ... 148 A2
Shirley DE6 ... 200 B4
Stanton DE6 ... 183 D3
Staveley S43 ... 78 B2
Willington DE65 ... 242 A3
Hall Leys La DE73 ... 245 E1
Hall Meadow Croft S20 ... 59 F3
Hall Meadow Dr S20 ... 59 F3
Hall Meadow Gr S20 ... 59 F3
Hall Meadow Rd SK13 ... 10 B1
Hall Pk DE73 ... 244 A3
Hall Rd Aldercar NG16 ... 182 B2
Brimington S43 ... 96 C4
Marchington ST14 ... 224 C1
Rolleston DE13 ... 239 F2
Hall Rise Ashbourne DE6 ... 173 E2
Darley Dale DE4 ... 127 E2
Hall St Alfreton DE55 ... 159 D2
Derby DE24 ... 233 D4
New Mills SK22 ... 33 D4
Swadlincote DE11 ... 256 A1
Hall Terr S45 ... 131 E2
Hall The DE4 ... 154 B3
Hall View S41 ... 95 F3
Hall Wlk S42 ... 115 E1
Hall's Ct SK13 ... 10 B1
Hall's Row 1 S40 ... 95 E1
Hallahan Gr ST4 ... 269 E2
Hallam Ct S18 ... 76 A4
Hallam Fields DE74 ... 247 D1
Hallam Fields Jun Sch DE7 ... 208 C3
Hallam Fields Rd DE7 ... 209 D2
Hallam St ST4 ... 269 F1
Hallam Way DE7 ... 207 E4
Hallamway NG19 ... 136 B1
Hallcliff La S42 ... 93 F1
Hallcroft Ave DE12 ... 262 A2
Hallcroft Rd DE7 ... 208 C4
Halldale La DE4 ... 127 F2
Hallfield Cl S42 ... 115 D2
Hallfield Rd DE55 ... 148 A2
Hallfieldgate La DE55 ... 146 B1
Hallfields Rd
Swadlincote, Newhall DE11 ... 255 F2
Swadlincote, Stanton DE11 ... 255 E2
Hallflash La S44 ... 116 A4
Hallgate La S45 ... 132 A1
Hallington Dr DE75 ... 181 E1
Hallmoor Rd DE4 ... 127 E2
Hallowes Ct S18 ... 57 D1
Hallowes Dr S18 ... 76 B4
Hallowes La S18 ... 76 A4
Hallowes Rise S18 ... 76 B4
Halls La NG16 ... 195 D4
Halls Rd NG9 ... 223 E3
Hallsteads SK17 ... 47 F1
Hallsteads Cl SK17 ... 47 F1
Hallum Ct DE7 ... 194 C2
Hallworth Wlk S21 ... 58 C1
Hallyburton Cl S2 ... 43 E3
Hallyburton Dr S2 ... 43 E3
Hallyburton Rd S2 ... 43 E3
Halsteads The DE6 ... 163 D1
Halstock Dr DE24 ... 233 E4
Halton Cl S41 ... 76 C1
Hambledon Cl S40 ... 95 E3
Hambledon Dr DE24 ... 231 E1
Hambleton Ave S42 ... 131 F3
Hambleton Cl NG10 ... 223 D1
Hamblin Cres DE24 ... 231 F2
Hamill Cl S42 ... 131 F4
Hamilton Cl Beeston NG9 ... 223 F1
Derby DE3 ... 217 F2
Hamilton Dr
Nottingham NG7 ... 268 A1
Swadlincote DE11 ... 256 B3
Hamilton Fields DE15 ... 248 A1
Hamilton Gr DE11 ... 256 B3
Hamilton Rd
Burton u T DE15 ... 248 A1
Derby, Rose Hill DE23 ... 218 C1
Derby, Spondon DE21 ... 220 C3
Long Eaton NG10 ... 223 E1
Hamilton St ST4 ... 269 F1
Hamilton Terr DE65 ... 242 A3
Hamlet La DE55 ... 160 A3
Hamlet The Heanor DE75 ... 181 F2
South Normanton DE55 ... 160 A3
Hammersmith DE5 ... 169 E2
Hammonds Ct DE4 ... 165 F4
Hampden St Derby DE23 ... 232 A4
Eastwood NG16 ... 195 E4
Nottingham NG1 ... 268 A2
Hampshire Cl SK13 ... 17 F4
Hampshire Ct NG16 ... 171 D2
Hampshire Dr NG10 ... 223 D3
Hampshire Rd DE21 ... 219 E4
Hampstead Dr DE22 ... 218 A3
Hampton Cl Beeston NG9 ... 223 F2
Derby DE21 ... 220 C3
West Hallam DE7 ... 207 E4
Hampton St S41 ... 115 E4
Hanbury Ave DE65 ... 227 E1
Hanbury Cl
Chesterfield S40 ... 95 D3
Dronfield S18 ... 56 C1
Hanbury Hill DE13 ... 238 A3
Hanbury Rd DE21 ... 219 F3
Hancock St ST4 ... 269 F2
Hand's Rd DE75 ... 182 A1
Handby St S41 ... 115 E4
Handel St Derby DE24 ... 232 B4
Nottingham NG3 ... 268 C2
Handford Ct DE22 ... 218 B3
Handford St DE22 ... 218 B3
Handley La
Clay Cross S45 ... 131 D1
Edensor DE45 ... 91 D1
Stretton DE55 ... 145 F4
Handley Rd S43 ... 77 E3
Handsacre Cl DE11 ... 255 F2
Handyside St DE1 ... 267 B4
Hangar Hill S80 ... 82 A3
Hanger Bank DE72 ... 246 A4
Hanley Cl SK12 ... 32 B3
Hanley St 13 NG1 ... 268 A2
Hanover Sq DE22 ... 218 A3
Hansard Gate DE21 ... 267 D3
Hanslynn DE72 ... 233 F2
Hanstubbin Rd NG16 ... 171 F3
Hanwell Way DE22 ... 218 A3
Harbin Rd DE12 ... 253 E1
Harborough Ave S2 ... 44 A4
Harby Ave NG19 ... 136 B3
Harcourt Pl DE74 ... 247 D2
Harcourt Rd DE14 ... 253 F4
Harcourt St Derby DE1 ... 267 B2
Mansfield NG18 ... 268 C3
Hard La S26 ... 61 F4
Hardacre Cl DE73 ... 252 A4
Hardhurst Rd Derby DE24 ... 233 D3
Unstone S18 ... 76 C3
Hardie Ave DE55 ... 160 A3
Hardie Pl S43 ... 97 E4
Hardince St ST4 ... 269 F1
Harding Terr ST4 ... 269 E1
Harding's La SK17 ... 138 A3
Hardmeadow La S45 ... 130 A1
Hardstoft Rd
Holmewood S45 ... 132 C1
Pilsley S45 ... 132 C1
Hardwick Ave
Chesterfield S43 ... 77 E2
Derby DE22 ... 204 B2
Shirebrook NG20 ... 119 F2
West Hallam DE7 ... 207 F4
Hardwick Cl Clowne S43 ... 81 D2
Dronfield S18 ... 57 E1
Holmewood S42 ... 132 C4
Ripley DE5 ... 169 E2
Hardwick Ct NG10 ... 235 F2
Hardwick Dr Derby DE3 ... 217 F1
Long Duckmanton S44 ... 97 E2
Hardwick Hall S44 ... 133 F2
Hardwick Hall Ctry Pk S44 ... 133 F3
Hardwick Inf & Jun Schs DE23 ... 219 D1
Hardwick La S45 ... 129 E3
Hardwick Mount SK17 ... 85 E4
Hardwick Old Hall S44 ... 133 F2
Hardwick Park Nature Wlk S44 ... 133 E2
Hardwick Pl DE7 ... 208 B3
Hardwick Rd NG7 ... 268 A1
Hardwick Sq E SK17 ... 85 E4
Hardwick Sq N SK17 ... 85 E4
Hardwick Sq S SK17 ... 85 D4
Hardwick Sq W SK17 ... 85 D4
Hardwick St Buxton SK17 ... 85 D4
Chesterfield S41 ... 266 B4
Derby DE24 ... 232 B4
Langwith NG20 ... 119 F4
Mansfield NG18 ... 268 C4
Shirebrook NG20 ... 120 A2
Tibshelf DE55 ... 148 A4
Hardwick View Rd S42 ... 132 C4
Hardwick's Yd S40 ... 95 F1
Hardy Barn DE75 ... 194 A4
Hardy Cl Kimberley NG16 ... 195 F4
Long Eaton NG10 ... 236 B3
Hardy Cres DE5 ... 181 D4
Hardy Pl NG19 ... 268 A4
Hardy St Alfreton DE55 ... 158 C3
Kimberley NG16 ... 195 F4
Nottingham NG7 ... 268 A2
Hardybarn La SK17 ... 86 B4
Harebell Cl DE21 ... 206 A2
Harehedge La DE13 ... 240 A1
Harehill Cres S42 ... 114 B2
Harehill Rd S40 ... 114 C4
Hareholme St NG19 ... 268 B4
Harepit Cl DE24 ... 233 D3
Harewood Cres S42 ... 131 D3
Harewood Ct NG10 ... 223 D2
Harewood Rd Derby DE22 ... 204 B2
Holymoorside S42 ... 113 E3
Hargate Hill La SK13 ... 16 C4
Hargate Rd SK17 ... 84 C3
Hargrave Ave DE72 ... 221 E3
Hargreaves La ST17 ... 269 D3
Harlaxton Dr
Long Eaton NG10 ... 237 D4
Nottingham NG7 ... 268 A1
Harlech Cl Derby DE21 ... 221 D3
Ilkeston DE7 ... 194 B2
Harlequin Ct NG16 ... 182 B2
Harlesden Ave DE22 ... 218 A4
Harlesthorpe Ave S43 ... 80 C3
Harlesthorpe La S43 ... 80 C3
Harlow Cl Derby DE24 ... 232 C2
Mansfield Woodhouse NG19 ... 136 B3
Harlow Ct DE7 ... 207 E4
Harold Ave NG16 ... 182 A2
Harold St NG2 ... 268 C1
Harperhill Cl S40 ... 114 C4
Harpfield Rd ST4 ... 269 D1
Harpole Cl DE55 ... 169 F4
Harport Dr S45 ... 131 F1
Harpswell Cl DE22 ... 204 C1
Harpur Ave Derby DE73 ... 231 D4
Ticknall DE73 ... 251 D2
Harpur Hill Prim Sch SK17 ... 85 E2
Harpur Hill Rd SK17 ... 85 E2
Harrier Rd DE56 ... 179 E3
Harrier Way DE24 ... 231 F2
Harriet St DE23 ... 219 D2
Harriett St NG9 ... 223 E4
Harrimans Dr DE72 ... 235 F4
Harringay Gdns DE22 ... 218 B3
Harrington Ave DE72 ... 221 E1
Harrington Jun Sch NG10 ... 223 D1
Harrington Rd Derby DE23 ... 218 B1
Sheffield S2 ... 43 D4
Harrington St
Derby, Allenton DE24 ... 232 C3
Derby, Normanton DE23 ... 232 A4
Draycott DE72 ... 235 D4
Long Eaton NG10 ... 236 A3
Mansfield NG18 ... 268 B3
Harris Ave DE5 ... 169 E1
Harris Cl DE5 ... 169 E1
Harris Rd Buxton SK17 ... 85 E2
Stafford ST 16 ... 269 F4
Harris St ST4 ... 269 E2
Harrison Cl DE14 ... 254 A4
Harrison Dr DE4 ... 154 C1
Harrison La
Lodge Moor S10 ... 42 C4
Tibshelf DE55 ... 147 F3
Harrison Rd
Mansfield NG18 ... 268 A3
Stapleford NG9 ... 223 E4
Harrison St DE22 ... 218 C2
Harrogate Cres DE21 ... 205 E1
Harrop La S10 ... 42 C3
Harrop White Rd NG19 ... 268 A4
Harrots La SK17 ... 137 E3
Harrow Dr DE14 ... 254 B4
Harrow Rd DE11 ... 256 A4
Harrow St DE24 ... 219 F1
Harrowby St ST 16 ... 269 F4
Hart Ave NG10 ... 223 D3
Hartfield Cl S41 ... 115 D4
Hartford Cl S8 ... 43 D2
Hartford Rd S8 ... 43 D2
Harthill Field Rd S26 ... 62 A2
Harthill Inf & Jun Sch S26 ... 61 F3
Harthill La S43 ... 61 F1
Harthill Rd Sheffield S13 ... 44 A4
Thorpe Salvin S80 ... 62 B4
Hartill St ST4 ... 269 F2
Hartington CE Prim Sch SK17 ... 137 E3
Hartington Cl DE7 ... 207 F4
Hartington Ct Clowne S43 ... 81 D2
Dronfield S18 ... 57 D1
Hartington Dr Chinley SK23 ... 34 C1
Creswell S80 ... 81 E1
Hartington Ind Est S43 ... 78 C2
Hartington Pl DE7 ... 194 C3
Hartington Rd Buxton SK17 ... 85 D4
Chesterfield S41 ... 96 B1
Dronfield S18 ... 57 D1
Hartington St Derby DE23 ... 267 B1
Langwith NG20 ... 119 F4
Hartington View S43 ... 78 C2
Hartington Way DE3 ... 217 E1
Hartland Dr DE23 ... 231 F3
Hartland Way S41 ... 77 D1
Hartley St S2 ... 43 D4
Hartopp Ave S2 ... 43 E3
Hartopp Cl S2 ... 43 E3
Hartopp Dr S2 ... 43 E3
Hartopp Rd S2 ... 43 E3
Hartshay Hill DE5 ... 169 E1
Hartshill Rd
Hartshorne DE11 ... 257 D2
Stoke-on-T ST4 ... 269 D2
Hartshorne CE Prim Sch DE11 ... 257 D3
Hartshorne Rd Derby DE23 ... 231 E3
Repton DE65 ... 249 F4
Woodville DE11 ... 256 C2
Hartside Cl 11 S40 ... 95 E3
Hartside Gdns 1 NG10 ... 236 A4
Hartwell St NG3 ... 268 B2
Hartwood Dr NG9 ... 209 E1
Harvest Hill DE11 ... 256 A4
Harvest Way Derby DE21 ... 206 B2
2 Old Brampton S40 ... 95 D3
Harvey Close Mews S8 ... 43 D2
Harvey Clough Rd S8 ... 43 D2
Harvey Croft NG9 ... 209 E2
Harvey Ct S44 ... 98 C1
Harvey Pl ST14 ... 210 A1
Harvey Rd Branston DE14 ... 254 A4
Castle Donington DE74 ... 247 D1
Chesterfield S41 ... 96 C1
Derby DE24 ... 232 C3
Harwood Ave DE14 ... 253 F4
Harwood Cl S2 ... 43 D4
Harwood St S2 ... 43 D4
Hasgill Cl DE21 ... 206 B2
Haslam Cres S8 ... 56 C3
Haslam Ct S44 ... 98 C1
Haslam St NG7 ... 268 A1
Haslam's La DE22 ... 205 D1
Hasland Hall Com Sch S41 ... 115 E4
Hasland Inf Sch S41 ... 115 E4
Hasland Jun Sch S41 ... 115 E4
Hasland Rd S41 ... 115 E4
Haslemere Ct DE23 ... 219 D1
Haslemere Rd NG10 ... 236 A4
Haslin Rd SK17 ... 85 E1
Hassall Rd DE65 ... 227 E1
Hassock La N DE75 ... 194 A4
Hassock La S DE75 ... 194 B3
Hassocky La Calow S44 ... 116 A3
Temple Normanton S44 ... 116 A3
Hassop Rd Calver S32 ... 72 A1
Derby DE21 ... 220 A4
Hassop DE45 ... 90 B1
Staveley S43 ... 78 C2
Hastilar Cl S2 ... 44 A4
Hastilar Rd S2 ... 44 A4
Hastilar Rd S S13 ... 44 B4
Hasting St DE74 ... 247 D1
Hastings Cl
Breedon on t H DE73 ... 252 C1
Chesterfield S40 ... 95 E3
Hastings Rd Buxton SK17 ... 85 E2
Swadlincote DE11 ... 256 A2
Hastings St DE23 ... 219 D1
Haston Dr DE55 ... 170 B4
Hatchmere Cl DE21 ... 206 A1
Hatfield Ave NG10 ... 223 D2
Hatfield Rd DE24 ... 232 C3
Hathaway Cl S42 ... 131 D3
Hathern Cl Calow S43 ... 96 C2
Derby DE23 ... 231 F3
Long Eaton NG10 ... 236 B3
Hathersage Ave
Derby DE23 ... 231 F4
Long Eaton NG10 ... 235 F3
Hathersage Cres SK13 ... 9 F1
Hathersage Dr
Glossop SK13 ... 17 F4
Somercotes DE55 ... 170 A4
Hathersage Rd Bamford S33 ... 40 A1
Totley S11 ... 54 B3
Hathersage Sta S32 ... 53 D4
Hatherton St ST 16 ... 269 F4
Hatton Cl S18 ... 75 E4
Hatton Crofts NG10 ... 236 B3
Hatton Ct DE73 ... 252 A4
Hatton Dr S40 ... 95 D3
Haulton Dr DE74 ... 247 D2
Havelock Gdns NG3 ... 268 B2
Havelock Rd DE23 ... 232 A4
Havelock St Ilkeston DE7 ... 208 C4
Ripley DE5 ... 169 F1
Haven Baulk Ave DE23 ... 230 C4
Haven Baulk La DE23 ... 230 C4
Haven Ct DE24 ... 233 E3
Havercroft Tr S21 ... 60 A4
Hawfield La
Burton u T DE15 ... 248 B2
Newton Solney DE15 ... 248 C2
Hawk Green Rd SK6 ... 23 D2
Hawk Rd SK22 ... 33 F4
Hawk's Dr DE15 ... 248 B2
Hawke St DE22 ... 218 B3
Hawkeshead Ave S18 ... 56 C1
Hawkhill Rd S32 ... 71 E3
Hawking La S44 ... 133 D4
Hawkins Ct DE7 ... 194 C2
Hawkins Dr DE56 ... 168 A2
Hawkins St ST4 ... 269 F1
Hawkshead Ave DE21 ... 205 E1
Hawksley Ave S40 ... 95 F2
Hawksley Dr
Darley Dale DE4 ... 127 D2
Rolleston DE13 ... 240 A2
Hawksway S21 ... 59 D2
Hawksworth St NG3 ... 268 C2
Hawley St S18 ... 58 A1
Hawleys Cl DE4 ... 143 F3
Hawthorn Ave
Breaston DE72 ... 235 F4
Creswell S80 ... 81 F1
Derby DE24 ... 233 D4
Glapwell S44 ... 134 A4
Mastin Moor S43 ... 79 E2
Netherseal DE12 ... 264 C4
Ripley DE5 ... 180 B4
Stapleford NG9 ... 223 E3
Hawthorn Bank Hadfield SK13 ... 9 F2
New Mills SK22 ... 33 D3
Hawthorn Cl Ashbourne DE6 ... 185 E4
Chinley SK23 ... 34 C1
Clowne S43 ... 80 B2
Denstone ST14 ... 196 C3
Doveridge DE6 ... 211 D1
Hilton DE65 ... 228 B1
Hope S33 ... 39 D2
Hawthorn Cr DE65 ... 230 B1
Hawthorn Cres DE15 ... 254 C4
Hawthorn Dr DE4 ... 155 D3
Hawthorn Gr SK14 ... 9 E3
Hawthorn Rd
Castle Donington DE74 ... 247 D3
Eckington S21 ... 59 D1
Hawthorn Rise DE11 ... 255 F4
Hawthorn St DE24 ... 232 B4
Hawthorn Way ST17 ... 269 F3
Hawthorne Ave
Borrowash DE72 ... 221 E1
Dronfield S18 ... 57 D2
Long Eaton NG10 ... 236 B3
Shirebrook NG20 ... 119 E2
Shirland DE55 ... 146 B3
Stoke-on-T ST4 ... 269 D1
Tibshelf DE55 ... 148 A4
Hawthorne Cl
Barlborough S43 ... 80 A3
Kilburn DE56 ... 179 F1
Killamarsh S21 ... 60 B3
Stretton DE55 ... 145 E4
Hawthorne Rd NG16 ... 160 B2
Hawthorne Rise NG16 ... 195 D2
Hawthorne St S40 ... 266 B1
Hawthorne Way S40 ... 94 C3
Hawthornes Ave DE55 ... 159 F3
Hawthorns The
Belper DE56 ... 179 E3
Chapel-en-le-F SK23 ... 47 D2
Little Eaton DE21 ... 205 E4
Hawton Cl NG19 ... 135 F1
Hawtrey Gdns DE24 ... 233 D3
Haxby Cl S13 ... 44 C3
Haxby Pl S13 ... 44 C3
Haxby St S13 ... 44 C3
Hay La Ashover S45 ... 145 D4
Scropton DE65 ... 226 C3
Spout DE56 ... 166 B3
Wirksworth DE56 ... 166 B3
Hay Wain La DE11 ... 256 A4
Haybrook Ct S17 ... 55 F3
Haycroft Cl NG19 ... 136 C3
Hayden Fold SK13 ... 16 B4
Haydn Rd DE21 ... 219 F4
Haydock Cl NG16 ... 195 F4
Haydock Park Rd DE24 ... 232 C4
Hayes Ave Breaston DE72 ... 235 D4
Derby DE72 ... 231 E4
Hayes Cl Pinxton NG16 ... 160 B2
West Hallam DE7 ... 207 F4
Hayes Con Ctr The DE55 ... 170 A3
Hayes Cres DE55 ... 169 F4
Hayes Ct S20 ... 59 F3
Hayes Dr S20 ... 59 F3
Hayes Farm Ct DE73 ... 251 D2
Hayes La DE55 ... 169 F4
Hayes The DE65 ... 230 B1
Hayes Wood Rd DE7 ... 193 D1
Hayfield Cl Belper DE56 ... 179 D3
Sheffield S8 ... 56 C4
Staveley S43 ... 78 C2
Wingerworth S42 ... 114 C2
Hayfield Cres S12 ... 44 B2
Hayfield Dr S12 ... 44 B2
Hayfield Pl S12 ... 44 B2
Hayfield Prim Sch SK22 ... 25 E2
Hayfield Rd
Chapel-en-le-F SK23 ... 47 D4
Chinley SK23 ... 35 D2
New Mills SK22 ... 24 C1
Hayfield Rd E SK23 ... 47 E3
Hayfield View S21 ... 59 E2
Hayford Way S43 ... 78 C1
Hayley Croft DE56 ... 190 C1
Hayling Cl DE7 ... 194 B2
Haynes Ave NG9 ... 209 E3
Hays Cl DE7 ... 194 B1
Hays La DE6 ... 164 C1
Hays The DE65 ... 227 E1
Haywards Cl SK13 ... 10 B2
Haywood Cl DE24 ... 233 D3
Haywood St NG2 ... 268 C1
Hayworth Rd NG10 ... 223 D3
Hazel Ave Derby DE23 ... 231 E3
Killamarsh S21 ... 60 B3
Lower Pilsley S45 ... 132 A2
Hazel Cl Ashbourne DE6 ... 185 E4
Dronfield S18 ... 76 A4
Findern DE65 ... 230 C1
Heanor DE75 ... 181 E1
Stoke-on-T ST4 ... 269 D1
Swadlincote DE11 ... 256 A3
Hazel Cres NG20 ... 119 E2
Hazel Ct S18 ... 76 A4
Hazel Dr Chesterfield S40 ... 114 C4
Derby DE21 ... 221 D3
Wingerworth S42 ... 115 D2
Hazel Gr Calver S32 ... 72 B1
Duffield DE56 ... 190 C2
Mansfield Woodhouse NG19 ... 136 A3
Mastin Moor S43 ... 79 E2
Matlock DE4 ... 143 E3
South Normanton DE55 ... 160 A3
Hazel Rd S21 ... 59 E1
Hazelbadge Cres S12 ... 44 C2
Hazelby Rd S80 ... 100 C4
Hazeldene Cl DE56 ... 190 C3
Hazelhurst S41 ... 115 E3
Hazelhurst Ave S41 ... 96 A3
Hazelhurst La S41 ... 96 A3
Hazelmere Rd S80 ... 81 E2
Hazelrigg Cl DE74 ... 246 C2
Hazeltree Cl DE5 ... 180 B4
Hazelwood Cl 7 S18 ... 56 B1
Hazelwood Hill DE56 ... 190 B4
Hazelwood Rd
Burton u T DE15 ... 254 C3
Derby DE21 ... 219 F4
Duffield DE56 ... 190 B3
Hazelwood DE56 ... 190 B3
Hazlebarrow Cl S8 ... 57 E3
Hazlebarrow Cres S8 ... 57 E4
Hazlebarrow Ct S8 ... 57 D4
Hazlebarrow Dr S8 ... 57 D4
Hazlebarrow Gr S8 ... 57 E4
Hazlebarrow Rd S8 ... 57 D4
Hazlehurst La S8 ... 57 F4
Hazletarrow Prim Schs S8 ... 57 E3
Headingley Ct DE23 ... 231 E4
Headland Cl S43 ... 96 C4
Headland Rd S43 ... 96 C4
Heage La DE65 ... 229 E4
Heage Prim Sch DE56 ... 168 B1
Heage Rd DE5 ... 169 E1
Healaugh Way S40 ... 115 D4
Heale St S43 ... 80 C2
Heanor Gate Ind Est DE75 ... 193 E4
Heanor Gate Rd
Heanor DE75 ... 193 E4
Shipley DE75 ... 193 E4
Heanor Gate Sch DE75 ... 181 E1

Heanor Langley Mill & District Meml Hospl
DE75 .... **181** F1
Heanor Rd Codnor DE5 .... **181** D4
  Denby DE5 .... **181** D2
Heanor Rd, DE75 .... **181** E1
Heanor Rd
  Heanor, Loscoe DE75 ...... **181** E4
  Ilkeston DE7 .... **194** B2
  Smalley DE7 .... **193** D4
Hearthcote Rd DE11 .... **256** A2
Hearthstone La DE4 .... **143** E1
Heath Ave Derby DE23 ..... **218** B1
  Killamarsh S21 .... **60** B3
Heath Cross ST14 .... **210** A1
Heath Ct DE24 .... **231** F2
Heath Fields Prim Sch
DE65 .... **227** E1
Heath Gdns DE72 .... **236** A4
Heath Gr SK17 .... **85** E3
Heath La Blackfordby DE11 .. **257** E1
  Findern DE65 .... **242** B4
  Hartshorne DE11 .... **257** F2
  Smisby LE65 .... **258** A3
  Ticknall LE65 .... **258** A3
Heath Park Rd SK17 .... **85** E3
Heath Prim Sch S44 ...... **116** C1
Heath Rd Burton u T DE15 .. **254** C4
  Glossop SK13 .... **10** B1
  Hollmewood S44 .... **116** C1
  Williamthorpe S42 .... **132** C4
  Ripley DE5 .... **169** F1
  Uttoxeter ST14 .... **210** A1
Heath St SK17 .... **85** D3
Heath The NG16 .... **195** D4
Heath View SK17 .... **85** F1
Heath Way DE65 .... **227** E1
Heathcoat Sq NG1 .... **268** B2
Heathcote Cl DE24 .... **233** E3
Heathcote Dr S41 .... **115** F4
Heather Ave S44 .... **116** C1
Heather Bank Cl SK13 ...... **17** D4
Heather Cl Calow S44 .... **97** D2
  Derby DE24 .... **231** E1
  Mansfield NG18 .... **268** B3
  South Normanton DE55 .... **160** A2
  Swanwick DE55 .... **170** A4
Heather Cres
  Breaston DE72 .... **235** F4
  Derby DE72 .... **231** E3
Heather Gr SK14 .... **9** E3
Heather Lea Ave S17 .... **55** E4
Heather Lea Pl S17 .... **55** E4
Heather Vale Cl S41 .... **115** F4
Heather Way S42 .... **113** E4
Heatherley Dr NG19 .... **136** C1
Heatherley Prim Sch
NG19 .... **136** C1
Heathervale Rd S41 .... **115** E4
Heathfield DE4 .... **143** E4
Heathfield Ave
  Chesterfield S40 .... **95** E2
  Ilkeston DE7 .... **209** D4
Heathfield Cl Dronfield S18 .. **75** F4
  Wingerworth S42 .... **115** D2
Heathfield Gdns DE55 ..... **148** A4
Heathfield Nook Rd SK17 ... **85** F1
Heathfield Rd S12 .... **44** B2
Heathlands Dr ST14 .... **210** A1
Heaton 20 S18 .... **56** B1
Heaton St S40 .... **95** E1
Heavygate La DE56 .... **177** F4
Hebden Cl DE23 .... **230** C3
Hebden Dr SK13 .... **17** F4
Hebrides Cl DE24 .... **231** E2
Heddon Bar NG19 .... **136** C2
Hedge Gr DE11 .... **256** A4
Hedgebank Ct DE21 .... **206** B2
Hedgerow Gdns DE21 ...... **206** B2
Hedingham Way DE3 .... **230** B4
Hedley Cl DE55 .... **170** B4
Hedley Dr S43 .... **96** B4
Heeley Arches S8 .... **43** D4
Heeley Bank Inf & Jun Sch
S2 .... **43** D4
Heeley Bank Rd S2 .... **43** D4
Heeley Grn S2 .... **43** D3
Heigham Cl DE24 .... **232** B2
Heights of Abraham DE4 .. **143** D1
Helmsdale Cl NG18 .... **268** A3
Helmsley Ave S20 .... **59** F4
Helmton Dr S8 .... **43** D2
Helmton Rd S8 .... **43** D1
Helston Cl
  Chesterfield S41 .... **115** D4
  Derby DE24 .... **233** D3
  Linton DE12 .... **261** E3
Helvellyn Way NG10 .... **223** D1
Heming Ave S45 .... **132** B1
Hemington Cty Sch DE74 .. **247** E3
Hemington Hill DE74 .... **247** E2
Hemington La DE74 .... **247** F3
Hemlock Ave
  Long Eaton NG10 .... **223** E1
  Stapleford NG9 .... **223** F4
Hemlock Cl DE21 .... **206** A2
Hemlock La DE7 .... **208** B3
Hemp Yd DE6 .... **165** D1
Hemper Gr S8 .... **56** B4
Hemper La S8 .... **56** B3
Hemsley Dr NG16 .... **182** B2
Hemsworth Prim Sch S8 ... **43** E1
Hemsworth Rd S8 .... **43** E1
Hendon Way DE22 .... **218** A3
Henley Ave S8 .... **57** E4
Henley Gdns NG9 .... **209** F1
Henley Gn DE22 .... **217** F3
Henley Way DE7 .... **207** E4

Henmore Pl DE6 .... **173** E1
Henmore Trad Est DE6 ... **173** D1
Hennymoor Cl S80 .... **82** A3
Hennymoor La S80 .... **82** B1
Henry Ave
  Mansfield Woodhouse
  NG19 .... **136** A3
  Matlock DE4 .... **143** E3
Henry Bradley Inf Sch
S43 .... **96** C4
Henry Cres DE55 .... **159** E2
Henry Prince CE Fst Sch
The DE6 .... **184** B4
Henry St Chesterfield S41 .... **96** A4
  Derby DE1 .... **267** A4
  Eckington S21 .... **59** E2
  Glossop SK13 .... **10** B1
  Grassmoor S42 .... **115** F2
  Nottingham NG2 .... **268** C1
  Ripley DE5 .... **169** E1
Henshaw Ave DE7 .... **208** B3
Henshaw Pl DE7 .... **194** C2
Herbert Rd ST17 .... **269** E3
Herbert St Burton u T DE15 .. **248** A2
  Fenton ST4 .... **269** F1
  Mansfield NG18 .... **268** B3
Herbert Strutt Prim Sch
DE56 .... **178** C1
Herdings Ct S12 .... **44** A2
Herdings Prim Sch S14 ... **43** F1
Herdings Rd S12 .... **44** A2
Herdings View S12 .... **44** A2
Hereford Ave NG19 .... **136** B3
Hereford Cl SK17 .... **85** E2
Hereford Cres DE11 .... **256** B3
Hereford Dr S43 .... **96** C4
Hereford Rd Buxton SK17 ... **85** E2
  Derby DE21 .... **219** E4
Hereward's Rd S8 .... **43** E1
Herewood Cl NG20 .... **119** F2
Heritage Com Sch S43 ..... **80** B2
Heritage Dr S43 .... **80** B3
Heritage Mint Sch DE4 ... **143** E2
Heritage Way DE15 .... **248** A1
Hermitage Ave
  Borrowash DE72 .... **221** E1
  Mansfield NG18 .... **268** A3
  Somercotes DE55 .... **170** B3
Hermitage Ct DE21 .... **206** A1
Hermitage La NG18 .... **268** A3
Hermitage Park Way
  DE11 .... **256** A4
Hermitage Sq NG2 .... **268** C1
Hermitage Wlk
  Ilkeston DE7 .... **208** C3
  Nottingham NG7 .... **268** A1
Hermon St NG7 .... **268** A2
Hernstone La SK17 .... **49** D1
Heron Dr DE11 .... **256** C2
Heron Way DE3 .... **218** A1
Heronswood Dr DE21 ...... **220** B3
Herriot Dr S40 .... **266** C1
Heskey Cl NG3 .... **268** B2
Hessey St S13 .... **44** C3
Hewers Holt S43 .... **80** A3
Hewett St NG20 .... **120** B3
Hewitt Pl S26 .... **61** F3
Hexham Ave DE7 .... **209** D2
Hexham Wlk DE21 .... **205** F1
Hey St NG10 .... **236** B2
Heydon Cl DE56 .... **179** D3
Heyford Ct DE75 .... **182** A1
Heysbank Rd SK12 .... **32** B3
Heyward St NG18 .... **268** C4
Heywood St Brimington S43 .. **96** C4
  Mansfield NG18 .... **268** C4
Heyworth Rd SK23 .... **47** E3
Heyworth St DE22 .... **218** B3
Hibbert Rd NG18 .... **268** C4
Hibbert St SK22 .... **33** D3
Hickings La NG9 .... **223** F4
Hickingwood La S43 .... **81** D3
Hickinwood Cres S43 .... **80** C3
Hickleton Cl DE5 .... **169** E1
Hickling Cl DE24 .... **232** B2
Hickling Ct NG18 .... **268** C4
Hickton Rd DE55 .... **169** F3
Hide La SK17 .... **137** F4
Hide St ST4 .... **269** E2
Hides Gn S44 .... **99** D1
Higg La DE4, DE56 .... **167** D3
Higger La S32 .... **52** C4
Higgins Rd DE11 .... **255** F3
High Bank DE5 .... **180** C1
High Bank Rd DE15 .... **248** A2
High Cross Biggin SK17 .... **138** A3
  Hartington SK17 .... **137** F3
High Cross St 4 NG1 ...... **268** B2
High Edge Dr DE56 .... **179** F4
High Edge Mews DE56 ..... **179** D3
High Hazel Cl S45 .... **131** F2
High Hazel Wlk S45 .... **131** F2
High Hazels Rd S43 .... **80** A3
High Hill Rd SK22 .... **24** B1
High Holborn DE7 .... **194** C2
High Holborn Rd
  Codnor DE5 .... **170** A1
  Ripley DE5 .... **170** A1
High La Charlesworth SK13 ... **16** C4
  Glossop SK13 .... **16** C4
  Highlane S12 .... **44** C1
  Holloway, Dethick Common
  DE4 .... **144** C1
  Holloway, Upper Holloway
  DE4 .... **156** B3
  Holymoorside S42 .... **113** F3
High La Central DE7 .... **193** F1
High La E DE7 .... **208** A4

High La W DE7 .... **193** F1
High Lea Rd SK22 .... **33** D4
High Lees Rd S43 .... **80** C1
High Meadow Cl DE5 ...... **180** B4
High Pavement
  Belper DE56 .... **179** D2
  Nottingham NG1 .... **268** B1
High Peak Coll of F Ed
  SK17 .... **85** E2
High Pk ST16 .... **269** D3
High Rd DE55 .... **157** F2
High Ridge
  Mansfield NG19 .... **136** C1
  Matlock DE4 .... **143** E4
High Spania NG16 .... **195** F4
High St Alfreton DE55 ..... **159** D2
  Apperknowle S18 .... **58** A1
  Barlborough S43 .... **80** A4
  Belper DE56 .... **179** D2
  Bolsover S44 .... **99** D1
  Bonsall DE4 .... **142** B1
  Brimington S43 .... **96** C4
  Brinsley NG16 .... **171** E1
  Buxton SK17 .... **85** D4
  Calver S32 .... **72** A1
  Castle Donington DE74 .... **247** D1
  Chapel-en-le-F SK23 .... **47** D3
  Chesterfield, New Whittington
  S41 .... **77** E2
  Chesterfield, Stonegravels
  S40 .... **266** B3
  Clay Cross S45 .... **131** E2
  Clowne S43 .... **80** B2
  Codnor DE5 .... **181** D4
  Derby DE73 .... **233** D1
  Dore S17 .... **55** E4
  Doveridge DE6 .... **211** D1
  Dronfield S18 .... **57** D1
  Eckington S21 .... **59** E2
  Heanor, Loscoe DE75 ...... **181** E2
  Heanor, Newlands DE75 ... **181** F1
  Ilkeston DE7 .... **208** C4
  Kilburn DE56 .... **192** A4
  Killamarsh S21 .... **60** B3
  Kimberley NG16 .... **195** F3
  Linton DE12 .... **261** E3
  Long Eaton NG10 .... **236** C4
  Longnor SK17 .... **121** E3
  Mansfield NG18 .... **268** B3
  Mansfield Woodhouse
  NG19 .... **136** B2
  Marchington ST14 .... **224** C1
  Melbourne DE73 .... **252** A4
  Mosborough S20 .... **59** E4
  New Mills SK22 .... **33** E4
  Nottingham NG1 .... **268** B1
  Pleasleyhill NG19 .... **135** D3
  Repton DE65 .... **242** B1
  Riddings DE55 .... **170** B3
  Ripley DE5 .... **169** E1
  Rocester ST14 .... **196** C2
  Somercotes DE55 .... **170** B4
  South Normanton DE55 .... **160** A3
  Stapleford NG9 .... **223** F4
  Staveley S43 .... **78** C1
  Stonebroom DE55 .... **147** D2
  Stoney Middleton S32 ...... **71** F2
  Swadlincote, Church Gresley
  DE11 .... **256** B2
  Swadlincote, Newhall DE11 .. **256** A3
  Swanwick DE55 .... **169** F4
  Tibshelf DE55 .... **148** A4
  Ticknall DE73 .... **251** D2
  Tideswell SK17 .... **69** E2
  Tutbury DE13 .... **239** E3
  Whitwell S80 .... **81** F3
  Woodville DE11 .... **256** C1
High St E SK13 .... **10** B1
High St W SK13 .... **10** A1
High Tor DE4 .... **143** D1
High Tor Rd DE4 .... **143** D1
High Trees S17 .... **55** E4
High View Cl S41 .... **96** B1
High View Rd DE55 .... **160** B4
High View Sch & Tech Ctr
DE21 .... **205** F1
High Wood Fold SK6 .... **23** E4
Higham La
  Hackingknife SK14 .... **15** D4
  Morton DE55 .... **146** C2
Highashes La S45 .... **113** F1
Highbank SK13 .... **9** F4
Highbank Rd SK13 .... **17** F4
Highbury Cl DE22 .... **217** F3
Highbury Rd S41 .... **95** F3
Highcliffe Ave NG20 .... **119** E2
Highcroft Cl NG10 .... **236** C3
Higher Albert St S41 ...... **266** B4
Higher Barn Rd SK13 .... **9** F2
Higher Halsteads SK17 ..... **47** F2
Higher Sq SK13 .... **10** A4
Highfield DE45 .... **108** C4
Highfield Ave
  Chesterfield S41 .... **95** F3
  Dove Holes SK17 .... **47** F1
  Mansfield NG19 .... **136** A1
  Shirebrook NG20 .... **119** E3
Highfield Cl Bakewell DE45 .. **109** E3
  Heanor DE75 .... **181** D3
  Mansfield NG19 .... **136** A1
Highfield Cotts DE21 ...... **219** F3
Highfield Dr
  Bakewell DE45 .... **109** E3
  Ilkeston DE7 .... **208** A3
  Matlock DE4 .... **143** E4
  South Normanton DE55 .... **160** A3
Highfield Gdns Derby DE22 **218** C4
  Hollingworth SK14 .... **9** E3

Highfield Hall Sch S41 ...... **95** F3
Highfield La Biggin SK17 .. **138** A2
  Chesterfield S41 .... **95** F3
  Derby DE21 .... **219** F3
  Hartington SK17 .... **137** F3
  Weston Underwood DE6 .. **188** C3
Highfield Mews DE21 ...... **219** F3
Highfield Pl S2 .... **43** D4
Highfield Prim Sch NG10 .. **223** E1
Highfield Rd
  Ashbourne DE6 .... **185** D4
  Belper DE56 .... **178** C1
  Bolsover S44 .... **99** D1
  Chesterfield S41 .... **266** A4
  Derby, Little Chester DE22 .. **218** C4
  Derby, Littleover DE23 .... **231** E4
  Glossop SK13 .... **17** E4
  Hayfield SK22 .... **25** E2
  Hulland Ward DE6 .... **175** F2
  Kilburn DE56 .... **191** F4
  Little Eaton DE21 .... **205** E4
  Marple SK6 .... **23** D3
  Swadlincote DE11 .... **256** A2
  Swanwick DE55 .... **169** E4
Highfield St
  Long Eaton NG10 .... **223** E1
  Swadlincote DE11 .... **256** A2
Highfield Terr
  Chesterfield S41 .... **95** F3
  Mansfield NG18 .... **268** B3
  New Mills SK22 .... **33** E4
Highfield View Rd S41 .... **95** F3
Highfield Way
  Mansfield NG18 .... **268** B3
  Ripley DE5 .... **180** B4
Highfields Codnor DE5 .... **181** D4
  Peak Dale SK17 .... **67** D3
Highfields Cres S18 .... **76** A4
Highfields Dr
  Holmewood S42 .... **132** B4
  Linton DE12 .... **261** E3
Highfields Lower Sch DE4 **143** E2
Highfields Rd S18 .... **76** A4
Highfields Sch DE4 .... **143** F4
Highfields Way S42 .... **132** B4
Highgate Dr Dronfield S18 .. **76** B4
  Shipley DE7 .... **194** B2
Highgate Gn DE22 .... **218** A3
Highgate La S18 .... **76** B4
Highgate Rd SK22 .... **25** F1
Highgrove Cl DE13 .... **240** B1
Highgrove Dr DE73 .... **232** C1
Highland Buxton SK17 .... **85** E3
  Mansfield Woodhouse NG19 **136** B2
Highland Rd S43 .... **77** E2
Highlands Dr DE15 .... **248** A2
Highlands Pl S41 .... **76** C1
Highlightley La S18 .... **75** E3
Highlow Cl S40 .... **95** E3
Highstairs La DE55 .... **146** B4
Highstool La S17 .... **106** A3
Highurst St NG7 .... **268** A2
Highview SK13 .... **17** D4
Highway La DE6 .... **151** F1
Highwood Ave DE56 .... **179** E1
Highwood Cl SK13 .... **17** D4
Highwood La S80 .... **81** E3
Highwood Pl S21 .... **59** E2
Higson Ave ST4 .... **269** E2
Hilary Cl DE6 .... **179** F3
Hilcote La DE55 .... **148** A1
Hilcote St DE55 .... **160** A3
Hilderstone Cl DE24 .... **233** E3
Hill Brow DE1 .... **267** B2
Hill Cl Derby DE21 .... **220** C2
  Stanley DE7 .... **193** D1
  Turnditch DE56 .... **177** D1
Hill Crest Crich DE4 .... **157** D1
  Shirebrook NG20 .... **119** E2
Hill Crest Rd DE21 .... **219** E4
Hill Cross DE45 .... **108** C4
Hill Cross Ave DE23 .... **231** E4
Hill Cross Dr DE23 .... **231** D4
Hill Fields DE55 .... **160** A2
Hill Gr S43 .... **78** A2
Hill Green Cl DE12 .... **260** B2
Hill Nook Cl DE73 .... **233** D1
Hill Park Cl DE23 .... **218** A1
Hill Rd Ashover S45 .... **129** F2
  Eckington S21 .... **59** F2
  Heanor DE75 .... **181** E1
Hill Rise NG9 .... **209** E4
Hill Rise Cl DE23 .... **231** E4
Hill Sq The DE22 .... **205** D1
Hill St Burton u T DE15 .... **254** C4
  Clay Cross S45 .... **131** E2
  Donisthorpe DE12 .... **262** C1
  Pleasleyhill NG19 .... **135** D3
  Ripley DE5 .... **169** E2
  Sheffield S2 .... **43** D4
  Stoke-on-T ST4 .... **269** E2
  Swadlincote, Church Gresley
  DE11 .... **256** B2
  Swadlincote, Newhall DE11 .. **255** F3
Hill The Derby DE22 .... **205** D1
  Glapwell S44 .... **118** A1
Hill Top Bolsover S44 .... **99** D1
  Castle Donington DE74 .... **247** D1
  Derby DE21 .... **205** F2
Hill Top Ave NG20 .... **119** F2
Hill Top Inf Sch DE6 ...... **185** E4
Hill Top Rd DE55 .... **170** B3
Hill Top Rise SK23 .... **45** E4
Hill View Duffield DE56 ... **190** B2
  Repton DE65 .... **242** C1
  Whaley Bridge SK23 .... **45** E4
Hill View Cl DE21 .... **192** A4
Hill View Gr DE21 .... **220** C3

Hill View Rd S43 .... **96** C4
Hillary Pl DE7 .... **208** A3
Hillberry DE5 .... **170** A1
Hillberry Rise S40 .... **114** C3
Hillberry Rise S40 .... **114** C3
Hillcliff La DE56 .... **176** C1
Hillcrest DE13 .... **239** D3
Hillcrest Ave
  Burton u T DE15 .... **248** A2
  Hulland Ward DE6 .... **175** F2
  South Normanton DE55 .... **160** A2
Hillcrest Dr Codnor DE5 ... **181** D4
  Kilburn DE56 .... **192** A4
Hillcrest Gr S43 .... **78** C2
Hillcrest Rd S41 .... **115** E4
Hillcreste Dr DE73 .... **232** C2
Hillcroft Dr DE72 .... **221** E2
Hillend SK14 .... **9** D1
Hillend La S14 .... **9** D1
Hillfield La DE13 .... **240** C1
Hillfield Rd NG9 .... **209** F1
Hillfoot Rd S17 .... **55** E3
Hillhead La SK17 .... **85** F1
Hillhouses La S42 .... **114** C2
Hillman Dr S43 .... **97** E4
Hillmoor St NG19 .... **135** E2
Hillock The S32 .... **72** C1
Hills Croft DE6 .... **164** A1
Hills Rd DE72 .... **235** E4
Hills The S33 .... **51** D3
Hillsdale Rd DE15 .... **248** A3
Hillside Ashover S45 .... **130** A2
  Buxton SK17 .... **85** E2
  Castle Donington DE74 .... **247** D2
  Findern DE65 .... **230** B1
  Holloway DE4 .... **156** A3
  Langley Mill NG16 .... **182** A2
  Middleton (Nr Wirksworth)
  DE4 .... **154** B2
  Mosborough S20 .... **59** E4
  Tutbury DE13 .... **239** E3
  Whitwell S80 .... **81** F3
Hillside Ave Ashbourne DE6 **173** E2
  Derby DE21 .... **220** A3
  Dronfield S18 .... **76** A4
Hillside Cl Disley SK12 ...... **32** B3
  Hadfield SK13 .... **9** F2
  Whitwell S80 .... **81** F3
Hillside Cres DE21 .... **220** C2
Hillside Ct DE73 .... **252** C1
Hillside Dr Chesterfield S40 .. **95** E1
  Long Eaton NG10 .... **236** A4
  Mastin Moor S43 .... **79** E2
Hillside Gr Marple SK6 ...... **15** D1
  Sandiacre NG10 .... **223** D3
Hillside La DE4 .... **152** C1
Hillside Rd Derby DE21 .... **220** C2
  Linton DE12 .... **261** E4
Hillside Rise S40 .... **178** C1
Hillside View SK22 .... **33** D4
Hillsway
  Derby, Chellaston DE73 ... **232** C2
  Derby, Littleover DE23 .... **218** A1
  Shirebrook NG20 .... **119** E2
Hilltop DE56 .... **168** A4
Hilltop Cl S44 .... **118** A1
Hilltop La DE6 .... **215** E3
Hilltop Rd Ashover S45 .... **129** F3
  Chesterfield S41 .... **77** D1
  Dronfield S18 .... **76** A4
  Glossop SK13 .... **10** A2
  Pinxton NG16 .... **160** B2
  Wingerworth S42 .... **114** B2
Hilltop Way S18 .... **76** A4
Hilltops View DE4 .... **143** E3
Hillview Ct NG19 .... **136** B2
Hillwood Dr S13 .... **17** F4
Hilton Cl Derby DE3 .... **217** E1
  Long Eaton NG10 .... **235** F2
  Swadlincote DE11 .... **256** A4
Hilton Park Dr DE55 ..... **170** B4
Hilton Prim Sch DE55 .... **228** B1
Hilton Rd Eggington DE65 .. **241** D4
  Etwall DE65 .... **229** D2
  New Mills SK6 .... **32** A4
  Stoke-on-T ST4 .... **269** D2
Hincley Ct DE4 .... **110** C1
Hind Ave DE72 .... **235** E4
Hindersitch La DE4 .... **156** B1
Hindscarth Cres DE3 ...... **217** F1
Hinton Gr SK14 .... **15** D4
Hipley Cl S40 .... **95** D3
Hipper St S40 .... **266** B2
Hipper St S S40 .... **266** B2
Hipper St W S40 .... **95** F1
Hixon's La DE7 .... **208** A1
Hoades St S42 .... **131** E4
Hoargate La DE6 .... **200** C1
Hob Hill DE56 .... **190** A4
Hob La Kirk Ireton DE56 ... **176** B4
  Totley S18 .... **55** F1
Hobart Cl Burton u T DE15 **248** B1
  Derby DE3 .... **217** F1
Hobart Dr NG9 .... **209** F1
Hobhouse Rd NG19 .... **135** E1
Hobkirk Dr DE24 .... **231** F1
Hobsic Cl NG16 .... **182** B4
Hobsic La NG16 .... **171** F4
Hobson Dr DE7 .... **208** C3
Hobson Moor Rd SK14 ...... **9** D4
Hockerley Ave S23 .... **45** E4
Hockerley Cl SK23 .... **45** E4
Hockerley La SK23 .... **45** E4
Hockley NG1 .... **268** B1
Hockley La Fallgate S45 ... **130** A1
  Wingerworth S42 .... **115** D2

Hockley Way DE55 159 D1
Hodge Beck Cl DE24 233 E3
Hodge Fold SK14 15 F4
Hodge La Ashover S45 128 C4
Broadbottom SK14 15 F4
Marchington ST14 224 A1
Hodmire La S44 133 F4
Hodthorpe Cl DE21 206 A1
Hodthorpe Prim Sch S80 82 B3
Hogarth Cl NG9 223 F3
Hogarth Rd SK6 23 D4
Hogarth Rise S18 75 F4
Hogarth St NG3 268 C2
Hoggbarn La NG16 181 E3
Hoggs Field NG16 182 C1
Hogshaw Villas Rd
1 SK17 85 E4
Hoillant Sq DE6 175 F2
Holbeach Dr S40 114 C4
Holbeck Ave S44 99 E1
Holbeck Cl S41 266 C4
Holbeck La S80 101 E4
Holbeck St S80 81 E1
Holbein Cl S18 75 F4
Holborn Ave NG2 268 C1
Holborn Dr DE22 218 A4
Holborn View DE5 170 A1
Holbrook Ave
Mosborough S20 59 F4
North Wingfield S42 132 A4
Holbrook CE Prim Sch
DE56 191 E4
Holbrook Cl
Chesterfield S40 114 B4
Pleasley NG19 135 D3
Holbrook Dr S13 44 A3
Holbrook Gn S20 60 A4
Holbrook Pl S43 97 E3
Holbrook Rd Belper DE56 178 C1
Derby DE24 233 D3
Sheffield S13 44 A4
Holbrook St DE75 182 A1
Holbrook View DE56 192 A4
Holbrook Way S42 132 A4
Holburn Ave S18 57 D1
Holcombe St DE23 219 D1
Holden Ave DE72 246 A4
Holden Gdns NG9 223 F3
Holden St Mansfield NG18 268 B3
Nottingham NG7 268 A2
Holderness Cl DE24 231 E1
Holdings The DE11 256 A1
Holdon Croft DE12 260 B3
Holestone Gate Rd S45 129 E1
Holker Ave SK17 85 E4
Holkham Cl DE7 194 B2
Holland Cl DE55 146 C3
Holland Meadow NG10 236 B3
Holland Pl S2 43 D4
Holland Rd Chesterfield S41 76 C1
Sheffield S2 43 D4
Hollens Way S40 95 D3
Hollies Cl Clifton DE6 184 C3
Dronfield S18 76 B4
Newton Solney DE15 248 C4
Hollies Cres NG7 268 A1
Hollies Dr SK6 23 D3
Hollies La Great Cubley DE6 198 B2
Roston DE6 198 B2
Hollies Rd DE22 204 B2
Hollies The
Eastwood NG16 182 C1
Sandiacre NG10 223 D3
Hollin Cl S41 95 E4
Hollin Cross La SK13 17 E4
Hollin Dr SK23 47 D3
Hollin Hill S43 81 D2
Hollindale Dr S12 44 B3
Hollington Cl DE21 219 F4
Hollingwood Cres S43 78 A1
Hollingwood Prim Sch
S43 78 A1
Hollingworth Ave NG10 223 D2
Hollingworth Prim Sch
SK14 9 E3
Hollinhey Terr SK14 9 E3
Hollins Ave SK17 85 D4
Hollins La Crich DE4 157 D2
Gamesley SK13 9 E1
Marple SK6 23 E4
Hollins Mews SK13 9 E1
Hollins Mt SK6 23 D4
Hollins Spring Ave S18 76 A4
Hollins Spring Rd S18 76 A4
Hollins St SK17 85 D4
Hollins The DE4 156 A3
Hollins Wood Cl DE4 156 A3
Hollinsclough CE
Prim Sch SK17 104 B1
Hollinsclough Rake SK17 104 A1
Hollinsend Ave S12 44 B3
Hollinsend Pl S12 44 B3
Hollinsend Rd S12 44 A3
Hollinsmoor Rd SK22 24 B4
Hollinwood Rd Disley SK12 32 B3
Marple SK6 23 D1
Hollis La Chesterfield S41 266 C2
Denstone ST14 196 A3
Hollis St DE24 233 D4
Hollow Cres DE15 248 B2
Hollow Gate S33 51 D4
Hollow La Burton u T DE15 248 B2
Mayfield DE6 172 B1
Mosborough S20 59 F3
Hollow Of The Moor SK17 87 F2
Hollow Rd DE73 252 C2
Hollow Stone 9 NG1 268 B1
Hollow The Bamford S33 40 A2
Castle Donington DE74 247 D2
Derby, Littleover DE74 231 E4
Derby, Mickleover DE3 230 B4
Holloway DE4 156 A3
Roston DE6 197 F3
Holloway Rd Derby DE24 232 C3
Duffield DE56 190 C2
Hollowford Rd S33 38 A2
Hollowford Training &
Conference Ctr S33 38 B2
Hollowood Ave DE23 231 E4
Hollows The NG10 237 D4
Holly Ave Breaston DE72 222 C1
Ripley DE5 180 B4
Holly Bank SK14 9 E3
Holly Brook Way DE23 230 C3
Holly Bush La DE56 191 D3
Holly Cl Ashbourne DE6 185 E4
Draycott DE72 235 D4
Killamarsh S21 60 B3
Holly Ct Derby DE3 217 E1
Mansfield NG19 136 C1
Woodville DE11 256 C1
Holly Gdns S12 44 B3
Holly Gn DE15 254 C4
Holly Gr Sheffield S12 44 B3
Swanwick DE55 169 F4
Holly Hill Rd NG16 171 F3
Holly House Sch S41 77 D2
Holly La Alderwasley DE56 167 E2
Tansley DE4 144 A2
Holly Rd Kimberley NG16 195 F4
Mansfield NG19 136 C1
Uttoxeter ST14 210 A1
Holly St DE15 254 C4
Hollybank Ave S12 44 B3
Hollybank Cl Sheffield S12 44 B3
Swadlincote DE11 256 A4
Hollybank Cres
Sheffield S12 44 B3
Stoke-on-T ST4 269 E1
Hollybank Dr S12 44 B3
Hollybank Rd S12 44 B3
Hollybank Way S12 44 B3
Hollybrook Way DE23 230 C3
Hollybush Cl DE12 264 C4
Hollyhouse Dr DE55 160 A3
Hollyhurst La DE6 212 A3
Hollyhurst Row DE55 170 C3
Hollymoor Dr DE73 232 C1
Hollythorpe Cl S41 115 E4
Hollythorpe Cres S8 43 D2
Hollythorpe Rd S8 43 D2
Hollythorpe Rise S8 43 D2
Hollywell Ave DE5 181 D4
Hollywell Prim Sch NG16 195 F4
Hollywell St S41 266 B3
Hollywood Rd SK6 23 F4
Holm Ave DE21 205 D4
Holm Cl S18 56 B1
Holm La DE55 158 A2
Holme Cl Hatton DE65 227 E1
Holloway DE4 156 A3
Ilkeston DE7 194 B1
Holme Croft DE7 207 F4
Holme Farm Ave DE15 254 C4
Holme Hall Cres S40 95 D3
Holme Hall Prim Sch S40 95 D3
Holme La Bakewell DE45 109 E4
Derby DE21 220 B2
Holme Park Ave S40 95 D4
Holme Rd Chesterfield S41 96 A3
Matlock Bath DE4 143 D1
Holme Woods La HD7 2 C3
Holmebank Cl S40 95 F2
Holmebank E S40 95 F2
Holmebank W S40 95 F2
Holmefield Cres DE7 209 D4
Holmefield Rd S80 82 A3
Holmes Bank DE6 184 B4
Holmes Cl NG16 182 A2
Holmes Rd DE72 235 E4
Holmes St Derby DE23 219 D1
Heanor DE75 181 E1
Holmesdale Cl S18 57 E2
Holmesdale Inf Sch S18 57 E1
Holmesdale Rd S18 57 E2
Holmesfield Cl DE4 144 A3
Holmesfield Dr Derby DE3 217 F1
Shipley DE75 194 A4
Holmesfield Rd S18 56 A1
Holmewood Dr NG16 195 D4
Holmewood Ind Pk S42 116 B1
Holmfield Buxton SK17 84 C3
Derby DE23 231 F4
Holmgate Prim Sch S45 131 D2
Holmgate Rd S42 130 C2
Holmley Bank S18 57 D2
Holmley La S18 57 D2
Holmoak Cl DE21 206 A2
Holmshaw Dr S13 44 C4
Holmshaw Gr S13 44 C4
Holmwood Terr 2 SK17 85 E4
Holroyd Ave NG2 268 C1
Holt Ave DE24 233 E3
Holt Dr DE4 142 C4
Holt La Holloway DE4 156 A4
Matlock DE4 143 D2
Holt Rd DE4 127 F1
Holt's La DE13 239 D3
Holtlands Dr DE24 232 C3
Holy Rosary RC Prim Sch
The DE15 248 A2
Holyhead Dr DE21 206 A2
Holymoor Rd S42 113 F4
Holymoorside Prim Sch
S42 113 E4
Holyoake Ave S13 44 C4
Holyrood Cl DE21 221 D3
Holywell DE45 109 E3
Holywell La DE45 125 D3
Holywell Rd DE7 194 B2
Home Farm Cl DE72 221 E3
Home Farm Dr DE22 205 D2
Home Fm Ct NG16 171 E3
Homecroft Dr NG16 171 F4
Homeport Mews S41 266 B4
Homer Dr SK6 23 D4
Homestead NG16 182 A2
Homestead Rd SK12 32 B3
Honeycroft Cl DE56 179 D1
Honeycroft Ct DE55 160 A2
Honeyfield Dr DE5 180 C4
Honeysuckle Cl DE11 256 A3
Honeysuckle View DE15 255 D4
Honeywall ST4 269 E2
Honeywall La DE6 183 F4
Honingham Rd DE7 194 B2
Hook La ST14 210 A3
Hoole St S41 115 E4
Hooley Cl NG10 236 A3
Hooley St NG16 171 F3
Hoon Rd DE65 239 E4
Hoonwell La DE6 175 F3
Hooton St NG2 268 C2
Hop Inge The S26 61 F3
Hope Ave DE3 217 E1
Hope Dr NG7 268 A1
Hope Prim Sch S33 39 D2
Hope Rd Hope S33 39 E1
Thornhill S33 39 E1
Hope St Chesterfield S40 95 F2
Derby DE1 267 C2
Glossop SK13 10 C1
Ilkeston DE7 208 C4
Mansfield NG18 268 C3
Melbourne DE73 252 A4
Hope Sta S33 39 E2
Hope Terr DE4 143 D1
Hope Valley Coll S33 38 C2
Hopedale Rd S12 44 B2
Hopefield Ave S12 44 B2
Hopetoun St DE23 232 A4
Hopewell Rd DE4 143 E3
Hopewell Wlk DE7 194 C3
Hopkins Ct NG16 182 C2
Hopping Hill DE56 190 C4
Hopping Hill Terr E DE56 191 D4
Hopping Hill Terr W DE56 191 D4
Hopping La DE45 125 D2
Hopton Cl DE21 206 A1
Hopwell Rd DE72 222 A1
Hopwell Sch DE72 221 F3
Horace Ave NG9 223 E3
Horderns La SK23 47 D3
Horderns Park Rd SK23 47 D3
Horderns Rd SK23 47 D3
Horeston Cotts DE7 192 A4
Hornbeam Cl Derby DE21 205 F1
Ilkeston DE7 209 D4
Hornbeams The ST14 210 A1
Hornby Row ST4 269 E2
Horncastle Rd DE21 205 E1
Horner Rd S8 43 D4
Hornscroft Rd S44 99 D1
Hornsea Rd DE21 205 E1
Hornthorpe Rd S21 59 E1
Horridge St DE7 194 C2
Horse Fair Ave SK23 47 D3
Horse Shoes The DE74 247 E2
Horsecroft Cl DE7 194 B1
Horsehead La S44 99 E1
Horseshoe Ave SK17 47 F1
Horsewood Rd S40 114 A4
Horsley CE Prim Sch
DE21 191 F3
Horsley Cl S40 95 D3
Horsley Cres
Holbrook DE56 191 E4
Langley Mill NG16 182 A2
Horsley La DE21 191 F2
Horsley Rd Horsley DE21 191 F3
Kilburn DE56 191 F3
Horsley Woodhouse Prim
Sch DE7 192 B3
Horsleygate La S18 74 C4
Horsleygate Rd S17, S18 74 A4
Horton Cl
28 Mosborough S20 59 F4
Swanwick DE55 169 F4
Horton Dr S20 59 F4
Horton St DE23 219 E1
Horwood Ave DE23 218 B1
Hoselett Field Rd NG10 236 C3
Hospital La DE3 230 A4
Hoten Rd NG2 268 C1
Houfton Cres S44 98 C2
Houfton Rd S44 98 C2
Houghton Ave DE7 194 B2
Houghton Ct DE21 205 F1
Houldsworth Cres S44 98 C1
Houldsworth Dr S41 96 C1
Hoult St DE22 218 B2
Houndkirk Rd S11 54 B4
Hounds Gate NG7 268 A1
Hounslow Rd DE22 218 A3
Houston Cl DE21 220 A3
Hoveton Cl DE24 232 B2
How La S33 38 B2
Howard Cl Glossop SK13 10 A1
Long Eaton NG10 223 F1
Howard Dr Chesterfield S41 77 D1
North Wingfield S42 131 F3
Howard Rd NG19 268 A4
Howard St Derby DE23 218 C1
Glossop SK13 10 B1
Nottingham NG3 268 B2
Howden Cl Derby DE3 217 E1
Staveley S43 78 C2
Howden Rd SK22 24 B1
Howe St DE22 218 B3
Howells Pl S43 79 D2
Howitt Cres ST14 210 A1
Howitt St Heanor DE75 181 F1
Long Eaton NG10 236 C4
Howth Cl DE21 220 A2
Hoylake Ave S40 114 B4
Hoylake Cl NG19 136 C3
Hoylake Ct DE3 217 E2
Hoylake Dr DE3 217 E2
Hoyland Ct DE56 179 F3
Hubert Shaw Cl DE24 232 C2
Huckerby Rd DE7 194 B1
Hucklow Ave
Chesterfield S40 266 A1
North Wingfield S42 132 A4
Staveley S43 97 E4
Hucklow Ct DE21 206 A2
Hucknall Ave S40 95 E2
Hudson Cl S26 61 F4
Hudson Mount S44 118 A4
Hudson St NG3 268 C2
Hufton's Ct DE75 194 A4
Hufton's Dr DE75 194 A4
Hugh La S33 51 D4
Hugh St SK13 10 A1
Hulland CE Prim Sch DE6 175 F2
Hulland St DE1 267 D1
Hulland View DE22 204 B1
Hulme St ST4 269 D2
Humber Cl DE24 233 E3
Humber Rd NG10 223 E1
Humbleton Dr DE22 218 A3
Humphrey Rd S8 56 C4
Hundall La Chesterfield S41 77 D2
Unstone S18 77 D4
Hunger La DE6 188 C2
Hungerhill La S42, S45 113 D2
Hungry La Bradwell S33 51 D3
Hathersage S32 53 D4
Hunloke Ave S40 95 F1
Hunloke Cres S40 95 F1
Hunloke Park Prim Sch
S42 115 D2
Hunloke Rd S42 132 C4
Hunloke View S42 115 D2
Hunsoon Rd S21 59 E2
Hunstone Ave S8 57 D4
Hunt Ave DE75 181 F1
Hunt La S45 145 D4
Hunter Dr DE56 191 F4
Hunter Rd DE56 179 E3
Hunter's La S13 44 B3
Hunters Croft DE24 231 F1
Hunters Dr ST4 269 D1
Hunters Gn SK23 34 C1
Hunters La SK13 16 C4
Hunters Way ST4 269 E1
Huntingdon Ave S44 99 D1
Huntingdon Ct DE73 252 A4
Huntingdon Dr
Castle Donington DE74 247 D2
Nottingham NG7 268 A1
Huntingdon Gn DE21 219 E3
Huntingdon Jun & Inf
Schs NG3 268 B2
Huntingdon Rd DE15 254 B4
Huntingdon St NG3 268 B2
Huntingdon Way NG9 223 F1
Huntingdon Wlk NG10 223 D3
Huntley Ave Derby DE21 220 C3
Stoke-on-T ST4 269 E1
Huntley Cl S43 97 D4
Hunts La DE12 264 C4
Huntsman Rd S43 78 C1
Huntspill Rd DE65 228 C1
Hurdlow Mews SK13 9 E1
Hurds Hollow DE4 143 D3
Hurker Rise DE4 143 E4
Hurl Dr S12 43 F3
Hurley Ct DE7 207 F4
Hurlfield Ave S12 44 A3
Hurlfield Campus S2 43 F3
Hurlfield Ct S12 44 A3
Hurlfield Dr S12 43 F3
Hurlfield Hill S2 43 F3
Hurlfield Rd S12 43 F3
Hurst Dr Burton u T DE13 240 C1
Stanley DE7 207 E3
Hurst La DE55 146 A3
Hurst Lea Rd SK22 33 E4
Hurst Rd SK13 10 C1
Hurst Rise DE4 143 E3
Hurstbrook Cl SK13 10 C1
Hurstclough La
Bamford S32 40 B1
Hathersage S33 40 B1
Huss's La NG10 236 C4
Hut La S21 60 C2
Hutchings Cres S43 80 B3
Hutchinson Gn NG3 268 B2
Huthwaite CE Inf Sch
NG17 148 C1
Huthwaite La DE55 148 B1
Hutmoor Butts DE45 107 D2
Hutton St Derby DE24 232 C3
Nottingham NG2 268 C1
Hyde Bank Rd SK22 33 E4
Hyde Park Rd DE22 218 A3
Hyde Rd SK14 9 D2
Hyde Way SK14 9 D2
Hydro Cl DE45 91 F3
Hylton Cl DE14 254 A4
Hyndley Rd S44 98 C2

Ian Ave DE4 165 F4
Ians Way S40 95 E2
Ibbotsons Croft S32 53 D4
Ibsley Cl DE24 233 E3
Ida's Rd S21 59 E2
Ilam Cl S43 97 E3
Ilam Ct DE6 185 E4
Ilam Sq DE7 194 C3
Ilford Cl DE7 194 B2
Ilford Rd DE22 218 A3
Ilford Wlk DE22 218 A3
Ilion St NG19 135 F1
Ilkeston Com Hospl DE7 194 B2
Ilkeston Rd Heanor DE75 193 F4
Nottingham NG7 268 A2
Sandiacre NG10 223 E4
Sandiacre NG10 223 E4
Smalley DE7 192 C1
Stanton-by-D DE7 208 C2
Stapleford NG9 209 F1
Trowell NG9 209 E3
Ilkeston Sch DE7 208 B4
Immingham Gr S43 78 B1
Imperial Ct DE22 204 B3
Imperial Rd DE4 143 D3
Inchwood Cl NG9 223 F1
Independent Hill DE55 158 C2
Industrial St DE23 219 D1
Infirmary Rd S41 266 C4
Ingestre Rd ST17 269 E3
Ingham Dr DE3 230 B4
Ingham Rd NG10 223 E1
Ingle Cl DE21 220 C3
Ingle's Channel DE56 178 C2
Ingleborough Gdns
8 NG10 236 A4
Ingleby Ave DE23 231 F4
Ingleby Cl
16 Dronfield S18 56 B1
Swadlincote DE11 256 A2
Ingleby La DE73 251 D3
Ingleby Rd NG10 235 F2
Inglefield Rd DE7 209 D3
Ingleton Rd S41 115 D4
Inglewood ST17 269 D3
Inglewood Ave DE3 217 E2
Inglis St ST4 269 F2
Ingliston Cl DE24 233 E3
Inkerman Rd NG16 171 F3
Inkerman St NG16 171 F3
Inkersall Dr S20 59 F4
Inkersall Green Rd S43 97 E4
Inkersall Prim Sch S43 97 E4
Inkersall Rd S43 97 F4
Inn La DE22 204 A4
Inns La DE55 157 F2
Institute La DE55 159 D2
Instow Dr DE23 231 E3
Instow Rise NG3 268 B2
Intake Ave NG18 268 A3
Intake Farm Fst Sch
NG19 268 A4
Intake Fst & Mid Sch S12 44 A3
Intake La Bakewell DE45 109 F2
Cromford DE4 155 D3
Holloway DE4 155 F2
Intakes La DE6 188 B4
Inverary Cl DE24 231 F2
Invernia Cl DE23 231 F3
Iona Cl Derby DE24 231 F2
Tibshelf DE55 147 F3
Iona Dr NG9 209 E1
Ireland Cl S43 78 C1
Ireland St S43 78 C1
Ireton St NG7 268 A2
Iron Cliff Rd S44 98 C2
Iron Gate DE1 267 B3
Irongate S40 266 B3
Ironside Cl S14 43 E2
Ironside Pl S14 43 F2
Ironside Rd S14 43 F2
Ironside Wlk S14 43 E1
Ironville & Codnor Park
Prim Sch NG16 170 C2
Ironwalls La DE13 239 E3
Irvine Cl DE24 231 E2
Irving Pl DE24 232 C4
Isaac's La NG9 223 E4
Isabella St NG1 268 B1
Islay Cl NG9 209 E2
Islay Rd DE24 231 F2
Isleworth Dr DE22 217 F3
Ismay Rd DE21 219 F3
Ivan Brook Cl 17 S18 56 B1
Ivanhoe Cl S42 115 E1
Ivatt Dr NG2 268 C1
Iveagh Wlk DE55 170 C3
Ivonbrook Cl DE4 142 A4
Ivy Cl Chesterfield S41 77 D1
Donisthorpe DE12 262 C1
Willington DE65 242 A3
Ivy Ct Derby DE3 217 E1
Hilton DE65 228 B1
Sheffield S8 43 E1
Ivy Gr DE5 169 E1
Ivy House Specl Sch
DE23 219 E1
Ivy La Eastwood NG16 182 C1
Elton DE4 140 C3
Ivy Lodge Cl DE15 254 C4
Ivy Spring Cl S42 115 D2
Ivy Sq DE23 219 E1
Ivybridge Cl DE21 206 B2
Ivycroft SK13 9 F2

Ivyside Cl S21 60 B3
Ivyside Gdns S21 60 B3

Jack's La ST14 224 C1
Jackass La DE56 167 D2
Jacklin Cl DE14 254 A3
Jacksdale Cl DE22 204 B1
Jacksdale Prim Sch NG16 171 D2
Jackson Ave Derby DE3 218 A1
Ilkeston DE7 208 C4
Sandiacre NG10 223 D3
Tupton S42 131 E4
Jackson Rd
Bramley-Vale S44 117 F1
Clay Cross S45 131 F2
Matlock DE4 143 D3
Jackson St Derby DE22 218 C2
Glossop SK13 17 E4
Mottram in L SK14 9 D2
Padfield SK13 10 B3
Jackson Tor Rd DE4 143 D3
Jackson's La Heage DE56 179 E4
Pentrich DE5 169 D4
Jacksons Edge Rd SK12 32 A3
Jacksons La Belper DE56 190 C4
Etwall DE65 229 E1
Jackys La S26 61 F3
Jacobean Ct DE15 248 B2
Jagger's La S32 52 C4
Jaggers La Ashover S45 128 C3
Darley Dale DE4 128 C3
Jago Ave S43 81 D2
James Andrew Cl S8 56 C4
James Andrew Cres S8 56 C4
James Andrew Croft S8 56 C4
James Cl DE1 218 C3
James St Chesterfield S41 96 A3
Glossop SK13 17 E4
Kimberley NG16 195 F3
Somercotes DE55 170 B4
Stoke-on-T ST4 269 E1
Swadlincote DE11 256 B3
James's La DE6 215 E1
Jane La SK23 34 A1
Jap La DE45 110 C4
Jarnett The SK17 107 D4
Jarvey's La DE22 217 F4
Jarvis Rd DE24 231 F1
Jasmin Cl NG20 119 E3
Jasmine Cl
Burton u T DE15 255 D4
Derby DE21 220 A3
Swanwick DE55 169 F4
Jaspers La DE4 153 D1
Jaunty Ave S12 44 B2
Jaunty Cl S12 44 A2
Jaunty Cres S12 44 B2
Jaunty Dr S12 44 A2
Jaunty La S12 44 A2
Jaunty Mount S12 44 B2
Jaunty Pl S12 44 A2
Jaunty Rd S12 44 B2
Jaunty View S12 44 B2
Jaunty Way S12 44 A2
Jaw Bones Hill S40 115 D4
Jawbone La DE73 252 B4
Jebb's La Idridgehay DE56 176 C4
Shottle DE56 177 D4
Jedburgh Cl Derby DE24 231 F1
Nottingham NG3 268 B2
Jefferson Pl DE24 232 C4
Jeffery St S2 43 D3
Jeffrey La S33 51 D3
Jeffries Ave DE4 156 C1
Jeffries La DE4 156 C1
Jellicoe St NG20 101 D1
Jemison Cl DE23 230 C4
Jenford St NG18 268 A3
Jennison St NG19 136 A1
Jenny's Ct DE56 179 E3
Jephson Rd DE14 254 A4
Jeremy Cl ST4 269 D1
Jermyn Ave S12 44 C2
Jermyn Cl S12 44 C2
Jermyn Cres S12 44 C2
Jermyn Dr S12 44 C2
Jermyn Way S12 44 C2
Jerningham St ST16 269 D4
Jersey Gdns NG3 268 C2
Jersey Rd S2 43 D4
Jervis Ct DE7 194 C2
Jervis Pl S43 97 D3
Jesses La DE56 178 B4
Jessop Ave NG16 170 C2
Jessop Dr DE24 231 F1
Jessop St Codnor DE5 181 D4
Ripley DE5 181 D4
Jinny Cl DE65 239 E4
Joan Ave DE75 181 F1
Joan La S33 40 B2
Jodrell Ave DE56 179 E2
Jodrell Meadow SK23 45 F4
Jodrell Rd SK23 45 E4
Jodrell St SK22 33 D4
John Bank La DE45 108 C4
John Berrysford Cl DE21 219 F3
John Dalton St SK13 9 F3
John Davies Prim Sch NG17 148 C2
John Duncan Sch SK17 66 A1
John Eaton's Almshouses S8 43 D1
John F Kennedy Gdns DE21 220 B3
John Flamsteed Com Sch DE5 180 A1
John Kennedy Gdn SK14 9 D4
John Kennedy Rd SK14 9 D2
John King Inf Sch NG16 160 B2
John King Workshop Mus NG16 160 B2
John Lombe Dr DE1 219 D4
John O'Gaunts Way DE56 179 E2
John of Rolleston Prim Sch DE13 240 A2
John Port Cl DE65 229 E2
John Port L Ctr DE65 229 D2
John Port Sch DE65 229 D2
John St Alfreton DE55 159 D2
Brimington S43 96 C4
Chesterfield S40 95 F2
Clay Cross S45 131 E2
Clowne S43 80 B2
Compstall SK6 15 D2
Creswell S80 81 F1
Derby DE1 267 C2
Eckington S21 59 E2
Glossop SK13 17 E4
Heanor DE75 181 E1
Ilkeston DE7 194 C1
Marple SK6 23 D3
Matlock DE4 143 D3
North Wingfield S42 131 F4
Somercotes DE55 170 B4
Stafford ST 16 269 F4
Swadlincote, Albert Village DE11 256 B1
Swadlincote, Lower Medway DE11 256 B3
Swadlincote, Newhall DE11 255 F3
John Turner Rd DE4 127 E2
Johnnygate La S18 75 D2
Johnson Ave DE24 232 C4
Johnson Dr DE75 181 F1
Johnson La
Idridgehay DE56 176 C4
Sheldon DE45 107 F3
Johnson Rd ST14 210 A1
Johnson St SK23 45 F4
Johnson Way SK23 47 E3
Johnstone Cl S40 266 A1
Jolly La DE6 175 D4
Jones St SK13 10 A3
Jordan Ave DE13 240 C1
Jordan St SK13 10 C1
Jordanthorpe Gn S8 57 E3
Jordanthorpe Parkway S8 57 E3
Jordanthorpe Sch S8 57 D3
Jordanthorpe View S8 57 E4
Joseph St Belper DE56 178 C2
Derby DE23 219 D1
Eckington S21 59 E2
Marple SK6 23 D3
Joseph Wright Terr DE1 267 B4
Joyce Ave NG9 223 F2
Jubalton Cl DE24 232 C3
Jubilee Ave DE5 169 E1
Jubilee Cl DE73 252 A4
Jubilee Cres Clowne S43 81 D2
Killamarsh S21 60 C4
Whitwell S80 81 F3
Jubilee Ct Belper DE56 179 D1
Wirksworth DE4 165 F4
Jubilee Gdns
New Mills SK22 33 E4
Whitwell S80 81 F3
Jubilee Pl S80 81 F3
Jubilee Rd
Chapel-en-le-F SK23 47 D3
Derby DE24 232 C2
Whitwell S80 81 F3
Jubilee Sq DE6 184 B4
Jubilee St
Kimberley NG16 195 F4
New Mills SK22 33 E4
Nottingham NG2 268 C1
Jubilee Terr DE12 262 C1
Judith Gr ST4 269 F1
Judy Hill DE4 127 F1
Julia Cres DE55 146 C2
Julian Cl DE7 209 D3
Julie Ave DE75 182 A1
Jumble Rd S11 42 C1
Junction Rd NG10 237 D3
Junction St DE1 218 C2
Juniper Ct NG16 195 E4
Juniper Rise S21 60 B3
Jura Ave DE5 169 E1
Jury St DE1 267 A3

Katherine Dr NG9 223 F2
Katrine Wlk DE24 231 F2
Kay Dr DE11 255 F3
Kean Pl DE24 232 C4
Kearsley Rd S2 43 D4
Kearyn St ST4 269 E1
Keats Ave DE23 218 A1
Keats Cl NG10 236 A3
Keats Dr DE11 256 B3
Keats Rd Chesterfield S41 95 F4
Stonebroom DE55 146 C2
Keats Way S42 115 F2
Keats Wlk DE55 146 C2
Keble Cl Burton u T DE15 248 B1
Derby DE1 267 C1
Kedleston Cl
Burton u T DE13 240 B1
Derby DE22 204 B1
Long Eaton NG10 236 A3
Ripley DE5 169 E2
Kedleston Dr DE7 194 B2
Kedleston Gdns DE1 267 A4
Kedleston Hall DE22 203 F3
Kedleston Old Rd DE22 218 B4
Kedleston Rd Buxton SK17 85 E4
Derby DE22 204 A3
Quarndon DE22 204 A3
Weston Underwood DE22 203 F4
Kedleston St DE1 267 A4
Keeling La DE4 126 A1
Keepers La S18 75 F2
Kegworth Ave DE23 231 E3
Keilder Ct S40 95 E1
Kelburn Ave S40 95 E1
Keldholme La DE24 233 E3
Kelham Gn NG3 268 C2
Kelham Rd NG19 268 A4
Kelmoor Rd DE24 233 D4
Kelsons Ave SK17 85 E3
Kelstedge La S45 129 E3
Kelvedon Gdns NG3 268 C2
Kelvin Cl NG9 223 E3
Kemble Pl DE24 232 C4
Kemp Cl S21 60 B3
Kemp Rd SK6 23 E4
Kempton Cl NG16 195 F4
Kempton Park Rd DE24 232 B4
Kempton Rd DE15 248 A2
Kendal Cl SK17 85 E2
Kendal Dr S18 56 C1
Kendal Rd S41 95 F4
Kendal Wlk DE21 205 E1
Kendon Ave DE23 231 F3
Kendray Cl DE56 179 E3
Kendricks Cl DE11 257 D4
Kenilworth Ave DE23 231 F4
Kenilworth Dr DE7 208 B3
Kenilworth Rd
Nottingham NG7 268 A1
Ripley DE5 169 E1
Kenmere Cl S45 131 E1
Kenmore Cl NG19 268 A3
Kenmore Gdns NG3 268 B2
Kennack Cl DE55 160 B3
Kennedy Ave
Long Eaton NG10 236 B3
Mansfield Woodhouse NG19 136 B2
Kennedy Cl DE21 220 A4
Kennedy Dr NG9 209 F1
Kennet Paddock NG19 136 B2
Kennet Vale S40 95 E3
Kenneth Gr SK17 84 C3
Kenning St S45 131 E2
Kenninghall Cl S2 43 E4
Kenninghall Dr S2 43 E4
Kenninghall Pl S2 43 E4
Kenninghall Rd S2 43 E4
Kensal Rise DE22 218 A3
Kensington Ave DE75 181 E1
Kensington Cl NG19 136 C3
Kensington Gdns DE7 208 C4
Kensington Jun Sch DE7 209 D4
Kensington Rd
Burton u T DE15 248 A2
Sandiacre NG10 223 D2
Kensington St Derby DE1 267 A3
Ilkeston DE7 208 C3
Kent Ave NG16 171 D2
Kent House Cl S12 58 C4
Kent Rd Burton u T DE15 254 C3
Eastwood NG16 195 E4
Glossop SK13 10 B1
Sheffield S8 43 D3
Kent St Chesterfield S41 115 E4
Derby DE21 219 F4
Nottingham NG1 268 B2
Kent's Bank Rd SK17 85 E3
Kentmere Cl 1 S18 56 C1
Kentwood Rd NG2 268 C1
Kenwell Dr S17 56 A3
Kenyon Rd S41 96 C1
Keppel Ct DE7 194 C2
Kepple Gate DE5 180 C4
Kernel Cl DE23 231 D4
Kerry Dr DE7 192 C3
Kerry St DE21 219 F4
Kerry's Yd DE56 191 F4
Kershaw St SK13 17 E4
Kershope Dr DE21 206 A2
Kerwin Cl S17 55 E4
Kerwin Dr S17 55 E4
Kerwin Rd S17 55 E4
Kestrel Ave DE11 256 C2
Kestrel Cl Ilkeston DE7 208 C2
Killamarsh S21 60 A4
Marple SK6 23 D2
Kestrel Dr S21 59 D2
Kestrel Hts NG16 170 C2
Kestrel Way DE15 248 B2
Kestrels Croft DE24 231 F2
Keswick Ave DE23 231 F3
Keswick Cl DE7 208 B3
Keswick Ct NG10 223 D1
Keswick Dr S41 95 E4
Keswick Pl S8 56 C4
Keswick St NG2 268 C1
Ketton Ave S8 43 D2
Kevin Cl DE21 220 A4
Kew Cres Heanor DE75 182 A1
Sheffield S12 44 A1
Kew Gdns DE22 218 A3
Key St NG2 268 C2
Keyhaven Cl DE21 219 E4
Keynsham Cl DE24 232 C4
Keys Rd DE55 159 D1
Keys St DE1 267 C4
Keyworth Cl NG19 268 A4
Kibworth Cl DE21 220 A4
Kidd Rd SK13 17 F3
Kidsley Cl 7 S40 95 D3
Kilbourn St NG3 268 B2
Kilburn Inf & Jun Schs DE56 191 F4
Kilburn La DE56 179 F2
Kilburn Rd Belper DE56 179 E2
Sheffield S8 56 C4
Kilburn Toll Bar DE56 179 F1
Kilburn Way DE11 255 F3
Kildale Gdns S20 59 E4
Kildare Rd DE21 220 A2
Kildonan Gr S12 44 B2
Killamarsh Inf Sch S21 60 C4
Killamarsh Jun Sch S21 60 C4
Killamarsh La S21 61 D3
Killingworth Ave DE24 231 F2
Killis La Belper DE56 179 E1
Holbrook DE56 191 E4
Kiln Bent Rd HD7 3 D3
Kiln Cl DE7 193 F1
Kiln Croft DE65 229 E2
Kiln La Hadfield SK13 10 A3
Parwich DE6 151 E1
Kiln Way DE11 256 B2
Kilnsey Ct DE23 230 C3
Kilvington Ave S13 44 A4
Kilvington Cres S13 44 A4
Kilvington Rd S13 44 A4
Kimberley Cl NG16 195 F3
Kimberley Dr DE15 248 B2
Kimberley Prim Sch NG16 195 F3
Kimberley Rd DE72 221 D1
Kinder Cl SK13 17 D4
Kinder Cres DE56 168 A3
Kinder Dr SK6 23 D3
Kinder Gr SK17 85 D3
Kinder Rd Hayfield SK22 25 E1
Staveley S43 97 D3
Kinder Row SK22 25 F1
Kinder View SK22 33 E4
Kinder Way SK17 85 F4
Kinder Wlk DE22 218 C2
King Alfred St DE22 267 A2
King Charles Ct SK13 17 E4
King Charles St
8 NG1 268 A1
King Ecgbert Lower Sch S17 55 E3
King Ecgbert Rd S17 55 F3
King Ecgbert Upper Sch S17 55 F3
King Edward Ave SK13 10 B1
King Edward Fst Sch NG18 268 C3
King Edward Gdns NG10 223 D3
King Edward St
Nottingham NG1 268 B2
Sandiacre NG10 223 D3
Shirebrook NG20 119 F2
Wirksworth DE4 166 A4
King Edward VI High Sch ST17 269 D3
King George Ave DE7 208 C4
King George St
Wessington DE55 157 F4
Wirksworth DE4 165 F4
King St Alfreton DE55 158 C2
Ashbourne DE6 173 E1
Bakewell DE45 109 E3
Belper DE56 178 C2
Brimington S43 77 F1
Broadbottom SK14 16 A4
Burton u T DE14 254 B4
Clay Cross S45 131 E2
Clowne S43 80 C2
Derby DE1 267 B4
Duffield DE56 190 C2
Eastwood NG16 182 C1
Glossop SK13 17 E4
Hodthorpe S80 82 B3
Hollingworth SK14 9 E3
Ilkeston DE7 194 C1
Long Eaton NG10 236 B4
Mansfield NG18 268 C4
Mansfield Woodhouse NG19 136 B1
Middleton (Nr Wirksworth) DE4 154 B3
Nottingham NG1 268 B2
Pinxton NG16 160 B2
South Normanton DE55 159 F3
Tibshelf DE55 148 A4
Warsop Vale NG20 120 B3
King St N S41 96 A4
King St S S40 115 D4
King William Ctr NG16 170 C2
King William St NG16 170 C2
King's Cl SK17 85 E4
King's Mead Cl DE1 267 A4
King's Mead Wlk DE1 267 A4
King's Mills La DE72 245 F3
King's Pl NG1 268 B1
King's Rd SK17 85 E4
Kingfisher Ave DE11 256 C2
Kingfisher Ho S41 77 D2
Kingfisher Wlk DE24 231 F1
Kings Cl Carsington DE4 164 C4
Clowne S43 80 C2
Creswell S80 81 F1
Heanor DE75 181 E1
Kings Coppice S17 55 E3
Kings Croft DE22 204 C2
Kings Ct DE1 267 B4
Kings Dr Brinsley NG16 182 C4
Derby DE3 218 A1
Kings Gate DE74 247 F2
Kings Hill DE4 153 D1
Kings Mews S21 59 F2
Kings Rd Sandiacre NG10 223 D3
Swadlincote DE11 256 A3
Kings Way S80 82 B3
Kingsbury Cl DE15 248 A2
Kingsbury Rd DE22 218 A3
Kingsclere Ave DE21 206 A1
Kingscroft Cl S17 55 F4
Kingsdale Cl NG10 236 A3
Kingsfield Ind Est DE4 165 F3
Kingsfield Rd DE4 165 F4
Kingsgate S32 72 B1
Kingsland Ave ST4 269 D1
Kingsland Cl DE21 205 F1
Kingsley Ave
Chesterfield S40 114 C4
Mansfield Woodhouse NG19 136 B3
Kingsley Cl NG19 136 B2
Kingsley Cres
Long Eaton NG10 236 A2
Stonebroom DE55 146 C2
Kingsley Ct NG19 136 B3
Kingsley Rd DE22 204 B2
Kingsley St DE24 231 F3
Kingsmead Ave NG9 209 E1
Kingsmead Hospl ST16 269 E4
Kingsmead Ind Est DE22 218 B3
Kingsmede Ave S40 95 E1
Kingsmoor Fields SK13 10 B2
Kingsmoor Rd SK13 10 B1
Kingsmuir Rd DE3 217 E2
Kingsthorpe Cl NG19 136 C1
Kingston Ave Ilkeston DE7 209 D2
Stafford ST 16 269 F4
Kingston Ct DE7 207 E4
Kingston Rd
Burton u T DE15 248 B1
Mansfield NG18 268 C4
Kingston St DE1 218 C4
Kingsway Derby DE22 218 A3
Heanor DE75 181 E1
Ilkeston DE7 209 D3
Stafford ST16 269 D3
Stoke-on-T ST4 269 E2
Kingsway Cres DE56 192 A4
Kingsway Hospl DE3 218 A2
Kingsway Ind Est DE22 218 B3
Kingsway Park Cl DE22 218 B3
Kingsway Ret Pk DE22 218 B3
Kingswood Ave DE56 179 E3
Kingswood Cl S41 95 E4
Kinross Ave DE21 219 E4
Kintyre Dr 11 DE24 231 E2
Kipling Cl S18 76 B4
Kipling Dr DE3 217 E1
Kipling Rd S41 95 F4
Kipling St 4 NG18 268 B4
Kirby La DE4 142 A4
Kirk Cl DE5 180 B4
Kirk Dale Ave DE21 220 C2
Kirk Hallam Com Sch DE7 208 B3
Kirk Ireton CE Prim Sch DE6 165 D1
Kirk Langley CE Prim Sch DE6 202 C1
Kirk Leys Ave N DE21 220 C2
Kirk Leys Ave S DE21 220 C2
Kirk St DE1 219 D4
Kirk's La DE56 179 D2
Kirkby Ave Ilkeston DE7 208 C3
Sheffield S12 44 A2
Kirkby Dr S12 44 A2
Kirkby Rd S12 44 A2
Kirkby View S12 44 A2
Kirkby Way S12 44 A2
Kirkcroft Ave S21 60 B4
Kirkcroft Dr S21 60 B3
Kirkcroft La S21 60 B3
Kirkdale Cl S40 115 D4
Kirkdale Gdns NG10 236 A3
Kirkdale Rd NG10 236 A3
Kirkewhite Ave NG10 236 B4
Kirkfield Dr DE72 235 E4
Kirkham Cl DE75 181 E1
Kirkham Dr NG9 223 F1
Kirkham La DE56 168 A4
Kirkham St ST4 269 E1
Kirkhill Sch S2 43 E4
Kirkistown Cl DE24 233 E3
Kirkland Ave NG18 268 A3
Kirkland Cl DE74 247 D2
Kirkland La ST4 269 E1
Kirkland Way 13 DE24 231 E2
Kirkman Rd DE75 181 E2
Kirkstead Cl Derby DE21 206 A1
Pinxton NG16 160 B2
Kirkstead Jun Sch NG16 160 B2
Kirkstead Rd NG16 160 B2
Kirkstone Ct NG10 223 D1
Kirkstone Rd Buxton SK17 85 E2
Chesterfield S41 95 E4
Kirton Ave NG10 236 B4
Kishfield La SK23 45 D3
Kissingate L Ctr NG20 119 F2
Kitchener Ave DE23 231 F4
Kitchener Dr NG18 268 C3
Kitchener Terr NG20 101 D1
Kitson Ave NG16 171 E2
Knab Rd DE4 127 F2
Knabhall La DE4 144 B3
Knapp Ave NG16 182 C1
Knifesmithgate S40 266 B3
Knight Ave ST 16 269 F4
Knight's La Bretby DE15 249 D3
Repton DE15 249 D3

Knighton St S42 131 F3
Knights Cl DE24 231 F1
Knights Ct DE13 240 C1
Knightsbridge DE22 218 A3
Knightwake Rd SK22 33 D4
Kniveton CE Prim Sch DE6 163 E1
Kniveton La DE6 174 B2
Kniveton Pk DE7 208 B4
Knob Fields DE11 261 F4
Knob La DE56 166 B3
Knoll Cl DE23 231 D4
Knoll St SK22 33 D4
Knoll The Chesterfield S40 94 C1
Dronfield S18 57 E2
Mansfield NG18 268 A3
Shirebrook NG20 119 E2
Swadlincote DE11 256 A3
Tansley DE4 144 A3
Knowes Cl SK17 85 F4
Knowes Cres SK17 85 E4
Knowl Ave DE56 178 C3
Knowl St ST4 269 E2
Knowle Ave SK23 47 D3
Knowle Rd SK6 23 E3
Knowle Top S20 59 F4
Knowles Hill DE13 240 A2
Knowles Ind Est SK23 33 E2
Knowleston Pl DE4 143 E2
Knutsford Gn DE21 205 E1
Kye La S26 61 F3
Kyle Gr DE21 206 A2
Kynance Cl Derby DE24 233 E3
South Normanton DE55 160 B3

Laburnam Cl S80 81 F1
Laburnham Ct S44 97 D2
Laburnham Ave NG20 119 F3
Laburnum Cl Bolsover S44 99 E1
Darley Dale DE4 127 D2
Sandiacre NG10 223 D4
South Normanton DE55 160 A4
Laburnum Cres Derby DE22 204 B2
Swanwick DE55 170 A4
Laburnum Gr Derby DE22 218 A3
Killamarsh S21 60 B3
Mansfield Woodhouse NG19 136 A2
Laburnum Rd
Burton u T DE15 254 C3
Swadlincote DE11 256 A3
Laburnum St S43 78 A1
Laburnum Way DE65 229 E2
Laceby Ct NG19 136 C2
Lacey Cl DE7 194 B2
Lacey Fields Rd DE75 182 A1
Ladbroke Gdns DE22 217 F3
Ladies Spring Dr S17 56 A4
Ladies Spring Gr S17 56 A4
Ladle End La DE12 253 E1
Lady Field Rd S80 62 B4
Lady Grove Rd DE4 127 F1
Lady Lea Rd DE21 192 A3
Lady Ley Hill DE21 192 A3
Lady Manners Sch DE45 109 E2
Lady Mantle Cl DE73 232 C1
Ladybank Rd Derby DE3 217 E1
Mosborough S20 59 E3
Ladybank View S21 59 E2
Ladybower Cl DE11 256 A1
Ladybower Ct 9 S17 56 A3
Ladybower Dr S32 53 D4
Ladybower La S43 97 E4
Ladybower Rd DE21 220 C2
Ladybrook La NG18 268 A4
Ladybrook Pl NG19 268 A4
Ladycroft SK17 66 B1
Ladycroft Paddock DE22 204 C2
Ladycross Inf Sch NG10 223 D3
Ladyfields DE11 256 B3
Ladyflatts Rd DE4 165 F4
Ladygrove Cotts DE23 219 D2
Ladylea Rd NG10 236 A2
Ladypit Rd SK23 33 F2
Ladysmith Rd DE72 221 D1
Ladythorne Ave SK6 23 D3
Ladywell Cl DE13 240 C1
Ladywell Ct DE56 179 D2
Ladywood Ave DE56 179 D3
Ladywood Dr S40 95 E4
Ladywood Prim Sch DE7 208 B3
Ladywood Rd Dale DE7 208 B3
Ilkeston DE7 208 B3
Lake Ave Heanor DE75 181 E2
Mansfield NG19 268 A4
Lake Dr Derby DE23 231 F4
Doveridge DE6 211 D1
Lake Side Doveridge DE6 211 D1
Hadfield SK13 10 A3
Lakeside Ashbourne DE6 173 E1
Bakewell DE45 109 D4
Wingerworth S42 114 C1
Lakeside Ave NG10 236 B3
Lakeside Cres NG10 236 B3
Lakeside Dr DE23 231 D4
Lakeside Inf Sch NG10 236 B3
Lamartine St NG3 268 B2
Lamb Cres DE5 169 F1
Lamb Hill Cl S13 44 B4
Lambcroft Rd NG16 160 B2
Lambe Ct DE23 267 C1
Lambgates SK13 10 A3
Lambhouse La DE56 177 F3
Lambley Dr DE22 204 B1
Lambourn Ct DE22 205 D2
Lambourn Dr DE22 205 D2
Lambourne Ave DE6 185 E4
Lambpart La S33 50 B3
Lambrook Cl DE3 217 E1
Lambton Cl DE7 194 C2
Lammascote Rd ST16 269 E4
Lampad Cl DE73 252 A4
Lampeter Cl DE21 206 A1
Lanark St DE21 219 F4
Lancaster Ave
Sandiacre NG10 223 D2
Stapleford NG9 223 F4
Lancaster Dr DE13 239 D3
Lancaster Rd S41 95 F4
Lancaster Sports Ctr DE1 267 B4
Lancaster St S44 117 F1
Lancaster Wlk DE21 221 D3
Lancelot Cl S40 114 B4
Lancelot Dr DE13 240 C1
Lancing Rd S2 43 D4
Landau Forte Coll DE1 267 C4
Lander La DE56 179 D2
Landmere Cl DE7 194 B2
Landon Cl S40 114 A4
Landsdown Gr NG10 223 F1
Landseer Cl Dronfield S18 56 C1
Sheffield S14 43 E1
Landseer Dr Marple SK6 23 E4
Sheffield S14 43 F1
Landseer Pl S14 43 F1
Landseer Wlk S14 43 F1
Lane Head Longnor SK17 121 D4
Stoney Middleton S32 71 E2
Lane Head Rd Totley S17 55 E2
Whaley Bridge SK23 45 E3
Lane The Awsworth NG16 195 E2
Spinkhill S21 60 B1
Lanes The DE4 155 D2
Lanesend Cotts SK23 46 A4
Laneside Ave NG9 223 F1
Laneside Cl SK23 47 D3
Laneside Rd New Mills SK22 33 F4
Rowarth SK22 24 C3
Laneward Cl DE7 194 B2
Lang Rd DE24 232 C3
Langdale Cl S40 94 C3
Langdale Dr Derby DE21 205 E1
Dronfield S18 57 E2
Long Eaton NG10 236 A3
Langdale Sq S43 96 B4
Langdon Cl NG10 223 D1
Langer Cl DE14 254 A3
Langer Field Ave S40 115 D4
Langer La
Chesterfield S40, S42 114 C3
Wingerworth S40, S42 114 C3
Langford Rd Derby DE3 217 E2
Mansfield NG19 268 A3
Langham Pl NG18 268 A4
Langhurst Rd S40 95 E2
Langley Ave Ilkeston DE7 194 B3
Somercotes DE55 170 B4
Langley Cl
3 Chesterfield S40 95 D3
Mansfield NG19 135 F1
Langley Ct SK13 10 A3
Langley Dr SK13 17 F4
Langley Inf Sch DE75 182 A1
Langley Mill CE Inf Sch NG16 182 A2
Langley Mill Jun Sch NG16 182 A2
Langley Mill Sta NG16 182 A2
Langley Pk NG16 182 A2
Langley Rd DE21 220 C2
Langley St DE22 218 B3
Langsett Dr DE73 233 D1
Langsett La SK13 9 E1
Langstone Ave S44 99 E1
Langton Hollow NG16 171 E3
Langtree Ave S41 77 D1
Langwith Bassett Prim Sch NG20 119 F4
Langwith Ctry Pk NG20 100 C1
Langwith Dr NG20 100 C1
Langwith Maltings NG20 119 F4
Langwith Rd Bolsover S44 118 B4
Shirebrook NG20 119 F3
Lansbury Ave
Mastin Moor S43 79 D2
Pilsley S45 132 B1
Lansbury Dr DE55 160 A3
Lansbury Rd S21 59 E2
Lanscombe Park Rd DE22 204 C1
Lansdowne Ave S41 95 F3
Lansdowne Rd
Branston DE14 253 F4
Brimington S43 96 B4
Buxton SK17 66 A1
Swadlincote DE11 256 A2
Lansing Gdns DE21 220 A3
Lant La DE4 144 A4
Lantern View SK22 24 A1
Lapwing Cl DE24 231 F1
Larch Ave Killamarsh S21 60 B3
Mansfield Woodhouse NG19 136 A3
Ripley DE5 169 E1
Shirebrook NG20 119 E2
Larch Cl DE22 204 B2
Larch Cres NG16 182 C1
Larch Dr NG10 223 D4
Larch Rd Eckington S21 59 D1
Kilburn DE56 192 A4
Swadlincote DE11 255 F3
Larch Way Chesterfield S40 95 E3
Glossop SK13 17 F4
Larchdale Cl DE55 160 A2
Larges St DE1 218 C3
Lark Cl DE23 231 E3
Larkdale St NG7 268 A2
Larkhill DE55 169 F4
Larkhill Cl DE55 169 F4
Larkhill Cres DE24 231 F2
Larkin Cl DE24 232 A3
Larklands Ave DE7 209 D4
Larklands Inf Sch DE7 209 D4
Larkspur Cl
Mansfield NG19 136 B1
South Normanton DE55 160 A2
Larkspur Ct DE21 206 A2
Larkstone La DE6 149 D1
Larpit Gn S80 82 A3
Lascelles Rd SK17 85 D4
Lashley Cl DE21 205 F1
Latham Cl DE15 248 B1
Lathbury Cl DE21 205 E1
Lathkil Dr DE55 159 F3
Lathkil Gr SK17 85 E4
Lathkill Ave Derby DE24 233 E4
Ilkeston DE7 194 C3
Staveley S43 97 E3
Lathkill Cl Sheffield S13 44 B4
West Hallam DE7 207 F4
Lathkill Dale DE11 255 F1
Lathkill Dr Ashbourne DE6 185 F4
Ripley DE5 180 B3
Selston NG16 171 F4
Lathkill Gr Clay Cross S45 131 E1
Tibshelf DE55 147 F3
Lathkill Rd Derby DE21 219 F4
Sheffield S13 44 B4
Lathkilldale Cres NG10 236 A3
Latimer Cl DE23 230 C4
Latimer St DE24 232 B3
Latrigg Cl DE3 217 F1
Lauder Cl DE24 231 F1
Launceston Rd DE24 233 D3
Laund Ave DE56 179 D3
Laund Cl DE56 179 D3
Laund Hill DE56 179 D3
Laund Nook DE56 179 D3
Launds Ave NG16 171 E4
Laurel Ave
Long Duckmanton S44 97 E2
Mansfield NG19 136 C1
Mansfield NG18 268 C3
Ripley DE5 169 E1
Laurel Cl Eckington S21 59 E1
Shirebrook NG20 119 E3
Swanwick DE55 170 A4
Laurel Cres Brimington S43 78 A1
Long Eaton NG10 236 B3
Smalley DE7 192 C3
Laurel Dr S21 60 B3
Laurel Garth Cl S41 77 D2
Laurel Gr Burton u T DE15 254 C3
South Normanton DE55 160 A2
Laurence Cl S41 77 D1
Laurie Pl DE24 232 C4
Lavender Rd DE55 170 A4
Lavender Row DE22 204 C1
Laverdene Ave S17 55 F2
Laverdene Cl S17 55 F2
Laverdene Dr S17 55 F2
Laverdene Rd S17 55 F2
Laverdene Way S17 55 F2
Laverick Rd NG16 171 D2
Lawn Ave Derby DE65 204 B1
Etwall DE65 229 E3
Lawn Cl DE75 181 F1
Lawn Heads Ave DE23 218 B1
Lawn Mill Rd NG16 195 F4
Lawn Prim Sch DE22 204 B1
Lawn Rd ST17 269 D3
Lawn The S18 57 D1
Lawn Villas S44 97 D1
Lawnfold SK13 9 F2
Lawnlea Cl DE23 231 F3
Lawns Dr DE11 256 A4
Lawns The
Aston-on-T DE72 246 A4
Rolleston DE13 240 A2
Uttoxeter ST14 210 A1
Lawnside DE21 220 C3
Lawnswood Cl DE23 231 E4
Lawrence Ave
Awsworth NG16 195 E2
Breaston DE72 235 E4
Derby DE21 220 A4
Eastwood NG16 182 C1
Holmewood S42 116 B1
Mansfield Woodhouse NG19 136 A2
Ripley DE5 180 B4
Lawrence Dr NG16 182 B4
Lawrence St Derby DE23 231 F4
Long Eaton NG10 236 B4
Sandiacre NG10 223 D4
Stafford ST17 269 E3
Stapleford NG9 223 E3
Lawson Ave NG10 236 C4
Lawson St NG7 268 A2
Laxfield Cl S40 114 B4
Layton Ave NG18 268 B4
Layton Burroughs
8 NG18 268 B4
Layton Dr S41 77 D1
Lea Cl DE22 204 C2
Lea Cres DE55 170 B3
Lea Dr
Derby, Chaddesden DE21 219 F3
Derby, Mickleover DE3 217 F2
Lea La NG16 171 F3
Lea Main Rd DE4 156 A4
Lea Moor Rd DE4 156 C4
Lea Prim Sch DE4 156 A4
Lea Rd Cromford DE4 155 E3
Dronfield S18 57 D1
Hayfield SK22 25 E2
Holloway DE4 156 A4
Lea St SK22 33 D4
Lea Vale DE55 160 A2
Lea Wood Croft DE4 156 A3
Leabrook Rd S18 56 B1
Leabrooks Ave NG19 136 B3
Leabrooks Rd DE55 170 B4
Leacroft Rd Derby DE23 219 D1
Winster DE4 141 E3
Leadale Ave DE55 170 A4
Leadale Cres NG19 136 C3
Leadbeater Ave ST4 269 D1
Leadbeater Rd S12 44 A2
Leafenden Cl DE22 205 D2
Leafgreen La DE23 231 E3
Leafield Rd SK12 32 B3
Leafy La DE75 181 F1
Leake St DE22 218 B3
Leam Glen NG19 136 B1
Leamington Cl DE23 218 B1
Leamington Dr DE55 160 A3
Leamington Rd DE14 253 F4
Leamington St DE5 169 F1
Leamoor Ave DE55 170 A4
Lean Town SK13 17 E3
Leander Cl DE23 231 E4
Leander Rise DE15 255 D4
Leaper St DE1 218 C3
Leapley La Alkmonton DE6 199 E2
Yeaveley DE6 199 E2
Leas Ave NG19 135 D3
Leas Park Jun Sch NG19 136 B2
Leas Rd NG19 136 B2
Leashaw Crich DE4 156 B2
Holloway DE4 156 B2
Leashaw Rd Crich DE4 156 B2
Holloway DE4 156 B2
Leaside Rd ST4 269 D1
Leason St ST4 269 E2
Leathersley La
Scropton DE6 226 B1
Sudbury DE6 226 B1
Leaway The NG20 119 E2
Leawood Gdns DE21 206 A2
Leawood Pump Ho DE4 155 F2
Leawood Rd DE11 256 B4
Leche Cft DE56 179 E2
Lechlade Cl DE7 207 E4
Ledbury Chase DE24 231 E1
Ledbury Pl DE21 205 E1
Ledo Ave DE5 169 E1
Lee Cres DE7 209 D4
Lee Dale SK17 85 E2
Lee Farm Cl DE73 232 C1
Lee Head SK13 16 B3
Lee La DE75 182 A1
Lee Mount SK13 17 E4
Lee Rd S41 96 C1
Lee Vale Dr SK13 16 B4
Leebangs Rd SK14 16 A4
Leech Ct NG16 195 D4
Leedhams Croft DE12 259 E4
Leeds Pl DE1 267 D2
Leeds Rd S81 63 F4
Leefield Rd SK23 47 D3
Leek Rd Buxton SK17 84 C3
Longnor SK17 121 D3
Stoke-on-T ST4 269 F2
Leeming La NG19, NG20 136 C4
Leeming La N NG19 136 C3
Leeming La S NG19 136 B1
Leeming Pk NG19 136 B2
Leeming St NG18 268 B4
Leen Valley Dr NG20 119 F2
Lees Brook Com Sch DE21 220 A4
Lees Hall Ave S8 43 D2
Lees Hall Pl S8 43 D3
Lees Hall Rd S8 43 D2
Lees Hill St NG2 268 C1
Lees House Ct S8 43 D2
Lees La DE55 159 F3
Lees Nook S8 43 D2
Lees Rd DE4 126 C2
Lees Row SK13 10 B3
Lees The DE24 233 E3
Leese St ST4 269 E2
Leeside Rd S33 40 B2
Leeswood Cl S41 95 E4
Leeway DE21 220 B2
Leicester Dr SK13 17 F4
Leicester St
Burton u T DE14 254 B4
Derby DE22 218 C2
Long Eaton NG10 236 C3
Leigh Rd Beeston NG9 223 F2
Disley SK12 32 A3
Leigh Way S42 131 F4
Leighton Dr Marple SK6 23 E4
Sheffield S14 43 F2
Leighton Pl S14 43 F2
Leighton Rd S14 43 F2
Leighton St NG3 268 C2
Leighton View S2 43 F3
Leisure La SK17 137 F3
Leman St DE22 218 C2
Lemont Rd S17 55 F2
Leniscar Ave DE75 181 E2
Lennox St NG1 268 B2
Lens Rd DE22 204 B1
Lenthall Inf Sch S18 57 D2
Lenton Ave Derby DE21 219 F3
Nottingham NG7 268 A1
Lenton Rd NG7 268 A1
Lenton St NG10 223 E4
Leominster Dr DE21 206 A1
Leonard Cl Derby DE23 267 B1
Sheffield S2 44 A4
Leonard St DE23 267 C1
Leopold St Derby DE1 267 B2
Long Eaton NG10 236 B4
Leslie Ave NG16 195 F3
Leslie Cl DE23 230 C4
Lesser La SK17 85 F4
Level La SK17 84 B3
Leven Cl DE24 231 F1
Levens Way S41 95 F4
Leveret Cl DE73 233 D1
Leverton Rd NG19 268 A4
Lewcote La DE7 194 A1
Lewis Cl NG3 268 B2
Lewis St Derby DE23 218 C1
Stoke-on-T ST4 269 E2
Lewiston Rd DE21 220 A3
Lexington Rd DE21 220 B3
Ley Ave DE55 159 D2
Ley Croft Hatton DE65 227 E1
Mansfield Woodhouse NG19 136 B3
Ley Gdns DE55 159 D2
Ley La
Mansfield Woodhouse NG19 136 B2
Marple SK6 23 E4
Leyburn Cl S40 95 F3
Leycote Way DE56 179 D3
Leyfield Rd S17 55 E4
Leygate View SK22 33 D4
Leyland Cl NG9 223 F1
Leyland Ct DE1 218 C4
Leyland Gdns DE1 218 C4
Leyland St DE1 218 C4
Leylands DE22 218 C4
Leylands La SK14 15 F4
Leys Ct DE56 179 E2
Leys Field Gdns DE73 233 D1
Leys Jun Sch DE55 159 E2
Leys La DE4 154 A4
Leys The Little Eaton DE21 191 E1
Swadlincote DE11 255 F3
Leytonstone Dr DE22 218 A3
Lichfield Ave DE11 256 C3
Lichfield Cl NG9 223 F2
Lichfield Ct ST17 269 E3
Lichfield Dr DE24 233 D4
Lichfield Rd
Barton Turn DE14 253 E2
Branston DE14 253 E2
Chesterfield S40 114 B4
Stafford ST17 269 E3
Lichford Rd S2 43 E3
Lickpenny La DE4 144 C2
Lid La DE6 197 F4
Liddle St ST4 269 E1
Lidgate Cl DE3 217 E1
Liffs Rd Alsop en le D DE6 150 B4
Biggin SK17 138 B1
Light Alders La SK12 32 A3
Lightfoot Rd ST14 210 A1
Lightwood Ave 3 SK17 85 E4
Lightwood House Hospl S8 43 F1
Lightwood La
Middle Handley S21 77 F4
Sheffield S14 43 F1
Lightwood Rd Buxton SK17 66 A1
Marsh Lane S21 58 C1
Lilac Ave DE22 218 A3
Lilac Cl Derby DE24 233 D3
Holmewood S44 116 C1
Lilac Gr Bolsover S44 99 E1
Burton u T DE15 254 C3
Glapwell S44 134 A4
Heanor DE75 181 F1
Market Warsop NG20 120 C4
Shirebrook NG20 119 F3
South Normanton DE55 160 A2
Lilac Mews DE7 194 B2
Lilac St S43 78 A1
Lilac Way Derby DE22 204 B1
Shirland DE55 146 B1
Lilian Prime Cl DE24 233 D4
Lilley St DE24 233 D3
Lillymede Cl S40 114 C3
Lilybank Cl DE4 143 E3
Lilypools The DE73 252 A4
Limb La S17 55 E4
Limbersitch La DE65 227 F3
Lime Ave
Derby, Breadsall Hilltop DE21 205 E1
Derby, Rose Hill DE1 267 A1
Duffield DE56 190 C3
Langley Mill NG16 182 B1
New Mills SK22 24 B1
Ripley DE5 169 E1
Staveley S43 78 C1
Lime Cl Calow S44 97 D2
Doveridge DE6 224 A4
Hatton DE65 227 E1
Pinxton NG16 160 B2
Lime Cres Belper DE56 179 D1
Market Warsop NG20 120 C4
Lime Gr Ashbourne DE6 185 E4
Burton u T DE15 254 C3
Darley Dale DE4 127 E2
Derby DE21 220 A3
Draycott DE72 234 C4
Long Eaton NG10 236 B4
Sandiacre NG10 223 D3
South Normanton DE55 160 A3
Stapleford NG9 223 E3

Lime Grove Ave DE4 143 E3
Lime Grove Wlk DE4 143 E3
Lime Kiln La Marple SK6 23 D3
Turnditch DE56 189 D4
Lime La Derby DE21 206 A2
Morley DE7 206 B3
Lime Rd S21 59 D1
Lime St Ilkeston DE7 208 C4
Stoke-on-T ST4 269 E1
Lime Terr NG10 236 B4
Lime Tree Ave
Darley Dale DE4 127 D2
Glapwell S44 134 A4
Killamarsh S21 60 B3
Mansfield Woodhouse NG19 136 A3
Swadlincote DE11 256 A4
Lime Tree Gr
Clay Cross S45 131 F1
Long Duckmanton S44 97 E2
Lime Tree Pl NG18 268 C3
Lime Tree Rd DE4 143 E3
Lime Wlk DE23 218 B1
Limecroft View S42 115 D2
Limedale Ave DE21 206 A2
Limekiln Fields Rd S44 99 D2
Limerick Rd DE21 220 A2
Limes Ave Derby DE3 217 E1
Nether Langwith NG20 101 D1
Limes Cl The DE4 143 E3
Limes Cres NG20 119 E3
Limes Pk DE5 169 E1
Limes The DE7 193 F2
Limestone Terr NG19 136 A2
Limetree Cl S43 96 C3
Limetree Rise DE7 208 B3
Limmen Gdns NG3 268 C2
Limpenny St NG7 268 A2
Linacre Ave S45 131 E1
Linacre Rd Chesterfield S40 95 D3
Old Brampton S40 95 D3
Linacre Way SK13 17 F4
Linacres Dr DE73 233 D1
Linbery Cl DE55 158 A2
Lincoln Ave Derby DE24 233 D4
Sandiacre NG10 223 D2
Lincoln Cir NG7 268 A1
Lincoln Cl Stapleford NG9 209 F1
Tibshelf DE55 148 A3
Lincoln Dr NG19 136 B2
Lincoln Gn DE73 232 C1
Lincoln Rd DE15 254 B4
Lincoln St Alfreton DE55 158 C2
Chesterfield S40 115 D4
Nottingham NG3 268 B2
Tibshelf DE55 148 A3
Lincoln Way Glossop SK13 17 F4
Swadlincote DE11 256 C3
Lindale Rd S41 76 B1
Linden Ave
Chesterfield S40 95 D1
Clay Cross S45 131 E1
Dronfield S18 57 D2
Linden Cl DE56 192 A4
Linden Ct S45 131 E1
Linden Dr S41 115 E3
Linden Gr Matlock DE4 143 E3
Sandiacre NG10 223 D4
Shirebrook NG20 119 F2
Stapleford NG9 223 F3
Linden Park Gr S40 95 E2
Linden Rd S80 81 F1
Linden St Mansfield NG19 136 A1
Shirebrook NG20 119 F2
Linden Way SK6 32 A4
Lindford Cl DE21 205 F2
Lindisfarne Cl 8 DE24 231 E2
Lindisfarne Ct 5 S40 95 E1
Lindisfarne Rd S18 76 A4
Lindley St Mansfield NG18 268 B4
Selston NG16 171 E3
Lindon Dr DE24 233 E3
Lindrick Cl Derby DE3 217 F1
Mansfield Woodhouse NG19 136 B3
Lindrick Gdns S40 114 B4
Lindsay Cl NG18 268 B3
Lindsey Cl DE21 219 F3
Lindum Gr NG2 268 C1
Lindway La
Brackenfield DE55 145 D1
Crich DE55 145 D1
Ling La S44 118 B2
Ling Rd S40 114 B4
Lingfield Rd DE14 253 F4
Lingfield Rise DE3 217 E2
Lingfoot Ave S8 57 D3
Lingfoot Cl S8 57 D3
Lingfoot Cres S8 57 E3
Lingfoot Dr S8 57 E3
Lingfoot Pl S8 57 D3
Lingfoot Wlk S8 57 E3
Linglongs Ave SK23 45 E3
Linglongs Rd SK23 45 E3
Lings Cres S42 132 A4
Linkmel Rd NG16 182 B2
Links Cl DE24 231 F2
Links Rd
Chapel-en-le-F SK23 46 C3
Dronfield S18 76 A4
Linley La S12 44 B3
Linley Rd ST4 269 D2
Linmell St NG3 268 C2
Linnet Cl DE21 220 C3
Linnet Ho S41 77 D2
Linscott Cl S41 95 E4
Linshaws Rd HD7 3 F3
Linton Prim Sch DE12 261 E3
Linton Rd Chesterfield S40 114 B4
Linton DE11 261 F4
Rosliston DE12 260 C3
Linwood Cres NG16 182 C1
Linwood Ct NG19 136 C2
Lion St ST4 269 E2
Lionel Gr ST4 269 D1
Lipp Ave S21 60 B4
Liskeard Dr DE22 204 B2
Lismore Ct 5 DE24 231 E2
Lismore Gr SK17 85 D4
Lismore Park SK17 85 D4
Lismore Rd Buxton SK17 85 D4
Sheffield S8 43 D3
Lissett Ave DE7 208 C4
Lister Ave S12 44 A2
Lister Cl Derby DE3 218 A2
Sheffield S12 44 A2
Lister Cres S12 44 A2
Lister Dr S12 44 A2
Lister Gate NG1 268 B1
Lister Pl S12 44 A2
Lister Way S12 44 A2
Liston Dr DE22 218 C4
Litchen Cl DE7 194 C1
Litchfield Cl NG10 237 D4
Litchurch La DE24 219 E1
Litchurch St DE1 267 C1
Little Acre NG19 136 C3
Little Bolehill DE4 155 D1
Little Breck DE55 160 A2
Little Bridge St DE1 218 C3
Little Brind Rd S40 95 D4
Little Debdale La NG19 135 F1
Little Eaton Prim Sch DE21 205 E4
Little Fen DE55 147 F3
Little Hallam Hill DE7 208 C3
Little Hallam La DE7 209 D3
Little La
Ashford in t W DE45 89 F1
Kimberley NG16 195 F3
Litton SK17 69 F2
Pleasleyhill NG19 135 D3
Sheffield S12 44 A3
Shirebrook NG20 119 E2
Sutton in A NG17 148 C1
Thorpe Salvin S80 63 D3
Tibshelf DE55 148 A3
Little London DE4 156 A3
Little Longstone Cl DE3 217 F1
Little Lunnon NG11 237 F3
Little Meadow Rd DE73 233 D1
Little Morton Rd S42, S45 132 A3
Little Norton Ave S8 57 D4
Little Norton Dr S8 57 D4
Little Norton La S8 57 D4
Little Norton Way S8 57 D4
Little Thorn Ind Est DE11 256 C1
Little Wood Dr S12 44 A2
Little Wood Rd S12 44 A2
Little Woodbury Dr DE23 230 C3
Littlebrook Cl SK13 10 A2
Littledale Cl DE21 206 B2
Littlefield La Ellastone DE6 183 D1
Snelston DE6 184 A2
Littlefield Rd DE65 227 E4
Littlefields SK14 9 D2
Littlemoor Chesterfield S41 95 E4
Eckington S21 59 F2
Littlemoor Cres S41 95 E4
Littlemoor Ctr 2 S41 95 F4
Littlemoor La DE4 143 F1
Littlemoor Rd SK14 9 D1
Littleover Com Sch DE23 230 C4
Littleover Cres DE23 218 B1
Littleover La DE23 231 F4
Littleton Cl ST 16 269 F4
Littlewell La DE7 208 C1
Littlewood La NG19 136 A3
Littleworth NG18 268 C3
Litton CE Prim Sch SK17 69 F2
Litton Cl Belper DE56 179 D3
Ilkeston DE7 194 C2
Staveley S43 97 E4
Litton Dr DE21 220 C2
Litton Mews SK13 9 F1
Litton Rd NG19 136 C2
Liverpool Rd ST4 269 E2
Liverpool St Derby DE21 219 F4
Nottingham NG3 268 C2
Liversage Pl DE1 267 C2
Liversage Rd DE1 267 C2
Liversage St DE1 267 C2
Livingstone Rd DE23 218 C1
Lloyd St Derby DE22 218 B3
Stafford ST16 269 E4
Loads Rd S42 113 D4
Loadshead La S42 112 B4
Lochinvar Cl DE21 220 C2
Lock Cl DE7 208 B3
Lock La Long Eaton NG10 236 B2
Sandiacre NG10 223 E2
Locke Way ST 16 269 F4
Lockington Cl DE73 232 C1
Lockington Rd DE74 247 E3
Locko Ct DE21 220 B3
Locko La S45 132 C2
Locko Rd Dale DE21 220 C4
Derby DE21 220 C4
Pilsley S45 132 B2
Lockoford La
Chesterfield, Stonegravels S41 96 A3
Chesterfield, Tapton S41 96 B3
Lockoford Rd S41 96 A3
Lockside SK6 23 D3
Lockton Ave DE75 193 F4
Lockwood Rd DE22 204 B2
Lode La DE6 149 F2
Lodge Ave DE6 185 D4
Lodge Bank SK13 10 A3
Lodge Cl Calow S43 97 D2
Duffield DE56 190 C2
Etwall DE65 229 E2
Lodge Ct SK14 9 D2
Lodge Dr Belper DE56 178 C3
Wingerworth S42 115 D2
Lodge Est DE72 246 A4
Lodge Farm Cl S40 114 B4
Lodge Hill DE13 239 F2
Lodge La Aldercar NG16 181 F4
Alstonefield DE6 149 D2
Derby, Little Chester DE1 267 A4
Derby, Spondon DE21 220 B2
Mackworth DE6, DE22 203 E3
Shottle DE56 177 E4
Lodge Mews DE72 246 A4
Lodge Moor Rd S10 42 C4
Lodge Pl S43 97 E3
Lodge Rd Eastwood NG16 195 D4
Long Eaton NG10 236 B3
Mapperley DE7 193 F2
Netherseal DE12 261 E1
Stoke-on-T ST4 269 D2
Lodge St DE72 235 D4
Lodge The Hadfield SK13 10 A3
Tideswell SK17 69 E1
Lodge Way DE3 217 E1
Lodge Wlk S43 97 E3
Lohengrin Ct DE13 240 C1
Lombard St DE22 217 F3
Lomond Ave DE24 231 F1
London Rd Buxton SK17 85 E3
Castle Donington DE74 247 D4
Derby DE24 219 E1
Nottingham NG2 268 B1
Shardlow DE72 234 C1
Sheffield, Heeley S8 43 D3
Sheffield, Highfield S2 43 D4
Stoke-on-T ST4 269 E1
London Rd S S2 43 D4
London St S43 77 E2
Long Acre View S20 60 A4
Long Bridge La DE24 232 B4
Long Croft DE72 246 A4
Long Eaton Com Sch NG10 236 B4
Long Eaton Lower Sch NG10 236 B3
Long Eaton Sta NG10 236 A3
Long Hill Buxton SK17, SK23 65 E2
Darley Dale DE4 127 E2
Whaley Bridge SK17, SK23 65 E2
Long La Alstonefield DE6 149 D3
Ashover S42 130 A3
Chapel-en-le-F SK23 47 D2
Charlesworth SK13 16 B4
Killamarsh S21 60 C3
Kirk Langley DE6 202 A1
Lees DE6 202 A1
Longford DE6 200 C1
Shipley DE75 194 B3
Shirebrook NG20 119 F2
Taddington SK17 87 F3
Thurvaston DE6 201 E1
Trusley DE6 201 E1
West Handley S21 77 E4
Whaley Bridge SK23 46 B2
Long Lane CE Prim Sch DE6 201 F1
Long Meadow
Great Cubley DE6 198 C1
Mansfield Woodhouse NG19 136 B3
Long Meadow Rd DE55 158 C2
Long Rake DE45 123 E2
Long Row Belper DE56 178 C2
Nottingham NG1 268 B1
Shardlow DE72 235 D1
Long Row Prim Sch DE56 178 C3
Long Row W NG1 268 B1
Long Shambles S40 266 B3
Long St DE15 254 C4
Longacre Rd S18 76 A4
Longacre Way S20 60 A4
Longbow Cl DE13 240 B1
Longbow Gr DE13 240 B1
Longbridge La
Heanor DE75 181 E2
Peak Dale SK17 67 D2
Longclough Dr SK13 17 D4
Longcourse La S44 98 A1
Longcroft Ave S18 56 B1
Longcroft Cl S42 131 E4
Longcroft Cres 2 S18 56 B1
Longcroft Rd S18 56 B1
Longcroft View S80 82 A3
Longdale NG19 136 C1
Longdale Dr SK14 9 D2
Longdale Gdns SK14 9 D2
Longden Cl NG9 209 F1
Longden St NG3 268 C2
Longdendale High Sch SK14 9 E3
Longedge Gr S42 115 D2
Longedge La S42 114 C2
Longedge Rise S42 115 D2
Longfield Cres DE7 208 C3
Longfield La DE7 208 C3
Longfield Rd ST4 269 D2
Longford Cl Derby DE22 204 B1
8 Sheffield S17 56 A3
Longford Cres S17 56 A3
Longford Dr S17 55 F2
Longford La DE6 214 C4
Longford Parochial CE Prim Sch DE6 214 B4
Longford Rd S17 56 A2
Longford Spinney S17 55 F2
Longford St DE22 218 C4
Longhedge La
Burton u T DE13 239 F1
Pleasley NG19 134 C3
Longhurst La SK6 23 E3
Longhurst View S80 81 F3
Longlands S44 99 D1
Longlands Dr SK22 33 D4
Longlands La DE65 230 B1
Longlands Rd
New Mills SK22 33 D4
Swadlincote DE11 256 B4
Longley La DE21 220 B3
Longload La DE4 154 C3
Longmeade Dr SK23 47 D2
Longmoor Gdns NG10 223 D1
Longmoor La
Breaston DE72 222 C1
Sandiacre NG10 223 D2
Longmoor Prim Sch NG10 223 E2
Longmoor Rd Glossop SK13 17 D4
Long Eaton NG10 223 D1
Longnor Mews SK13 9 E1
Longreave La DE45 90 B2
Longrose La DE6 163 D1
Longshaw Cl
North Wingfield S42 131 F3
Staveley S43 97 E4
Longshaw Ctry Pk S32 54 A2
Longside Rd S42 112 C3
Longson Rd SK23 47 E3
Longster La NG20 120 B2
Longstock Cl DE21 205 F1
Longstone CE Prim Sch DE45 89 F2
Longstone Cres S12 44 B2
Longstone La DE45 89 F1
Longstone Rise DE56 179 D3
Longstone Wlk DE1 267 A2
Longthorpe Cl DE23 231 D4
Longwalls La DE56 178 B3
Longwood Inf Sch NG16 160 B1
Longwood Rd NG16 160 C1
Lons Inf Sch DE5 169 E1
Lonsdale Dr NG9 223 F1
Lonsdale Gr DE4 142 C4
Lonsdale Pl DE22 218 B2
Lonsdale Rd
Branston DE14 254 A4
Pilsley S45 132 A1
Lonsdale St ST4 269 E1
Loosemore Dr S12 43 F3
Lord Haddon Rd DE7 194 C1
Lord Nelson St NG2 268 C1
Lord Roberts Rd S40 266 B1
Lord St Derby DE24 232 B3
Glossop SK13 10 B1
Hollingworth SK14 9 E2
Mansfield NG18 268 B3
Nottingham NG2 268 C1
Lords Cl S44 99 D1
Lordship La ST4 269 F2
Lordsmill St S41 266 C2
Lorne Cl S18 56 B1
Lorne St DE22 218 C2
Lorraine Cl DE24 232 C2
Loscoe CE Prim Sch DE75 181 E2
Loscoe Grange DE75 181 E2
Loscoe Rd Derby DE21 206 A1
Heanor DE75 181 E1
Loscoe-denby La DE5, DE75 181 D2
Losk Cnr S44 118 B1
Losk La S44 118 B2
Lothian Pl
Castle Donington DE74 247 D2
Derby DE21 219 F4
Lothlorien Cl DE23 231 D4
Loudon St DE23 219 D2
Loudoun Pl DE74 247 D2
Loughborough Ave NG2 268 C1
Loundes Rd S18 76 C3
Loundsley Ct S40 94 C2
Loundsley Green Rd S40 95 E3
Lount La DE13 239 F1
Lousie Greaves La DE21 220 C3
Louvain Rd DE23 218 B1
Louwil Ave NG19 136 C3
Lovatt Cl DE13 240 C1
Lovatt St ST4 269 E2
Love La DE55 147 E2
Low Cl DE6 189 D1
Low Comm S21 79 E4
Low Lea Rd SK6 23 D3
Low Leighton Rd SK22 33 E4
Low Meadow SK23 45 E4
Low Pavement
Chesterfield S40 266 B3
4 Nottingham NG1 268 B1
Low's La DE7 209 D1
Lowburn Rd S13 44 B4
Lowdham St NG3 268 C2
Lowe St Derby DE24 232 C3
Stoke-on-T ST4 269 E2
Lowedges Cres S8 56 C3
Lowedges Dr S8 56 C3
Lowedges Pl S8 57 D3
Lowedges Prim Sch S8 56 C3
Lowedges Rd S8 56 C3
Lower Bagthorpe NG16 171 F2
Lower Bank SK13 17 E4
Lower Barn Rd SK13 9 F2
Lower Bloomsgrove Rd DE7 194 C1
Lower Brook St NG10 236 C4
Lower Chapel St
18 Ilkeston DE7 194 C1
Stonebroom DE55 147 D2
Lower Clara Mount Rd DE75 182 A1
Lower Cres ST4 269 D2
Lower Dale Rd DE23 218 C1
Lower Dr DE55 169 E4
Lower Dunstead Rd
Aldercar NG16 182 A2
Langley Mill NG16 182 A2
Lower Eaves View SK23 47 E3
Lower Eldon St NG2 268 C1
Lower Eley St DE1 267 A1
Lower Fold SK6 23 D4
Lower Gladstone St DE75 181 F1
Lower Gn DE65 230 B1
Lower Granby St DE7 194 C1
Lower Greenshall La SK12 32 C3
Lower Grove Rd S40 266 A3
Lower Hague SK22 32 C4
Lower Hall Cl DE56 191 E3
Lower Hardwick St 1 SK17 85 D4
Lower High St DE13 239 E4
Lower La SK23 34 B1
Lower Macclesfield Rd SK23 45 F3
Lower Mantle Cl S45 131 E2
Lower Maples DE75 194 A4
Lower Market St SK14 16 A4
Lower Middleton St DE7 195 D1
Lower Nelson St DE75 181 E1
Lower Orchard St NG9 223 E4
Lower Park St NG9 223 E3
Lower Parliament St NG1 268 B1
Lower Rd DE22 217 F4
Lower Somercotes DE55 170 C4
Lower Sq SK13 10 A4
Lower St DE6 224 A4
Lower Stanton Rd DE7 208 C3
Lower Strines Rd SK6 23 D3
Lower Terr Rd SK17 69 D3
Lower Whitworth Rd DE7 208 C3
Lowerlea SK12 32 B3
Lowery Dr SK6 23 D4
Lowes Hill DE5 169 E2
Lowes La DE73 244 B4
Lowfield Ave S12 58 C4
Lowfield Ct S2 43 D4
Lowfield Prim Sch S2 43 D4
Lowfields S43 79 D1
Lowgates S43 79 D1
Lowlands Lea DE75 181 F1
Lowlands Rd DE56 179 D2
Lowndes Cl ST4 269 D1
Lowry Ct SK14 9 D2
Lowry Dr S18 56 C1
Lowside S32 72 B1
Lowside Cl S32 72 A1
Loxley Cl Chesterfield S40 95 D2
Derby DE21 206 A1
Loxton Ct DE3 217 E2
Loyne Cl DE24 231 F1
Lucas La DE65 228 C1
Lucas Rd S41 95 F3
Lucas Terr SK22 25 E2
Luccombe Dr DE24 233 E3
Lucerne Rd DE21 206 B2
Ludborough Wlk NG19 136 C2
Ludgate St DE13 239 E3
Ludgate Wlk DE22 217 F3
Ludham Cl S41 95 F4
Ludham Gdns S41 95 F4
Ludlam Ave NG16 195 D4
Ludlow Cl DE21 220 C3
Ludworth Prim Sch SK6 23 D4
Luke La DE6 201 F4
Lukesland Ave ST4 269 D1
Lullington Rd
Clifton Campville B79 263 F2
Overseal DE12 262 A2
Lulworth Cl DE23 231 E3
Lulworth Ct NG16 195 F4
Lum's Hill Rise DE4 143 E3
Lumb La Hazelwood DE56 178 A2
Northwood DE4 127 D3
Lumber La DE6 176 B1
Lumsdale Cres DE4 143 E3
Lumsdale Rd Matlock DE4 143 F3
Staveley S43 97 E4
Luna Croft S12 43 F1
Lundie Cl DE24 231 E1
Lundy Rd S18 76 A4
Lune Meadow NG19 136 C2
Lupin Cl DE21 206 B2
Lupin Way S44 97 D2
Lupton Cres S8 56 C3
Lupton Dr S8 56 C3
Lupton Rd S8 56 C3
Lupton Wlk S8 57 D3
Lwr Bank Cl SK13 9 F2
Lychgate Cl DE21 205 E1
Lydden Cl S43 96 C4
Lydford Ave S41 77 D1
Lydford Rd DE55 159 D3
Lydgate S32 71 F3
Lydgate Dr S42 114 C2
Lydia Gdns NG16 182 C1
Lydstep Cl DE21 206 B1
Lyle Cl NG16 195 F4
Lyme Hall SK12 32 A1

Lyme Park Ctry Pk SK12 32 A1
Lyme Pk SK23 34 C1
Lyme Rd SK12 32 A3
Lymefield Terr SK14 16 A4
Lymewood Dr SK12 32 B3
Lynam Cl S45 131 F2
Lynam Rd Fritchley DE56 168 B4
South Wingfield DE56 168 B4
Lynam St ST4 269 E2
Lyncroft Ave DE5 169 F1
Lyndale Dr DE5 181 D4
Lynden Ave NG10 236 B3
Lyndhurst Gr DE21 220 A3
Lyndhurst Rd NG2 268 C1
Lyndhurst St DE23 219 D1
Lyne Ave SK13 17 D4
Lynholmes Rd DE4 143 E3
Lynmouth Dr DE7 194 B2
Lynne Cl SK13 17 F4
Lynton Cl DE5 169 E2
Lynton Rd DE56 168 A2
Lynton St DE22 218 C2
Lynwood Cl
Branston DE14 253 F4
19 Dronfield S18 56 B1
Lynwood Rd
Branston DE14 253 F4
Derby DE24 231 F2
Lytham Cl DE21 205 E1
Lyttelton St DE22 218 B3
Lytton Cl NG3 268 C2
Lytton St ST4 269 F2

Macaulay St DE24 232 A3
Macclesfield Main Rd SK17 84 B3
Macclesfield Old Rd SK17 84 B3
Macclesfield Rd
Buxton SK17 85 D3
Whaley Bridge SK23 45 E3
Macdonald Cl S42 115 F2
Macdonald Sq DE7 208 B3
Machins Ct S18 57 D1
Mackenzie St DE22 218 B3
Mackinley Ave NG9 209 F1
Macklin St DE1 267 B3
Mackworth Coll DE1 267 B2
Mackworth Tertiary Coll DE22 218 A3
Maclagan St ST4 269 E1
Macready Pl DE24 232 C4
Macworth Rd DE1 218 C3
Maddock La DE4 153 D1
Madehurst Gdns S2 43 D4
Madehurst Rd S2 43 D4
Madehurst Rise S2 43 D4
Madehurst View S2 43 D4
Madeley Ct DE3 217 E1
Madeley St DE23 219 D1
Madin Dr S43 97 D3
Madin St Chesterfield S41 266 B4
Tupton S42 131 E4
Madison Ave DE21 219 F4
Madras Rd DE15 248 B2
Mag La Idridgehay DE56 176 B3
Whaley NG20 100 B3
Magnolia Way DE55 170 A4
Magson St NG3 268 C2
Maguere Ave SK13 10 A3
Maid Marian Way NG1 268 B1
Maidstone Dr DE24 232 C3
Maidwell Cl DE56 179 E3
Main Ave Derby DE22 204 C3
Totley S17 55 F2
Main Rd Aston DE6 226 A2
Bamford S33 40 A2
Bradwell S33 51 D4
Brailsford DE6 201 F4
Crich DE4 156 B1
Elvaston DE72 234 A3
Flagg SK17 106 C3
Grindleford S32 72 B4
Hathersage S32 53 D4
Heath S44 117 D1
Holmesfield S18 75 D4
Marsh Lane S21 58 C2
Morton DE55 147 D3
Nether Langwith NG20 101 D1
Old Brampton S42 94 C4
Pentrich DE5 169 E3
Renishaw S21 79 D4
Ridgeway S12 58 C4
Ripley DE5 169 D2
Shirland DE55 146 B1
Smalley DE7 192 C2
Somercotes DE55 170 C3
Stretton DE55 146 B3
Stretton DE55 146 B3
Sudbury DE6 225 F3
Taddington SK17 88 A2
Underwood Green NG16 171 F1
Unstone S18 76 C4
Wensley DE4 127 E1
West Handley S21 77 E4
Westwood NG16 171 D2
Main St Awsworth NG16 195 E3
Blackfordby DE11 257 E1
Bolsover S44 117 F4
Branston DE14 253 F4
Breaston DE72 235 E4
Breedon on t H DE73 252 C1
Brinsley NG16 171 E1
Burnaston DE65 229 F3
Burton u T, Stapenhill DE15 254 C4
Burton u T, Stretton DE13 240 C1
Caldwell DE12 260 C4

Main St continued
Calver S32 72 B1
Chelmorton SK17 106 A4
Church Broughton DE65 227 D4
Clifton Campville B79 263 F1
Coton in t E DE12 260 B2
Eastwood NG16 182 C1
Eggington DE65 241 D3
Elvaston DE72 234 B3
Etwall DE65 229 D2
Findern DE65 230 B1
Great Longstone DE45 90 A2
Hartshorne DE11 257 D3
Hemington DE74 247 E3
Hilton DE65 228 B1
Horsley Woodhouse DE7 192 B3
Kimberley NG16 195 F3
Kirk Ireton DE6 165 D1
Linton DE12 261 E3
Lockington DE74 247 F3
Long Eaton NG10 236 C4
Mapperley DE7 193 F2
Melbourne DE73 245 E1
Middleton (Nr Wirksworth) DE4 154 B2
Milton DE65 243 D1
Moira DE11 256 B1
Netherseal DE12 264 C4
Newton DE55 148 A2
Newton Solney DE15 248 C4
Over Haddon DE45 109 D1
Overseal DE12 262 A2
Palterton S44 118 A3
Repton DE65 242 B1
Rosliston DE12 260 B3
Scarcliffe S44 118 C3
Shirebrook NG20 119 E2
Smisby LE65 257 F2
South Normanton DE55 160 A3
Stanton-by-D DE7 222 C4
Sutton in A NG17 148 C2
Swadlincote DE12 255 F3
Tatenhill DE13 253 D4
Ticknall DE73 251 D3
Walton-on-T DE12 253 E1
Weston-on-T DE72 245 F3
Whaley Thorns S44 101 D1
Wilson DE73 252 C3
Winster DE4 141 E3
Maine Dr DE21 220 A3
Mais Cl DE4 144 A3
Makeney Rd Belper DE56 191 D3
Duffield DE56 190 C1
Holbrook DE56 191 E3
Malbon's Yd DE6 173 E1
Malcolm Gr DE23 230 C4
Malcolm St DE23 219 D1
Malham Cl S40 95 E3
Malham Gdns S20 59 E4
Malham Gr S20 59 F4
Malham Rd DE23 230 C3
Malia Rd S41 96 B3
Malin Cl DE24 233 D3
Malinscommon La DE56 166 B2
Malkin St S41 266 C3
Mallard Cl Killamarsh S21 60 A4
Shirebrook NG20 119 F2
Mallatratt Pl NG19 136 A3
Malmesbury Ave DE11 256 B3
Malpas Rd DE4 143 D3
Malson Way S41 95 F3
Malt Mill La ST16 269 E4
Maltby Ave DE55 146 C3
Maltby Cl DE22 204 C1
Malthouse Cl
Eastwood NG16 182 C1
Wirksworth DE4 154 C2
Malthouse Ct DE6 173 E1
Malthouse La Ashover S45 129 F2
Froggatt S32 72 B3
Hatton DE65 227 E2
Nether Heage DE56 168 A1
Malthouse Rd S80 82 A3
Maltings The
Burton u T DE15 248 A1
Shardlow DE72 235 D1
Maltmill La NG1 268 B1
Malton Pl DE21 205 E1
Malvern Ave DE15 248 A1
Malvern Cl Derby DE3 217 E2
Stafford ST17 269 F3
Malvern Gdns
5 Long Eaton NG10 236 A4
Matlock DE4 143 D3
Malvern Rd S40 95 F2
Malvern Rise SK13 10 A3
Malvern Way DE21 205 E1
Manchester La DE11 257 E3
Manchester Rd Buxton SK17 65 F1
Chapel-en-le-F SK23 46 C3
Tideswell SK17 69 D3
Tintwistle SK13 9 F4
Manchester St Derby DE22 218 B3
Long Eaton NG10 236 B3
Manifold Ave
Ashbourne DE6 173 E1
Staveley S43 97 E4
Manifold Dr Derby DE24 233 D4
Selston NG16 171 F4
Manitoba Way NG16 171 F4
Manknell Rd S41 96 A4
Manners Ave DE7 194 B1
Manners Cl SK23 34 B1
Manners Ind Est DE7 194 C1
Manners Rd DE7 194 C1
Manners St DE7 209 D3
Manning View DE7 194 C1
Mannion Cres NG10 236 A3

Manor Ave Brimington S43 96 C4
Derby DE23 218 B2
Stapleford NG9 223 E4
Manor Bglws S18 56 C1
Manor Cl Brassington DE4 153 D1
Newton DE55 148 A2
Pilsley S45 132 B1
Swadlincote DE15 255 D3
Manor Coll S40 266 A3
Manor Comp Lower Sch NG19 136 A1
Manor Comp Mid Sch NG19 136 B3
Manor Comp Upper Sch NG19 136 B3
Manor Court Rd S44 98 C2
Manor Cres
Burton u T DE15 255 D3
Chesterfield S40 95 E2
Dronfield S18 56 C1
Manor Croft DE5 169 E2
Manor Ct Barrow u T DE73 244 A3
Breaston DE72 235 F4
Clowne S43 80 C2
Somercotes DE55 170 C3
Manor Ct St ST4 269 D1
Manor Dr Brimington S43 96 C4
Chesterfield S40 95 E2
Netherseal DE12 264 C3
Manor Farm Ct S80 81 F3
Manor Farm Mews
Burnaston DE65 229 F3
Long Duckmanton S44 98 A2
Manor Farm Rd DE72 246 A4
Manor Fields Dr DE7 208 B4
Manor Gr S43 80 A4
Manor House Rd NG10 236 C3
Manor Inf Sch S43 96 C3
Manor Leigh DE72 235 F4
Manor Park Ct DE3 218 A2
Manor Park Rd SK13 10 C1
Manor Park View SK13 10 C1
Manor Park Way DE3 218 A2
Manor Pk DE72 221 D1
Manor Rd Ashbourne DE6 173 E2
Barlborough S43 80 A4
Barton in F NG11 237 F3
Belper DE56 178 C2
Borrowash DE72 221 D1
Calow S43 96 C3
Chesterfield S40 95 E2
Derby, California DE23 218 B1
Derby, Chellaston DE73 232 C1
Eastwood NG16 182 C1
Harthill S26 61 F4
Ilkeston DE7 194 C1
Killamarsh S21 60 C3
Mansfield Woodhouse NG19 136 A2
South Wingfield DE55 157 F2
Swadlincote DE15 255 D3
Whaley Bridge SK23 45 F3
Manor St Glossop SK13 10 B1
Nottingham NG2 268 C1
Manor View S20 59 F4
Manse Ave S80 100 B4
Manse Cl S80 100 B4
Mansell Cl ST16 269 D3
Mansfeldt Cres S41 95 F3
Mansfeldt Rd S41 95 F3
Mansfield Comm Hospl NG18 268 B3
Mansfield Dr S12 44 B3
Mansfield Gr NG1 268 A2
Mansfield Rd
Alfreton DE55 159 D2
Bramley-Vale S44 117 F1
Brinsley NG16 182 C2
Chesterfield S44 115 F3
Clowne S43 80 C1
Creswell S80 81 F1
Derby DE1 219 D4
Eastwood NG16 182 C2
Glapwell S44 134 B4
Heanor DE75 182 A1
Heath S44 117 D2
Killamarsh S21, S26 60 C3
Mansfield Woodhouse NG19 136 B1
Market Warsop NG20 120 C1
Nottingham NG1 268 B2
Palterton S44 118 A3
Scarcliffe S44 118 B3
Selston NG16 171 F4
Sheffield S12 44 B3
South Normanton DE55 160 B3
Temple Normanton S42 116 B2
Tibshelf DE55 148 A4
Worksop S80 82 C4
Mansfield St Derby DE1 267 B5
Somercotes DE55 170 B4
Mansfield Woodhouse Sta NG19 136 A2
Mansfields Croft DE65 229 D2
Manton Cl DE11 255 F3
Manvers Ave DE5 169 F1
Manvers Ct NG20 120 A2
Manvers Rd S44 97 D2
Manvers St
1 Mansfield NG18 268 B4
Mansfield Woodhouse NG19 136 A2
Market Warsop NG20 120 A2
Nottingham NG2 268 C1
Ripley DE5 169 F1
Manystones La DE4 153 D2
Maple Ave Derby DE23 231 E3
Disley SK12 33 D3
Ripley DE5 180 B4
Sandiacre NG10 223 D4

Maple Cl Doveridge DE6 211 D1
Mansfield NG19 136 C1
Maple Dr Ashbourne DE6 185 E4
Belper DE56 179 D1
Creswell S80 81 F1
Derby, Boulton DE24 233 D3
Derby, Chellaston DE73 233 D1
Killamarsh S21 60 B3
South Normanton DE55 160 A2
Maple Gdns DE75 181 E1
Maple Gr Breaston DE72 235 F4
Burton u T DE15 254 C3
Derby DE72 204 B3
Glapwell S44 134 A4
Maple Rd DE11 256 A3
Maple St S43 97 D4
Maple Way DE14 254 A4
Maplebeck Ct DE1 267 B5
Mapletoft Ave NG19 136 A3
Mapleton Ave DE21 205 F1
Mapleton Rd
Ashbourne DE6 173 D1
Draycott DE72 235 D4
Mapperley CE Prim Sch DE7 193 F2
Mapperley La DE7 193 F1
Mapperley Rd 6 S18 56 B1
Marchington Cl DE22 204 C1
Marchington Ind Est ST14 224 C1
Marchwood Cl S40 95 F2
Marchwood Ct ST4 269 D1
Marcus St DE1 219 D4
Mardale Cl S41 76 C1
Maree Cl DE24 231 F2
Marfleet Cl DE3 217 E2
Margaret Ave Derby DE21 219 F3
Ilkeston DE7 208 C4
Long Eaton NG10 223 F1
Sandiacre NG10 223 D2
Margaret St DE1 267 B5
Margreave Rd DE21 219 F4
Marham Cl NG2 268 C1
Marigold Cl DE21 206 A2
Marina Dr
Derby, Allenton DE24 232 C3
Derby, Spondon DE21 220 B3
Marina Rd DE7 193 D4
Marion Ct SK17 85 E3
Marjorie Rd DE21 219 F4
Marjory La DE6 213 E2
Mark St NG10 223 E3
Mark's Cl DE23 231 E3
Markeaton La DE22 218 A4
Markeaton Prim Sch DE22 218 C4
Markeaton St DE22 218 C3
Market Cl Shirebrook NG20 119 F2
South Normanton DE55 160 A3
Market Pl Ashbourne DE6 173 E1
Belper DE56 179 D2
Bolsover S44 99 D1
5 Buxton SK17 85 D4
Castleton S33 38 B1
Chapel-en-le-F SK23 47 D3
Chesterfield S40 266 B3
Codnor DE5 181 D4
Crich DE4 156 C1
Cromford DE4 155 D3
Ilkeston DE7 208 C4
Ironville NG16 170 C2
Long Eaton NG10 236 C4
Longnor SK17 121 D3
Mansfield NG18 268 B4
Mansfield Woodhouse NG19 136 B2
Melbourne DE73 252 A4
Mottram in L SK14 9 D2
Riddings DE55 170 C3
Ripley DE5 169 E1
Somercotes DE55 170 B4
South Normanton DE55 160 A3
Staveley S43 78 C1
Sutton in A NG17 148 C2
Tideswell SK17 69 E2
Wirksworth DE4 165 F4
Market Sq 10 Stafford ST16 269 E4
Tideswell SK17 69 E2
Market St Bakewell DE45 109 E3
Broadbottom SK14 16 A4
Buxton SK17 85 D4
Castle Donington DE74 247 D2
Chapel-en-le-F SK23 47 D3
Clay Cross S45 131 E2
Disley SK12 32 B3
Draycott DE72 235 D4
Eckington S21 59 E2
Glossop SK13 10 B1
Hayfield SK22 25 E2
Heanor DE75 181 F1
Hollingworth SK14 9 E3
Ilkeston DE7 208 C4
Ironville NG16 170 C2
Mansfield NG18 268 B4
Mottram in L SK14 9 D2
New Mills SK22 33 D4
Nottingham NG1 268 B1
Shirebrook NG20 119 F2
South Normanton DE55 160 A3
Stafford ST16 269 E4
Staveley S43 78 C1
Sutton in A NG17 148 C2
Swadlincote DE11 256 A2
Swadlincote, Church Gresley DE11 256 A1
Whaley Bridge SK23 45 F4
Markham Cres S43 78 C1
Markham Ct DE21 205 F1

Markham La S44 98 A2
Markham Rd
Chesterfield S40 266 B2
Long Duckmanton S44 98 A3
Markham Rise S45 131 D2
Markland Ave S43 81 D2
Markland La S80 81 D1
Markland View S80 81 E2
Marlborough Cres DE15 255 D4
Marlborough Dr DE56 179 E3
Marlborough Rd
Breaston DE72 235 E4
Buxton SK17 85 D4
Derby DE24 232 B4
Long Eaton NG10 223 F1
Mansfield NG19 135 F1
Marlborough St ST4 269 F1
Marlow Brow SK13 10 A2
Marlow Cres DE7 207 E4
Marlow St 5 Buxton SK17 85 E4
5 Hadfield SK13 10 A3
Marlpit La Bolsover S44 99 E2
Denstone ST14 196 B3
Ellastone DE6 183 D1
Sutton on t H DE6 228 A4
Marlpool Inf Sch DE75 194 A4
Marlpool Jun Sch DE75 182 A1
Marple Rd SK13 16 A3
Marple Sta SK6 23 D4
Marples Ave NG19 136 C3
Marriott Ave NG18, NG19 268 A4
Marrison Dr S21 60 B3
Marsden Cl DE56 190 C2
Marsden Pl 2 S40 95 E1
Marsden St
Chesterfield S40 266 B3
Derby DE24 232 C4
Hadfield SK13 10 A2
Marsh Ave Dronfield S18 57 D2
Hope S33 38 C2
Marsh Cl S20 59 E3
Marsh Green La S45 129 F2
Marsh Hall La SK23 46 C3
Marsh Hollow DE6 200 C3
Marsh La Belper DE56 179 D3
New Mills SK22 33 E3
Stanton DE6 183 E4
Marsh Lane Cres DE56 179 D2
Marsh Lane Prim Sch S21 58 C2
Marsh View S21 59 D1
Marshall Dr NG9 223 F4
Marshall St Alfreton DE55 159 D2
Heanor DE75 181 F1
Marsham Dr SK6 23 D3
Marshaw Cl DE3 217 F1
Marshes The S33 38 C2
Marshfield Gr S43 79 D1
Marshgreen Cl DE24 233 E3
Marston SK17 106 A4
Marston Brook DE65 228 C1
Marston Cl Belper DE56 179 E3
Derby DE23 231 E3
Dronfield S18 75 E4
Marston Cres S17 55 F3
Marston La Doveridge DE6 211 E2
Hatton DE65 239 E4
Marston on D DE65 228 A1
Rolleston DE13 240 A2
Marston Montgomery Prim Sch DE6 211 F4
Marston Old La DE65 239 E4
Marston Rise DE15 254 C4
Martin Ct S21 59 E2
Martin Dr Derby DE21 220 A4
Stafford ST16 269 D4
Martin Rise S21 59 E2
Martin St ST16 269 E4
Martin's La DE13 238 A2
Martindale Ct DE56 179 E3
Martins La S42 131 D4
Martlet Ave SK12 32 B3
Mary Ann St S41 76 C2
Mary Howitt Inf Com Sch DE75 181 E1
Mary St Eckington S21 59 E2
Whaley Thorns NG20 101 D1
Mary Swanwick Prim Sch S41 77 D2
Maryfield Wlk ST4 269 D2
Maryland Ct
Stapleford NG9 209 F1
Swadlincote DE11 256 A4
Maryland Rd DE21 220 A3
Marylebone Cres DE22 218 A3
Masefield Ave Derby DE23 231 F4
Holmewood S42 116 B1
Swadlincote DE11 256 B3
Masefield Dr ST17 269 D3
Masefield Rd S13 44 B4
Mason Cres S13 44 B4
Mason Gr S13 44 B4
Mason Rd DE7 194 B1
Mason St S80 81 F3
Masonic Pl NG1 268 A2
Masons Gr SK13 10 A3
Massey Gdns NG3 268 C2
Masson Cl S40 95 E3
Masson Rd DE4 143 D1
Masterson St ST4 269 F1
Mastin Ave S43 80 B3
Mather's Way S42 115 E1
Matlock Ave NG18 268 B3
Matlock Bath Holy Trinity CE Prim Sch DE4 155 D4
Matlock Bath Sta DE4 143 D1
Matlock Ct NG10 235 F3
Matlock Dr S43 97 E3
Matlock Gn DE4 143 E2

Matlock Inf & Jun Sch DE4 143 E3
Matlock Rd
Ambergate DE56 167 F2
Ashover S45 113 F2
Belper DE56 178 C4
Brackenfield DE55 145 E1
Brackenfield DE55 145 E1
Derby DE21 205 F1
Holymoorside S42 114 A4
Wessington DE55 157 F4
Matlock St DE45 109 E3
Matlock Sta DE4 143 D3
Mattersey Ct NG19 136 A1
Matthew Cl SK13 9 F4
Matthew Holland Comp Sch NG16 171 F4
Matthew St DE24 232 C3
Matthew Way DE23 230 C4
Matthews Ct NG9 209 F1
Matthews Fold S8 43 E1
Matthews La S8 43 E1
Maude St S21 59 E2
Maugerhay S8 43 E1
Maunleigh NG19 136 C1
Mawfa Ave S14 43 E1
Mawfa Cres S14 43 E1
Mawfa Dr S14 43 E1
Mawfa Rd S14 43 E1
Mawkin La NG16 160 C3
Maws La NG16 195 F4
Mawstone La DE45 125 D2
Max Rd DE21 219 F4
Maxey Pl S8 43 D3
Maxtoke Rd NG7 268 A1
Maxwell Ave DE22 218 B4
Maxwell Pl ST4 269 D2
Maxwell St DE72 235 F4
May Ave S41 77 E2
May South DE7 194 B2
May St Derby DE22 218 C2
Ilkeston DE7 194 C2
Maybank Cl SK23 35 D1
Mayfair DE11 255 F3
Mayfair Ave NG18 268 C3
Mayfair Cres DE22 217 F3
Mayfield Ave Heanor DE75 181 F1
Kilburn DE56 192 A4
Mayfield DE6 184 B4
Mayfield Dr
Burton u T DE15 255 D4
North Wingfield S42 131 F3
Stapleford NG9 209 F1
Mayfield Gr NG10 223 F1
Mayfield Place E ST4 269 D1
Mayfield Place W ST4 269 D1
Mayfield Rd
Ashbourne DE6 173 D1
Burton u T DE15 248 A2
Chesterfield S40 95 E1
Derby DE21 219 F4
Lodge Moor S10 42 C4
Marple SK6 15 D1
Mayfield Terr
Hathersage S32 53 D4
Mayfield DE6 184 B3
Mayflower Ct NG20 119 F2
Mayflower Rd NG16 195 D4
Mayhall Ave NG19 136 A2
Maylands DE72 221 D1
Maylands Ave DE72 235 F4
Maynard Rd
Chesterfield S40 266 A1
Nether Padley S32 53 E1
Maynestone Rd SK23 34 C3
Maypole Hill DE11 256 A3
Maypole La DE23 230 C4
McAdam Cl DE15 248 A1
McGough Mews DE24 232 A3
McMahon Ave S43 97 D3
McNeil Gr DE72 235 D4
Mead Cl DE24 231 F2
Mead Cres DE15 255 D3
Mead Wlk DE15 255 D3
Meadow Ave Codnor DE5 181 D4
Mansfield NG18 268 C3
Peak Dale SK17 67 D3
Meadow Bank Glossop SK13 16 C4
Hollingworth SK14 9 E3
Mansfield Woodhouse NG19 136 C3
South Normanton DE55 160 A4
Meadow Cl Bolsover S44 118 A4
Breaston DE72 235 F4
Chesterfield S43 77 E1
Derby DE21 220 C2
Dove Holes SK17 47 F1
Draycott DE72 235 D4
Dronfield S18 57 E2
Eastwood NG16 182 C2
Findern DE65 230 B1
Horsley Woodhouse DE7 192 B3
Repton DE65 242 C1
Stoney Middleton S32 72 A2
Tibshelf DE55 148 A4
Whaley Bridge SK23 45 E4
Meadow Cotts NG19 136 B2
Meadow Cres DE74 247 D1
Meadow Croft S42 132 B4
Meadow Ct Belper DE56 178 C2
Chesterfield S43 77 E2
Kilburn DE56 192 A4
South Normanton DE55 159 F2
Meadow Farm Com Prim Sch DE21 220 A2
Meadow Gr Newton DE55 148 A2
Totley S17 55 F2
Meadow Grove Rd S17 55 E2
Meadow Head Ave S8 56 C4
Meadow Head Dr S8 56 C4
Meadow La
Burton u T DE13 248 A4
Derby, Chaddesden DE21 219 F3
Derby, The Holmes DE1 267 D3
Disley SK12 32 B3
Dove Holes SK17 47 F1
Long Eaton NG10 236 C4
Newton DE55 159 F4
Repton DE65 243 D2
Roston DE6 197 E4
Swadlincote DE11 256 A3
Tideswell SK17 69 D1
Meadow Lane Ind Est DE55 159 D3
Meadow Nook DE24 233 E3
Meadow Rd
Awsworth NG16 195 E3
Clay Cross S45 131 D3
Derby, The Holmes DE1 267 C3
Derby, Wilmorton DE24 219 F1
Ripley DE5 169 F1
Meadow Rise
Brassington DE4 153 D1
Church Broughton DE65 227 D4
Glossop SK13 16 C4
Old Brampton S40 94 C2
Meadow St Ilkeston DE7 194 C1
Ironville NG16 170 C3
New Mills SK22 33 E4
Meadow Vale DE56 190 B2
Meadow View
Bolsover S43 80 C2
Chesterfield S40 114 A4
Darley Dale DE4 142 C4
Doveridge DE6 224 B4
Holmewood S42 132 B4
Rolleston DE13 240 B2
South Wingfield DE55 157 F3
Meadow View Cl DE21 206 A2
Meadow View Rd
Sheffield S8 56 C4
Swadlincote DE11 255 F3
Meadow Way Derby DE73 233 D1
Swadlincote DE11 256 A3
Meadowbank Way NG16 182 B2
Meadowbrook Ind Est S20 60 A4
Meadowcroft SK14 9 D2
Meadowcroft Gdns S20 59 F4
Meadowcroft Glade S20 59 F4
Meadowcroft Rise S20 59 F4
Meadowfield SK23 45 E4
Meadowfield Cl SK13 9 F2
Meadowgrass Cl DE23 231 D3
Meadowhead S8 57 D4
Meadowhead Sec Sch S8 57 D4
Meadowhill Rd S41 115 E4
Meadowlands S44 99 E1
Meadowlark Gr DE21 206 A1
Meadows Com Sch S41 77 D2
Meadows Croft DE56 190 B2
Meadows Ind Est The DE21 219 E3
Meadows Prim Sch The DE56 190 B2
Meadows Rd SK22 25 E1
Meadows The
Chesterfield S40 94 C3
Heanor DE75 181 F3
Old Brampton S40 95 D3
Swanwick DE55 169 F4
Uttoxeter ST14 210 A1
Meadowside Disley SK12 33 D3
Mayfield DE6 184 B3
Whaley Bridge SK23 45 E4
Meadowside Cl
Shirley DE6 200 B4
Wingerworth S42 115 D2
Meads The S8 57 D4
Meadway Dr S17 55 E4
Meadway The S17 55 E4
Meakin St S41 115 E4
Meal Hill Rd HD7 2 C4
Meal St SK22 33 E4
Mear Dr DE72 221 D1
Mear Greaves La DE15 248 A2
Mease La B79 263 D1
Mease The DE65 228 C1
Measham Rd
Donisthorpe DE12 265 E3
Moira DE12 262 C2
Stretton en le F DE12 265 F1
Meath Ave DE21 220 A2
Meden Ave NG19 134 C4
Meden Bank NG19 135 D3
Meden Cl NG19 135 D3
Meden Rd NG19 136 B2
Meden Sq NG19 135 D3
Medina Cl DE24 233 E3
Medlock Cl S40 114 A4
Medlock Rd S40 114 B4
Medway Dr DE22 205 D3
Meerbrook Cl DE21 206 A1
Meerbrook Pl DE7 208 B3
Meersbrook Park Rd S8 43 D3
Meersbrook Rd S8 43 D3
Megaloughton La DE21 220 B2
Megdale DE4 143 D3
Melandra Castle Rd SK13 9 E1
Melandra Ct DE22 218 C2
Melandra Rd SK13 9 F2
Melanie Cl SK13 17 D4
Melbourn Cl DE56 190 C2
Melbourne Ave
Burton u T DE15 248 B2
Dronfield S18 56 A1
Melbourne Cl Belper DE56 179 D1
Derby, Allestree DE3 204 B1
Derby, Mickleover DE3 217 F2
Melbourne Ct NG10 235 F2
Melbourne Hall DE73 252 A4
Melbourne Inf Sch DE73 252 A4
Melbourne Jun Sch DE73 252 A4
Melbourne La
Breedon on t H DE73 252 C1
Ticknall DE73 251 E3
Melbourne Rd NG9 209 F1
Melbourne St Derby DE1 267 B1
Mansfield Woodhouse NG19 136 B3
Melbreak Cl DE3 217 F1
Melfort Cl DE24 231 F1
Meliden Way ST4 269 D1
Melling Cl S40 114 C4
Mellington Cl S8 43 E1
Mellor Dr ST14 210 A1
Mellor La Barlow S18 75 F1
Chapel-en-le-F SK23 47 D3
Mellor Rd Branston DE14 254 A4
New Mills SK22 24 B2
Mellor St DE24 232 C3
Mellor Way S40 115 D4
Mellor's La DE56 191 E3
Melrose Ave NG18 268 C3
Melrose Cl Chesterfield S40 95 E2
Derby DE24 231 F1
Meltham La S41 96 A3
Melton Ave Derby DE73 231 E3
Melbourne DE73 252 A4
Melton Ct Sandiacre NG10 223 D3
Somercotes DE55 170 B3
Melville Cl DE6 175 F2
Melville Cres S43 96 C2
Melville Ct DE65 229 D2
Melville Gdns NG3 268 C2
Melville St NG1 268 B1
Memorial Rd DE22 204 B2
Mendip Cl NG10 223 D1
Mendip Cres S40 95 D2
Mendip Ct DE21 205 F1
Menin Rd DE22 204 B1
Mentmore Cl DE55 170 A4
Mercaston Cl S40 95 D3
Mercaston La
Hulland Ward DE6 188 A2
Mackworth DE6, DE22 203 D4
Weston Underwood DE6, DE22 203 D4
Mercaston Rd DE21 219 F4
Mercer Cres DE55 159 E2
Merchant Ave DE21 220 B2
Merchant St Derby DE22 218 C3
Shirebrook NG20 120 A2
Mercia Cl DE65 239 E4
Mercia Dr Dore S17 55 F3
Willington DE65 242 A3
Mercian Mews DE21 220 B2
Meredith Ct NG9 209 F1
Mereoak La DE11 257 F4
Meridian Cl DE7 194 C2
Merlin Cl DE56 179 E3
Merlin Cres DE14 253 F4
Merlin Gn DE24 231 E2
Merlin Way Ilkeston DE7 208 C2
Woodville DE11 256 C2
Merrial Cl DE45 109 E2
Merrick Cl S40 95 E3
Merridale Rd DE23 231 E4
Merrill Coll DE24 232 C2
Merrill Lower Sch DE24 232 C3
Merrill Way DE24 232 B3
Merrybower Cl DE24 231 E2
Merrydale Rd DE15 255 D4
Mersey Bank Rd SK13 9 F2
Merthyr Ct DE21 206 A1
Merton Ct NG9 209 F1
Mervyn Rd DE15 248 A2
Metcalfe Cl DE24 233 D4
Metcalfe Way S21 60 B3
Meteor Ctr The DE21 205 E1
Methley Cl S2 43 F3
Metro Ave DE55 148 A2
Mettesford DE4 143 E3
Meverill Rd SK17 69 E3
Mevril Rd SK23 45 F3
Mewies Cl DE12 253 E1
Mews The DE73 252 A4
Meynell Cl Burton u T DE15 248 A1
Chesterfield S40 95 E1
Meynell Ct DE22 204 B1
Meynell Rd NG10 236 B3
Meynell Rise DE6 173 E2
Meynell St Derby DE23 218 C1
Swadlincote DE11 256 A1
Meynell Way S21 60 B3
Meyrick Rd ST17 269 E3
Michael Cl S42 115 D3
Michael House-Rudolf Steiner Sch DE75 194 A3
Michael's La DE6 183 E3
Michelle Cl DE24 231 E2
Michigan Cl DE21 220 B3
Michlow Dr S33 51 D4
Michlow La S33 51 D4
Micklebring Cl DE5 169 E1
Micklecroft Gdns DE23 230 C4
Mickledon Cl 3 NG10 236 A4
Mickleover Prim Sch DE3 217 E1
Mickleross Cl DE3 217 E2
Mickleton Cl DE11 256 A1
Mickley Inf Sch DE55 146 B2
Mickley La Dronfield S17 55 F2
Shirland DE55 146 B3
Totley S17 55 F2
Middle Friars ST17 269 E3
Middle Hay Cl S14 43 F2
Middle Hay Pl S14 43 F2
Middle Hay Rise S14 43 F2
Middle Hay View S14 43 F2
Middle Hill NG1 268 B1
Middle La S45 131 F2
Middle Ox Cl S20 59 F3
Middle Ox Gdns S20 59 F3
Middle Pavement
Chesterfield S40 266 B3
5 Nottingham NG1 268 B1
Middle Rd S42 114 C1
Middle Shambles S40 266 B3
Middle St S44 118 B4
Middlebeck Cl DE73 232 C1
Middlecroft L Ctr S43 97 E4
Middlecroft Rd S43 97 E4
Middlefield Cl S17 55 E4
Middlefield Croft S17 55 E4
Middlegate Field Dr S80 82 A3
Middleton Ave
Codnor DE5 181 D3
Derby DE23 218 B1
Middleton Dr S43 97 D3
Middleton La S32 71 E2
Middleton Prim Sch DE4 154 B2
Middleton Rd
Ilkeston DE7 209 D3
Mansfield Woodhouse NG19 136 B3
Middleton St
Awsworth NG16 195 E2
Cossall DE7 195 D1
Derby DE23 219 D1
Middleton Top Visitor's Ctr DE4 154 B2
Midhill Rd S2 43 D4
Midland Ave NG9 223 E3
Midland Ct S41 115 D4
Midland Pl DE1 267 D2
Midland Railway Ctr DE5 169 F2
Midland Rd Derby DE1 267 D1
Eastwood NG16 182 C1
Heanor DE75 181 F1
Swadlincote DE11 256 A2
Midland Road Ind Est DE11 256 A3
Midland St NG10 236 C4
Midland Terr
Ambergate DE56 167 F2
Barrow Hill S43 78 A2
Blackwell DE55 147 E1
Chesterfield S41 115 D4
New Mills SK22 33 E4
Midland View S42 131 F4
Midland Way S43 80 A3
Midway DE22 204 C1
Midway Ctr S45 131 E2
Midway Rd DE11 256 B3
Midworth St NG18 268 B3
Mikado Rd NG10 236 B3
Milbank Cl DE3 217 F3
Milburn Gdns DE21 206 A2
Milbury Cl DE21 205 F1
Mile Ash La DE22 204 C1
Milford DE45 109 E3
Milford Ave NG10 223 D2
Milford Dr DE7 194 B2
Milford Prim Sch DE56 190 C4
Milford Rd Duffield DE56 190 C2
Staveley S43 97 E3
Milford St DE1 218 C4
Milken La S45 130 A2
Mill Brow Broadbottom SK14 16 A4
Marple SK6 23 E4
Mill Brow Rd SK6 23 F4
Mill Cl Borrowash DE72 221 E1
Findern DE65 230 B1
Kilburn DE56 192 A4
Newton Solney DE15 248 C4
Swadlincote DE11 256 B3
Swanwick DE55 169 F4
Mill Cliff SK17 85 E4
Mill Cres Whitwell S80 82 A3
Wingerworth S42 115 E2
Mill Croft DE3 217 E2
Mill Farm Cl S32 72 B1
Mill Fleam DE65 228 C1
Mill Gn S43 78 C1
Mill Hil Sch DE5 180 C4
Mill Hill Elvaston DE24 233 E2
Long Duckmanton S44 117 D3
Mill Hill Dr DE15 248 A2
Mill Hill La Breaston DE72 222 C1
Burton u T DE15 248 A2
Derby DE23 267 A1
Mill Hill Rd DE23 267 A1
Mill Holme DE55 160 A2
Mill La Ashbourne DE6 173 F1
Belper DE56 179 D2
Bolsover, Limekiln Field S44 99 D2
Bolsover, Shuttlewood S44 98 C4
Bradbourne DE6 163 D3
Castleton S33 38 B2
Chesterfield S40 95 E1
Clay Cross S42, S45 130 C3
Codnor DE5 181 D4
Common Side S18 75 E2
Cossall NG16 195 E1
Derby DE74 217 E2
Doveridge DE6 211 D1
Dronfield S18 57 D1
Eyam S32 71 F3
Foston DE6 226 B4
Grassmoor S42 115 E2
Hartington SK17 137 E3
Hathersage S32 52 C4
Mill La continued
Heath S44 117 D1
Hilton DE65 228 B1
Holloway DE4 156 A3
Millthorpe S18 74 C3
Pinxton NG16 160 B1
Renishaw S21 60 A1
Roston DE6 197 E4
Sandiacre NG10 223 E3
Scropton DE65 226 C1
Shirley DE6 200 B4
Stainsby S44 133 E4
Totley S17 55 F3
Whitwell S80 82 A3
Wingerworth S42 115 E2
Mill Meadow Way DE65 229 D2
Mill Moor Cl DE73 232 C1
Mill Mus DE4 155 D4
Mill Rd Cromford DE4 155 D3
Heanor DE75 194 A4
Stapleford NG9 223 E4
Mill St Bakewell DE45 109 E3
Belper DE56 179 D2
Chesterfield S41 266 C3
Clowne S43 80 C2
Common Side S18 75 E2
Coton in t E DE12 260 B2
Derby DE1 218 C3
Glossop SK13 10 B1
Hayfield SK22 25 E2
Ilkeston DE7 194 C1
Mansfield NG18 268 C3
Rocester ST14 197 D2
Stafford ST16 269 E4
Stoney Middleton S32 72 A2
Mill Stream Cl S40 95 E1
Mill Wlk Bolsover S44 99 D2
Whitwell S80 82 A3
Mill Yd DE55 170 B4
Millash La S80 82 A2
Millbank Heanor DE75 194 A4
Stafford ST16 269 E4
Millbank Cl DE7 194 B2
Millbank Dr ST14 197 D2
Millbrook SK14 9 F3
Millcross La S18 75 F2
Milldale Ave SK17 84 C3
Milldale Cl Chesterfield S40 95 E3
Ripley DE5 180 B3
Milldale Ct Ashbourne DE6 185 E4
Belper DE56 179 D2
Milldale Rd Derby DE21 220 C2
Long Eaton NG10 236 A3
Totley S17 55 F3
Milldam La DE6 186 C4
Miller Ave S43 79 E2
Millers Dale Cl DE56 179 E3
Millers Gn DE4 165 F3
Millers La DE55 145 F1
Millersdale Ave DE7 194 C3
Millersdale Cl DE15 248 A3
Millersdale Ct SK13 10 C1
Millersdale Way SK17 85 D3
Millfield DE72 235 D1
Millfield Cl DE7 194 B2
Millfield Croft DE11 256 A4
Millfield Rd Ilkeston DE7 209 D4
Kimberley NG16 195 F4
Millfield St DE11 257 D1
Millom Pl DE21 205 E1
Mills Cl DE72 235 D4
Mills Ct DE4 156 C1
Millstone Cl 21 S18 56 B1
Millstone La DE55 169 E4
Millthorpe La S18 75 D3
Milltown SK13 10 B1
Millview Cl NG2 268 C1
Millway NG19 136 B1
Millway La DE6 149 F2
Milnbank Ave SK17 85 E4
Milner Ave Codnor DE5 181 D4
Draycott DE72 235 D4
Milner Rd NG10 236 B4
Milnhay Rd Heanor NG16 182 B1
Langley Mill NG16 182 B1
Milton Ave Alfreton DE55 159 E2
Ilkeston DE7 194 C2
Shirland DE55 146 B2
Swadlincote DE11 256 B3
Milton Cres S40 115 D4
Milton La SK23 46 A3
Milton Pl S43 78 C1
Milton Rd Derby DE65 217 E2
Ilkeston DE7 194 C2
Repton DE65 242 B1
Milton St Derby DE22 218 B2
Ilkeston DE7 194 C2
Long Eaton NG10 236 B4
Mansfield NG18 268 B4
Nottingham NG1 268 B2
Milward Rd DE75 181 E1
Mimosa Cres DE23 231 F3
Miners Hill DE4 153 D1
Minimum Terr S40 266 A2
Minshall St ST4 269 F1
Minster Rd DE21 205 F1
Minster Way DE55 169 F4
Mint Cl NG10 236 A4
Minton Rd DE74 246 C2
Minton St ST4 269 D2
Mires La
Great Longstone DE45 90 A2
Litton SK17 70 A2
Mires The Alstonefield DE6 149 D2
Birchover DE4 126 A1

Miriam Ave S40 .... 114 A4
Miry La DE65 .... 227 E2
Misterton Cl DE22 .... 204 C1
Misterton Ct NG19 .... 136 A1
Mitcham Wlk DE22 .... 218 A3
Mitchell Ave NG16 .... 182 A2
Mitchell St Clowne S43 ...... 80 C2
Long Eaton NG10 .... 236 C4
Mitchell Terr DE7 .... 209 D3
Mitchell Way S43 .... 77 F2
Mitre Dr DE65 .... 242 B1
Mitre (Repton School)
The DE65 .... 242 B1
Moat Bank DE15 .... 248 B1
Moat St DE11 .... 256 A1
Moat The DE74 .... 247 D2
Model Village S80 .... 100 C4
Model Village Prim Sch
NG20 .... 119 F2
Moffatt Rd S2 .... 43 D4
Moira Cl DE21 .... 220 A4
Moira Dale DE74 .... 247 E2
Moira Rd
Donisthorpe DE12 .... 262 C1
Moira DE11 .... 262 C4
Overseal DE12 .... 262 A2
Woodville DE11 .... 256 C1
Moira St DE73 .... 252 A4
Moisty La
Marchington ST14 .... 224 B2
Stoney Middleton S32 ...... 71 D2
Molineux Ave S43 .... 78 B1
Molineux St DE23 .... 219 D1
Molloy Pl S8 .... 43 D3
Molloy St S8 .... 43 D3
Monarch Dr DE21 .... 206 B2
Moncrieff Cres DE21 ...... 220 A4
Mondello Dr DE24 .... 233 E3
Monk Rd DE55 .... 159 D1
Monk St Derby DE22 ...... 267 A2
Tutbury DE13 .... 239 E4
Monk's Rd SK13 .... 17 F3
Monks Cl Derby DE24 .... 231 E2
Ilkeston DE7 .... 209 D4
Monks' Rd SK13 .... 16 C3
Monks Way S81 .... 63 F4
Monksdale Cl SK17 .... 69 D2
Monksdale La SK17 .... 68 C1
Monkton Cl DE7 .... 194 B2
Monkwood Rd S41 .... 95 E4
Monmouth St DE21 .... 219 E3
Monnies End S43 .... 80 B3
Monpelier Cl DE14 .... 254 A4
Monsal Ave S41 .... 85 E4
Monsal Cres Staveley S43 .... 97 D3
Tibshelf DE55 .... 147 F3
Monsal Dr Derby DE21 .... 220 C2
South Normanton DE55 .... 159 F3
Monsal Gr SK17 .... 85 E4
Monsaldale Cl
Burton u T DE15 .... 248 A2
Long Eaton NG10 .... 236 A3
Monsall Ave DE7 .... 194 C3
Monsdale La DE6 .... 151 F1
Monsom La DE65 .... 242 B2
Montagu St SK6 .... 15 D1
Monteith Pl DE74 .... 247 D2
Montford Mews DE74 ..... 247 D2
Montfort St NG7 .... 268 A2
Montgomery Cl DE65 ..... 228 C1
Montgomery St NG7 ...... 268 A2
Montpelier DE22 .... 204 B4
Montpelier Pl SK17 .... 66 B1
Montpelier Rd DE56 ...... 167 F2
Montrose Cl DE24 .... 231 F2
Montrose Ct NG9 .... 209 F1
Montrose Pl S18 .... 56 B1
Montrose Sq NG19 .... 136 A3
Monument Hill NG16 ..... 170 C2
Monument La NG16 .... 170 C2
Monyash CE Prim Sch
DE45 .... 107 E1
Monyash Cl Derby DE21 .... 220 A4
Ilkeston DE7 .... 194 C4
Staveley S43 .... 97 E4
Monyash Mews SK13 .... 9 E1
Monyash Rd
Bakewell DE45 .... 109 E3
Over Haddon DE45 .... 109 D1
Monyash Way DE56 .... 179 D3
Moonpenny Way S18 .... 57 D1
Moor Cres S20 .... 59 E4
Moor Dr DE24 .... 233 D3
Moor End DE21 .... 220 C3
Moor End Rd SK6 .... 24 A3
Moor Farm Ave S20 .... 59 D4
Moor Farm Garth S20 .... 59 E4
Moor Farm Rd E DE6 .... 185 F4
Moor Farm Rd W DE6 ... 185 F4
Moor Farm Rise S20 .... 59 D4
Moor La Aston-on-T DE72 .... 246 A4
Barrow u T DE73 .... 244 A4
Bolsover S44 .... 99 D1
Bonsall DE4 .... 142 A1
Callow DE4 .... 165 D2
Calow S44 .... 116 B4
Chelmorton SK17 .... 87 F1
Dale DE7 .... 207 F1
Darley Dale DE4 .... 127 E2
Derby DE24 .... 232 B3
Elton DE4 .... 140 C3
Flagg DE45 .... 106 C2
Kirk Ireton DE6 .... 165 D2
Kirk Langley DE6 .... 202 C1
Little Eaton DE21 .... 191 F1

Moor La continued
Mansfield NG18 .... 268 A3
Ockbrook DE72 .... 221 E3
Osmaston DE6 .... 185 F3
Scarcliffe S44 .... 119 D4
Taddington SK17 .... 87 F1
Youlgreave DE45 .... 125 D3
Moor Lane Fst Sch NG18 .. 268 A3
Moor Rd Ashover S45 .... 129 F2
Breadsall DE7 .... 205 F3
Brinsley NG16 .... 182 C4
Great Longstone DE45 ..... 89 F3
Moor Rise DE56 .... 191 E4
Moor St Derby DE21 ...... 220 C3
Mansfield NG18 .... 268 B3
Moor The Brinsley NG16 .... 182 B4
Middleton (Nr Wirksworth)
DE4 .... 154 B2
Moor Valley
Mosborough S20 .... 59 D4
Sheffield S20 .... 44 C1
Moor View Rd S43 .... 79 D1
Mooracre La S44 .... 99 E1
Moorbridge La NG9 ...... 209 E1
Moorbrook La S33 .... 50 C4
Moore Cl S42 .... 116 B1
Moore St DE23 .... 219 D2
Mooredge Dr DE4 .... 143 E3
Mooredge Rd DE4 .... 157 D1
Moorend DE4 .... 111 E2
Moores Ave NG10 .... 223 E4
Moorfield DE4 .... 143 E4
Moorfield Ave Bolsover S44 .. 99 D1
Holbrook DE56 .... 191 E4
Moorfield Cres NG10 ..... 223 D3
Moorfield Ct NG9 .... 209 F1
Moorfield La NG20 .... 100 C3
Moorfield Prec SK14 .... 9 E3
Moorfield Sq S44 .... 99 D1
Moorfield St SK14 .... 9 E3
Moorfield Terr SK14 .... 9 E3
Moorfields Ave NG16 .... 182 C2
Moorgate DE22 .... 217 F3
Moorgate Ave NG19 ..... 134 C4
Moorgate Cres S18 .... 76 A4
Moorgate St NG7 .... 268 A2
Moorhaigh La NG19 ..... 135 D2
Moorhall DE45 .... 109 E3
Moorhead Ave DE24 ..... 232 C3
Moorhead Prim Sch DE24 .. 232 C3
Moorings The SK12 .... 32 C3
Moorland Ave NG9 .... 223 E3
Moorland Cl NG19 .... 268 A4
Moorland Dr S44 .... 116 C1
Moorland La NG19 .... 268 A4
Moorland Rd Derby DE3 .. 217 E2
Hathersage S32 .... 53 D4
Moorland View
Apperknowle S18 .... 58 A1
Sheffield S20 .... 44 A1
Moorland View Rd S40 .... 95 E1
Moorlands Cl NG10 ...... 223 D1
Moorlands La Bonsall DE4 .. 142 A2
Froggatt S32 .... 72 B3
Moorlawn Ave S42 .... 113 F4
Moorpark Ave S40 .... 114 B4
Moorpool Cres DE56 .... 191 E4
Moorside Cl Cromford DE4 .. 155 D3
Mosborough S20 .... 59 E4
Moorside Cres DE24 ...... 231 F2
Moorside La DE56 .... 191 E4
Moorsyde Rd ST4 .... 269 D1
Moorthorpe Gdns S20 .... 44 C1
Moorthorpe Gn S20 .... 44 C1
Moorthorpe Way S20 .... 44 C1
Moortop Rd S21 .... 58 A1
Moorview Cl Brimington S43 .. 96 B4
Wingerworth S42 .... 115 D2
Moorview Ct 14 S17 .... 56 A3
Moorway NG21 .... 205 F2
Moorway Croft DE23 .... 231 D4
Moorway La DE23 .... 231 D4
Moorways Sports Ctr
DE24 .... 232 B3
Moorwood Ave S17 .... 55 E1
Moorwoodmoor La S45 .. 157 E3
Moray Ct NG16 .... 195 F4
Moray Pl S18 .... 56 B1
Mordaunt Rd S2 .... 43 F3
Morden Gn DE22 .... 218 A3
Morden Rd NG16 .... 195 E4
Morefern Dr DE21 .... 205 F1
Moreland St NG2 .... 268 C1
Moreland Terr NG2 ...... 268 C1
Morland Dr S14 .... 43 F2
Morland Dr S14 .... 43 F2
Morland Pl S14 .... 43 F2
Morland Rd Birch Vale SK22 .. 25 D1
Sheffield S14 .... 43 F2
Morledge DE1 .... 267 C3
Morleston St DE23 .... 267 C1
Morley Almshouses La
DE7 .... 206 A4
Morley Ave S40 .... 95 E2
Morley Cl Belper DE56 .... 179 F3
Dronfield S18 .... 56 B1
Morley Dr DE7 .... 194 B2
Morley La
Breadsall DE7, DE21 ..... 205 F4
Little Eaton DE7, DE21 ... 205 F4
Stanley DE7 .... 207 D3
Morley Prim Sch DE7 .. 206 B4
Morley Rd DE21 .... 206 B1
Morley St Derby DE22 .... 218 B3
Glossop SK13 .... 17 E4
Morleyfields Cl DE5 ...... 169 F1
Morlich Dr DE24 .... 231 F3
Morningside Cl DE24 .... 232 B2

Mornington Cl NG10 .... 223 E3
Mornington Cres DE22 .. 218 A3
Mornington Rd S42 ...... 132 B4
Mornington Rise DE4 ... 143 E2
Morpeth Gdns DE21 ..... 205 E1
Morrell Wood Dr DE56 .. 179 E3
Morris Ave S41 .... 95 F3
Morris Dr S41 .... 95 F3
Mortimer St DE24 .... 232 B4
Mortimer Wilson Sch
DE55 .... 159 D2
Morton Ave S45 .... 131 D2
Morton La S21 .... 58 B1
Morton Prim Sch DE55 .. 147 D3
Morton Rd Pilsley S45 .... 147 E4
Shirland DE55 .... 146 B3
Morton St NG19 .... 135 F1
Morven Ave Bolsover S44 .. 99 D1
Mansfield Woodhouse
NG19 .... 136 A1
Morven St S80 .... 100 C4
Mosborough Inf & Jun Sch
S20 .... 59 E4
Mosborough Moor S20 .... 59 D4
Mosbrough Rd S13 .... 44 A4
Moscar Cross Rd S6 ...... 31 F3
Mosedale Cl DE24 .... 232 C4
Moseley St DE5 .... 169 E1
Moses La DE7 .... 206 C3
Moses View S81 .... 63 F4
Mosley Dr ST14 .... 210 A1
Mosley Rd SK17 .... 85 D3
Moss Dr S21 .... 60 B3
Moss Edge Rd HD7 .... 3 E4
Moss La Broadbottom SK14 .. 15 F4
Hulland Ward DE6 .... 175 F2
Ripley DE5 .... 169 E2
Moss Rd Ilkeston DE7 .... 208 C4
Totley S17 .... 55 D2
Moss Rise Pl S21 .... 59 E2
Moss St Derby DE22 ...... 218 C2
Hollingworth SK14 .... 9 E3
Moss View S20 .... 59 E3
Moss View Rd SK23 .... 47 E3
Moss Way S20 .... 59 E4
Mossbank Cl SK13 .... 9 F2
Mossborough Hall Dr S20 .. 59 F3
Mossbrook Sch S8 ...... 57 E4
Mossdale Ave S20 .... 59 E4
Mostyn Ave S41 .... 218 B1
Mottistone Cl DE24 ...... 233 E3
Mottram CE Prim Sch SK14 .. 9 D4
Mottram Old Rd SK14 ... 15 D4
Mottram Rd
Broadbottom SK14 .... 16 A4
Mottram in L SK14 .... 9 D2
Mouldridge La
Aldwark DE4 .... 139 F1
Ballidon DE4 .... 139 F1
Moult Ave DE21 .... 220 C2
Moulton Cl Belper DE56 .. 179 E3
Swanwick DE55 .... 169 F4
Mound Rd S40 .... 266 B1
Mount Ave ST4 .... 269 D2
Mount Carmel St DE23 .. 267 A1
Mount Cres DE55 .... 160 A2
Mount Hooton Rd NG7 .. 268 A2
Mount Milner NG18 ..... 268 C3
Mount Pleasant
Ashford in t W DE45 ..... 108 C4
Castle Donington DE74 .. 247 D2
Ilkeston DE7 .... 194 C2
Mansfield NG18 .... 268 B4
Ripley DE5 .... 169 E1
Somercotes DE55 .... 170 B3
Mount Pleasant CE Prim
Sch ST4 .... 269 F1
Mount Pleasant Dr
Belper DE56 .... 178 C3
Heage DE56 .... 179 F4
Mount Pleasant La DE12 .. 265 D2
Mount Pleasant Rd
Grindleford S32 .... 72 B4
Linton DE11 .... 261 F4
Repton DE65 .... 242 C1
Swadlincote DE11 .... 256 A1
Mount Rd Bretby DE15 .. 249 D2
Hackingknife SK14 .... 15 D3
Hartshorne DE11 .... 257 D2
Linton DE11 .... 261 E4
Mount Row DE7 .... 269 E4
Mount Sch for the Deaf
ST4 .... 269 D2
Mount St Breaston DE72 .. 235 F4
Burton u T DE15 .... 248 A2
Derby DE1 .... 267 B1
Glossop SK13 .... 17 E4
Heanor DE75 .... 181 F1
Mansfield NG19 .... 268 B4
Nottingham NG1 .... 268 A1
5 Stafford ST16 .... 269 E4
Stapleford NG9 .... 223 F4
Mount St Mary's RC Coll
S21 .... 60 B1
Mount The NG9 .... 223 E3
Mount View Ave S8 .... 43 D2
Mount View Cl NG18 .... 268 C3
Mount View Gdns S8 ..... 43 D2
Mount View Rd S8 .... 43 D2
Mountbatten Ct DE7 .... 194 C2
Mountcastle St S41 .... 95 F4
Mountcastle Wlk S41 ..... 95 F4
Mountfield Ave NG10 ... 223 D2
Mountfield Pl ST4 .... 269 F1
Mountfield Way DE24 ... 233 E2
Mountford Ave DE4 ...... 165 F4
Mountford Cl DE21 ...... 206 A1
Mountford Croft S17 ...... 55 F3

Mouselow Cl SK13 .... 9 F1
Mowbray St DE24 .... 232 B4
Moy Ave DE24 .... 231 F1
Moyne Gdns DE73 .... 245 D4
Mudhurst La SK12 .... 32 C1
Muggington CE Prim Sch
DE6 .... 188 C1
Muirfield Cl S41 .... 96 A3
Muirfield Dr DE3 .... 217 F1
Muirfield Way NG19 ..... 136 C3
Mulberry Cl Belper DE56 .. 179 D2
Wingerworth S42 .... 115 D2
Mulberry Mews DE5 ..... 180 B3
Mulberry Rd S21 .... 59 D1
Mulberry Way Hilton DE65 .. 228 C1
Killamarsh S21 .... 60 A3
Mull Ct 9 DE24 .... 231 E2
Mullberries Ct DE22 ..... 204 C2
Mullion Pl DE24 .... 233 D3
Mumford Dr DE6 .... 185 E4
Mundella Pl S8 .... 43 D2
Mundella Prim Sch S8 .. 43 D2
Mundy CE Jun Sch DE75 .. 181 F1
Mundy Cl DE1 .... 218 C3
Mundy St Derby DE1 ..... 218 C3
Heanor DE75 .... 181 F1
Ilkeston DE7 .... 194 C1
Mundy's Dr DE75 .... 193 F4
Munro Cl S21 .... 60 B3
Munro St ST4 .... 269 D1
Munster Terr ST4 .... 269 D1
Murray Park Com Sch DE3 217 F2
Murray Rd Derby DE3 ... 217 F2
Killamarsh S21 .... 60 C4
Murray St Derby DE24 ... 232 C4
Mansfield NG18 .... 268 B3
Murrayfield Dr S20 .... 59 F3
Musard Pl S43 .... 78 B1
Musard Way S21 .... 60 B3
Muse La Boylestone DE6 .. 213 D1
Church Broughton DE6 .. 213 D1
Mushroom La DE11 ...... 262 B4
Muskham Ave DE7 .... 194 C2
Muskham Ct NG19 .... 136 A1
Musters St NG20 .... 120 A2
Muswell Rd DE24 .... 217 F3
Mycock La DE45 .... 106 C3
Myers Cl DE24 .... 231 F2
Mynd The NG19 .... 136 C3
Mynors St S16 .... 269 D2
Myrtle Ave Long Eaton NG10 236 B3
Stapleford NG9 .... 223 F3
Myrtle Cl NG20 .... 119 E3
Myrtle Gr S43 .... 78 A1
Myrtle Rd S2 .... 43 D4
Myrtle Springs S12 .... 43 F3
Myrtle Springs Sch S12 .. 43 F2
Mytham Bridge S33 .... 40 A1

Nabb La ST14 .... 196 A2
Nailers Way DE56 .... 179 E3
Nailor La DE4 .... 142 B2
Nairn Ave DE21 .... 219 E4
Nairn Cl DE24 .... 231 E2
Nairn Dr S18 .... 56 B1
Namur Cl DE22 .... 218 B2
Nan Gell's Hill DE4 ...... 155 D2
Napier Cl DE3 .... 217 F2
Napier St Derby DE22 .... 218 B3
Fenton ST4 .... 269 F1
Narlow La DE6 .... 161 F1
Narrow La Denstone ST14 .. 196 B3
Ticknall DE73 .... 250 C2
Narrowleys La S45 .... 129 F2
Naseby Cl DE3 .... 217 F2
Naseby Dr NG10 .... 236 C2
Naseby Rd DE56 .... 179 E2
Nathaniel Rd NG10 ...... 236 C3
National Stone Ctr DE4 .. 154 C2
National Tramway Mus
DE4 .... 156 C1
Navan Rd S2 .... 44 A4
Neal Ct NG10 .... 182 A2
Neale Bank S43 .... 96 B4
Neale St NG10 .... 236 C4
Near Meadow NG10 ...... 236 C3
Nearwell Cl SK23 .... 46 C3
Nearwood Dr DE21 ...... 205 F2
Needham St DE5 .... 181 D4
Needwood Ave NG9 ..... 209 E1
Needwood Ct DE13 .... 239 E3
Neighwood Cl NG9 ...... 223 F1
Neilson St DE24 .... 232 C4
Nelper Cres DE7 .... 209 D3
Nelson Cl DE3 .... 217 F2
Nelson Pl DE11 .... 257 F2
Nelson Rd ST4 .... 269 F4
Nelson St Burton u T DE15 .. 248 B2
Chesterfield S41 .... 96 A3
Derby DE1 .... 267 D1
Fenton ST4 .... 269 F1
Ilkeston DE7 .... 194 C2
Long Eaton NG10 .... 236 B3
Nottingham NG1 .... 268 B1
Swadlincote DE11 .... 256 A3
Nene Cl DE13 .... 240 B1
Nesbit St S44 .... 118 A4
Nesfield Cl Chesterfield S41 .. 95 E4
Derby DE24 .... 233 E4
Nesfield Rd DE7 .... 194 C1
Ness Wlk DE22 .... 204 C2
Nether Ave S21 .... 60 B3
Nether Blindlow La SK17 .. 106 A3
Nether Cl Duffield DE56 .. 190 C3
Eastwood NG16 .... 182 C2
Swanwick DE55 .... 169 F4
Wingerworth S42 .... 115 D1

Nether Croft Cl S43 .... 96 C4
Nether Croft Rd 5 S43 .. 96 C4
Nether Gdns DE21 .... 165 F4
Nether La Brassington DE4 .. 163 F4
Hazelwood DE56 .... 190 A4
Holbrook DE56 .... 191 E3
Kirk Ireton DE56 .... 176 A4
Nether Springs Rd S44 ... 98 C2
Nether Thorpe Rd S80 ... 63 D3
Nether Way DE4 .... 127 E2
Netherclose St DE23 ..... 219 D1
Nethercroft La S45 .... 131 F2
Netherdene Rd S18 .... 57 D1
Netherfield Cl S43 .... 79 D1
Netherfield La DE74 ..... 247 F4
Netherfield Rd
Chapel-en-le-F SK23 ...... 47 E3
Chesterfield S40 .... 114 A4
Long Eaton NG10 .... 236 B2
Sandiacre NG10 .... 223 D2
Netherfields Cres S18 ..... 76 A4
Nethergreen Ave S21 ..... 60 B4
Nethergreen Gdns S21 ... 60 B4
Netherleigh Ct S40 .... 95 D2
Netherleigh Rd S40 .... 95 D2
Nethermoor Ave S21 ..... 60 B4
Nethermoor Cl S21 .... 60 B4
Nethermoor Dr S21 ...... 60 B4
Nethermoor La S21 .... 60 B4
Nethermoor Rd
Nether Moor S42 .... 115 D1
Tupton S42 .... 131 E4
Wingerworth S42 .... 115 D1
Netherseal Rd
Chilcote DE12 .... 264 C2
Clifton Campville B79 .... 263 F1
Netherside S33 .... 51 D4
Netherside Dr DE73 ...... 233 D1
Netherthorpe S43 .... 79 D1
Netherthorpe Cl
Killamarsh S21 .... 60 B4
Netherthorpe S43 .... 78 C1
Netherthorpe La S21 ..... 60 B4
Netherthorpe Rd S43 .... 78 C1
Netherthorpe Sch S43 .. 79 D1
Netherwood Ct DE22 .... 204 B2
Nettlefold Cres DE73 .... 245 D1
Nettleton La SK17 .... 85 E2
Nettleworth Inf Sch NG19 136 B2
Neville Cl DE13 .... 240 A2
Nevinson Ave DE23 ...... 231 E4
Nevinson Dr DE23 .... 231 E4
Nevis Cl Chesterfield S40 .. 95 E2
Derby DE24 .... 231 E1
New Barlborough Cl S43 .. 80 B3
New Bath Rd DE4 .... 155 D4
New Beetwell St S40 ..... 266 B2
New Bolsover Prim Sch
S44 .... 98 C1
New Breck Rd DE56 ..... 179 D2
New Church St S33 .... 51 D4
New Cl S32 .... 71 E3
New Cotts NG20 .... 101 F2
New Derby Rd NG16 .... 182 B1
New Eaton Rd NG9 ...... 223 F3
New England Way NG19 .. 135 E2
New Fall St NG17 .... 148 C2
New Garden St ST17 ..... 269 E4
New Hall Rd S40 .... 95 E1
New High St SK17 .... 85 E4
New Horwich Rd SK23 ... 45 F4
New Inn La DE21 .... 205 E4
New La Bradwell S33 ...... 50 C3
Hilcote DE55 .... 148 B1
New Lawn Rd DE7 .... 208 C4
New Linden St NG20 .... 120 A2
New Lumford DE45 ...... 109 E4
New Market St NG1 .... 85 D3
New Mill La NG19 .... 136 C2
New Mills Central Sta
SK22 .... 33 D4
New Mills Newtown Sta
SK22 .... 33 D3
New Mills Prim Sch SK22 33 D3
New Mills Rd
Chisworth SK13 .... 16 A2
Hayfield SK22 .... 25 D2
New Mills Sch The SK22 .. 33 E4
New Mount Cl DE24 ..... 231 E3
New Queen St S41 .... 266 B4
New Rd Apperknowle S18 .. 58 A1
Bamford S33 .... 40 A3
Barlborough S43 .... 80 A4
Barton in F NG11 .... 237 F3
Belper DE56 .... 178 C2
Boylestone DE6 .... 213 D2
Bradwell S33 .... 51 D2
Buxworth SK23 .... 34 A1
Coton in t E DE12 .... 260 B2
Crich DE4 .... 168 A4
Derby DE65 .... 205 D1
Eyam S32 .... 71 F3
Grindleford S32 .... 72 A3
Heage DE56 .... 179 E4
Hilton DE65 .... 228 C1
Holmesfield S18 .... 75 D3
Holymoorside S42 .... 113 E4
Idridgehay DE56 .... 176 C2
Ironville NG16 .... 170 C2
Middleton (Nr Wirksworth)
DE4 .... 154 A3
Ridgeway DE56 .... 168 A2
Somercotes DE5, NG16 .. 170 B1
Stapleford NG9 .... 209 E1
Swadlincote DE12 .... 255 F3
Tintwistle SK13 .... 9 F4
Uttoxeter ST14 .... 210 A1
Weston Underwood DE6 .. 188 B1

New Rd continued
Whaley Bridge, Buxworth SK23 33 F1
Whaley Bridge, Over Leigh SK23 45 F3
Wingerworth S42 114 C2
Wirksworth DE4 155 D2
Woodville DE11 256 C1
Youlgreave DE45 125 E3
New Rd (Baslow Rd) DE45 108 C4
New Row NG16 171 D3
New Sq S40 266 B3
New St Alfreton DE55 159 D2
Bakewell DE45 109 E3
Bolsover S44 99 D2
Broadbottom SK14 16 A4
Chesterfield S40 266 B2
Derby DE1 267 C2
Donisthorpe DE12 262 C1
Draycott DE72 235 D4
Grassmoor S42 115 F2
Hilcote DE55 160 B4
Little Eaton DE21 205 E4
Long Eaton NG10 236 C4
Matlock DE4 143 E3
Morton DE55 147 D3
Mosborough S20 60 A4
New Mills SK22 33 E4
Newton DE55 148 A2
North Wingfield S42 131 F3
Ockbrook DE72 221 E2
Peak Dale SK17 67 D3
Pilsley S45 132 B1
Ripley DE5 169 F1
Rosliston DE12 260 B3
Shirland DE55 146 B1
Somercotes DE55 170 B4
South Normanton DE55 160 A3
Stanley DE7 207 E3
Sutton in A NG17 148 C2
Swadlincote DE11 256 A1
Swanwick DE55 169 F4
Whitwell S80 81 F3
New St Bus Link S20 60 A4
New Station Rd S44 99 D1
New Terr Pleasley NG19 134 C3
Sandiacre NG10 223 D3
New Tythe St NG10 236 C4
New Whittington Prim Sch S41 77 E2
New Wye St SK17 85 E4
New Zealand La DE56 190 C1
New Zealand Sq DE22 218 B3
Newark S20 59 F4
Newark Cres NG2 268 C1
Newark Rd DE21 205 E1
Newark St NG2 268 C1
Newbarn Cl NG20 119 E1
Newbery Ave NG10 236 C3
Newbold Ave
Borrowash DE72 221 E1
Chesterfield S41 95 F3
Newbold Back La S40 95 E3
Newbold CE Prim Sch S41 95 F4
Newbold Cl DE73 232 C1
Newbold Com Sch
Chesterfield S41 95 F3
Chesterfield, Newbold S40 95 E3
Newbold Ct 1 S41 95 E4
Newbold Dr
Castle Donington DE74 247 D3
Chesterfield S41 95 F3
Newbold Rd S40 95 E3
Newborough Rd DE24 233 E3
Newbound La NG17 134 B1
Newboundmill La NG19 135 D3
Newbridge Cl DE7 207 E4
Newbridge Cres DE24 232 C2
Newbridge Ct S41 77 D1
Newbridge Dr S43 96 B4
Newbridge La S41 77 D1
Newbridge Rd DE56 168 A1
Newbridge St S41 77 D1
Newburgh Terr S32 72 B1
Newbury Dr DE13 240 B1
Newbury St DE24 232 C4
Newby Rd S41 95 E4
Newcastle Cir NG7 268 A1
Newcastle Dr NG7 268 A2
Newcastle La ST4 269 D1
Newcastle Rd ST4 269 D1
Newcastle St
2 Mansfield NG18 268 B4
Mansfield Woodhouse NG19 136 A2
Sutton in A NG17 148 C2
Newchase Bsns Pk DE23 219 D1
Newdigate St Derby DE23 232 A4
Ilkeston DE7 209 D3
Kimberley NG16 195 F3
Nottingham NG7 268 A2
West Hallam DE7 207 E4
Newell Way DE4 127 E2
Newfield Cres S17 55 E4
Newfield Croft S17 55 E4
Newfield Farm Cl S12 43 F3
Newfield Green Rd S2 43 E3
Newfield La S17 55 E4
Newfield Rd DE15 248 A2
Newfield Sec Sch (Boys) S8 43 E2
Newfield Sec Sch (Girls) S8 43 E2
Newgate Cl DE73 233 D1
Newgate Fst Sch NG18 268 C4
Newgate La NG18 268 C4
Newgates La NG19 134 C1
Newhall Inf Sch DE11 255 F4
Newhall Jun Sch DE11 255 F4
Newhall Rd DE11 256 B3
Newhall St Edward's RC Prim Sch DE11 256 A3
Newham Ave DE5 169 E1
Newham Cl DE75 182 A1
Newhaven Ave NG19 136 A2
Newhaven Cl S40 95 D1
Newhaven Rd DE21 220 A3
Newholme Hospl DE45 109 F4
Newland Dale S41 266 B4
Newland Gdns S41 95 F3
Newland St DE1 267 A3
Newlands Ave
Chesterfield S40 95 E2
Sheffield S12 44 A3
Newlands Cl DE11 256 A1
Newlands Cres DE55 148 A2
Newlands Dr Hadfield SK13 9 F2
Heanor DE75 181 F2
Sheffield S12 44 A3
Somercotes DE55 170 B3
Newlands Gr S12 44 A3
Newlands Rd Sheffield S12 44 A3
Somercotes DE55 170 B2
Newlyn Dr Derby DE23 231 F4
South Normanton DE55 160 B3
Newlyn Pl S8 43 D2
Newman Dr DE14 254 A4
Newmanleys Rd NG16 194 C4
Newmanleys Rd S NG16 194 C4
Newmarket Ct DE24 219 F1
Newmarket Dr DE24 232 C4
Newmarket La S45 130 C2
Newmarket Way NG9 223 F1
Newport Cres NG19 135 F1
Newport Ct DE24 233 E3
Newport Rd ST16 269 D3
Newquay Pl DE24 233 E3
Newshaw La SK13 9 F2
Newstead Ave Derby DE21 219 F3
Sheffield S12 44 C2
Newstead Cl
5 Dronfield S18 56 B1
Sheffield S12 44 C2
Newstead Dr S12 44 C1
Newstead Gr
Nottingham NG1 268 A2
Sheffield S12 44 C2
Newstead Pl S12 44 C1
Newstead Rd
Long Eaton NG10 223 E2
Sheffield S12 44 C1
Newstead Rd S DE7 194 B2
Newstead Rise S12 44 C1
Newstead Terr SK17 85 D3
Newstead Way S12 44 C1
Newton Cl Belper DE56 179 E3
Newton Solney DE15 248 C4
Newton Dr NG9 223 F3
Newton La DE15 248 C4
Newton Leys DE15 248 B2
Newton Park Cl DE11 256 A4
Newton Prim Sch DE55 148 A2
Newton Rd
Burton u T DE15 248 A3
Tibshelf DE55 147 F2
Newton Solney CE Inf Sch DE15 248 C4
Newton St NG18 268 C3
Newton's La NG16 195 D2
Newton's Wlk DE22 218 C4
Newtondale Ave NG19 136 C1
Newtons Croft Cres S43 80 A3
Newtonwood La DE55 148 A3
Newtown Cty Prim Sch SK22 33 D3
Nicholas Cl DE21 220 C3
Nicholas St S41 115 E4
Nicholls St ST4 269 E1
Nicholson Ct SK17 69 E2
Nicholson Pl S8 43 D3
Nicholson Rd S2 43 D3
Nicholson's Row NG20 119 F2
Nicklaus Cl DE14 254 A4
Nicola Gdns DE23 231 E2
Nicolas Cl SK17 85 F4
Nidderdale Ct DE24 233 E3
Nields Way SK6 23 E2
Nightingale Ave NG19 135 D2
Nightingale Cl
Clay Cross S45 131 F1
Holloway DE4 155 F3
Ripley DE5 169 E1
Nightingale Dr
Mansfield NG19 135 F1
Woodville DE11 256 C2
Nightingale Inf Sch DE24 232 B4
Nightingale Jun Sch DE24 232 B4
Nightingale Rd DE24 232 B4
Nile St NG1 268 B2
Nine Ladies DE4 126 B2
Ninelands Rd S32 53 D4
No Man's Heath Rd DE12 264 C2
No Man's La Risley DE7 222 B4
Sandiacre DE7 222 B4
Nobel Cl S80 81 F1
Noble St DE1 267 D1
Nodder Rd S13 44 B4
Nodin Hill La DE56 168 A2
Noel St Derby DE22 218 B3
Mansfield NG18 268 B4
Noel-Baker Com Sch DE24 232 C2
Nook End Rd DE75 181 E1
Nook The Barrow u T DE73 244 A3
Heanor DE75 181 E2
Holbrook DE56 191 E4
Shirebrook NG20 119 E2
Stoney Middleton S32 72 A2
Nooning La DE72 234 C4
Norbriggs Prim Sch S43 79 D2
Norbriggs Rd S43 79 E1
Norburn Dr S21 60 B3
Norbury CE Prim Sch DE6 197 F4
Norbury Cl Chesterfield S40 95 D3
Derby DE22 204 C1
Sheffield S8 56 C4
Norbury Cres DE23 231 E3
Norbury Ct DE22 204 B1
Norbury Hollow DE6 183 E1
Norbury Way DE56 179 E3
Norfolk Ave S42 115 F1
Norfolk Cl S40 114 A4
Norfolk Ct NG19 136 C3
Norfolk Dr NG18 268 B4
Norfolk Fst Sch S2 43 F4
Norfolk Gdns DE22 218 C4
Norfolk Mid Sch S2 43 F4
Norfolk Rd Burton u T DE15 254 B4
Long Eaton NG10 223 F1
Norfolk Sch S2 43 F4
Norfolk Sq SK13 10 B1
Norfolk St Derby DE23 219 D1
Glossop SK13 10 B1
Norfolk Wlk NG10 223 D3
Norgreave Way S20 59 F4
Norman Ave DE23 231 F4
Norman Cl NG3 268 B2
Norman Cres DE7 194 C2
Norman Keep DE13 239 E3
Norman Rd Ripley DE5 169 E1
Somercotes DE55 170 C4
Tutbury DE13 239 E3
Norman St Ilkeston DE7 194 C2
Kimberley NG16 195 F4
Normandy Rd DE65 228 C1
Normanton Ave DE55 159 E2
Normanton Gr S13 44 C3
Normanton Hill S13 44 B3
Normanton Inf Sch DE23 231 F4
Normanton Jun Sch DE23 231 F4
Normanton La DE23 231 D4
Normanton Rd DE23 267 B1
Normanton Sch SK17 85 D4
Normanton Spring Ct S13 44 C3
Normanton Spring Rd S13 44 C3
Normanton Village Inf Sch DE23 231 F4
North Ave Ashbourne DE6 173 D1
Derby, Darley Abbey DE3 205 D2
Derby, Mickleover DE3 217 F1
Sandiacre NG10 223 D3
North Brook Rd SK13 9 F2
North Castle St ST16 269 D4
North Church St
Bakewell DE45 109 E3
1 Nottingham NG1 268 B2
North Circus St NG7 268 A2
North Cl Derby DE65 217 F2
South Normanton DE55 159 F3
Tintwistle SK13 9 F4
Unstone S18 76 C3
Willington DE65 242 A3
North Cres Killamarsh S21 60 C4
Long Duckmanton S44 98 A3
North Derbyshire Tertiary Coll S43 80 C2
North Derbyshire Tertiary Coll (Markland Campus) S80 81 F2
North End DE4 154 C1
North Farm Cl S26 61 F4
North Gr S44 98 A3
North La
Belper, Farnah Green DE56 178 B1
Belper, Milford DE56 190 C4
North La DE6 187 F2
North Leys DE6 173 D1
North Moor View S43 96 C4
North Par Derby DE1 267 B4
Matlock Bath DE4 143 D1
North Rd Buxton SK17 66 B1
Calow S44 96 C2
Clowne S43 80 C2
Glossop SK13 10 B2
Hayfield SK22 25 E2
Long Eaton NG10 236 B3
Nottingham NG7 268 A1
North Row DE22 205 D1
North Sherwood St NG1 268 B2
North Side S42 115 E1
North St Alfreton DE55 159 D2
Blackwell DE55 147 F1
Bramley-Vale S44 117 E1
Burton u T DE15 248 A2
Clay Cross S45 131 D3
Cromford DE4 155 D3
Derby, Little Chester DE1 267 B5
Derby, Littleover DE23 218 B1
9 Ilkeston DE7 194 C1
Langley Mill NG16 182 A2
Market Warsop NG20 120 B2
Melbourne DE73 252 A4
North Wingfield S42 131 F3
Nottingham NG2 268 C1
Pinxton NG16 160 B2
Somercotes DE55 170 B3
South Normanton DE55 159 F3
Stoke-on-T ST4 269 E2
North St continued
Swadlincote DE11 256 A3
Whaley Thorns NG20 101 D1
North Staffs Hospl Ctr (Outpatients Dept) ST4 269 D2
North Staffs Royal Infmy ST4 269 D2
North Terr S41 115 D4
North View DE4 168 A4
North View St S44 98 C2
North Walls ST16 269 E4
North Wingfield Inf & Jun Sch S42 131 F4
North Wingfield Rd S42 115 F2
Northacre Rd DE21 206 A1
Northam Dr DE5 169 E2
Northampton St NG3 268 C2
Northcliffe Rd DE6 173 E1
Northcote Ave Sheffield S2 43 D3
Stoke-on-T ST4 269 E2
Northcote Rd S8 43 D3
Northcote St NG10 236 C4
Northedge La S42 130 A4
Northern Ave S2 43 F4
Northern Comm S18 56 A1
Northern Dr NG9 209 E2
Northern Rd DE75 181 E1
Northfield Derby DE24 231 E2
Kilburn DE56 179 F1
Northfield Ave
Ilkeston DE7 194 C1
Long Eaton NG10 236 A2
Mansfield Woodhouse NG19 136 A2
Rocester ST14 197 D2
Northfield Cl ST14 210 A1
Northfield Cres NG9 223 F2
Northfield Inf & Jun Sch NG19 136 A3
Northfield Jun Sch S18 57 E2
Northfield La
Mansfield Woodhouse NG19 135 F2
Mansfield Woodhouse NG19 136 A3
Palterton S44 118 B3
Northfield Pk NG19 136 A3
Northfield Rd NG9 223 F2
Northfields Clowne S43 80 C2
Long Eaton NG10 236 A2
Northgate St 6 DE7 194 C1
Northlands S26 61 F4
Northmead Dr DE3 218 A2
Northmoor Cl 7 S43 96 C4
Northumberland Cl NG3 268 B2
Northumberland Rd DE15 254 B4
Northumberland St DE23 218 C1
Northwood Ave
Darley Dale DE4 127 E2
Derby DE21 219 F4
Northwood La
Ellastone DE6 183 E2
Northwood DE4 127 D3
Northwood Rise DE6 185 E4
Northwood St NG9 223 E4
Norton Ave Bolsover S44 98 C3
Chesterfield S40 114 A4
Sheffield S8, S12 43 F1
Norton Church Glebe S8 43 E1
Norton Church Rd S8 43 D1
Norton Coll S8 57 D4
Norton Free Sch S8 43 E1
Norton Green Cl S8 43 E1
Norton La S8 57 D4
Norton Lawns S8 43 E1
Norton Lees Cl S8 43 D2
Norton Lees Cres S8 43 D2
Norton Lees La S8 43 D2
Norton Lees Rd S8 43 D2
Norton Lees Sq S8 43 D2
Norton Mews S8 43 E1
Norton Park Ave S8 57 D4
Norton Park Cres S8 57 D4
Norton Park Dr S8 57 D4
Norton Park Rd S8 57 D4
Norton Park View S8 57 D4
Norwell Ct NG19 136 A1
Norwich Cl NG19 136 B3
Norwich St DE21 219 F4
Norwood Ave S41 115 F3
Norwood Cl
Chesterfield S41 115 F3
Derby DE22 218 A3
Norwood Cres S21 60 C4
Norwood High Sch S17 55 F3
Norwood Ind Est S21 60 C4
Norwood Pl S21 60 C4
Notintone St NG2 268 C1
Nottingham Cl S42 115 D2
Nottingham Dr S42 115 D2
Nottingham High Sch NG1 268 A2
Nottingham High Sch for Girls NG1 268 A2
Nottingham La
Ironville NG16 170 C3
Somercotes DE55, NG16 170 C3
Nottingham Midland Sta NG1 268 B1
Nottingham Rd
Alfreton DE55 159 D1
Ashby-de-la-Z LE65 258 C1
Belper DE56 179 D2
Borrowash DE72 221 E1
Breedon on t H DE73 252 B1
Codnor DE5 181 E4
Derby, Chaddesden DE21 219 F3
Derby, Little Chester DE1 267 C4
Nottingham Rd continued
Derby, Spondon DE21 220 C2
Eastwood, Bailey Grove NG16 182 C1
Eastwood, Giltbrook NG16 195 E4
Ilkeston DE7 209 D3
Long Eaton NG10 236 C4
Mansfield NG18 268 B3
Ripley DE5 169 F1
Selston NG16 171 F3
Somercotes DE55 159 D1
Stapleford, Stanton Gate NG9 223 F4
Stapleford, Trowell NG9 209 F3
Tansley DE4 144 A2
Trowell NG9 209 F3
Nottingham Trent Univ NG1 268 A2
Nowill Ct S8 43 D3
Nowill Pl S8 43 D3
Nugent Gdns NG3 268 C2
Nun's St DE1 218 C3
Nunbrook Gr SK17 85 E4
Nunn Brook Rd NG17 148 C1
Nunn Brook Rise NG17 148 C1
Nunn Cl NG17 148 C1
Nunsfield Dr DE24 233 D4
Nunsfield Rd SK17 66 B1
Nursery Ave
Sandiacre NG10 222 C3
West Hallam DE7 207 F4
Nursery Cl
Borrowash DE72 221 D1
Glossop SK13 17 E4
Swadlincote DE11 256 A3
Nursery Croft DE4 165 F3
Nursery Ct NG18 268 C4
Nursery Dr SK17 66 B1
Nursery Gdns DE55 160 B2
Nursery Hollow DE7 208 C3
Nursery La SK17 84 C3
Nursery St Mansfield NG18 268 C4
Stoke-on-T ST4 269 E1
Nutbrook Cres DE7 208 B2
Nuthall Cir DE7 208 B2
Nuttall Cl DE55 158 C2
Nuttall St DE55 158 C2
Nuttall Terr S44 117 E1
Nutwood Cl DE22 205 D2
Oadby Rise DE23 231 F3
Oak Ave Aldercar NG16 182 A3
Disley SK12 33 D3
Mansfield NG18 268 C4
Ripley DE5 180 B4
Sandiacre NG10 223 D4
Shirebrook NG20 119 E2
Oak Bank SK12 33 D3
Oak Bank Ave S41 77 D1
Oak Bank Cl NG18 268 B4
Oak Cl Chapel-en-le-F SK23 47 E3
Derby DE72 204 C2
Duffield DE56 190 C1
Killamarsh S21 60 B3
Linton DE11 261 F4
Mottram in L SK14 9 D2
Ockbrook DE72 221 E3
Pinxton NG16 160 B2
Oak Cres Ashbourne DE6 185 E4
Derby DE23 231 E4
Wingerworth S42 114 C2
Oak Dr Alfreton DE55 159 D2
Derby, Boulton DE24 233 D3
Derby, Mickleover DE65 217 F1
Doveridge DE6 211 D1
Eastwood NG16 182 C1
Hilton DE65 228 B1
Oak La DE6 212 B2
Oak Lodge Dr NG16 195 F4
Oak Rd Denstone ST14 196 B3
Elvaston DE72 233 F2
Grassmoor S42 115 F2
Matlock DE4 143 E3
Sheffield S12 44 A1
Oak St Brimington S43 78 A1
Derby DE23 219 D1
Glossop SK13 10 B1
Mosborough S20 59 E4
Sheffield S8 43 D4
Swadlincote DE11 256 A1
Oak Tree Ave S44 134 A4
Oak Tree Cl S44 97 E2
Oak Tree Cres NG19 136 A2
Oak Tree Ct DE72 221 E1
Oak Tree Gdns DE4 144 A2
Oak Tree Rd S43 80 C1
Oakamoor Cl S40 95 D3
Oakbank Ct S17 55 F3
Oakdale Cl S45 131 F1
Oakdale Rd DE55 160 A2
Oakdell S18 57 E2
Oakerthorpe Rd DE4 155 D1
Oakes Park Sch S8 43 E1
Oakes Park View S14 43 E1
Oakes The SK13 17 D4
Oakes's Row NG16 170 C3
Oakfield Ave S40 95 D1
Oakfield Ct DE7 193 D1
Oakfield Dr NG10 223 D2
Oakfield Rd Hadfield SK13 9 F2
Stapleford NG9 223 E4
Oakfields DE13 238 A2
Oakham Cl DE21 205 E1
Oakham Way DE7 194 C2
Oakhill Rd S18 57 E2

Oakhurst Cl DE56 178 B3
Oakland Ave
Long Eaton NG10 236 B3
Sutton in A NG17 148 C1
Oakland Cres DE55 170 B3
Oakland St DE55 159 D2
Oakland Terr NG10 236 B3
Oaklands Ave Derby DE23 231 E3
Heanor DE75 182 A1
Marple SK6 23 E4
Oaklands Cl DE5 180 B1
Oaklands Dr ST17 269 D3
Oaklands Rd Etwall DE65 229 E2
Swadlincote DE11 256 A3
Oaklands The DE55 160 A2
Oaklands Way DE73 252 A4
Oaklea SK17 85 E3
Oaklea Way S42 131 D3
Oakleigh Ave Derby DE21 219 F3
Swadlincote DE11 255 F3
Oakley Ave S40 95 F2
Oakley's Rd NG10 236 C4
Oakley's Rd W NG10 236 B3
Oakover Dr DE22 204 B1
Oakridge DE21 220 A4
Oakridge Cl NG19 136 C1
Oaks Ave Creswell S80 100 B4
Hayfield SK22 25 E1
Oaks Farm La S44 97 D1
Oaks La Ashover S45 129 E3
Old Brampton S42 94 A4
Oaks Rd DE65 242 A3
Oaks The DE21 205 E4
Oaksedge La DE4 144 A3
Oakside Way DE21 206 A2
Oakstedge La S45 145 D4
Oaktree Ave DE24 232 A4
Oaktree Cl DE55 170 A4
Oaktree Rd DE55 148 B1
Oakwell Cres DE7 208 C4
Oakwell Dr DE7 208 C4
Oakwood SK13 16 C4
Oakwood Cl DE65 231 E1
Oakwood District Ctr
DE21 206 A1
Oakwood Dr DE21 206 A1
Oakwood Inf Sch DE24 233 D3
Oakwood Jun Sch DE24 233 D3
Oakwood Rd SK12 32 B3
Oakworth Cl S20 59 F3
Oakworth Dr S20 59 E3
Oakworth Gr S20 59 E3
Oakworth View S20 59 E3
Oardale Rd NG18 268 A4
Oarr La S18 56 B1
Oat Hill DE4 165 F4
Oats Orch S20 59 E3
Occupation Cl S43 80 A3
Occupation La
North Wingfield S42 131 F4
Sheffield S12 44 C2
Woodville DE11 256 C1
Occupation Rd
Chesterfield S41 95 F4
Moira DE11 262 B4
New Houghton NG19 134 C4
Ochard St DE7 208 C4
Ochbrook Ct DE7 194 C2
Ockbrook Sch DE72 221 E3
Oddfellows Cotts 8 SK17 85 D4
Oddfellows Rd S32 53 D4
Oddfellows Terr S32 53 D4
Oddford La DE4 127 E1
Odom Ct S8 43 D3
Offcote Cres DE6 173 E2
Offerton Ave DE23 231 F4
Offridge Cl S43 80 C1
Ogden St SK14 16 A4
Ogle Dr NG7 268 A1
Ogston La
Brackenfield DE55 146 A2
Shirland DE55 146 A2
Ogston New Rd DE55 145 F2
Okeover Ave DE6 173 E1
Oker Ave DE4 127 D2
Oker Dr DE4 127 D2
Oker La DE4 142 B3
Oker Rd DE4 142 A4
Oker Terr DE4 142 A4
Old Bakery Cl S41 77 D1
Old Bank DE6 184 B4
Old Barn Cl DE21 205 E4
Old Chester Rd DE1 219 D4
Old Church La DE22 204 B3
Old Coach Rd DE4 143 F2
Old Coalpit La SK17 86 C1
Old Colliery La S42 132 C4
Old Coppice Side DE75 193 F4
Old Dam La SK17 49 E2
Old Derby Rd
Ashbourne DE6 185 E4
Eastwood NG16 182 B2
Old End DE12 265 F1
Old Gate HD7 2 C4
Old Gate Ave DE72 245 F3
Old Hackney La DE4 142 C4
Old Hall Ave
Derby, Alvaston DE24 233 D4
Derby, Littleover DE23 218 A1
Duffield DE56 190 C2
Whaley Bridge SK23 45 F2
Old Hall Cl
Darley Dale DE4 127 E2
Glossop SK13 10 B1
Old Hall Dr DE65 242 A3
Old Hall Gdns
Stoney Middleton S32 72 A2
Swadlincote DE11 256 A1
Old Hall Jun Sch S40 95 E1
Old Hall La
Church Broughton DE65 227 D4
Marple SK6 23 E3
Mottram in L SK14 9 D3
Whitwell S80 81 F3
Old Hall Mills Bsns Pk
DE21 205 E4
Old Hall Rd
Chesterfield S40 95 E2
Derby DE23 218 B1
Old Hall Sq 3 SK13 10 A3
Old Hartshay Hill DE5 169 E1
Old Hay Gdns S17 55 E3
Old Hay La S17 55 E3
Old Highcliff La DE56 177 D2
Old Hill Ashbourne DE6 173 E1
Bolsover S44 99 D1
Old House Mus DE45 109 E3
Old House Rd S40 95 E3
Old La Derby DE22 205 D1
Mosborough S20 60 A4
Shottle DE56 177 D3
Wirksworth DE4 154 C1
Old Lenton St NG1 268 B2
Old Lime Ct DE4 143 E3
Old Longhill Rd SK17 65 D2
Old Manor Rd NG19 136 B2
Old Mansfield Rd DE21 205 E1
Old Market Pl
Mansfield NG18 268 B4
South Normanton DE55 160 A3
Old Market Sq NG1 268 B1
Old Mill Cl Duffield DE56 190 C2
Pilsley S45 132 B1
Old Mill Dr S40 95 D4
Old Mill La NG19 136 C1
Old Park Ave S8 56 B4
Old Park Rd S8 56 B4
Old Peverel Rd S44 98 A2
Old Pit La DE7 193 D3
Old Pond The DE75 194 A4
Old Rd Branston DE14 253 F4
Buxton SK23 65 E3
Chesterfield S40 95 E2
Darley Dale DE4 127 E1
Furness Vale SK23 33 E2
Heage DE56 179 F4
Ladder Hill SK23 46 A1
Mottram in L SK14 9 D3
Old Brampton S40 95 E2
Tintwistle SK13 10 A4
Whaley Bridge SK23 45 F3
Old School Cl S44 117 E1
Old School La
Chesterfield S44 96 C1
Pleasley NG19 135 D3
Old St SK14 16 A4
Old Station Cl DE4 126 C4
Old Station Yd S43 96 B4
Old Storth La DE55 160 A2
Old Terr NG19 134 C2
Old Vicarage Cl DE23 218 B1
Old Vicarage La DE22 204 B3
Old Vicarage Sch The
DE22 205 D2
Old Whieldon Rd ST4 269 F1
Old Whittington La S18 76 C3
Oldbury Cl DE21 206 A1
Olde Derwent Ave DE4 143 D2
Oldfield Dr DE11 256 B3
Oldfield La Hilton DE65 241 D4
Hognaston DE6 164 A1
Kirk Ireton DE6 164 C1
Snelston DE6 184 A2
Wensley DE4 142 A4
Oldhay Cl S17 55 E3
Oldicote La DE15 248 C2
Oldknow Rd SK6 23 D3
Oldmill St ST4 269 F2
Oldridge Cl S40 95 D3
Oldwell Cl S17 55 E2
Olga Rd NG3 268 C2
Olive Ave Long Eaton NG10 223 F1
Shirebrook NG20 119 E3
Olive Cres S12 44 A1
Olive Gr DE21 219 F3
Olive Grove Rd S2 43 D4
Olive Rd S20 59 E4
Olive St DE22 218 C2
Olive Terr SK14 16 A4
Oliver Cl Heanor DE75 182 A1
Nottingham NG7 268 A2
Oliver Rd Ilkeston DE7 208 B3
Stoke-on-T ST4 269 D2
Oliver St NG7 268 A2
Olivet Rd S8 43 D2
Olivier St DE23 219 D1
Ollersett Ave SK22 33 E4
Ollersett La SK22 24 C1
Ollersett View Hospl
SK22 33 E4
Olton Rd DE3 217 E2
Onslow Rd DE3 217 F2
Onward Cotts SK17 85 E4
Opal Cl DE21 206 A1
Openacre NG16 170 C2
Openwood Rd DE56 179 F2
Openwoodgate DE56 179 E2
Orange Cl NG20 119 F3
Orange St DE55 159 D2
Orby Cl NG3 268 C2
Orchard Ave
Castle Donington DE74 247 D2
Whaley Bridge SK23 45 E4
Orchard Bsns Pk
Ilkeston DE7 194 B1
Sandiacre NG10 223 E3
Orchard Cl Barlborough S43 80 A4
Belper DE56 191 D4
Bolsover S44 99 D1
Breaston DE72 235 F4
Clowne S43 80 C2
Derby DE23 231 E4
Elvaston DE24 233 E2
Hilton DE65 228 B1
Melbourne DE73 252 A4
Ockbrook DE72 221 E2
Ripley DE5 181 D4
Shirebrook NG20 119 F3
Uttoxeter ST14 210 A1
Walton-on-T DE12 253 E1
West Hallam DE7 207 F4
Willington DE65 242 A3
Orchard Cotts DE56 190 C2
Orchard Cres
Glapwell S44 134 A4
Swanwick DE55 169 E4
Orchard Ct Derby DE21 220 C3
Langley Mill NG16 182 A2
Orchard Cty Prim Sch
DE74 247 D2
Orchard Dr Creswell S80 81 F1
Gamesley SK13 9 F1
Orchard La
Darley Dale DE4 142 C4
Wyaston DE6 185 E1
Orchard Lee S26 61 F3
Orchard Pl S21 60 B3
Orchard Rd Compstall SK6 15 D1
Matlock Bath DE4 143 D1
Somercotes DE55 170 B3
Whaley Bridge SK23 45 E4
Orchard Rise DE75 181 F1
Orchard Sq 26 S18 56 B1
Orchard St
Derby, Little Chester DE1 267 A4
Derby, Mickleover DE3 217 E1
Kimberley NG16 195 F3
Langley Mill NG16 182 A2
Long Eaton NG10 236 C4
Mansfield NG19 136 A1
Stafford ST17 269 E3
Stapleford NG9 223 E4
Swadlincote DE11 255 F3
Orchard The Belper DE56 179 D2
Codnor DE5 170 A1
Horsley Woodhouse DE7 192 B3
Stanton-by-D DE7 222 C4
Stramshall ST14 210 A2
Youlgreave DE45 125 E3
Orchard View
Bolsover S44 117 F4
Mansfield Woodhouse
NG19 136 A2
Orchard View Rd S40 95 E2
Orchard Way Derby DE73 232 C1
Sandiacre NG10 223 D2
Orchards The
Derby DE22 204 B2
Westwood NG16 171 D2
Orchards Way S40 95 E1
Orchid Cl Burton u T DE15 255 D4
Calow S44 97 D2
Ordish Ave DE21 219 F3
Ordley La DE6 183 F4
Oregon Way DE21 220 B3
Orford Ave SK12 32 B3
Organ Way SK14 9 E3
Oriel Ct DE1 267 C1
Oriel St ST4 269 E2
Orkney Cl DE24 231 E2
Orly Ave DE74 247 D1
Ormesby Cl S18 56 B1
Ormond Cl
Chesterfield S40 114 A4
Sheffield S8 57 D3
Ormond Dr S8 57 D3
Ormond Rd S8 57 D4
Ormond Way S8 57 D4
Ormonde St NG16 182 A2
Ormonde Terr NG16 182 A2
Ormsby Rd S41 95 F4
Ormskirk Rise DE21 220 C2
Orpean Way NG9 223 F1
Orpen Dr S14 43 F1
Orpen Way S14 43 F1
Orwins Cl 5 S41 95 E4
Osborne Cl NG10 223 D2
Osborne Croft S26 61 F3
Osborne Pl SK13 10 A3
Osborne Rd Derby DE23 219 E2
Stoke-on-T ST4 269 D2
Osborne St DE15 248 A2
Osmaston CE Prim Sch
DE6 185 F2
Osmaston Cl NG10 235 F3
Osmaston Park Ind Est
DE24 232 C4
Osmaston Rd DE23 219 D1
Osmaston St NG10 223 E3
Osmond Rd S21 59 E2
Osprey Cl Burton u T DE15 248 B2
Derby DE24 231 F1
Ossington Cl NG1 268 B2
Osterly Gn DE22 218 A3
Ostrich La DE6 163 D1
Oswestry Cl DE21 206 A2
Otter St DE1 219 D4
Otterburn Dr DE22 204 B1
Oulton Cl DE24 232 B2
Oundle Dr Ilkeston DE7 209 D4
Mansfield NG19 135 E1
Our Lady's RC Prim Sch
ST4 269 F1
Ousley La DE6 183 E3
Out La S44 132 C3
Outfield Rd DE15 254 C4
Outgang La
Mansfield Woodhouse
NG19 136 B2
Pleasley NG19 135 D3
Outlands Rd S33 50 C3
Outram Ct DE5 169 F1
Outram Rd S41 95 F3
Outram St DE5 169 F1
Outram Way DE24 231 F1
Outseats Dr DE55 159 D2
Oval Ct DE23 231 E4
Oval The ST17 269 E3
Over Haddon Craft Ctr
DE45 109 D1
Over Hill Rd Buxworth SK23 34 A3
Chinley SK23 34 A3
Over La Baslow DE45 91 F3
Belper DE56 179 F3
Hazelwood DE56 178 A1
Overcroft Rise S17 55 E2
Overdale DE4 143 E3
Overdale Ave SK17 85 E4
Overdale Cl NG10 236 A3
Overdale Gdns S17 55 E3
Overdale Rd Derby DE23 218 C1
Disley SK12 32 C3
Overdale Rise S17 55 E3
Overend Cl S14 43 E2
Overend Dr S14 43 E2
Overend Rd S14 43 E2
Overend Way S14 43 E2
Overlees S18 75 E2
Overseal Manor Sch DE12 262 A2
Overseal Prim Sch DE12 262 A2
Oversetts Ct DE11 255 F3
Oversetts Rd DE11 255 F3
Overstone Cl DE56 179 E2
Overton Cl S43 78 C2
Owen Ave NG10 237 D3
Ower Bar Rd S17 54 A2
Owers Ave DE75 193 F4
Owlcotes View S44 118 A4
Owler Car La S8, S18 57 F3
Owlers La DE23 218 B1
Owlston Cl NG16 182 C2
Owlswick Cl DE23 231 D4
Owlthorpe Ave S20 59 D4
Owlthorpe Cl S20 59 D4
Owlthorpe Dr S20 59 D4
Owlthorpe Gr S20 59 D4
Owlthorpe La S20 59 D4
Owlthorpe Rise S20 59 D4
Ox Cl S45 131 E2
Ox Close Ave S17 56 A3
Ox Hill S20 60 A3
Oxbury Rd NG16 195 F4
Oxclose Dr S18 56 B1
Oxclose La
Alsop en le D DE6 150 B1
Dronfield S18 56 B1
Mansfield Woodhouse
NG19 136 A2
Radmanthwaite NG19 135 E2
Oxcroft Est S44 99 E4
Oxcroft La Bolsover S44 99 D3
Elmton S44 99 F4
Oxcroft Way S43 80 A3
Oxenhope Cl DE23 230 C4
Oxford Cl S43 96 C4
Oxford Cres ST4 269 E2
Oxford St Blackwell DE55 147 F1
Bramley-Vale S44 117 F1
Derby, Litchurch DE1 267 C1
Derby, Spondon DE21 220 C3
Eastwood NG16 182 C1
Ilkeston DE7 208 C4
Long Eaton NG10 236 B4
Mansfield Woodhouse
NG19 136 B1
Nottingham NG1 268 A1
Ripley DE5 169 E1
Stoke-on-T ST4 269 E2
Swadlincote DE11 256 A1
Oxley Rd DE15 248 A2
Oxmead DE6 184 B4
Oxpasture La NG20 100 A3
Oxton Cl NG19 268 A4
Oxwich Ct DE21 206 A1
Ozier Holt NG10 236 B3

Pack Horse Rd DE73 252 A4
Packenham Bvd DE65 227 D2
Packer's Row S40 266 B3
Packman La S26 62 B3
Paddock Cl
Castle Donington DE74 246 C2
Wingerworth S42 114 C2
Paddock Cres S2 43 F3
Paddock Croft DE21 205 F1
Paddock La SK23 45 F3
Paddock The
Blackwell DE55 147 F1
Bolsover S44 99 D1
Burton u T DE15 248 A2
Buxton SK17 84 C4
Elvaston DE24 233 E2
Hadfield SK13 9 F3
Hollingworth SK14 9 F3
Ockbrook DE72 221 E2
Rolleston DE13 240 A2
Whaley Bridge SK23 45 F3
Paddock Way S18 57 D2
Paddocks Cl NG16 160 B2
Paddocks The
Mansfield Woodhouse
NG19 136 C3
Pilsley S45 132 B1
Sandiacre NG10 223 D3
Swadlincote DE11 255 F3
Woodthorpe S43 79 E2
Paddocks View NG10 236 A4
Padfield Cty Prim Sch
SK13 10 A3
Padfield Gate SK13 17 E4
Padfield Main Rd SK13 10 B3
Padget High Sch DE14 254 A4
Padley Cl Derby DE22 205 D3
Ripley DE5 169 E2
Padley Hill Mansfield NG18 268 B3
Nether Padley S32 53 F1
Padley Rd S32 53 E1
Padley Way S42 131 F3
Padley Wood La S45 147 D4
Padley Wood Rd S45 132 B1
Padstow Cl DE24 231 E2
Padstow Rd DE24 233 E3
Painter's La DE6 186 A2
Painters Way
Darley Dale DE4 127 E1
Winster DE4 141 E3
Paisley Cl S43 97 E4
Palace La DE56 166 B1
Palace Rd SK17 85 D4
Palatine Gr DE23 230 C4
Palatine St NG7 268 A1
Palerow La
Alderwasley DE56 166 C2
Spout DE56 166 C2
Pall Mall DE21 205 F2
Palladium Dr DE23 231 D3
Palm Cl DE23 218 A1
Palmbourne Ind Pk ST16 269 D4
Palmer Cl Branston DE14 254 A4
Stafford ST 16 269 F4
Palmer Cres S18 57 D1
Palmer Dr Stapleford NG9 223 E3
Swanwick DE55 169 F4
Palmerston Ct DE73 252 A4
Palmerston Gdns NG3 268 B2
Palmerston St Derby DE23 218 C1
Underwood Green NG16 171 F1
Westwood NG16 171 E2
Palterton La S44 117 E3
Palterton Prim Sch S44 118 A3
Pamela's Cl DE21 221 D3
Pankhurst Pl S45 131 E2
Panton Cl ST 16 269 F4
Parade The DE3 217 E1
Paradise St SK13 10 A3
Parcel Terr DE22 218 B3
Pares Way DE72 221 E3
Park Ave Ashbourne DE6 173 E1
Awsworth NG16 195 D3
Castle Donington DE74 246 C2
Darley Dale DE4 127 E2
Dronfield S18 57 D1
Eastwood NG16 182 C2
Furness Vale SK23 33 E2
Glapwell S44 118 B1
Holmesfield S18 75 D4
Ilkeston DE7 208 C4
Mansfield NG18 268 C4
Mansfield Woodhouse NG19 136 B2
Ripley DE5 169 F1
Scropton DE65 227 D3
Shirebrook NG20 119 F2
Stanley DE7 207 E3
Uttoxeter ST14 210 A1
Park Cl Chesterfield S40 115 D4
Glossop SK13 10 B1
Linton DE12 261 E3
Little Eaton DE21 205 D4
Matlock DE4 143 E2
Pinxton NG16 160 B1
Shirland DE55 146 C1
Stanton-by-D DE7 222 C4
Park Cres
Chapel-en-le-F SK23 47 D3
Doveridge DE6 211 D1
Eastwood NG16 182 C2
Furness Vale SK23 33 E2
Glossop SK13 10 A2
Heage DE56 179 F4
Ilkeston DE7 209 D4
Stafford ST17 269 E3
Park Ct Heanor DE75 181 F1
Mansfield NG18 268 C4
Swadlincote DE11 256 B3
Park Dene Dr SK13 10 B1
Park Dr Chesterfield S41 266 C1
Derby DE23 218 B1
Ilkeston DE7 208 C4
Nottingham NG7 268 A1
Sandiacre NG10 223 D2
Swanwick DE55 169 F3
Park Edge S32 52 C4
Park Farm Ctr DE22 204 B1
Park Farm Dr DE22 204 B1
Park Farm Mews S21 60 B1
Park Gr DE22 218 C4
Park Grange Cl S2 43 E4
Park Grange Dr S2 43 E4
Park Grange Mount S2 43 E4
Park Grange Rd S2 43 E4
Park Grange View S2 43 E4
Park Hall Ave S40 114 A4
Park Hall Cl S40 114 A4
Park Hall Gdns
Chesterfield S40 114 A4
Mansfield Woodhouse
NG19 136 B3

Park Hall La DE7 .... 207 E4
Park Hall Rd Denby DE5 ...... 180 A2
 Mansfield Woodhouse
 NG19 .... 136 B3
Park Head Rd DE4 .... 143 D3
Park Hill Awsworth NG16 ... 195 D3
 Eckington S21 .... 59 F2
Park Hill Cl SK22 .... 24 B1
Park Hill Dr DE23 .... 231 F4
Park House Prim Sch
 S45 .... 132 A2
Park Jun & Inf Schs The
 NG20 .... 119 F3
Park La
 Castle Donington DE74 .... 246 C2
 Chesterfield S41 .... 95 F4
 Darley Dale DE4 .... 127 E1
 Derby, Allestree DE22 ..... 204 C2
 Derby, Littleover DE23 .... 218 B1
 Holbeck NG20 .... 101 E3
 Mansfield NG18 .... 268 B3
 Over Haddon DE4 .... 110 B1
 Pentrich DE5 .... 169 D4
 Pinxton NG16 .... 160 B1
 Shirland DE55 .... 159 D4
 Shirley DE6 .... 200 B4
 South Wingfield DE55 ...... 157 E1
 Tutbury DE13 .... 239 D3
 Weston-on-T DE72 .... 245 F2
Park Leys Ct DE21 .... 220 C2
Park Mews
 Mansfield Woodhouse
 NG19 .... 136 B2
 Somercotes DE55 .... 170 B3
Park Mill Dr DE55 .... 159 E4
Park Pale The DE13 .... 239 E3
Park Ravine NG7 .... 268 A1
Park Rd Ashbourne DE6 .... 173 E1
 Bakewell DE45 .... 109 E3
 Belper DE56 .... 179 D1
 Buxton SK17 .... 85 D4
 Chapel-en-le-F SK23 .... 47 D3
 Chesterfield S40 .... 266 A1
 Chesterfield S40 .... 266 B2
 Derby, Mickleover DE3 ..... 217 E1
 Derby, Spondon DE21 ...... 220 B3
 Disley SK12 .... 32 A3
 Duffield DE56 .... 190 B2
 Hadfield SK13 .... 10 A2
 Heage DE56 .... 179 F4
 Holmewood S42 .... 116 C1
 Ilkeston DE7 .... 208 C4
 Linton DE12 .... 262 A3
 Mansfield Woodhouse
 NG19 .... 136 A2
 New Mills SK22 .... 33 E4
 Nottingham NG7 .... 268 A1
 Over Haddon DE45 .... 110 A1
 Ripley DE5 .... 169 F1
 Shirebrook NG20 .... 119 F3
 Stapleford NG9 .... 223 F4
 Swadlincote, Church Gresley
 DE11 .... 256 B1
 Swadlincote, Newhall DE12 . 255 E3
 Tupton S42 .... 131 E4
 Whaley Bridge SK23 .... 45 E3
Park Rise S18 .... 75 D4
Park Row Clay Cross S45 ... 131 E2
 Nottingham NG1 .... 268 A1
Park Side DE55 .... 170 B4
Park Spring Cl S2 .... 43 E4
Park Spring Dr S2 .... 43 E4
Park Spring Gr S2 .... 43 E4
Park Spring Pl S2 .... 43 E4
Park Spring Way S2 .... 43 E4
Park St Alfreton DE55 ...... 158 C2
 Barlborough S43 .... 80 A4
 Breaston DE72 .... 235 F4
 Chesterfield S40 .... 115 D4
 Derby DE1 .... 267 D2
 Heanor DE75 .... 181 E1
 Long Eaton NG10 .... 223 E1
 Mansfield Woodhouse
 NG19 .... 136 A2
 Ripley DE5 .... 169 F1
 Stafford ST17 .... 269 E3
 Stapleford NG9 .... 223 E3
 Swadlincote DE11 .... 256 A3
 Uttoxeter ST14 .... 210 B1
 Wessington DE55 .... 157 F4
Park Terr Glossop SK13 ...... 17 E4
 Northwood DE4 .... 127 D3
 Nottingham NG1 .... 268 A1
Park The Darley Dale DE4 .. 127 E2
 Mansfield NG18 .... 268 C4
 Mayfield DE6 .... 184 B4
Park Valley NG7 .... 268 A1
Park View
 Aston-on-T DE72 .... 246 A4
 Bakewell DE45 .... 109 E3
 Barlborough S43 .... 80 A4
 Chesterfield S41 .... 115 E4
 Clowne S43 .... 80 C3
 Heanor DE75 .... 181 E1
 Somercotes DE55 .... 170 B3
Park View Ave S20 .... 59 F4
Park View Cl DE22 .... 204 C2
Park View Ct S8 .... 43 E1
Park View Dr SK23 .... 47 D3
Park View Rise SK22 .... 24 B1
Park View Way NG18 .... 268 C3
Park Way DE65 .... 229 E2
Parker Ave S44 .... 96 C2
Parker Cl DE11 .... 267 A4
Parker Ctr DE21 .... 219 E4
Parker St DE1 .... 218 C4
Parker's Croft Rd ST17 ...... 269 E3
Parker's La NG19 .... 136 B2

Parkers Cl DE11 .... 257 D1
Parkers La S17 .... 55 E4
Parkfield Cl S2 .... 43 D4
Parkfield Cres DE12 .... 265 F1
Parkfield Cl SK17 .... 85 D4
Parkfield La DE6 .... 184 B2
Parkfields Dr DE22 .... 218 C4
Parkgate Cl S20 .... 59 D4
Parkgate Croft S20 .... 59 D4
Parkgate Dr S20 .... 59 D4
Parkgate La Staveley S21 .... 77 F3
 Unstone S21 .... 77 F3
Parkham Rd NG16 .... 195 F4
Parkhill La S21 .... 60 B1
Parkhouse Cl S45 .... 131 D2
Parkhouse Dr DE55 .... 159 F3
Parkhouse Rd S45 .... 132 A2
Parkin St DE55 .... 159 D2
Parkland Ave SK22 .... 24 B1
Parkland Dr S42 .... 115 D1
Parklands Dr DE73 .... 59 D4
Parklands Inf Sch NG10 .... 223 D1
Parks Ave DE55 .... 157 F2
Parkside Buxton SK17 .... 85 D4
 Heage DE56 .... 179 F4
Parkside Ave NG16 .... 236 A4
Parkside Cl NG16 .... 170 C2
Parkside Com Sch S40 ...... 266 A2
Parkside Dr Ironville NG16 . 170 C2
 Long Eaton NG10 .... 236 A4
Parkside Jun Sch DE6 .... 173 E1
Parkside La SK6 .... 23 E3
Parkside Rd DE21 .... 220 A3
Parkside Sh Ctr S21 .... 60 B4
Parkstone Ct DE3 .... 217 E1
Parkstone Delph S12 .... 44 A1
Parkview DE21 .... 205 E4
Parkville Cl SK17 .... 85 E3
Parkway Derby DE73 .... 232 C1
 New Mills SK22 .... 24 B1
 Whitwell S80 .... 82 A3
Parkway Ct S8 .... 56 C4
Parkway The DE4 .... 127 E2
Parkwood Sch DE55 .... 158 C2
Parliament Cl DE22 .... 218 C2
Parliament Rd NG19 .... 268 A4
Parliament St Derby DE22 . 218 C2
 Swadlincote DE11 .... 255 F3
Parsonage Cl S20 .... 59 E3
Parsonage Croft DE45 ...... 109 E3
Parsonage Gdns SK6 .... 23 D2
Parsons Cl SK17 .... 137 E3
Parsons Gate S33 .... 40 A3
Parsons Gr DE5 .... 180 B1
Partington Cl SK13 .... 10 C1
Partington Pk SK13 .... 10 B2
Partridge Cl S21 .... 59 D2
Partridge Dr DE11 .... 256 C2
Partridge Way DE3 .... 218 A2
Parture Gr S21 .... 59 E2
Parwich Cl S40 .... 95 D3
Parwich La DE4 .... 151 F4
Parwich Prim Sch DE6 ...... 151 E1
Parwich Rd S42 .... 131 F3
Pasteur Ave DE5 .... 169 E1
Pasture La Brassington DE4 . 152 B1
 Flagg SK17 .... 106 B3
 Hilcote DE55 .... 148 B1
 Long Eaton NG10 .... 237 D3
 Stonebroom DE55 .... 147 D2
Pasture Rd NG9 .... 209 E1
Pastures Ave DE23 .... 230 C4
Pastures Hill DE23 .... 231 D4
Pastures Hospl DE3 .... 230 A4
Pastures The
 Duffield DE56 .... 190 C2
 Eastwood NG16 .... 195 D4
 Mansfield Woodhouse
 NG19 .... 136 C3
 Repton DE65 .... 242 B1
 Swadlincote DE11 .... 255 F3
Paterson Ave DE21 .... 220 A3
Patmore Sq DE23 .... 231 F4
Paton Gr S43 .... 96 B4
Patrick Cl DE12 .... 261 E3
Patten Ct DE24 .... 232 A3
Patterdale Cl S18 .... 56 C1
Patterson Pl NG18 .... 268 C4
Pattison St S44 .... 98 C3
Paulet High Sch DE15 .... 254 C4
Paulson's Dr NG18 .... 268 B4
Pavilion Cl S43 .... 80 C1
Pavilion Gdns Buxton SK17 . 85 D4
 New Houghton NG19 .... 134 C4
Pavilion Rd Derby DE23 .... 231 E4
 Ilkeston DE7 .... 208 C4
Pavilion Workshops S42 .... 116 B1
Paxton Cl Derby DE3 .... 217 E1
 Matlock DE4 .... 143 D3
Paxton Ct S14 .... 43 F2
Paxton Gdns NG3 .... 268 C2
Paxton Rd S41 .... 96 B3
Payler Cl S2 .... 44 A4
Payne St DE22 .... 218 B3
Peach Ave Selston NG16 ... 171 F3
 South Normanton DE55 ... 160 A4
Peach St Derby DE22 .... 218 B3
 Heanor DE75 .... 181 E1
Peachey St NG1 .... 268 B2
Peacock Cl Hadfield SK13 .... 9 F2
 Killamarsh S21 .... 60 B3
Peacock Pl DE7 .... 194 B2
Peacock St NG18 .... 268 B3
Peacock Way DE55 .... 169 F4
Peacroft La DE65 .... 228 B1
Peafield La NG19 .... 136 C2
Peafield Lane Prim Sch
 NG19 .... 136 C2

Peak Ave DE55 .... 170 A3
Peak Cavern S33 .... 38 A1
Peak Dale Prim Sch SK17 ... 67 D3
Peak Forest CE Prim Sch
 SK17 .... 49 D2
Peak Pl S43 .... 97 E4
Peak Railway DE4 .... 143 D3
Peak Rd SK22 .... 33 E4
Peak The NG20 .... 119 F2
Peak View Clowne S43 .... 80 B3
 South Normanton DE55 .... 159 F3
Peak View Dr DE6 .... 173 E1
Peak View Rd S40 .... 95 E3
Peakdale Cl
 Long Eaton NG10 .... 236 A3
 Ripley DE5 .... 180 B3
Peakdale Cres S12 .... 44 C3
Peakdale Rd Hadfield SK13 ... 9 F2
 Marple SK6 .... 23 D2
Peakland View DE4 .... 127 D2
Peaknaze Cl SK13 .... 17 D4
Peaktor La DE4 .... 126 C4
Pear Tree Ave Ripley DE5 .. 180 B4
 Swadlincote DE55 .... 255 F4
Pear Tree Cl Brimington S43 . 97 D4
 Hadfield SK13 .... 9 F2
 Hartshorne DE11 .... 257 D4
 Killamarsh S21 .... 60 B3
 Marple SK6 .... 23 D4
Pear Tree Com Jun & Inf
 Schs DE23 .... 232 A4
Pear Tree Cres DE23 .... 232 A4
Pear Tree Dr Linton DE12 .. 261 E3
 Shirebrook NG20 .... 119 F3
Pear Tree Ind Pk DE23 ..... 232 A4
Pear Tree Rd S45 .... 132 B1
Pear Tree St DE23 .... 219 D1
Pear Tree Sta DE23 .... 232 A4
Pearce La S42 .... 114 B2
Pearl Bank DE6 .... 211 F4
Pearl Cl DE21 .... 206 A1
Pearl Way SK14 .... 9 D1
Peartree Ave S42 .... 114 C2
Peartree Cl DE74 .... 247 D2
Peartree Ct DE21 .... 205 E1
Peartree La NG17 .... 134 A1
Peas Hill Rd NG3 .... 268 B2
Pease Cl DE55 .... 159 D2
Pease Hill DE55 .... 159 D2
Peasehill DE5 .... 180 C4
Peasehill Rd DE5 .... 180 C4
Peasunhurst La S45 .... 113 D1
Peat La S36 .... 166 B2
Peatburn Ave DE75 .... 181 E1
Peatfield Rd Killamarsh S21 . 60 C4
 Stapleford NG9 .... 209 E1
Peats Cl DE6 .... 165 D1
Peckham Gdns DE22 .... 218 A3
Pedley Ave 1 S20 .... 59 F4
Pedley Dr 2 S20 .... 59 F4
Pedley St DE7 .... 208 C4
Peebles Cl DE24 .... 231 F1
Peel Cres NG19 .... 135 E1
Peel Rd NG19 .... 268 A4
Peel St Derby DE22 .... 218 B3
 Langley Mill NG16 .... 182 A2
 Long Eaton NG10 .... 236 C4
 Nottingham NG1 .... 268 A2
 Padfield SK13 .... 10 B3
 South Normanton DE55 .... 160 A3
 Stafford ST16 .... 269 D4
Peers Cl DE21 .... 206 A1
Peet St DE22 .... 218 C2
Pegasus Way DE65 .... 228 C1
Peggs Wlk DE23 .... 231 F4
Pegwell Cl DE23 .... 231 E4
Pelham Ave DE7 .... 194 C1
Pelham Cres NG7 .... 268 A1
Pelham St Derby DE22 ...... 218 C2
 Mansfield NG18 .... 268 C4
 11 Nottingham NG1 .... 268 B1
Pemberton St NG1 .... 268 B1
Pemberton The DE55 .... 160 A2
Pembleton Dr NG19 .... 135 E1
Pembrey Cl NG9 .... 209 E1
Pembroke Cl 7 S40 .... 95 E1
Pembroke Ct 6 S41 .... 95 F4
Pembroke Rd Dronfield S18 . 76 A4
 Shireoaks S81 .... 63 F4
Pembroke St DE21 .... 219 E4
Pen Cl DE55 .... 148 A2
Penalton Cl DE24 .... 232 C3
Pendean Cl DE55 .... 147 F1
Pendennis Cl DE24 .... 233 D3
Pendine Cl DE55 .... 160 B3
Pendlebury Dr DE3 .... 217 F1
Pendleside Way DE23 ...... 230 C4
Pendleton La DE56 .... 166 C4
Penfold Way DE55 .... 147 D3
Penge Rd DE22 .... 218 A4
Penhaligan's Cl DE73 .... 232 C1
Penine View DE56 .... 179 F4
Peniston Rise DE73 .... 252 A4
Penistone Gdns S45 .... 131 E1
Penkhull Inf Sch ST4 .... 269 E2
Penkhull New Rd ST4 .... 269 E1
Penkhull Terr ST4 .... 269 E1
Penkville St ST4 .... 269 E1
Penmore Cl S41 .... 115 E4
Penmore Gdns S41 .... 96 B1
Penmore La S41 .... 115 E4
Penmore St S41 .... 115 E4
Penn La DE73 .... 252 A4
Penn St DE56 .... 179 D2
Penncroft Dr S45 .... 131 E1
Penncroft La S45 .... 131 E2
Penniment La NG19 .... 135 D1

Pennine Ave DE55 .... 170 B4
Pennine Cl
 Long Eaton, New Sawley
 NG10 .... 236 B2
 Long Eaton, Wilsthorpe
 NG10 .... 223 D1
 Mansfield Woodhouse NG19 136 B2
 Newton DE55 .... 148 A2
 Sutton in A NG17 .... 148 C2
 Tibshelf DE55 .... 147 F3
Pennine Dr Selston NG16 .. 171 F4
 South Normanton DE55 .... 159 F3
Pennine Rd SK13 .... 17 C4
Pennine View S44 .... 118 A3
Pennine Way
 Chesterfield S40 .... 95 E3
 Grassmoor S42 .... 115 F2
 Swadlincote DE11 .... 256 A2
Pennine Way Jun Sch
 DE11 .... 256 A1
Penns Rd S2 .... 43 E3
Penny Acres Prim Sch S18 . 74 C4
Penny Engine La S21 .... 59 F2
Penny Gn S80 .... 82 A3
Penny La S17 .... 55 E3
Penny Long La DE22 .... 218 C4
Pennycress Cl DE23 .... 231 D4
Pennycroft La ST14 .... 210 B1
Pennycroft Rd ST14 .... 210 A1
Pennycrofts ST16 .... 269 E4
Pennyfields Bvd NG10 ...... 236 A4
Pennyfoot St NG1 .... 268 C1
Pennytown Ct DE55 .... 159 E1
Pennyunk La DE45 .... 89 F1
Pennywell Dr S42 .... 113 E4
Penrhyn Ave DE23 .... 218 B1
Penrhyn Cl NG3 .... 268 B2
Penrith Pl DE21 .... 205 E1
Penrose Cres S44 .... 97 E2
Pentagon The DE21 .... 219 E3
Pentewen Cl DE22 .... 204 C1
Penthorpe Cl S12 .... 44 A3
Pentland Cl
 5 Chesterfield S40 .... 95 E3
 Derby DE21 .... 206 A1
Pentland Gdns NG10 .... 223 D1
Pentland Rd S18 .... 56 B1
Pentrich Rd Ripley DE5 ..... 169 E1
 Swanwick DE55 .... 169 E4
Penzance Rd DE24 .... 233 D3
Pepper La DE7 .... 208 C1
Percy St Derby DE22 .... 218 C2
 Ilkeston DE7 .... 208 C4
Percy Wood Cl DE65 .... 228 B1
Peregrine Way S26 .... 61 F3
Peregrine Cl
 Burton u T DE15 .... 248 B2
 3 Derby DE24 .... 231 E2
Perlethorpe Ave
 Mansfield NG19 .... 136 A1
 Nottingham NG2 .... 268 C1
Perth Cl Burton u T DE15 .. 248 B1
 Derby DE3 .... 217 F2
 Mansfield Woodhouse
 NG19 .... 136 B3
Perth Dr NG9 .... 209 F1
Perth St Derby DE21 .... 205 E1
 Nottingham NG1 .... 268 B2
Peter Baines Ind Est DE22 . 267 A1
Peter More Hill S80 .... 81 F2
Peter St Ashbourne DE6 .... 173 E1
 Hadfield SK13 .... 10 A3
Peterborough St DE21 ...... 219 F4
Peterdale Cl S43 .... 96 C4
Peterdale Rd S43 .... 96 C4
Peterhouse Terr DE23 ...... 219 D1
Peterlee Pl DE24 .... 233 D3
Peters Ave S45 .... 131 D2
Peters Ct DE65 .... 227 E1
Petersgate NG10 .... 223 D1
Petersgate Cl NG10 .... 223 D1
Petersham Dr DE24 .... 233 E3
Petersham Rd NG10 .... 223 D1
Peterway DE55 .... 170 B4
Pettifor Terr DE55 .... 147 E1
Petty Close La DE6 .... 202 B1
Pettyclose La S41 .... 96 B3
Petworth Ave NG9 .... 223 F2
Pevensey Ave S41 .... 95 F3
Pevensey Ct S41 .... 95 F4
Peveril Ave Borrowash DE72 221 E1
 New Mills SK22 .... 24 B1
Peveril Cl Castleton S33 ..... 38 B1
 Darley Dale DE4 .... 127 E2
 Somercotes DE55 .... 170 B3
Peveril Cres
 Long Eaton NG10 .... 235 F3
 West Hallam DE7 .... 207 F4
Peveril Ct Glossop SK13 ..... 17 E4
 Ripley DE5 .... 169 E1
Peveril Dr Ilkeston DE7 ..... 194 B1
 Nottingham NG7 .... 268 A1
 Somercotes DE55 .... 170 B3
Peveril Gdns SK12 .... 33 D3
Peveril Mews SK12 .... 33 D3
Peveril Rd Buxton SK17 ...... 85 E4
 Castleton S33 .... 38 B1
 Chesterfield S41 .... 95 F4
 Eckington S21 .... 59 F2
 Tibshelf DE55 .... 147 F3
Peveril St DE24 .... 232 B3
Peverill Rd S44 .... 98 C2
Pewit Cl S42 .... 132 B4
Pewit La Pilsley DE55 .... 147 E3
 Tibshelf DE55 .... 147 E3
Pheasant Field Dr DE21 .... 221 D3
Pheasant Hill NG19 .... 136 A1
Philip Howard Rd SK13 ...... 17 E4

Philips Croft DE56 .... 190 C2
Philipway DE55 .... 170 B4
Phoenix Ct S12 .... 44 C1
Phoenix Rd S12 .... 44 C1
Phoenix St DE1 .... 267 B4
Phyllis Gr NG10 .... 236 C4
Pic Tor La DE4 .... 143 D2
Piccadilly Cotts S41 .... 96 B2
Piccadilly La DE6 .... 172 B1
Piccadilly Rd S41 .... 96 B2
Pickard La DE56 .... 168 B1
Pickering Ave NG16 .... 182 C1
Pickering Rise DE21 .... 205 E1
Pickford Pl SK23 .... 47 D3
Pickleys La DE6 .... 224 B4
Pickton Cl S40 .... 95 E1
Pictor Gr SK17 .... 85 E4
Pictor Rd SK17 .... 85 E4
Piddocks Rd DE15 .... 255 D3
Pig La DE4 .... 111 D2
Pighills La S18 .... 57 D2
Pike Cl S40 .... 95 D3
Pike View Cl SK23 .... 34 C1
Pike's La SK13 .... 17 D4
Pilcher Gate NG1 .... 268 B1
Pilgrim Ct S81 .... 63 F4
Pilgrim Pl ST16 .... 269 E3
Pilgrim St ST16 .... 269 E3
Pilgrims Way DE24 .... 231 E2
Pilhough La DE4 .... 126 B3
Pilhough Rd DE4 .... 126 C3
Pilkington's Yd S21 .... 59 F2
Pillar Butts DE4 .... 165 F4
Pilsley CE Prim Sch DE45 ... 91 E1
Pilsley Cl DE56 .... 179 E3
Pilsley Prim Sch S45 .... 132 B1
Pilsley Rd Clay Cross S45 .. 131 F2
 Morton DE55 .... 147 D3
Pimlico Derby DE22 .... 218 A3
 Ilkeston DE7 .... 208 C4
Pimm's Rd DE6 .... 217 D4
Pinch The DE6 .... 150 A1
Pinchom's Hill Rd DE56 .... 179 D2
Pincot Rd SK22 .... 33 E4
Pindale Ave S43 .... 97 E4
Pindale Rd Castleton S33 ... 38 C1
 Hope S33 .... 38 C1
Pinder St NG1 .... 268 B1
Pine Ave NG16 .... 182 A2
Pine Cl Branston DE14 ...... 254 A4
 Creswell S80 .... 81 F1
 Derby DE21 .... 220 A2
 Etwall DE65 .... 229 E2
 Killamarsh S21 .... 60 B3
 Mansfield Woodhouse
 NG19 .... 136 B3
 Ripley DE5 .... 169 E1
 Shirebrook NG20 .... 119 F3
 Smalley DE7 .... 192 C3
Pine Croft DE6 .... 185 E4
Pine Gr DE11 .... 255 F3
Pine St S43 .... 97 D4
Pine Tree Wlk NG16 .... 182 B3
Pine View Chesterfield S40 . 95 D2
 Clay Cross S45 .... 131 F2
Pine Wlk DE11 .... 261 F4
Pinecroft Ct DE21 .... 206 A1
Pines The DE72 .... 235 D3
Pinewood DE5 .... 181 D4
Pinewood Rd Belper DE56 . 178 C3
 Burton u T DE15 .... 254 C3
 Matlock DE4 .... 143 D4
Pinfold SK13 .... 9 F2
Pinfold Cl
 Holymoorside S42 .... 113 F4
 Repton DE65 .... 242 B1
 Tutbury DE13 .... 239 E3
Pinfold Cres SK17 .... 69 E2
Pinfold Hill S32 .... 72 C1
Pinfold La Bradley DE6 ..... 187 D4
 Repton DE65 .... 242 B1
 Stapleford NG9 .... 223 F4
Pinfold Rd SK17 .... 69 E2
Pinfold St S21 .... 59 E2
Pinfold The Belper DE56 ... 179 E3
 Elvaston DE72 .... 233 F2
 Glapwell S44 .... 118 A1
 Middleton DE45 .... 124 C2
Pinfold View DE45 .... 109 E3
Pingle DE22 .... 204 C2
Pingle Cres DE56 .... 178 C3
Pingle Farm Rd DE11 .... 255 F3
Pingle Grange S43 .... 96 C4
Pingle La Belper DE56 ...... 178 C3
 Carsington DE4 .... 164 C4
Pingle Rd S21 .... 60 C4
Pingle St DE11 .... 256 A3
Pingle The Derby DE21 ..... 220 C2
 Long Eaton NG10 .... 236 B4
 Melbourne DE73 .... 252 A4
Pingott La SK13 .... 10 A3
Pintail Dr DE24 .... 231 E2
Pinxton Gn NG16 .... 160 C2
Pinxton La
 Kirby-in-A NG17 .... 160 C3
 South Normanton DE55 ... 160 B3
Piper Ave S45 .... 131 F2
Piper La Holymoorside S40 . 94 C2
 Old Brampton S40 .... 94 C2
Pipeyard La S21 .... 59 E1
Pippenwell Rd SK17 .... 106 A4
Pippin Hill DE5 .... 180 C1
Pipworth La S21 .... 59 F2
Pit Close La DE73 .... 233 D1
Pit Farm DE55 .... 170 A2

Pit La Codnor DE5 181 D4
Crich DE4 157 D3
Ripley DE5 169 F1
Sheffield S12 44 A4
Shipley DE75 194 A3
Shirland DE55 158 B4
Pitch Cl S43 80 C1
Pitt Hill NG20 100 C1
Pitt St S21 59 E1
Pittar St DE22 267 A2
Pittlemere La SK17 50 A1
Pittywood Rd DE4 165 F4
Placket La DE4 141 D3
Plackett Cl DE72 235 E4
Plain The DE6 201 F4
Plains La DE56 178 A2
Plainspot Rd NG16 171 F1
Plaistow Green Rd DE4 156 C1
Plant La NG10 236 A2
Plantagenet St NG3 268 B2
Plantain Gdns DE23 231 E3
Plantation Cl S80 81 F3
Plantation Rd S8 43 D3
Plantations The 9 NG10 236 A4
Plantin Rise S20 59 F4
Plantin The S20 59 F4
Platt St Padfield SK13 10 A3
Pinxton NG16 160 B1
Platts Ave DE75 181 E1
Pleasant Ave S44 118 A4
Pleasant Cl S12 44 A3
Pleasant Pl S40 95 E2
Pleasant Rd S12 44 A3
Pleasant View SK6 15 D2
Plimsoll St DE22 218 B3
Plough Gate DE22 204 C1
Plough La NG1 268 C1
Ploughfield Cl DE23 231 D3
Plover Ave DE11 256 C2
Plover Way S44 96 C2
Plowman Ct NG9 223 E3
Plowright Cl S14 43 E3
Plowright Dr S14 43 E3
Plowright Mount S14 43 E3
Plowright Way S14 43 E3
Plucksbridge Rd SK6 23 D2
Plumbley Hall Mews S20 59 E3
Plumbley Hall Rd S20 59 E3
Plumbley La S12 59 D3
Plummer Rd DE11 256 A3
Plumptre NG16 182 A3
Plumptre Cl NG16 182 C1
Plumptre Sq NG1 268 B1
Plumptre St NG1 268 B1
Plumptre Way NG16 182 C1
Plymouth Ave NG16 160 C1
Pocknedge La S42 113 E4
Pole La Marple SK22 24 A2
New Mills SK22, SK6 24 A2
Pole's Rd DE6 217 D4
Pollard Dr NG18 268 C4
Pollards Oaks DE72 221 E1
Polly Froggat La S32 72 A1
Polyfields La S44 118 A4
Pond La Tupton S42 131 E4
Wingerworth S42 114 C2
Pond Rd DE56 191 E4
Pond St S40 266 B2
Pondwell Cnr S43 96 C4
Pondwell Dr S43 96 C4
Ponsonby Terr DE1 218 C3
Pontefract St DE24 232 B4
Pontypool Cl DE21 206 A1
Pool Cl Elvaston DE24 233 E2
Pinxton NG16 160 B1
Pool Rd DE73 252 B3
Pool St DE11 256 B1
Pool's La S21 77 E4
Poole St DE24 232 C3
Poole's Cavern SK17 84 C3
Poolsbrook Ave S43 98 A4
Poolsbrook Cres S43 98 A4
Poolsbrook Prim Sch S43 98 A4
Poolsbrook Rd S44 98 A3
Poolsbrook Sq S43 98 A4
Poolsbrook View S43 98 A4
Pope Carr Rd DE4 143 E3
Popham St NG1 268 B1
Poplar Ave Chesterfield S40 95 D1
Derby DE21 220 C3
Moira DE12 262 C1
New Mills SK22 24 B1
Ripley DE5 180 B4
Sandiacre NG10 223 D4
Swadlincote DE11 256 A3
Poplar Cl Derby DE24 233 D4
Dronfield S18 76 B4
Killamarsh S21 60 B3
Poplar Cres DE6 185 E4
Poplar Dr Glapwell S44 134 A4
Pleasleyhill NG19 135 D2
Poplar Nook DE22 204 C2
Poplar Rd Breaston DE72 235 F4
Eckington S21 59 E1
South Normanton DE55 160 A4
Poplar Row DE22 205 D1
Poplar St
Mansfield Woodhouse
NG19 136 B2
Nottingham NG1 268 C1
Poplar Terr SK23 47 D4
Poplar Way High Lane SK6 32 A4
Ilkeston DE7 208 B3
Poplars The Derby DE22 204 C2
Whitwell S80 82 A3
Porlock Cl 2 NG10 236 A4
Porlock Ct DE21 206 A1
Port Way DE21, DE56 191 E3
Porteous Cl DE4 127 E2
Porter La Matlock Bath DE4 154 C2
Middleton (Nr Wirksworth)
DE4 154 C2
Wirksworth DE4 154 C2
Porter Rd DE23 218 C1
Porter St S43 78 C1
Porter's La Derby DE21 205 F2
Findern DE65 230 B1
Porterhouse Rd DE5 169 F1
Porters Farm ST14 224 C1
Porthcawl Pl DE21 206 B1
Portland Ave Bolsover S44 99 D1
Branston DE14 254 A4
Creswell S80 81 F1
Portland Cl DE3 217 E1
Portland Cres Bolsover S44 99 D1
Mansfield Woodhouse
NG19 136 B2
Stapleford NG9 223 F3
Portland Ct Mews NG19 136 B2
Portland Gr SK23 34 C1
Portland Rd Beeston NG9 223 F1
Eastwood NG16 195 D4
Ilkeston DE7 194 C2
Long Eaton NG10 236 A2
New Mills SK22 24 B1
Nottingham NG7 268 A2
Shirebrook NG20 119 F2
Whaley Thorns NG20 101 D1
Portland Sq DE45 109 E3
Portland St Clowne S43 81 D2
Derby DE23 232 A4
Etwall DE65 229 D2
Mansfield NG18 268 B3
Mansfield Woodhouse
NG19 136 B2
New Houghton NG19 135 D4
Whitwell S80 81 F3
Portland Terr NG20 101 D1
Portman Chase DE24 231 E1
Portreath Dr DE22 204 C2
Portway Cl DE22 205 D2
Portway Dr DE13 239 E3
Portway Inf & Jun Sch
DE22 204 C2
Post St SK13 10 A3
Postern St 4 NG1 268 A1
Postmans La S42 116 B2
Posy La DE72 246 A4
Potato Pit Hill DE7 208 A1
Potlocks The DE65 242 B3
Potter Rd SK13 9 F2
Potter St Derby DE21 220 B2
Melbourne DE73 252 A4
Potters Cl S41 77 E1
Potters La DE4 157 D3
Potters Nook S81 63 F4
Potters Way DE7 209 D4
Pottery Cl DE56 179 E3
Pottery La Chesterfield S41 96 A4
Denby DE5 180 B2
Pottery Prim Sch DE56 179 E2
Poulson St ST4 269 E2
Poulter St NG20 100 C1
Poulton Dr NG2 268 C1
Poultry NG1 268 B1
Powell Dr S21 60 B3
Powell St DE23 218 C1
Powtrell Pl DE7 209 D3
Poynter Cl DE75 181 E1
Poynton Wood Cres S17 56 A3
Poynton Wood Glade S17 56 A3
Poyser Ave DE21 220 A4
Poyser La DE6 203 D1
Pratt Cl NG19 135 E1
Pratthall La DE56 166 A3
Premier Ave DE6 185 E4
Prescot Cl DE3 217 E1
Prescott Ave ST 16 269 F4
Press La S42 130 B3
Prestbury Cl DE21 206 A1
Prestom Ave DE55 159 D2
Preston Ave DE55 159 D2
Preston St S8 43 D4
Prestwood Ct ST17 269 E3
Prestwood La ST14 196 C4
Prestwood Park Dr DE11 256 B3
Pretoria St S44 98 C3
Previn Gdns NG3 268 C2
Pride Park Stad
(Derby FC) DE21 219 F2
Pride Parkway DE21 219 E2
Priestcliffe Rd SK17 87 F2
Priestland Ave DE21 220 B2
Priestley Ave DE55 146 B3
Primary Cl DE56 179 D2
Prime Ind Est DE23 219 D1
Prime Ind Pk DE23 219 E1
Prime Parkway DE1 267 C5
Primrose Ave NG16 171 F1
Primrose Cl Derby DE21 205 F2
Killamarsh S21 60 C4
South Normanton DE55 160 A4
Primrose Cres SK13 17 D4
Primrose Dr DE7 206 B4
Primrose Hill
Blackwell DE55 147 F1
Glossop SK13 17 D4
Primrose La Glossop SK13 17 D4
Killamarsh S21 60 C4
Little Hayfield SK22 25 E3
Marple SK6 24 A2
Primrose Meadow DE11 256 A4
Primrose Rise NG16 195 D4
Primrose St DE7 194 C2
Primula Way DE23 231 E2
Prince Charles Ave DE22 218 A3
Prince Edward Fst & Mid
Sch S2 44 A4
Prince of Wales Rd S2 44 A4
Prince St Ilkeston DE7 194 C2
Long Eaton NG10 236 B4
Prince's Rd Buxton SK17 85 E4
Stoke-on-T ST4 269 D2
Princes Dr DE23 218 A1
Princes Rd SK23 34 C1
Princes St Derby DE23 219 D1
Mansfield NG18 268 B3
4 Stafford ST16 269 E4
Princess Ave Linton DE12 261 E3
South Normanton DE55 160 A3
Princess Cl DE11 256 C1
Princess Ct S2 44 A4
Princess Dr
Borrowash DE72 221 D1
Sandiacre NG10 223 D2
Princess Pl S45 131 E1
Princess Rd Dronfield S18 57 D1
Uttoxeter ST14 210 A1
Princess St Brimington S43 96 C4
Chesterfield S40 266 A4
Eastwood NG16 182 C2
Glossop SK13 17 E4
Long Eaton NG10 236 B4
Swadlincote DE11 261 F4
Princess Way DE13 240 C1
Printers Fold SK14 9 E3
Printers Pk SK14 9 F3
Priors Barn Cl DE72 221 E1
Priorway Ave DE72 221 E1
Priorway Gdns DE72 221 E1
Priory Cl Derby DE73 245 D4
Ilkeston DE7 208 B3
Swadlincote DE11 256 A3
Tutbury DE13 239 D3
Yeaveley DE6 199 E3
Priory Ct S26 61 F3
Priory Gdns DE55 170 A4
Priory Lands DE13 240 C1
Priory Rd Alfreton DE55 159 D3
Eastwood NG16 182 C1
Mansfield Woodhouse NG19 136 A3
Priory Sq NG19 136 A2
Pritchard Dr NG9 223 F3
Pritchett Dr DE23 230 C4
Private Dr S43 78 A1
Progress Ct DE45 109 E3
Prospect Ave DE55 159 F3
Prospect Ct 13 Sheffield S17 56 A3
Sutton in A NG17 148 C1
Prospect Dr Belper DE56 178 C1
Matlock DE4 143 D3
Sheffield S17 55 F3
Shirebrook NG20 119 F2
Prospect Pl 5 S17 56 A3
Prospect Rd
Chesterfield S45 76 C1
Denby DE5 180 A1
Dronfield S18 57 E2
Heanor DE75 194 A4
Pilsley S45 132 B1
Sheffield, Lowfield S2 43 D4
Sheffield, Totley Rise S17 56 A3
Stafford ST16 269 F4
Prospect St Alfreton DE55 159 D2
Mansfield NG18 268 C3
Prospect Terr
Chesterfield S40 95 F2
Crich DE4 168 A4
Providence Ct DE11 256 C1
Providence Pl 12 DE7 194 C1
Providence Rd NG16 171 D2
Providence St DE5 180 C4
Provident St DE23 219 D1
Pryor Mede S26 61 F3
Pudding Bag La S45 129 F2
Pulborough Gdns DE23 231 D3
Pullman Cl S43 78 C2
Pullman Rd Derby DE21 219 F2
Nottingham NG2 268 C1
Pump Cl DE4 143 E2
Pump La DE6 211 D1
Pump St ST4 269 E2
Purbeck Ave S40 95 E2
Purbeck Cl NG10 236 A4
Purchase Ave DE75 181 E1
Purdy Meadow NG10 235 F3
Purseglove Dr SK17 69 E2
Purseglove Rd SK17 69 E2
Putney Cl DE22 217 F3
Pybus St DE22 218 B3
Pye Bridge Ind Est DE55 170 C3
Pye Hill Rd NG16 171 D2
Pyegrove SK13 10 C1
Pyegrove Rd SK13 10 C1
Pykestone Cl DE21 205 F1
Pym Leys NG10 235 F3
Pym St NG3 268 C2
Pynot Rd S41 77 D1
Pytchley Cl DE56 179 E2

Quadrant The Buxton SK17 85 D4
Totley S17 55 F3
Quaker Cl DE73 252 A4
Quaker La NG18 268 B3
Quaker Way NG18 268 B4
Quantock Cl DE24 231 E1
Quantock Rd NG10 223 D1
Quantock Way S40 95 D3
Quarn Dr DE22 204 B2
Quarn Gdns DE1 218 C4
Quarn St DE1 218 C4
Quarn Way DE1 218 C3
Quarndon Hts DE22 204 B2
Quarndon View DE22 204 B1
Quarry Ave ST4 269 D2
Quarry Bank DE4 143 D4
Quarry Bank Rd S41 96 B1
Quarry Berry La DE12 264 C1
Quarry Cl SK13 10 B1
Quarry Hill Marsh Lane S21 58 B1
Mosborough S20 59 D4
Stanton-by-D NG10 223 D4
Quarry Hill Ind Pk DE7 208 C2
Quarry Hill Rd DE7 208 C3
Quarry La Alton S42 130 B3
Brackenfield DE55 145 E3
Chesterfield S40 95 E1
Mansfield NG18 268 B3
Matlock DE4 143 F4
Stonebroom DE55 146 C2
Quarry Rd Apperknowle S18 58 A1
Belper DE56 178 C1
Birch Vale SK22 24 C1
Bolsover S44 99 D2
Killamarsh S21 60 B4
Morley DE7 192 A1
New Mills SK22 33 E4
Somercotes DE55 170 B4
Stoke-on-T ST4 269 D2
Totley S17 55 F3
Quarry Vale Gr S12 44 B2
Quarry Vale Rd S12 44 B2
Queen Anne St ST4 269 E2
Queen Elizabeth Ct DE6 173 D1
Queen Elizabeth Way DE7 208 B3
Queen Elizabeth's Gram
Sch DE6 173 E2
Queen Elizabeth's Lower
Sch Department DE6 185 E4
Queen Elizabeth's Sch
The NG19 136 A1
Queen Elizabeths Gram
Sch DE6 173 D1
Queen Mary Cl S2 44 A4
Queen Mary Gr S2 44 A4
Queen Mary Ct DE1 218 C4
Queen Mary Rd
Chesterfield S40 95 D1
Sheffield S2 44 A4
Queen St Belper DE56 179 D2
Brimington S43 77 F1
Chesterfield S40 266 A4
Clay Cross S45 131 E2
Creswell S80 81 F1
Derby DE1 267 B4
Eckington S21 59 F2
Glossop SK13 17 D4
Hadfield SK13 10 A2
Ilkeston DE7 208 C4
Ironville NG16 170 C2
Langley Mill NG16 182 B2
Long Eaton NG10 236 C4
Longnor SK17 121 D3
Mansfield NG18 268 B4
Marple SK6 23 D3
Middleton (Nr Wirksworth)
DE4 154 B3
Mosborough S20 59 E4
2 Nottingham NG1 268 B2
Pilsley S45 132 B1
Pinxton NG16 160 B2
Ripley DE5 181 D4
Somercotes DE55 170 B4
South Normanton DE55 159 F3
Staveley S43 97 E4
Swadlincote DE11 256 A1
Tideswell SK17 69 E2
Queen St N S41 96 A4
Queen Victoria Rd
Sheffield S17 55 F3
Totley S17 55 F3
Tupton S42 115 E1
Queen's Ave SK17 85 E4
Queen's Bridge Rd NG2 268 B1
Queen's Dr Belper DE56 178 C3
Glossop SK13 10 C1
Ilkeston DE7 208 C4
Swadlincote DE11 256 A3
Queen's Park Sports Ctr
S40 266 A2
Queen's Rd Buxton SK17 85 E4
Nottingham NG2 268 B1
Stoke-on-T ST4 269 D2
Queen's Sq NG16 182 C1
Queen's Way S42 115 E1
Queen's Wlk
Nether Langwith NG20 101 D1
Tupton S42 115 E1
Queens Ave Heanor DE75 181 E1
Ilkeston DE7 209 D3
Stanley DE7 207 E3
Queens Cl S80 82 B3
Queens Ct Creswell S80 81 F1
Draycott DE72 235 D4
Queens Dr Brinsley NG16 182 C4
Derby DE23 218 B1
Sandiacre NG10 223 D2
Queens L Ctr DE1 267 B4
Queens Rd Hodthorpe S80 82 B3
Sheffield S2 43 D4
Queens Rd N NG16 182 C1
Queens Rd S NG16 182 C1
Queens Rise DE13 239 E3
Queensferry Gdns DE24 232 C2
Queensland Cl DE3 217 E2
Queensland Cres DE15 248 B1
Queensview Dr DE5 181 D4
Queensville Ave ST17 269 F3
Queensville Bridge ST17 269 F3
Queensway
Castle Donington DE74 246 C2
Derby DE22 204 C1
Holmewood S42 116 C1
Melbourne DE73 252 A4
Pilsley S45 132 B1
Stafford ST16 269 E4
Stoke-on-T ST4 269 F1
Stonebroom DE55 146 C2
Quenby La DE5 169 F1
Quentin Rd SK23 47 E3
Quick Cl DE73 252 A4
Quick Hill Rd DE24 231 E1
Quillings Way DE72 221 E1
Quilow La DE6 185 F2
Quixhill Bank ST14 196 C4
Quixhill La ST14 196 C4
Quoit Gn S18 57 D1
Quorn Cl DE15 248 A1
Quorn Dr 5 S40 95 D3
Quorn Rise DE23 231 F3
Quorndon Cres NG10 236 B3

Rabown Ave DE23 231 E4
Racecourse Ind Est DE21 219 E4
Racecourse Mount S41 95 F4
Racecourse Rd S41 95 F4
Racecourse Rd E S41 96 A4
Racester Way S42 131 F3
Rad Meadows NG10 236 B3
Radbourne La DE22 217 F3
Radbourne Rd NG2 268 C1
Radbourne St Derby DE22 218 B3
Mansfield Woodhouse
NG19 136 C2
Radburn Ct NG9 209 F1
Radcliffe Ave DE21 219 F4
Radcliffe Dr DE22 218 B2
Radford Rd DE7 192 C3
Radford St Derby DE24 232 C4
1 Mansfield NG18 268 B3
Radmanthwaite Rd NG19 135 E2
Radnor Pl NG19 135 E2
Radnor St DE21 219 E4
Radstock Gdns DE21 205 F1
Radstone Cl DE21 206 A1
Raeburn Cl S14 43 F1
Raeburn Dr Beeston NG9 223 F1
Marple SK6 23 D4
Raeburn Pl S14 43 F2
Raeburn Rd S14 43 F2
Raeburn Way S14 43 F1
Raglan Ave DE22 218 B3
Raglan St DE55 159 D2
Railway Ave S80 100 B4
Railway Cotts NG16 195 F3
Railway Row NG16 170 C2
Railway Side DE11 256 A1
Railway St Glossop SK13 10 B1
Hadfield SK13 10 A3
Stafford ST16 269 D4
Railway Terr Buxton SK17 85 E4
Chesterfield S41 115 D4
Derby DE1 267 D2
Rain's La DE4 154 B2
Rainham Gdns DE24 233 D3
Rainier Dr DE21 220 A3
Rake Head Rd HD7 2 C4
Rake La DE45 124 B2
Rake The DE45 123 D3
Rakes La DE6 162 A3
Rakes Rd DE45 107 E1
Raleigh Cl DE7 194 C2
Raleigh Inf Sch NG7 268 A2
Raleigh Rd NG19 268 A4
Raleigh St Derby DE22 218 B3
Nottingham NG7 268 A2
Raliegh Rd S2 43 D3
Ralph Dr DE55 170 B4
Ralph Rd S43 79 D1
Ralston Croft S20 59 F3
Ralston Ct S20 59 E3
Ralston Gr S20 59 E3
Ralston Pl S20 59 E3
Rambler Cl DE11 256 A3
Ramblers Dr DE21 206 B2
Ramper Ave S43 80 C1
Ramscliff Ave DE12 265 F4
Ramsdean Cl DE21 219 E4
Ramsden Cl SK13 10 B1
Ramsden La HD7 3 D4
Ramsden Rd HD7 3 E4
Ramsey Ave S40 95 E1
Ramsey Cl NG9 209 F1
Ramsey St ST4 269 F1
Ramshaw Cl 6 S40 95 E4
Ramshaw Rd S18 76 C3
Ramshaw Way DE22 218 C2
Randall Dr DE11 256 A2
Randall Pl S2 43 D4
Randall St S21 59 D1
Randolph Rd DE23 231 F4
Ranelagh Gdns DE22 218 A4
Raneld Mount S40 114 B4
Rangemoor La DE6 183 E3
Rangemore Cl DE3 217 F2
Ranmoor Cl S41 115 E4
Ranmoor Hill S32 52 C4
Rannoch Cl
Derby, Allestree DE22 204 C2
Derby, Spondon DE21 220 C3
Rannoch Dr NG19 268 A3
Ranworth Cl DE24 232 B2
Ratcliffe Ave DE14 254 A4
Ratcliffe Gate NG18 268 C3
Ratcliffe St NG16 182 C1
Rauche Ct DE23 267 C1
Raven Ave DE55 147 F3

Raven Cl DE55 170 B3
Raven Oak Cl DE56 179 D2
Raven St DE22 218 C2
Ravencar Rd S21 59 D2
Ravenscourt Rd DE22 218 B3
Ravenscroft Ave S13 44 C4
Ravenscroft Cl S13 44 C4
Ravenscroft Cres S13 44 C4
Ravenscroft Ct S13 44 C4
Ravenscroft Dr
Derby DE21 219 F3
Sheffield S13 44 C4
Ravenscroft Oval S13 44 C4
Ravenscroft Pl S13 44 C4
Ravenscroft Rd S13 44 C4
Ravenscroft Way S13 44 C4
Ravensdale Ave
Long Eaton NG10 223 D1
Mansfield NG18 268 C4
Ravensdale Cl S43 97 E3
Ravensdale Inf & Jun Sch DE3 217 F2
Ravensdale Rd
Derby DE22 204 B2
Dronfield S18 56 B1
Mansfield NG18 268 C4
Ravenstor Rd DE4 154 C1
Ravenswood Rd S40 95 D3
Rawdon Cl DE74 247 D2
Rawdon Rd DE12 262 C3
Rawdon St DE23 218 C1
Rawlins Ct S18 57 E2
Rawlinson Ave DE23 232 A4
Rawson Gn DE56 179 F1
Ray St DE75 181 F1
Ray's Ave DE75 181 F1
Rayleigh Ave S43 96 B4
Raynald Rd S2 44 A4
Rayneham Rd DE7 194 B2
Raynesway DE21 220 A2
Raynesway Park Dr DE21 220 A1
Reader St DE21 220 C3
Rebecca St ST4 269 E2
Recreation Cl
Blackwell DE55 147 F1
Clowne S43 80 C2
Recreation Dr NG20 119 F1
Recreation Gd (Chesterfield FC) The S40 266 A4
Recreation Rd Calow S43 96 C3
New Houghton NG19 134 C4
Sandiacre NG10 223 D3
Shirebrook NG20 119 F2
Tideswell SK17 69 E2
Wirksworth DE4 165 F4
Recreation St
Long Eaton NG10 236 C4
Mansfield NG18 268 C4
Recreation Terr NG9 223 E3
Recreation View NG20 119 F3
Rectory Cl
Breedon on t H DE73 252 C1
Eckington S21 59 F2
Long Duckmanton S44 98 A2
Rectory Dr S42 114 C2
Rectory Farm Mews DE72 245 F2
Rectory Gdns
Aston-on-T DE72 246 A4
Harthill S26 61 F3
Killamarsh S21 60 B3
Rectory La Breadsall DE21 205 E3
Kirk Ireton DE6 165 D1
Stretton en le F DE12 265 F1
Rectory Pl NG11 237 F3
Rectory Rd Breaston DE72 235 F4
Clowne S43 80 C2
Killamarsh S21 60 B3
Long Duckmanton S44 98 A2
Staveley S43 78 C1
Reculver Cl DE23 231 E4
Red Barn Cl DE55 148 A2
Red Hill DE4 144 B2
Red Hill La DE4 144 B2
Red La Belper DE56 191 D3
Brinsley NG16 171 F1
Disley SK12 32 B3
Repton DE65 249 F3
South Normanton DE55 159 F2
Red Lion Hill DE4 153 D1
Red Lion Sq DE75 181 F1
Red Lion St ST16 269 E4
Redacre Cl S44 99 E1
Redbarn La DE55 148 A2
Redbrook Ave S41 115 D4
Redbury Cl DE1 218 C2
Redcar Gdns DE21 205 E1
Redcliffe Rd NG18 268 C3
Reddish Ave SK23 45 E3
Reddish La SK23 45 E3
Reddish Rd SK23 45 E3
Redfern Ave DE5 169 F1
Redfern Cl SK13 10 A3
Redfern Rd ST14 210 A1
Redfern St S42 131 E4
Redgap La SK17 86 A4
Redgate SK13 10 B2
Redgate Cl NG19 268 A4
Redgate Sch NG19 268 A4
Redgate St Mansfield NG19 268 A4
Pinxton NG16 160 B1
Redgrave Dr ST16 269 D3
Redgrove Way S40 114 B4
Redhill La DE13 239 D3
Redhill Lodge Rd DE11 256 A4
Redhill Prim Sch DE72 221 E3
Redhouse Cl S43 77 E2
Redhouse La SK12 32 C3
Redland Cl Derby DE24 231 F2
Ilkeston DE7 194 C2
Redmires Dr DE73 233 D1
Redmires Rd S10 42 A4
Redmoor Cl
Burton u T DE15 248 A2
Codnor DE5 170 A1
Redmoor La Disley SK12 33 D2
New Mills SK22 33 D3
Rednall Cl S40 95 D3
Redruth Pl DE24 233 E3
Redshaw St DE1 218 C4
Redstart Cl DE21 220 C3
Redthorn Rd S13 44 C4
Redvers Buller Rd S40 266 B1
Redway Croft DE73 252 A4
Redwing Croft DE23 231 E4
Redwood Dr DE15 255 D4
Redwood Inf Sch DE24 231 F2
Redwood Jun Sch DE24 231 F2
Redwood Rd DE24 231 F2
Reedman Rd NG10 236 A2
Reeves Rd DE23 219 D1
Regency Cl Derby DE23 231 E4
Glossop SK13 10 B1
Regent Ct NG16 170 C2
Regent St Clowne S43 80 B2
Derby DE1 267 C1
Glossop SK13 10 B1
Ilkeston DE7 208 C4
Kimberley NG16 195 F3
Langley Mill NG16 182 A2
Long Eaton NG10 236 B4
Mansfield NG18 268 B4
Nottingham NG1 268 A1
Padfield SK13 10 A3
Stapleford NG10 223 E3
Stoke-on-T ST4 269 E1
Swadlincote DE11 256 A1
Reginald Rd N DE21 219 F4
Reginald Rd S DE21 219 F3
Reginald St DE23 219 D1
Regis Cl DE21 206 A1
Registry St ST4 269 E2
Reigate Dr DE22 218 A4
Reigate Prim Sch DE22 217 F4
Rembrandt Dr S18 56 C1
Renals St DE23 267 B1
Reney Ave S8 56 B3
Reney Cres S8 56 B3
Reney Dr S8 56 B3
Reney Rd S8 56 C4
Reney Wlk S8 56 B3
Renfrew Ct NG19 268 A3
Renfrew St DE21 219 F4
Renishaw Hall Mus & Craft Ctr S21 59 F1
Renishaw Prim Sch S21 79 D4
Renishaw Rd S43 79 E2
Renshaw Dr DE11 255 F3
Rent Cl S41 95 F3
Repton Ave DE23 218 B1
Repton Cl S40 95 D3
Repton Ct NG19 136 C2
Repton Dr DE7 209 D4
Repton Pl 3 S18 56 B1
Repton Prep Sch DE65 243 E1
Repton Prim Sch DE65 242 C1
Repton Rd Hartshorne DE11 256 C4
Long Eaton NG10 235 F2
Newton Solney DE15 248 C4
Willington DE65 242 A3
Repton Sch DE65 242 B2
Reservoir Hill DE12 262 B4
Reservoir Rd SK23 45 E4
Reservoir Terr S40 95 F2
Resthaven DE11 256 A3
Retford Cl DE21 205 E1
Revill Cl DE7 194 B1
Revill Cres NG9 223 F4
Revolution House Mus S41 77 D1
Reynard Cres S21 79 D4
Reynards La SK17 137 F2
Reynolds Ave DE5 169 F1
Reynolds Cl S18 75 F4
Reynolds Dr SK6 23 D4
Rhodes Ave S41 95 F3
Rhodes Cotts S43 80 C2
Rhodes St SK13 10 A3
Rhodes Wlk NG18 268 A3
Rhodesia Rd S40 95 E1
Rhodeswood Dr SK13 10 A3
Rhuddlan Pl SK23 34 B1
Ribblesdale DE7 208 B3
Ribblesdale Cl DE22 204 B1
Ribblesdale Dr S12 59 D4
Ribblesdale Rd NG10 236 A3
Riber Ave DE55 170 B4
Riber Bank SK13 9 F1
Riber Cl Long Eaton NG10 236 B3
Staveley S43 97 E3
West Hallam DE7 207 F4
Riber Cres S45 131 D3
Riber Rd Holloway DE4 156 A4
Matlock DE4 143 E1
Riber Terr S40 266 A2
Riber View Cl DE4 144 A3
Riber Wildlife Pk DE4 143 E2
Richard La SK17 69 E2
Richard Wakefield CE Prim Sch DE13 239 E3
Richards Ave ST16 269 F4
Richards Ct S8 43 D3
Richards Rd S2 43 D4
Richardson Dr DE7 192 C3
Richardson Endowed Prim Sch DE7 192 C3
Richardson St DE22 218 B3
Richardsons La DE55 170 B3
Richmond Ave Derby DE72 231 E4
Ilkeston DE7 194 C2
Long Eaton DE72 236 A4
Sandiacre NG10 223 D2
Sheffield S13 44 C4
Richmond Cl
Chesterfield S40 114 C4
Hadfield SK13 10 A3
West Hallam DE7 207 E4
Richmond Coll of F Ed S13 44 B4
Richmond Ct DE65 242 B1
Richmond Dr Duffield DE56 190 B3
Mansfield Woodhouse NG19 136 B1
Richmond Gr S13 44 C4
Richmond Hall Ave S13 44 B4
Richmond Hall Cres S13 44 B4
Richmond Hall Dr S13 44 B4
Richmond Hall Rd S13 44 B4
Richmond Hall Way S13 44 B4
Richmond Hill Rd S13 44 B4
Richmond Park Rd S13 44 C4
Richmond Pl S13 44 B4
Richmond Rd
Derby, Chaddesden DE21 219 F3
Derby, Rose Hill DE23 219 D1
Sheffield S13 44 B4
Richmond St ST4 269 E2
Richworth Rd S13 44 C4
Rick St NG1 268 B2
Ricroft Rd SK6 15 D2
Ridd Way S42 115 D2
Riddings DE22 204 C2
Riddings Cl S2 44 A4
Riddings Inf Sch DE55 170 B3
Riddings Jun Sch DE55 170 B3
Riddings La S32 72 B2
Riddings St DE22 218 C2
Ridge Ave SK6 23 D2
Ridge Cl SK13 9 F2
Ridge Cres SK6 23 D2
Ridge End Fold SK6 23 D1
Ridge La SK23 65 E4
Ridge Rd Marple SK6 23 D2
Marsh Lane S21 58 C1
Ridge The Blackwell DE55 147 F1
Marple SK6 23 D2
Ridge Top La SK22 25 E1
Ridgedale Rd S44 118 A4
Ridgedale View DE5 169 E1
Ridgehill Ave S12 44 A3
Ridgehill Gr S12 44 A3
Ridgeway Derby DE73 245 D4
Dronfield S18 57 E2
Heanor DE75 193 F4
Ridgeway Ave Bolsover S44 99 E1
Derby DE23 231 E3
Ridgeway Cottage Ind Ctr S12 58 C4
Ridgeway Cres S12 44 A3
Ridgeway Dr Ilkeston DE7 208 A3
Sheffield S12 44 A3
Ridgeway Inf Sch DE23 231 E3
Ridgeway La DE56 168 B2
Ridgeway Moor S12 58 C3
Ridgeway Prim Sch S12 58 C4
Ridgeway Rd
Burton u T DE15 254 C4
Sheffield S12 44 A2
Ridgeway St NG3 268 C2
Ridgeway The SK12 32 B3
Ridgeways SK22 25 E1
Ridgewood Ct DE21 205 F1
Ridgewood Dr DE4 155 E3
Ridgway S43 80 C1
Ridgway W S43 80 C1
Riding Bank DE73 251 F3
Ridings Rd SK13 9 F3
Ridings The
Mansfield NG19 136 C1
Ockbrook DE72 221 E3
Ridley St ST4 269 F1
Ridley Wlk ST4 269 F1
Rigga La DE56 191 D1
Riggotts Way S42 94 C4
Riggs La DE6 212 A4
Rigley Ave 19 DE7 194 C1
Rigsby Ct DE3 217 E2
Riley Ave DE55 157 F4
Riley Back La S32 71 F3
Riley La DE5 169 D3
Rimsdale Cl DE24 231 F2
Ring-o-Bells La SK12 32 B3
Ringer La S43 80 C2
Ringer Way S43 80 C2
Ringinglow Rd S11 42 C2
Ringstone Way SK23 45 E4
Ringwood Ave
Chesterfield S41 95 F4
Hackingknife SK14 15 D4
Staveley S43 97 E4
Ringwood Cl DE21 219 F4
Ringwood Rd S43 96 C4
Ringwood View 9 S43 96 C4
Rink Dr DE11 256 A2
Ripley Hospl DE5 169 E1
Ripley Inf Sch DE5 180 B4
Ripley Jun Sch DE5 180 B4
Ripley Rd DE56 168 B3
Ripon Cres DE21 219 F4
Ripon Gdns SK17 85 E3
Risborrow Cl DE65 229 E2
Rise The Derby DE22 204 C1
Swadlincote DE11 255 F3
Whaley Bridge SK23 45 E3
Rises The SK13 9 F3
Risley Ct DE7 194 C2
Risley La DE72 222 B1
Risley Lower Gram CE Prim Sch DE72 222 C2
Ritson Cl NG3 268 B2
Rivenhall Cl DE23 230 C4
River St DE1 267 B4
River View Aldercar DE55 171 D3
Belper DE56 190 C4
Litton SK17 88 B4
Riverbank DE4 110 C1
Riverbank The DE65 242 A3
Riverbank Way SK13 17 F4
Riverdale Cl DE15 248 A3
Riversdale DE56 168 A2
Riversfield Dr ST14 196 C2
Riverside DE12 253 E1
Riverside Cl Calver S32 72 B1
Glossop SK13 10 B1
Riverside Cres S42 113 F4
Riverside Dr
Branston DE14 253 F4
Calver S32 72 B1
Riverside L Ctr ST16 269 E4
Riverside Rd DE21 219 E2
Riverside Way NG19 136 B3
Riverview Cotts SK13 17 E4
Riverway ST17 269 E3
Rivington Rd NG9 223 F1
Roadmeadow Cl DE6 185 E4
Robert Ave NG18 268 A3
Robert Cl S18 76 C3
Robert Rd S8 57 D4
Robert Sherborne Inf Sch The DE13 240 B2
Robert St DE1 267 C4
Robert Sutton High Sch DE15 255 D4
Roberts Ave NG17 148 C1
Roberts Dr DE55 159 D2
Roberts St Ilkeston DE7 209 D3
Nottingham NG2 268 C1
Robertson Rd SK17 85 D3
Robertson's Ave S44 98 A2
Robey Dr NG16 182 C2
Robian Way DE11 256 A2
Robin Croft Rd DE22 204 C2
Robin Hood Chase NG3 268 B2
Robin Hood Cl NG16 182 C1
Robin Hood Ind Est NG3 268 C2
Robin Hood Inf & Jun Sch NG19 136 A2
Robin Hood Pl DE11 256 B1
Robin Hood St NG3 268 C2
Robin Rd DE1 218 C4
Robin's Cross La DE65 249 F4
Robina Cl DE21 206 B2
Robina Dr NG16 195 E4
Robincroft S40 114 C4
Robincroft Rd S42 114 B2
Robinettes La NG16 195 E1
Robinlands La S33 38 A2
Robinscross DE72 221 D1
Robinson Ind Est DE23 219 D1
Robinson Rd DE11 256 A3
Robinson Way S21 60 B3
Robinson's Hill DE73 251 F3
Robridding Rd S45 129 D2
Robson Cl DE24 233 D4
Roby Lea DE74 246 C2
Roche 17 S20 59 F4
Rochester Cl Derby DE24 233 D3
Long Eaton NG10 236 A4
Rochley Cl DE21 205 F1
Rock Bank Buxton SK17 85 E2
Whaley Bridge SK23 45 F3
Rock Cres S45 131 D3
Rock Ct NG18 268 C4
Rock Dr NG7 268 A1
Rock Hill NG18 268 C3
Rock La S44 116 C3
Rock St Mansfield NG18 268 C3
New Mills SK22 33 E4
Rock Terr Bakewell DE45 109 E3
Buxton SK17 85 D3
Rock Valley NG18 268 C4
Rockbourne Cl DE24 233 E3
Rockcliffe Cl DE11 256 A1
Rockeries The DE56 168 C1
Rockfield Rd SK17 85 E4
Rockford Ct NG9 209 F1
Rockhall Terr SK22 25 F1
Rockhouse Rd DE24 233 D3
Rockingham 16 S20 59 F4
Rockingham Cl
Chesterfield S40 95 E2
Derby DE22 205 D2
4 Dronfield S18 56 B1
Rocklands The NG20 119 F2
Rockley Cl S40 114 C4
Rockley Way NG20 119 F2
Rocks The DE4 144 A3
Rockside Stps DE4 143 E3
Rockside View DE4 143 E4
Rod Moor Rd S18 56 A2
Roden St NG3 268 C2
Rodge Croft S41 77 D2
Rodger's La DE55 159 D3
Rodknoll La S42 93 E1
Rodney Cl DE65 228 C1
Rodney Way DE7 194 C2
Rodney Wlk DE23 230 C4
Rodsley Cl S40 95 D3
Rodsley Cres DE23 231 E3
Rodsley La Rodsley DE6 199 F4
Wyaston DE6 199 F4
Yeaveley DE6 199 F3
Rodwood Ave S43 80 A4
Roe Cross Rd SK14 9 D3
Roe Farm La DE21 219 F4
Roe Wlk DE23 219 D1
Roe's La DE4 157 D1
Roebuck Pl SK23 47 D3
Roebuck St ST4 269 F2
Roecar Cl S41 77 D1
Roehampton Dr
Derby DE22 218 A4
Stapleford NG9 209 E1
Rogers Ave S80 81 E1
Rogerstone Ave ST4 269 D1
Rolaine Cl NG19 136 B2
Rolleston Cres NG16 195 F4
Rolleston Dr NG16 195 D4
Rolleston La DE13 239 E3
Rollet Cl S2 44 A4
Rollins La SK6 15 D1
Roman Bank NG19 136 B2
Roman Rd DE1 219 D4
Roman Way DE72 221 E1
Romeley Cres S43 80 B2
Romford Way S43 78 A2
Romney Dr S18 56 C1
Romney Gdns S2 43 D3
Romsley Cl DE3 217 E2
Rona Cl Derby DE24 231 F2
Mansfield NG18 268 A3
Ronald Cl DE23 230 C4
Rood La Clowne S43 80 C2
Idridgehay DE56 176 C3
Rookery The NG18 268 B4
Roosevelt Ave Derby DE21 220 A3
Long Eaton NG10 236 B3
Rooth St NG18 268 B3
Roper Ave DE75 193 F4
Roper Hill S10 42 B4
Ropewalk Ind Ctr DE7 195 D1
Ropewalk The Heanor DE75 193 F4
Ilkeston DE7 195 D1
Nottingham NG7 268 A1
Stanley DE7 193 D1
Rosamond Ave S17 56 A3
Rosamond Cl S17 56 A3
Rosamond Dr S17 56 A3
Rosamond Glade S17 56 A3
Rosamond Pl S17 56 A3
Rosamond's Ride DE23 231 E4
Rose Ave Borrowash DE72 221 E1
Burton u T DE13 241 D1
Calow S44 97 D2
Clowne S43 81 D3
Ilkeston DE7 194 C1
Rose Bank Cl SK14 9 E3
Rose Cottage Dr NG17 148 C1
Rose Cotts S41 96 B1
Rose Cres S43 79 E2
Rose Ct Clay Cross S45 131 D2
Long Eaton NG10 223 D1
Rose End Ave DE4 155 D3
Rose Farm Prim Sch DE21 219 F4
Rose Hill Chesterfield S40 266 B3
Stafford ST16 269 D4
Swadlincote DE11 256 C2
Rose Hill E S40 266 B3
Rose Hill St DE23 219 D1
Rose Hill W S40 266 A3
Rose La
Mansfield Woodhouse NG19 136 B2
Ticknall DE73 251 D2
Rose Tree La DE11 255 F4
Rose Valley DE11 256 A3
Rose Way S21 60 B3
Rose Wood Cl S41 95 E4
Roseberry Ct DE21 206 A1
Rosebery Hill NG18 268 C3
Rosecroft Gdns DE11 256 B2
Rosedale Ave
Chesterfield S40 115 D4
Derby DE24 233 D3
Rosedale Cl NG10 236 A3
Rosedale View S40 114 A4
Rosedale Way NG19 136 C1
Roseheath Cl DE23 231 F3
Rosehill Ct S44 99 D1
Rosehill Inf Sch DE23 219 D2
Rosehill Sch NG3 268 C2
Roseleigh Cres DE11 255 F3
Rosemary Ave NG18 268 B4
Rosemary Dr DE24 233 D3
Rosemary St NG18 268 B4
Rosemoor La DE21 206 A1
Rosemount Ct DE22 204 B2
Rosengrave St DE1 267 B2
Rosette Cl DE21 206 B2
Rosewood Cl Derby DE24 233 E4
South Normanton DE55 160 A4
Rosewood Cres DE75 182 A1
Rosewood Rd DE15 254 C3
Rosier Cres DE55 170 A4
Rosling Way S44 97 E1
Rosliston CE Prim Sch DE12 260 B3
Rosliston Rd
Burton u T DE15 254 C4
Rosliston DE15 254 B2
Walton-on-T DE12 259 F4
Rosliston Rd S DE15 254 C3
Roslyn Cres S32 53 D4
Roslyn Rd S32 53 D4
Ross Wlk DE21 205 F1
Rossell Dr NG9 223 F3
Rossendale DE7 194 C2
Rossendale Cl S40 114 C4

Rosser Ave S12 ... 43 F1
Rossington Dr DE23 ... 230 C3
Rossington Rd NG2 ... 268 C2
Rosslyn Gdns DE24 ... 233 D3
Roston Cl 10 S18 ... 56 B1
Rothay Cl S18 ... 75 F4
Rothbourne Croft DE6 ... 151 E1
Rothbury Ave NG9 ... 209 E1
Rothbury Pl DE21 ... 205 F1
Rother Ave S43 ... 96 B4
Rother Cl S40 ... 114 C4
Rother Croft S42 ... 131 E4
Rother Jun Sch S40 ... 115 D4
Rother St S45 ... 132 B1
Rother Valley Way S20 ... 60 A4
Rother Way S41 ... 96 A3
Rotherham Cl S21 ... 60 C4
Rotherham Rd
Barlborough S43 ... 61 E1
Bolsover S44 ... 99 F1
Clowne S43 ... 80 C3
Eckington S20 ... 59 F3
Killamarsh S21 ... 60 C4
Mosborough S20 ... 59 F3
New Houghton NG19 ... 134 C4
Scarcliffe S44 ... 118 B4
Stony Houghton S44 ... 118 B2
Rotherham Rd N S20 ... 59 F4
Rotherside Rd S21 ... 59 F2
Rothervale Rd S40 ... 115 D4
Rotherwood Rd S21 ... 60 C4
Rothesay Cl DE24 ... 231 F2
Rothey Gr S40 ... 94 C3
Rothley Ave NG2 ... 268 C2
Rothwell La DE56 ... 179 D2
Rothwell Rd DE3 ... 217 E2
Rothwell St ST4 ... 269 D1
Rough Heanor Rd DE3 ... 218 A1
Rough La DE6 ... 186 B3
Roughpiece La DE56 ... 166 B3
Roughton Cl DE3 ... 230 B4
Round Hill Cl SK13 ... 9 F2
Round Way SK22 ... 33 E4
Rouse Cl ST16 ... 269 D3
Rouse St S45 ... 132 B1
Routh Ave DE74 ... 247 D1
Rowan Ave Ripley DE5 ... 180 B4
Stapleford NG9 ... 209 F1
Rowan Cl Creswell S80 ... 81 F1
Darley Dale DE4 ... 127 D2
Derby, Cherrytree Hill DE21 ... 220 A3
Derby, Sinfin DE24 ... 231 E2
Ilkeston DE7 ... 208 C3
Mansfield NG19 ... 136 B1
Rowan Croft NG17 ... 148 C2
Rowan Dr Kilburn DE56 ... 192 A4
Selston NG16 ... 171 E4
Shirebrook NG20 ... 119 E3
Shirland DE55 ... 146 B1
Rowan Park Cl DE23 ... 231 D4
Rowan Rd Eckington S21 ... 59 E1
Mastin Moor S43 ... 79 E2
Rowan Sch The S17 ... 55 F3
Rowan Tree Cl
Ashbourne DE6 ... 185 E4
Killamarsh S21 ... 60 B3
Rowan Tree Dell S17 ... 55 F2
Rowan Tree Rd S21 ... 60 A3
Rowan Wlk SK13 ... 9 F2
Rowbury Dr DE15 ... 248 A1
Rowdale Cres S12 ... 44 B3
Rowditch Ave DE22 ... 218 B2
Rowditch Pl DE22 ... 218 B2
Rowena Cl DE24 ... 232 C4
Rowland Ct DE55 ... 158 C2
Rowland Rd S2 ... 43 D4
Rowland St Alfreton DE55 ... 159 D2
Derby DE24 ... 232 C3
Rowley Ave ST17 ... 269 D3
Rowley Ct DE11 ... 256 A2
Rowley Gdns DE23 ... 231 E4
Rowley Hall Dr ST17 ... 269 D3
Rowley La DE23 ... 231 E4
Rowsley Ave Derby DE23 ... 231 E4
Long Eaton NG10 ... 236 A3
Rowsley CE Prim Sch
DE4 ... 126 C4
Rowsley Cres S43 ... 97 E4
Rowsley Mews SK13 ... 9 F1
Rowthorne Ave DE55 ... 170 A4
Rowthorne La
Ault Hucknall S44 ... 134 A4
Glapwell S44 ... 134 A4
Rowton Grange Rd SK23 ... 47 D3
Roxburgh Ave DE21 ... 219 F4
Roxton Ave S8 ... 56 C4
Roxton Ct NG16 ... 195 F4
Royal Ave NG10 ... 223 E1
Royal Cl DE72 ... 221 D1
Royal Croft Dr DE45 ... 91 F3
Royal Gate DE56 ... 179 E2
Royal Gr DE21 ... 206 B2
Royal Hill Rd DE21 ... 220 B3
Royal Oak Pl DE45 ... 109 E3
Royal Rd SK12 ... 32 B3
Royal Sch for the Deaf
DE22 ... 218 B3
Royale Cl S21 ... 59 F2
Roydon Cl DE3 ... 217 E2
Royle Ave SK13 ... 10 B1
Royston Cl Ashbourne DE6 ... 185 E4
Chesterfield S40 ... 114 A4
Royston Dr DE56 ... 179 E3
Rubens Cl Dronfield S18 ... 56 C1
Marple SK6 ... 23 E4
Ruby Paddocks NG16 ... 195 F3
Rudyard Ave DE21 ... 220 C3
Rufford Ave NG18 ... 268 C4
Rufford Cl S40 ... 95 F1
Rufford Dr NG19 ... 136 C2
Rufford Rd NG10 ... 236 A2
Ruffstone Cl DE56 ... 191 E4
Rugby Ave DE55 ... 159 E2
Rugby Cl DE14 ... 254 B4
Rugby St DE24 ... 219 F1
Rugeley Ave NG10 ... 237 D4
Ruislip Cl NG16 ... 195 F4
Rupert Rd DE21 ... 220 A4
Rupert St Ilkeston DE7 ... 195 D1
Lower Pilsley S45 ... 132 A2
Rush Leys NG10 ... 236 B3
Rushcliffe Ave DE21 ... 219 F3
Rushdale Ave Derby DE23 ... 231 E3
Sheffield S8 ... 43 D3
Rushdale Mount S8 ... 43 D3
Rushdale Rd S8 ... 43 D3
Rushdale Terr S8 ... 43 D3
Rushen Mount S40 ... 114 C3
Rushes The Hadfield SK13 ... 9 F2
Mansfield Woodhouse NG19 ... 136 B3
Rushleigh Ct S17 ... 55 E4
Rushley Ave S17 ... 55 E4
Rushley Cl S17 ... 55 E4
Rushley Dr S17 ... 55 E4
Rushley Rd S17 ... 55 E4
Rushpool Ave NG19 ... 136 B2
Rushton Cl SK6 ... 23 D3
Rushton Dr SK6 ... 23 D3
Rushup Cl DE22 ... 205 D3
Rushup La SK17 ... 48 B4
Rushy La NG10 ... 222 C3
Rushycroft SK14 ... 9 D2
Ruskin Ave NG10 ... 236 A3
Ruskin Rd Derby DE1 ... 218 C4
Mansfield NG19 ... 135 E1
Ruskin Sq S8 ... 43 D3
Ruskin Way DE23 ... 231 D4
Russel St ST16 ... 269 D4
Russell Gdns S42 ... 131 D3
Russell Pl NG1 ... 268 A2
Russell St Compstall SK6 ... 15 D2
Derby DE24 ... 219 E1
Long Eaton NG10 ... 223 E1
Nottingham NG7 ... 268 A2
Swadlincote DE11 ... 256 B2
Russet Cl Derby DE21 ... 206 A1
Hatton DE65 ... 227 E1
Ruston Cl Chesterfield S40 ... 95 D3
Swadlincote DE11 ... 256 A2
Rutherford Dr DE21 ... 205 F1
Rutherford Pl ST4 ... 269 D2
Ruthyn Ave S43 ... 80 A4
Rutland Ave Bolsover S44 ... 99 D1
Borrowash DE72 ... 221 E1
Matlock DE4 ... 143 E3
Ripley DE5 ... 181 D4
Rutland Cl DE15 ... 254 B3
Rutland Ct DE7 ... 194 B1
Rutland Dr DE3 ... 217 F2
Rutland Gr NG10 ... 223 E3
Rutland Pl DE56 ... 168 A3
Rutland Rd Chesterfield S40 ... 266 A3
Westwood NG16 ... 171 E2
Rutland Sq DE45 ... 109 E3
Rutland St Chesterfield S41 ... 77 D1
Derby DE23 ... 219 D1
Ilkeston DE7 ... 194 C1
Mansfield NG18 ... 268 C3
Matlock DE4 ... 143 E3
6 Nottingham NG1 ... 268 A1
Rutland Terr DE7 ... 194 C1
Rutland Way SK23 ... 34 B1
Ryal Cl DE72 ... 221 E3
Ryan Cl DE24 ... 231 F2
Rycroft CE Mid Sch ST14 ... 196 C2
Rycroft Rd DE74 ... 247 E3
Rydal Ave NG10 ... 223 D1
Rydal Cl Derby DE22 ... 204 C2
Dronfield S18 ... 56 B1
Rydal Cres S41 ... 95 F4
Rydal Way S45 ... 131 D2
Ryder Cl DE11 ... 255 F1
Rye Butts DE73 ... 232 C1
Rye Cl DE21 ... 205 F2
Rye Cres S45 ... 131 E2
Rye Flatt La S40 ... 95 E1
Rye Flatts La DE65 ... 227 E1
Ryecroft DE4 ... 127 E1
Ryecroft Glen Rd S17 ... 56 A4
Ryecroft St NG9 ... 223 F4
Ryecroft View S17 ... 55 E4
Ryedale Gdns DE23 ... 231 E3
Ryegrass Cl DE56 ... 179 E2
Ryegrass Rd DE21 ... 206 B1
Ryehill Ave S40 ... 95 D1
Ryemere Cl NG16 ... 182 C1
Rykneld Cl DE23 ... 230 C3
Rykneld Ct S45 ... 131 E2
Rykneld Dr DE23 ... 230 C4
Rykneld Prim Sch DE14 ... 253 F4
Rykneld Rd Derby DE23 ... 230 C3
Findern DE23 ... 230 C3
Rykneld Rise S42 ... 115 D2
Rykneld Way DE23 ... 230 C3
Ryknield Hill DE5 ... 180 A1
Ryknield Rd DE56 ... 192 A4
Rylah Hill S44 ... 118 A3
Rymill Dr DE21 ... 205 F1
Sabine St ST17 ... 269 E3
Sacheveral La DE4 ... 140 C2
Sacheveral Ave NG16 ... 160 B2
Sacheverel St DE1 ... 267 B2
Sackerville Tr S21 ... 60 A4
Sackville Cl S40 ... 114 A4
Sackville St DE23 ... 231 F4
Saddlers Cl NG19 ... 136 C1
Saddleworth Wlk DE24 ... 232 C2
Sadler Gate DE1 ... 267 B3
Sadler St NG19 ... 268 A4
Saffron Dr DE21 ... 206 A1
Sage Dr DE11 ... 256 C2
St Agnes Ave DE22 ... 204 B2
St Aidan's Ave S2 ... 43 E4
St Aidan's Cl S2 ... 43 F4
St Aidan's Dr S2 ... 43 F4
St Aidan's Mount S2 ... 43 F4
St Aidan's Pl S2 ... 43 F4
St Aidan's Rd S2 ... 43 F4
St Aidan's Way S2 ... 43 F4
St Alban's RC Prim Sch
DE21 ... 219 F3
St Albans Cl S42 ... 132 C4
St Albans Pl SK22 ... 33 E4
St Albans Rd DE22 ... 218 B2
St Albans St SK22 ... 33 E4
St Alkmund's Cl DE56 ... 190 C2
St Alkmund's Way DE1 ... 267 B4
St Alkmunds Way DE56 ... 190 C2
St Andrew St NG18 ... 268 C3
St Andrew's CE Prim Sch
DE7 ... 207 D3
St Andrew's CE Sch B79 ... 263 F1
St Andrew's CE/Meth
Prim Sch S18 ... 56 B1
St Andrew's Cl B79 ... 263 F1
St Andrew's Dr
Ilkeston DE7 ... 208 C4
Swanwick DE55 ... 169 F4
St Andrews Cl DE55 ... 170 A4
St Andrews Ct SK13 ... 10 A2
St Andrews Rise S40 ... 114 B4
St Andrews Specl Sch
DE21 ... 205 F1
St Andrews View DE21 ... 205 F1
St Andrews Wlk SK22 ... 33 E4
St Ann's Cl SK23 ... 46 C3
St Ann's St NG1 ... 268 B2
St Ann's Valley NG3 ... 268 C2
St Ann's Way NG3 ... 268 B2
St Ann's Well Rd NG3 ... 268 B2
St Anne's CE Prim Sch
DE45 ... 91 F3
St Anne's Cl Baslow DE45 ... 91 F3
Derby DE1 ... 218 C3
St Anne's La DE74 ... 247 D2
St Anne's RC Prim Sch
SK17 ... 66 A1
St Annes St SK14 ... 16 A4
St Anselms Sch DE45 ... 109 E3
St Augustine St DE23 ... 218 C1
St Augustines Ave S40 ... 115 D4
St Augustines Cres S40 ... 115 D4
St Augustines Dr S40 ... 266 B1
St Augustines Mount S40 ... 266 B1
St Augustines Rd S40 ... 115 D4
St Augustines Rise S40 ... 115 D4
St Austin's RC Prim Sch
ST17 ... 269 E3
St Barnabas La S2 ... 43 D4
St Barnabas Rd S2 ... 43 D4
St Barnabus RC Cath NG1 ... 268 A2
St Bartholomew's CE
Prim Sch SK17 ... 121 D4
St Benedict RC Sch DE22 ... 204 C1
St Benet's Sch DE56 ... 167 D4
St Bride's Wlk DE22 ... 218 A3
St Catherine St NG18 ... 268 C3
St Catherine's Rd DE11 ... 255 F3
St Catherines Prep Sch
SK6 ... 23 D4
St Cecilia Gdns NG3 ... 268 B2
St Chad's CE Inf Sch
DE23 ... 218 C2
St Chad's Cl
Denstone ST14 ... 196 B3
Draycott DE72 ... 235 D4
St Chad's Pl 11 ST16 ... 269 E4
St Chad's Rd Derby DE23 ... 218 C1
Nottingham NG3 ... 268 C2
St Charles Cl SK13 ... 9 F3
St Charles' RC Sch SK13 ... 9 F3
St Christopher Ave ST4 ... 269 D1
St Christopher St NG2 ... 268 C1
St Clare's Cl DE22 ... 218 B1
St Clare's Specl Sch DE3 ... 218 A1
St Cuthbert's Rd
Derby DE22 ... 218 B2
Nottingham NG3 ... 268 C2
St David's Cl DE22 ... 218 B2
St David's Rise S40 ... 114 B4
St Davids Rd B79 ... 263 F1
St Dominic's Jun Sch
ST4 ... 269 D2
St Edmund's Ave NG19 ... 136 B2
St Edmund's Cl DE22 ... 204 C2
St Edmunds CE Prim Sch
NG19 ... 136 B2
St Edward's CE Sch
DE74 ... 247 D2
St Edward's Rd DE74 ... 247 D1
St Edwards Ct DE11 ... 255 F3
St Elizabeth Cl S2 ... 43 D4
St Elizabeth's RC Prim
Sch DE56 ... 178 C3
St Elphins Sch DE4 ... 127 F1
St Francis Ley Ind Pk
DE23 ... 219 D1
St George's CE Prim Sch
SK22 ... 33 E4
St George's Pl DE56 ... 178 C2
St George's RC Prim Sch
DE23 ... 231 E4
St George's Rd ST17 ... 269 F3
St Georges Hospl ST16 ... 269 E4
St Georges Rd SK22 ... 33 E4
St Giles CE Prim Sch
Killamarsh S21 ... 60 B3
Matlock, Old Matlock DE4 ... 143 E2
Matlock, Starkholmes DE4 ... 143 E1
St Giles CE Sch S21 ... 60 B3
St Giles Cl S40 ... 115 D4
St Giles Rd DE23 ... 218 C1
St Giles Specl Sch DE21 ... 205 E1
St Giles Wlk DE4 ... 143 E2
St Hardulph's Prim Sch
DE73 ... 252 C1
St Helen's Cl
Chesterfield S41 ... 266 B4
Darley Dale DE4 ... 127 D2
Grindleford S32 ... 72 B4
St Helen's Cres NG9 ... 209 E2
St Helen's Croft S32 ... 72 B4
St Helen's Dr NG16 ... 171 E4
St Helen's La DE56 ... 166 A4
St Helen's St
Chesterfield S41 ... 266 B4
Derby DE1 ... 267 A4
St Helen's St NG7 ... 268 A2
St Helens Ave NG16 ... 160 B2
St Hugh's Cl DE22 ... 205 D1
St James Ave DE7 ... 209 D4
St James' CE Inf Sch
DE23 ... 267 C1
St James' CE Jun Sch
DE23 ... 219 D2
St James Cl Belper DE56 ... 179 E2
Chesterfield S41 ... 96 B1
Glossop SK13 ... 17 E4
Willington DE65 ... 242 B3
St James Ct NG10 ... 223 D2
St James' Dr NG16 ... 182 B4
St James' Sq SK22 ... 33 E4
St James' St
9 Buxton SK17 ... 85 D4
Derby, Rose Hill DE23 ... 219 D1
Derby, The Holmes DE1 ... 267 B3
Nottingham NG1 ... 268 A1
St James' Terr SK17 ... 85 D4
St James's Ct SK17 ... 85 E2
St James's St NG9 ... 223 E3
St James's Terr
5 Nottingham NG1 ... 268 A1
Stapleford NG9 ... 223 E3
St John Fisher RC Prim
Sch DE24 ... 233 E4
St John Houghton RC Sch
DE7 ... 208 B3
St John St Hayfield SK22 ... 25 E1
Mansfield NG18 ... 268 B4
St John's Ave DE21 ... 220 A3
St John's CE Mid Sch
NG18 ... 268 B4
St John's CE Prim Sch
Belper DE56 ... 179 D3
Ripley DE5 ... 169 F1
Stafford ST16 ... 269 F4
Stapleford NG9 ... 223 F4
St John's Cl Brinsley NG16 ... 171 E1
Derby DE22 ... 204 B2
St John's Dr Derby DE21 ... 220 A3
Kilburn DE56 ... 192 A4
Swadlincote DE11 ... 255 F3
St John's Mount S41 ... 95 F4
St John's Pl NG18 ... 268 B4
St John's Rd Belper DE56 ... 179 D2
Buxton SK17 ... 85 D4
Chesterfield S41 ... 95 F4
Dronfield S18 ... 76 C4
Ilkeston DE7 ... 209 D4
Matlock Bath DE4 ... 143 D2
Smalley DE7 ... 192 C3
Tideswell SK17 ... 69 E2
St John's St Ashbourne DE6 ... 173 E1
Long Eaton NG10 ... 236 B4
Wirksworth DE4 ... 165 F4
St John's Terr DE1 ... 218 C3
St John's Wlk ST 16 ... 269 F4
St Johns Cl Bamford S33 ... 40 A2
Chesterfield S40 ... 114 A4
Ripley DE5 ... 169 F1
St Johns Pl S43 ... 78 B1
St Johns Rd S43 ... 78 B1
St Jonn's Cres S43 ... 80 C2
St Joseph's Prep Sch NG1 ... 268 A2
St Joseph's RC Prim Sch
Derby DE23 ... 267 A1
Matlock DE4 ... 143 E3
Shirebrook NG20 ... 119 F3
Staveley S43 ... 97 E4
St Joseph's St DE4 ... 143 E3
St Katherine's La DE4 ... 110 C1
St Laurence Ct NG10 ... 236 C3
St Lawrence Ave S44 ... 118 B4
St Lawrence CE Prim Sch
NG10 ... 236 C3
St Lawrence Cl DE75 ... 181 F1
St Lawrence Rd S42 ... 131 F3
St Lawrence View S80 ... 81 F3
St Leonard's Ave ST17 ... 269 F3
St Leonard's Prim Sch
ST17 ... 269 F3
St Leonards Dr S41 ... 96 B1
St Leonards Pl DE55 ... 146 C1
St Luke's CE Prim Sch
SK13 ... 10 B1
St Luke's Sch S81 ... 63 F4
St Luke's St NG3 ... 268 C2
St Lukes Ct 7 S41 ... 95 F4
St Lukes Prim Sch SK17 ... 137 D4
St Margaret St NG18 ... 268 C3
St Margaret's Dr S40 ... 266 A3
St Margaret's RC Prim Sch
SK13 ... 16 B4
St Mark's Cl DE4 ... 155 D3
St Mark's Rd
Chesterfield S40 ... 95 F2
Derby DE21 ... 219 E3
St Marks St NG3 ... 268 B2
St Martin's Pl ST16 ... 269 E4
St Martin's Rd SK6 ... 23 D3
St Martin's Specl Sch
DE24 ... 232 C4
St Martin's Wlk S80 ... 82 B3
St Mary St DE7 ... 208 C4
St Mary's Ave DE72 ... 235 D4
St Mary's CE Fst Sch ST14 ... 210 A1
St Mary's Cl Derby DE24 ... 233 D3
Newton Solney DE15 ... 248 C4
St Mary's Cres ST14 ... 210 A1
St Mary's Ct DE1 ... 267 B4
St Mary's Dr DE13 ... 240 C1
St Mary's Gate
Chesterfield S41 ... 266 C3
Derby DE1 ... 267 B3
Nottingham NG1 ... 268 B1
7 Stafford ST16 ... 269 E4
Wirksworth DE4 ... 165 F4
St Mary's Gr 6 ST16 ... 269 E4
St Mary's Inf Sch S18 ... 76 C4
St Mary's Pl 8 ST16 ... 269 E4
St Mary's RC Prim Sch
Chesterfield S40 ... 266 A4
Derby DE1 ... 267 B4
Glossop SK13 ... 17 E4
Marple SK6 ... 23 D4
New Mills SK22 ... 33 D4
St Mary's RC Sch S40 ... 95 E4
St Mary's Rd Disley SK12 ... 32 B3
Glossop SK13 ... 17 E4
New Mills SK22 ... 33 D4
St Mary's Wlk NG16 ... 171 D2
St Marys Wharf Rd DE1 ... 219 D4
St Matthew's St DE14 ... 254 B4
St Matthew's Wlk DE22 ... 204 C1
St Matthias Rd NG3 ... 268 C2
St Mawes Cl DE22 ... 204 B2
St Mellion Cl DE3 ... 217 F1
St Michael's CE Prim Sch
S32 ... 53 D4
St Michael's Cl
Holbrook DE56 ... 191 E3
Shirley DE6 ... 200 B4
Willington DE65 ... 242 A3
St Michael's Dr
South Normanton DE55 ... 160 A4
Stretton en le F DE12 ... 265 F1
St Michael's La DE1 ... 267 B4
St Michaels Cl Crich DE4 ... 156 C1
Derby DE24 ... 233 E4
St Michaels View DE24 ... 233 E4
St Nicholas Cl DE22 ... 204 B1
St Nicholas St NG1 ... 268 B1
St Norbert Dr DE7 ... 208 B2
St Oswald Cres DE6 ... 173 E1
St Oswald's CE Inf Sch
DE6 ... 173 D1
St Oswald's Hospl DE6 ... 173 D1
St Pancras Way DE1 ... 267 C5
St Patrick's Pl 1 ST16 ... 269 E4
St Patrick's St 2 ST16 ... 269 E4
St Paul's CE Prim Sch
ST17 ... 269 E3
St Paul's Rd DE1 ... 219 D4
St Pauls Ave S41 ... 115 E3
St Peter & St Paul Sch
S41 ... 115 E4
St Peter's CE Fst Sch
ST14 ... 224 C1
St Peter's CE Jun Sch
DE23 ... 218 B1
St Peter's CE Prim Sch
Netherseal DE12 ... 264 C3
Stoke-on-T ST4 ... 269 E1
St Peter's Churchyard DE1 ... 267 B3
St Peter's Cl DE56 ... 178 C2
St Peter's Gate NG1 ... 268 B1
St Peter's Rd Buxton SK17 ... 66 B1
Derby DE73 ... 233 D1
Thorpe Salvin S80 ... 62 C4
St Peter's Sch NG18 ... 268 C3
St Peter's St DE1 ... 267 B3
St Peter's Way NG18 ... 268 C3
St Peters CE Sch DE6 ... 149 E2
St Peters Cl
Long Duckmanton S44 ... 98 A2
Stoke-on-T ST4 ... 269 E2
St Peters Croft DE56 ... 179 D2
St Peters High Sch ST4 ... 269 D2
St Philip Howard RC Sch
SK13 ... 17 D4
St Philip Neri's with St
Bede's RC Prim Sch
NG18 ... 268 B4
St Philip's Dr S41 ... 115 D4
St Philomena's Convent
Prim Sch DE1 ... 267 B4
St Quentin Cl Derby DE22 ... 218 B2
12 Sheffield S17 ... 56 A3
St Quentin Dr S17 ... 56 A3
St Quentin Mount S17 ... 56 A3
St Quentin Rise S17 ... 56 A3
St Quentin View S17 ... 56 A3
St Ronan's Ave DE56 ... 190 C1
St Stephen's Ave NG2 ... 268 C1
St Stephen's Cl DE23 ... 231 E3
St Stephen's Ct DE11 ... 256 C2

St Stephen's Rd NG2 268 C1
St Stephens Cl DE72 221 D1
St Swithin's Cl DE22 218 B2
St Theresa's RC Prim Sch S2 44 A4
St Thomas Cl DE55 147 F3
St Thomas More RC Sch SK17 85 D4
St Thomas of Canterbury Prim Sch S8 56 C4
St Thomas Pl ST4 269 D1
St Thomas Prim Sch ST4 269 D2
St Thomas RC Prim Sch DE7 208 C3
St Thomas Rd DE23 219 D1
St Thomas' St S40 95 E1
St Thomas St ST 16 269 F4
St Vincent Cl NG10 236 C3
St Werburgh's CE Prim Sch DE21 220 B3
St Werburgh's CE Prim Sch DE13 238 A2
St Werburgh's View DE21 220 B3
St Wilfrid's Rd Sheffield S2 43 D4
  West Hallam DE7 207 F4
St Wystan's Rd DE22 218 B2
St Wystans Sch DE65 242 B1
Salcey Cl DE55 169 F4
Salcey Dr NG9 209 E1
Salcey Sq 3 S40 95 E1
Salcombe Rd DE55 159 E3
Sale & Davys CE Prim Sch DE73 244 A3
Sale St DE23 219 D1
Sales Ave S42 131 E4
Sales La DE15 248 B2
Salford Gdns NG3 268 B2
Salisbury Ave
  Burton u T DE15 248 B2
  Chesterfield S41 95 F4
  Dronfield S18 76 A4
Salisbury Cl NG19 136 B2
Salisbury Cres S41 95 F4
Salisbury Dr Stafford ST 16 269 F4
  Swadlincote DE11 256 C3
Salisbury La DE73 252 A4
Salisbury Rd Dronfield S18 76 A4
  Mansfield NG19 268 A4
  Stafford ST 16 269 F4
Salisbury St Derby DE23 267 B1
  Hadfield SK13 10 A3
  Long Eaton NG10 236 C4
Sallyfield La DE6 183 F4
Sallywood Cl DE24 231 E1
Salmond Ave ST 16 269 F4
Salt Ave ST17 269 E3
Salt Rd ST17 269 E3
Saltburn Cl DE21 205 E1
Salter Cl DE74 246 C2
Salter St ST16 269 E4
Saltergate S40 266 B3
Saltergate La S30 40 B1
Salters La DE4 142 C2
Salvin Cres S43 80 C2
Samantha Ct DE21 206 A1
Sampson's La NG19 135 D2
Samuel Cl Mansfield NG19 268 A4
  Sheffield S2 43 E4
Samuel Dr S2 43 E4
Samuel Pl S2 43 E4
Samuel Rd S2 43 E4
Samuel St SK14 9 E2
Sand La DE6 211 D1
Sandalwood Cl DE24 233 E4
Sandalwood Rd DE15 254 C3
Sandbach Cl DE21 206 A1
Sandbed La DE56 179 E2
Sandby Croft S14 43 F1
Sandby Ct S14 43 F1
Sandby Dr Marple SK6 23 D4
  Sheffield S14 43 F1
Sandcliffe Pk DE11 256 B4
Sandcliffe Rd DE11 256 B3
Sandcroft Cl DE11 256 B3
Sandcroft Rd DE21 220 C3
Sanderson Rd DE21 220 A3
Sandfield Cl DE21 220 A4
Sandfield Rd NG9 223 F1
Sandford Ave NG10 236 C4
Sandford Brook DE65 228 C1
Sandgate Ave NG19 136 B2
Sandgate Cl DE24 233 D3
Sandgate Rd NG19 136 B2
Sandhall La DE56 166 C3
Sandham La DE5 169 E1
Sandhill La
  Charlesworth SK6 16 A1
  Marple SK6 15 F1
Sandhills Rd S44 99 E1
Sandiacre Rd NG9 223 E3
Sandiway Chesterfield S40 114 B4
  Glossop SK13 17 F4
Sandlands The DE11 256 B3
Sandown Ave DE3 217 E2
Sandown Cl
  Branston DE14 254 A4
  Eckington S21 59 D2
Sandown Rd Beeston NG9 223 F1
  Derby DE24 232 C4
Sandringham Ave DE15 248 A1
Sandringham Cl S44 97 D2
Sandringham Ct NG19 136 A3
Sandringham Dr
  Derby DE21 220 C3
  Mansfield Woodhouse NG19 136 A3
Sandringham Pl DE7 208 B3
Sandringham Rd
  Calow S44 97 D2
  Derby DE21 205 F1
  Mansfield Woodhouse NG19 136 C3
  Nottingham NG2 268 C1
  Sandiacre NG10 223 D2
Sands Cl S14 43 F2
Sandstone Ave S40 114 A4
Sandwood Cl DE55 148 A2
Sandy Cl S80 81 F3
Sandy La Caldwell DE12 261 D4
  Chisworth SK13 16 A2
  Crich DE4 167 F4
  Horsley DE21 192 A2
  Mansfield NG18 268 C4
  Matlock DE4 143 E4
Sandybank Cl SK13 9 F2
Sandybrook Cl DE6 173 E2
Sandycliffe Cl NG19 136 C1
Sandyford La
  Alderwasley DE56 166 C2
  Spout DE56 166 C2
Sandyhill Cl DE73 233 D1
Sandypits La DE65 229 E2
Sanforth St S41 96 A3
Santolina Dr DE21 205 F1
Sapperton Cl DE23 231 E3
Sapperton La
  Boylestone DE65 213 F1
  Church Broughton DE65 213 F1
Sarah Cl DE55 170 B4
Sargent Gdns NG3 268 C2
Sark Rd S2 43 D4
Sash St ST16 269 E4
Saundby Ave NG19 135 E1
Saundersfoot Way DE21 206 B1
Savage La S17 55 E4
Saville Cl NG9 223 F4
Saville House Sch NG19 136 A2
Saw Pit Ind Est DE55 148 B3
Saw Pit La DE55 148 A3
Sawley Jun & Inf Schs NG10 236 A3
Sawley Rd Breaston DE72 235 F3
  Draycott DE72 235 D4
Sawmills Ind Pk DE75 181 E2
Sawpit La DE65 227 E1
Saxon Cl DE15 254 C4
Saxon Croft DE65 242 B1
Saxon Gr DE65 242 A3
Saxon Rd S8 43 D4
Saxon St DE15 254 C4
Saxondale Ave DE3 217 E2
Saxton Ave DE75 181 F1
Scaddows La DE73 250 C2
Scalby Cl NG16 182 B1
Scaliot Cl SK22 33 D4
Scalpcliffe Rd DE15 248 A1
Scarborough Ave DE7 208 C4
Scarborough Rise DE21 205 E1
Scarborough St NG3 268 B2
Scarcliffe Cl DE24 232 C2
Scarcliffe La NG20 119 E4
Scarcliffe Prim Sch S44 118 C3
Scarcliffe St NG18 268 C4
Scarcliffe Terr NG20 101 D1
Scargill CE Prim Sch DE7 207 E4
Scargill Rd DE7 207 F4
Scargill Wlk NG16 182 C2
Scarsdale Ave
  Derby, Allestree DE23 204 B2
  Derby, California DE23 218 B1
Scarsdale Cl S18 76 A4
Scarsdale Cres S43 96 B4
Scarsdale Cross S18 57 D1
Scarsdale Hospl S40 266 B4
Scarsdale Pl 7 SK17 85 D4
Scarsdale Rd
  Chesterfield S41 96 A4
  Dronfield S18 57 D1
  Duffield DE56 190 C2
Scarsdale St S44 117 F4
Scarthin DE4 155 D3
Schofield Ct DE4 110 C1
School Ave S20 59 F4
School Board La S40 95 F2
School Cl Blackwell DE55 147 E1
  Fenny Bentley DE6 162 A1
  Moira DE11 256 B1
  Mosborough S20 59 F4
  Newton DE55 148 A2
  Shirland DE55 146 B1
  Stonebroom DE55 146 C2
School Croft DE55 170 B3
School House Hill DE56 168 B1
School La Ashbourne DE6 173 D1
  Baslow DE45 91 F3
  Beeley DE4 111 D2
  Brackenfield DE55 145 E1
  Castle Donington DE74 247 D2
  Compstall SK6 15 D2
  Crich DE4 157 D1
  Derby DE73 233 D1
  Dronfield S18 57 D1
  Hassop DE45 90 C3
  Hathersage S32 53 D4
  Heage DE56 168 B1
  Long Duckmanton S44 97 E2
  Mansfield Woodhouse NG19 136 B2
  Marsh Lane S21 58 C2
  Old Brampton S42 93 F2
  Ripley DE5 169 E1
  Rolleston DE13 240 B2
  Rowsley DE4 126 C4
  Sheffield, Greenhill S8 56 C4
  Sheffield, Norton S8 57 E4
  South Normanton DE55 160 A2
School La continued
  Stanton in P DE4 126 B3
  Stanton-by-D DE7 222 C4
  Sudbury DE6 225 F2
  Taddington SK17 87 F2
School Lane Cl S8 43 E1
School Rd Chesterfield S41 96 A4
  Matlock DE4 143 E3
  Peak Dale SK17 67 D3
  Uttoxeter ST14 210 A1
School Sq DE7 207 F4
School St Eckington S21 59 E2
  Moira DE12 262 C1
  Mosborough S20 59 E4
  Swadlincote DE11 256 A1
Schoolpiece La DE65 227 E4
Scotches The DE56 178 C3
Scotia Cl S2 43 F4
Scotia Dr S2 43 F4
Scotland St S80 81 F3
Scotswood Rd NG19 136 A3
Scott Cl S42 115 F2
Scott Cres DE55 146 C2
Scott Dr Belper DE56 179 F3
  Marple SK6 23 D4
  Somercotes DE55 170 B4
Scott St Derby DE23 218 C1
  Whaley Thorns NG20 101 D1
Scotts The DE11 261 E4
Scowerdons Cl S12 44 C3
Scowerdons Dr S12 44 C3
Scratta La S80 63 E1
Screetham La DE4 112 B1
Scropton Old Rd DE65 239 E4
Scropton Rd
  Hatton DE65 239 D4
  Scropton DE65 226 C1
Scropton Wlk DE24 232 C2
Sea Breeze Terr S13 44 C4
Seaburn Rd NG9 223 F1
Seaford Way DE7 194 C3
Seagrave Ave S12 44 A2
Seagrave Cl DE21 220 A4
Seagrave Cres S12 44 A2
Seagrave Dr S12 44 A2
Seagrave Rd S12 44 A2
Seal View DE12 261 E3
Seale St DE1 267 B5
Sealey Cl DE65 242 B3
Seals Rd DE12 262 C1
Sealwood La Linton DE12 261 F2
  Overseal DE12 261 F3
Seamer Rd NG16 195 F4
Seanor La S45 132 A2
Searl St DE1 218 C3
Searle Ave ST16 269 D3
Searson Ave S44 99 D1
Searston Ave S42 132 B4
Seascale Cl DE21 205 E1
Seaton Cl DE3 217 E2
Second Ave Derby DE73 245 D4
  Risley DE72 222 C3
Sedbergh Cres S41 95 E4
Sedgebrook Cl DE21 205 F1
Sedgebrook St NG19 136 C2
Sedgefield Gn DE3 217 E1
Sedgemoor Cl S40 95 D2
Sedgley Ave NG2 268 C2
Sedgwick St
  Langley Mill NG16 182 A2
  Westwood NG16 171 D2
Seely Rd NG7 268 A2
Sefton Ave NG9 223 F4
Sefton Cl DE15 248 A1
Sefton Rd DE21 219 F3
Sefton St SK13 17 E4
Selborne St DE24 219 E1
Selby Cl Beeston NG9 223 F2
  Chesterfield S40 114 B4
Selhurst Rd S41 95 F3
Selina Cl DE74 247 D2
Selkirk St DE21 219 F4
Selly Oak Gr S8 57 E3
Selly Oak Rd S8 57 E3
Selmer Ct S43 96 B4
Selston CE Inf Sch NG16 171 F3
Selston Rd NG16 171 D3
Selworthy Cl DE21 206 A1
Selwyn St Bolsover S44 118 B4
  Derby DE22 218 B3
  Stoke-on-T ST4 269 E1
Senners La SK17 87 D1
Serina Ave DE23 231 E4
Serlay La S26 61 F3
Serlby Dr S26 61 F3
Serlby Rise NG3 268 C2
Setcup La S21 59 E1
Sett Cl SK22 33 D4
Settlement The DE72 221 E3
Setts Way S42 115 D2
Seven Arches Way ST4 269 F2
Seven Oaks Rd DE7 209 D1
Sevenoaks Ave DE22 217 F3
Severals NG9 223 F4
Severn Cl DE13 240 B1
Severn Cres S42 132 A3
Severn Sq DE55 159 D2
Severn St DE24 232 C4
Severnale Cl DE22 205 D3
Severnlands Dr DE24 233 E2
Sewell Rd S20 59 F3
Sexton St SK13 9 F4
Seymour Cl DE22 218 B3
Seymour La S43 79 E1
Seymour Rd NG16 182 C1
Seymour St NG3 268 C2
Shacklecross Cl DE72 221 E1
Shady Gr DE65 228 B1
Shaftesbury Ave
  Chesterfield S40 95 E2
  Long Eaton NG10 236 A2
  Mansfield NG19 135 F1
  Sandiacre NG10 223 D3
Shaftesbury Cres DE23 219 D1
Shaftesbury St DE23 219 D1
Shaftesbury St S DE23 219 D1
Shafton Cl S45 131 F2
Shafton Wlk S45 131 F2
Shakespeare Ave
  Creswell S80 81 E1
  Mansfield Woodhouse NG19 136 A2
  Shirland DE55 146 B2
Shakespeare Cl
  Clay Cross S42 131 D3
  Repton DE65 242 B1
  Swadlincote DE11 256 B3
Shakespeare Cres S18 76 B4
Shakespeare Dr DE55 159 D2
Shakespeare Rd NG16 195 E3
Shakespeare St
  Derby DE24 232 A3
  Grassmoor S42 115 F2
  Holmewood S42 116 B1
  Long Eaton NG10 223 E1
  Nottingham NG1 268 B2
Shakespeare Villas NG1 268 B2
Shaldon Dr DE23 218 B1
Shalfleet Dr DE24 233 E3
Shallcross Ave SK23 45 F2
Shallcross Cres SK23 45 F2
Shallcross Rd SK23 45 F2
Shambles The S40 266 B3
Shamrock Pl S43 79 E2
Shamrock St DE23 218 C1
Shandwick Ct 14 DE24 231 E2
Shanklin Dr NG9 223 E4
Shannon Cl DE23 231 E3
Shap Cl 7 S40 95 E3
Shardlow Prim Sch DE72 234 C1
Shardlow Rd
  Aston-on-T DE72 246 B4
  Derby DE24 233 E3
Sharley Park L Ctr S45 131 E2
Sharman Cl
  Apperknowle S18 58 A1
  Stoke-on-T ST4 269 D2
Sharp Cl Ilkeston DE7 208 B3
  Long Eaton NG10 236 B3
Sharpe Ave S8 56 C4
Sharpswood Manor DE11 256 C2
Sharrard Cl S12 44 A3
Sharrard Dr S12 44 A3
Sharrard Gr S12 44 A3
Sharrard Rd S12 44 A3
Shatton La S33 51 F4
Shaw La Belper DE56 191 D4
  Hadfield SK13 9 F2
  Holloway DE4 156 B4
  Marston Montgomery DE6 198 A1
Shaw St Chesterfield S41 96 A4
  Derby DE22 218 C3
  Dronfield S18 57 E2
  Glossop SK13 17 E4
  Holmewood S42 116 B1
  Mottram in L SK14 9 D2
  Somercotes DE55 170 B3
Shaw St E DE7 209 D3
Shaw St W DE7 209 D3
Shaw's Row S40 95 E1
Shaw's Yd DE56 191 F4
Shawcroft DE6 173 E1
Shawcroft Ave DE55 170 B3
Shawfield Rd SK13 9 F2
Shaws Gn DE22 218 C3
Shaws Hill DE4 156 B1
Sheaf Bank S2 43 D4
Sheardhall Ave SK12 32 C3
Sheards Cl 7 S18 56 C1
Sheards Dr S18 56 C1
Sheards Way S18 56 C1
Shearwater Cl DE23 231 E4
Sheepbridge La
  Chesterfield S41 76 C1
  Mansfield NG18 268 A3
Sheepcote Rd S21 60 B3
Sheephill Rd S11 42 C1
Sheeplea La S45 129 F4
Sheepwash La S45 145 D4
Sheet Stores Ind Est NG10 236 B3
Sheffield City Poly S17 55 E2
Sheffield Hallam Univ S17 55 E2
Sheffield Pl DE1 267 D2
Sheffield Rd Baslow DE45 92 A4
  Chapel-en-le-F SK23 47 F4
  Chesterfield S41 96 A3
  Creswell S80 81 E2
  Dronfield S18 56 C2
  Eckington S21 59 F3
  Glossop SK13 10 C1
  Hathersage S32 53 D4
  Killamarsh S21 60 B4
  Mosborough S21 59 F3
  Renishaw S21 79 E4
  Sheffield S12 44 C1
  Unstone S18 76 C2
  Unstone S18 76 C2
  Whitwell S80 81 E2
Shelburne St ST4 269 E1
Sheldon Cl NG10 223 D2
Sheldon Ct DE24 232 C2
Sheldon Mews SK13 9 E1
Sheldon Rd
  Chesterfield S40 95 D3
  Heanor DE75 181 E3
Shelford Cl DE3 217 E2
Shelford Hill NG19 268 A3
Shelley Ave NG19 136 A2
Shelley Dr Derby DE24 232 A3
  Dronfield S18 76 B4
Shelley Gr DE55 146 C2
Shelley St S42 116 B1
Shelly Rd DE11 256 B3
Shelmory Cl DE24 232 C3
Shelton Cl NG19 135 F1
Shelton Dr DE24 232 C2
Shelton Jun & Inf Sch DE24 232 B2
Shelton Old Rd ST4 269 E2
Shelton St NG3 268 B2
Shenington Way DE21 206 A1
Shepherd St DE23 218 B1
Shepherd's La DE73 251 E3
Shepherd's Row S18 77 D4
Shepley St Chesterfield S40 95 E1
  Glossop SK13 10 C1
  Hadfield SK13 9 F2
Shepley's Yd S40 266 B3
Sheppard St ST4 269 E1
Shepton Cl DE7 194 B2
Sheraton Way SK17 66 A1
Sherbourne Ave S41 95 F4
Sherbourne Dr
  Belper DE56 179 E3
  Branston DE14 254 A4
Sherbrook Gr SK17 85 E3
Sherbrooke Rd SK12 32 B3
Sheridan Ct NG9 209 F1
Sheridan St Derby DE24 231 F3
  Stafford ST 16 269 F4
Sheriff Dr DE4 143 D3
Sheringham Dr NG18 268 C3
Sherman Cl DE65 228 C1
Sherriff's Lea NG9 223 F1
Sherston Cl DE21 206 A1
Sherwin Cl NG3 268 B2
Sherwin Rd NG9 209 F1
Sherwin St DE22 218 C4
Sherwood Ave
  Borrowash DE72 221 E1
  Creswell S80 81 E1
  Derby, Chaddesden DE21 219 F4
  Derby, Littleover DE23 231 E3
  Hope S33 39 D2
  Pinxton NG16 160 B2
  Shirebrook NG20 119 F2
Sherwood Chase S17 55 F3
Sherwood Copse SK17 69 E2
Sherwood Dr NG20 119 F2
Sherwood Fold SK13 16 B4
Sherwood Foresters Regiment Meml DE4 156 C2
Sherwood Hall L Ctr DE4 143 E2
Sherwood Pl 15 S18 56 B1
Sherwood Rd Buxton SK17 85 E3
  Dronfield S18 56 B1
  Killamarsh S21 60 C4
  Matlock DE4 143 E2
  Tideswell SK17 69 E2
Sherwood Rise
  Eastwood NG16 182 C1
  Mansfield Woodhouse NG19 136 C2
Sherwood St Bolsover S44 117 F4
  Chesterfield S40 266 C1
  Derby DE22 218 C2
  Mansfield NG18 268 B3
  Mansfield Woodhouse NG19 136 A1
  Newton DE55 148 A2
  Shirland DE55 146 B3
  Somercotes DE55 170 B4
  Sutton in A NG17 148 C2
Shetland Cl Derby DE21 219 E4
  Mansfield NG19 136 C1
Shetland Rd Dronfield S18 76 A4
  Tibshelf DE55 147 F3
Shields Cres DE74 246 C2
Shieling The DE65 227 E1
Shilling Way NG10 236 A4
Shiloh Rd SK22, SK6 24 A3
Shilton Cl ST4 269 D1
Shinwell Ave S43 97 D4
Shipley Cl DE14 254 A4
Shipley Ct DE7 194 B1
Shipley Ctry Pk DE75 193 F3
Shipley Ctry Pk Visitor Ctr DE75 193 F4
Shipley La Mapperley DE75 193 F3
  Shipley DE75 193 F3
Shipley Wlk DE24 232 C2
Shipman Ct S20 59 E4
Shipstone St DE7 209 D3
Shirburn Ave NG18 268 C4
Shire Hill Hospl SK13 10 C2
Shire La Heath S44 116 C2
  Long Duckmanton S44 116 C2
Shire Way SK13 10 C2
Shirebrook Com Sch NG20 119 E3
Shirebrook Dr SK13 17 F4
Shirebrook Rd S8 43 D3
Shireoaks DE56 178 B3
Shireoaks Comm S81 63 F4
Shireoaks Rd Dronfield S18 57 E1
  Shireoaks S80 63 F3
Shireoaks Row S81 63 F4
Shireoaks Sta S81 63 F4
Shires The NG19 136 C1
Shirland Prim Sch DE55 146 B1
Shirland St S41 266 B4

Shirley Cl
Castle Donington DE74 ...... 247 D2
Chesterfield S40 .... 95 D3
Hope S33 .... 39 D2
Shirley Cres DE72 .... 235 E4
Shirley La Rodsley DE6 .. 200 A3
Shirley DE6 .... 200 A3
Shirley Pk DE72 .... 246 A4
Shirley Rd Derby DE21 .... 205 F1
Ripley DE5 .... 169 E1
Swanwick DE55 .... 169 F4
Shirley St NG10 .... 236 A2
Shop La DE56 .... 168 B1
Shop Stones DE72 .... 221 E3
Shoreham St S2 .... 43 D4
Short Ave DE24 .... 204 C3

Short Brook Fst & Mid Sch
S20 .... 59 F4
Short Cl S42 .... 113 E4
Short Hill
Breedon on t H DE73 .... 252 C3
[8] Nottingham NG1 .... 268 B1
Short La DE74 .... 246 C2
Short Lands DE56 .... 179 D2
Short Row DE56 .... 178 C2
Short St Belper DE56 ..... 179 D2
Burton u T DE15 .... 254 C4

Short Street Inf Sch
DE15 .... 254 C4
Shortbrook Bank [19] S20 . 59 F4
Shortbrook Cl [14] S20 .... 59 F4
Shortbrook Croft [12] S20 . 59 F4
Shortbrook Dr [18] S20 ... 59 F4
Shortbrook Rd S20 .... 59 F4
Shortbrook Way [21] S20 .. 59 F4
Shortbrook Wlk [15] S20 .. 59 F4
Shortheath DE12 .... 262 B2
Shortheath Rd DE12 .... 262 C2
Shortlands The DE4 .... 143 D2
Shorts La S17 .... 55 D3
Shortwood Cl NG1 .... 268 B1
Shorwell DE24 .... 233 E3
Shottle Wlk DE24 .... 232 C2
Shotwoodhill La DE13 .... 240 A3
Shrewsbury Cl DE21 ...... 206 B1
Shrewsbury Rd
Burton u T DE13 .... 240 C1
Stafford ST17 .... 269 E3
Shrewsbury St SK13 ...... 10 B1
Shropshire Ave
Derby DE21 .... 219 F4
Westwood NG16 .... 171 E2
Shropshire Dr SK13 .... 17 F4
Shrubbery The DE11 ...... 257 D1
Shuckstone La DE4 .... 156 C3
Shudehill SK22 .... 25 E2
Shuttlewood Rd S44 ...... 99 D2
Shutts La DE55 .... 109 E2
Sibthorpe St NG18 .... 268 B3
Sicklebrook La S18 .... 57 F2
Sickleholme S33 .... 40 A1
Siddals La DE22 .... 204 C2
Siddals Rd DE1 .... 267 C2
Siddals St DE15 .... 248 A2
Siddons St DE24 .... 233 D4
Side End La SK23 .... 45 D1
Sides La DE6 .... 184 A3
Sideway Rd ST4 .... 269 E1
Sidings The DE21 .... 220 A2
Sidings Way DE55 .... 147 E1
Sidlaw Cl [6] S40 .... 95 E3
Sidmouth Cl DE24 .... 233 E4
Sidney Cl DE3 .... 217 F2
Sidney St Derby DE1 ...... 267 C1
Kimberley NG16 .... 195 F3
Long Eaton NG10 .... 236 B3
Siemens Rd ST17 .... 269 E3
Silk Hill SK23 .... 45 F4
Silk Mill La DE13 .... 239 E3
Silk St SK13 .... 10 C1
Silken Holme DE55 .... 160 A2
Silkstone Cl Sheffield S12 . 44 C2
Swadlincote DE11 .... 256 A1
Silkstone Cres S12 .... 44 C2
Silkstone Pl S12 .... 44 C2
Silkstone Rd S12 .... 44 C2
Sillitoe Pl ST4 .... 269 E1
Silver Birch Cres DE55 .. 159 E4
Silver Hill Rd DE23 .... 219 D1
Silver La Elvaston DE72 .. 234 A3
Marchington ST14 .... 224 C1
Silver Mill Rd S2 .... 43 D4
Silver Spring SK14 .... 15 D4
Silverburn Dr DE21 .... 206 A1
Silverdale NG9 .... 223 F3
Silverdale Ave NG19 ...... 136 A4
Silverdale Cl S41 .... 76 C1
Silverhill DE13 .... 240 B1
Silverhill La NG17 .... 148 C4
Silverhill Prim Sch DE3 .. 217 E2
Silverhill Rd DE21 .... 220 C2
Silverlands SK17 .... 85 E4
Silverlands Cl SK17 .... 85 E4
Silverlands Pk SK17 .... 85 E4
Silverton Dr DE24 .... 231 E1
Silvey Gr DE21 .... 220 B2
Simcoe Leys DE73 .... 233 D1
Simcrest Ave S21 .... 60 B3
Simmondley Gr SK13 ...... 17 D4
Simmondley La SK13 ...... 17 D4
Simmondley New Rd SK13 . 17 D4
Simmondley Prim Sch
SK13 .... 17 D4
Simon Fields Cl DE7 ...... 193 D1
Simonburn Ave ST4 .... 269 D2

Simons Cl SK13 .... 17 D4
Simons Wlk SK13 .... 17 D4
Simpson St DE24 .... 232 C3
Sims Ave DE1 .... 218 C3
Sims Croft S41 .... 77 E2
Sinclair Cl Derby DE24 ... 231 F2
Heanor DE75 .... 193 E4
Heanor DE75 .... 232 B2
Sinfin Ave DE24 .... 232 B2
Sinfin Central Sta DE24 .. 232 A3
Sinfin Com Sch DE24 ..... 231 F2
Sinfin Fields Cres DE24 .. 232 B3
Sinfin La Barrow u T DE73 . 244 A3
Derby DE24 .... 231 F2
Sinfin Moor La
Derby, Chellaston DE73 ..... 232 C1
Derby, Sinfin DE73 .... 231 F2
Sinfin North Sta DE24 .... 232 A3
Sinfin Prim Sch DE24 ..... 231 F3
Sir Frank Whittle Rd DE21 . 219 E4
Sir Harold Jackson Prim
Sch S17 .... 56 A3
Sir Henry's La DE73 .... 252 A2
Sir Josephs La DE4 .... 127 D2
Sir William Hill Rd S32 ... 71 E4
Siskin Cl DE24 .... 231 E2
Sisley Ave NG9 .... 223 F3
Sister's La DE72 .... 221 E3
Sitch La Callow DE4 .... 165 D2
Thornsett SK22 .... 24 C2
Sitch Rd DE4 .... 142 B4
Sitwell [20] S80 .... 59 F4
Sitwell Ave S40 .... 266 A1
Sitwell Cl DE21 .... 220 B2
Sitwell Dr DE56 .... 192 A4
Sitwell Grange La
Pilsley S45 .... 147 E4
Tibshelf S45 .... 147 E4
Sitwell St
Derby, Spondon DE21 .... 220 C2
Derby, The Holmes DE1 ..... 267 B2
Eckington S21 .... 59 E2
Sitwell Villas DE55 .... 146 C3
Skeavington's La DE7 ..... 194 C3
Skegby La DE18, NG19 .... 268 A3
Skegby Mount NG18 .... 268 A3
Skeldale Dr S40 .... 115 D4
Skelton Rd S8 .... 43 D3
Skelwith Cl S41 .... 95 E4
Sketchley St NG3 .... 268 C2
Ski 2000 Ilkeston NG16 .. 195 D1
Skiddaw Cl [9] S40 .... 95 E3
Skiddaw Dr DE3 .... 217 F1
Skinner St S80 .... 81 E1
Skipton Cl DE7 .... 194 B2
Skipton Gn DE21 .... 205 E1
Skye Gdns DE55 .... 147 F3
Skylark Way DE24 .... 231 E2
Slack La Ashover S45 ...... 129 E1
Brailsford DE6 .... 187 E1
Chesterfield S40 .... 95 D2
Derby, Darley Abbey DE22 . 204 C1
Derby, New Zealand DE22 .. 218 B3
Hartshorne DE11 .... 257 D3
Mayfield DE6 .... 184 B4
Nether Heage DE56 .... 168 B2
Ripley DE5 .... 169 E1
Shipley DE75 .... 193 F4
Somercotes DE55 .... 170 B3
Wessington DE55 .... 157 E4
Slack's La S45 .... 132 B1
Slackey La DE12 .... 262 B2
Slacks La SK22 .... 25 E3
Slade Cl Etwall DE65 ...... 229 E2
South Normanton DE55 ..... 160 A2
Slade Fields ST14 .... 210 A1
Slade Hollow La DE6 ...... 201 D2
Slade La DE6 .... 202 C4
Slag La S43 .... 77 E3
Slaidburn Cl DE3 .... 217 F1
Slaley La DE4 .... 154 B4
Slaley View Rd S43 .... 80 A3
Slaney Cl DE24 .... 232 C4
Slant Cl SK13 .... 17 E4
Slant La NG19 .... 136 A2
Slant The DE24 .... 119 E2
Slate St S2 .... 43 D4
Slatelands Ave SK13 ...... 17 D4
Slatelands Rd SK13 .... 17 D4
Slatepit La
Barlow S32, S42 .... 93 E4
Old Brampton S32, S42 ..... 93 E4
Slater Ave DE22 .... 218 C3
Slater Cres DE4 .... 165 F4
Slater St S45 .... 131 E2
Slayley Hill S43 .... 80 B2
Slayley View S43 .... 80 B3
Slaypit La S80 .... 62 B3
Sledgegate La DE4 .... 156 A4
Sledmere Cl DE24 .... 233 E4
Sleepy La DE73 .... 245 E1
Sleetmoor La
Somercotes DE55 .... 170 A4
Swanwick DE55 .... 170 A4
Sleights La NG16 .... 160 B1
Slindon Croft DE24 .... 233 E3
Slipperlow La SK17 .... 87 F1
Sloade La S12 .... 58 C3
Sloane Rd DE22 .... 218 A3
Sly Rd NG7 .... 268 A2
Small Gate NG19 .... 136 C3
Small Knowle End SK17 .. 67 E3
Small Meer Cl DE73 .... 232 C1
Small Thorn Pl DE11 ...... 256 C1
Smalldale Cotts SK17 ..... 67 E4
Smalldale Head Rd S33 .. 50 C4
Smalldale Rd Sheffield S12 . 44 B2
Smalldale SK17 .... 67 E4
Smalley Dr DE21 .... 206 A2

Smalley Mill Rd
Horsley DE21 .... 192 A2
Smalley DE7 .... 192 A2
Smallman St ST16 .... 269 E4
Smeath Rd NG16 .... 171 F1
Smeckley Wood Cl S18 ... 76 B2
Somercotes DE55 .... 159 E1
Smedley Ave Ilkeston DE7 . 209 D3
Somercotes DE55 .... 159 E1
Smedley Cl DE65 .... 241 D3
Smedley Pl SK13 .... 10 C1
Smedley St DE4 .... 143 D3
Smedley St E DE4 .... 143 E3
Smedley St W DE4 .... 143 D4
Smedley's Ave NG10 ...... 223 D3
Smeeton St DE75 .... 182 A1
Smelter Wood Ave S13 ... 44 C4
Smelter Wood Cl S13 ..... 44 C4
Smelter Wood Cres S13 .. 44 C4
Smelter Wood Ct S13 ..... 44 C4
Smelter Wood Dr S13 ..... 44 C4
Smelter Wood La S13 ..... 44 C4
Smelter Wood Pl S13 ...... 44 C4
Smelter Wood Rd S13 ..... 44 C4
Smelter Wood Rise S13 .. 44 C4
Smelter Wood Way S13 ... 44 C4
Smeltinghouse La S18 .... 75 F2
Smisby Rd LE65 .... 258 A1
Smisby Way DE24 .... 232 C2
Smith Ave Codnor DE5 .... 170 A1
Melbourne DE73 .... 245 D1
Staveley S43 .... 97 E4
Smith Cres S41 .... 96 B1
Smith Dr NG16 .... 182 A2
Smith Rd DE4 .... 143 D3
Smith-Hall La DE6 .... 188 A4
Smithfield Ave
Chesterfield S41 .... 115 E4
Trowell NG9 .... 209 E2
Smithfield Rd S12 .... 44 A2
Smithpool Rd ST4 .... 269 F1
Smithson Ave S44 .... 99 D1
Smithurst Rd NG16 .... 195 D4
Smithy Ave S45 .... 131 E2
Smithy Cl Glossop SK13 .. 10 B1
Parwich DE6 .... 151 E1
Smithy Croft S18 .... 56 B1
Smithy Fold SK13 .... 10 B1
Smithy Hill S33 .... 51 D4
Smithy Knoll Rd S32 ...... 72 B1
Smithy La
Clifton Campville B79 .... 263 F1
Marple SK6 .... 15 F1
Smithy Meadows S32 ..... 53 D4
Smithy Pl S42 .... 115 F1
Smithy Row NG1 .... 268 B1
Smuse La DE4 .... 143 F2
Snake La DE56 .... 190 C2
Snake Rd S33 .... 28 B4
Snape Hill S18 .... 57 D2
Snape Hill Dr S18 .... 57 D1
Snape Hill La S18 .... 57 D1
Snapehill Cl S18 .... 57 D2
Snapehill Cres S18 .... 57 D2
Snapes La DE6 .... 184 A1
Sneinton Bvd NG2 .... 268 C1
Sneinton CE Prim Sch The
NG2 .... 268 C1
Sneinton Hermitage NG2 . 268 C1
Sneinton Hollows NG2 .... 268 C1
Sneinton Rd NG2 .... 268 C1
Snelsmoor La DE73 .... 233 D1
Snelston Cl S18 .... 56 B1
Snelston Cres DE23 .... 218 B1
Snipe Cl S42 .... 113 E4
Snipesmoor La DE6 .... 185 F4
Snitterton Rd DE4 .... 143 D3
Snow Hill ST16 .... 269 E4
Snowberry Ave DE56 ...... 179 D2
Snowdon La S21 .... 58 A2
Snowdrop Valley DE4 ..... 168 A4
Snowfield View DE4 .... 165 F3
Snows Yd ST16 .... 269 D4
Soaper La S18 .... 57 D1
Soarbank Cl NG16 .... 195 F4
Society Pl DE23 .... 219 D1
Soft Water La S33 .... 51 D4
Solney Cl DE11 .... 255 F2
Soloman Pk NG16 .... 195 D1
Soloman Rd NG16 .... 195 D1
Solomons View SK14 ...... 85 E4
Solway Cl DE21 .... 206 A1
Solway Rise S18 .... 56 B1
Somerby Way DE21 .... 205 F1
Somercotes Hill DE55 .... 170 B4
Somercotes Inf Sch DE55 . 170 B4
Somercotes Rd S12 .... 44 B3
Somerlea Park Jun Sch
DE55 .... 170 B4
Somersal Cl DE24 .... 232 C2
Somersall Cl S40 .... 95 D1
Somersall La S40 .... 95 D1
Somersall Park Rd S40 ... 95 D1
Somersall St NG19 .... 268 A4
Somersall Willows S40 ... 95 D1
Somersby Ave S40 .... 114 A4
Somerset Cl Buxton SK17 . 85 F4
Long Eaton NG10 .... 237 D4
Somerset Dr S43 .... 97 D4
Somerset Rd DE15 .... 254 B3
Somerset St DE21 .... 219 E4
Somme Rd DE22 .... 204 A2
Sookholme Cl NG20 .... 119 F2
Sookholme La NG20 .... 120 C3
Sookholme Rd
Market Warsop NG20 .... 120 C1
Shirebrook NG20 .... 119 F2
Soresby St S40 .... 266 B3
Sorrel Dr DE11 .... 256 C4

Sough La Bolehill DE4 .... 155 D1
Taddington SK17 .... 87 E1
Wirksworth DE4 .... 154 C1
Sough Rd DE55 .... 160 A4
Soughley La S10 .... 42 B4
South Ave Buxton SK17 ... 85 D4
Derby, Chellaston DE73 ..... 232 C2
Derby, Darley Abbey DE22 . 205 D2
Derby, Littleover DE23 ...... 218 B1
Derby, Spondon DE21 .... 220 C2
Shirebrook NG20 .... 119 F2
South Brae Cl DE23 .... 231 E4
South Broadway St DE14 . 254 B4
South Church St DE45 .... 109 E3
South Cl Tintwistle SK13 .. 9 F4
Unstone S18 .... 76 C3
South Cres Bolsover S44 . 99 D1
Killamarsh S21 .... 60 C4
Long Duckmanton S44 ...... 98 A3
South Darley CE Prim Sch
DE4 .... 142 A4
South Dr
Derby, Chellaston DE73 ..... 232 C2
Derby, Cherrytree Hill DE21 . 220 A3
Derby, Little Chester DE1 .. 218 C4
Derby, Littleover DE3 .... 218 A1
Swadlincote DE11 .... 255 F3
South East Derbyshire Coll
Heanor DE75 .... 181 F1
Ilkeston DE7 .... 208 C3
South Farm Ave S26 ...... 61 F3
South Hill Rolleston DE13 . 240 B2
Stretton DE55 .... 145 F4
South Hill La DE55 .... 145 F3
South Lodge Ct S40 .... 95 D2
South Marlow St SK13 .... 10 A2
South Oak St DE14 .... 254 A4
South Par
Matlock Bath DE4 .... 143 D1
[1] Nottingham NG1 .... 268 B1
South Park Ave DE4 ...... 127 E2
South Pl
Chesterfield, Brampton S40 . 95 E1
Chesterfield, Stonegravels
S40 .... 266 B2
Ripley DE5 .... 169 E1
South Rd NG7 .... 268 A1
South Sherwood St NG1 .. 268 B2
South St
Ashbourne DE6 .... 173 E1
Blackwell DE55 .... 147 F1
Buxton SK17 .... 85 D4
Chesterfield S40 .... 266 B2
Derby DE1 .... 218 C3
Draycott DE72 .... 235 D4
Eastwood, Bailey Grove
NG16 .... 182 C1
Eastwood, Giltbrook NG16 . 195 E4
Ilkeston DE7 .... 208 C4
Long Eaton NG10 .... 236 C4
Melbourne DE73 .... 252 A4
Mosborough S20 .... 59 E3
Pilsley S45 .... 132 B1
Somercotes DE55 .... 170 B3
South Normanton DE55 ..... 160 A3
Stafford ST16 .... 269 D4
Swanwick DE55 .... 169 F4
Woodville DE11 .... 257 D1
South St N S43 .... 77 E2
South Terr ST4 .... 269 E1
South Uxbridge St DE14 .. 254 A4
South View Bamford S33 .. 40 A2
Mayfield DE6 .... 184 B3
Mosborough S20 .... 60 A4
New Mills SK22 .... 33 D4
Whitwell S80 .... 81 F3
South View Rd SK13 .... 17 F4
South View Wlk ST14 ..... 196 C2
South Walls ST16 .... 269 E4
South Wingfield Prim Sch
DE55 .... 157 F2
South Wolf St ST4 .... 269 E2
Southall St S8 .... 43 D3
Southampton St NG3 ...... 268 C2
Southard's La S80 .... 62 C3
Southbrook Cl SK13 .... 9 F2
Southcote Dr S8 .... 56 C4
Southcroft Alfreton DE55 . 159 D2
Buxton SK17 .... 85 D4
Derby DE23 .... 231 E2
Southdown Ave S40 .... 95 E3
Southdown Cl DE24 .... 231 E1
Southend S42 .... 115 F1
Southey St NG7 .... 268 A2
Southfield Ave S41 .... 115 E3
Southfield Cl S80 .... 81 F3
Southfield Dr Dronfield S18 . 76 B4
South Normanton DE55 ..... 160 B3
Southfield Ind Site S80 .. 82 A2
Southfield La S80 .... 82 A2
Southfield Mount S18 ..... 76 B4
Southfields Clowne S43 ... 80 C2
Long Eaton NG10 .... 236 C4
Southfields Ave NG16 ..... 160 B2
Southgate S21 .... 59 F2
Southgate Cl DE21 .... 217 E2
Southgate Cres S43 .... 80 C3
Southgate Ct S21 .... 59 F2
Southgate Inf Sch DE24 .. 232 C4
Southgate Way S43 .... 78 C2
Southmead Way DE3 ...... 218 A2
Southmoor S43 .... 96 C2
Southwark Cl DE24 .... 219 F1
Southwell Rd NG1 .... 268 C1
Southwood Ave S18 .... 76 A4
Southwood Dr S43 .... 80 C2
Southwood House Specl
Sch DE56 .... 191 E3

Southwood St DE24 .... 232 B1
Sovereigh Gr NG10 .... 236 A4
Sovereign Way
Derby DE21 .... 206 B2
Heanor DE75 .... 181 F1
Sowbrook Brook DE7 ...... 208 B2
Sowbrook La DE7 .... 208 C2
Sowter Rd DE1 .... 267 B4
Spa Brook Cl S12 .... 44 C2
Spa Brook Dr S12 .... 44 C3
Spa Croft DE55 .... 147 F3
Spa La
Chesterfield, Hady S41 ...... 266 C2
Chesterfield, Stonegravels
S41 .... 266 C2
Derby DE1 .... 267 C3
Spa View Ave S12 .... 44 C2
Spa View Dr S12 .... 44 C2
Spa View Pl S12 .... 44 C2
Spa View Rd S12 .... 44 C2
Spa View Terr S12 .... 44 C2
Spa View Way S12 .... 44 C2
Spalden Ave DE6 .... 173 E2
Spalding Rd NG3 .... 268 C2
Spang La NG17 .... 148 C2
Spaniel Row [2] NG1 ...... 268 B1
Spanker La DE56 .... 168 A1
Spanker Terr DE56 .... 168 B1
Spark St ST4 .... 269 E2
Spark Terr ST4 .... 269 E2
Sparrow Cl DE24 .... 231 E2
Sparrowbusk Cl S43 ...... 80 A3
Speedwell SK13 .... 9 F4
Speedwell Cl Derby DE21 . 206 B2
Tintwistle SK13 .... 9 F4
Woodville DE11 .... 256 C2
Speedwell Ind Est S43 ... 78 C1
Speedwell Inf Sch S43 ... 78 C1
Speighthill Cres S42 ...... 114 C2
Spenbeck Dr DE22 .... 205 D3
Spencer Ave Belper DE56 . 179 D2
Derby DE21 .... 232 B2
Sandiacre NG10 .... 223 D3
Woodthorpe S43 .... 79 D1
Spencer Cl DE13 .... 240 B1
Spencer Cres NG9 .... 223 F4
Spencer Dr DE55 .... 170 B4
Spencer Gr SK17 .... 85 D3
Spencer Rd Belper DE56 . 179 D2
Buxton SK17 .... 85 D3
Chapel-en-le-F SK23 .... 46 C3
Sheffield S2 .... 43 D4
Stoke-on-T ST4 .... 269 F2
Spencer St Bolsover S44 . 117 F4
Chesterfield S40 .... 266 B4
Derby DE24 .... 233 D4
Mansfield NG18 .... 268 B3
Stanley DE7 .... 193 D1
Spend La Mappleton DE6 . 173 D3
Thorpe DE6 .... 161 F1
Spender Cl DE6 .... 185 E4
Sperry Cl NG16 .... 171 F3
Spindletree Dr DE21 ...... 205 F1
Spinkhill Ave S13 .... 44 B4
Spinkhill Dr S13 .... 44 B4
Spinkhill Immaculate
Conception Prim Sch S21 . 60 B2
Spinkhill La S21 .... 60 A1
Spinkhill Rd Killamarsh S21 . 60 C2
Sheffield S13 .... 44 B4
Spinnerbottom SK22 ...... 24 C1
Spinners Way DE56 .... 179 E3
Spinney Cl Derby DE22 ... 205 D1
Glossop SK13 .... 10 B1
Mansfield Woodhouse NG19 . 136 C3
Spinney Cres NG9 .... 223 F2
Spinney Dr NG10 .... 223 E1
Spinney Hill DE73 .... 252 A4
Spinney Rd Branston DE14 . 253 F4
Derby, Chaddesden DE21 .. 219 F4
Derby, St Luke's DE22 ...... 218 C2
Ilkeston DE7 .... 208 C3
Long Eaton NG10 .... 223 E1
Spinney Rise NG9 .... 223 F2
Spinney The Belper DE56 . 179 D3
Borrowash DE72 .... 221 E1
Castle Donington DE74 ..... 247 D2
Ripley DE5 .... 169 E2
Shirebrook NG20 .... 119 F2
Stanton-by-D NG10 .... 222 C4
Spire Hollin SK13 .... 10 B1
Spital Gdns S41 .... 96 B1
Spital La S41 .... 96 B1
Spitewinter La S18, S32 .. 93 E4
Spittal DE7 .... 247 D2
Spittal Gn S44 .... 118 A4
Spittal Hill DE74 .... 247 D2
Spode St ST4 .... 269 E1
Spondon Sta DE21 .... 220 B2
Spooner Dr S21 .... 60 B3
Spooner La S32 .... 72 B3
Spoonley Wood Ct DE23 . 230 C4
Sporton Cl DE55 .... 160 A4
Sporton La DE55 .... 160 A4
Spotswood Cl S14 .... 43 F2
Spotswood Dr S2 .... 43 F3
Spotswood Mount S14 .... 43 F2
Spotswood Pl S14 .... 43 F2
Spotswood Rd S14 .... 43 F2
Spout La Spout DE56 ...... 166 B2
Tansley DE4 .... 144 A2
Spridgeon Cl NG10 .... 223 D1
Spring Bank
Great Longstone DE45 ...... 90 A2
Peak Dale SK17 .... 67 E2
Spring Bank Rd
Chesterfield S40 .... 266 A3
New Mills SK22 .... 33 E4

Spring Cl Belper DE56 .... 178 C3
Bradwell S33 .... 51 D4
Breaston DE72 .... 235 E4
Renishaw S21 .... 79 E4
Swadlincote DE11 .... 256 A1
Spring Cl Dell S14 .... 43 F2
Spring Cl Mount S14 .... 43 F2
Spring Cl View S14 .... 43 F2
Spring Cottage Rd DE12 .. 262 B3
Spring Dale Gdns DE6 ..... 209 E2
Spring Garden Terr DE7 .. 194 C1
Spring Gdns Buxton SK17 .... 85 E4
Derby DE21 .... 219 F4
Hadfield SK13 .... 10 A3
Spring Hill Kimberley NG16 .. 195 F3
Mansfield Woodhouse
NG19 .... 136 A2
Whitwell S80 .... 82 A3
Spring Hollow DE56 .... 190 B4
Spring House Cl S40 .... 94 C3
Spring La Elmton NG20 ...... 99 F3
Heanor DE75 .... 181 F1
Sheffield S2 .... 43 F4
Shireoaks S80 .... 63 F3
Spring Mount SK22 .... 33 E4
Spring Pl S40 .... 266 B3
Spring Rd DE55 .... 170 C1
Spring Rise SK13 .... 16 C4
Spring St Broadbottom SK14 .. 16 A4
Derby DE22 .... 218 C2
Glossop SK13 .... 10 A1
Hollingworth SK14 .... 9 E3
Swadlincote DE11 .... 262 A4
Whitwell S80 .... 82 A3
Spring The NG10 .... 236 B3
Spring Vale Rd
Brimington S43 .... 96 C4
Hayfield SK22 .... 25 F1
Spring Water Dr SK13 .... 9 F2
Spring Wood Cl S41 .... 95 E4
Springbank SK13 .... 9 F3
Springdale Ct DE3 .... 217 F1
Springfarm Rd DE15 .... 248 A1
Springfield
Charlesworth SK13 .... 16 B3
Derby DE23 .... 218 A1
Springfield Ave
Ashbourne DE6 .... 185 E4
Chesterfield S40 .... 95 E2
Heanor DE75 .... 181 D3
Long Eaton NG10 .... 236 C4
Sandiacre NG10 .... 223 D2
Shirebrook NG20 .... 119 F3
Springfield Cl Clowne S43 .... 80 C2
Crich DE4 .... 157 D1
Eckington S21 .... 59 E2
Hadfield SK13 .... 9 F2
Swadlincote DE11 .... 256 A3
Springfield Cres
Bolsover S44 .... 98 C2
Somercotes DE55 .... 170 B4
Springfield Ct NG9 .... 209 F1
Springfield Dr DE56 .... 190 B2
Springfield Gdn DE7 .... 194 C1
Springfield Jun Sch DE11 . 256 B3
Springfield Prim Sch
Derby DE21 .... 220 B3
Stoke-on-T ST4 .... 269 D2
Springfield Rd Bradwell S33 . 51 D4
Common Side S18 .... 75 E2
Derby, Chellaston DE73 ..... 232 C1
Derby, Cherrytree Hill DE21 . 220 A3
Etwall DE65 .... 229 D2
Holmewood S42 .... 132 C4
Repton DE65 .... 242 B1
Swadlincote DE11 .... 256 A3
Springfield Rise DE4 .... 143 E3
Springfield Terr
Hayfield SK22 .... 25 E1
Ripley DE5 .... 169 F1
Springfield View DE5 .... 169 E1
Springfields Rd ST4 .... 269 D1
Springhill DE11 .... 257 D4
Springhill Way DE5 .... 181 D4
Springmeadow SK13 .... 16 B4
Springvale Cl S45 .... 131 E1
Springvale Rd S45 .... 131 E1
Springwell Com Sch S43 .... 97 C4
Springwell Hill S21 .... 77 F3
Springwell St NG17 .... 148 C1
Springwood SK13 .... 16 C4
Springwood Ct S43 .... 77 E2
Springwood Dr DE21 .... 206 A1
Springwood Farm Rd DE11 256 A4
Springwood L Ctr DE21 .... 206 A1
Springwood Rd S8 .... 43 D3
Springwood St S42 .... 116 A2
Sprinkswoods La DE6 .... 184 C3
Spruce Ave NG16 .... 171 E3
Spruce Rise S21 .... 60 B3
Spurr St S2 .... 43 D4
Square The Bretby DE15 .. 249 D2
Buxton SK17 .... 85 D4
Clay Cross S45 .... 131 F2
Derby, Darley Abbey DE3 .. 205 D1
Derby, Mickleover DE3 ...... 217 E1
Eyam S32 .... 71 F3
Marchington ST14 .... 224 C1
Monyash DE45 .... 107 E1
Squiers View ST4 .... 269 F2
Squires Way DE23 .... 231 D4
Squirrel La DE73 .... 252 C2

Stable Cl DE4 .... 156 A3
Stable La DE6 .... 149 D1
Stables Ct S44 .... 99 E1
Stables St DE22 .... 218 B3
Stacey Rd NG19 .... 135 E1

Staden Bsns Pk SK17 .... 85 F3
Staden La SK17 .... 85 F2
Stadium Ind Pk NG10 .... 236 C4
Stadmoor Ct DE73 .... 232 C1
Staffa Dr DE55 .... 147 F3
Stafford Cl
1 Dronfield S18 .... 56 B1
Glossop SK13 .... 17 F4
Smalley DE7 .... 192 C3
Stafford Coll ST16 .... 269 D4
Stafford Coll
(The Oval Annexe) ST17 . 269 E3
Stafford Cres DE4 .... 165 F4
Long Eaton NG10 .... 236 C4
Mansfield NG19 .... 268 A4
New Mills SK22 .... 24 B1
Stafford ST16 .... 269 E4
Stafford Sta ST16 .... 269 D3
Staffordshire General
Hospl ST16 .... 269 F4
Staffordshire General
Infmy ST16 .... 269 D4
Staffordshire Univ ST4 ..... 269 F2
Staines Cl DE3 .... 217 E1
Stainforth St NG19 .... 136 B1
Stainsbro' La Callow DE4 .. 165 D3
Carsington DE4 .... 165 D3
Stainsby Ave Heanor DE75 .. 193 F4
Horsley Woodhouse DE7 ... 192 C3
Stainsby Cl S42 .... 132 C4
Staithes Wlk DE21 .... 205 E1
Staker La DE3 .... 230 B3
Stalybridge Ctry Pk SK15 ... 4 A2
Stalybridge Rd SK14 .... 9 D2
Stamer St ST4 .... 269 E1
Stamford Cl NG10 .... 236 C2
Stamford St
Awsworth NG16 .... 195 E2
Derby DE24 .... 232 B3
Heanor DE75 .... 181 F1
3 Ilkeston DE7 .... 194 C1
Stamps Cl DE15 .... 248 B2
Stanage Gn DE3 .... 217 F1
Stanage Rise S12 .... 44 C3
Stanage Way S40 .... 94 C3
Stancliffe Ave DE4 .... 127 E2
Stancliffe Hall Sch DE4 .. 127 D3
Stancliffe View DE4 .... 127 D2
Stand House Fst Sch S2 .. 44 A4
Stand Rd S41 .... 95 F4
Standard Hill 7 NG1 .... 268 A1
Standard St ST4 .... 269 F1
Standing Butts Cl DE12 ... 259 E4
Standlow La DE6 .... 163 E1
Stanedge Rd DE45 .... 109 D3
Stanford Rd S8 .... 56 C4
Stanford St NG1 .... 268 B1
Stanford Way S40 .... 114 A4
Stanhope Glade DE15 ...... 256 A4
Stanhope Rd Derby DE3 .. 217 F2
Sheffield S12 .... 44 B3
Swadlincote DE11 .... 256 A3
Stanhope St
Bramley-Vale S44 .... 117 F1
Burton u T DE15 .... 248 A2
Derby DE23 .... 219 D1
Ilkeston DE7 .... 209 D3
Long Eaton NG10 .... 236 B4
Nottingham NG1 .... 268 B1
Stanton-by-D NG10 .... 222 C4
Stanier Way DE21 .... 220 A2
Staniforth Ave S21 .... 59 D2
Stanleigh Rd DE12 .... 262 A4
Stanley Ave Ripley DE5 .... 169 F1
Staveley S43 .... 97 D4
Stanley Cl Derby DE22 ..... 218 C4
Ilkeston DE7 .... 208 C4
Netherseal DE12 .... 264 C4
Woodville DE11 .... 256 C2
Stanley Comm Prim Sch
DE7 .... 193 D1
Stanley Cres ST14 .... 210 A1
Stanley Dr NG9 .... 209 F1
Stanley Hall La SK12 .... 32 B3
Stanley La NG17 .... 133 E1
Stanley Matthews Sports
Ctr ST4 .... 269 F2
Stanley Pl NG1 .... 268 A2
Stanley Rd
Derby, Allenton DE24 .... 232 C3
Derby, Cherrytree Hill DE21 220 A3
Sheffield S8 .... 43 D3
Stoke-on-T ST4 .... 269 D2
Stanley St Chesterfield S41 .. 96 B1
Derby DE22 .... 218 B3
Ilkeston DE7 .... 208 C4
Killamarsh S21 .... 60 B4
Long Eaton NG10 .... 236 C4
Somercotes DE55 .... 170 B4
Swadlincote DE11 .... 256 B2
Stanshope La DE6 .... 149 E1
Stanstead Rd DE3 .... 217 E2
Stanton Ave DE56 .... 179 D2
Stanton Cl DE4 .... 127 D2
Stanton Cres S12 .... 44 B2
Stanton Gate DE7 .... 209 E1
Stanton Hill DE73 .... 251 E3
Stanton Moor View DE4 .. 142 C4
Stanton Pl Mansfield NG18 . 268 B4
New Houghton NG19 .... 134 C2
Stanton Prim Sch DE15 ... 255 D3
Stanton Rd Ashbourne DE6 .. 185 E4
Burton u T DE15 .... 254 C4
Ilkeston DE7 .... 208 C4
Sandiacre NG10 .... 223 D4
Stanton St Derby DE23 .... 218 C1
New Houghton NG19 .... 134 C4

Stanton Vale Specl Sch
DE7 .... 208 C3
Stanton View DE45 .... 109 E2
Stanton-in-Peak CE Prim
Sch DE4 .... 126 B3
Stantonhall La DE4 .... 126 B4
Stanwood Dr S40 .... 114 A4
Stanyforth St SK13 .... 10 A2
Stapleford La NG9 .... 223 F2
Stapleford Rd
Stapleford NG9 .... 209 E2
Trowell NG9 .... 209 E2
Stapleton Rd DE7 .... 194 C2
Starch La NG10 .... 223 E4
Starcross Ct DE3 .... 217 E2
Starkholmes Rd DE4 .... 143 E1
Starkie Ave DE74 .... 246 C2
Start La SK23 .... 45 D4
Starthe Bank DE75 .... 181 F1
Statham Ave S42 .... 131 E4
Statham St DE22 .... 218 C4
Station App Buxton SK17 .... 85 D4
Derby DE1 .... 267 C2
Duffield DE56 .... 190 C2
Hathersage S32 .... 53 D4
Station Back La S41 .... 266 C3
Station Cl DE73 .... 232 C1
Station Ct 10 DE7 .... 194 C1
Station Dr DE12 .... 262 C2
Station Hill NG19 .... 136 A2
Station La Apperknowle S18 .. 58 A1
Chesterfield S43 .... 77 C1
Codnor DE5 .... 181 D3
Ironville NG16 .... 170 C2
Shatton S33 .... 40 A1
Walton-on-T DE12 .... 253 E1
Station La Ind Est S41 ..... 77 D1
Station New Rd S42 .... 131 E4
Station Rd Ambergate DE56 . 167 F2
Ashbourne DE6 .... 173 D1
Awsworth NG16 .... 195 E3
Bakewell DE45 .... 109 F3
Bamford S33 .... 40 A1
Barton Turn DE13 .... 253 D1
Birch Vale SK22 .... 25 D1
Bolsover S44 .... 98 C2
Borrowash DE72 .... 221 D1
Breadsall DE21 .... 205 F2
Brimington S43 .... 96 B4
Brimington, New Brimington
S43 .... 78 A1
Buxton SK17 .... 85 E4
Buxworth SK23 .... 34 A1
Chapel-en-le-F SK23 .... 47 D3
Chesterfield, Old Whittington
S41 .... 77 D1
Chesterfield S41 .... 266 C3
Chinley SK23 .... 34 B1
Clowne S43 .... 80 C2
Darley Dale DE4 .... 127 E1
Denby DE5 .... 180 A2
Derby, Chellaston DE73 ..... 232 C1
Derby, Mickleover DE74 .... 217 E2
Derby, Spondon DE21 ...... 220 B2
Dove Holes SK17 .... 47 F1
Draycott DE72 .... 235 D4
Duffield DE56 .... 190 C2
Eckington S21 .... 59 F2
Furness Vale SK23 .... 33 E2
Great Longstone DE45 .... 89 F2
Hadfield SK13 .... 10 A3
Hathersage S32 .... 53 D4
Hatton DE65 .... 227 E1
Heanor NG16 .... 182 A1
Hemington DE74 .... 247 D3
Hemington DE74 .... 247 E3
Hope S33 .... 39 E2
Ilkeston DE7 .... 194 C1
Killamarsh S21 .... 60 A3
Kimberley NG16 .... 195 F3
Langley Mill NG16 .... 182 A1
Little Eaton DE21 .... 205 E4
Long Eaton NG10 .... 236 C4
Mansfield NG18 .... 268 B3
Marple SK6 .... 23 D4
Melbourne DE73 .... 252 B4
Morton DE55 .... 147 D3
Mosborough S20 .... 59 F4
New Mills SK22 .... 33 D4
North Wingfield S42 .... 131 F3
Pilsley S45 .... 132 B1
Rolleston DE13 .... 240 B2
Sandiacre NG10 .... 223 E3
Scarcliffe S44 .... 118 C3
Selston NG16 .... 160 C1
Shirebrook NG20 .... 119 F3
Spinkhill S21 .... 60 B1
Stafford ST16 .... 269 D3
Stanley DE7 .... 207 E3
Strines SK6 .... 23 E1
Tibshelf DE55 .... 147 F3
West Hallam DE7 .... 207 E4
Whitwell S80 .... 82 A3
Woodville DE11 .... 256 C1
Station St Ashbourne DE6 .. 173 D1
Cossall S43 .... 195 D1
Glossop SK13 .... 10 B1
Long Eaton NG10 .... 236 C4
Mansfield NG18 .... 268 B3
Mansfield Woodhouse NG19 136 A2
Nottingham NG1 .... 268 B1
Swadlincote DE11 .... 261 F4
Station View NG20 .... 119 F2
Station Wlk 6 SK17 .... 85 E4
Staunton Ave DE23 .... 231 F3
Staunton Cl DE74 .... 247 D2
Staunton Harold Hall Craft
& Ferrous Ctr LE65 .... 258 C4

Staunton La DE73 .... 251 D1
Staveley Cl DE24 .... 232 C2
Staveley Jun Sch S43 .... 78 C1
Staveley La Barrow Hill S43 .. 78 A3
Eckington S21 .... 59 F1
Staveley Rd
Chesterfield S43 .... 77 F2
Long Duckmanton S44 .... 97 F2
Poolsbrook S43 .... 98 A4
Sheffield S8 .... 43 D4
Staverton Dr DE3 .... 217 E2
Stead St S21 .... 59 E2
Steam Mill La DE5 .... 181 D4
Steel La NG10 .... 99 D1
Steel St ST4 .... 269 D2
Steel's La S44 .... 118 A3
Steele Ave S43 .... 97 D3
Steele Ct SK17 .... 85 D4
Steep La S42 .... 114 A2
Steep Turnpike DE4 .... 143 E3
Steeping Cl S43 .... 96 C4
Steeple Cl DE21 .... 205 F1
Steeple Grange DE4 .... 154 C2
Steetley La Whitwell S80 ..... 63 F2
Worksop S80 .... 63 F2
Stella St NG18 .... 268 B3
Stenson Ave DE23 .... 231 F3
Stenson Fields Prim Com
Sch DE24 .... 231 E1
Stenson Rd
Derby, Littleover DE23, DE24 .. 231 E2
Derby, Sinfin DE23, DE24 .. 231 E2
Stenton Rd S8 .... 56 C4
Stephens Rd DE14 .... 254 A4
Stephenson Pl
Chesterfield S40 .... 266 B3
Clay Cross S45 .... 131 D2
Stephenson Rd S43 .... 78 C1
Stepping Cl DE22 .... 218 C3
Stepping La DE22 .... 218 C3
Sterland St S40 .... 95 F2
Sterndale Cl S17 .... 69 F2
Sterndale La SK17 .... 69 F2
Sterndale Moor SK17 .... 105 F3
Sterndale Rd NG10 .... 236 A3
Sterry Cl S43 .... 80 C1
Steven Cl NG9 .... 223 F2
Stevenage Cl DE24 .... 232 C3
Stevens La DE72 .... 235 E4
Stevens Rd NG10 .... 223 D3
Stevenson Ave DE72 .... 235 D4
Stevenson Jun Sch NG9 .. 223 F4
Stevenson Pl DE23 .... 231 D4
Stevenson Rd DE6 .... 224 A4
Steward Gate S33 .... 40 A3
Stewart Cl Branston DE14 .. 254 A3
Derby DE21 .... 220 C3
Stewart St Fenton ST4 ..... 269 F1
Somercotes DE55 .... 170 B3
Stile Croft DE4 .... 154 B3
Stiles Cl SK13 .... 9 F3
Stiles Rd DE24 .... 233 D4
Stillman Cl S41 .... 115 C4
Stinting La
Mansfield NG19 .... 136 C1
Shirebrook NG20 .... 119 E1
Stirland St DE5 .... 170 A1
Stirling Ave NG19 .... 268 A3
Stirling Cl DE21 .... 219 E4
Stirling Gr NG16 .... 195 F4
Stock La ST14 .... 224 B1
Stockbrook Rd DE22 .... 218 B2
Stockbrook St DE22 .... 218 C2
Stocker Ave DE24 .... 233 E4
Stockley La S44 .... 117 F1
Stockley View S44 .... 118 A4
Stockport Rd
Broadbottom SK14 .... 15 E4
Marple SK6 .... 23 D3
Stocks Green Ct S17 .... 55 E2
Stocks Green Dr S17 .... 55 E2
Stocks Rd NG16 .... 195 F4
Stocks The SK13 .... 10 A4
Stockton Dr SK23 .... 34 C1
Stockwell Gate NG18 .... 268 B3
Stoddard Dr DE75 .... 181 F1
Stoke Cl DE56 .... 179 F3
Stoke Recn Ctr ST4 .... 269 E1
Stoke-on-Trent Sixth
Form Coll ST4 .... 269 F2
Stoke-on-Trent Sta ST4 .. 269 E2
Stollard St S45 .... 131 E2
Stone Bridge Rd NG3 ...... 268 C2
Stone Cl DE21 .... 220 C3
Stone Cross La NG18 .... 268 B4
Stone Furlong Rd DE45 ..... 91 F3
Stone Hill Rd DE23 .... 218 C1
Stone La S43 .... 77 E2
Stone Meadows NG10 ...... 236 C3
Stone Rd S18 .... 57 E2
Stone Row Chesterfield S40 .. 95 E1
Marple SK6 .... 23 D3
Stone St Mosborough S20 .. 59 E4
Stoke-on-T ST4 .... 269 E2
Stonebench La SK17 .... 106 B2
Stonebridge Ct Ind Est
NG3 .... 268 C2
Stonebroom La DE55 .... 147 D3
Stonebroom Prim Sch
DE55 .... 147 D2
Stonebroom Wlk DE24 ..... 232 C2
Stonechat Cl DE23 .... 218 A2
Stonecliff Terr SK17 .... 85 E4
Stonecroft Rd S17 .... 55 F4
Stonedale Cl S20 .... 59 E4
Stonegravels Croft S20 ...... 59 F3
Stonegravels La S41 .... 96 A3
Stonegravels Way S20 .... 59 F3

Stoneheads Rise SK23 ...... 45 E4
Stonehill DE74 .... 247 D1
Stoneholes Dr S45 .... 131 F1
Stoneleigh St NG7 .... 268 A2
Stoneleigh Way DE55 ...... 169 E1
Stoneley Cl S12 .... 44 A1
Stoneley Cres S12 .... 44 A1
Stoneley Dell S12 .... 44 A1
Stoneley Dr S12 .... 44 A1
Stonelow Cres S18 .... 57 E1
Stonelow Cty Jun Sch The
S18 .... 57 E1
Stonelow Gn S18 .... 57 E1
Stonelow Rd S18 .... 57 E1
Stonepit La DE6 .... 164 A2
Stoneridge SK13 .... 9 F3
Stonerows La DE55 .... 145 E3
Stonesby Cl DE21 .... 205 F1
Stonesdale Ct DE24 .... 233 E3
Stonewell La SK17 .... 137 E3
Stoney Cl DE45 .... 109 E2
Stoney Cross DE21 .... 220 C2
Stoney Flatts Cres DE21 .. 220 A4
Stoney Hill 155 D1
Stoney La Brinsley NG16 .. 182 B3
Derby DE21 .... 220 C3
Hognaston DE6 .... 164 A1
Littlemoor S42 .... 130 B2
Selston NG16 .... 171 F4
Stretton en le F DE12 .... 265 F1
Trowell NG9 .... 209 D3
Stoney Middleton CE Prim
Sch S32 .... 71 F2
Stoney St NG1 .... 268 B1
Stoney Way DE4 .... 143 E2
Stoney Wood Dr DE4 .... 156 B1
Stoneycroft La S42 .... 114 A3
Stoneydale Cl DE11 .... 255 F3
Stoneyland Dr SK22 .... 33 D4
Stony La DE56 .... 191 E3
Stony Ridge Rd S17 .... 54 B3
Stonyhurst Ct DE24 .... 232 C2
Stoodley Pike Gdns DE22 . 204 B1
Stoops Cl S40 .... 95 E3
Stoppard Cl DE7 .... 194 B1
Storer La DE56 .... 166 A2
Stores Rd DE21 .... 219 D4
Storforth La S41 .... 115 D4
Storforth Lane Terr S41 ... 115 C4
Storforth Lane Trad Est
S40 .... 115 D4
Stormont Cl DE55 .... 160 A2
Stornoway Cl DE24 .... 231 E2
Storrs Rd S40 .... 95 D1
Stort Sq NG19 .... 136 B1
Storth Bank SK13 .... 16 C4
Storth La DE55 .... 160 A2
Storth Meadow Rd SK13 ... 16 C4
Storthfield Way DE55 ...... 160 A2
Stour Cl S43 .... 96 C4
Stourdale Cl NG10 .... 236 A3
Stourport Dr DE73 .... 233 D2
Stow Ct NG9 .... 136 C2
Stowmarket Dr DE21 .... 219 E4
Stradbroke Ave S13 .... 44 B4
Stradbroke Cl S13 .... 44 C4
Stradbroke Cres S13 .... 44 C4
Stradbroke Dr S13 .... 44 C4
Stradbroke Pl S13 .... 44 C4
Stradbroke Prim Sch S13 . 44 B4
Stradbroke Rd S13 .... 44 C4
Stradbroke Rise S40 .... 114 B4
Stradbroke Way S13 .... 44 C4
Stradbroke Wlk S13 .... 44 B4
Strand DE1 .... 267 B3
Strand Arc DE1 .... 267 B3
Stranfaer Cl DE55 .... 170 A4
Stranraer Cl NG19 .... 136 B3
Stratford Cl DE65 .... 242 B1
Stratford Rd DE21 .... 205 E2
Stratford St DE7 .... 194 C2
Strathallan Cl DE4 .... 127 E2
Strathaven Ct DE21 .... 220 C3
Strathglen Cl NG16 .... 195 F4
Strathmore Ave DE24 ...... 233 D3
Stratton Rd S44 .... 99 D1
Straw La DE55 .... 146 B4
Strawberry Bank NG17 .... 148 C2
Strawberry La
Blackfordby DE11 .... 257 D1
Rosliston DE12 .... 260 B3
Strawberry Lee La S17 ...... 55 D3
Streatham Rd DE22 .... 218 A3
Street Farm Cl S26 .... 61 F3
Street La Denby DE5 .... 180 A3
Ripley DE5 .... 180 A3
Street Lane Prim Sch DE5 180 A1
Street The SK17 .... 64 B3
Streetfield Cres S20 .... 59 E3
Streetfield La S20 .... 59 F3
Streetfields S20 .... 59 F3
Strelley Ave S20 .... 180 B4
Stretfield Rd S33 .... 39 D1
Strettea La DE55 .... 146 B1
Stretton Cl DE3 .... 217 E1
Stretton Handley CE Prim
Sch DE55 .... 145 E4
Stretton Rd Clay Cross S45 .. 131 E1
Morton DE55 .... 146 C3
Stretton DE55 .... 146 B4
Stretton View DE12 .... 265 F3
Striding Edge Cl NG10 .... 223 D1
Strines Rd S6 .... 23 D2
Strines Sta SK6 .... 23 E1
Stroma Cl DE24 .... 231 F2

Strutt St Belper DE56 178 C2
Derby DE23 219 D1
Stuart Cl S41 96 B3
Stuart St DE1 267 B4
Stubben Edge La S45 130 B1
Stubbin Wood Sch NG20 119 F3
Stubbing Rd S40 114 C4
Stubbins La SK23 34 B1
Stubbins Wood NG20 119 F3
Stubbins Wood La NG20 119 F3
Stubley Cl S18 56 C2
Stubley Croft S8 56 C4
Stubley Dr S18 56 C1
Stubley Hollow S18 56 C2
Stubley La S18 56 C1
Stubley Pl S18 56 C1
Stubwood Hollow ST14 196 B3
Studbrook Cl DE74 246 C2
Studfarm Cl DE73 252 C1
Sturge Croft S2 43 D3
Sturges La DE72 233 F2
Sturgess St ST4 269 E1
Sturston Rd DE6 173 E1
Stychfields ST17 269 E3
Sudbury Ave Ilkeston DE7 209 D4
Sandiacre NG10 223 D3
Sudbury Cl Chesterfield S40 95 D3
Derby DE1 218 C3
Sudbury Ct NG10 235 F2
Sudbury Hall & Mus DE6 225 E3
Sudbury Mews NG16 182 C1
Sudbury Pk DE6 225 E4
Sudbury Prim Sch DE6 225 F2
Sudbury St DE1 218 C3
Sudhall Cl S41 95 E4
Suff La NG16 160 B2
Suffolk Ave DE21 219 F4
Suffolk Rd DE15 254 B4
Sugworth Rd S6 31 F3
Summer Cross SK17 69 D2
Summer Dr DE4 165 F4
Summer La Totley S17 55 E2
Wirksworth DE4 165 F4
Summer Leys La NG2 268 B1
Summer St ST4 269 E1
Summer Wood Ct DE23 231 E4
Summerbottom SK14 16 A4
Summerbrook Ct DE22 218 C2
Summerfield Cres S43 96 C4
Summerfield Rd
Chesterfield S40 266 A1
Dronfield S18 57 D2
Summerfields Way DE7 194 B2
Summerfields Way S DE7 194 B1
Summerley Lower Rd S18 57 F1
Summerley Rd S18 57 F1
Summerskill Gn S43 97 E4
Summerwood La S18 56 C1
Summerwood Pl 8 S18 56 C1
Summit Dr NG20 119 F2
Sumner St SK13 17 E4
Sumners Pl SK13 10 A1
Sun La DE4 156 C1
Sun St Derby DE22 267 A2
Woodville DE11 256 C1
Sunart Cl DE24 231 F1
Sunbourne Ct NG7 268 A2
Sundew Cl DE21 220 C2
Sundown Ave DE23 231 E3
Sundown Cl SK22 33 D4
Sundown Pl S13 44 C4
Sundown Rd S13 44 C4
Suningdale Cl DE13 240 B1
Sunlaws St SK13 17 D4
Sunlea Cres NG9 223 F3
Sunningdale Ave
Derby DE21 220 B3
Heanor DE75 193 F4
Sunningdale Cl S40 114 C4
Sunningdale Dr DE7 208 A3
Sunningdale Rise S40 114 B4
Sunninghill Cl DE7 207 E4
Sunny Bank
Great Longstone DE45 90 A2
Tibshelf DE55 147 F3
Sunny Bank Gdns DE56 178 C1
Sunny Bank La SK17 69 E2
Sunny Banks SK13 17 D4
Sunny Brook Cl S43 80 C2
Sunny Gr DE21 220 A3
Sunny Hill DE56 190 C4
Sunny Springs S41 266 B4
Sunnybank DE4 110 C1
Sunnyfield SK17 85 F1
Sunnyhill Ave DE23 231 F3
Sunnyside Swadlincote DE11 255 F4
Whitwell S80 82 A3
Sunnyside Rd ST14 210 A1
Sunnyvale Ave S17 55 F2
Sunnyvale Rd S17 55 E2
Surbiton Cl DE22 218 A3
Surbiton Ct DE7 207 E4
Surgery La DE4 157 D1
Surrey Dr NG19 268 A4
Surrey St Derby DE22 218 B3
Glossop SK13 10 B1
Sussex Cir DE21 219 F4
Sussex Rd DE15 254 C3
Sussex Way NG10 223 D3
Sutherland Rd DE23 219 D1
Sutherland St ST4 269 F1
Sutton Ave DE73 232 C2
Sutton Cl DE22 218 B3
Sutton Cres S43 97 E4
Sutton Ct NG16 182 C1
Sutton Dr Derby DE24 232 C2
Stoke-on-T ST4 269 D1
Sutton Hall Rd S44 117 F4
Sutton La Etwall DE65 229 D3
Hatton DE65 227 F2
Hilton DE65 228 B2
Long Duckmanton S44 116 C4
Sutton Rd
Church Broughton DE65 227 E4
Mansfield NG18 268 A3
Sutton in A NG17 148 C2
Sutton Road Fst Sch NG18 268 A3
Sutton Scarsdale Hall S44 117 D3
Sutton View S44 118 A4
Sutton Way SK13 10 A3
Suttons La SK6 23 D3
Swaddale Ave S41 96 A3
Swaddale Cl S41 96 A3
Swadlincote La DE11 255 F1
Swadlincote Rd DE11 256 C2
Swadlincote Ski Ctr DE11 256 B2
Swalebank Cl S40 115 D4
Swaledale Ct DE24 233 E3
Swallow Cl DE3 218 A2
Swallow House Cres SK22 25 E2
Swallow House La SK22 25 E2
Swallow Rd DE11 256 C2
Swallowdale Rd DE24 231 E2
Swan Cl ST16 269 D3
Swan La NG19 136 A2
Swan St ST4 269 E2
Swanbourne Cl S41 96 B1
Swanmore Rd DE23 231 D4
Swann Yd NG17 148 C2
Swanson Ave NG17 148 C2
Swanwick Ave NG20 119 F2
Swanwick Gdns DE21 206 A1
Swanwick Hall Sch DE55 169 F4
Swanwick Hill DE55 169 F4
Swanwick Prim Sch DE55 169 E3
Swanwick Rd DE55 170 A4
Swanwick St S41 77 D1
Swarkestone Dr DE23 231 E3
Swarkestone Rd
Barrow u T DE73 244 A3
Derby DE73 244 C4
Swathwick Cl S42 114 C2
Swathwick La S42 114 B2
Swayfield Cl DE3 217 E2
Sweetbriar Cl DE24 233 D3
Swift Cl Derby DE3 218 A2
Woodville DE11 256 C2
Swift Ct NG16 182 C1
Swinburne St Derby DE1 267 B1
Nottingham NG3 268 C2
Swinderby Dr DE21 206 A1
Swindon Cl NG16 195 E4
Swiney Way NG9 223 F1
Swinger La S45 129 E4
Swinney Bank DE56 179 D3
Swinney La DE56 179 D3
Swinscoe Hill DE6 172 A1
Swinscoe Way S40 95 D3
Swinson Cl ST14 197 D2
Sycamore Ave
Chesterfield S40 95 F1
Creswell S80 81 F1
Derby DE65 204 B2
Dronfield S18 57 D2
Findern DE65 230 C1
Glapwell S44 134 A4
Ripley DE5 180 B4
Swadlincote DE11 256 A4
Sycamore Cl Bolsover S44 99 E1
Buxton SK17 66 A1
Etwall DE65 229 E2
Linton DE12 261 E3
Mapperley DE7 193 F2
New Mills SK22 24 C1
Pinxton NG16 160 B2
Selston NG16 171 E4
Shirland DE55 146 B2
Sycamore Cotts DE6 151 E1
Sycamore Cres NG10 223 D4
Sycamore Dr Calow S44 96 C2
Ilkeston DE7 209 D4
Killamarsh S21 60 B3
Sycamore Jun & Inf Schs NG3 268 B2
Sycamore La
Barlborough S43 80 A3
Brimington S43 78 A1
Sycamore Rd
Awsworth NG16 195 E3
Brimington S43 78 A1
Burton u T DE15 254 C3
Castle Donington DE74 247 D3
Chapel-en-le-F SK23 47 D2
Long Eaton NG10 236 B3
Mansfield Woodhouse
NG19 136 B3
Matlock DE4 143 D3
Mayfield DE6 184 B4
Thornsett SK22 24 C1
Sycamore St
Market Warsop NG20 120 C3
Mosborough S20 59 E4
Sycamores The
Eastwood NG16 182 C1
Hadfield SK13 9 F2
South Normanton DE55 160 A3
Syda La S42 93 F1
Syday La S21 79 F4
Sydenham Rd DE22 218 A4
Sydney Cl NG19 136 B3
Sydney St Chesterfield S40 95 F2
Draycott DE72 235 D4
Sydnope Hill DE4 128 A3
Syerscote La B79 263 D1
Sylvan Cl S41 266 C1
Sylvan Cliff SK17 85 E4
Sylvan Dr S42 131 D3
Sylvan Pk SK17 85 E4
Sylvester St NG18 268 A3
Sylvia Rd S18 76 B3
Sywell Cl DE55 169 F4
Tabley Gdns SK6 23 D2
Taddington Cl DE21 219 F4
Taddington & Priestcliffe CE Prim Sch SK17 87 F2
Taddington Rd
Chesterfield S40 95 D3
Derby DE21 205 F1
Taft Ave NG10 223 D3
Tagg La DE45 107 D1
Taggs Knoll S33 40 A2
Taghole La DE6 188 C1
Tailby Dr DE65 242 A3
Talbot Cres S41 115 E4
Talbot Dr NG9 209 E1
Talbot House Sch SK13 10 B1
Talbot Pl DE12 265 F4
Talbot Rd Glossop SK13 10 B1
Stafford ST17 269 E3
Talbot St Chesterfield S41 115 E4
Derby DE1 218 C3
Glossop SK13 10 B1
Nottingham NG1 268 A2
Pinxton NG16 160 B1
Swadlincote DE11 256 A1
Talgarth Cl DE21 206 B1
Tamar Ave DE22 204 B2
Tamworth Rd
Castle Donington DE74 235 F1
Long Eaton NG10 236 B3
Stretton en le F DE12 265 F1
Tamworth St DE56 190 C2
Tamworth Terr DE56 190 C2
Tanner's La DE65 242 B2
Tansley Ave DE7 193 D1
Tansley Dr S40 95 D3
Tansley Prim Sch DE4 144 A2
Tansley Rd S42 131 F3
Tansley Rise DE21 205 F1
Tansley Way S43 97 E3
Tants Meadow DE56 191 F3
Tantum Ave DE75 181 E2
Tanyard Cl DE74 247 D2
Tap La S40 266 A3
Taplow Cl DE3 217 E1
Tapton La S41 266 C3
Tapton Lock Hill S41 96 A3
Tapton Terr S41 266 C4
Tapton Vale S41 96 B3
Tapton View Rd S41 95 F3
Tapton Way S44 96 C2
Tarina Cl DE73 233 D1
Tarnside Fold SK13 17 D4
Tarporley Gr ST4 269 D1
Tasman Cl DE3 217 F2
Tatenhill La
Branston DE14 253 E4
Tatenhill DE13 253 D4
Tatham's La DE7 194 C1
Tattersall Wlk NG19 136 C2
Tattershall Dr NG7 268 A1
Tattle Hill DE7 207 F1
Taunton Cl DE24 233 E4
Tavern Rd SK13 9 F2
Taverners Cres DE23 231 E4
Tavistock Ave DE5 169 E1
Tavistock Cl DE24 231 E2
Tavistock Sq DE55 159 D3
Tawney Croft DE4 144 A2
Tawny Way DE23 231 D4
Taxal & Fernilee CE Contr Prim Sch SK23 45 E3
Taxal Lodge Sch SK23 45 E3
Taxal Moor Rd SK23 45 E2
Tay Cl Derby DE24 231 E1
Dronfield S18 56 B1
Tay Wlk DE22 204 C2
Taylor Cres
Chesterfield S41 96 B1
Stapleford NG9 223 F4
Taylor La DE75 181 E2
Taylor St Derby DE24 219 F1
Hollingworth SK14 9 E2
Ilkeston DE7 194 C1
Taylor's La Spout DE56 166 A2
Trusley DE6 215 F3
Tayside Cl DE24 231 E2
Teal Cl NG20 119 E2
Tealby Wlk NG19 136 C2
Tean Cl DE15 248 A1
Tedder Ave SK17 85 E2
Tedgness Rd S32 53 F1
Tedworth Ave DE24 231 E1
Teesdale Rd
Long Eaton NG10 236 A3
Mosborough S12 58 C4
Telegraph St ST17 269 E3
Telford Cl DE3 217 F1
Telford Cres S43 78 C1
Telford Rd SK6 23 D2
Telmah Cl DE13 240 B1
Temperance Hill DE55 145 F4
Temperance St SK14 16 A4
Templar Cl DE24 231 E2
Temple Ave SK13 10 B3
Temple Normanton Bsns Pk S42 116 A2
Temple Normanton Prim Sch S42 116 B2
Temple Rd Buxton SK17 85 D3
Matlock Bath DE4 143 D1
Temple St Derby DE23 219 D2
Fenton ST4 269 F1
Padfield SK13 10 B3
Temple View SK17 85 E4
Temple Wlk DE4 143 D1
Ten Foot Cl SK13 10 A1
Tenant St DE1 267 B3
Tennessee Rd DE21 220 A4
Tennis Dr NG7 268 A1
Tennyson Ave
Chesterfield S40 266 A3
Mansfield Woodhouse NG19 136 B1
Swadlincote DE11 256 B3
Tennyson Rd S80 81 E1
Tennyson Sq NG16 195 E2
Tennyson St Derby DE24 232 B4
Holmewood S42 116 B1
Ilkeston DE7 194 C2
7 Mansfield NG18 268 B4
Nottingham NG7 268 A2
Shirland DE55 146 B3
Tennyson Way S42 115 F2
Tenter Cl NG10 236 B3
Tenter La Heage DE56 168 B1
Mansfield NG18 268 B3
Tenterbanks ST16 269 D4
Tern Ave DE11 256 C2
Terrace La NG19 134 C3
Terrace Rd Buxton SK17 85 D4
Chapel-en-le-F SK23 47 D3
Mansfield NG18 268 C4
Tideswell SK17 69 E2
Terrace The DE4 143 F4
Terret Gr SK17 84 B3
Terrey Rd S17 55 F3
Terry Pl DE24 232 C4
Tetford Wlk NG19 136 C2
Teversal Ave NG19 135 D2
Tevery Cl NG9 223 F4
Teviot Pl DE21 206 A1
Tewkesbury Ave NG19 136 B2
Tewkesbury Cres DE21 219 E4
Tewkesbury Dr NG16 195 F4
Tewkesbury Rd NG10 236 C3
Thackeray Rd DE55 146 C2
Thackeray St DE24 232 A3
Thames Cl DE22 217 F3
Thanet Dr DE24 233 D3
Thanet St S45 131 E2
Thatchers La DE4 144 A2
Theatre La S41 266 C3
Theatre Sq NG1 268 B2
Theatre Yd S40 266 B3
Thickley Cl NG20 119 F2
Thirlmere Ave DE22 204 C2
Thirlmere Cl NG10 223 D1
Thirlmere Dr S18 57 D1
Thirlmere Rd
Chesterfield S41 95 E4
Long Eaton NG10 223 D1
Thirlwell Rd S8 43 D3
Thirsk Pl DE24 232 B4
Thirteen Row S44 118 A3
Thistle Cl NG16 195 D4
Thistle Green Cl DE75 182 A1
Thistledown Cl DE22 205 D1
Thistley Hough ST4 269 D1
Thistley Hough High Sch ST4 269 D2
Thomas Cl NG3 268 B2
Thomas Cook Cl DE73 252 A4
Thomas St Compstall SK6 15 D1
Glossop SK13 10 C1
Thompson Cl S41 96 A4
Thompson St
Chesterfield S41 96 A4
Langley Mill NG16 182 A2
Thomson Dr DE5 181 D4
Thoresby Ave NG20 119 F2
Thoresby Cl Derby DE21 206 A1
Ripley DE5 169 F1
Thoresby Cres DE72 234 C4
Thoresby Pl S43 97 E3
Thoresby Rd
Long Eaton NG10 236 B3
Mansfield Woodhouse NG19 136 A2
Thoresby St NG18 268 B4
Thoresey Ave S43 81 D2
Thorn Ave NG19 135 F1
Thorn Cl DE22 204 B2
Thorn Dr NG16 195 D4
Thorn St Derby DE23 218 C1
Woodville DE11 256 C1
Thorn Tree Gdns NG16 182 C2
Thorn Tree La Bretby DE15 255 F4
Swadlincote DE15 255 F4
Thornborough Cl S2 43 E4
Thornborough Pl S2 43 E4
Thornborough Rd S2 43 E4
Thornbridge Ave S12 44 B2
Thornbridge Cl S12 44 B2
Thornbridge Cres
Chesterfield S40 115 D3
Sheffield S12 44 C2
Thornbridge Dr S12 44 B2
Thornbridge Gr S12 44 B2
Thornbridge Hall Training Coll DE45 89 F1
Thornbridge La S12 44 C2
Thornbridge Pl S12 44 B2
Thornbridge Rise S12 44 C2
Thornbridge Sch S12 44 B1
Thornbridge Way S12 44 C2
Thornbrook Rd SK23 47 E3
Thornburrow Dr ST4 269 D2
Thorncliffe Ave DE4 127 D3
Thorncliffe Rd SK13 9 F2
Thorndene Cl S41 96 A3
Thorndike Ave DE24 233 D4
Thorndon Cl DE3 230 B4
Thorndon Way S40 114 B4
Thorne Cl S40 94 C2
Thornecliffewood SK14 9 E3
Thornell Cl SK23 47 E3
Thornescroft Gdns DE14 254 A4
Thorness Cl DE24 233 E3
Thornewill Dr DE13 240 C1
Thorneywood Rd NG10 236 C4
Thornfield Ave S40 95 D1
Thornhill La S33 39 F2
Thornhill Rd
Derby, California DE22 218 B2
Derby, Littleover DE23 218 B1
Thornsett SK22 24 C1
Thornsett Ave SK17 85 F4
Thornsett Cl SK17 85 F4
Thornsett Gdns S17 55 F4
Thornsett Prim Sch SK22 24 C2
Thornton Pl S18 56 B1
Thornton Rd ST4 269 F2
Thorntree Cl DE72 222 C1
Thorntree La DE1 267 B3
Thornway SK6 32 A4
Thornwood Cl SK17 85 D4
Thoroton St NG7 268 A2
Thorp Cl S2 43 D4
Thorpe Ave Dronfield S18 57 E2
Whitwell S80 81 F3
Thorpe Cl
9 Chesterfield S41 95 F4
Stapleford NG9 223 E4
Thorpe Croft DE4 156 A3
Thorpe Downs Rd DE11 256 A1
Thorpe Dr DE3 217 F2
Thorpe Hill Dr DE75 193 F4
Thorpe House Ave S8 43 D2
Thorpe House Rd S8 43 D2
Thorpe House Rise S8 43 D2
Thorpe La S80 63 E3
Thorpe Leys NG10 236 B3
Thorpe Rd Eastwood NG16 182 C2
Harthill S26 62 A4
Thorpe St Glossop SK13 10 C1
Ilkeston DE7 194 C2
Thorpe Way DE56 179 D3
Thorpe's Rd Heanor DE75 181 E1
Shipley DE75 193 E4
Thorpelands Ave NG19 136 C1
Thorpelands Dr DE22 204 C1
Thorpleigh Rd S43 79 D1
Three Gates DE56 178 C1
Throstle Nest Way DE6 201 F4
Thrumpton Ave NG10 237 D4
Thrumpton Hall NG11 237 D2
Thrushton Cl DE65 230 B1
Thruxton Cl DE24 233 E3
Thunderpit La S32 71 D2
Thurcaton Way DE55 148 A2
Thurgarton Ct DE6 173 E1
Thurgarton St NG2 268 C1
Thurland St 12 NG1 268 B1
Thurlby Ct NG19 136 C2
Thurlow Ct DE21 206 A1
Thurman St DE7 209 D3
Thurrows Way DE73 233 D1
Thurstan Ave S8 56 C4
Thurston Ave DE55 170 B4
Thurstone Furlong DE73 232 C1
Thurvaston Rd DE6 197 F1
Thyme Cl DE23 231 E2
Tiber Cl DE24 233 E3
Tibshelf Inf Sch DE55 148 A4
Tibshelf Rd Blackwell DE55 147 E1
Holmewood S42 132 C4
Tibshelf Sch DE55 148 A4
Tickham Ave DE24 231 E1
Ticknall La Denby DE5 180 A1
Hartshorne DE11 257 D4
Ticknall Parochial Sch DE73 251 D3
Ticknall Wlk DE23 231 F3
Tideswell Cl S43 97 E4
Tideswell Ct NG18 268 C4
Tideswell Gn DE11 255 F3
Tideswell La S32 71 D3
Tideswell Rd DE21 205 F1
Tiger Yd DE6 173 D1
Tilbury Pl DE24 233 D1
Tillotson Cl S8 43 D3
Tillotson Rise S8 43 D3
Tilson Ave ST4 269 D2
Tilton Gr DE7 208 B3
Timber La S45 132 C3
Timbersbrook Cl DE21 206 A1
Timsbury Ct DE21 205 F1
Tinderbox La DE65 229 F3
Tinkerley La
Idridgehay DE6 165 E1
Kirk Ireton DE56 165 E1
Tinkley La S42 130 B2
Tinsell Brook DE65 228 C1
Tinsley Rd NG16 182 B1
Tintagel Cl
Burton u T DE13 240 C1
Derby DE23 219 D1
Tintwistle CE Prim Sch SK13 10 A4
Tip Tree Cl NG16 195 F4
Tipnall Rd DE74 247 D2
Tipper's La DE65 227 D4
Tippett Ct NG3 268 C2
Tipping St ST16 269 E4

Tiree Cl Derby DE24 .... 231 F2
Stapleford NG9 .... 209 E1
Tibshelf DE55 .... 147 F3
Tissington Cl S40 .... 95 D3
Tissington Dr DE21 .... 206 A2
Titchfield Ave NG19 .... 136 B2
Titchfield St Creswell S80 ..... 81 F1
Mansfield NG19 .... 268 B4
Whitwell S80 .... 81 F3
Tithe Barn Cl ST17 .... 69 E2
Tithe Barn La S17 .... 269 F4
Tithe Barn Rd ST 16 .... 269 F4
Tithebarn La DE6 .... 215 E3
Titterton St ST4 .... 269 F1
Tiverton Cl DE3 .... 217 E2
Tivoli Gdns DE1 .... 218 C4
Tixall Rd ST16, ST18 .... 269 F4
Toadmoor La DE56 .... 167 F2
Tobermory Way DE24 .... 231 E2
Todbrook Cl SK23 .... 45 E3
Todd St SK13 .... 17 E4
Tolkien Way ST4 .... 269 E2
Toll Bar Ave S12 .... 43 F3
Toll Bar Cl S12 .... 43 F3
Toll Bar Dr S12 .... 43 F3
Toll Bar Rd S12 .... 43 F3
Tollbridge Rd S43 .... 79 D1
Tollemache Cl SK14 .... 9 D3
Tollemache Rd SK14 .... 9 D3
Tollhouse Hill 12 NG1 .... 268 A2
Tom La
  Chapel-en-le-F SK23 .... 46 B3
  Staveley S44 .... 97 F3
Tomlinson Ind Est DE21 .... 205 E1
Tomwood Rise SK13 .... 16 B3
Tonbridge Dr DE24 .... 233 D3
Tonge La DE74 .... 252 C2
Tongue La SK17 .... 85 F4
Tongue La Ind Est SK17 ...... 85 F4
Tontine Rd S40 .... 266 B2
Toothill La NG18 .... 268 C4
Toothill Rd NG18 .... 268 B4
Top Farm Ct DE56 .... 191 F4
Top Fingle Cl S43 .... 96 C4
Top Hag La DE56 .... 168 A3
Top La Crich DE4 .... 156 B1
  Mansfield NG19 .... 135 D1
  Old Brampton S42 .... 93 F2
  Shottle DE56 .... 166 B1
Top Lons DE56 .... 176 A4
Top Manor Cl DE72 .... 221 E3
Top Meadow DE11 .... 256 A4
Top Rd Calow S44 .... 97 D2
  Wingerworth S42 .... 114 B1
Top Row NG16 .... 171 D3
Tophill La DE4 .... 153 E4
Tophole Rd S33 .... 50 C2
Topley Gdns DE21 .... 205 F1
Toppham Dr S8 .... 56 C3
Toppham Rd S8 .... 56 C3
Toppham Way S8 .... 56 C3
Topshill La DE6 .... 165 D1
Tor Ave DE55 .... 170 B3
Tor Rise DE4 .... 143 D2
Tor View Rise DE4 .... 155 D3
Torksey Wlk NG19 .... 136 C2
Torr St SK17 .... 85 D4
Torr Top St SK22 .... 33 E4
Torrance Cl DE14 .... 254 A3
Torridon Cl DE24 .... 231 F2
Torrs Valley SK22 .... 33 E4
Torrvale Rd SK22 .... 33 D4
Tors The DE4 .... 156 C1
Torside Way SK13 .... 10 A3
Torwood Dr S8 .... 56 C4
Totley All Saints CE Prim
  Sch S17 .... 55 E2
Totley Brook Cl S17 .... 55 E3
Totley Brook Croft S17 ...... 55 E3
Totley Brook Glen S17 .... 55 E3
Totley Brook Gr S17 .... 55 E3
Totley Brook Rd S17 .... 55 F3
Totley Brook Way S17 .... 55 E3
Totley Cty Inf & Jun Sch
  S17 .... 55 E2
Totley Grange Cl S17 .... 55 E2
Totley Grange Dr S17 .... 55 E2
Totley Grange Rd S17 .... 55 E2
Totley Hall La S17 .... 55 E2
Totley La S17 .... 56 A3
Totley Mews SK13 .... 9 E1
Totley Mnt S43 .... 96 B4
Toton Banks Road Inf Sch
  NG9 .... 223 F1
Toton Cty Jun Sch NG9 ..... 223 F1
Toton La Beeston NG9 .... 223 F3
  Stapleford NG9 .... 223 F3
Toulmin Dr DE11 .... 256 A2
Tower Bsns Pk S45 .... 131 E2
Tower Cl Sheffield S2 .... 43 E4
  Somercotes DE55 .... 170 B4
Tower Cres S44 .... 118 C4
Tower Dr S2 .... 43 E4
Tower Rd Burton u T DE15 .. 248 A1
  Hartshorne DE11 .... 257 D3
Tower St DE24 .... 232 B4
Tower View Prim Sch
  DE15 .... 248 B2
Towers La S32 .... 40 C1
Towle Cl DE72 .... 221 E1
Towle St NG10 .... 236 A2
Towles Pastures DE74 .... 247 D2
Town End
  Apperknowle S18 .... 58 A1
  Bolsover S44 .... 99 D1
  Buxton SK17 .... 66 C1
  Shirland DE55 .... 146 B1
Town End Rd DE72 .... 235 D4

Town End Sch DE55 .... 147 F3
Town Fold SK6 .... 23 D4
Town Gate S33 .... 51 D4
Town Hall Yd DE6 .... 173 E1
Town La Bradwell S33 .... 51 D4
  Charlesworth SK13 .... 16 B3
  Newton DE55 .... 148 A2
Town St Brassington DE4 ... 153 D1
  Duffield DE56 .... 190 C2
  Holbrook DE56 .... 191 E3
  Marple SK6 .... 23 D4
  Pinxton NG16 .... 160 C2
  Sandiacre NG10 .... 223 D3
Town The DE21 .... 205 E4
Town View NG16 .... 195 F4
Townfield La S33 .... 39 F1
Townhead La S33 .... 39 F2
Townhead Rd S17 .... 55 E4
Townscliffe La SK6 .... 23 E3
Townsend Gr DE73 .... 233 D1
Townside Cl NG10 .... 236 A2
Towson Ave NG16 .... 182 B1
Trade St ST4 .... 269 E2
Trafalgar Rd
  Long Eaton NG10 .... 236 B3
  Stoke-on-T ST4 .... 269 D2
Trafalgar Sq NG10 .... 236 C4
Traffic St Derby DE1 .... 267 C2
  Nottingham NG2 .... 268 B1
Traffic Terr
  Barrow Hill S43 .... 78 A2
  Chesterfield S41 .... 115 D4
Trafford Way DE23 .... 231 E4
Tranmere Ave S45 .... 131 E2
Transvaal Terr S44 .... 118 A3
Travers Rd NG10 .... 223 D3
Travey Rd S2 .... 44 A4
Treak Cliff Cavern S33 .... 37 F2
Tredcroft St SK13 .... 17 D4
Tredegar Dr DE21 .... 206 A1
Treeneuk Cl S40 .... 95 D2
Trefoil Ct DE23 .... 231 D4
Tregaron Cl DE21 .... 206 B1
Tregony Way DE24 .... 231 E2
Trelawney Rd S45 .... 131 E2
Trenchard Ave ST 16 .... 269 F4
Trenchard Dr SK17 .... 85 E2
Trent Ave Buxton SK17 .... 85 E2
  Willington DE65 .... 242 B3
Trent Bridge Ct DE23 .... 231 E4
Trent Cl Derby DE65 .... 231 E1
  Nottingham NG2 .... 268 C1
  Willington DE65 .... 242 B3
Trent Coll NG10 .... 236 B4
Trent Dr DE23 .... 231 E3
Trent Gr Alfreton DE55 ..... 159 D1
  Dronfield S18 .... 57 D2
Trent La
  Castle Donington DE74 ..... 247 D3
  Long Eaton NG10 .... 236 C3
  Melbourne DE73 .... 245 E1
  Newton Solney DE15 .... 248 C4
  Weston-on-T DE72 .... 245 F2
Trent Rd Ilkeston DE7 .... 208 B2
  Nottingham NG2 .... 268 C1
Trent Rise DE21 .... 220 C2
Trent St Derby DE24 .... 233 D4
  Long Eaton NG10 .... 236 C4
  Nottingham NG1 .... 268 B1
Trent Valley Rd ST4 .... 269 D1
Trent Wlk NG19 .... 136 C2
Trenton Cl NG9 .... 209 F1
Trenton Dr NG10 .... 237 D4
Trenton Green Dr DE21 .... 220 A3
Trenton Grn DE21 .... 220 A3
Tresillian Cl DE22 .... 204 C1
Tressall Cl DE7 .... 209 D4
Trevelyn Cl DE15 .... 248 B1
Treveris Cl DE21 .... 220 C2
Trevone Ave NG9 .... 223 F3
Trevose Cl S40 .... 114 B4
Triangle The DE7 .... 209 D3
Trickett Cl S33 .... 38 B2
Trinity Cl
  Chesterfield S40 .... 266 A4
  Ilkeston DE7 .... 194 C2
Trinity Gr DE11 .... 256 A2
Trinity Sq NG1 .... 268 B2
Trinity St DE1 .... 267 C2
Trinkey La S32 .... 72 A2
Tristram Gr DE13 .... 240 E1
Troon Cl Burton u T DE13 .. 240 B1
  Chesterfield S40 .... 114 B4
  Derby DE23 .... 231 D4
  Kimberley NG16 .... 195 F4
Trot La SK17 .... 70 A3
Trough La NG16 .... 195 F4
Troughbrook Hill S43 .... 97 D4
Troughbrook Rd S43 .... 78 A1
Trowbridge Cl DE21 .... 205 F1
Trowell Ave DE7 .... 209 D3
Trowell CE Sch NG9 .... 209 E2
Trowell Gr
  Long Eaton NG10 .... 223 E1
  Stapleford NG9 .... 209 F2
Trowell Park Dr NG9 .... 209 E1
Trowell Rd NG9 .... 209 E1
Trowels La DE22 .... 218 B2
Trueman St DE7 .... 194 C2
Truman Cl NG3 .... 268 B2
Truman St Cossall DE7 ...... 195 D1
  Kimberley NG16 .... 195 E4
Truro Cl DE11 .... 256 C3
Truro Cres DE21 .... 219 F4
Trusley Gdns DE23 .... 231 E3
Trusley Wlk NG19 .... 136 C2
Trustley Cl DE14 .... 254 A4
Tuckers La NG18 .... 268 A4

Tudor Cl
  Long Eaton NG10 .... 223 F1
  Stoke-on-T ST4 .... 269 E1
Tudor Falls DE75 .... 181 F2
Tudor Field Cl DE73 .... 233 D1
Tudor Pl DE7 .... 208 B3
Tudor Rd DE21 .... 220 A3
Tudor Rise B79 .... 263 F1
Tudor St S43 .... 78 C1
Tudor Way DE11 .... 256 A3
Tudorhouse Cl DE11 .... 256 A4
Tuffolds Cl S2 .... 44 A4
Tufnell Gdns DE22 .... 218 A4
Tulip Rd NG16 .... 195 D3
Tulla Cl DE24 .... 231 F1
Tullis Cl ST16 .... 269 D3
Tunnel Rd NG7 .... 268 A1
Tunnel Yd DE6 .... 173 D1
Tunstall Cl S40 .... 95 E1
Tunstall Way S40 .... 95 E1
Tupton Hall Sch S42 .... 131 E4
Tupton Prim Sch S42 .... 115 E1
Tupton Way S42 .... 116 B1
Turf Lea Rd SK6 .... 23 D1
Turlowfields La DE6 .... 175 E4
Turnberry Cl
  Chesterfield S40 .... 114 B4
  Ilkeston DE7 .... 194 B1
Turnbury Cl DE14 .... 254 A4
Turncliffe Cl SK17 .... 84 C3
Turnditch CE Prim Sch
  DE56 .... 177 D1
Turner Ave NG16 .... 182 A2
Turner Cl
  4 Dronfield S18 .... 56 C1
  Stapleford NG9 .... 223 F3
Turner Dr
  Eastwood NG16 .... 195 D4
  Staveley S43 .... 97 D4
Turner Rd NG10 .... 236 B2
Turner St DE24 .... 232 C3
Turners La DE55 .... 170 A4
Turnlee Cl SK13 .... 17 E4
Turnlee Dr SK13 .... 17 E4
Turnlee Rd SK13 .... 17 E4
Turnley Rd DE55 .... 160 B3
Turnoaks Bsns Pk S40 ...... 115 D3
Turnoaks La S40 .... 115 D4
Turnpike Cl DE4 .... 143 E3
Turton Cl NG16 .... 182 A2
Tutbury & Hatton Sta
  DE6 .... 239 E4
Tutbury Rd
  Burton u T DE13 .... 240 A1
  Rolleston DE13 .... 240 A1
Tuxford Cl DE21 .... 206 A1
Tuxford Wlk NG3 .... 268 C2
Twentylands DE13 .... 240 B2
Twentywell Dr S17 .... 56 A3
Twentywell La S17 .... 56 A3
Twentywell Rd S17 .... 56 A3
Twentywell Rise S17 .... 56 A3
Twentywell View S17 .... 56 A3
Twickenham Cl S20 .... 59 F3
Twickenham Cres S20 .... 59 F3
Twickenham Ct S20 .... 59 F3
Twickenham Dr DE22 .... 218 A3
Twickenham Glade S20 ...... 59 F3
Twickenham Glen S20 .... 59 F3
Twickenham Gr S20 .... 59 F3
Twin Oaks Cl DE23 .... 230 C4
Twisses Bank DE6 .... 213 D1
Twyford Cl Heanor DE75 ... 193 E4
  Swadlincote DE11 .... 255 F1
  West Hallam DE7 .... 207 E4
  Willington DE65 .... 242 B3
Twyford Rd
  Barrow u T DE73 .... 244 A3
  Long Eaton NG10 .... 235 F2
  Willington DE65 .... 242 A3
Twyford St DE23 .... 267 B1
Tylney Rd S40 .... 114 A4
Tyndale Chase DE24 .... 231 E1
Tyndall Pl ST4 .... 269 D2
Tynedale Cl NG10 .... 236 A3
Tynefield Ct DE65 .... 229 D1
Tynefield Mews DE65 .... 229 D1
Tynsel Parkes CE Fst Sch
  ST14 .... 210 A1
Tythe The DE11 .... 256 A4
Uffa Magna DE3 .... 217 E1
Ulley Cres S13 .... 44 A4
Ulley Rd S13 .... 44 A4
Ullswater Ave S20 .... 59 F3
Ullswater Cl Derby DE21 ... 205 E1
  Dronfield S18 .... 56 C1
  Mosborough S20 .... 59 F3
Ullswater Dr
  Derby DE21 .... 220 C3
  Dronfield S18 .... 56 C1
Ullswater Pk 6 S18 .... 56 C1
Ullswater Pl S18 .... 56 C1
Ulster Terr ST4 .... 269 E1
Ulverston Rd S41 .... 95 E4
Underhall DE4 .... 127 C1
Underhill Ave DE23 .... 231 F4
Underhill Cl DE23 .... 231 F3
Underhill Rd S43 .... 80 A3
Underpass The DE1 .... 267 C4
Undertown La DE6 .... 197 E3
Underwood CE Sch NG16 .. 171 F1
Underwood Terr DE7 .... 143 D4
Union Rd
  Ilkeston DE7 .... 208 C4
  New Mills SK22 .... 33 E4
  Nottingham NG1 .... 268 B2
  Swadlincote DE11 .... 256 A1

Union St Ashbourne DE6 .... 173 D1
  Glossop SK13 .... 17 E4
  Harthill S26 .... 61 F3
  Long Eaton NG10 .... 236 C4
  Mansfield NG18 .... 268 B4
  Melbourne DE73 .... 252 A4
  South Normanton DE55 ... 159 F3
Unity Cl DE11 .... 256 A1
Unity Wlk ST4 .... 17 E4
Univ of Derby DE22 .... 204 B1
Univ of Derby (Sch of Art
  & Design) DE1 .... 267 B2
Univ of Sheffield
  (Research Labs) SK17 ...... 85 D1
Unstone Dronfield By-Pass
  S18 .... 75 F4
Unstone Hill S18 .... 76 B4
Unstone Jun Sch S18 .... 76 C4
Unstone Rd S18 .... 76 C2
Unthank La S17, S18 .... 74 B2
Upchurch Cl DE3 .... 217 E2
Upland Rise S40 .... 95 E1
Uplands Ave DE23 .... 231 E3
Uplands Gdns DE23 .... 218 C1
Uplands Rd Glossop SK13 ... 17 E4
  Hackingknife SK14 .... 15 D3
Upper Albert Rd S8 .... 43 D3
Upper Bainbridge St DE23 219 D2
Upper Barn Cl DE75 .... 181 F1
Upper Blindlow La S17 ..... 106 A3
Upper Boundary Rd DE22 . 218 C2
Upper College St 10 NG1 . 268 A2
Upper Cres ST4 .... 269 D2
Upper Croft S45 .... 131 F2
Upper Croft Cl S43 .... 96 C4
Upper Dale Rd DE23 .... 218 C1
Upper Dunstead Rd NG16 . 182 A2
Upper Eldon St NG2 .... 268 C1
Upper End Rd SK17 .... 67 E2
Upper Furlong St ST4 ...... 269 F1
Upper Greenhill Gdns DE4 143 E3
Upper Hall Cl DE56 .... 191 E3
Upper Hollow DE23 .... 218 B1
Upper King St S43 .... 77 F1
Upper La DE6 .... 175 F2
Upper Mantle Cl S45 .... 131 E2
Upper Marehay Rd DE5 ... 180 B3
Upper Moor St S40 .... 95 D1
Upper Nelson St DE75 ...... 181 E1
Upper Newbold Cl S40 .... 95 D4
Upper Orchard St NG9 ...... 223 E4
Upper Parliament St NG1 . 268 B2
Upper School La S18 .... 76 A4
Upper Town La DE4 .... 126 A1
Upper Valley Rd S8 .... 43 D3
Upper Wellington St NG10 223 E1
Upper Yeld Rd DE45 .... 109 E2
Uppermoor Rd DE24 .... 232 C3
Upperthorpe Rd S21 .... 60 B3
Upperthorpe Villas S21 ...... 60 B3
Uppertown La DE4 .... 142 B1
Upperwood Rd DE4 .... 143 D1
Upton Cl DE75 .... 182 A1
Upton Mount NG19 .... 135 F1
Upwood Cl S40 .... 95 D3
Upwoods Rd DE6 .... 211 D1
Utah Cl DE65 .... 228 C1
Uttoxeter New Rd DE22 ... 218 B2
Uttoxeter Old Rd DE22 .... 218 C3
Uttoxeter Rd Derby DE65 . 217 F1
  Hatton DE65 .... 227 D1
  Hilton DE65 .... 228 B1
  Scropton DE65 .... 226 C2
Vale Cl Bolsover S44 .... 99 D1
  Dronfield S18 .... 57 D1
Vale Dr NG20 .... 119 F1
Vale House Dr SK13 .... 10 A3
Vale Mills DE22 .... 218 C2
Vale Rd Hartshorne DE11 .. 257 D2
  Mansfield Woodhouse NG19 136 A2
  Swadlincote DE11 .... 256 A3
Vale St ST4 .... 269 E2
Vale The DE7 .... 194 C2
Valentine Ave NG16 .... 171 F4
Valerian Cl SK17 .... 85 E4
Valerie Rd DE72 .... 246 A4
Vallance St NG19 .... 136 A2
Valley Cl S45 .... 132 A2
Valley Dr S21 .... 60 B4
Valley Gdns SK14 .... 15 F4
Valley Rd Bolsover S44 ..... 118 A4
  Broadbottom SK14 .... 15 F4
  Chesterfield S41 .... 96 B1
  Clay Cross S45 .... 131 D2
  Common Side S18 .... 75 E2
  Derby, Cherrytree Hill DE21 220 A3
  Derby, Littleover DE23 ..... 218 B1
  Glossop SK13 .... 16 C4
  Hayfield SK22 .... 25 F1
  Ilkeston DE7 .... 208 C3
  Killamarsh S21 .... 60 B4
  Kimberley NG16 .... 195 E4
  Mastin Moor S43 .... 79 E2
  Overseal DE12 .... 262 A2
  Sheffield S8 .... 43 D3
  Shirebrook NG20 .... 119 F3
Valley Rise Common Side S18 75 E2
  Swadlincote DE11 .... 256 A3
Valley View Belper DE56 ... 179 D1
  Ilkeston DE7 .... 208 C3
Valley View Cl
  Chesterfield S41 .... 115 F4
  Eckington S21 .... 59 E1
Valley View Dr DE7 .... 193 D1
Valley View Rd DE55 .... 170 B2
Vancouver Ave DE21 .... 220 B2
Vancouver Dr DE15 .... 248 B3

Vanguard Rd NG10 .... 236 B3
Vanguard Trad Est S40 ..... 115 D4
Varley St DE24 .... 232 B3
Vaughan Pl NG20 .... 119 F3
Vaughan Rd SK23 .... 45 F3
Vaughan Way ST17 .... 269 D3
Vauxhall Ave DE22 .... 218 A4
Venture Cres DE55 .... 159 D1
Verbena Dr DE23 .... 231 E2
Vere Cl DE65 .... 242 A3
Vermont Dr DE21 .... 220 B3
Verney St NG19 .... 134 C4
Verney Way NG19 .... 134 C4
Vernon Ct NG20 .... 120 A2
Vernon Dr Bakewell DE45 . 109 D4
  Derby DE21 .... 220 C2
Vernon Gn DE45 .... 109 D4
Vernon Rd Chesterfield S40 . 95 E2
  Dore S17 .... 55 F3
  Stoke-on-T ST4 .... 269 E2
Vernon Rise S42 .... 115 F1
Vernon St Derby DE1 .... 218 C3
  Ilkeston DE7 .... 194 C2
  11 Nottingham NG1 .... 268 A2
  Shirebrook NG20 .... 120 A2
Vernongate DE1 .... 218 C3
Veronica Dr NG16 .... 195 E4
Vestry Rd DE21 .... 205 F2
Vetchfield Cl DE24 .... 231 F1
Via Gellia Rd DE4 .... 154 B4
Vicar La Chesterfield S40 .. 266 B3
  Tibshelf DE55 .... 148 A3
Vicarage Ave Derby DE23 . 218 C1
  Ilkeston DE7 .... 194 B2
Vicarage Cl Belper DE56 ... 179 D2
  Burton u T DE15 .... 248 A2
  Heath S44 .... 117 D1
  Holmesfield S18 .... 75 D4
  Nottingham NG3 .... 268 B2
  Shirebrook NG20 .... 119 F2
  Smalley DE7 .... 192 C3
  Swanwick DE55 .... 169 F4
Vicarage Ct DE3 .... 217 E1
Vicarage Dr Derby DE21 ... 220 A4
  Stramshall ST14 .... 210 A2
Vicarage Gdns Heanor DE75 181 F1
  Swadlincote DE11 .... 256 B2
Vicarage La
  Ashford in t W DE45 .... 108 C4
  Dore S17 .... 55 E4
  Duffield DE56 .... 190 C2
  Hayfield SK22 .... 25 E1
  Ironville NG16 .... 170 C2
  Little Eaton DE21 .... 205 E4
  Rowsley DE4 .... 110 C1
Vicarage Mews DE55 .... 170 C3
Vicarage Rd Belper DE56 .. 190 C4
  Derby, Chellaston DE73 ... 232 C1
  Derby, Mickleover DE73 .. 217 E1
  Stoke-on-T ST4 .... 269 D2
  Swadlincote DE11 .... 256 B2
  Woodville DE11 .... 256 C1
Vicarage St DE7 .... 194 B2
Vicarage Way ST17 .... 269 D3
Vicarage Wlk DE12 .... 260 B3
Vicarwood Ave Derby DE22 204 C1
  Holbrook DE56 .... 191 E4
Victor Ave DE22 .... 218 C4
Victor Cres NG10 .... 223 E2
Victor Rd S17 .... 55 F4
Victoria Ave
  Borrowash DE72 .... 221 D1
  7 Buxton SK17 .... 85 E4
  Draycott DE72 .... 235 D4
  Hadfield SK13 .... 10 A3
  Heanor DE75 .... 181 E1
  Netherthorpe S43 .... 79 D2
  Nottingham NG2 .... 268 C1
Victoria Cl DE3 .... 217 F2
Victoria Cotts DE55 .... 159 E1
Victoria Cres NG16 .... 170 C2
Victoria Ct Ilkeston DE7 ... 194 C1
  Mansfield NG18 .... 268 B3
  Matlock DE4 .... 143 E3
Victoria Ctr NG1 .... 268 B2
Victoria Dr DE55 .... 147 F1
Victoria Gr S43 .... 96 C3
Victoria Hall Gdns DE4 .... 143 E3
Victoria Park Rd
  Buxton SK17 .... 85 E4
  Calow S43 .... 96 C3
Victoria Rd Bamford S33 .... 40 A2
  Draycott DE72 .... 235 D4
  Pinxton NG16 .... 160 B2
  Ripley DE5 .... 169 E1
  Sandiacre NG10 .... 223 D3
  Selston NG16 .... 171 F3
  Stafford ST16 .... 269 D4
Victoria Sq DE6 .... 173 E1
Victoria St Alfreton DE55 . 159 D2
  Bolsover S44 .... 118 A4
  Brimington S43 .... 77 F1
  Castle Donington DE74 .... 247 D3
  Chesterfield S41 .... 266 B4
  Clay Cross S45 .... 131 E2
  Creswell S80 .... 81 F1
  Derby DE1 .... 267 B3
  Dronfield S18 .... 56 C1
  Glossop SK13 .... 17 E4
  Ilkeston DE7 .... 194 C1
  Ironville NG16 .... 170 C2
  Langley Mill NG16 .... 182 B2
  Long Eaton NG10 .... 236 A3
  Melbourne DE73 .... 252 A4
  New Mills SK22 .... 33 D3

Victoria St continued
Nottingham NG1 .... 268 B1
Ripley DE5 .... 169 F1
Shirebrook NG20 .... 119 F2
Somercotes DE55 .... 170 B4
South Normanton DE55 .... 160 A3
Stafford ST16 .... 269 E4
Stapleford NG9 .... 223 E4
Victoria St N S41 .... 76 C1
Victoria St W S40 .... 95 E1
Victoria Terr DE55 .... 148 A4
Victoria Wlk S42 .... 115 E1
Victory Ave DE5 .... 169 F1
Victory Cl NG10 .... 236 B3
Victory Dr NG19 .... 136 C1
Victory Rd DE24 .... 232 A3
View Rd S2 .... 43 D4
Viewdales Cl DE6 .... 175 F1
Viking Bsns Ctr DE11 .... 256 C2
Vikinglea Cl S2 .... 44 A4
Vikinglea Dr S2 .... 44 A4
Vikinglea Rd S2 .... 44 A4
Villa St Draycott DE72 .... 235 D4
Stoke-on-T ST4 .... 269 E1
Village Com Sch DE23 .... 231 F4
Village Ct DE56 .... 190 C2
Village St DE23 .... 231 F4
Village The Dale DE7 .... 207 F1
West Hallam DE7 .... 207 F4
Villas Rd Bolsover S44 .... 98 C2
Toadmoor DE56 .... 167 F2
Villas The Stoke-on-T ST4 .... 269 E1
Whaley Thorns NG20 .... 101 D2
Villiers Cl S2 .... 43 F3
Villiers Dr S2 .... 43 F3
Vincent Ave Derby DE21 .... 220 C2
Ilkeston DE7 .... 208 C4
Vincent Cl DE56 .... 192 A4
Vincent Cres S40 .... 95 D1
Vincent St DE23 .... 218 C1
Vine Cl DE23 .... 231 D4
Vine Cres NG10 .... 223 D3
Vine Farm Cl DE7 .... 208 B3
Vine Row ST4 .... 269 E1
Vinebank St ST4 .... 269 E1
Viola Cl DE21 .... 206 B2
Violet La DE15 .... 254 C4
Violet Lane Sch DE15 .... 254 C4
Violet St DE23 .... 218 C1
Violet Way DE15 .... 255 D4
Virginsalley La DE6 .... 184 B1
Vista The NG9 .... 223 F3
Vivian St Bolsover S44 .... 98 C3
Derby DE1 .... 219 D4
Vulcan St DE23 .... 219 D1
Vyse Dr NG10 .... 236 B3

Wade Ave Derby DE23 .... 218 B1
Ilkeston DE7 .... 209 D4
Wade Dr DE3 .... 217 F1
Wade St DE23 .... 218 B1
Wadebridge Gr DE24 .... 233 E3
Wadham St ST4 .... 269 E2
Wadhurst Gdns NG3 .... 268 B2
Wadsworth Ave S12 .... 44 B3
Wadsworth Cl S12 .... 44 B3
Wadsworth Dr S12 .... 44 B3
Wadsworth Rd Sheffield S12 .... 44 B3
Stapleford NG9 .... 223 F4
Wagstaff La NG16 .... 171 E3
Wain Ave S42 .... 132 A4
Wain Dr ST4 .... 269 D1
Wain Way S42 .... 132 A4
Waingroves Prim Sch DE5 .... 181 D4
Waingroves Rd
Codnor DE5 .... 181 D3
Ripley DE5 .... 181 D4
Wainwood Rise ST4 .... 269 D1
Wainwright Ave S13 .... 44 B4
Wainwright Cres S13 .... 44 B4
Wakami Cres DE73 .... 233 D2
Wakefield Ave DE13 .... 239 D3
Wakefield Croft DE7 .... 194 B2
Wakelyn Cl DE72 .... 234 C1
Walbrook Rd DE23 .... 218 C1
Walcote Cl DE56 .... 179 E3
Walden Rd S2 .... 43 D4
Waldene Dr DE24 .... 233 D3
Waldley La DE6 .... 211 E4
Waldorf Ave DE24 .... 233 D4
Waldorf Cl DE24 .... 233 D4
Walford Rd Killamarsh S21 .... 60 B3
Rolleston DE13 .... 240 B2
Walgrove Ave S40 .... 95 F1
Walgrove Rd S40 .... 95 E1
Walk Cl DE72 .... 235 D4
Walk Mill Rd SK22 .... 25 E1
Walk The DE56 .... 192 A4
Walkden St NG18 .... 268 B4
Walker Ave DE5 .... 169 F1
Walker Gr NG9 .... 223 F4
Walker La DE1 .... 267 A4
Walker St Hadfield SK13 .... 10 A2
Nottingham NG2 .... 268 C1
Walkers Ave NG16 .... 182 C3
Walkers La S21 .... 60 B3
Wall Ditch DE6 .... 149 D1
Wall Rd DE14 .... 254 A4
Wall St Buxton SK17 .... 85 E4
Ripley DE5 .... 169 E1
Wallace St DE22 .... 218 B3
Wallfields Cl DE65 .... 230 B1
Wallis Cl DE72 .... 235 D4
Wallis Rd NG18 .... 268 C4
Walls La S80 .... 81 D4
Walnut Ave Derby DE24 .... 233 D4
Shireoaks S81 .... 63 F4
Walnut Cl
Aston-on-T DE72 .... 246 A4
Barrow u T DE73 .... 244 A3
Burnaston DE65 .... 229 F3
Derby DE73 .... 245 D4
Ilkeston DE7 .... 209 D4
Repton DE65 .... 243 D1
Swadlincote DE11 .... 256 A3
Walnut Dr S21 .... 60 B3
Walnut Rd DE56 .... 179 D2
Walnut St DE24 .... 232 B4
Walpole St DE21 .... 219 E3
Walseker La S26 .... 61 E4
Walsham Ct DE21 .... 205 E1
Walter Evans CE Prim Sch DE22 .... 204 C1
Walter St Derby DE1 .... 218 C4
Draycott DE72 .... 234 C4
Nottingham NG7 .... 268 A2
Walters Cres NG16 .... 171 E3
Waltham Ave DE24 .... 231 F2
Walthamstow Dr DE22 .... 218 A3
Waltheof Rd S2 .... 44 A4
Walton Ave Derby DE24 .... 232 C2
Nottingham NG2, NG3 .... 268 C2
Walton Back La
Chesterfield S40 .... 114 A4
Holymoorside S42 .... 113 F4
Walton Cl Chesterfield S40 .... 114 A4
Dronfield S18 .... 56 B1
Swadlincote DE11 .... 256 A2
Walton Cres
Ashbourne DE6 .... 173 E1
Chesterfield S40 .... 95 F1
Fenton ST4 .... 269 F1
Walton Ct Sheffield S8 .... 56 C4
West Hallam DE7 .... 207 E4
Walton Dr Chesterfield S40 .... 95 F1
Derby DE23 .... 231 F4
Walton Drive Ct S40 .... 95 F1
Walton Fields Rd S40 .... 95 E1
Walton Hill DE74 .... 247 D2
Walton Hospl S40 .... 114 C4
Walton Rd Chesterfield S40 .... 95 E1
Derby DE21 .... 219 F3
Walton-on-T DE15 .... 254 B3
Walton St NG10 .... 223 E1
Walton Way S42 .... 114 C2
Walton Wlk S40 .... 95 F1
Walton-on-Trent CE Prim Sch DE12 .... 259 E4
Wansbeck Cl NG7 .... 268 A2
Wansfell Cl DE3 .... 217 F1
Wapentake La DE56 .... 165 E1
Warburton Cl S2 .... 43 E4
Warburton Gdns S2 .... 43 E4
Warburton Rd S2 .... 43 E4
Ward Dr DE55 .... 170 B4
Ward La Barlborough S43 .... 80 A4
Disley SK12 .... 32 C2
Ward Pl Mansfield NG18 .... 268 A3
Sheffield S8 .... 43 D4
Ward St Derby DE22 .... 218 C2
Tupton S42 .... 131 E4
Ward's La Breaston DE72 .... 235 E4
King's Newton DE73 .... 245 D1
Melbourne DE73 .... 244 C2
Ward's Yd S40 .... 266 B2
Wardgate Way S40 .... 95 D3
Wardlow Ave DE21 .... 220 A4
Wardlow Cl S40 .... 114 C4
Wardlow Mews SK13 .... 9 E1
Wardlow Rd Ilkeston DE7 .... 194 C2
Sheffield S12 .... 44 B3
Wardwick DE1 .... 267 B3
Warehouse La S33 .... 38 B2
Warhurst Fold 2 SK13 .... 10 A3
Warmbrook DE4 .... 165 F4
Warmbrook Jun Sch SK23 .... 47 E3
Warmbrook Rd SK23 .... 47 E3
Warminster Cl S8 .... 43 D2
Warminster Cres S8 .... 43 D2
Warminster Dr S8 .... 43 D2
Warminster Gdns S8 .... 43 D2
Warminster Pl S8 .... 43 D1
Warminster Rd S8 .... 43 D2
Warmwells La DE5 .... 180 B3
Warner St Chesterfield S41 .... 266 C1
Derby, Mickleover DE3 .... 217 E1
Derby, St Luke's DE22 .... 218 C2
Warney Rd DE4 .... 127 E1
Warren Ave NG9 .... 223 E4
Warren Ave Extension NG9 .... 223 E4
Warren Cl Burton u T DE13 .... 240 C1
Pilsley S45 .... 132 B1
Warren Cres S21 .... 58 C1
Warren Ct NG9 .... 223 E4
Warren Dr DE12 .... 261 E3
Warren La Branston DE14 .... 253 F4
Castle Donington DE74 .... 236 A1
Warren Lea SK6 .... 15 D1
Warren Rise S18 .... 57 E2
Warren St DE24 .... 232 C4
Warren Wlk S21 .... 58 C1
Warrendale Ct DE73 .... 233 D1
Warser Gate NG1 .... 268 B1
Warsop Rd NG19 .... 136 B2
Warsop Vale Jun Mix & Inf Sch NG20 .... 120 B2
Warwick Ave DE23 .... 218 B1
Warwick Cl Branston DE14 .... 253 F4
Glossop SK13 .... 17 F4
Swadlincote DE11 .... 256 C3
Warwick Dr DE7 .... 194 B2
Warwick Gdns DE56 .... 179 E3
Warwick Rd
Long Eaton NG10 .... 237 D4
Somercotes DE55 .... 159 E1
Warwick St
Chesterfield S40 .... 115 D4
Derby DE24 .... 219 E1
Wasdale Ave S20 .... 59 F3
Wash Gn DE56, DE4 .... 166 A4
Wash House La S40 .... 95 E1
Washbrook La DE6 .... 161 F2
Washford Rd DE65 .... 228 C1
Washhouse Bottom SK17 .... 69 F4
Washington Ave DE21 .... 220 A3
Washington Cl DE73 .... 252 A4
Washington Dr
Mansfield NG18 .... 268 A3
Stapleford NG9 .... 209 F1
Wasnidge Cl NG3 .... 268 B2
Watburn Rd SK22 .... 24 B1
Water La Bakewell DE45 .... 109 E3
Bamford S33 .... 40 A2
Bolsover S44 .... 117 F4
Cromford DE4 .... 155 D3
Eyam S32 .... 71 F3
Hollingworth SK14 .... 9 E3
Mansfield NG19 .... 135 D2
Middleton (Nr Wirksworth) DE4 .... 154 B3
South Normanton DE55 .... 160 A3
Stony Houghton NG19 .... 118 C1
Tideswell SK17 .... 68 C3
Wirksworth DE4 .... 165 F4
Water Meadow La S40 .... 95 D4
Water Meadows The DE73 .... 244 B3
Water Orton Cl NG9 .... 223 F2
Water St Bakewell DE45 .... 109 E3
Buxton SK17 .... 85 D4
Glossop SK13 .... 10 C1
Stafford ST16 .... 269 E4
Stoke-on-T ST4 .... 269 E1
Watercress La S45 .... 131 E1
Waterfoot Cotts SK14 .... 9 D2
Waterfoot La SK23 .... 45 E3
Waterford Dr DE21 .... 220 A2
Watergo La DE23 .... 230 C4
Watering La DE56 .... 191 E3
Wateringbury Gr S43 .... 78 C1
Waterloo Cl DE55 .... 160 B4
Waterloo Cres NG7 .... 268 A2
Waterloo Ct DE1 .... 267 C5
Waterloo La NG9 .... 209 F3
Waterloo Pl DE11 .... 256 A2
Waterloo Prom NG7 .... 268 A2
Waterloo Rd
Matlock Bath DE4 .... 143 D1
Nottingham NG7 .... 268 A2
Waterloo St
Bramley-Vale S44 .... 117 F1
Clay Cross S45 .... 131 E2
Watermeade S21 .... 59 D1
Watermeadow Cl NG19 .... 136 B3
Watermeadow Rd DE24 .... 233 D3
Watermeadows The NG10 .... 236 A4
Waterpark Rd DE6 .... 224 A4
Waters Edge SK6 .... 23 D4
Waterside Baslow DE45 .... 91 E3
Burton u T DE15 .... 254 C4
Hadfield SK13 .... 10 A3
Ironville NG16 .... 170 C2
Marple SK6 .... 23 D3
Waterside Cl Derby DE22 .... 205 D1
Sandiacre NG10 .... 223 D2
Waterside Jun Sch DE15 .... 254 C4
Waterside Rd
Burton u T DE15 .... 254 B4
Disley SK12 .... 32 C4
New Mills SK22 .... 32 C4
Walton-on-T DE15 .... 254 B4
Waterswallows La SK17 .... 66 C2
Waterswallows Rd SK17 .... 66 C1
Waterthorpe Cl 9 S20 .... 59 F4
Waterthorpe Cres S20 .... 59 F4
Waterthorpe Gdns 6 S20 .... 59 F4
Waterthorpe Glade S20 .... 59 F4
Waterthorpe Glen 8 S20 .... 59 F4
Waterthorpe Rise 7 S20 .... 59 F4
Waterway The NG10 .... 223 E2
Watery La Ashbourne DE6 .... 184 C4
Bretby DE15 .... 249 E2
Clifton DE6 .... 184 C4
Ellastone DE6 .... 183 D2
Scropton DE65 .... 226 C1
Swadlincote DE11 .... 255 E3
Thurvaston DE6 .... 215 E3
Watford Bridge Ind Est SK22 .... 24 B1
Watford Bridge Rd SK22 .... 24 B1
Watford La SK22 .... 24 B1
Watford Rd Buxton SK17 .... 84 C4
New Mills SK22 .... 24 B1
Watford St ST4 .... 269 F2
Watkin Ave SK13 .... 9 F2
Watkin St Fenton ST4 .... 269 F1
Nottingham NG3 .... 268 B2
Watkinson St DE75 .... 181 E1
Watnall Cres NG19 .... 268 A4
Watson Ave Heanor DE75 .... 181 F1
Mansfield NG18 .... 268 C4
Watson La S42 .... 114 B2
Watson Rd DE7 .... 194 B1
Watson St Derby DE1 .... 218 C3
Derby DE1 .... 218 C4
Stoke-on-T ST4 .... 269 E2
Watten Cl DE24 .... 231 F1
Watts Gn DE45 .... 108 C4
Waveney Cl DE22 .... 205 D3
Waverley House Sch NG7 .... 268 A2
Waverley St Derby DE24 .... 232 B4
Long Eaton NG10 .... 236 C4
Nottingham NG7 .... 268 A2
Tibshelf DE55 .... 148 A4
Wayfaring Rd DE21 .... 206 A1
Wayford Ave S41 .... 266 C1
Wayside S43 .... 96 B4
Wayside Cl S42 .... 132 A4
Wayside Ct S43 .... 96 B4
Wayzgoose Dr DE21 .... 219 E3
Weaddow La DE45 .... 124 C1
Weakland Cl S12 .... 44 C2
Weakland Cres S12 .... 44 C2
Weakland Dr S12 .... 44 C2
Weakland Way S12 .... 44 C2
Weather Hill La HD7 .... 3 F4
Weathern Field DE12 .... 261 E3
Weaver Cl Ashbourne DE6 .... 185 E4
Crich DE4 .... 156 C1
Weaver Rd ST14 .... 210 A1
Weavers Cl Belper DE56 .... 179 E3
Borrowash DE72 .... 221 E1
Weavers Gn DE3 .... 217 E1
Weavers The ST14 .... 196 B3
Weaving Ave S33 .... 38 B1
Webster Ave NG16 .... 182 C1
Webster Croft S41 .... 77 D1
Webster Ct S40 .... 95 F3
Webster St DE1 .... 267 A2
Wedgewood Cl DE15 .... 248 A1
Wedneshough SK14 .... 9 E3
Weekday Cross NG1 .... 268 B1
Weighbridge Rd NG18 .... 268 C3
Weightman Dr NG16 .... 195 D4
Weir Bank DE15 .... 254 C3
Weirfield Rd DE22 .... 205 D1
Weirside DE6 .... 184 B4
Welbeck Ave Buxton SK17 .... 85 E3
Ilkeston DE7 .... 208 B3
Welbeck Cl 23 Dronfield S18 .... 56 B1
Nottingham NG3 .... 268 B2
Staveley S43 .... 97 E3
Welbeck Ct S43 .... 80 C2
Welbeck Dr S42 .... 114 C2
Welbeck Gdns NG9 .... 223 F2
Welbeck Gr DE22 .... 204 B2
Welbeck Rd Bolsover S44 .... 99 D1
Long Eaton NG10 .... 223 E2
Mansfield Woodhouse NG19 .... 136 B2
Welbeck St Creswell S80 .... 81 F1
Mansfield NG18 .... 268 B4
Whitwell S80 .... 82 A3
Welbury Gdns S20 .... 59 F3
Welby St ST4 .... 269 F1
Welch Ave NG9 .... 223 F4
Welch St ST4 .... 269 E2
Welfare Ave S40 .... 95 E2
Welfare Cl NG20 .... 119 F2
Welfitt Gr NG20 .... 101 D1
Well Banks DE6 .... 165 D1
Well Cl DE6 .... 175 F2
Well Gate SK13 .... 10 C1
Well La Belper DE56 .... 190 C4
Blackfordby DE11 .... 257 D1
Holymoorside S42 .... 112 C4
Repton DE65 .... 242 B1
Shirland DE55 .... 146 B2
Well Rd S8 .... 43 D3
Well Row SK14 .... 16 A4
Well Spring Cl 6 S43 .... 96 C4
Well St Brassington DE4 .... 152 C1
Derby DE1 .... 267 B5
Elton DE4 .... 140 C4
New Mills SK22 .... 33 D4
Ripley DE5 .... 169 E1
Welland Cl Burton u T DE15 .... 248 A3
Derby DE3 .... 217 E2
Welland Rd DE65 .... 228 B1
Wellcarr Rd S8 .... 43 D1
Wellcroft Cl NG18 .... 268 A3
Welldon St DE5 .... 181 D2
Weller St ST4 .... 269 D2
Wellesley Ave DE23 .... 231 E4
Wellfield DE4 .... 143 E3
Wellfield Cl S12 .... 44 C1
Wellfield St DE4 .... 143 E3
Wellgate La DE45 .... 109 D1
Wellhead Rd S8 .... 43 D3
Wellington Cir 1 NG1 .... 268 A1
Wellington Cl DE4 .... 143 E4
Wellington Cres DE1 .... 267 D2
Wellington Ct DE56 .... 178 C2
Wellington Pl NG16 .... 182 C1
Wellington Rd DE14 .... 253 F4
Wellington Sq NG7 .... 268 A2
Wellington St
Chesterfield S43 .... 77 E2
Derby DE1 .... 267 D2
Eastwood NG16 .... 182 C2
Heanor DE75 .... 181 E2
Long Eaton NG10 .... 223 E1
Matlock DE4 .... 143 E3
Nottingham NG3 .... 268 B2
Ripley DE5 .... 169 F1
Stapleford NG9 .... 223 E3
Wellington Villas NG7 .... 268 A2
Wells Cl NG19 .... 136 B2
Wells Ct DE23 .... 230 C4
Wells Rd DE3 .... 217 F1
Wells St S44 .... 118 B4
Wellspring Cl
Barlborough S43 .... 80 A3
Wingerworth S42 .... 115 D2
Wellspring Dale NG9 .... 223 F3
Wellwood Rd DE11 .... 256 A3
Welney Cl DE3 .... 230 B4
Welshpool Pl S40 .... 95 E2
Welshpool Rd DE21 .... 205 E1
Welwyn Ave
Derby, Allestree DE24 .... 204 B2
Derby, Alleton DE24 .... 232 C2
Mansfield Woodhouse NG19 .... 136 C2
Welwyn Cl Chesterfield S40 .... 95 E2
Sheffield S12 .... 44 A2
Welwyn Rd S12 .... 44 A2
Wembley Gdns DE22 .... 218 A3
Wendover Cl DE3 .... 217 E1
Wenham La NG17 .... 148 C2
Wenlock Cl Chesterfield S40 .... 95 E2
Derby DE3 .... 217 F1
Eastwood NG16 .... 195 E4
Wenlock Cres S40 .... 95 E2
Wenlock Dr S42 .... 115 F2
Wensley Dr DE21 .... 220 C2
Wensley Rd
North Wingfield S42 .... 131 F3
Winster DE4 .... 141 E3
Wensley Way S43 .... 97 E4
Wensleydale Cl NG19 .... 136 C1
Wensleydale Rd NG10 .... 236 A3
Wensleydale Wlk DE24 .... 233 E4
Wentworth Ave S40 .... 114 C4
Wentworth Cl Derby DE3 .... 217 F1
Mansfield NG19 .... 136 C1
Wentworth Croft DE75 .... 182 A2
Wentworth Ct NG16 .... 195 F3
Wentworth Dr DE13 .... 240 B1
Wentworth Rd S8 .... 56 C4
Wentworth St DE7 .... 195 D1
Werburgh Cl DE21 .... 220 B2
Werburgh St DE22 .... 218 C2
Werneth Low Ctry Pk SK14 .... 15 D4
Werneth Low Rd SK14 .... 15 D3
Werneth Rd SK13 .... 17 D4
Wesley La DE72 .... 221 E3
Wesley Pl NG9 .... 223 F4
Wesley Rd Ambergate DE56 .... 167 F2
Derby DE24 .... 233 D3
Stonebroom DE55 .... 146 C2
Wesley St Glossop SK13 .... 10 C1
Hadfield SK13 .... 10 A3
Ilkeston DE7 .... 194 C2
Langley Mill NG16 .... 182 B2
Wesleyan Chapel Wlk NG9 .... 223 E4
Wessex Gdns S17 .... 55 E3
Wessington Dr S43 .... 97 E4
Wessington La DE55 .... 158 A3
Wessington Mews
Derby DE22 .... 204 C1
Gamesley SK13 .... 9 F1
Wessington Prim Sch DE55 .... 157 F4
West Ave
Derby, Chellaston DE73 .... 232 C2
Derby, Little Chester DE1 .... 267 A4
Draycott DE72 .... 234 C4
Hilton DE65 .... 228 B1
Ripley DE5 .... 169 E1
Sandiacre NG10 .... 223 D3
Stapleford NG9 .... 223 F4
Stoke-on-T ST4 .... 269 D2
West Bank Matlock Bath DE4 .... 143 D1
Stoke-on-T ST4 .... 269 E1
Toadmoor DE56 .... 168 A1
Winster DE4 .... 141 D3
West Bank Ave Crich DE4 .... 156 C1
Derby DE22 .... 218 C4
Mansfield NG18, NG19 .... 268 B4
West Bank Cl DE22 .... 218 C4
West Bank Lea NG19 .... 136 A1
West Bank Link NG19 .... 136 A1
West Bank Rd DE22 .... 204 C3
West Bank Wynd NG18 .... 268 B4
West Bars S40 .... 266 A3
West Cl Derby DE22 .... 204 C1
Stafford ST 16 .... 269 F4
West Cres
Long Duckmanton S44 .... 98 A3
Matlock DE4 .... 143 D3
West Croft Ave DE23 .... 231 E3
West Croft Cl DE45 .... 125 D3
West Dr Derby DE3 .... 217 E1
Doveridge DE6 .... 211 D1
Tintwistle SK13 .... 9 F4
West Edge Cl S45 .... 129 E2
West End Alfreton DE55 .... 159 D2
Barlborough S43 .... 80 A4
Brassington DE4 .... 152 C1
Broadbottom SK14 .... 15 F4
Elton DE4 .... 140 C3
Pinxton NG16 .... 160 B2
Wirksworth DE4 .... 165 F4
West End Cl DE55 .... 159 D2
West End Cres DE7 .... 208 B4
West End Dr Ilkeston DE7 .... 208 B4
Shardlow DE72 .... 234 C1
West End St NG9 .... 223 E3
West End View S21 .... 59 E1
West Gate Holme HD7 .... 3 F4
Long Eaton NG10 .... 236 C4
Mansfield NG18 .... 268 B4
West Gr DE24 .... 232 B3
West Hill Codnor DE5 .... 181 D4
Mansfield NG18 .... 268 B4
West Hill Ave NG18 .... 268 B4
West Hill Dr NG18 .... 268 B4
West Hill Pk NG19 .... 136 A2
West Hill Way NG18 .... 268 B4
West Lawn DE65 .... 230 B1
West Lea S40 .... 95 D1
West Lea Cotts S43 .... 80 B2
West Lees Rd S33 .... 40 A2
West Nottingham Coll of F Ed NG18 .... 268 B4
West Par ST4 .... 269 F1

West Park Com Sch DE21 . **220 B3**
West Park Rd DE22 .... 218 C4
West Rd Buxton SK17 .... 85 D3
  Derby DE21 .... 220 B3
West Row DE22 .... 205 D1
West Service Rd DE21 .... 220 A2
West St Bramley-Vale S44 .... 117 E1
  Burton u T DE15 .... 248 A2
  Chesterfield S40 .... 266 A4
  Clay Cross S45 .... 131 D2
  Clowne S43 .... 81 D3
  Creswell S80 .... 81 E1
  Dronfield S18 .... 56 C1
  Eckington S21 .... 59 E1
  Heanor DE75 .... 181 E1
  Ilkeston DE7 .... 208 C4
  Langley Mill NG16 .... 182 A2
  Nottingham NG2 .... 268 C1
  Somercotes DE55 .... 170 B3
  South Normanton DE55 .... 159 F3
  Stonebroom DE55 .... 146 C2
  Swadlincote DE11 .... 256 A2
  Tintwistle SK13 .... 9 F4
  Warsop Vale NG20 .... 120 B2
  Whaley Thorns NG20 .... 101 D2
West Terr **8** DE7 .... 194 C1
West View Barlborough S43 ... 80 A3
  Bolsover S44 .... 118 A4
  Mayfield DE6 .... 184 B3
  Rocester ST14 .... 197 D2
  Staveley S43 .... 78 B1
West View Ave DE23 .... 231 D4
West View Cl S17 .... 55 F3
West View La S17 .... 55 F3
West View Rd S41 .... 95 F3
West Way DE55 .... 159 E1
West Way ST17 .... 269 D3
West Way Gn ST17 .... 269 D3
Westacre Dr DE11 .... 255 F1
Westbank Cl S18 .... 57 D2
Westbourne Ave DE55 .... 147 D2
Westbourne Gr S40 .... 95 D2
Westbourne Pk DE22 .... 217 F4
Westbridge Rd S43 .... 80 A4
Westbrook Cl
  Chapel-en-le-F SK23 .... 47 E3
  Chesterfield S40 .... 94 C1
Westbrook Dr S40 .... 94 C1
Westbrook Specl Sch
  NG10 .... **236 B4**
Westbury Gdns DE56 .... 179 E3
Westbury St DE22 .... 218 C2
Westby La Awsworth NG16 .. 195 E2
  Kimberley NG16 .... 195 E2
Westcroft Cres S20 .... 59 E4
Westcroft Dr S20 .... 59 E4
Westcroft Gdns S20 .... 59 E4
Westcroft Glen S20 .... 59 E4
Westcroft Gr S20 .... 59 E4
Westcross Ave NG9 .... 223 F4
Westdale Cl NG10 .... 236 A3
Westdale Rd
  Mansfield NG19 .... 136 A1
  Westwood NG16 .... 171 E2
Westdene Ave DE24 .... 232 B3
Westerlands NG9 .... 223 F3
Western Ave DE55 .... 169 E4
Western Dr DE75 .... 193 F4
Western La SK23 .... 46 A4
Western Rd
  Derby, Mickleover DE3 ..... 217 F1
  Derby, Rose Hill DE23 ...... 219 D2
Western Terr NG7 .... 268 A1
Westfield Ave
  Chesterfield S40 .... 95 D1
  Heanor DE75 .... 181 F1
Westfield Bank S43 .... 80 A4
Westfield Campus S20 .... **59 E4**
Westfield Cl Chesterfield S40 .. 95 D1
  Ilkeston DE7 .... 208 B3
  Mansfield NG19 .... 268 A4
Westfield Cres S20 .... 59 E4
Westfield Ctr S20 .... 59 E4
Westfield Dr Blackwell DE55 . 147 F1
  Ilkeston DE7 .... 194 B1
  Mansfield NG19 .... 268 A4
Westfield Gdns S40 .... 95 D1
Westfield Inf Sch S40 .... **95 D1**
Westfield La Barlborough S43 . 79 F4
  Mansfield NG19 .... 268 A4
  Middle Handley S21 .... 77 F4
Westfield Northway S20 ... 59 F4
Westfield Rd Dronfield S18 ... 76 B4
  Killamarsh S21 .... 60 B3
  Swadlincote DE11 .... 256 A3
Westfield Southway S20 .... 59 F4
Westgate St NG3 .... 268 C2
Westgreen Ave DE24 .... 232 B3
Westhall Rd DE3 .... 217 E2
Westhead Ave ST 16 .... 269 F4
Westhill La S42 .... 115 F2
Westhorpe Ave NG2 .... 268 C1
Westhorpe Dr NG10 .... 236 B4
Westhouses Prim Sch
  DE55 .... **147 E1**
Westland Dr NG16 .... 160 B2
Westland Gdns S20 .... 59 E4
Westland Gr **3** S20 .... 59 F4
Westland Rd S20 .... 59 F4
Westland St S14 .... 269 E2
Westleigh NG19 .... 136 B3
Westleigh Ave DE22 .... 218 B3
Westleigh Ct S40 .... 95 F3
Westley Cres DE21 .... 191 E1
Westminster Ave NG10 .... 223 F4
Westminster St DE24 .... 232 C4
Westmoor Rd S43 .... 96 C2
Westmorland Cl DE21 .... 219 E3

Westmorland Way NG16 .. 171 D2
Weston Bank DE6 .... 211 F4
Weston Cl S40 .... 95 D3
Weston Cres NG10 .... 235 F2
Weston Park Ave DE24 .... 232 C2
Weston Park Gdns DE24 .. 232 B2
Weston Rd Aston-on-T DE72 246 A4
  Stafford ST16, ST18 .... 269 F4
  Weston-on-T DE72 .... 245 F3
Weston Rise DE72 .... 245 D4
Weston Spot Cl DE5 .... 180 B4
Weston St Heanor DE75 .... 194 A4
  Swadlincote DE11 .... 256 A2
**Weston-on-Trent
Parochial Prim Sch**
  DE72 .... **245 F2**
Westthorpe Rd S21 .... 60 B3
Westward Cl ST14 .... 210 A1
Westwell Pl S20 .... 59 E3
Westwick Cres S8 .... 56 B4
Westwick Gr S8 .... 56 C4
Westwick La S42 .... 94 B1
Westwick Rd S8 .... 56 C4
Westwick St DE7 .... 209 D3
Westwood Ave S43 .... 97 E4
Westwood Cl S43 .... 97 E3
Westwood Dr Derby DE4 ... 232 B3
  Staveley S43 .... 97 E3
Westwood La S43 .... 96 C2
Westwood Pk DE11 .... 255 F3
Westwood Rd Calow S44 .... 97 D2
  Nottingham NG2 .... 268 C1
Wetherby Cl NG16 .... 195 F4
Wetherby Rd DE24 .... 232 C4
Wetherel Rd DE15 .... 248 B1
Wetlands La S44 .... 96 C2
Weyacres DE72 .... 221 E1
Weybridge Cl DE7 .... 207 E4
Whaley Bridge Prim Sch
  SK23 .... **45 F4**
Whaley Bridge Sta SK23 ... **45 F4**
Whaley Comm S44 .... 100 B2
Whaley La SK23 .... 45 E4
Whaley Rd NG20 .... 100 C1
**Whaley Thorns Heritage
Ctr** NG20 .... **101 D2**
Whaley Thorns Prim Sch
  NG20 .... **101 D2**
Whalley Ave ST4 .... 269 D1
Wharf La Chesterfield S41 .. 266 B4
  Staveley S43 .... 78 C2
Wharf Pl ST4 .... 269 F2
Wharf Rd Nottingham NG7 . 268 A1
  Pinxton NG16 .... 160 B1
  Whaley Bridge SK23 .... 45 F4
Wharf The DE72 .... 235 D1
Wharfdale Rd NG10 .... 236 A3
Wharfedale Cl DE22 .... 205 D2
Wharmby Ave NG19 .... 135 E2
Wharncliffe Cl SK13 .... 9 F2
Wharncliffe Rd DE7 .... 208 C4
Whatstandwell Sta DE4 ... 156 B1
Wheal La Sheldon SK17 .... 107 E4
  Taddington SK17 .... 107 E4
Wheatbridge Rd S40 .... 266 A3
Wheatcroft SK13 .... 9 F2
Wheatcroft Cl
  Clay Cross S45 .... 131 E1
  Wingerworth S42 .... 115 D2
Wheatcroft La S44 .... 156 C4
Wheatcroft Way DE21 ..... 205 E1
Wheatfield Cres NG19 .... 136 C3
Wheatfield Way S40 .... 94 C3
Wheathill Cl Calow S43 ..... 96 C2
  Chesterfield S40 .... 94 C3
Wheathill La S41 .... 96 B2
Wheatland Cl DE24 .... 231 E1
Wheatlands DE11 .... 256 A4
Wheatlands La DE45 .... 91 E3
Wheatlands Rd
  Burton u T DE15 .... 254 C4
  Wingerworth S42 .... 114 C2
Wheatley Ave
  Somercotes DE55 .... 159 E1
  Stoke-on-T ST4 .... 269 D1
Wheatley Cl NG19 .... 136 C1
Wheatley Gdns DE4 .... 127 E1
Wheatley La DE15 .... 248 B2
Wheatley Rd DE4 .... 127 E2
Wheatsheaf Cl DE21 .... 206 B1
Wheatsheaf La DE4 .... 156 C1
Wheatsheaf Rd SK23 .... 45 F3
Wheeldon Ave
  Belper DE56 .... 179 D2
  Derby DE22 .... 218 C4
Wheeldon Cres S43 .... 96 B4
Wheeldon Way DE6 .... 175 F2
Wheeler Gate NG1 .... 268 B1
Whenby Cl DE3 .... 217 E1
Whernside Cl DE24 .... 233 E3
Wheston Bank SK17 .... 69 D3
Whetmorhurst Rd SK6 ...... 23 F2
Whieldon Cres ST4 .... 269 F1
Whieldon Rd ST4 .... 269 F1
Whilton Cres DE7 .... 207 E4
Whilton Ct DE56 .... 179 C2
Whinacre Cl S8 .... 57 D3
Whinacre Pl S8 .... 57 D3
Whinacre Wlk S8 .... 57 D3
Whinbush Ave DE4 .... 232 C3
Whinney Bank NG19 .... 136 B2
Whinney Hill NG19 .... 136 B2
Whiston St DE23 .... 219 D1
Whitaker Gdns DE23 .... 218 C1
Whitaker Rd DE23 .... 218 C1
Whitaker St DE23 .... 219 D1
Whitburn Rd NG9 .... 223 F2
Whitby Ave DE21 .... 205 E1

Whitcombe Pl DE5 .... 169 E1
White Edge Cl S40 .... 95 E3
White Edge Dr DE45 .... 91 F3
White Gate Rd HD7 .... 3 E4
White Gates DE5 .... 181 D4
White Hart St NG18 .... 268 B4
White Hart Yd DE56 .... 191 F4
White Knowle Pk SK17 ...... 85 E3
White Knowle Rd SK17 ...... 85 E3
White La Highlane S12 .... 44 B1
  Sheffield S12 .... 44 B1
  Shottle DE56 .... 177 E2
White Leas S40 .... 95 D2
White Leas Ave S42 .... 132 A4
White Lion Sq DE7 .... 208 C4
White Lion St ST17 .... 269 E3
White Lodge La DE45 .... 91 F3
White Rd
  Netherthorpe S43 .... 79 D2
  New Mills SK22 .... 24 B1
White St DE22 .... 218 C4
White Thorns Cl S8 .... 57 D3
White Thorns Dr S8 .... 57 D3
White Thorns View S8 .... 57 D3
White Tor Rd DE4 .... 143 E1
White Woods Way DE4 .... 143 D2
White's La DE55 .... 170 A4
Whitebank Cl S41 .... 266 C1
Whitecarr La
  Ashover DE55 .... 145 D2
  Brackenfield DE55 .... 145 D2
Whitecotes Cl S40 .... 114 C4
Whitecotes La S40 .... 114 C4
Whitecotes Pk S40 .... 114 C4
Whitecotes Prim Sch S40 **114 C4**
Whitecroft Rd SK6 .... 23 E1
Whitecross Ave SK17 .... 69 E2
Whitecross Gdns DE1 ...... 218 C4
Whitecross Rd SK17 .... 69 E3
Whitecross St DE1 .... 218 C3
Whitefield La Ashover S45 . 129 D3
  Chelmorton SK17 .... 106 B4
Whitehall Terr SK23 .... 34 B1
Whitehead Cl DE7 .... 194 B1
Whitehead Dr NG16 .... 182 B4
Whitehead St S43 .... 78 C1
Whitehough Head La SK23 . 46 C4
Whitehouse CI DE24 .... 232 B2
Whitehouse Rise DE56 .... 178 C3
Whitehouses S41 .... 266 C1
Whitehurst St DE24 .... 232 B4
Whitelea La DE4 .... 144 A3
Whiteleas Rd SK23 .... 45 E2
Whiteley Rd DE5 .... 180 C4
Whitelow La Dore S17 .... 55 D4
  Ible DE4 .... 153 F4
Whitely Cl NG9 .... 223 F4
Whitemoor Hall DE56 ...... 179 E3
Whitemoor La DE56 .... 179 E3
Whites Cl DE55 .... 159 D1
Whites Croft View S43 .... 80 A3
Whiteway DE22 .... 204 C1
Whitewell Gdns DE24 ...... 233 E3
Whitewells La DE56 .... 178 B4
Whitewells Rd DE56 .... 167 F1
Whitfield Ave SK13 .... 17 E4
Whitfield CE Prim Sch
  SK13 .... **17 D4**
Whitfield Cross SK13 .... 17 E4
Whitfield La DE45 .... 124 C1
Whitfield Pk SK13 .... 17 E4
Whiting Ave NG9 .... 223 F1
Whiting St S8 .... 43 D3
Whitle Bank Rd SK22 .... 24 A1
Whitle Rd SK22 .... 24 B1
Whitley Way DE6 .... 185 F4
Whitmore Ave S42 .... 115 F1
Whitmore Rd DE21 .... 219 F3
Whitstable Cl DE23 .... 231 E4
Whittaker La DE21 .... 191 E1
Whitting Mews S41 .... 76 C1
Whitting Valley Rd S41 ..... 77 D1
Whittington Hall Hospl
  S41 .... **77 E2**
Whittington Hill S41 .... 77 D1
Whittington La S41 .... 76 C3
Whittington Rd
  Chesterfield S43 .... 77 F2
  Staveley S43 .... 77 F2
Whittington St DE24 .... 232 B3
Whittington Way S41 .... 77 D1
Whittlebury Dr DE23 .... 230 C4
Whitton Pl S44 .... 98 A3
Whitwell Rd S80 .... 63 D2
Whitworth Ave DE4 .... 127 E2
Whitworth Hospl DE4 ..... **142 C4**
Whitworth Rd
  Chesterfield S41 .... 96 A3
  Darley Dale DE4 .... 127 D2
  Ilkeston DE7 .... 208 C3
  Northwood DE4 .... 127 D2
Whiwell Prim Sch S80 ..... **82 A3**
Whysall St DE75 .... 181 F1
Whyteleafe Gr DE21 .... 206 A1
Wickens Pl S43 .... 79 D2
Wickersley Cl DE22 .... 204 C1
Wickets The DE15 .... 254 C4
Wickfield Cl S12 .... 44 C3
Wickfield Dr S12 .... 44 C3
Wickfield Gr S12 .... 44 C3
Wickfield Pl S12 .... 44 C3
Wickfield Rd S12 .... 44 C3
Wicksteed Cl DE56 .... 179 E3
Widdop Cl S13 .... 44 B4
Widdop Croft S13 .... 44 B4
Widdybank Cl DE22 .... 204 B1
Wideshaft DE11 .... 256 B2
Widmerpool St NG16 ...... 160 B1

Wigley Cl NG3 .... 268 C2
Wigley Prim Sch S42 .... **93 F2**
Wigley Rd S43 .... 97 E3
Wigmore Cl DE3 .... 217 E2
Wilberforce Rd NG19 ...... 135 E1
Wilbury Dr S12 .... 44 A3
Wilcox Ave NG19 .... 136 A3
Wild Hill NG17 .... 148 C4
Wild La DE4 .... 157 D2
Wild St DE22 .... 218 B3
Wildaygreen La S18 .... 75 D1
Wilderbrook La DE56 .... 178 A4
Wilders Lea Ct DE56 .... 179 D1
Wildhay La DE6 .... 183 E4
Wildman St NG7 .... 268 A2
Wildpark La DE6 .... 202 B3
Wildsmith St DE24 .... 233 D4
Wilford Rd NG2 .... 268 B1
Wilford St NG2 .... 268 B1
Wilfred Pl ST4 .... 269 D2
Wilfred St DE23 .... 219 D1
Wilhallow La NG16 .... 171 F1
Wilkin Hill S18 .... 75 F1
Wilkins Dr DE24 .... 232 C4
Wilkinson Cl
  Chesterfield S40 .... 115 D3
  Pleasley NG19 .... 135 D3
Wilkinson Dr S43 .... 97 D4
Will Shore's La DE4 .... 142 B3
Willcock Rd DE14 .... 254 A4
Willerbley Rd DE4 .... 143 E1
Willersley Ct **3** S41 .... 95 E4
Willersley Rd DE4 .... 155 E4
Willesden Ave DE22 .... 218 A4
Willetts Rd DE21 .... 220 A4
William Allitt Sch DE11 .... **255 F4**
William Ave NG16 .... 182 C1
William Booth Inf Sch
  NG2 .... **268 C1**
William Cl S20 .... 59 E3
William Cres S20 .... 59 E3
**William Gilbert Endowed
Prim Sch** DE56 .... **190 C2**
**William Howitt Jun Com
Sch** DE75 .... **181 E1**
William Levick Prim Sch
  S18 .... **56 B1**
William Lilley Inf Sch
  NG9 .... **223 E3**
William Nadins Way DE11 . 255 F2
William Newton Cl DE65 .. 241 D3
William Rd NG9 .... 223 E4
William Rhodes Prim Sch
  S40 .... **266 A1**
**William Shrewsbury Prim
Sch** DE13 .... **240 C1**
William St Belper DE56 .... 178 C2
  Chesterfield S41 .... 96 A3
  Derby DE1 .... 218 C3
  Eckington S21 .... 59 E2
  Long Eaton NG10 .... 223 E1
William St N S41 .... 76 C1
Williams Cl DE55 .... 170 B3
Williamson Ave SK17 .... 66 B1
Williamson Cres SK23 .... 45 E4
Williamson Rd SK23 .... 45 E4
Williamson St NG19 .... 268 A4
Williamthorpe Cl S42 ...... 132 A4
Williamthorpe Ind Pk
  S42 .... **116 B1**
Williamthorpe Rd S42 ..... 132 A4
Willington Prim Sch
  DE65 .... **242 A3**
Willington Rd Etwall DE65 . 229 E2
  Findern DE65 .... 242 B4
  Repton DE65 .... 242 A2
Willington Sta DE65 .... **242 A3**
Willn St DE23 .... 218 C1
Willoughby Ave NG10 ..... 223 E2
Willoughby Cl DE72 .... 235 F4
Willoughby St DE7 .... 195 D1
Willow Ave
  Long Eaton NG10 .... 223 E1
  Ripley DE5 .... 180 B4
  Shirebrook NG20 .... 119 E3
  Stapleford NG9 .... 223 E3
Willow Brook Cl DE65 ..... 228 B1
Willow Cl Alfreton DE55 ... 159 D3
  Aston-on-T DE72 .... 246 A4
  Creswell S80 .... 81 F1
  Derby DE72 .... 204 C1
  Pilsley S45 .... 132 B1
  South Normanton DE55 ... 160 A3
Willow Croft DE24 .... 233 E2
Willow Ct S44 .... 97 D2
Willow Dr
  Chapel-en-le-F SK23 .... 47 D3
  Mastin Moor S43 .... 79 E2
  Swadlincote DE11 .... 255 F4
Willow Farm Ct DE65 ...... 230 B1
Willow Garth Rd S41 .... 95 E4
Willow Gr Belper DE56 ..... 179 D1
  Willington DE65 .... 242 A3
Willow Meadow Rd DE6 .. 185 E4
Willow Pl DE15 .... 254 C4
Willow Rd
  Castle Donington DE74 .... 247 D3
  Killamarsh S21 .... 60 B3
Willow Rise NG10 .... 223 D3
Willow Row DE1 .... 267 A4
Willow St DE55 .... 146 B1
Willow Terr S43 .... 80 C1
Willow Way DE4 .... 127 D2
Willowbath La DE4 .... 165 F4
Willowbrook Grange DE73 233 D1
Willowcroft Rd DE21 ...... 220 C2
Willowdale Ave ST4 .... 269 F1
Willowfields DE65 .... 228 B1

Willowherb Cl DE24 .... 231 F1
Willowpit La DE65 .... 228 C3
Willows Ave DE55 .... 159 D3
Willows The
  Hulland Ward DE6 .... 175 F2
  Pleasley NG19 .... 135 D3
Willowsend Cl DE65 .... 230 B1
Willridding La DE6 .... 183 E4
Wilson Ave DE23 .... 231 E4
Wilson Rd DE23 .... 231 E4
Wilmans Wlk SK13 .... 10 A3
Wilmington Ave DE24 ..... 233 D3
Wilmore Rd DE24 .... 232 A3
Wilmorton Prim Sch
  DE24 .... **219 F1**
Wilmorton Tertiary Coll
  DE24 .... **219 F1**
Wilmot Ave Derby DE21 ... 219 F3
  Weston-on-T DE72 .... 245 F3
Wilmot Dr DE7 .... 192 C3
Wilmot Rd Belper DE56 ... 179 D2
  Swadlincote DE11 .... 256 A2
Wilmot St Derby DE1 .... 267 B2
  Heanor DE75 .... 181 F1
  Ilkeston DE7 .... 194 C1
  Long Eaton NG10 .... 236 A3
  Matlock DE4 .... 143 D3
Wilmslow Dr DE21 .... 206 A1
Wilne Ave NG10 .... 236 A2
Wilne Cl NG10 .... 235 F2
Wilne La Breaston DE72 .... 235 E2
  Shardlow DE72 .... 235 D1
Wilne Rd Draycott DE72 ... 235 D3
  Long Eaton NG10 .... 235 F2
Wilshaw Cl SK23 .... 47 E3
Wilson Ave Blackwell DE55 . 147 F1
  Clowne S43 .... 80 C3
  Heanor DE75 .... 181 D2
Wilson Cl Burnaston DE3 ... 230 B4
  Clay Cross S45 .... 131 E1
Wilson Dr DE55 .... 170 B4
Wilson La S44 .... 117 D1
Wilson Pl S8 .... 43 D4
Wilson Rd Derby DE21 ..... 219 F4
  Dronfield S18 .... 57 E2
  Eastwood NG16 .... 182 C1
Wilson Rise DE73 .... 252 C3
Wilson St Alfreton DE55 ... 159 D2
  Derby DE1 .... 267 B2
  Dronfield S18 .... 76 A4
  Pinxton NG16 .... 160 B2
  Radmanthwaite NG19 ...... 135 E1
Wilson's Terr SK13 .... 17 D4
Wilsthorpe Rd
  Breaston DE72 .... 235 F4
  Derby DE21 .... 220 A4
  Long Eaton NG10 .... 236 A3
Wilsthorpe Sch NG10 ..... **223 D1**
Wilton Cl DE24 .... 231 E1
Wilton Pl DE7 .... 194 C1
Wilton St **7** DE7 .... 194 C1
Wiltshire Ave NG16 .... 171 D2
Wiltshire Dr SK13 .... 17 F4
Wiltshire Rd DE21 .... 219 F4
Wimbledon Rd DE22 .... 218 A4
Wimborne Cres S41 .... 95 F4
Wimbourne Cl DE73 .... 233 D1
Wimpole Gdns DE22 .... 218 A3
Wimsey Way DE55 .... 159 D1
Wincanton Cl DE24 .... 219 E1
Winchcombe Dr DE15 ..... 248 A1
Winchcombe Way DE21 ... 206 A1
Winchester Cres DE7 .... 209 D4
Winchester Dr
  Burton u T DE14 .... 254 B4
  Linton DE12 .... 261 E3
  Mansfield Woodhouse NG19 136 B2
  Swadlincote DE11 .... 256 B3
Winchester Rd S41 .... 95 F4
Windermere Ave
  Dronfield S18 .... 56 C1
  Ilkeston DE7 .... 208 B3
Windermere Cres DE22 ... 204 C2
Windermere Dr DE21 ...... 220 C3
Windermere Gdns NG10 .. 223 D1
Windermere Rd
  Chesterfield S41 .... 95 E4
  Clay Cross S45 .... 131 D2
  Long Eaton NG10 .... 223 D1
Windlea Rd DE55 .... 170 B3
Windley Cres DE22 .... 204 C1
Windley Dr DE7 .... 194 B2
Windley La
  Idridgehay DE56 .... 176 C3
  Turnditch DE56 .... 177 D1
  Windley DE56 .... 189 F4
Windley Sch NG7 .... **268 A2**
Windmill Ave DE56 .... 192 A4
Windmill Cl Bolsover S44 .... 99 D2
  Castle Donington DE74 .... 247 D1
  Elvaston DE24 .... 233 E2
  Ockbrook DE72 .... 221 E3
Windmill Dr ST14 .... 224 C2
Windmill Greenway S20 .... 59 F3
Windmill Hill La DE22 ..... 218 B3
Windmill La
  Alderwasley DE56 .... 166 C3
  Ashbourne DE6 .... 173 E2
  Belper DE56 .... 179 D2
  Eyam S32 .... 71 E3
  Mansfield NG18 .... 268 C4
  Nottingham NG2 .... 268 C2
  Snelston DE6 .... 184 C1
  Unstone S18 .... 77 D3
Windmill Rd DE65 .... 229 D2

Windmill Rise
Belper DE56 .... 179 D3
Somercotes DE55 .... 170 B4
South Normanton DE55 .... 159 F3
Windmill St DE11 .... 256 A1
Windmill View DE56 .... 179 F4
Windrush Cl DE22 .... 205 D3
Windses Est S32 .... 53 E1
Windsmoor Rd NG16 .... 182 B4
Windsmoor St ST4 .... 269 E1
Windsor Ave Derby DE73 .... 231 D4
Melbourne DE73 .... 252 A4
Windsor Cl
Ashbourne DE6 .... 173 E2
Borrowash DE72 .... 221 E1
⁴ Chesterfield S40 .... 95 E1
Heanor DE75 .... 181 F2
Swadlincote DE11 .... 256 A3
Swanwick DE55 .... 170 A4
Trowell NG9 .... 209 D3
Windsor Cres
Ilkeston DE7 .... 208 C2
Stapleford NG9 .... 223 F4
Windsor Ct Derby DE3 .... 217 E1
Sandiacre NG10 .... 223 D2
West Hallam DE7 .... 207 E4
Windsor Dr Derby DE21 ..... 221 D3
Dronfield S18 .... 56 B1
Wingerworth S42 .... 114 C2
Windsor Gdns NG18 .... 268 C3
Windsor Park Rd SK17 ...... 85 E4
Windsor Rd Buxton SK17 ... 85 E4
Linton DE12 .... 261 E3
Mansfield NG18 .... 268 C3
Uttoxeter ST16 .... 210 A1
Windsor St NG9 .... 223 F4
Windsor Wlk S41 .... 115 E4
Windy Fields Rd S42 .... 113 E4
Windy House La S2 .... 44 A4
Windy La DE21 .... 191 E1
Windyridge SK17 .... 121 D3
Winfield St S6 .... 15 D1
Wingerworth Ave S8 .... 56 B4
Wingerworth Cotts S42 .... 115 F2
Wingerworth Park Rd
DE21 .... 220 C3
Wingerworth St S42 .... 115 F2
Wingfield Cl S18 .... 56 B1
Wingfield Cres S12 .... 44 B3
Wingfield Dr Derby DE21 ... 205 F1
Ilkeston DE7 .... 194 B2
Wingfield Gr SK13 .... 17 F4
Wingfield Rd
Alfreton DE55 .... 158 C2
Tupton S42 .... 131 E4
Winhill Rd SK22 .... 24 B1
Winkburn Rd NG18, NG19 ... 268 A4
Winn La DE6 .... 174 C4
Winnat Pl S43 .... 97 E4
Winnats S33 .... 37 F1
Winnats Cl Chesterfield S40 ... 95 E3
Glossop SK13 .... 17 F4
Winney Hill S26 .... 61 F3
Winney La S26 .... 61 F2
Winnington Rd SK6 .... 23 D4
Winshill Inf Sch DE15 .... 248 A3
Winslow Ave SK14 .... 9 D1
Winslow Grn DE21 .... 220 B3
Winster CE Prim Sch DE4 . 141 E3
Winster Cl Belper DE56 ..... 179 D3
Clay Cross S45 .... 131 D3
Winster Gn DE11 .... 255 F3
Winster Gr SK17 .... 85 F4
Winster La DE4 .... 140 C3
Winster Market Ho DE4 ... 141 E3
Winster Mews SK13 .... 9 F1
Winster Rd Derby DE21 ..... 205 F1
Staveley S43 .... 97 E4
Winster Sq S17 .... 85 F4
Winster Way NG10 .... 235 F3
Winston Cl NG9 .... 223 F4
Winter Closes NG16 .... 171 F1
Winterbourne Dr NG9 ...... 209 F1
Wintercroft La DE11 .... 161 F1
Wintergreen Dr DE23 .... 230 C3
Winton Sq ST4 .... 269 E2
Wintonfield St ST4 .... 269 F2
Wire La DE55 .... 148 A2
Wirksmoor Rd SK22 .... 33 D4
Wirksworth CE Inf Sch
DE4 .... 165 F4
Wirksworth Hall Gdns
DE4 .... 165 F4
Wirksworth Ind Est DE4 ... 154 C2
Wirksworth Inf Sch DE4 ... 154 C1
Wirksworth Jun Sch DE4 . 155 D1
Wirksworth Rd
Duffield DE56 .... 190 B2
Idridgehay DE56 .... 176 C3
Ilkeston DE7 .... 208 B2
Kirk Ireton DE6 .... 165 D1
Shottle DE56 .... 177 E2
Windley DE56 .... 177 E2
Wisbech Cl S40 .... 114 C4
Wisgreaves Rd DE24 .... 232 C4
Wishing Stone Way DE4 .... 143 F3

Witham Cl S41 .... 96 B3
Witham Ct S40 .... 95 E2
Witham Dr DE23 .... 231 E3
Witney Cl DE24 .... 232 B4
Witney St S8 .... 43 D4
Wittering Cl NG10 .... 236 C3
Woburn Cl
^ Blackwell DE55 .... 147 F1
Swanwick DE55 .... 169 F4
Woburn Croft NG10 .... 223 D2
Woburn La NG19 .... 135 E2
Woburn Pl Derby DE22 ...... 218 A3
Radmanthwaite NG19 ... 135 E2
Woburn Rd NG19 .... 135 E2
Wolds Rise DE4 .... 143 E4
Wolfa St DE22 .... 218 C2
Wolfcote Cl S45 .... 131 E1
Wolfe Cl S40 .... 95 E1
Wolfe St S40 .... 269 E1
Wolfscote Dale DE11 .... 255 F1
Wollaton Ave S17 .... 56 A3
Wollaton Dr ⁷ S17 .... 56 A3
Wollaton Rd Derby DE21 ... 219 F4
Sheffield S17 .... 56 A3
Wollaton Rd S DE21 .... 205 F1
Wollaton St NG1 .... 268 A2
Wollen Cl S80 .... 81 F1
Wolseley Rd Sheffield S2 ... 43 D4
Stafford ST16 .... 269 F4
Wolverhampton Rd ST17 ... 269 E3
Wolverley Grange DE24 .... 233 E3
Wood Ave Creswell S80 ..... 81 E1
Sandiacre NG10 .... 223 D3
Wood Cl S42 .... 114 B2
Wood Croft DE23 .... 231 E4
Wood End Rd DE75 .... 181 F1
Wood Gdns SK22 .... 25 E2
Wood La Belper DE56 .... 190 C4
Creswell S80 .... 100 B4
Hanbury DE13 .... 238 A2
Hayfield SK22 .... 25 E2
Holloway DE4 .... 144 A1
Horsley Woodhouse DE7 ... 192 B3
Ible DE4 .... 153 F3
Idridgehay DE56 .... 176 C4
Kniveton DE6 .... 163 D1
Market Warsop NG20 .... 120 C4
Pentrich DE5 .... 169 D2
Pleasley NG20 .... 119 F1
Scarcliffe S44 .... 118 C3
Shirebrook NG20 .... 119 F1
Smalley DE7 .... 192 B3
Swadlincote DE11 .... 256 A4
Wood Nook La NG16 .... 171 F3
Wood Rd
Derby, Chaddesden DE21 ... 220 A4
Derby, Oakwood DE21 .... 205 F1
Derby, Spondon DE21 .... 221 D3
Wood St Alfreton DE55 ..... 159 E3
Codnor DE5 .... 181 D4
Derby DE1 .... 267 C4
Eastwood NG16 .... 182 C2
Glossop SK13 .... 17 E4
Hollingworth SK14 ...... 9 E3
Holmewood S42 .... 116 C1
Ilkeston DE7 .... 194 C1
Mansfield NG18 .... 268 B4
New Mills SK22 .... 33 D4
Nottingham NG7 .... 268 A2
Ripley DE5 .... 169 E1
Somercotes DE55 .... 170 B4
Swadlincote DE11 .... 256 A1
Wirksworth DE4 .... 165 F4
Wood St N DE55 .... 159 E3
Wood's Hospl SK13 .... 10 B2
Woodale Cl DE23 .... 230 C3
Woodall La S26 .... 61 E3
Woodall Rd S21 .... 60 C3
Woodall Service Area
S21 .... 61 D3
Woodbeck Ct DE21 .... 206 A1
Woodberry Ave ST4 .... 269 D1
Woodberry Cl ST4 .... 269 D1
Woodborough Rd
Mansfield NG19 .... 135 F1
Nottingham NG3 .... 268 B2
Woodbourne Rd SK22 .... 33 D3
Woodbridge Cl DE21 .... 232 C1
Woodbridge Jun Sch
DE55 .... 159 D2
Woodbridge Rise S40 .... 114 A4
Woodbrook SK23 .... 45 F4
Woodbrook Ct SK23 .... 45 F4
Woodchester Dr DE24 ...... 233 E3
Woodcock Gr SK13 .... 10 C1
Woodcock Rd SK13 .... 11 D1
Woodcote Way DE23 .... 231 D4
Woodfall La DE56 .... 189 F2
Woodfield Cl SK13 .... 9 F3
Woodfield Dr Ripley DE5 .... 181 D4
Swadlincote DE11 .... 256 B3
Woodfield Rd NG16 .... 160 B2
Woodford Rd DE22 .... 218 A4
Woodford Way S43 .... 78 A2
Woodgate Dr DE73 .... 233 D1
Woodhall Dr DE23 .... 230 C4
Woodhead La S45 .... 130 B1
Woodhead Rd Glossop SK13 . 10 B3
Holme HD7 .... 2 C3

Woodhead Rd continued
Sheffield S2 .... 43 D4
Tintwistle SK13 .... 10 A4
Woodhouse Ct NG19 .... 136 B1
Woodhouse La
Barlborough S43 .... 79 F3
Bolsover S44 .... 98 C2
Mastin Moor S43 .... 79 E3
Rowsley DE4 .... 126 C4
Scropton DE65 .... 226 C4
South Normanton DE55 ... 159 F3
Winster DE4 .... 141 E3
Woodhouse Rd
Kilburn DE56 .... 192 A4
Mansfield NG18 .... 268 B4
Woodhouse St
Nottingham NG3 .... 268 C2
Stoke-on-T ST4 .... 269 E1
Swadlincote DE11 .... 256 B2
Woodhouse West Fst &
Mid Sch S13 .... 44 C3
Woodhurst Cl DE21 .... 219 E4
Woodland Ave
Borrowash DE72 .... 221 E1
Ilkeston DE7 .... 194 B2
Sutton in A NG17 .... 148 C2
Woodland Dr
Scropton DE6 .... 226 B2
Sheffield S12 .... 44 A1
Woodland Gr Clowne S43 .... 81 D2
Mansfield Woodhouse
NG19 .... 136 B2
Woodland Pl S17 .... 55 F3
Woodland Rd Derby DE22 .. 218 C4
Sheffield S8 .... 43 D2
Swadlincote DE11 .... 255 D2
Woodland View Dore S17 ... 56 A4
Sheffield S12 .... 44 A1
Whaley Thorns NG20 ... 101 D2
Woodland Views ST14 ...... 224 C1
Woodland Way
Clay Cross S42 .... 131 D3
Eastwood NG16 .... 182 C1
Woodland Wlk S40 .... 94 C3
Woodlands Brimington S43 ... 96 B4
Wirksworth DE4 .... 165 F4
Woodlands Ave
Breaston DE72 .... 235 F4
Derby DE24 .... 232 C2
Woodlands Brow DE6 .... 173 E2
Woodlands Cl
Little Eaton DE21 .... 205 D4
Melbourne DE73 .... 252 A4
Tintwistle SK13 .... 9 F3
Woodlands Com Sch
DE22 .... 204 B2
Woodlands Cres DE12 ...... 262 A2
Woodlands Gr S42 .... 131 D3
Woodlands La Derby DE73 .. 245 D4
Quarndon DE22 .... 204 B3
Woodlands Rd
Chapel-en-le-F SK23 .... 47 D2
Derby DE22 .... 204 C3
Disley SK12 .... 32 A3
New Mills SK22 .... 33 D4
Overseal DE12 .... 262 A2
Woodlands The
Mansfield NG19 .... 136 A1
Melbourne DE73 .... 252 A4
Whaley Thorns NG20 ... 101 D2
Woodlands Way DE73 ...... 252 A4
Woodlands Yd DE73 .... 245 D4
Woodlea Gr DE21 .... 205 E4
Woodleigh Cl S40 .... 94 C3
Woodmans Croft DE65 ..... 227 E1
Woodminton Dr DE73 ...... 232 C2
Woodnook Cl S40 .... 95 D2
Woodnook La S40 .... 94 C3
Woodnook Way S40 .... 94 C2
Woodpecker Hill DE7 .... 208 A1
Woodrising Cl DE21 .... 206 A2
Woodroffe Wlk DE23 .... 231 F4
Woodrove Ave S13 .... 44 A4
Woodrove Cl S13 .... 44 A4
Woods La Burton u T DE15 .. 248 A1
Derby DE22 .... 267 A1
Woodseats Rd S13 .... 16 A3
Woodshop La DE73 .... 244 B3
Woodside Buxton SK17 ..... 85 E4
Eastwood NG16 .... 182 C2
Horsley DE7 .... 192 B2
Woodside Ave
Holmesfield S18 .... 75 D4
Killamarsh S21 .... 60 C4
Woodside Cl
Bakewell DE45 .... 109 E3
Chesterfield S40 .... 95 D2
Woodside Cres
Ilkeston DE7 .... 194 B3
Long Eaton NG10 .... 236 A4
Woodside Dr
Bakewell DE45 .... 109 E3
Derby DE24 .... 205 D2
Woodside Pl S45 .... 131 D2
Woodside Rd
Sandiacre NG10 .... 223 D3
Shirebrook NG20 .... 119 F3
Shireoaks S81 .... 63 F4
Woodside St SK22 .... 33 D3

Woodside View S18 .... 75 D4
Woodsorrel Dr DE21 .... 206 A2
Woodstock Cl DE22 .... 204 B2
Woodstock Dr S41 .... 115 E4
Woodstock Rd NG9 .... 223 F2
Woodstock Rise S41 .... 115 E4
Woodthorpe Ave
Clay Cross S45 .... 131 D2
Derby, Allenton DE24 ... 232 C2
Derby, Chaddesden DE21 ... 219 F3
Woodthorpe CE Prim Sch
S43 .... 79 E1
Woodthorpe Cl
Bolsover S44 .... 98 C4
Sheffield S2 .... 44 A4
Woodthorpe Cres S13 ...... 44 B4
Woodthorpe Rd
Bolsover S44 .... 98 C4
Sheffield S13 .... 44 B4
Woodthorpe S43 .... 79 E1
Woodthorpe Sec Sch
S13 .... 44 B4
Woodvale Cl S40 .... 114 A4
Woodview Cl S42 .... 114 C1
Woodview Rd DE11 .... 255 F3
Woodville CE Jun Sch
DE11 .... 256 C1
Woodville Inf Sch DE11 ... 256 C1
Woodville Rd
Hartshorne DE11 .... 257 D3
Overseal DE12 .... 262 A2
Woodward's Pl DE11 .... 256 B2
Woodwards Cl DE72 .... 221 E1
Woodyard La DE65 .... 226 C3
Woolaton La SK17 .... 138 B1
Wooley Cl S42 .... 131 D4
Wooliscroft Way DE7 .... 194 B1
Woolley Bridge Rd SK13 .... 9 E3
Woolley Cl SK14 .... 9 E2
Woolley La
Hollingworth SK14 ...... 9 E3
Hollingworth, Woolley SK14 ... 9 E2
Woolley Mill La SK13 .... 9 F4
Woolley Rd DE4 .... 143 D3
Woolley Yd DE4 .... 141 E3
Woolpack La NG1 .... 268 B1
Woolrych St DE23 .... 218 C1
Woolsthorpe Cres DE7 ..... 208 B2
Woosnam Cl DE14 .... 254 A3
Worcester Ave NG19 .... 136 B3
Worcester Cres DE21 .... 219 F4
Worcester Gr S13 .... 17 F4
Worcester Mews NG19 ..... 136 B3
Worcester Rd DE15 .... 254 C3
Wordsworth Ave
Derby DE24 .... 231 F3
Mansfield Woodhouse
NG19 .... 136 A2
Swadlincote DE11 .... 256 B3
Wordsworth Dr DE24 .... 232 A3
Wordsworth Pl S18 .... 76 B4
Wordsworth Rd
Awsworth NG16 .... 195 E3
Chesterfield S41 .... 95 F4
Works La S44 .... 97 D2
Works Rd S43 .... 78 A1
Worksop Rd
Mastin Moor S43 .... 79 E2
Nottingham NG3 .... 268 C2
Thorpe Salvin S80 ...... 62 C4
Whitwell S80 .... 81 F3
Worrall Ave NG10 .... 223 F1
Worthington La DE73 ...... 252 C1
Wortley Ave NG9 .... 209 E2
Wortley Cl DE7 .... 209 D4
Wortley Ct S33 .... 51 D4
Wragley Way DE24 .... 231 E1
Wray Cl NG3 .... 268 C2
Wreakes La S18 .... 56 C1
Wren Cl DE11 .... 256 C2
Wren Nest Rd SK13 .... 10 A1
Wren Nest Terr SK13 .... 10 B1
Wren Park Cl
Belper DE56 .... 178 B3
Chesterfield S40 .... 114 C4
Findern DE65 .... 230 B1
Ridgeway S12 .... 58 C4
Wren Park Prim Sch
DE3 .... 218 A1
Wrenpark Rd S42 .... 114 B2
Wretham Cl DE3 .... 230 B4
Wright Ave DE5 .... 169 F1
Wright St DE5 .... 181 D4
Wroxham Ct DE24 .... 232 B2
Wulfric Cl S2 .... 43 F4
Wulfric Pl S2 .... 43 F4
Wulfric Rd Eckington S21 ... 59 E2
Sheffield, Deep Pit S2 .. 43 F4
Sheffield, Manor Estate S2 ... 44 A4
Wyaston Cl DE22 .... 204 C1
Wyaston Rd
Ashbourne DE6 .... 185 E3
Osmaston DE6 .... 185 E3
Wybersley Rd
High Lane SK6 .... 32 A4
Marple SK6 .... 23 D1
Wychwood Dr NG9 .... 209 E1
Wycliffe Rd DE55 .... 159 D2
Wye Bank DE45 .... 109 F3

Wye Bank Gr DE45 .... 109 F3
Wye Dale DE11 .... 255 F1
Wye Gr SK17 .... 85 D4
Wye Head Cl SK17 .... 84 C4
Wye St Buxton SK17 .... 85 E4
Derby DE24 .... 233 D4
Wye Terr DE4 .... 126 C4
Wyedale Cl Bakewell DE45 .. 109 F2
Buxton SK17 .... 85 D3
Wyedale Cres DE45 .... 109 F2
Wyedale Ct ⁵ S41 .... 95 F4
Wyedale Dr DE45 .... 109 F2
Wyedale View DE45 .... 109 F2
Wyelands Cl SK17 .... 84 C4
Wyming Brook Dr S10 ...... 42 A4
Wynd The S21 .... 79 E4
Wyndale Dr DE7 .... 208 B3
Wyndham Cres DE15 .... 248 B2
Wyndham St DE24 .... 233 D4
Wynton Ave DE24 .... 232 C4
Wyntor Ave DE4 .... 141 E3
Wynward Cl DE7 .... 194 B2
Wysall Cl NG19 .... 135 F1
Wystan Ct DE65 .... 242 B1
Wyston Brook DE65 .... 228 B1
Wythburn Rd S41 .... 95 E4
Wyver La DE56 .... 178 C4
Wyvern Ave NG10 .... 236 B3
Wyvern Cl Eastwood NG16 .. 195 D4
Matlock DE4 .... 143 D3
Wyvern Gdns S17 .... 55 F3
Wyvern Way DE21 .... 220 A2

Yardley Cl DE55 .... 169 F4
Yardley Way DE56 .... 179 E2
Yarncliff Cl S40 .... 95 E3
Yarrow Cl DE24 .... 231 F1
Yates Ave DE72 .... 246 A3
Yates St SK22 .... 33 E4
Yates St DE23 .... 219 D1
Yeaman St ST4 .... 269 E1
Yeardsley Ave SK23 .... 33 E2
Yeardsley Gn SK23 .... 45 E4
Yeardsley La SK23 .... 33 E2
Yeld Cl DE45 .... 109 E2
Yeld Rd DE45 .... 109 E3
Yeld The DE45 .... 109 E3
Yeldersley Cl S40 .... 95 D3
Yeldersley La
Brailsford DE6 .... 187 D1
Osmaston DE6 .... 186 C3
Yelt La DE6 .... 224 B4
Yeoman Park Sch NG19 ... 136 B2
Yeoman St DE4 .... 142 B1
Yeovil Cl DE24 .... 233 E4
Yerley Hill DE6 .... 172 B3
Yew Tree Ave DE72 .... 221 E3
Yew Tree Cl S45 .... 129 F2
Yew Tree Dr
Chesterfield S40 .... 114 A4
Clay Cross S42 .... 131 D3
Killamarsh S21 .... 60 B3
Shirebrook NG20 .... 119 E3
Sutton in A NG17 .... 148 C1
Yew Tree Gdns DE12 .... 260 B3
Yew Tree Hill DE4 .... 156 A3
Yew Tree La Bradley DE6 ... 186 C4
Elvaston DE72 .... 233 F2
Yew Tree Rd Hatton DE65 .. 227 E1
Rosliston DE12 .... 260 B3
Swadlincote DE11 .... 255 F4
Yewdale Gr DE21 .... 206 B2
Yews Cl DE73 .... 233 D1
Yewtree Dr DE24 .... 233 E4
Yewtree Cres DE15 .... 254 C4
Yokecliffe Ave DE4 .... 165 F4
Yokecliffe Cres DE4 .... 165 F4
Yokecliffe Dr DE4 .... 165 F4
Yokecliffe Hill DE4 .... 165 F4
York Ave Sandiacre NG10 ... 223 D2
Westwood NG16 .... 171 D2
York Cl DE11 .... 256 B3
York Cres S44 .... 117 F1
York Pl North Wingfield S42 . 132 A4
Shireoaks S81 .... 63 F4
York Rd Derby DE21 .... 219 F4
Long Eaton NG10 .... 223 E1
Shirebrook NG20 .... 119 F2
Swadlincote DE11 .... 256 A1
York St Chesterfield S41 .... 115 E4
Derby DE1 .... 218 C3
Glossop SK13 .... 10 C1
Mansfield NG18 .... 268 B2
Nottingham NG3 .... 268 B2
York Terr Glossop SK13 ..... 17 E4
Pinxton NG16 .... 160 B1
Yorke St NG19 .... 136 A1
Yorkshire Way SK13 .... 17 F4
Youlgreave All Saints CE
Prim Sch DE45 .... 125 E3
Youlgreave Cl DE21 .... 205 F1
Youlgreave Cres SK13 ...... 9 E1
Youlgreave Dr S12 .... 44 B3
Young St DE23 .... 218 C1
Younger St ST4 .... 269 F1
Yoxall Ave ST4 .... 269 D2
Ypres Rd DE22 .... 204 B1

Zetland Cres DE24 .... 231 E1

os Ordnance Survey

STREET ATLASES on CD-ROM

The Interactive Street Atlases are CD-ROM versions of the Ordnance Survey/Philip's Street Atlases. They have a wide range of software features, additional levels of mapping, and are remarkably easy to use.

Searches can be carried out for street names and buildings, towns and villages, National Grid references, Postcode districts and sectors, and for page-grid references from the printed Atlases.

You can move around the mapping with no breaks at page boundaries, and scale bars, keys and locator maps can be displayed or hidden. You can measure distances along complex routes, add bookmarks,

draw over the mapping with a range of tools, and create hotspots connected to database tables. You can print sections of mapping, and the price includes a licence to make 1,500 prints.

The Interactive Street Atlases can be used effectively together with the printed atlases – for example, you can always see on which page of the printed Atlas a section of electronic mapping appears.

Network licences and discounts for bulk purchases are available. Prices subject to change without notice.

You can obtain the Atlases by mail order direct from the publisher:

Mapping includes:

◆ **General Map for orientation**
◆ **County Map showing major routes**
◆ **Road Map showing the majority of roads and streets, and highlighting through routes**
◆ **Street Map, the full mapping from the printed Street Atlases, which forms a "seamless" map of the whole region and can be magnified**

Tel: 01933 443863
Fax: 01933 443849

Philip's Direct,
27 Sanders Road, Wellingborough,
Northants NN8 4NL

Available now:

◆ **Berkshire** (£150 + VAT)
◆ **Hertfordshire** (£150 + VAT)

More titles coming soon!

---

os Ordnance Survey

Updated annually

MOTORING ATLAS
Britain

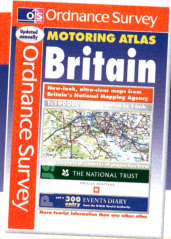

The best-selling *OS Motoring Atlas Britain* uses unrivalled and up-to-date mapping from the Ordnance Survey digital database. The exceptionally clear mapping is at a large scale of 3 miles to 1 inch (Orkney/Shetland Islands at 5 miles to 1 inch).

A special feature of the atlas is its wealth of tourist and leisure information. It contains comprehensive directories, including descriptions and location details, of the properties of the National Trust in England and Wales, the National Trust for Scotland, English Heritage and

Historic Scotland. There is also a useful diary of British Tourist Authority Events listing more than 300 days out around Britain during the year.

Available from all good bookshops or direct from the publisher:
Tel: 01933 443863

The atlas includes:

◆ **112 pages of fully updated mapping**
◆ **45 city and town plans**
◆ **8 extra-detailed city approach maps**
◆ **route-planning maps**
◆ **restricted motorway junctions**
◆ **local radio information**
◆ **distances chart**
◆ **county boundaries map**
◆ **multi-language legend**

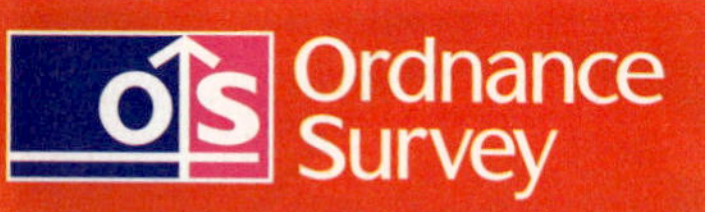

STREET ATLASES ORDER FORM

The Street Atlases are available from all good bookshops or by mail order direct from the publisher. Orders can be made in the following ways. **By phone** Ring our special Credit Card Hotline on **01933 443863** during office hours (9am to 5pm) or leave a message on the answering machine, quoting your full credit card number plus expiry date and your full name and address. **By post or fax** Fill out the order form below (you may photocopy it) and post it to: **Philip's Direct, 27 Sanders Road, Wellingborough, Northants NN8 4NL** or fax it to: **01933 443849**. Before placing an order by post, by fax or on the answering machine, please telephone to check availability and prices.

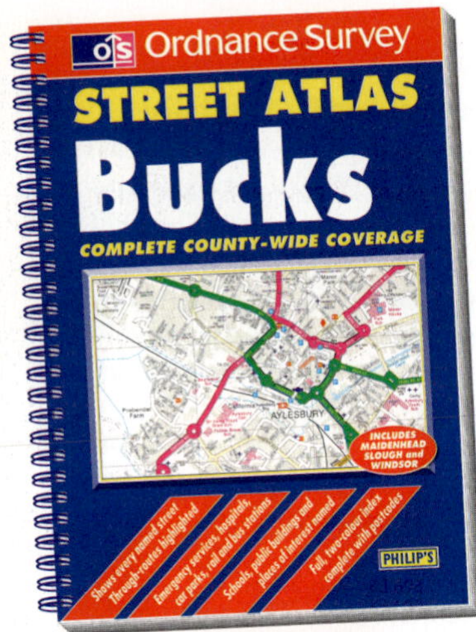

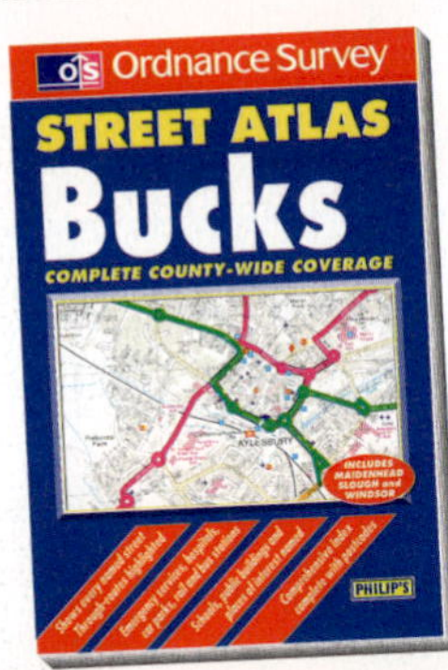

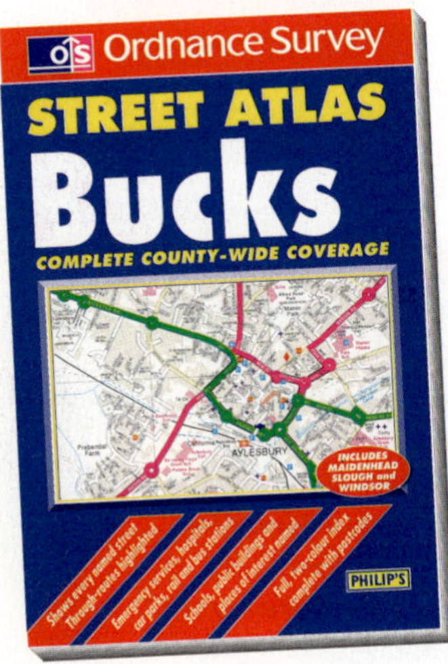

COLOUR TOWN AND CITY EDITIONS

	PAPERBACK	
	Quantity @ £3.50 each	£ Total
WARRINGTON, WIDNES, RUNCORN	☐ 0 540 07588 4	➤ ☐
NORTHWICH, WINSFORD, MIDDLEWICH	☐ 0 540 07589 2	➤ ☐
DERBY	☐ 0 540 07608 2	➤ ☐
PEAK DISTRICT TOWNS	☐ 0 540 07609 0	➤ ☐

COLOUR EDITIONS

	HARDBACK	SPIRAL	POCKET	
	Quantity @ £10.99 each	Quantity @ £8.99 each	Quantity @ £4.99 each	£ Total
BERKSHIRE	☐ 0 540 06170 0	☐ 0 540 06172 7	☐ 0 540 06173 5	➤ ☐
MERSEYSIDE	☐ 0 540 06480 7	☐ 0 540 06481 5	☐ 0 540 06482 3	➤ ☐
	Quantity @ £12.99 each	Quantity @ £8.99 each	Quantity @ £4.99 each	£ Total
SURREY	☐ 0 540 06435 1	☐ 0 540 06436 X	☐ 0 540 06438 6	➤ ☐
	Quantity @ £12.99 each	Quantity @ £9.99 each	Quantity @ £4.99 each	£ Total
BUCKINGHAMSHIRE	☐ 0 540 07466 7	☐ 0 540 07467 5	☐ 0 540 07468 3	➤ ☐
DURHAM	☐ 0 540 06365 7	☐ 0 540 06366 5	☐ 0 540 06367 3	➤ ☐
HERTFORDSHIRE	☐ 0 540 06174 3	☐ 0 540 06175 1	☐ 0 540 06176 X	➤ ☐
EAST KENT	☐ 0 540 07483 7	☐ 0 540 07276 1	☐ 0 540 07287 7	➤ ☐
WEST KENT	☐ 0 540 07366 0	☐ 0 540 07367 9	☐ 0 540 07369 5	➤ ☐
EAST SUSSEX	☐ 0 540 07306 7	☐ 0 540 07307 5	☐ 0 540 07312 1	➤ ☐
WEST SUSSEX	☐ 0 540 07319 9	☐ 0 540 07323 7	☐ 0 540 07327 X	➤ ☐
TYNE AND WEAR	☐ 0 540 06370 3	☐ 0 540 06371 1	☐ 0 540 06372 X	➤ ☐
SOUTH YORKSHIRE	☐ 0 540 06330 4	☐ 0 540 06331 2	☐ 0 540 06332 0	➤ ☐
	Quantity @ £12.99 each	Quantity @ £9.99 each	Quantity @ £5.50 each	£ Total
GREATER MANCHESTER	☐ 0 540 06485 8	☐ 0 540 06486 6	☐ 0 540 06487 4	➤ ☐
	Quantity @ £12.99 each	Quantity @ £9.99 each	Quantity @ £5.99 each	£ Total
CHESHIRE	☐ 0 540 07507 8	☐ 0 540 07508 6	☐ 0 540 07509 4	➤ ☐
DERBYSHIRE	☐ 0 540 07531 0	☐ 0 540 07532 9	☐ 0 540 07533 7	➤ ☐

STREET ATLASES ORDER FORM

COLOUR EDITIONS

	HARDBACK	SPIRAL	POCKET	
	Quantity @ £12.99 each	Quantity @ £9.99 each	Quantity @ £5.99 each	£ Total
SOUTH HAMPSHIRE	☐ 0 540 07476 4	☐ 0 540 07477 2	☐ 0 540 07478 0	➤ ☐
NORTH HAMPSHIRE	☐ 0 540 07471 3	☐ 0 540 07472 1	☐ 0 540 07473 X	➤ ☐
OXFORDSHIRE	☐ 0 540 07512 4	☐ 0 540 07513 2	☐ 0 540 07514 0	➤ ☐
WEST YORKSHIRE	☐ 0 540 06329 0	☐ 0 540 06327 4	☐ 0 540 06328 2	➤ ☐
	Quantity @ £14.99 each	Quantity @ £9.99 each	Quantity @ £5.99 each	£ Total
LANCASHIRE	☐ 0 540 06440 8	☐ 0 540 06441 6	☐ 0 540 06443 2	➤ ☐

BLACK AND WHITE EDITIONS

	HARDBACK	SOFTBACK	POCKET	
	Quantity @ £10.99 each			£ Total
WARWICKSHIRE	☐ 0 540 05642 1	—	—	➤ ☐
	Quantity @ £12.99 each	Quantity @ £9.99 each	Quantity @ £4.99 each	Total
BRISTOL AND AVON	☐ 0 540 06140 9	☐ 0 540 06141 7	☐ 0 540 06142 5	➤ ☐
CARDIFF, SWANSEA & GLAMORGAN	☐ 0 540 06186 7	☐ 0 540 06187 5	☐ 0 540 06207 3	➤ ☐
EDINBURGH & East Central Scotland	☐ 0 540 06180 8	☐ 0 540 06181 6	☐ 0 540 06182 4	➤ ☐
EAST ESSEX	☐ 0 540 05848 3	☐ 0 540 05866 1	☐ 0 540 05850 5	➤ ☐
WEST ESSEX	☐ 0 540 05849 1	☐ 0 540 05867 X	☐ 0 540 05851 3	➤ ☐
NOTTINGHAMSHIRE	—	☐ 0 540 05859 9	☐ 0 540 05860 2	➤ ☐
STAFFORDSHIRE	☐ 0 540 06134 4	☐ 0 540 06135 2	☐ 0 540 06136 0	➤ ☐
	Quantity @ £12.99 each	Quantity @ £9.99 each	Quantity @ £5.99 each	£ Total
GLASGOW & West Central Scotland	☐ 0 540 06183 2	☐ 0 540 06184 0	☐ 0 540 06185 9	➤ ☐

➤

Post to: Philip's Direct,
27 Sanders Road, Wellingborough,
Northants NN8 4NL

◆ Free postage and packing

◆ All available titles will normally be dispatched within 5 working days of receipt of order but please allow up to 28 days for delivery

☐ Please tick this box if you do not wish your name to be used by other carefully selected organisations that may wish to send you information about other products and services

Registered Office: 25 Victoria Street, London SW1H 0EX

Registered in England number: 3396524

I enclose a cheque / postal order, for a **total** of ☐

made payable to *Reed Book Services,* or please debit my

☐ Access ☐ American Express ☐ Visa ☐ Diners

account by ☐

Account no

☐☐☐☐ ☐☐☐☐ ☐☐☐☐ ☐☐☐☐

Expiry date ☐☐ ☐☐

Signature..

Name...

Address...

....

....

....POSTCODE

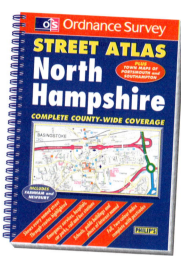

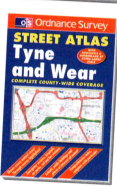

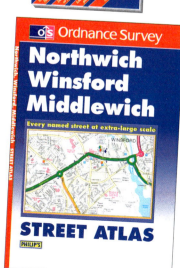